U0875171

北京昂首走进新世纪

“九五”时期，是北京市认真贯彻中央一系列指示精神，确立首都经济发展战略并取得重大突破的重要时期；是积极探索和实践现代化国际城市发展之路，首都功能不断增强、国际地位空前提高的重要时期；也是全市经济发展成效显著、城市建设阔步前进、人民生活提前跨入小康、社会经济生活出现历史性重大变化的时期。

摘自《北京市国民经济和社会发展第十五年计划纲要》

国民经济持续快速健康发展

喜庆的北京夜晚

居民的"菜篮子"里四季鲜菜不断

充满生机的京郊大地

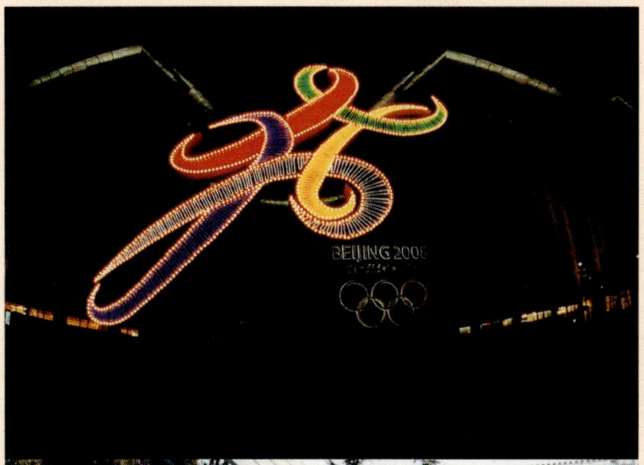

申奥标志耸立街头

绿色奥运科技奥运深入人心

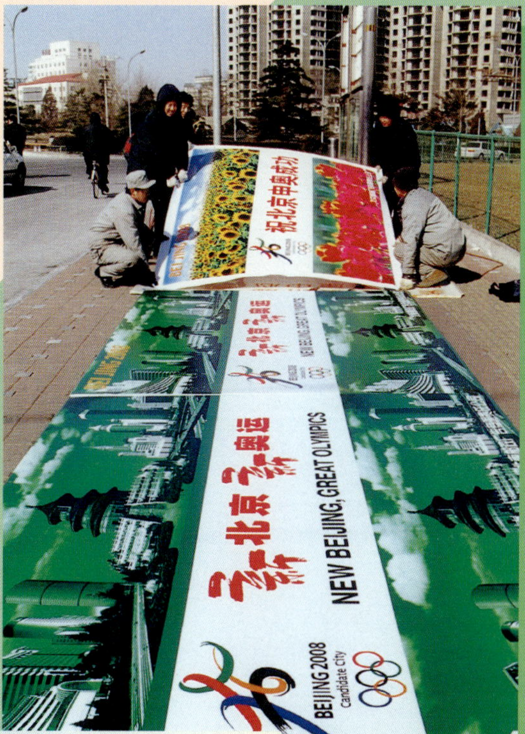

北京街头悬挂申奥宣传品

被评为"九十年代十大建筑之一的北京奥林匹克体育中心及亚运村

万众一心盼奥运 2008

北京市第五次

普查服务社

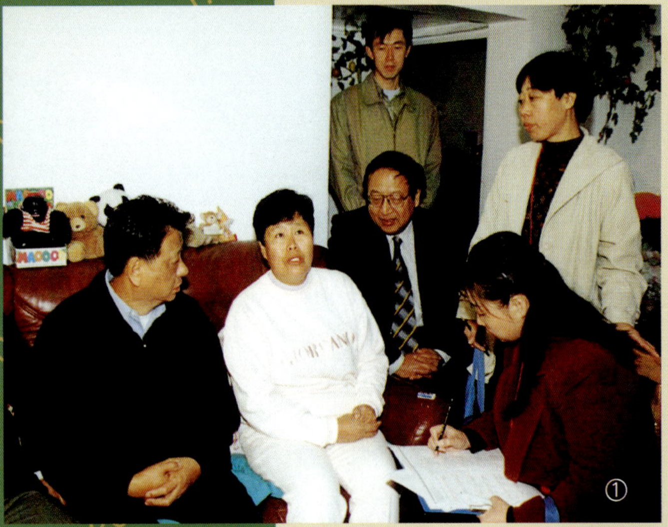

①

②

③

① 国务委员、国务院秘书长王忠禹同志、国家统计局局长朱之鑫同志到通州区入户检查人口普查登记工作

② 刘淇市长参加国务院第五次人口普查电视电话会议

③ 孟学农常务副市长参加国务院人口普查电视电话会议北京分会场会议

④ 孟学农常务副市长参加人口普查宣传咨询活动

⑤ 北京市统计局副局长、市人口普查办公室主任顾兖州接受外国记者有关人口普查问题的采访

④

⑤

全国人口普查取得圆满成功

会　社会支持普查

根据国务院的决定，我市于2000年11月1日进行了第五次全国人口普查的登记工作。在国务院和北京市政府的领导下，在全市各有关单位和广大人民群众的积极支持配合下，经过十万名普查工作人员的艰苦努力，圆满地完成了人口普查的现场登记和复查任务，主要数据的快速汇总工作已经结束。据快速汇总结果，全市总人口为1381.9万人，与1990年7月1日0时第四次全国人口普查的1081.9万人相比，十年零四个月共增加了300万人，增长27.7%。平均每年增加29万人，年平均增长率为2.4%。

摘自北京市统计局《2000年北京市第五次全国人口普查主要数据公报》

⑥ 中国人寿北分公司为北京所有人口普查工作人员提供人身意外伤害保险

⑦ 全国著名劳动模范李素丽义务为北京第五次人口普查拍摄电视公益广告

⑧ 朝阳区人口普查办公室举办人口普查知识竞赛

⑨ 北京市第五次全国人口普查新闻发布会

⑩ 北京市第五次全国人口普查办公室在全国最大的图书大厦——西单图书大厦向市民免费发放人口普查公报

北京市园林局大步跨

北京市园林局主要职责：研究拟订城市园林绿化地方性法规、规章草案及实施办法。研究拟订园林行业发展战略和方针政策；制定城市园林绿化发展规划和年度计划并监督实施；制定园林绿化专业规划和绿地系统详细规划；指导城区和有关部门制定园林绿化计划。组织审定重点园林绿化工程项目的规划设计方案，并负责监督实施；审核城市园林绿地和风景名胜区内建设项目的规划设计方案并监督实施；审核城市重点建设项目设计方案中的园林绿地比例和布局。负责本市新建公园和风景名胜区建设的立项、验收和定级工作；负责公园和风景名胜区资源的调查评估和等级评定工作；制定公园和风景名胜区的管理标准并组织实施；负责管理市属公园。负责绿化补偿费、居住区绿化建设费和公共绿地建设费的收缴管理工作；依法审批占用城市绿地和伐移城市树木事项；负责园林绿化的行政执法工作。制定园林绿化养护的质量等级、定额标准和古树名木保护等级标准，组织重点绿地养护的招标工作并监督实施。

进新世纪

认定园林绿化设计、施工和养护单位资质；制定园林绿化建设项目的工程质量标准、定额标准并组织实施。负责群众性园林绿化工作；宣传动员、组织指导单位和个人认养绿地的活动；负责组织园林绿化检查和宣传工作；组织园林绿化成果普查和资源调查评估工作。制定园林绿化科技发展规划、科研计划并组织重点科研项目研究 组织科技成果鉴定、申报和推广工作；开展生物多样性保护工作。制定园林绿化行业人才培养规划并组织实施；负责组织园林专业教育和岗位培训工作；负责园林专业技术职称、等级的考核评定工作。

2000年市园林局计划植树170万株，种草100万平方米，完成绿化面积2550公顷。实际完成植树1199万株（城区187万株、隔离地区1012万株），种草215万平方米，完成绿化面积2929公顷（隔离地区绿化2666公顷、城市其它绿化263公顷）。完成宣武区手帕口北街绿地、朝阳区阳光广场绿地、水碓绿地、海淀区中华世纪坛绿地、石景山绿化广场等11块总面积34.35公顷的城市集中大绿地的建设。各办事处500平方米小绿地建设任务完成110处，总面积14公顷。全市160个单位庭院和60个居住小区进行了绿化美化整治，居住区新增绿化面积87公顷。完成长河、双紫支渠、京密引水渠昆玉段等水系配套绿化美化工程，新增绿地65公顷。对中关村路（原白颐路）等重点大街结合环境综合整治进行了绿化美化改造。

绿染

▲ 绿化广场

▲ 小区绿地

◀ 街道绿地

首都绿化委员会办公室

京城

▲ 绿色通道

▲ 西单文化广场

首都绿化委员会办公室
百花山人工造
密云水库水源涵养林
福荫

▲ 滨河公园

▲ 河道绿化

◀ 城市隔离地区绿化

百姓

构筑地

推

北京城市铁路已于1999年底开工，目前已进入紧张的施工高潮，预计2002年6月西段建成运营。

国务院和北京市有关领导为北京城市铁路开工奠基

复八线建成通车典礼

地铁总公司在古城车辆段实行轮乘制改革试点

北京市地下铁道总公司

下动脉

动京城飞奔

北京地下铁道是我国第一条现代化城市交通设施。建成通车三十年来，对缓解首都交通压力，方便人民生活，促进首都城市建设和经济发展发挥了重要的作用。

北京市地下铁道总公司是一个现代化技术密集型的国有大型企业，具有地上、地下建筑，车辆、供电、通信、信号、线路、机电设备、列车运行和行车组织自动化系统等各类专业技术；拥有整套自动化程度较高的行车指挥和运行保安系统 有独立的供电系统、通信系统、空气调节系统、给排水和照明系统。

北京地铁现有一号线和环线，共计54公里，39个运营车站。年运量4.8亿人次，日均运量120万人次。总运量占全市公交总量的12.1%。北京市地铁目前在按照北京市总体规划方案中城市轨道交通的网络规划，加快建设步伐，在新世纪初，将陆续建成40.8公里的北京城市铁路，17公里的八通线和27.7公里的地铁五号线。

新世纪、新北京、新地铁。北京地铁在未来的五至十年内将有一个突飞猛进的发展，将成为首都现代化交通的重要骨干。

铁车辆厂制造新型地铁WVF电动客车

本版由北京市地下铁道总公司供稿

文/摄 贾 鹏 李传利

绿岸穿南北 碧水绕京城

北京是座依水而建的文明古都，又是因水而兴的现代国际化大都市。1998年4月至2000年9月，北京市组织了城市水系中心区综合治理工程，通过清淤、截污，水利设施新建和改造、拆迁、绿化等措施，先后治理了北线的长河、双紫支渠、六海、筒子河、昆玉河、南线的玉渊潭经南护城河到高碑店湖。治理河道50公里，湖泊13处，清淤190万方，改扩建闸、桥、坝等建筑物27座，铺设污水管线60公里，增加水面15万平方米，形成绿地150公顷。开辟露天游泳场6处，接待群众40万人次。昆明湖至北京展览馆后湖，昆明湖至玉渊潭，玉渊潭经南护城河至高碑店湖共36公里河道实现通航，累计接待游客35万人次。水系沿线的水利文物进行了有效保护。“水清、流畅、岸绿、通航”的治理目标已经实现。

按照首都总体规划要求，城市周边地区的水环境治理工作已经展开，“绿岸穿南北、碧水绕京城”的景观已开始实现。

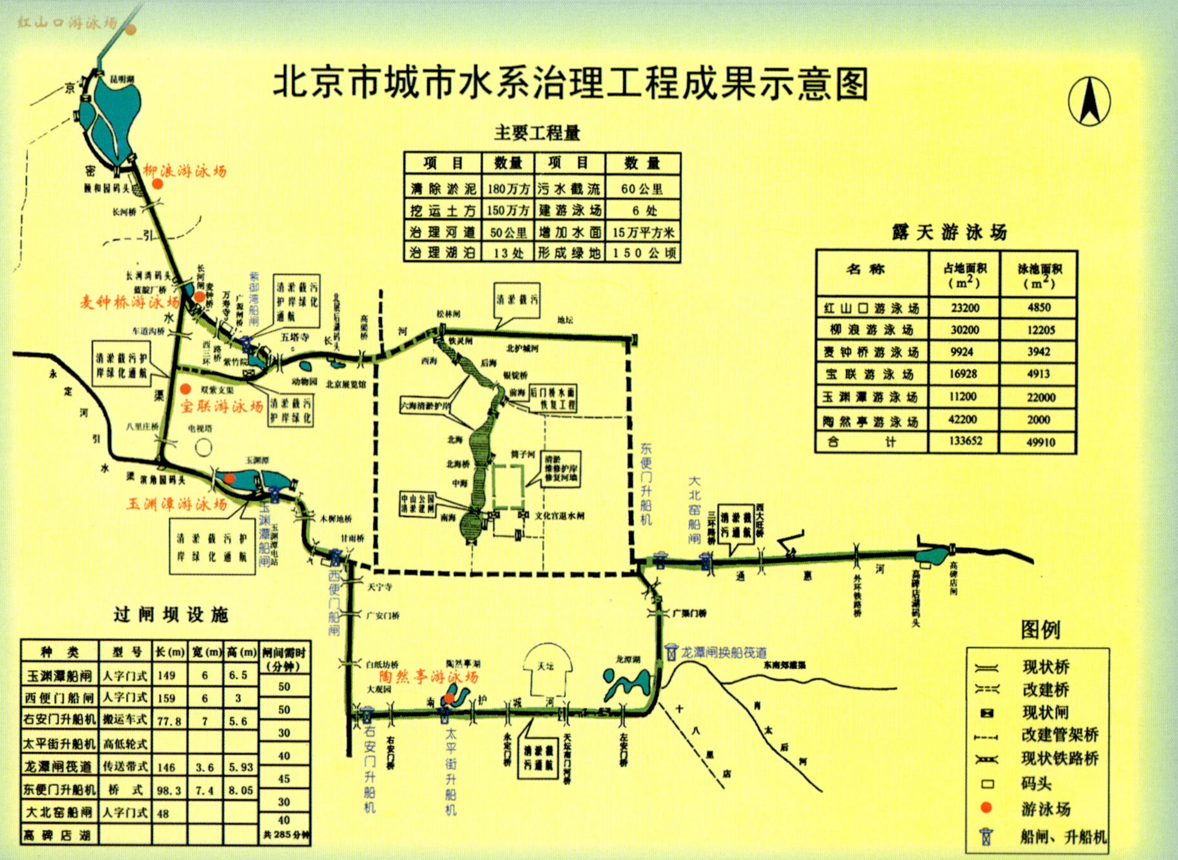

主要工程量

项目	数量	项目	数量
清除淤泥	180万方	污水截流	60公里
挖运土方	150万方	建游泳场	6处
治理河道	50公里	增加水面	15万平方米
治理湖泊	13处	形成绿地	150公顷

露天游泳场

名称	占地面积（m^2）	泳池面积（m^2）
红山口游泳场	23200	4850
柳浪游泳场	30200	12205
麦钟桥游泳场	9924	3942
宝联游泳场	16928	4913
玉渊潭游泳场	11200	22000
陶然亭游泳场	42200	2000
合计	133652	49910

过闸坝设施

种类	型号	长(m)	宽(m)	高(m)	闸间需时（分钟）
玉渊潭船闸	人字门式	149	6	6.5	50
西便门船闸	人字门式	159	6	3	50
右安门升船机	搬运车式	77.8	7	5.6	30
太平街升船机	高低轮式				40
龙潭闸筏道	传送带式	146	3.6	5.93	45
东便门升船机	桥式	98.3	7.4	8.05	30
大北窑船闸	人字门式	48			40
高碑店湖					共285分钟

北京市水利局

① 市委书记贾庆林同志参观农机精品展

② 岳福洪副市长参观北京市农业局小汤山特菜基地

新职能、新作风、新形象

——北京市农业局

③ 农业部领导考察北京市“放心菜”销售试点专柜

④ 北京市农作物引种育种中心

政府机构改革后，随着畜牧、水产、农机政府职能的划入，北京市农业局迎来了历史进程中的又一个春天，成为主管本市种植业、畜牧业、水产业和农业机械化工作的市政府直属机构，承担着农业行政执法、科技推广、质量检测和信息服务等方面的职能。

2000年，北京市农业局的科技人员和干部、职工为全面提高郊区农业整体水平，大力推进农业结构战略性调整，加快农民增收步伐，使郊区农业实现“九五”计划的战略目标做出应有的贡献。

北京郊区种植业由传统二元结构向三元结构转变，蔬菜种植面积发展到90万亩，花卉、药材种植面积突破了10万亩，饲草种植面积达到27.7万亩。养殖业发展快速，产值占大农业产值比重达到50%。“六种农业”收效显著，实现净增加值10亿元，比上年翻一番。农业科技的推广应用和先进技术装备水平明显提高，近11万农民经过培训获得绿色证书。北京大力发展绿色农业，在全国率先启动农产品安全体系建设。农业局作为执法主体的法律、法规、规章共87部，农业执法力度加大，执法行为规范，有效地保护农民的合法利益。

春风又绿京郊大地，北京市农业局的新思路、新作风、新形象在为京郊率先基本实现农业现代化的征途中发挥更大的作用。

“九五”期间，北京市种植业、畜牧业、水产业蓬勃发展

北京迈向国际一流旅游城市

改革开放20多年来，北京旅游业迅猛发展，已具备了相当的产业规模，形成了国际旅游为中心、国内旅游为基础，二者并重发展的格局。

北京市人民政府在《关于同意<北京市旅游发展总体规划>》的批复中指出：“旅游业是符合北京城市性质，适合首都特点的重要产业，是首都经济新的增长点。加快旅游业发展，对推动全市经济增长，提高市民生活质量，保护古都风貌和历史文化资源，建设现代化国际城市具有重要意义。各区县政府、各有关部门要加强协作，密切配合，积极支持旅游业的发展，保证《旅游总体规划》的顺利实施。”

按照《北京市旅游发展总体规划》，北京市在“十五”期间至2020年旅游业发展的总体目标是：将北京建设成为具有东方特色的一流国际旅游城市和具有首都风貌的国内首位旅游中心城市。

北京统计年鉴

BEIJING STATISTICAL YEARBOOK

2001

北京市统计局编

COMPILED BY BEIJING
MUNICIPAL STATISTICAL BUREAU

中国统计出版社
China Statistics Press

(京)新登字 041 号

图书在版编目（CIP）数据

北京统计年鉴，2001/北京市统计局编.-北京：中国统计出版社，2001.7
ISBN 7-5037-3495-7

Ⅰ.北… Ⅱ.北… Ⅲ.社会经济统计-统计资料-北京-2001-年鉴 Ⅳ.C832.1-54

中国版本图书馆 CIP 数据核字（2001）第 028988 号

北京统计年鉴-2001

作　　者/ 北京市统计局
责任编辑/ 蔡启新
E-mail/ yearbook@stats.gov.cn
出版发行/ 中国统计出版社
通信地址/ 北京市西城区三里河月坛南街 75 号　中国统计出版社
电　　话/（010）63262295
印　　刷/ 北京理工大学印刷厂
经　　销/ 新华书店
开　　本/ 889×1194 毫米/ 16 开本
字　　数/ 200 万字
印　　张/ 44.25 印张　　彩插/3 印张
印　　数/ 0001-2000 册
版　　别/ 2001 年 6 月第 1 版
版　　次/ 2001 年 6 月第 1 次印刷
书　　号/ ISBN 7-5037-3495-7/C・1867
定　　价/ 280.00 元

中国统计版图书，版权所有，侵权必究。

中国统计版图书，如有印装错误，本社发行部负责调换。

《北京统计年鉴》编辑委员会

主　　任：唐　龙、柳纪纲

副 主 任：邹兰春、徐　风、潘　璠、顾兖州、王晓沙、侯小维、韩暖生

编辑委员：（以姓氏笔画为序）

刁满庆、刘亚力、刘建伟、李　萍、李宏丽、邬春仙、吴万标、邵建民、张继斌、郑　新、潘健民、魏小真

总 编 辑：于秀琴

责任编辑：张雪原、朱燕南

编辑人员：丁文斌、王　敏、邢志宏、石平平、虞京平、栗瑞梅、李艳春、庞江倩、胡欣洁、乔丽娜、马云松、王乐强、孟素洁、张小洁、朱亦军、孔　雷、周　博、周　锐、穆卫红、杨朝宇、李力红、邢宏丽、贾　薇、金顺爱、张培农、程书芳、周　娟、王顺昌、肖玉清、杨莅群、王孝廉、刘小红、何建红、高　云、崔小凤、牛小慧、张　健、邓永旭、任　虹、刘红红、薛清华、王宝生、钱　岩、郎　华、毕宁宁、林　涛、王丽英、夏沁芳

英文翻译：朱燕南

统计图绘制：朱燕南

彩页设计：张雪原

Editorial Board and Staff

Ⅰ. Editorial Board

Chairman: Tang Long, Liu Jigang

Vice-chairmen: Zou Lanchun, Xu Feng, Pan Fan, Gu Yanzhou, Wang Xiaosha, Hou Xiaowei, Han Nuansheng

Editorial Board: (in order of strokes of Chinese surname)

Diao Manqing, Liu Yali, Liu Jianwei, Li Ping, Li Hongli, Wu Chunxian, Wu Wanbiao, Shao Jianmin, Zhang Jibin, Zheng Xin, Pan Jianmin, Wei Xiaozhen

Ⅱ.Editorial Staff

Editor-in-chief: Yu Xiuqin

Coordinator: Zhang Xueyuan，Zhu Yannan

Editorial Staff: Ding Wenbin, Wang Min, Xing Zhihong, Shi Pingping, Yu Jingping, Li Ruimei, Li Yanchun, Pang Jiangqian, Hu Xinjie, Qiao Lina, Ma Yunsong, Wang Leqiang, Meng Sujie, Zhang Xiaojie, Zhu Yijun, Kong Lei, Zhou Bo, Zhou Rui, Mu Weihong, Yang Zhaoyu, Li Lihong, Xing Hongli, Jia Wei, Jin Shunai,Zhang Peinong, Cheng Shufang, Zhou Juan, Wang Shunchang, Xiao Yuqing, Yang Liqun, Wang Xiaolian, Liu Xiaohong, He Jianhong, Gao Yun, Cui Xiaofeng, Niu Xiaohui, Zhang Jian, Deng Yongxu, Ren Hong, Liu Honghong, Xue Qinghua, Wang Baosheng, Qian Yan, Lang Hua, Bi Ningning, Lin Tao, Wang Liying, Xia Qinfang

English Translator: Zhu Yannan

Statistical Chart: Zhu Yannan

Color Page Design: Zhang Xueyuan

编 辑 说 明

1、《北京统计年鉴》是一部按年连续出版的大型统计资料书。本书通过大量的统计数据，真实地记录了北京市一年来社会经济和科技方面的发展变化情况，是国内外各界人士了解北京认识北京的重要资料工具书。

2、《北京统计年鉴—2001》为全部中英文对照版；并配有电子版统计年鉴，具备制图和快速查询的功能，而且可通过转换键实现中英文切换，以增强图书版统计年鉴的功能，满足各方面读者的爱好和习惯，紧跟当前电子信息化的步伐。内容上增加了第五次人口普查手工汇总资料、个体私营经济资料、新建体育场馆资料、环境保护资料、最低生活保障、工资及失业保障金资料，丰富了旅游事业统计内容，并根据实际情况调整了少量统计指标和统计表。每个细目都针对主要指标制作了统计图并编排了指标解释。

3、年鉴正文分为两部分——文章选编和统计图表。第一部分登载了北京市2000年暨“九五”期间国民经济和社会发展统计公报和2000年北京市第五次全国人口普查主要数据公报；第二部分统计图表分综合，人口，劳动力和工资，固定资产投资及房地产业，农业和农村经济，工业，能源生产和消费，建筑业，交通运输、邮电通信业，批发零售贸易及餐饮业，对外经济贸易，旅游业，金融、保险，物价，教育、文化，科技，卫生、体育，城市公用事业，人民生活，社会福利、政法及其他，服务业，企业及企业集团情况，开发区情况，区县资料等24个细目；在附录部分中还分列了北京市自改革开放以来的主要经济数据、各类市场情况、世界各国及香港、澳门资料等。

4、本年鉴的资料来源大部分为年度统计报表，部分来自抽样调查，世界各国及香港、澳门数据来自相关统计资料。

5、本年鉴对以前发表的统计资料重新进行了核实，相应地调整了部分数据。读者在使用历史资料时，如数据有出入，请以本年鉴为准。

6、本年鉴采用的国民经济行业分类是按照中华人民共和国国家标准《国民经济行业分类和代码》划分的；登记注册类型是按照1998年9月国家统计局、国家工商行政管理局颁发的《关于划分企业登记注册类型的规定》划分的；使用的度量衡单位均采用国家统一的标准计量单位。

7、统计资料若无年份说明，均为2000年当年数据。

8、各表分组数相加与总计数略有差额，因四舍五入之故。

9、本年鉴使用的符号说明：“…”表示数据不足该表最小单位数；“空格”表示该项指标数据不详或没有数据；“#”表示其中项。

Preface

1. Beijing Statistical Yearbook is a regular large-scale statistical reference book published yearly. With a vast amount of statistical data, the book can keep you abreast of new developments in Beijing on various aspects, including society, science and technology, etc.. It is really an important and efficient reference book for people of various circles in and outside China to know and understand Beijing.

2. Based on the original style, Beijing Statistical Yearbook 2001 is a radical revision of its predecessor.

• To support the opening to outside of Beijing and meet the foreigners' needs for their business and investment in Beijing, Beijing Statistical Yearbook 2001 is published in complete Chinese-English edition.

• To meet various interests and habits of users and reinforce the functions of the yearbook, Beijing Statistical Yearbook 2001 has its electronic edition published simultaneously with additional functions like charting, quick search, shift between Chinese and English in search by Shift key, etc..

• The content is enriched by additions on the statistics for hand-collection of the 2000 population census of Beijing, individual and private economy, newly-built stadiums and gymnasiums, environment protection, lowest wage,cost-of-living and unemployment insurance, and add some statistics in tourism chapter.

• For the convenience of using, chart and explanatory of main indicators are added to every chapter.

3. The yearbook has two parts: Articles and Statistical Graph. The first part consists of Statistical Communiqué on the 2000 (the Period of the 9`th Five-year Plan)National Economic and Social Development of Beijing and Communiqué on Major Figures of the 2000 Population Census of Bijing. The second part consists of all the 24 chapters concerning General Survey, Population, Labor Force and Wage, Investment in Fixed Assets and Real Estate, Agriculture and Rural Economy, Industry, Energy Production and Consumption, Construction, Transportation, Posts and Telecommunications, Wholesale, Retail and Catering Trades, Foreign Economy and Trade, Tourism, Banking and Insurance, Price, Education and Culture, Technology, Health and Sports, Municipal Public Utilities, People's Livelihood, Social Welfare, Politics, Law and Others, Services, Statistics for Enterprise and enterprise Group, Beijing Development Zone,General Survey of Districts and Counties, etc.. You can find also in the second part as the content of appendix that the economic data from 1978 to 2000, conditions of various markets and data of counties and territories ,Hongkong and Macao, etc..

4. Most of data in this yearbook sources are from annual reports, a small part sources form sample survey, data of countries, Hongkong and Macao from some related statistics.

5. Some of the published data are changed in this yearbook according to our checking, therefore, data in this yearbook are reliable whenever you find different data in other publications.

6. The sector classification of national economy in this yearbook is in line with State Standard Classification and Code of National Economy by Sector of the People's Republic of China. The classification of registration status is in line with the Provisions on Classification of Registration Status of Enterprises issued by State Statistical Bureau and State Administrative Bureau for Industry and Commerce. The units of weights and measures adopted in the yearbook are all national standard units of weights and measures.

7. Data of each table refers to that of 2000 if there is no year mark.

8. Sum of numbers of each group may be not equal to the total because of rounding up.

9. Special symbols in this yearbook: "…" indicates the amount is too small to be recorded in the table; " blank space" indicates missing case; "#" indicates an item(indicator) among the previous one.

目　录
CONTENTS

文章选编
ARTICLES

统计图表
STATISTICAL GRAPH AND CHART

综　合
GENERAL SURVEY

主要统计指标统计图

GRAPH OF MAIN STATISTICAL INDICATORS

批发零售贸易业及餐饮业

WHOLESALE，RETAIL AND CATERING

科 技

SCIENCE AND TECHNOLOGY

社会福利、政法及其他

SOCIAL WELFARE，POLITICS AND LAW AND OTHERS

北京统计年鉴——2001

BEIJING STATISTICAL YEARBOOK

文 章 选 编

A R T I C L E S

北京市统计局2000年暨“九五”期间
国民经济和社会发展统计公报

2001年2月2日

2000年，在市委、市政府的领导下，全市人民团结进取，奋发努力，在扩大内需、调整结构和深化改革等各方面取得显著成效，全市经济持续、快速、健康增长，社会发展全面进步，就业形势基本稳定，人民生活水平继续提高，全面完成了“九五”计划，提前实现了现代化建设第二步战略目标。在经济发展中，结构调整的任务还很艰巨，经济增长的质量有待进一步提高。

一、综合经济

经济实力：经济增长步伐继续加快。2000年全市实现国内生产总值2460.5亿元，比上年增长11%，经济增长率连续四年稳步上升。人均国内生产总值达到2.2万元（折合美元2700美元），比上年增长10.3%，比1995年增长61%。全面完成了“九五”时期经济和社会发展计划，五年间，全市经济年均增速达到10%；全市国内生产总值累计超过10000亿元，比“八五”时期增加1.2倍（现价）。

经济结构：产业结构调整取得明显成效。全市第一产业实现增加值90亿元，比上年增长4%，初步结束了长期低速徘徊的局面；第二产业935.8亿元，增长11.4%；第三产业1434.7亿元，增长11.1%，增速减缓的局面初步扭转。农业、工业和第三产业增速分别比上年提高1.5、0.4和2个百分点。三次产业比重由1995年的5.8%、44.1%和50.1%变化为3.7%、38%和58.3%，第三产业比重继续提高。五年间，第一、第二和第三产业年均增速分别为1.2%、9.7%和11%。

所有制结构逐步完善。在全市国内生产总值中，国有、集体经济所占比重从1995年的80.4%下降到2000年的68.2%，其中国有经济比重仍然高达57.5%，特别是在交通运输、邮电通信、金融保险等国民经济的重要行业和关键领域，国有经济比重均在95%以上。国有、集体经济以外的其他所有制经济发展势头强劲，增加值比重从1995年的19.6%迅速上升到31.8%，年均增速高达23.3%，比国有、集体经济年均增速高17.9个百分点，对经济增长的贡献率从1995年的40.2%上升到58.4%。

三大需求：投资与消费需求进一步扩大，外需不足的矛盾出现明显缓解。

固定资产投资需求：以政府为主导的投资继续对启动经济发挥重要作用。为增加投资促进经济增长，市政府近两年相继确定了67项和50项重点工程，全年完成全社会固定资产投资1297.4亿元，比上年增长10.8%，其中地方投资完成979.5亿元，增长17.8%。全市在实施扩大内需的三年间累计投资达到3623.6亿元，年均增速为11.9%，投资重点是城市基础设施项目和房地产项目，分别占投资总规模的26.9%和36.5%。“九五”期间，全社会累计投资总量达到5461.7亿元，相当于“八五”时期全市投资总量的2.3倍，城市面貌发生了巨变。

消费需求：最终消费需求趋向活跃。全年实现社会消费品零售额1443.3亿元，比上年增长9.9%，扣除价格因素，实际增长11.1%。城市、农村消费市场同步增长，城镇实现消费品零售额1231.1亿元，增长9.8%，农村实现212.2亿元，增长10.7%。“九五”期间消费呈现稳步发展势头，五年累计实现社会消费品零售额5927亿元，比“八五”时期增长1.1倍，年平均增长11.8%。消费结构升级，消费领域扩大。以“吃穿用”为主的商品消费比重从九十年代初期的90%左右下降到60%左右，服务性消费比重上升到40%左右。住房“货币化”取代福利分房，激活了住宅消费市场。全年实现商品房销售额470.7亿元，比上年增长53.1%；个人住宅销售额336.4亿元，占商品房销售额的71.5%，比上年增长1.6倍，反映出房地产业从投资和消费两个方面对经济增长的促进作用。

出口需求：外贸出口高速增长。全市海关出口总额达到119.7亿美元，比上年增长20.8%；地方企业出口46.3亿美元，比上年增长41.8%，增速分别比上年提高26.7和26.6个百分点。经济外向度有所提高，地方企业出口额占全市国内生产总值的比重达到16%，比1995年提高2.5个百分点。机电产品出口占50%以上，主要是电子及通信产品。

市场价格：价格止跌回升，通货紧缩趋势得到有效遏制。居民消费价格指数为103.5%，比上年提高2.9个百分点。零售价格指数为98.9%，下降的幅度大大减小。工业品出厂价格指数为102.5%，比上年提高4.8个百分点。

增长质量：经济运行质量有所改善。社会劳动生产率有所提高，全年为40073元/人，按现价计算，比上年增长14%；其中，第一产业12178.6元/人，增长3.8%；第二产业43607元/人，增长12.2%；第三产业44077元/人，增长15.8%。

地方财政收入持续快速增长。全年地方财政收入342.4亿元，比上年增长22.7%。其中，增值税、营业税、企业所得税、个人所得税全面增长，增幅分别为15.7%、15.7%、16.2%和22.9%。“九五”期间累计实现财政收入1182亿元，比“八五”时期增加1.5倍，年均增速达到24.3%。

国有大中型企业改制脱困“三年两目标”全面实现。190户国有大中型骨干企业提前一个月完成改制目标，153个企业初步建立了现代企业制度，企业改制面达到80.5%。列入三年脱困目标的400户国有及国有控股大中型工业企业经济效益回升，全年经济效益综合指数为115.98%；实现利润51.7亿元，比上年增长38.4%；亏损企业明显减少，年末亏损企业亏损面为14.5%。

科技进步：经济增长的科技含量提高。科技进步对全市经济增长的贡献率达52.5%，比1995年提高9.4个百分点。其中第一产业科技进步贡献率达54.6%，提高了7个百分点；第二产业47.7%，提高6.2个百分点；第三产业52.9%，提高9个百分点。

国务院《关于建设中关村科技园区有关问题的批复》极大地促进了中关村科技园区的发展，新的创业热潮蓬勃兴起。全年新认定高新技术企业2261家，比上年增长1倍，累计已达8224家；全区高新技术企业完成增加值326亿元，比上年增长44.2%（现价）；上缴税费61.7亿元，增长51.2%。出口创汇19.4亿美元，增长1倍。

二、城市建设

基础设施投资：基础设施的瓶颈制约明显缓解。全年完成基础设施投资351.9亿元，比上年增长16.3%，占全市固定资产投资的比重为29.5%，比上年上升1.3个百分点。50项重点工程建设进展顺利，到年末开工项目47个，其中12个项目基本建成。全年完成重点项目投资245.3亿元，占全市投资的20.6%。“九五”期间累计完成基础设施投资达到1382.1亿元，比“八五”期间增长1.8倍，年均增长19.7%。地铁复八线、平安大街、京昌、京沈高速公路等一批道路工程全面完成。

环境保护和治理：环境保护和治理取得重要进展。能源结构改善，全年低硫煤使用量达到500万吨。严格机动车排放标准，日夜路检合格率超过80%。实施降尘绿化措施，防治颗粒物污染，空气质量明显好转，全年空气污染指数三级及好于三级的天气天数占全年天数的93.7%，二级和好于二级的天数达到48.4%。二氧化硫、二氧化氮、总悬浮颗粒物、一氧化碳浓度分别比上年下降11%、8%、3%和7%。工业污染源全部达标排放，5000多家污染工业企业完成达标验收。城市水系环境治理进展顺利，初步实现了“水清、岸绿、流畅、通航”。玉渊潭、南护城河、通惠河—高碑店湖的水系综合整治任务完成并实现通航。全市污水处理率达到40%，比1995年提高20.6个百分点；年末城市垃圾无害化处理率达到81.5%，比1995年提高60个百分点。积极开展大规模和高标准绿化工作。市区绿化隔离带增加2666公顷。年末，全市城市人均占有公共绿地9.7平方米；全市林木覆盖率43%，城市绿化覆盖率36.5 %。加强城市环境综合整治，市容市貌明显改观。大范围改善首都圈生态环境的工作开始起步。

公共交通：公共交通能力显著增强。年末，全市公共交通运营车辆达到1.35万辆，比1995年增加近8000辆；客运出租车营运车辆达到6.5万辆，比1995年增加8000多辆。公交运营线路总长度接近17000公里，比1995年增长2.7倍，其中公共交通总公司当年新辟公共电汽车线路49条，调整延长线路52条。城市公共交通共运送乘客40.8亿人次（不含出租车），其中公共电汽车运送乘客34.7亿人次，占85%；地铁4.4亿人次，占10.8%；出租汽车客运量6.2亿人次。

公用事业：城市公用事业稳步发展。全年自来水销售量8亿吨，比1995年增加1亿吨；集中供热面积达到10000万平方米，比1995年增加近3000万平方米；全年用电量达到330亿千瓦小时，比1995年增长48%；燃气用户295.7万户，比1995年增加60万户。

三、主要行业

农业：农业结构调整取得成效。全市农业增加值比上年增长4%，是“九五”以来增速最高的年份，比1995年增长8%。农业总产值中养殖业比重达到50.6%，比1995年提高5个百分点。各类经济作物占用耕地面积的比重由1995年的21%上升到28%。全年粮食产量为144.2万吨，主要农副产品产量实现较大幅度提高，肉类、蔬菜、牛奶产量均比上年增长10%以上。涌现了以“锦绣大地”为代表的一批闻名全国的现代农业示范基地。

工业：整体实力和竞争力明显增强。全市工业实现增加值737亿元，比上年增长13.2%。“九五”期间工业年平均增速达到9.9%，五年累计实现增加值3126.8亿元，比“八五”时期增长74.5 %（现价）。

高新技术产业成为带动工业增长的龙头。全年高新技术产业实现工业增加值213.5亿元，占全市工业的比重为28.9%，比上年上升3.5个百分点；占全市国内生产总值的比重达到8.6%，比上年提高1个百分点，对工业增长的贡献率保持在60%左右。

工业增长中近40%靠出口生产带动。全市工业企业完成出口产值310.1亿元，比上年增长1.3倍，占全市工业的比重达到13.6%，同比提高6.4个百分点。出口的工业品以电子通信产品为主。

国有及国有控股工业快速发展。全年国有及国有控股工业企业实现增加值达到 512.8 亿元，比上年增长 17.2%，占全市工业的比重达到 74.3%。外商及港澳台企业成为推动工业增长的重要力量，全年实现增加值 311.4 亿元，增长 24.6%，占全市工业的比重达到 45.1%。

工业经济效益状况全面好转。全市规模以上工业实现销售收入 2575.7 亿元，比上年增长 31.6%。工业产销率达到 98.51%，比上年提高 1.74 个百分点。工业经济效益综合指数达到 117.9%，比上年提高 12.2 个百分点。实现利润 110.8 亿元，比上年增长 65.5%，其中盈利企业盈利额为 147.3 亿元，增长 39.8%，亏损企业亏损额 36.4 亿元，下降 5 %。

建筑业：建筑业稳步发展。全年建筑业实现增加值 198.8 亿元，比上年增长 2.1 %。"九五"期间累计实现增加值 857.8 亿元，比"八五"期间增加 1.3 倍。全市建筑施工面积 6995.9 万平方米，比上年增长 6.7%，比 1995 年增长 26.6%；竣工面积 2358.2 万平方米，比上年增长 1.6%，五年累计竣工 9644.3 万平方米，比"八五"期间增长 55.4%。强化建筑工程招投标制，加强合同管理，全市取得合法开工手续的招标工程的合同备案率达到 100%。工程质量明显提高，全市工程优良品率达 55.3%，比上年提高 6.1 个百分点。加强建筑队伍管理，积极发展专业施工企业。年末，全市拥有四级及四级以上的建筑施工企业 1771 个，比 1995 年末增长 11.6 %。全市建筑企业施工科技含量提高，技术装备率和动力装备率分别达到 8233 元/人和 6 千瓦/人，比 1995 年增长 38.4%和 93.5%。

交通运输业：交通运输业发展出现新格局。全年交通运输业实现增加值 69.5 亿元，比上年增长 6%。全年货物运输量 27827.9 万吨，比上年下降 1.6%；旅客运输量 18526.7 万人次，比上年增长 24.6%。"九五"期间，公路运量分别占货运量的 90.8%和客运量的 62%；铁路运量占货运量的 8.9%和客运量的 31.6%。

邮电通信业：邮电通信业持续高速发展。全年实现增加值 123.4 亿元，比上年增长 21%。全年邮电业务总量达到 219.5 亿元，比上年增长 39.1%。订销报纸 15.2 亿份，发送函件 5.8 亿件，收寄特快专递 790 万件，分别比上年增长 4.1%、5.5%和 1.7%。年末全市公众网固定电话交换机容量达 630 万门，比上年增长 12.7%。年末全市固定电话用户 439 万户，移动电话用户 266 万户，分别比上年增长 16.8 %和 43%。全市公众网固定电话普及率达到 50.8 部/百人，其中市区电话普及率达到 66.4 部/百人，分别比上年增长 11.9%和 9%。随着科学技术水平的提高和数字化网络化经济进入中国市场，电子政务、电子商务等数字技术迅猛发展，年末电子计算机互联网用户达到 56.3 万户。全市信息化水平居于全国首位。

商业：多元化竞争格局促进商业持续繁荣。全年批发零售贸易和餐饮业实现增加值 222.6 亿元，比上年增长 6.9%。"九五"期间累计实现增加值 1030.4 亿元，比"八五"时期扩大 75.8%。贸易流通量扩大。全年社会商品购进总值 2808.4 亿元，增长 20.7%；商品销售总值 3263.2 亿元，增长 22.5%。与 1995 年相比，商品购进总值增长 60.7%，商品销售总值增长 80%。大中型商业企业经济效益有所改善，实现销售收入 2300.7 亿元，比上年增长 23.4 %；实现利润 34.7 亿元，增长 50.6 %。

新型商业快速发展。到年末，全市以超市便利店为主体的连锁企业达 127 家，连锁店铺近 1300 家。五年间，全市商业总体布局和商业设施按照国际化、现代化大都市的要求发展，形成多处有较大规模、有良好购物环境和文化氛围的商业文化中心。

金融保险业：金融业稳健有序发展。全年金融保险业实现增加值 378.2 亿元，比上年增长 16.9%。金融存款稳定增加，年末全市地方级金融机构存款余额 9705 亿元，比年初增加 1434.7 亿元，新增额比上年增长 0.4%。贷款力度加大，年末全市贷款余额 5944.6 亿元，比年初增加 1116.1 亿元，新增额比上年增长 99.5%。全年累计回笼现金 167.2 亿元，比上年增长 3.2 倍。

保险市场稳步发展。全年完成国内外保险业务收入 88 亿元，比上年增长 1.8%，比 1995 年增长 2.3 倍。人身险实现保费收入 58.1 亿元，比上年下降 2.3%；财产险实现保费收入 30 亿元，增长 10.6%。全年保险理赔总额 18.7 亿元，比上年下降 41.5%；综合赔付率 21.3%。

证券交易量大幅增长。全年证券交易机构实现交易额 14457 亿元，比上年增长 32.5%；其中股票交易额 9136.5 亿元，增长 66%；国债交易额 600 亿元，增长 6.6%。全年证券市场融资 480.3 亿元。

房地产业：供需市场全面活跃。全年实现增加值 80.4 亿元，比上年增长 14.6%。全年完成房地产投资 522.1 亿元，比上年增长 23.9%，占全社会固定资产投资的比重达到 40.2%。五年累计完成房地产投资 1979.5 亿元，比"八五"时期增长 2.5 倍。全年房地产施工面积 4455 万平方米；竣工面积 1365.6 万平方米。五年累计竣工 4762.6 万平方米，比"八五" 时期增长 1.3 倍。

商品房市场交易活跃。全年销售商品房 955.8 万平方米，比上年增长 75.6%；其中销售商品住宅 897.1 万平方米，增长 85.1%。"九五"期间累计销售商品房 2415.6 万平方米，比"八五"期间增长 1.8 倍；其中销售商品住宅 2198 万平方米，增长 1.7 倍。五年实现商品房销售额 1250.5 亿元，比"八五"期间增长 4.6 倍；其中销售商品住宅 1031.5 亿元，增长 4.4 倍。

四、外向型经济

外贸进出口：外贸进出口规模进一步扩大。据海关统计，全年全市完成进出口总值496.2亿美元，比上年增长44.4%。"九五"期间累计进出口总值为1741.9亿美元，其中出口总值为501.1亿美元。地方企业进出口总值116.5亿美元，比上年增长38.8%；"九五"期间进出口377.7亿美元，比"八五"期间增长88.9%；其中出口152.7亿美元，比"八五"期间增长71.9%。

利用外资：利用外资工作取得显著成绩。全年全市新批外资项目1149项，合同外资金额43.4亿美元，分别比上年增长77.6%和1.4倍。实际利用外资完成30.1亿美元，比上年增长2.5 %。"九五"时期，共签订利用外资项目4100项，协议外资金额129.8亿美元，项目平均规模达316.6万美元，比"八五"时期扩大200多万美元。实际利用外资五年累计达136.7亿美元，比"八五"时期增长1.4倍。利用外资在形式上更加多样化，初步形成了全方位、多层次、宽领域开放格局。

对外承包工程和劳务合作：对外服务贸易领域又有新的拓展。全年新签对外承包工程和劳务合作合同额1.61亿美元，完成营业额1.98亿美元。年末在外人数1169人。

旅游：旅游业健康发展。全年接待海外旅游者282.1万人次，比上年增长11.8%；旅游外汇收入27.7亿美元，比上年增长10.8%。全市接待国内旅游者1.02亿人次，旅游收入496亿元，均比上年增长10%。形成了国际国内旅游两者同步发展的格局。

全市宾馆饭店接待宾客能力增强。年末，全市共有旅游定点饭店456家，其中星级饭店407家，客房数达到8.4万间，比1995年末增加2.5万间。

开发区：各类开发区成为吸引高科技项目和外资的重点区域。全年科技园区、开发区和工业小区新增建成区土地面积0.42平方公里，累计达到27.7平方公里。年内招商企业1813家，比上年增加701家。入区企业大部分集中在高科技和外资项目，日本三洋、美国通用等一批重点项目相继签约、动工。累计入区企业13288家，其中投产企业11281家。全年各类开发区共实现增加值395亿元，比上年增长40.3%（现价），比1995年增长3倍。实现总收入1979.4亿元，增长68.7%；实现利润75.5亿元，增长13.5%；上缴税费85.4亿元，增长59.3 %。

五、社会事业

科学技术：科技实力进一步加强。年末，北京地区拥有科技活动人员24万人。全年投入科技活动经费（内部支出）230亿元，比上年增长14.3%。"九五"期间累计投入893亿元，比"八五"时期增长近1倍。研究与发展经费投入106亿元，占国内生产总值的比重由1995年的2.5%提高到4.3%。积极促进科技成果产业化，全年北京地区技术市场技术合同成交总金额达到140.3亿元，比上年增长52%。"九五"期间，加强技术创新，促进高科技成果产业化，五年累计技术合同成交总金额突破400亿元，比"八五"时期增长近1.5倍。专利申请量突破10336件，比上年增长33.8%。

教育：坚持把教育放在优先发展的战略地位。全年地方财政收入中用于教育事业费的支出为60.1亿元，比上年增长22%；五年地方财政收入中累计用于教育事业费的支出为216.2亿元，比"八五"期间增加1.9倍。全社会教育经费投入200亿元，比1995年增长1倍多，占当年国内生产总值的比重达到8%，比1995年提高2.3个百分点。五年累计全社会教育经费投入达到700多亿元。积极增加教育需求，招生规模扩大。全市高中阶段教育招收新生13.3万人，初中毕业生升学率达到95%。普通高中和职业高中招生比例达到5：5。北京地区高校招收研究生2.3万人，比上年增长37.5%；招收本科生7.5万人，增长26.8%；成人高校招生10.4万人，增长17.8%。本市18—22岁人口高等教育基本入学率达到40%，居全国之首。教育资源配置优化，规模效益提高。经过调整，目前全市普通高校59所，比上年减少5所；成人高校61所，减少8所；中等职业学校393所，减少29所；小学2169所，减少183所。普通高校本专科生校均规模4789人，比上年增加1132人。高校后勤社会化改革全面推进，大学生校外公寓开工100万平方米。全面修订面向21世纪教育教学计划，改革招生考试制度，九年义务教育成果继续巩固。

文化：文化事业呈现蓬勃生机。全年文化产业增加值107亿元， 占国内生产总值的比重为4.4%。年末，全市共有文化产业单位3800多个，拥有文艺团体近40个，演出8564场次；图书馆24个，博物馆112家。"九五"期间，创作了一批优秀剧目和作品，其中有《风雨同仁堂》等作品荣获全国"五个一工程"奖。新闻出版事业健康发展。北京人民广播电台七个系列台平均每日播音时间达到130小时，北京电视台平均每周播出时间达到435小时，分别比"八五"时期增长27.6%和43.2%。北京有线广播电视网络扩大，已拥有用户168万户，全市43%的居民可以收看到40个频道的电视节目。年末，北京地区出版的报纸达到247种，平均期印数3520万份，分别比1995年增长2.9%和下降7.9%；出版的杂志达到2273种，平均期印数6116万份，分别比1995年增长20.6%和21.9%；全市出版图书54797种，总印数113352万册（张），分别比1995年增长41.2%和36.0%。

卫生：全市医疗水平明显提高。年末全市共有医疗卫生机构6176个，医院床位6.9万张，卫生技术人员10.3万人。

与 1995 年相比，医疗卫生机构增加 1221 个，医院床位增加 0.5 万张，卫生技术人员减少 1.3 万人。城乡居民整体健康指标水平位于发展中国家前列，有的已接近发达国家水平。

体育：群众健身与竞技体育相互促进，成绩突出。群众体育蓬勃发展，全市经常参加体育锻炼的人口达到 480 万人，占全市常住人口的比重达到 40%；大中小学生体育锻炼达标率达到 95%以上。体育锻炼成为人民“科学、健康、文明”生活方式的一部分。竞技体育成绩优异。年末，全市有专业体育运动员 1981 人，比 1995 年增加 181 人。全市共举办竞技体育比赛 1500 场，观众达到 430 万人次。全市参加国际、国内比赛的运动员 1353 人次，获得奖牌 157 枚，其中金牌 56 枚，银牌 50 枚。第 27 届奥运会上，中国奥运代表团有 24 名北京籍运动员入选，夺得奖牌 5 枚。“九五”期间，全市运动员在国际、国内比赛中共获得奖牌 836.5 块，其中金牌 342 块，银牌 269.5 块。

六、人口、就业与人民生活

人口：全市人口总量增长有所减缓。年末公安部门统计的户籍人口为 1107.5 万人，比上年增长 0.7%；比 1995 年增加 37.2 万人，年均增长 0.69 %，低于“八五”期间 0.04 个百分点。

就业及社会保障：就业形势基本稳定。年末，全市从业人员 614 万人，其中第一、二、三产业从业人员分别为 73.9 万人、214.6 万人和 325.5 万人。第三产业成为吸纳就业的重要领域，产业人员所占比重由 1995 年的 48.7%上升到 53%。全市职工人数 454 万人，比上年下降 1.8%，比 1995 年下降 8.7%。年末城镇登记失业率为 0.75%，失业人员就业率 72.63%，下岗职工就业率 69.68%，实现了既定目标。“九五”期间，“再就业工程”成就突出，共分流安置下岗和社会人员近 50 万人。

社会保障制度逐步完善。全市参加养老保险的职工及退休人员达到 391.6 万人，比 1995 年增加 130 多万人；参加失业保险的职工 306 万人，比 1995 年增加 86 万人；地方企业参加大病统筹的职工和退休人员 232.6 万人， 比 1995 年增加 57.6 万人。三项保险统筹基金的收缴率均达到 95%以上。

居民收入：城乡居民收入水平较快增长。全市职工平均工资 15600 元，比上年增长 13.2%，扣除价格因素，实际增长 9.4%。城镇居民人均可支配收入 10349.7 元，比上年增长 12.7%，扣除价格因素，实际增长 8.9%。“九五”期间年均实际递增 7.1%。全年人均消费性支出为 8493.5 元， 比上年增长 13.5%，扣除价格因素，实际增长 9.5%，五年年均实际递增 6.2%。城镇居民恩格尔系数 36.3%，比 1995 年降低 12.2 个百分点。农民收入实现了 1995 年以来的最高增速，全年人均纯收入 4687 元，比上年增长 8.6%，扣除价格因素，实际增长 7.3%，五年平均实际递增 6.2 %。农民人均生活消费性支出 3441.3 元，比上年增长 9.9%，五年平均递增 5.5%。“九五”时期城乡居民总体生活水平已经开始从小康向富裕迈进。

居民储蓄：城乡居民储蓄稳定增加。年末储蓄余额 2923.2 亿元，比年初增加 242.5 亿元，其中城镇居民储蓄存款余额 2663.3 亿元，比年初增加 234.3 亿元。“九五”时期城乡居民储蓄增加 1669.2 亿元，比“八五”时期增长 62.5%。

居民住房：住房条件得到明显改善。全市完成住宅投资 372.5 亿元，比上年增长 5.3%；住宅竣工面积 1499.7 万平方米。“九五”期间累计完成住宅投资 1422 亿元，累计竣工 5979.9 万平方米，分别比“八五”期间增长 1.6 倍和 61.3%。全年竣工经济适用住宅 176 万平方米。危房改造拆迁 63 万平方米，拆迁居民 2.5 万户；五年累计拆迁 215 万平方米，拆迁居民 8.3 万户。城镇居民人均住房使用面积 16.2 平方米，比上年增加 0.3 平方米；比 1995 年增加 2.9 平方米；农村居民人均生活用房面积 28.9 平方米，比上年增加 0.3 平方米，比 1995 年增加 3.9 平方米。

附 1　公报注释：

1、本公报数据为初步统计数。

2、本公报中增加值为现价，除注明外，增长速度均按可比价计算。

3、因全国第五次人口普查数据仍在核查，普查结果将按国务院统一要求另行发布。

附 2　2000 年经济发展统计表:

指标名称	单 位	2000 年	2000 年为 1999 年%
社会消费品零售额	亿元	1443.3	109.9
吃	亿元	410.2	109.5
穿	亿元	173.0	111.2
用	亿元	810.9	109.3
主要农副产品产量			
粮食总产量	万吨	144.2	71.7

指标名称	单 位	2000年	2000年为1999年%
蔬菜总产量	万吨	489.1	114.6
肉类总产量	万吨	56.3	114.4
鲜蛋总产量	万吨	16.0	101.3
牛奶总产量	万吨	30.3	126.3
水产品总产量	万吨	7.5	100.0
出栏猪	万头	415.6	103.7
主要工业产品产量			
成品钢材	万吨	696.7	105.0
发电量	亿千瓦小时	145.3	107.9
供热量	万百万千焦	3654.0	101.8
液化石油气	万吨	40.0	109.1
化肥 （折纯）	万吨	6.8	82.6
水泥	万吨	827.0	104.5
乙烯	万吨	65.5	96.4
载货汽车	辆	104667	114.9
彩色显象管	万只	534.4	116.3
显示器	万部	205.6	376.5
移动通信设备	万部（信道）	1421.6	222.6
微型计算机	万部	257.8	187.6
移动电话机	万部	1549.6	268.8
程控交换机	万线	1019.4	133.4
房间空调器	万台	31.4	141.2
饮料酒	万吨	185.6	124.4
方便主食品	吨	71673	113.8
乳制品	吨	20579	148.4
各种运输方式运量（北京地区）：			
货物运输量	万吨	27827.9	98.4
铁路（预计）	万吨	2612.0	101.1
公路	万吨	25122.0	98.0
民航	万吨	33.6	112.4
旅客运输量	万人次	18526.7	124.6
铁路（预计）	万人次	4589.0	109.2
公路	万人次	13009.0	131.7
民航	万人次	928.7	117.9
居民消费价格指数(以上年为100)		103.5	
食品类		97.9	
衣着类		102.6	
家庭设备及用品		96.3	
医疗保健		113.5	
交通和通讯工具类		92.3	
娱乐教育文化用品类		97.8	
居住		117.9	
服务项目		116.2	
商品零售价格指数(以上年为100)		98.9	

指标名称	单　位	2000 年	2000 年为 1999 年%
城镇居民耐用消费品拥有量(每百户):			
空调器	台	69.9	139.5
淋浴热水器	个	74.4	110.9
彩电	台	145.5	102.9
电冰箱	台	107.4	104.5
洗衣机	台	102.8	103.2
家用电脑	台	32.1	136.6
微波炉	台	58.4	119.7
脱排油烟机	台	112.4	178.7
电炊具	台	104.0	124.3

STATISTICAL COMMUNIQUE ON THE 2000 (THE PERIOD OF THE 9TH FIVE-YEAR PLAN) NATIONAL ECONOMIC AND SOCIAL DEVELOPMENT OF THE CITY OF BEIJING

February 2, 2001

In 2000, under the leadership of Beijing municipal Party committee of the Communist Party of China and Beijing Municipal government, all people of the city united to keep forging ahead and worked hard for the prosperity of the country. Remarkable results were yielded on the expansion of domestic demand and the deepening of reform. The economy of Beijing had a sustained, rapid and healthy growth. Social development progressed fully. The employment situation kept stable basically. Living standards of the people continued to improve. The 9th Five-Year Plan was fulfilled in all aspects, with the second-step strategic aim for modernization construction met ahead of schedule. In the economic development, the task of structural adjustment was still arduous. The quality of economic growth had much room for further improvement.

Ⅰ.General

Economic strength: The pace of economic growth continued to speed up. In 2000, the gross domestic product (GDP) of Beijing was 246.05 billion yuan, up by 11 percent over the previous year. The economic growth rate has risen steadily for consecutive four years. The per capita GDP reached 22,000 yuan (2,700 US dollars equivalent), up 10.3 percent over the previous year and 61 percent over 1995. The economic and social development plan for the period of the 9th Five-Year Plan was fulfilled roundly. During the five years, the annually average growth rate of the economy of Beijing was 10 percent; the accumulative GDP of Beijing exceeded one trillion yuan, with the aggregate GDP up 1.2 fold on the period of the 8th Five-Year Plan.

Economic structure: Obvious results were achieved in the adjustment of industrial structure. In 2000, the added value of the primary industry was 9 billion yuan, up by 4 percent over the previous year, representing an elementary end of the situation of long-period pacing up and down at low speed; the added value of the secondary industry was 93.58 billion yuan, up by 11.4 percent, and that of the tertiary industry was 143.47 billion yuan, up by 11.1 percent, elementarily reversing the downward trend of growth rate. The growth rate of the agriculture, industry and tertiary industry rose 1.5, 0.4 and 2 percentage points respectively on the previous year. The proportion of three industries changed from 5.8 percent, 44.1 percent and 50.1 percent respectively in 1995 to 3.7 percent, 38 percent and 58.3 percent respectively in 2000. The proportion of the tertiary industry kept on increasing. During the five years, the annually average growth rate of the primary, secondary and tertiary industry was 1.2 percent, 9.7 percent and 11 percent respectively.

Structure of ownership has been perfect gradually. State-owned economy and collective economy accounted for 68.2 percent of Beijing's GDP, declined as compared with 80.4 percent in 1995. The proportion of State-owned economy was still up to 57.5 percent. Especially in the important sectors and key fields of the national economy including transportation, post and telecommunications, banking and insurance, the proportion of State-owned economy was more than 95 percent. Economies in other ownership other than State-owned economy or collective economy tended to grow strongly, of which the added value accounted for 31.8 percent of the GDP of Beijing, soared from 19.6 percent in 1995, with the annually average growth rate standing at 23.3 percent, 17.9 percentage points higher than that of the State-owned and collective economies. The contribution rate to the growth of national economy rose from 40.2 percent in 1995 to 58.4 percent.

Three demands: The investment and consumer demands were further expanded. Contradictions caused by insufficient foreign demand were dulled distinctly.

Demand for fixed assets investment: The government-leading investment continued to play an important role in stirring the economy. To increase the investment and push forward economic growth, the Municipal Government set 67 and 50 key projects in succession in the last two years. In 2000, the completed investment in fixed assets of Beijing totaled 129.74 billion yuan, up 10.8

percent over the previous year. Of this total, the investment of local units was 97.95 billion yuan, up 17.8 percent. The accumulative investment completed in the three years during which domestic demand was expanded reached 362.36 billion yuan, with an annually average growth rate of 11.9 percent. The investment focused on the urban infrastructure facilities and real estate projects, accounting for 26.9 percent and 36.5 percent respectively of the total investment. During the period of the 9th Five-Year Plan, the aggregate investment of Beijing reached 546.17 billion yuan, 2.3 times as much as that in the period of the 8th Five-Year Plan. Tremendous changes took place on the appearance of the city.

Consumer demand: The end-consumer demand tended to be thriving. In 2000, the retail sales of consumer commodities of the whole year reached 144.33 billion yuan, up 9.9 percent, a real increase of 11.1 percent if eliminating the price factor. The consumer markets in urban and rural areas grew at the same pace. The retail sales in urban areas stood at 123.11 billion yuan, up 9.8 percent, in rural areas, 21.22 billion yuan, up 10.7 percent. During the period of the 9th Five-Year Plan, consumption tended to grow steadily. The accumulative retail sales of consumer commodities reached 592.7 billion yuan in the five years, up 1.1 fold on that of the period of the 8th Five-Year Plan, with the annually average growth rate at 11.8 percent. The consumer structure was upgraded and the consumer area broadened. The proportion of "food, clothing and daily use commodities" consumer declined from some 90 percent in the early 1990s to 60 percent around, with that of service consumer up to 40 percent around. Monetized housing substituted for the welfare housing, activating the market of house consumer. In 2000, the sales of marketable houses reached 47.07 billion yuan, up 53.1 percent over the previous year; that of individual houses was 33.64 billion yuan, accounting for 71.5 percent of that of marketable houses, up 1.6 fold on the previous year, reflecting that the real estate sector played a promoting role in the economic growth on the aspects both investment and consumer.

Export demand: Foreign trade export grew at a high speed. In 2000, the export volume of Beijing totaled 11.97 billion US dollars, up 20.8 percent over the previous year. The exports of local enterprises reached 4.63 billion US dollars, up 41.8 percent over the previous year. The growth rate rose by 26.7 percentage points and 26.6 percent points respectively from that in the previous year. The economy was much export oriented to some extent. The export volume of local enterprises accounted for 16 percent of Beijing's GDP, 2.5 percentage points higher than that 1995; that of electromechanical products accounted for 50 percent over, which mainly included electronic and communications products.

Price: Price reversed from declining to rising. The deflation trend was kept within limits effectively. The household consumer prices index of the year was 103.5 percent, 2.9 percentage points higher than the previous year. The index for retail prices was 98.9 percent, representing a great reduction of declining rate. The index of mill prices of industrial products was 102.5 percent, 4.8 percentage points higher than the previous year.

Quality of growth: The quality of economic operation improved to some extent. In 2000, the social labor productivity increased a little to 40073 yuan per person, up 14 percent over the previous year as calculated at current price. Of which, for the primary industry, 12178.6 yuan per person, up 3.8 percent; for the secondary industry, 43607 yuan per person, up 12.2 percent, and for the tertiary industry , 44077 yuan per person, up 15.8 percent.

The financial revenue of local governments rose at a sustained and high speed. The financial revenue of local governments totaled 34.24 billion yuan in the year, up 22.7 percent over the previous year. Of which, the Value-added tax, sales tax, business income tax and individual income tax increased completely, up 15.7 percent, 15.7 percent, 16.2 percent and 22.9 percent respectively. The accumulated financial revenue in the period of the 9th Five-Year Plan was 118.2 billion yuan, up 1.5 fold on that in the period of the 8th Five-Year Plan, an annually average growth rate of 24.3 percent..

The "two targets in three years" for the transformation of operational mechanism and difficulty relief in large- and medium-sized State-owned enterprises were achieved fully. 190 large- and medium-sized State-owned backbone enterprises met their goals of transformation of operational mechanism one month ahead of schedule. 153 enterprises established modern enterprise system initially. There were 80.5 percent of businesses involved in the transformation of operational mechanism. Increase was seen in the economic efficiency of 400 large- and medium-sized State-owned or State-holding enterprises involved in the three-year difficulty relief target. The overall index of economic efficiency of the year was 115.98 percent. Profits garnered in the year reached 5.17 billion yuan, up 38.4 percent over the previous year. Deficit enterprises reduced in number obviously. At the end of the year, the proportion of deficit enterprises was 14.5 percent.

Scientific and technologic advance: The economic growth contained more scientific factors. In 2000, the contribution rate of scientific and technologic advance to the economic growth was 52.5 percent, up 9.4 percentage points from that in 1995. Of which, the contribution rate of scientific and technologic advance of the primary industry was 54.6 percent, an increase of 7 percentage points; of the secondary industry, 47.7 percent, an increase of 6.2 percentage points; of the tertiary industry, 52.9 percent, an increase of 9 percentage points.

The State Council's Reply and Ratification on Problems of Building the Zhongguancun High-Tech Park greatly promoted the development of Zhongguancun High-Tech Park. A new great upsurge of pioneering rose up luxuriantly. The number of enterprises that were recognized as high-tech ones in the year was doubled to 2261, pushing the total to 8224 in number. The added value of high-tech enterprises in the Park was 32.6 billion yuan in the year, up by 44.2 percent (calculated at current price). Taxes and fees turned in amounted to 6.17 billion yuan, up 51.2 percent. The amount of foreign exchanges earned from export was doubled to 1.94 billion US dollars.

Ⅱ.Urban Construction

Investment in infrastructure facilities: Bottleneck restrict of infrastructure facilities were relaxed distinctly. In 2000, the investment in the infrastructure facilities totaled 35.19 billion yuan, up 16.3 percent over the previous year, accounting for 29.5 percent of the fixed assets investment of Beijing, representing an increase of 1.3 percentage points from that in the previous year. 50 key projects were constructed smoothly. By the end of 2000, the construction of 47 projects was commenced, 12 of them were completed basically. The investment in key projects was 24.53 billion yuan in the year, accounting for 20.6 percent of the investment of the city. During the period of the 9th Five-Year Plan, the accumulative investment in infrastructure facilities was 138.21 billion yuan, up 1.8 fold on that in the period of the 8th Five-Year Plan, with an annual average growth rate of 19.7 percent. A group of road projects including the Fuxingmen-Bawangfen subway line, Ping'an Avenue, Beijing-Changping Expressway and Beijing-Shenyang Expressway were completed fully.

Environmental protection and control: Significant progress was made in the environmental protection and control. Improvement was achieved in the energy structure. In 2000, five million tons of low-sulfur coal was used. Standards for the tail-gas of motor vehicles were strictly controlled. The up-to-standard rate of day and night road inspection exceeded 80 percent. Dust reduction afforestation was adopted as a measure to prevent pollution caused by granules, resulting in the distinct improvement of the air quality. Days in which the index of air pollution was at level III or up accounted for 93.7 percent of the total of the year, and that in which the index of air pollution was at level II or up, 48.4 percent. The concentration of sulfur oxide, nitrous oxide, total floating granules and carbon monoxide declined by 11 percent, 8 percent, 3 percent and 7 percent respectively over the previous year. Discharge in all sources of industrial pollution was up to the standard. More than 5000 enterprises engaged in pollution industry were checked and accepted in compliance with standards. Control on the urban water system environment progressed smoothly. The goal of "clear water, green bank, smooth and open to navigation" was met initially. Synthetic control on the water systems including Yuyuantan Lake, South Huchenghe River, Tonghuihe River-Gaobeidian Lake, which have been open to navigation, was completed basically. The rate of sewage disposal of the year was 40 percent, 20.6 percentage points higher than that in 1995. At the end of the year, the rate of harmless disposal of garbage in Beijing was 81.5 percent, 60 percentage points higher than that in 1995. Large-scale and high-level afforestation work developed vigorously. The area of afforestation separation zones in urban area increased 2666 hectare. At the end of the year, the per capita public green land area was 9.7 square meters; 43 percent of the city was covered by trees and forest. 36.5 percent of the urban area was greenly covered. Comprehensive environmental control in the whole city was strengthened. The appearance of Beijing improved markedly. Wide-range improvement on the ecological environment around the Capital was launched.

Mass transit: The capacity of mass transit was reinforced remarkably. At the end of the year, public transit vehicles in the city totaled 13,500 in number, nearly 8,000 more than that of 1995; taxis totaled 65,000 in number, an increase of more than 8000 from than of 1995. The total length of public transit lines approached 17,000 kilometers, up 2.7 fold on that of 1995. Of the total, 49 lines for public buses and trolley buses were newly added in the year by the Public Transit Corporation, 52 lines were adjusted and extended. Urban public transportation vehicles (excluding taxis) transported passengers of 4.08 billion person-times in the year, of which, 3.47 billion person-times were by buses trolley buses, accounting for 85 percent; 440 million person-times were by subways, accounting for 10.8 percent; 620 million passengers were transported by taxis.

Public utilities: The public utilities of the city developed steadily. In 2000, 800 million tons of water was sold, an increase of one million tons from that in 1995. The concentrating heating area reached 100 million square meters, an increase of nearly 30 million square meters from that in 1995. The total utilized electricity was 33 billion kilowatt-hours in the year, up 48 percent over 1995. Fired gas users numbered 2.957 million, an increase of 600,000 in number from that in 1995.

III. Main Sectors

Agriculture: Achievements were scored in the adjustment of agricultural structure. In 2000, the added value of Beijing's agriculture increased by 4 percent over the previous year, representing a year in which the growth rate being the fastest since the period of the 9th Five-Year Plan, and up 8 percent over 1995. Of the total output value of agriculture, the fish-breeding and poultry-raising sector accounted for 50.6 percent, 5 percentage points higher than that of 1995. The area of cash crops accounted for 28 percent of that of cultivated land, up against 21 percent in 1995. The grain output totaled 1.442 million tons in the year. The output of major agricultural products and by-products rose drastically. Each of the output of meat, vegetable and milk increased by 10-20 percent over the previous year. A group of nationally well-known modern agricultural demonstration bases came forth, represented by Beautiful Land.

Industry: The overall strength and competitiveness was enhanced evidently. In 2000, the total added value of the industrial sector was 73.7 billion yuan, up 13.2 percent over the previous year. During the period of the 9th Five-Year Plan, the annually average growth rate of the industrial sector was 9.9 percent. The five-year added value accumulated to 312.68 billion yuan, with the aggregate figure up 74.5 percent over that in the period of the 8th Five-Year Plan.

New and high-tech industry has constituted a main force in driving up the industrial growth. In 2000, the added value of high-tech industry was 21.35 billion yuan, a proportion of 28.9 percent of the total of Beijing's industrial sector, and 3.5 percentage points higher than that in the previous year; a proportion of 8.6 percent of the total GDP of Beijing, 1 percentage point higher than that in the previous year. The contribution rate to the industrial growth kept 60 percent aroung.

Nearly 40 percent of the industrial growth was driven by export production. In 2000, the export output value of Beijing was 31.01 billion yuan, accounting for 13.6 percent of the total of Beijing's industrial sector, and 6.3 percentage points higher than that in the last year. Exported industrial products mainly included electronic and communications products.

State-owned and State holding industries developed rapidly. In 2000, the added value of State-owned and State holding businesses was 51.28 billion yuan, up by 17.2 percent over the previous year, and taking 74.3 percent in the total of Beijing's industrial sector. Enterprises from foreign countries, Hong Kong, Macao and Taiwan became substantial forces in driving up the industrial growth, with their total added value standing at 31.14 billion yuan, up 24.6 percent, and accounting for 45.1 percent of the total of Beijing's industrial sector.

The economic efficiency in the industrial sector has been taking a turn for the better in all aspects. In 2000, the industrial sales of Beijing registered 257.57 billion yuan, up 31.6 percent over the last year. The production-marketing ratio was 98.51 percent, 1.74 percentage points higher than that in the last year. The aggregative index number of the economic efficiency of industrial sector was 117.9 percent, 12.2 percentage points higher than the previous year. Total profits achieved in 2000 reached 11.08 billion yuan, up 65.5 percent over the previous year. Of this total, the profits of profit-making enterprises were 14.73 billion yuan, up 39.8 percent, and the losses of losing enterprises were 3.64 billion yuan, down by 5 percent.

Construction: The construction sector developed steadily. In 2000, the total added value of the construction sector was 19.88 billion yuan, up 2.1 percent over the previous year. The added value accumulated in the period of the 9th Five-Year Plan was 85.78 billion yuan, up 1.3 fold on the period of the 8th Five-Year Plan. The construction floor space in Beijing was 69.959 million square meters in 2000, up by 6.7 percent over the previous year, and 26.6 percent over 1995. The completed floor space in Beijing was 23.582 million square meters in 2000, up by 1.6 percent over the previous year, that accumulated in the five years amounted to 96.443 million square meters, up 55.4 percent over that in the period of the 8th Five-Year Plan. The public bidding system was developed in 2000, with the contract management strengthened. One hundred percent of contracts for bidding projects with legally authorized commencement procedures were put on records. The quality of construction projects improved evidently. In 2000, excellent and good projects in the whole city accounted for 55.3 percent of the total, 6.1 percentage points higher than the previous year. Construction teams were controlled with more strict standards. Professional construction businesses developed actively. At the end of the year, construction businesses at level 4 and up numbered 1771, up by 11.6 percent from that at the end of 1995. The scientific concentration in the construction of building businesses in Beijing was enhanced. The rate of technical equipment and power equipment was 8233 yuan/person and 6KW/person respectively, up by 38.4 percent and 93.5 percent respectively from 1995.

Transportation: A new pattern emerged in the development of transportation sector. In 2000, the total added value of the transportation sector was 6.95 billion yuan, up by 6 percent over the previous year. The total volume of freight transportation was 278.279 million tons, down by 1.6 percent over the previous year; that of passenger transportation was 185.267 million person-times, up by 24.6 percent over the previous year. During the period of the 9th Five-Year Plan, the transportation volume by highways accounted for 90.8 percent and 62 percent respectively of the freight transportation and passenger transportation; that by railways accounted for 8.9 percent and 31.6 percent respectively of the freight transportation and passenger transportation.

Posts and telecommunications: The posts and telecommunications sector registered sustained and high-speed development. In 2000, the total added value of the posts and telecommunications sector was 12.34 billion yuan, up by 21 percent over the previous year. The business transactions of postal and telecommunications service totaled 21.95 billion yuan in the year, up by 39.1 percent over the previous year. 1.52 billion copies of newspaper were subscribed and sold in the year; 580 million copies of correspondence were sent; 7.90 million copies of EMS were received and sent; up 4.1 percent, 5.5 percent and 1.7 percent respectively over the previous year. At the end of 2000, the exchanges of fixed telephones in public network increased their capacity to 6.30 million gates, up by 12.7 percent over the previous year. By the end of the year, fixed telephones subscribers in Beijing numbered 4.39 million, and cellular phone users, 2.66 million, up by 16.8 percent and 43 percent over the previous year. There were 50.8 fixed telephones of public network per 100-population in Beijing, and 66.4 telephones per 100 urban inhabitants, up by 11.9 percent and 9 percent respectively over the previous year. With the enhancement of scientific and technological level as well as the access of digital and network economy to China' market, the e-government and e-commerce and other digital technologies developed rapidly. By the end of 2000, Internet users of Beijing totaled 563,000. The informatization level of Beijing ranked first in the country.

Commerce: Diversified competitions promoted the sustained boom of the commerce sector. In 2000, the total added value of the wholesale and retail trades and catering industry was 22.26 billion yuan, up 6.9 percent over the previous year. During the period of the 9th Five-Year Plan, the accumulated added value registered 103.04 billion yuan, up 75.8 percent over the period of the 8th Five-Year Plan. The volume of trade circulation increased. The overall value of purchased commodities in the whole year reached 280.84 billion yuan, up 20.7 percent; that of sold commodities reached 326.32 billion yuan, up 22.5 percent. As compared with 1995, the overall value of purchased commodities rose by 60.7 percent, and that of sold commodities, rose by 80 percent. The economic benefits in large- and medium-sized commercial businesses improved a little, with the sales reaching 230.07 billion yuan, up by 23.4 percent over the previous year, and the profits, 3.47 billion yuan, up by 50.6 percent.

New type commerce grew rapidly. By the end of the year, chain businesses taking supermarket and convenience stores as main body numbered 127, with chain stores approaching 1300 in number. During the five years, the overall commercial layout and commercial facilities developed in compliance with the requirements for international modern metropolis. Larger-scaled commercial and cultural centers were built in many places, which were provided with fine shopping environment and cultural atmosphere.

Banking and insurance: The banking sector developed steadily, healthily and orderly. In 2000, the total added value of the banking and insurance sector was 37.82 billion yuan, up 16.9 percent over the previous year. Saving deposits increased steadily. At the end of the year, the saving deposits in the banking institutions of Beijing totaled 970.5 billion yuan, 143.47 billion yuan more than that at the beginning of the year. The increased saving deposits rose by 0.4 percent on the last year. More loans could be available. At the end of 2000, the loans in Beijing totaled 594.46 billion yuan in Beijing, an increase of 111.61 billion yuan from that at the beginning of the year. The increased loans rose by 99.5 percent compared with that in the last year. Funds returned in the year accumulated to 16.72 billion yuan, up 3.2 fold on the previous year.

The insurance market grew steadily. In 2000, the insurance premium in domestic and foreign insurance institutions totaled 8.8 billion yuan, up 1.8 percent over the previous year, and up 2.3 fold on that in 1995. The premium of life insurance was 5.81 billion yuan, down by 2.3 percent over the previous year; of property insurance, 3.0 billion yuan, up 10.6 percent. The insurance companies paid an indemnity of 1.87 billion yuan as reparations in insurance programs, down by 41.5 percent over the previous year, with the overall loss ratio at 21.3 percent.

The transaction volume of securities increased sharply. The turnover of all stock institutions totaled 1445.7 billion yuan, up 32.5 percent over the previous year. Of this total, the turnover of stocks was 913.65 billion yuan, up 66 percent; that of treasury bonds was

60.0 billion yuan, up 6.6 percent. A total of 48.03 billion yuan funds were raised on the financial market.

Real Estate: Both of the supply and demand markets flourished fully. In 2000, the total added value of the real estate sector was 8.04 billion yuan, up by 14.6 percent over the previous year. Also in 2000, the investment in the real estate sector totaled 52.21 billion yuan, up by 23.9 percent over the previous year, with the proportion in the fixed assets investment of the year at 40.0 percent. The accumulated investment in the five years registered 197.95 billion yuan, up 2.5 fold on that in the period of the 8th Five-Year Plan. In 2000, the total construction floor space of the real estate sector reached 44.55 million square meters. Floor space of buildings completed in the year was 13.656 million square meters. The accumulated floor space of buildings completed during the five years reached 47.626 million square meters, up 1.3 fold on that in the period of the 8th Five-Year Plan.

The transaction on the marketable house market was flourishing. The total floor space of marketable houses sold in 2000 was 9.558 million square meters, up 75.6 percent over the previous year. Of this total, the floor space of marketable residential houses was 8.971 million square meters, up 85.1 percent. During the period of the 9th Five-Year Plan, the accumulated floor space of marketable houses sold totaled 24.156 million square meters, up 1.8 fold on that in the period of the 8th Five-Year Plan. Of this total, the floor space of marketable residential houses was 21.98 million square meters, up 1.7 fold. The sales of marketable houses in the five years reached 125.05 billion yuan, up 4.6 fold on that in the period of the 8th Five-Year Plan; of which, the sales of marketable residential houses stood at 103.15 billion yuan, up 4.4 fold.

IV. Export-oriented Economy

Foreign trade import & export: The scale of foreign trade import and export was further expanded. According to Beijing Customs, the total import & export value in 2000 was 49.62 billion US dollars, up by 44.4 percent over the previous year. During the period of the 9th Five-Year Plan, the accumulative import & export value was 174.19 billion US dollars, Of which, the total export value was 50.11 US dollars. The total import & export value of local businesses was 11.65 billion US dollars, up 38.8 percent over the previous year. During the period of the 9th Five-Year Plan, the accumulative import & export value of local businesses was 37.77 billion US dollars, up 71.9 percent against the period of the 8th Five-Year Plan. Of which, the total export value was 15.27 billion US dollars, up 82.4 percent as compared with that in the period of the 8th Five-Year Plan.

Utilization of foreign capitals: Notable achievements were made in the utilization of foreign capitals. The city approved 1149 foreign-invested projects in the year, with the contracted foreign capitals amounting to 4.34 billion US dollars, up 77.6 percent and 1.4 fold respectively on the previous year. The foreign capitals actually utilized in 2000 reached 3.01 billion US dollars, up 2.5 percent over the previous year. During the period of the 9th Five-Year Plan, 4100 foreign-funded projects were signed, with the agreed foreign capitals amounting to 12.98 billion US dollars. The average volume of these projects was 3.166 million US dollars, an increase of more than 2 million US dollars from that in the period of the 8th Five-Year Plan. The foreign capitals actually utilized in the five years accumulated to 13.67 billion US dollars, up 1.4 fold on the period of the 8th Five-Year Plan. There were more diversified forms for use of foreign capitals. Beijing has been open to the outside world in all sides, multiple levels and a wide range.

Foreign-contracted Construction Projects and Labor Service Collaboration: Foreign services and trade expanded to new fields. In 2000, the amount of newly signed contracts for foreign-contracted construction projects and labor service collaboration was 161 million US dollars. The completed turnover totaled 198 million US dollars. By the end of 2000, 1169 Chinese workers were working overseas.

Tourism: Healthy progress was scored in tourism. In 2000, Beijing received 2.821 million tourists from overseas, up by 11.8 percent over the previous year. The foreign exchange incomes from tourism totaled 2.77 billion US dollars, up 10.8 percent over the previous year. In the year, Beijing also received 102 million tourists from other provinces and regions of China, earning 49.6 billion yuan of incomes from tourism, each rising 10 percent over the previous year. The international tourism and national tourism grew synchronously.

The reception capacity of hotels in Beijing was elevated. At the end of the year, the total number of specially designated hotels was 456, of which, 406 were star-level ones. The guest rooms totaled 84,000, an increase of 25,000 in number from that at the end of 1995.

Development Zones: Various development zones became key regions to attract high-tech projects and foreign capitals. In 2000, the newly built science & tech parks, development zones and industrial zones covered an area of 0.42 square kilometer, bringing the total area of these zones to 27.7 square kilometers. During the year, 1813 enterprises landed in these zones of the city, 701 more than the figure in the previous year. Enterprises landed in these zones mainly focused on high-tech and foreign-funded projects. A group of key projects including Sanyo and GM signed and started their construction one after another. The total number of enterprises landed in the zones accumulated to 13288, of which, 11281 have been put into production. The added value realized in the development zones of Beijing was 39.5 billion yuan, up 40.3 percent (at current price) on the previous year and 2 fold on 1995. The total income was 197.94 billion yuan, up 68.7 percent, the profits, 7.55 billion yuan, up 13.5 percent, and the fees and taxes, 8.54 billion yuan, up 59.3 percent.

V. Social Works

Science and Technology: The scientific and technical strength was further enhanced. At the end of 2000, a total of 240,000 people were engaged in scientific and technological activities in Beijing. Expenditures input in scientific and technological activities (internal expenditures) amounted to 23 billion yuan in the year, up 14.3 percent over the previous year. During the period of the 9th Five-Year Plan, an accumulative amount of 89.3 billion yuan was invested in such activities, almost doubling the figure in the period of the 8th Five-Year Plan. The expenditure on research and development (R&D) was 10.6 billion yuan, accounting for 4.3 percent of the GDP of Beijing as compared with 2.5 percent in 1995. Industrialization of scientific and technological results was pushed forward actively. The total value of technical contracts signed on technical markets reached 14.03 billion yuan, up 52 percent over the previous year. During the period of the 9th Five-Year Plan, the technical innovation was enhanced, with the industrialization of scientific and technological results promoted. The total value of technical contracts accumulated in the five years topped 40 billion yuan, up nearly 1.5 fold on that in the period of the 8th Five-Year Plan. Patents applied in the year topped 10336 in number, up 33.8 percent over the previous year.

Education: The City has adhered to play education on a strategic position for preferential development. In 2000, the financial input into education from local fiscal revenues increased by 22 percent to 6.01 billion yuan. In the five years, the accumulated financial input into education from local fiscal revenues was 21.62 billion yuan, up 1.9 fold on that in the period of the 8th Five-Year Plan. Education expenditures of Beijing totaled 20 billion yuan, up more than one fold on 1995, accounting for 8 percent of the GDP of the year, 2.3 percentage points higher than that of 1995. In the five years, education expenditures accumulated to more than 70 billion yuan. Education demand was enhanced actively. More students were enrolled. In 2000, 133,000 new students were enrolled in senior high school. 95 percent of the students who graduated from junior high school entered senior high school. The ratio between the new entrants of regular senior high school and the vocational senior high school was 5:5. There were 23,000 new entrants of graduate students in colleges and universities in Beijing, up 37.5 percent over the previous year. The number of enrolled regular four-year college students totaled 75,000 in the year, up 26.8 percent. There were 104,000 new entrants of adult colleges and universities in the year, up 17.8 percent. The basic rate of the population aged from 18 to 22 years entering institutions of higher education reached 40 percent, top of China. The allocation of educational resources was optimized. The scaled efficiency improved increasingly. Upon adjustment, regular colleges and universities in Beijing numbered 59, a reduction of 5 from the previous year; adult colleges and universities numbered 61, a reduction of 8; secondary vocational and technical schools numbered 393, a reduction of 29; and primary schools numbered 2169, a reduction of 183. The average number of students for four-year college courses and technical courses was 4789, an increase of 1132 from the previous year. Socialized reform was pushed forward fully on the logistics in colleges and universities. The floor space of the construction work commenced for exterior apartments of college students was 1 million square meters. The 21st-century-oriented education and teaching program was revised fully. The enrollment and examination system was reformed, with the achievements of 9-year compulsive education solidified.

Culture: The cultural work was vigorous. In 2000, the added value of cultural industry in Beijing was 10.7 billion yuan, a proportion of 4.4 percent in Beijing's GDP. At the end of the year, a total of over 3800 units were engaged in cultural industry in Beijing. There were nearly 40 literary groups in Beijing performed 8564 times; there were 24 libraries and 112 museums. During the period of the 9th Five-Year Plan, a group of excellent programs and works were created, of which, *Hardships of Tongrentang* and other works won the national prize of "Five One Project". Journalism developed healthily. The average daily broadcasting time of the 7 stations of Radio Beijing was 130 hours, and the average weekly telecast time of BTV was 435 hours, up 27.6 percent and 43.2 percent respectively from that in the period of the 8th Five-Year Plan. The cable radio and TV network was expanded, with users numbering 1.68 million. 43 percent of Beijing inhabitants could teleview 40 channels. At the end of the year, 247 categories of newspapers and periodicals were published in Beijing, with an average impression of 35.20 million copies per issue, up by 2.9 percent and down by 7.9 percent respectively from that of 1995. 2273 categories of magazines were published in the year, with an average impression of 61.16 million copies per issue, up by 20.6 percent and 21.9 percent respectively from that of 1995. 54797 categories of books were published in Beijing, with a total impression of 1133.52 million copies, up by 41.2 percent and 36.0 percent respectively from that of 1995.

Public Health: The medical level of Beijing was elevated distinctly. At the end of 2000, there were 6176 health-care institutions in Beijing, with a total of 69,000 beds and 103,000 health workers. As compared with 1995, health-care institutions increased by 1221; beds, increased by 5000; health worker, decreased by 13,000 in number. The overall level of heath indexes for the residents in urban and rural areas led developing countries, some close to that of developed countries.

Sports: The public body-building and the athletic sports pushed forward each other. Mass sports developed vigorously. 4.80 million people in Beijing took part in physical training frequently in the year, accounting for 40 percent of the total permanent resident population of Beijing. More than 95 percent of the students in primary school and junior high school as well as colleges and universities reached the standard of physical training. Physical training became a part of the "scientific, healthy and civilized " life style of the people. Excellent results were made for athletic sports. At the end of the year, there were 1981 professional athletes in Beijing, an increase of 181 in number from 1995. In 2000, a total of 1500 sport games were held in Beijing, attracting 4.30 million audiences. 1353 athletes participated in international and national sport games in the year, winning 157 medals including 56 gold medals and 50 silver medals. At the 27th Olympic Games, 24 athletes of Beijing natives were selected for the Olympic delegation of China who won five medals. During the period of the 9th Five-Year Plan, athletes of Beijing won 836.5 medals in international and national sports games, including 342 gold ones and 269.5 silver ones.

VI. Population, Employment and People's Life

Population: The increase of aggregate population of Beijing slowed down to some extent. According to the Public Security department, the registered permanent population totaled 11.075 million at the end of the year, up 0.7 percent over the previous year; rose by 372,000 on 1995, an annually average growth rate of 0.69 percent, 0.04 percentage point lower than that in the period of the 8th Five-Year Plan.

Employment and Social Security: The employment had a basically stable situation. By the end of 2000, the total of employed people in Beijing numbered 6.14 million, of which, 739,000 people were employed in the primary industry, 2.146 million people were engaged in the secondary industry and 3.255 million people in the tertiary industry. The tertiary industry has constituted an important field to absorb employees. People employed in the tertiary industry accounted for 53 percent of the total, up as compared with 48.7 percent in 1995. In 2000, there were 4.54 million workers in Beijing, down by 1.8 percent from that in the previous year and 8.7 percent from that in 1995. At the end of the year, the urban unemployment rate as calculated from unemployment registration was 0.75 percent. The employment rate of unemployed workers was 72.63 percent, that of laid-off workers, 69.68 percent, reaching the set target. During the period of the 9th Five-Year Plan, outstanding achievements were scored in the reemployment program. Nearly 500,000 laid-off and idle people in society were employed in other positions or newly employed.

The social security system became perfect step by step. 3.916 million workers and retired workers participated in the retirement security program in the year, an increase of more than 130,000 people from that in 1995. 3.06 million staff and workers participated in the unemployment security program, an increase of 860,000 people from that in 1995. 2.326 million workers and retired workers of local enterprises participated in the general health care program for major diseases, an increase of 576,000 xxx in number from that in 1995. More than 95 percent of the general funds for each of the three programs were received.

Household Income: Household income increased rapidly. In 2000, the annual per capita salary of Beijing's staff and workers was 15600 yuan, up by 13.2 percent over the previous year, a real increase of 9.4 percent if eliminating the price factor. The annual per capita disposable income of urban households reached 10349.7 yuan, up 12.7 percent over the previous year, a real increase of 8.9 percent if eliminating the price factor, with the annual average growth rate standing at 7.1 percent in the period of the 9th Five-Year Plan. The annual per capita living expenses of urban residents in Beijing reached 8493.5 yuan, up 13.5 percent over the previous year, a real increase of 9.5 percent if eliminating the price factor, and the actual annual growth rate averaging 6.2 percent in the five years. Of the urban resident's living expenses, those on food accounted for 36.3 percent, 12.2 percentage points lower than that in 1995.

The income of households in rural areas increased rapidly, reaching the largest growth rate since 1995. The annual per capita net income of rural households was 4687 yuan, up 8.6 percent over the previous year, a real increase of 7.3 percent if eliminating the price factor, with the actual annual growth rate averaging 6.2 percent in the five years; The per capita living expenses of rural households reached 3441.3 yuan, up by 9.9 percent over the previous year, with the annual growth rate averaging 5.5 percent in the five years. In the period of the 9th Five-Year Plan, overall household living standard began to go up from well-to-do standard toward well-off standard.

Savings of Inhabitants: Savings deposits of urban and rural residents increased steadily. At the end of 2000, saving deposits of Beijing totaled 292.32 billion yuan, 24.25 billion yuan more than that at the beginning of the year. Of the total, those of urban residents were 266.33 billion yuan, 23.43 billion yuan more than that at the beginning of the year. During the period of the 9th Five-Year Plan, the savings deposits of urban and rural residents increased 166.92 billion yuan, up 62.5 percent from that in the period of the 8th Five-Year Plan.

Houses of Inhabitants Housing conditions improved evidently. In 2000, Beijing's investment in residential buildings totaled 37.25 billion yuan, up 5.3 percent over the previous year. The floor space of residential buildings completed in the year was 14.997 million square meters. In the period of the 9th Five-Year Plan, the accumulative total of the investment in residential buildings reached 142.2 billion yuan, and that of the floor space of residential buildings completed was 59.799 million square meters, up 1.6 fold and 61.3 percent respectively on that in the period of the 8th Five-Year Plan. The floor space of economic and suitable houses completed in the year totaled 1.76 million square meters. The floor space of dilapidated buildings reconstructed or removed in the year was 630,000 square meters, with 25,000 households removed. The accumulative floor space of dilapidated buildings reconstructed or removed in the five years reached 2.15 million square meters, with 83,000 households removed. The average per capita usable floor area for urban residents rose increased to16.2 square meters in the year, 0.3 square meter more than the previous year and 2.9 square meters more than 1995. The average per capita living area of rural residents' houses increased to 28.9 square meters, 0.3 square meter more than the previous year and 3.9 square meters more than 1995.

Annex 1 Notes:

a) All figures in the Communique are preliminary statistics.

b) Figures in value terms on added value quoted in the Communique are at current prices, whereas growth rates are calculated at comparable prices unless otherwise indicated.

c) As figures from the 5th Nationwide Census are still under checking, the conclusion on the Census will be published separately in accordance with the uniform requirements of the State Council.

Annex 2 Statistical Statements of the Economic Development 2000

Name of Index	Unit	2000	2000 as % of 1999
Retail Sales of Consumer Commodities	Billion yuan	144.33	109.9
Foodstuffs	Billion yuan	41.02	109.5
Clothing	Billion yuan	17.30	111.2
Daily use commodities	Billion yuan	81.09	109.3
Output of Major Agricultural Products and Byproducts			
Grain	10,000tons	144.2	71.7
Vegetable	Ditto	489.1	114.6
Meat	Ditto	56.3	114.4
Fresh egg	Ditto	16.0	101.3
Milk	Ditto	30.3	126.3

Name of Index	Unit	2000	2000 as % of 1999
Aquatic product	Ditto	7.5	100.0
Pig slaughtered	10,000 heads	415.6	103.7
Output of Major Industrial Products			
Steel product	10,000 tons	696.7	105.0
Electricity generated	Billion kwh	14.53	107.9
Heating supplied	10,000 million kjs	3654	101.8
LPG	10,000 tons	40.0	109.1
Fertilizer	Ditto	6.8	82.6
Cement	Ditto	827.0	104.5
Ethylene	Ditto	65.5	96.4
Motor truck	Nos.	104667	114.9
Color teletron	10,000 pieces	534.4	116.3
Display	10,000 sets	205.6	376.5
Mobile communications equipment	10,000sets (channels)	1421.6	222.6
Micro computer	10,000 sets	257.8	187.6
Cellular phone	10,000 sets	1549.6	268.8
Program-controlled exchanger	10,000 lines	1019.4	133.4
Air conditioner	10,000 sets	31.4	141.2
Liquor	10,000 tons	185.6	124.4
Instant food	Ton	71673	113.8
Milky product	Ton	20579	148.4
Total Volume of Transportation by Various Means (In Beijing)			
Of Freight Transportation	10,000 tons	27827.9	98.4
Railway (anticipated)	10,000 tons	2612.0	101.1
Highway	10,000 tons	25122.0	98.0
Airway	10,000 tons	33.6	112.4
Of Passenger Transportation	10,000 person-times	18526.7	124.6
Railway (anticipated)	10,000 person-times	4589.0	109.2
Highway	10,000 person-times	13009.0	131.7
Civil aviation	10,000 person-times	928.7	117.9
Commodity Retail Price Index (Previous Year=100)		98.9	
Household Consumer Price Index (Previous Year=100)		103.5	
Foodstuffs		97.9	
Clothing		102.6	
Household equipment and commodities		96.3	
Health care commodities		113.5	
Transportation & communication tools		92.3	
Entertainment, education & cultural commodities		97.8	
Housing		117.9	
Service items		116.2	
Durable Consumer Goods Held by Households (per-hundred)			

Name of Index	Unit	2000	2000 as % of 1999
Air conditioner	Sets.	69.9	139.5
Shower heater	Nos.	74.4	110.9
Color TV	Sets	145.5	102.9
Refrigerator	Sets	107.4	104.5
Washer	Nos.	102.8	103.2
Personal computer	Sets	32.1	136.6
Microwave oven	Sets	58.4	119.7
Kitchen ventilator	Sets	112.4	178.7
Electric cooker	Sets	104.0	124.3

2000年北京市第五次全国人口普查主要数据公报

北 京 市 统 计 局

2001 年 4 月 5 日

根据国务院的决定，我市于 2000 年 11 月 1 日进行了第五次全国人口普查的登记工作。在国务院和北京市政府的领导下，在全市各有关单位和广大人民群众的积极支持配合下，经过十万名普查工作人员的艰苦努力，圆满地完成了人口普查的现场登记和复查任务，主要数据的快速汇总工作已经结束。目前，普查的全部资料正在进行电子计算机数据处理，现将主要数据的快速汇总结果公布如下：

一、全市总人口

全市总人口为 1381.9 万人，与 1990 年 7 月 1 日 0 时第四次全国人口普查的 1081.9 万人相比，十年零四个月共增加了 300 万人，增长 27.7%。平均每年增加 29 万人，年平均增长率为 2.4%。

二、自然增长

普查时点前一年，即 1999 年 11 月 1 日至 2000 年 10 月 31 日全市出生人口为 8.1 万人，人口出生率为 6.0‰；死亡人口为 7.0 万人，人口死亡率为 5.1‰；自然增加人口为 1.1 万人，人口自然增长率为 0.9‰。

三、家庭户人口

全市共有家庭户 417.6 万户，家庭户人口为 1214.5 万人，占总人口的 87.9%，平均每个家庭户的人口为 2.9 人，比 1990 年第四次全国人口普查的 3.2 人减少了 0.3 人。

四、人口地区分布

全市人口地区分布如下：

东 城 区	53.6 万人
西 城 区	70.7 万人
崇 文 区	34.6 万人
宣 武 区	52.6 万人
朝 阳 区	229.0 万人
丰 台 区	136.9 万人
石景山区	48.9 万人
海 淀 区	224.0 万人
门头沟区	26.7 万人
房 山 区	81.4 万人
通 州 区	67.4 万人
顺 义 区	63.7 万人
昌 平 区	61.5 万人
大 兴 县	67.2 万人
平 谷 县	39.7 万人
怀 柔 县	29.6 万人
密 云 县	42.0 万人
延 庆 县	27.5 万人

五、性别构成

全市人口中，男性为720.6万人，占总人口的52.1%；女性为661.3万人，占总人口的47.9%。性别比（以女性为100，男性对女性的比例）为109.0，高于1990年第四次全国人口普查的107.0。

六、年龄构成

全市人口中，0--14岁的人口为187.8万人，占总人口的13.6%； 15--64岁的人口为1078.6万人，占总人口的78.0%；65岁及以上的人口为115.5万人，占总人口的8.4%。与1990年第四次全国人口普查相比，0--14岁人口的比重下降了6.6个百分点，65岁及以上人口的比重上升了2.1个百分点。

七、民族构成

全市人口中，汉族人口为1322.9万人，占总人口的95.7%；各少数民族人口为59万人，占总人口的4.3%。与1990年第四次全国人口普查相比，汉族人口增加了282.4万人，增长27.1%；各少数民族人口增加了17.6万人，增长42.5%。

八、各种受教育程度人口

全市6周岁及6周岁以上人口中，接受大学（指大专以上）教育的232.8万人，占17.5%；接受高中（含中专、职高等）教育的319.9万人，占24.1%；接受初中教育的475.3万人，占35.8%；接受小学教育的234.3万人，占17.7%（以上各种受教育程度的人包括各类学校的毕业生、肄业生和在校生）。

与1990年第四次全国人口普查相比，每10万人中拥有各种受教育程度的人数有如下变化：受过大学教育的由9300人上升为16843人；受过高中教育的由18978人上升为23151人；受过初中教育的由30551人上升为34391人；受过小学教育的由22579人下降为16956人。

全市人口中，文盲人口（指15周岁及15周岁以上不识字或识字很少的人）为58.5万人，与1990年第四次全国人口普查相比，文盲率由10.9%下降为4.9%，下降了6个百分点。

九、城乡人口

全市人口中，居住在城镇的人口为1071.6万人，占总人口的77.5%；居住在乡村的人口为310.3万人，占总人口的22.5%。与1990年第四次全国人口普查相比，城镇人口占总人口的比重上升了4.1个百分点。

注：1、本公报为初步汇总数。

2、普查登记以2000年11月1日0时（北京时间）为标准时间，普查登记的对象是具有中华人民共和国国籍并在中华人民共和国境内大陆上常住的人。

3、全市总人口中，包括离开户口登记地半年以上的外地来京人员，不包括户籍人口中离京半年以上的人。

4、家庭户人口中，不包括相互之间没有家庭成员关系、集体居住的人。

5、全市人口地区分布数为各区县实际登记数；全市总人口中包括根据事后质量抽查推算的漏报人数。

6、文盲率是指文盲人口占15周岁及15周岁以上人口的比例。

7、城乡人口是按国家统计局1999年发布的《关于统计上划分城乡的规定（试行）》计算的。

COMMUNIQUE ON MAJOR FIGURES OF THE 2000 POPULATION CENSUS OF BEIJING

Beijing Statistics Bureau

April 5, 2001

According to decision of the State Council, Beijing carried out its fifth national census on November 1st, 2001. Thanks to the leadership of State Council and Beijing municipal government as well as the support and cooperation from extensive masses, the field enumeration and post-enumeration check were completed successfully through the painstaking efforts and hard work of one hundred thousand census workers. AT present, all data colleted through the census are undergoing computer processing. The advanced tabulation of the major figures has completed and the results are released as follows:

I. Total Population of Beijing

Beijing has a population of 13.819 million. Compared with the population of 10.819 million from the 1990 national census (with zero o'clock of July 1st, 1990 as the reference time), it increased by 3 million in number, or 27.7 percent over the past ten years and four months. The average annual growth was 290,000 persons, or a growth rate of 2.4 percent.

II. Natural Growth of Population

During the one-year period before the time point of this census, i.e. from November 1, 1999 to October 31, 2000, 81,000 babies were born, representing a birth rate of 6.0 per mill; 70,000 people died, representing a death rate of 5.1 per mill. The natural population growth was 11,000 persons, or a growth rate of 0.9 per mill.

III. Population of Family Households

There were 4.176 million family households in Beijing, with a population of 12.145 million persons, accounting for 87.9 percent of the total population of Beijing. The average size of a family household was 2.9 persons, or 0.3 persons less as against the 3.2 persons of the 1990 population census.

IV. District Distribution of Population

The population distribution in different districts and counties of Beijing is shown as follows:

Districts & Counties	Population(person)
Dongcheng District	536,000
Xicheng District	707,000
Chongwen District	346,000
Xuanwu District	526,000
Chaoyang District	2,290,000
Fengtai District	1,369,000
Shijingshan District	489,000
Haidian District	2,240,000
Mentougou District	267,000
Fangshan District	814,000
Tongzhou District	674,000
Shunyi District	637,000

Districts & Counties	Population(person)
Changping District	615,000
Daxing County	672,000
Pinggu County	397,000
Huairou County	296,000
Miyun County	420,000
Yanqing County	275,000

V. Sex Composition

Of the people enumerated in Beijing, 7.206 million or 52.1 percent were males, while 6.613 million or 47.9 percent were females. The sex ratio (female=100) was 109.0, higher than the 107.0 from the 1990 population census.

VI. Age Composition

Of the people enumerated in Beijing, 1.878 million persons were in the age group of 0-14, accounting for 13.6 percent of the total population; 10.786 million persons in the age group of 15-64, accounting for 78.0 percent and 1.155 million persons in the age group of 65 and over, accounting for 8.4 percent. As compared with the results of the 1990 population census, the share of people in the age group of 0-14 was down by 6.6 percentage points, and that for people aged 65 and over was up by 2.1 percentage points.

VII. Composition of Ethnic Groups

Of the people enumerated in Beijing, 13.229 million persons or 95.7 percent were of Han ethnic group, and 590,000 persons or 4.3 percent were of various minority ethnic groups. Compared with the 1990 population census, the population of Han people increased by 2.824 million persons, or 27.1 percent; while the population of various minority ethnic groups increased by 176,000 persons, or 42.5 percent.

VIII. Composition of Educational Attainment

Of the people aged 6 and over in Beijing, 2.328 million persons or 17.5 percent had finished university education (referring to junior college and above); 3.199 million persons or 24.1 percent had received senior secondary education (including secondary technical school education and vocational senior middle school education); 2.343 million persons or 17.7 percent had had primary education (the educated persons included graduates and students in various schools).

Compared with the 1990 population census, the following changes have taken place in the number of people with various education attainments per every 100,000 people: number of people with university education increased to 16,843 from 9300; number of people with senior secondary education increased to 23,151 from 18,987; number of people with junior secondary education increased from 30,551 to 34,391; and number of people with primary education decreased from 22,579 to 16,956.

Of the people enumerated in Beijing, 585,000 persons were illiterate (i.e. people over 15 years old who cannot read or can read very little). Compared with the 10.9 percent of illiterate people in the 1990 population census, the proportion has dropped to 4.9 percent, or down by 6 percentage points.

IX. Urban and Rural Population

In Beijing, there were 10.716 million urban residents, accounting for 77.5 percent of the total population; and rural residents numbered 3.103 million, accounting for 22.5 percent. Compared with the 1990 population census, the proportion of urban residents rose by 4.1 percentage points.

Note:

a) All figures in the Communiqué are preliminary results.

b) Population enumerated, with zero o'clock of November 1, 2000 (Beijing Time) as the reference time, refers to people with citizenship of the People's Republic of China and with permanent residence on the mainland of P.R.C.

c) The total population of Beijing includes persons who came to Beijing from other provinces and regions in the country and had not been in their household registry jurisdictional areas for more than half a year, and does not include those who are permanent residents of Beijing and had not been in Beijing for more than half a year.

d) Population of family households does not include those who are not related to one another and live as single persons in a non-family household.

e) Calculation of the population distributed in different districts and counties of Beijing is based on the actual population enumerated in different districts and counties; the figure of the total population of Beijing includes the under-reported population estimated by a post-enumeration sample check.

f) The proportion of illiterate people refers to the proportion of illiterate people to the people aged 15 and over.

g) Calculation of urban and rural population is based on the Proposal Regulation on Statistical Classification of Urban and Rural Areas released by the National Bureau of Statistics in 1999.

北京统计年鉴——2001

BEIJING STATISTICAL YEARBOOK

统 计 图 表

STATISTICAL GRAPH AND CHART

综　合 1

GENERAL SURVEY

国内生产总值 （单位：亿元）
Gross Domestic Product (100 million yuan)

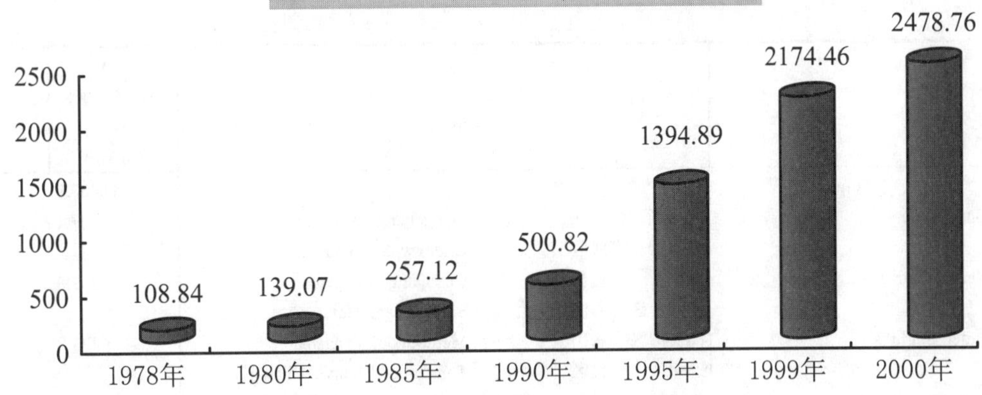

国内生产总值产业构成
Industry Composition of Gross Domestic Product

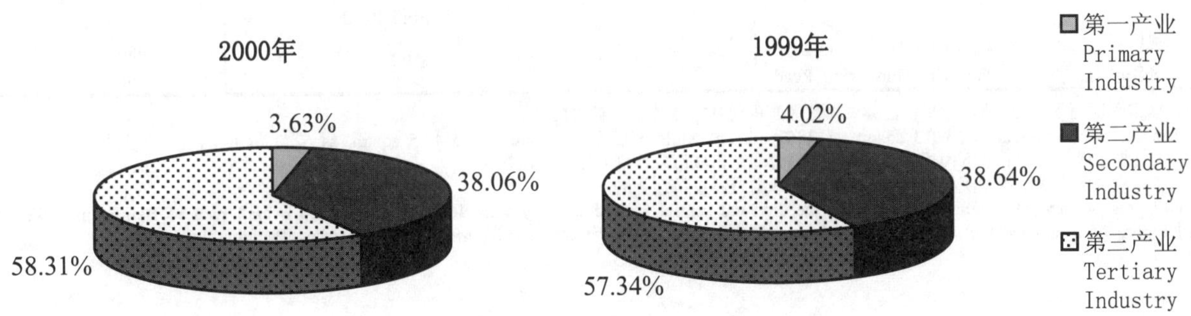

地方财政收支 （单位：亿元）
Local Financial Revenue and Expenditure (100 million yuan)

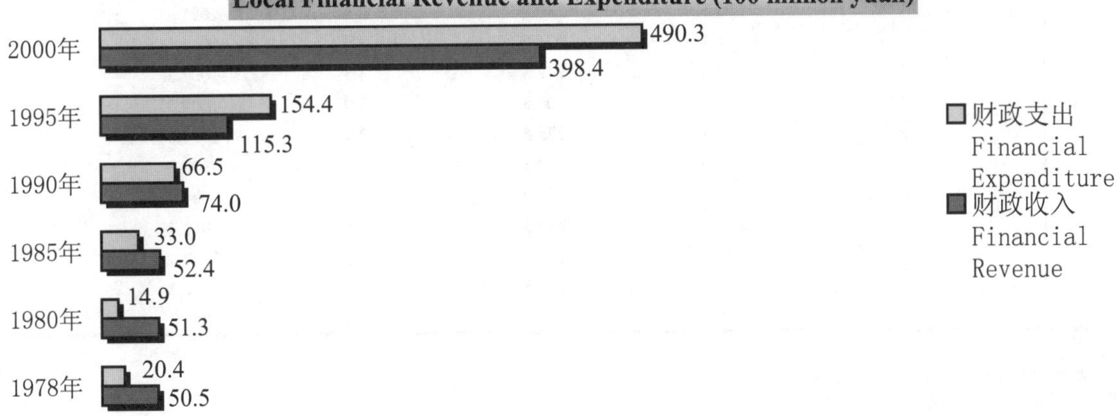

1-1 土 地 面 积
LAND AREA

项目	Item	范围	Scope	面积(平方公里) Area (sq.km)	比重(%) Proportion (%)
全 市	**Total**			**16807.8**	**100**
城 区	City Proper	东城区、西城区、崇文区、宣武区	Dongcheng, Xicheng, Chongwen, Xuanwu	87.1	0.5
近郊区	Near Suburbs	朝阳区、丰台区、石景山区、海淀区	Chaoyang, Fengtai, Shijingshan, Haidian	1282.8	7.6
远郊区	Outer Suburbs	门头沟区、房山区、通州区、顺义区、昌平区	Mentougou, Fangshan, Tongzhou, Shunyi, Changping	6473.8	38.5
各 县	Counties	大兴县、平谷县、怀柔县、密云县、延庆县	Daxing, Pinggu, Huairou, Miyun,Yanqing	8964.1	53.4
规划市区	**Programmed Scope of the City**			**1041.0**	**6.2**
		东：定福庄	East：Dingfuzhuang		
		南：南苑	South：Nanyuan		
		西：石景山	West：Shijingshan		
		北：清河	North：Qinghe		
市区中心地区	Central Part of the City	边缘大体在四环路内外	The edge is roughly around the Fourth Ring Road	289.8	1.7
建成区	Completed Part			490.1	2.9
三环路以内	Within The Third Ring Road			158.0	0.9

附：全市平原面积6390.3平方公里，占38%。山区面积10417.5平方公里，占62%。
Appendix：Area of plain is 6390.3 sq.km, as 38% of total while area of mountain is 10147.5 sq.km, as 62% of total.
注：1.规划市区、市中心地区面积是1992年重新修订北京市城市总体规划后确定的数字。
2.建成区面积是市规划院根据1989年航空遥感照射资料重新计算的。
a) Figures on area of programmed scope of the city and central part of the city were in line with revised overall plan of Beijing in 1992.
b) Figure of completed part was recalculated according to data of air remote sensing irradiation by Beijing Planning Institution.

1-2 气 象
METEOROLOGY

月份 Month	降水量(毫米) Precipitation (mm)	平均气温(℃) Average Temperature (℃)	日照时数(时) Hours of Sunshine (hour)	平均风速(米/秒) Average Wind Speed (mile/second)	平均气压(百帕) Average Pressure (100 pa)	大风日数(日) Days of Strong Wind (day)
全 年 Total	**371.1**	**12.8**	**2667.2**	**2.5**	**1012.7**	**10**
1	11.9	-6.4	170.9	2.6	1027.4	1
2	0	-1.5	230.8	2.4	1021.8	1
3	8.8	8.1	275.5	3.4	1014.1	3
4	18.3	14.6	248.8	3.3	1007.3	4
5	37.7	20.4	304.8	2.9	1004.5	0
6	19.0	26.7	275.2	2.4	1001.8	1
7	61.5	29.6	232.3	2.4	998.4	0
8	150.5	25.7	186.9	2.0	1004.0	0
9	18.4	21.8	239.3	1.8	1010.7	0
10	35.2	12.6	170.0	2.2	1017.5	0
11	9.7	3.0	159.5	2.3	1022.7	0
12	0.1	-0.6	173.2	2.3	1021.8	0

附：1.无霜期204天。
2.年极端最高气温39.4℃，出现日期7月1日。
3.年极端最低气温-15℃，出现日期1月16日。
a) Annual frost-free period is 204 days.
b) Annual utmost highest air temperature is 39.4℃,on the 1st of July.
c) Annual utmost lowest air temperature is −15℃,on the 16th of January.

1-3 行 政 区 划
ADMINISTRATIVE DIVISIONS

单位：个 (number)

地 区 Region		镇 Town	乡 Township	街道办事处 Urban Subdistrict Office	居家委员会 Neighborhood Committee	村民委员会 Village Committee
全 市	**Total**	**142**	**70**	**123**	**4438**	**4039**
城 区	**City Propers**			**35**	**978**	
东 城 区	Dongcheng			10	285	
西 城 区	Xicheng			10	298	
崇 文 区	Chongwen			7	156	
宣 武 区	Xuanwu			8	239	
近 郊 区	**Near Suburbs**	**1**	**40**	**70**	**2690**	**340**
朝 阳 区	Chaoyang		24	22	1055	169
丰 台 区	Fengtai		6	16	356	81
石景山区	Shijingshan			10	208	11
海 淀 区	Haidian	1	10	22	1071	79
远 郊 区	**Outer Suburbs**	**81**	**10**	**18**	**557**	**1870**
门头沟区	Mentougou	9	1	4	104	189
房 山 区	Fangshan	19	8	7	133	463
通 州 区	Tongzhou	18	1	4	152	480
顺 义 区	Shunyi	19		2	44	425
昌 平 区	Changping	16		1	124	313
各 县	**Counties**	**60**	**20**		**213**	**1829**
大 兴 县	Daxing	14			50	547
平 谷 县	Pinggu	12	5		36	273
怀 柔 县	Huairou	10	5		32	287
密 云 县	Miyun	13	6		61	345
延 庆 县	Yanqing	11	4		34	377

1-4 全部法人单位数(按所在地分)
TOTAL INSTITUTIONAL UNITS (BY REGION)

单位：个 (unit)

地区	Region	合计 Total	中央单位 of Central	市属单位 of City	区县属单位 of District and County
全市	**Total**	**95950**	**11041**	**10262**	**74647**
城区	**City Propers**	**23547**	**4204**	**3267**	**16076**
东城区	Dongcheng	8982	1443	903	6636
西城区	Xicheng	7852	2138	1079	4635
崇文区	Chongwen	3058	236	544	2278
宣武区	Xuanwu	3655	387	741	2527
近郊区	**Near Suburbs**	**45915**	**6044**	**5836**	**34035**
朝阳区	Chaoyang	17390	1720	2876	12794
丰台区	Fengtai	8868	976	972	6920
石景山区	Shijingshan	2381	146	246	1989
海淀区	Haidian	17276	3202	1742	12332
远郊区	**Outer Suburbs**	**15442**	**527**	**751**	**14164**
门头沟区	Mentougou	1775	38	68	1669
房山区	Fangshan	3221	197	127	2897
通州区	Tongzhou	4199	116	206	3877
顺义区	Shunyi	2945	55	89	2801
昌平区	Changping	3302	121	261	2920
各县	**Counties**	**11046**	**266**	**408**	**10372**
大兴县	Daxing	5073	133	264	4676
平谷县	Pinggu	1315	20	25	1270
怀柔县	Huairou	1763	39	29	1695
密云县	Miyun	1475	42	37	1396
延庆县	Yanqing	1420	32	53	1335

1-5 全部法人、产业活动单位数(按所在地分)
TOTAL INSTITUTIONAL UNITS AND ESTABLISHMENTS (BY REGION)

单位：个 (unit)

地区	Region	法人单位数 合计 Institutional Units	单产业法人 Single Sector	多产业法人 Multi-sector	多产业法人单位的产业活动单位数 Establishments of Multi-sector Institutional Units
全市	**Total**	**95950**	**92926**	**3024**	**14538**
城区	**City Propers**	**23547**	**22652**	**895**	**4206**
东城区	Dongcheng	8982	8723	259	1290
西城区	Xicheng	7852	7492	360	1668
崇文区	Chongwen	3058	2955	103	526
宣武区	Xuanwu	3655	3482	173	722
近郊区	**Near Suburbs**	**45915**	**44737**	**1178**	**5886**
朝阳区	Chaoyang	17390	16708	682	2917
丰台区	Fengtai	8868	8659	209	1266
石景山区	Shijingshan	2381	2307	74	417
海淀区	Haidian	17276	17063	213	1286
远郊区	**Outer Suburbs**	**15442**	**14804**	**638**	**2970**
门头沟区	Mentougou	1775	1624	151	736
房山区	Fangshan	3221	3078	143	695
通州区	Tongzhou	4199	4047	152	717
顺义区	Shunyi	2945	2894	51	156
昌平区	Changping	3302	3161	141	666
各县	**Counties**	**11046**	**10733**	**313**	**1476**
大兴县	Daxing	5073	4961	112	475
平谷县	Pinggu	1315	1273	42	274
怀柔县	Huairou	1763	1687	76	370
密云县	Miyun	1475	1444	31	89
延庆县	Yanqing	1420	1368	52	268

注：多产业法人单位的产业活动单位在本市有14538个,有29个在外省市。

Note: Of total establishments of multi-sector institutional units, there are 14538 in local and 29 in outports.

1-6 全部法人、产业活动单位数
TOTAL INSTITUTIONAL UNITS AND ESTABLISHMENTS

单位：个 (unit)

项目	Item	法人单位数合计 Institutional Units	单产业法人 Single Sector	多产业法人 Multi-sector	多产业法人单位的产业活动单位数 Establishments of Multi-sector Institutional Units
总计	**Total**	**95950**	**92926**	**3024**	**14567**
按登记注册类型分	**Grouped by Registration Status**				
内资经济	Domestic Investment Economy	90123	87137	2986	14364
国有经济	State-owned	24948	23224	1724	9053
集体经济	Collective-owned	25768	25136	632	4404
股份合作企业	Share Holding	4925	4883	42	135
联营经济	Joint-owned	915	895	20	79
国有独资公司	State-owned Funded Company	246	228	18	68
其他有限责任公司	Other Limited-Liability Corporations	10214	10141	73	229
股份有限公司	Share Holding Corporations Ltd.	1535	1498	37	217
私营经济	Private	15240	15189	51	171
其他	Others	6332	5943	389	8
港澳台商投资经济	Hongkong,Macao and Taiwan Funded	2320	2304	16	53
与港澳台商合资经营	Joint Venture with Hongkong, Macao and Taiwan	1577	1566	11	34
与港澳台商合作经营	Cooperative with Hongkong, Macao and Taiwan	231	229	2	6
港、澳、台商独资经济	Hongkong,Macao and Taiwan Funded	493	491	2	6
港澳台商投资股份有限公司	Hongkong,Macao and Taiwan Share Holding Corporations Ltd.	19	18	1	7
外商投资经济	Foreign Funded	3507	3485	22	150
中外合资经营	Chinese-Foreign Joint Venture	2018	2001	17	134
中外合作经营	Chinese-Foreign Cooperative	294	293	1	4
外资(独资)经济	Foreign Funded	1177	1174	3	11
外商投资股份有限公司	Foreign Share Holding Corporation Ltd.	18	17	1	1
按单位类别分	**Grouped by Type of Units**				
农业	Agriculture	820	786	34	152
工业	Industry	19422	19096	326	1351
建筑业	Construction	3501	3367	134	558
运输邮电业	Transportation,Posts and Tele-communications	490	448	42	278
批发零售贸易及餐饮业	Wholesale, Retail and Catering	25060	24142	918	6539
服务业	Services	28608	28036	572	3348
行政事业及其他	Administrative Units,Institutions and Others	18049	17051	998	2341
按隶属关系分	**Grouped by Administrative Relationship**				
中央属	Central	11041	10515	526	2363
市属	City	10262	9691	571	2737
区县属	Districts and Counties	18215	17125	1090	6434
街道属	Subdistrict	3763	3636	127	816
镇属	Town	4810	4711	99	375
乡属	Township	2348	2277	71	301
居委会属	Neighborhood Committee	3240	2962	278	789
村委会属	Village Committee	11246	11132	114	284
其他	Others	31025	30877	148	468
按地理位置分	**Grouped by Geographic Position**				
二环路以内	Within the Second Ring Road	17298	16683	615	2977
二环路至三环路	the Second-third Ring Road	20265	19637	628	2851
三环路至四环路	the Third-Fourth Ring Road	16424	15995	429	1974
四环路以外	Beyond the Fourth Ring Road	41963	40611	1352	6736
按执行会计制度分	**Grouped by Accounting System Executed**				
企业	Enterprises	78378	76324	2054	
事业	Institutions	7640	7184	456	
机关	Agencies and Organizations	1486	1417	69	
其他	Others	8446	8001	445	

1-7 企业法人单位数
ENTERPRISE INSTITUTIONAL UNITS

单位：个 (unit)

项目	Item	法人单位合计 Institutional Unit	项目	Item	法人单位合计 Institutional Unit
总　计	**Total**	**78378**	**按登记注册类型分**	**Grouped by Registration Status**	
城　区	**City Propers**	**19898**	内资企业	Domestic Investment Enterprises	72560
东城区	Dongcheng	7760	国有企业	State-owned	15683
西城区	Xicheng	6459	集体企业	Collective-owned	23831
崇文区	Chongwen	2466	股份合作企业	Share Holding Cooperative	4914
宣武区	Xuanwu	3213	联营企业	Joint-owned	908
近郊区	**Near Suburbs**	**39596**	国有独资公司	State-owned Funded Company	243
朝阳区	Chaoyang	15022	其他有限责任公司	Other Limited-Liability Corporations	10213
丰台区	Fengtai	7658			
石景山区	Shijingshan	1871	股份有限公司	Share Holding Corporations Ltd.	1535
海淀区	Haidian	15045			
远郊区	**Outer Suburbs**	**11187**	私营企业	Private	15149
门头沟区	Mentougou	1126	其他内资企业	Others	84
房山区	Fangshan	2186	港澳台商投资企业	Hongkong,Macao and Taiwan Funded	2318
通州区	Tongzhou	3262			
顺义区	Shunyi	2153	与港澳台商合资经营企业	Joint Venture with Hongkong, Maocao and Taiwan	1577
昌平区	Changping	2460			
各　县	**Counties**	**7697**	与港澳台商合作经营企业	Cooperative with Hongkong, Macao and Taiwan	230
大兴县	Daxing	4122			
平谷县	Pinggu	766	港、澳、台商独资企业	Hongkong,Macao and Taiwan Funded	492
怀柔县	Huairou	1222			
密云县	Miyun	837	港澳台商投资股份有限公司	Hongkong,Macao and Taiwan Share Holding Corporations Ltd.	19
延庆县	Yanqing	750			
按营业状况分	**Grouped by Business**				
营　业	Going on	68093	外商投资企业	Foreign Funded	3500
停　业	Closed	5122	中外合资经营企业	Chinese-Foreign Joint Venture	2017
筹　建	Preparation	2770	中外合作经营企业	Chinese-Foreign Cooperative	291
当年撤销	Recall in this Year	1246	外资(独资)企业	Foreign Funded	1174
其　他	Others	1147	外商投资股份有限公司	Foreign Share Holding Corporations Ltd.	18
按开业时间分	**Grouped by Set up Time**		**按地理位置分**	**Grouped by Location**	
1949年以前	Before 1949	191	二环路以内	Within the Second Ring Road	14732
	1950——1965	1665	二环路至三环路	Between the Second-third Ring Road	17474
	1966——1979	2009			
	1980——1989	10675	三环路至四环路	Between the Third-Fourth Ring Road	14004
1990年以后	After 1990	63838			
按企业规模分	**Grouped by Size**		四环路以外	Beyond the Fourth Ring Road	32168
大　型	Large	715	**按控股情况分**	**Grouped by Share Holding Conditions**	
中　型	Medium	2310			
小　型	Small	45062	# 国有绝对控股	State-owned Relative Holding	17579
			国有相对控股	State-owned Absolute Holding	1579

1-8 国民经济各行业法人和产业活动单位数(按行业分)

INSTITUTIONAL UNITS AND ESTABLISHMENTS(BY SECTOR)

单位：个 (unit)

行业	Sector	法人单位数合计 Institutional Units	单产业法人 Single Sector	多产业法人 Multi-sector	多产业法人单位的产业活动单位数 Establishments of Multi-sector Institutional Units
合　计	**Total**	**95950**	**92926**	**3024**	**14567**
农　业	Agriculture	382	369	13	72
林　业	Forestry	70	58	12	26
畜牧业	Animal Husbandry	319	311	8	57
渔　业	Fishery	49	48	1	11
农、林、牧、渔服务业	FFAF Services	524	501	23	95
煤炭采选业	Coal Mining and Dressing	185	182	3	67
石油和天然气开采业	Petroleum and Natural Gas Extraction				
黑色金属矿采选业	Ferrous Metals Mining and Dressing	20	20		1
有色金属矿采选业	Nonferrous Metals Mining and Dressing	16	16		3
非金属矿采选业	Nonmetal Minerals Mining and Dressing	258	258		15
其他矿采选业	Other Minerals Mining and Dressing	2	2		
食品加工业	Food Processing	573	564	9	49
食品制造业	Food Making	635	629	6	45
饮料制造业	Beverage Making	282	279	3	10
烟草制造业	Tobacco Processing	4	4		
纺织业	Textile	479	463	16	51
服装及其他纤维制品制造业	Garments and Other Fiber Products	941	917	24	74
皮革、毛皮、羽绒及其制品业	Leather,Furs,Down and Related Products	175	172	3	11
木材加工及竹、藤、棕、革制品业	Timber Processing,Bamboo,Cane, Palm Fiber and Straw Products	246	244	2	19
家具制造业	Furniture Manufacturing	549	546	3	16
造纸及纸制品业	Papermaking and Paper Products	506	505	1	10
印刷业、记录媒介的复制	Printing and Record Medium Reproduction	1001	980	21	57
文教体育用品制造业	Stationery,Education and Sports Goods	231	228	3	6
石油加工及炼焦业	Petroleum Processing and Coking	111	109	2	5
化学原料及化学制品制造业	Raw Chemical Materials and Chemical Products	1376	1364	12	63
医药制造业	Medical and Pharmaceutical Products	286	280	6	15
化学纤维制造业	Chemical Fiber	44	44		

1-8 续表 1 continued

单位：个 (unit)

行业	Sector	法人单位数合计 Institutional Units	单产业法人 Single Sector	多产业法人 Multi-sector	多产业法人单位的产业活动单位数 Establishments of Multi-sector Institutional Units
橡胶制品业	Rubber Products	126	119	7	13
塑料制品业	Plastic Products	737	730	7	30
非金属矿物制品业	Nonmetal Mineral Products	1738	1716	22	102
黑色金属冶炼及压延加工业	Smelting and Processing of Ferrous Metals	81	76	5	27
有色金属冶炼及压延加工业	Smelting and Processing of Nonferrous Metals	151	148	3	8
金属制品业	Metal Products	2205	2188	17	107
普通机械制造业	Ordinary Machinery	1228	1210	18	84
专业设备制造业	Special Purpose Equipment	1052	1025	27	91
交通运输设备制造业	Transportation Equipment	1297	1261	36	162
武器弹药制造业	Weapons and Ammunition	11	7	4	5
电气机械及器材制造业	Electric Equipment and Machinery	912	893	19	61
电子及通信设备制造业	Electronic and Telecommunications Equipment	817	804	13	25
仪器仪表及文化办公用机械制造业	Instruments,Meters,Cultural and Office Machinery	476	472	4	13
其他制造业	Other Manufacturing	583	562	21	69
电力、蒸汽、热水的生产和供应业	Electricity,Steam,Hot Water Production and Supply	64	58	6	20
煤气生产和供应业	Gas Production and Supply	12	10	2	5
自来水的生产和供应业	Tap Water Production and Supply	12	11	1	12
土木工程建筑业	Civil Engineering	1423	1324	99	395
线路、管道和设备安装业	Lines,Pipelines and Equipment Installation	825	799	26	86
装修装饰业	Fitting and Decoration	1253	1244	9	77
地质勘查业	Geological Prospecting	55	52	3	3
水利管理业	Water Conservancy	186	167	19	27
铁路运输业	Railway Transport	24	22	2	80
公路运输业	Highway Transport	382	348	34	136
管道运输业	Pipeline Transport	1	1		
水上运输业	Waterway Transport	3	3		
航空运输业	Air Transport	8	8		
交通运输辅助业	Transport Supporting and Auxiliary Services	279	277	2	26
其他交通运输业	Other Transport	12	12		3
仓储业	Storage	249	246	3	21
邮电通信业	Posts and Telecommunications	67	61	6	62
食品、饮料、烟草和家庭用品批发业	Wholesale of Food, Beverage, Tobacoo and Household Articles	5069	4885	184	575

1-8 续表 2 continued

单位：个 (unit)

行业	Sector	法人单位数合计 Institutional Units	单产业法人 Single Sector	多产业法人 Multi-sector	多产业法人单位的产业活动单位数 Establishments of Multi-sector Institutional Units
能源、材料和机械电子设备批发业	Wholesale of Energy, Materials and Electronic Equipment	5040	4934	106	424
其他批发业	Other Wholesale Trade	855	840	15	56
零售业	Retail Trade	11535	11003	532	4453
商业经纪与代理业	Commercial Brokerage and Agencies	75	72	3	5
餐饮业	Catering	2560	2479	81	1031
金融业	Banking	911	656	255	1419
保险业	Insurance	50	50		
房地产开发与经营业	Real Estate Development and Operation	897	881	16	37
房地产管理业	Real Estate Management	1173	1140	33	75
房地产代理与经纪业	Real Estate Brokerage and Agency	106	106		2
公共服务业	Public Services	1395	1346	49	165
居民服务业	Resident Services	1843	1763	71	733
旅馆业	Hotels	1724	1673	51	394
租赁服务业	Leasing Services	398	394	4	49
旅游业	Tourism	378	372	6	25
娱乐服务业	Recreational Services	349	345	4	40
信息、咨询服务业	Information and Consultancy Services	6243	6221	22	107
计算机应用服务业	Computer Application Services	2558	2553	5	15
其他社会服务业	Other Social Services	1508	1475	33	126
卫 生	Health	671	658	13	45
体 育	Sports	133	128	5	11
社会福利保障业	Social Welfare	187	184	3	18
教 育	Education	2950	2695	255	1355
文化艺术业	Culture and Arts	1369	1329	40	80
广播电影电视业	Radio,Film,Television	175	169	6	11
科学研究业	Scientific Research	558	532	26	45
综合技术服务业	Polytechnical Services	7909	7883	26	83
国家机关	Government Organs	1570	1491	79	101
政党机关	Party Organs	97	96	1	1
社会团体	Social Bodies	481	469	12	18
基层群众自治组织	Masses Autonomous Body	8375	7928	447	448
其他行业	Other Sectors	1284	1229	55	92

1-9 全市个体、私营经济基本情况

STATISTICS FOR INDIVIDUAL AND PRIVATE ECONOMY

单位：万元 (10000 yuan)

项目 Item		私营 Private			个体 Individuals		
		2000	1999	2000年为1999年% 2000 as % of 1999	2000	1999	2000年为1999年% 2000 as % of 1999
工商登记注册 *	**Registered in Department of Industry and Commerce**						
户数 （户）	Number of Households (household)	102787	83203	123.5	245241	257416	95.3
从业人员 （人）	Employed Persons (person)	90785	83906	108.2	345332	359077	96.2
注册资本	Registered Capital	10362744	6738222	153.8	266766	275772	96.7
地税税收	**Taxes to Local Tax Department**						
户数 （户）	Number of Households (household)	26163	47323	55.3			
入库税收合计	Taxes Put into National Treasury	159995	84916	188.4	11191	11856	94.4
#营业税	Business Tax	74864	35757	209.4	5334	5689	93.8
国税税收	**Taxes to National Tax Department**						
户数 （户）	Number of Households (household)				58370	51620	113.1
纳税总金额	Total Taxes Paid	54421	36155	150.5	35134	34677	101.3
#增值税	Increased Value Tax	54398	36151	150.5	29008	22385	129.6
单位代码发放 *	**Institution Code Sent out**						
户数 （户）	Number of Households (household)	12277	10780	113.9			
工业总产值	**Gross Output Value of Industry**				**668073**	**456497**	**146.3**
商品销售额	**Sales Value**				**2533837**	**2308924**	**109.7**
固定资产投资完成额	**Investment in Fixed Assets Completed**	**14075**	**20096**	**70.0**			

注：1.私营工商登记注册从业人员不含自然人有限公司从业人员。
2.固定资产投资完成额为私营个体合计数。
3.*为时点累计数。

a) Employed persons registered of private economy exclude those of limited company established by natural persons.
b) Investment in fixed assets completed is total data of private and individual economy.
c) Data with * indicates the accumulative one at the year-end.

1-10 国民经济主要指标
MAJOR INDICATORS FOR NATIONAL ECONOMY

项目		Item		2000	1999	2000年为1999年% 2000 as % of 1999
人口		**Population**				
年末常住户籍人口	(万人)	Year-end Permanent Residents Registered	(10000 persons)	1107.5	1099.8	100.7
劳动力		**Labor Force**				
从业人员	(万人)	Employment	(10000 persons)	619.3	618.6	100.1
# 职工人数	(万人)	Staff and Workers	(10000 persons)	434.2	438.0	99.1
国内生产总值	**(亿元)**	**Gross Domestic Product**	**(100 million yuan)**	**2478.8**	**2174.5**	**111.0**
工农业总产值 (1990年不变价,亿元)		**Gross Output Value of Industry and Agriculture (at 1990 constant prices, 100 million yuan)**		**2902.6**	**2224.9**	**130.5**
全社会固定资产投资	**(亿元)**	**Total Investment in Fixed Assets**	**(100 million yuan)**	**1297.4**	**1170.6**	110.8
# 固定资产投资	(亿元)	Investment in Fixed Assets	(100 million yuan)	1192.6	1072.9	111.2
# 基本建设投资	(亿元)	Capital Construction	(100 million yuan)	447.0	432.7	103.3
更新改造投资	(亿元)	.Innovation	(100 million yuan)	185.9	175.2	106.1
房地产开发投资	(亿元)	Real Estate Development	(100 million yuan)	522.1	421.5	123.9
财政		**Finance**				
财政收入	(亿元)	Revenue	(100 million yuan)	398.4	320.4	124.3
财政支出	(亿元)	Expenditures	(100 million yuan)	490.3	398.5	123.0
物价		**Price Indices**				
居民消费价格总指数	(%)	Consumer Price Index	(%)	103.5	100.6	
商品零售价格总指数	(%)	Retail Price Index	(%)	98.9	98.8	
职工工资		**Wages of Staff and Workers**				
职工工资总额	(亿元)	Total Wages	(100 million yuan)	695.5	614.5	113.2
职工平均工资	(元)	Average Wage	(yuan)	15726	13778	114.1
居民消费水平	**(元)**	**Per Capita Consumption**	**(yuan)**	**7326**	**5784**	**124.5**
非农业居民	(元)	Non-Agricultural	(yuan)	9054	7040	127.7
农业居民	(元)	Agricultural	(yuan)	3601	3168	108.3
农村经济		**Rural Economy**				
农林牧渔业总产值 (1990年不变价,亿元)		Gross Output Value of Farming,Forestry,Animal Husbandry and Fishery(at 1990 constant prices)	(100 million yuan)	112.6	99.6	113.1
乡镇集体企业数	(个)	Number of Township and Village Enterprises	(unit)	11961	13428	89.1
乡镇企业从业人数	(万人)	Employment of Township and Village Enterprises	(10000 persons)	68.2	69.3	98.4
乡镇企业总收入	(亿元)	Total Revenue of Township and Village Enterprises	(100 million yuan)	660.2	589.2	112.1
工业		**Industry**				
工业总产值(1990年不变价，不含个体工业，亿元)		Gross Output Value (at 1990 constant prices,excluding individual industry,100 million yuan)		2722.8	2081.0	130.8
轻工业	(亿元)	Light Industry	(100 million yuan)	648.4	556.1	116.6
重工业	(亿元)	Heavy Industry	(100 million yuan)	2074.3	1524.9	136.0

1-10 续表 1 continued

项目	Item	2000	1999	2000年为1999年% 2000 as % of 1999
独立核算工业企业全员劳动生产率(按增加值计算，元/人)	Overall Labor Productivity of Enterprises with Independent Accounting System (according to added value,yuan/person)	51469	36347	141.6
独立核算工业企业主要财务指标	Major Financial Indicators for Enterprises with Independent Accounting System			
固定资产原价 (亿元)	Original Value of Fixed Assets (100 million yuan)	2531.6	2312.1	109.5
利税总额 (亿元)	Total Pre-tax Profits (100 million yuan)	256.1	184.6	138.7
运输邮电	**Transportation,Posts and Telecommunications**			
货物周转量 (亿吨公里)	Freight Ton-Kilometers (100 million ton-km)	299.6	283.9	105.5
铁路 (亿吨公里)	Railways (100 million ton-km)	200.2	192.9	103.8
公路 (亿吨公里)	Highways (100 million ton-km)	82.6	75.4	109.5
民航 (亿吨公里)	Civil Aviation (100 million ton-km)	16.8	15.5	108.4
管道 (亿吨公里)	Pipelines (100 million ton-km)	0.04	0.02	200.0
旅客周转量 (亿人公里)	Passenger-Kilometers (100 million passenger-km)	314.0	270.1	116.3
铁路 (亿人公里)	Railways (100 million passenger-km)	62.7	58.0	108.1
公路 (亿人公里)	Highways (100 million passenger-km)	52.8	40.1	131.7
民航 (亿人公里)	Civil Aviation (100 million passenger-km)	198.5	172.1	115.3
邮电业务总量 (亿元)	Business Volume of Posts and Telecommunication Services (100 million yuan)	214.7	165.9	129.4
全市电话交换机总容量 (万门)	Total Capacity of Telephone Exchanges (10000 lines)	803.7	748.3	107.4
商　业	**Commerce**			
社会消费品零售额 (亿元)	Total Retail Sales of Consumer Goods (100 million yuan)	1443.3	1313.3	109.9
批发零售贸易业 (亿元)	Wholesale and Retail (100 million yuan)	1025.5	926.2	110.7
餐饮业 (亿元)	Catering (100 million yuan)	86.4	81.3	106.3
其他 (亿元)	Others (100 million yuan)	331.4	305.8	108.4
商业饮食业服务业营业网点 (万个)	Outlets of Commerce,Catering and Services (10000)	23.6	24.4	96.7
# 商业 (万个)	Commerce (10000)	17.5	17.7	98.9
饮食业 (万个)	Catering (10000)	2.9	3.2	90.6
服务业 (万个)	Services (10000)	3.3	3.5	94.3
对外经济贸易和旅游	**Foreign Economy,Trade and Tourism**			
地方企业进出口总额 (亿美元)	Total Import and Export of Local Enterprises (USD 100 million)	116.5	84.4	138.8
进口额 (亿美元)	Total Imports (USD 100 million)	70.2	51.8	135.6
出口额 (亿美元)	Total Exports (USD 100 million)	46.3	32.6	141.9
新批三资企业数 (个)	Number of Foreign-funded Enterprises (unit)	1149	647	177.6
协议外资金额 (亿美元)	Total Amount of Foreign Capital in the Signed Agreements (USD 100 million)	43.4	18.3	2.4倍

1-10 续表 2 continued

项目		Item		2000	1999	2000年为1999年% 2000 as % of 1999
实际利用外资	(亿美元)	Total Amount of Foreign Capital Actually Used	(USD 100 million)	30.1	29.4	102.4
# 外商直接投资	(亿美元)	Foreign Direct Investments	(USD 100 million)	24.6	22.3	110.3
接待入境旅游人数	(万人次)	Number of International Tourists	(10000 person.times)	282.1	252.4	111.8
金融保险		**Banking and Insurance**				
银行存款增加额	(亿元)	Adding Deposits of Banks	(100 million yuan)	1364.4	1376.9	99.1
银行贷款增加额	(亿元)	Adding Loans of Banks	(100 million yuan)	1084.8	513.4	2.1倍
城乡居民储蓄存款余额	(亿元)	Saving Deposits of Urban and Rural Residents	(100 million yuan)	2923.2	2680.7	109.0
城镇	(亿元)	Urban	(100 million yuan)	2663.3	2429.0	109.6
农村	(亿元)	Rural	(100 million yuan)	259.9	251.6	103.3
保险公司保险费收入	(亿元)	Premiums Income of Insurance Company	(100 million yuan)	88	86.5	101.8
教 育		**Education**				
毕业生数	(万人)	Number of Graduates	(10000 persons)	51.0	50.1	101.8
研究生	(人)	Postgraduates	(person)	13238	12241	108.1
高等学校	(万人)	Institutions of Higher Education	(10000 persons)	5.2	5.0	104.0
中等职业技术教育	(万人)	Secondary Vocational Technical Education	(10000 persons)	8.5	7.9	107.6
普通中学	(万人)	Regular Secondary School	(10000 persons)	18.7	19.4	96.4
小学	(万人)	Primary Schools	(10000 persons)	18.5	17.6	105.1
文 化		**Culture**				
公共图书馆藏书	(万册)	Collection of Public Libraries	(10000 copies)	3020	2934	102.9
艺术剧团国内演出场次	(场)	Times of Domestic Performance of Art Troup	(time)	7610	8564	88.9
科 技		**Science and Technology**				
科技人员	(万人)	Personnel	(10000 persons)	119.2	136.1	87.6
卫 生		**Health**				
医院病床数	(万张)	Hospitals Beds	(10000)	6.5	6.3	103.2
卫生技术人员数	(万人)	Medical Technical Personnel	(10000 persons)	11.6	11.7	99.1
# 医生	(万人)	Doctors	(10000 persons)	5.2	5.3	98.1
护师(士)	(万人)	Senior and Junior Nurses	(10000 persons)	4	4	100.0
城市公用事业		**Urban Public Utilities**				
用电量	(亿千瓦时)	Electricity Consumption	(100 million kwh)	331.8	297.3	111.6
自来水销售量	(亿吨)	Sales of Tap Water	(100 million tons)	7.5	7.8	96.5
居民燃气用户	(万户)	Households of Access to Gas	(10000)	291.9	259.8	112.4
城市公共交通客运量	(亿人次)	Passengers Carried of City Public Transport	(100 million person.times)	40.7	42.7	95.3
城市大型立交桥	(座)	Large Flyovers	(unit)	149	141	105.7
城市绿化覆盖率	(%)	Coverage Rate of Urban Green Area	(%)	36.5	36.3	
城市居民人均住房使用面积	(平方米)	Per Capita Using Space of Rooms of Urban Residents	(sq.m)	16.8	15.9	105.5
农村居民人均住房面积	(平方米)	Per Capita Floor Space of Rooms of Rural Residents	(sq.m)	28.9	28.6	101.0

1-11 国民经济主要指标比例关系
PROPORTIONS OF MAIN NATIONAL ECONOMIC INDICATORS

项目	Item	绝对值(万元) Value(10000 yuan) 2000	1999	构成(%) Composition(%) 2000	1999
全市从业人员 (人)	**Total Employment (person)**	**6192927**	**6185812**	**100**	**100**
第一产业	Primary Industry	729236	745270	11.8	12.0
第二产业	Secondary Industry	2081583	2161961	33.6	35.0
第三产业	Tertiary Industry	3382108	3278581	54.6	53.0
国内生产总值	**Gross Domestic Product**	**24787600**	**21744600**	**100**	**100**
第一产业	Primary Industry	899700	874800	3.6	4.0
第二产业	Secondary Industry	9435100	8402300	38.1	38.7
第三产业	Tertiary Industry	14452800	12467500	58.3	57.3
固定资产投资	**Investment in Fixed Assets**	**6705682**	**6513968**	**100**	**100**
第一产业	Primary Industry	29771	16647	0.4	0.3
第二产业	Secondary Industry	1572750	1793558	23.5	27.5
第三产业	Tertiary Industry	5103161	4703763	76.1	72.2
固定资产投资拨贷款	**Allocations and Loans on Investment in Fixed Assets**	**6579371**	**6575841**	**100**	**100**
国家预算内资金	State Budgetary Appropriation	1066856	1356504	16.2	20.6
国内贷款	Domestic Loans	1349943	969362	20.5	14.7
利用外资	Foreign Capital	144025	344867	2.2	5.2
自筹资金	Self-raised Funds	3749061	3590697	57.0	54.7
# 股票	Stocks	95591	35411	1.5	0.5
其他资金	Other Capital	269486	314411	4.1	4.8
工农业总产值(现价)	**Gross Output Value of Industry and Agriculture (at current prices)**	**29694010**	**23746033**	**100**	**100**
工业	Industry	27742156	21902616	93.4	92.2
农业	Agriculture	1951854	1843427	6.6	7.8
工业总产值 (不含个体工业，现价)	**Gross Output Value of Industry(excluding individual industry,at current prices)**	**27074083**	**21446119**	**100**	**100**
轻工业	Light Indutry	6852281	6106775	25.3	28.5
重工业	Heavy Industry	20221802	15339344	74.7	71.5
农业总产值(现价)	**Gross Output Value of Agriculture(at current prices)**	**1951853.6**	**1843426.7**	**100**	**100**
种植业	Farming	910949.5	911918.7	48.4	49.4
林业	Forestry	53956.6	41868.4	2.8	2.3
牧业	Animal Husbandry	905626.9	810859.3	46.4	44.0
渔业	Fishery	81320.6	78779.6	4.2	4.3
货运量 (万吨)	**Freight Traffic (10000 tons)**	**30716.7**	**28274.8**	**100**	**100**
铁路	Railways	2611.7	2582.8	8.5	9.1
公路	Highways	28010	25635.0	91.2	90.7
民航	Civil Aviation	34.7	29.9	0.1	0.1
管道	Pipelines	60.3	27.1	0.2	0.1
客运量 (万人)	**Passenger Traffic (10000 persons)**	**18396.1**	**14866.4**	**100**	**100**
铁路	Railways	4458.4	4200.5	24.2	28.3
公路	Highways	13009	9878.0	70.7	66.4
民航	Civil Aviation	928.7	787.9	5.0	5.3
社会消费品零售总额	**Retail Sales of Consumer Goods**	**14433001**	**13133233**	**100**	**100**
批发零售贸易业	Wholesale and Retail	10255131	9261776	71.1	70.5
餐饮业	Catering	864010	812690	6.0	6.2
制造业	Manufacturing	868870	798169	6.0	6.1
其他	Others	2444990	2260598	16.9	17.2
# 农民对非农民	Peasants Saling to Non-Peasants	64181	76180	0.4	0.6
地方财政收入相当于国内生产总值的比例 (%)	**The Proportion of Local Financial Revenue in Gross Domestic Product (%)**	**16.1**	**14.7**		
地方基建支出占地方财政收入的比例 (%)	**The Proportion of Local Capital Construction Expenditures in Local Financial Revenue (%)**	**14.4**	**14.2**		

1-12 按登记注册类型分国民经济主要指标比例关系
PROPORTIONS OF MAIN NATIONAL ECONOMIC INDICATORS BY REGISTERED TYPE

项目	Item	绝对值 Value 2000	1999	构成(%) Composition(%) 2000	1999
全市从业人员 (人)	**Total Employment (person)**	**6186012**	**6185812**	**100**	**100**
国 有	State-Owned	2662057	2876190	43.0	46.5
集 体	Collective Owned	482580	496790	7.8	8.0
其 他	Others	1173706	950148	19.0	15.4
城镇个体、私营	Urban Individuals	244311	237293	3.9	3.8
农村劳动者	Rural Labor Force	1630273	1625391	26.4	26.3
固定资产投资 (万元)	**Investment in Fixed Assets (10000 yuan)**	**6705682**	**6513968**	**100**	**100**
国 有	State-Owned	6098510	5840694	90.9	89.7
集 体	Collective Owned	63576	129955	0.9	2.0
联 营	Joint Owned	2888	3531	…	0.1
股份合作企业	Share Holding Enterprises	16011	17477	0.2	0.3
股份有限公司	Share Holding Company	135769	75301	2.0	1.2
有限责任公司	Limited-liability Company	82288	24492	1.2	0.4
其他内资企业	Others	975		…	
中外合资经营	Chinese-foreign Joint Venture	173545	157469	2.6	2.4
中外合作经营	Chinses-foreign Cooperative	4586	4787	0.1	0.1
外商(独资)企业	Foreign Enterprises	19080	15580	0.3	0.2
外商投资股份有限公司	Foreign Funded Share Holding Company	13080	1126	0.2	…
港澳台合资经营	Joint Venture with HongKong, Macao and Taiwan	24734	93003	0.4	1.4
港澳台合作经营	Cooperative from HongKong,Macao and Taiwan	63675	138083	0.9	2.1
港澳台商独资	HongKong,Macao and Taiwan Enterprises	5985	10470	0.1	0.2
港澳台商投资股份有限公司	Hongkong,Macao and Taiwan Funded Share Holding Company	980	2000	…	…
工业总产值 (不含个体工业,现价, 万元)	**Gross Output Value of Industry(excluding individual industry,at current prices, 10000 yuan)**	**27074083**	**21446119**	**100**	**100**
国 有	State-Owned	7885866	7695460	29.1	35.9
集 体	Collective Owned	2626223	2631668	9.7	12.3
私 营	Private	281555	371298	1.0	1.7
联 营	Joint Owned	2022769	285789	7.5	1.3
股份合作企业	Share Holding Enterprises	360373	243651	1.3	1.1
股份有限公司	Share Holding Company	555716	918343	2.1	4.3
有限责任公司	Limited-liability Company	1657570	1278151	6.1	6.0
其他内资企业	Others	587	428	…	…

1-12 续表 continued

项目	Item	绝对值 Value 2000	绝对值 Value 1999	构成(%) Composition(%) 2000	构成(%) Composition(%) 1999
中外合资经营	Chinese-foreign Joint Venture	7079682	5186351	26.1	24.2
中外合作经营	Chinses-foreign Cooperative	194527	145261	0.7	0.7
外商(独资)企业	Foreign Enterprises	789463	431159	2.9	2.0
外商投资股份有限公司	Foreign Funded Share Holding Company	144629	151826	0.5	0.7
港澳台合资经营	Joint Venture with HongKong, Macao and Taiwan	1393668	1198653	5.1	5.6
港澳台合作经营	Cooperative from HongKong,Macao and Taiwan	51984	36024	0.2	0.2
港澳台商独资	HongKong,Macao and Taiwan Enterprises	2024841	861265	7.5	4.0
港澳台商投资股份有限公司	Hongkong,Macao and Taiwan Funded Share Holding Company	4630	10792	…	0.1
建筑业总产值 (万元)	**Gross Output Value of Construction (10000 yuan)**	**7274774.1**	**6814102.3**	**100**	**100**
国有	State-Owned	3259032.4	3529404.9	44.8	51.9
集体	Collective Owned	1576469.4	1536494.5	21.7	22.5
私营	Private	109687.1	54127.0	1.5	0.8
联营	Joint Owned	31721.9	20733.4	0.4	0.3
股份合作企业	Share Holding Enterprises	206518.7	176854.1	2.8	2.6
股份有限公司	Share Holding Company	120207.9	688383.0	1.7	10.1
有限责任公司	Limited-liability Company	1629968.8	567656.5	22.4	8.3
其他内资企业	Others	92114.9	8158.2	1.3	0.1
外商投资企业	Foreign Funded Enterprises	148082.8	131615.7	2.0	1.9
港澳台商投资企业	Hongkong,Macao and Taiwan Funded Enterprises	100970.2	100675.0	1.4	1.5
大中型批发零售贸易业消费品零售额 (万元)	**Retail Sales Consumer Goods of Large and Medium Wholesale and Retail Sales (10000 yuan)**	**6611447**	**5554995**	**100**	**100**
国有	State-Owned	2749739	2551678	41.6	45.8
集体	Collective Owned	920083	792314	13.9	14.3
股份有限公司	Share Holding Company	838158	727343	12.7	13.1
其他内资企业	Other Domestic Investment Enterprises	1563559	1027252	23.6	18.5
外商投资企业	Foreign Funded Enterprises	486966	413869	7.4	7.5
港澳台商投资企业	Hongkong,Macao and Taiwan Funded Enterprises	52943	42539	0.8	0.8

1-13 北 京 一 日

A DAY IN BEIJING

项　目		Item		2000	1999
生产量		**Output**			
国内生产总值	(当年价格，万元)	Gross Domestic Product	(at current prices, 10000 yuan)	67911.2	59574.2
工业总产值	(当年价格，万元)	Gross Output Value of Industry	(at current prices, 10000 yuan)	76005.9	60007.2
原　煤	(吨)	Coal	(ton)	15150.6	21700.2
发电量	(万千瓦时)	Electricity	(10000 kwh)	3979.6	3922.7
钢	(吨)	Steel	(ton)	22011.6	20122.3
农业总产值	(当年价格，万元)	Gross Output Value of Agriculture	(at current prices,10000 yuan)	5347.5	5050.5
独立核算建筑施工企业建筑业总产值	(万元)	Gross Output Value of Construction Enterprises with Independent Accounting System	(10000 yuan)	19930.9	18668.8
新建住宅竣工面积	(万平方米)	Floor Space of New Residence Completed	(10000 sq.m)	4.1	4.2
货运量	(包括管道，万吨)	Freight Traffic	(including pipelines, 10000 tons)	84.2	77.5
客运量	(万人)	Passenger Traffic	(10000 persons)	50.4	40.0
社会消费品零售总额	(万元)	Retail Sales of Consumer Goods	(10000 yuan)	39542.5	35981.5
地方企业海关出口额	(万美元)	Exports of Local Enterprises	(USD 10000)	1267.6	893.4
财政收入	(万元)	Financial Revenue	(10000 yuan)	10914.8	8779.5
旅游外汇收入	(万美元)	Foreign Exchange Income from Tourism	(USD 10000)	758.4	683.8
消费量		**Consumption**			
粮　食	(吨)	Grain	(ton)	2331.2	4765.5
猪　肉	(吨)	Pork	(ton)	725.2	878.2
牛羊肉	(吨)	Beef and Mutton	(ton)	175.6	276.1
鲜　蛋	(吨)	Fresh Eggs	(ton)	362.7	322.0
水产品	(吨)	Aquatic Products	(ton)	533.4	625.1
食用植物油	(吨)	Edible Vegetable Oil	(ton)	1220.7	937.2
鲜　菜	(吨)	Fresh Vegetable	(ton)	8138.0	10105.9
生活用水(自来水厂)	(万吨)	Residential Use of Tap Water	(10000 tons)	161.2	165.1
其　他		**Others**			
市内公共交通客运量	(万人次)	Urban Passenger Traffic	(10000 person.times)	1114.2	1169.1
接待入境旅游人数	(人次)	Foreign Tourists Received	(person.time)	7728.5	6914.9
邮寄函件	(万件)	Mail Delivery	(10000)	158.1	150.9
拍发公众电报	(万份)	Telegrams	(10000)	0.1	0.2
城乡居民储蓄存款	(万元)	Saving Deposit of Urban and Rural Residents	(10000 yuan)	6645.0	10780.2
出生人口	(人)	Birth Population	(person)	198	172
死亡人口	(人)	Death Population	(person)	213	169
登记结婚对数	(对)	Marriage Registered	(couple)	218	226
离婚对数	(对)	Registered Divorces	(couple)	73	65

1-14 平均每人主要社会经济活动
SELECTED INDICATORS ON PER CAPITA SOCIAL AND ECONOMIC ACTIVITIES

项目		Item		2000	1999
国内生产总值	**(当年价格,元)**	**Gross Domestic Product**	**(at current prices,yuan)**	**22460**	**19846**
工农业总产值	**(1990年不变价,元)**	**Gross Output Value of Industry and Agriculture**	**(at 1990 constant prices, yuan)**	**26298.8**	**20306.0**
财政收入	**(元)**	**Financial Revenue**	**(yuan)**	**3609.6**	**2924.6**
房屋建筑竣工面积	**(平方米)**	**Floor Space of Building Completed**	**(sq.m)**	**2.1**	**2.1**
# 新建住宅	(平方米)	New Residence	(sq.m)	1.4	1.4
工　业		**Industry**			
工业总产值	(1990年不变价，元)	Gross Output Value of Industry	(at 1990 constant prices,yuan)	25278.3	19396.7
主要工业产品产量		Output of Major Products			
布	(米)	Cloth	(meter)	11.0	13.5
彩色电视机(百人)	(台)	Color Television(100 persons)	(unit)	0.1	1.1
原　煤	(千克)	Coal	(kg)	501.0	722.9
发电量	(千瓦时)	Electricity	(kwh)	1316.1	1306.7
钢	(千克)	Steel	(kg)	727.9	670.3
农　业		**Agriculture**			
农业总产值	(1990年不变价，元)	Gross Output Value of Agriculture	(at 1990 constant prices,yuan)	1020.5	909.2
主要农产品产量		Output of Major Products			
粮　食	(千克)	Grain	(kg)	130.6	183.4
肉　类	(千克)	Meat	(kg)	51.0	45.2
鲜　蛋	(千克)	Fresh Eggs	(kg)	14.5	14.4
鲜　菜	(千克)	Fresh Vegetable	(kg)	441.5	389.5
水产品	(千克)	Aquatic Products	(kg)	6.8	6.9
牛　奶	(千克)	Milk	(kg)	27.5	21.9
干鲜果	(千克)	Dry and Fresh Fruit	(kg)	55.2	51.5
商　业		**Commerce**			
社会消费品零售总额	(元)	Retail Sales of Consumer Goods	(yuan)	13076.9	11986.2
# 吃的商品	(元)	Food	(yuan)	3716.8	3417.9
穿的商品	(元)	Clothing	(yuan)	1567.6	1420.5
用的商品	(元)	Daily Used Articles	(yuan)	7346.7	6772.9
主要消费品零售量		Retail Sales of Major Consumer Goods in Quantity			
粮　食	(千克)	Grain	(kg)	77.1	115.3
食用植物油	(千克)	Edible Vegetable Oil	(kg)	40.4	29.3
猪　肉	(千克)	Pork	(kg)	24.0	24.2
鲜　蛋	(千克)	Fresh Eggs	(kg)	12.0	10.5
水产品	(千克)	Aquatic Products	(kg)	17.6	20.8
邮　电		**Posts and Telecommunications**			
邮寄函件	(件)	Mail Delivery	(unit)	52.3	50.3
城市公用事业		**Urban Public Utilities**			
日生活用水量	(千克)	Daily Residential Use of Water	(kg)	240.2	250.1
城市居民居住面积	(平方米)	Living Space of Urban Residents	(sq.m)	11.15	10.63
平均每千人拥有公共交通车辆	(辆)	Possession of Public Traffic Vehicles Per 1000 Persons	(unit)	1.28	1.14
乘坐公共电汽车次数	(人次)	Times of Riding in Bus or Trolley	(person.time)	329.1	345.4
公共绿地面积	(平方米)	Public Green Areas	(sq.m)	9.7	9.1
卫　生		**Health**			
平均每千人拥有医生	(人)	Number of Doctors Per 1000 Persons	(person)	4.66	4.79
平均每千人拥有医院床位	(张)	Number of Beds Per 1000 Persons	(unit)	6.25	6.15
人民生活		**Pepople's Livelihood**			
职工年平均工资	(元)	Annual Average Wage	(yuan)	15726	13778
居民家庭可支配收入	(元)	Annual Discretionary Income of Urban Residents	(yuan)	10349.7	9182.8
农民家庭纯收入	(元)	Annual Net Income of Rural Residents	(yuan)	4687.0	4316.4
城乡居民储蓄存款余额	(元)	Savings Deposit of Urban and Rural Residents	(yuan)	26394.6	24374.1
城镇居民	(元)	Urban	(yuan)	35011.1	32508.4
农村居民	(元)	Rural	(yuan)	7494.5	7136.5

1-15 总　产　出
TOTAL OUTPUT

单位：万元　　(10000 yuan)

项目	Item	2000	1999	2000年为1999年% 2000 as % of 1999
总　计	**Total**	**80264500**	**70888300**	**110.9**
第一产业	Primary Industry	1951800	1843400	107.2
第二产业	Secondary Industry	38783500	33691000	112.7
工　业	Industry	30855700	26284500	114.2
建筑业	Construction	7927800	7406500	105.2
第三产业	Tertiary Industry	39529200	35353900	108.1
# 交通运输、仓储及邮电业	Transportation,Storage,Posts and Telecommunications	4780500	4649300	104.3
批发和零售贸易、餐饮业	Wholesale,Retail and Catering Trade	5044100	3980300	109.0

注：绝对数按现价计算，发展速度按可比价格计算(下同)。

Note: The data in terms of value are calculated at current prices,while the related indices are calculated at comparable prices (The followings are the same).

1-16 国民生产总值
GROSS NATIONAL PRODUCT

单位：万元　　(10000 yuan)

项目	Item	2000	1999	2000年为1999年% 2000 as % of 1999	构成(%) Composition(%) 2000	1999
国民生产总值	**Gross National Product**	**24793200**	**21749700**	**111.0**		
国内生产总值	**Gross Domestic Product**	**24787600**	**21744600**	**111.0**	**100**	**100**
第一产业	**Primary Industry**	**899700**	**874800**	**104.0**	**3.6**	**4.0**
第二产业	**Secondary Industry**	**9435100**	**8402300**	**111.4**	**38.1**	**38.7**
工　业	Industry	7453200	6493400	113.2	30.1	29.9
建筑业	Construction	1981900	1908900	102.1	8.0	8.8
第三产业	**Tertiary Industry**	**14452800**	**12467500**	**111.1**	**58.3**	**57.3**
农林牧渔服务业	FFAF Services	22500	22700	95.6	0.1	0.1
地质勘探业、水利管理业	Geological Prospecting and Water Conservancy	53300	46000	111.9	0.2	0.2
交通运输、仓储及邮电业	Transportation,Storage, Posts and Telecommunications	1901200	1675400	110.9	7.7	7.7
批发和零售贸易、餐饮业	Wholesale,Retail and Catering	2185400	2104300	105.0	8.8	9.7
金融保险业	Banking and Insurance	3788900	3163700	116.4	15.3	14.5
房地产业	Real Estate	773700	694500	109.5	3.1	3.2
社会服务业	Social Services	1911800	1477400	111.1	7.7	6.8
卫生、体育、社会福利事业	Health,Sports and Social Welfare	431900	335900	118.9	1.7	1.5
教育、文艺、广播电影电视事业	Education,Culture,Art,Radio, Film and Television	1484200	1199500	117.2	6.0	5.5
科学研究和综合技术服务业	Scientific Research and Poly-technical Services	1028700	1011700	97.8	4.2	4.7
国家政党机关、社会团体	Government Organs,Party Organs and Social Bodies	700100	579100	117.1	2.8	2.7
其他	Others	171100	157300	105.3	0.7	0.7
国外(地区)净要素收入	**Net Income of Essential Factor from Foreign Country(Territory)**	**5600**	**5100**	**108.7**		
人均国内生产总值(元)	**Per Capita Gross Domestic Products (yuan)**	**22460**	**19846**	**110.2**		

1-17 国内生产总值构成项目
COMPOSITION OF GROSS DOMESTIC PRODUCT

单位：万元 (10000 yuan)

项目	Item	增加值 Added Value	劳动者报酬 Compensation for Labors	固定资产折旧 Depreciation of Fixed Asset	生产税净额 Net Taxes on Production	营业盈余 Operating Surplus
国内生产总值	**Gross Domestic Product**	**24787600**	**11310200**	**3040400**	**4309300**	**6127700**
第一产业	**Primary Industry**	**899700**	**546100**	**7100**	**62200**	**284300**
第二产业	**Secondary Industry**	**9435100**	**4516400**	**1728000**	**1642600**	**1548100**
工　业	Industry	7453200	3247800	1399100	1491900	1314400
建筑业	Construction	1981900	1268600	328900	150700	233700
第三产业	**Tertiary Industry**	**14452800**	**6247700**	**1305300**	**2604500**	**4295300**
农林牧渔服务业	FFAF Services	22500	17300	600	3000	1600
地质勘探业、水利管理业	Geological Prospecting and Water Conservancy	53300	35300	3500	20300	-5800
交通运输、仓储及邮电业	Transportation,Storage, Posts and Telecommunications	1901200	519800	130700	866700	384000
批发和零售贸易、餐饮业	Wholesale,Retail and Catering	2185400	1097000	-48100	236300	900200
金融保险业	Banking and Insurance	3788900	430100	386700	120000	2852100
房地产业	Real Estate	773700	344900	300700	389200	-261100
社会服务业	Social Services	1911800	1165200	242300	409200	95100
卫生、体育、社会福利事业	Health,Sports and Social Welfare	431900	369000	1900	59700	1300
教育、文艺、广播电影电视事业	Education,Culture,Art,Radio,Film and Television	1484200	1012700	118000	187700	165800
科学研究和综合技术服务业	Scientific Research and Poly-technical Services	1028700	654200	97100	158000	119400
国家政党机关、社会团体	Government Organs,Party Organs and Social Bodies	700100	546100	12000	139900	2100
其　他	Others	171100	56100	59900	14500	40600

1-18 按支出法计算的国内生产总值
GROSS DOMESTIC PRODUCT BY EXPENDITURE APPROACH

单位：万元 (10000 yuan)

项目	Item	2000	1999	2000年为1999年% 2000 as % of 1999
国内生产总值	**Gross Domestic Product**	**24787600**	**21744600**	**111.0**
最终消费	Final Consumption Expenditure	12213300	9541400	123.9
居民总消费	Household Consumption	8085300	6337600	125.4
农业居民	Agricultural	1259200	1125200	106.6
非农业居民	Non-Agricultural	6826100	5212400	130.1
政府消费	Government Consumption	4128000	3203800	121.3
资本形成总额	Gross Capital Formation	15173800	15261600	96.1
固定资产形成总额	Completed Fixed Assets	13769800	12334600	110.6
存货增加	Changes in Inventories	1404000	2927000	47.8
货物和服务净出口	Net Export of Goods and Services	-2599500	-3058400	

1-19 居民总消费水平
HOUSEHOLD CONSUMPTION

单位：元 (yuan)

项目	Item	2000	1999	2000年为1999年% 2000 as % of 1999
全市居民总消费水平	**All Households**	**7326**	**5784**	**124.5**
农业居民	Agricultural	3601	3168	108.3
非农业居民	Non-Agricultural	9054	7040	127.7
农业居民与非农业居民对比 (以农业居民为100)	**Ratio of Consumption of Agricultural to Non-Agricultural(Agricultural=100)**	**1: 2.5**	**1:2.2**	

1-20 最终消费
FINAL CONSUMPTION EXPENDITURE

单位：万元 (10000 yuan)

项目	Item	2000	1999	2000年为1999年% 2000 as % of 1999
最终消费	**Final Consumption Expenditure**	**12213300**	**9541400**	**123.9**
居民消费	**Household Consumption**	**8085300**	**6337600**	**125.4**
农业居民	Agricultural	1259200	1125200	106.6
自给性消费	Self-sufficiency	29900	68300	46.1
商品性消费	Commodity	799400	675000	119.7
文化生活及服务性消费	Culture and Services	275500	234100	105.5
住房及水电消费	Residence,Water and Electricity	154400	147800	92.1
# 住房消费	Residence	84700	80400	87.7
非农业居民	Non-Agricultural	6826100	5212400	130.1
商品性消费	Commodity	3936700	3107200	130.2
文化生活及服务性消费	Culture and Services	2182600	1732600	107.2
住房及水电消费	Residence,Water and Electricity	706800	372600	160.9
# 住房消费	Residence	557200	269400	165.2
政府消费	**Government Consumption**	**4128000**	**3203800**	**121.3**

1-21 主要社会经济效益指标
MAJOR ECONOMIC EFFICIENCY INDICATORS

项目	Item		2000	1999
社会劳动生产率(当年价格)	(元/人) **Overall Labor Productivity (at current prices)**	**(yuan/person)**	**40026**	**35152**
第一产业	(元/人) Primary Industry	(yuan/person)	12338	11738
第二产业	(元/人) Secondary Industry	(yuan/person)	45327	38864
第三产业	(元/人) Tertiary Industry	(yuan/person)	42733	38027
资本形成率（投资率）	(%) **Rate of Capital Formation**	(%)	**61.2**	**70.2**
消费率	(%) **Consumption Rate**	(%)	**49.3**	**43.9**
总产出中间投入率	(%) **Intermediate Input/Total Output**	(%)	**69.1**	**69.3**
第一产业	(%) Primary Industry	(%)	53.9	52.5
第二产业	(%) Secondary Industry	(%)	75.7	75.1
第三产业	(%) Tertiary Industry	(%)	63.4	64.7
增加值率	(%) **GDP/Total Output**	(%)	**30.9**	**30.7**
第一产业	(%) Primary Industry	(%)	46.1	47.5
第二产业	(%) Secondary Industry	(%)	24.3	24.9
第三产业	(%) Tertiary Industry	(%)	36.6	35.3

1-22 1999 年国民经济总体帐户
OVERALL ACCOUNT OF NATIONAL ECONOMY OF 1999

1-22-1 生产帐户
PRODUCTION ACCOUNT

单位：亿元 (100 million yuan)

劳动者报酬	Compensation for Labors	1053.1	总产出	Total Output	7233.8
工资及工资性收入	Wages and Related Income	953.5	减：中间消耗	Subtract: Intermediate Consumption	5059.3
单位社会保险付款	Employer's Contribution of Social Securities	99.6			
生产税净额	Net Taxes on Production	294.9			
生产税	Production Taxes	348.7			
减：生产补贴	Subtract: Production Subsidies	53.8			
亏损补贴	Losing Subsidies	44.1			
价格补贴	Price Subsidies	9.7			
固定资产折旧	Depreciation of Fixed Assets	400.6			
营业盈余	Earnings Surplus	425.9			
增加值分配	**Distribution of Value Added**	**2174.5**	**增加值**	**Value Added**	**2174.5**

1-22-2 收入分配及支出帐户
INCOME DISTRIBUTION AND EXPENDITURE ACCOUNT

单位：亿元 (100 million yuan)

财产收入支付	Payment for Property Income	1312.1	营业盈余	Earnings Surplus	425.9
利息支出	Interest	600.8	固定资产折旧	Depreciation of Fixed Asset	400.6
红利支出	Dividend	15.8	财产收入	Property Income	1562.0
土地租金支出	Land Rental		利息收入	Interest	600.8
其他支出	Others	695.5	红利收入	Dividend	179.6
经常转移支出	Payment for Current Transfer	381.6	土地租金收入	Land Rental	
收入税支出	Income Taxes	106.8	其他收入	Others	781.6
财政经常性拨款支出	Fiscal Current Allocation		劳动者报酬	Compensation for Labors	1053.1
社会保险付款支出	Payment to Social Security	99.6	工资及工资性收入	Wages and Related Income	953.5
社会补助支出	Allowance	11.3	单位社会保险付款	Employer's Contribution of Social Securities	99.6
其他经常转移支出	Others	163.9			
可支配总收入	Total Disposable Income	2519.5	生产税净额	Net Taxes on Production	294.9
最终消费	Final Consumption Expenditure	954.2	生产税	Production Tax	348.7
居民消费	Household Consumption	633.8	减：生产补贴	Subtract: Production Subsidies	53.8
政府消费	Government Consumption	320.4	亏损补贴	Losing Subsidies	44.1
总储蓄	Savings	1565.3	价格补贴	Price Subsidies	9.7
			经常转移收入	Current Transfer Income	476.7
			收入税收入	Income Tax	106.8
			财政经常性拨款收入	Fiscal Current Allocation	
			社会保险付款收入	Social Security Payment	99.6
			社会补助收入	Allowance	11.3
			其他经常转移收入	Others	259.0
支出和总储蓄	**Expenditure and Savings**	**4213.2**	**收　入**	**Income**	**4213.2**

1-22-3 资 本 帐 户
CAPITAL ACCOUNT

单位：亿元　　(100 million yuan)

固定资产形成总额	Gross Fixed Capital Formation	1233.5	总储蓄	Total Savings	1565.3
存货增加	Changes in Inventories	292.7	资本转移收入净额	Capital Transfer,Net	
其他非金融资产获得减处置	Minus Items from Other Non-financial Capital		资本转移收入	Capital Transfer Income	152.2
			投资性补助收入	Investment Allowance	152.2
资金余缺	Surplus or Shortage of Capital	39.2	其他资本转移收入	Others	
			减：资本转移支出	Subtract：Capital Transfer Expenditure	152.2
统计误差	Statistical Discrepancy	-0.1			
			投资性补助支出	Investment Allowance	152.2
			其他资本转移支出	Others	
资本运用	**Capital Utilization**	**1565.3**	**资本筹集**	**Capital Source**	**1565.3**

1-22-4 金 融 帐 户
FINANCIAL ACCOUNT

单位：亿元　　(100 million yuan)

国内金融交易	Domestic Financial Transaction	3715.7	国内金融交易	Domestic Financial Transaction	3720.7
通货	Currency in Circulation	143.3	通货	Currency in Circulation	
存款	Deposits	1436.0	存款	Deposits	1394.5
短期存款	Short-term	854.2	短期存款	Short-term	854.2
长期存款	Long-term	581.8	长期存款	Long-term	540.3
贷款	Loans	666.3	贷款	Loans	666.3
短期贷款	Short-term	482.1	短期贷款	Short-term	482.1
长期贷款	Long-term	184.2	长期贷款	Long-term	184.2
证券(不含股票)	Securities(excluding stock)	189.9	证券(不含股票)	Securities(excluding stock)	472.9
短期证券	Short-term		短期证券	Short-term	
长期证券	Long-term	189.9	长期证券	Long-term	472.9
股票及其他股权	Stock and Other Stock Ownership	271.2	股票及其他股权	Stock and Other Stock Ownership	813.7
保险准备金	Reserves for Insurance Business		保险准备金	Reserves for Insurance Business	
其他金融资产	Other Financial Capital	1009.0	其他负债	Other Liabilities	373.3
国际资本往来	International Capital Flow	40.1	国际资本往来	International Capital Flow	-4.1
短期资本	Short-term	22.2	短期资本	Short-term	-2.9
长期资本	Long-term	17.9	长期资本	Long-term	-1.2
国际储备资产	Assets in International Reserves		资金余缺	Surplus or Shortage of Capital	39.2
金融资产净增额	**Net Increase of Financial Capital**	**3755.8**	**负债净增额与资金余缺**	**Net Increase of Liability and Surplus or Shortage of Capital**	**3755.8**

1-22-5 期末资产负债帐户
YEAR-END BALANCE ACCOUNT

单位：亿元 (100 million yuan)

非金融资产	Non-financial Capital	13855.4	负债	Liabilities	16415.6
固定资产	Fixed Assets	9555.7	国内金融负债	Domestic Financial Liabilities	16001.7
存货	Inventories	2629.6	通货	Currency in Circulation	
其他非金融资产	Others	1670.1	存款	Deposits	9061.3
金融资产	Financial Capital	18202.5	短期存款	Short-term	4287.2
国内金融资产	Domestic Financial Capital	18202.5	长期存款	Long-term	4774.1
通货	Currency in Circulation	203.7	贷款	Loans	4055.2
存款	Deposits	9061.3	短期贷款	Short-term	2977.0
短期存款	Short-term	4287.2	长期贷款	Long-term	1078.2
长期存款	Long-term	4774.1	证券(不含股票)	Securities(excluding stock)	7.8
贷款	Loans	4055.2	短期证券	Short-term	0.1
短期贷款	Short-term	2977.0	长期证券	Long-term	7.7
长期贷款	Long-term	1078.2	股票及其他股权	Stock and Other Stock Ownership	2742.2
证券(不含股票)	Securities(excluding stock)	1576.1	保险准备金	Reserves for Insurance Business	47.7
短期证券	Short-term	387.5	其他负债	Others	87.5
长期证券	Long-term	1188.6	国外金融负债	Foreign Financial Liabilities	413.9
股票及其他股权	Stock and Other Stock Ownership	3022.4	短期负债	Short-term	142.5
保险准备金	Reserves for Insurance Business		长期负债	Long-term	271.4
其他金融资产	Others	47.7	资产负债差额	Balance of Assets and Liabilities	15642.3
国外金融资产	Foreign Financial Capital	236.1			
短期资本	Short-term Capital				
长期资本	Long-term Capital				
储备资产	Reserves		**负债与资产负债差额**	**Liabilities and Balance of Capital and Liabilities**	**32057.9**
资　产	**Capital**	**32057.9**			

1-23 1999 年资产负债表

单位：亿元

项目	Item	非金融部门 Non-financial Enterprises 使用 Utilization	非金融部门 Non-financial Enterprises 来源 Source	金融部门 Financial Institutions 使用 Utilization	金融部门 Financial Institutions 来源 Source
非金融资产	**Non-financial Capital**	**7888.18**		**308.97**	
固定资产	Fixed Assets	4798.27		255.71	
固定资产净值	Net Value	3827.33		175.26	
固定资产原值	Original Value	5564.03		232.94	
减：累计折旧	Subtract：Accumulative Depreciation	1736.70		57.68	
在建工程	Projects under Construction	871.88		80.11	
固定资产清理	Liquidation Fixed Assets	74.28		0.33	
待处理固定资产净损失	Net Losing of Fixed Assets Unsettled	24.78		0.01	
存货	Inventories	2552.85			
产成品和商品库存	Finished Products and Commodity Stock	1231.30			
其他资产	Others	537.06		53.26	
无形资产	Intangible Assets	249.76		8.92	
金融资产与负债	**Financial Assets and Liabilities**	**6875.46**	**6913.81**	**4910.2**	**9188.86**
国内金融资产与负债	Domestic Financial Assets and Liabilities	6875.46	6651.40	4910.2	9109.28
通　货	Currency in Circulation	41.38		2.68	
存　款	Deposits	5208.8		46.15	9061.34
短期存款	Short-term	3266.78		32.31	4287.19
# 财政存款	Financial				77.06
长期存款	Long-term	1942.02		13.84	4774.15
贷　款	Loans		3827.52	4055.17	
短期贷款	Short-term		2931.16	2976.95	
# 财政借款	Financial				
长期贷款	Long-term		896.36	1078.22	
股票及其他股权	Stock and Other Stock Ownership	1220.72	2742.18	139.57	
证　券(不含股票)	Securities(excluding stock)	161.79	7.50	712.78	0.27
短期证券	Short-term	110.78		197.73	0.10
#政府债券	Government	101.92		160.16	
长期证券	Long-term	51.01	7.50	515.05	0.17
# 政府债券	Government	44.91		204.93	
保险准备金	Reserves for Insurance Business	18.85			47.67
其　他	Others	223.92	74.20		
国外金融资产与负债	Foreign Financial Assets and Liabilities		262.41		79.58
短期资本	Short-term Capital		52.36		73.61
长期资本	Long-term Capital		210.05		5.97
资产负债差额	**Balance of Assets and Liabilities**		**7849.83**		**-3969.69**

1999 BALANCE SHEET

(100 million yuan)

政府部门 Governments		住户部门 Households		国内省外 Non-local		国外 Rest of the World		合计 Total	
使用 Utilization	来源 Source	使用 Utilization	来源 Source	使用 Utilization	来源 Source	使用 Utilization	来源 Source	使用 Utilization	来源 Source
1137.70		**3446.09**						**12780.94**	
1111.35		3390.38						9555.71	
1111.35		3390.38						8504.32	
1239.23		4521.32						11557.5	
127.88		1130.94						3053.20	
								951.99	
								74.61	
								24.79	
20.98		55.71						2629.54	
		43.77						1275.07	
5.37								595.69	
								258.68	
1817.48	**270.57**	**4599.36**	**42.33**		**2200.83**	**413.90**		**18616.40**	**18616.40**
1817.48	198.66	4599.36	42.33		2200.83			18202.50	18202.50
12.88		146.79			203.73			203.73	203.73
430.57		3421.97						9061.34	9061.34
338.77		681.64						4287.19	4287.19
77.06								77.06	77.06
91.80		2740.33						4774.15	4774.15
	185.32		42.33					4055.17	4055.17
	40.38		5.41					2976.95	2976.95
	144.94		36.92					1078.22	1078.22
1354.32		307.77			280.20			3022.38	3022.38
7.54		694.01			1568.35			1576.12	1576.12
2.44		76.53			387.38			387.48	387.48
1.98		72.87			336.93			336.93	336.93
5.10		617.48			1180.97			1188.64	1188.64
3.67		561.35			814.86			814.86	814.86
		28.82						47.67	47.67
12.17	13.34				148.55			236.09	236.09
	71.91					413.90		413.90	413.90
	16.54					142.51		142.51	142.51
	55.37					271.39		271.39	271.39
	2684.61		**9077.56**		**-2200.83**		**413.90**		**12780.94**

1-24 地方财政收入
LOCAL FINANCIAL REVENUE

项目	Item	绝对数（万元）Value(10000 yuan) 2000	1999	2000年为1999年% 2000 as % of 1999	构成（%）Composition(%) 2000	1999
总计	**Total**	**3983895**	**3204406**	**124.3**	**100**	**100**
一般预算财政收入	**General Budgetary Financial Revenue**	**3449968**	**2813661**	**122.6**	**86.6**	**87.8**
# 增值税	Increased Value Tax	459557	397193	115.7	11.5	12.4
营业税	Business Tax	1490539	1288567	115.7	37.4	40.2
个人所得税	Private Income Tax	563847	458826	122.9	14.2	14.3
城市维护建设税	City Maintenance Tax	173539	152725	113.6	4.4	4.8
固定资产投资方向调节税	Adjusting Tax of Investment in Fixed Assets	21388	69530	30.8	0.5	2.2
农牧业税和耕地占用税类	Tax for Farming and Animal Husbandry and Cultivated Land Occupation	15697	16989	92.4	0.4	0.5
企业所得税	Enterprise Income Tax	616582	530721	116.2	15.5	16.6
国有资产经营收益	Business Income of State-owned Assets	1135	1992	57.0	0.0	0.1
国有企业计划亏损补贴类	Losing Subsidies of Planning of State-owned Enterprises	-541807	-570789	94.9	-13.6	-17.8
企业所得税退税	Returned Tax of Income Tax of Enterprises	-36314	-70786	51.3	-0.9	-2.2
罚没收入、行政性收费	Forfeit and Administrative Fee	144792	110037	131.6	3.6	3.4
基金预算收入合计	**Total Fund Budgetary Income**	**533927**	**390745**	**136.6**	**13.4**	**12.2**

1-25 地方财政支出
LOCAL FINANCIAL EXPENDITURE

项目	Item	绝对数（万元）Value(10000 yuan) 2000	1999	2000年为1999年% 2000 as % of 1999	构成（%）Composition(%) 2000	1999
总计	**Total**	**4903419**	**3985328**	**123.04**	**100**	**100**
一般预算财政支出	**General Budgetary Financial Expenditure**	**4429969**	**3551932**	**124.72**	**90.34**	**89.13**
# 基本建设支出	Capital Construction	574884	454629	126.45	11.72	11.41
企业挖潜改造资金	Innovation Funds of Enterprises	327083	311385	105.04	6.67	7.81
科技三项费用	Science and Technology Promotion	38441	39002	98.56	0.78	0.98
流动资金	Circulating Funds	6627	15831	41.86	0.14	0.40
农林水气等部门事业费	Agriculture, Forestry, Water Conservancy and Meteorology	39582	36765	107.66	0.81	0.92
支援农村生产支出	Supporting Agricultural Production	98712	78727	125.39	2.01	1.98
城市维护费	City Maintenance	237058	171160	138.50	4.83	4.29
工业交通等部门的事业费	Fees of Industrial and Transportation Departments	20127	14424	139.54	0.41	0.36
文体广播事业费	Fees of Culture and Radio	92628	76074	121.76	1.89	1.91
教育事业费	Fees of Education	600709	492233	122.04	12.25	12.35
卫生经费	Funds of Health	285305	227743	125.27	5.82	5.71
科学事业费	Fees of Science	62070	49106	126.40	1.27	1.23
行政管理费	Government Administration	209237	159947	130.82	4.27	4.01
公检法司支出	Public Security Agency, Procuratorial Agency and Court of Justice	335916	263718	127.38	6.85	6.62
抚恤和社会福利救济费	Pensions and Relief Funds for Social Welfare	111436	80220	138.91	2.27	2.01
政策性补贴支出	Policy Subsidies	91891	97992	93.77	1.87	2.46
基金支出合计	**Funds Expenditure**	**473450**	**433396**	**109.24**	**9.66**	**10.87**

主 要 统 计 指 标 解 释

国内生产总值 是按市场价格计算的国内生产总值的简称。它是一个国家（地区）所有常住单位在一定时期内生产活动的最终成果。国内生产总值有三种表现形式，即价值形态、收入形态和产品形态。从价值形态看，它是所有常住单位在一定时期内所生产的全部货物和服务价值超过同期投入的全部非固定资产货物和服务价值的差额，即所有常住单位的增加值之和；从收入形态看，它是所有常住单位在一定时期内所创造并分配给常住单位和非常住单位的初次分配收入之和；从产品形态看，它是最终使用的货物和服务减去进口货物和服务。在实际核算中，国内生产总值的三种表现形态表现为三种计算方法，即生产法、收入法和支出法。三种方法分别从不同的方面反映国内生产总值及其构成。

三次产业 根据社会生产活动历史发展的顺序对产业结构的划分，产品直接取自自然界的部门称为第一产业，对初级产品进行再加工的部门成为第二产业。为生产和消费提供各种服务的部门称为第三产业。它是世界上通用的产业结构分类，但各国的划分不尽一致。我国的三次产业划分是：

第一产业：农业（包括种植业、林业和渔业）。

第二产业：工业（包括采掘工业、制造业、自来水、电力、蒸汽、热水、煤气）和建筑业。

第三产业：除第一、第二产业以外的其他各业。由于第三产业包括的行业多、范围广，根据我国的实际情况第三产业可分为两大部门：一是流通部门，二是服务部门。具体又可分为四个层次：

第一层次：流通部门，包括交通运输业、邮电通讯业、商业、饮食业、物资供销业和仓储业。

第二层次：为生产和生活服务的部门，包括金融、保险业、地质普查业、房地产业、公用事业，居民服务业，咨询服务业和综合技术服务业，农、林、牧、渔、服务业和水利业，公路、内河（湖）航道养护业等。

第三层次：为提高科学文化水平和居民素质服务的部门，包括教育、文化、广播电视，科学研究、卫生、体育和社会福利事业。

第四层次：为社会公共需要服务的部门，包括国家机关、社会团体，以及军队和警察等。

可比价格 指在不同时期的价值指标对比时，扣除了价格变动的因素，以确切反映物量的变化。按可比价格计算有两种方法：一种是直接用产量乘某一年的不变价格计算；另一种是用价格指数换算。

不变价格 指用同类产品的年平均价格作为固定价格，来计算各年产品价值。按不变价格计算的产品价值消除了价格变动因素，不同时期对比可以反映生产的发展速度。新中国成立后，随着工农业产品价格水平的变化，国家统计局先后五次制定了全国统一的工业产品不变价格和农业产品不变价格，从 1949 年到 1952 年使用 1952 年工（农）业产品不变价格，从 1957 年到 1971 年使用 1957 年不变价格，从 1971 年到 1981 年使用 1970 年不变价格，从 1981 年到 1990 年使用 1980 年不变价格，从 1990 年开始使用 1990 年不变价格。

支出法国内生产总值 指一个国家（或地区）所有常住单位在一定时期内用于最终消费、资本形成总额，以及货物和服务的净出口总额，它反映本期生产的国内生产总值的使用构成。

最终消费 指常住单位在一定时期内对于货物和服务的全部最终消费支出，也就是常住单位为满足物质、文化和精神生活的需要，从本国经济领土和国外购买的货物和服务的支出。它不包括非常住单位在本国经济领土内的消费支出。最终消费分为居民消费和政府消费。

（一）居民消费：指常住住户在一定时期内对于货物和服务的全部最终消费支出。居民关于货物的最终消费支出在货物的所有权发生变化时记录，关于服务的最终支出在服务提供的时候记录。居民消费支出按市场价格计算，即按居民支付的购买者价格计算，货物的购买价格是购买者取得交货所支付的价格，它包括购买者支付的运输和商业费用。居民支出除了直接以货币形式购买的货物和服务的消费支出外，还包括以其他方式获得的货物和服务的消费支出，即所谓的虚拟消费支出。居民虚拟消费支出包括如下几种类型：单位以实物报酬及实物转移的形式提供给劳动者的货物和服务；住户生产并由本住户消费了的货物和服务，其中自有住房服务；金融机构提供的金融媒介服务；保险公司提供的保险服务。

（二）政府消费 指政府部门为全社会提供的公共服务的消费支出和免费或以较低的价格向居民住户提供的货物和服务的净支出，前者等于政府服务的产出价值减去政府单位所获得的经营收入的价值，政府服务的产出价值等于它的经常性业务支出加上固定资产折旧；后者等于政府部门向居民住户提供的货物和服务的市场价值减去向居民住户收取的价值。

资本形成总额 指常住单位在一定时期内获得减去处置的固定资产和存货的净值，包括固定资产形成总额和存货增加两项。

（一）固定资产形成总额　指常住单位在一定时期内购置、转入和自产自用的固定资产价值，扣除固定资产的销售和转出后的价值。可分为有形固定资产形成总额和无形固定资产形成总额。有形固定资产形成总额包括一定时期内完成的建筑工程、安装工程和设备工器具购置（减处置）价值，以及土地改良、新增役、种、奶、毛、娱乐用牲畜和新增经济林木价值。无形固定资产形成总额包括矿藏的勘探、计算机软件、娱乐和文学艺术品原件等获得价值。

（二）存货增加　指常住单位在一定时期内存货实物量变动的市场价值即期末价值减期初价值的差额。存货增加可以是正值，也可以是负值，正值表示存货上升，负值表示存货下降。它包括生产单位购进的原材料、燃料和储备物资等存货，以及生产单位生产的产成品、在制品和半成品等存货等。

货物和服务净出口　指货物和服务出口减货物和服务进口的差额。出口包括常住单位向非常住单位出售或无偿转让的各种货物和服务的价值；进口包括常住单位从非常住单位购买或无偿得到的各种货物和服务的价值。由于服务活动的提供与使用同时发生，因此服务的进出口业务并不发生出入境现象，一般把常住单位从国外得到的服务作为进口，非常住单位从本国得到的服务作为出口。货物的出口和进口都按离岸价格计算。

净出口　指出口与进口的差额。出口包括常住单位向非常住单位出售或无偿转让的各种货物和服务的总值；进口包括常住单位从非常住单位购买或无偿得到的各种货物和服务的总值。由于服务活动提供与使用同时发生，因此服务的进出口业务并不发生出入境现象，应把常住单位从国外得到的服务作为进口，反之，非常住单位从我国得到的服务作为出口。

劳动者报酬　劳动者报酬是指劳动者因从事生产活动所获得的全部报酬。它包括劳动者获得的各种形式工资、奖金和津贴，既包括货币形式的，也包括实物形式的，它还包括劳动者所享受的公费医疗和医药卫生费、上下班交通补贴和单位支付的社会保险费等。单位支付的社会保险费，就是单位直接支付给负责社会保险的政府单位（一般指劳动部门）的社会保险金或为本单位职工离退休、发生死亡、伤残、医疗保险等而支付的保险费。对于个体经济来说，其所有者所获得的劳动报酬和经营利润不易区分，这两部分统一作为劳动者报酬处理。

生产税净额　指生产税减生产补贴后的差额。生产税指政府对生产单位生产、销售和从事经营活动以及因从事生产活动使用某些生产要素，如固定资产、土地、劳动力所征收的各种税、附加费和规费。具体包括销售税金及附加、增值税、管理费中开支的各种税、应交纳的养路费、排污费和水电费附加、烟酒专卖上缴政府的专项收入等。生产补贴与生产税相反，是政府对生产单位的单方面收入转移，因此视为负生产税处理，包括政策亏损补贴、粮食系统价格补贴、外贸企业出口退税收入等。

固定资产折旧　指一定时期内为弥补固定资产损耗按照核定的固定资产折旧率提取的固定资产折旧，或按国民经济核算统一规定的折旧率虚拟计算的固定资产折旧。它反映了固定资产在当期生产中的转移价值。各种类型企业和企业化管理的事业单位的固定资产折旧指实际计提并计入成本费用中的折旧费；不计提折旧的单位，如政府机关、非企业化管理的事业单位和居民住房的固定资产折旧则是按照统一规定的折旧率和固定资产原值计算的虚拟折旧。原则上，固定资产折旧应按固定资产的重置价值来计算，但是我国目前尚不具备对全社会固定资产进行重估价的基础，所以暂时只能采用上述方法来计算。

营业盈余　指常住单位创造的增加值扣除劳动者报酬、生产税净额和固定资产折旧后的余额。它相当于企业的经营利润加上生产补贴，但要扣除从利润中开支的工资和福利以及从税后利润中提取的公益金等。

登记注册类型　以在工商行政管理机关登记注册的各类企业为划分对象。行政机关、事业单位和社会团体及其他经济组织参照执行。

国有企业　指企业全部资产归国家所有，并按国家有关法律规定登记注册的非公司制的经济组织。不包括有限责任公司中的国有独资公司。

集体企业　指企业资产归集体所有，并按国家有关法律规定登记注册的经济组织。

股份合作企业　以合作制为基础，由企业职工共同出资入股，吸收一定比例的社会资产投资组建，实行自主经营、自负盈亏，共同劳动，民主管理，按劳分配与按股分红相结合的一种集体经济组织。

联营企业　指两个及两个以上相同或不同所有制的企业法人或事业单位法人，按自愿、平等、互利的原则，共同投资组成的经济组织。包括国有联营、集体联营、国有与集体联营和其他联营企业。

有限责任公司　指根据国家有关法律规定登记注册，由两个以上，五十个以下的股东共同出资，公司以其全部资产对其债务承担责任的经济组织。包括国有独资公司以及其他有限责任公司。

股份有限公司　指根据国家有关法律规定登记注册，其全部注册资本由等额股份构成并通过发行股票筹集资本的经济组织。

私营企业　指由自然人投资设立或由自然人控股，以雇佣劳动为基础的盈利性经济组织。包括按照有关法律、条例规定登记注册的私营独资企业、私营合伙企业、私营有限责任公司和私营股份有限公司。

其他企业 指上述单位之外的其他内资经济组织。

港、澳、台商投资企业 指港澳台地区投资者依照中华人民共和国有关涉外经济的法律、法规，以合资、合作、独资、股份有限公司的形式在内地设立的企业。凡其中港澳台股本占公司注册资本比例小于 25%的，属于内资企业中的股份有限公司。

外商投资企业 指外国企业或外国人依照中华人民共和国有关涉外经济的法律、法规，以合资、合作、独资、股份有限公司的形式在中国内地投资设立的企业。凡其中外资股本占公司注册资本比例小于 25%的，属于内资企业中的股份有限公司。

Explanatory Notes On Main Statistical Indicators

Gross Domestic Product refers to gross domestic product calculated at market prices, which is the final products of all resident units in a country （or region） during a certain period of time. Gross domestic product is expressed in three different forms, i. e. value added, income, and products respectively. The form of value added refers to the total value of all products and services produced by all resident units during a certain period of time minus total value of input of non-fixed assets materials and services, or the summation of the value added by each of the resident units; the form of income refers to the total income created by each resident unit and distributed Primarily to all resident and non-resident units; the form of products refers to the total of final goods and services minus imports of goods and services. In the practice of national accounting, gross domestic product is calculated with three approaches, i. e. product approach, income approach, and expenditure approach respectively to reflect gross domestic product and its composition from different aspects.

Three Industries An industry structure classified according to the historical evolution of economic activity. Primary industry refers to extraction of natural resources ; secondary industry involves processing of primary products; and tertiary industry provides various kinds of services for production and consumption. The classification is universal although it varies to some extent form country to country. Each industry in China comprises:

Primary industry: Agriculture（including farming, forestry and fishery）.

Secondary industry: Industry（including mining and quarrying, manufacturing , water supply, electricity generation and supply, steam, hot water, gas）and Construction .

Tertiary industry: all other industries not included in primary or secondary industry.

Due to the fact that tertiary industry involves in a large variety of industries in China, it is divided into two groups: circulation groups, and service groups and further into four levels:

The first level: Circulation department, including transportation, posts and telecommunications, commerce, catering, material distribution, and storage.

The second level: Service department providing production and consumption services, including banking, insurance, geological survey, real estates, public utilities, service for residents, consulting service, and comprehensive technical services, and service for agriculture, forestry, animal husbandry, fishery, water conservancy, and maintenance of roads and inland water ways, etc.

The third level: Service department for upgrading scientific, educational and cultural level of the people, including education , culture, broadcasting , television, scientific research, public health, sports, and social welfare, etc.

The fourth level: Department providing public goods, including government organs, social organizations, armies, and policemen.

Comparable Prices are applied when comparing indicators of value over time to reflect accurately the changes in real term. Two methods are used for calculating comparable price indicators: 1. Multiplying the output of products by their constant prices of a certain year; 2. Conversion of the data in current prices by relevant price index.

Constant Prices refers to the average price of a given product in a certain year, which is used for comparison of output value over time. As the output value at constant prices removes the factor of price changes, it reflects the trend of production development over time. Since 1949, with the changes in general price level, the State Statistical Bureau has issued nationally unified constant prices five times: the 1952 constant prices for 1949-1957; the 1957 constant prices for 1958-1970; the 1970 constant prices for 1971-1981; the 1980 constant prices for 1981-1990; and the 1990 constant prices have been used since 1991.

GDP Calculated with Expenditure Approach refers to total expenditure on final consumption, total capital formation and net export of goods and services by resident units of a country in a certain period of time. It reflects the composition of GDP by its uses.

Final Consumption refers to the total expenditure of resident units on final consumption of goods and services in a certain period, namely the expenditure of the resident units on goods and services from domestic economic territory and abroad to meet the needs of material, cultural and spiritual life. It excludes the consumption expenditure of non-resident units in the economic territory of the country. The final consumption is classified into private consumption and government consumption.

（1）Private consumption refers to the total expenditure of households on the final consumption of goods and services in a certain period of time. The expenditure of households on final consumption of goods is recorded when the change of the ownership of goods happens. The expenditure of residents on the final consumption of services is recorded when the services is provided. The expenditure of private consumption is calculated at market prices, namely the purchasers' prices which the households pay; the purchasers' prices of goods are the prices the households pay when they obtain the goods, including the transport and commercial expenses paid by the households. In addition to the expenditure on consumption of goods and services with cash, there are other expenditures on goods and services obtained in other ways, i. e. the so-called fictitious expenditure on consumption, is also included in the expenditure of private consumption. The fictitious expenditure of private consumption includes the following cases: （a）the goods and services provided to private by the units as remuneration or benefit; （b）consumption of self-produced goods and services, in which the services refer only to the services provided by the residential buildings owned by the households; （c）the financial intermediary services provided by the financial institutions; （d）the insurance services provided by the insurance companies.

（2）Government consumption refers to the expenditure on the consumption of the public services provided by the government to the whole society and the net expenditure on the goods and services provided by the government to the households free charge or at lower prices. The former equals to the actual output value of the government services minus the value of operating income obtained by the government department. （The output value of the government services equals to its current operating expenditure plus the depreciation of its fixed assets）. The latter equals to the market value of the goods and services provided by the government to the households minus the value received by the government from the households.

Total Capital Formation refers to the net amount of that the fixed assets and inventory acquired minus those disposed, including the net incremental fixed assets and the net incremental inventory.

（1）Net incremental fixed assets refers to the value of fixed assets purchased, transferred in and self-produced by the resident units deducting the value of fixed assets sold and transferred out in a certain period. It can be classified into net incremental tangible assets and net incremental intangible assets. The net incremental tangible assets include the value of the construction projects, installation projects completed and the equipment, apparatus and instruments purchased as well as the value of land improved, the incremental value of draught animals, breeding stock, milk, wool and recreational animals and the economic forest in a certain period. The net incremental intangible assets includes the prospecting of minerals, the acquisition of computer softwares, the originals of recreational, literary and art works.

（2）Net incremental inventory refers to the market value of the change in inventory in a certain period, i.e, the difference of inventory value between the beginning and the end of the period . The net incremental inventory can be positive or negative. A positive value indicates the net increase in inventory while a negative value indicates the net decrease in inventory. The inventory includes the raw materials, fuels and reserve materials purchased by the production units as well as the inventory of finished products, semi-finished products, work-in-progress, etc.

Net Export of Goods and Services refers to the difference between the exports and the imports of goods and services. The exports include the value of various goods and services sold or voluntary transferred by the resident units to the non-resident units. The imports include the value of various goods and services purchased or gratuitously acquired by the resident units from the non-resident units. Because the provision and the use of services happen simultaneously, the import and export of services are not necessarily to cross the border of a country. The services received by the resident units from abroad are usually regarded as imports while the services received by non-resident units are usually regarded as exports . The exports and imports of goods are calculated at

FOB.

Laborers' Remuneration refers to all the incomes earned by the laborers from their productive activities, which include wages, bonuses and allowances the laborers received in various forms, including incomes in money and in kind . It also includes the free medical services and the medicine subsidies provided to the laborers as well as traffic subsidies and social insurance fee paid by the laborers' working units for them. The social insurance fee paid by the laborers' working units refers to the social insurance fee paid directly by the working units to the government department （usually the department of labor ） or the insurance fee paid by the enterprises and institutions for the retirement, death, and medical injury treatment of the staff and workers. For the individual economy, since the laborers' remuneration is not easily distinguished from the operating profit , both are treated as laborers' remuneration.

Net Taxes on Production refers to the difference between the taxes and the subsidies on production. The taxes on production refers to the various taxes, extra charges and fees levied on the production units on their production, sale and business activities as well as on some factors in production, such as fixed assets, land and labor force. In detail,, they include sales tax and extra charges, value added tax, various taxes paid from overhead, road toll, sewage charges, extra charges on water and electric power consumed, special revenue turned over to the government by the monopolized trade of tobacco and liquor, etc. In contrast to the taxes on production , the subsidies on production is an unilateral revenue transfer from the government to the production units and is therefore treated as the negative taxes on production. They include subsidies on the loss due to implementation of government policies, price subsidies to the grain institutions, foreign trade corporations' export rebates, etc.

Depreciation of Fixed Assets refers to the depreciation of fixed assets drawn in accordance with the stipulated depreciation rate for the purpose of compensating the wear loss of the fixed assets, or the depreciation of fixed assets calculated in a fictitious way in accordance with the stipulated unified depreciation rate in the national economic accounting system. It reflects the transferred value of the fixed assets in the production of the current period. The depreciation of fixed assets in various enterprises and institutions managed as enterprises refers to the depreciation expenses actually drawn and recorded as cost. In the units which do not draw the depreciation expenses, such as government organs, institutions not managed as enterprises as well as the houses of residents, the depreciation of fixed assets is the fictitious depreciation, which is calculated in accordance with the stipulated unified depreciation rate. In principle, the depreciation of fixed assets should be calculated on the basis of the re-purchased value of the fixed assets. However, it is not feasible to re-evaluate all the fixed assets in China. Therefore, the above-mentioned methods are temporarily adopted at present.

Operating Surplus refers to the net value of that the value added created by the resident units deducting the laborers' remuneration, net taxes on production and the depreciation of fixed assets. It is equivalent to the business profit of the enterprises plus subsidies on production , but the wages and welfare expenses paid from the profits and the public welfare fund drawn from the post-tax profits should be deducted.

Registered Type refers to type that all kinds of enterprises registered in administrative organ of industry and commerce. And registered type of government organs, party organs, institutions, social bodies and other economic organizations will be in light of the above.

State-owned Enterprises refers to non-company economic organizations with enterprises' assets owned by the state and registered according to related laws of the state, exclude state-owned sole-funds company of limited-liability company.

Collective-owned Enterprises refers to economic organizations with enterprises' assets owned by collectives and registered according to related laws of the state.

Share Holding Cooperative Enterprises refers to collective-owned economic organizations founded on bases of cooperative system and funded by shares of staff and workers and social assets in a certain proportion. They carry out rules of voluntary, equality, personal responsibility for profit and loss, working together, democratic management, combine distribution according to work with sharing profits according to shares.

Joint Enterprises refers to economic organizations funded by two or above institutional units with same or different ownership on the basis of voluntary, equality and mutual benefit , include state-owned joint, collective-owned joint, state-collective joint and other joint enterprises.

Limited-liability Company refers to economic organizations funded by two-fifty shareholders and registered according to related laws of the state, include state-owned sole-funds company and other limited-liability companies.

Share Holding Company refers to economic organizations registered according to related laws of the state and their total capital composed with same quota shares and collected by issuing shares.

Private Owned Enterprises refers to profit-making economic organizations founded on bases of wage labor and funded or share held by personnel, include sole-funded enterprises, cooperative enterprises, limited-liability company and share holding company registered according to related laws of the state.

Other Enterprises refers to other domestic investment economic organizations excluding the above.

Hongkong,Macao and Taiwan Funded Enterprises refers to enterprises established by entrepreneurs from Hongkong, Macao and Taiwan within the territory of mainland China according to related economic laws and regulations of the People's Republic of China in forms of joint ventures, cooperative sole-funded and share holding company. And those proportion of shares capital of Hongkong, Macao and Taiwan in registered capital less than 25% will be part of share holding company of domestic invested enterprises.

Foreign Funded Enterprises refers to enterprises established by foreign entrepreneurs within the territory of mainland China according to related economic laws and regulations of the People's Republic of China in forms of joint ventures, cooperative sole-funded and share holding company. And those proportion of foreign shares capital in registered capital less than 25% will be part of share holding company of domestic invested enterprises.

人　口 2

POPULATION

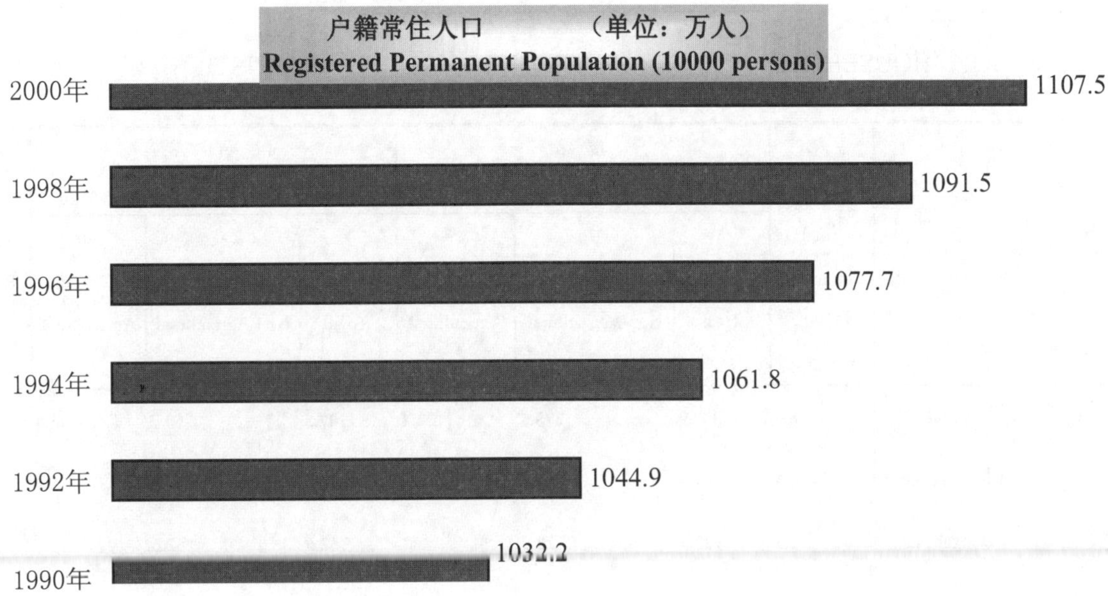
户籍常住人口　（单位：万人）
Registered Permanent Population (10000 persons)
2000年
1107.5
1998年
1091.5
1996年
1077.7
1994年
1061.8
1992年
1044.9
1990年
1032.2

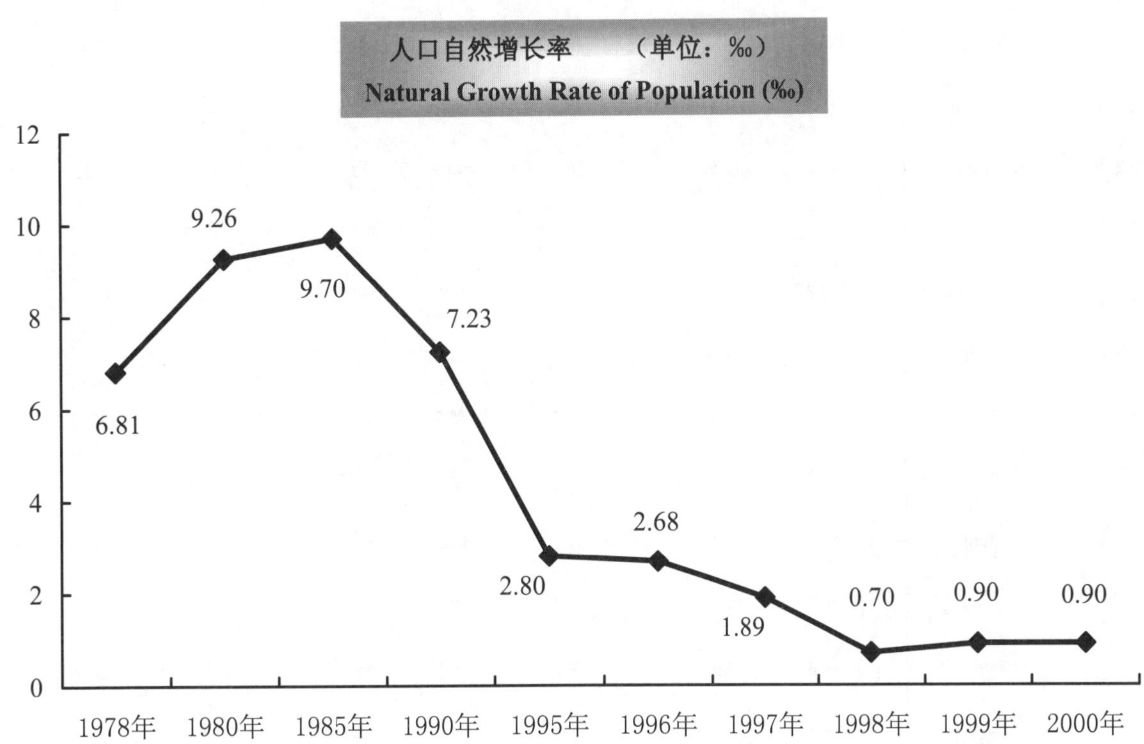
人口自然增长率　（单位：‰）
Natural Growth Rate of Population (‰)
12
10
8
6
4
2
0
6.81
9.26
9.70
7.23
2.80
2.68
1.89
0.70
0.90
0.90
1978年
1980年
1985年
1990年
1995年
1996年
1997年
1998年
1999年
2000年

2-1 户 数 及 人 口 数(户籍统计)
HOUSEHOLD AND POPULATION(REGISTERED STATISTICS)

地区 Region		总人口(万人) Total Population (10000 persons)	户数(万户) Households(10000 households)			常住人口(万人) Permanent Residents(10000 persons)			暂住人口(万人) Temporary Residents (10000 persons)
			合计 Total	非农业户 Non-Agricultural	农业户 Agricultural	合计 Total	非农业户 Non-Agricultural	农业户 Agricultural	
全 市	**Total**	**1278.0**	**397.9**	**275.5**	**122.4**	**1107.5**	**760.7**	**346.8**	**170.5**
城 区	**City Propers**	**266.3**	**87.7**	**87.7**	**…**	**238.2**	**238.2**	**…**	**28.1**
东城区	Dongcheng	71.3	23.5	23.5		62.6	62.6		8.7
西城区	Xicheng	85.6	28.2	28.2	…	78.1	78.1	…	7.5
崇文区	Chongwen	46.2	15.7	15.7	…	41.3	41.3	…	4.9
宣武区	Xuanwu	63.2	20.3	20.3	…	56.2	56.2	…	7.0
近郊区	**Near Suburbs**	**537.3**	**152.4**	**132.2**	**20.2**	**429.2**	**381.9**	**47.3**	**108.1**
朝阳区	Chaoyang	189.7	56.9	48.7	8.2	152.2	133.5	18.7	37.5
丰台区	Fengtai	110.3	31.4	25.3	6.1	82.2	67.5	14.7	28.1
石景山区	Shijingshan	41.5	11.5	10.8	0.7	33.2	31.6	1.6	8.3
海淀区	Haidian	195.8	52.6	47.4	5.2	161.6	149.3	12.3	34.2
远郊区	**Outer Suburbs**	**277.8**	**91.9**	**35.9**	**56.0**	**253.9**	**91.2**	**162.7**	**23.9**
门头沟区	Mentougou	25.5	9.1	5.9	3.2	23.4	15.3	8.1	2.1
房山区	Fangshan	78.3	25.6	9.7	15.9	74.3	27.0	47.3	4.0
通州区	Tongzhou	65.2	23.1	8.6	14.5	59.7	19.1	40.6	5.5
顺义区	Shunyi	59.3	18.3	4.8	13.5	53.7	11.8	41.9	5.6
昌平区	Changping	49.5	15.8	6.9	8.9	42.8	18.0	24.8	6.7
各 县	**Counties**	**196.6**	**65.9**	**19.7**	**46.2**	**186.2**	**49.4**	**136.8**	**10.4**
大兴县	Daxing	58.9	17.2	6.0	11.2	52.8	15.6	37.2	6.1
平谷县	Pinggu	39.9	12.8	3.8	9.0	38.7	9.7	29.0	1.2
怀柔县	Huairou	28.3	10.2	3.3	6.9	26.3	8.2	18.1	2.0
密云县	Miyun	42.2	15.5	3.9	11.6	41.5	9.7	31.8	0.7
延庆县	Yanqing	27.3	10.2	2.7	7.5	26.9	6.2	20.7	0.4

2-2 人　口　密　度(户籍统计)
POPULATION DENSITY(REGISTERED STATISTICS)

地　区 Region		常住人口 (万人) Permanent Population (10000 persons)	土地面积 (平方公里) Land Area (sq.km)	人口密度 (人／平方公里) Population Density (person/sq.km)
全　市	**Total**	**1107.5**	**16807.8**	**658**
城　区	**City Proper**	**238.2**	**87.1**	**27332**
市中心最稠密街道	The Densest Streets			
天坛街道	Tiantan Street	6.9	1.3	52995
椿树街道	Chunshu Street	5.0	1.0	49853
前门街道	Qianmen Street	4.8	1.1	43263
大栅栏街道	Dashanlan Street	5.4	1.3	41626
崇文门外街道	Chongwenmen Street	4.5	1.1	40504
东 城 区	Dongcheng	62.6	24.7	25328
西 城 区	Xicheng	78.1	30.0	26048
崇 文 区	Chongwen	41.3	15.9	25969
宣 武 区	Xuanwu	56.2	16.5	33980
近 郊 区	**Near Suburbs**	**429.2**	**1282.8**	**3337**
朝 阳 区	Chaoyang	152.2	470.8	3232
丰 台 区	Fengtai	82.2	304.2	2704
石景山区	Shijingshan	33.2	81.8	3919
海 淀 区	Haidian	161.6	426.0	3795
远 郊 区	**Outer Suburbs**	**253.9**	**6478.0**	**392**
门头沟区	Mentougou	23.4	1331.3	176
房 山 区	Fangshan	74.3	1866.7	398
通 州 区	Tongzhou	59.7	870.0	687
顺 义 区	Shunyi	53.7	980.0	548
昌 平 区	Changping	42.8	1430.0	299
各　县	**Counties**	**186.2**	**8959.9**	**208**
大 兴 县	Daxing	52.8	1012.0	521
平 谷 县	Pinggu	38.7	1075.0	360
怀 柔 县	Huairou	26.3	2557.3	103
密 云 县	Miyun	41.5	2335.6	178
延 庆 县	Yanqing	26.9	1980.0	136

2-3 常住人口性别构成及性别比(户籍统计)
SEX COMPOSITION AND SEX RATIO OF PERMANENT RESIDENTS (REGISTERED STATISTICS)

地 区	Region	常住人口(万人) Permanent Population(10000 persons) 合 计 Total	男 Male	女 Female	性别比 (女=100) Sex Ratio (female=100)
全 市	**Total**	**1107.5**	**560.1**	**547.4**	**102.3**
城 区	**City Propers**	**238.2**	**120.0**	**118.2**	**101.6**
东城区	Dongcheng	62.6	31.2	31.4	99.3
西城区	Xicheng	78.1	39.1	39.0	100.2
崇文区	Chongwen	41.3	20.6	20.7	99.9
宣武区	Xuanwu	56.2	29.1	27.1	107.6
近郊区	**Near Suburbs**	**429.2**	**219.9**	**209.3**	**105.0**
朝阳区	Chaoyang	152.2	77.5	74.7	103.7
丰台区	Fengtai	82.2	41.9	40.3	103.9
石景山区	Shijingshan	33.2	17.5	15.7	111.1
海淀区	Haidian	161.6	83.0	78.6	105.7
远郊区	**Outer Suburbs**	**253.9**	**126.7**	**127.2**	**99.5**
门头沟区	Mentougou	23.4	12.2	11.2	109.0
房山区	Fangshan	74.3	37.4	36.9	101.1
通州区	Tongzhou	59.7	29.4	30.3	97.0
顺义区	Shunyi	53.7	26.4	27.3	97.0
昌平区	Changping	42.8	21.3	21.5	98.7
各 县	**Counties**	**186.2**	**93.5**	**92.7**	**100.9**
大兴县	Daxing	52.8	26.4	26.4	100.0
平谷县	Pinggu	38.7	19.3	19.4	99.9
怀柔县	Huairou	26.3	13.3	13.0	102.2
密云县	Miyun	41.5	20.9	20.6	101.2
延庆县	Yanqing	26.9	13.6	13.3	102.7

2-4 户籍人口自然变动人数(户籍统计)
NATURAL CHANGE OF REGISTERED POPULATION(REGISTERED STATISTICS)

单位：人 (person)

地 区	Region	出生人数 Number of Birth 2000	1999	死亡人数 Number of Death 2000	1999	自然增加人数 Number of Natural Growth 2000	1999
全 市	**Total**	**72168**	**62757**	**77587**	**61598**	**-5419**	**1159**
城 区	**City Propers**	**9682**	**9213**	**16651**	**14594**	**-6969**	**-5381**
东城区	Dongcheng	2696	2588	4044	3786	-1348	-1198
西城区	Xicheng	3501	3270	5296	4378	-1795	-1108
崇文区	Chongwen	1489	1391	3093	2628	-1604	-1237
宣武区	Xuanwu	1996	1964	4218	3802	-2222	-1838
近郊区	**Near Suburbs**	**24498**	**21161**	**23441**	**20417**	**1057**	**744**
朝阳区	Chaoyang	8923	7525	9126	7886	-203	-361
丰台区	Fengtai	4954	4213	5207	4654	-253	-441
石景山区	Shijingshan	1602	1512	1880	1578	-278	-66
海淀区	Haidian	9019	7911	7228	6299	1791	1612
远郊区	**Outer Suburbs**	**20116**	**17349**	**20897**	**17048**	**-781**	**301**
门头沟区	Mentougou	1862	1483	2395	1670	-533	-187
房山区	Fangshan	6240	5730	5541	4846	699	884
通州区	Tongzhou	4627	3650	4501	4166	126	-516
顺义区	Shunyi	3891	3388	4297	4125	-406	-737
昌平区	Changping	3496	3098	4163	2241	-667	857
各 县	**Counties**	**17872**	**15034**	**16598**	**9539**	**1274**	**5495**
大兴县	Daxing	5405	4497	3843	2842	1562	1655
平谷县	Pinggu	3283	2906	3395	1870	-112	1036
怀柔县	Huairou	2682	1926	2130	1618	552	308
密云县	Miyun	3747	3271	4925	1286	-1178	1985
延庆县	Yanqing	2755	2434	2305	1923	450	511

2-5 人 口 变 动(户籍统计)

POPULATION CHANGE(REGISTERED STATISTICS)

单位：人 (person)

项目	Item	2000	1999
自然变动	**Natural Change**		
自然增加	Natural Increase	-5419	1159
非农业人口	Non-agricultural Population	-3051	-1418
农业人口	Agricultural Population	-2368	2577
出 生	Birth	72168	62757
非农业人口	Non-agricultural Population	39731	35251
农业人口	Agricultural Population	32437	27506
死 亡	Death	77587	61598
非农业人口	Non-agricultural Population	42782	36669
农业人口	Agricultural Population	34805	24929
机械变动	**Non-natural Change**		
机械增加	Non-natural Increase	89109	68845
非农业人口	Non-agricultural Population	82906	63083
农业人口	Agricultural Population	6203	5762
市外迁入	Move in from outside	141548	113369
非农业人口	Non-agricultural Population	130162	103450
农业人口	Agricultural Population	11386	9919
迁往市外	Move out	52439	44524
非农业人口	Non-agricultural Population	47256	40367
农业人口	Agricultural Population	5183	4157

2-6 2000年人口实际自然变动情况

ACTUAL NATURAL CHANGE OF POPULATION

项目	Item		常住人口 Permanent Residents
自然变动人数(人)	Natural Change of Population	(person)	
出生人数	Number of Birth		80766
死亡人数	Number of Death		69642
自然增加人数	Natural Increase of Population		11124
自然变动率 (‰)	Natural Growth Rate	(‰)	
出生率	Birth Rate		6.2
死亡率	Death Rate		5.3
自然增长率	Natural Growth Rate		0.9

注：本表数据为2000年北京市第五次全国人口普查快速汇总数据推算数字。

Note: Data of this table was estimated through the quick collections of 2000 Beijing Population Census.

2-7 计 划 生 育 状 况
FAMILY PLANNING

项　目		Item		2000	1999	2000年比1999年增、减 2000 compared with 1999
全　市		**Total**				
计划内生育	(人)	Within Plan	(person)	78860	70727	8133
计划生育率	(%)	Family Planning Rate	(%)	97.2	98.4	-1.2
已婚育龄妇女人数	(人)	Number of Women of Childbearing Age	(person)	2299188	2298077	1111
实际采取节育措施人数	(人)	Number of Women Controlled Birth	(person)	2025294	2042666	-17372
独生子女领证率	(%)	Acceptance Rate of Only-child Certificate	(%)	66.0	64.7	1.2
城　市		**City**				
计划生育率	(%)	Family Planning Rate	(%)	98.9	99.7	-0.8
已婚育龄妇女人数	(人)	Number of Women of Childbearing Age	(person)	1429554	1420880	8674
实际采取节育措施人数	(人)	Number of Women Controlled Birth	(person)	1234590	1232457	2133
独生子女领证率	(%)	Acceptance Rate of Only-child Certificate	(%)	80.1	78.3	1.8
农　村		**Rural**				
计划生育率	(%)	Family Planning Rate	(%)	94.9	96.8	-1.9
已婚育龄妇女人数	(人)	Number of Women of Childbearing Age	(person)	869634	877197	-7563
实际采取节育措施人数	(人)	Number of Women Controlled Birth	(person)	790704	810209	-19505
独生子女领证率	(%)	Acceptance Rate of Only-child Certificate	(%)	42.7	42.8	-0.1

资料来源：北京市计划生育委员会。
Data source: Beijing Birth Control Committee.

2-8 北京市各区县人口数
POPULATION OF DISTRICTS AND COUNTIES

单位：万人　　　　(10000 persons)

地　区	Region	合 计 Total	男 Male	女 Female	性别比(女=100) Sex Ratio(female=100)
全　市	**Total**	**1356.9**	**707.6**	**649.3**	**109.0**
东城区	Dongcheng	53.6	26.9	26.6	101.3
西城区	Xicheng	70.7	36.0	34.6	104.1
崇文区	Chongwen	34.6	17.3	17.3	100.3
宣武区	Xuanwu	52.6	27.2	25.4	107.0
朝阳区	Chaoyang	229.0	121.7	107.3	113.5
丰台区	Fengtai	136.9	72.0	64.9	110.9
石景山区	Shijingshan	48.9	26.0	22.9	113.6
海淀区	Haidian	224.0	119.6	104.4	114.5
门头沟区	Mentougou	26.7	13.8	12.8	107.8
房山区	Fangshan	81.4	42.2	39.2	107.7
通州区	Tongzhou	67.4	33.9	33.4	101.5
顺义区	Shunyi	63.7	32.5	31.1	104.4
昌平区	Changping	61.5	32.8	28.6	114.7
大兴县	Daxing	67.2	35.1	32.1	109.3
平谷县	Pinggu	39.7	19.8	19.9	99.3
怀柔县	Huairou	29.6	15.2	14.4	106.2
密云县	Miyun	42.0	21.1	20.9	100.9
延庆县	Yanqing	27.5	14.2	13.3	106.5

注：1.自表2-8起，数据均来源于2000年北京市第五次全国人口普查快速汇总资料。
2.全市及各区县的数据为2000年11月1日零时的实际登记数。
a) From table 2-8, data was gained through the quick collections of 2000 Beijing Population Census.
b) Data of total, districts and counties is that actually rigistered at zero hour on the 1st, November in 2000.

2-9 北京市各区县户数、人口数
HOUSEHOLD AND POPULATION OF DISTRICTS AND COUNTIES

地区 Region		户数（万户） Households(10000 households)			人口数（万人） Population(10000 persons)			家庭户平均每户人数（人） Average Persons Per Household (person)
		合计 Total	家庭户 Family-household	集体户 Collective-household	合计 Total	家庭户 Family-household	集体户 Collective-household	
全　市	**Total**	**442.2**	**410.0**	**32.2**	**1356.9**	**1192.5**	**164.4**	**2.9**
东城区	Dongcheng	17.8	17.0	0.8	53.6	48.9	4.6	2.9
西城区	Xicheng	24.4	23.1	1.4	70.7	63.1	7.6	2.7
崇文区	Chongwen	12.2	11.8	0.4	34.6	32.8	1.8	2.8
宣武区	Xuanwu	18.1	17.4	0.7	52.6	48.1	4.5	2.8
朝阳区	Chaoyang	77.2	71.3	5.8	229.0	198.1	30.9	2.8
丰台区	Fengtai	46.2	43.2	2.9	136.9	121.7	15.3	2.8
石景山区	Shijingshan	16.7	15.3	1.4	48.9	43.0	6.0	2.8
海淀区	Haidian	72.6	61.5	11.1	224.0	170.8	53.2	2.8
门头沟区	Mentougou	9.0	8.7	0.3	26.7	25.6	1.0	2.9
房山区	Fangshan	24.9	23.7	1.2	81.4	75.2	6.2	3.2
通州区	Tongzhou	21.3	20.6	0.8	67.4	63.1	4.3	3.1
顺义区	Shunyi	19.0	18.0	1.0	63.7	58.5	5.1	3.3
昌平区	Changping	19.4	17.2	2.2	61.5	49.7	11.8	2.9
大兴县	Daxing	19.2	18.1	1.1	67.2	60.2	6.9	3.3
平谷县	Pinggu	11.5	11.3	0.2	39.7	38.5	1.1	3.4
怀柔县	Huairou	9.9	9.5	0.4	29.6	27.9	1.7	2.9
密云县	Miyun	13.9	13.6	0.3	42.0	40.8	1.2	3.0
延庆县	Yanqing	9.1	8.9	0.2	27.5	26.5	1.0	3.0

2-10 北京市各区县民族人口状况
POPULATION FOR NATIONALITY OF DISTRICTS AND COUNTIES

地区 Region		合计（万人） Total (10000 persons)	汉族 Han		其他民族 Other Nationalitities	
			人口数（万人） Population (10000 persons)	比重（%） Proportion (%)	人口数（万人） Population (10001 persons)	比重（%） Proportion (%)
全　市	**Total**	**1356.9**	**1299.0**	**95.7**	**57.9**	**4.3**
东城区	Dongcheng	53.6	50.1	93.6	3.4	6.4
西城区	Xicheng	70.7	66.5	94.1	4.2	5.9
崇文区	Chongwen	34.6	33.0	95.2	1.6	4.8
宣武区	Xuanwu	52.6	48.7	92.6	3.9	7.4
朝阳区	Chaoyang	229.0	217.7	95.1	11.3	4.9
丰台区	Fengtai	136.9	132.2	96.5	4.7	3.5
石景山区	Shijingshan	48.9	47.5	97.0	1.5	3.0
海淀区	Haidian	224.0	213.9	95.5	10.1	4.5
门头沟区	Mentougou	26.7	26.3	98.7	0.3	1.3
房山区	Fangshan	81.4	79.3	97.4	2.1	2.6
通州区	Tongzhou	67.4	64.8	96.2	2.5	3.8
顺义区	Shunyi	63.7	61.9	97.2	1.8	2.8
昌平区	Changping	61.5	59.5	96.8	1.9	3.2
大兴县	Daxing	67.2	64.6	96.2	2.6	3.8
平谷县	Pinggu	39.7	39.4	99.4	0.3	0.6
怀柔县	Huairou	29.6	27.3	92.2	2.3	7.8
密云县	Miyun	42.0	39.7	94.4	2.3	5.6
延庆县	Yanqing	27.5	26.6	96.4	1.0	3.6

2-11 北京市各区县人口年龄状况
POPULATION FOR AGE OF DISTRICTS AND COUNTIES

单位：万人 (10000 persons)

地区	Region	合计 Total	分年龄段人口 Population Grouped by Age 0-5	6-14	15-64	65岁及以上 65 years old and above
全市	**Total**	**1356.9**	**54.5**	**130.0**	**1059.1**	**113.4**
东城区	Dongcheng	53.6	1.5	4.6	41.0	6.6
西城区	Xicheng	70.7	1.9	5.8	54.2	8.8
崇文区	Chongwen	34.6	1.0	3.1	26.2	4.4
宣武区	Xuanwu	52.6	1.3	4.4	40.4	6.4
朝阳区	Chaoyang	229.0	8.5	16.4	186.0	18.1
丰台区	Fengtai	136.9	5.6	10.8	109.7	10.8
石景山区	Shijingshan	48.9	2.1	3.8	39.3	3.8
海淀区	Haidian	224.0	8.0	15.6	184.2	16.2
门头沟区	Mentougou	26.7	1.3	2.8	20.2	2.4
房山区	Fangshan	81.4	4.0	10.9	61.1	5.4
通州区	Tongzhou	67.4	2.8	8.6	50.7	5.4
顺义区	Shunyi	63.7	2.7	9.2	46.8	4.9
昌平区	Changping	61.5	2.7	5.3	49.4	4.1
大兴县	Daxing	67.2	3.4	8.8	50.5	4.5
平谷县	Pinggu	39.7	2.0	6.8	27.4	3.4
怀柔县	Huairou	29.6	1.6	3.5	22.0	2.4
密云县	Miyun	42.0	2.4	5.6	30.5	3.5
延庆县	Yanqing	27.5	1.6	4.0	19.6	2.4

2-12 北京市各区县人口受教育程度状况
POPULATION FOR EDUCATION LEVEL OF DISTRICTS AND COUNTIES

单位：万人 (10000 persons)

地区	Region	6周岁及以上人口 Population at and above 6 years old	未上过学人口 Never Attending School	扫盲班 Illiteracy-eliminate Class	小学 Primary School Level	初中 Junior Middle School Level	高中 Senior Middle School Level	大专及以上 College Level and above
全市	**Total**	**1302.5**	**58.2**	**4.8**	**230.1**	**466.7**	**314.1**	**228.5**
东城区	Dongcheng	52.1	1.7	0.2	6.7	14.6	17.0	11.9
西城区	Xicheng	68.7	1.9	0.2	8.3	18.5	20.7	19.1
崇文区	Chongwen	33.6	1.6	0.1	5.1	10.6	11.4	4.8
宣武区	Xuanwu	51.3	1.9	0.2	7.2	15.4	17.0	9.6
朝阳区	Chaoyang	220.5	6.4	0.7	31.1	75.3	59.0	47.9
丰台区	Fengtai	131.3	5.1	0.5	20.8	48.1	36.7	20.2
石景山区	Shijingshan	46.9	1.7	0.2	6.8	15.0	14.8	8.5
海淀区	Haidian	216.0	4.8	0.6	25.2	57.9	51.1	76.5
门头沟区	Mentougou	25.3	1.8	0.1	5.7	9.8	6.4	1.5
房山区	Fangshan	77.4	4.6	0.3	19.3	34.9	14.2	4.2
通州区	Tongzhou	64.6	3.3	0.3	16.7	29.9	10.6	3.7
顺义区	Shunyi	60.9	4.1	0.3	15.0	29.7	9.3	2.6
昌平区	Changping	58.8	3.0	0.3	10.4	24.5	12.8	7.8
大兴县	Daxing	63.8	3.9	0.2	15.4	28.9	10.9	4.5
平谷县	Pinggu	37.7	3.6	0.1	11.0	16.1	5.7	1.1
怀柔县	Huairou	28.0	2.4	0.2	6.6	11.1	5.9	1.8
密云县	Miyun	39.6	4.0	0.2	10.6	16.6	6.6	1.6
延庆县	Yanqing	26.0	2.6	0.2	8.2	9.7	4.0	1.3

2-13 北京市各区县文盲人口数
NUMBER OF ILLITERACY OF DISTRICTS AND COUNTIES

地区 Region		15周岁及以上人口 (万人) Population of 15 years old and above (10000 persons)	# 文盲人口 (万人) Illiteracy (10000 persons)	文盲率 (%) Illiteracy Rate (%)
全　市	**Total**	1172.5	57.5	4.9
东城区	Dongcheng	47.5	1.8	3.7
西城区	Xicheng	62.9	1.9	3.1
崇文区	Chongwen	30.5	1.6	5.1
宣武区	Xuanwu	46.9	1.8	3.9
朝阳区	Chaoyang	204.1	6.3	3.1
丰台区	Fengtai	120.5	5.0	4.1
石景山区	Shijingshan	43.0	1.7	4.0
海淀区	Haidian	200.4	4.5	2.3
门头沟区	Mentougou	22.6	1.8	7.9
房山区	Fangshan	66.5	4.5	6.8
通州区	Tongzhou	56.1	3.2	5.7
顺义区	Shunyi	51.7	4.0	7.7
昌平区	Changping	53.5	3.0	5.7
大兴县	Daxing	55.0	3.9	7.0
平谷县	Pinggu	30.8	3.6	11.6
怀柔县	Huairou	24.4	2.4	9.7
密云县	Miyun	34.0	4.0	11.6
延庆县	Yanqing	22.0	2.6	11.6

主 要 统 计 指 标 解 释

人口数 指一定时点、一定地区范围内有生命的个人的总和。年度统计的年末人口数是指每年 12 月 31 日 24 时的人口数。

出生率 指在一定时期内（通常为一年）出生人数与同期平均人数(或期中之数)的比率，一般用千分率表示。计算公式：

$$出生率=\frac{年出生人数}{年平均人数}\times 1000‰$$

出生人数是指活产，即脱离母体时（不管怀孕月数），有过呼吸或其他生命现象的活婴儿总和。

年平均人数是年初、年底人口数的平均数，也可用年中人口数代替。

死亡率 指在一定时期内（通常为一年）一定地区的死亡人数与同期平均人数（或期中人数）之比，一般用千分率表示。计算公式：

$$死亡率=\frac{年死亡人数}{年平均人数}\times 1000‰$$

人口自然增长率 指在一定时期内（通常为一年）人口自然增加数（出生人数减死亡人数）与该时期内平均人数（或期中人数）之比，一般用千分率表示。计算公式：

$$人口自然增长率=\frac{本年出生人数—本年死亡人数}{年平均人数}\times 1000‰$$

人口自然增长率=人口出生率—人口死亡率

Explanatory Notes On Main Statistical Indicators

Total Population refers to the total number of people alive at a certain point of time within a given area. Year-end total population is that at 24:00 on 31st of December.

Birth Rate refers to the ratio of the number of births to the average population during a certion period of time (usually a year), which is often expressed in ‰. The following formula is used:

$$\text{Birth Rate}=\frac{\text{Number of Birth}}{\text{Average Population}}\times 1000‰$$

Number of Birth refers to live births, i. e. the births when babies had showed any vital phenomena regardless of the length of pregnancy.

Average Population is the average of population at the beginning of a year and that at the end of the year. Sometimes it is substituted for with the mid-year population.

Death Rate refers to the ratio of the number of deaths to the average population （or mid-year population）during a certain period of time (usually one year), which is often expressed in ‰. The following formula is used:

$$\text{Death Rate}=\frac{\text{Number of Deaths}}{\text{Average Population}}\times 1000‰$$

Natural Growth Rate of Population refers to the ratio of the natural increase in population （number of births minus number of deaths ）in a certain period of time （usually a year）to the average population （or mid-year population）of the same period, which is often expressed in ‰. The following formulas are applied:

$$\text{Natural Growth Rate of Population} = \frac{\text{Number of Births} - \text{Number of Deaths}}{\text{Average Population}} \times 1000‰$$

Natural Growth Rate of Population = Birth Rate − Death Rate

3 劳动力和工资

LABOR FORCE AND WAGE

全市从业人员（按产业分）（单位：万人）
Employed Persons (by Indutry, 10000 persons)

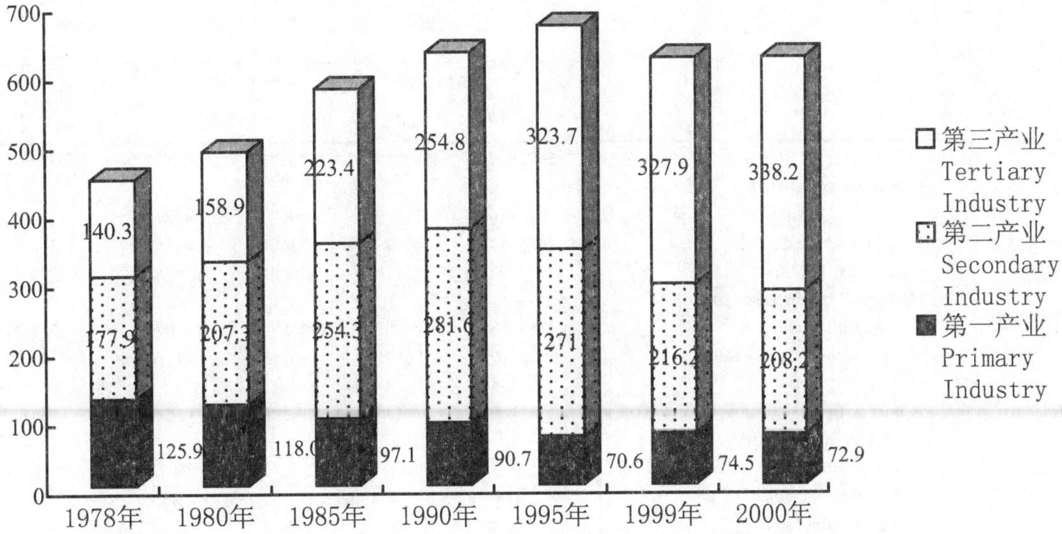

职工平均工资　　（单位：元）
Average Wage of Staff and Workers (yuan)

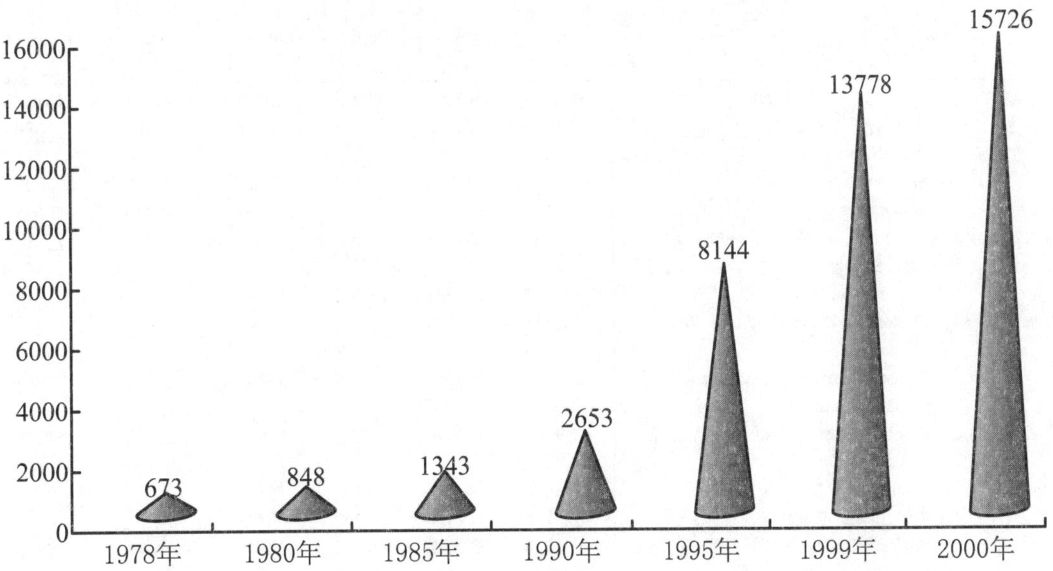

3-1 全市从业人员(按产业、部类分)

EMPLOYED PERSONS BY INDUSTRY AND DEPARTMENT

项目	Item	2000 合计 Total	2000 城市 Urban	2000 农村 Rural	1999 合计 Total	1999 城市 Urban	1999 农村 Rural
人数 (人)	**Number of Persons (person)**	**6192927**	**4562654**	**1630273**	**6185812**	**4560421**	**1625391**
按产业分	**Grouped by Industry**						
第一产业	Primary Industry	729236	29659	699577	745270	31671	713599
第二产业	Secondary Industry	2081583	1556979	524604	2161961	1632380	529581
第三产业	Tertiary Industry	3382108	2976016	406092	3278581	2896370	382211
按部类分	**Grouped by Department**						
物质生产部门	Material Production	3139608	1776083	1363525	3241076	1866276	1374800
非物质生产部门	Nonmaterial Production	3053319	2786571	266748	2944736	2694145	250591
构成 (%)	**Composition (%)**	**100**	**100**	**100**	**100**	**100**	**100**
按产业分	**Grouped by Industry**						
第一产业	Primary Industry	11.8	0.7	42.9	12.0	0.7	43.9
第二产业	Secondary Industry	33.6	34.1	32.2	35.0	35.8	32.6
第三产业	Tertiary Industry	54.6	65.2	24.9	53.0	63.5	23.5
按部类分	**Grouped by Department**						
物质生产部门	Material Production	50.7	38.9	83.6	52.4	40.9	84.6
非物质生产部门	Nonmaterial Production	49.3	61.1	16.4	47.6	59.1	15.4

3-2 全市从业人员(按登记注册类型分)

EMPLOYED PERSONS BY REGISTRATION STATUS

单位：人 (person)

行业	Sector	合计 Total	国有经济 State-owned	集体经济 Collective Owned	其他经济 Others	城镇私营劳动者 Urban Private	城镇个体劳动者 Urban Individuals	农村劳动者 Rural Labors
总计	**Total**	**6192927**	**2662057**	**482580**	**1173706**	**42447**	**201864**	**1630273**
农、林、牧、渔业	Farming,Forestry,Animal Husbandry and Fishery	729236	22708	916	5246	399	390	699577
采掘业	Excavation	30948	25066	84	666	40	20	5072
制造业	Manufacturing	1341884	492122	86559	366191	10730	10515	375767
电力、煤气及水的生产和供应业	Electricity,Gas,Water Production and Supply	40238	31765	566	7569			338
建筑业	Construction	653362	248783	161336	97831	1506	646	143260
地质勘查业水利管理业	Geological Prospecting and Water Conservancy	15151	14477	461	46			167
交通运输、仓储及邮电通信业	Transportation,Storage,Post and Telecommunication	328789	159390	6509	17209	382	5955	139344
批发和零售贸易餐饮业	Wholesale,Retail Trade and Catering Services	891905	196996	85839	199655	20332	157869	231214
金融、保险业	Finance and Insurance	71246	49087	6636	15523			
房地产业	Real Estate Trade	125113	49614	4177	69183			2139
社会服务业	Social Services	693546	312092	70795	250841	8086	25971	25761
卫生体育和社会福利业	Health Care,Sports and Social Welfare	159343	126222	30238	2488			395
教育、文化艺术和广播电影电视业	Education,Culture,Art,Radio,Film and Television	418712	397377	7599	12260			1476
科学研究和综合技术服务业	Scientific Research and Polytechnical Services	327345	200934	14741	111386			284
国家机关、政党机关和社会团体	Government Agencies,Party Agencies and Social Organizations	247244	246832	333	79			
其他行业	Others	118865	88592	5791	17533	972	498	5479

3-3 城镇单位从业人员年末人数

YEAR-END EMPLOYED PERSONS IN URBAN UNITS

单位：人 (person)

项目	Item	从业人员 Employed Persons	在岗职工 Staff and Workers at their Posts	聘用留用的离退休人员 Retired and VCSR Engaged and Kept on	聘用的外籍及港澳台方人员 Personnel of Foreign,Hong-kong,Macao and Taiwan	人事档案关系保留在原单位人员 Personnel Organizational Affiliation Reserved
总计	**Total**	**4318343**	**3979251**	**140679**	**4983**	**193430**
按登记注册类型分	**Grouped by Registration Status**					
内资经济	Domestic Investment Economy	3937987	3649904	128951	671	158461
国有经济	State-owned	2662057	2557580	51534	415	52528
集体经济	Collective-owned	482580	417302	39788	11	25479
联营经济	Joint-owned	40217	36506	1492	2	2217
股份有限公司	Share Holding Corporations Ltd.	139703	125799	4299	14	9591
有限责任公司	Limited-Liability Corporations	341967	287165	14294	72	40436
股份合作企业	Share Holding	85028	74133	4751	34	6110
其他经济	Others	186435	151419	12793	123	22100
外商投资经济	Foreign Funded	238462	209419	5518	3057	20468
港、澳、台商投资经济	Hongkong,Macao and Taiwan Funded	141894	119928	6210	1255	14501
按隶属关系分	**Grouped by Administrative Relationship**					
# 中央	Central	1183421	1111860	32628	940	37993
地方	Local	2547578	2380842	63768	2073	100895
按行业分	**Grouped by Sector**					
农、林、牧、渔业	Farming,Forestry,Animal Husbandry and Fishery	28870	28477	170	24	199
# 农业	Farming	5209	5048	30	16	115
采掘业	Excavation	25816	25756	60		
制造业	Manufacturing	944872	895612	19198	1235	28827
电力、煤气及水的生产和供应业	Electricity,Gas,Water Production and Supply	39900	39325	200		375
建筑业	Construction	507950	486860	11159	104	9827
地质勘查业水利管理业	Geological Prospecting and Water Conservancy	14984	14766	164		54
交通运输、仓储及邮电通信业	Transportation,Storage,Posts and Telecommunications	183108	175243	1130	138	6597
# 交通运输业	Transportation	131509	127492	513	75	3429
邮电通信业	Posts and Telecommunications	42922	39516	529	56	2821
批发和零售贸易餐饮业	Wholesale, Retail Trade and Catering Services	482490	425790	15987	304	40409
# 批发业	Wholesale Trade	179040	158080	6820	103	14037
零售业	Retail Trade	230813	206013	7543	55	17202
餐饮业	Catering Services	67262	56634	1532	139	8957
金融、保险业	Finance and Insurance	71246	69662	647	72	865
房地产业	Real Estate Trade	122974	103153	8649	292	10880
社会服务业	Social Services	633728	553857	25990	1416	52465
# 公共服务业	Public Services	183835	166743	3116	8	13968
居民服务业	Resident Services	50465	45403	1849	32	3181
旅馆业	Hotels	115939	103006	4737	403	7793
卫生体育和社会福利业	Health Care,Sports and Social Welfare	158948	134075	20789	50	4034
# 卫生	Health Care	123800	120383	2435	42	940
体育	Sports	8778	7915	182	8	673
教育、文化艺术和广播电影电视业	Education,Culture,Art, Radio,Film and Television	417236	394567	12278	557	9834
教育	Education	324423	309748	9264	420	4991
文化艺术业	Culture and Art	73826	68669	2335	84	2738
广播电影电视业	Radio,Film and Television	18987	16150	679	53	2105
科学研究和综合技术服务业	Scientific Research and Polytechnical Services	327061	284198	19027	398	23438
科学研究业	Scientific Research	127694	122506	4594	10	584
综合技术服务业	Polytechnical Services	199367	161692	14433	388	22854
国家机关、政党机关和社会团体	Government Agencies,Party Agencies and Social Organizations	247244	242554	3215		1475
其他行业	Others	111916	105356	2016	393	4151

注：城镇单位从业人员年末人数与报国家统计局劳动工资年报口径一致，不含城镇个体、私营企业、农村从业人员。

Note:Data in this table is in accordance to the annual bulletin of labors and wages reported to state statistical bureau, not include urban individuals, private and rural employed persons.

3-4 职 工 人 数
NUMBER OF STAFF AND WORKERS

单位：人 (person)

项目	Item	2000	1999	2000年为1999年% 2000 as % of 1999
总计	**Total**	**4342480**	**4379854**	**99.1**
按登记注册类型分	**Grouped by Registration Status**			
内资经济	Domestic Investment Economy	4001474	4071320	98.3
国有经济	State-owned	2830026	3029773	93.4
集体经济	Collective-owned	459877	496005	92.7
联营经济	Joint-owned	44234	51806	85.4
股份有限公司	Share Holding Corporations Ltd.	132496	220136	60.2
有限责任公司	Limited-Liability Corporations	306055	210413	145.5
股份合作企业	Share Holding	76428	61712	123.8
其他经济	Others	152358	1475	
外商投资经济	Foreign Funded	217594	191480	113.6
港、澳、台商投资经济	Hongkong,Macao and Taiwan Funded	123412	117054	105.4
按隶属关系分	**Grouped by Administrative Relationship**			
# 中央	Central	1170539	1223360	95.7
地方	Local	2679914	2775852	96.5
按行业分	**Grouped by Sector**			
农、林、牧、渔业	Farming,Forestry,Animal Husbandry and Fishery	31116	33677	92.4
# 农业	Farming	5525	4755	116.2
采掘业	Excavation	28143	30895	91.1
制造业	Manufacturing	1073278	1154474	93.0
电力、煤气及水的生产和供应业	Electricity,Gas,Water Production and Supply	40200	41752	96.3
建筑业	Construction	533146	514461	103.6
地质勘查业水利管理业	Geological Prospecting and Water Conservancy	15313	16958	90.3
交通运输、仓储及邮电通信业	Transportation,Storage,Posts and Telecommunications	188299	196556	95.8
# 交通运输业	Transportation	134898	135400	99.6
邮电通信业	Posts and Telecommunications	42757	44786	95.5
批发和零售贸易餐饮业	Wholesale, Retail Trade and Catering Services	480428	524923	91.5
# 批发业	Wholesale Trade	179371	188593	95.1
零售业	Retail Trade	235169	266686	88.2
餐饮业	Catering Services	60030	64230	93.5
金融、保险业	Finance and Insurance	71916	72295	99.5
房地产业	Real Estate Trade	106876	92148	116.0
社会服务业	Social Services	584862	528425	110.7
# 公共服务业	Public Services	174320	163069	106.9
居民服务业	Resident Services	48275	44599	108.2
旅馆业	Hotels	108045	111180	97.2
卫生体育和社会福利业	Health Care,Sports and Social Welfare	135451	133016	101.8
# 卫生	Health Care	121326	120619	100.6
体育	Sports	8221	7977	103.1
教育、文化艺术和广播电影电视业	Education,Culture,Art, Radio,Film and Television	401179	411604	97.5
教育	Education	314538	324070	97.1
文化艺术业	Culture and Art	70418	70073	100.5
广播电影电视业	Radio,Film and Television	16223	17461	92.9
科学研究和综合技术服务业	Scientific Research and Polytechnical Services	291778	258752	112.8
科学研究业	Scientific Research	127601	135602	94.1
综合技术服务业	Polytechnical Services	164177	123150	133.3
国家机关、政党机关和社会团体	Government Agencies,Party Agencies and Social Organizations	251317	304918	82.4
其他行业	Others	109178	65000	168.0

3-5 从业人员人数增减情况
CHANGES IN NUMBER OF EMPOLYED PERSONS

单位：人 (person)

项目	Item	2000 合计 Total	2000 #中央单位 Central	2000 #地方单位 Local	1999 合计 Total	1999 #中央单位 Central	1999 #地方单位 Local
净增人数	**Net Increase**	**-167746**	**-38251**	**-166299**	**-191459**	**-46261**	**-144793**
增加人数	**Number of Persons Increased**	**627298**	**120607**	**337164**	**587689**	**120473**	**352019**
从农村招收	Recruited from Rural Area	216367	29526	114752	211348	39438	124414
从城镇招收	Recruited from Urban Area	78479	11309	31114	64597	9685	28024
录用的退伍军人	Employment of Demobilized Soldiers	5929	1251	3906	5018	1373	3205
录用大中专技校毕业生	Employment of Graduate	60193	21570	30936	61239	19700	35411
不在岗职工重新上岗	Staff and Workers Rework after off their Posts	18721	2272	15791	25742	2374	22674
调入人数	Job Changes	135176	34572	72288	115535	24549	73933
# 市外调入	from Outside Beijing	16694	3252	5991	8658	2436	3138
其他	Others	112433	20107	68377	104210	23354	64358
减少人数	**Number of Persons Decreased**	**795044**	**158858**	**503463**	**779148**	**166734**	**496812**
离休退休退职	Retire and Quit	116897	28338	85416	78223	24261	52510
开除除名辞退	Be Discharged	59333	14803	27119	71545	24357	32100
终止解除合同	Contract Expiration	288008	43396	177565	277914	40088	186080
在岗职工无岗	Staff and Workers at their posts but have no work	41297	5825	35182	54867	6865	47052
调出人数	Job Changes	143393	39070	85302	145232	38164	86692
# 调往市外	to Outside Beijing	8813	1893	1788	12815	2692	2328
其他	Others	146116	27426	92879	151367	32999	92378

3-6 城镇新增就业人数
INCREMENTAL EMPLOYMENT IN URBAN AREA

单位：人 (person)

项目	Item	2000	1999	2000年为1999年% 2000 as % of 1999
总计	**Total**	**124567**	**116841**	**106.6**
国有经济	State-Owned Economy	54631	52766	103.5
集体经济	Collective-Owned Economy	5790	6340	91.3
个体经济	Individuals	3509	18285	19.2
其他经济	Others	60637	39450	153.7

3-7 国民经济各行业职工人数(按隶属关系、登记注册类型分)

单位：人

行业	Sector	全市 Total	# 中央 Central	# 地方 Local
总计	**Total**	**4342480**	**1170539**	**2679914**
农、林、牧、渔业	**Farming,Forestry,Animal Husbandry and Fishery**	**31116**	**1688**	**28774**
# 农、林、牧、渔服务业	FFAF Services	5525	99	5081
采掘业	**Excavation**	**28143**	**38**	**28105**
制造业	**Manufacturing**	**1073278**	**178471**	**838759**
食品加工业	Food Processing	18773	869	16439
食品制造业	Food Making	34176	1626	28527
饮料制造业	Beverage Making	26352	377	24802
烟草制造业	Tobacco Processing	836		836
纺织业	Textile Industry	51044	70	50363
服装及其他纤维制品制造业	Garments and Other Fiber Products	42715	2063	32348
皮革、毛皮、羽绒及其制品业	Leather,Furs,Down and Related Products	8142	48	7381
木材加工及竹、藤、棕、革制品业	Timber Processing,Bamboo,Cane,Palm Fiber and Straw Products	3785	665	2593
家具制造业	Furniture Manufacturing	9206	810	3989
造纸及纸制品业	Papermaking and Paper Products	10873	267	10013
印刷业、记录媒介的复制	Printing and Record Medium Reproduced	40910	22909	15946
文教体育用品制造业	Stationery,Education and Sports Goods	10002	63	8924
石油加工及炼焦业	Petroleum Processing and Coking Products	51196	44454	6580
化学原料及化学制品制造业	Raw Chemical Materials and Chemical Products	44946	1588	40493
医药制造业	Medical and Pharmaceutical Products	26452	2114	23518
化学纤维制造业	Chemical Fibers	4418	41	4300
橡胶制品业	Rubber Products	11724	338	11318
塑料制品业	Plastic Products	18881	739	16214
非金属矿物制品业	Nonmetal Mineral Products	61051	2130	56360
黑色金属冶炼及压延加工业	Smelting and Pressing Ferrous Metals	153966	65	153792
有色金属冶炼及压延加工业	Smelting and Pressing of Nonferrous Metals	3863	27	3748
金属制品业	Metal Products	30889	1208	24904
普通机械制造业	Ordinary Machinery	63081	9692	50950
专业设备制造业	Special Purpose Equipment	58189	12549	42749
交通运输设备制造业	Transportation Equipment	106534	41016	62370
武器弹药制造业	Weapons and Ammunition	11625	11625	
电气机械及器材制造业	Electric Equipment and Machine	52772	8194	41804
电子及通信设备制造业	Electronic and Telecommunication	76624	8488	65336
仪器仪表及文化办公用机械制造业	Instruments,Meters,Cultural and Official Machinery	24187	4102	18966
其他制造业	Other Manufacturing	16066	334	13196
电力、煤气及水的生产和供应业	**Electricity,Gas and Water Production and Supply**	**40200**	**9969**	**30231**
电力、蒸气、热水的生产和供应业	Electricity,Steam and Hot Water Production and Supply	25533	9969	15564
煤气生产和供应业	Gas Production and Supply	8383		8383
自来水的生产和供应业	Water Production and Supply	6284		6284
建筑业	**Construction**	**533146**	**111628**	**283032**
土木工程建筑业	Civil Engineering	439861	84198	245034
线路、管道和设备安装业	Circuit,Pipeline and Equipment Installation	59413	24141	26063
建筑物的装修装饰业	Buildings Fitting up and Decoration	33872	3289	11935
地质勘查业、水利管理业	**Geological Prospecting and Water Conservancy**	**15313**	**6078**	**9235**
地质勘查业	Geological Prospecting	5838	5153	685
水利管理业	Water Conservancy	9475	925	8550

NUMBER OF STAFF AND WORKERS BY SECTOR
(BY ADMINISTRATIVE RELATIONSHIP AND REGISTRATION STATUS)

(person)

国有经济 State-Owned	# 中 央 Central	# 地 方 Local	集体经济 Collective Owned	其他经济 Others
2830026	**1028335**	**1729009**	**459877**	**1052577**
24987	**1152**	**23835**	**900**	**5229**
3022		3022	304	2199
27396	**38**	**27358**	**85**	**662**
608977	**151415**	**457292**	**103891**	**360410**
9567	38	9529	421	8785
13305	213	13078	1295	19576
11896	96	11800	1266	13190
				836
29796		29779	4327	10721
7754	1999	5755	8059	26902
3699		3699	2145	2298
1936	613	1323	496	1353
1100	240	860	964	7142
5819	171	5648	937	4117
30071	21494	8521	4587	6252
4302	26	4276	1704	3996
50457	44360	6097	307	432
27059	408	26647	2366	15521
15521	1699	13822	1224	9707
2845	1	2844	113	1460
6487	273	6214	2368	2869
5726	319	5407	3621	9534
23151	1291	21860	9661	28239
147539		147539	900	5527
2044	27	2017	425	1394
8169	718	7423	7626	15094
38169	4373	33796	8932	15980
29267	11131	18136	4087	24835
58983	35691	23155	11748	35803
11625	11625			
23627	7387	16240	9488	19657
22280	3626	18640	4594	49750
13343	3590	9753	3603	7241
3440	6	3434	6427	6199
32130	**8491**	**23639**	**512**	**7558**
17520	8491	9029	512	7501
8326		8326		57
6284		6284		
287124	**86260**	**148660**	**154079**	**91943**
253347	72663	129754	127094	59420
28138	12156	14790	17881	13394
5639	1441	4116	9104	19129
14806	**6032**	**8774**	**461**	**46**
5792	5107	685		46
9014	925	8089	461	

3-7 续表 1 continued

单位：人

行业	Sector	全市 Total	# 中央 Central	# 地方 Local
交通运输、仓储及邮电通信业	**Transportation,Storage,Posts and Telecommunications**	**188299**	**130880**	**53767**
铁路运输业	Railway	64014	63796	218
公路运输业	Highway	28010	2563	24469
管道运输业	Pipeline	91	91	
航空运输业	Airway	10093	10093	
交通运输辅助业	Transport Supporting ans Auxiliary Services	32690	11260	20317
仓储业	Storage	10644	1908	8178
邮电通信业	Posts and Telecommunications	42757	41169	585
批发和零售贸易餐饮业	**Wholesale,Retail Trade and Catering Services**	**480428**	**58990**	**309082**
批发业	Wholesale Trade	179371	38513	105913
零售业	Retail Trade	235169	12892	171810
商业经纪与代理业	Commercial Management and Agency	5858	4399	1301
餐饮业	Catering Trade	60030	3186	30058
金融、保险业	**Finance and Insurance**	**71916**	**67773**	**3096**
金融业	Finance	66796	63466	2397
保险业	Insurance	5120	4307	699
房地产业	**Real Estate Trade**	**106876**	**16349**	**65587**
房地产开发与经营业	Real Estate Development	30641	2127	21201
房地产管理业	Real Estate Management	75006	14214	43566
房地产代理与经纪业	Real Estate Brokerage and Agency	1229	8	820
社会服务业	**Social Services**	**584862**	**106005**	**357772**
公共设施服务业	Public Facilities Utilities	174320	7533	152194
# 市内公共交通业	Public Transportation in City	117756	5813	101546
# 市内公共汽电车业	Public Bus and Trolleybus	58822		58703
园林绿化业	Gardens Afforest	18957	322	18345
环境卫生业	Environmental Sanitation	22101	112	20321
市政工程管理业	Municipal Engineering Management	7897	37	7314
居民服务业	Resident Services	48275	2892	15049
旅馆业	Hotels	108045	40116	51647
租赁服务业	Leasing	7426	1077	4871
旅游业	Tourism	11218	3570	7056
娱乐服务业	Recreation	8491	1415	3367
信息、咨询服务业	Information and Consultancy Services	65985	19503	18162
# 广告业	Advertisement	9342	2616	1539
计算机应用服务业	Computer Application Services	50611	4661	33791
其他社会服务业	Other Social Services	110491	25235	71635
# 市场管理服务业	Market Management Services	19884	531	18755
卫生、体育和社会福利业	**Health Care,Sports and Social Welfare**	**135451**	**41058**	**93570**
卫生	Health Care	121326	37866	82975
体育	Sports	8221	2824	5119
社会福利	Social Welfare	5904	368	5476
教育、文化艺术及广播电影电视业	**Education,Culture and Arts, Radio,Film and Television**	**401179**	**147641**	**247601**
教育	Education	314538	85795	226238
高等教育	Higher Education	108151	75509	32274
普通高等教育	Ordinary Higher Education	95850	69509	26269
成人高等教育	Adult Higher Education	12301	6000	6005

3-7 续表 2 continued

(person)

国有经济 State-Owned			集体经济 Collective Owned	其他经济 Others
	# 中 央 Central	# 地 方 Local		
165694	**123977**	**41562**	**6564**	**16041**
64014	63796	218		
19966	1518	18448	5114	2930
				91
10093	10093			
23103	7651	15297	514	9073
8812	1531	7281	684	1148
39706	39388	318	252	2799
224753	**43848**	**176012**	**87384**	**168291**
98749	30648	66710	29992	50630
103038	7709	92470	46584	85547
5135	4158	959		723
17831	1333	15873	10808	31391
50358	**49478**	**790**	**6944**	**14614**
47601	46721	790	6944	12251
2757	2757			2363
47204	**7575**	**39255**	**3673**	**55999**
12850	1633	11097	915	16876
33846	5934	27658	2724	38436
508	8	500	34	687
301795	**74657**	**215382**	**64386**	**218681**
128264	4586	123343	9904	36152
79796	3727	75745	7610	30350
58679		58679	24	119
17503	286	17217	54	1400
19725	19	19699	259	2117
6886		6886	449	562
9960	1125	8720	28874	9441
57121	26071	22997	7842	43082
2455	940	1504	1073	3898
7084	3213	3781	481	3653
1526	555	966	487	6478
19482	13919	5223	5069	41434
2221	1644	555	1094	6027
6907	3751	3136	1871	41833
68996	20497	45712	8785	32710
1917	199	1718	590	17377
124449	**40723**	**83726**	**9784**	**1218**
111682	37593	74089	9066	578
7606	2824	4782	74	541
5161	306	4855	644	99
387630	**146677**	**240846**	**5651**	**7898**
305695	85488	220100	5260	3583
107591	75462	32057	91	469
95850	69509	26269		
11741	5953	5788	91	469

3-7 续表 3 continued

单位：人

行业	Sector	全市 Total	# 中央 Central	# 地方 Local
中等教育	Secondary School Education	106261	3627	102053
中等专业学校	Specialized Secondary Schools	12595	974	11571
普通中学	Regular Secondary Schools	75148	2231	72386
农业、职业中学	Agricultural and Vocational Schools	11485	4	11481
技工学校	Technical Schools	2932	213	2719
成人中等学校	Adult Secondary Schools	3696	160	3536
工读学校	Schools for Juvenile Delinquents	405	45	360
初等教育	Primary Education	72181	978	71055
小学校	Primary Schools	72155	978	71055
成人初等学校	Adult Primary Schools	26		
学前教育	Preschool Education	11676	1537	9803
特殊教育	Special Education	901	144	735
其他教育	Other Education	15368	4000	10318
文化艺术业	Culture and Arts	70418	50856	16496
艺术	Arts	8356	4872	3460
出版	Publication	39306	34769	4301
文物保护	Historical Relics Preservation	5145	3018	2070
图书馆	Library	3073	1915	1158
档案馆	Archives	1035	667	368
群众文化	Mass Culture	4619	480	4078
新闻	News	4123	4102	21
文化艺术经纪与代理业	Brokers and Agents for Cultural and Arts Activities	1783	423	646
其他文化艺术业	Others	2978	610	394
广播电影电视业	Radio,Film and Television	16223	10990	4867
广播	Radio	5004	3944	1060
电影	Film	5077	3277	1559
电视	Television	6142	3769	2248
科学研究和综合技术服务	**Scientific Research and Polytechical Services**	**291778**	**157010**	**116127**
科学研究业	Scientific Research	127601	114800	11110
自然科学研究	Natural Science Research	79066	70213	7952
社会科学研究	Social Science Research	7526	7105	403
其他科学研究	Other Scientific Research	41009	37482	2755
综合技术服务业	Polytechnical Services	164177	42210	105017
气象	Atmospheric	2729	2545	184
地震	Seismology	1138	1061	77
测绘	Surveying and Mapping	2472	1129	1343
技术监督	Technology Supervisor	7665	4260	3193
海洋环境	Sea and Ocean Environments	299	299	
环境保护	Environmental Protection	1635	230	1339
技术推广和科技交流服务业	Technology Promotion and Exchange Services	15215	3120	9224
工程设计业	Engineering Design	22550	14573	7435
其他综合技术服务业	Other Polytechnical Services	110474	14993	82222
国家机关、政党机关和社会团体	**Government Agencies,Party Agencies and Social Organizations**	**251317**	**64418**	**186103**
国家机关	Government Agencies	230138	49483	179872
政党机关	Party Agencies	10310	6812	3498
社会团体	Social Organizations	10869	8123	2733
其他行业	**Other Sectors**	**109178**	**72543**	**29073**

3-7 续表 4 continued

(person)

国有经济 State-Owned	# 中 央 Central	# 地 方 Local	集体经济 Collective Owned	其他经济 Others
103164	3585	99579	1942	1155
12143	974	11169	285	167
72825	2189	70636	1382	941
11485	4	11481		
2637	213	2424	260	35
3669	160	3509	15	12
405	45	360		
72033	978	71055		148
72033	978	71055		122
				26
9081	1537	7544	2290	305
879	144	735	22	
12947	3782	9130	915	1506
66373	50323	16050	274	3771
8213	4803	3410	50	93
38807	34600	4207	84	415
5060	3018	2042		85
3033	1915	1118		40
1035	667	368		
4544	480	4064	14	61
4123	4102	21		
775	161	614	22	986
783	577	206	104	2091
15562	10866	4696	117	544
5004	3944	1060		
4714	3209	1505	36	327
5844	3713	2131	81	217
193258	**152836**	**38601**	**10814**	**87706**
126965	114435	10867	489	147
78503	69848	7754	489	74
7508	7105	403		18
40954	37482	2710		55
66293	38401	27734	10325	87559
2646	2545	101		83
1136	1061	75		2
2284	1129	1155	41	147
7061	4198	2863	66	538
299	299			
851	220	631	39	745
5212	2616	2571	1294	8709
19127	13839	5288	852	2571
27677	12494	15050	8033	74764
250996	**64133**	**186080**	**269**	**52**
230138	49483	179872		
10310	6812	3498		
10548	7838	2710	269	52
88469	**71043**	**17197**	**4480**	**16229**

3-8 国民经济各行业在岗职工人数(按用工期限分)

单位：人

行业	Sector	全市 Total	# 女性 Female	比重(%) Proportion (%)	长期职工 Permanent Workers	临时职工 Temporary Workers
总计	**Total**	**3979251**	**1499745**	**37.7**	**3433242**	**546009**
农、林、牧、渔业	**Farming,Forestry,Animal Husbandry and Fishery**	**28477**	**10808**	**38.0**	**22698**	**5779**
# 农、林、牧、渔服务业	FFAF Services	5048	2226	44.1	3524	1524
采掘业	**Excavation**	**25756**	**5039**	**19.6**	**25568**	**188**
制造业	**Manufacturing**	**895612**	**345537**	**38.6**	**824882**	**70730**
食品加工业	Food Processing	15898	6215	39.1	13079	2819
食品制造业	Food Making	30461	15280	50.2	23907	6554
饮料制造业	Beverage Making	24271	8866	36.5	21638	2633
烟草制造业	Tobacco Processing	818	365	44.6	817	1
纺织业	Textile Industry	38122	24533	64.4	36536	1586
服装及其他纤维制品制造业	Garments and Other Fiber Products	36382	26726	73.5	27699	8683
皮革、毛皮、羽绒及其制品业	Leather,Furs,Down and Related Products	5086	3062	60.2	4309	777
木材加工及竹、藤、棕、革制品业	Timber Processing,Bamboo,Cane, Palm Fiber and Straw Products	2788	997	35.8	2330	458
家具制造业	Furniture Manufacturing	8854	2470	27.9	6351	2503
造纸及纸制品业	Papermaking and Paper Products	8096	3807	47.0	6244	1852
印刷业、记录媒介的复制	Printing and Record Medium Reproduced	37266	18344	49.2	34916	2350
文教体育用品制造业	Stationery,Education and Sports Goods	8759	4328	49.4	7525	1234
石油加工及炼焦业	Petroleum Processing and Coking Products	40147	12738	31.7	40014	133
化学原料及化学制品制造业	Raw Chemical Materials and Chemical Products	38062	14452	38.0	35476	2586
医药制造业	Medical and Pharmaceutical Products	24897	12808	51.4	24146	751
化学纤维制造业	Chemical Fibers	2468	1155	46.8	2358	110
橡胶制品业	Rubber Products	7707	3288	42.7	6077	1630
塑料制品业	Plastic Products	14319	6220	43.4	11367	2952
非金属矿物制品业	Nonmetal Mineral Products	54216	15732	29.0	48191	6025
黑色金属冶炼及压延加工业	Smelting and Pressing Ferrous Metals	126768	32497	25.6	126178	590
有色金属冶炼及压延加工业	Smelting and Pressing of Non-ferrous Metals	3310	981	29.6	3194	116
金属制品业	Metal Products	26155	7073	27.0	21897	4258
普通机械制造业	Ordinary Machinery	49894	16773	33.6	47503	2391
专业设备制造业	Special Purpose Equipment	49879	15394	30.9	45132	4747
交通运输设备制造业	Transportation Equipment	86828	27307	31.4	83622	3206
武器弹药制造业	Weapons and Ammunition	10364	3294	31.8	10174	190
电气机械及器材制造业	Electric Equipment and Machine	43675	17158	39.3	40580	3095
电子及通信设备制造业	Electronic and Telecommunication	66631	27743	41.6	63774	2857
仪器仪表及文化办公用机械制造业	Instruments,Meters,Cultural and Office Machinery	20658	9126	44.2	19489	1169
其他制造业	Other Manufacturing	12833	6805	53.0	10359	2474
电力、煤气及水的生产和供应业	**Electricity,Gas and Water Production and Supply**	**39325**	**13550**	**34.5**	**38533**	**792**
电力、蒸气、热水的生产和供应业	Electricity,Steam and Hot Water Production and Supply	25026	8055	32.2	24462	564
煤气生产和供应业	Gas Production and Supply	8368	3265	39.0	8340	28
自来水的生产和供应业	Water Production and Supply	5931	2230	37.6	5731	200
建筑业	**Construction**	**486860**	**65486**	**13.5**	**302385**	**184475**
土木工程建筑业	Civil Engineering	396284	50649	12.8	243760	152524
线路、管道和设备安装业	Lines,Pipelines and Equipment Installation	57178	9546	16.7	40161	17017
建筑物的装修装饰业	Fitting and Decoration	33398	5291	15.8	18464	14934
地质勘查业、水利管理业	**Geological Prospecting and Water Conservancy**	**14766**	**3812**	**25.8**	**13385**	**1381**

STAFF AND WORKERS AT THEIR POSTS BY SECTOR (BY TYPE OF STAFF AND WORKERS)

(person)

# 全市国有经济 Total State-owned Economy	长期职工 Permanent Workers	临时职工 Temporary Workers	# 地方国有经济 Local State-Owned Economy	长期职工 Permanent Workers	临时职工 Temporary Workers
2557580	**2328493**	**229087**	**1513598**	**1411507**	**102091**
22572	**18274**	**4298**	**21439**	**17236**	**4203**
2549	2140	409	2549	2140	409
25010	**24913**	**97**	**24972**	**24875**	**97**
480248	**465410**	**14838**	**351589**	**339714**	**11875**
7265	6157	1108	7227	6119	1108
9926	8280	1646	9699	8229	1470
11259	10840	419	11166	10790	376
20595	20502	93	20578	20485	93
5788	5098	690	4083	3728	355
1645	1243	402	1645	1243	402
1218	1107	111	894	783	111
864	730	134	711	579	132
3214	3081	133	3046	2952	94
27054	25998	1056	7724	7346	378
3617	3486	131	3591	3460	131
39425	39423	2	5548	5547	1
21369	20404	965	20986	20070	916
14278	13880	398	12653	12512	141
929	928	1	928	928	
3245	2603	642	3120	2480	640
3258	2934	324	2940	2668	272
20314	18374	1940	19064	17268	1796
121121	120932	189	121121	120932	189
1507	1494	13	1480	1479	1
6236	5757	479	5653	5314	339
28300	27728	572	24342	23823	519
22705	22327	378	13142	12886	256
48112	47230	882	16818	16411	407
10364	10174	190			
18100	17266	834	11172	10369	803
15244	14658	586	12000	11502	498
10849	10516	333	7817	7557	260
2447	2260	187	2441	2254	187
31255	**30591**	**664**	**22777**	**22229**	**548**
17013	16549	464	8535	8187	348
8311	8311		8311	8311	
5931	5731	200	5931	5731	200
243884	**180491**	**63393**	**113321**	**101992**	**11329**
212089	154962	57127	95611	87652	7959
26411	22924	3487	13812	12812	1000
5384	2605	2779	3898	1528	2370
14260	**12918**	**1342**	**8666**	**7395**	**1271**

3-8 续表 1 continued

单位：人

行业	Sector	全市 Total	# 女性 Female	比重 (%) Proportion (%)	长期职工 Permanent Workers	临时职工 Temporary Workers
地质勘查业	Geological Prospecting	5346	1547	28.9	5311	35
水利管理业	Water Conservancy	9420	2265	24.0	8074	1346
交通运输、仓储及邮电通信业	**Transportation,Storage,Posts and Telecommunications**	**175243**	**50219**	**28.7**	**156365**	**18878**
铁路运输业	Railway	60696	10790	17.8	60696	
公路运输业	Highway	24291	6464	26.6	19702	4589
管道运输业	Pipeline	91	24	26.4	91	
航空运输业	Airway	10084	4150	41.2	9991	93
交通运输辅助业	Transportation Subsidiary Services	32330	9296	28.8	20364	11966
仓储业	Storage	8235	2319	28.2	7584	651
邮电通信业	Posts and Telecommunications	39516	17176	43.5	37937	1579
批发和零售贸易餐饮业	**Wholesale,Retail Trade and Catering Services**	**425790**	**212622**	**49.9**	**363161**	**62629**
批发业	Wholesale Trade	158080	62273	39.4	141429	16651
零售业	Retail Trade	206013	119293	57.9	182595	23418
商业经纪与代理业	Commercial Brokerage and Agency	5063	1935	38.2	4792	271
餐饮业	Catering Trade	56634	29121	51.4	34345	22289
金融、保险业	**Finance and Insurance**	**69662**	**36307**	**52.1**	**67540**	**2122**
金融业	Finance	64596	33931	52.5	62508	2088
保险业	Insurance	5066	2376	46.9	5032	34
房地产业	**Real Estate**	**103153**	**37838**	**36.7**	**82222**	**20931**
房地产开发与经营业	Real Estate Development and Operation	29910	10175	34.0	26903	3007
房地产管理业	Real Estate Management	72021	27099	37.6	54173	17848
房地产代理与经纪业	Real Estate Brokerage and Agency	1222	564	46.2	1146	76
社会服务业	**Social Services**	**553857**	**198736**	**35.9**	**456748**	**97109**
公共设施服务业	Public Utilities	166743	57209	34.3	153726	13017
# 市内公共交通业	Public Transportation in City	110941	36699	33.1	107379	3562
# 市内公共汽电车业	Public Bus and Trolleybus	54410	27743	51.0	53307	1103
园林绿化业	Gardens Afforest	18546	7696	41.5	16304	2242
环境卫生业	Environmental Sanitation	21991	7901	35.9	18114	3877
市政工程管理业	Municipal Engineering Management	7754	2102	27.1	6538	1216
居民服务业	Resident Services	45403	14922	32.9	16202	29201
旅馆业	Hotels	103006	51787	50.3	83356	19650
租赁服务业	Leasing	6577	1674	25.5	5581	996
旅游业	Tourism	10712	4631	43.2	9196	1516
娱乐服务业	Recreation	8458	4304	50.9	5597	2861
信息、咨询服务业	Information and Consultancy Services	64318	27264	42.4	55956	8362
# 广告业	Advertisement	9280	4111	44.3	7780	1500
咨询服务业	Consultancy Services					
计算机应用服务业	Computer Application Services	50293	18201	36.2	48019	2274
其他社会服务业	Other Social Services	98347	18744	19.1	79115	19232
# 市场管理服务业	Market Management Services	10665	4580	42.9	7154	3511
卫生、体育和社会福利业	**Health Care,Sports and Social Welfare**	**134075**	**88401**	**65.9**	**124445**	**9630**
卫生	Health Care	120383	82134	68.2	112389	7994
体育	Sports	7915	3013	38.1	6839	1076
社会福利保障业	Social Welfare	5777	3254	56.3	5217	560
教育、文化艺术及广播电影电视业	**Education,Culture and Arts, Radio, Film and Television**	**394567**	**212414**	**53.8**	**366500**	**28067**
教育	Education	309748	176012	56.8	288345	21403
高等教育	Higher Education	106856	46501	43.5	95052	11804
普通高等教育	Ordinary Higher Education	94705	40653	42.9	84533	10172
成人高等教育	Adult Higher Education	12151	5848	48.1	10519	1632

3-8 续表 2 continued

(person)

# 全市国有经济 Total State-owned Economy	长期职工 Permanent Workers	临时职工 Temporary Workers	# 地方国有经济 Local State-Owned Economy	长期职工 Permanent Workers	临时职工 Temporary Workers
5300	5265	35	626	621	5
8960	7653	1307	8040	6774	1266
153706	**139022**	**14684**	**36865**	**25424**	**11441**
60696	60696		218	218	
17061	13287	3774	15892	12162	3730
10084	9991	93			
22760	13684	9076	15171	7812	7359
6636	6264	372	5274	4973	301
36469	35100	1369	310	259	51
187569	**173287**	**14282**	**141953**	**131507**	**10446**
83861	78425	5436	53838	50251	3587
84466	79339	5127	74521	70482	4039
4341	4288	53	644	618	26
14901	11235	3666	12950	10156	2794
48460	**46701**	**1759**	**778**	**747**	**31**
45757	44014	1743	778	747	31
2703	2687	16			
44969	**37049**	**7920**	**37117**	**31252**	**5865**
12335	11071	1264	10600	9438	1162
32128	25521	6607	26019	21365	4654
506	457	49	498	449	49
287158	**253254**	**33904**	**203019**	**186121**	**16898**
122793	113708	9085	117939	109146	8793
74983	73103	1880	70978	69253	1725
54268	53167	1101	54268	53167	1101
17113	15104	2009	16836	14878	1958
19615	16211	3404	19589	16185	3404
6764	5920	844	6764	5920	844
8409	6860	1549	7172	5905	1267
53627	40524	13103	20092	16880	3212
1771	1502	269	828	774	54
6646	5840	806	3431	2749	682
1522	1147	375	964	770	194
18458	16905	1553	4561	4169	392
2177	1910	267	527	465	62
6613	6420	193	3093	3051	42
67319	60348	6971	44939	42677	2262
1613	1371	242	1417	1179	238
123323	**114655**	**8668**	**82985**	**77278**	**5707**
110925	103531	7394	73496	68748	4748
7302	6520	782	4697	4209	488
5096	4604	492	4792	4321	471
381464	**355120**	**26344**	**236740**	**223846**	**12894**
301309	280976	20333	216926	205831	11095
106296	94557	11739	31895	28509	3386
94705	84533	10172	26188	23374	2814
11591	10024	1567	5707	5135	572

3-8 续表 3 continued

单位：人

行业	Sector	全市 Total	# 女性 Female	比重 (%) Proportion (%)	长期职工 Permanent Workers	临时职工 Temporary Workers
中等教育	Secondary School Education	104670	62060	59.3	100317	4353
中等专业学校	Specialized Secondary Schools	12390	6577	53.1	11583	807
普通中学	Regular Secondary Schools	74166	45261	61.0	71513	2653
农业、职业中学	Agricultural and Vocational Schools	11209	6842	61.0	10818	391
技工学校	Technical Schools	2854	1333	46.7	2608	246
成人中等学校	Adult Secondary Schools	3657	1898	51.9	3418	239
工读学校	Schools for Juvenile Delinquents	394	149	37.8	377	17
初等教育	Primary Education	70922	50166	70.7	69109	1813
小学校	Primary Schools	70896	50146	70.7	69083	1813
成人初等学校	Adult Primary Schools	26	20	76.9	26	
学前教育	Preschool Education	11186	10362	92.6	10364	822
特殊教育	Special Education	898	636	70.8	841	57
其他教育	Other Education	15216	6287	41.3	12662	2554
文化艺术业	Culture and Arts	68669	30123	43.9	62945	5724
艺术	Arts	7781	2958	38.0	7182	599
出版	Publication	38711	17064	44.1	35849	2862
文物保护	Historical Relics Preservation	5119	2101	41.0	4486	633
图书馆	Library	2914	1847	63.4	2831	83
档案馆	Archives	1032	523	50.7	964	68
群众文化	Mass Culture	4315	2050	47.5	3817	498
新闻	News	4123	1510	36.6	3794	329
文化艺术经纪与代理业	Brokers and Agents for Cultural and Arts Activities	1777	814	45.8	1543	234
其他文化艺术业	Others	2897	1256	43.4	2479	418
广播电影电视业	Radio,Film and Television	16150	6279	38.9	15210	940
广播	Radio	5003	2106	42.1	4816	187
电影	Film	5008	1849	36.9	4676	332
电视	Television	6139	2324	37.9	5718	421
科学研究和综合技术服务	**Scientific Research and Polytechnical Services**	**284198**	**103487**	**36.4**	**272543**	**11655**
科学研究业	Scientific Research	122506	47310	38.6	118387	4119
自然科学研究	Natural Science Research	75174	28942	38.5	72847	2327
社会科学研究	Social Science Research	7485	2949	39.4	7259	226
其他科学研究	Other Scientific Research	39847	15419	38.7	38281	1566
综合技术服务业	Polytechnical Services	161692	56177	34.7	154156	7536
气象	Atmospheric	2715	1128	41.5	2511	204
地震	Seismology	1104	387	35.1	1085	19
测绘	Surveying and Mapping	1961	625	31.9	1921	40
技术监督	Technology Supervisor	7557	2749	36.4	7105	452
海洋环境	Sea and Ocean Environments	299	106	35.5	299	
环境保护	Environmental Protection	1597	519	32.5	1518	79
技术推广和科技交流服务业	Technology Promotion and Exchange Services	14866	5340	35.9	13208	1658
工程设计业	Engineering Design	21961	8882	40.4	21257	704
其他综合技术服务业	Other Polytechnical Services	109632	36441	33.2	105252	4380
国家机关、政党机关和社会团体	**Government Agencies,Party Agencies and Social Organizations**	**242554**	**74347**	**30.7**	**233695**	**8859**
国家机关	Government Agencies	221530	66627	30.1	213683	7847
政党机关	Party Agencies	10286	3319	32.3	9673	613
社会团体	Social Organizations	10738	4401	41.0	10339	399
其他行业	**Other Sectors**	**105356**	**41142**	**39.1**	**82572**	**22784**

3-8 续表 4 continued

(person)

# 全市国有经济 Total State-owned Economy	长期职工 Permanent Workers	临时职工 Temporary Workers	# 地方国有经济 Local State-Owned Economy	长期职工 Permanent Worker	临时职工 Temporary Workers
101589	97398	4191	98030	94089	3941
11952	11145	807	10978	10252	726
71845	69316	2529	69671	67301	2370
11209	10818	391	11205	10814	391
2559	2348	211	2348	2137	211
3630	3394	236	3479	3253	226
394	377	17	349	332	17
70774	68986	1788	69827	68070	1757
70774	68986	1788	69827	68070	1757
8953	8271	682	7421	6846	575
876	819	57	735	678	57
12821	10945	1876	9018	7639	1379
64659	59513	5146	15173	13688	1485
7651	7087	564	2989	2821	168
38214	35378	2836	4136	3784	352
5034	4402	632	2025	1682	343
2874	2791	83	1108	1037	71
1032	964	68	368	356	12
4243	3761	482	3768	3346	422
4123	3794	329	21	21	
773	683	90	614	524	90
715	653	62	144	117	27
15496	14631	865	4641	4327	314
5003	4816	187	1060	980	80
4649	4350	299	1450	1338	112
5844	5465	379	2131	2009	122
185872	**179360**	**6512**	**36975**	**35407**	**1568**
121874	117758	4116	9832	9343	489
74615	72291	2324	6962	6517	445
7467	7241	226	386	379	7
39792	38226	1566	2484	2447	37
63998	61602	2396	27143	26064	1079
2632	2428	204	101	101	
1102	1083	19	75	74	1
1773	1737	36	1146	1110	36
6953	6518	435	2828	2518	310
299	299				
814	791	23	625	604	21
4899	4461	438	2389	2195	194
18547	18043	504	5205	4936	269
26979	26242	737	14774	14526	248
242233	**233377**	**8856**	**178762**	**171985**	**6777**
221530	213683	7847	172626	166103	6523
10286	9673	613	3476	3372	104
10417	10021	396	2660	2510	150
85597	**64071**	**21526**	**15640**	**14499**	**1141**

3-9 职 工 工 资 总 额
TOTAL WAGES OF STAFF AND WORKERS

单位：万元 (10000 yuan)

项 目	Item	2000	1999	2000年为1999年% 2000 as % of 1999
总 计	**Total**	**6954671**	**6144815**	**113.2**
按登记注册类型分	**Grouped by Registration Status**			
内资经济	Domestic Investment Economy	6058223	5413102	111.9
国有经济	State-owned	4535963	4200008	108.0
集体经济	Collective-owned	466867	447507	104.3
联营经济	Joint-owned	56493	58615	96.4
股份有限公司	Share Holding Corporations Ltd.	232480	310687	74.8
有限责任公司	Limited-Liability Corporations	509318	329420	154.6
股份合作企业	Share Holding	82148	64890	126.6
其他经济	Others	174954	1975	
外商投资经济	Foreign Funded	632579	491122	128.8
港、澳、台商投资经济	Hongkong,Macao and Taiwan Funded	263870	240590	109.7
按隶属关系分	**Grouped by Administrative Relationship**			
# 中央	Central	2242969	2021963	110.9
地方	Local	4003047	3584429	111.7
按行业分	**Grouped by Sector**			
农、林、牧、渔业	Farming,Forestry,Animal Husbandry and Fishery	35057	33176	105.7
# 农业	Farming	4924	4023	122.4
采掘业	Excavation	30014	31586	95.0
制造业	Manufacturing	1452663	1391474	104.4
电力、煤气及水的生产和供应业	Electricity,Gas,Water Production and Supply	89508	75340	118.8
建筑业	Construction	682589	636356	107.3
地质勘查业水利管理业	Geological Prospecting and Water Conservancy	25586	20947	122.1
交通运输、仓储及邮电通信业	Transportation,Storage,Posts and Telecommunications Services	339790	310646	109.4
# 交通运输业	Transportation	220223	199018	110.7
邮电通信业	Posts and Telecommunications	105659	92562	114.1
批发和零售贸易餐饮业	Wholesale,Retail Trade and Catering Services	684460	654041	104.7
# 批发业	Wholesale Trade	298758	271636	110.0
零售业	Retail Trade	297442	296538	100.3
餐饮业	Catering Trade	68441	70712	96.8
金融、保险业	Finance and Insurance	171286	171295	100.0
房地产业	Real Estate	198142	162611	121.9
社会服务业	Social Services	978863	787261	124.3
居民服务业	Resident Services	42950	37359	115.0
旅馆业	Hotels	169053	163319	103.5
卫生体育和社会福利业	Health Care,Sports and Social Welfare	289994	236459	122.6
# 卫生	Health Care	263167	218039	120.7
体育	Sports	16732	12204	137.1
教育、文化艺术和广播电影电视业	Education,Culture,Art, Radio,Film and Television	733753	631553	116.2
教育	Education	548456	471097	116.4
文化艺术业	Culture and Art	142298	123041	115.7
广播电影电视业	Radio,Film and Television	43000	37414	114.9
科学研究和综合技术服务业	Scientific Research and Polytechnical Services	591100	435699	135.7
科学研究业	Scientific Research	244171	214128	114.0
综合技术服务业	Polytechnical Services	346928	221571	156.6
国家机关、政党机关和社会团体	Government Agencies,Party Agencies and Social Organizations	445925	426797	104.5
其他行业	Others	205941	139574	147.5

3-10 职 工 平 均 工 资
AVERAGE WAGE OF STAFF AND WORKERS

单位：元 (yuan)

项 目	Item	2000	1999	2000年为1999年% 2000 as % of 1999
总 计	**Total**	**15726**	**13778**	**114.1**
按登记注册类型分	**Grouped by Registration Status**			
内资经济	Domestic Investment Economy	14816	13043	113.6
国有经济	State-owned	15483	13483	114.8
集体经济	Collective-owned	9844	8928	110.3
联营经济	Joint-owned	11850	11070	107.0
股份有限公司	Share Holding Corporations Ltd.	17858	14732	121.2
有限责任公司	Limited-Liability Corporations	17309	15870	109.1
股份合作企业	Share Holding	11368	10600	107.2
其他经济	Others	12431	14045	88.5
外商投资经济	Foreign Funded	29832	25571	116.7
港、澳、台商投资经济	Hongkong,Macao and Taiwan Funded	21759	20468	106.3
按隶属关系分	**Grouped by Administrative Relationship**			
# 中央	Central	18760	16132	116.3
地方	Local	14466	12650	114.4
按行业分	**Grouped by Sector**			
农、林、牧、渔业	Farming,Forestry,Animal Husbandry and Fishery	10692	9127	117.1
# 农业	Farming	8626	8116	106.3
采掘业	Excavation	10276	9476	108.4
制造业	Manufacturing	13062	11759	111.1
电力、煤气及水的生产和供应业	Electricity,Gas,Water Production and Supply	19673	16510	119.2
建筑业	Construction	12275	11644	105.4
地质勘查业水利管理业	Geological Prospecting and Water Conservancy	16289	13079	124.5
交通运输、仓储及邮电通信业	Transportation,Storage,Posts and Telecommuni-cations Services	18000	15328	117.4
# 交通运输业	Transportation	16335	14134	115.6
邮电通信业	Posts and Telecommunications	24559	20635	119.0
批发和零售贸易餐饮业	Wholesale,Retail Trade and Catering Services	13781	12273	112.3
# 批发业	Wholesale Trade	16069	14208	113.1
零售业	Retail Trade	12123	10888	111.3
餐饮业	Catering Trade	11502	11058	104.0
金融、保险业	Finance and Insurance	23697	24450	96.9
房地产业	Real Estate	19188	18012	106.5
社会服务业	Social Services	16612	14880	111.6
居民服务业	Residents Services	8956	8403	106.6
旅馆业	Hotels	15347	14329	107.1
卫生体育和社会福利业	Health Care,Sports and Social Welfare	21657	17832	121.5
# 卫生	Health Care	21935	18112	121.1
体育	Sports	20498	15527	132.0
教育、文化艺术和广播电影电视业	Education,Culture,Art, Radio,Film and Television	18256	15365	118.8
教育	Education	17371	14553	119.4
文化艺术业	Culture and Art	20424	17623	115.9
广播电影电视业	Radio,Film and Television	26030	21396	121.7
科学研究和综合技术服务业	Scientific Research and Polytechnical Services	20555	16582	124.0
科学研究业	Scientific Research	18907	15439	122.5
综合技术服务业	Polytechnical Services	21898	17860	122.6
国家机关、政党机关和社会团体	Government Agencies,Party Agencies and Social Organizations	17726	14078	125.9
其他行业	Others	19483	21726	89.7

3-11 国民经济各行业职工工资总额及平均工资

行业	Sector	工资总额(万元) Total Wages (10000 yuan)	# 中央 Central	# 地方 Local	国有经济 State-owned
总计	**Total**	**6954671**	**2242969**	**4003047**	**4535963**
农、林、牧、渔业	**Farming,Forestry,Animal Husbandry and Fishery**	**35057**	**3038**	**31391**	**28909**
# 农、林、牧、渔服务业	FFAF Services	4924	299	4291	2752
采掘业	**Excavation**	**30014**	**87**	**29927**	**29337**
制造业	**Manufacturing**	**1452663**	**294877**	**1086806**	**782753**
食品加工业	Food Processing	22077	1666	18476	9419
食品制造业	Food Making	52324	4313	42905	14965
饮料制造业	Beverage Making	35314	405	33035	16236
烟草制造业	Tobacco Processing	3343		3343	
纺织业	Textile Industry	46960	74	46241	27033
服装及其他纤维制品制造业	Garments and Other Fiber Products	39153	2190	28471	7177
皮革、毛皮、羽绒及其制品业	Leather,Furs,Down and Related Products	5977	114	5098	2209
木材加工及竹、藤、棕、革制品业	Timber Processing,Bamboo,Cane,Palm Fiber and Straw Products	4186	590	3133	1559
家具制造业	Furniture Manufacturing	8600	706	3939	860
造纸及纸制品业	Papermaking and Paper Products	12734	408	11674	5711
印刷业、记录媒介的复制	Printing and Record Medium Reproduced	57828	35618	19022	43030
文教体育用品制造业	Stationery,Education and Sports Goods	12694	133	11304	5762
石油加工及炼焦业	Petroleum Processing and Coking Products	95012	83462	11406	94104
化学原料及化学制品制造业	Raw Chemical Materials and Chemical Products	64000	3149	56337	33961
医药制造业	Medical and Pharmaceutical Products	45946	4689	40010	23520
化学纤维制造业	Chemical Fibers	4087	261	3775	2139
橡胶制品业	Rubber Products	10529	378	10101	4982
塑料制品业	Plastic Products	18196	1009	15263	4514
非金属矿物制品业	Nonmetal Mineral Products	77403	3001	71240	27654
黑色金属冶炼及压延加工业	Smelting and Pressing Ferrous Metals	212651	43	212515	203687
有色金属冶炼及压延加工业	Smelting and Pressing of Nonferrous Metals	6207	14	6121	1929
金属制品业	Metal Products	31529	1271	25974	8678
普通机械制造业	Ordinary Machinery	72006	16201	52666	39104
专业设备制造业	Special Purpose Equipment	75370	16024	52687	34796
交通运输设备制造业	Transportation Equipment	133818	60064	70351	72130
武器弹药制造业	Weapons and Ammunition	14794	14794		14794
电气机械及器材制造业	Electric Equipment and Machine	65991	11277	51440	32104
电子及通信设备制造业	Electronic and Telecommunication	174164	24993	142728	30996
仪器仪表及文化办公用机械制造业	Instruments,Meters,Cultural and Office Machinery	33246	7372	23897	16403
其他制造业	Other Manufacturing	16524	657	13653	3297
电力、煤气及水的生产和供应业	**Electricity,Gas and Water Production and Supply**	**89508**	**32037**	**57471**	**72434**
电力、蒸气、热水的生产和供应业	Electricity,Steam and Hot Water Production and Supply	65176	32037	33138	48150
煤气生产和供应业	Gas Production and Supply	13912		13912	13863
自来水的生产和供应业	Water Production and Supply	10421		10421	10421
建筑业	**Construction**	**682589**	**174145**	**379943**	**378066**
土木工程建筑业	Civil Engineering	540977	117501	321280	312842
线路、管道和设备安装业	Lines,Pipelines and Equipment Installation	104176	51362	44404	58927
建筑物的装修装饰业	Fitting and Decoration	37436	5282	14259	6297
地质勘查业、水利管理业	**Geological Prospecting and Water Conservancy**	**25586**	**10590**	**14996**	**25060**
地质勘查业	Geological Prospecting	10345	8629	1716	10257
水利管理业	Water Conservancy	15241	1961	13280	14803

TOTAL WAGES AND AVERAGE WAGE OF STAFF AND WORKERS BY SECTOR

# 中 央 Central	# 地 方 Local	集体经济 Collective-Owned	其他经济 Others	平均工资（元） Average Wage (yuan)	国有经济 State-owned	集体经济 Collective-Owned	其他经济 Others
1921232	**2549670**	**466867**	**1951841**	**15726**	**15483**	**9844**	**19165**
2358	**26551**	**918**	**5230**	**10692**	**10828**	**9572**	**10193**
	2752	358	1814	8626	8289	11779	8703
87	**29249**	**53**	**625**	**10276**	**10307**	**6564**	**9429**
228526	**553896**	**88018**	**581891**	**13062**	**12151**	**7907**	**16315**
46	9373	446	12212	10707	8230	10684	13947
177	14728	910	36449	14622	10135	6225	18637
78	16157	1282	17796	13047	12725	10309	13623
			3343	37149			37149
	27019	2843	17084	8717	8636	5734	9701
2101	5076	4614	27363	9113	8665	5425	10453
	2209	1423	2344	6779	5572	6129	9265
525	1034	358	2269	10305	7473	7429	15189
164	696	868	6872	9899	7544	8418	10545
283	5428	860	6163	11196	9235	8037	14959
33426	9544	3851	10947	13944	14049	8302	17644
54	5709	1548	5384	12464	13132	8550	13506
83061	11043	555	353	18348	18401	24019	8604
490	33465	2955	27084	13483	11755	11540	16912
2849	20671	1383	21043	17167	14778	11098	21913
9	2130	303	1645	7445	5980	14647	9641
318	4663	1929	3618	8735	7392	7795	12743
335	4180	3117	10564	9121	7212	7895	10844
1967	25687	8214	41535	11520	10733	7986	13338
	203687	781	8182	13614	13611	8641	14489
14	1915	450	3829	15542	9030	10020	27172
763	7892	5542	17309	9503	8719	6800	11482
6059	33046	8100	24802	10756	9381	8548	15714
13642	21154	3792	36782	12484	10822	8520	15475
44652	27318	9416	52273	11969	11769	7317	13887
14794				12752	12752		
10035	22069	8527	25361	11880	11031	8307	15675
6597	24390	4639	138529	23500	13373	9286	30156
6075	10328	3897	12946	13167	11258	9992	19097
12	3285	5416	7811	9933	9138	7772	12892
28320	**44113**	**764**	**16311**	**19673**	**19451**	**14912**	**21052**
28320	19829	764	16263	21248	21427	14912	21145
	13863		48	16487	16541		8490
	10421			16316	16316		
135806	**202258**	**164997**	**139526**	**12275**	**12124**	**10748**	**15383**
103182	170858	130616	97519	11857	11547	10344	16508
30441	27416	26654	18595	15218	16247	14160	13913
2182	3983	7727	23412	11947	13544	9176	12819
10502	**14558**	**438**	**88**	**16289**	**16492**	**9322**	**20974**
8541	1716		88	17012	16984		20974
1961	12842	438		15833	16167	9322	

3-11 续表 1 continued

行业 Sector		工资总额(万元) Total Wages(10000 yuan)	# 中央 Central	# 地方 Local	国有经济 State-owned
交通运输、仓储及邮电通信业	**Transportation,Storage,Posts and Telecommunications**	**339790**	**253667**	**71873**	**291234**
铁路运输业	Railway	98016	97822	194	98016
公路运输业	Highway	31451	5177	25191	21967
管道运输业	Pipeline	189	189		
航空运输业	Airway	28101	28101		28101
交通运输辅助业	Transportation Subsidiary Services	62466	24126	35572	42227
仓储业	Storage	13909	3003	10162	11246
邮电通信业	Posts and Telecommunications	105659	95249	753	89677
批发和零售贸易餐饮业	**Wholesale,Retail Trade and Catering Services**	**684460**	**160102**	**389326**	**349318**
批发业	Wholesale Trade	298758	112222	139038	184497
零售业	Retail Trade	297442	26696	208554	127882
商业经纪与代理业	Commercial Brokerage and Agency	19819	17402	2019	18207
餐饮业	Catering Trade	68441	3782	39715	18733
金融、保险业	**Finance and Insurance**	**171286**	**155950**	**10915**	**111231**
金融业	Finance	155379	142570	8787	103461
保险业	Insurance	15907	13381	2128	7771
房地产业	**Real Estate**	**198142**	**34073**	**122232**	**82512**
房地产开发与经营业	Real Estate Development and Operation	75240	5667	53121	29564
房地产管理业	Real Estate Management	119775	28400	67328	51663
房地产代理与经纪业	Real Estate Brokerage and Agency	3127	7	1783	1285
社会服务业	**Social Services**	**978863**	**209760**	**564941**	**456002**
公共设施服务业	Public Utilities	251710	8975	230969	212486
# 市内公共交通业	Public Transportation in City	149007	5060	138012	123264
# 市内公共汽电车业	Public Bus and Trolleybus	93367		93138	93113
园林绿化业	Gardens Afforest	36312	427	35547	33865
环境卫生业	Environmental Sanitation	39664	333	36041	35469
市政工程管理业	Municipal Engineering Management	15313	108	14673	13280
居民服务业	Resident Services	42950	4443	17666	12717
旅馆业	Hotels	169053	66149	82909	75996
租赁服务业	Leasing	8211	2349	3852	3403
旅游业	Tourism	20654	9142	10610	14014
娱乐服务业	Recreation	13990	2583	5640	2297
信息、咨询服务业	Information and Consultancy Services	157786	51451	36342	43072
# 广告业	Advertisement	21949	8622	2800	5566
计算机应用服务业	Computer Application Services	178992	12707	107784	15336
其他社会服务业	Other Social Services	135517	51963	69169	76681
# 市场管理服务业	Market Management Services	29337	796	28014	3026
卫生、体育和社会福利业	**Health Care,Sports and Social Welfare**	**289994**	**96116**	**191701**	**271882**
卫生	Health Care	263167	89418	172423	247422
体育	Sports	16732	6076	10393	15685
社会服务保障业	Social Welfare	10095	623	8885	8776
教育、文化艺术及广播电影电视业	**Education,Culture and Arts, Radio,Film and Television**	**733753**	**291316**	**433484**	**713812**
教育	Education	548456	155432	388349	535120
高等教育	Higher Education	196039	135830	59469	195167
普通高等教育	Ordinary Higher Education	173663	125326	48258	173663
成人高等教育	Adult Higher Education	22376	10504	11210	21505

3-11 续表 2 continued

# 中 央 Central	# 地 方 Local	集体经济 Collective-Owned	其他经济 Others	平均工资 (元) Average Wage (yuan)	国有经济 State-owned	集体经济 Collective-Owned	其他经济 Others
233813	**57033**	**6710**	**41846**	**18000**	**17391**	**9571**	**29265**
97822	194			15422	15422		
2123	19844	4999	4485	10661	10281	9116	16916
			189	21217			21217
28101				28079	28079		
14148	27690	695	19545	19730	18031	12892	25373
2388	8859	750	1912	12717	12294	10653	17626
89230	447	266	15715	24559	22437	9375	56714
124890	**218556**	**87613**	**247529**	**13781**	**14653**	**9391**	**15002**
92272	90516	32164	82097	16069	17494	10064	16928
14666	109692	46474	123086	12123	11702	9240	14350
16604	1587		1612	33586	34859		23781
1349	16760	8975	40733	11502	10170	8133	13556
108244	**2597**	**7385**	**52669**	**23697**	**21716**	**10628**	**37320**
100473	2597	7385	44533	23117	21355	10628	37692
7771			8137	31381	28043		35407
14286	**67334**	**4755**	**110875**	**19188**	**17497**	**13436**	**21092**
4121	24880	1442	44234	24935	22573	15246	27421
10159	41176	3230	64882	16619	15392	12623	18049
7	1278	83	1759	30688	25912	24321	35975
140623	**302637**	**57810**	**465051**	**16612**	**14394**	**8860**	**22443**
4643	207525	8396	30828	13729	14987	9031	9556
3232	119754	4684	21058	11893	13428	6721	7939
	93113	25	230	13050	13041	9694	19464
365	33501	55	2392	17736	17859	8431	16551
24	35429	213	3982	17894	18033	7885	17879
	13280	704	1329	19024	19097	12962	24078
1614	10946	19941	10291	8956	12752	6915	11257
36270	29752	8340	84717	15347	12996	10002	19546
2029	1358	1025	3782	11211	12875	9196	10607
8534	5347	417	6223	18387	18814	8259	18977
721	1571	508	11186	15452	13026	10212	16465
33085	8859	6570	108144	24899	21708	12933	28127
4374	1182	1672	14711	24001	23828	15557	25655
9857	5458	3254	160402	38128	20409	17182	42732
43868	31821	9359	49478	12332	11383	9665	15064
518	2509	623	25687	14161	15193	9228	14232
95627	**176255**	**15435**	**2677**	**21657**	**22107**	**15790**	**23401**
89013	158409	14113	1632	21935	22417	15620	28632
6076	9609	54	994	20498	20627	6969	20623
539	8237	1268	51	17520	17527	19131	5547
288974	**424715**	**7707**	**12234**	**18256**	**18327**	**13675**	**17994**
154583	380414	7218	6118	17371	17415	13664	19258
135714	59375	520	351	18022	18024	59817	8583
125326	48258			18007	18007		
10388	11117	520	351	18140	18164	59817	8583

3-11 续表 3 continued

行业	Sector	工资总额(万元) Total Wages (10000 yuan)	# 中央 Central	# 地方 Local	国有经济 State-owned
中等教育	Secondary School Education	190785	8148	181362	185477
中等专业学校	Specialized Secondary Schools	22859	1793	21006	22195
普通中学	Regular Secondary Schools	134877	5549	128114	130716
农业、职业中学	Agricultural and Vocational Schools	20711	7	20704	20711
技工学校	Technical Schools	5049	431	4618	4598
成人中等学校	Adult Secondary Schools	6451	266	6185	6418
工读学校	Schools for Juvenile Delinquents	838	103	735	838
初等教育	Primary Education	116259	1969	113962	115932
小学校	Primary Schools	116224	1969	113962	115932
成人初等学校	Adult Primary Schools	36			
学前教育	Preschool Education	18153	2559	14907	15065
特殊教育	Special Education	1446	190	1237	1427
其他教育	Other Education	25773	6735	17412	22051
文化艺术业	Culture and Arts	142298	105785	32750	136795
艺术	Arts	13479	8141	5304	13314
出版	Publication	92168	78422	13388	90771
文物保护	Historical Relics Preservation	9370	5584	3654	9187
图书馆	Library	5308	3567	1741	5303
档案馆	Archives	2011	1176	835	2011
群众文化	Mass Culture	7397	785	6479	7248
新闻	News	6039	6010	30	6039
文化艺术经纪与代理业	Brokers and Agents for Cultural and Arts Activities	2289	804	829	1348
其他文化艺术业	Others	4236	1297	489	1574
广播电影电视业	Radio,Film and Television	43000	30099	12386	41897
广播	Radio	9627	7368	2259	9627
电影	Film	7936	5629	1941	7413
电视	Television	25436	17101	8186	24856
科学研究和综合技术服务	**Scientific Research and Polytechnical Services**	591100	314257	236646	377233
科学研究业	Scientific Research	244171	221929	19689	242738
自然科学研究	Natural Science Research	156892	141726	13620	155537
社会科学研究	Social Science Research	11742	10998	726	11724
其他科学研究	Other Scientific Research	75537	69205	5343	75478
综合技术服务业	Polytechnical Services	346928	92328	216957	134495
气象	Atmospheric	5279	4992	287	5201
地震	Seismology	1517	1403	114	1514
测绘	Surveying and Mapping	5162	1573	3589	4706
技术监督	Technology Supervisor	15239	8091	6734	13737
海洋环境	Sea and Ocean Environments	441	441		441
环境保护	Environmental Protection	2661	503	2078	1441
技术推广和科技交流服务业	Technology Promotion and Exchange Services	37205	5570	16678	7914
工程设计业	Engineering Design	52934	33924	18022	45154
其他综合技术服务业	Other Polytechnical Services	226490	35831	169457	54389
国家机关、政党机关和社会团体	**Government Agencies,Party Agencies and Social Organizations**	445925	117241	327423	445502
国家机关	Government Agencies	408628	90996	316391	408628
政党机关	Party Agencies	16940	10571	6369	16940
社会团体	Social Organizations	20358	15674	4663	19934
其他行业	**Other Sectors**	205941	95711	53973	120678

3-11 续表 4 continued

# 中 央 Central	# 地 方 Local	集体经济 Collective-Owned	其他经济 Others	平均工资 (元) Average Wage (yuan)	国有经济 State-owned	集体经济 Collective-Owned	其他经济 Others
8038	177440	2898	2410	17984	18005	14970	21232
1793	20402	478	186	17487	17583	16967	11117
5438	125278	1975	2187	18028	18028	14226	23742
7	20704			18441	18441		
431	4167	422	28	17783	18012	16804	8114
266	6152	23	9	17350	17389	15542	7618
103	735			20600	20600		
1969	113962		328	15862	15847		23232
1969	113962		292	15860	15847		23543
			36	20959			20959
2559	12506	2481	607	15577	16614	10772	21436
190	1237	19		15983	16161	8838	
6113	15894	1299	2423	17163	17129	13904	20043
104561	32234	338	5165	20424	20620	14248	16705
8056	5258	47	118	16068	16140	8678	13766
77594	13176	184	1213	23593	23536	21196	29375
5584	3603		183	17776	17714		21511
3567	1736		5	17118	17309		1351
1176	835			19241	19241		
785	6463	17	132	16286	16136	11787	36721
6010	30			14237	14237		
553	795	27	914	16706	18267	15616	14864
1235	338	63	2599	16016	20706	9747	14282
29829	12068	152	951	26030	26397	13007	17936
7368	2259			19297	19297		
5536	1877	29	494	15333	15567	7321	13208
16925	7931	123	457	40031	40608	15960	29272
301179	73332	16310	197556	20555	19269	14628	24495
220887	19323	1252	181	18907	18890	24080	14244
140684	13308	1252	104	19515	19489	24080	15006
10998	726		18	15524	15529		12826
69205	5289		59	18341	18346		13501
80292	54010	15058	197376	21898	19992	14166	24511
4992	209		79	19191	19486		9585
1403	111		3	12690	12690		13000
1573	3132	69	387	20765	20415	18757	26885
7823	5914	98	1404	19783	19320	15316	26543
441				14408	14408		
448	993	69	1152	17093	17089	18216	17036
3998	3874	1592	27699	25419	14537	11605	35416
31561	13593	1375	6406	23025	22986	15324	26156
28053	26184	11855	160247	21611	19592	14418	23284
116879	327383	349	74	17726	17732	12795	13660
90996	316391			17755	17755		
10571	6369			16034	16034		
15312	4622	349	74	18754	18935	12795	13660
91119	29204	7604	77659	19483	14113	16772	49594

3-12 国民经济各行业在岗职工工资总额及平均工资

行业	Sector	工资总额（万元）Total Wages (10000 yuan)	# 中央 Central	# 地方 Local	国有经济 State-owned
总计	**Total**	**6639343**	**2172173**	**3798373**	**4374563**
农、林、牧、渔业	**Farming,Forestry,Animal Husbandry and Fishery**	**33585**	**3020**	**29966**	**27659**
# 农、林、牧、渔服务业	FFAF Services	4663	294	4045	2576
采掘业	**Excavation**	**28989**	**87**	**28902**	**28312**
制造业	**Manufacturing**	**1350044**	**279146**	**1004729**	**721291**
食品加工业	Food Processing	20233	1643	17018	8342
食品制造业	Food Making	50359	4292	41078	13670
饮料制造业	Beverage Making	34007	397	31795	15859
烟草制造业	Tobacco Processing	3324		3324	
纺织业	Textile Industry	41773	74	41069	23568
服装及其他纤维制品制造业	Garments and Other Fiber Products	36332	2008	26215	6266
皮革、毛皮、羽绒及其制品业	Leather,Furs,Down and Related Products	4955	93	4117	1510
木材加工及竹、藤、棕、革制品业	Timber Processing,Bamboo,Cane,Palm Fiber and Straw Products	3841	508	2884	1308
家具制造业	Furniture Manufacturing	8287	668	3730	804
造纸及纸制品业	Papermaking and Paper Products	11293	387	10314	4462
印刷业、记录媒介的复制	Printing and Record Medium Reproduced	54521	33280	18202	40485
文教体育用品制造业	Stationery,Education and Sports Goods	12091	105	10779	5472
石油加工及炼焦业	Petroleum Processing and Coking Products	90426	79440	10843	89896
化学原料及化学制品制造业	Raw Chemical Materials and Chemical Products	58085	2192	51735	30106
医药制造业	Medical and Pharmaceutical Products	43407	4645	37932	22604
化学纤维制造业	Chemical Fibers	3257	107	3100	1480
橡胶制品业	Rubber Products	9224	268	8907	3950
塑料制品业	Plastic Products	15532	823	12829	3455
非金属矿物制品业	Nonmetal Mineral Products	73152	2967	67238	25933
黑色金属冶炼及压延加工业	Smelting and Pressing Ferrous Metals	199633	39	199502	191250
有色金属冶炼及压延加工业	Smelting and Pressing of Nonferrous Metals	5562	14	5489	1738
金属制品业	Metal Products	28987	996	23886	7543
普通机械制造业	Ordinary Machinery	65314	14930	47490	34764
专业设备制造业	Special Purpose Equipment	69843	15026	48875	31478
交通运输设备制造业	Transportation Equipment	124317	57533	63555	67269
武器弹药制造业	Weapons and Ammunition	14013	14013		14013
电气机械及器材制造业	Electric Equipment and Machine	60241	11159	46092	28592
电子及通信设备制造业	Electronic and Telecommunication	162887	24316	132655	27432
仪器仪表及文化办公用机械制造业	Instruments,Meters,Cultural and Office Machinery	30014	6689	21580	15080
其他制造业	Other Manufacturing	15133	535	12494	2964
电力、煤气及水的生产和供应业	**Electricity,Gas and Water Production and Supply**	**89092**	**31963**	**57129**	**72051**
电力、蒸气、热水的生产和供应业	Electricity,Steam and Hot Water Production and Supply	64874	31963	32912	47882
煤气生产和供应业	Gas Production and Supply	13907		13907	13859
自来水的生产和供应业	Water Production and Supply	10310		10310	10310
建筑业	**Construction**	**655952**	**166554**	**362660**	**360699**
土木工程建筑业	Civil Engineering	520878	112706	306596	296988
线路、管道和设备安装业	Lines,Pipelines and Equipment Installation	99225	48891	42293	57799
建筑物的装修装饰业	Fitting and Decoration	35849	4957	13771	5913
地质勘查业、水利管理业	**Geological Prospecting and Water Conservancy**	**25171**	**10259**	**14912**	**24645**
地质勘查业	Geological Prospecting	9984	8305	1679	9896
水利管理业	Water Conservancy	15186	1954	13233	14749

TOTAL WAGES AND AVERAGE WAGE OF STAFF AND WORKERS AT THEIR POSTS IN DIFFERENT TRADES

				平均工资 (元) Average Wage (yuan)			
# 中 央 Central	# 地 方 Local	集体经济 Collective-Owned	其他经济 Others		国有经济 State-owned	集体经济 Collective-Owned	其他经济 Others
1874409	**2436653**	**428014**	**1836766**	**16350**	**16431**	**10005**	**18926**
2344	**25315**	**915**	**5011**	**11303**	**11583**	**9578**	**10271**
	2576	358	1729	9109	9381	11779	8355
87	**28224**	**52**	**625**	**10821**	**10869**	**6603**	**9429**
216950	**504022**	**76305**	**552447**	**14423**	**13901**	**9105**	**16572**
46	8295	444	11448	12012	10072	10773	14045
177	13433	889	35800	15792	12218	6642	18491
77	15782	1139	17009	13575	12941	11880	14368
			3324	37436			37436
	23554	2075	16130	10006	10070	8380	10164
1919	4347	3809	26257	10029	10190	7009	10655
	1510	1192	2253	8820	8232	8887	9226
446	862	295	2238	11870	8978	10104	15050
142	661	825	6659	9978	9183	8745	10265
280	4182	801	6030	12418	10876	8891	14743
31339	9094	3526	10511	14467	14707	8636	17293
54	5418	1427	5192	13699	14897	10365	13749
79400	10495	190	340	22057	22266	8605	8448
469	29632	1962	26016	14541	13222	9296	17269
2806	19797	1293	19511	17300	15440	10526	21157
1	1479	156	1621	8606	7640	7581	9874
218	3732	1845	3429	10284	9358	8239	13669
332	3123	2592	9485	10437	9880	8376	11440
1943	23990	7901	39318	12255	11618	8590	13957
	191250	752	7631	15255	15285	9063	15523
14	1724	407	3417	16159	10853	9411	24268
543	6977	4736	16708	10401	9930	7922	11687
5707	29057	7097	23453	12059	10774	9842	15972
12805	18673	3386	34979	13224	12084	9273	15133
42497	24617	8028	49020	13299	13092	8587	14968
14013				13648	13648		
9966	18625	7559	24091	13239	12685	9567	15992
6190	21232	4138	131317	25282	16205	11951	29820
5555	9525	3244	11690	13946	12540	11537	17491
11	2953	4597	7572	11708	11364	10623	12643
28249	**43801**	**734**	**16307**	**19807**	**19622**	**14346**	**21046**
28249	19632	734	16258	21368	21610	14346	21139
	13859		48	16511	16565		8490
	10310			16640	16640		
132029	**189030**	**159388**	**135865**	**12899**	**13480**	**10486**	**15274**
99944	158605	128160	95730	12660	12991	10240	16602
30086	26643	23559	17868	14957	16693	12764	13478
2000	3783	7669	22267	11654	13633	9136	12351
10171	**14474**	**438**	**88**	**16607**	**16827**	**9338**	**20974**
8217	1679		88	17877	17853		20974
1954	12795	438		15866	16202	9338	

3-12 续表 1 continued

行业	Sector	工资总额(万元) Total Wages (10000 yuan)	# 中央 Central	# 地方 Local	国有经济 State-owned
交通运输、仓储及邮电通信业	**Transportation,Storage,Posts and Telecommunications**	**327030**	**245785**	**68272**	**281544**
铁路运输业	Railway	95203	95009	194	95203
公路运输业	Highway	28350	4107	23285	20138
管道运输业	Pipeline	189	189		
航空运输业	Airway	28095	28095		28095
交通运输辅助业	Transportation Subsidiary Services	61868	23819	35362	41979
仓储业	Storage	12215	2749	8766	9887
邮电通信业	Posts and Telecommunications	101110	91816	665	86241
批发和零售贸易餐饮业	**Wholesale,Retail Trade and Catering Services**	**633162**	**152276**	**357018**	**326506**
批发业	Wholesale Trade	275738	108078	125812	172947
零售业	Retail Trade	276095	23805	194334	118917
商业经纪与代理业	Commercial Brokerage and Agency	19026	16828	1815	17548
餐饮业	Catering Trade	62303	3565	35058	17093
金融、保险业	**Finance and Insurance**	**168792**	**154361**	**10109**	**110170**
金融业	Finance	153330	141102	8304	102475
保险业	Insurance	15462	13259	1804	7695
房地产业	**Real Estate**	**188022**	**32955**	**117085**	**80448**
房地产开发与经营业	Real Estate Development and Operation	71961	5549	51185	28992
房地产管理业	Real Estate Management	113167	27399	64225	50172
房地产代理与经纪业	Real Estate Brokerage and Agency	2894	7	1675	1285
社会服务业	**Social Services**	**926907**	**200921**	**532559**	**440553**
公共设施服务业	Public Utilities	241738	7249	223192	205724
# 市内公共交通业	Public Transportation in City	141408	4710	130976	117074
# 市内公共汽电车业	Public Bus and Trolleybus	88156		87941	87916
园林绿化业	Gardens Afforest	35891	415	35200	33569
环境卫生业	Environmental Sanitation	39359	168	35932	35372
市政工程管理业	Municipal Engineering Management	15226	108	14592	13200
居民服务业	Resident Services	40725	4140	16223	12005
旅馆业	Hotels	161791	63718	79370	72686
租赁服务业	Leasing	7370	2311	3292	2986
旅游业	Tourism	19886	8946	10215	13652
娱乐服务业	Recreation	12535	2427	5253	2223
信息、咨询服务业	Information and Consultancy Services	148038	49131	33467	41294
# 广告业	Advertisement	20935	8367	2657	5405
计算机应用服务业	Computer Application Services	169593	11920	100938	14382
其他社会服务业	Other Social Services	125231	51080	60609	75601
# 市场管理服务业	Market Management Services	22317	778	21043	2896
卫生、体育和社会福利业	**Health Care,Sports and Social Welfare**	**287832**	**95783**	**190664**	**271057**
卫生	Health Care	262232	89203	171940	246863
体育	Sports	16154	5959	9935	15498
社会服务保障业	Social Welfare	9445	620	8790	8695
教育、文化艺术及广播电影电视业	**Education,Culture and Arts, Radio,Film and Television**	**722903**	**287273**	**428251**	**705916**
教育	Education	542441	154335	384499	531218
高等教育	Higher Education	194646	134980	59302	194210
普通高等教育	Ordinary Higher Education	172918	124610	48230	172918
成人高等教育	Adult Higher Education	21728	10370	11072	21292

3-12 续表 2 continued

# 中 央 Central	# 地 方 Local	集体经济 Collective-Owned	其他经济 Others	平均工资(元) Average Wage (yuan)	国有经济 State-owned	集体经济 Collective-Owned	其他经济 Others
227152	**54004**	**5394**	**40092**	**18558**	**18037**	**9012**	**28350**
95009	194			15736	15736		
1906	18232	3955	4257	11509	11576	8457	16635
			189	21217			21217
28095				28103	28103		
14049	27543	681	19207	19758	18186	12690	24970
2266	7621	530	1798	14289	14070	10790	17442
85827	415	227	14642	24578	22643	8115	52838
121122	**199968**	**79241**	**227415**	**14396**	**16301**	**9708**	**14403**
89440	81971	28991	73801	16909	19296	10860	15786
14219	101416	41572	115606	12811	13114	9427	14318
16148	1385		1477	37720	40129		22019
1316	15195	8679	36531	11090	10948	8013	12285
107197	**2588**	**7189**	**51433**	**23789**	**21969**	**10685**	**36532**
99502	2588	7189	43666	23260	21615	10685	37065
7695			7767	30703	28104		33800
13860	**65792**	**4262**	**103311**	**18836**	**17815**	**12999**	**20106**
4020	24462	1333	41637	24424	22997	14564	26119
9833	40052	2847	60148	16319	15651	12193	17208
7	1278	83	1527	28600	26004	28514	31227
136829	**291467**	**52795**	**433560**	**16549**	**14479**	**8518**	**22365**
4443	201000	7032	28982	13644	14956	7657	9524
3114	113707	4461	19873	11796	13270	6441	8035
	87916	25	215	12895	12887	9694	18346
353	33216	52	2269	17877	18064	8355	15859
24	35331	202	3785	17848	18088	7474	16997
	13200	704	1322	19267	19330	12962	24904
1606	10245	19211	9510	8972	14004	6852	10827
35245	27873	7697	81408	15352	13148	10387	19070
2006	964	915	3469	11651	16354	9551	9794
8421	5100	410	5824	18457	19342	8212	18104
682	1538	498	9813	13914	12653	10212	14508
31675	8519	5624	101120	23966	21888	12072	26440
4263	1131	1560	13969	23033	23552	14568	24409
9416	4948	3059	152152	36371	19859	16151	40581
43336	31278	8349	41282	12825	11437	9431	18192
505	2391	597	18823	20371	17445	9336	21749
95310	**175747**	**14723**	**2052**	**21717**	**22244**	**15438**	**17966**
88814	158049	13973	1396	22027	22520	15774	24496
5959	9539	50	606	20568	21239	6512	12622
536	8159	701	50	16771	17608	11640	5390
285307	**420486**	**6604**	**10384**	**18265**	**18394**	**12612**	**15306**
153705	377390	6209	5014	17417	17511	12653	15792
134923	59208	90	346	18108	18151	10364	8471
124610	48230			18145	18145		
10313	10978	90	346	17814	18196	10364	8471

3-12 续表 3 continued

行业 Sector		工资总额（万元）Total Wages (10000 yuan)	# 中央 Central	# 地方 Local	国有经济 State-owned
中等教育	Secondary School Education	188416	8068	179271	183692
中等专业学校	Specialized Secondary Schools	22725	1793	20872	22071
普通中学	Regular Secondary Schools	133123	5475	126630	129529
农业、职业中学	Agricultural and Vocational Schools	20450	7	20443	20450
技工学校	Technical Schools	4926	430	4496	4482
成人中等学校	Adult Secondary Schools	6368	261	6108	6336
工读学校	Schools for Juvenile Delinquents	824	103	721	824
初等教育	Primary Education	115317	1952	113045	114997
小学校	Primary Schools	115282	1952	113045	114997
成人初等学校	Adult Primary Schools	36			
学前教育	Preschool Education	17871	2555	14693	15003
特殊教育	Special Education	1446	190	1237	1427
其他教育	Other Education	24744	6589	16951	21890
文化艺术业	Culture and Arts	138965	104077	31597	134097
艺术	Arts	12871	7936	4906	12724
出版	Publication	90516	77164	13012	89269
文物保护	Historical Relics Preservation	9296	5576	3627	9152
图书馆	Library	5153	3422	1730	5148
档案馆	Archives	2006	1171	835	2006
群众文化	Mass Culture	7083	784	6249	7019
新闻	News	6039	6010	30	6039
文化艺术经纪与代理业	Brokers and Agents for Cultural and Arts Activities	2177	781	829	1336
其他文化艺术业	Others	3824	1233	378	1405
广播电影电视业	Radio,Film and Television	41497	28862	12155	40601
广播	Radio	9627	7367	2259	9627
电影	Film	7860	5588	1920	7352
电视	Television	24010	15906	7976	23622
科学研究和综合技术服务	**Scientific Research and Polytechnical Services**	**565462**	**306723**	**221320**	**368945**
科学研究业	Scientific Research	240230	218902	18878	238827
自然科学研究	Natural Science Research	153664	139250	12929	152330
社会科学研究	Social Science Research	11707	10972	724	11697
其他科学研究	Other Scientific Research	74858	68680	5225	7480
综合技术服务业	Polytechnical Services	325232	87822	202442	1301
气象	Atmospheric	5232	4956	276	5154
地震	Seismology	1492	1379	113	1489
测绘	Surveying and Mapping	4559	979	3580	4105
技术监督	Technology Supervisor	14615	7711	6577	13394
海洋环境	Sea and Ocean Environments	441	441		441
环境保护	Environmental Protection	2532	445	2015	1394
技术推广和科技交流服务业	Technology Promotion and Exchange Services	34922	5158	15328	7595
工程设计业	Engineering Design	51360	32889	17590	44585
其他综合技术服务业	Other Polytechnical Services	210078	33863	156964	5196
国家机关、政党机关和社会团体	**Government Agencies,Party Agencies and Social Organizations**	**438975**	**114229**	**323512**	**438563**
国家机关	Government Agencies	402059	88237	312607	402059
政党机关	Party Agencies	16901	10568	6333	16901
社会团体	Social Organizations	20016	15424	4572	19604
其他行业	**Other Sectors**	**197426**	**90836**	**51284**	**116205**

3-12 续表 4 continued

				平均工资			
		集体经济 Collective-Owned	其他经济 Others	(元) Average Wage (yuan)	国有经济 State-owned	集体经济 Collective-Owned	其他经济 Others
# 中 央 Central	# 地 方 Local						
7987	175704	2881	1843	18004	18080	15015	16255
1793	20278	468	186	17622	17714	17402	11117
5394	124134	1975	1620	18003	18080	14257	17610
7	20443			18643	18643		
430	4052	415	28	17771	18022	16617	8114
261	6075	23	9	17339	17378	15542	7618
103	721			20800	20800		
1952	113045		320	15945	15932		22695
1952	113045		284	15944	15932		22933
			36	20959			20959
2555	12448	2314	554	15950	16756	11764	19570
190	1237	19		16032	16212	8838	
6097	15749	904	1950	16638	17166	9912	16145
103002	31095	252	4617	20462	20752	11781	14979
7853	4870	36	112	16478	16550	9686	12971
76468	12800	126	1121	23534	23514	14800	27147
5576	3576		144	17737	17749		16992
3422	1725		5	17449	17654		1351
1171	835			19287	19287		
784	6235	14	50	16706	16740	13027	13938
6010	30			14237	14237		
540	795	19	823	15963	18147	10924	13473
1177	228	58	2361	14931	20574	8995	13016
28600	12000	142	753	25255	25715	12389	14295
7367	2259			19299	19299		
5496	1857	25	482	15436	15710	6645	12898
15738	7884	117	271	37805	38592	15224	17712
295867	**70470**	**14085**	**182433**	**20186**	**19567**	**12802**	**22643**
217860	18532	1250	153	19340	19327	24216	12082
138208	12636	1250	85	20051	20030	24216	12371
10972	724		10	15562	15577		7427
68680	5171		58	18689	18695		13109
78007	51938	12835	182279	20860	20024	12240	22660
4956	197		79	19117	19411		9585
1379	110		3	12818	12818		13000
979	3126	69	385	23250	23063	18757	26710
7572	5823	96	1125	19236	19121	15040	21266
441				14408	14408		
414	980	46	1093	16498	16954	12319	16172
3879	3679	1303	26024	24442	14688	9906	33356
31087	13498	1260	5515	22915	23372	14082	22582
27300	24525	10061	148056	20218	19241	12363	21531
113877	**323472**	**340**	**73**	**18106**	**18113**	**12437**	**13450**
88237	312607			18178	18178		
10568	6333			16032	16032		
15072	4532	340	73	18668	18859	12437	13450
88058	**27792**	**5550**	**75671**	**19409**	**14096**	**12850**	**50582**

3-13 分地区职工人数、平均工资
NUMBER OF STAFF AND WORKERS,AVERAGE WAGE BY REGION

地 区	Region	职工人数(人) Staff and Workers(person) 2000	1999	平均工资(元) Average Wage(yuan) 2000	1999
全 市	**Total**	**4342480**	**4379854**	**15726**	**13778**
城 区	**City Propers**	**1318613**	**1438411**	**16304**	**14371**
东城区	Dongcheng	407531	420837	17940	15410
西城区	Xicheng	502923	589542	17016	15490
崇文区	Chongwen	132134	143293	14856	12698
宣武区	Xuanwu	276025	284739	13360	11492
近郊区	**Near Suburbs**	**2229210**	**2181546**	**16541**	**14431**
朝阳区	Chaoyang	797117	834011	17691	15309
丰台区	Fengtai	424086	334082	13275	11711
石景山区	Shijingshan	272703	290592	12711	11077
海淀区	Haidian	735304	722861	18702	16061
远郊区	**Outer Suburbs**	**499260**	**482485**	**12583**	**11285**
门头沟区	Mentougou	63553	66826	11655	9905
房山区	Fangshan	149876	134203	14030	12922
通州区	Tongzhou	88397	89869	11618	9859
昌平区	Changping	113616	112996	11232	10494
顺义区	Shunyi	83818	78591	13532	9730
各 县	**Counties**	**287933**	**275207**	**12588**	**10892**
大兴县	Daxing	119799	109476	14050	11592
平谷县	Pinggu	43713	47726	9910	8937
怀柔县	Huairou	38842	37411	13277	11575
密云县	Miyun	49427	47392	11684	9946
延庆县	Yanqing	36152	33202	11691	10293
外 地	**Nonlocal**	**7464**	**2205**	**5765**	**9656**

3-14 在岗职工人数、工资
NUMBER AND WAGE OF STAFF AND WORKERS AT THEIR POSTS

项目	Item	人数（人）Number (person)	工资总额（万元）Total Wages (10000 yuan)	平均工资（元）Average Wage (yuan)
总计	**Total**	**3979251**	**6639343**	**16350**
按登记注册类型分	**Grouped by Registration Status**			
内资经济	Domestic Investment Economy	3649904	5785136	15475
国有经济	State-owned	2557580	4374563	16431
集体经济	Collective-owned	417302	428014	10005
联营经济	Joint-owned	36506	51736	13086
股份有限公司	Share Holding Corporations Ltd.	125799	221281	17762
有限责任公司	Limited-Liability Corporations	287165	470106	17122
股份合作企业	Share Holding	74133	77514	11126
其他经济	Others	151419	161921	11579
外商投资经济	Foreign Funded	209419	605978	29621
港、澳、台商投资经济	Hongkong,Macao and Taiwan Funded	119928	248229	21082
按隶属关系分	**Grouped by Administrative Relationship**			
# 中央	Central	1111860	2172173	19059
地方	Local	2380842	3798373	15397
按行业分	**Grouped by Sector**			
农、林、牧、渔业	Farming,Forestry,Animal Husbandry and Fishery	28477	33585	11303
# 农业	Farming	5048	4663	9109
采掘业	Excavation	25756	28989	10821
制造业	Manufacturing	895612	1350044	14423
电力、煤气及水的生产和供应业	Electricity,Gas,Water Production and Supply	39325	89092	19807
建筑业	Construction	486860	655952	12899
地质勘查业水利管理业	Geological Prospecting and Water Conservancy	14766	25171	16607
交通运输、仓储及邮电通信业	Transportation,Storage,Posts and Telecommunications Services	175243	327030	18558
# 交通运输业	Transportation	127492	213705	16889
邮电通信业	Posts and Telecommunications Services	39516	101110	24578
批发和零售贸易餐饮业	Wholesale,Retail Trade and Catering Services	425790	633162	14396
# 批发业	Wholesale Trade	158080	275738	16909
零售业	Retail Trade	206013	276095	12811
餐饮业	Catering Trade	56634	62303	11090
金融、保险业	Finance and Insurance	69662	168792	23789
房地产业	Real Estate	103153	188022	18836
社会服务业	Social Services	553857	926907	16549
# 居民服务业	Resident Services	45403	40725	8972
旅馆业	Hotels	103006	161791	15352
卫生体育和社会福利业	Health Care,Sports and Social Welfare	134075	287832	21717
# 卫生	Health Care	120383	262232	22027
体育	Sports	7915	16154	20568
教育、文化艺术和广播电影电视业	Education,Culture,Art, Radio,Film and Television	394567	722903	18265
教育	Education	309748	542441	17417
文化艺术业	Culture and Art	68669	138965	20462
广播电影电视业	Radio,Film and Television	16150	41497	25255
科学研究和综合技术服务业	Scientific Research and Polytechnical Services	284198	565462	20186
科学研究业	Scientific Research	122506	240230	19340
综合技术服务业	Polytechnical Services	161692	325232	20860
国家机关、政党机关和社会团体	Government Agencies,Party Agencies and Social Organizations	242554	438975	18106
其他行业	Others	105356	197426	19409

3-15 分地区从业人员人数、劳动报酬
NUMBER AND REMUNERATION OF EMPLOYED PERSONS BY REGION

地区	Region	人数(人) Number of Employed Persons (person)	劳动报酬(元) Remuneration (yuan)
全　市	**Total**	4318343	7073675
城　区	**City Propers**	1339507	2217628
东城区	Dongcheng	418606	747439
西城区	Xicheng	507967	879178
崇文区	Chongwen	123958	203479
宣武区	Xuanwu	288976	387532
近郊区	**Near Suburbs**	2222378	3836166
朝阳区	Chaoyang	794785	1503730
丰台区	Fengtai	417546	583182
石景山区	Shijingshan	227914	339915
海淀区	Haidian	782133	1409338
远郊区	**Outer Suburbs**	476345	650180
门头沟区	Mentougou	59710	75469
房山区	Fangshan	145064	219098
通州区	Tongzhou	82625	102380
昌平区	Changping	82615	121442
顺义区	Shunyi	106331	131791
各　县	**Counties**	276866	365477
大兴县	Daxing	115764	169009
平谷县	Pinggu	39859	44540
怀柔县	Huairou	37916	51745
密云县	Miyun	48204	56872
延庆县	Yanqing	35123	43312
外　地	**Nonlocal**	3247	4225

主 要 统 计 指 标 解 释

从业人员 指从事一定社会劳动并取得劳动报酬或经营收入的人员。包括：（1）全部在岗职工（2）再就业的离退休人员（3）私营业主（4）个体户主（5）私营和个体从业人员（6）乡镇企业从业人员（7）农村从业人员（8）其他从业人员（包括民办教师、宗教职业者、现役军人等人事档案关系保留在原单位的人员）

这一指标反映了一定时期内全部劳动力资源的实际利用情况，是研究我国基本国情国力的重要指标。

职工 指在国有经济、城镇集体经济、联营经济、股份合作经济、股份有限公司、有限责任公司、外商和港、澳、台商投资经济、其他经济及其附属机构工作，并由其支付工资或生活费的各类人员。

职工工资总额 指各单位在一定时期内直接支付给本单位全部在岗职工的劳动报酬总额和不在岗职工的生活费。

工资总额的计算原则应以直接支付给职工的全部劳动报酬为根据。各单位支付给职工的劳动报酬以及其他根据有关规定支付的工资，不论是计入成本的还是不计入成本的，不论是按国家规定列入计征奖金税项目的，还是未列入计征奖金税项目的，不论是以货币形式支付的还是以实物形式支付的，均包括在工资总额内。

职工平均工资 指企业、事业、机关单位的职工在一定时期内平均每人所得的货币工资额。它表明一定时期职工工资收入的高低程度，是反映职工工资水平的主要指标。计算公式为：

$$\text{职工平均工资} = \frac{\text{报告期实际支付的全部职工工资总额}}{\text{报告期全部职工平均人数}}$$

Explanatory Notes On Main Statistical Indicators

Employment refers to the persons who are engaged in social labor and receive payment or earn business income, including:(1) all staff and workers at their posts, (2) re-employed retirees , (3) owners of private enterprises, (4) owners of individual business, (5) employed persons in private enterprises and individual business, (6) employed persons in the township and village enterprises, (7) employed persons in agriculture, (8) other employed persons （including teachers in the schools run by the local people , people engaged in religious profession and the servicemen, etc. whose organizational affiliation reserved in reformer units）.

This indicator reflects the actual utilization of total labor force during a certain period of time and is often used for the research on China's economic affairs and national power.

Staff and Workers refer to the persons who work in （and receive payment and living expenses therefrom）enterprises and institutions of state-owned,collective-owned,share holding cooperative,share holding company,limited-liability company, and foreign, Hongkong, Macao, Taiwan funded, and other types of ownership and their affiliated units.

Total Wages of Staff and Workers refer to the total remuneration payment to staff and workers at their posts and living expenses to staff and workers not at their posts in various units during a certain period of time.

The calculation of total wages is based on the total remuneration payment to the staff and workers. Therefore, all the wages and salaries and other payments to staff and workers are included in the total wages regardless of their sources, categories, and forms（in kind or cash）.

Average Wage of Staff and Workers refers to the average wage in money terms per employed person during a certain period of time for staff and workers in enterprises, institutions and government agencies, which reflects the general level of wage income during a certain period of time, and is calculated as follows:

$$\text{Average Wage of Staff and Workers} = \frac{\text{Total Wages of Staff and Workers}}{\text{Average Number of Staff and Workers}}$$

固定资产投资及房地产业

4

INVESTMENT IN FIXED ASSETS AND REAL ESTATE

全社会固定资产投资　　　（单位：亿元）
Total Investment in Fixed Assets (100 million yuan)

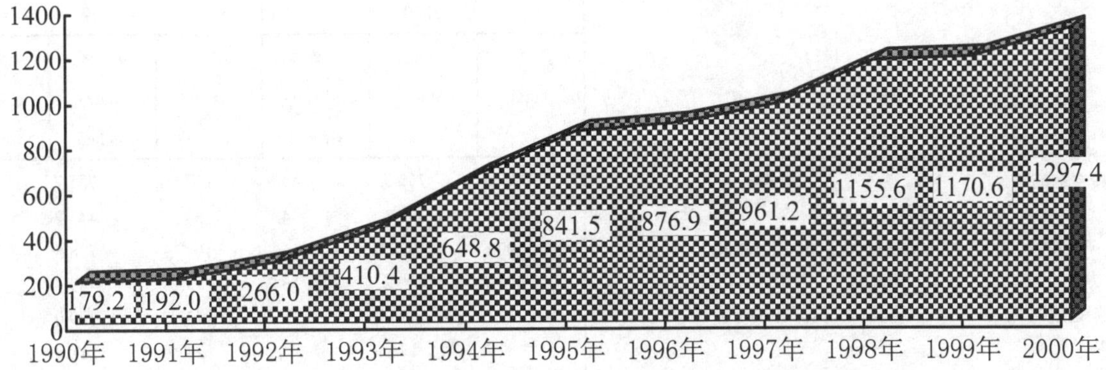

城市基础设施占全社会固定资产投资比重（单位：%）
Percentage of Municipal Infrastructure in Total Fixed Assets (%)

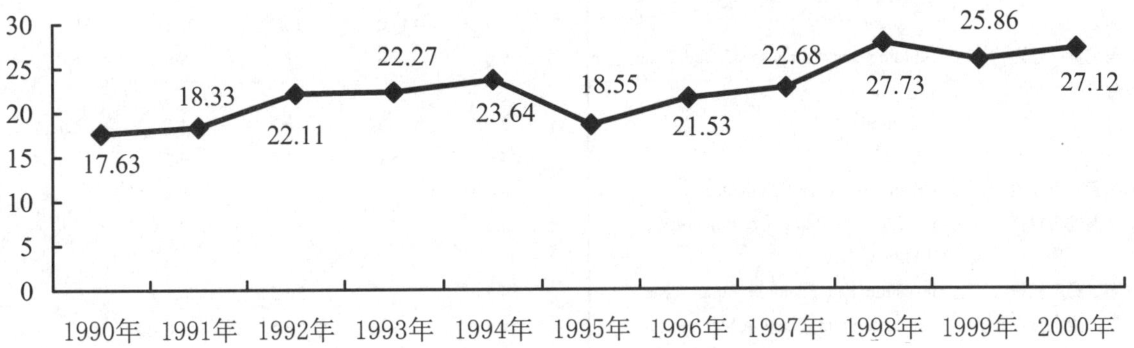

商品房屋建设（单位：万平方米）
Commercial Buildings (10000 sq.m)

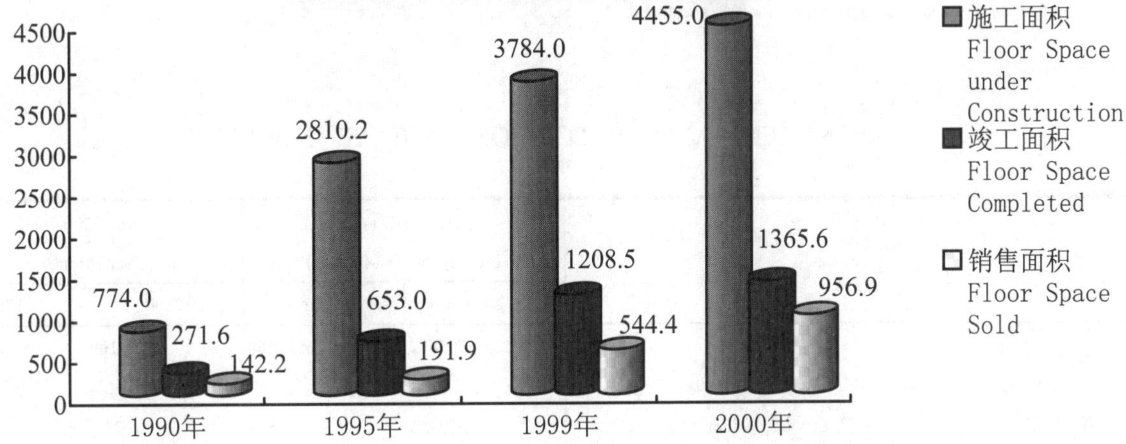

4-1 全社会固定资产投资额
TOTAL INVESTMENT IN FIXED ASSETS

单位：亿元 (100 million yuan)

项目	Item	2000 合计 Total	2000 # 国有 State-owned	2000 # 集体 Collective-owned	1999 合计 Total	1999 #国有 State-owned	1999 # 集体 Collective-owned
投资总额	**Total**	**1297.4**	**765.8**	**45.0**	**1170.6**	**735.7**	**55.8**
# 地方	Local	979.5	491.3	44.7	831.8	445.2	55.4
固定资产投资	Investment in Fixed Assets	1192.6	758.0	16.7	1072.9	728.8	28.0
# 地方	Local	876.7	485.2	16.7	735.9	439.7	27.5
基本建设投资	Capital Construction	447.0	405.2		432.7	389.0	
中央	Central	182.2	174.9		242.0	218.7	
地方	Local	264.8	230.3		190.7	170.3	
更新改造措施	Innovation	185.9	173.3		175.2	164.6	
中央	Central	96.0	93.7		64.6	63.8	
地方	Local	89.9	79.6		110.6	100.8	
全民其他	Others of the Whole People Ownership	31.3	31.3		30.5	30.5	
城镇集体	Urban Collective	6.3		6.3	13.0		13.0
房地产开发	Real Estate Development	522.1	148.2	10.4	421.5	144.7	15.0
# 地方	Local	484.4	144.0	10.4	391.1	138.1	14.5
零星固定资产建造及购置	Building and Purchase of Odd Fixed Assets	9.6	7.8	1.8	9.0	6.9	2.1
中央	Central	2.0	1.7	0.3	1.8	1.4	0.4
地方	Local	7.6	6.1	1.5	7.2	5.5	1.7
城镇私营、个体投资	Urban Private and Individual	8.4			8.2		
城镇私人建房投资	Individual Building Construction in Urban Area	2.3			2.3		
农村固定资产投资	Investment in Fixed in Rural Assets	84.5		26.5	78.2		25.7
非农户固定资产投资	Investment in Fixed Assets Non-agriculture Households	55.4		26.5	54.8		25.7
农户固定资产投资	Investment in Fixed Assets of Agriculture Households	29.1			23.4		
# 私人建房	Individual Building Construction	18.0			12.5		

注：自1999年，年报国家统计制度对固定资产投资统计范围进行了调整，增加城镇私营、个体投资统计，调整扩大农村固定资产投资统计范围。

Note: According to state statistical rules, statistical range of investment in fixed assets has been adjusted-adding data of urban private and individual units, expanding the range of rural investment.

4-2 产业投资及比重
INVESTMENT AND PROPORTION BY TYPE INDUSTRY

项目	Item	投资额 (万元) Investment(10000 yuan)		比重 (%) Proportion(%)	
		2000	1999	2000	1999
总计	**Total**	**6705682**	**6513968**	**100**	**100**
第一产业	Primary Industry	29771	16647	0.4	0.3
第二产业	Secondary Industry	1572750	1793558	23.5	27.5
第三产业	Tertiary Industry	5103161	4703763	76.1	72.2

注：本表不含房地产投资。

Note: Data of this table exclude investment in real estate.

4-3 全市固定资产投资额

INVESTMENT IN FIXED ASSETS OF THE CITY

单位：万元 (10000 yuan)

项目 Item		2000 合计 Total	2000 # 基本建设 Capital Construction	2000 # 更新改造 Technical Updating and Trans-formation	1999 合计 Total	1999 # 基本建设 Capital Construction	1999 # 更新改造 Technical Updating and Trans-formation
投资额	**Total**	**6705682**	**4469841**	**1859435**	**6513968**	**4327251**	**1752093**
按构成分	**Grouped by Use of Funds**						
建筑安装工程	Construction and Installation	3802253	2848995	706918	4005057	2914124	761921
设备工器具购置	Purchases of Equipments and Instruments	1435822	470923	958599	1281769	560222	705686
其他	Others	1467607	1149923	193918	1227142	852905	284486
按用途分	**Grouped by User**						
农林牧渔业用	Farming,Forestry,Animal Husbandry and Fishery	24154	24035	119	6953	6451	502
工业、建筑业用	Industry,Construction	1318950	742561	564078	1480297	1022237	427910
商业、运输邮电业用	Commerce,Transportation, Posts and Telecommunications	1225997	284745	622416	1268980	419591	546617
住宅	Residential Buildings	842324	780316	38937	1173016	1040232	58954
其他	Others	3294257	2638184	633885	2584722	1838740	718110
更新改造投资按用途分	**Grouped by Purpose of Investment in Innovation**						
增产	Increasing Production	272231		272231	126065		126065
节约能源	Energy Saving	7865		7865	12668		12668
其他节约	Other Saving Measures	3195		3195	2070		2070
增加品种	Increasing Varieties	35428		35428	40554		40554
提高产品质量	Improving Quality of Products	84798		84798	36506		36506
三废治理	Environmental Protection	144095		144095	139807		139807
其他	Others	1311823		1311823	1394423		1394423
按建设性质分	**Grouped by Type of Construction**						
新建	New Construction	1695082	1359129	12329	1596842	1294950	10618
改建和扩建	Repconstruction and Expansion	4372427	2761146	1579511	4093048	2481402	1536248
单纯建造生活设施	Living Installation	364151	282699	63705	573259	480117	36560
迁建和恢复	Movement and Recovery	106133	64939	39601	103995	65063	34830
单纯购置设备	Purchase of Equipment	167889	1928	164289	146824	5719	133837

注：本表及以下各表包括基本建设、更新改造和其他投资，不含房地产开发投资。

Note：This table and its followings include capital construction,innovation and other investment,exclude real estate development investment.

4-3 续表 continued

单位：万元 (10000 yuan)

项目 Item		2000 合计 Total	2000 #基本建设 Capital Construction	2000 #更新改造 Technical Updating and Trans-formation	1999 合计 Total	1999 #基本建设 Capital Construction	1999 #更新改造 Technical Updating and Trans-formation
按建设项目规模分	**Grouped by Size of Construction Projects**						
基本建设大中型项目	Large and Medium Projects of Capital Construction	859785	859785		774239	774239	
基本建设小型项目	Small Projects of Capital Construction	3608128	3608128		3547293	3547293	
更新改造限额以上项目	Projects of Innovation above the Limits	862491		862491	744704		744704
更新改造限额以下项目	Projects of Innovation below the Limits	832655		832655	873552		873552
其他	Others	542623	1928	164289	574180	5719	133837
按企业登记注册类型分	**Grouped by Registration Status of Enterprises**						
内资企业	Domestic Investment Enterprises	6400017	4189212	1834399	6091450	3945320	1711506
国有企业	State-owned	6098510	4052521	1733159	5840694	3890475	1645550
集体企业	Collective-owned	63576			129955		
联营企业	Joint Owned	2888	2788	100	3531	3531	
股份合作企业	Share Holding	16011	16011		17477	9951	7526
股份有限公司	Share Holding Corporations Ltd.	135769	65701	70068	75301	27384	47917
有限责任公司	Limited-Liability Corporations	82288	51326	30962	24492	13979	10513
其他企业	Others	975	865	110			
港澳台商投资企业	Hongkong,Macao and Taiwan Funded Enterprises	95374	87629	7745	243556	235279	8277
港澳台合资经营	Joint Venture	24734	17969	6765	93003	86806	6197
港澳台合作经营	Cooperative	63675	63675		138083	138003	80
港澳台商独资企业	Hongkong,Macao and Taiwan Enterprises	5985	5985		10470	10470	
港澳台商投资股份有限公司	Hongkong,Macao and Taiwan Share Holding Corporations Ltd.	980		980	2000		2000
外商投资企业	Foreign Funded Enterprises	210291	193000	17291	178962	146652	32310
中外合资经营	Joint Venture	173545	157154	16391	157469	125257	32212
中外合作经营	Cooperative	4586	3686	900	4787	4787	
外资(独资)企业	Foreign Enterprises	19080	19080		15580	15580	
外商投资股份有限公司	Foreign Share Holding Corporation Ltd.	13080	13080		1126	1028	98

4-4 地方固定资产投资额
LOCAL INVESTMENT IN FIXED ASSETS

单位：万元　　　　(10000 yuan)

项目	Item	2000			1999		
		合计 Total	# 基本建设 Capital Construction	# 更新改造 Technical Updating and Trans-formation	合计 Total	# 基本建设 Capital Construction	# 更新改造 Technical Updating and Trans-formation
投资额	**Total**	**3923508**	**2647629**	**899473**	**3447454**	**1907191**	**1105639**
按构成分	**Grouped by Use of Funds**						
建筑安装工程	Construction and Installation	2189656	1508371	434945	2207536	1311404	567120
设备工器具购置	Purchases of Equipments and Instruments	609544	239307	363937	485490	166200	303429
其他	Others	1124308	899951	100591	754428	429587	235090
按用途分	**Grouped by User**						
农林牧渔业用	Farming,Forestry,Animal Husbandry and Fishery	24154	24035	119	6953	6451	502
工业、建筑业用	Industry,Construction	769554	490214	267029	732267	396362	305755
商业、运输邮电业用	Commerce,Transportation, Posts and Telecommunications	438715	96153	23726	574675	198463	73440
住宅	Residential Buildings	327697	284643	19983	436896	323831	39235
其他	Others	2363388	1752584	588616	1696663	982084	686707
更新改造投资按用途分	**Grouped by Purpose of Investment in Innovation**						
增产	Increasing Production	88712		88712	98680		98680
节约能源	Energy Saving	7330		7330	10495		10495
其他节约	Other Saving Measures	50		50	2056		2056
增加品种	Increasing Varieties	25647		25647	35595		35595
提高产品质量	Improving Quality of Products	38429		38429	27802		27802
三废治理	Environmental Protection	125217		125217	112456		112456
其他	Others	614088		614088	818555		818555
按建设性质分	**Grouped by Type of Construction**						
新建	New Construction	1378142	1046400	8118	1264448	963044	10130
改建和扩建	Repconstruction and Expansion	2131127	1397844	701513	1719280	713070	930812
单纯建造生活设施	Living Installation	195824	157465	20612	298943	209992	32369
迁建和恢复	Movement and Recovery	87114	45920	39601	58090	19158	34830
单纯购置设备	Purchase of Equipment	131301		129629	106693	1927	97498

4-4 续表 continued

单位：万元 (10000 yuan)

项目	Item	2000 合计 Total	2000 # 基本建设 Capital Construction	2000 # 更新改造 Technical Updating and Trans-formation	1999 合计 Total	1999 # 基本建设 Capital Construction	1999 # 更新改造 Technical Updating and Trans-formation
按建设项目规模分	**Grouped by Size of Construction Projects**						
基本建设大中型项目	Large and Medium Projects of Capital Construction	630810	630810		403065	403065	
基本建设小型项目	Small Projects of Capital Construction	2016819	2016819		1502199	1502199	
更新改造限额以上项目	Projects of Innovation above the Limits	570794		570794	664089		664089
更新改造限额以下项目	Projects of Innovation below the Limits	199050		199050	344052		344052
其他	Others	506035		129629	534049	1927	97498
按企业登记注册类型分	**Grouped by Registration Status of Enterprises**						
内资企业	Domestic Investment Enterprises	3685489	2434646	874437	3258035	1757424	1065987
国有企业	State-owned	3411803	2303345	795628	3015453	1703227	1007557
集体企业	Collective-owned	63576			129955		
联营企业	Joint Owned	2888	2788	100	3531	3531	
股份合作企业	Share Holding	16011	16011		9951	9951	
股份有限公司	Share Holding Corporations Ltd.	110504	62701	47803	75301	27384	47917
有限责任公司	Limited-Liability Corporations	79732	48936	30796	23844	13331	10513
其他企业	Others	975	865	110			
港澳台商投资企业	Hongkong,Macao and Taiwan Funded Enterprises	39164	31419	7745	95655	87378	8277
港澳台合资经营	Joint Venture	22326	15561	6765	36197	30000	6197
港澳台合作经营	Cooperative	9873	9873		46988	46908	80
港澳台商独资企业	Hongkong,Macao and Taiwan Enterprises	5985	5985		10470	10470	
港澳台商投资股份有限公司	Hongkong,Macao and Taiwan Share Holding Corporations Ltd.	980		980	2000		2000
外商投资企业	Foreign Funded Enterprises	198855	181564	17291	93764	62389	31375
中外合资经营	Joint Venture	171439	155048	16391	73501	42224	31277
中外合作经营	Cooperative	4286	3386	900	4057	4057	
外资(独资)企业	Foreign Enterprises	19080	19080		15580	15580	
外商投资股份有限公司	Foreign Share Holding Corporation Ltd.	4050	4050		626	528	98

4-5 固定资产投资财务拨贷款额
FINANCIAL ALLOCATIONS AND LOANS FOR INVESTMENT IN FIXED ASSETS

单位：万元 (10000 yuan)

项目 Item		2000 合计 Total	2000 # 基本建设 Capital Construction	2000 # 更新改造 Technical Updating and Trans-formation	1999 合计 Total	1999 # 基本建设 Capital Construction	1999 # 更新改造 Technical Updating and Trans-formation
上年结余资金	**Balance of Last Year**	**1567658**	**1458960**	**98705**	**1015427**	**837265**	**150039**
本年拨款贷款	**Allocations and Loans in this Year**	**6579371**	**4336119**	**1953834**	**6575841**	**4488073**	**1712951**
国家预算内资金	State Appropriations	1066856	925610	137246	1356504	1175077	170927
国内贷款	Domestic Loans	1349943	871143	310916	969362	650658	161034
债　券	Bonds						
利用外资	Foreign Investment	144025	142255	1770	344867	239544	105323
自筹资金	Fundraising	3749061	2147565	1488111	3590697	2148398	1248068
# 股票	Stocks	95591	34576	61015	35411	3533	31878
其他资金	Others	269486	249546	15791	314411	274396	27599

4-6 地方固定资产投资财务拨贷款额
FINANCIAL ALLOCATIONS AND LOANS FOR LOCAL INVESTMENT IN FIXED ASSETS

单位：万元 (10000 yuan)

项目 Item		2000 合计 Total	2000 # 基本建设 Capital Construction	2000 # 更新改造 Technical Updating and Trans-formation	1999 合计 Total	1999 # 基本建设 Capital Construction	1999 # 更新改造 Technical Updating and Trans-formation
上年结余资金	**Balance of Last Year**	**558043**	**457205**	**90845**	**507037**	**350408**	**128506**
本年拨款贷款	**Allocations and Loans in this Year**	**3781647**	**2557657**	**934572**	**3485301**	**1971159**	**1139325**
国家预算内资金	State Appropriations	446814	317710	125104	468305	301639	156166
国内贷款	Domestic Loans	1010398	726293	116221	585946	302769	125507
债　券	Bonds						
利用外资	Foreign Investment	111277	111100	177	220315	131487	88828
自筹资金	Fundraising	1982144	1188184	680575	1957320	1020147	742942
# 股票	Stocks	64371	3356	61015	33555	3130	30425
其他资金	Others	231014	214370	12495	253415	215117	25882

4-7 城市基础设施投资额
MUNICIPAL INFRASTRUCTURE INVESTMENT

项目	Item	投资额（万元）Investment(10000 yuan) 全市 Total	# 地方 Local	比重(%) Proportion(%) 全市 Total	# 地方 Local
全市总计	**Total**	**3519275**	**2512746**	**100**	**100**
能源	**Energy**	**532116**	**282564**	**15.1**	**11.2**
电力	Electricity	266473	16921	7.6	0.7
供热	Heat	60704	60704	1.7	2.4
供气	Gas	124542	124542	3.5	4.9
供水	Water	80397	80397	2.3	3.2
公共服务业	**Public Services**	**1550298**	**1550298**	**44.1**	**61.7**
市内公共交通	Public Traffic	197704	197704	5.6	7.9
# 市内公交电汽车	Buses and Trolleys	79454	79454	2.3	3.2
出租汽车	Taxies	21065	21065	0.6	0.8
园林绿化	Parks and Green Areas	18180	18180	0.5	0.7
环境卫生	Environmental Sanitation	5718	5718	0.2	0.2
市政工程管理	Municipal Construction	1328696	1328696	37.8	52.9
其他公共服务业	Others				
交通运输	**Transportation**	**447598**	**325474**	**12.7**	**13.0**
铁路	Railway	2837		0.1	
公路	Highway	321808	321808	9.1	12.9
管道运输	Pipeline				
航空	Aviation	18009		0.5	
其他	Others	104944	3666	3.0	0.1
邮政电信	**Posts and Telecommunications**	**636611**	**2178**	**18.1**	**0.1**
邮政	Posts	7911	618	0.2	
电信	Telecommunications	628700	1560	17.9	0.1
其他	**Others**	**352652**	**352232**	**10.0**	**14.0**
水利	Water Conservancy	112405	112145	3.2	4.5
环境保护	Environmental Protection	193833	193833	5.5	7.7
其他	Others	46414	46254	1.3	1.8

4-8 能源及交通投资额
INVESTMENT IN ENERGY AND TRANSPORTATION

单位：万元 (10000 yuan)

项目	Item	全市 Total 2000	1999	# 地方 Local 2000	1999
全市固定资产投资总额	**Investment in Fixed Assets of the City**	**6705682**	**6513968**	**3923508**	**3447454**
# 能源、交通投资额	Investment in Energy and Transportation	1804191	2041641	566849	637311
占全市投资额比重 (%)	Proportion (%)	26.8	31.3	14.4	18.5
能源投资额	Investment in Energy	577931	959216	216276	275314
占全市投资额比重 (%)	Proportion (%)	8.6	14.7	5.5	8.0
运输、邮电投资额	Investment in Transportation,Posts and Telecommunications	1226260	1082425	350573	361997
占全市投资额比重 (%)	Proportion (%)	18.2	16.6	8.9	10.5
在能源投资中	**Of the Investment in Energy**				
煤(国家统配煤矿)	Coal(State Collieries)	2076	4113	2076	4113
电(公用电厂及小水电)	Electricity(Public Power Plants and Hydropower Stations)	321143	599915	18966	19713
油品(炼油厂原油加工)	Oil Products(Crude Oil Processing of Refinery)	66661	108708	7183	5008
燃料气(液化石油气、焦炉煤气)	Fuel Gas(Liquefied Petroleum Gas,Gas)	124994	101718	124994	101718
热气(公用局)	Heat(Public Utilities Bureau)	63057	144762	63057	144762
在运输投资中	**Of Investment in Transportation**				
铁路	Railway	54728	35472		
公路	Highway	342853	332676	342853	332676
航空	Aviation	21046	15339	981	850
邮政、电信	Posts and Telecommunications	682042	568966	2178	4696
交通运输辅助业	Transportation Subsidiary Services	125591	129972	4561	23775

4-9 施工及投入生产(或交付使用)的项目数
NUMBER OF PROJECTS UNDER CONSTRUCTION AND PUT INTO USE (OR PUT INTO OPERATION)

单位：个 (unit)

项目	Item	全市 Total 2000	全市 Total 1999	#地方 Local 2000	#地方 Local 1999
全市施工项目	**Total Projects under Construction**	**2533**	**2878**	**1442**	**1596**
# 本年新开工	Started this Year	1417	1406	793	809
全部竣工投产项目	Total Projects Completed and Put into Use	1309	1474	737	852
建设项目投产率 (%)	Rate of Projects Completed and Put into Use (%)	51.7	51.2	51.1	53.4
基本建设施工项目	**Capital Construction Projects under Construction**	**1210**	**1194**	**769**	**729**
# 本年新开工	Started this Year	508	426	385	327
全部竣工投产项目	Total Projects Completed and Put into Use	486	438	330	315
建设项目投产率 (%)	Rate of Projects Completed and Put into Use (%)	40.2	36.7	42.9	43.2
更新改造措施施工项目	**Innovation Projects under Construction**	**1240**	**1558**	**590**	**741**
# 本年新开工	Started this Year	873	927	372	429
全部竣工投产项目	Total Projects Completed and Put into Use	780	965	364	466
建设项目投产率 (%)	Rate of Projects Completed and Put into Use (%)	62.9	61.9	61.7	62.9
其他投资施工项目	**Other Projects under Construction**	**83**	**126**	**83**	**126**
# 本年新开工	Started this Year	36	53	36	53
全部竣工投产项目	Total Projects Completed and Put into Use	43	71	43	71
建设项目投产率 (%)	Rate of Projects Completed and Put into Use (%)	51.8	56.3	51.8	56.3

4-10 全市固定资产投资额及新增固定资产(按行业分)

INVESTMENT IN FIXED ASSETS AND ITS INCREMENTAL FIXED ASSETS (BY SECTOR)

单位：万元 (10000 yuan)

行业	Sector	投资额 Investment 合计 Total	中央 Central	地方 Local	新增固定资产 Incremental Fixed Assets 合计 Total	中央 Central	地方 Local
总计	**Total**	**6705682**	**2782174**	**3923508**	**6931803**	**3870370**	**3061433**
农、林、牧、渔业	**Farming,Forestry,Animal Husbandry and Fishery**	**36193**	**264**	**35929**	**27910**	**8464**	**19446**
农业	Farming	11767		11767	7971		7971
林业	Forestry	16773		16773	3084		3084
畜牧业	Animal Husbandry	1231		1231	441		441
农、林、牧、渔服务业	FFAF Services	6422	264	6158	16414	8464	7950
采掘业	**Excavation**	**11741**		**11741**	**6744**		**6744**
煤炭采选业	Coal Mining and Dressing	2076		2076	859		859
黑色金属矿采选业	Ferrous Metals Mining and Dressing	9474		9474	5835		5835
铁矿采选业	Iron Mining and Dressing	9474		9474	5835		5835
非金属矿采选业	Nonmetal Minerals Mining and Dressing	191		191	50		50
土砂石开采业	Sand and Stone Mining and Dressing	191		191	50		50
制造业	**Manufacturing**	**877621**	**348986**	**528635**	**625549**	**277531**	**348018**
食品加工业	Food Processing	821		821			
屠宰及肉类蛋类加工业	Butcher, Meat and Egg	821		821			
食品制造业	Food Making	5316		5316	1972		1972
糕点、糖果制造业	Pastry and Candy	320		320	200		200
乳制品制造业	Diary Products	430		430	430		430
调味品制造业	Flavorings	2901		2901	197		197
其他食品制造业	Other Foods	1665		1665	1145		1145
饮料制造业	Beverage Making	31245		31245	30903		30903
酒精及饮料酒制造业	Alcohol and Beverage Wine	29795		29795	29453		29453
软饮料制造业	Soft Drink	1450		1450	1450		1450
烟草加工业	Tobacco Making	7301		7301			
纺织业	Textile Industry	7740		7740	18759		18759
棉纺织业	Cotton Textile	3271		3271	4660		4660
毛纺织业	Woolen Textile	1422		1422			
针织品业	Knitting Textile	2367		2367	13419		13419
其他纺织业	Others	680		680	680		680
服装及其他纤维制品制造业	Garments and Other Fiber Products	6907		6907	6652		6652
服装制造业	Garment Industry	5337		5337	5752		5752
制鞋业	Shoes Making	1570		1570	900		900
皮革、毛皮、羽绒及其制品业	Leather,Furs,Down and Related Products	11020		11020	6496		6496
制革业	Leather Making	1470		1470			
皮革制品制造业	Leathers and Related Products	9550		9550	6496		6496
木材加工及竹、藤、棕、草制品业	Timber Processing,Bamboo,Cane, Palm Fiber and Straw Products	2175		2175	4136		4136
人造板制造业	Artificial Board	1265		1265			

4-10 续表1 continued

单位：万元 (10000 yuan)

行业	Sector	投资额 Investment 合计 Total	中央 Central	地方 Local	新增固定资产 Incremental Fixed Assets 合计 Total	中央 Central	地方 Local
木制品业	Wooden Products	910		910	4136		4136
家具制造业	Furniture Industry	4512		4512	5578		5578
木制家具制造业	Wooden Furniture	3581		3581	4079		4079
金属家具制造业	Metal Furniture	47		47	671		671
其他家具制造业	Other Furniture	884		884	828		828
造纸及纸制品业	Papermaking and Paper Products	265		265	5165		5165
纸浆制造业	Paper Pulp	65		65	5165		5165
纸制品业	Paper Products	200		200			
印刷业、记录媒介的复制	Printing and Record Medium Reproduced	30766	11199	19567	35472	13951	21521
印刷业	Printing	30535	10968	19567	31328	9807	21521
记录媒介的复制	Record Medium Reproduced	231	231		4144	4144	
文教体育用品制造业	Stationery,Education and Sports Goods	8319		8319	2790		2790
文化用品制造业	Stationery	5186		5186	848		848
乐器及其他文娱用品制造业	Music Instruments and Other Stationery Goods	1768		1768	1762		1762
玩具制造业	Toys	1365		1365	180		180
石油加工及炼焦业	Petroleum Processing and Coking Products	66661	59478	7183	75825	75825	
原油加工业	Petroleum Processing	55867	55867		68977	68977	
石油制品业	Petroleum Products	3611	3611		6848	6848	
炼焦业	Coking Products	7183		7183			
化学原料及化学制品制造业	Raw Chemical Materials and Chemical Products	211333	187767	23566	131620	123234	8386
基本化学原料制造业	Elementary Raw Chemical Materials	5810		5810	1324		1324
化学肥料制造业	Chemical Fertilizer	621		621	621		621
有机化学产品制造业	Organic Chemical Products	184298	180324	3974	14279	10194	4085
合成材料制造业	Synthetic Materials	5338	4577	761	113040	113040	
专用化学产品制造业	Special Purpose Chemical Products	2474		2474	2157		2157
日用化学产品制造业	Daily Use Chemical Products	12792	2866	9926	199		199
医药制造业	Medical and Pharmaceutical Products	59089	20292	38797	49433	16961	32472
化学药品制剂制造业	Original Chemical Medicine	40249	13300	26949	39834	13000	26834
中药材及中成药加工	Raw Material and Products of Chinese Medicine	8153	2162	5991	2097		2097
生物制品业	Biological Products	10687	4830	5857	7502	3961	3541
化学纤维制造业	Chemical Fiber	2150	1770	380	2150	1770	380
合成纤维制造业	Synthetic Fibers	2150	1770	380	2150	1770	380
橡胶制品业	Rubber Products	2617		2617			
轮胎制造业	Tire	1250		1250			
橡胶板、管、棒材制造业	Board,Pipe and Stick Products	387		387			
其他橡胶制品业	Others	980		980			
塑料制品业	Plastic Products	2028		2028			
塑料薄膜制造业	Plastic Film	1628		1628			
塑料 板、管、棒材制造业	Board,Pipe and Stick Products	400		400			
非金属矿物制品业	Nonmetal Mineral Products	49641	6829	42812	33371	8583	24788
水泥制造业	Cement	17515		17515	6713		6713

4-10 续表2 continued

单位：万元 (10000 yuan)

行业	Sector	投资额 Investment 合计 Total	中央 Central	地方 Local	新增固定资产 Incremental Fixed Assets 合计 Total	中央 Central	地方 Local
水泥制品和石棉水泥制品业	Cement Products and Asbestos Cement Products	4355	1371	2984	1771	1421	350
砖瓦、石灰和轻质建筑材料制造业	Brick,Tile,Lime and Light Construction Material	17566	4823	12743	21277	6327	14950
玻璃及玻璃制品业	Glass and Glass Products	1089		1089	2295		2295
陶瓷制品业	Ceramics Products	2300		2300			
耐火材料制品业	Refractory Products	6181		6181	480		480
其他类未包括的非金属矿物制品业	Others	635	635		835	835	
黑色金属冶炼及压延加工业	Smelting and Pressing Ferrous Metals	39988		39988	26097		26097
炼铁业	Puddling	10543		10543	12337		12337
炼钢业	Steelmaking	868		868	238		238
钢压延加工业	Steel Pressing	28577		28577	13522		13522
有色金属冶炼及压延加工业	Smelting and Pressing of Nonferrous Metals	1626		1626	2968		2968
有色金属压延加工业	Nonferrous Metals Pressing	1626		1626	2968		2968
金属制品业	Metal Products	9393		9393	3114		3114
金属结构制造业	Metal Structure	48		48			
铸铁管制造业	Tube of Cast Iron	239		239	239		239
工具制造业	Tools	1031		1031			
集装箱和金属包装物品制造业	Container and Metal Cover	900		900			
建筑用金属制品业	Products for Construct Use	7175		7175	2875		2875
普通机械制造业	Ordinary Machinery	39445		39445	16085		16085
锅炉及原动机制造业	Boiler and Motive Machine	7655		7655	2833		2833
金属加工机械制造业	Metal Processing Machine	10528		10528	412		412
通用设备制造业	Universal Equipment	3076		3076	517		517
轴承、阀门制造业	Bearings and Valve	326		326	326		326
其他通用零部件制造业	Other Universal Components and Parts	13965		13965	11324		11324
铸锻件制造业	Casting and Malleation	3895		3895	673		673
专用设备制造业	Equipment for Special Purpose	26464	3475	22989	19517	926	18591
机电工业专用设备制造业	Equipment for Engine and Electricity	1529	1239	290	880	590	290
石化及其他工业专用设备制造业	Equipment for Petroleum and Other Sector of Industry	9382		9382	13411		13411
轻纺工业专用设备制造业	Equipment for Light-textile Industry	961		961	693		693
农、林、牧、渔,水利业机械制造业	Machines for Farming,Forestry, Animal Husbandry,Fishing and Irrigation	250		250			
医疗器械制造业	Medical Machines	3808		3808	4197		4197
其他专用设备制造业	Other Special Purpose Equipments	10534	2236	8298	336	336	
交通运输设备制造业	Transport Equipment	65327	36707	28620	30378	14608	15770
铁路运输设备制造业	Railway Transportation	12580	12014	566	9081	8815	266
汽车制造业	Motor Vehicles	22018		22018	14543		14543
航空航天器制造业	Aviation and Spaceflight	24246	24246		5793	5793	
交通运输设备修理业	Transport Equipment Repairing	6483	447	6036	961		961

4-10 续表3 continued

单位：万元 (10000 yuan)

行业	Sector	投资额 Investment			新增固定资产 Incremental Fixed Assets		
		合计 Total	中央 Central	地方 Local	合计 Total	中央 Central	地方 Local
电气机械及器材制造业	Electric Equipment and Appliances	20419	300	20119	14223	300	13923
电机制造业	Generator	1214		1214	1214		1214
输配电及控制设备制造业	Electricity Transmit,Distribution and Control Equipment	14520		14520	4288		4288
电工器材制造业	Electrical Appliances	600	300	300	300	300	
日用电器制造业	Daily Use Electrical Appliances	4085		4085	8421		8421
电子及通信设备制造业	Electronic and Telecommunication Equipment	148870	14203	134667	91219	18349	72870
通信设备制造业	Telecommunication Equipment	21793	1172	20621	2086	806	1280
广播电视设备制造业	Radio and Television Equipment	3281		3281	1001		1001
电子计算机制造业	Computer	23260	12408	10852	31925	17033	14892
电子器件制造业	Electronic Device	83617		83617	48313		48313
电子元件制造业	Electronic Cell	8027		8027	2629		2629
日用电子器具制造业	Daily Use Electronic Appliances	5765		5765	251		251
其他电子设备制造业	Other Electronic Machines	3127	623	2504	5014	510	4504
仪器仪表及文化、办公用机械制造业	Instruments,Meters,Cultural and Office Machinery	13393	5006	8387	10657	2664	7993
通用仪器仪表制造	General Instruments and Meters	5360	2677	2683	5487	903	4584
专用仪器仪表制造业	Special Purpose Instruments	3658	2102	1556	1537	652	885
电子测量仪器制造业	Electronic Survey Instrument	2288		2288	2524		2524
计量器具制造业	Measuring Implements	327	227	100	1109	1109	
钟表制造业	Horologium	360		360			
其他制造业	Other Manufacturing	830		830	609		609
工艺美术品制造业	Art Products	154		154	209		209
其他生产、生活用品制造业	Others	676		676	400		400
电力、煤气及水的生产和供应业	**Electricity,Gas and Water Production and Supply**	**591655**	**302177**	**289478**	**1391206**	**875358**	**515848**
电力、蒸气、热水的生产和供应业	Electricity,Steam and Hot Water Production and Supply	384200	302177	82023	1088845	875358	213487
电力生产业	Electricity Production	55435	50152	5283	45737	45642	95
电力供应业	Electricity Supply	265708	252025	13683	839945	829716	10229
蒸气、热水生产和供应业	Steam and Hot Water Production and Supply	63057		63057	203163		203163
煤气生产和供应业	Gas Production and Supply	124994		124994	66533		66533
煤气生产业	Gas Production	452		452			
煤气供应业	Gas Supply	124542		124542	66533		66533
自来水的生产和供应业	Water Production and Supply	82461		82461	235828		235828
自来水生产业	Water Production	60336		60336	193039		193039
自来水供应业	Water Supply	22125		22125	42789		42789
建筑业	**Construction**	**91733**	**40701**	**51032**	**96572**	**36445**	**60127**
土木工程建筑业	Civil Engineering Construct	78812	27980	50832	88549	28942	59607
房屋建筑业	Building Construction	64162	13330	50832	76849	17242	59607
铁路、公路、遂道、桥梁建筑业	Railways,Highways,Tunnels and Bridges Construction	10150	10150		8200	8200	
堤坝、电站、码头建筑业	Dikes and Dams,Power Station and Wharves	3500	3500		3500	3500	
其他土木工程建筑业	Other Civil Engineering Construction	1000	1000				
线路、管道和设备安装业	Lines,Pipelines and Equipments Installation	12921	12721	200	8023	7503	520

4-10 续表4 continued

单位：万元　　　　(10000 yuan)

行业	Sector	投资额 Investment 合计 Total	中央 Central	地方 Local	新增固定资产 Incremental Fixed Assets 合计 Total	中央 Central	地方 Local
线路、管道安装业	Lines and Pipelines Installation	9360	9360		4400	4400	
设备安装业	Equipments Installation	3561	3361	200	3623	3103	520
地质勘业、水利管理业	**Geological Prospecting and Water Conservancy**	**114078**	**1573**	**112505**	**18260**	**1523**	**16737**
地质勘察业	Geological Prospecting	360	360		570	570	
矿产地质勘察业	Minerals Prospecting	270	270		570	570	
工程地质勘察设计业	Geological Prospecting and Design	90	90				
水利管理业	Water Conservancy	113718	1213	112505	17690	953	16737
交通运输、仓储及邮电通信业	**Transportation,Storage,Posts and Telecommunications**	**1244291**	**880128**	**364163**	**1926857**	**1354551**	**572306**
铁路运输业	Railways	54728	54728		54874	54874	
公路运输业	Highways	342853		342853	560447		560447
汽车运输业	Motor Vehicles	342853		342853	560447		560447
航空运输业	Aviations	21046	20065	981	18239	16408	1831
航空客货运输业	Passenger and Freight Transportation	20065	20065		16408	16408	
交通运输辅助业	Transportation Subsidiary Services	125591	121030	4561	696339	691778	4561
公路管理及养护业	Highway Management and Maintenance	4561		4561	4561		4561
机场及航空运输辅助业	Airport and Logistics of Aviation	121030	121030		691778	691778	
仓储业	Storage	18031	4441	13590	16470	12563	3907
邮电通信业	Posts and Telecommunications	682042	679864	2178	580488	578928	1560
邮政业	Posts	9881	9263	618	6950	6950	
电信业	Telecommunications	672161	670601	1560	573538	571978	1560
批发和零售贸易餐饮业	**Wholesale,Retail Trade and Catering Services**	**81584**	**3784**	**77800**	**176813**	**90434**	**86379**
食品、饮料、烟草和家庭用品批发业	Wholesale of Food,Beverage, Tobacco and Family Use Goods	21994	1818	20176	45538	16651	28887
食品、饮料、烟草批发业	Food,Beverage and Tobacco	7190	1818	5372	18450	16651	1799
纺织品、服装和鞋帽批发业	Textile,Garments,Shoes and Hats	2077		2077			
日用百货批发业	Daily Use Goods	12177		12177	26288		26288
五金交电化工批发业	Hardware,Electrical Appliance and Chemical	550		550	800		800
能源、材料、机械和电子设备批发业	Wholesale of Energy,Materials Machine and Electronic Equipment	13572	206	13366	16180		16180
能源批发业	Energy	6708		6708	7730		7730
化工材料批发业	Chemical Materials	420		420	5300		5300
建筑材料批发业	Building Materials	5321		5321	2652		2652
金属材料批发业	Ferrous Materials	455		455	498		498
机械、电子设备批发业	Machine and Electronic Equipment	596	206	390			
再生物资回收批发业	Recovery of Reclaimed Materials	72		72			
其他批发业	Other Wholesale Trade	3606	1000	2606	79203	73063	6140
图书报刊批发业	Books,Newspaper and Magazines	492	492		334	334	

4-10 续表5 continued

单位：万元 (10000 yuan)

行业	Sector	投资额 Investment 合计 Total	中央 Central	地方 Local	新增固定资产 Incremental Fixed Assets 合计 Total	中央 Central	地方 Local
农业生产资料批发业	Agricultural Capital Goods	1906		1906	5440		5440
其他类未包括的批发	Others	1208	508	700	73429	72729	700
零售业	Retail Trade	40026	160	39866	34732	720	34012
食品、饮料和烟草零售业	Food,Beverage and Tobacco	9485		9485	9310		9310
日用百货零售业	Daily Use Goods	16842	160	16682	16060	720	15340
纺织品、服装和鞋帽零售业	Textile,Garments,Shoes and Hats	1538		1538	2074		2074
药品及医疗器械零售业	Medicines and Medical Instruments	572		572			
图书报刊零售业	Books,Newspaper and Magazines	223		223			
其他零售业	Others	11366		11366	7288		7288
商业经纪与代理业	Commercial Brokerage and Agencies	600	600				
餐饮业	Catering Trade	1786		1786	1160		1160
正餐	Dinner	1786		1786	1160		1160
金融、保险业	**Finance and Insurance**	**80290**	**80290**		**56179**	**56179**	
金融业	Finance	79418	79418		55303	55303	
中央银行	Central Bank	23552	23552		48986	48986	
商业银行	Commercial Bank	53802	53802				
其他非银行金融业	Other Non-bank Finance	2064	2064		6317	6317	
保险业	Insurance	872	872		876	876	
房地产业	**Real Estate**	**9149**		**9149**	**7568**		**7568**
房地产管理业	Management	9149		9149	7568		7568
社会服务业	**Social Services**	**1636668**	**38324**	**1598344**	**726416**	**32706**	**693710**
公共服务业	Public Services	1461526		1461526	638960		638960
市内公共交通业	Urban Public Traffic	233449		233449	138216		138216
园林绿化业	Gardens Afforest	20596		20596	15044		15044
环境卫生业	Environmental Sanitation	10139		10139	46572		46572
市政工程管理业	Municipal Engineering Management	1196811		1196811	438535		438535
其他公共服务业	Others	386		386	386		386
居民服务业	Resident Services	5189		5189	8155		8155
沐浴业	Bath	3500		3500	6692		6692
殡葬业	Funeral and Interment Services	882		882	120		120
旅馆业	Hotels	115794	16050	99744	40063	2547	37516
租赁服务业	Leasing	219	219		23200	23200	
旅游业	Tourism	8481	1793	6688	6010	221	5789
娱乐服务业	Recreation	18836		18836	240		240
信息、咨询服务业	Information and Consultancy	10271	9271	1000	2600		2600
其他类未包括的信息咨询服务业	Others	10271	9271	1000	2600		2600
计算机应用服务业	Computer Application	10188	9738	450	7188	6738	450
软件开发咨询业	Software Development Consultancy	10188	9738	450	7188	6738	450
其他社会服务业	Other Social Services	6164	1253	4911			
市场管理服务业	Market Management	1253	1253				
其他类未包括的社会服务业	Others	4911		4911			
卫生体育和社会福利业	**Health Care,Sports and Social Welfare**	**86524**	**33604**	**52920**	**88144**	**24623**	**63521**
卫生	Health Care	68629	28703	39926	63341	15951	47390

4-10 续表6 continued

单位：万元 (10000 yuan)

行业 Sector		投资额 Investment 合计 Total	中央 Central	地方 Local	新增固定资产 Incremental Fixed Assets 合计 Total	中央 Central	地方 Local
医院	Hospitals	59423	26264	33159	61663	15951	45712
卫生防疫站	Sanitation and Antiepidemic Stations	3810		3810			
妇幼保健所(站)	Maternity and Child Care Institutions	1678		1678	1678		1678
药品检验所(室)	Mediine Test	2439	2439				
其他医院	Other Hospitals	1223		1223			
体育	Sports	11334	4901	6433	16562	8672	7890
社会福利保障业	Social Welfare and Security	6561		6561	8241		8241
社会福利业	Social Welfare	6191		6191	8241		8241
其他类未包括的社会福利保障业	Others	370		370			
教育、文化艺术及广播电影电视业	**Education,Culture and Arts,Radio,Film and Television**	**632641**	**454695**	**177946**	**610977**	**486181**	**124796**
教育	Education	460605	355278	105327	456753	373306	83447
高等教育	Higher Education	376087	347642	28445	375209	358759	16450
中等教育	Secondary School Education	62442	5687	56755	65372	12036	53336
初等教育	Primary Education	6985		6985	6022		6022
特殊教育	Special Education	1450		1450			
其他教育	Other Education	13641	1949	11692	10150	2511	7639
文化艺术业	Culture and Arts	146776	79723	67053	123412	85046	38366
艺术	Arts	46404	46404		7276	7276	
出版	Publication	17945	17745	200	15060	14860	200
文物保护	Historical Relics Preservation	1002		1002	803		803
图书馆	Libraries	9448	2770	6678	7300	7300	
群众文化	Mass Culture	7142	3800	3342	5153	3623	1530
新闻	News	7004	7004		5901	5901	
其他文化艺术业	Others	57831	2000	55831	81919	46086	35833
广播电影电视业	Radio,Film and Television	25260	19694	5566	30812	27829	2983
广播	Radio	3583	262	3321	317	317	
电影	Film	4968	3080	1888	9323	6835	2488
电视	Television	16709	16352	357	21172	20677	495
科学研究和综合技术服务业	**Scientific Research and Polytechnical Services**	**473940**	**243405**	**230535**	**391914**	**179877**	**212037**
科学研究业	Scientific Research	241405	222946	18459	178304	171004	7300
自然科学研究	Natural Science	205826	195889	9937	140135	140135	
社会科学研究	Social Science	11660	11660		11737	11737	
其他科学研究	Others	23919	15397	8522	26432	19132	7300
综合技术服务业	Polytechnical Services	232535	20459	212076	213610	8873	204737
气象	Meteorology	1437	1237	200	1897	1697	200
地震	Earthquake	290		290	490		490
测绘	Map	3583	2685	898	898		898
技术监督	Technology Control	1338	939	399	1801	470	1331
环境保护	Environment Protection	195833		195833	195008		195008
技术推广和科技	Technology Spreading and Scientific	5869	3000	2869	1191		1191
工程设计业	Engineering Design	15482	12398	3084	10743	6706	4037
其他综合技术服务业	Others	8703	200	8503	1582		1582
国家机关、政党机关和社会团体	**Government Agencies,Party Agencies and Social Organizations**	**536503**	**330732**	**205771**	**639472**	**415893**	**223579**
国家机关	Government Agencies	426079	228695	197384	529871	317389	212482
政党机关	Party Agencies	72249	69362	2887	36243	36243	
社会团体	Social Organizations	38175	32675	5500	73358	62261	11097
其他行业	**Other Sectors**	**201071**	**23511**	**177560**	**141222**	**30605**	**110617**
企业管理机构	Administrative Organs of Enterprises	72406	23247	49159	81100	30501	50599
其他类未包括的行业	Others	128665	264	128401	60122	104	60018

4-11 全市基本建设投资额及新增固定资产(按行业分)

INVESTMENT IN CAPITAL CONSTRUCTION AND ITS INCREMENTAL FIXED ASSETS (BY SECTOR)

单位：万元 (10000 yuan)

行业	Sector	投资额 Investment			新增固定资产 Incremental Fixed Assets		
		合计 Total	中央 Central	地方 Local	合计 Total	中央 Central	地方 Local
总计	**Total**	**4469841**	**1822212**	**2647629**	**4959611**	**3180339**	**1779272**
农、林、牧、渔业	**Farming,Forestry,Animal Husbandry and Fishery**	**36193**	**264**	**35929**	**27910**	**8464**	**19446**
农业	Farming	11767		11767	7971		7971
林业	Forestry	16773		16773	3084		3084
畜牧业	Animal Husbandry	1231		1231	441		441
农、林、牧、渔服务业	FFAF Services	6422	264	6158	16414	8464	7950
采掘业	**Excavation**	**3188**		**3188**	**64**		**64**
黑色金属矿采选业	Ferrous Metals Mining and Dressing	3188		3188	64		64
铁矿采选业	Iron Mining and Dressing	3188		3188	64		64
制造业	**Manufacturing**	**394822**	**105967**	**288855**	**411041**	**219468**	**191573**
食品加工业	Food Processing	300		300			
屠宰及肉类蛋类加工业	Butcher, Meat and Egg	300		300			
食品制造业	Food Making	1785		1785	1145		1145
糕点、糖果制造业	Pastry and Candy	120		120			
其他食品制造业	Other Foods	1665		1665	1145		1145
饮料制造业	Beverage Making	1939		1939	1929		1929
酒精及饮料酒制造业	Alcohol and Beverage Wine	639		639	629		629
软饮料制造业	Soft Drink	1300		1300	1300		1300
纺织业	Textile Industry	3895		3895	18033		18033
棉纺织业	Cotton Textile	3171		3171	4660		4660
针织品业	Knitting Textile	44		44	12693		12693
其他纺织业	Others	680		680	680		680
服装及其他纤维制品制造业	Garments and Other Fiber Products	5428		5428	5578		5578
服装制造业	Garment Industry	4028		4028	4678		4678
制鞋业	Shoes Making	1400		1400	900		900
皮革、毛皮、羽绒及其制品业	Leather,Furs,Down and Related Products	7215		7215	3798		3798
皮革制品制造业	Leathers and Related Products	7215		7215	3798		3798
木材加工及竹、藤、棕、草制品业	Timber Processing,Bamboo,Cane, Palm Fiber and Straw Products	922		922	4136		4136
人造板制造业	Artificial Board	300		300			
木制品业	Wooden Products	622		622	4136		4136
家具制造业	Furniture Industry	4414		4414	4358		4358
木制家具制造业	Wooden Furniture	3530		3530	3530		3530
其他家具制造业	Other Furniture	884		884	828		828
造纸及纸制品业	Papermaking and Paper Products	265		265	5165		5165
纸浆制造业	Paper Pulp	65		65	5165		5165
纸制品业	Paper Products	200		200			
印刷业、记录媒介的复制	Printing and Record Medium Reproduced	19576	2931	16645	23529	5733	17796
印刷业	Printing	19345	2700	16645	19385	1589	17796
记录媒介的复制	Record Medium Reproduced	231	231		4144	4144	
文教体育用品制造业	Stationery,Education and Sports Goods	1018		1018	1645		1645

4-11 续表1 continued

单位：万元 (10000 yuan)

行业	Sector	投资额 Investment 合计 Total	中央 Central	地方 Local	新增固定资产 Incremental Fixed Assets 合计 Total	中央 Central	地方 Local
文化用品制造业	Stationery	221		221	848		848
乐器及其他文娱用品制造业	Music Instruments and Other Stationery Goods	797		797	797		797
石油加工及炼焦业	Petroleum Processing and Coking Products	23437	23437		53861	53861	
原油加工业	Petroleum Processing	23437	23437		53861	53861	
化学原料及化学制品制造业	Raw Chemical Materials and Chemical Products	20422	8167	12255	108907	108064	843
基本化学原料制造业	Elementary Raw Chemical Materials	400		400			
有机化学产品制造业	Organic Chemical Products	5405	5300	105			
合成材料制造业	Synthetic Materials	762	1	761	108064	108064	
专用化学产品制造业	Special Purpose Chemical Products	1258		1258	839		839
日用化学产品制造业	Daily Use Chemical Products	12597	2866	9731	4		4
医药制造业	Medical and Pharmaceutical Products	49800	18097	31703	41208	14623	26585
化学药品制剂制造业	Original Chemical Medicine	37012	13300	23712	36044	13000	23044
中药材及中成药加工	Raw Material and Products of Chinese Medicine	5484	2162	3322			
生物制品业	Biological Products	7304	2635	4669	5164	1623	3541
化学纤维制造业	Chemical Fiber	380		380	380		380
合成纤维制造业	Synthetic Fibers	380		380	380		380
橡胶制品业	Rubber Products	387		387			
橡胶板、管、棒材制造业	Board, Pipe and Stick	387		387			
塑料制品业	Plastic Products	400		400			
塑料 板、管、棒材制造业	Board, Pipe and Stick	400		400			
非金属矿物制品业	Nonmetal Mineral Products	19787	3281	16506	9829	3631	6198
水泥制造业	Cement	2062		2062	1400		1400
水泥制品和石棉水泥制品业	Cement Products and Asbestos Cement Products	4355	1371	2984	1771	1421	350
砖瓦、石灰和轻质建筑材料制造业	Brick,Tile,Lime and Light Construction Material	5744	1275	4469	5823	1375	4448
玻璃及玻璃制品业	Glass and Glass Products	1080		1080			
耐火材料制品业	Refractory Products	5911		5911			
其他类未包括的非金属矿物制品业	Others	635	635		835	835	
黑色金属冶炼及压延加工业	Smelting and Pressing Ferrous Metals	1249		1249			
钢压延加工业	Steel Pressing	1249		1249			
有色金属冶炼及压延加工业	Smelting and Pressing of Nonferrous Metals	1090		1090	1990		1990
有色金属压延加工业	Nonferrous Metals Pressing	1090		1090	1990		1990
金属制品业	Metal Products	8254		8254	2875		2875
金属结构制造业	Metal Structure	48		48			
工具制造业	Tools	1031		1031			
建筑用金属制品业	Products for Construct Use	7175		7175	2875		2875
普通机械制造业	Ordinary Machinery	30218		30218	13790		13790
锅炉及原动机制造业	Boiler and Motive Machine	3645		3645	1949		1949
金属加工机械制造业	Metal Processing Machine	6177		6177			
通用设备制造业	Universal Equipment	3031		3031	517		517
其他通用零部件制造业	Other Universal Components and Parts	13965		13965	11324		11324
铸锻件制造业	Casting and Malleation	3400		3400			
专用设备制造业	Equipment for Special Purpose	12971	2400	10571	7714	500	7214
机电工业专用设备制造业	Equipment for Engine and Electricity	500	500		500	500	
石化及其他工业专用设备制造业	Equipment for Petroleum and Other Sector of Industry	1800		1800	3830		3830
轻纺工业专用设备制造业	Equipment for Light-textile Industry	268		268			

4-11 续表2 continued

单位：万元 (10000 yuan)

行业	Sector	投资额 Investment			新增固定资产 Incremental Fixed Assets		
		合计 Total	中央 Central	地方 Local	合计 Total	中央 Central	地方 Local
农、林、牧、渔、水利业机械制造业	Machines for Farming,Forestry,Animal Husbandry,Fishing and Irrigation	250		250			
医疗器械制造业	Medical Machines	1955		1955	3384		3384
其他专用设备制造业	Other Equipments for Special Purpose	8198	1900	6298			
交通运输设备制造业	Transport Equipments	42322	28746	13576	14672	11383	3289
铁路运输设备制造业	Railway Transport	4053	4053		5590	5590	
汽车制造业	Motor Vehicles	8561		8561	3289		3289
航空航天器制造业	Aviation and Spaceflight	24246	24246		5793	5793	
交通运输设备修理业	Transport Equipments Repairing	5462	447	5015			
电气机械及器材制造业	Electric Equipment and Appliances	3466	300	3166	614	300	314
电机制造业	Electrical Machinery	314		314	314		314
输配电及控制设备制造业	Electricity Transmit,Distribution and Control Equipment	2552		2552			
电工器材制造业	Electric Appliances	600	300	300	300	300	
电子及通信设备制造业	Electronic and Telecommunication Equipment	124198	13837	110361	80112	18349	61763
通信设备制造业	Telecommunication Equipment	12856	806	12050	806	806	
电子计算机制造业	Computer	23260	12408	10852	31925	17033	14892
电子器件制造业	Electronic Device	81261		81261	43067		43067
电子元件制造业	Electronic Cell	1232		1232			
日用电子器具制造业	Daily Use Electronic Appliances	3162		3162			
其他电子设备制造业	Other Electronic Machines	2427	623	1804	4314	510	3804
仪器仪表及文化、办公用机械制造业	Instruments,Meters,Cultural and Office Machinery	7072	2811	4261	4804	2664	2140
通用仪器仪表制造	General Instruments and Meters	1647	482	1165	1123	903	220
专用仪器仪表制造业	Special Purpose Instruments	3658	2102	1556	1537	652	885
电子测量仪器制造业	Electronic Survey Instrument	1080		1080	1035		1035
计量器具制造业	Measuring Implements	327	227	100	1109	1109	
钟表制造业	Hirologium	360		360			
其他制造业	Other Manufacturing	652		652	609		609
工艺美术品制造业	Art Products	154		154	209		209
其他生产、生活用品制造业	Others	498		498	400		400
电力、煤气及水的生产和供应业	**Electricity,Gas and Water Production and Supply**	**508470**	**251069**	**257401**	**1291623**	**828368**	**463255**
电力、蒸气、热水的生产和供应业	Electricity,Steam and Hot Water Production and Supply	314715	251069	63646	1029982	828368	201614
电力生产业	Electricity Production	2612	2612		2190	2190	
电力供应业	Electricity Supply	260575	248457	12118	834842	826178	8664
蒸气、热水生产和供应业	Steam and Hot Water Production and Supply	51528		51528	192950		192950
煤气生产和供应业	Gas Production and Supply	122510		122510	63183		63183
煤气生产业	Gas Production	452		452			
煤气供应业	Gas Supply	122058		122058	63183		63183
自来水的生产和供应业	Water Production and Supply	71245		71245	198458		198458
自来水生产业	Water Production	56330		56330	189724		189724
自来水供应业	Water Supply	14915		14915	8734		8734

4-11 续表3 continued

单位：万元 (10000 yuan)

行业	Sector	投资额 Investment			新增固定资产 Incremental Fixed Assets		
		合计 Total	中央 Central	地方 Local	合计 Total	中央 Central	地方 Local
建筑业	**Construction**	**62663**	**33613**	**29050**	**76687**	**26862**	**49825**
土木工程建筑业	Civil Engineering Construct	52721	23871	28850	71385	22080	49305
房屋建筑业	Building Construction	41497	12647	28850	65864	16559	49305
铁路、公路、遂道、桥梁建筑业	Railways,Highways,Tunnels and Bridges Construction	6724	6724		2021	2021	
堤坝、电站码头建筑业	Dikes and Dams,Power Station and Wharves	3500	3500		3500	3500	
其他土木工程建筑业	Others	1000	1000				
线路、管道和设备安装业	Lines,Pipelines and Equipments Installation	9942	9742	200	5302	4782	520
线路、管道安装业	Lines and Pipelines Installation	9360	9360		4400	4400	
设备安装业	Equipments Installation	582	382	200	902	382	520
地质勘察业、水利管理业	**Geological Prospecting and Water Conservancy**	**38157**	**1573**	**36584**	**1523**	**1523**	
地质勘察业	Geological Prospecting	360	360		570	570	
矿产地质勘察业	Minerals Prospecting	270	270		570	570	
工程地质勘察设计业	Geological Prospecting and Design	90	90				
水利管理业	Water Conservancy	37797	1213	36584	953	953	
交通运输、仓储及邮电通信业	**Transportation,Storage,Posts and Telecommunications**	**276018**	**249988**	**26030**	**805227**	**792873**	**12354**
铁路运输业	Railways	25109	25109		35524	35524	
公路运输业	Highways	8386		8386	4161		4161
汽车运输业	Motor Vehicles	8386		8386	4161		4161
航空运输业	Aviations	14447	13466	981	11270	9439	1831
航空客货运输业	Passenger and Freight Transportation	13466	13466		9439	9439	
交通运输辅助业	Transportation Subsidiary Services	118692	117797	895	689640.	688745	895
公路管理及养护业	Highway Management and Maintenance	895		895	895		895
机场及航空运输辅助业	Airport and Logistics of Aviation	117797	117797		688745	688745	
仓储业	Storage	17529	3939	13590	15968	12061	3907
邮电通信业	Posts and Telecommunications	91855	89677	2178	48664	47104	1560
邮政业	Posts	9881	9263	618	6950	6950	
电信业	Telecommunications	81974	80414	1560	41714	40154	1560
批发和零售贸易餐饮业	**Wholesale,Retail Trade and Catering Services**	**60575**	**3784**	**56791**	**149787**	**90434**	**59353**
食品、饮料、烟草和家庭用品批发业	Wholesale of Food,Beverage, Tobacco and Family Use Goods	17140	1818	15322	39990	16651	23339
食品、饮料、烟草批发业	Food,Beverage and Tobacco	6990	1818	5172	18450	16651	1799
纺织品、服装和鞋帽批发业	Textile,Garments,Shoes and Hats	500		500			
日用百货批发业	Daily Use Goods	9600		9600	21540		21540
五金交电化工批发业	Hardware,Electrical Appliance and Chemical	50		50			
能源、材料、机械和电子设备批发业	Wholesale of Energy,Materials Machine and Electronic Equipments	9559	206	9353	14040		14040
能源批发业	Energy	6008		6008	7580		7580
化工材料批发业	Chemical Materials	420		420	5300		5300
建筑材料批发业	Building Materials	2470		2470	662		662
金属材料批发业	Ferrous Materials	455		455	498		498
机械、电子设备批发业	Machine and Electronic Equipments	206	206				

4-11 续表4 continued

单位：万元 (10000 yuan)

行业	Sector	投资额 Investment 合计 Total	中央 Central	地方 Local	新增固定资产 Incremental Fixed Assets 合计 Total	中央 Central	地方 Local
其他批发业	Others	2045	1000	1045	73763	73063	700
图书报刊批发业	Books,Newspaper and Magazines	492	492		334	334	
农业生产资料批发业	Agricultural Capital Goods	345		345			
其他类未包括的批发	Others	1208	508	700	73429	72729	700
零售业	Retail Trade	29445	160	29285	20834	720	20114
食品、饮料和烟草零售业	Food,Beverage and Tobacco	8287		8287	8712		8712
日用百货零售业	Daily Use Goods	13717	160	13557	7772	720	7052
纺织品、服装和鞋帽零售业	Textile,Garments,Shoes and Hats	1500		1500	1500		1500
药品及医疗器械零售业	Medicines and Medical Instruments	572		572			
图书报刊零售业	Books,Newspaper and Magazines	223		223			
其他零售业	Others	5146		5146	2850		2850
商业经纪与代理业	Commercial Brokerage and Agencies	600	600				
餐饮业	Catering Trade	1786		1786	1160		1160
正餐	Dinner	1786		1786	1160		1160
金融、保险业	**Finance and Insurance**	**80290**	**80290**		**56179**	**56179**	
金融业	Finance	79418	79418		55303	55303	
中央银行	Central Bank	23552	23552		48986	48986	
商业银行	Commercial Bank	53802	53802				
其他非银行金融业	Other Non-bank Finance	2064	2064		6317	6317	
保险业	Insurance	872	872		876	876	
房地产业	**Real Estate**	**9009**		**9009**	**7118**		**7118**
房地产管理业	Management	9009		9009	7118		7118
社会服务业	**Social Services**	**1387802**	**38134**	**1349668**	**550776**	**32706**	**518070**
公共服务业	Public Services	1275782		1275782	489990		489990
市内公共交通业	Urban Public Traffic	111801		111801	15187		15187
园林绿化业	Gardens Afforest	19614		19614	15044		15044
环境卫生业	Environmental Sanitation	10139		10139	46572		46572
市政工程管理业	Municipal Engineering Management	1133842		1133842	412801		412801
其他公共服务业	Others	386		386	386		386
居民服务业	Resident Services	5189		5189	8155		8155
沐浴业	Bath	3500		3500	6692		6692
殡葬业	Funeral and Interment Services	882		882	120		120
旅馆业	Hotels	55068	15860	39208	14109	2547	11562
租赁服务业	Leasing	219	219		23200	23200	
旅游业	Tourism	8005	1793	6212	5534	221	5313
娱乐服务业	Recreation	16916		16916			
信息、咨询服务业	Information and Consultancy	10271	9271	1000	2600		2600
咨询服务业	Consultancy Services						
其他类未包括的信息咨询服务业	Others	10271	9271	1000	2600		2600
计算机应用服务业	Computer Application	10188	9738	450	7188	6738	450
软件开发咨询业	Software Development Consultancy	10188	9738	450	7188	6738	450
其他社会服务业	Other Social Services	6164	1253	4911			
市场管理服务业	Market Management	1253	1253				
其他类未包括的社会服务业	Others	4911		4911			
卫生体育和社会福利业	**Health Care,Sports and Social Welfare**	**78168**	**30434**	**47734**	**83837**	**21973**	**61864**
卫生	Health Care	62232	25533	36699	59110	13301	45809
医院	Hospitals	53026	23094	29932	57432	13301	44131

4-11 续表5 continued

单位：万元 (10000 yuan)

行业	Sector	投资额 Investment			新增固定资产 Incremental Fixed Assets		
		合计 Total	中央 Central	地方 Local	合计 Total	中央 Central	地方 Local
卫生防疫站	Sanitation and Antiepidemic Stations	3810		3810			
妇幼保健所(站)	Maternity and Child Care Institutions	1678		1678	1678		1678
药品检验所(室)	Medicine Test	2439	2439				
其他医院	Other Hospitals	1223		1223			
体育	Sports	9397	4901	4496	16562	8672	7890
社会福利保障业	Social Welfare and Securation	6539		6539	8165		8165
社会福利业	Social Welfare	6169		6169	8165		8165
其他类未包括的社会服务业	Others	370		370			
教育、文化艺术及广播电影电视业	**Education,Culture and Arts,Radio,Film and Television**	**608471**	**451695**	**156776**	**601619**	**486181**	**115438**
教育	Education	455458	355278	100180	450726	373306	77420
高等教育	Higher Education	376087	347642	28445	375209	358759	16450
中等教育	Secondary School Education	58037	5687	52350	60087	12036	48051
初等教育	Primary Education	6985		6985	6022		6022
特殊教育	Special Education	1450		1450			
其他教育	Other Education	12899	1949	10950	9408	2511	6897
文化艺术业	Culture and Arts	127753	76723	51030	120081	85046	35035
艺术	Arts	46404	46404		7276	7276	
出版	Publication	17945	17745	200	15060	14860	200
文物保护	Historical Relics Preservation	1002		1002	803		803
图书馆	Libiaries	9448	2770	6678	7300	7300	
群众文化	Mass Culture	4142	800	3342	5153	3623	1530
新闻	News	7004	7004		5901	5901	
其他文化艺术业	Others	41808	2000	39808	78588	46086	32502
广播电影电视业	Radio,Film and Television	25260	19694	5566	30812	27829	2983
广播	Radio	3583	262	3321	317	317	
电影	Film	4968	3080	1888	9323	6835	2488
电视	Television	16709	16352	357	21172	20677	495
科学研究和综合技术服务业	**Scientific Research and Polytechnical Services**	**264285**	**233722**	**30563**	**189038**	**172546**	**16492**
科学研究业	Scientific Research	229781	213263	16518	170973	163673	7300
自然科学研究	Natural Science	194202	186206	7996	132804	132804	
社会科学研究	Social Science	11660	11660		11737	11737	
其他科学研究	Others	23919	15397	8522	26432	19132	7300
综合技术服务业	Polytechnical Services	34504	20459	14045	18065	8873	9192
气象	Meteorologe	1437	1237	200	1897	1697	200
地震	Earthquake	290		290	490		490
测绘	Map	3583	2685	898	898		898
技术监督	Technology Control	1338	939	399	1801	470	1331
环境保护	Environment Protection	825		825			
技术推广和科技交流服务业	Technology Spreading and Scientific Technical Exchanges	5869	3000	2869	1191		1191
工程设计业	Engineering Design	14945	12398	2547	10206	6706	3500
其他综合技术服务业	Others	6217	200	6017	1582		1582
国家机关、政党机关和社会团体	**Government Agencies,Party Agencies and Social Organizations**	**504788**	**328649**	**176139**	**599389**	**414065**	**185324**
国家机关	Government Agencies	397875	226612	171263	500885	315561	185324
政党机关	Party Agencies	72249	69362	2887	36243	36243	
社会团体	Social Organizations	34664	32675	1989	62261	62261	
其他行业	**Other Sectors**	**156942**	**13030**	**143912**	**107793**	**28697**	**79096**
企业管理机构	Administrative Organs of Enterprises	51308	12870	38438	72730	28697	44033
其他类未包括的行业	Others	105634	160	105474	35063		35063

4-12 全市更新改造投资额及新增固定资产(按行业分)

INVESTMENT IN INNOVATION AND ITS INCREMENTAL FIXED ASSETS (BY SECTOR)

单位：万元 (10000 yuan)

行业	Sector	投资额 Investment 合计 Total	中央 Central	地方 Local	新增固定资产 Incremental Fixed Assets 合计 Total	中央 Central	地方 Local
总计	**Total**	**1859435**	**959962**	**899473**	**1388694**	**690031**	**698663**
采掘业	**Excavation**	**5335**		**5335**	**4106**		**4106**
煤炭采选业	Coal Mining and Dressing	1276		1276	767		767
黑色金属矿采选业	Ferrous Metals Mining and Dressing	3868		3868	3289		3289
铁矿采选业	Iron Mining and Dressing	3868		3868	3289		3289
非金属矿采选业	Nonmetal Minerals Mining and Dressing	191		191	50		50
土沙石开采业	Sand and Stone Mining and Dressing	191		191	50		50
制造业	**Manufacturing**	**471282**	**243019**	**228263**	**206147**	**58063**	**148084**
食品加工业	Food Processing	521		521			
屠宰及肉类蛋类加工业	Butcher, Meat and Egg	521		521			
食品制造业	Food Making	3269		3269	827		827
糕点、糖果制造业	Pastry and Candy	200		200	200		200
乳制品制造业	Dairy Products	430		430	430		430
调味品制造业	Flavorings	2639		2639	197		197
饮料制造业	Beverage Making	29306		29306	28974		28974
酒精及饮料酒制造业	Alcohol and Beverage Wine	29156		29156	28824		28824
软饮料制造业	Soft Drink	150		150	150		150
烟草加工业	Tobacco Processing	7301		7301			
纺织业	Textile Industry	3571		3571	726		726
棉纺织业	Cotton Textile	100		100			
毛纺织业	Woolen Textile	1148		1148			
针织品业	Knitting Textile	2323		2323	726		726
服装及其他纤维制品制造业	Garments and Other Fiber Products	912		912	677		677
服装制造业	Garment Industry	912		912	677		677
皮革、毛皮、羽绒及其制品业	Leather,Furs,Eider Down and Related Products	3273		3273	1023		1023
制革业	Leather Making	1470		1470			
皮革制品制造业	Leather Products	1803		1803	1023		1023
木材加工及竹、藤、棕、草制品业	Timber Processing,Bamboo,Cane, Palm Fiber and Straw Products	1253		1253			
人造板制造业	Artificial Board	965		965			
木制品业	Wooden Products	288		288			
家具制造业	Furniture Industry	98		98	1220		1220
木制家具制造业	Wood Furniture	51		51	549		549
金属家具制造业	Metal Furniture	47		47	671		671

4-12 续表1 continued

单位：万元 (10000 yuan)

行业	Sector	投资额 Investment 合计 Total	中央 Central	地方 Local	新增固定资产 Incremental Fixed Assets 合计 Total	中央 Central	地方 Local
印刷业、记录媒介的复制	Printing and Record Medium Reproduced	9871	8268	1603	10621	8218	2403
印刷业	Printing	9871	8268	1603	10621	8218	2403
文教体育用品制造业	Stationery,Education and Sports Goods	7301		7301	1145		1145
文化用品制造业	Stationery	4965		4965			
乐器及其他文娱用品制造业	Music Instruments and Other Stationery Goods	971		971	965		965
玩具制造业	Toys	1365		1365	180		180
石油加工及炼焦业	Petroleum Processing and Coking Products	43224	36041	7183	21964	21964	
原油加工业	Petroleum Processing	32430	32430		15116	15116	
石油制品业	Petroleum Products	3611	3611		6848	6848	
炼焦业	Coking Products	7183		7183			
化学原料及化学制品制造业	Raw Chemical Materials and Chemical Products	190418	179600	10818	21520	15170	6350
基本化学原料制造业	Elementary Raw Chemical Materials	5410		5410	1324		1324
化学肥料制造业	Chemical Fertilizer	621		621	621		621
有机化学产品制造业	Organic Chemical Products	178893	175024	3869	14279	10194	4085
合成材料制造业	Synthetic Materials	4576	4576		4976	4976	
专用化学产品制造业	Special Purpose Chemical Products	918		918	320		320
医药制造业	Medical and Pharmaceutical Products	6904	2195	4709	8225	2338	5887
化学药品制剂制造业	Original Chemical Medicine	2040		2040	3790		3790
中药材及中成药加工	Raw Material and Products of Chinese Medicine	2669		2669	2097		2097
生物制品业	Biological Products	2195	2195		2338	2338	
化学纤维制造业	Chemical Fiber	1770	1770		1770	1770	
合成纤维制造业	Synthetic Fibers	1770	1770		1770	1770	
橡胶制品业	Rubber Products	2230		2230			
轮胎制造业	Tire Manufacturing	1250		1250			
其他橡胶制品业	Others	980		980			
塑料制品业	Plastic Products	1628		1628			
塑料薄膜制造业	Plastic Film	1628		1628			
非金属矿物制品业	Nonmetal Mineral Products	29854	3548	26306	23542	4952	18590
水泥制造业	Cement	15453		15453	5313		5313

4-12 续表2 continued

单位：万元 (10000 yuan)

行业 Sector		投资额 Investment 合计 Total	中央 Central	地方 Local	新增固定资产 Incremental Fixed Assets 合计 Total	中央 Central	地方 Local
砖瓦、石灰和轻质建筑材料制造业	Brick,Tile,Lime and Light Construction Material	11822	3548	8274	15454	4952	10502
玻璃及玻璃制品业	Glass and Glass Products	9		9	2295		2295
陶瓷制品业	Ceramics Products	2300		2300			
耐火材料制品业	Refractory Products	270		270	480		480
黑色金属冶炼及压延加工业	Smelting and Pressing of Ferrous Metals	38739		38739	26097		26097
炼铁业	Puddling	10543		10543	12337		12337
炼钢业	Steelmaking	868		868	238		238
钢压延加工业	Steel Pressing	27328		27328	13522		13522
有色金属冶炼及压延加工业	Smelting and Pressing of Nonferrous Metals	536		536	978		978
有色金属压延加工业	Nonferrous Metals Pressing	536		536	978		978
金属制品业	Metal Products	1139		1139	239		239
铸铁管制造业	Tube of Cast Iron	239		239	239		239
集装箱和金属包装物品制造业	Container and Metal Cover	900		900			
普通机械制造业	Ordinary Machinery	7409		7409	2295		2295
锅炉及原动机制造业	Boiler and Motive Machine	2192		2192	884		884
金属加工机械制造业	Metal Processing Machine	4351		4351	412		412
通用设备制造业	Universal Equipments	45		45			
轴承、阀门制造业	Bearings and Valve	326		326	326		326
铸锻件制造业	Casting and Malleation	495		495	673		673
专用设备制造业	Equipments for Special Purpose	12800	1075	11725	11110	426	10684
机电工业专用设备制造业	Equipments for Engine and Electricity	1029	739	290	380	90	290
石化及其他工业专用设备制造业	Equipments for Petroleum and Other Sector of Industry	7582		7582	9581		9581
医疗器械制造业	Medical Machines	1853		1853	813		813
其他专用设备制造业	Other Equipments for Special Purpose	2336	336	2000	336	336	
交通运输设备制造业	Transport Equipments	22125	7961	14164	14826	3225	11601
铁路运输设备制造业	Railway Transport	8527	7961	566	3491	3225	266
汽车制造业	Motor Vehicles	12577		12577	10374		10374
交通运输设备修理业	Transport Equipments Repairing	1021		1021	961		961

4-12 续表3 continued

单位：万元 (10000 yuan)

行业	Sector	投资额 Investment 合计 Total	中央 Central	地方 Local	新增固定资产 Incremental Fixed Assets 合计 Total	中央 Central	地方 Local
电气机械及器材制造业	Electric Equipment and Appliances	16053		16053	12709		12709
输配电及控制设备制造业	Electricity Transmit,Distribution and Control Equipments	11968		11968	4288		4288
日用电器制造业	Daily Use Electrical Appliances	4085		4085	8421		8421
电子及通信设备制造业	Electronic and Telecommunication Equipments	23782	366	23416	10141		10141
通信设备制造业	Telecommunication Equipments	8937	366	8571	1280		1280
广播电视设备制造业	Radio and Television Equipments	3281		3281	1001		1001
电子器件制造业	Electronic Device	2166		2166	4980		4980
电子元件制造业	Electronic Cell	6795		6795	2629		2629
日用电子器具制造业	Daily Use Electronic Appliance	2603		2603	251		251
仪器仪表及文化、办公用机械制造业	Instruments,Meters,Cultural and Office Machinery	5817	2195	3622	5518		5518
通用仪器仪表制造	General Instruments and Meters	3713	2195	1518	4364		4364
电子测量仪器制造业	Electronic Survey Instruments	704		704	1154		1154
其他制造业	Others	178		178			
其他生产、生活用品制造	Other Goods for Production and Life	178		178			
电力、煤气及水的生产和供应业	**Electricity,Gas and Water Production and Supply**	**81620**	**51108**	**30512**	**98018**	**46990**	**51028**
电力、蒸气、热水的生产和供应业	Electricity,Steam and Hot Water Production and Supply	67920	51108	16812	57298	46990	10308
电力生产业	Electricity Production	52823	47540	5283	43547	43452	95
电力供应业	Electricity Supply	3568	3568		3538	3538	
蒸气、热水生产和供应业	Steam and Hot Water Production and Supply	11529		11529	10213		10213
煤气生产和供应业	Gas Production and Supply	2484		2484	3350		3350
煤气供应业	Gas Supply	2484		2484	3350		3350
自来水的生产和供应业	Water Production and Supply	11216		11216	37370		37370
自来水生产业	Water Production	4006		4006	3315		3315
自来水供应业	Water Supply	7210		7210	34055		34055
建筑业	**Construction**	**11273**	**7088**	**4185**	**13768**	**9583**	**4185**
土木工程建筑业	Civil Engineering Construct	8294	4109	4185	11047	6862	4185
房屋建筑业	Building Construction	4868	683	4185	4868	683	4185

4-12 续表4 continued

单位：万元 (10000 yuan)

行业	Sector	投资额 Investment 合计 Total	中央 Central	地方 Local	新增固定资产 Incremental Fixed Assets 合计 Total	中央 Central	地方 Local
铁路、公路、遂道、桥梁建筑业	Railways,Highways,Tunnels and Bridges Construction	3426	3426		6179	6179	
线路、管道和设备安装业	Lines,Pipelines and Equipments Installation	2979	2979		2721	2721	
线路、管道安装业	Lines and Pipelines Installation	2979	2979		2721	2721	
设备安装业	Equipments Installation						
地质勘查业、水利管理业	**Geological Prospecting and Water Conservancy**	**75921**		**75921**	**16737**		**16737**
水利管理业	Water Conservancy	75921		75921	16737		16737
交通运输、仓储及邮电通信业	**Transportation,Storage,Posts and Telecommunications**	**658382**	**630140**	**28242**	**598062**	**561678**	**36384**
铁路运输业	Railways	29619	29619		19350	19350	
公路运输业	Highways	26221		26221	34363		34363
汽车运输业	Motor Vehicles	26221		26221	34363		34363
航空运输业	Aviations	6599	6599		6969	6969	
航空客货运输业	Passenger and Freight Transportation	6599	6599		6969	6969	
交通运输辅助业	Logistic Support for Transportation	5254	3233	2021	5054	3033	2021
公路管理及养护业	Highway Management and Maintenance	2021		2021	2021		2021
机场及航空运输辅助业	Airport and Logistics of Aviation	3233	3233		3033	3033	
仓储业	Storage	502	502		502	502	
邮电通信业	Posts and Telecommunications	590187	590187		531824	531824	
电信业	Telecommunications	590187	590187		531824	531824	
批发和零售贸易餐饮业	**Wholesale,Retail Trade and Catering Services**	**5442**		**5442**	**3312**		**3312**
食品、饮料、烟草和家庭用品批发业	Wholesale of Food,Beverage,Tobacco and Family Use Goods	200		200			
食品、饮料、烟草批发业	Food,Beverage and Tobacco	200		200			
能源、材料、机械和电子设备批发业	Wholesale of Energy,Materials Machine and Electronic Equipment	3941		3941	2140		2140
能源批发业	Energy	700		700	150		150
建筑材料批发业	Building Materials	2851		2851	1990		1990
机械电子设备批发业	Machine and Electronic Equipments	390		390			
零售业	Retail Trade	1301		1301	1172		1172
食品、饮料和烟草零售业	Food,Beverage and Tobacco	1198		1198	598		598
日用百货零售业	Daily Use Goods	65		65			

4-12 续表5 continued

单位：万元 (10000 yuan)

行业	Sector	投资额 Investment 合计 Total	中央 Central	地方 Local	新增固定资产 Incremental Fixed Assets 合计 Total	中央 Central	地方 Local
纺织品、服装和鞋帽零售业	Textile,Garments,Shoes and Hats	38		38	574		574
社会服务业	**Social Services**	**245858**	**190**	**245668**	**174312**		**174312**
公共服务业	Public Services	185744		185744	148970		148970
市内公共交通业	Urban Public Traffic	121648		121648	123029		123029
园林绿化业	Gardens Afforest	982		982			
市政工程管理业	Municipal Engineering Management	62969		62969	25734		25734
旅馆业	Hotels	60114	190	59924	25342		25342
卫生体育和社会福利业	**Health Care,Sports and Social Welfare**	**8356**	**3170**	**5186**	**4307**	**2650**	**1657**
卫生	Health Care	6397	3170	3227	4231	2650	1581
医院	Hospitals	6397	3170	3227	4231	2650	1581
体育	Sports	1937		1937			
社会福利保障业	Social Welfare and Security	22		22	76		76
社会福利业	Social Welfare	22		22	76		76
教育、文化艺术及广播电影电视业	**Education,Culture and Arts,Radio,Film and Television**	**23270**	**3000**	**20270**	**7758**		**7758**
教育	Education	4247		4247	4427		4427
中等教育	Secondary School Education	3505		3505	3685		3685
其他教育	Other Education	742		742	742		742
文化艺术业	Culture and Arts	19023	3000	16023	3331		3331
群众文化	Mass Culture	3000	3000				
其他文化艺术业	Others	16023		16023	3331		3331
科学研究和综合技术服务业	**Scientific Research and Polytechnical Services**	**207169**	**9683**	**197486**	**202876**	**7331**	**195545**
科学研究业	Scientific Research	11624	9683	1941	7331	7331	
自然科学研究	Natural Science	11624	9683	1941	7331	7331	
综合技术服务业	Polytechnical Services	195545		195545	195545		195545
环境保护	Environment Protection	195008		195008	195008		195008
工程设计业	Engineering Design	537		537	537		537
国家机关、政党机关和社会团体	**Government Agencies,Party Agencies and Social Organizations**	**28204**	**2083**	**26121**	**28986**	**1828**	**27158**
国家机关	Government Agencies	28204	2083	26121	28986	1828	27158
其他行业	**Other Sectors**	37323	10481	26842	30305	1908	28397
企业管理机构	Administrative Organs of Enterprises	16237	10377	5860	6164	1804	4360
其他类未包括的行业	Others	21086	104	20982	24141	104	24037

4-13 新增生产能力(或效益)
INCREMENTAL PRODUCTION CAPACITY(OR EFFICIENCY)

能力名称		Production Capacity		合计 Total	国有 State-owned	集体 Collective-owned
天然气管输	(公里)	Natural Gas Pipeline Carrying	(km)	103.0	103.0	
	(亿立方米／年)		(100 million cu.m/year)	2.0	2.0	
润滑油（综合能力）	(万吨／年)	Lube	(10000 tons/year)	5.0	0.0	
油罐容量	(万立方米)	Capacity of Oilcan	(10000 cu.m)	20.0	20.0	
锻压钢材	(万吨／年)	Smithing Steel Products	(10000 tons/year)	2.3	2.3	
输电线路长度	(11万伏及以上,公里)	Length of Transmit Electricity Line	(over 11,0000 volts,km)	412.1	412.1	
变电设备能力	(11万千伏安及以上)	Capacity of Transformer Equipments	(over 11,0000 volts)	565.5	565.5	
水泥	(万吨／年)	Cement	(10000 tons/year)	65.0	65.0	
家具	(万件／年)	Furniture	(10000/year)	1.3	1.3	
烧碱	(吨／年)	Caustic Soda	(ton/year)	100000.0	100000.0	
磷肥	(吨／年)	Phosphate	(ton/year)	5000.0	5000.0	
合成橡胶	(吨／年)	Synthetic Rubber	(ton/year)	30000.0	30000.0	
输液	(万瓶/年)	Infusion	(10000 bottles/year)	1000.0		
胶囊剂	(万粒/年)	Capsule	(10000/year)	3000.0		
其它内燃机制造	(台／年)	Other Internal Combustion Engine	(unit/year)	43000.0		
	(万千瓦／年)		(10000 kw/year)	245.0		
医疗器械制造	(台／年)	Medical Appliances	(unit/year)	500.0		
集成电路	(万块／年)	Integrated Circuit	(10000/year)	70.0		
微型电子计算机	(万部／年)	Micro-Computer	(10000/year)	200.0	200.0	
# 便携式微型计算机	(万部／年)	Portable	(10000/year)	21.0	21.0	
电子计算机外部设备	(台／年)	Outer Equipments of Computer	(unit/year)	2500000.0		
化学纤维	(吨／年)	Chemical Fibre	(ton/year)	1000.0		
# 合成纤维	(吨／年)	Synthetic Fibre	(ton/year)	1000.0		
其他乳制品	(吨／年)	Other Dairy Products	(ton/year)	12000.0	12000.0	
啤酒	(万吨／年)	Beer	(10000 tons/year)	8.8	8.8	
软饮料	(吨／年)	Soft Drink	(ton/year)	40000.0	40000.0	
瓶装（或罐装）饮用水	(吨／年)	Bottle(Canister)-packing	(ton/year)	40000.0	40000.0	
皮鞋	(万双／年)	Leather Shoes	(10000 pairs/year)	10.0	10.0	
服装	(万件／年)	Garment	(10000/year)	40.0		20.0
塑料制品	(万吨/年)	Plastic Products	(10000 tons/year)	0.2	0.2	
家用洗衣机	(万台／年)	Household Washing Machines	(10000/year)	10.0	10.0	
房间空气调节器	(万台／年)	House Air Conditioner	(10000/year)	15.0	15.0	
新建公路	(公里)	Highway New Built	(km)	99.0	99.0	

4-13 续表 continued

能力名称		Production Capacity		合计 Total	国有 State-owned	集体 Collective-owned
# 高速公路	(公里)	Express Highway	(km)	66.0	66.0	
一级公路	(公里)	First-grade Highways	(km)	31.0	31.0	
改建公路	(公里)	Reconstructed Highways	(km)	23.0	23.0	
# 一级公路	(公里)	First-grade	(km)	17.0	17.0	
# 二级公路	(公里)	Second-grade	(km)	6.0	6.0	
飞机购置	(架)	Plane Purchasing	(unit)	2.0	0.0	
候机楼	(座)	Waiting Building	(unit)	2.0	1.0	
	(平方米)		(sq.m)	327928.0	326500.0	
造林面积	(万亩)	Afforestation Area	(10000 mu)	19.1	19.1	
有效灌溉面积	(万亩)	Irrigated Areas	(10000 mu)	14.1	14.1	
粮食仓库	(万公斤)	Grain Storehouse	(10000 kg)	14988.0	14988.0	
	(平方米)		(sq.m)	41636.0	41636.0	
高等院校：学生席位	(个)	Institutions of Higher Education: Student Seats	(unit)	5585.0	5585.0	
建筑面积	(平方米)	Floor Space	(sq.m)	95703.0	95703.0	
中等院校：学生席位	(个)	Secondary Schools: Student Seats	(unit)	4758.0	4258.0	
建筑面积	(平方米)	Floor Space	(sq.m)	40563.0	37563.0	
小学校：学生席位	(个)	Primary Schools: Student Seats	(unit)	2180.0	2180.0	
建筑面积	(平方米)	Floor Space	(sq.m)	16006.0	16006.0	
其他学校：学生席位	(个)	Other Schools: Student Seats	(unit)	4750.0	4750.0	
建筑面积	(平方米)	Floor Space	(sq.m)	28677.0	28677.0	
公共图书馆藏书量	(万册(件))	Volumes of Public Libraries	(10000 volumes)	30.0	30.0	
阅览室座席	(个)	Seats of Reading Room	(unit)	200.0	200.0	
建筑面积	(平方米)	Floor Space	(sq.m)	2129.0	2129.0	
影剧院座席	(个)	Seats of Theatre	(unit)	700.0	700.0	
建筑面积	(平方米)	Floor Space	(sq.m)	4205.0	4205.0	
医院病床	(张)	Hospital Beds	(unit)	1502.0	1502.0	
宾馆旅馆招待所客房数	(间)	Guest Rooms of Hotels	(room)	357.0	269.0	88.0
	(平方米)		(sq.m)	22067.0	17800.0	4267.0
城市自来水供水能力	(万吨/日)	Urban Tap Water Supplying Capacity	(10000 tons/day)	30.0	30.0	0.0
城市自来水管道长度	(公里)	Length of City Tap Water Pipelines	(km)	66.0	66.0	
城市公共交通车辆购置	(辆)	Purchase of Public Traffic Vehicles	(unit)	1029.0	1029.0	
城市道路扩建长度	(公里)	Expanded Length of Highways	(km)	61.6	61.6	
城市道路扩建面积	(万平方米)	Expanded Area of Highways	(10000 sq.m)	227.7	227.7	
城市排水管道铺设长度	(公里)	Length of Paved Drainage Pipeline	(km)	7.4	7.4	
城市污水处理能力	(万吨/日)	Disposal Capability	(10000 tons/day)	59.5	59.5	
城市永久性桥梁	(座)	Perpetual Bridges	(unit)	27.0	27.0	

4-14 房屋建筑施工及竣工面积

FLOOR SPACE OF BUILDINGS UNDER CONSTRUCTION AND COMPLETED

单位：万平方米 (10000 sq.m)

项目	Item	2000	1999	占竣工面积(%) Proportion in Floor Space Completed(%) 2000	1999
施工总面积	**Floor Space of Buildings under Construction**	**6995.9**	**6556.5**		
竣工总面积	**Floor Space of Buildings Completed**	**2358.2**	**2321.4**	**100**	**100**
在竣工总面积中:	**Of the Floor Space Completed**				
按用途分	**Grouped by Use**				
# 厂房	Plant	93.9	72.4	4.0	3.1
仓库	Storehouse	19.0	19.1	0.8	0.8
办公室	Office	157.2	42.3	6.7	1.8
家属住宅	Families Residence	1098.1	1375.1	46.6	59.2
单身宿舍	Benchelor Quarters	40.0	25.7	1.7	1.1
教育用房	Education	63.5	68.8	2.7	3.0
科研用房	Scientific Research	22.3	36.5	0.9	1.6
医疗用房	Medical	15.8	27.0	0.7	1.2
商业营业用房	Commerce	88.1	86.6	3.7	3.7
礼堂、俱乐部	Assembly Hall and Club	4.2	3.6	0.2	0.2
影剧院	Theater and Cinema	0.4	2.0	0.0	0.1
托儿所、幼儿园	Nursery and Kindergarten	5.0	9.0	0.2	0.4
旅馆、招待所	Hotel	14.5	16.6	0.6	0.7
按隶属关系分	**Grouped by Administrative Relationship**				
中　央	Central	555.1	572.0	23.5	24.6
地　方	Local	437.5	540.9	18.6	23.3
# 国　有	State-owned	353.9	414.3	15.0	17.8
集　体	Collective-owned	32.8	63.2	1.4	2.7
房地产开发企业	Real Estate Development Enterprises	1365.6	1208.5	57.9	52.1
按地区分	**Grouped by Region**				
城　区	City Propers	448.8	430.7	19.0	18.6
近郊区	Near Suburbs	1324.6	1357.7	56.2	58.5
远郊区	Outer Suburbs	584.8	533.0	24.8	22.9

4-15 经济适用房

ECONOMIC AND SUITABLE HOUSES

项目 Item	合计 Total 2000	1999	# 住宅 Residence 2000	1999
完成投资 (万元) Investment Completed (10000 yuan)	479707	370959	379519	280415
施工面积 (万平方米) Floor Space of Buildings under Construction (10000 sq.m)	358.7	350.3	324.9	310.2
竣工面积 (万平方米) Floor Space of Buildings Completed (10000 sq.m)	195.7	129.1	176.0	122.9
竣工套数 (套) Suites of Rooms Completed (suite)	16575	12901	16575	12901
销售面积 (万平方米) Floor Space of Buildings Sold (10000 sq.m)	168.2	45.8	168.2	45.8
销售套数 (套) Suites of Rooms Sold (suite)	14924	4995	14924	4995
预售面积 (万平方米) Floors Space of Buildings Sold in advance (10000 sq.m)	108.2	53.8	108.2	53.8
预售套数 (套) Suites of Rooms Sold in advance (suite)	10964	5101	10964	5101

4-16 房屋建筑每平方米造价
COST PER SQ.M OF BUILDINGS

项目	Item	2000	1999	2000年比1999年增(+)减(-) Increase or Decrease
平均造价	**Average Cost**	2009	**1929**	**80**
# 厂房	Plant	2036	2111	-75
仓库	Storehouse	1541	1614	-73
办公室	Office	3125	2124	1001
家属住宅	Families Residence	1502	1452	50
单身宿舍	Benchelor Quarters	1687	1488	199
教育用房	Education	1607	2051	-444
科研用房	Scientific Research	2930	2105	825
医疗用房	Medical	2300	2577	-277
商业营业用房	Commerce	2371	2299	72
礼堂、俱乐部	Assembly Hall and Club	2473	4528	-2055
影剧院	Theater and Cinema	1895	3566	-1671
托儿所、幼儿园	Nursery and Kindergarten	1679	1548	131
旅馆、招待所	Hotel	2900	3336	-436

4-17 新建住宅竣工面积
FLOOR SPACE OF NEW RESIDENTIAL BUILDINGS COMPLETED

单位：万平方米 (10000 sq.m)

项目 Item		1949-2000 合计 Total	2000	占新建住宅面积(%) Proportion in Floor Space of New Residential Buildings(%) 合计 Total	2000
总计	**Total**	**18451.4**	**1499.7**	**100**	**100**
平房	Single-storey House	823.6	9.5	4.5	0.6
楼房	Storied Building	17627.8	1490.2	95.5	99.4
二～三层	2-3 Stories	958.5	42.3	5.2	2.8
四～五层	4-5 Stories	3254.4	72.1	17.6	4.8
六～八层	6-8 Stories	7936.7	546.1	43.0	36.4
九层以上	Over 9 Stories	5478.2	829.7	29.7	55.2
在总计中	**Of Total**				
城区	City Proper	3024.1	214.5	16.4	14.3
近郊区	Near Suburb	11984.6	863.4	65.0	57.6
远郊区	Outer Suburb	3442.7	421.8	18.6	28.1

4-18 农村集体及城乡私人建房面积
BUILDING CONSTRUCTION BY RURAL COLLECTED-OWNED UNITS,URBAN AND RURAL INDIVIDUALS

单位：万平方米、间 (10000 sq.m,room)

项目 Item		2000年 建成房屋面积 Floor Space of Buildings in 2000	#住宅面积 Floor Space of Residence	#住宅间数 Rooms of Residence	1999年 建成房屋面积 Floor Space of Buildings in 1999	#住宅面积 Floor Space of Residence	#住宅间数 Rooms of Residence
总计	**Total**	**797.4**	**491.2**	**409333**	**742.6**	**471.6**	**393000**
城镇私人建房	Urban Individuals	33.9	33.9	28250	35.6	31.6	26333
农村集体建房	Rural Collective-owned Units	763.5	457.3	381083	707.0	440.0	366667
非农户	Agriculture	313.0	83.8	69833	365.0	131.0	109167
农户	Non-agriculture	450.5	373.5	311250	342.0	309.0	257500

4-19 基本建设大中型项目一览表

单位：万元

建设项目名称 Construction Project	建设地址 Address	国民经济行业 Sector	隶属关系 Administrative Relationship	建设性质 Type of Construction	建设阶段 Stage	开工年月 Beginning Time	投产年月 Operating Time	计划总投资 Total Investment
总计								**5194477**
一、列入国家正式计划项目								**2135441**
北京供电公司"9950"工程	北京市	电力供应业	中央	扩建	施工	199712		127203
北京大学211工程	北京市	普通高等教育	中央	扩建	施工	199510		61206
清华大学211工程	北京市	普通高等教育	中央	扩建	施工	199612		42299
中国人民大学211工程	北京市	普通高等教育	中央	扩建	施工	199702		13246
北京科技大学211工程	北京市	普通高等教育	中央	扩建	施工	199706	200012	9212
北京师范大学211工程	北京市	普通高等教育	中央	扩建	施工	199810		7670
北方交通大学211工程	北京市	普通高等教育	中央	扩建	施工	199806		9044
中国农业大学211工程	北京市	普通高等教育	中央	扩建	施工	199701	200012	4100
北京林业大学211工程	北京市	普通高等教育	中央	扩建	施工	199705		5180
中国地质大学211工程	北京市	普通高等教育	中央	扩建	施工	199812		2417
北京邮电大学211工程	北京市	普通高等教育	中央	扩建	施工	199807		12000
北京大学医学部211工程	北京市	普通高等教育	中央	扩建	施工	199612		3150
北京理工大学211工程	北京市	普通高等教育	中央	扩建	施工	199612		31050
北京航空航天大学211工程	北京市	普通高等教育	中央	扩建	施工	199703	200009	19032
对外经济贸易大学211工程	北京市	普通高等教育	中央	单建	施工	199712	200002	2500
中国石油大学（北京）211工程	北京市	普通高等教育	中央	扩建	施工	199603	200003	8454
文化部文化设施建设管理中心天桥剧场翻修扩建工程	北京市	艺术	中央	扩建	施工	199611		19800
中央美术学院学院迁建工程	北京市	普通高等教育	中央	迁建	施工	199812		45470
北京市中央音乐学院附中迁建工程	北京市	普通高等教育	中央	迁建	施工	199812		20123
中国社会科学院中心图书馆工程	北京市	社会科学研究	中央	扩建	施工	200003		11449
北京大学第一医院外科病房楼工程	北京市	综合医院	中央	扩建	施工	200005		44600
北京市燃气集团有限责任公司陕北天然气进京市内工程	北京市	煤气供应业	市属	新建	施工	199602		390000
北京市自来水集团公司第九水厂扩建工程(三期)	北京市	自来水生产业	市属	扩建	施工	199712		291278
北京市公联公司南西北四环路	北京市	市政工程管理业	市属	新建	施工	199805		696500
华北电力集团公司顺义50万输变电工程	北京市	电力供应业	中央	新建	施工	199906		190284
民航华北局空中交通管理局北京区域管制中心	北京市	机场及航空运输辅助业	中央	新建	施工	200010		68174
二、列入国家收尾计划项目								**1535162**
首都机场扩建指挥部首都机场航站区扩建工程	北京市	机场及航空运输辅助业	中央	扩建	施工	199510	200012	872041
华能国际电力开发公司北京分公司华能北京电厂	北京市	火力发电业	中央	新建	收尾	199404		663121
三、未列入国家计划项目								**1523874**
北京市市政总公司高碑店污水处理厂二期工程	北京市	市政工程管理业	市属	扩建	施工	199711	200012	112000
文化部文化设施管理中心戏曲学院	北京市	普通高等教育	中央	新建	施工	199804	200008	37489
中国医学科学院北京协和医院扩建工程	北京市	综合医院	中央	扩建	施工	198509		53158
中国作家协会中国现代文学馆	北京市	社会团体	中央	新建	施工	199801	200012	15000
北京燕山石化有限公司丁基橡胶装置	北京市	合成橡胶制造业	中央	扩建	施工	199711	200012	109977
北京市首钢矿业公司水厂铁矿扩建	北京市	铁矿采选业	市属	扩建	施工	198612		299406
北京市首钢日电电子有限公司技术升级三期	北京市	集成电路制造业	市属	扩建	施工	199910		94400
北京地铁建设公司地铁复八线工程	北京市	轨道交通业	市属	新建	施工	198805		757174
北京市密云水库安全加固工程	北京市	水利管理业	市属	改建	施工	199808		45270

LARGE AND MEDIUM PROJECTS OF CAPITAL CONSTRUCTION

(10000 yuan)

本年计划投资 Planning Investment of this Year	自年初累计完成投资 Accumulative Investment Since Year-Beginning	建筑工程 Construction	安装工程 Installation	设备购置 Purchase of Equip-ments	本年新增固定资产 Incremental Fixed Assets	年初累计资金来源合计 Accumulative Fund Source Since Year-Beginning	建筑规模和新增生产能力(或效益) Construction Size and Incremental Productive Capital(or Benefit) 名称 Item	计算单位 Counting Unit	建设规模 Size	新增能力累计 Accumulative Incremental Capacity	# 本年 of this Year
839789	**859785**				**1410932**	**709392**					
648274	**637930**				**431720**	**562175**					
15000	14000				2641	14000	输电线路长	公里	283		
6743	6256				8699	5241					
5791	4154				34809	1625					
1366	1674				630	843					
8722	7980				9492	8517					
3510	3510				3510	3510					
7815	7815				7390	7815					
92	330				330	92					
1000	900				900	1000					
1389	652				652	1389					
4410	200					720					
315	315				315						
13586	13586				25111	13586					
5500	5380				7064	1500					
574	574				3074	274					
20	20				20	20					
4125	4125					4125	影剧院：座	个	1200		
12661	10111				85	12661					
5123	2972					5123	中等学校：	个	500		
5000	4289					2300					
2200	3496				500	2200	疗养院、所	张	531		
69000	57210				57726	59319	天然气管输	公里	340		103
30000	54844				188418	39124	城市自来水	万吨／日	50		25
400000	388565					331759	城市道路扩	公里	50		45
42232	42232				79754	41232	输电线路长	公里	244		44
2100	2740				600	4200					
61395	**78203**				**662166**	**38488**					
60695	77503				661176	38488	候机楼	座	1		1
700	700				990						
130120	**143652**				**317046**	**108729**					
24507	24507				108590		城市污水处理能力	万吨／日	50		50
6834	6834				40185	6834					
4026	3939					4026	医院病床	张	841		
2687	2687				17076						
1	1				108064		合成橡胶	吨／年	30000		30000
4600	3188				64	3188	铁矿开采	万吨／年	1050		
23610	44681				43067	44681					
60465	54425					50000					
3390	3390										

4-20 国家及北京市重点工程一览表

单位：万元

建设项目名称 Construction Project	国民经济行业 Sector	隶属关系 Administrative Relationship	建设性质 Type of Construction	建设阶段 Stage	开工年月 Beginning Time	投产年月 Operating Time	计划总投资 Total Investment
重大项目合计							**14322425**
一、基础设施项目							**8072542**
地铁“复—八”线工程	轨道交通	市属	新建	施工	198805		757174
陕甘宁天然气进京市内工程	煤气供应	市属	新建	施工	199602		390000
高碑店热电厂市内供热管网工程	蒸气热水	市属	新建	施工	199412		368032
第九水厂三期	自来水生产	市属	扩建	施工	199712		291278
北京城市电网建设、改造“9950”工程	电力供应	市属	扩建	施工	199512		740000
南中轴路（南三环--南四环）	市政工程管理	市属	新建	施工	200010		8300
酒仙桥污水处理厂	市政工程管理	市属	新建	施工	199905		57000
北京城市快速轨道交通工程	轨道交通	市属	新建	施工	199912		657000
南、西、北四环路工程	市政工程管理	市属	新建	施工	199912		696500
广安大街改扩建工程	市政工程管理	市属	改建	施工	200008		340000
中关村地区道路工程	市政工程管理	区属	改建	施工	199912		71300
清河污水处理厂及配套管线	市政工程管理	市属	新建	施工	200003		90170
路网加密工程	市政工程管理	区属	改建	施工	200005		123100
106国道北京段（京开高速公路）	汽车运输	市属	新建	施工	199903		271196
阿苏卫垃圾填埋场二期工程	环境卫生业	市属	扩建	施工	199912		12000
市区燃煤锅炉置换项目	环境保护	区属	改建	施工	199901		665000
西单基础设施改造工程	房地产开发	区属	改建	施工	199812		344000
德外大街改扩建工程	市政工程管理	市属	改建	筹建			87600
西外大街改造（西直门--紫竹桥）	市政工程管理	市属	改建	施工	200012		80000
永定河滞洪水库	水利管理	市属	扩建	施工	200011		83215
地铁五号线	轨道交通	市属	新建	施工	200009		1200000
地铁八通线	轨道交通	市属	新建	施工	200012		330000
第十水厂	自来水生产	市属	新建	筹建			270000
清河治理工程	水利管理业	市属	改建	施工	200009		54577
凉水河水系污水截留管线	市政工程管理	市属	扩建	施工	200012		51300
城市污水回用工程	市政工程管理	市属	扩建	施工	200004		33800
二、公共文化、科技、教育等大型公建项目							**4415535**
北京植物园展览温室	园林绿化业	市属	扩建	施工	199806		26000
中国银行总行大厦	金融业	中央	新建	施工	199608		300000
中国建筑文化中心	其它文化艺术	中央	新建	施工	199705	200010	36800
中华民族园二期	园林绿化业	区属	扩建	施工	199712		30000
首都图书馆新馆	图书馆	市属	新建	施工	199712		26000
中华世纪坛	其它文化艺术	市属	新建	施工	199903		41595
东方广场	房地产开发	区属	新建	施工	199409		1618500
北大生物城工程	生物制品业	中央	新建	施工	200007		80000
中关村西区改造	房地产开发	区属	新建	施工	200011		1000000
中关村软件园	软件开发咨询	区属	新建	筹建			180000
国家大剧院工程	艺术	中央	新建	施工	200004		360000
首都博物馆新馆	文物保护	市属	新建	筹建			115000
北京世界贸易中心	社会团体	市属	新建	筹建			440000
大学生公寓	房地产开发	市属	单建	施工	199910		150000
北京儿童医院门诊楼	专科医院	市属	扩建	施工	200009		11640
三、工业技改及土地开发项目							**674348**
数字技术开发中心和背投式大屏幕彩色电视机规模化	通信设备制造	市属	扩建	施工	200003		19940
太阳能利用产业化工程	玻璃制品业	市属	新建	施工	200009		19000
首钢日电电子有限公司技术升级	集成电路制造	市属	扩建	施工	199910		94440
广渠门外五厂搬迁		市属	迁建	筹建			500000
琉璃河水泥厂技术改造二期工程	水泥制造业	市属	扩建	施工	200007		40968
四.住宅开发项目							1160000
回龙观文化居住区	房地产开发	市属	单建	施工	199812		280000
天通苑住宅小区	房地产开发	区属	单建	施工	199904		240000
牛街危改小区二期	房地产开发	区属	单建	筹建			280000
西二旗住宅区	房地产开发	区属	单建	施工	200011		360000

MAJOR PROJECTS OF STATE AND BEIJING

(10000 yuan)

本年计划投资 Planning Investment of this Year	自年初累计完成投资 Accumulative Investment Since Year-Beginning	建筑工程 Construction	安装工程 Installation	设备、工器具购置 Purchase of Equipments and Implements	本年新增固定资产 Incremental Fixed Assets	建筑规模和新增生产能力(或效益) Construction Size and Incremental Productive Capital(or Benefit)				
						名称 Item	计算单位 Counting Unit	建设规模 Size	新增能力累计 Accumulative Incremental Capacity	# 本年 of this Year
2993836	**2453384**	**1029273**	**60926**	**244165**	**1198813**					
1998093	**1726413**	**707004**	**45902**	**149050**	**789193**					
60465	54425	17345	3026	7549		地铁	公里	13.5	1.8	
69000	57210	24897	1897	11708	57726	天然气管	公里	304.0	219.0	103.0
39170	48602	30407	85	77	80216					
30000	54844	37018	2817	5612	188418	自来水	万吨／日	50.0	50.0	25.0
44000	21917	13617		5300		输电线路	公里	294.0		
3800	2500	2500				城市道路	公里	2.4		
21691	26800	16503	440	8109		污水处理	万吨/日	20.0		
270000	48136	17936				轻轨铁路	公里	40.9		
400000	500205	318745				城市道路	公里	49.5	45.0	45.0
192620	341963	7000			165000	城市道路	公里	6.1		
40000	69920	38320			68620	城市道路	公里	13.0		
33400	22687	3610				污水处理	万吨／日	20.0		
64600	20180	6464			15180	城市道路	公里	8.5		
138400	115817	61817				高速公路	公里	42.2		
3000	3000	2400	100	200		垃圾处理	吨／日	2000.0		
126037	215669	56654	37537	110425	211997					
93000	23679	8288								
68000	4062	121				城市道路	公里	1.2		
52200	15430	1102			2000	城市道路	公里	2.0		
28500	7249					水库容量	亿立方米	0.5		
8185	1389	300		6		地铁	公里	27.7		
20000	3564			64	36	地铁	公里	18.0		
105000						自来水	万吨／日	50.0		
38225	33194	16394								
15000	8970	634				排水管道	公里	21.0		
33800	25001	24932				排水管道	公里	35.0		
544333	**447926**	**150674**	**14743**	**46875**	**52292**					
4000	3004	688	688	404						
120000	53802	18087	6560	26764						
12000	2000	2000			46086					
4000	1354	1269			5191					
5000	6678	6499				藏书量	万册（件）	400.0		
23883	17266	13923	90	2309						
120000	117323	57173	7405	17278						
9000	2623	1918		120	1015					
140000	143505									
300	289									
37750	41909	4948				坐席	个	6200.0		
10000										
6600										
50000	57411	43757								
1800	762	412								
153610	**58821**	**9768**	**281**	**48240**	**43067**					
10000	4000	3468								
23610	44681	2300	281	42100	43067					
100000										
20000	10140	4000		6140		水泥	万吨／年	60.0		
297800	220224	161827			314261					
38800	62379	44227			74261					
151000	151000	117600			240000					
42000	5800									
66000	1045									

4-21 房地产开发企业基本情况
BASIC INFORMATION OF REAL ESTATE DEVELOPMENT ENTERPRISES

项目	Item	企业单位个数(个) Number of Enterprises (unit)	资本金合计(万元) Total Capital (10000 yuan)	资产总计(万元) Total Assets (10000 yuan)	年末职工人数(人) Staff and Workers (year-end) (person)
总计	**Total**	**893**	**6275945**	**36828433**	**42837**
按企业登记注册类型分	**Grouped by Registration Status**				
内资企业	Domestic Investment Enterprises	624	2804220	20152426	28384
国有企业	State-owned	231	971449	11616448	14489
集体企业	Collective-owned	25	63984	531283	1592
联营企业	Joint Owned	4	4200	48420	88
股份合作企业	Share Holding	13	40323	246013	688
股份有限公司	Share Holding Corporations Ltd.	62	839691	2242182	3129
有限责任公司	Limited Liability Corporations	249	790001	4829139	6873
其他企业	Others	40	94572	638941	1525
港澳台商投资企业	Hongkong,Macao and Taiwan Funded Enterprises	181	2473115	12278541	10515
港澳台合资经营	Joint Venture	81	814822	3600218	3324
港澳台合作经营	Cooperative	96	1638383	8503364	7044
港澳台商独资企业	Hongkong,Macao and Taiwan Enterprises	3	19910	101817	146
港澳台商投资股份有限公司	Hongkong,Macao and Taiwan Funded Share Holding Corporations Ltd.	1		73142	1
外商投资企业	Foreign Funded Enterprises	88	998610	4397466	3938
中外合资经营	Joint Venture	31	401060	1620607	1981
中外合作经营	Cooperative	55	466550	2067121	1747
外资(独资)企业	Foreign Enterprises				
外商投资股份有限公司	Foreign Funded Share Holding Corporations Ltd.	2	131000	709738	210
按隶属关系分	**Grouped by Administrative Relationship**				
中央单位	Central	92	593798	3420759	4065
地方单位	Local	801	5682147	33407674	38772
按资质等级分	**Grouped by Grade**				
一级	First-grade	35	573586	7260033	6401
二级	Second-grade	58	320704	3065500	3721
三级	Third-grade	37	183806	1354534	1740
四级	Fourth-grade	4	6010	22774	80
五级	Fifth-grade				
无级	No-grade	748	5117590	24727385	30523
兼营	Part-time Operating	11	74249	398207	372
按营业状况分	**Grouped by Business Condition**				
营业	Going on	799	5840373	35456137	41201
停业	Closed down	15	97626	270269	321
筹建	Preparing to Establish	66	305125	1010531	1114
当年撤消	Cancel in this Year				
其他	Others	13	32821	91496	201

4-22 房地产开发企业开发情况
REAL ESTATE DEVELOPMENT

单位：万元,平方米 (10000 yuan,sq.m)

项目	Item	全市 合计 Total	# 国有企业 State-Owned	# 三资企业 Foreign Funded	按隶属关系分 Grouped by Administrative Relationship 中央单位 Central Unit	地方单位 Local Unit
计划总投资	Total Planned Investment	38396147	13072342	13489425	2593025	35803122
自开始建设至本年度累计完成投资	Accumulative Investment Completed from Beginning to the End of this Year	20438837	6279545	8845660	1564813	18874024
本年完成投资合计	Investment Completed This Year	5220737	1482066	1584871	377069	4843668
# 商品房建设投资	Commercial House	3328132	979883	972862	249689	3078443
土地开发投资	Land Development	292821	120466	55240	10747	282074
土地购置费	Purchase of Land	575796	129269	201850	72612	503184
本年完成投资按用途分	Grouped by Purpose of Investment Completed This Year					
住　宅	Residential Buildings	2882583	756486	696155	141664	2740919
办公楼	Office	452191	70558	272661	63720	388471
商业营业用房	Commerce	306195	53308	158522	54038	252157
其　他	Others	1579768	601714	457533	117647	1462121
本年土地开发	Land Development This Year					
完成开发土地面积	Land Space Developed	4601374	1667672	442867	7292	4594082
开发土地面积	Land Space under Development	2504553	1391135	246661	129800	2374753
购置土地面积	Land Space Purchased	5390349	1948639	789726	201596	5188753
房屋建筑施工和竣工面积	Floor Space of Buildings under Construction or Completed					
施工面积	Floor Space of Buildings under Construction	44550029	15082089	12743878	2595903	41954126
# 住　宅	Residential Buildings	29715204	10478503	6241679	1218307	28496897
竣工面积	Floor Space of Buildings Completed	13655990	5483776	3233926	637316	13018674
# 住　宅	Residential Buildings	10136624	4144022	1880136	360371	9776253
销售面积	Floor Space of Selling House	9568966	3816063	1897729	397212	9171754
# 住　宅	Residential Buildings	8982150	3695565	1548177	354954	8627196
# 个　人	to Individuals	7727084	3052892	1330560	270846	7456238
销售额	Sales	4707247	1445809	1660379	286629	4420618
# 住　宅	Residential Buildings	4093363	1385272	1200657	226379	3866984
# 个　人	to Individuals	3346298	1113871	947332	178182	3168116
平均销售价格	Selling Price	4919	3789	8749	7216	4820
# 住　宅	Residential Buildings	4557	3748	7755	6378	4482

主 要 统 计 指 标 解 释

全社会固定资产投资 固定资产投资是全社会固定资产再生产的主要手段。通过建造和购置固定资产的活动，国民经济不断采用先进技术装备，建立新兴部门，进一步调整经济结构和生产力的地区分布，增强经济实力，为改善人民物质文化生活创造物质条件。这对我国的社会主义现代化建设具有重要意义。全社会固定资产投资包括基本建设项目、更新改造项目、国有单位其他投资、城镇集体经济、联营经济、股份制经济、城镇私营经济、城镇个体经济、外商投资经济、港澳台投资经济及其他经济类型投资单位，各种经济类型的房地产开发企业、城镇和工矿区私人建房、农村投资。

基本建设项目 是指批准包括在一个总体设计范围内进行建设，由一个或若干个设计文件规定的有内在联系的单项工程所组成。经济上实行统一核算，行政上有独立组织形式，实行统一管理的基本建设单位。通常以一个企业、事业、行政单位或独立工程作为一个基本建设项目。包括（1）列入中央和各级地方本年基本建设计划的建设项目，以及虽未列入本年基本建设计划，但使用以前年度基本建设结转资金（包括基建库存设备和材料）在本年继续施工的建设项目；（2）本年基本建设计划内投资与更新改造计划内投资结合安排的新建项目和新增生产能力（或工程效益）达到大中型项目标准的扩建项目，以及为改变生产力布局而进行的全厂性迁建项目；（3）国有单位既未列入基建计划，也未列入更新改造计划的总投资在 50 万元及以上的新建、扩建、恢复项目和为改变生产力布局而进行的全厂性迁建项目，以及行政、事业单位增建业务用房和生活福利设施的项目。

更新改造项目 是指经有权单位批准，具有独立的设计文件或项目建议书，能独立发挥效益的工程。更新改造项目大体上相当于基本建设项目的单项工程。包括：（1）列入中央和各级地方本年更新改造计划的项目和虽未列入本年更新改造计划，但使用上年更新改造结转资金（包括库存设备和材料）；（2）本年更新改造计划内投资与基本建设计划内投资结合安排的对企、事业单位原有设施进行技术改造或更新的项目，和增建主要生产车间、分厂等其新增生产能力（或工程效益）未达到大中型项目标准的项目，以及由于城市环境保护和安全生产的需要而进行的迁建项目；（3）国有企、事业单位既未列入基建计划也未列入更新改造计划，总投资在 50 万元及以上的属于改建或更新改造性质的项目，以及由于城市环境保护和安全生产的需要而进行的迁建工程。

国有单位其他投资 是指国有单位按规定不列入基本建设计划和更新改造计划管理的，总投资在 50 万元及以上的投资。包括（1）用油田维护费和石油开发基金进行的油田维护和开发工程；（2）煤炭、铁矿、森工等采掘采伐业用维简费进行的开拓延伸工程；（3）交通部门用公路养路费对原有公路、桥梁进行的改造工程；（4）商业部门用简易建筑费建造的仓库工程。

城镇集体经济投资 是指包括县及县以上人民政府所在地建制镇地域内的城镇集体经济单位，总投资在 50 万元及以上建造和购置固定资产的投资。

房地产开发 包括各种经济类型的房地产开发公司、商品房建设公司及其他房地产开发单位统一开发的包括统建、代建、拆迁、还建的住宅、厂房、仓库、饭店、宾馆、度假村、写字楼、办公楼等房屋建筑物和配套的服务设施、土地开发工程，如道路、给水、排水、供电、供热、通讯、平整场地等基础设施工程的投资。包括非房地产企业实际从事房地产开发或经营活动，不包括单纯的土地交易活动。

城镇私营、个体经济投资 是指包括县及县以上人民政府所在地建制镇地域内的全部城镇私营、个体经济的固定资产投资。城镇私营经济投资包括总投资 2 万元及以上的建造和购置固定资产的投资；城镇个体经济投资包括总投资 2000 元及以上的建造和购置固定资产的投资。

零星固定资产投资 是指包括除基本建设项目、更新改造项目、国有单位其他投资、城镇集体经济投资以外的，总投资在 50 万元及以下的建造和购置固定资产的投资。

城镇和工矿区私人建房投资 是指包括市、县城、镇、工矿区所辖范围内的全部私人建房投资，不论其房主是否系本地常住户口均应包括。

农村投资 是指县及县以上人民政府所在地建制镇地域以外的全部农村固定资产投资。包括非农户投资和农户投资。非农户投资包括使用年限一年以上、单位价值 200 元以上的建造和购置固定资产的投资；农户投资包括使用年限一年以上、单位价值 50 元以上建造和购置固定资产的投资。

固定资产投资的资金来源 根据固定资产投资的资金来源不同，分为上年末结余资金、本年资金来源和各项应付款。本年资金来源包括国家预算内资金、国内贷款、债券、利用外资、自筹资金和其他资金来源六种。

国家预算内资金 分为财政拨款和财政安排的贷款两部分。包括中央财政的基本建设基金、专项支出、收回再贷、贴息资金，财政安排的挖潜革新改造和新产品试制支出、城建支出、商业部门简易建筑支出、不发达地区发展基金等基金中用于固定资产投资的自决；地方财政中由国家统筹安排的资金等。

国内贷款 指报告期企、事业单位向银行及非银行金融机构借入的用于固定资产投资的各种国内借款。国内贷款包括：银行利用自有资金及吸收的存款发放的贷款、上级主管部门拨入的国内贷款、国家专项贷款（包括煤代油贷款、劳改煤矿专项贷款等），地方财政专项资金安排的贷款、国内储备贷款、周转贷款等。

债券 是企业（公司）或金融机构通过发行各种证券筹集到的用于固定资产投资的资金，包括由银行代理国家专业投资公司发行的重点企业证券和重点建设证券。

利用外资 指报告期收到的用于固定资产建造和购置的境外资金。包括外商直接投资、对外借款（外国政府贷款、国际金融组织贷款、出口信贷、外国银行商业贷款、对外发行债券和股票）及外商其他投资（包括补偿贸易和加工装配中由外商提供的设备价款、国际租赁）。不包括我国自有外汇资金。国家统借统还的外资，是指由我国政府出面同外国政府、团体或金融组织签定贷款协议、并负责偿还本息的国外贷款。

自筹资金 指建设单位报告期收到的，由各地区、各部门及企事业单位筹集用于固定资产投资的预算外资金。包括中央各部门、各级地方和企事业单位的自有资金。股票是指股份制企业通过发行股票筹集到的用于固定资产投资的资金。

其他资金来源 指报告期收到的除以上各种资金之外其他用于固定资产投资的资金。包括社会集资、个人资金、无偿捐赠的资金及其他单位拨入的资金等。

固定资产投资按国民经济行业分 根据现有企业、事业、行政单位和基本建设项目建成投产后的主要产品或主要用途及社会经济活动性质来确定。基本建设按建设项目划分国民经济行业，一般情况下，一个基本建设项目只能属于一种国民经济行业；更新改造、国有经济单位其他投资、城镇集体、城镇私营、城镇个体经济根据整个企业、事业单位所属的行业来划分，一个企业、事业单位只能属于一种国民经济行业。

固定资产投资按建设性质分 建设项目的建设性质一般分为新建、扩建、改建、单纯建造生活设施、迁建、恢复、单纯购置。基本建设按建设项目划分建设性质，更新改造、国有单位其他投资、城镇集体、城镇私营、城镇个体按整个企业、事业单位的建设情况确定建设性质。

新建 一般是指从无到有、“平地起家”开始建设的单位或独立工程。有的单位原有基础很小，经过建设后其新增加的固定资产价值超过原有固定资产价值（原值）三倍以上的也算新建。

扩建 是指为扩大原有产品的生产能力（或效益）或增加新的产品生产能力，而增建主要生产车间（或主要工程）、独立的生产线、分厂的企业；行政、事业单位在原单位增建业务用房（如学校增建教学用房、医院增建门诊部或病房、行政机关增建办公楼等）也作为扩建。

改建 是指现有企业、事业单位不增建主要生产车间、分厂等，而对原有设施进行技术改造或更新为了技术进步（包括相应配套的辅助性生产、生活福利设施）的作为改建；为适应市场变化的需要，而改变企业的主要产品种类，或原有产品生产作业线由于各工序之间能力不平衡，为填平补齐充分发挥原有生产能力而增建不增加本单位主要产品设计能力的车间，也作为改建。

单纯建造生活设施 是指在不扩建、改建生产性工程和业务用房的情况下，单纯建造职工住宅、托儿所、子弟学校、医务室、浴室、食堂等生活福利设施。

固定资产投资按用途分 固定资产投资按用途分为农林牧渔业用、工业建筑业用、商业运输邮电业用、住宅和其他五部分，是研究不同用途的固定资产投资之间比例关系的重要指标。基本建设项目、更新改造限额以上项目、国有单位其他投资、城镇集体、城镇私营、城镇个体投资按单项工程确定，更新改造限额以下投资单位按项目确定。

固定资产投资按构成分 固定资产投资活动按其工作内容和实现方式分为建筑安装工程，设备、工具、器具购置，其他费用三个部分。

建筑安装工程（建安工作量） 指各种房屋、建筑物的建造工程和各种设备、装置的安装工程。包括各种房屋建造工程，各种用途设备基础和各种工业窑炉的砌筑工程；为施工而进行的各种准备工作和临时工程以及完工后的清理工作等；铁路、道路的铺设，矿井的开凿及石油管道的架设等；水利工程；防空地下建筑等特殊工程；以及各种机械设备的安装工程；为测定安装工程质量，对设备进行的试行工作。在安装工程中，不包括被安装设备本身的价值。

设备、工具、器具购置 指购置或自制达到固定资产标准的设备、工具、器具的价值，固定资产的标准按财务部门规定。新建及扩建单位的新建车间按照设计和计划要求购置或自制的全部设备、工具、器具，不论是否达到固定资产标准均计入“设备、工具、器具购置”中。

其他费用　指在固定资产建造和购置过程中发生的，除上述几项以外的各种应摊入固定资产的费用。它包括两种性质的费用，一种是属于增加固定资产的费用，主要有：建设单位管理费，土地、青苗等补偿费和安置补助费、勘察设计费，研究试验费、农林单位牲畜购置费、各种经济林木的营造费、办公和生活家具、器具购置费、引进技术和进口设备项目的其他费用、联合试运转费等；一种是属于不增加固定资产的费用，主要有：施工机械转移费、生产职工培训费、农业开荒费用及报废工程损失费等。

施工项目　指报告期内曾进行建筑或安装工程施工活动的建设项目。施工项目分为报告期正式施工项目、报告期收尾项目和以前年度全部停缓建项目。正式施工项目包括报告期内新开工项目、报告期以前开工跨入报告期继续施工的项目以及报告期施工过并在报告期内全部建成投产或停缓建的项目。

新增生产能力或工程效益　指通过固定资产投资活动而增加的设计能力或工程效益，它是用实物形态表示的固定资产投资的成果。新增生产能力的计算，是以能独立发挥生产能力或效益的单项工程（或项目）为对象。当建设项目（或单项工程）建成，经有关部门鉴定合格，正式移交投入生产，即可计算新增生产能力或工程效益。计算新增生产能力或工程效益有以下几种表现形式：1．以建设项目（单位工程）建成投产后的年产能力表示。如煤炭开采、石油开采等；2．以建设项目（单项工程）建成投产后处理原料的能力表示。如选矿工程的处理矿石能力，洗煤厂年洗原煤能力等；3．以新增的主要设备数量或容量表示。如棉纺锭数，发电机组容量等。4．以建筑物容积、容量、面积或长度表示。如水库容量、铁路公路里程等。

新增生产能力的数量一般按设计能力计算。设计能力是指设计文件中规定的在正常情况下能够达到的生产能力，而不论投产后的实际产量如何。以设备数量、建筑物容积、面积、长度等表示的新增生产能力（或工程效益），则按建成的实际数量计算。

城市基础设施投资　城市基础设施包括第二产业中的电力、煤气及水的生产和供应业；第三产业中的水利业、铁路运输、公路运输、管道运输、航空运输、邮电通信、公共服务和环境保护等。

房屋施工面积　是指报告期内施工的全部房屋建筑面积。包括报告期新开工的面积、报告期施工过并在报告期竣工的面积，以及以前年度已停建在报告期继续施工的面积。房屋建筑面积是从房屋外墙线算起的各层平面面积的总和，包括房屋结构（如柱、墙）占用的面积和地下室面积。多层建筑按各自然层面积总和计算，包括房屋内的楼隔层，突出墙面的眺望间、门斗、有柱雨罩的面积。不包括突出墙面结构的构件、艺术装饰等所占的面积，如台阶等。凹阳台、挑阳台按其水平投影面积一半计算建筑面积。

房屋竣工面积　指在报告期内房屋建筑按照设计要求已全部完工，达到住人和使用条件，经验收鉴定合格（或达到竣工验收标准），正式移交使用单位的建筑面积。

房屋面积竣工率　指一定时期内房屋竣工面积占同期房屋施工面积的比率。它是从房屋建筑施工速度的角度反映投资效果和建筑业经济效益的指标。

新增固定资产　指通过投资活动所形成的新的固定资产价值。包括已经建成投入生产或交付使用的工程价值和达到固定资产标准的设备、工具、器具的价值及有关应摊入的费用。它是以价值形式表示的固定资产投资成果的综合性指标，可以综合反映不同时期、不同部门、不同地区的固定资产投资成果。

建设项目投产率　指一定时期内全部建成投产项目个数占同期正式施工项目个数的比率。它是从建设项目建设速度的角度反映投资效果的指标。

Explanatory Notes On Main Statistical Indicators

Total Investment in Fixed Assets　Investment in fixed assets is essential for reproduction of fixed assets. By means of construction and purchase of fixed assets, more advanced technologies and equipments are adopted in the national economy, and new sectors are established, which promote the adjustment of economic structure and the regional distribution of production and enhance the economic strengths so as to provide the material conditions for improving people's livelihood. This is significant for speeding up the socialist modernization in China.Total investment in fixed assets includes projects of capital construction, replacement & innovation, other investment by the state-owned units, the investment by the urban collective units, the investment by the joint-owned units, the share holding units, urban private and individual units, the investment by the foreign funds and Hongkong, Macao and Taiwan units and other investment units, the investment of real estate development enterprises, personal house building in urban areas and the jurisdiction of city, and rural investment.

Investment in Capital Construction Capital construction refers to the new construction projects or extension projects and the related work of the enterprises, institutions or administrative units mainly for the purpose of expanding production capacity or improving project efficiency. It includes: (1) Projects listed in the capital construction plan of the central government and the local governments at various levels in current year as well as the on-going projects from previous years' plan of capital construction and carried forward the investment to this year (including the equipments and materials kept in stock of the capital construction); (2) New construction projects arranged in both the plan of capital construction and the plan of replacement & innovation; Extension projects with the newly increased production capacity (or project efficiency) up to the standard of a large and medium-sized project; and the projects of moving the whole factory to a new site so as to improve the distribution of productive forces; (3) New construction projects, extension projects or restoration projects with the total investment at and above 500 thousand RMB by the state-owned units, though listed neither in the plan of capital construction nor in the plan of replacement & innovation; the projects in the state-owned units of moving the whole factory to a new site so as to improve the distribution of productive forces; and the projects of additional business houses by the administrative units and institutions and welfare facilities by the administrative units.

Investment in Replacement & Innovation: Replacement & innovation refers to the renewal or technological upgrade of the original fixed assets by the enterprises and institutions as well as the corresponding supplementary projects and works (excluding major overhaul and maintenance). It includes: (1) Projects listed in the replacement & innovation plan of the central government and the local governments at various levels in current year as well as the on-going projects from previous years, replacement & innovation plan with the investment carried forward to this year; (2)Replacement or innovation projects arranged both in the plan of replacement & innovation and in the plan of capital construction; Extension projects(main workshops or a branch of the factory)with the newly increased production capacity (or project efficiency) below the standard of a large and medium-sized project; and the projects of moving the whole factory to a new site so as to meet the requirements of urban environmental protection or safe production; (3) Replacement or innovation projects with the total investment at and above 500 thousand RMB by the state-owned units, though listed neither in the plan of capital construction nor in the plan of replacement & innovation; Projects in state-owned units of moving a whole factory to new site so as to meet the requirements of urban environmental protection or safe production.

Other Investment by State-owned Units refers to investment by stated-owned units at and above 500 thousand RMB which not listed in capital construction and replacement & innovation plan. It includes: (1) Projects of oil fields maintenance and exploitation with the oil fields maintenance funds and petroleum development funds; (2) Opening and extending projects with the maintenance funds in coal, ore and other mining enterprises and logging enterprises; (3) Reconstruction of the original highways and bridges with the highway maintenance funds in the department of communications; (4) Construction of warehouses with the funds of simple construction in the commercial department.

Investment by Urban Collective Units refers to investment by urban collective units at and above 500 thousand RMB on building and purchasing fixed assets.

Investment in Real Estate Development includes the investment by the real estate development companies, commercial buildings construction companies and other real estate development units of various types of ownership in the construction of buildings, such as residential buildings, factory buildings, warehouses, hotels, guesthouses, holiday villages, office buildings, and the complementary service facilities and land development projects, such as road, water supply, water drainage, power supply, heating, telecommunications, land leveling and other infrastructures. It covers the activities of the non-real estate companies in real estate development or management, but excludes the activities in simple land transactions.

Investment by Urban Private and Individual Units refers to investment by all urban private and individual units. Investment by urban private units includes that at and above 20 thousand RMB on building and purchasing fixed assets and investment by urban individual units includes that at and above 2000 RMB on building and purchasing fixed assets.

Odd Investment in Fixed Assets refer to investment above 20 thousand RMB and below 500 thousand RMB on building and purchasing fixed assets except investment in capital construction, replacement & innovation, investment by state-owned units and urban collective units.

Investment in Personal House in Urban Area, Industrial and Mining Area refers to investment in personal house of city, county,town, industrial and mining area.

Rural Investment It includes investment by agricultural and non-agricultural households. Investment by non-agricultural households includes that on building and purchasing fixed assets which unit value at 200 RMB, using limits above one year. Investment by agricultural households includes that on building and purchasing fixed assets which unit value above 50 RMB, using limits above one year.

Sources of Funds for Investment in Fixed Assets are classified into: (a) balance of funds brought forward from the previous year, （b） subtotaled sources of funds in this year and （c） various payable funds. The subtotaled sources of funds in this year is further divided into six categories: state budgetary appropriation, domestic loans, bonds, foreign investment, self-raised funds, and others.

State Budgetary Appropriation are classified into financial allocations and loans, includes the central capital construction fund, special expenditure, reloans after drawn back, discount fund, funds from finance on innovation, new products development, city construction, simply construction of commercial department and development fund of developing area, funds overall arranged by state of local finance.

Domestic Loans refer to various funds borrowed by enterprises and institutions from banks and non-bank financial institutions during the reference period for the purpose of investment in fixed assets. Domestic loans include loans issued by bands from their self-owned funds and deposit, loans appropriated by higher responsible authorities, special loans by government（including loan for replacing petroleum with coal, special loan for reform-through-labor coal mines ）, loans arranged by local government from special funds, domestic reserve loan, and working loan, etc..

Bonds refer to funds raised by enterprises （companies ） or financial institutions through issuing various bonds for the purpose of investment in fixed assets, The bonds include Key Enterprise Bond and Key Construction Program Bonds issued by the banks on behalf of the state specialized investment companies.

Foreign Investment refers to foreign funds received during the reference period for the purpose of building and purchasing fixed assets, including direct investment, loans and other foreign investment, excluding self-owned foreign exchange. Foreign funds borrowed and managed by the government refer to foreign loan borrowed by the government from foreign government, organizations, or financial institutions under official agreements and the government is responsible for the repayment of the principal and the interests.

Self-raised Funds refer to extra-budgetary funds received by each region, department, enterprise and institution on investment in fixed assets, including self-owned funds of central departments, local enterprises and institutions. Stocks refer to funds raised by share holding enterprises through issuing stocks for the purpose of investment in fixed assets.

Other Funds Sources refer to funds received during the reference period which are not included in the above-mentioned source, including social fund raising, individual funds, contribution gratis and funds allocated by other units..

Investment in Fixed Assets by Sector The classification of construction projects by sector is determined by the major products or the purpose of the projects when they are put into use, and by the nature of their social economic activities. The investment in capital construction is classified according to construction projects, In general, one project only belong to one sector. While investment in replacement & innovation, other investment by state-owned units and urban collective, private and individual units are classified according to the sector which the whole enterprise or institution belongs to. In general, one enterprise or institution can only belong to one sector.

Investment in Fixed Assets by Type of Construction The investment projects in general can be classified into new construction, expansion, reconstruction, building living construction, moving away, purchasing and restoration. For capital construction the type of construction is determined by the project. For investment in replacement & innovation and for other investment by state-owned and collective-owned units, urban private and individual units, the type of construction is determined by the enterprise or the institution.

New construction in general refers to newly constructed units or independent projects; some of expansions are also considered as new constructions in the case that the value of the original fixed assets is quite small, and the value of increased fixed assets exceeds the original ones over three times,.

Expansion refers to construction of new major production workshop or projects, independent production line, or construction branch of a factory so as to increase the production capacity and efficiency of the original products. Newly constructed business houses in institutions and administrative organizations (such as the newly constructed teaching buildings in schools, clinics or bed building in hospitals, and office buildings in administrative organizations, etc.) are classified as expansions.

Reconstruction refers to technical upgrade and renewal of the existing equipment and technical conditions undertaken by enterprises and institutions for the purposes of technological advancement, improvement in product quality, enlarging variety of products, promoting new generation of products, reducing productive consumption and cost, promoting comprehensive utilization of resources, strengthening treatment of waste gas, wastewater and solid wastes, and safety in production, etc. through application of new technologies and techniques, use of new equipment and new materials (including accessory facilities for production or for living and welfare purposes). Construction of new workshops for easing the bottleneck limits rather than increasing production capacity is also considered as reconstruction.

Building Living Construction refers to Building welfare constructions such as residence, kingdergarden, schools, clinics, canteens and so on for staff and workers with no expansion,reconstruting productive projects and business buildings.

Investment in Fixed Assets by Industry can be classified into five fields, i. e. construction for FFAF; industry and construction; commerce,transportation,posts and telecommunications; residence and others, which reflects important proportions of investment among different industries. The industry of the investment in capital construction, replacement & innovation above quota, other investment in fixed assets by state-owned units, urban collective units, urban private and individual units is determined according to the individual projects. The industry of the investment in replacement & innovation below quota is determined according to the relevant projects.

Investment in Fixed Assets by Composition refers to the three major parts of investment activities, i. e. construction and installation, purchase of equipment and instrument, and other expenses.

Construction and installation (work load of construction and installation) refers to the construction of various houses and buildings and installation of various kinds of equipment and instruments, including construction of various houses, equipment foundations and industrial kilns and stoves, preparation in advance and clearing up afterwards for project construction, pavement of railways and roads, drilling of mines and putting up of oil pipes, construction for water conservancy, underground constructions for air defense and other special projects, installation of various machinery equipment, trial running for testing the quality of installation. The value of equipment installed is not included in the value of installation projects.

Purchase of equipment and instruments refers to the total value of equipment, tools, and vessels purchased or self-produced which come up to standards for fixed assets. Equipment, tools and vessels purchased or self-produced for new workshops by newly established or expanded units are categorized as "purchase of equipment and instruments" no matter whether they come up to the standards for fixed assets or not.

Other expenses refers to expenses on building and purchasing fixed assets except the above items, which consist of two categories: one results in the increase of fixed assets, including administration expenses of construction units, compensation for the loss of land and young crops, subsidies for moving, and expenses on geological prospecting and designing, research and testing, purchase of animals by agricultural and forestry units, planting and operating of various economic forest, purchase of office and home furniture, purchase of instruments and vessels, introduction of technology and imports of equipment, and joint trial running; the other does not result in the increase of fixed assets, including expenses on transportation of construction machines, training of staff and workers , opening up waste land, and loss of discarded projects.

Projects under Construction refer to projects having construction and installation activities undertaken in the reference period, including projects under construction or winding up in the reference period, stop or delayed from previous period. Projects under construction including those started in the reference period, or continued from previous period, or completed and put into production or suspended in the reference period.

Newly Increased Production Capacity or Project Efficiency refers to the increase of designed capacity and project efficiency through investment in fixed assets, which reflects the accomplishment of investment in fixed assets in kind. The statistics of newly increased production capacity is based on individual project with possibility of operating independently. A project is counted as newly increased production capacity when it is completed and checked and accepted and put into use. The newly increased production capacity and project efficiency are usually expressed in one of the following terms: (1) annual production capacity , such as extraction of coal and petroleum;(2)raw material processing capacity, such as ore dressing capacity of ore dressing projects, the dressing, capacity of a coal washer; (3) number or capacity of major equipment increased, such as the number of cotton spindles increased and the capacity of generating sets increased;(4)physical measures of construction, such as volume, capacity, area, and length, for instance, the capacity of reservoirs, the length of railways or highways.

Newly increased production capacity in terms of quantity is calculated at designed capacity in general, which refers to the production capacity or project efficiency of a project under normal conditions supposed in construction documents regardless of the actual output.

Investment in urban infrastructure facilities include the production and supply of electricity, gas and tap water in the secondary industry and water conservancy, railway transportation, highway transportation, pipeline transportation, air transportation, posts and telecommunications, public services, environmental protection in the tertiary industry.

Floor Space of Buildings under Construction refers to total floor of buildings under construction, including those of buildings started in the reference period, or continued from previous period, constructed and completed in the reference period and reconstruction in the reference period. It is total of each story of buildings calculated from the outside line of building walls, including the space occupied by constructions like pillars or walls and basements. The floor space of space of multi-story building is the totaled floor space of each story, including area occupied by separating walls, watching rooms, doorways, and pillars, excluding protruding wall structures, artistic decoration, etc.(for example, flight of steps). The space of porch and balcony is counted by half of the projection area.

Floor Space of Buildings Completed refers to the total floor space of the completed buildings, which have met the designed using or living conditions, passed the check and accepted by the users in the reference period.

Percentage of Floor Space of Buildings Completed refers to the ratio of the floor space of buildings completed to the floor space of buildings under construction in the same period, which reflects the investment result and economic efficiency of the construction industry from the point of the construction speed.

Incremental Fixed Assets refer to the newly increased value of fixed assets through investment, including the value of projects completed and put into use, the value of equipment, tool and vessels considered as fixed assets as well as the relevant expenses accounted as investment in fixed assets. This is a comprehensive indicator of investment in fixed assets, reflecting the achievements of investment in fixed assets in given periods, given sectors or given regions.

Rate of Construction Projects Put into Use refers to the ratio of the number of construction projects completed and put into use to the number of projects under construction in the same period, which reflects the investment efficiency from the point of the construction speed.

农业及农村经济 5

AGRICULTURE AND RURAL ECONOMY

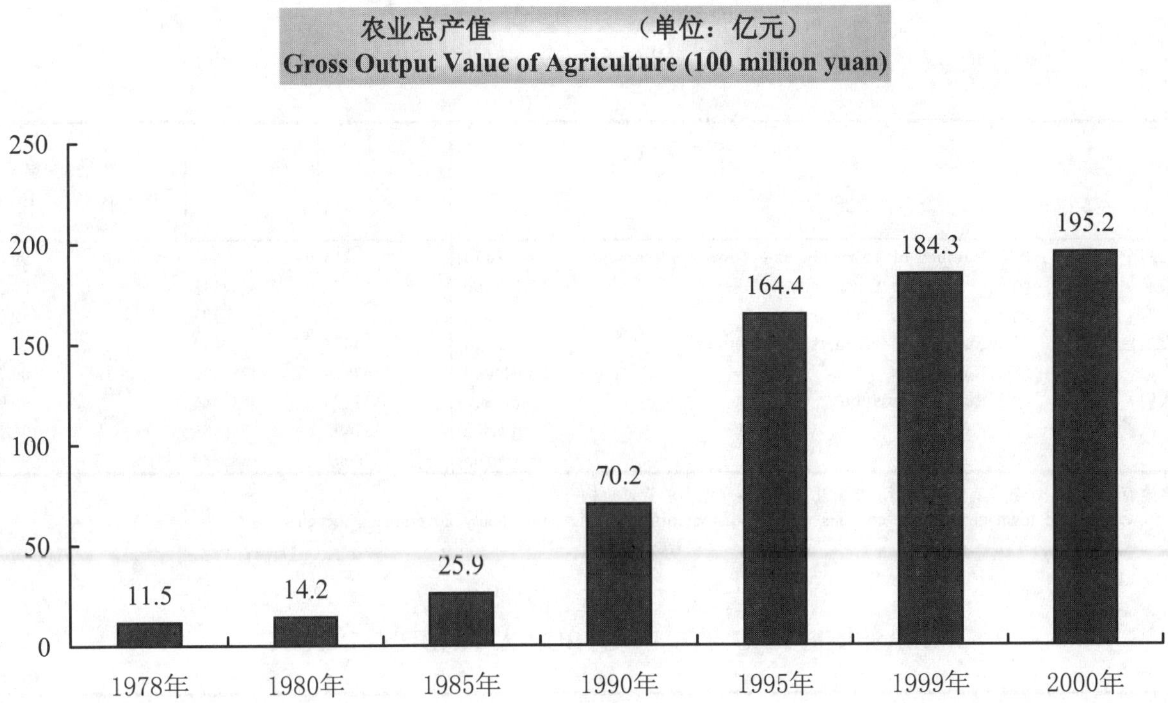
农业总产值 （单位：亿元）
Gross Output Value of Agriculture (100 million yuan)
250
200
150
100
50
0
11.5
14.2
25.9
70.2
164.4
184.3
195.2
1978年
1980年
1985年
1990年
1995年
1999年
2000年

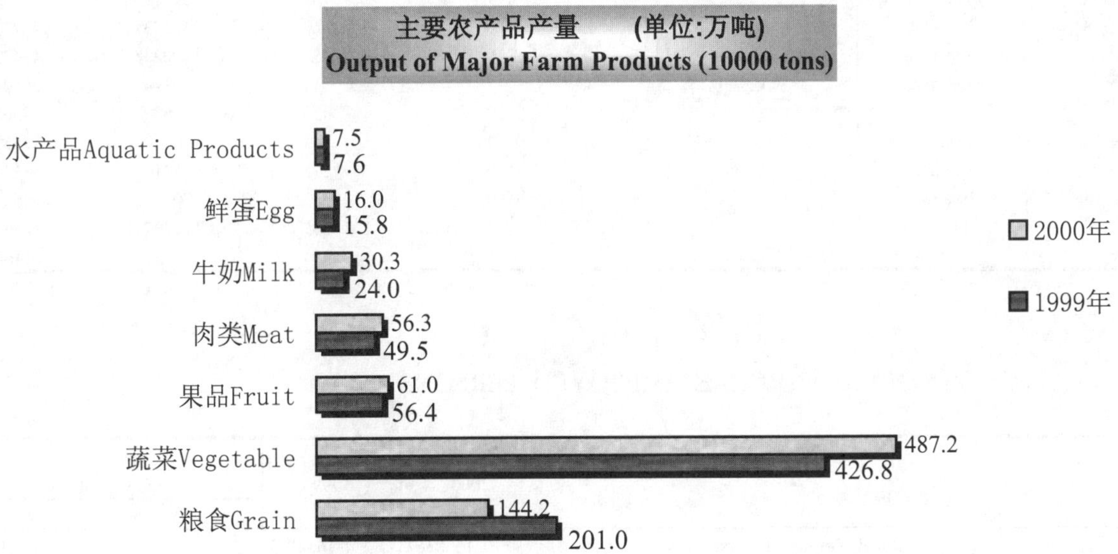
主要农产品产量 (单位:万吨)
Output of Major Farm Products (10000 tons)
水产品Aquatic Products
7.5
7.6
鲜蛋Egg
16.0
15.8
牛奶Milk
30.3
24.0
肉类Meat
56.3
49.5
果品Fruit
61.0
56.4
蔬菜Vegetable
487.2
426.8
粮食Grain
144.2
201.0
2000年
1999年

5-1 农 村 基 层 组 织 情 况
RURAL GRASSROOTS UNITS

项 目 Item				2000	1999	2000年为1999年% 2000 as % of 1999
乡镇政府个数	**(个)**	**Number of Township and Town Governments**	**(unit)**	**215**	**239**	**90.0**
乡政府	(个)	Township Governments	(unit)	71	118	60.2
镇政府	(个)	Town Governments	(unit)	144	121	119.0
村民委员会个数	**(个)**	**Number of Villagers' Committees**	**(unit)**	**4043**	**4043**	
乡村户数	**(户)**	**Households**	**(household)**	**1267975**	**1259270**	**100.7**
乡村人口	**(人)**	**Rural Population**	**(person)**	**3637493**	**3639366**	**99.9**
男	(人)	Male	(person)	1757492	1755986	100.1
女	(人)	Female	(person)	1880001	1883380	99.8

注：乡政府、镇政府个数含有农村的街道办事处和区县政府派出的管理机构。
Note: Township and town government contains rural subdistrict offices,district and county government agencies.

5-2 郊区县基层组织情况
GRASSROOTS UNITS IN SUBURBS AND COUNTIES

单位：个 (unit)

项 目	Item	乡 政 府 Township Government	镇 政 府 Town Government	村民委员会 Villagers' Committee	乡村户数 (户) Rural Household (household)	乡村人口 (人) Rural Population (person)
全 市	**Total**	**71**	**144**	**4043**	**1267975**	**3637493**
朝 阳 区	Chaoyang	24		169	90692	213076
丰 台 区	Fengtai	6		81	60672	155199
石景山区	Shijingshan	1		12	7084	15836
海 淀 区	Haidian	10	1	79	58933	145308
门头沟区	Mentougou	1	9	189	34572	95638
房 山 区	Fangshan	8	20	463	163673	487719
通 州 区	Tongzhou	1	18	483	149023	414736
昌 平 区	Changping		17	313	96144	268076
顺 义 区	Shunyi		19	426	135682	423027
大 兴 县	Daxing		14	547	116418	385596
平 谷 县	Pinggu	5	12	275	96310	313757
怀 柔 县	Huairou	5	10	287	70134	186278
密 云 县	Miyun	6	13	345	112707	321625
延 庆 县	Yanqing	4	11	374	75931	211622

5-3 乡 村 从 业 人 员
RURAL EMPLOYED PERSONS

单位：人 (person)

项 目	Item	2000	1999	构 成 (%) Composition(%) 2000	1999
乡村从业人员	**Rural Employed Persons**	**1658367**	**1652709**	**100**	**100**
# 种植业	Planting	534683	572041	32.3	34.6
林 业	Forestry	61848	48984	3.7	3.0
牧 业	Animal Husbandry	88185	77777	5.3	4.7
渔 业	Fishery	11985	12032	0.7	0.7
农村工业	Industry	335184	348580	20.2	21.1
乡镇工业	Township and Town Industry	118164	132736	7.1	8.0
村及村以下工业	Industry at Village Level and below	217020	215844	13.1	13.1
农村建筑业	Construction	139405	127270	8.4	7.7
农村运输业	Transportation	132516	118797	8.4	7.2
农村商业、饮食业	Commerce and Catering	121495	102991	7.3	6.2

5-4 郊区县乡村从业人员

RURAL EMPLOYED PERSONS IN SUBURBS AND COUNTIES

单位：人 (person)

项目 Item		从业人员 Employed Persons 2000	1999	# 种植业从业人员 Employed Persons of Planting 2000	1999
全市	**Total**	**1658367**	**1652709**	**696701**	**710834**
朝阳区	Chaoyang	97376	90957	19119	18432
丰台区	Fengtai	72542	71394	19861	18303
石景山区	Shijingshan	7007	7638	1186	1281
海淀区	Haidian	54121	61383	11041	15299
门头沟区	Mentougou	42332	43210	12916	11729
房山区	Fangshan	223141	213154	77297	78131
通州区	Tongzhou	183734	184599	80316	82852
昌平区	Changping	118524	118142	45544	47761
顺义区	Shunyi	184199	189018	58347	62788
大兴县	Daxing	195532	191692	124309	127421
平谷县	Pinggu	150456	149169	81568	79235
怀柔县	Huairou	81885	81752	36432	36330
密云县	Miyun	154363	156813	76389	78604
延庆县	Yanqing	93155	93788	52376	52668

5-5 郊区国内生产总值

GROSS DOMESTIC PRODUCT OF SUBURBS

单位：万元 (10000 yuan)

项目 Item		2000	1999	2000年为1999年% 2000 as % of 1999	构成(%) Composition(%) 2000	1999
总计	**Total**	**5478259.1**	**4869831.5**	**112.5**	**100**	**100**
第一产业	**Primary Industry**	**899676.5**	**874786.3**	**102.8**	**16.4**	**18.0**
第二产业	**Secondary Industry**	**2237645.0**	**1943080.2**	**115.2**	**40.9**	**39.9**
# 工业	Industry	1714606.2	1486978.1	115.3	31.3	30.5
第三产业	**Tertiary Industry**	**2340937.6**	**2051965.0**	**114.1**	**42.7**	**42.1**
农林牧渔服务业	Services of FFAF	21400.6	19525.0	109.6	0.4	0.4
地质勘查及水利管理业	Geographic Prospect and Water Conservancy	7194.2	4687.9	153.5	0.1	0.1
交通运输、仓储及邮电通信业	Transportation,Storge, Posts and Telecommunications	351962.9	304261.9	115.7	6.4	6.2
批发零售贸易及餐饮业	Wholesales,Retail Sale and Catering	461745.4	409050.9	112.9	8.4	8.4
金融保险业	Finance and Insurance	228851.3	216089.0	105.9	4.2	4.4
房地产业	Real Estate	338643.3	241247.3	140.4	6.2	5.0
社会服务业	Social Services	376720.6	354346.4	106.3	6.9	7.3
卫生、体育及社会福利事业	Health,Sports and Social Welfares	67448.0	58941.6	114.4	1.2	1.2
教育、文化及广播电影电视业	Education,Culture, Radio,Film and Television	161637.0	145764.1	110.9	3	3.0
科学研究及综合技术服务业	Scientific Research and Polytechnic Services	23757.6	22996.0	103.3	0.4	0.5
国家机关、党政机关及社会团体	Government Agencies,Party Agencies and Social Organizations	144797.2	134040.7	108.0	2.6	2.8
其他行业	Others	156779.5	141014.2	111.2	2.9	2.9

注：“郊区国内生产总值”统计口径：近郊区为乡及乡以下农村部分；远郊区（县）为县及县以下所属部分(下表同)。

Note: Gross domestic product of near suburbs is that produced by units of rural area at township level and below,and that of outer suburbs and counties is produced by units at county level and below(the following is the same).

5-6 郊区国内生产总值构成项目

STRUCTURE OF GROSS DOMESTIC PRODUCT OF SUBURBS

单位：万元 (10000 yuan)

项目	Item	增加值 Added Value	劳动者报酬 Compensation for Labors	生产税净额 Net Taxes on Production	固定资产折旧 Depreciation on Fixed Assets	营业盈余 Operating Surplus
总计	**Total**	**5478259.1**	**2596295.7**	**601593.4**	**922266.9**	**1358103.1**
第一产业	**Primary Industry**	**899676.5**	**546089.2**	**7129.5**	**62199.0**	**284258.8**
第二产业	**Secondary Industry**	**2237645.0**	**1003685.1**	**417051.4**	**338722.6**	**478185.9**
# 工业	Industry	1714606.2	711164.2	353231.9	291456.7	358753.4
第三产业	**Tertiary Industry**	**2340937.6**	**1046521.4**	**177412.5**	**521345.3**	**595658.4**
农林牧渔服务业	Services of FFAF	21400.6	14241.2	592.2	3454.2	3113.0
地质勘查及水利管理业	Geographic Prospect and Water Conservancy	7194.2	5068.4	293.9	2166.8	-334.9
交通运输、仓储及邮电通信业	Transportation,Storge,Posts and Telecommunications	351962.9	159296.5	28699.3	67436.1	96531.0
批发零售贸易及餐饮业	Wholesales,Retail Sale and Catering Services	461745.4	247458.6	49962.3	53482.6	110841.9
金融保险业	Finance and Insurance	228851.3	27004.2	18079.8	8708.9	175058.4
房地产业	Real Estate	338643.3	25711.3	29791.6	243878.3	39262.1
社会服务业	Social Services	376720.6	170118.5	38902.4	70988.9	96710.8
卫生、体育及社会福利事业	Health,Sports and Social Welfares	67448.0	55040.3	559.6	6973.1	4875.0
教育、文化及广播电影电视业	Education,Culture,Radio,Film and Television	161637.0	139297.4	964.9	22323.2	-948.5
科学研究及综合技术服务业	Scientific Research and Poly-technic Services	23757.6	12643.3	1681.9	7216.1	2216.3
国家机关、党政机关及社会团体	Government Agencies,Party Agencies and Social Organizations	144797.2	116838.8	814.0	18380.4	8764.0
其他行业	Others	156779.5	73802.9	7070.6	16336.7	59569.3

5-7 农业总产值

GROSS OUTPUT VALUE OF AGRICULTURE

单位：万元 (10000 yuan)

项目	Item	总产值（1990年不变价格） Gross Output Value (at 1990 constant prices) 2000	1999	2000年为1999年% 2000 as % of 1999	总产值（现价） Gross Output Value (at current prices) 2000	1999	2000年为1999年% 2000 as % of 1999
总计	**Total**	**1126303.3**	**996231.2**	**113.1**	**1951854**	**1843427**	**105.9**
种植业	**Planting**	**543426.2**	**492854.1**	**110.3**	**910949.5**	**911918.7**	**99.9**
谷物	Cereal	70582.8	106059.8	66.6	174949.2	263270.8	66.5
豆类	Beans	5753.5	2825.5	203.6	15020.3	6422.3	233.9
经济作物	Cash Crops	10662.1	9974.3	106.9	16991.4	15385.5	110.4
蔬菜、瓜类	Vegetable and Melon	312771.6	236078	132.5	518870.3	450075.4	115.3
桑、水果	Mulberry and Fruit	114707.2	95109.7	120.6	139936	120034.9	116.6
其他	Others	28949.0	42806.8	67.6	45182.3	56729.8	79.7
林业	**Forestry**	**22208.7**	**18127.5**	**122.5**	**53956.6**	**41868.4**	**128.9**
牧业	**Animal Husbandry**	**503656.4**	**434137.3**	**116.0**	**905626.9**	**810859.3**	**111.7**
家畜繁殖增重	Weight Increase of Domestic Animals Breeding	229935.9	201134	114.3	455395	416181.3	109.4
# 养猪	Hogs	166171.7	146503.3	113.4	334963.6	312604.6	107.2
家禽饲养	Poultry Raising	155734	125294.5	124.3	279065.6	230150.6	121.3
活的畜禽产品	Live Animal and Poultry Production	117140.9	104513.3	112.1	169224	157746.5	107.3
# 鲜蛋	Fresh Eggs	68930.0	70284.7	98.1	67009	79319.2	84.5
其他	Others	845.6	3195.5	26.5	1942.3	6780.9	28.7
渔业	**Fishery**	**57012.0**	**51112.3**	**111.6**	**81320.6**	**78779.6**	**103.2**

5-8 农林牧渔业中间消耗
INTERMEDIATE INPUT OF FARMING,FORESTRY,ANIMAL HUSBANDRY AND FISHERY

单位：万元 (10000 yuan)

项目	Item	2000	1999	2000年为1999年% 2000 as % of 1999
农林牧渔业生产中间消耗总计	**Total**	**1052177**	**968640**	**108.6**
农业中间消耗合计	**Farming**	**407965**	**409488**	**99.6**
种植业中间消耗	Planting	402987	398638	101.1
中间物质消耗	Intermediate Material Input	355963	346490	102.7
# 用种量	Seeds	52324.8	42857.3	122.1
肥　料	Fertilizer	124417	118560	104.9
农　药	Farm Chemical	15372.3	15069.6	102.0
对非物质生产部门劳务支出	Services Expenditure to Non-material Production Departments	47023.9	52148.5	90.2
其他农业中间消耗	Others	4978	10849.5	45.9
中间物质消耗	Intermediate Material Input	4530.2	10411.9	43.5
对非物质生产部门劳务支出	Services Expenditure to Non-material Production Departments	447.8	437.6	102.3
林业中间消耗合计	**Forestry**	**22989.8**	**14156.9**	**162.4**
中间物质消耗	Intermediate Material Input	20831.7	12629.5	164.9
# 农　药	Farm Chemical	744.4	835.4	89.1
对非物质生产部门劳务支出	Services Expenditure to Non-material Production Departments	2158.1	1527.4	141.3
牧业中间消耗合计	**Animal Husbandry**	**571386**	**497374**	**114.9**
中间物质消耗	Intermediate Material Input	547925	473748	115.7
# 饲料、饲草	Forage and Forage Grass	465404	408246	114.0
对非物质生产部门劳务支出	Services Expenditure to Non-material Production Departments	23461.2	23625.2	99.3
渔业中间消耗合计	**Fishery**	**49836.4**	**47622.2**	**104.6**
中间物质消耗	Intermediate Material Input	47792.7	44255.0	108.0
# 饲　料	Forage	31931.3	29616.7	107.8
对非物质生产部门劳务支出	Services Expenditure to Non-material Production Departments	2043.7	3367.2	60.7

5-9 耕　地　面　积
CULTIVATED AREAS

项目	Item	面　积 (公顷) Area (hectare)		构　成 (%) Composition(%)	
		2000	1999	2000	1999
合　计	**Total**	**329248**	**338384**	**100**	**100**
按水利状况分	**Grouped by Irrigation Conditions**				
水　田	Irrigated Field	29168.0	29536.7	8.9	8.7
旱　地	Non-irrigated Farmland	300079.7	308848	91.1	91.3
# 水浇地	Irrigated Land	241331.5	246525	73.3	72.9
# 菜　地	Vegetable Plot				
按当年使用分	**Grouped by Using in this Year**				
粮食作物	Grain Crops	191430.9	240510	58.1	71.1
经济作物	Cash Crops	17447.1	11876.1	5.3	3.5
蔬　菜	Vegetable	50824.7	43157.7	15.5	12.8
其　他	Others	69545.0	42840.4	21.1	12.6

5-10 国有农场基本情况
BASIC STATISTICS ON STATE FARMS

项目 Item			2000	1999	2000年为1999年% 2000 as % of 1999
农场数	(个) Number of Farms	(unit)	15	15	100.0
年末固定职工	(人) Number of Full-time Staff(year-end)	(person)	31108	38719	80.3
耕地面积	(公倾) Cultivated Land	(hectare)	2420	2752	87.9
农业总产值 (1990年不变价)	(万元) Gross Output Value of Agriculture (at 1990 constant prices)	(10000 yuan)	23833	26102	91.3
工业总产值 (1990年不变价,万元)	Gross Output Value of Industry (at 1990 constant prices)	(10000 yuan)	120904	121288	99.7
主要农产品产量	Yield of Major Farm Products	(ton)			
粮　食	(吨) Grain	(ton)	4393	6840	64.2
蔬　菜	(吨) Vegetable	(ton)	500	1295	38.6
牛　奶	(吨) Milk	(ton)	126884	126000	100.7
# 商品量	(吨) Commodity	(ton)	123077	122336	100.6
干鲜果品	(吨) Dry and Fresh Fruit	(ton)	2726	3421	79.7
大中型拖拉机	(台) Large and Medium Tractors	(unit)	60	155	38.7
小型拖拉机	(台) Mini-Tractors	(unit)	35	41	85.4
载重汽车	(辆) Trucks	(unit)	81	252	32.1
销售收入	(万元) Sales Revenue	(10000 yuan)	270547	299017	90.5
利　润	(万元) Profits	(10000 yuan)	4254	3339	127.4
税　金	(万元) Taxes	(10000 yuan)	13245	10662	124.2

注：本表数据由市农场局提供。
Note: Data of this table is provided by Beijing Municipal Farm Bureau.

5-11 主要农作物播种面积及产量
SOWN AREAS AND YIELD OF MAJOR FARM CROPS

项目	Item	2000			1999		
		播种面积 (公顷) Sown Areas (hectare)	单　产 (公斤／公顷) Unit Yield (kg/hectare)	总产量 (吨) Total Yield (ton)	播种面积 (公顷) Sown Areas (hectare)	单　产 (公斤／公顷) Unit Yield (kg/hectare)	总产量 (吨) Total Yield (ton)
粮　食	**Grain**	**308257.8**	**4676.7**	**1441627**	**409708.0**	**4905.4**	**2009793**
按季节分	Grouped by Season						
夏　粮	Summer Grain	121764.5	5492.1	668739	168195.4	5680.1	955362
秋　粮	Autumn Grain	186493.3	4144.3	772888	241512.6	4365.9	1054431
按品种分	Grouped by Variety						
稻　谷	Rice	14062.9	6654.0	93575	19152.7	6755	129377
冬小麦	Winter Wheat	121686.7	5494.5	668508	168039.7	5683.2	955003
玉　米	Corn	135808.1	4323.0	587098	198111.3	4374.0	866539
薯　类	Tubers	6039.2	5003.6	30218	5222.2	4591.9	23980
大　豆	Soybean	22054.4	2136.2	47112	10376.4	1948.5	20218
棉　花	**Cotton**	**1587.6**	**983.2**	**1561**	**1857.9**	**1016.2**	**1888**
油　料	**Oil-bearing Crops**	**15438.2**	**2461.0**	**37993**	**10427.1**	**2647.0**	**27601**
# 花　生	Peanuts	12825.9	2622.5	33636	9859.4	2736.9	26984
蔬　菜	**Vegetable**	**107818.2**	**45367.6**	**4891457**	**93517.9**	**45635.3**	**4267718**
瓜　类	**Melon**	**8068.6**	**51175.4**	**412914**	**5457.3**	**53775.9**	**293471**
# 西　瓜	Watermelon	7061.3	53291.2	376305	5032.9	54911.3	276363

5-12 郊区县粮食、油料占耕地面积

THE PROPORTION OF GRAIN,OIL-BEARING CROPS IN CULTIVATED AREA OF SUBURBS AND COUNTIES

单位：公顷 (hectare)

地区	Region	粮食 Grain			油料 Oil-bearing Crops		
		2000	1999	2000年为1999年% 2000 as % of 1999	2000	1999	2000年为1999年% 2000 as % of 1999
全市	**Total**	**191431.0**	**240510.2**	**79.6**	**13940.2**	**9723.4**	**143.4**
朝阳区	Chaoyang	4489.0	6872.1	65.3	1.0		
丰台区	Fengtai	1944.9	2191.1	88.8	1.3		
海淀区	Haidian	4388.7	5037.8	87.1			
门头沟区	Mentougou	2396.1	2482.7	96.5			
房山区	Fangshan	26677.1	31593.1	84.4	1219.9	683.0	178.6
通州区	Tongzhou	25275.1	37115.4	68.1	1264.6	634.7	199.2
昌平区	Changping	16051.4	18789.4	85.4	50.2	12.2	411.5
顺义区	Shunyi	27165.1	40119.9	67.7	1166.5	339.3	343.8
大兴县	Daxing	25542.9	29962.9	85.3	3990.3	3582.2	111.4
平谷县	Pinggu	10502.0	13661.6	76.9	611.9	254.5	240.4
怀柔县	Huairou	10329.3	12463.9	82.9	1087.1	672.8	161.6
密云县	Miyun	14875.7	16075.4	92.5	4233.5	3477.5	121.7
延庆县	Yanqing	21390.9	23444.5	91.2	313.9	67.2	467.1
农场局	Municipal Farm Bureau	402.8	700.4	57.5			

5-13 郊区县蔬菜、西瓜占耕地面积

THE PROPORTION OF VEGETABLE,WATERMELON IN CULTIVATED AREA OF SUBURBS AND COUNTIES

单位：公顷 (hectare)

地区	Region	蔬菜 Vegetable			西瓜 Watermelon		
		2000	1999	2000年为1999年% 2000 as % of 1999	2000	1999	2000年为1999年% 2000 as % of 1999
全市	**Total**	**50824.7**	**43157.7**	**117.8**	**4955.5**	**3399.8**	**145.8**
朝阳区	Chaoyang	2519.3	2209.9	114.0	4.1	0.3	1366.7
丰台区	Fengtai	1598.5	1982.7	80.6			
石景山区	Shijingshan		113.3				
海淀区	Haidian	995.3	1424.5	69.9			
门头沟区	Mentougou	353.3	430.7	82.0			
房山区	Fangshan	2359.1	2113.1	111.6	458.9	68.9	666.0
通州区	Tongzhou	8942.9	6764.1	132.2	238.3	212.5	112.1
昌平区	Changping	1719.4	1554.5	110.6	55.7		
顺义区	Shunyi	9113.4	7069.9	128.9	892.9	437.3	204.2
大兴县	Daxing	11626.0	9765.3	119.1	3139.8	2549.8	123.1
平谷县	Pinggu	3652.8	2958.8	123.5	117.9	108.2	109.0
怀柔县	Huairou	960.2	781.8	122.8	10.3	1.3	792.3
密云县	Miyun	1420.5	1320.9	107.5	18.1	16.9	107.1
延庆县	Yanqing	5564.0	4630.1	120.2	19.5	4.6	423.9
农场局	Municipal Farm Bureau		38.1				

5-14 郊区县粮食、油料播种面积
SOWN AREAS OF GRAIN,OIL-BEARING CROPS IN SUBURBS AND COUNTIES

单位：公顷 (hectare)

地区	Region	粮食 Grain			油料 Oil-bearing Crops		
		2000	1999	2000年为1999年% 2000 as % of 1999	2000	1999	2000年为1999年% 2000 as % of 1999
全市	**Total**	**308257.8**	**409708.0**	**75.2**	**15438.2**	**10427.0**	**148.1**
朝阳区	Chaoyang	7348.8	11808.3	62.2	2.0		
丰台区	Fengtai	2833.2	3202.3	88.5	1.3		
海淀区	Haidian	4693.6	5505.9	85.3			
门头沟区	Mentougou	3350.2	3959.6	84.6			
房山区	Fangshan	44419.3	52813.1	84.1	1266.7	705.6	179.5
通州区	Tongzhou	43761.4	72695.4	60.2	1363.9	653.5	208.7
昌平区	Changping	25950.1	32169.7	80.7	58.1	18.5	314.1
顺义区	Shunyi	50399.4	77087.7	65.4	1304.3	348.0	374.8
大兴县	Daxing	45107.9	54235.7	83.2	4700.7	3996.3	117.6
平谷县	Pinggu	18636.1	25724.6	72.4	649.7	276.1	235.3
怀柔县	Huairou	16369.5	19859.1	82.4	1189.1	679.5	175.0
密云县	Miyun	22226.0	25172.2	88.3	4583.7	3678.3	124.6
延庆县	Yanqing	22356.8	24191.1	92.4	318.7	71.2	447.6
农场局	Municipal Farm Bureau	805.5	1283.3	62.8			

5-15 郊区县蔬菜、西瓜播种面积
SOWN AREAS OF VEGETABLE,WATERMELON IN SUBURBS AND COUNTIES

单位：公顷 (hectare)

地区	Region	蔬菜 Vegetable			西瓜 Watermelon		
		2000	1999	2000年为1999年% 2000 as % of 1999	2000	1999	2000年为1999年% 2000 as % of 1999
全市	**Total**	**107818**	**93517.9**	**115.3**	**7061.3**	**5032.8**	**140.3**
朝阳区	Chaoyang	5303.5	4713.1	112.5	4.5	0.7	642.9
丰台区	Fengtai	3817.9	3894.9	98.0			
石景山区	Shijingshan	240.7	241.2	99.8			
海淀区	Haidian	2708.5	3326.5	81.4			
门头沟区	Mentougou	751.5	822.1	91.4			
房山区	Fangshan	5572.9	4994.3	111.6	482.5	80.3	600.9
通州区	Tongzhou	19037.6	15607.7	122.0	476.5	425.1	112.1
昌平区	Changping	3150.1	3046.5	103.4	68.1		
顺义区	Shunyi	18520	14800.8	125.1	1744.3	874.6	199.4
大兴县	Daxing	25703.7	22007.5	116.8	3968.9	3390.7	117.1
平谷县	Pinggu	7983.1	7108.5	112.3	233.7	216.3	108.0
怀柔县	Huairou	1854.7	1746.6	106.2	16.5	2.7	611.1
密云县	Miyun	3074.9	3102.3	99.1	32.5	33.9	95.9
延庆县	Yanqing	10090.7	8048.1	125.4	33.8	8.5	397.7
农场局	Municipal Farm Bureau	8.4	57.8	14.5			

5-16 郊区县粮食、油料总产量

TOTAL YIELD OF GRAIN,OIL-BEARING CROPS IN SUBURBS AND COUNTIES

单位：吨 (ton)

地区	Region	粮食 Grain 2000	粮食 Grain 1999	粮食 Grain 2000年为1999年% 2000 as % of 1999	油料 Oil-bearing Crops 2000	油料 Oil-bearing Crops 1999	油料 Oil-bearing Crops 2000年为1999年% 2000 as % of 1999
全市	**Total**	**1441627**	**2009793**	**71.7**	**37993**	**27601**	**137.7**
朝阳区	Chaoyang	39194	65881	59.5	2		
丰台区	Fengtai	8396	10872	77.2	2		
海淀区	Haidian	29726	36288	81.9			
门头沟区	Mentougou	5517	8386	65.8			
房山区	Fangshan	207294	271848	76.3	3196	1485	215.2
通州区	Tongzhou	223945	382884	58.5	3191	1579	202.1
昌平区	Changping	117642	162680	72.3	161	75	214.7
顺义区	Shunyi	238879	377797	63.2	3661	1316	278.2
大兴县	Daxing	231121	282632	81.8	14444	11367	127.1
平谷县	Pinggu	71601	108511	66.0	1202	518	232.1
怀柔县	Huairou	78361	112824	69.5	3929	2635	149.1
密云县	Miyun	54206	94459	57.4	7670	8548	89.7
延庆县	Yanqing	146155	140166	104.3	535	78	685.9
农场局	Municipal Farm Bureau	4393	6884	63.8			

注：各区县粮食总产量之和不等于全市合计数。

Note: The sum of output of grain of suburbs and counties is not equal to the total.

5-17 郊区县蔬菜、西瓜总产量

TOTAL YIELD OF VEGETABLE,WATERMELON IN SUBURBS AND COUNTIES

单位：吨 (ton)

地区	Region	蔬菜 Vegetable 2000	蔬菜 Vegetable 1999	蔬菜 Vegetable 2000年为1999年% 2000 as % of 1999	西瓜 Watermelon 2000	西瓜 Watermelon 1999	西瓜 Watermelon 2000年为1999年% 2000 as % of 1999
全市	**Total**	**4891457**	**4267718**	**114.6**	**376305**	**276363**	**136.2**
朝阳区	Chaoyang	174157	176573	98.6	184	30	613.3
丰台区	Fengtai	143524	155205	92.5			
石景山区	Shijingshan	9148	8825	103.7			
海淀区	Haidian	107313	139312	77.0			
门头沟区	Mentougou	21878	22989	95.2			
房山区	Fangshan	239703	206200	116.3	26604	3585	742.1
通州区	Tongzhou	866332	756107	114.6	30431	27919	109.0
昌平区	Changping	127478	122148	104.4	2641		
顺义区	Shunyi	1009775	850208	118.8	90421	44855	201.6
大兴县	Daxing	1112582	984891	113.0	208845	186253	112.1
平谷县	Pinggu	360682	330697	109.1	13752	11880	115.8
怀柔县	Huairou	54240	51183	106.0	710	140	507.1
密云县	Miyun	183116	159061	115.1	1445	1286	112.4
延庆县	Yanqing	481029	423024	113.7	1272	415	306.5
农场局	Municipal Farm Bureau	500	1295	38.6			

5-18 蔬菜播种面积及产量
SOWN AREA AND YIELD OF VEGETABLE

项　目	Item	播种面积 (公顷) Sown Areas(hectare)	总 产 量 (吨) Total Yield(ton)
合　计	**Total**	**107818.2**	**4891457.1**
叶菜类	Vegetable with Leaf	44879.8	2239489.0
# 大白菜	Chinese Cabbage	17475.3	1106886.0
小白菜	Pakchoi	1582.7	57560.0
元白菜	Cabbage	5445.5	250518.7
油　菜	Rape	2130.6	70606.5
菠　菜	Spinach	2560.3	83821.5
芹　菜	Calery	3108.9	179368.0
茄果菜类	Aggplant and Fruit-vegetable	16359.3	744098.5
# 茄　子	Aggplant	5044.7	216938.0
西红柿	Tomato	6634.0	346871.0
青　椒	Chili	2394.1	91991.5
瓜菜类	Melon-vegetable	13157.3	644604.9
# 黄　瓜	Cucumber	6996.4	332721.9
冬　瓜	Wax Guard	2152.3	134274.8
块根、块茎菜类	Vegetable with Lump-root or Bine	10968.2	437197.9
# 萝　卜	Radish	6506.0	296668.9
土　豆	Potato	3000.1	82341.0
菜用豆类	Vegetable-bean	7655.9	260736.7
# 四季豆	Kidney Bean	2945.3	101727.7
豇　豆	Cowpea	2580.4	85933.0
葱蒜类	Onion and Garlic	7492.8	323589.1
# 葱	Onion	3179.3	134646.0
韭　菜	Leek	2466.5	118894.1
水生菜类	Aquatic Vegetable	1348.9	29791.0
# 莲　藕	Lotus	1116.5	24766.0
其它蔬菜类	Others	5956.0	211950.0

5-19 郊区县粮食耕地面积单位产量

YIELD OF GRAIN PER HECTARE CULTIVATED AREA IN SUBURBS AND COUNTIES

地　区 Region		2000 耕地面积 (公顷) Cultivated Areas (hectare)	2000 单产 (公斤/公顷) Unit Yield (kg/hectare)	2000 总产量 (吨) Total Yield (ton)	1999 耕地面积 (公顷) Cultivated Areas (hectare)	1999 单产 (公斤/公顷) Unit Yield (kg/hectare)	1999 总产量 (吨) Total Yield (ton)
全　市	**Total**	**191431.0**	**7530.8**	**1441627**	**240510**	**8356.4**	**2009793**
朝阳区	Chaoyang	4489.0	8731.1	39194	6872	9586.9	65881
丰台区	Fengtai	1944.9	4316.9	8396	2191	4962.1	10872
海淀区	Haidian	4388.7	6773.3	29726	5038	7202.9	36288
门头沟区	Mentougou	2396.1	2302.5	5517	2483	3377.4	8386
房山区	Fangshan	26677.1	7770.5	207294	31593	8604.7	271848
通州区	Tongzhou	25275.1	8860.3	223945	37115	10316.2	382884
昌平区	Changping	16051.4	7329.1	117642	18789	8658.3	162680
顺义区	Shunyi	27165.1	8793.6	238879	40120	9416.7	377797
大兴县	Daxing	25542.9	9048.3	231121	29963	9432.7	282632
平谷县	Pinggu	10502.0	6817.8	71601	13662	7942.5	108511
怀柔县	Huairou	10329.3	7586.3	78361	12464	9052.0	112824
密云县	Miyun	14875.7	3643.9	54206	16075	5876.1	94459
延庆县	Yanqing	21390.9	6832.6	146155	23445	5978.5	140166
农场局	Municipal Farm Bureau	402.8	10906.2	4393	700	9834.3	6884

5-20 郊区县蔬菜耕地面积单位产量

YIELD OF VEGETABLE PER HECTARE CULTIVATED AREA IN SUBURBS AND COUNTIES

地　区 Region		2000 耕地面积 (公顷) Cultivated Areas (hectare)	2000 单产 (公斤/公顷) Unit Yield (kg/hectare)	2000 总产量 (吨) Total Yield (ton)	1999 耕地面积 (公顷) Cultivated Areas (hectare)	1999 单产 (公斤/公顷) Unit Yield (kg/hectare)	1999 总产量 (吨) Total Yield (ton)
全　市	**Total**	**50824.7**	**96241.7**	**4891457**	**43157.7**	**98886.6**	**4267718**
朝阳区	Chaoyang	2519.3	69129.1	174157	2209.9	79900.9	176573
丰台区	Fengtai	1598.5	89786.7	143524	1982.7	78279.6	155205
石景山区	Shijingshan			9148	113.3	77890.6	8825
海淀区	Haidian	995.3	107819.8	107313	1424.5	97797.1	139312
门头沟区	Mentougou	353.3	61924.7	21878	430.7	53375.9	22989
房山区	Fangshan	2359.1	101607.8	239703	2113.1	97581.8	206200
通州区	Tongzhou	8942.9	96873.7	866332	6764.1	111782.4	756107
昌平区	Changping	1719.4	74141.0	127478	1554.5	78577.0	122148
顺义区	Shunyi	9113.4	110801.1	1009775	7069.9	120257.4	850208
大兴县	Daxing	11626.0	95697.7	1112582	9765.3	100856.2	984891
平谷县	Pinggu	3652.8	98741.2	360682	2958.8	111767.3	330697
怀柔县	Huairou	960.2	56488.2	54240	781.8	65468.2	51183
密云县	Miyun	1420.5	128909.5	183116	1320.9	120418.7	159061
延庆县	Yanqing	5564.0	86453.8	481029	4630.1	91363.9	423024
农场局	Municipal Farm Bureau			500	38.1	33989.5	1295

5-21 畜 牧 业 生 产
ANIMALS HUSBANDRY

项目 Item			2000 合计 Total	2000 #国有集体 State-Owned and Collective-Owned	1999 合计 Total	1999 #国有集体 State-Owned and Collective-Owned	2000年为1999年% 2000 as % of 1999 合计 Total	2000年为1999年% 2000 as % of 1999 #国有集体 State-Owned and Collective-Owned
大牲畜		Large Animals						
年末总头数	(万头)	Total (year-end,10000 heads)	23.6		19.0		124.2	
#役 畜		Draught Animals	3.5		4.1		85.4	
牛		Cattle and Buffaloes	18.8		13.6		138.2	
马		Horses	0.6		0.7		85.7	
骡		Mules	1.5		1.8		83.3	
驴		Donkeys	2.7		2.9		93.1	
乳 牛		Cows						
年末总头数	(头)	Total (year-end,head)	94912.0	42699.0	64411.0	39638.0	147.4	107.7
#成乳牛		Adult Cows	63879.0		42716.0		149.5	
牛奶总产量	(万吨)	Cow Milk (10000 tons)	30.3	13.6	24.0	16.7	126.3	81.4
肉 牛		Beef Cattle						
全年出栏	(头)	Slaughtered Cattle (head)	172652.0		134899.0		128.0	
折净肉	(吨)	Converted into Beef (ton)	32681.4		23905.0		136.7	
羊		Sheep and Goats						
全年出栏羊	(万只)	Slaughtered Sheep and Goats (10000 heads)	103.9		88.2		117.8	
折净肉	(吨)	Converted into Mutton (ton)	15590		13462.0		115.8	
年末存栏	(万只)	Livestock on Hand (year-end,10000 heads)	120.1		103.1		116.5	
山 羊	(万只)	Goats (10000 heads)	51.3		47.9		107.1	
绵 羊	(万只)	Sheep (10000 heads)	68.8		55.2		124.6	
猪		Hogs						
全年出栏猪	(万头)	Slaughtered Fattened Hogs (10000 heads)	415.6	166.4	400.9	198.1	103.7	84.0
折带骨肉	(万吨)	Converted into Pork with Bone (10000 tons)	29.1		28.6		101.7	
年末存栏	(万头)	Livestock on Hand (year-end,10000 heads)	250.0	97.2	248.3	116.8	100.7	83.2
家 禽		Poultry						
年末存栏	(万只)	Livestock on Hand (year-end,10000 heads)	3369.2		3135.1		107.5	
鸭		Ducks	502.1		364.8		137.6	
肉 鸡		Chickens	1461.0	601.5	1349.5	564.5	108.3	106.6
产蛋鸡		Hens	1406.1	483.8	1420.8	512.1	99.0	94.5
产蛋量	(万吨)	Poultry Eggs (10000 tons)						
#鸡 蛋		Eggs	15.6		15.5		100.6	
年末养兔	**(万只)**	**Rabbits (year-end,10000 heads)**	**80.2**		**35.0**		**229.0**	
养 蜂		Bees						
年末养蜂	(万箱)	Bees (year-end,10000 boxes)	8.4		6.9		121.7	
蜂蜜产量	(吨)	Honey (ton)	2604.5		1838.9		141.6	

5-22 林业及干鲜果品生产
FORESTRY,DRY AND FRESH FRUIT PRODUCTION

项目		Item		2000	1999	2000年为1999年% 2000 as % of 1999
林业生产		**Forestry**				
本年造林面积	(公顷)	Afforestation Area this Year	(hectare)	26093.2	30198.1	86.4
育苗面积	(公顷)	Nursery Garden Area	(hectare)	7294.7	4920.2	148.3
# 本年新育	(公顷)	New Growing this Year	(hectare)	3382.8	1462.0	231.4
果类生产		**Fruit**				
干鲜果总产量	(吨)	Output of Dry and Fresh Fruit	(ton)	609721	564301.0	108.1
干 果	(吨)	Dry Fruit	(ton)	23814.0	23724.0	100.4
# 核 桃	(吨)	Walnut	(ton)	8816.0	8030.0	109.8
板 栗	(吨)	Chinese Chestnut	(ton)	9016.0	10578.0	85.2
鲜 果	(吨)	Fresh Fruit	(ton)	585907	540577.0	108.4
# 苹 果	(吨)	Apple	(ton)	157654	151717.0	103.9
梨	(吨)	Pear	(ton)	102693	98705.0	104.0
葡 萄	(吨)	Grape	(ton)	33961.4	23070.0	
柿 子	(吨)	Persimmon	(ton)	54561.0	48979.0	111.4
桃	(吨)	Peach	(ton)	197476	179614.0	110.0
年末实有果园面积	**(公顷)**	**Orchard Area(year-end)**	**(hectare)**	**85336.0**	**64008.1**	**133.3**

5-23 水 产 品 生 产
AQUATIC PRODUCTS

项目		Item		2000	1999	2000年为1999年% 2000 as % of 1999
现有水面面积	**(公顷)**	**Area of Water Surface**	**(hectare)**	**23494.5**	**24451.1**	**96.1**
# 已利用水面面积	(公顷)	Utilized Area	(hectare)	22760.6	23605.4	96.4
大水库	(公顷)	Large Reservoir	(hectare)	13053.3	13853.3	94.2
中、小水库	(公顷)	Medium and Small Reservoirs	(hectare)	1927.0	1931.0	99.8
坑 塘	(公顷)	Puddle and Pond	(hectare)	7720.7	7777.9	99.3
# 鱼种池	(公顷)	Fish Fry Pond	(hectare)	893.0	1011.6	88.3
鱼种生产量	**(万尾)**	**Output of Fish Fry**	**(10000 pieces)**	**12513.1**	**13873.4**	**90.2**
放养鱼种	**(万尾)**	**Fish Fry Breed**	**(10000 pieces)**	**16526.2**	**16213.7**	**101.9**
成鱼捕捞量	**(吨)**	**Adult Fish Catched**	**(ton)**	**75044**	**75555.5**	**99.3**
# 大水库	(吨)	in Large Reservoirs	(ton)	4513.6	4178.6	108.0
中、小水库	(吨)	in Medium and Small Reservoirs	(ton)	722.0	837.3	86.2
坑 塘	(吨)	in Puddle and Pond	(ton)	67275.6	68479.8	98.3
# 鱼类商品量	(吨)	Commodity Fish	(ton)	45232.9	66265.5	68.3

5-24 主要农产品产量
OUTPUT OF MAJOR FARM PRODUCTS

单位：吨 (ton)

项目	Item	2000	1999	2000年为1999年% 2000 as % of 1999
蔬菜产量	**Yield of Vegetable**	**4891457.1**	**4267718**	**114.6**
#特菜	Special Vegetable	278364	199340	139.7
干鲜果品产量	**Yield of Dry and Fresh Fruit**	**609720.8**	**564301**	**108.1**
#干果产量	Dry Fruit	23814	23724	100.4
鲜果产量	Fresh Fruit	585906.8	540577	108.4
肉类总产量	**Output of Meat**	**562806**	**494879**	**113.7**
#猪肉	Pork	290927	285509	101.9
牛肉	Beef	32681.4	23905	136.7
羊肉	Mutton	15590	13462	115.8
牛奶产量	**Output of Cow Milk**	**303312.4**	**240112**	**126.3**
鲜蛋产量	**Output of Fresh Eggs**	**160165.2**	**157902**	**101.4**
#鸡蛋	Eggs	156144.7	155213	100.6
鸭蛋	Duck's Eggs	3765.5	2669	141.1
淡水鱼产量	**Output of Freshwater Fish**	**75044**	**75555.5**	**99.3**

5-25 郊区县副食品产量
OUTPUT OF NON-STAPLE FOOD IN SUBURBS AND COUNTIES

地区	Region	蔬菜 (吨) Vegetable (ton)	鲜蛋 (吨) Fresh Eggs (ton)	牛奶 (吨) Cow Milk (ton)	干鲜果 (吨) Dry and Fresh Fruit (ton)	成鱼捕捞量 (吨) Adult Fish Catched (ton)	生猪出栏 (头) Slaughtered Fattened Hog (head)	蛋鸡存栏 (万只) Hens on Hand (10000 heads)
全市	**Total**	**4891457**	**160165.2**	**303312**	**609720.8**	**75044**	**4156079**	**1406.1**
朝阳区	Chaoyang	174157	491	**8058**	924	5271.3	251753	4.8
丰台区	Fengtai	143524	4718	4205	4772	339.8	67223	39.1
石景山区	Shijingshan	9148	1586	2022	999	40	28667	9.4
海淀区	Haidian	107313	2212	2619	11187	2710	53036	12.9
门头沟区	Mentougou	21878	1096	4123	6461	450	33022	9.1
房山区	Fangshan	239703	14048	12181	67480	2100	344896	169.0
通州区	Tongzhou	866332	13725	22919	42441	11668.9	443301	96.0
昌平区	Changping	127478	6938	17595	55005	8048.3	246146	59.6
顺义区	Shunyi	1009775	21340.2	20790.4	45616.8	16072.5	1418711	198.8
大兴县	Daxing	1112582	29441	27847	95488	4812.6	395543	208.7
平谷县	Pinggu	360682	22666	1055	150145	14365	260623	236.9
怀柔县	Huairou	54240	7648	19339	45818	2045	195410	74.6
密云县	Miyun	183116	19549	10679	35905	4308.7	320078	181.3
延庆县	Yanqing	481029	12692	22996	45236	2811.9	152505	92.9
农场局	Municipal Farm Bureau	500	2015	126884	2243		45165	13.0

5-26 设施农业面积及产量
AREAS AND OUTPUT OF FACILITY-AGRICULTURE

项目	Item	设施农业面积（亩）Areas of Facility-agriculture (mu)	设施农业产量（吨）Output of Facility-agriculture (ton)
合计	**Total**	**295758**	
按类型划分	Grouped by Type		
#温室	Hothouse	37791	
日光温室	Sunshine-hothouse	45362	
大棚	Large Shed	71673	
中、小棚	Medium and Small Shed	113708	
阳畦	Sunshine Bed	27224	
按品种划分	Grouped by Variety		
#蔬菜	Vegetable	211457	1274332
花卉	Flowers	11532	
瓜类	Melons	56591	221819
果类	Fruits	7128	5375

5-27 农村劳动生产率
RURAL LABOR PRODUCTIVITY

项目	Item	2000	1999	2000年为1999年% 2000 as % of 1999
每一农村从业人员创造产值（按各业从业人员分别计算）	**Output Value Per Person Employed (calculated separately by sectors)**			
每一农村从业人员创造农村社会总产值（元）	Rural Gross Output Value Per Person Employed (yuan)	63860	55897	114.2
每一农村从业人员创造农业总产值（元）	Gross Output Value of Agriculture Per Person Employed (yuan)	28016	25927	108.1
每一农村从业人员创造工业总产值（元）	Gross Output Value of Industry Per Person Employed (yuan)	148631	122959	120.9
每一农村从业人员创造建筑业总产值（元）	Gross Output Value of Construction Per Person Employed (yuan)	121865	110017	110.8
每一农村从业人员创造运输业总产值（元）	Gross Output Value of Transportation Per Person Employed (yuan)	65075	63709	102.1
每一农村从业人员创造商业、饮食业总产值（元）	Gross Output Value of Commerce and Catering Per Person Employed (yuan)	90163	92205	97.8
每一农业从业人员生产的农产品产量（按农林牧渔从业人员合计计算）	**Yield of Farm Products Per Person Employed (calculated by total persons employed of farming, forestry,animal husbandry and fishery)**			
粮食（公斤）	Grain (kg)	2069	2827	73.2
油料（公斤）	Oil-bearing Crops (kg)	55	39	141.0
蔬菜（公斤）	Vegetable (kg)	7021	6002	117.0
水果（公斤）	Fruit (kg)	840	761	110.4
猪牛羊肉（公斤）	Pork,Beef and Mutton (kg)	487	454	107.3
牛奶（公斤）	Cow Milk (kg)	435	338	128.7
鲜蛋（公斤）	Fresh Eggs (kg)	230	222	103.6
淡水鱼（公斤）	Fresh-water Fish (kg)	108	106	101.9

5-28 农业生产条件
PRODUCTIVE CONDITIONS OF AGRICULTURE

项目		Item		2000	1999 1998	2000年为1999年% 2000 as % of 1999
主要农业机械拥有量		**Possession of Major Agricultural Machinery**				
农业机械总动力	(万千瓦)	Total Power of Agricultural Machinery	(10000 kw)	399.2	410.4	97.3
大中型拖拉机	(混合台)	Large and Medium Tractors	(unit)	11781.2	11852.0	99.4
小型拖拉机	(台)	Mini-Tractors	(unit)	25004.0	27295.0	91.6
机引农具	(台)	Towing Farm Machinery	(unit)			
机动喷雾器	(部)	Motorized Sprayer	(unit)	14019	13542	103.5
机动插秧机	(台)	Motorized Rice Transplanter	(unit)	268	317	84.5
联合收割机	(台)	Combine Harvester	(unit)	4485	4528	99.1
机动脱粒机	(台)	Motorized Sheller	(unit)	13228	13324	99.3
米面加工机	(台)	Processing Machine of Rice and Flour	(unit)	8945	9549	93.7
机动挤奶器	(台)	Motorized Milker	(unit)	440	185	237.8
饲料粉碎机	(台)	Fodder Grinder	(unit)	5384	4957	108.6
载重汽车	(辆)	Truck	(unit)	15520	16884	91.9
农业机械作业面积		**Operation Area with Agricultural Machinery**				
机耕面积	(公顷)	Cultivated Area by Machine	(hectare)	228279	258867	88.2
占全部耕地面积比重	(%)	as Percentage of Total	(%)	69.3	76.5	
机播面积	(公顷)	Sown Area by Machine	(hectare)	189436	293687	64.5
占播种面积比重	(%)	as Percentage of Sown Area	(%)	41.4	55.7	
机收面积	(公顷)	Harvest Area by Machine	(hectare)	167840	245827	68.3
占播种面积比重	(%)	as Percentage of Harvest Area	(%)	36.7	46.6	
农村用电量及小水电		**Rural Electricity Consumption and Small Hydropower Station**				
农村用电量	(万千瓦小时)	Rural Electricity Consumption	(10000 kwh)	572257	330069	173.4
# 农业生产用	(万千瓦小时)	For Agricultural Productive Use	(10000 kwh)	135587	125650	107.9
乡镇、村办企业用	(万千瓦小时)	For Township and Village Enterprises Use	(10000 kwh)	106716	94226	113.3
农村小水电站	(处)	Rural Small Hydropower Station	(unit)	40	43	93.0
发电量	(万千瓦小时)	Generated Energy	(10000 kwh)	1737.3	1633.2	106.4
农田水利		**Irrigation and Water Conservancy**				
排灌用动力机械	(台)	Power-driven Irrigation Machinery	(unit)	74016	62900	117.7
	(万千瓦)		(10000 kwh)	68.4	68.4	
机(电)井	(眼)	Motor-pumped Well	(unit)	43017	44505	96.7
# 已配套	(眼)	Completed Set	(unit)			
扬水站(固定机电排灌站)	(处)	Pumping Station	(unit)	4855	4861	99.9
有效灌溉面积	(公顷)	Irrigated Areas	(hectare)	322660	322120	100.2
占耕地面积		as Percentage of Cultivated Areas	(%)	98.0	95.3	
化肥施用量(折纯)		**Consumption of Chemical Fertilizer (converted into pure)**				
化肥施用量	(吨)	Consumption of Chemical Fertilizers	(ton)	179282	190291	94.2
氮　肥	(吨)	Nitrogenous Fertilizer	(ton)	104518	115940	90.1
磷　肥	(吨)	Phosphate Fertilizer	(ton)	10335.3	10851	95.2
钾　肥	(吨)	Potash Fertilizer	(ton)	3625.8	3922	92.4
每公顷耕地施用量	(公斤)	Consumption Per Hectare Cultivated Areas	(kg)	363.0	562	64.6

注：农村小水电站是指乡村两级小水电实有数。农村用电量为市供电局提供。

Note: Data of rural small hydropower station refers to actual number of small hydropower at township and Village level.Data on consumption of electricity is provided by Beijing Municipal Power Supply Bureau.

5-29 乡镇集体企业各业基本情况
BASIC STATISTICS ON SECTORS OF TOWN AND TOWNSHIP ENTERPRISES

行业 Sector	企业个数（个）Number of Enterprises (unit)		从业人员（人）Persons Employed (person)		总收入（万元）Total Revenue (10000 yuan)		利润总额（万元）Total Profits (10000 yuan)		税金（万元）Taxes (10000 yuan)
	数量 Number	占% Proportion	数量 Number	占% Proportion	数量 Number	占% Proportion	数量 Number	占% Proportion	
合计 Total	**11961**	**100**	**681886**	**100**	**6602498**	**100**	**357639**	**100**	**235859**
农业 Agriculture	446	3.7	15274	2.2	147402	2.2	19259	5.4	2210
工业 Industry	7909	66.1	427726	62.7	3639939	55.1	177205	49.5	146542
交通运输业 Transportation	285	2.4	12644	1.9	88033	1.3	3664	1.0	3126
施工建筑业 Construction	784	6.6	135366	19.9	1120666	17.0	65487	18.3	42660
商品流通业 Commerce	1300	10.9	31022	4.5	1008896	15.3	32029	9.0	15116
旅游饮服业 Tourism,Catering and Services	1015	8.5	48274	7.1	439347	6.7	39364	11.0	18652
其他 Others	222	1.8	11580	1.7	158215	2.4	20631	5.8	7553

5-30 乡镇集体企业出口供货情况
GOODS SUPPLIES FOR EXPORT OF TOWN AND TOWNSHIP ENTERPRISES

单位：万元 (10000 yuan)

行业	Sector	出口产品交货总额 Total Amount on Delivery of Exports		直接出口 Direct Export		间接出口 Indirect Export	
		2000	1999	2000	1999	2000	1999
合计	**Total**	**519645**	**453277**	**356422**	**311906**	**163223**	**141371**
化工	Chemical Products	7811	3424	2786	2354	5025	1070
机械	Machinery	51296	18833	42171	15230	9125	3603
矿产	Mineral Products	4618	1731	550	712	4068	1019
轻工	Light Industry	66458	84620	35395	48900	31063	35720
食品	Food	10911	6880	3786	1041	7125	5839
土产	Local Products	230	4435		4266	230	169
畜产	Livestock Products	7467	5642	7317	5617	150	25
纺织	Textile	53280	39954	42599	27752	10681	12202
服装	Garment	223644	194290	160417	143384	63227	50906
工艺品	Handicraft	41519	29923	33057	22038	8462	7885
其他	Others	52411	63545	28344	40612	24067	22933

5-31 乡镇企业主要产品产量
MAJOR PRODUCTS OUTPUT OF TOWN AND TOWNSHIP ENTERPRISES

产品名称 Products				2000	1999	2000年为1999年% 2000 as % of 1999
发电量	(万千瓦时)	Electricity	(10000 kwh)	3432.0	4328.0	79.3
原 煤	(万吨)	Raw Coal	(10000 tons)	245.0	376.6	65.1
塑料制品	(吨)	Plastic Products	(ton)	58504.0	48161.0	121.5
泵	(台)	Pump	(unit)	20458.0	10109.0	202.4
水 泥	(万吨)	Cement	(10000 tons)	267.0	255.0	104.7
砖	(亿块)	Brick	(100 million pieces)	49.5	49.9	99.2
石 灰	(万吨)	Lime	(10000 tons)	132.0	152.7	86.4
水磨石	(万平方米)	Terrazzo	(10000 sq.m)	36.0	52.2	69.0
水泥预制构件	(万立方米)	Cement Prefabricated Components	(10000 sq.m)	251.0	166.9	150.4
棉 布	(万米)	Cotton Cloth	(10000 meters)	4895.0	8250.0	59.3
服 装	(万件)	Garment	(10000)	8483.0	6664.0	127.3
布 鞋	(万双)	Cloth Shoes	(10000 pairs)	214.0	265.0	80.8
白 酒	(吨)	White Sprite	(ton)	1513.0	1995.0	75.8
家 具	(万件)	Furniture	(10000)	702.0	349.0	201.1

5-32 郊区县乡镇集体企业主要经济指标
MAIN ECONOMIC INDICATORS FOR TOWN AND TOWNSHIP ENTERPRISES IN SUBURBS AND COUNTIES

地区	Region	企业个数 (个) Number of Enterprises (unit)	从业人员 (人) Persons Employed (person)	总收入 (万元) Total Revenue (10000 yuan)	利润总额 (万元) Total Profits (10000 yuan)	人均利润 (元) Profit Per Capita (yuan)	税金 (万元) Taxes (10000 yuan)	# 所得税 (万元) Income Tax (10000 yuan)
全 市	**Total**	**11961**	**681886**	**6602498**	**357639**	**5245**	**235859**	**52983**
朝阳区	Chaoyang	1462	79028	778953	23721	3002	26665	5417
丰台区	Fengtai	1179	64084	659581	53389	8331	20655	5195
石景山区	Shijingshan	216	8104	138968	3768	4650	2827	709
海淀区	Haidian	904	.39353	483547	19294	4903	16697	3012
门头沟区	Mentougou	537	15915	142186	7872	4946	4261	1155
房山区	Fangshan	1151	81061	680527	35549	4385	22594	5061
通州区	Tongzhou	1576	72841	593885	34507	4737	21132	5773
昌平区	Changping	1018	45163	397173	24378	5398	15314	2629
顺义区	Shunyi	835	82276	588941	29211	3550	22182	4298
大兴县	Daxing	1340	63289	737973	42294	6683	30236	5111
平谷县	Pinggu	711	49820	535862	37486	7524	19205	4134
怀柔县	Huairou	550	31828	532861	31263	9822	19471	7498
密云县	Miyun	259	26493	147603	4927	1860	7045	1154
延庆县	Yanqing	223	22631	184438	9980	4410	7575	1837

5-33 郊区县乡镇个体、私营企业主要经济指标

MAIN ECONOMIC INDICATORS FOR RURAL INDIVIDUAL AND JOINT ENTERPRISES IN SUBURBS AND COUNTIES

地区 Region		企业个数 (个) Number of Enterprises (unit)	从业人员 (人) Persons Employed (person)	总收入 (万元) Total Revenue (10000 yuan)	利润总额 (万元) Total Profits (10000 yuan)	人均利润 (元) Profit Per Capita (yuan)	税金 (万元) Taxes (10000 yuan)	# 所得税 (万元) Income Tax (10000 yuan)
全　市	**Total**	**106793**	**332231**	**2988566**	**262610**	**7904**	**67082**	**14375**
朝阳区	Chaoyang	36	1033	10678	318	3078	244	20
丰台区	Fengtai	1150	3012	29876	3659	12148	1395	315
石景山区	Shijingshan	395	1868	13074	1314	7034	419	43
海淀区	Haidian	2731	15196	139484	6989	4599	4268	254
门头沟区	Mentougou	8166	16441	119927	16301	9915	1985	269
房山区	Fangshan	32752	95459	1111577	101679	10652	13247	1321
通州区	Tongzhou	12501	43103	279956	36696	8514	12510	2717
昌平区	Changping	2214	6580	39984	4344	6602	1612	203
顺义区	Shunyi	12276	52294	306946	26577	5082	11412	4779
大兴县	Daxing	11539	28452	256168	21392	7519	4240	983
平谷县	Pinggu	2137	9197	51321	3921	4263	1061	231
怀柔县	Huairou	5668	14775	284218	19755	13371	6295	2141
密云县	Miyun	10249	32174	226385	14356	4462	5045	440
延庆县	Yanqing	4979	12647	118972	5309	4198	3349	659

5-34 农村劳动力转移情况
STATISTICS ON RURAL LABOR FORCE TRANSFERRING

项目	Item	合计 Total 数量（人） Number (person)	合计 Total 构成（%） Composition (%)	平原 Plain 数量（人） Number (person)	平原 Plain 构成（%） Composition (%)	山区 Mountain Area 数量（人） Number (person)	山区 Mountain Area 构成（%） Composition (%)
调查户劳动力转移人数	**Labor Force Transferring of Household in Surveyed**	**878**	**100**	**683**	**100**	**195**	**100**
当年转移的劳动力	**Labor Force Transferred in This Year**	**172**	**19.6**	**132**	**19.3**	**40**	**20.5**
转移劳动力素质情况	**Quality Level of Labor Force Transferring**						
性别构成	Sex Composition						
男劳动力	Male	542	61.7	423	61.9	119	61.0
# 整劳动力	Full Labor Force	459	52.3	361	52.9	98	50.3
女劳动力	Female	336	38.3	260	38.1	76	39.0
# 整劳动力	Full Labor Force	275	31.3	213	31.2	62	31.8
文化程度	Educational Level						
小学及以下文化程度	at Primary School Level and below	57	6.5	42	6.1	15	7.7
初中文化程度	at Junior Middle School Level	520	59.2	398	58.3	122	62.6
中专文化程度	at Specialized Secondary School Level	264	30.1	214	31.3	50	25.6
大专及以上文化程度	at Junior College Level and above	37	4.2	29	4.3	8	4.1
接受专业培训情况	Taking Professional Training						
接受专业培训	Trained	299	34.1	235	34.4	64	32.8
未接受专业培训	No Trained	579	65.9	448	65.6	131	67.2
转移劳动力行业分布	**Sector Transfer to**						
农牧渔业	Farming,Animal Husbandry and Fishery	9	1.0	8	1.2	1	0.5
工业	Industry	301	34.3	258	37.8	43	22.1
建筑业	Construction	56	6.5	42	6.2	14	7.2
交通运输业	Transportation and Posts	107	12.2	83	12.1	24	12.3
邮电通讯业	Posts and Telecommunications	8	0.9	6	0.9	2	1.0
商业饮食业	Commerce and Catering Trades	102	11.6	79	11.6	23	11.8
服务业	Services	132	15.0	102	14.8	30	15.4
文教卫生	Culture,Education and Health	37	4.2	28	4.1	9	4.6
其他	Others	126	14.3	77	11.3	49	25.1
转移地域	**Region Transfer To**						
本市内转移	Within Local City	875	99.7	681	99.7	194	99.5
转向外省市	To Nonlocal	3	0.3	2	0.3	1	0.5
调查户当年返回农业的劳动力	**Labor Force Back to Agriculture in This Year of Households in Survey**	**3**	**0.3**	**2**	**0.3**	**1**	**0.5**

注：本表数据是在郊区750个农户中调查取得。

Note: Data of this table was gained from 750 farm households survey.

5-35 乡村劳动力构成
COMPOSITION OF RURAL LABOR FORCE

项目	Item	合计 Total 数量(人) Number (person)	合计 Total 构成(%) Composition (%)	平原 Plain 数量(人) Number (person)	平原 Plain 构成(%) Composition (%)	山区 Mountain Area 数量(人) Number (person)	山区 Mountain Area 构成(%) Composition (%)
调查村整半劳动力	**Full and Half Labor Force in Village Surveyed**	**1770**	**100**	**1284**	**100**	**486**	**100**
按性别分	Grouped by Sex						
男劳动力	Male	921	52.0	669	52.1	252	51.8
# 整劳动力	Full Labor Force	717	40.5	521	40.6	196	40.3
女劳动力	Female	849	48.0	615	47.9	234	48.2
# 整劳动力	Full Labor Force	568	32.1	412	32.1	156	32.1
按文化程度分	Grouped by Educational Level						
文盲或半文盲	Illiteracy and Half-illiteracy	34	1.9	25	1.9	9	1.8
小学程度	at Primary School Level	203	11.5	147	11.4	56	11.5
初中程度	at Junior Middle School Level	1050	59.3	762	59.3	288	59.3
中专程度	at Specialized Secondary School Level	436	24.6	316	24.7	120	24.7
大专及以上程度	at Junior College Level and above	47	2.7	34	2.7	13	2.7
按是否接受过专业培训分	Grouped by Whether Received Specialized Training						
受过各种专业培训	Received All Kinds of Specialized Training	449	25.4	326	25.4	123	25.3
未接受专业培训	Never Received Specialized Training	1321	74.6	958	74.6	363	74.7

注：本表数据是在郊区750个农户中调查取得。
Note: Data of this table was gained from 750 farm households survey.

5-36 农村平均每人拥有固定资产投资情况
INVESTMENT IN FIXED ASSETS PER CAPITA OF COUNTRY

单位：元，平方米 (yuan,sq.m)

项目	Item	合计 Total	乡(镇)所有 Of Township	村组所有 Of Village	农户所有 Of Household
本年新增固定资产原值	**Original Value of Incremental Fixed Assets**	**2163.2**	**503.0**	**819.5**	**840.7**
本年固定资产投资完成额	**Investment in Fixed Assets Completed in this year**	**2321.3**	**523.0**	**950.1**	**848.2**
按资金来源分	Grouped by Source of Funds				
自筹资金	Self-raised	1956.6	413.1	820.7	722.8
银行信用社贷款	Loan from Bank and Credit Cooperative	117.7	45.5	72.2	
其他来源	Others	247.0	64.4	57.2	125.4
按资金投向分	Grouped by Use of Funds				
农业	Agriculture	261.6	29.7	122.1	109.8
工业	Industry	431.0	125.4	305.6	
建筑业	Construction	400.2	80.9	138.5	180.8
交通运输业	Transportation	117.4	10.2	54.2	53.0
邮电通讯业	Posts and Telecommunications	0.4	0.2	0.2	
批发零售贸易业	Wholesale and Retail Trade	128.0	47.6	31.9	48.5
社会服务业	Social Services	60.8	17.5	37.8	5.5
文化教育事业	Culture and Education	27.6	15.2	12.4	
卫生体育社会福利业	Health,Sports and Social Welfare	41.9	36.9	5.0	
其他	Others	852.4	159.4	242.4	450.6
本年施工房屋面积	**Floor Space of Buildings under Construction in this Year**	**2.5**	**0.4**	**0.8**	**1.3**
# 住宅	Residential Buildings	1.4	0.1	0.2	1.1
本年竣工房屋面积	**Floor Space of Buildings Completed in this Year**	**2.1**	**0.2**	**0.6**	**1.2**
# 住宅	Residential Buildings	1.3	0.04	0.2	1.0
本年竣工房屋投资完成额	**Investment of Buildings Completed in this Year**	**973.1**	**151.9**	**267.4**	**553.8**
# 住宅	Residential Buildings	596.0	27.8	64.7	503.4

注：本表数据是在郊区80个乡镇、250个村、750个农户及所在村中调查取得。

Note: Data of this table was gained from the survey of 80 towns, 250 villages and 750 farm households.

5-37 农村经济收入与分配

INCOME AND DISTRIBUTION OF RURAL ECONOMY

单位：万元 (10000 yuan)

项目	Item	2000	1999	2000年为1999年% 2000 as % of 1999
营业收入	**Operation Income**	**12868661.6**	**11188467.2**	**115.0**
农 业	Agriculture	674691.9	663178.8	101.7
# 粮食	Grain	173967.0	249007.7	69.9
林 业	Forestry	111492.0	99695.5	111.8
牧 业	Animal Husbandry	665653.6	562019.7	118.4
渔 业	Fishery	67914.1	58158.0	116.8
工 业	Industry	4447320.0	3899783.2	114.0
交通运输业	Transportation	1100352.3	989193.5	111.2
建筑业	Construction	1677572.7	1430955.1	117.2
商业、饮食业	Commerce and Catering	2334589.2	1950388.5	119.7
服务业	Services	988305.3	844027.9	117.1
其 他	Others	800770.5	691067.0	115.9
营业成本	**Operation Cost**	**11336974.0**	**9903286.7**	**114.5**
农 业	Agriculture	607481.5	589759.7	103.0
# 粮食	Grain	139961.8	187476.4	74.7
林 业	Forestry	101216.9	86991.3	116.4
牧 业	Animal Husbandry	633297.8	540204.0	117.2
渔 业	Fishery	65731.5	60937.9	107.9
工 业	Industry	3881064.8	3413093.5	113.7
交通运输业	Transportation	1036055.6	956514.7	107.2
建筑业	Construction	1493475.4	1246755.4	119.8
商业、饮食业	Commerce and Catering	2078785.8	1766741.9	117.7
服务业	Services	838471.0	704861.9	118.9
其 他	Others	601393.7	537424.4	111.9
营业利润	**Operation Profits**	**715058.6**	**583410.5**	**122.6**
利润总额	**Total Profits**	**771432.7**	**661737.8**	**116.6**
税后利润	**Net Profits**	**704072.5**	**602434.1**	**116.9**
可供分配的利润	**Profit to be Divided**	**692073.6**	**560407.5**	**123.5**
未分配利润	**Retained Profits**	**137798.3**	**73334.8**	**187.9**

5-38 郊区规模乡镇发展情况

STATISTICS FOR SCALE TOWN AND TOWNSHIPS IN SUBURBS AND COUNTIES

乡镇名称 Name	总人口(人) Population (person)	总劳动力(人) Labor Force(person)	农村社会总产值(万元) Rural Gross Output Value (10000 yuan)	乡镇企业个数(个) Town and Township Enterprises (unit)	乡镇企业总收入(万元) Total Revenue of Town and Township Enterprises (10000 yuan)	乡镇企业利润总额(万元) Total Profits of Town and Township Enterprises (10000 yuan)
小红门乡	17811	8595	116403.2	234	99413.0	2892.0
十八里店乡	29139	13534	53717.7	144	57491.0	2527.0
南磨房乡	4519	2322	158454.1	46	183000.0	8543.0
高碑店乡	30138	2703	111194.6	132	122918.0	7721.0
平房乡	17091	8489	64422.0	86	24861.0	693.0
金盏乡	9790	4123	55333.7	52	38395.0	889.0
来广营乡	9095	3923	65309.4	97	53892.0	265.0
洼里乡	8105	3808	52447.2	76	79049.1	7858.8
黑庄户乡	11028	4112	53405.1	30	24736.0	3782.5
卢沟桥乡	39477	20109	127476.0	395	226853.0	24603.0
花乡	38575	21041	152262.0	284	280613.0	19143.0
长辛店乡	19344	6618	55333.2	108	31518.6	-460.0
石景山农委	15836	7007	62952.7	216	138968.0	3059.0
四季青乡	44366	13334	69380.1	269	133209.0	22245.0
永定镇	17580	7789	69988.8	657	77438.0	4727.0
周口店地区	27507	9698	143404.0	129	169216.0	13037.0
琉璃河地区	24082	11245	110879.6	677	75494.3	2675.0
房山城关镇	30606	13166	195961.4	2731	320554.7	7499.0
良乡镇	75904	11962	132982.0	2834	202504.0	1976.0
阎村镇	28426	10310	118405.5	1041	127801.0	19642.0
交道镇	20282	6664	96587.0	38	88203.0	4026.0
窦店镇	19389	7451	152608.4	1316	163368.0	6898.0
石楼镇	29004	12696	75281.7	53	21682.1	382.6
张坊镇	21598	10548	50029.8	11	50726.0	3178.0
青龙湖镇	19088	9132	61209.7	842	44539.0	778.5
韩村河镇	16014	7160	225105.0	1283	179162.0	
通州城关镇	34310	12457	126764.0	2413	166423.0	20189.0
梨园镇	24709	5897	97402.6	1031	80679.0	7215.8
徐辛庄镇	24123	10077	69138.0	1204	44910.0	3839.0
宋庄镇	28361	14504	156451.0	1786	150088.0	6707.0
张家湾镇	26205	10134	103043.6	193	77493.0	3308.0
郭县镇	30658	15826	88087.0	1086	64200.0	2932.0
牛堡屯镇	24369	11817	73695.6	730	52483.0	2854.0
次渠镇	21845	10429	53582.2	299	35123.0	2580.0
马驹桥镇	23090	11004	51182.0	579	35045.0	997.0
仁和地区	35606	16288	156269.5	2096	135313.0	3630.0
后沙峪地区	15295	5502	72948.8	588	11787.0	4270.0

注：规模乡镇是指农村社会总产值达到5亿元的乡镇(续表同）。
Note: Town and townships refer to those their rural gross output value amount to 500 million yuan(the continued is the same).

5-38 续表 continued

乡 镇 名 称 Name	总 人 口(人) Population (person)	总劳动力(人) Labor Force(person)	农村社会总产值(万元) Rural Gross Output Value (10000 yuan)	乡镇企业个数(个) Town and Township Enterprises (unit)	乡镇企业总收入(万元) Total Revenue of Town and Township Enterprises (10000 yuan)	乡镇企业利润总额(万元) Total Profits of Town and Township Enterprises (10000 yuan)
天竺地区	13621	6641	63648.5	55	30157.0	1050.0
杨镇地区	41930	17319	90680.9	1011	42591.0	2323.0
南法信地区	11937	5988	69962.9	390	54136.0	5084.0
马坡地区	15330	7845	64036.6	168	50820.0	4326.0
高丽营镇	19494	8855	63130.8	67	55085.0	1748.0
李桥镇	30037	11717	110054.3	1067	82457.0	6114.0
南彩镇	30639	14550	75428.9	122	41748.0	3604.0
大孙各庄镇	25775	11736	116377.9	93	48025.0	6223.0
张镇	21936	9984	75620.4	147	23920.4	2041.7
木林镇	34063	12946	65953.8	94	15709.0	879.0
北小营镇	28272	11474	143772.6	9	84177.0	9433.0
赵全营镇	22356	9513	86405.3	50	15303.0	1279.2
马池口镇	21903	8618	53982.2	97	35020.0	691.0
沙河镇	21687	8836	103713.8	137	36846.0	2318.0
回龙观镇	15423	6886	51585.0	76	46218.0	2780.0
小汤山镇	23208	11777	56142.0	58	24108.0	639.0
北七家镇	26741	9818	75684.0	59	32240.0	1872.0
黄村镇	46077	22530	175457.0	350	99491.0	6797.0
西红门镇	17112	8046	126902.0	242	211806.0	20068.0
旧宫镇	11514	4303	109653.9	183	95350.0	568.0
青云店镇	31573	15932	55387.0	152	29839.3	333.0
采育镇	29437	14736	54912.6	94	20844.0	540.0
庞各庄镇	38587	21335	113940.2	66	77768.0	2164.0
魏善庄镇	28537	15419	50630.9	55	20812.0	2187.5
瀛海镇	18194	8371	70679.9	176	37496.0	998.0
亦庄乡	21407	10729	111458.2	133	62342.2	3169.9
东高村镇	30698	12914	60510.7	55	71605.3	5865.0
峪口镇	28620	13606	76060.8	257	45000.4	1532.4
马坊镇	17671	9154	92739.9	345	101851.0	12087.0
马昌营镇	15325	7643	64089.3	54	57533.0	3350.5
怀柔镇	23161	9995	211856.0	128	295049.0	16081.0
北房镇	15472	7622	83819.0	368	51022.0	3471.0
杨宋镇	14071	4555	75053.6	282	76753.0	4508.0
庙城镇	15521	5238	89001.6	164	78010.0	3494.0
桥梓镇	18077	6930	93047.8	96	75789.0	2991.0
西田各庄镇	38417	16486	53777.7	1239	36784.0	521.0
太师屯镇	39793	18465	77243.0	667	35212.0	1450.0
延庆镇	33449	15984	90660.6	11	24473.0	1227.0
旧县镇	21404	9846	68007.5	690	53733.0	3103.0
张山营镇	225879	11463	54376.9	15	23012.0	662.0

主要统计指标解释

农业总产值　是以货币表现的农、林、牧、渔业全部产品的总量，它反映一定时期内农业生产总规模和总成果。

农、林、牧、渔业的统计范围包括国有经济各种专业农（农、林、牧、渔）场以及国家各级机关团体学校、部队；集体所有制的乡、镇、村各级办农场；工矿企业经营的农、林、牧、渔业，农村各种经济组织和农户经营的农林牧渔业和农民家庭兼营的商品性工业等。

（1）农业　包括种植业和其他农业。

种植业　包括谷物、豆类、薯类、棉、油料、糖料、麻类、烟叶、蔬菜、药材、瓜类和其他农作物的种植，以及茶园、桑园、果园的生产经营。

其他农业　包括采集野生植物的果实、纤维、树胶、树脂、油料以及柴草、野生药材、菌类等及农民家庭兼营的商品性工业。

（2）林业　包括林木的栽培（不包括茶园、桑园和果园的栽培、管理和收获等活动）、林产品的采集和村及村以下合作经济组织和农户的竹木采伐。

（3）牧业　包括除渔业养殖以外的一切动物饲养和放牧以及野生动物的捕猎和饲养。

（4）渔业　包括水生动物和海藻类植物的养殖和捕捞。

农业总产值的计算方法通常是按农林牧渔业产品及其副产品的产量分别乘以各自单位产品价格求得，少数生产周期较长，当年没有产品或产品产量不易统计的，则采用间接方法匡算其产值，然后将四业产品产值相加即为农业总产值。

1957 年以前的农业总产值中包括了厩肥和农民自给性手工业（如农民自制衣服、鞋、袜，自己从事粮食初步加工等）。1958 年及以后的农业总产值，林业中增加了村及村以下竹木采伐产值；牧业中取消费厩肥产值；副业中取消了农民自给性手工业产值；渔业中增加了海洋捕捞水产品产值。1980 年及以后的农业总产值，在副业中增加了农民家庭兼营工业商品部分的产值。从 1984 年起村及村以下办工业产值划归工业。从 1993 年起，取消副业。将野生动物的捕猎划入牧业，野生植物采集和农民家庭兼营商品性工业划归农业。

耕地面积　指年初可以用来种植农作物、经常进行耕锄的田地，除包括熟地、当年新开荒地、连续撂荒未满三年的耕地和当年的休闲地（轮歇地）外，还包括以种植农作物为主并附带种植桑树、茶树、果树和其他林木的土地，以及沿海、沿湖地区已围垦利用的“海涂”、“湖田 ”等面积。但不包括属于专业性的桑园、茶园、果园、果木苗圃、林地、芦苇地、天然或人工草地面积。

农作物播种面积　指实际播种或移植有农作物的面积。凡是实际种植有农作物的面积，不论种植在耕地上还是种植在非耕地上，均包括在农作物播种面积中。在播种季节基本结束后，因遭灾而重新改种和补种的农作物面积，也包括在内。

有效灌溉面积　指具有一定的水源，地块比较平整，灌溉工程或设备已经配套，在一般年景下当年能够进行正常灌溉的耕地面积。

农业机械总动力　指主要用于农、林、牧、渔业的各种动力机械的动力总和。包括耕作机械、排灌机械、收获机械、农用运输机械、植物保护机械、牧业机械、渔业机械和其他农用机械[内燃机按引擎马力折成瓦（特）计算，电动机按功率折成瓦（特）计算]。不包括专门用于乡、镇、村、组办工业、基本建设、非农业运输、科学实验和教学等非农业生产方面用的动力机械与作业机械。

乡村从业人员　指乡村人口中 16 岁以上实际参加生产经营活动并取得实物或货币收入的人员，既包括劳动年龄内经常参加劳动的人员，也包括超过劳动年龄但经常参加劳动的人员。但不包括户口在家的在外学生、现役军人和丧失劳动能力的人，也不包括待业人员和家务劳动者。从业人员年龄为 16 岁以上。从业人员按从事主业时间最长（时间相同按收入）分为农业从业人员、工业从业人员、建筑业从业人员、交运仓储及邮电通讯业从业人员、批零贸易及餐饮业从业人员、其它从业人员人员。

期初（末）畜禽存栏头（只）数　指本期期初（末）农村各种合作经济组织和国营农场、农民个人、机关、团体、学校、工矿企业、部队等单位以及城镇居民饲养的大牲畜、猪、羊、家禽等禽畜的存栏头（只）数。

乡镇企业　即原来农村人民公社和生产大队两级集体经济举办的社队企业。在农村政社组织管理体制分设以后，除了乡、村合作经济组织办企业外，又出现了部分农民联营或其他形式的合作企业和个体企业。1984 年 3 月确定将这类企业统称“乡镇企业”。

乡镇企业单位一般应拥有固定的组织、生产场所、生产设备和从业人员；有核算制度，承担经济责任和纳税义务；是一个比较稳定的经济实体。

Explanatory Notes On Main Statistical Indicators

Gross Output of Agriculture refers to the total volume of products of farming, forestry, animal husbandry and fishery in value terms, which reflects the total scale and total result of agricultural production during a given period of time.

The statistical coverage of farming, forestry, animal husbandry and fishery are as follows:

In terms of ownership, China's agriculture includes specialized state farms（farming, forestry, animal husbandry and fishery), farms managed by various government organs, organizations, schools, research institutions, and army; farms managed by rural collective organizations at levels of township, town, and village; farming, forestry, animal husbandry, fishery run by mining and industrial enterprises; farming, forestry, animal husbandry and fishery and some commodity industries run by individual farmers.

（1）Farming includes cultivation of farm crops and other agricultural activities .

Cultivation includes the cultivation of grain crops, beans, tubers, cotton, oil-bearing crops, sugar crops, fiber crops, tobacco, vegetables, medicinal herbs, melons and gourds, and cultivation and management of tea plantations, mulberry fields and orchards.

Other agricultural activities includes gathering fruits, fiber, oil, gum and resin of wild plants, firewood and firegrass, wild medicinal herbs, fungus plants, and commodity industries of the rural households.

（2）Forestry refers to planting various kinds of trees（excluding tea plantations, mulberry fields and orchards）, gathering of forest products, and felling of bamboo and trees by villages and other cooperative organizations under villages.

（3）Animal husbandry refers to raising and grazing of all animals except fishery and aquaculture, and hunting and raising of wild animals.

（4）Fishery refers to cultivation and catching of fish and other aquatic animals and cultivation and collection of seaweed and other aquatic plants.

Gross output value of agriculture is obtained by first multiplying the output of each product or by-product by its price, resulting in the output value of each single item. For a small number of products, annual output of which is not available or difficult to get due to the long production/ growing process involved, the output value is estimated through an indirect approach. The sum of output value of all products of farming, forestry, animal husbandry, and fishery is then equal to the gross output value of agriculture.

Prior to 1957, China's gross agricultural output value included barnyard manure and handicraft products for self-consumption（clothes, shoes, stockings, and initial grain processing undertaken by peasants）. Since 1958, felling of bamboo and trees by villages and other cooperative organizations under villages had been added to forestry; value of barnyard manure had been removed from animal husbandry; self-consumed handicrafts had been removed from sideline productions; while the output value of industries run by villages and cooperative organizations under village had been added in sideline productions and the output value of fish catches by motor fishing boats had been added to fishery. Since 1980, the value of handicraft products made for sale by households had been added to sideline productions. Since 1984, industry run by villages and cooperative organizations under villages has been put in the sector of industry. Since 1993, the subdivision of sideline productions has been canceled, and the hunting of wild animals has been classified into animal husbandry, and the gathering of wild plants and commodity industry run by rural households has been put in farming.

Cultivated Area（Area under cultivation） refers to farmland which is plowed constantly for growing crops, including cultivated land, newly cultivated land in the current year, farmland left without cultivation for less than three years and fallow land in the current year, rotation land, farmland for crops but growing also a few fruit trees, mulberry trees and other trees and cultivated seashore land and lake land, etc. The land of mulberry fields, tea plantations, orchards, nurseries of young plants, forestland, reed land, natural and man-made grassland are not included in cultivated land.

Sown Area of Crops refers to area of land sown or transplanted with crops regardless of being in cultivated area or non-cultivated area. Area of land resown after natural disasters is also included in.

Irrigated Area refers to areas that are effectively irrigated, i. e. level land which has water source and complete sets of irrigation facilities and is able to provide adequate water for irrigation under normal conditions.

Total Power of Farm Machinery refers to total mechanical power of machinery used in farming, forestry, animal husbandry, and fishery, including plow, irrigation and drainage, harvesting, transport, plant protection, stock breeding, forestry and fishery. The horsepower of internal combustion engines is converted into watts and the power of electric motors is converted into watts. Machinery employed for non-agricultural industry, construction, transportation, scientific experiments and teaching is excluded.

Rural Employment refers to persons above 16-year-old who actually engaged in production and get income in kind or money income, including those usually engaged in production within or beyond labor-age and excluding students outside whose residence card at home, serviceman, disabilities, people waiting for employment and houseworkers. Employment can be divided into six categories by period of engaging in major labor: employment of agriculture, employment of industry, employment of construction, employment of transportation, storage, posts and telecommunications, employment of wholesale, retail sales and catering and other employment.

Number of Livestock or Poultry on Hand at the Beginning（or End ）of the reference Period refers to the total number of big animals, pigs, sheep, fowls, etc. raised by rural cooperative organizations, army, and urban residents at the beginning （or end ） of the reference period.

Township Enterprises refer to enterprises originally run by the collective economies at the people's commune and the production brigade levels. After the rural administrative system reform, besides the enterprises run by townships and villages, farmers' cooperative or other types of cooperative enterprises and private enterprises had appeared in the rural areas. In March 1984, all the aforesaid enterprises were defined as the “township enterprises.”

Township Enterprises should have fixed organization, production sites, production equipment and employees, and also have accounting systems, undertake economic responsibilities and pay taxes. So, they are relatively stable economic entities.

北京统计年鉴——2001

BEIJING STATISTICAL YEARBOOK

工 业

6

INDUSTRY

工业总产值　　（单位：亿元）
Gross Output Value of Industry (100 million yuan)

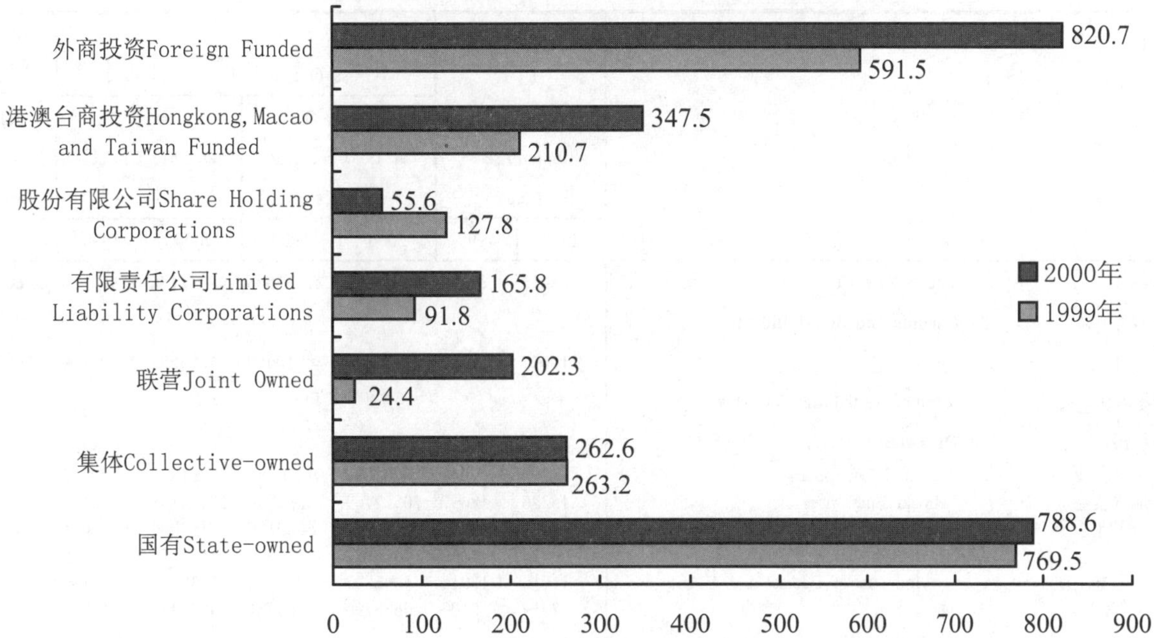

主要工业产品产量

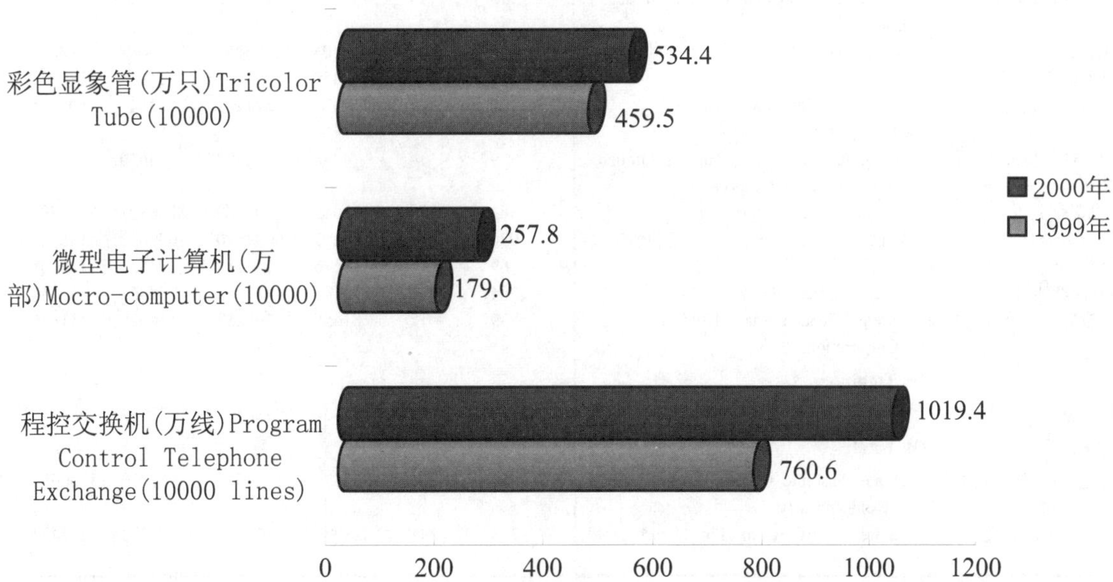

6-1 工业企业单位数和工业总产值、销售产值

NUMBER OF INDUSTRIAL ENTERPRISES, GROSS OUTPUT VALUE AND SALES

单位：万元 (10000 yuan)

项目	Item	企业单位数(个) Number of Enterprises (unit)		工业总产值 Gross Output Value of Industry				销售产值(当年价格) Sales (at current prices)
				1990年不变价 at 1990 constant prices		当年价格 at current prices		
		2000	1999	2000	1999	2000	1999	
全市合计	**The Whole City**	**28815**	**32870**	**27899677**	**21253006**	**27742156**	**21902616**	**26634287**
(含个体工业)	**(include Individual Industry)**							
总　计	**Total**	**16027**	**19682**	**27227811**	**20810067**	**27074083**	**21446119**	**25992893**
(不含个体工业)	**(exclude Individual Industry)**							
在总计中：	**Of Total:**							
中央企业	Central Enterprises	801	1045	6705042	7520169	7561927	7190947	7365682
地方企业	Local Enterprises	15226	18637	20522769	13289899	19512156	14255145	18627211
工业系统	Industry System	1027	1554	7226770	6260106	7194080	6446674	6855146
非工业系统	Non-Industry System	724	1059	1011387	841069	1507510	1316985	1503117
区县工业	Industry of District and County	11016	13915	5648822	5082944	5938148	5376153	5671882
其他	Others	2459	2109	6635790	1105781	4872418	1115333	4597066
在总计中：	**Of Total:**							
内资企业	Domestic Investment Enterprises	13732	16990	12242980	11352883	15390660	13424788	14886778
国有企业	State-Owned	1981	2829	5376433	5920611	7885866	7695460	7776397
集体企业	Collective Owned	8030	10738	2437420	2510989	2626223	2631668	2477569
股份合作企业	Share Holding	834	826	326434	228015	360373	243651	337809
私营企业	Private Owned	207	1524	363395	355227	281555	371298	262152
联营企业	Joint Owned	725	302	1704213	296764	2022769	285789	1968840
有限责任公司	Limited Liability Corporations	192	553	1505722	1113691	1657570	1278151	1558939
股份有限公司	Share Holding Corporations	1755	206	528809	927143	555716	918343	504495
其他企业	Others	8	12	554	445	587	428	576
港澳台商投资企业	Hongkong,Macao and Taiwan Funded Enterprises	913	1114	5192816	2750595	3475123	2106734	3308916
港澳台合资经营	Joint Venture	655	821	1525804	1185884	1393668	1198653	1329838
港澳台合作经营	Cooperative	40	52	49450	32999	51984	36024	50456
港澳台商独资企业	Hongkong,Macao and Taiwan Enterprises	209	227	3613076	1521209	2024841	861265	1924202
港澳台商投资股份有限公司	Hongkong,Macao and Taiwan Funded Share Holding Corporations	9	14	4486	10503	4630	10792	4420
外商投资企业	Foreign Funded Enterprises	1382	1578	9792015	6706589	8208301	5914596	7797199
中外合资经营	Joint Venture	920	1087	8834261	6048510	7079682	5186351	6819454
中外合作经营	Cooperative	69	71	196516	144254	194527	145261	190644
外资(独资)企业	Foreign Enterprises	384	408	679783	417572	789463	431159	640610
外商投资股份有限公司	Foreign Funded Share Holding Corporations	9	12	81456	96253	144629	151826	146491
在总计中：	**Of Total:**							
农村企业	Rural Enterprises	7667	9627	3095331	2924508	3272622	3083423	3109718
在总计中：	**Of Total:**							
国有绝对控股企业	State Absolute Controlling Share Hold Industry	2636	4266	16866391	13029642	16641070	13500616	16198965
国有相对控股企业	State Relative Controlling Share Hold Industry	253	247	828289	1301641	840283	1282492	802222

注：1.本资料除"主要工业产品生产总量"(全社会)及标明者外，均为不含个体的独立核算工业企业统计范围。

2.全市合计(含个体工业)中的不变价工业总产值及销售产值为折算数。

3.2000年企业单位数为年报统计范围工业企业,1999年企业单位数为工商局注册登记企业。

a) Data of this chapter refers to industrial enterprises with independent accounting system(except individuals),except the table of "major products output" (refers to total)and items with note.

b) Data of gross output value at constant prices and sales of the whole city(include individual)is that converted.

c) Enterprises in 2000 refers to those of annual-report, and enterprises of 1999 refers to those registered in industrial and commercial bureau.

6-1 续表 1 continued

单位：万元 (10000 yuan)

项目	Item	企业单位数(个) Number of Enterprises (unit) 2000	1999	工业总产值 Gross Output Value of Industry 1990年不变价 at 1990 constant prices 2000	1999	当年价格 at current prices 2000	1999	销售产值(当年价格) Sales (at current prices)
在总计中：	**Of Total:**							
轻工业	Light Industry	7830	9559	6484495	5560892	6852281	6106775	6608416
以农产品为原料	Using Farm Products as Raw Materials	4689	5713	3837702	3261405	4353867	3934752	4198790
以非农产品为原料	Using Non-Farm Products as Raw Materials	3141	3846	2646792	2299486	2498414	2172023	2409626
重工业	Heavy Industry	8197	10123	20743317	15249176	20221802	15339344	19384477
采掘工业	Excavation	382	502	120627	114320	216172	191301	215447
原料工业	Raw Material	1048	1277	4046705	3379893	6728664	4920776	6677276
加工工业	Processing	6767	8344	16575985	11754963	13276966	10227267	12491754
在总计中：	**Of Total:**							
大型企业	Large Enterprises	215	217	14171278	7705996	13481429	8266005	13103639
中型企业	Medium Enterprises	266	292	2054756	2441733	2266435	2448433	2169127
小型企业	Small Enterprises	15546	19173	11001778	10662339	11326220	10731681	10720127
在总计中：	**Of Total:**							
煤炭采选业	Coal Mining and Dressing	145	194	68749	57035	157507	125320	160364
石油和天然气开采业	Petroleum and Natural Gas Extraction		1		138		138	
黑色金属矿采选业	Ferrous Metals Mining and Dressing	19	19	9042	10985	14196	17541	13982
有色金属矿采选业	Nonferrous Metals Mining and Dressing	13	16	6789	4213	7019	4284	5846
非金属矿采选业	Nonmetal Minerals Mining and Dressing	202	271	35760	42089	37132	44210	34939
其他矿采选业	Other Minerals Mining and Dressing	2	2	223	291	254	270	252
食品加工业	Food Processing	461	573	447742	447626	581871	629688	587653
食品制造业	Food Making	523	668	596951	421002	755338	547637	719421
饮料制造业	Beverage Making	240	271	792145	556623	729222	634867	685815
烟草加工业	Tobacco Processing	2	4	46485	45142	83914	70101	84453
纺织业	Textile Industry	397	516	424333	380403	461319	403711	440670
服装及其他纤维制品制造业	Garments and Other Fiber Products	792	985	459497	426799	532150	491168	521293
皮革、毛皮、羽绒及其制品业	Leather,Furs,Down and Related Products	142	174	47020	45513	57331	56009	56774
木材加工及竹藤、棕、草制品业	Timber Processing,Bamboo Cane,Palm Fiber and Straw Products	199	247	68288	45373	72198	53141	71031
家具制造业	Furniture Manufacturing	457	547	150467	146877	159586	152044	156758
造纸及纸制品业	Papermaking and Paper Products	429	525	203261	186889	218787	200846	210411
印刷业，记录媒介的复制	Printing and Record Medium Reproduced	891	1011	404785	352979	494236	468519	483446

6-1 续表 2 continued

单位：万元 (10000 yuan)

项目	Item	企业单位数(个) Number of Enterprises (unit) 2000	1999	工业总产值 Gross Output Value of Industry 1990年不变价 at 1990 constant prices 2000	1999	当年价格 at current prices 2000	1999	销售产值(当年价格) Sales (at current prices)
文教体育用品制造业	Stationery,Educational and Sports Goods	207	242	85599	96264	104467	114157	101251
石油加工及炼焦业	Petroleum Processing and Coking Products	86	110	1162161	898414	2618221	1445224	2596259
化学原料及化学制品	Raw Chemical Materials and Chemical Product	1117	1358	1297718	1179687	1406604	1177497	1372396
医药制造业	Medical and Pharmaceutical Products	220	254	581535	496184	540637	450470	508109
化学纤维制造业	Chemical Fibers	34	45	43149	59162	35102	41838	34219
橡胶制品业	Rubber Products	101	139	155440	153245	136561	135539	116197
塑料制品业	Plastic Products	625	736	309296	271760	300265	268703	288471
非金属矿物制品	Nonmetal Mineral Products	1484	1780	924431	872528	1091759	1042200	1056980
黑色金属冶炼及压延加工业	Smelting and Pressing of Ferrous Metals	67	79	1315513	1041863	1806555	1494973	1803373
有色金属冶炼及压延加工业	Smelting and Pressing of Nonferrous Metals	117	151	119852	95351	124946	98028	121074
金属制品业	Metal Products	1865	2282	731054	639080	718249	638648	687800
普通机械制造业	Ordinary Machinery Manufacturing	1004	1247	519489	464901	536636	489141	521546
专用设备制造业	Equipments for Special Purposes Manufacturing	814	1007	1191953	944247	1172957	973475	1129636
交通运输设备制造业	Transportation Equipment Manufacturing	1081	1344	951619	1053515	1062303	1186733	1030743
武器弹药制造业	Weapon and Ammunition Manufacturing	9	9	69780	54806	93921	70696	93564
电气机械及器材制造	Electric Equipment and Machinery	775	930	1052609	914764	944425	867126	904731
电子及通信设备制造	Electronic and Telecommunications	606	763	12034394	7551449	8467298	5643635	7885207
仪器仪表及文化、办公用机械制造	Instruments,Meters,Cultural and Office Machinery	355	486	407348	369142	410260	366497	388522
其他制造业	Other Manufacturing	475	605	157855	158902	160415	153180	143824
电力、蒸汽、热水的生产和供应业	Electricity,Steam and Hot Water Production and Supply	55	66	264311	233833	752540	688150	752074
煤气生产和供应业	Gas Production and Supply	7	12	38184	39131	81596	75521	80803
自来水的生产和供应业	Tap Water Production and Supply	9	13	52987	51862	146308	125230	143012

6-2 主 要 工 业 产 品 生 产 总 量
OUTPUT OF MAIN INDUSTRIAL PRODUCTS

主要工业产品名称 Products			本年生产量 Output in this Year
原 煤	(吨) Coal	(ton)	5529980
铁矿石成品矿	(吨) Iron Ore Products	(ton)	6051981
发电量	(万千瓦小时) Electricity	(10000 kwh)	1452564
火 电	(万千瓦小时) Thermal Power	(10000 kwh)	1366187
供热量	(万百万千焦) Heating Supply	(10 billion kilo-joule)	3654
自来水生产量	(万吨) Tap Water Production	(10000 tons)	78151
大 米	(吨) Rice	(ton)	11736
小麦粉	(万吨) Wheat Flour	(10000 tons)	36
食用植物油	(吨) Edible Vegetable Oil	(ton)	82677
配混合饲料	(吨) Mixed Feed	(ton)	745981
乳制品	(吨) Dairy Products	(ton)	20579
方便主食品	(吨) Convenient Staple Food	(ton)	71673
罐 头	(吨) Canned Food	(ton)	23
白 酒	(吨) Liquor	(ton)	70034
啤 酒	(吨) Beer	(ton)	1771827
软饮料	(吨) Soft Drink	(ton)	662451
冷冻饮品	(吨) Frozen Drink	(ton)	25410
卷 烟	(箱) Cigarettes	(case)	170678
合成纤维	(吨) Synthetic Fiber	(ton)	16270
纱	(吨) Yarn	(ton)	40924
布	(万米) Cloth	(10000 m)	12183
# 棉 布	(万米) Cotton Cloth	(10000 m)	9233
混纺交织布	(万米) Blend Cloth	(10000 m)	2930
纯化纤布	(万米) Pure Chemical Fiber Cloth	(10000 m)	20
绒线(毛线)	(吨) Knitting Wool	(ton)	845
呢 绒	(万米) Woolen Piece Goods	(10000 m)	939
丝织品	(万米) Silk Fabrics	(10000 m)	54
服 装	(万件) Garments	(10000)	9879
锯 材	(立方米) Sawn Timber	(cu.m)	6506
家 具	(件) Furniture	(unit)	2721403
人造板	(立方米) Artificial Wooden Board	(cu.m)	137964
机制纸	(吨) Machine-made Paper	(ton)	31011
机制纸板	(吨) Machine-made Paperboard	(ton)	74951
体育用品及用具	(千元) Sports Goods and Appliance	(1000 yuan)	117065
工艺美术制品	(千元) Handicrafts	(1000 yuan)	258832
汽 油	(吨) Gasoline	(ton)	1462001

6-2 续表1 continued

单位 ：吨 (ton)

主要工业产品名称	Products	本年生产量 Output in this Year
柴 油	Diesel Oil	1839240
润滑油	Lubricating Oil	321763
燃料油	Fuel Oil	789475
焦 炭	Coke	4020711
硫酸(折100%)	Sulfuric Acid(100%)	79703
氢氧化钠(烧碱)(折100%)	Caustic Soda(100%)	151428
碳化钙(电石)(折 300升/千克)	Calcium Carbide(300 liters/kg)	5277
合成氨	Synthetic Ammonia	72771
农用氮、磷、钾化学肥料(折纯)	Chemical Fertilizer(pure)	67939
乙 烯	Ethylene	655159
纯 苯	Pure Benzene	105129
油 漆	Paint	15127
染 料	Dyestuff	3763
塑料树脂及共聚物	Plastic Resin and Copolymer	850536
合成橡胶	Synthetic Rubber	128510
合成纤维单体	Synthetic Fiber(Monomer)	51431
合成纤维聚合物	Synthetic Fiber(Polymerizate)	3021
合成洗涤剂	Synthetic Detergents	36716
化学原料药	Chemical Raw Medicine	3461
轮胎外胎 (条)	Tires (unit)	1977873
塑料制品	Plastic Products	109957
# 农业用薄膜	Film for Farm Use	16037
水 泥 (万吨)	Cement (10000 tons)	827
平板玻璃 (重量箱)	Plate Glass (wt.case)	4321030
生 铁	Pig Iron	7732371
钢	Steel	8034228
成品钢材	Steel Products	6966882
# 普通中型钢材	Ordinary Rolled-Steel,Medium	215274
普通小型钢材	Ordinary Rolled-Steel,Small	2579943
优质钢型钢材	High Quality Section Steel	319873
线 材	Wire Rod	2918140
中厚钢板	Medium Steel Plate	524017
钢 带	Steel Band	287284
无缝钢管	Seamless Steel Pipe	1187
焊接钢管	Welded Steel Pipe	111134
铁合金	Ferroalloy	20043
铜	Copper	231

6-2 续表2 continued

主要工业产品名称 Products			本年生产量 Output in this Year
铜加工材	(吨) Copper Products	(ton)	12048
铝　材	(吨) Aluminum Products	(ton)	23482
日用精铝制品	(吨) Daily-use Refined Aluminum Products	(ton)	410
金属切削机床	(台) Metal-Cutting Machine Tools	(unit)	2497
# 高精度机床	(台) High-Precision Machine Tools	(unit)	128
数控机床	(台) Numerical Control Machine Tools	(unit)	568
大型机床	(台) Large Machine Tools	(unit)	31
小型拖拉机	(台) Mini-tractor	(unit)	3907
汽　车	(辆) Motor Vehicle	(unit)	125260
# 载货汽车	(辆) Trucks	(unit)	104667
公路汽车	(辆) Highway Motor Vehicle	(unit)	15621
轿车	(辆) Cars	(unit)	4867
摩托车	(辆) Motorcycle	(unit)	2645
发电设备	(千瓦) Generating Equipment	(kw)	150000
绝缘制品	(吨) Insulating Products	(ton)	5523
家用洗衣机	(台) Household Washing Machines	(unit)	210006
家用电冰箱	(台) Household Refrigerators	(unit)	35963
房间空气调节器	(台) House Air Conditioner	(unit)	313832
程控交换机	(线) Program Control Telephone Exchange	(line)	10194341
电子计算机	(部) Computer	(unit)	785
微型电子计算机	(部) Micro-computer	(unit)	2578488
彩色显象管	(只) Tricolor Tube	(unit)	5344277
半导体集成电路	(万块) Semiconductor Integrated Circuit	(10000)	23684
电子元件	(万只) Electronic Cell	(10000)	1651987
彩色电视机	(部) Color TV Set	(unit)	5630
录相机	(部) Video Recorder	(unit)	980000
收录放机	(部) Recorder	(unit)	253541
自动化仪表及系统	(台) Automatic Meters and System	(unit)	1178543
光学仪器	(台) Optical Instrument	(unit)	64391
照相机	(台) Camera	(unit)	551909
表	(只) Clock	(unit)	780454

6-3 全部独立核算工业企业主要经济指标

单位：万元

项目	Item	企业单位个数(个) Number of Enterprises (unit)	#亏损企业 Loss-making Enterprises	工业总产值(当年价格) Gross Output Value of Industry (at current prices)	新产品产值 Value of New Products	工业总产值(1990年不变价格) Gross Output Value of Industry (at 1990 constant prices)	工业增加值(生产法) Added Value of Industry (with production method)
总　计	**Total**	16027	3630	27074083	5892487	27227811	7452255
在总计中：	**Of Total:**						
中央企业	Central Enterprises	801	285	7561927	2223964	6705042	1837889
地方企业	Local Enterprises	15226	3345	19512156	3668523	20522769	5614367
工业系统	Industry System	1027	269	7194080	1319231	7226770	2067472
非工业系统	Non-Industry System	724	209	1507510	16274	1011387	544819
区县工业	Industry of District and County	11016	1908	5938148	163534	5648822	1859226
其他	Others	2459	959	4872418	2169484	6635790	1142850
在总计中：	**Of Total:**						
内资企业	Domestic Investment Enterprises	13732	2615	15390660	2052038	12242980	4751148
国有企业	State-Owned	1981	512	7885866	688211	5376433	2497087
集体企业	Collective Owned	8030	1278	2626223	46575	2437420	801199
股份合作企业	Share Holding	834	151	360373	10589	326434	108629
联营企业	Joint Owned	207	46	281555	27681	363395	40844
有限责任公司	Limited-Liability Corporations	725	187	2022769	403730	1704213	637527
股份有限公司	Share Holding Corporations	192	44	1657570	822253	1505722	481441
私营企业	Private Owned	1755	396	555716	52999	528809	184192
其他企业	Others	8	1	587		554	229
港澳台商投资企业	Hongkong,Macao and Taiwan Funded Enterprises	913	425	3475123	1858822	5192816	753000
港澳台合资经营	Joint Venture	655	290	1393668	238063	1525804	360515
港澳台合作经营	Cooperative	40	17	51984		49450	20259
港澳台商独资企业	Hongkong,Macao and Taiwan Enterprises	209	112	2024841	1620759	3613076	371559
港澳台商投资股份有限公司	Hongkong,Macao and Taiwan Funded Share Holding Corporations	9	6	4630		4486	666
外商投资企业	Foreign Funded Enterprises	1382	590	8208301	1981627	9792015	1948107
中外合资经营	Joint Venture	920	367	7079682	1877269	8834261	1544638
中外合作经营	Cooperative	69	17	194527	3941	196516	59830
外资(独资)企业	Foreign Enterprises	384	204	789463	86231	679783	281609
外商投资股份有限公司	Foreign Funded Share Holding Corporations	9	2	144629	14187	81456	62030
在总计中：	**Of Total:**						
农村企业	Rural Enterprises	7667	919	3272622	7246	3095331	1007072
在总计中：	**Of Total:**						
国有绝对控股企业	State Absolute Controlling Share Hold Industry	2636	719	16641070	4473662	16866391	4427338
国有相对控股企业	State Relative Controlling Share Share Hold Industry	253	99	840283	144498	828289	272634
在总计中：	**Of Total:**						
轻工业	Light Industry	7830	1920	6852281	441834	6484495	2353121
以农产品为原料	Using Farm Products as Raw Materials	4689	1191	4353867	140689	3837702	1513443
以非农产品为原料	Using Non-Farm Products as Raw Materials	3141	729	2498414	301146	2646792	839678
重工业	Heavy Industry	8197	1710	20221802	5450653	20743317	5099134
采掘工业	Excavation	382	31	216172		120627	96925
原料工业	Raw Material	1048	224	6728664	471857	4046705	1859974
加工工业	Processing	6767	1455	13276966	4978796	16575985	3142235
在总计中：	**Of Total:**						
大型企业	Large Enterprises	215	49	13481429	3568202	14171278	3310532
中型企业	Medium Enterprises	266	54	2266435	745900	2054756	794034
小型企业	Small Enterprises	15546	3527	11326220	1578385	11001778	3347690

MAIN INDICATORS FOR INDUSTRIAL ENTERPRISES WITH INDEPENDENT ACCOUNTING SYSTEM

(10000 yuan)

工业销售产值(当年价格) Sales Value of Industry (at current price)	出口交货值 Delivery Value of Exports	全部从业人员年平均人数(人) Average Number of Persons Employed (person)	资产负债 Assets and Liabilities						
			流动资产合计 Circulating Funds	应收帐款净额 Accounts Receivable	存货 Stock	产成品 Finished Products	流动资产平均余额 Average Balance of Circulating Funds	长期投资 Longterm Investment	固定资产合计 Fixed Assets
25992893	2554681	1456026	21731195	5566291	6647350	2416969	20429255	3103969	19268171
7365682	750582	203035	4829596	1318669	1192822	321639	5010457	819065	5458694
18627211	1804100	1252991	16901599	4247622	5454528	2095330	15418798	2284905	13809476
6855146	803577	458859	7456633	1932705	2390270	861592	7411062	1811737	7401640
1503116	19999	88375	1531188	398464	353515	112742	1317146	126312	2313705
5671882	445311	610815	4384795	920610	1795821	835709	4077526	226322	3164872
4597066	535213	94942	3528983	995842	914922	285287	2613065	120534	929259
14886778	555961	1203612	14129062	2719384	4458617	1711378	13809839	3006286	15717495
7776397	285270	567822	7214849	1301672	2276820	707130	7732654	1816274	9870613
2477569	141111	374716	1970353	392420	914416	464278	1855510	128894	1233769
337809	20765	39964	234409	47093	96395	46560	212015	19848	143090
262152	5059	28193	334771	55788	138205	59636	326895	51427	252486
1968840	51735	92636	1933940	448804	459028	198564	1739452	633932	3159898
1558939	39074	50623	2060951	396987	411197	170740	1611982	340002	874643
504495	12875	49483	379539	76590	162441	64453	331112	15909	182845
576	72	175	250	30	115	18	219		152
3308916	251721	87926	2265948	535072	760363	271359	1739285	44766	826527
1329838	210171	68200	1268966	363453	451172	174437	1126919	29830	699591
50456	8987	3267	46912	11193	15225	6667	40477	938	33390
1924202	32278	15883	940422	158834	290128	87710	562732	13565	88740
4420	285	576	9648	1592	3839	2545	9157	433	4806
7797199	1747000	164488	5336186	2311835	1428370	434233	4880131	52918	2724148
6819454	1602537	127746	4545176	2021173	1197663	349878	4231872	50767	2194127
190644	20878	5255	123724	30906	49930	22520	104721	201	95864
640610	94965	24432	613361	240429	161909	51510	490434	1015	290641
146491	28621	7055	53925	19328	18868	10324	53104	934	143516
3109718	314247	383386	2060411	458647	964027	499129	1921550	83260	1390498
16198965	1401548	758794	13525713	3258592	3880155	1289990	13351412	2798767	14970704
802222	94010	29032	659645	154754	182504	54218	572726	47448	516482
6608416	710952	589883	5899273	1044016	2062524	941498	5585135	667990	4928030
4198790	460738	401294	3543945	594355	1265130	572603	3335120	398124	2889613
2409626	250214	188589	2355328	449661	797394	368895	2250015	269866	2038418
19384477	1843730	866143	15831923	4522274	4584826	1475471	14844120	2435979	14340141
215447	29385	46499	230587	94604	32677	19868	227682	27892	175854
6677276	183151	255333	4357140	837506	1191437	318544	4458520	1119607	9288731
12491754	1631195	564311	11244197	3590165	3360712	1137058	10157918	1288480	4875556
13103639	1236550	506061	9474442	2431418	2841910	893991	9763063	1705901	12309132
2169127	199400	129368	2336271	543046	553547	233688	2125354	622543	1732492
10720127	1118732	820597	9920483	2591826	3251893	1289289	8540838	775525	5226546

6-3 续表 1 continued

单位：万元

项目	Item	资产负债 固定资产原价合计 Original Value of Fixed Assets	# 生产经营用 For Productive Use	累计折旧 Accumulative Depreciation	#本年折旧 Depreciation in this Year	固定资产净值年平均余额 Average Net Value of Fixed Assets	无形资产及递延资产 Intangible and Deferred Assets
总 计	**Total**	25316408	20976587	8674040	1224388	16021620	1827469
在总计中：	**Of Total:**						
中央企业	Central Enterprises	7218302	6353661	2666490	357957	4491863	203331
地方企业	Local Enterprises	18098107	14622926	6007550	866431	11529757	1624137
工业系统	Industry System	10155949	8872282	3821014	462409	6273814	919838
非工业系统	Non-Industry System	2897109	1898727	741668	127107	1881149	60593
区县工业	Industry of District and County	3958899	3190265	1133126	179002	2677960	360555
其他	Others	1086150	661652	311743	97913	696835	283152
在总计中：	**Of Total:**						
内资企业	Domestic Investment Enterprises	20470597	17054399	7090855	908113	12942504	1256431
国有企业	State-Owned	13275784	10917610	5078407	575751	8080361	485434
集体企业	Collective Owned	1623187	1286135	545647	71251	1029588	113884
股份合作企业	Share Holding	178550	140543	50830	9397	129267	16134
联营企业	Joint Owned	339502	216235	106982	10011	228283	26538
有限责任公司	Limited-Liability Corporations	3805972	3492179	902277	176934	2710198	501260
股份有限公司	Share Holding Corporations	1044635	834808	369100	54226	612047	87675
私营企业	Private Owned	202784	166719	37580	10536	152609	25506
其他企业	Others	185	171	33	8	152	
港澳台商投资企业	Hongkong,Macao and Taiwan Funded Enterprises	1026970	877968	304890	55594	696347	255237
港澳台合资经营	Joint Venture	880309	772020	265890	43835	600999	101037
港澳台合作经营	Cooperative	38668	23999	7864	2166	32249	3306
港澳台商独资企业	Hongkong,Macao and Taiwan Enterprises	101994	77458	29622	9353	58577	150128
港澳台商投资股份有限公司	Hongkong,Macao and Taiwan Funded Share Holding Corporations	5998	4491	1514	241	4523	766
外商投资企业	Foreign Funded Enterprises	3818841	3044221	1278295	260681	2382769	315800
中外合资经营	Joint Venture	3165374	2488446	1100455	216956	1942775	239816
中外合作经营	Cooperative	111946	73124	30346	8101	63464	13681
外资(独资)企业	Foreign Enterprises	360629	303553	88799	23972	242199	42819
外商投资股份有限公司	Foreign Funded Share Holding Corporations	180892	179097	58695	11652	134331	19485
在总计中：	**Of Total:**						
农村企业	Rural Enterprises	1754399	1416561	505474	82541	1183413	113804
在总计中：	**Of Total:**						
国有绝对控股企业	State Absolute Controlling Share Hold Industry	19786710	16608898	6989643	906620	12394595	1107259
国有相对控股企业	State Relative Controlling Share Share Hold Industry	757810	666342	281189	31665	449512	69446
在总计中：	**Of Total:**						
轻工业	Light Industry	6462132	4312094	1988961	349781	4253891	671556
以农产品为原料	Using Farm Products as Raw Materials	3817703	3034773	1208862	187783	2503255	281247
以非农产品为原料	Using Non-Farm Products as Raw Materials	2644429	1277321	780099	161998	1750636	390309
重工业	Heavy Industry	18854276	16664494	6685079	874607	11767729	1155913
采掘工业	Excavation	243183	68308	83410	11165	163908	7557
原料工业	Raw Material	12288483	11741803	4405893	557443	7638735	653858
加工工业	Processing	6322610	4854383	2195776	306000	3965087	494497
在总计中：	**Of Total:**						
大型企业	Large Enterprises	16508453	13850315	5948130	782189	10287451	863690
中型企业	Medium Enterprises	2176167	1919554	702077	105434	1400070	223300
小型企业	Small Enterprises	6631788	5206719	2023833	336765	4334099	740480

6-3 续表 2 continued

(10000 yuan)

#无形资产 Intangible Assets	其他资产 Other Assets	资产总计 Total Assets	流动负债合计 Liquid Liabilities	短期借款 Shortterm Loans	长期负债合计 Long-term Liabilities	长期借款 Longterm Loans	负债合计 Total Liabilities	所有者权益 Creditors' Equity	实收资本 Contributed Capital	国家资本 State
Assets and Liabilities										
950540	196498	46127325	19748023	6775159	6867220	4547388	26763977	19363348	12959106	4869047
151758	22989	1133676	4147934	1107510	3001059	1096844	7180964	4152712	2313522	1177936
798782	173509	34793649	15600089	5667649	3866162	3450544	19583013	15210636	10645584	3691111
313859	51666	17641513	7459588	3112732	2694822	2488952	10207167	7434346	4612459	1551692
41038	17220	4049018	1169265	250248	259828	223021	1445995	2603023	2012604	1577093
195476	56984	8193543	4203859	1506436	679975	533341	4911374	3282169	2694107	397393
248409	47639	4909575	2767376	798233	231537	205229	3018476	1891099	1326413	164933
477083	34784	34144073	13005972	4432693	6768187	3895628	19243947	14900126	8760442	4309452
213105	9711	19396881	7401874	2621795	3898584	1877813	11316713	8080169	4386671	2821546
47078	7436	3454336	1892466	584265	355316	280448	2274532	1179804	925286	33774
12715	1178	414663	231983	62756	27866	18851	263308	151355	116918	7929
7829	858	666091	374071	108378	95157	76646	471499	194592	146574	22246
113809	7524	6236554	1635226	570822	1545326	1446881	3182592	3053962	2270658	1221201
64756	6286	3369557	1163815	389977	218910	172864	1395803	1973753	713095	202280
17792	1788	605587	306409	94698	27026	22125	339372	266215	200909	465
	2	404	128	2			128	276	332	10
214300	41953	3434431	2206474	679869	210722	186881	2429750	1004681	945232	161943
69336	35762	2135185	1302591	527941	131897	111736	1442285	692900	796860	160051
1888	1884	86431	39727	10638	2779	2481	42514	43917	30550	1630
142559	4287	1197142	856194	140313	72876	72321	933820	263322	112599	
517	21	15673	7961	977	3170	343	11131	4542	5222	262
259158	119761	8548821	4535578	1662597	488312	464879	5090280	3458541	3253432	397652
211563	99574	7129460	3861685	1485027	431413	404232	4354289	2775171	2523697	378092
11588	3161	236630	88436	21070	6537	6307	95733	140897	117673	8003
25354	15281	963125	519930	133170	59397	53334	583752	379373	492371	11178
10653	1746	219606	65528	23331	-9034	1006	56506	163100	119691	378
62380	27465	3675452	1959309	761659	298623	229983	2275840	1399612	1166643	38842
415737	73877	32476321	12314369	4330971	5884338	3754912	18246013	14230307	8119473	4409475
51315	20877	1313898	519869	189134	63047	50992	627932	685966	582568	165024
436129	82173	12249033	5627780	2186387	1122403	905863	6784413	5464620	4543649	1493388
178668	50630	7163558	3401581	1381111	537528	383234	3963498	3200060	2735023	766928
257461	31544	5085475	2226199	805277	584875	522630	2820915	2264560	1808626	726459
514412	114325	33878292	14120243	4588772	5744818	3641525	19979564	13898728	8415457	3375659
1075	305	442195	189435	70494	63542	54106	253010	189185	108717	83943
232525	-5692	15413643	4384284	1568694	4320967	2523449	8733092	6680551	3929957	2439489
280811	119712	18022454	9546525	2949583	1360309	1063969	10993462	7028992	4376784	852228
306151	19767	24372932	9186386	3546765	5037138	3057958	14236972	10135960	5680532	3018653
134965	11011	4925616	1855301	597818	453812	342357	2309167	2616449	1576787	892310
509424	165720	16828776	8706336	2630576	1376271	1147073	10217838	6610938	5701787	958084

6-3 续表 3 continued

单位：万元

项目	Item	资产负债 Assets and Liabilities				
		集体资本 Collective	法人资本 Institutional Units	个人资本 Individuals	港澳台资本 Hongkong, Macao and Taiwan	外商资本 Foreign
总　计	**Total**	936617	3979751	528940	598707	2046044
在总计中：	**Of Total:**					
中央企业	Central Enterprises	32625	935610	28157	31209	107985
地方企业	Local Enterprises	903992	3044141	500783	567499	1938059
工业系统	Industry System	124007	2006544	124970	114280	690967
非工业系统	Non-Industry System	18462	148108	19957	44368	204617
区县工业	Industry of District and County	730924	626040	235877	240966	462907
其他	Others	30600	263449	119979	167884	579568
在总计中：	**Of Total:**					
内资企业	Domestic Investment Enterprises	777342	3119696	510111	3228	40612
国有企业	State-Owned	22402	1458113	78590	1572	4448
集体企业	Collective Owned	630499	172775	82555	683	4999
股份合作企业	Share Holding	25620	39187	44002	42	138
联营企业	Joint Owned	33341	87393	2450		1144
有限责任公司	Limited-Liability Corporations	36363	945157	52579	425	14932
股份有限公司	Share Holding Corporations	19764	339511	136589		14950
私营企业	Private Owned	9354	77444	113141	506	
其他企业	Others		117	205		
港澳台商投资企业	Hongkong,Macao and Taiwan Funded Enterprises	55516	190345	8107	487492	41828
港澳台合资经营	Joint Venture	54433	181015	7627	360467	33267
港澳台合作经营	Cooperative	390	4567	480	21548	1934
港澳台商独资企业	Hongkong,Macao and Taiwan Enterprises		2465		103882	6252
港澳台商投资股份有限公司	Hongkong,Macao and Taiwan Funded Share Holding Corporations	693	2298		1595	374
外商投资企业	Foreign Funded Enterprises	103758	669710	10721	107987	1963604
中外合资经营	Joint Venture	93709	563811	9496	72226	1406362
中外合作经营	Cooperative	7342	8171	412	14315	79432
外资(独资)企业	Foreign Enterprises	236	10049	372	20218	450317
外商投资股份有限公司	Foreign Funded Share Holding Corporations	2472	87679	441	1228	27493
在总计中：	**Of Total:**					
农村企业	Rural Enterprises	507140	294525	121035	72085	133017
在总计中：	**Of Total:**					
国有绝对控股企业	State Absolute Controlling Share Hold Industry	66402	3007816	213152	116964	305665
国有相对控股企业	State Relative Controlling Share Share Hold Industry	13830	77418	12380	58939	254977
在总计中：	**Of Total:**					
轻工业	Light Industry	441995	1004365	219226	358629	1026046
以农产品为原料	Using Farm Products as Raw Materials	267489	561249	142627	252984	743746
以非农产品为原料	Using Non-Farm Products as Raw Materials	174506	443115	76600	105645	282300
重工业	Heavy Industry	494622	2975387	309713	240078	1019998
采掘工业	Excavation	16155	5972	2183		464
原料工业	Raw Material	70201	1201829	73700	34239	110500
加工工业	Processing	408266	1767586	233831	205839	909035
在总计中：	**Of Total:**					
大型企业	Large Enterprises	48463	1677984	110303	105301	719829
中型企业	Medium Enterprises	79426	427716	59991	39708	77636
小型企业	Small Enterprises	808728	1874051	358646	453698	1248580

6-3 续表 4 continued

(10000 yuan)

损益及分配 Profits,Loss and Distribution										
产品销售收入 Sales Revenue	产品销售成本 Cost of Sales	产品销售费用 Expenses of Sales	产品销售税金及附加 Sales Tax and Extra Charges	产品销售利润 Sales Profits	管理费用 Overhead Cost	税金 Taxes	财产保险费 Premium of Property	劳动待业保险费 Premium for Employment Insurance	财务费用 Financial Expenses	利息支出 Expenses of Interest
28213557	23380075	1176328	264793	3392361	2297601	65584	20859	314237	504718	464090
7963488	6866275	148484	96605	852124	483190	10332	5231	67001	114196	108686
20250069	16513800	1027844	168188	2540237	1814410	55252	15628	247236	390521	355403
8083709	6717449	313526	46992	1005742	886674	29403	8601	195831	249938	244706
1719757	1455633	90030	45009	129086	159628	5651	1334	21277	13787	12676
5534996	4404047	361809	68248	700891	465565	15730	4470	25991	92208	74202
4911607	3936672	262478	7940	704517	302543	4468	1223	4137	34588	23819
16673800	13998647	536613	235889	1902651	1598803	50302	15212	299513	383833	359409
9198204	7784243	198494	193980	1021487	976829	29717	8380	234476	236154	234401
2461325	2055603	92856	15670	297197	215041	7192	1881	19601	44725	35068
331329	276898	16059	1768	36604	25013	668	258	1252	4543	3709
287352	241044	14697	1583	30029	42205	1525	369	7376	8803	7732
2146594	1838998	93441	9934	204220	190450	5319	2926	28238	58731	53974
1743564	1417432	72093	10107	243931	108145	5092	1186	8000	25596	20470
504867	383977	48944	2840	69106	41046	789	213	569	5280	4055
566	452	29	8	77	75	1				-1
3217677	2583000	176523	3885	454270	194954	2108	1451	3289	24582	15803
1333858	1126320	76373	3700	127465	97994	1648	1263	2768	19677	15576
51040	35114	4674	1	11251	5020	82	36	46	646	550
1828577	1418495	94974	173	314935	91239	358	143	399	4191	-386
4202	3071	502	10	619	701	19	9	77	67	63
8322081	6798429	463193	25019	1035440	503844	13174	4196	11435	96303	88878
7129180	5933029	333408	23465	839278	384867	11662	3531	10455	83913	80255
191547	134759	22103	13	34673	16777	303	66	132	2895	1287
855901	626772	99323	1364	128442	96533	1037	542	582	7328	5302
145453	103869	8358	177	33048	5667	173	57	266	2166	2034
2986363	2487002	128972	16743	353646	185912	6607	1998	2249	47609	35006
17962500	15249013	521355	219640	1972492	1462068	42410	13975	280141	364613	351386
839444	640580	63193	2426	133245	86629	1735	903	4095	9211	7834
6799974	5167942	553063	120933	958036	759253	21644	8047	83554	132506	116972
4346926	3282092	376342	104216	584277	473963	13808	5658	54200	87951	79214
2453048	1885851	176721	16717	373759	285290	7836	2389	29354	44555	37757
21413583	18212133	623265	143860	2434325	1538348	43940	12812	230683	372211	347118
219951	163605	15588	2174	38583	34552	764	33	17208	4842	4282
7650822	6724718	96568	102273	727264	504457	17668	7257	103651	203239	196030
13542811	11323809	511110	39413	1668478	999339	25508	5523	109824	164131	146807
14806810	12677249	396526	166172	1566863	1093688	35128	11367	221078	304516	294351
2301506	1879020	82721	50829	288937	236329	8580	1785	39151	41021	38287
11105241	8823805	697082	47792	1536561	967584	21876	7707	54007	159180	131452

6-3 续表 5 continued

单位：万元

项目	Item	损益及分配 Profits,Loss and Distribution 营业利润 Operating Profits	投资收益 Investment Income	补贴收入 Subsidy Income	营业外收入 Out-business Income	营业外支出 Out-business Expenditure	利润总额 Total Profits
总计	Total	851206	160183	182502	339567	262190	1270874
在总计中：	Of Total:						
中央企业	Central Enterprises	350444	41604	27872	22338	69896	357668
地方企业	Local Enterprises	500761	118579	154629	317229	192294	913206
工业系统	Industry System	26167	79454	65370	219104	140750	243088
非工业系统	Non-Industry System	-29382	6855	74718	25803	14519	64799
区县工业	Industry of District and County	189296	20597	7301	33039	25019	238492
其他	Others	314681	11673	7240	39283	12005	366827
在总计中：	Of Total:						
内资企业	Domestic Investment Enterprises	234513	160544	181541	251419	201612	603660
国有企业	State-Owned	-7031	104231	112140	199013	172539	206980
集体企业	Collective Owned	69649	3459	6041	15655	10797	87766
股份合作企业	Share Holding	9293	710	547	3685	1449	13328
联营企业	Joint Owned	-9752	1576	803	14283	2091	5386
有限责任公司	Limited-Liability Corporations	3008	22221	57132	10773	8439	84847
股份有限公司	Share Holding Corporations	144581	28285	2196	7484	5094	177985
私营企业	Private Owned	24763	63	2681	523	1203	27364
其他企业	Others	2			3		5
港澳台商投资企业	Hongkong,Macao and Taiwan Funded Enterprises	167214	92	51	15909	8984	177990
港澳台合资经营	Joint Venture	15163	877	51	5922	5204	18869
港澳台合作经营	Cooperative	5785	85		4933	58	10936
港澳台商独资企业	Hongkong,Macao and Taiwan Enterprises	146401	-870		5024	3716	148273
港澳台商投资股份有限公司	Hongkong,Macao and Taiwan Funded Share Holding Corporations	-135			30	6	-87
外商投资企业	Foreign Funded Enterprises	449479	-453	910	72240	51594	489224
中外合资经营	Joint Venture	381452	-827	28	61636	49603	405126
中外合作经营	Cooperative	15149	47	728	865	621	16186
外资(独资)企业	Foreign Enterprises	27512	327	154	9457	2137	39974
外商投资股份有限公司	Foreign Funded Share Holding Corporations	25367			281	-767	27938
在总计中：	Of Total:						
农村企业	Rural Enterprises	127272	1638	2401	9235	9665	134838
在总计中：	Of Total:						
国有绝对控股企业	State Absolute Controlling Share Hold Industry	403619	150613	169018	250544	193835	755897
国有相对控股企业	State Relative Controlling Share Share Hold Industry	46171	1456	475	5971	3009	52334
在总计中：	Of Total:						
轻工业	Light Industry	200035	63495	39480	103773	68093	324138
以农产品为原料	Using Farm Products as Raw Materials	102577	36143	14778	75604	36789	182384
以非农产品为原料	Using Non-Farm Products as Raw Materials	97458	27352	24702	28169	31303	141754
重工业	Heavy Industry	651170	96689	143022	235795	194097	946736
采掘工业	Excavation	2517	476	11847	1374	3144	13843
原料工业	Raw Material	67735	21567	100418	63721	117161	128532
加工工业	Processing	580919	74646	30757	170700	73792	804362
在总计中：	Of Total:						
大型企业	Large Enterprises	305143	100373	144088	211389	190747	547516
中型企业	Medium Enterprises	100230	42219	14136	38724	10027	188206
小型企业	Small Enterprises	445833	17592	24277	89454	61415	535151

6-3 续表 6 continued

(10000 yuan)

应交所得税 Income Tax Payable	应付利润 Profits Payable	亏损企业亏损额 Total Losing of Lossmaking Enterprises	利税总额 Total Pre-tax Profits	工资，福利费，增值税 Wages,Welfares and Added Value Tax 本年应付工资总额 Total Wags Payable	本年应付福利费总额 Total Welfares Payable	本年应交增值税 Added Value Tax	本年进项税额 Tax Include in Purchasing Cost	本年销项税额 Tax Include in Sales Cost	工业中间投入合计 Intermediate Input of Industry
260474	242779	450235	2561091	1901482	310850	1025424	3252929	4106548	20647252
77193	44060	59381	670610	383317	64832	216337	939134	1133164	5940375
183281	198719	390854	1890481	1518165	246018	809087	2313796	2973384	14706877
86028	80987	163020	659441	710552	121547	369362	1194596	1500345	5495970
16775	1044	31903	191437	135969	21951	81630	179447	255678	1044321
50779	52671	116965	540452	494497	68047	233712	548381	766245	4312634
29698	64017	78966	499151	177148	34474	124385	391372	451116	3853952
188737	90759	203021	1539839	1408363	203135	700289	2215068	2851994	11339800
104345	37127	92080	793869	817502	122365	392909	1308529	1662929	5781688
23699	30239	48986	201417	272035	34539	97982	245843	332572	1923006
3223	2902	5381	26599	31958	3631	11504	35399	45469	263248
2510	2989	4970	16169	30294	4005	9200	37934	46118	249910
15517	8673	36632	195896	138327	20731	101115	245917	341379	1486357
34524	6066	5427	255098	75564	12935	67006	287346	349744	1243135
4917	2760	9538	50739	42521	4922	20534	54071	73720	392059
1	4	6	53	161	8	40	29	65	398
9849	13186	61692	284443	133491	22942	102568	268930	325378	2824691
8369	11786	51770	69940	87751	15762	47371	138866	185859	1080523
528	1063	973	13990	3947	700	3054	5248	8038	34778
897	358	8609	200461	41177	6398	52015	124313	130844	1705297
55	-20	340	52	615	82	129	503	637	4093
61888	138834	185522	736809	359629	84773	222566	768932	929177	6482760
54667	128607	145794	607267	283602	65720	178676	642669	762318	5713720
2642	5274	2282	25447	12300	2178	9248	17631	24061	143945
4519	6217	37325	71158	52555	14333	29820	100481	129959	537674
59	-1264	122	32937	11173	2541	4822	8151	12838	87422
25539	35662	30333	252238	276000	33119	100656	277572	365120	2366206
182594	125785	199808	1635575	1175854	188000	660038	2196499	2756069	12873770
6867	19670	26971	90983	67704	13678	36224	71947	103068	603872
84382	70600	190060	780740	640983	101155	335669	657555	962534	4834830
51205	35633	125563	505410	428475	68776	218810	421615	615574	3059234
33177	34967	64497	275329	212508	32378	116859	235940	346960	1775596
176092	172180	260176	1780351	1260499	209696	689755	2595374	3144014	15812422
1002	2082	802	25214	42948	13023	9197	12989	21032	128444
79871	30602	47135	554199	456013	64003	323395	1130414	1430278	5192085
95219	139496	212238	1200938	761539	132670	357163	1451971	1692704	10491893
132326	101243	146349	1245255	867158	146556	531567	1836994	2240973	10702464
33047	2256	30209	342543	177752	29226	103508	255681	356581	1575909
95101	139281	273677	973293	856573	135069	390349	1160254	1508994	8368880

6-4 全部独立核算工业企业主要经济指标(按行业分)

单位：万元

项目	Item	企业单位个数(个) Number of Enterprises (unit)	#亏损企业 Loss-making Enterprises	工业总产值(当年价格) Gross Output Value of Industry (at current prices)	新产品产值 Value of New Products	工业总产值(1990年不变价格) Gross Output Value of Industry (at 1990 constant prices)	工业增加值(生产法) Added Value of Industry (with production method)
煤炭采选业	Coal Mining and Dressing	145	9	157507		68749	77809
黑色金属矿采选业	Ferrous Metals Mining and Processing	19		14196		9042	4341
有色金属矿采选业	Nonferrous Metals Mining and Processing	13	1	7019		6789	2203
非金属矿采选业	Nonmetal Minerals Mining and Processing	202	19	37132		35760	12453
其他矿采选业	Other Minerals Mining and Processing	2	1	254		223	108
食品加工业	Food Processing	461	126	581871	8422	447742	104166
食品制造业	Food Making	523	161	755338	13945	596951	305496
饮料制造业	Beverage Making	240	90	729222	1775	792145	265602
烟草加工业	Tobacco Processing	2	1	83914	1957	46485	57089
纺织业	Textile Industry	397	100	461319	20974	424333	130720
服装及其他纤维制品制造业	Garments and Other Fiber Products	792	232	532150	558	459497	174304
皮革、毛皮、羽绒及其制品业	Leather,Furs,Down and Related Products	142	40	57331	38	47020	16987
木材加工及竹、藤、棕、草制品业	Timber Processing,Bamboo,Cane,Palm Fiber and Straw Products	199	41	72198		68288	18828
家具制造业	Furniture Manufacturing	457	99	159586	71	150467	47494
造纸及纸制品业	Papermaking and Paper Products	429	83	218787	27	203261	75965
印刷业、记录媒介的复制	Printing and Record Medium Reproduced	891	177	494236	37423	404785	211549
文教、体育用品制造	Stationery,Educational and Sports Goods	207	54	104467	8483	85599	33295
石油加工及炼焦业	Petroleum Processing and Coking Products	86	18	2618221	254141	1162161	368250
化学原料及化学制品制造业	Raw Chemical Materials and Chemical Products	1117	238	1406604	75125	1297718	390494
医药制造业	Medical and Pharmaceutical Products	220	51	540637	77118	581535	253045
化学纤维制造业	Chemical Fibers	34	10	35102		43149	4544
橡胶制品业	Rubber Products	101	23	136561	8148	155440	32467
塑料制品业	Plastic Products	625	150	300265	14433	309296	76850
非金属矿物制品业	Nonmetal Mineral Products	1484	222	1091759	90731	924431	371771
黑色金属冶炼及压延加工业	Smelting and Pressing of Ferrous Metals	67	20	1806555	121088	1315513	622648
有色金属冶炼及压延加工业	Smelting and Pressing of Nonferrous Metals	117	25	124946	41274	119852	24311
金属制品业	Metal Products	1865	371	718249	6122	731054	208124
普通机械制造业	Ordinary Machinery Manufacturing	1004	184	536636	44912	519489	173804
专用设备制造业	Equipments for Special Purposes Manufacturing	814	210	1172957	454931	1191953	312689
交通运输设备制造业	Transportation Equipment Manufacturing	1081	296	1062303	176645	951619	283459
武器弹药制造业	Weapon and Ammunition Manufacturing	9	2	93921	6753	69780	39776
电气机械及器材制造	Electric Equipment and Machinery	775	171	944425	193308	1052609	261463
电子及通信设备制造	Electronic and Telecommunications	606	178	8467298	4E+06	12034394	1731699
仪器仪表及文化、办公用机械制造业	Instruments,Meters,Cultural and Office Machinery Manufacturing	355	94	410260	103075	407348	121158
其他制造业	Other Manufacturing	475	119	160415	1408	157855	63023
电力、蒸汽、热水的生产和供应业	Electricity,Steam and Hot Water Production and Supply	55	10	752540	10196	264311	449555
煤气生产和供应业	Gas Production and Supply	7	1	81596		38184	66573
自来水的生产和供应	Water Production and Supply	9	3	146308		52987	58147

MAIN INDICATORS FOR INDUSTRIAL ENTERPRISES WITH INDEPENDENT ACCOUNTING SYSTEM(BY SECTOR)

(10000 yuan)

工业销售产值(当年价格) Sales Value of Industry (at current price)	出口交货值 Delivery Value of Exports	全部从业人员年平均人数(人) Average Number of Persons Employed (person)	资产负债 Assets and Liabilities: 流动资产合计 Circulating Funds	应收帐款净额 Accounts Receivable	存货 Stock	产成品 Finished Products	流动资产平均余额 Average Balance of Circulating Funds	长期投资 Longterm Investment	固定资产合计 Fixed Assets
160364	28224	37952	165185	81584	19784	12206	178980	10667	133125
13982		2861	37839	8150	7255	3735	31474	2555	23180
5846		742	11057	550	286	167	1165	13297	2015
34939	1160	4874	16268	4239	5251	3692	15777	1373	17141
252		37	233	80	102	69	283		205
587653	10281	25325	277625	71368	79325	29380	276892	11411	267359
719421	19769	45177	515757	79804	123628	55195	426020	64933	404212
685815	11387	35520	605841	78013	192997	45960	576587	54591	657705
84453	2163	910	21165	338	6422	105	22883	3042	31289
440670	149234	62355	432195	68793	196213	102845	458748	47396	310824
521293	199381	89468	444824	81586	214057	115124	417093	23877	238979
56774	15703	11029	105333	15619	31728	16417	96049	7646	50366
71031	1209	7154	81053	13660	37098	20707	67485	2812	73176
156758	25428	20311	132185	17180	75321	34308	122117	1811	72169
210411	7120	21757	178448	45483	55340	25184	178230	10353	162666
483446	166	63118	352748	55550	102579	33423	334782	32813	480024
101251	19104	14633	115669	19844	53082	21323	111688	5724	55884
2596259	16007	41853	994627	169810	284216	66496	1209982	73512	1372388
1372396	61396	67015	1065072	227216	333689	152767	969148	157721	1432509
508109	24996	32861	690459	115242	227472	128754	662974	217669	364994
34219	122	3630	34028	5145	14901	6492	32546	93	39160
116197	19991	11351	98501	37508	42465	27425	92625	5897	123497
288471	13067	28339	273082	62000	100411	48956	264559	40824	301658
1056980	37047	127005	1141554	284006	400151	226939	1043486	232033	1064767
1803373	101673	103979	1273339	166821	521098	76516	1306181	492878	2368358
121074	4842	7092	217146	22370	31198	12266	133517	28662	60687
687800	44470	75177	586872	122535	245565	125061	539364	27680	404463
521546	57512	76997	842194	185571	351353	118012	848990	65359	567292
1129636	60109	72351	1145825	205011	451024	192536	1023681	153795	535065
1030743	18496	113931	1266657	307822	515155	122529	1571261	286263	895715
93564	105	10629	85643	11485	30801	3855	79307	24559	99794
904731	47124	63889	1031379	358887	337754	129577	1053673	74825	472942
7885207	1497154	88094	5910159	2285785	1280422	353839	4739341	566174	1516641
388522	42940	29388	478815	84721	169935	60343	457436	60271	156584
143824	17300	22540	161857	31187	68745	37057	142925	9241	83131
752074		22115	683891	196837	20321	568	693287	275004	3293862
80803		8483	105655	38143	9670	21	112496	8565	502366
143012		6084	151015	6348	10537	7125	136226	8645	631981

6-4 续表 1 continued

单位：万元

项目	Item	资产负债 固定资产原价合计 Original Value of Fixed Assets	# 生产经营用 For Productive Use	累计折旧 Accumulative Depreciation	#本年折旧 Depreciation in this Year	固定资产净值年平均余额 Average Net Value of Fixed Assets	无形资产及递延资产 Intangible and Deferred Assets
煤炭采选业	Coal Mining and Dressing	193858	26831	65743	9152	125017	3167
黑色金属矿采选业	Ferrous Metals Mining and Processing	22343	20821	8144	863	20312	2567
有色金属矿采选业	Nonferrous Metals Mining and Processing	1833	794	245	135	1515	16
非金属矿采选业	Nonmetal Minerals Mining and Processing	24560	19310	9081	979	16704	1754
其他矿采选业	Other Minerals Mining and Processing	257	221	52	21	165	52
食品加工业	Food Processing	349903	280675	111108	16293	241127	20152
食品制造业	Food Making	552793	433331	171503	29347	362303	49371
饮料制造业	Beverage Making	816742	668914	208654	35209	545262	68303
烟草加工业	Tobacco Processing	42117	41481	16019	2194	28826	571
纺织业	Textile Industry	461500	360264	178058	19653	291180	32602
服装及其他纤维制品制造业	Garments and Other Fiber Products	305750	243107	96788	13711	199728	24510
皮革、毛皮、羽绒及其制品业	Leather,Furs,Down and Related Products	60589	49557	17608	1747	44116	7916
木材加工及竹、藤、棕、草制品业	Timber Processing,Bamboo,Cane,Palm Fiber and Straw Products	84889	72345	17642	5429	63432	7978
家具制造业	Furniture Manufacturing	93630	75724	25397	5508	66363	6494
造纸及纸制品业	Papermaking and Paper Products	197038	149822	50165	8123	141973	26573
印刷业、记录媒介的复制	Printing and Record Medium Reproduced	704626	548835	260593	46186	436348	8527
文教、体育用品制造	Stationery,Educational and Sports Goods	73453	62103	25163	3810	52735	11458
石油加工及炼焦业	Petroleum Processing and Coking Products	2296441	2101691	1212814	107633	1086879	91149
化学原料及化学制品制造业	Raw Chemical Materials and Chemical Products	1877217	1662301	530818	115539	1364052	413745
医药制造业	Medical and Pharmaceutical Products	423857	318349	123177	21290	272980	72925
化学纤维制造业	Chemical Fibers	60578	52586	23426	1810	38462	12317
橡胶制品业	Rubber Products	138574	126533	49269	5828	85503	15530
塑料制品业	Plastic Products	383971	254528	111976	16352	274232	34371
非金属矿物制品业	Nonmetal Mineral Products	1333602	1096179	431264	64189	883028	166776
黑色金属冶炼及压延加工业	Smelting and Pressing of Ferrous Metals	3358984	3353486	1488418	127989	1923000	73213
有色金属冶炼及压延加工业	Smelting and Pressing of Nonferrous Metals	76553	61940	32106	2932	44568	29886
金属制品业	Metal Products	511011	398112	155551	24626	342471	35238
普通机械制造业	Ordinary Machinery Manufacturing	717851	541426	247286	29422	462083	50641
专用设备制造业	Equipments for Special Purposes Manufacturing	639164	479634	211487	30353	407853	58356
交通运输设备制造业	Transportation Equipment Manufacturing	1263208	926048	498056	59235	718920	42330
武器弹药制造业	Weapon and Ammunition Manufacturing	129372	87332	41359	2508	102150	1471
电气机械及器材制造	Electric Equipment and Machinery	641461	499250	218494	47791	454169	69367
电子及通信设备制造	Electronic and Telecommunications	1918640	1414841	634934	119640	1103718	177749
仪器仪表及文化、办公用机械制造业	Instruments,Meters,Cultural and Office Machinery Manufacturing	225208	172620	85909	8944	137385	15556
其他制造业	Other Manufacturing	114458	78362	41852	3573	68275	21260
电力、蒸汽、热水的生产和供应业	Electricity,Steam and Hot Water Production and Supply	3775309	3654797	920140	173994	2649239	36566
煤气生产和供应业	Gas Production and Supply	624328	603195	145697	24828	383586	
自来水的生产和供应	Water Production and Supply	820741	39246	208044	37553	581966	137012

6-4 续表 2 continued

(10000 yuan)

Assets and Liabilities										
			流动负债		长期负债					
#无形资产 Intangible Assets	其他资产 Other Assets	资产总计 Total Assets	合计 Liquid Liabilities	短期借款 Shortterm Loans	合计 Long-term Liabilities	长期借款 Longterm Loans	负债合计 Total Liabilities	所有者权益 Creditors' Equity	实收资本 Contributed Capital	国家资本 State
958	138	312283	134997	44449	47377	41362	182400	129883	63670	52070
		66141	35646	22306	5899	5229	41545	24596	14523	12342
16	12	26398	3398	70	3511	3511	6909	19489	19534	19142
48	143	36680	15116	3669	6756	4004	21878	14801	10521	390
52	12	502	205				205	297	298	
12093	9976	586522	305419	120751	43672	33826	353296	233226	250357	102828
25507	11827	1046099	510419	182359	81679	73637	593283	452816	623444	50434
56607	6243	1392684	539512	246594	69141	58737	611636	781048	472991	166521
484		56067	-1141	85	214	6027	-927	56994	41744	41711
21591	2956	825973	479328	234582	97977	64246	577937	248036	256414	47684
13185	5798	737987	451949	140901	40156	25655	497312	240675	265544	25106
744	474	171736	111284	35700	17213	14186	129903	41833	46565	1507
4075	3104	168122	82921	30032	28988	25608	112504	55618	53952	1828
3411	792	213450	130362	44048	11336	9813	142205	71246	71024	3531
13895	2250	380290	193314	83114	42173	30339	236792	143498	119324	19302
3537	5044	879155	283660	67364	107004	50518	396168	482987	363623	207822
8068	2397	191132	117045	47016	12667	13165	129875	61257	54269	12626
77798	669	2532345	1130447	317927	214274	190388	1357528	1174816	511623	502241
41178	21140	3090188	1032586	443341	1099230	1E+06	2136765	953423	569828	293838
60256	4514	1350560	556017	294226	45746	30591	603196	747364	419152	122073
1871	3	85602	39766	21566	40413	37734	80252	5350	19399	1761
12402	90	243514	120692	39727	70945	64859	192178	51336	45847	6801
11569	4059	653995	370296	133760	71043	63550	442519	211476	213303	16549
109548	17365	2622495	1161718	343233	352740	280446	1528108	1094387	834550	240035
55988	-15341	4192447	1442529	660507	337473	418241	1781542	2410905	1138015	671225
3447	231	336611	101420	50628	24947	17886	126499	210112	86527	39013
25205	6839	1061092	598119	207017	93139	74048	700639	360453	400537	38892
25856	24313	1549803	812513	255706	166324	133654	982893	566910	470041	56912
33429	4890	1897942	943002	284080	102572	58921	1051048	846894	418304	69819
28205	7299	2498264	1290806	360848	300193	246010	1602179	896085	808599	241369
5		211467	87258	34737	21680	12656	108939	102528	44449	36865
23749	16802	1665315	953956	367902	161726	132932	1116861	548455	516572	37880
103234	46465	8217188	4539933	1E+06	378116	304945	4972751	3244437	1457375	284186
10801	3697	714931	360014	85863	49519	28944	411014	303917	208957	46396
11424	1650	277138	142246	35830	21439	11965	164472	112666	89163	13029
14509	21	4289345	548461	39016	2493554	723752	3042014	1247331	1060103	467284
		616585	27567	84	21799	6469	49826	566759	409713	408865
135795	627	929280	95245	11941	184587	193185	279833	649447	509256	509173

6-4 续表 3 continued

单位：万元

项目	Item	资产负债 Assets and Liabilities				
		集体资本 Collective	法人资本 Institutional Units	个人资本 Individuals	港澳台资本 Hongkong, Macao and Taiwan	外商资本 Foreign
煤炭采选业	Coal Mining and Dressing	8718	2365	517		
黑色金属矿采选业	Ferrous Metals Mining and Processing	2137	8	36		
有色金属矿采选业	Nonferrous Metals Mining and Processing	387	5			
非金属矿采选业	Nonmetal Minerals Mining and Processing	4732	3594	1629		176
其他矿采选业	Other Minerals Mining and Processing	11				288
食品加工业	Food Processing	16306	41794	15866	34649	38914
食品制造业	Food Making	13711	78492	8574	56480	415753
饮料制造业	Beverage Making	15656	102528	28737	44314	115235
烟草加工业	Tobacco Processing	34				
纺织业	Textile Industry	44665	101785	18028	28093	16158
服装及其他纤维制品制造业	Garments and Other Fiber Products	71098	75604	20927	23863	48946
皮革、毛皮、羽绒及其制品业	Leather,Furs,Down and Related Products	21969	14394	3208	1298	4190
木材加工及竹、藤、棕、草制品业	Timber Processing,Bamboo,Cane,Palm Fiber and Straw Products	4157	28470	2307	3445	13746
家具制造业	Furniture Manufacturing	20273	22562	8073	7550	9036
造纸及纸制品业	Papermaking and Paper Products	18607	20674	4568	19352	36821
印刷业、记录媒介的复制	Printing and Record Medium Reproduced	35248	51040	7529	21162	40822
文教、体育用品制造	Stationery,Educational and Sports Goods	12523	14227	2271	4372	8249
石油加工及炼焦业	Petroleum Processing and Coking Products	5299	2056	728	118	1181
化学原料及化学制品制造业	Raw Chemical Materials and Chemical Products	38110	129657	29049	16360	62814
医药制造业	Medical and Pharmaceutical Products	9569	162629	38728	16141	70012
化学纤维制造业	Chemical Fibers	2277	12553	1191	271	1346
橡胶制品业	Rubber Products	7486	21004	303	2675	7578
塑料制品业	Plastic Products	47529	75926	8886	13286	51128
非金属矿物制品业	Nonmetal Mineral Products	105887	305835	14501	14862	153431
黑色金属冶炼及压延加工业	Smelting and Pressing of Ferrous Metals	14014	375294	37025	26868	13589
有色金属冶炼及压延加工业	Smelting and Pressing of Nonferrous Metals	3902	27320	13184	243	2865
金属制品业	Metal Products	87974	101111	43597	65375	63589
普通机械制造业	Ordinary Machinery Manufacturing	69861	182046	13043	4822	143358
专用设备制造业	Equipments for Special Purposes Manufacturing	32815	192846	57918	19360	45545
交通运输设备制造业	Transportation Equipment Manufacturing	73614	364277	17487	22543	89308
武器弹药制造业	Weapon and Ammunition Manufacturing	6	7578			
电气机械及器材制造	Electric Equipment and Machinery	67785	242489	25509	32453	110456
电子及通信设备制造	Electronic and Telecommunications	39281	525252	89555	89232	429870
仪器仪表及文化、办公用机械制造业	Instruments,Meters,Cultural and Office Machinery Manufacturing	13614	81778	8075	25085	34008
其他制造业	Other Manufacturing	23767	27119	4314	4352	16582
电力、蒸汽、热水的生产和供应业	Electricity,Steam and Hot Water Production and Supply	3017	585246	3507		1050
煤气生产和供应业	Gas Production and Supply	580	196	71		
自来水的生产和供应	Water Production and Supply				83	

6-4 续表 4 continued

(10000 yuan)

损益及分配 Profits,Loss and Distribution										
产品					管理				财务	
销售收入 Sales Revenue	产品销售成本 Cost of Sales	产品销售费用 Expenses of Sales	产品销售税金及附加 Sales Tax and Extra Charges	产品销售利润 Sales Profits	费用 Overhead Cost	税金 Taxes	财产保险费 Premium of Property	劳动待业保险费 Premium for Employment Insurance	费用 Financial Expenses	利息支出 Expenses of Interest
168459	122298	13290	1153	31718	30027	623	2	16875	3149	2786
14236	10960	400	490	2387	1285	64	6	118	1247	1241
5889	4680	120	22	1066	723	6		35	-45	-78
31063	25359	1768	504	3432	2500	72	25	180	487	333
240	211	10	4	15	18				3	
577510	507665	30311	818	38716	38281	1221	568	2828	8891	7783
712800	474976	132321	3791	101712	82549	2572	744	5828	9978	8761
699302	455757	88474	54411	100660	63643	2209	764	3492	16202	15071
84505	37279	1264	36434	9528	4951	67	196	2040	61	199
430698	360814	15300	1238	53347	50584	1489	512	10287	19343	17930
494820	412784	33434	1127	47475	50178	1241	793	4996	9330	7577
54964	44921	3864	162	6017	12448	288	98	2824	3499	3005
71482	58060	3449	202	9771	8021	154	80	549	1815	1717
145707	122535	8566	499	14108	11921	385	229	341	1860	1535
208300	165473	10854	553	31420	22927	736	282	2455	4898	4392
510969	392885	11141	2896	104047	80025	2229	812	13375	4800	4006
109071	87787	6642	322	14320	16147	400	202	2451	3118	2893
2873142	2576837	24613	77462	194230	161439	3510	3834	20937	37262	36642
1404067	1155218	64721	13911	170217	120895	3071	2554	15656	37299	34998
675467	423095	87545	3188	161639	90458	2724	854	7306	14292	12322
37032	34493	664	154	1720	3192	228	38	958	3044	2928
117599	101317	3947	3677	8659	12044	257	130	2174	-2225	3702
293782	254000	11280	675	27827	32358	1180	106	3134	7120	7540
1041856	849286	41342	5563	145665	118143	4076	1262	17093	33919	31443
2229691	1950881	23519	11883	243409	168323	8009	312	59287	83759	81026
122876	104651	2367	254	15604	10232	242	58	901	1331	1048
672449	564813	27462	3335	76841	63618	1614	482	6292	10849	7289
538390	432344	23383	1974	80689	87850	2669	672	13790	20302	18486
1159048	924069	52476	4313	178190	127556	5467	974	14058	12287	10458
1191831	1015818	32987	11181	131844	175248	4174	1049	28594	34178	32326
83444	70433	457	42	12512	17553	237	65	4404	2025	2042
907059	710874	59845	2028	134312	100610	2450	795	10234	17918	15115
8805223	7461834	317912	8370	1017107	389333	6659	1733	22943	62317	48595
425253	338803	22635	2950	60866	57621	1322	257	7041	4920	4792
143231	102896	15294	1152	23888	24686	494	191	3056	2003	1399
845344	699673	2445	6757	136468	25964	1532	81	2154	34526	34101
201344	211195	3	802	-10657	14801	726	85	3201	-603	-648
125417	113105	222	496	11594	19450	1190	15	2350	-440	-663

6-4 续表 5 continued

单位：万元

项目	Item	损益及分配 Profits,Loss and Distribution 营业利润 Operating Profits	投资收益 Investment Income	补贴收入 Subsidy Income	营业外收入 Out-business Income	营业外支出 Out-business Expenditure	利润总额 Total Profits
煤炭采选业	Coal Mining and Dressing	745	197	11733	989	2820	11515
黑色金属矿采选业	Ferrous Metals Mining and Processing	453			109	221	341
有色金属矿采选业	Nonferrous Metals Mining and Processing	394	209		3	3	603
非金属矿采选业	Nonmetal Minerals Mining and Processing	965	69	114	271	98	1424
其他矿采选业	Other Minerals Mining and Processing	-6			2	3	-6
食品加工业	Food Processing	-5717	238	5212	917	1369	-296
食品制造业	Food Making	15123	1572	909	9847	3231	25483
饮料制造业	Beverage Making	24246	20216	6014	8985	5128	42588
烟草加工业	Tobacco Processing	4664	296		30	1	4989
纺织业	Textile Industry	-7660	1150	199	33165	17839	6204
服装及其他纤维制品制造业	Garments and Other Fiber Products	324	1050	248	2289	1763	2683
皮革、毛皮、羽绒及其制品业	Leather,Furs,Down and Related Products	-2300	-294	36	4226	676	1142
木材加工及竹、藤、棕、草制品业	Timber Processing,Bamboo,Cane,Palm Fiber and Straw Products	232		114	1140	1718	154
家具制造业	Furniture Manufacturing	1257	-57	85	488	355	2866
造纸及纸制品业	Papermaking and Paper Products	5809	4124	385	7711	2472	15480
印刷业、记录媒介的复制	Printing and Record Medium Reproduced	37154	632	537	6609	3128	42326
文教、体育用品制造	Stationery,Educational and Sports Goods	-1201	406	19	1243	510	-45
石油加工及炼焦业	Petroleum Processing and Coking Products	-3423	4406	21611	1530	5532	7411
化学原料及化学制品制造业	Raw Chemical Materials and Chemical Products	24145	14542	23456	2525	2960	62160
医药制造业	Medical and Pharmaceutical Products	80540	19399	1391	1805	18083	85492
化学纤维制造业	Chemical Fibers	-3483	2	102	329	608	-3658
橡胶制品业	Rubber Products	-743	2	1641	739	356	1940
塑料制品业	Plastic Products	-5255	700	168	8890	2197	2764
非金属矿物制品业	Nonmetal Mineral Products	10602	4204	6073	22002	14944	30446
黑色金属冶炼及压延加工业	Smelting and Pressing of Ferrous Metals	19535	6589	5	52747	55365	23644
有色金属冶炼及压延加工业	Smelting and Pressing of Nonferrous Metals	6785	3515	34	1197	579	11123
金属制品业	Metal Products	9054	1118	4793	7735	6101	7026
普通机械制造业	Ordinary Machinery Manufacturing	-15309	174	766	25895	11844	3079
专用设备制造业	Equipments for Special Purposes Manufacturing	54312	4734	3097	16378	5186	76035
交通运输设备制造业	Transportation Equipment Manufacturing	-63627	5738	4147	27079	10349	-31176
武器弹药制造业	Weapon and Ammunition Manufacturing	-3226	1597	1929	204	708	19
电气机械及器材制造	Electric Equipment and Machinery	30636	3331	1199	22421	2758	54085
电子及通信设备制造	Electronic and Telecommunications	560596	56300	7403	57706	28683	665949
仪器仪表及文化、办公用机械制造业	Instruments,Meters,Cultural and Office Machinery Manufacturing	23101	3692	463	6281	2880	30725
其他制造业	Other Manufacturing	5256	251	754	2116	1614	6999
电力、蒸汽、热水的生产和供应业	Electricity,Steam and Hot Water Production and Supply	77179	-963	31011	3713	49544	61722
煤气生产和供应业	Gas Production and Supply	-23110	912	25300	94	33	3163
自来水的生产和供应	Water Production and Supply	-6842	135	21557	159	533	14475

6-4 续表 6 continued

(10000 yuan)

应交所得税 Income Tax Payable	应付利润 Profits Payable	亏损企业亏损额 Total Lossing of Lossmaking Enterprises	利税总额 Total Pre-tax Profits	工资，福利费，增值税 Wages,Welfares and Added Value Tax					
				本年应付工资总额 Total Wags Payable	本年应付福利费总额 Total Welfares Payable	本年应交增值税 Added Value Tax	本年进项税额 Tax Include in Purchasing Cost	本年销项税额 Tax Include in Sales Cost	工业中间投入合计 Intermediate Input of Industry
590	1510	355	20169	35871	12477	7501	10591	17638	87198
33	65		1218	2748	220	387	1779	2136	10242
109	11		673	491	28	48	75	105	4864
266	495	400	3162	3785	296	1234	518	1100	25913
4		12	15	33	2	17	19	36	163
3326	5009	18370	12008	26738	5132	11486	36831	47251	489192
7842	-3173	32042	76944	64401	11703	47670	65617	114905	497512
10457	3805	26537	148795	44794	8639	51796	69299	118766	515417
596		17	50071	3170	1398	8647	5790	13995	35472
2164	3309	11437	21668	55246	7271	14227	51864	62019	344826
2237	3272	12511	17184	74992	10444	13374	52532	62832	371220
804	1084	2352	3208	8403	1498	1904	4976	6878	42249
215	322	2908	3484	6682	661	3129	7359	8924	56498
776	1272	5001	7581	16989	1498	4217	14630	17183	116309
2758	6143	5366	26645	20338	3005	10613	22827	32814	153435
13128	13689	8381	79109	74846	13439	33888	52496	75525	316574
1086	886	5080	4968	16526	2751	4692	11704	16014	75864
27664	21306	1029	141468	86871	11891	56595	412124	464996	2306566
19152	10431	20840	148715	85605	15110	72644	161728	231986	1088754
14253	1576	5367	137178	58976	8252	48498	64457	110420	336090
40	1	4016	-2340	3214	445	1164	5293	6106	31722
596	694	2695	10651	11273	1770	5034	14325	18717	109128
1859	1804	11167	12611	27677	4105	9172	34356	41184	232587
8005	3984	22111	88997	132327	18039	52988	89232	138849	772977
31593	677	5755	158907	205329	25084	123380	470073	579111	1307286
1296	86	521	13251	7801	933	1875	13336	15098	102510
5285	6798	31808	34511	65516	9432	24150	72829	92892	534275
2230	3642	23741	26038	81492	11583	20985	61007	80025	383817
16920	19786	18023	123461	86496	12444	43113	205497	245074	903382
6803	9619	77795	19977	143117	24764	39972	156528	189356	818816
319		2327	913	14293	1592	851	2728	3398	54996
6375	16104	20670	92206	72110	10514	36093	104008	142732	719055
54815	101590	42518	841552	219411	51724	167233	837257	907203	6902832
3832	2714	4675	52816	50360	8520	19141	48557	67174	308243
2603	4046	5548	15778	21182	3215	7627	12693	20720	105019
10174	212	18587	133199	50482	7962	64719	56447	117360	367704
10	10	77	12045	11461	1570	8079	19803	27876	23102
263		198	22255	10437	1445	7284	1744	8151	95445

6-5 全部独立核算工业企业主要经济分析指标

单位：%

项目	Item	企业亏损面 Loss-making Enterprises as % of Total	总资产贡献率 Ratio of Total Assets to Industrial Output Value	资产保值增值率 Changing Rate of Net Assets
总　计(不含个体工业)	**Total(exclude individual industry)**	**22.65**	**6.82**	**116.10**
在总计中:	**Of Total:**			
中央企业	Central Enterprises	35.58	6.91	107.04
地方企业	Local Enterprises	21.97	6.80	118.85
工业系统	Industry System	26.19	5.14	109.66
非工业系统	Non-Industry System	29.03	5.52	119.09
区县工业	Industry of District and County	17.32	7.64	112.25
其他	Others	39.00	14.04	176.30
在总计中:	**Of Total:**			
内资企业	Domestic Investment Enterprises	19.04	5.72	117.35
国有企业	State-Owned	25.85	5.13	95.39
集体企业	Collective Owned	15.92	6.33	91.95
股份合作企业	Share Holding	18.11	7.68	111.98
联营企业	Joint Owned	22.22	3.56	102.32
有限责任公司	Limited Liability Corporations	25.79	4.57	190.50
股份有限公司	Share Holding Corporations	22.92	11.55	232.42
私营企业	Private Owned	22.56	11.10	161.03
其他企业	Others	12.50	6.30	41.32
港澳台商投资企业	Hongkong,Macao and Taiwan Funded Enterprises	46.55	9.77	115.01
港澳台合资经营	Joint Venture	44.27	4.14	100.68
港澳台合作经营	Cooperative	42.50	17.44	145.03
港澳台商独资企业	Hongkong,Macao and Taiwan Enterprises	53.59	21.97	176.11
港澳台商投资股份有限公司	Hongkong,Macao and Taiwan Funded Share Holding Corporations	66.67	0.72	82.73
外商投资企业	Foreign Funded Enterprises	42.69	10.21	111.32
中外合资经营	Joint Venture	39.89	10.06	106.56
中外合作经营	Cooperative	24.64	12.83	147.54
外资(独资)企业	Foreign Enterprises	53.13	9.65	172.02
外商投资股份有限公司	Foreign Funded Share Holding Corporations	22.22	14.01	87.52
在总计中:	**Of Total:**			
农村企业	Rural Enterprises	13.29	7.97	105.30
在总计中:	**Of Total:**			
国有绝对控股企业	State Absolute Controlling Share Hold Industry	27.28	6.30	116.15
国有相对控股企业	State Relative Controlling Share Hold Industry	39.13	6.79	121.15
在总计中:	**Of Total:**			
轻工业	Light Industry	24.52	7.30	105.47
以农产品为原料	Using Farm Products as Raw Materials	25.40	8.11	102.48
以非农产品为原料	Using Non-Farm Products as Raw Materials	23.21	6.15	110.00
重工业	Heavy Industry	20.86	6.64	120.90
采掘工业	Excavation	8.12	6.78	101.55
原料工业	Raw Material	21.37	5.04	118.73
加工工业	Processing	21.50	8.06	123.68
在总计中:	**Of Total:**			
大型企业	Large Enterprises	22.79	6.57	115.33
中型企业	Medium Enterprises	20.30	8.64	148.36
小型企业	Small Enterprises	22.69	6.70	107.93

MAIN INDICATORS ON ECONOMIC BENEFIT OF INDUSTRIAL ENTERPRISES WITH INDEPENDENT ACCOUNTING SYSTEM

(%)

资产负债率 Assets-Liabilities Ratio	流动资产周转率(次) Turnover Rate of Circulating Assets (time)	成本费用利润率 Ratio of Profits to Industrial Cost	全员劳动生产率(元) Overall Labor Productivity (yuan)	产品销售率 Proportion of Products Sold	增加值率 Ratio of Value Added to Gross Output Value	人均销售收入(元) Sales Revenue Per Capita (yuan)	流动比率 Circulating Assets/ Liquid Liabilities	速动比率 Quick-circulating Assets/ Liquid Liabilities
58.02	**1.38**	**4.65**	**51469**	**96.01**	**24.91**	**193771**	**110.04**	**76.38**
63.36	1.59	4.70	91028	97.40	22.26	392222	116.43	87.68
56.28	1.31	4.62	45059	95.46	25.91	161614	108.34	73.38
57.86	1.09	2.98	45309	95.29	26.72	176170	99.96	67.92
36.07	1.38	3.65	61994	99.77	35.25	185434	121.18	89.41
59.94	1.36	4.48	30608	95.52	25.85	90617	104.30	61.59
61.48	1.88	8.09	121047	94.35	21.64	517327	127.52	94.46
56.36	1.21	3.65	39695	96.73	28.22	138531	108.64	74.35
58.34	1.19	2.25	44223	98.61	30.50	161991	97.47	66.71
65.85	1.33	3.64	21502	94.34	25.38	65685	104.12	55.80
63.50	1.56	4.13	27334	93.74	24.61	82907	101.05	59.49
70.79	0.88	1.76	14568	93.11	12.72	101923	89.49	52.55
51.03	1.23	3.89	69206	97.33	28.62	231724	118.27	90.20
41.42	1.08	10.96	95636	94.05	25.23	344421	177.09	141.75
56.04	1.52	5.71	37431	90.78	26.59	102028	123.87	70.85
31.68	2.58	0.90	13159	98.13	33.87	32343	195.31	105.47
70.75	1.85	5.97	86120	95.22	18.35	365953	102.70	68.23
67.55	1.18	1.43	53157	95.42	21.84	195580	97.42	62.78
49.19	1.26	24.06	62358	97.06	33.14	156229	118.09	79.76
78.00	3.25	9.22	235245	95.03	15.57	1151279	109.84	75.95
71.02	0.46	-2.00	11628	95.46	11.48	72951	121.19	72.97
59.54	1.71	6.22	119098	94.99	21.62	505938	117.65	86.16
61.07	1.68	6.02	121592	96.32	19.83	558075	117.70	86.69
40.46	1.83	9.17	114491	98.00	26.95	364504	139.90	83.44
60.61	1.75	4.82	115907	81.15	33.21	350320	117.97	86.83
25.73	2.74	23.27	88415	101.29	39.62	206170	82.29	53.50
61.92	1.55	4.73	26415	95.02	25.26	77894	105.16	55.96
56.18	1.35	4.30	58674	97.34	24.64	236724	109.84	78.33
47.79	1.47	6.54	94434	95.47	28.87	289144	126.89	91.78
55.39	1.22	4.90	40114	96.44	29.88	115277	104.82	68.18
55.33	1.30	4.32	37925	96.44	30.41	108323	104.19	66.99
55.47	1.09	5.93	44773	96.45	28.97	130074	105.80	69.98
58.97	1.44	4.56	59202	95.86	23.11	247229	112.12	79.65
57.22	0.97	6.33	20962	99.66	41.58	47302	121.72	104.47
56.66	1.72	1.71	73253	99.24	25.92	299641	99.38	72.21
61.00	1.33	6.19	55995	94.09	21.41	239988	117.78	82.58
58.41	1.52	3.78	65784	97.20	23.13	292589	103.14	72.20
46.88	1.08	8.41	61722	95.71	30.74	177904	125.92	96.09
60.72	1.30	5.03	41024	94.65	25.57	135331	113.95	76.59

6-6 全部独立核算国有工业企业主要经济指标

单位：万元

项　目 Item		企业单位个数（个） Number of Enterprises (unit)	#亏损企业 Loss-making Enterprises	工业总产值（当年价格） Gross Output Value of Industry (at current prices)	新产品产值 Value of New Products	工业总产值（1990年不变价格） Gross Output Value of Industry (at 1990 constant prices)	工业增加值（生产法） Added Value of Industry (with production method)
总　计	**Total**	1981	512	7885866	688211	5376433	2497087
在总计中：	**Of Total:**						
中央企业	Central Enterprises	405	129	3833520	398058	2050833	1002595
地方企业	Local Enterprises	1576	383	4052346	290153	3325600	1494492
工业系统	Industry System	302	48	2775922	280335	2357203	984099
非工业系统	Non-Industry System	356	102	601121	4249	370940	259102
区县工业	Industry of District and County	899	226	667838	5570	590044	246963
其他	Others	19	7	7466		7414	4328
在总计中：	**Of Total:**						
轻工业	Light Industry	971	273	1667816	118596	1451911	694871
以农产品为原料	Using Farm Products as Raw Materials	636	176	1177057	76302	1024468	491608
以非农产品为原料	Using Non-Farm Products as Raw Materials	335	97	490759	42294	427443	203263
重工业	Heavy Industry	1010	239	6218051	569615	3924522	1802216
采掘工业	Excavation	16	3	92570		38150	59192
原料工业	Raw Material	131	20	4627779	268512	2489480	1281973
加工工业	Processing	863	216	1497702	301103	1396893	461051
在总计中：	**Of Total:**						
大型企业	Large Enterprises	130	23	6360419	457108	4103474	1933169
中型企业	Medium Enterprises	155	21	689805	59301	540066	296954
小型企业	Small Enterprises	1696	468	835643	171802	732893	266964

MAIN INDICATORS FOR STATE-OWNED INDUSTRIAL ENTERPRISES WITH INDEPENDENT ACCOUNTING SYSTEM

(10000 yuan)

工业销售产值(当年价格) Sales Value of Industry (at current price)	出口交货值 Delivery Value of Exports	全部从业人员年平均人数(人) Average Number of Persons Employed (person)	资产负债 Assets and Liabilities						
			流动资产合计 Circulating Funds	应收帐款净额 Accounts Receivable	存货 Stock	产成品 Finished Products	流动资产平均余额 Average Balance of Circulating Funds	长期投资 Longterm Investment	固定资产合计 Fixed Assets
7776397	285270	567822	7214849	1301672	2276820	707130	7732654	1816274	9870613
3767733	26704	156363	2502761	494837	693374	189908	2929320	379051	4243786
4008664	258566	411459	4712088	806835	1583446	517221	4803335	1437223	5626827
2728812	232148	289507	3509719	615447	1194013	376016	3714314	1339893	4040010
612644	6670	51089	638082	108166	181679	69220	551193	52412	964710
659740	19748	70454	561328	82675	206266	71595	536118	44566	619960
7469		409	2960	548	1488	390	1710	353	2147
1631901	98901	175448	1966083	245457	588146	262719	1918969	425245	2281909
1151390	74882	123136	1250715	169154	389818	176379	1204556	274267	1181292
480512	24019	52312	715369	76303	198328	86341	714413	150979	1100617
6144496	186369	392374	5248766	1056215	1688674	444410	5813685	1391028	7588704
97380	28123	26859	173023	79556	17792	8545	178265	25848	127746
4615218	115978	160837	2515131	407455	764825	139829	2768385	605920	5884897
1431898	42267	204678	2560613	569205	906057	296036	2867035	759260	1576061
6281396	235162	383336	5149073	935256	1654542	462231	5845593	1256759	8552062
671132	29807	75283	940700	118314	254317	104804	873317	428369	652771
823869	20300	109203	1125076	248103	367961	140094	1013744	131146	665780

6-6 续表 1 continued

单位：万元

项目 Item		资产负债：固定资产原价合计 Original Value of Fixed Assets	# 生产经营用 For Productive Use	累计折旧 Accumulative Depreciation	#本年折旧 Depreciation in this Year	固定资产净值年平均余额 Average Net Value of Fixed Assets	无形资产及递延资产 Intangible and Deferred Assets
总计	Total	13275784	10917610	5078407	575751	8080361	485434
在总计中：	Of Total:						
中央企业	Central Enterprises	5582757	5099075	2127670	260256	3410745	119064
地方企业	Local Enterprises	7693027	5818535	2950737	315496	4669616	366370
工业系统	Industry System	5674048	4808935	2361073	231078	3325324	294617
非工业系统	Non-Industry System	1235649	368132	359211	53101	826688	18777
区县工业	Industry of District and County	781017	639716	230037	31210	515380	52372
其他	Others	2314	1752	416	107	2225	605
在总计中：	Of Total:						
轻工业	Light Industry	3038610	1635586	946721	147705	1933530	185385
以农产品为原料	Using Farm Products as Raw Materials	1601573	1214717	538793	70282	1017216	83029
以非农产品为原料	Using Non-Farm Products as Raw Materials	1437038	420869	407928	77424	916314	102356
重工业	Heavy Industry	10237173	9282024	4131685	428046	6146831	300049
采掘工业	Excavation	183900	23420	68970	8233	118998	5285
原料工业	Raw Material	7964576	7706192	3252132	343463	4676435	149224
加工工业	Processing	2088698	1552412	810583	76350	1351397	145541
在总计中：	Of Total:						
大型企业	Large Enterprises	11546142	9568442	4470723	503765	6954473	324758
中型企业	Medium Enterprises	846430	667816	306822	38191	555815	96579
小型企业	Small Enterprises	883211	681353	300861	33795	570073	64098

6-6 续表 2 continued

(10000 yuan)

Assets and Liabilities										
			流动负债		长期负债合计					
#无形资产 Intan-gible Assets	其他资产 Other Assets	资产总计 Total Assets	合计 Liquid Liabilities	短期借款 Shortterm Loans	长期负债合计 Longterm Liabilities	长期借款 Longterm Loans	负债合计 Total Liabilities	所有者权益 Creditors' Equity	实收资本 Contributed Capital	国家资本 State
213105	9711	19396881	7401874	2621795	3898584	1877813	11316713	8080169	4386671	2821546
96405	8526	7253187	2471353	674945	2511453	604222	4994875	2258313	1212579	971824
116700	1185	12143694	4930521	1946850	1387131	1273591	6321838	5821856	3174092	1849723
94016	-6292	9177948	3877113	1653029	1133831	1054938	5012613	4165335	2128231	969268
7656	5542	1679523	556016	120693	163731	153696	721023	958500	728530	676814
14524	1891	1280116	494564	172511	89488	64908	585293	694823	315934	202913
505	43	6107	2829	617	81	49	2909	3198	1398	728
60860	9533	4868156	1888279	795607	543944	424184	2437119	2431037	1448710	1067472
37884	7368	2796671	1148555	470596	254069	161219	1407314	1389357	712410	469320
22976	2165	2071485	739724	325011	289875	262965	1029805	1041680	736300	598152
152245	178	14528725	5513595	1826188	3354640	1453629	8879593	5649132	2937961	1754075
		331901	138280	59059	57324	49282	195603	136298	85345	83116
102239	-14671	9140500	2769006	1004116	2690575	964205	5459773	3680728	1679296	1227932
50006	14849	5056323	2606309	763014	606742	440143	3224217	1832106	1173320	443026
162763	-4501	15278151	5334464	2017053	3467162	1558863	8802733	6475418	3262872	2122500
36045	7356	2125775	948146	327145	244768	197594	1192915	932860	570324	387753
14296	6856	1992955	1119264	277597	186654	121356	1321064	671891	553476	311293

6-6 续表 3 continued

单位：万元

项目 Item	集体资本 Collective	法人资本 Institutional Units	个人资本 Individuals	港澳台资本 Hongkong, Macao and Taiwan	外商资本 Foreign
	资产负债 Assets and Liabilities				
总计 Total	22402	1458113	78590	1572	4448
在总计中： Of Total:					
中央企业 Central Enterprises	2733	237163	580	279	
地方企业 Local Enterprises	19669	1220950	78010	1293	4448
工业系统 Industry System	14058	1084692	55217	993	4002
非工业系统 Non-Industry System	536	50203	320	210	446
区县工业 Industry of District and County	5067	85576	22288	90	
其他 Others	7	478	185		
在总计中： Of Total:					
轻工业 Light Industry	9869	333841	35879	1203	446
以农产品为原料 Using Farm Products as Raw Materials	7440	200084	34126	993	446
以非农产品为原料 Using Non-Farm Products as Raw Materials	2429	133757	1753	210	
重工业 Heavy Industry	12533	1124272	42711	369	4002
采掘工业 Excavation	101	2098	30		
原料工业 Raw Material	519	415560	35195	90	
加工工业 Processing	11913	706614	7486	279	4002
在总计中： Of Total:					
大型企业 Large Enterprises	6734	1062179	70465	993	
中型企业 Medium Enterprises	6587	166455	5527		4002
小型企业 Small Enterprises	9082	229479	2597	579	446

6-6 续表 4 continued

(10000 yuan)

损益及分配 Profits,Loss and Distribution										
产品					管理				财务	
销售收入 Sales Revenue	产品销售成本 Cost of Sales	产品销售费用 Expenses of Sales	产品销售税金及附加 Sales Tax and Extra Charges	产品销售利润 Sales Profits	费用 Overhead Cost	税金 Taxes	财产保险费 Premium of Property	劳动待业保险费 Premium for Employment Insurance	费用 Financial Expenses	利息支出 Expenses of Interest
9198204	7784243	198494	193980	1021487	976829	29717	8380	234476	236154	234401
4336486	3749454	39394	85384	462254	350741	6763	4258	60707	68592	66556
4861718	4034788	159100	108596	559234	626088	22954	4123	173769	167562	167845
3543253	3008403	93823	25924	415103	475445	17249	2660	151819	151356	152448
667197	555054	24697	42122	45324	75865	2934	785	13561	5271	5430
646847	468687	39281	40502	98377	74187	2764	672	8384	10932	9968
4421	2645	1299	48	429	591	8	6	5	3	
1917925	1435310	104939	89947	287729	287713	9277	3061	59977	49048	46411
1373512	1006341	73128	82998	211045	197459	6211	2379	41790	31279	29883
544412	428969	31811	6948	76685	90254	3067	682	18187	17768	16528
7280279	6348933	93555	104033	733758	689115	20440	5319	174498	187107	187991
100494	69372	9940	935	20247	29321	574	16	17167	3565	3254
5370803	4733734	38437	92468	506164	335778	12153	3998	84823	137162	132916
1808983	1545827	45178	10630	207348	324017	7713	1306	72509	46380	51821
7706443	6648362	124546	141843	791692	724656	23193	6588	188704	199621	199363
672250	469318	32730	45633	124569	124114	3293	999	29003	19199	18801
819511	666563	41218	6504	105226	128058	3231	793	16768	17334	16237

6-6 续表 5 continued

单位：万元

项目 Item		损益及分配 Profits,Loss and Distribution 营业利润 Operating Profits	投资收益 Investment Income	补贴收入 Subsidy Income	营业外收入 Out-business Income	营业外支出 Out-business Expenditure	利润总额 Total Profits
总计	Total	-7031	104231	112140	199013	172539	206980
在总计中：	Of Total:						
中央企业	Central Enterprises	95477	35650	25784	12869	61780	90655
地方企业	Local Enterprises	-102507	68581	86357	186144	110760	116325
工业系统	Industry System	-104872	47593	41997	162098	93478	38561
非工业系统	Non-Industry System	-24476	4249	42765	19594	12651	29604
区县工业	Industry of District and County	26812	16730	1475	4451	4630	47989
其他	Others	29	10	119	2	1	171
在总计中：	Of Total:						
轻工业	Light Industry	33507	50653	33867	64605	30565	130772
以农产品为原料	Using Farm Products as Raw Materials	38844	34255	10486	57474	24256	103102
以非农产品为原料	Using Non-Farm Products as Raw Materials	-5337	16398	23381	7131	6309	27671
重工业	Heavy Industry	-40538	53578	78274	134408	141975	76208
采掘工业	Excavation	-9377	466	11733	1230	2390	2333
原料工业	Raw Material	63811	12239	47469	57029	109293	62180
加工工业	Processing	-94972	40873	19072	76149	30292	11695
在总计中：	Of Total:						
大型企业	Large Enterprises	-23916	72781	100229	159065	159966	116701
中型企业	Medium Enterprises	30202	29572	2198	22377	5390	81610
小型企业	Small Enterprises	-13317	1878	9713	17572	7184	8669

6-6 续表 6 continued

(10000 yuan)

				工资，福利费，增值税 Wages,Welfares and Added Value Tax					
应交所得税 Income Tax Payable	应付利润 Profits Payable	亏损企业亏损额 Total Loss-ing of Loss-making Enterprises	利税总额 Total Pre-tax Profits	本年应付工资总额 Total Wags Payable	本年应付福利费总额 Total Welfares Payable	本年应交增值税 Added Value Tax	本年进项税额 Tax Include in Purchasing Cost	本年销项税额 Tax Include in Sales Cost	工业中间投入合计 Intermediate Input of Industry
104345	37127	92080	793869	817502	122365	392909	1308529	1662929	5781688
45809	27722	28542	308931	264853	40655	132892	540465	659633	2963817
58535	9405	63539	484938	552649	81710	260017	768064	1003295	2817871
39017	3528	41759	247157	422067	62351	182671	635770	797015	1974493
10202	1205	9374	105957	67706	10619	34232	75811	109449	376251
9298	4649	12378	131336	62192	8632	42845	56176	96281	463719
18	23	28	489	685	108	270	307	550	3407
34276	12791	35162	334930	215864	33806	114211	185902	283175	1087156
23693	9930	16857	272142	155957	26275	86042	138845	210067	771491
10584	2860	18305	62788	59907	7531	28169	47057	73108	315665
70069	24336	56918	458939	601638	88559	278698	1122627	1379754	4694532
19	118	37	8258	28365	11734	4990	6940	11751	38368
61002	20543	2505	366625	325032	42816	211976	874518	1071197	3557782
9047	3676	54376	84056	248242	34009	61731	241168	296806	1098382
82559	31251	51989	569975	614591	93508	311430	1155072	1432707	4738680
15429	2313	7700	172830	96511	15049	45587	70919	114481	438438
6357	3563	32391	51064	106400	13808	35891	82538	115741	604570

6-7 全部独立核算国有工业企业主要经济分析指标

单位：%

项目	Item	企业亏损面 Loss-making Enterprises as % of Total	总资产贡献率 Ratio of Total Assets to Industrial Output Value	资产保值增值率 Changing Rate of Net Assets
总计	**Total**	**25.85**	**5.13**	**95.39**
在总计中：	**Of Total:**			
中央企业	Central Enterprises	31.85	5.03	92.41
地方企业	Local Enterprises	24.30	5.20	96.60
工业系统	Industry System	15.89	4.33	110.94
非工业系统	Non-Industry System	28.65	5.36	56.99
区县工业	Industry of District and County	25.14	11.30	117.91
其他	Others	36.84	7.62	297.77
在总计中：	**Of Total:**			
轻工业	Light Industry	28.12	7.83	112.17
以农产品为原料	Using Farm Products as Raw Materials	27.67	11.07	114.79
以非农产品为原料	Using Non-Farm Products as Raw Materials	28.96	3.71	108.85
重工业	Heavy Industry	23.66	4.27	89.63
采掘工业	Excavation	18.75	3.50	98.83
原料工业	Raw Material	15.27	5.27	90.30
加工工业	Processing	25.03	2.54	87.71
在总计中：	**Of Total:**			
大型企业	Large Enterprises	17.69	5.00	104.17
中型企业	Medium Enterprises	13.55	8.41	87.59
小型企业	Small Enterprises	27.59	2.84	56.52

MAIN INDICATORS ON ECONOMIC BENEFIT OF STATE-OWNED INDUSTRIAL ENTERPRISES WITH INDEPENDENT ACCOUNTING SYSTEM

(%)

资产负债率 Assets-Liabilities Ratio	流动资产周转率(次) Turnover Rate of Circulating Assets (time)	成本费用利润率 Ratio of Profits to Industrial Cost	全员劳动生产率(元) Overall Labor Productivity (yuan)	产品销售率 Proportion of Products Sold	增加值率 Ratio of Value Added to Gross Output Value	人均销售收入(元) Sales Revenue Per Capita (yuan)	流动比率 Circulating Assets/ Liquid Liabilities	速动比率 Quick-circulating Assets/ Liquid Liabilities
58.34	**1.19**	**2.25**	**44223**	**98.61**	**30.50**	**161991**	**97.47**	**66.71**
68.86	1.48	2.15	64479	98.28	25.24	277335	101.27	73.21
52.06	1.01	2.33	36525	98.92	35.47	118158	95.57	63.45
54.62	0.95	1.03	34183	98.30	35.16	122389	90.52	59.73
42.93	1.21	4.48	51000	101.92	40.47	130595	114.76	82.08
45.72	1.21	8.09	35249	98.79	31.30	91811	113.50	71.79
47.63	2.59	3.77	106412	100.04	31.97	108093	104.63	52.03
50.06	1.00	6.97	39827	97.85	40.96	109316	104.12	72.97
50.32	1.14	7.88	40148	97.82	41.36	111544	108.89	74.95
49.71	0.76	4.86	39073	97.91	39.99	104070	96.71	69.90
61.12	1.25	1.04	46188	98.82	27.77	185544	95.20	64.57
58.93	0.56	2.08	22161	105.20	61.60	37415	125.13	112.26
59.73	1.94	1.19	80153	99.73	26.11	333928	90.83	63.21
63.77	0.63	0.60	22652	95.61	31.03	88382	98.25	63.48
57.62	1.32	1.52	50713	98.76	30.06	201036	96.52	65.51
56.12	0.77	12.65	39666	97.29	35.98	89296	99.21	72.39
66.29	0.81	1.02	24583	98.59	27.52	75045	100.52	67.64

6-8 全部独立核算集体工业企业主要经济指标

单位：万元

项目	Item	企业单位个数（个） Number of Enterprises (unit)	#亏损企业 Loss-making Enterprises	工业总产值（当年价格） Gross Output Value of Industry (at current prices)	新产品产值 Value of New Products	工业总产值（1990年不变价格） Gross Output Value of Industry (at 1990 constant prices)	工业增加值（生产法） Added Value of Industry (with production method)
总　计	**Total**	8030	1278	2626223	46575	2437420	801199
在总计中：	**Of Total:**						
中央企业	Central Enterprises	177	71	145217	5108	95116	39670
地方企业	Local Enterprises	7853	1207	2481006	41467	2342304	761529
工业系统	Industry System	295	99	95245	8081	100795	30751
非工业系统	Non-Industry System	137	27	25432	1700	20880	15155
区县工业	Industry of District and County	7265	1021	2297690	27620	2159460	684470
其他	Others	156	60	62639	4066	61169	31153
在总计中：	**Of Total:**						
农村企业	Rural Enterprises	6143	666	1957835	1242	1831577	599893
在总计中：	**Of Total:**						
轻工业	Light Industry	3638	591	1129483	11657	1061748	345864
以农产品为原料	Using Farm Products as Raw Materials	2113	328	744113	4617	662540	224105
以非农产品为原料	Using Non-Farm Products as Raw Materials	1525	263	385371	7040	399208	121758
重工业	Heavy Industry	4392	687	1496740	34919	1375673	455335
采掘工业	Excavation	331	23	77803		57375	31719
原料工业	Raw Material	522	97	307235		258478	72743
加工工业	Processing	3539	567	1111702	34919	1059820	350874
在总计中：	**Of Total:**						
大型企业	Large Enterprises	6	4	62913	5846	71672	6125
中型企业	Medium Enterprises	36	17	79361	1976	62381	30165
小型企业	Small Enterprises	7988	1257	2483949	38753	2303367	764910

MAIN INDICATORS FOR COLLECTIVE-OWNED INDUSTRIAL ENTERPRISES WITH INDEPENDENT ACCOUNTING SYSTEM

(10000 yuan)

工业销售产值(当年价格) Sales Value of Industry (at current price)	出口交货值 Delivery Value of Exports	全部从业人员年平均人数(人) Average Number of Persons Employed (person)	资产负债 Assets and Liabilities 流动资产合计 Circulating Funds	应收帐款净额 Accounts Receivable	存货 Stock	产成品 Finished Products	流动资产平均余额 Average Balance of Circulating Funds	长期投资 Longterm Investment	固定资产合计 Fixed Assets
2477569	141111	374716	1970353	392420	914416	464278	1855510	128894	1233769
131502		10526	126101	25138	40303	8086	108998	17591	36197
2346067	141111	364190	1844252	367282	874113	456193	1746513	111303	1197572
92444	10498	21374	148476	27127	64311	35615	140673	23432	102628
24157		3445	39512	5686	17031	2948	38494	903	17371
2166860	130613	335233	1579559	318075	765950	405324	1498969	83798	1064817
62606		4138	76705	16394	26821	12306	68377	3170	12756
1838864	123175	268107	1168504	233157	581407	315082	1114792	50731	762186
1071382	114405	173574	754878	142245	365490	193520	720004	47848	516662
701967	93053	116072	449556	86670	210624	109209	427683	28266	325551
369415	21352	57502	305323	55575	154866	84311	292322	19582	191111
1406187	26706	201142	1215474	250175	548926	270759	1135506	81046	717107
75589	101	16952	42216	10907	11770	8527	39116	1909	42096
283730	2689	23140	227897	41807	102755	42146	211308	17728	165893
1046868	23917	161050	945361	197462	434401	220087	885082	61409	509118
59374	1100	8036	76293	18206	38389	12914	75235	2907	80088
68661	4366	12971	90202	14930	41911	21666	86874	8468	77095
2349535	135645	353709	1803857	359284	834116	429699	1693401	117519	1076587

6-8 续表 1 continued

单位：万元

项目 Item		资产负债 固定资产原价合计 Original Value of Fixed Assets	# 生产经营用 For Productive Use	累计折旧 Accumulative Depreciation	#本年折旧 Depreciation in this Year	固定资产净值年平均余额 Average Net Value of Fixed Assets	无形资产及递延资产 Intangible and Deferred Assets
总　计	Total	1623187	1286135	545647	71251	1029588	113884
在总计中：	Of Total:						
中央企业	Central Enterprises	51172	41170	22980	4868	29314	461
地方企业	Local Enterprises	1572015	1244965	522667	66383	1000275	113423
工业系统	Industry System	126052	91756	46783	4036	81012	12960
非工业系统	Non-Industry System	16253	10526	6492	1462	8505	577
区县工业	Industry of District and County	1416296	1135346	465278	60146	902599	94823
其他	Others	13414	7337	4114	739	8159	5063
在总计中：	Of Total:						
农村企业	Rural Enterprises	1025037	822037	327207	47232	656879	35734
在总计中：	Of Total:						
轻工业	Light Industry	662482	524826	221130	31486	425538	38471
以农产品为原料	Using Farm Products as Raw Materials	425000	347840	143282	21560	269015	21495
以非农产品为原料	Using Non-Farm Prqducts as Raw Materials	237482	176986	77848	9926	156524	16976
重工业	Heavy Industry	960704	761309	324517	39765	604050	75414
采掘工业	Excavation	52057	40407	13108	2642	39048	1393
原料工业	Raw Material	200463	170206	51943	6619	144757	21464
加工工业	Processing	708184	550696	259467	30503	420246	52557
在总计中：	Of Total:						
大型企业	Large Enterprises	106424	95131	34553	2114	73899	38327
中型企业	Medium Enterprises	106199	84864	43858	5118	61094	4655
小型企业	Small Enterprises	1410563	1106140	467235	64019	894595	70902

6-8 续表 2 continued

(10000 yuan)

Assets and Liabilities										
#无形资产 Intangible Assets	其他资产 Other Assets	资产总计 Total Assets	流动负债合计 Liquid Liabilities	短期借款 Shortterm Loans	长期负债合计 Long-term Liabilities	长期借款 Longterm Loans	负债合计 Total Liabilities	所有者权益 Creditors' Equity	实收资本 Contributed Capital	国家资本 State
47078	7436	3454336	1892466	584265	355316	280448	2274532	1179804	925286	33774
171	485	180834	96733	7460	7988	3649	105314	75520	27117	1680
46907	6952	3273502	1795733	576805	347328	276799	2169218	1104284	898169	32094
2193	320	287816	155227	35460	47028	31999	202473	85343	77778	1805
69	16	58380	41064	4535	7017	690	59513	-1133	4976	1159
39702	6614	2829610	1564906	527217	286552	237977	1864984	964626	801229	28708
4943	2	97696	34536	9593	6731	6133	42248	55448	14186	422
19692	5716	2022871	1065417	384984	178031	141201	1254123	768748	599261	20932
18445	3726	1361585	746695	264953	127818	99419	879130	482455	396810	14290
11141	2723	827590	454536	173021	78471	58298	535812	291778	235586	9222
7303	1003	533995	292159	91933	49347	41121	343317	190677	161223	5068
28633	3711	2092752	1145771	319311	227498	181028	1395403	697349	528476	19484
308	293	87908	38875	9668	4683	3489	43591	44317	18576	271
16610	220	433202	234228	62758	76323	72396	325309	107893	77544	7149
11715	3197	1571642	872669	246886	146493	105144	1026503	545140	432356	12065
12830		197615	111936	32783	42459	38823	154395	43220	28392	111
1823		180420	99542	40269	23727	19301	123269	57151	56552	1454
32425	7436	3076302	1680988	511212	289130	222324	1996869	1079433	840342	32210

6-8 续表 3 continued

单位：万元

项目	Item	资产负债 Assets and Liabilities 集体资本 Collective	法人资本 Institutional Units	个人资本 Individuals	港澳台资本 Hongkong, Macao and Taiwan	外商资本 Foreign
总计	**Total**	630499	172775	82555	683	4999
在总计中：	**Of Total:**					
中央企业	Central Enterprises	22623	2743	71		
地方企业	Local Enterprises	607876	170032	82484	683	4999
工业系统	Industry System	61274	13889	809		
非工业系统	Non-Industry System	2756	1048	12		
区县工业	Industry of District and County	539211	148912	78716	683	4999
其他	Others	4635	6183	2947		
在总计中：	**Of Total:**					
农村企业	Rural Enterprises	382200	126816	63686	628	4999
在总计中：	**Of Total:**					
轻工业	Light Industry	269900	77936	32294	326	2065
以农产品为原料	Using Farm Products as Raw Materials	154966	54559	15360	8	1471
以非农产品为原料	Using Non-Farm Products as Raw Materials	114933	23377	16934	318	594
重工业	Heavy Industry	360600	94839	50261	358	2934
采掘工业	Excavation	15154	1622	1529		
原料工业	Raw Material	49647	10287	10104	358	
加工工业	Processing	295799	82929	38628		2934
在总计中：	**Of Total:**					
大型企业	Large Enterprises	25328	1260	1693		
中型企业	Medium Enterprises	48421	5922	398	358	
小型企业	Small Enterprises	556750	165593	80465	326	4999

6-8 续表 4 continued

(10000 yuan)

损益及分配 Profits,Loss and Distribution										
产品					管理				财务	
产品销售收入 Sales Revenue	产品销售成本 Cost of Sales	产品销售费用 Expenses of Sales	产品销售税金及附加 Sales Tax and Extra Charges	产品销售利润 Sales Profits	管理费用 Overhead Cost	税金 Taxes	财产保险费 Premium of Property	劳动待业保险费 Premium for Employment Insurance	财务费用 Financial Expenses	利息支出 Expenses of Interest
2461325	2055603	92856	15670	297197	215041	7192	1881	19601	44725	35068
153734	131435	3597	857	17846	14922	226	78	977	57	28
2307591	1924168	89259	14813	279351	200119	6965	1802	18624	44668	35040
104188	86726	4363	572	12526	25539	776	190	5552	3782	3697
25689	20236	1551	176	3727	4482	48	23	337	484	235
2116466	1778442	80964	13668	243392	164474	6113	1584	12687	39667	30428
61248	38764	2381	397	19706	5624	28	5	48	735	680
1790904	1510425	61969	11234	207276	105991	4548	1112	1118	27803	19863
1046458	878113	47369	6101	114875	89073	3051	1071	9460	19027	14677
685020	576450	32617	4031	71923	51653	1777	745	4950	12239	9852
361438	301664	14752	2070	42952	37420	1274	326	4510	6788	4825
1414867	1177490	45487	9569	182322	125968	4141	810	10141	25698	20391
73429	53744	5088	1017	13580	4423	181	16	25	949	770
298328	263458	5046	905	28919	22195	418	164	512	5441	4806
1043110	860288	35352	7647	139823	99350	3542	630	9604	19308	14815
55812	49384	454	140	5833	5069	138	62	877	3763	3782
67238	56380	2467	515	7875	13031	382	159	3074	2658	2097
2338275	1949838	89934	15015	283488	196941	6672	1659	15650	38305	29189

6-8 续表 5 continued

单位：万元

项目	Item	营业利润 Operating Profits	投资收益 Investment Income	补贴收入 Subsidy Income	营业外收入 Out-business Income	营业外支出 Out-business Expenditure	利润总额 Total Profits
		损益及分配 Profits,Loss and Distribution					
总计	**Total**	69649	3459	6041	15655	10797	87766
在总计中：	**Of Total:**						
中央企业	Central Enterprises	5271	444	6	490	770	5526
地方企业	Local Enterprises	64379	3015	6036	15165	10027	82240
工业系统	Industry System	-9482	358	26	3691	1361	-6546
非工业系统	Non-Industry System	-1585	-32	353	131	226	-1321
区县工业	Industry of District and County	61803	2688	3328	11240	8334	74119
其他	Others	13643	1	2329	103	106	15988
在总计中：	**Of Total:**						
农村企业	Rural Enterprises	78991	1303	1853	4787	4886	84619
在总计中：	**Of Total:**						
轻工业	Light Industry	26232	1649	2162	6454	4842	31824
以农产品为原料	Using Farm Products as Raw Materials	20313	1282	1463	2345	2646	22617
以非农产品为原料	Using Non-Farm Products as Raw Materials	5919	367	699	4109	2196	9207
重工业	Heavy Industry	43417	1811	3879	9201	5955	55942
采掘工业	Excavation	8127	10	114	143	316	8181
原料工业	Raw Material	4376	278	86	513	737	5581
加工工业	Processing	30913	1522	3679	8546	4902	42180
在总计中：	**Of Total:**						
大型企业	Large Enterprises	-1498			77	169	-1590
中型企业	Medium Enterprises	-3813	127	50	2746	555	-1123
小型企业	Small Enterprises	74960	3332	5991	12832	10073	90479

6-8 续表 6 continued

(10000 yuan)

应交所得税 Income Tax Payable	应付利润 Profits Payable	亏损企业亏损额 Total Loss-ing of Loss-making Enterprises	利税总额 Total Pre-tax Profits	工资，福利费，增值税 Wages,Welfares and Added Value Tax 本年应付工资总额 Total Wags Payable	本年应付福利费总额 Total Welfares Payable	本年应交增值税 Added Value Tax	本年进项税额 Tax Include in Purchasing Cost	本年销项税额 Tax Include in Sales Cost	工业中间投入合计 Intermediate Input of Industry
23699	30239	48986	201417	272035	34539	97982	245843	332572	1923006
2452	3885	1563	14276	10607	2098	7893	19603	25273	113440
21247	26354	47424	187141	261428	32441	90089	226241	307299	1809566
499	946	8491	-1215	19578	2586	4758	12491	16813	69252
222	132	2128	-22	6575	934	1125	2829	3132	11403
19441	24998	35559	165928	231621	27890	78141	207252	277732	1691360
1085	278	1246	22450	3654	1031	6065	3669	9622	37551
15934	23578	12527	160108	180906	20674	64254	170779	227691	1422197
10454	11284	20039	77311	117575	14685	39387	110470	145049	823006
7171	8207	10915	52398	75851	8891	25750	74978	97545	545757
3283	3077	9125	24914	41725	5794	13637	35492	47504	277249
13245	18955	28947	124106	154459	19854	58595	135374	187523	1100000
926	1891	659	12238	13554	1177	3040	1824	4072	49124
2385	4659	4046	16510	18903	2782	10025	37845	45957	244516
9934	12405	24242	95358	122002	15895	45531	95705	137494	806360
64		1776	243	6636	761	1693	8010	9673	58481
786	447	3597	3705	11528	1399	4312	7028	11146	53509
22850	29792	43613	197469	253871	32379	91976	230806	311753	1811016

6-9 全部独立核算"三资"工业企业主要经济指标

单位：万元

项目 Item		企业单位个数(个) Number of Enterprises (unit)	#亏损企业 Loss-making Enterprises	工业总产值(当年价格) Gross Output Value of Industry (at current prices)	新产品产值 Value of New Products	工业总产值(1990年不变价格) Gross Output Value of Industry (at 1990 constant prices)	工业增加值(生产法) Added Value of Industry (with production method)
总计	**Total**	2295	1015	11683424	3840449	14984831	2701107
在总计中：	**Of Total:**						
中央企业	Central Enterprises	153	70	2703126	1266798	3869590	429447
地方企业	Local Enterprises	2142	945	8980298	2573650	11115241	2271660
工业系统	Industry System	292	98	2698088	593010	3209819	735671
非工业系统	Non-Industry System	165	64	507591	2306	374128	151894
区县工业	Industry of District and County	951	363	1683522	50303	1669467	510524
其他	Others	734	420	4091097	1928031	5861827	873571
在总计中：	**Of Total:**						
轻工业	Light Industry	1362	620	2785416	211381	2640658	925054
以农产品为原料	Using Farm Products as Raw Materials	887	417	1712400	20220	1493689	577966
以非农产品为原料	Using Non-Farm Products as Raw Materials	475	203	1073016	191162	1146969	347088
重工业	Heavy Industry	933	395	8898008	3629067	12344173	1776053
采掘工业	Excavation	2	2	1471		2718	282
原料工业	Raw Material	108	46	361455	666	310875	98535
加工工业	Processing	823	347	8535082	3628401	12030581	1677236
在总计中：	**Of Total:**						
大型企业	Large Enterprises	51	17	5507639	2656856	8662761	1033954
中型企业	Medium Enterprises	38	8	718229	336188	693572	136025
小型企业	Small Enterprises	2206	990	5457557	847404	5628498	1531128

MAIN INDICATORS FOR FOREIGN FUNDED INDUSTRIAL ENTERPRISES WITH INDEPENDENT ACCOUNTING SYSTEM

(10000 yuan)

工业销售产值(当年价格) Sales Value of Industry (at current price)	出口交货值 Delivery Value of Exports	全部从业人员年平均人数(人) Average Number of Persons Employed (person)	资产负债 Assets and Liabilities						
			流动资产合计 Circulating Funds	应收帐款净额 Accounts Receivable	存货 Stock	产成品 Finished Products	流动资产平均余额 Average Balance of Circulating Funds	长期投资 Longterm Investment	固定资产合计 Fixed Assets
11106115	1998720	252414	7602133	2846907	2188733	705591	6619416	97683	3550675
2663858	707780	19135	1290304	663613	291542	62029	1173514	8127	409330
8442257	1290940	233279	6311830	2183294	1897191	643563	5445902	89557	3141346
2442228	508745	69741	2065240	894856	656805	209626	2022502	13962	1318861
503308	13329	15295	330712	90359	89524	24583	299507	25273	253079
1635832	256958	102580	1358296	343614	502244	221660	1219447	31342	979884
3860889	511908	45663	2557582	854465	648618	187694	1904446	18980	589522
2727261	459606	144719	2152291	472306	717969	306027	1998429	52687	1536431
1693408	259477	107060	1364874	250463	469761	195328	1262190	49117	1082710
1033854	200128	37659	787417	221843	248208	110699	736240	3570	453721
8378854	1539115	107695	5449842	2374601	1470763	399565	4620987	44997	2014245
1479	1160	117	883	402	126	15	741		524
360791	18249	13195	245228	83198	66594	24215	217158	484	311278
8016583	1519705	94383	5203731	2291001	1404044	375335	4403088	44513	1702443
5239548	955556	45668	2603995	1087998	698130	198622	2395396	15919	1272850
711739	140733	14169	523641	288279	119862	50904	462396	9165	178474
5154828	902431	192577	4474498	1470630	1370741	456065	3761624	72600	2099351

6-9 续表 1 continued

单位：万元

项目 Item		资产负债 固定资产原价合计 Original Value of Fixed Assets	# 生产经营用 For Productive Use	累计折旧 Accumulative Depreciation	#本年折旧 Depreciation in this Year	固定资产净值年平均余额 Average Net Value of Fixed Assets	无形资产及递延资产 Intangible and Deferred Assets
总 计	**Total**	4845811	3922188	1583185	316275	3079116	571037
在总计中：	**Of Total:**						
中央企业	Central Enterprises	592539	363032	195822	43296	398489	32616
地方企业	Local Enterprises	4253272	3559157	1387363	272979	2680627	538422
工业系统	Industry System	1941945	1809211	731343	106949	1111356	136003
非工业系统	Non-Industry System	362802	284663	115414	22665	231424	36816
区县工业	Industry of District and County	1198930	994745	317735	62006	864617	149441
其他	Others	749595	470538	222871	81359	473230	216162
在总计中：	**Of Total:**						
轻工业	Light Industry	2052277	1611597	645348	139699	1388239	349056
以农产品为原料	Using Farm Products as Raw Materials	1434226	1171832	439564	80308	958281	146984
以非农产品为原料	Using Non-Farm Products as Raw Materials	618051	439765	205784	59391	429958	202072
重工业	Heavy Industry	2793534	2310591	937837	176576	1690877	221981
采掘工业	Excavation	725	691	201	53	481	179
原料工业	Raw Material	384660	371700	115485	24451	249766	51502
加工工业	Processing	2408149	1938200	822150	152072	1440630	170300
在总计中：	**Of Total:**						
大型企业	Large Enterprises	1830422	1428693	627910	131330	1130412	108719
中型企业	Medium Enterprises	220615	203619	75719	15255	153564	29834
小型企业	Small Enterprises	2794774	2289877	879556	169691	1795141	432484

6-9 续表 2 continued

(10000 yuan)

Assets and Liabilities										
#无形资产 Intangible Assets	其他资产 Other Assets	资产总计 Total Assets	流动负债合计 Liquid Liabilities	短期借款 Shortterm Loans	长期负债合计 Long-term Liabilities	长期借款 Longterm Loans	负债合计 Total Liabilities	所有者权益 Creditors' Equity	实收资本 Contributed Capital	国家资本 State
473457	161714	11983252	6742052	2342466	699034	651760	7520030	4463222	4198664	559595
28725	13849	1754225	1042520	334247	75225	89321	1124271	629954	366669	77563
444732	147866	10229027	5699532	2008219	623809	562439	6395760	3833268	3831995	482032
119665	56728	3590795	1845314	736377	232890	202371	2128848	1461947	1449024	237648
31445	10815	656693	298713	102331	30362	29675	333265	323427	379489	84466
97415	39864	2558826	1374577	575275	190091	166782	1571248	987579	1090438	115173
196207	40459	3422713	2180928	594236	170466	163611	2362399	1060315	913044	44745
300272	60877	4151342	2122932	844050	308473	272923	2448824	1702518	2084596	276928
110846	34130	2677815	1364981	595238	166226	137523	1542419	1135396	1475781	227937
189426	26747	1473526	757951	248811	142248	135400	906404	567122	608815	48992
173185	100838	7831911	4619120	1498416	390561	378837	5071207	2760704	2114068	282667
99	12	1598	744	150	200	200	944	653	728	
46975	7868	616361	255387	83420	38630	42863	294250	322111	307666	54374
126111	92958	7213952	4362989	1414847	351731	335774	4776013	2437940	1805675	228293
103193	23823	4025305	2205426	822347	195368	197971	2412870	1612436	1285027	123389
27682	3204	744318	458043	144095	39723	22392	497819	246499	207510	51484
342583	134688	7213629	4078583	1376024	463944	431396	4609342	2604287	2706127	384722

6-9 续表 3 continued

单位：万元

项目 Item		资产负债 Assets and Liabilities				
		集体资本 Collective	法人资本 Institutional Units	个人资本 Individuals	港澳台资本 Hongkong, Macao and Taiwan	外商资本 Foreign
总计	Total	159275	860055	18828	595479	2005432
在总计中：	Of Total:					
中央企业	Central Enterprises	3509	146682		30930	107985
地方企业	Local Enterprises	155766	713373	18828	564550	1897447
工业系统	Industry System	8399	412466	5209	113287	672015
非工业系统	Non-Industry System	6030	40446	247	44128	204171
区县工业	Industry of District and County	128382	154405	10439	240101	441938
其他	Others	12955	106056	2933	167034	579323
在总计中：	Of Total:					
轻工业	Light Industry	99480	316628	12678	356240	1022642
以农产品为原料	Using Farm Products as Raw Materials	67686	175243	11706	251628	741582
以非农产品为原料	Using Non-Farm Products as Raw Materials	31794	141385	972	104612	281060
重工业	Heavy Industry	59795	543427	6150	239239	982790
采掘工业	Excavation	264				464
原料工业	Raw Material	9748	98521	732	33792	110500
加工工业	Processing	49783	444906	5418	205448	871826
在总计中：	Of Total:					
大型企业	Large Enterprises	459	351993		104308	704879
中型企业	Medium Enterprises	8627	33712	703	39350	73634
小型企业	Small Enterprises	150189	474350	18125	451821	1226920

6-9 续表 4 continued

(10000 yuan)

损益及分配 Profits,Loss and Distribution										
产品					管理				财务	
销售收入 Sales Revenue	产品销售成本 Cost of Sales	产品销售费用 Expenses of Sales	产品销售税金及附加 Sales Tax and Extra Charges	产品销售利润 Sales Profits	费用 Overhead Cost	税金 Taxes	财产保险费 Premium of Property	劳动待业保险费 Premium for Employment Insurance	费用 Financial Expenses	利息支出 Expenses of Interest
11539757	9381429	639715	28903	1489710	698798	15282	5647	14724	120885	104681
2661650	2333149	68647	4288	255566	68427	2333	416	1056	19621	19022
8878107	7048279	571068	24616	1234144	630371	12948	5231	13668	101264	85659
2568446	2041922	143575	11533	371416	208494	5981	2230	7208	43406	41941
514417	385874	52433	385	75724	46027	1099	506	2341	7168	5697
1593801	1207297	165301	8138	213065	145569	2238	1540	1884	25203	20610
4201443	3413186	209759	4560	573939	230281	3630	955	2235	25487	17411
2690610	1975682	298244	17856	398828	275849	7112	2988	6897	44203	38395
1657834	1214685	202767	12900	227482	174125	4630	2083	4728	34738	31318
1032776	760997	95477	4956	171346	101724	2483	905	2169	9465	7077
8849147	7405747	341471	11048	1090882	422949	8169	2659	7827	76682	66286
1479	991	265	4	220	133	1	1		135	127
365686	296787	11856	224	56818	25658	453	194	617	6205	5300
8481982	7107968	329350	10820	1033844	397158	7716	2464	7210	70342	60859
5209792	4388850	207818	16240	596884	205934	6195	1434	2217	48577	43831
729880	640864	26192	134	62690	41656	846	307	932	7945	8052
5600085	4351714	405705	12530	830136	451208	8240	3907	11575	64363	52797

6-9 续表 5 continued

单位：万元

项目 Item		损益及分配 Profits,Loss and Distribution 营业利润 Operating Profits	投资收益 Investment Income	补贴收入 Subsidy Income	营业外收入 Out-business Income	营业外支出 Out-business Expenditure	利润总额 Total Profits
总计	Total	616693	-361	960	88148	60578	667214
在总计中：	Of Total:						
中央企业	Central Enterprises	175232	307		6410	3800	180490
地方企业	Local Enterprises	441461	-668	960	81738	56777	486724
工业系统	Industry System	130414	-848		30349	38851	129177
非工业系统	Non-Industry System	18638	482		2896	1365	21809
区县工业	Industry of District and County	45726	318	956	12410	6118	58910
其他	Others	246683	-620	4	36083	10443	276828
在总计中：	Of Total:						
轻工业	Light Industry	91408	612	801	18270	26385	90071
以农产品为原料	Using Farm Products as Raw Materials	22836	437	789	12252	6718	33067
以非农产品为原料	Using Non-Farm Products as Raw Materials	68572	175	12	6018	19667	57004
重工业	Heavy Industry	525285	-973	160	69878	34193	577143
采掘工业	Excavation	-48					-48
原料工业	Raw Material	22409	-8	4	1808	2165	22075
加工工业	Processing	502924	-965	156	68070	32028	555116
在总计中：	Of Total:						
大型企业	Large Enterprises	348112	-679		34314	23613	366836
中型企业	Medium Enterprises	17747	-99		7008	2363	22244
小型企业	Small Enterprises	250834	417	960	46826	34602	278134

6-9 续表 6 continued

(10000 yuan)

				工资，福利费，增值税 Wages,Welfares and Added Value Tax					
应交所得税 Income Tax Payable	应付利润 Profits Payable	亏损企业亏损额 Total Lossing of Loss-making Enterprises	利税总额 Total Pre-tax Profits	本年应付工资总额 Total Wags Payable	本年应付福利费总额 Total Welfares Payable	本年应交增值税 Added Value Tax	本年进项税额 Tax Include in Purchasing Cost	本年销项税额 Tax Include in Sales Cost	工业中间投入合计 Intermediate Input of Industry
71737	152020	247214	1021252	493120	107715	325135	1037862	1254554	9307452
12900	11808	12770	219845	71192	15390	35067	270875	304862	2308746
58837	140212	234444	801407	421928	92325	290067	766987	949693	6998706
26461	68039	101627	245378	150015	37819	104668	256297	322217	2067085
4525	-935	18843	48110	32813	6590	25914	45698	68228	381613
8665	13256	51271	135757	118696	21746	68710	155409	222340	1241708
19186	59852	62703	372162	120404	26170	90775	309583	336908	3308300
22874	37817	113832	243953	218192	41859	136026	233438	362719	1996388
13736	12567	85015	131226	149512	28113	85259	148672	229015	1219692
9138	25250	28817	112728	68680	13747	50768	84766	133704	776696
48863	114203	133382	777298	274928	65856	189108	804424	891836	7311064
		48	-42	226	30	3		3	1192
559	3171	16703	36393	19719	3545	14094	38201	49537	277013
48303	111033	116631	740947	254983	62281	175012	766223	842296	7032859
33120	63104	81763	523551	138058	36284	140475	404177	454178	4614159
2934	-729	15898	41039	27400	4579	18661	72324	89992	600865
35683	89645	149553	456662	327661	66853	165998	561360	710385	4092427

6-10 独立核算大中型工业企业主要经济指标

单位：万元

项　目 Item		企业单位个数(个) Number of Enterprises (unit)	#亏损企业 Loss-making Enterprises	工业总产值(当年价格) Gross Output Value of Industry (at current prices)	新产品产值 Value of New Products	工业总产值(1990年不变价格) Gross Output Value of Industry (at 1990 constant prices)	工业增加值(生产法) Added Value of Industry (with production method)
总　计	**Total**	481	103	15747863	4314102	16226034	4104566
在总计中:	**Of Total:**						
中央工业	Central Industry	114	22	6468291	1850193	5765104	1496735
地方工业	Local Industry	367	81	9279572	2463909	10460930	2607830
工业系统	Industry System	209	36	5619954	898901	5486340	1583791
非工业系统	Non-Industry System	39	6	676567	3375	382362	311445
区县工业	Industry of District and County	91	30	797837	5809	770808	250454
其他	Others	28	9	2185214	1555823	3821420	462140
在总计中:	**Of Total:**						
内资企业	Domestic Investment Enterprises	392	78	9521996	1321058	6869701	2934587
国有企业	State-Owned	285	44	7050224	516409	4643540	2230123
集体企业	Collective Owned	42	21	142274	7822	134053	36290
股份合作企业	Share Holding	3		25546		29115	4713
联营企业	Joint Owned	15	3	156635	17994	245051	3147
有限责任公司	Limited Liability Corporations	27	7	1045903	186731	793240	282873
股份有限公司	Share Holding Corporations	16	1	1088439	592102	1013662	374437
私营企业	Private Owned	4	2	12975		11041	3003
港澳台商投资企业	Hongkong,Macao and Taiwan Funded Enterprises	28	8	1849256	1447306	3473908	324493
港澳台合资经营	Joint Venture	23	8	218227	5734	235709	39407
港澳台合作经营	Cooperative	3		12088		12088	4722
港澳台商独资企业	Hongkong,Macao and Taiwan Enterprises	2		1618941	1441572	3226111	280364
港澳台商投资股份有限公司	Hongkong,Macao and Taiwan Funded Share Holding Corporations						
外商投资企业	Foreign Funded Enterprises	61	17	4376611	1545739	5882425	845486
中外合资经营	Joint Venture	50	15	4150462	1543460	5724637	756046
中外合作经营	Cooperative	2		51494	2276	49595	12221
外资(独资)企业	Foreign Enterprises	7	2	64903	3	63698	28371
外商投资股份有限公司	Foreign Funded Share Holding Corporations	2		109752		44496	48848
在总计中:	**Of Total:**						
农村企业	Rural Enterprises	19	6	93444		81776	24649
在总计中:	**Of Total:**						
轻工业	Light Industry	213	52	2300978	291692	2305837	868503
以农产品为原料	Using Farm Products as Raw Materials	144	35	1394522	89158	1246177	578680
以非农产品为原料	Using Non-Farm Products as Raw Materials	69	17	906456	202534	1059661	289823
重工业	Heavy Industry	268	51	13446885	4022411	13920197	3236063
采掘工业	Excavation	4		90689		36590	58741
原料工业	Raw Material	44	7	5849959	314828	3324566	1619913
加工工业	Processing	220	44	7506238	3707583	10559041	1557409
在总计中:	**Of Total:**						
大型企业	Large Enterprises	215	49	13481429	3568202	14171278	3310532
中型企业	Medium Enterprises	266	54	2266435	745900	2054756	794034

MAIN INDICATORS FOR LOCAL LARGE AND MEDIUM INDUSTRIAL ENTERPRISES WITH INDEPENDENT ACCOUNTING SYSTEM

(10000 yuan)

工业销售产值(当年价格) Sales Value of Industry (at current price)	出口交货值 Delivery Value of Exports	全部从业人员年平均人数(人) Average Number of Persons Employed (person)	资产负债 Assets and Liabilities: 流动资产合计 Circulating Funds	应收帐款净额 Accounts Receivable	存货 Stock	产成品 Finished Products	流动资产平均余额 Average Balance of Circulating Funds	长期投资 Longterm Investment	固定资产合计 Fixed Assets
15272766	1435950	635429	11810713	2974464	3395457	1127680	11888417	2328444	14041624
6346516	717131	154044	3718440	1092011	865606	239070	4048621	492834	4737139
8926250	718819	481385	8092273	1882453	2529851	888610	7839795	1835610	9304486
5329727	503844	369092	5927167	1476220	1888781	680814	5960220	1720609	6389399
670745	8008	41915	691779	140742	173239	50534	635336	50913	1906239
788672	51840	59934	606181	109331	232126	73191	580116	41649	702352
2137106	155127	10444	867146	156161	235705	84070	664124	22439	306496
9321479	339660	575592	8683077	1598188	2577466	878154	9030625	2303361	12590300
6952528	264969	458619	6089773	1053570	1908859	567035	6718911	1685128	9204833
128035	5466	21007	166495	33137	80300	34580	162109	11375	157182
25738		1424	12868	3276	3303	600	12962	183	19988
142811	63	13802	225089	36055	97688	40534	222501	44063	161318
1038686	43540	50998	1069620	283271	236270	116605	993467	311139	2455679
1021741	21304	28901	1110656	186009	246622	117021	912598	251473	583366
11941	4319	841	8575	2870	4424	1779	8077		7935
1811727	15135	14464	800984	185537	222264	78164	664190	16392	184773
206623	8019	9747	278947	88362	76181	24873	266327	5140	157220
10210	7116	751	6870	3339	2347	1679	6474		3531
1594894		3966	515167	93836	143736	51612	391389	11252	24022
4139560	1081155	45373	2326652	1190740	595728	171363	2193602	8692	1266552
3903800	1032934	38294	2231122	1169563	557826	156332	2093093	8427	1048170
49528	8676	1255	25359	5695	11258	6171	29158	21	25384
72373	14163	1432	47142	10644	18154	3163	49405		102714
113859	25382	4392	23029	4839	8490	5697	21945	244	90284
90709	37407	8554	69298	12379	31464	17327	67892	1636	43729
2227954	276556	166459	2445926	347196	726704	317768	2368603	469262	2743840
1335674	120671	111320	1427222	213299	442050	190157	1342003	259096	1444220
892281	155886	55139	1018704	133897	284654	127611	1026601	210166	1299620
13044812	1159393	468970	9364787	2627269	2668753	809912	9519813	1859183	11297785
95570	28123	26552	161517	78858	17332	8316	176521	12534	126660
5827584	161170	204030	3412327	685842	965896	234483	3639056	805227	8439421
7121658	970099	238388	5790943	1862569	1685525	567113	5704237	1041422	2731703
13103639	1236550	506061	9474442	2431418	2841910	893991	9763063	1705901	12309132
2169127	199400	129368	2336271	543046	553547	233688	2125354	622543	1732492

6-10 续表 1 continued

单位：万元

项目	Item	资产负债 固定资产原价合计 Original Value of Fixed Assets	# 生产经营用 For Productive Use	累计折旧 Accumu-lative Depre-ciation	#本年折旧 Depre-ciation in this Year	固定资产净值年平均余额 Average Net Value of Fixed Assets	无形资产及递延资产 Intangible and Deferred Assets
总计	**Total**	18684620	15769869	6650207	887623	11687521	1086989
在总计中：	**Of Total:**						
中央工业	Central Industry	6302986	5610334	2401227	312972	3867511	147954
地方工业	Local Industry	12381633	10159535	4248980	574651	7820010	939035
工业系统	Industry System	8726685	7652082	3299936	398486	5416867	790684
非工业系统	Non-Industry System	2369980	1493544	564884	99787	1562287	23135
区县工业	Industry of District and County	892463	753502	263502	33865	586348	87093
其他	Others	392506	260408	120658	42514	254509	38123
在总计中：	**Of Total:**						
内资企业	Domestic Investment Enterprises	16633583	14137557	5946579	741039	10403546	948436
国有企业	State-Owned	12392573	10236258	4777545	541957	7510288	421337
集体企业	Collective Owned	212623	179995	78412	7232	134993	42982
股份合作企业	Share Holding	23286	21795	7405	1352	17522	1658
联营企业	Joint Owned	226508	134474	77895	6425	147232	17985
有限责任公司	Limited Liability Corporations	3006583	2830075	717890	139231	2136802	420380
股份有限公司	Share Holding Corporations	762353	727200	284582	44669	449907	43124
私营企业	Private Owned	9658	7761	2849	173	6802	970
港澳台商投资企业	Hongkong,Macao and Taiwan Funded Enterprises	214465	186410	71473	12746	138502	22421
港澳台合资经营	Joint Venture	181003	153680	62062	9809	117970	20634
港澳台合作经营	Cooperative	3766	3034	268	174	3531	
港澳台商独资企业	Hongkong,Macao and Taiwan Enterprises	29696	29696	9143	2762	17001	1787
港澳台商投资股份有限公司	Hongkong,Macao and Taiwan Funded Share Holding Corporations						
外商投资企业	Foreign Funded Enterprises	1836573	1445902	632156	133839	1145474	116132
中外合资经营	Joint Venture	1545675	1203462	547904	114202	949338	86850
中外合作经营	Cooperative	33989	12514	11043	2792	23932	6414
外资(独资)企业	Foreign Enterprises	126570	100507	27128	8033	85197	12191
外商投资股份有限公司	Foreign Funded Share Holding Corporations	130338	129420	46081	8812	87006	10677
在总计中：	**Of Total:**						
农村企业	Rural Enterprises	56427	53332	17718	2430	37882	3577
在总计中：	**Of Total:**						
轻工业	Light Industry	3641560	2095588	1133992	204530	2358149	268775
以农产品为原料	Using Farm Products as Raw Materials	1943263	1505739	641202	92394	1256053	123417
以非农产品为原料	Using Non-Farm Products as Raw Materials	1698297	589850	492790	112137	1102097	145358
重工业	Heavy Industry	15043060	13674280	5516215	683093	9329372	818214
采掘工业	Excavation	181962	22126	68146	8075	117960	5113
原料工业	Raw Material	11272653	10892581	4136125	510600	6945936	580296
加工工业	Processing	3588445	2759574	1311944	164417	2265475	232805
在总计中：	**Of Total:**						
大型企业	Large Enterprises	16508453	13850315	5948130	782189	10287451	863690
中型企业	Medium Enterprises	2176167	1919554	702077	105434	1400070	223300

6-10 续表 2 continued

(10000 yuan)

Assets and Liabilities										
#无形资产 Intangible Assets	其他资产 Other Assets	资产总计 Total Assets	流动负债合计 Liquid Liabilities	短期借款 Shortterm Loans	长期负债合计 Long-term Liabilities	长期借款 Longterm Loans	负债合计 Total Liabilities	所有者权益 Creditors' Equity	实收资本 Contributed Capital	国家资本 State
441116	30778	29298549	11041687	4144583	5490950	3400315	16546139	12752410	7257319	3910963
124239	9127	9105493	3291230	972442	2676087	786886	5972548	3132945	1428275	966725
316877	21651	20193056	7750457	3172142	2814863	2613429	10573591	9619465	5829044	2944237
230589	9875	14837735	6105803	2706999	2444422	2295980	8558216	6279519	3442967	1385549
17955	5113	2677179	451690	85301	193786	185276	645484	2031695	1550443	1414211
35373	3780	1441055	543398	206228	147042	106295	690471	750584	380122	126916
32961	2884	1237087	649566	173613	29614	25879	679420	557667	455513	17562
310242	3752	24528926	8378218	3178141	5255860	3179951	13635451	10893475	5764782	3736090
198808	2855	17403926	6282610	2344198	3711930	1756457	9995648	7408278	3833195	2510253
14653		378035	211478	73053	66186	58123	277664	100371	84944	1565
1658		34696	26031	2610	1396	1090	27428	7269	3240	
2403		448456	264117	80332	76412	63370	340530	107926	77054	8600
63507	62	4256881	975667	431319	1226499	1151375	2202167	2054714	1356467	1128718
28306	828	1989448	608939	242575	171037	147402	780240	1209208	405462	86859
906	6	17485	9376	4055	2400	2134	11776	5710	4420	95
18906	4746	1029315	674842	193036	37325	25375	712199	317116	200252	61574
17764	4646	466586	278848	149836	37325	25375	316205	150382	175836	61574
	100	10501	6044	3200			6044	4456	2065	
1142		552228	389950	40000			389950	162278	22351	
111968	22281	3740308	1988627	773406	197765	194989	2198489	1541819	1292285	113299
83491	20792	3395360	1910109	746728	200303	190664	2122509	1272850	1053391	105614
6414	-10	57168	20408	7220	1590	1390	21998	35170	37665	7685
11866	1499	163546	32933	13727	5992	2935	38925	124621	131373	
10197		124234	25177	5731	-10121		15057	109177	69856	
2147	772	119012	60608	29557	14991	8242	75599	43413	34961	2634
136133	10598	5938400	2288689	1088241	635737	510752	2924719	3013682	2145217	1027219
89953	8263	3262217	1279656	615496	280181	190405	1559878	1702339	1211265	477689
46179	2335	2676183	1009033	472745	355555	320347	1364841	1311342	933952	549529
304984	20180	23360148	8752998	3056342	4855213	2889563	13621420	9738728	5112102	2883744
		305824	133756	58997	54646	46653	188402	117422	66106	64410
193392	-14397	13222875	3593730	1363103	3917474	2146512	7511204	5711671	3066706	2299188
111592	34577	9831449	5025512	1634243	883094	696398	5921814	3909635	1979291	520146
306151	19767	24372932	9186386	3546765	5037138	3057958	14236972	10135960	5680532	3018653
134965	11011	4925616	1855301	597818	453812	342357	2309167	2616449	1576787	892310

6-10 续表 3 continued

单位：万元

项　　目 Item		资　产　负　债 Assets and Liabilities				
		集　体 资　本 Collective	法　人 资　本 Institutional Units	个　人 资　本 Individuals	港澳台 资　本 Hongkong, Macao and Taiwan	外　商 资　本 Foreign
总　计	**Total**	127890	2105700	170294	145009	797464
在总计中：	**Of Total:**					
中央工业	Central Industry	1154	385826	23116	6944	44510
地方工业	Local Industry	126736	1719874	147178	138065	752955
工业系统	Industry System	59334	1518719	117053	54279	308033
非工业系统	Non-Industry System	6320	48212	110	3492	78099
区县工业	Industry of District and County	60787	111228	24015	25953	31225
其他	Others	296	41716	6000	54341	335598
在总计中：	**Of Total:**					
内资企业	Domestic Investment Enterprises	118803	1719995	169591	1351	18952
国有企业	State-Owned	13321	1228634	75992	993	4002
集体企业	Collective Owned	73749	7182	2091	358	
股份合作企业	Share Holding	2356	95	789		
联营企业	Joint Owned	12372	56082			
有限责任公司	Limited Liability Corporations	9759	217590	400		
股份有限公司	Share Holding Corporations	7200	208334	88119		14950
私营企业	Private Owned	47	2078	2200		
港澳台商投资企业	Hongkong,Macao and Taiwan Funded Enterprises	315	28974	703	107903	783
港澳台合资经营	Joint Venture	210	28974	403	83892	783
港澳台合作经营	Cooperative	105		300	1660	
港澳台商独资企业	Hongkong,Macao and Taiwan Enterprises				22351	
港澳台商投资股份有限公司	Hongkong,Macao and Taiwan Funded Share Holding Corporations					
外商投资企业	Foreign Funded Enterprises	8772	356730		35755	777729
中外合资经营	Joint Venture	6672	289575		23755	627776
中外合作经营	Cooperative					29981
外资(独资)企业	Foreign Enterprises				12000	119373
外商投资股份有限公司	Foreign Funded Share Holding Corporations	2100	67156			600
在总计中：	**Of Total:**					
农村企业	Rural Enterprises	16307	8307	37	3562	4115
在总计中：	**Of Total:**					
轻工业	Light Industry	67319	452524	54713	78140	465302
以农产品为原料	Using Farm Products as Raw Materials	38614	237036	42169	53709	362048
以非农产品为原料	Using Non-Farm Products as Raw Materials	28705	215488	12544	24431	103254
重工业	Heavy Industry	60570	1653176	115581	66869	332163
采掘工业	Excavation	101	1564	30		
原料工业	Raw Material	4636	684495	47592	13693	17102
加工工业	Processing	55833	967117	67958	53176	315061
在总计中：	**Of Total:**					
大型企业	Large Enterprises	48463	1677984	110303	105301	719829
中型企业	Medium Enterprises	79426	427716	59991	39708	77636

6-10 续表 4 continued

(10000 yuan)

损益及分配 Profits,Loss and Distribution										
产品					管理				财务	
销售收入 Sales Revenue	产品销售成本 Cost of Sales	产品销售费用 Expenses of Sales	产品销售税金及附加 Sales Tax and Extra Charges	产品销售利润 Sales Profits	费用 Overhead Cost	税金 Taxes	财产保险费 Premium of Property	劳动待业保险费 Premium for Employment Insurance	费用 Financial Expenses	利息支出 Expenses of Interest
17108316	14556270	479246	217000	1855800	1330017	43708	13152	260230	345538	332638
6913357	6030830	95976	89969	696582	376323	8839	4395	61671	96028	92125
10194959	8525439	383270	127032	1159218	953693	34869	8758	198559	249509	240512
6495495	5481949	212660	38160	762727	709884	24243	7134	176492	224445	219099
899422	801787	26828	42993	27813	79169	3524	602	13701	3858	3011
775711	584200	44396	43817	103298	67709	4965	705	7475	14686	13397
2024332	1657503	99386	2062	265380	96931	2137	317	891	6520	5005
11168644	9526556	245236	200627	1196226	1082427	36667	11412	257081	289016	280754
8378693	7117680	157276	187476	916261	848770	26486	7587	217707	218820	218164
123049	105765	2921	655	13708	18100	520	221	3951	6420	5879
25627	23564	442	107	1514	2023	65	17	208	240	239
164121	143250	7744	989	12139	26358	913	205	5667	5891	5586
1245575	1121011	36035	5118	83412	119261	4368	2584	23905	38702	35693
1218770	1004424	39884	6227	168235	66933	4303	798	5641	18564	15036
12809	10863	934	55	957	981	13		2	380	157
1713005	1432557	81219	1001	198228	69983	475	195	392	5817	5459
209546	180329	7874	962	20381	17711	385	187	391	6810	6464
10022	6568	1564	1	1889	669	26	6	2	139	127
1493438	1245660	71782	38	175958	51603	64	2		-1132	-1132
4226667	3597157	152791	15372	461346	177607	6567	1545	2757	50705	46425
3998003	3437106	132465	15205	413227	162786	6224	1486	2716	45778	44586
48984	29493	12111		7380	5181	1	26	18	2089	712
65823	49263	3631		12928	7997	307	34	23	2462	868
113858	81295	4584	168	27811	1642	35			376	259
89899	70864	7279	227	11530	6826	186	33	7	1589	973
2512995	1885090	156084	97989	373832	335987	11510	3709	58646	68068	63754
1561301	1128670	101414	91461	239756	213718	7823	2510	38702	39923	38385
951694	756420	54669	6528	134076	122269	3688	1199	19944	28145	25369
14595321	12671179	323163	119012	1481968	994030	32198	9443	201584	277469	268883
98250	67571	9696	926	20057	28991	573	16	17140	3647	3335
6780563	5981699	66513	98762	633589	435858	16110	6577	100537	178179	173909
7716508	6621910	246954	19323	828322	529181	15514	2850	83907	95644	91639
14806810	12677249	396526	166172	1566863	1093688	35128	11367	221078	304516	294351
2301506	1879020	82721	50829	288937	236329	8580	1785	39151	41021	38287

6-10 续表 5 continued

单位：万元

项目	Item	损益及分配 Profits,Loss and Distribution 营业利润 Operating Profits	投资收益 Investment Income	补贴收入 Subsidy Income	营业外收入 Out-business Income	营业外支出 Out-business Expenditure	利润总额 Total Profits
总　计	**Total**	405373	142592	158224	250114	200775	735723
在总计中：	**Of Total:**						
中央工业	Central Industry	297729	42131	27119	15998	66964	299924
地方工业	Local Industry	107644	100461	131105	234116	133811	435799
工业系统	Industry System	-39435	78790	60672	192590	114128	173262
非工业系统	Non-Industry System	-47066	4891	68938	21745	11866	36642
区县工业	Industry of District and County	29991	16152	1417	7151	3603	52170
其他	Others	164154	628	78	12630	4214	173725
在总计中：	**Of Total:**						
内资企业	Domestic Investment Enterprises	39514	143370	158224	208791	174798	346643
国有企业	State-Owned	6286	102353	102427	181442	165355	198311
集体企业	Collective Owned	-5311	127	50	2823	724	-2713
股份合作企业	Share Holding	-498			2285	100	1687
联营企业	Joint Owned	-13982	1396	70	13360	1254	-349
有限责任公司	Limited Liability Corporations	-54222	20339	54355	3792	4249	20016
股份有限公司	Share Holding Corporations	107644	19155	1321	5078	3083	130115
私营企业	Private Owned	-403			12	33	-424
港澳台商投资企业	Hongkong,Macao and Taiwan Funded Enterprises	126115	-853		4098	4359	124929
港澳台合资经营	Joint Venture	-1405	-151		841	1684	-2470
港澳台合作经营	Cooperative	1081				4	1077
港澳台商独资企业	Hongkong,Macao and Taiwan Enterprises	126439	-703		3257	2671	126322
港澳台商投资股份有限公司	Hongkong,Macao and Taiwan Funded Share Holding Corporations						
外商投资企业	Foreign Funded Enterprises	239744	75		37225	21618	264151
中外合资经营	Joint Venture	211418	75		29234	22011	227417
中外合作经营	Cooperative	194			445	23	616
外资(独资)企业	Foreign Enterprises	2593			7494	605	9481
外商投资股份有限公司	Foreign Funded Share Holding Corporations	25540			52	-1022	26636
在总计中：	**Of Total:**						
农村企业	Rural Enterprises	2891	8		125	395	2652
在总计中：	**Of Total:**						
轻工业	Light Industry	51734	58696	29999	73801	33299	159035
以农产品为原料	Using Farm Products as Raw Materials	40315	33953	7098	56717	25858	97444
以非农产品为原料	Using Non-Farm Products as Raw Materials	11419	24743	22901	17084	7441	61591
重工业	Heavy Industry	353639	83895	128226	176312	167475	576688
采掘工业	Excavation	-9315	274	11733	1229	2387	2206
原料工业	Raw Material	61217	19732	100118	58581	111480	117275
加工工业	Processing	301737	63889	16375	116502	53609	457207
在总计中：	**Of Total:**						
大型企业	Large Enterprises	305143	100373	144088	211389	190747	547516
中型企业	Medium Enterprises	100230	42219	14136	38724	10027	188206

6-10 续表 6 continued

(10000 yuan)

应交所得税 Income Tax Payable	应付利润 Profits Payable	亏损企业亏损额 Total Loss-ing of Loss-making Enterprises	利税总额 Total Pre-tax Profits	工资，福利费，增值税 Wages,Welfares and Added Value Tax: 本年应付工资总额 Total Wags Payable	本年应付福利费总额 Total Welfares Payable	本年应交增值税 Added Value Tax	本年进项税额 Tax Include in Purchasing Cost	本年销项税额 Tax Include in Sales Cost	工业中间投入合计 Intermediate Input of Industry
165373	103499	176559	1587798	1044910	175781	635075	2092675	2597554	12278372
64929	31645	25661	558780	295794	49416	168887	809593	964136	5140443
100444	71853	150897	1029019	749116	126365	466188	1283082	1633418	7137929
70857	53252	118543	514401	573683	96799	302980	1047233	1287436	4339143
9991	-20722	3632	126977	71414	11655	47341	98625	142254	412463
10729	5226	12578	143516	59973	9977	47530	77929	123045	594912
8867	34097	16144	244125	44045	7934	68338	59295	80684	1791411
129319	41124	78898	1023208	879451	134919	475939	1616173	2053385	7063348
97988	33564	59689	742805	711102	108557	357017	1225991	1547188	5177118
849	447	5374	3948	18164	2160	6006	15037	20819	111990
557	58		3067	1981	269	1274	3164	4437	22106
984	657	2456	5484	18106	2368	4844	27768	32091	158332
3211	1717	9867	83423	78751	12409	58289	137570	196705	821319
25696	4681	917	184427	50629	9084	48085	205131	250147	762087
34		595	54	719	72	424	1512	1999	10396
1456	2387	11319	181892	42114	6064	55962	43430	55253	1580726
1438	1312	11319	7402	16139	2585	8910	25595	34601	187730
	1075		1672	1026	137	594	1121	1715	7960
18			172819	24949	3341	46459	16714	18937	1385037
34598	59988	86342	382697	123345	34799	103174	433071	488917	3634299
34232	57308	83780	337647	105303	29344	95025	417683	465725	3489442
50	272		3725	5118	1306	3109	4186	7190	42381
263	2344	2561	12131	5603	2102	2649	6286	8694	39181
53	65		29196	7320	2046	2392	4916	7308	63295
293	1537	1508	6218	9557	2114	3340	6847	10181	72134
42054	11161	61007	400979	239193	41286	143955	237561	361884	1576430
27471	-7218	40517	289131	163474	30473	100226	155497	238654	916067
14582	18379	20490	111848	75719	10813	43729	82064	123230	660363
123319	92338	115552	1186819	805717	134495	491120	1855114	2235671	10701943
4	118		8087	28116	11706	4954	6717	11493	36902
70836	24333	10626	501212	403530	56257	285174	1022926	1293998	4515220
52479	67887	104926	677521	374071	66532	200992	825472	930180	6149820
132326	101243	146349	1245255	867158	146556	531567	1836994	2240973	10702464
33047	2256	30209	342543	177752	29226	103508	255681	356581	1575909

6-11 独立核算大中型工业企业主要经济指标(按行业分)

单位：万元

项目	Item	企业单位个数(个) Number of Enterprises (unit)	#亏损企业 Loss-making Enterprises	工业总产值(当年价格) Gross Output Value of Industry (at current prices)	新产品产值 Value of New Products	工业总产值(1990年不变价格) Gross Output Value of Industry (at 1990 constant prices)	工业增加值(生产法) Added Value of Industry (with production method)
煤炭采选业	Coal Mining and Dressing	1		82811		31906	56041
黑色金属矿采选业	Ferrous Metals Mining and Processing	1		7673		4547	2629
非金属矿采选业	Nonmetal Minerals Mining and Processing	2		205		137	71
食品加工业	Food Processing	12	1	104279		66935	9873
食品制造业	Food Making	11	4	114819	3	78594	54146
饮料制造业	Beverage Making	13	5	450179	1439	531723	187929
烟草加工业	Tobacco Processing	1		83645	1957	46215	57037
纺织业	Textile Industry	17	5	145965	16998	125695	35759
服装及其他纤维制品制造业	Garments and Other Fiber Products	13	5	69807		53047	21433
皮革、毛皮、羽绒及其制品业	Leather,Furs,Down and Related Products	5		2810		2149	-149
木材加工及竹、藤、棕、草制品业	Timber Processing,Bamboo,Cane,Palm Fiber and Straw Products	2	1	6231		3910	933
家具制造业	Furniture Manufacturing	1	0	1992		2527	642
造纸及纸制品业	Papermaking and Paper Products	6	2	39183		35849	14310
印刷业、记录煤介的复制	Printing and Record Medium Reproduced	49	10	240300	37373	170370	120091
文教、体育用品制造	Stationery,Educational and Sports Goods	6	2	36699	710	24846	12393
石油加工及炼焦业	Petrolume Processing and Coking	2	1	2425853	138618	1050903	333145
化学原料及化学制品制造业	Raw Chemical Materials and Chemical Products	21	8	844878	47749	730051	203911
医药制造业	Medical and Pharmaceutical Products	21	1	256105	41762	296042	125053
化学纤维制造业	Chemical Fibers	1	1	13462		16525	-78
橡胶制品业	Rubber Products	5	3	59505	99	82981	11402
塑料制品业	Plastic Products	13	5	53370	4982	55847	7672
非金属矿物制品业	Nonmetal Mineral Products	32	5	397320	77560	339094	123043
黑色金属冶炼及压延加工业	Smelting and Pressing of Ferrous Metals	5	2	1766271	119771	1278886	616396
有色金属冶炼及压延加工业	Smelting and Pressing of Nonferrous Metals	4		36019	18355	34945	6925
金属制品业	Metal Products	14	6	66493	2420	82276	16850
普通机械制造业	Ordinary Machinery Manufacturing	27	6	179308	20260	165974	60513
专用设备制造业	Equipments for Special Purposes Manufacturing	31	5	748019	407099	770629	172860
交通运输设备制造业	Transportation Equipment Manufacturing	40	14	735515	159240	623779	188295
武器弹药制造业	Weapon and Ammunition Manufacturing	5	1	93711	6753	69570	39680
电气机械及器材制造	Electric Equipment and Machinery	26	3	263379	86167	378830	52378
电子及通信设备制造	Electronic and Telecommunications	48	3	5416009	3061106	8621536	1009219
仪器仪表及文化、办公用机械制造业	Instruments,Meters,Cultural and Office Machinery Manufacturing	24	2	157397	62177	166647	44978
其他制造业	Other Manufacturing	9	2	9830		7802	2926
电力、蒸汽、热水的生产和供应业	Electricity,Steam and Hot Water Production and Supply	10		651335	1507	214674	413544
煤气生产和供应业	Gas Production and Supply	2		79854		37331	65768
自来水的生产和供应	Water Production and Supply	1		107632		23261	36950

MAIN INDICATORS FOR LARGE AND MEDIUM INDUSTRIAL ENTERPRISES WITH INDEPENDENT ACCOUNTING SYSTEM(BY SECTOR)

(10000 yuan)

工业销售产值(当年价格) Sales Value of Industry (at current price)	出口交货值 Delivery Value of Exports	全部从业人员年平均人数(人) Average Number of Persons Employed (person)	资产负债 Assets and Liabilities: 流动资产合计 Circulating Funds	应收帐款净额 Accounts Receivable	存货 Stock	产成品 Finished Products	流动资产平均余额 Average Balance of Circulating Funds	长期投资 Longterm Investment	固定资产合计 Fixed Assets
87628	28123	24744	130499	74424	12183	6331	150154	8736	102391
7625		1412	27469	3879	4428	1387	22032	2555	18302
318		396	3550	556	721	599	4334	1243	5967
105491		2713	31597	6855	6177	2149	31559	1150	40057
98006	421	7727	118667	12005	15402	8883	57718	10650	121437
425047	8426	22992	325753	38050	101899	11771	308588	41047	509021
84166	2163	888	20901	159	6338	50	22618	3042	31209
140755	54835	25256	201711	32897	79835	44031	244074	26499	166848
72640	39811	9097	82883	24963	24809	15821	83555	7881	35896
2927	286	3241	49375	8020	4855	1625	44006	4605	22787
6298		1736	19714	4880	11890	10269	19857	1796	10565
1992		135	689	429	75		692		392
41166	2627	4240	71327	9632	18854	9836	74046	9720	73549
236785		23317	182670	28695	47722	13098	180136	21199	307162
36834	2213	4466	37556	8423	14816	7051	42281	4530	30907
2410351	14931	37544	855461	143038	230974	52577	1097447	66804	1308725
830471	52801	29209	559284	117949	181286	87452	522268	93961	1162507
241305	16539	16420	436603	41097	152705	91647	421641	211238	240127
13636		951	12318	2614	7253	3790	13536		21249
41752	4387	5261	59162	23956	27413	20166	56898	5440	91555
52528	78	4843	77498	14928	22233	9091	77618	25234	125494
387669	9132	39751	583383	146326	153678	77414	551918	212770	559969
1766688	99129	101108	1220292	154999	508017	71454	1253933	489512	2346244
35933	502	1340	38669	8064	6911	1935	16469	15242	23406
67627	9863	6205	96870	19591	29379	13953	93214	2827	64867
178000	19363	29829	422985	90736	152508	44033	448619	47167	314390
714857	48382	33605	611597	99350	252570	124444	543281	133066	336046
712968	9491	72309	943387	227874	385175	76467	1263907	251222	686975
93353	105	10354	81293	9407	30498	3855		24555	98976
252673	31278	21037	293688	61875	92873	41200	381013	54849	158248
5128182	969883	44610	3240899	1306054	689561	229842	2824340	463373	907496
152547	5580	14969	213779	35934	80117	32425	213817	46026	97620
9397	5601	2202	15189	1658	9875	5623	14061	1771	17463
651202		18431	517398	175673	13132	555	506226	22640	2907093
79061		8330	104560	37704	9382	7	111675	8490	501430
104890		4761	122039	1771	9914	6851	112003	7607	595256

6-11 续表 1 continued

单位：万元

项目	Item	资产负债 固定资产原价合计 Original Value of Fixed Assets	# 生产经营用 For Productive Use	累计折旧 Accumulative Depreciation	#本年折旧 Depreciation in this Year	固定资产净值年平均余额 Average Net Value of Fixed Assets	无形资产及递延资产 Intangible and Deferred Assets
煤炭采选业	Coal Mining and Dressing	159351		59567	7412	95656	1299
黑色金属矿采选业	Ferrous Metals Mining and Processing	14945	14945	5437	577	15545	2517
非金属矿采选业	Nonmetal Minerals Mining and Processing	7665	7181	3143	86	6759	1297
食品加工业	Food Processing	44252	40253	13988	1957	29361	1398
食品制造业	Food Making	173337	122357	54699	8519	119542	19057
饮料制造业	Beverage Making	646447	521863	168501	26961	428489	43845
烟草加工业	Tobacco Processing	42002	41367	15984	2188	28747	571
纺织业	Textile Industry	260170	184936	110789	10819	157798	15945
服装及其他纤维制品制造业	Garments and Other Fiber Products	47468	31822	17538	1624	29628	1342
皮革、毛皮、羽绒及其制品业	Leather,Furs,Down and Related Products	28305	22991	8223	623	22677	1554
木材加工及竹、藤、棕、草制品业	Timber Processing,Bamboo,Cane,Palm Fiber and Straw Products	15312	10057	5322	143	10286	44
家具制造业	Furniture Manufacturing	562	559	169	51	394	
造纸及纸制品业	Papermaking and Paper Products	81451	55396	18741	3450	60513	19458
印刷业、记录媒介的复制	Printing and Record Medium Reproduced	457292	362746	179095	29138	280009	3648
文教、体育用品制造	Stationery,Educational and Sports Goods	39216	36832	14179	1777	29816	2806
石油加工及炼焦业	Petrolume Processing and Coking	2212540	2089128	1187067	106694	1040327	90473
化学原料及化学制品制造业	Raw Chemical Materials and Chemical Products	1550493	1452344	438524	99962	1148873	377467
医药制造业	Medical and Pharmaceutical Products	292737	228132	85734	13677	185739	38007
化学纤维制造业	Chemical Fibers	27001	25857	6105	910	21583	9792
橡胶制品业	Rubber Products	96704	88299	38046	3123	60055	11964
塑料制品业	Plastic Products	157841	85329	44694	3791	120494	18787
非金属矿物制品业	Nonmetal Mineral Products	705709	546096	248330	29308	462928	111993
黑色金属冶炼及压延加工业	Smelting and Pressing of Ferrous Metals	3333560	3330459	1483214	127345	1902644	60912
有色金属冶炼及压延加工业	Smelting and Pressing of Nonferrous Metals	29323	26369	11778	935	17182	26367
金属制品业	Metal Products	81581	56711	31264	4246	53851	4910
普通机械制造业	Ordinary Machinery Manufacturing	397467	284130	143051	12581	249211	17624
专用设备制造业	Equipments for Special Purposes Manufacturing	385448	282835	129459	16375	248097	25493
交通运输设备制造业	Transportation Equipment Manufacturing	1001580	723220	411036	47104	549413	23926
武器弹药制造业	Weapon and Ammunition Manufacturing	128463	87162	41268	2495	102092	1471
电气机械及器材制造	Electric Equipment and Machinery	239202	170053	98533	29436	175758	25834
电子及通信设备制造	Electronic and Telecommunications	1151525	897837	364747	76410	696349	104891
仪器仪表及文化、办公用机械制造业	Instruments,Meters,Cultural and Office Machinery Manufacturing	142065	117063	57147	4403	84994	4388
其他制造业	Other Manufacturing	22178	16744	7354	694	14562	5019
电力、蒸汽、热水的生产和供应业	Electricity,Steam and Hot Water Production and Supply	3310870	3206413	805241	151847	2307180	11258
煤气生产和供应业	Gas Production and Supply	623408	602385	145482	24778	382874	
自来水的生产和供应	Water Production and Supply	777152		196763	36185	548094	1632

6-11 续表 2 continued

(10000 yuan)

Assets and Liabilities										
#无形资产 Intangible Assets	其他资产 Other Assets	资产总计 Total Assets	流动负债合计 Liquid Liabilities	短期借款 Shortterm Loans	长期负债合计 Long-term Liabilities	长期借款 Longterm Loans	负债合计 Total Liabilities	所有者权益 Creditors' Equity	实收资本 Contributed Capital	国家资本 State
		242925	106023	40518	44227	39052	150249	92676	52269	52070
		50842	24367	17546	5794	5124	30161	20682	12341	12341
		12056	3367	933	4625	2477	7992	4065	1496	
752	34	74236	31591	14908	3831	3667	35422	38813	27546	16886
10069	1119	270930	109310	52693	23253	21384	132563	138366	251292	5919
38578	2628	922294	277823	121724	45459	38312	323290	599004	325003	117525
484		55723	-1316		153	5966	-1162	56885	41711	41711
12192		411002	251684	143183	64864	42383	316548	94454	93071	19683
461	3152	131155	66824	22958	12722	5840	79546	51609	45903	7970
		78321	49016	15606	9633	9211	58648	19672	16531	
	1121	33239	20253	2960	1652		21905	11334	11924	
		1081	279				279	802	600	
10131	262	174316	97786	52638	29240	20373	127027	47289	56572	9769
2166	15	514693	132497	27661	72982	30697	205480	309213	216546	164169
1484		75799	54585	32383	5445	7054	60030	15769	13972	384
77251	651	2322113	997202	310230	208255	186742	1205457	1116656	466449	466159
16344	2	2193221	625885	315318	1025947	1004972	1651832	541390	282160	186681
32097	489	926464	363592	232296	28691	18621	392284	534181	252140	94777
		43359	16150	8464	25807	25863	41957	1402	5607	
11557		168122	87418	27026	66018	62251	153437	14685	18804	130
4051	633	247646	152084	70759	32161	31012	184246	63400	63043	5064
65700	5204	1473319	593481	190937	234419	188791	828454	644866	390964	179374
43832	-15887	4101073	1400802	649719	335048	416290	1735850	2365223	1082427	663364
920		103684	14190	4618	17921	14428	32110	71574	45983	37283
3138	1239	170713	118390	57630	22047	12682	140437	30277	56432	18550
13031	9171	811337	421833	138343	126144	101567	547978	263359	200306	23060
7036	526	1106728	521772	155823	59600	30740	581396	525332	185661	33810
17136	4543	1910053	950751	282193	241452	200730	1196728	713325	592355	202858
5		206295	83038	34737	21680	12656	104718	101577	43504	36126
8108	459	533077	256626	104977	63226	42879	320091	212986	164805	8514
46075	14101	4730759	2561468	925456	268919	218039	2838339	1892419	653783	139534
3298	610	362423	170946	47283	35602	20557	206716	155708	99209	32079
3912	708	40150	17080	7844	3907	2767	21019	19131	10401	3246
10537		3458389	413230	35220	2214608	447369	2627838	830551	594287	449705
		614480	26604		21794	6469	48398	566082	408861	408861
771		726533	25055		113826	123353	138881	587653	473363	473363

6-11 续表 3 continued

单位：万元

项目	Item	资产负债 Assets and Liabilities				
		集体资本 Collective	法人资本 Institutional Units	个人资本 Individuals	港澳台资本 Hongkong, Macao and Taiwan	外商资本 Foreign
煤炭采选业	Coal Mining and Dressing	101	68	30		
黑色金属矿采选业	Ferrous Metals Mining and Processing					
非金属矿采选业	Nonmetal Minerals Mining and Processing		1496			
食品加工业	Food Processing	376	6458			3826
食品制造业	Food Making	107	25218	20	12000	2E+05
饮料制造业	Beverage Making	4234	67599	20360	22486	92799
烟草加工业	Tobacco Processing					
纺织业	Textile Industry	4597	68053	403		335
服装及其他纤维制品制造业	Garments and Other Fiber Products	12297	23042	333	1660	600
皮革、毛皮、羽绒及其制品业	Leather,Furs,Down and Related Products	9052	7479			
木材加工及竹、藤、棕、草制品业	Timber Processing,Bamboo,Cane,Palm Fiber and Straw Products		11924			
家具制造业	Furniture Manufacturing		360		240	
造纸及纸制品业	Papermaking and Paper Products	3103	5464	28	10458	27750
印刷业、记录煤介的复制	Printing and Record Medium Reproduced	3216	14332	740	5379	28710
文教、体育用品制造	Stationery,Educational and Sports Goods	3500	9580	201	219	87
石油加工及炼焦业	Petrolume Processing and Coking	210			80	
化学原料及化学制品制造业	Raw Chemical Materials and Chemical Products	2384	63771	12222		17102
医药制造业	Medical and Pharmaceutical Products	215	99722	30082	993	26351
化学纤维制造业	Chemical Fibers		5607			
橡胶制品业	Rubber Products	3070	15604			
塑料制品业	Plastic Products	2654	33294			22031
非金属矿物制品业	Nonmetal Mineral Products	12027	161295	14	1041	37213
黑色金属冶炼及压延加工业	Smelting and Pressing of Ferrous Metals	4338	364397	36715	13613	
有色金属冶炼及压延加工业	Smelting and Pressing of Nonferrous Metals		8700			
金属制品业	Metal Products	8332	8477		16696	4378
普通机械制造业	Ordinary Machinery Manufacturing	6426	106929	361		63530
专用设备制造业	Equipments for Special Purposes Manufacturing	7216	105398	36214	1245	1778
交通运输设备制造业	Transportation Equipment Manufacturing	12848	301716	5417	11463	58053
武器弹药制造业	Weapon and Ammunition Manufacturing		7378			
电气机械及器材制造	Electric Equipment and Machinery	14530	88031		8007	45723
电子及通信设备制造	Electronic and Telecommunications	8667	298632	25292	22814	158843
仪器仪表及文化、办公用机械制造业	Instruments,Meters,Cultural and Office Machinery Manufacturing	474	49545	660	16123	328
其他制造业	Other Manufacturing	3914	1549	1200	493	
电力、蒸汽、热水的生产和供应业	Electricity,Steam and Hot Water Production and Supply		144582			
煤气生产和供应业	Gas Production and Supply					
自来水的生产和供应	Water Production and Supply					

6-11 续表 4 continued

(10000 yuan)

损益及分配 Profits,Loss and Distribution										
产品销售收入 Sales Revenue	产品销售成本 Cost of Sales	产品销售费用 Expenses of Sales	产品销售税金及附加 Sales Tax and Extra Charges	产品销售利润 Sales Profits	管理费用 Overhead Cost	税金 Taxes	财产保险费 Premium of Property	劳动待业保险费 Premium for Employment Insurance	财务费用 Financial Expenses	利息支出 Expenses of Interest
90516	61295	9556	721	18944	27432	505		16852	2752	2440
7415	6002	137	204	1073	799	51		114	833	835
319	274	3	2	40	760	17	16	174	61	61
104845	97738	1699	87	5322	3835	119	66	417	603	604
89258	67193	14238	2195	5633	14136	1739	80	2427	2403	2272
436905	279789	43045	48727	65343	45182	1840	504	3044	8484	8176
84219	37009	1257	36434	9519	4934	67	196	2040	53	191
140016	113133	3262	558	23062	28042	931	260	8294	13022	12573
71260	56822	7164	81	7194	9344	253	105	2074	1194	1161
2601	2801	191	3	-395	6110	156	52	1952	2428	2215
5664	4616	93	28	927	1814	48	40	441	573	571
1992	1630	24		338	162			36	-2	-2
41123	36908	3489	24	702	10692	335	163	2193	2492	2214
274055	201332	2891	1803	68028	51657	1443	529	11318	2311	2200
42793	34111	2175	188	6319	6599	243	117	1768	2118	2122
2679171	2418061	12410	76655	172045	145611	3238	3476	20146	35712	35139
841373	720054	27413	7209	86698	71372	2181	2113	12408	29074	28581
432062	296198	43375	2254	90236	57546	1184	706	6578	10991	9544
15222	14159	418	62	583	1341	31	9	561	1714	1713
45270	42181	2103	2452	-1466	6303	173	81	1810	-3288	2791
57148	51132	2599	66	3351	12424	551	-123	2441	4479	4356
419973	343774	17552	1769	56878	61893	1781	821	13819	21016	20690
2194366	1917659	23001	11772	241934	164303	7935	308	59177	83072	80433
37222	31214	690	38	5281	4086	79	25	546	337	334
67136	55805	2729	59	8544	9298	272	71	1510	2680	2318
178478	144601	5840	841	27196	43516	1493	380	11124	12396	10948
713330	584841	25145	2068	101276	65917	4189	660	10089	6344	5613
849401	729211	16913	9624	93653	131252	3117	634	25316	26891	26358
83202	70204	457	42	12499	17237	237	65	4404	2070	2087
248277	208904	14007	450	24916	37629	1165	372	5705	7517	6560
5659779	4881362	184640	3052	590725	213837	4111	1107	18078	39643	32708
153657	126937	8250	430	18041	25482	791	120	5195	3099	3065
12488	9700	1003	241	1544	4038	98	56	857	402	339
740852	600585	1481	5613	133174	21273	1485	67	1928	23204	22833
199602	209710		797	-10905	14557	698	76	3194	-620	-656
87329	99328		453	-12452	9608	1153	2	2203	-522	-745

6-11 续表 5 continued

单位：万元

项目	Item	损益及分配 Profits,Loss and Distribution 营业利润 Operating Profits	投资收益 Investment Income	补贴收入 Subsidy Income	营业外收入 Out-business Income	营业外支出 Out-business Expenditure	利润总额 Total Profits
煤炭采选业	Coal Mining and Dressing	-9177	197	11733	933	2162	2194
黑色金属矿采选业	Ferrous Metals Mining and Processing	133			57	180	11
非金属矿采选业	Nonmetal Minerals Mining and Processing	-270	77		239	44	1
食品加工业	Food Processing	940	5	1014	256	111	2202
食品制造业	Food Making	-8540	705		1518	1005	-7320
饮料制造业	Beverage Making	15221	20517	5861	7345	2400	35638
烟草加工业	Tobacco Processing	4681	296		30	1	5006
纺织业	Textile Industry	-10525	992	120	30392	17104	-112
服装及其他纤维制品制造业	Garments and Other Fiber Products	601	-98	64	217	441	366
皮革、毛皮、羽绒及其制品业	Leather,Furs,Down and Related Products	-2936	-364		3785	378	161
木材加工及竹、藤、棕、草制品业	Timber Processing,Bamboo,Cane,Palm Fiber and Straw Products	-1386			402	50	-1034
家具制造业	Furniture Manufacturing	179					179
造纸及纸制品业	Papermaking and Paper Products	-10831	4087		7109	1804	-1560
印刷业、记录媒介的复制	Printing and Record Medium Reproduced	28857	1105	78	5141	2164	33085
文教、体育用品制造	Stationery,Educational and Sports Goods	228	147		806	232	943
石油加工及炼焦业	Petrolume Processing and Coking	-9627	3548	21599	1038	4379	996
化学原料及化学制品制造业	Raw Chemical Materials and Chemical Products	-8669	12889	22283	1006	1621	25917
医药制造业	Medical and Pharmaceutical Products	38647	18597	289	1020	822	57737
化学纤维制造业	Chemical Fibers	-1716			36	380	-2060
橡胶制品业	Rubber Products	-4325	2	1410	643	181	-2136
塑料制品业	Plastic Products	-10188	302	1	6748	851	-3987
非金属矿物制品业	Nonmetal Mineral Products	-11927	4216	5180	17583	11244	3791
黑色金属冶炼及压延加工业	Smelting and Pressing of Ferrous Metals	22343	6550	5	51894	55218	25574
有色金属冶炼及压延加工业	Smelting and Pressing of Nonferrous Metals	1266	730		625	65	2556
金属制品业	Metal Products	-2021	11		2121	2180	-9875
普通机械制造业	Ordinary Machinery Manufacturing	-21702	-248	602	20862	9845	-9282
专用设备制造业	Equipments for Special Purposes Manufacturing	33838	4167	2640	9660	2910	48673
交通运输设备制造业	Transportation Equipment Manufacturing	-53120	5458	3917	23527	7410	-22369
武器弹药制造业	Weapon and Ammunition Manufacturing	-2967	1597	1929	204	708	278
电气机械及器材制造	Electric Equipment and Machinery	-10470	2804	890	14777	1399	5598
电子及通信设备制造	Electronic and Telecommunications	391742	48463	635	32127	22178	5E+05
仪器仪表及文化、办公用机械制造业	Instruments,Meters,Cultural and Office Machinery Manufacturing	1316	3134	220	4417	1728	7359
其他制造业	Other Manufacturing	-868	91		929	77	229
电力、蒸汽、热水的生产和供应业	Electricity,Steam and Hot Water Production and Supply	90930	1532	30898	2537	49441	76717
煤气生产和供应业	Gas Production and Supply	-23095	912	25300	94	29	3182
自来水的生产和供应	Water Production and Supply	-21186	172	21557	38	35	546

6-11 续表 6 continued

(10000 yuan)

应交所得税 Income Tax Payable	应付利润 Profits Payable	亏损企业亏损额 Total Loss-ing of Loss-making Enterprises	利税总额 Total Pre-tax Profits	工资，福利费，增值税 Wages,Welfares and Added Value Tax					
				本年应付工资总额 Total Wags Payable	本年应付福利费总额 Total Welfares Payable	本年应交增值税 Added Value Tax	本年进项税额 Tax Include in Purchasing Cost	本年销项税额 Tax Include in Sales Cost	工业中间投入合计 Intermediate Input of Industry
	118		7824	26181	11488	4909	5335	10066	31679
3			223	1614	175	9	1382	1390	5053
1			39	321	43	37		37	170
555	1138	418	4227	3313	753	1939	5913	7962	96345
774	-21648	11656	1428	12741	2020	6553	8686	13816	67226
7693	1258	16875	121737	30091	5950	37372	39082	75498	299622
596			50075	3144	1394	8635	5753	13947	35243
783	2316	4417	6446	26426	3840	6000	19172	22910	116206
253	1236	1526	2693	11381	2351	2247	4852	6945	50620
23			243	2149	277	79	472	529	3037
		1037	-702	1411	176	304	632	1004	5602
22	158		321	233	37	142	197	339	1492
48	-1962	2011	-83	6919	1486	1453	5668	6937	26327
10777	10252	2303	56735	43407	9335	21846	28236	39744	142055
434	564	493	3227	6155	871	2096	6067	8105	26402
25359	20244	141	128467	84808	11237	50817	380510	429778	2143525
10117	2966	9556	77227	46809	9594	44101	102353	146097	685068
8835	289	505	84901	34200	4174	24910	44102	66406	155963
		2060	-1377	1254	176	621	2151	2761	14161
1		2136	1645	6157	864	1329	7169	8368	49432
13		4427	-2101	7329	1132	1820	8375	9209	47518
3144	-2627	7243	28288	53185	7767	22728	42602	65841	297006
31282	52	2675	159910	202981	24756	122565	465422	573689	1272440
89			3150	1771	186	556	3841	4391	29650
245	272	12785	-8180	7083	1180	1636	8640	10001	51280
348	148	14257	-243	36642	5939	8198	20894	29241	126993
11131	15723	5785	76676	42216	5800	25935	158608	181456	601094
4703	5691	55818	13387	105413	19836	26132	116665	135577	573352
319		2068	1171	14157	1535	851	2728	3398	54882
483	355	8743	13999	26125	3486	7951	33335	40550	218953
35681	66099	6741	582075	116278	25679	122503	477915	517094	4529293
1760	654	671	16867	19788	2204	9078	18769	27788	121497
109	201	216	1114	2432	400	644	1239	1935	7548
9668	4		138377	40969	6889	56047	44553	100972	293838
			12020	11289	1555	8042	19618	27660	22128
123			5991	8542	1198	4992	1740	6114	75674

6-12 规模以上工业企业主要经济指标

单位：万元

项目	Item	企业单位个数(个) Number of Enterprises (unit)	工业总产值（当年价格） Gross Output Value of Industry (at current prices)	# 新产品产值 Value of New Products
总计	**Total**	4572	25653086	5884826
在总计中：	**Of Total:**			
中央企业	Central Enterprises	542	7536769	2223925
地方企业	Local Enterprises	4030	18116317	3660901
工业系统	Industry System	597	7153250	1318548
非工业系统	Non-Industry System	458	1490995	16141
区县工业	Industry of District and County	2512	4780117	159432
其他	Others	463	4691955	2166780
在总计中：	**Of Total:**			
内资企业	Domestic Investment Enterprises	3565	14143587	2046311
国有企业	State-Owned	1980	7885724	688211
集体企业	Collective Owned	899	1753404	45278
股份合作企业	Share Holding	114	273798	10316
联营企业	Joint Owned	71	262917	27681
有限责任公司	Limited Liability Corporations	234	1957019	403107
股份有限公司	Share Holding Corporations	83	1639714	820160
私营企业	Private Owned	184	371010	51559
港澳台商投资企业	Hongkong,Macao and Taiwan Funded Enterprises	364	3394976	1857769
港澳台合资经营	Joint Venture	283	1336053	237010
港澳台合作经营	Cooperative	18	49340	
港澳台商独资企业	Hongkong,Macao and Taiwan Enterprises	61	2006743	1620759
港澳台商投资股份有限公司	Hongkong,Macao and Taiwan Funded Share Holding Corporations	2	2841	
外商投资企业	Foreign Funded Enterprises	643	8114523	1980745
中外合资经营	Joint Venture	462	7017316	1876440
中外合作经营	Cooperative	32	191515	3941
外资(独资)企业	Foreign Enterprises	142	761424	86178
外商投资股份有限公司	Foreign Funded Share Holding Corporations	7	144268	14187
在总计中：	**Of Total:**			
农村企业	Rural Enterprises	1137	2341987	6768
在总计中：	**Of Total:**			
国有绝对控股企业	State Absolute Controlling Share Hold Industry	2330	16601803	4473272
国有相对控股企业	State Relative Controlling Share Hold Industry	100	824093	144407

注：规模以上工业企业是指年销售收入500万元及以上的工业企业。

MAIN INDICATORS FOR INDUSTRIAL ENTERPRISES IN SCALE

(10000 yuan)

工业总产值 (1990年不变价格) Gross Output Value of Industry (at 1990 constant prices)	工业销售产值 Sales Value of Industry	# 出口交货值 Delivery Value of Exports	从业人员平均人数 (人) Average Number of Persons Employed (person)	工业增加值 Added Value of Industry
25858371	24646096	2516517	1132627	6993173
6681455	7340658	749940	196720	1832690
19176916	17305438	1766577	935907	5160483
7187831	6813827	801438	445261	2056788
996106	1486709	19521	83947	539448
4534367	4581649	414945	346564	1477052
6458612	4423253	530673	60135	1087195
11041033	13709030	534724	915415	4335653
5376303	7775917	285270	567398	2497087
1602810	1654352	124388	157326	508690
241984	255799	20014	21277	79287
345283	242724	4261	22973	34775
1640489	1906483	50832	80674	616198
1487257	1542805	39044	47462	476428
346907	330950	10916	18305	123188
5116205	3233037	244893	72004	732458
1471408	1274503	204914	56784	346692
47049	47877	8884	2709	19574
3595050	1907779	30941	12232	365777
2698	2878	154	279	415
9701132	7704030	1736900	145208	1925062
8774154	6757333	1596257	114729	1530841
193332	187944	20878	4634	59016
652551	612572	91145	18840	273343
81095	146182	28621	7005	61862
2201474	2236060	290771	184901	694512
16829817	16157522	1400675	750597	4420633
812338	787299	93065	25437	269681

Note: Industrial enterprises in scale refer to the enterprises which sales revenue 5 million yuan and above.

6-12 续表 1 continued

单位：万元

项目 Item		企业单位个数(个) Number of Enterprises (unit)	工业总产值（当年价格） Gross Output Value of Industry (at current prices)	# 新产品产值 Value of New Products
在总计中：	**Of Total:**			
轻工业	Light Industry	2248	6151514	438857
以农产品为原料	Using Farm Products as Raw Materials	1486	3934951	138738
以非农产品为原料	Using Non-Farm Products as Raw Material	762	2216563	300118
重工业	Heavy Industry	2324	19501572	5445969
采掘工业	Excavation	48	179000	
原料工业	Raw Material	347	6633264	471593
加工工业	Processing	1929	12689308	4974377
在总计中：	**Of Total:**			
大型企业	Large Enterprises	208	13481219	3568199
中型企业	Medium Enterprises	247	2262820	745900
小型企业	Small Enterprises	4117	9909047	1570726
在总计中：	**Of Total:**			
煤炭采选业	Coal Mining and Dressing	14	145274	
黑色金属矿采选业	Ferrous Metals Mining and Dressing	4	12003	
有色金属矿采选业	Nonferrous Metals Mining and Dressing	5	4303	
非金属矿采选业	Nonmetal Minerals Mining and Dressing	25	17421	
食品加工业	Food Processing	207	544630	8422
食品制造业	Food Making	186	716056	13222
饮料制造业	Beverage Making	77	710318	1775
烟草加工业	Tobacco Processing	1	83645	1957
纺织业	Textile Industry	145	424866	20974
服装及其他纤维制品制造业	Garments and Other Fiber Products	230	462821	535
皮革、毛皮、羽绒及其制品业	Leather,Furs,Down and Related Products	37	42893	38
木材加工及竹、藤、棕、草制品业	Timber Processing,Bamboo,Cane, Palm Fiber and Straw Products	33	58255	
家具制造业	Furniture Manufacturing	90	115136	
造纸及纸制品业	Papermaking and Paper Products	84	170368	
印刷业，记录媒介的复制	Printing and Record Medium Reproduced	321	411855	37423

6-12 续表 2 continued

(10000 yuan)

工业总产值 (1990年不变价格) Gross Output Value of Industry (at 1990 constant prices)	工业销售产值 Sales Value of Industry	# 出口交货值 Delivery Value of Exports	从业人员平均人数 (人) Average Number of Persons Employed (person)	工业增加值 Added Value of Industry
5805857	5940753	680828	424885	2126949
3434959	3798633	441255	295501	1375838
2370898	2142119	239573	129384	751111
20052514	18705344	1835689	707742	4866224
90011	180042	29284	34321	81901
3953801	6587542	182284	240848	1827354
16008702	11937760	1624120	432573	2956969
14171069	13103084	1236550	504837	3311190
2051608	2165885	199400	125306	794152
9635694	9377127	1080567	502484	2887831
60936	147241	28123	30589	72173
7029	11955		2122	3462
4106	4278		292	1252
17941	16569	1160	1318	5014
411917	551443	9776	20934	94086
559954	680161	19769	36386	294900
771627	666992	11374	31771	256975
46215	84166	2163	888	57037
388874	407094	143181	51036	119231
393862	455129	190676	64307	149630
33903	43081	14256	6981	13220
54501	57761	729	4207	14573
107181	114584	25057	10487	31535
157189	165150	6570	12167	60973
326339	405226	20	41121	183866

6-12 续表 3 continued

单位：万元

项目	Item	企业单位个数(个) Number of Enterprises (unit)	工业总产值(当年价格) Gross Output Value of Industry (at current prices)	# 新产品产值 Value of New Products
文教体育用品制造业	Stationery,Educational and Sports Goods	53	88224	8028
石油加工及炼焦业	Petroleum Processing and Coking	33	2610073	254141
化学原料及化学制品	Raw Chemical Materials and Chemical Products	302	1301447	74496
医药制造业	Medical and Pharmaceutical Products	115	527681	76011
化学纤维制造业	Chemical Fibers	15	31747	
橡胶制品业	Rubber Products	30	127290	8148
塑料制品业	Plastic Products	179	237334	14433
非金属矿物制品	Nonmetal Mineral Products	315	927922	90468
黑色金属冶炼及压延加工业	Smelting and Pressing of Ferrous Metals	23	1802720	121088
有色金属冶炼及压延加工业	Smelting and Pressing of Nonferrous Metals	44	113804	41274
金属制品业	Metal Products	328	524363	5934
普通机械制造业	Ordinary Machinery Manufacturing	252	443402	44851
专用设备制造业	Equipments for Special Purposes Manufacturing	262	1113504	454070
交通运输设备制造业	Transportation Equipments Manufacturing	336	990355	176454
武器弹药制造业	Weapon and Ammunition Manufacturing	7	93904	6753
电气机械及器材制造	Electric Equipments and Machinery	257	881807	192989
电子及通信设备制造	Electronic and Telecommunications	299	8431914	4117312
仪器仪表及文化、办公用机械制造	Instruments,Meters,Cultural and Office Machinery	134	383111	102443
其他制造业	Other Manufacturing	84	124572	1390
电力、蒸汽、热水的生产和供应业	Electricity,Steam and Hot Water Production and Supply	33	751237	10196
煤气生产和供应	Gas Production and Supply	3	80526	
自来水的生产和供应	Tap Water Production and Supply	9	146308	

6-12 续表 4 continued

(10000 yuan)

工业总产值 (1990年不变价格) Gross Output Value of Industry (at 1990 constant prices)	工业销售产值 Sales Value of Industry	# 出口交货值 Delivery Value of Exports	从业人员平均人数 (人) Average Number of Persons Employed (person)	工业增加值 Added Value of Industry
69879	85633	17589	10284	29003
1154415	2588458	16007	40971	365486
1194345	1274044	59954	51381	356394
569134	495895	24952	30067	248851
39819	30932	67	2957	3349
146456	107106	19403	8995	29164
248177	228405	12899	17015	58450
771077	907636	35777	84866	313407
1311851	1799450	101629	103206	621369
108651	110728	4622	5670	21078
541615	502614	41592	35652	148167
427577	433198	55085	55390	144983
1135855	1075497	59700	59936	293033
880807	961381	18369	96623	261277
69763	93547	105	10608	39766
990501	842845	46448	50158	241302
11998921	7851383	1496486	81790	1725123
381237	362398	42164	24713	112085
123013	110656	10814	11534	49715
263327	750716		21711	448998
37389	79733		8410	66105
52987	143012		6084	58147

6-13 个体经营工业主要指标

MAIN INDICATORS ON INDIVIDUAL ENTERPRISES

单位：万元 (10000 yuan)

项 目 Item		企 业 单位数 (个) Number of Enterprise (unit)	从业人员 年末人数 (人) Employment (year-end) (person)	工业总产值 (当年价格) Gross Output Value of Industry (at current prices)	上缴税金 Taxes Turned Over	自有资金 Self-own Capital
总 计	**Total**	**12788**	**82433**	**668073**	**17553**	**116688**
在总计中：	**Of Total:**					
轻 工 业	Light Industry	9616	56360	440311	11483	79545
重 工 业	Heavy Industry	3172	26073	227762	6070	37143
在总计中：	**Of Total:**					
城镇个体工业	Urban Individual Enterprises	2418	7274	61707	2708	7817
农村个体工业	Rural Individual Enterprises	10370	75159	606366	14845	108871

6-14 大中型工业企业按销售收入排序
ARRANGING IN SALES REVENUE ORDER OF LARGE AND MEDIUM INDUSTRIAL ENTERPRISES

序号 No.	企业名称	Enterprise
1	中国石化集团北京燕山石油化工有限公司	Beijing Yanshan Petrochemical Group Co.,Ltd
2	首钢总公司	Shougang Group
3	北京诺基亚移动通信有限公司	Beijing Nokia Mobile Telecom Munications Ltd.
4	联想（北京）有限公司	LEGEND(Beijing) Group Co.,Ltd
5	北京化学工业集团有限责任公司	Beijing Chemical Industry Group Corp.
6	中国华北电力集团公司(在京单位)	NORTH China Power Group Co.
7	北京诺基亚航星通讯系统有限公司	Beijing Noka Hang Xing Telecom Munications Systems Co.,Ltd.
8	北京国际交换系统有限公司	Beijing International Switching Corp.
9	北汽福田车辆股份有限公司	Beiqifutian Auto Corp.
10	北京松下彩色显像管有限公司	Beijing National Color Kinescope Co.,Ltd
11	中国北京同仁堂集团公司	Tongrentang Group Co.
12	北京燕京啤酒集团公司	Beijing Yanjing Beer Group Corp.
13	北京松下通信设备有限公司	Beijing Matsushita Communictian Equipment
14	北京东方电子集团股份有限公司	Beijing Orient Electronics Group CO.,LTD.
15	北京邮电通信设备厂	Beijing Post&Telecom Equipment Factory
16	清华同方股份有限公司	Tsinghua TongFang CO.,LTD
17	北京市燃气集团有限责任公司	Beijing Gas Group Co.,Ltd.
18	北京建筑材料集团有限责任公司	Beijing Building Materials Group Corp.
19	北京市汽车修理公司	Beijing Automobile Repair Company
20	北京飞机维修工程有限公司	Aircraft Maintenanc And Engineering Corporation Beijing
21	北京京能热电股份有限公司	Beijing JingNeng Thermal Towercoltd Co.,Ltd.
22	北京朗讯科技光缆有限公司	Lucent Technolojief Fiber Optic Cable Co.,Ltd.
23	北京化二股份有限公司	Beijing Huaer Co.,Ltd.
24	北京北大方正电子有限公司	Beijing Founder Electronics Co.,Ltd.
25	航卫通用电器医疗系统有限公司	Ge HangWei Medical Systems Company Ltd.
26	北京市热力集团有限责任公司	Beijing District Fleating Group Go.,Ltd.
27	北京吉普汽车有限公司	Beijing Jeep Corp.
28	北京矿务局	Beijing Mining Ministry
29	北京牡丹电子集团公司	Beijing Peony Electronics Group Co.
30	北京市自来水集团有限责任公司	Beijing Running Water Group Corp.
31	北京卷烟厂	Beijing Tobacco Factory
32	北京福田车辆股份有限公司怀柔汽车厂	Beijing Futian Auto Corp.Huairou Auto Factory
33	北京大唐发电股份有限公司	Beijing Datang Electric Power Co.,Ltd
34	北京村田电子有限公司	Beijing Murata Electronics Co.,Ltd.
35	北京ＪＶＣ电子产业有限公司	Beijng JVC Electronics Industrial Co.,Ltd.
36	北京松下电子部品有限公司	Beijing Matsushita Electronics Components Co.,Ltd.
37	北京汽车摩托车联合制造公司	Beijing Automobile & Motorcycle Union Manufacturing Co
38	北新建材（集团）有限公司	Beijing New Building Materials Co.,Ltd
39	北京印钞厂	Beijing Printing Bill Factory.
40	北京可口可乐饮料有限公司	Beijing Coca-Cola Beverage Co.,Ltd.
41	北京首钢宝生带钢厂	Beijing Shougang Posheng Strip Co.,Ltd.
42	北京京棉集团有限责任公司	Beijing jingmian Group Corp.
43	北京华北电力实业总公司	North China Power Industry Corp.
44	北京市顺义区肉类联合加工厂	Beijing Shunyi District Meat United Processing Factory
45	北京市客车总厂	Beijing Coach General Factory
46	首都航天机械公司	Capital Aviation Machinery Co.
47	北京市三露厂	CHINA Beijing Sanlu Factory
48	北京二七车辆厂	Beijing Erqi Auto Factory.
49	邮电部北京邮票厂	Beijing Postage Stamp Printing Flouse.
50	北京轻型汽车有限公司	Beijing Light Automobile Co., Ltd

6-14 续表 continued

序 号 No.	企 业 名 称	Enterprise
51	中国大恒（集团）有限公司	China Daheng Group,Inc.
52	北人印刷机械股份有限公司	Beiren Printing mechanic Corp.
53	北京四通松下电工有限公司	Beijing STONE Matsushita Electric Works Ltd.
54	北京二七机车厂	Beijing Erqi Auto Factory.
55	清华紫光股份有限公司	TsingHua Unisplendour Corp.Ltd.
56	北京古桥电器公司	Beijing GuQiao Electric Co.
57	北京星海乐器有限责任公司	Beijing XingHai Musical Instruments Company Ltd.
58	北京双鹤药业股份有限公司	Beijing Double-crane Medicine CO.,LTD
59	北京顺美服装股份有限公司	Beijing Smart Garments CO.,LTD.
60	北京北方车辆制造厂	Beijing North Auto Factory.
61	北京恩布拉科雪花压缩机有限公司	Beijing Embraco Snowflake Compressor Company Led.
62	北京电力设备总厂	Beijing Power Equipment Group.
63	北内集团总公司	Beinei Group Corp.
64	拜耳医药保健有限公司	Bayer Healthcare Company LTD.
65	北京市顺义宏利钢管有限公司	Beijing Shunyi Hongli Steel Tube Ltd.
66	北京北化精细化学品有限责任公司	Beijing Beihua Fine Chemicals CO.,Ltd.
67	北京万东医疗装备股份有限公司	Beijing Wandong Medical Equipment CO.,Ltd
68	北京欧陆太平洋制罐有限公司	Beijing CCE Pacific CAN Co.,Ltd.
69	北京第一机床厂	Beijing 1ST Machine Tool Factory.
70	北京市液化石油气公司	Beijing Liquefied Petroleum Gas Company
71	北京北方华德车辆制造有限责任公司	Beijing North HuaDe Vehicle Co.,Ltd.
72	北京市牛栏山酒厂	Beijing Niulanshan Wine Factory.
73	北京玻璃集团公司	Beijing Glass Group Co.
74	北京万辉药业集团	Beijing Wanhui Pharmaceutical Group
75	北京吉乐电子集团有限公司	Beijing JiLe Electroncs Group Co.,Ltd.
76	北京轮胎厂	Beijing Tire Factory(Beijing Capital Tire CO.,Ltd.)
77	北京兆维电子(集团)有限责任公司	Beijing C&W Electronics(Group) CO.,LTD.
78	北京王致和食品集团有限公司	Beijing WangZhiHe Food Group Co.,Ltd.
79	SMC(中国)有限公司	SMC(China) CO.,Ltd
80	中国纺科院机械厂	China Textile Academy Ma Chinery Plant
81	北京水泥厂有限责任公司	Beijing Cement Plant Co.,Ltd.
82	北京爱立信通信系统有限公司	Beijing Ericsson Communication System CO.,Ltd.
83	北京ABB电气传动系统有限公司	ABB Beijing Drive Systems Co.,Ltd.
84	北京星航机电设备厂	Beijing XingHang Mechanical-Electrical Equipment Plant
85	北京航星机器制造公司	Beijing Hangxing Machine Building Corp.
86	北京第三制药厂	Beijing 3RD Pharmaceutical Factory.
87	北京红星酿酒集团公司	Beijing Red Star Wine-Marking Group Company.
88	北京化工实验厂	Beijing Chemical Engineering Experimental Plant
89	北京三环亚太啤酒有限公司	Beijing Three Ring Asia Pacific Beer CO.,LTD.
90	北京天海工业有限公司	Beijing Tianhai Industry CO.,Ltd
91	北京市电机总厂	Beijing General Electrical Machinery Factory.
92	北京燕化高新技术股份有限公司	Beijing Yanhua Updated High-teeh Co.,Ltd.
93	北京正大饲料有限公司	Beijing Chia Tai Feedmill Ltd.
94	北京起重机器厂	Beijing Crane Factory.
95	国营华北光学仪器厂	North CHINA Optical Instrument Factory.
96	北京广东健力宝饮料有限公司	Beijing Guangdong Jianlibao Beverage CO.,Ltd
97	北京市东方罗门哈斯有限公司	Beijing Eastern Tohm&Haas CO.,Ltd.
98	北京青云航空仪表有限公司	Beijing Qingyun Air Meter CO.,Ltd
99	北京保温瓶工业公司	Beijing Vacuum Bottle Industry Corp.
100	和路雪(中国)有限公司	Wau's (China) Co.,Ltd.

6-15 大中型工业企业按利税总额排序

ARRANGING IN TOTAL PRE-TAX PROFITS OF LARGE AND MEDIUM INDUSTRIAL ENTERPRISES

序号 No.	企业名称	Enterprise
1	联想（北京）有限公司	LEGEND(Beijing) Group Co.,Ltd
2	首钢总公司	Shougang Group
3	中国石化集团北京燕山石油化工有限公司	Beijing Yanshan Petrochemical Group Co.,Ltd
4	北京诺基亚移动通信有限公司	Beijing Noka Mobile Telecom Munications Ltd.
5	北京燕京啤酒集团公司	Beijing Yanjing Beer Group Corp.
6	北京国际交换系统有限公司	Beijing International Switching Corp.
7	中国华北电力集团公司(在京单位)	NORTH China Power Group Co.
8	北京卷烟厂	Beijing Tobacco Factory
9	北京朗讯科技光缆有限公司	Lucent Technolojief Fiber Optic Cable Co.,Ltd.
10	北京松下通信设备有限公司	Beijing Matsushita Communictian Equipment
11	北京京能热电股份有限公司	Beijing JingNeng Thermal Towercoltd Co.,Ltd.
12	北京市三露厂	CHINA Beijing Sanlu Factory
13	北京松下彩色显像管有限公司	Beijing National Color Kinescope Co.,Ltd
14	北京大唐发电股份有限公司	Beijing Datang Electric Power Co.,Ltd
15	清华同方股份有限公司	Tsinghua TongFang CO.,LTD
16	中国北京同仁堂集团公司	Tongrentang Group Co.
17	北京双鹤药业股份有限公司	Beijing Double-crane Medicine CO.,LTD
18	北京化学工业集团有限责任公司	Beijing Chemical Industry Group Corp.
19	北京诺基亚航星通讯系统有限公司	Beijing Noka Hang Xing Telecom Munications Systems Co.,Ltd.
20	北京东方电子集团股份有限公司	Beijing Orient Electronics Group CO.,LTD.
21	北汽福田车辆股份有限公司	Beiqifutian Auto Corp.
22	北京飞机维修工程有限公司	Aircraft Maintenanc And Engineering Corporation Beijing
23	航卫通用电器医疗系统有限公司	Ge HangWei Medical Systems Company Ltd.
24	北京化二股份有限公司	Beijing Huaer Co.,Ltd
25	北京印钞厂	Beijing Printing Bill Factory.
26	北京市牛栏山酒厂	Beijing Niulanshan Wine Factory.
27	北京华北电力实业总公司	North China Power Industry Corp.
28	邮电部北京邮票厂	Beijing Postage Stamp Printing Flouse.
29	清华紫光股份有限公司	TsingHua Unisplendour Corp.Ltd.
30	北京建筑材料集团有限责任公司	Beijing Building Materials Group Corp.
31	北京万辉药业集团	Beijing Wanhui Pharmaceutical Group
32	北京市燃气集团有限责任公司	Beijing Gas Group Co.,Ltd.
33	清华紫光（集团）总公司	Tsinghua ZiGuang (Group) Corp.
34	北京村田电子有限公司	Beijing Murata Electronics Co.,Ltd.
35	北京邮电通信设备厂	Beijing Post&Telecom Equipment Factory
36	北京福田车辆股份有限公司怀柔汽车厂	Beijing Futian Auto Corp.Huairou Auto Factory
37	北京矿务局	Beijing Mining Ministry
38	北京北方华德车辆制造有限责任公司	Beijing North HuaDe Vehicle Co.,Ltd.
39	北人印刷机械股份有限公司	Beiren Printing mechanic Corp.
40	北京可口可乐饮料有限公司	Beijing Coca-Cola Beverage Co.,Ltd.
41	北京红星酿酒集团公司	Beijing Red Star Wine-Marking Group Company.
42	北京北大方正电子有限公司	Beijing Founder Electronics Co.,Ltd.
43	北京汽车摩托车联合制造公司	Beijing Automobile & Motorcycle Union Manufacturing Co
44	北京市汽车修理公司	Beijing Automobile Repair Company
45	北京松下电子部品有限公司	Beijing Matsushita Electronics Components Co.,Ltd.
46	北京市热力集团有限责任公司	Beijing District Fleating Group Go.,Ltd.
47	中国大恒（集团）有限公司	China Daheng Group,Inc.
48	北新建材（集团）有限公司	Beijing New Building Materials Co.,Ltd
49	北京市自来水集团有限责任公司	Beijing Running Water Group Corp.
50	北京燕化高新技术股份有限公司	Beijing Yanhua Updated High-teeh Co.,Ltd.

6-15 续 表 continued

序 号 No.	企 业 名 称	Enterprise
51	北京天坛生物制品股份有限公司	Beijing Tiantan Biological Product CO.,LTD
52	北京万东医疗装备股份有限公司	Beijing Wandong Medical Equipment CO.,Ltd
53	北京三环亚太啤酒有限公司	Beijing Three Ring Asia Pacific Beer CO.,LTD.
54	北京ABB电气传动系统有限公司	ABB Beijing Drive Systems Co.,Ltd.
55	康明斯发动机(北京)有限公司	Cummins Engine (Beijing) Co.,Ltd.
56	北京兆维电子(集团)有限责任公司	Beijing C&W Electronics(Group) CO.,LTD.
57	北京日邦印刷有限公司	Beijing Ribang Printing CO.,Ltd
58	北京京棉集团有限责任公司	Beijing jingmian Group Corp.
59	中科实业集团（控股）公司	Industry Group(Holding) Corp.of CAS
60	北京电子管厂	Beijing Electron Tube Factory
61	北京普莱克斯实用气体有限公司	Beijing Pulaikesi Practical Gas CO.,Ltd
62	SMC(中国)有限公司	SMC(China) CO.,Ltd
63	北京星海乐器有限责任公司	Beijing XingHai Musical Instruments Company Ltd.
64	北京中融安全印务公司	Beijing Zhongrong Safety Printing Corp.
65	北京四通松下电工有限公司	Beijing STONE Matsushita Electric Works Ltd.
66	拜耳医药保健有限公司	Bayer Healthcare Company LTD.
67	北人集团公司	Beiren Group Corp.
68	北京王致和食品集团有限公司	Beijing WangZhiHe Food Group Co.,Ltd.
69	北京二七车辆厂	Beijing Erqi Auto Factory.
70	北京二七机车厂	Beijing Erqi Auto Factory.
71	北京正元保健品厂	Beijing Zhengyuan Health Articles Factory
72	北京中科三环高技术股份有限公司	Beijing Three Ring Asia High-tech CO.,LTD. Of CAS
73	北京吉乐电子集团有限公司	Beijing JiLe Electroncs Group Co.,Ltd.
74	北京市顺义区肉类联合加工厂	Beijing Shunyi District Meat United Processing Factory
75	北京ＪＶＣ电子产业有限公司	Beijng JVC Electronics Industrial Co.,Ltd.
76	乐天四通食品有限公司	Lotte Stone Foods Co.,Ltd.
77	新华通讯社印刷厂	The Xinhua News Agency Printing Factory.
78	北京市客车总厂	Beijing Coach General Factory
79	北京恩布拉科雪花压缩机有限公司	Beijing Embraco Snowflake Compressor Company Led.
80	经济日报印刷厂	Economic Daily Priting Factory.
81	北京航星机器制造公司	Beijing Hangxing Machine Building Corp.
82	北京第一机床厂	Beijing 1ST Machine Tool Factory.
83	北京电力设备总厂	Beijing Power Equipment Group.
84	北京旅行车股份有限公司	Beijign Caravan Corp.
85	北京水泥厂有限责任公司	Beijing Cement Plant Co.,Ltd
86	北京广东健力宝饮料有限公司	Beijing Guangdong Jianlibao Beverage CO.,Ltd.
87	美航快速彩色印刷公司	Meihang Quick Color Printing Corp.
88	北京宝岛包装印刷有限公司	Beijing Baodao Packing & Printing CO.,Ltd
89	北京日用化学二厂	Beijing 2ND Daily Chemistry Factory.
90	北京玻璃集团公司	Beijing Glass Group Co.
91	北京豪特耐集中供热设备有限公司	Beijing Haotenai Central Heat Supply Equipment CO.,Ltd
92	北京华环电子有限公司	Beijing Huahuan Electron CO.,Ltd
93	北京青云航空仪表有限公司	Beijing Qingyun Air Meter CO.,Ltd
94	中国纺科院机械厂	China Textile Academy Ma Chinery Plant
95	北京中生生物工程高技术公司	Beijing Zhongsheng Biological Project High Technology Co.
96	国营华北光学仪器厂	North CHINA Optical Instrument Factory.
97	北京轮胎厂	Beijing Tire Factory(Beijing Capital Tire CO.,Ltd.)
98	广播电影电视部设备制造厂	Equipment Factory of National Radio,Film and Television Department
99	北京维根制衣有限公司	Beijing Wagon Garments Co.,Ltd
100	北京四环生物工程制品厂	Beijing Fourrings Bioengineering Products Factory

6-16 大中型工业企业按总资产贡献率排序
ARRANGING IN RATIO OF PRE-TAX PROFITS TO TOTAL CAPITAL ORDER OF LARGE AND MEDIUM ENTERPRISES

序号 No.	企业名称	Enterprise
1	北京卷烟厂	Beijing Tobacco Factory
2	北京正元保健品厂	Beijing Zhengyuan Health Articles Factory
3	北京朗讯科技光缆有限公司	Lucent Technolojief Fiber Optic Cable Co.,Ltd.
4	北京北方华德车辆制造有限责任公司	Beijing North HuaDe Vehicle Co.,Ltd.
5	北京市三露厂	CHINA Beijing Sanlu Factory
6	北京松下通信设备有限公司	Beijing Matsushita Communictian Equipment
7	康明斯发动机(北京)有限公司	Cummins Engine (Beijing) Co.,Ltd.
8	北京南常肉食机械有限公司	Beijing Nanchang Meat Machinery CO.,Ltd
9	美航快速彩色印刷公司	Meihang Quick Color Printing Corp.
10	联想（北京）有限公司	LEGEND(Beijing) Group Co.,Ltd
11	航卫通用电器医疗系统有限公司	Ge HangWei Medical Systems Company Ltd.
12	北京京能热电股份有限公司	Beijing JingNeng Thermal Towercoltd Co.,Ltd.
13	北京ABB电气传动系统有限公司	ABB Beijing Drive Systems Co.,Ltd.
14	北京首安工业消防工程有限公司	Beijing Shouan Industrial Fire Engineering CO.,Ltd
15	北京中生生物工程高技术公司	Beijing Zhongsheng Biological Project High Technology
16	北京市牛栏山酒厂	Beijing NiuLanshan Wine Factory.
17	北京宝岛包装印刷有限公司	Beijing Baodao Packing & Printing CO.,Ltd
18	北京天坛京伟家具有限公司	Beijing Tiantan Jingwei Furniture CO.,Ltd
19	北京日邦印刷有限公司	Beijing Ribang Printing CO.,Ltd
20	北京华环电子有限公司	Beijing Huahuan Electron CO.,Ltd
21	清华紫光股份有限公司	TsingHua Unisplendour Corp.Ltd.
22	北京大唐发电股份有限公司	Beijing Datang Electric Power Co.,Ltd
23	北京双燕商标彩印厂	Beijing Double-swallow Trademark Color Printing Factor
24	北京中融安全印务公司	Beijing Zhongrong Safety Printing Corp.
25	北京村田电子有限公司	Beijing Murata Electronics Co.,Ltd.
26	邮电部北京邮票厂	Beijing Postage Stamp Printing Flouse.
27	北京航天石化技术装备工程公司	Beijing Hangtian Petrochemical Technological Equipment
28	北京维根制衣有限公司	Beijing Weigen Garment CO.,Ltd
29	北京燕化高新技术股份有限公司	Beijing Yanhua Updated High-teeh Co.,Ltd.
30	北京双鹤药业股份有限公司	Beijing Double-crane Medicine CO.,LTD
31	北京华北电力实业总公司	North China Power Industry Corp.
32	北京福田车辆股份有限公司怀柔汽车厂	Beijing Futian Auto Corp.Huairou Auto Factory
33	北京红星酿酒集团公司	Beijing Red Star Wine-Marking Group Company.
34	经济日报印刷厂	Economic Daily Printing Factory.
35	北京协和制药二厂	Beijing Xiehe 2ND Pharmaceutical Factory
36	北京燕京啤酒集团公司	Beijing Yanjing Beer Group Corp.
37	北京北大方正电子有限公司	Beijing Founder Electronics Co.,Ltd.
38	北京诺基亚移动通信有限公司	Beijing Nokia Mobile Telecom Munications Ltd.
39	北京博飞仪器股份有限公司	Beijing Bofei Instrument CO.,Ltd
40	北京四环生物工程制品厂	Beijing Sihuan Pharmaceutical Factory.
41	北京国际交换系统有限公司	Beijing International Switching Corp.
42	中国中医研究院实验药厂	China Traditional Chinese Medicine Research Institute
43	北京雨润食品有限公司	Beijing Yurun Food Co.,Ltd.
44	北京中医药大学药厂	Beijing Traditional Chinese Medicine College
45	北京印钞厂	Beijing Printing Bill Factory.
46	北京燕达皇冠盖有限公司	Beijing Yanda Huangguangai CO.,Ltd
47	北京豪特耐集中供热设备有限公司	Beijing Haotenai Central Heat Supply Equipment CO.,Ltd
48	新华通讯社印刷厂	The Xinhua News Agency Printing Factory.
49	北京市礼花厂	Beijing Fireworks Display Factory
50	广播电影电视部设备制造厂	Equipment Factory of National Radio,Film and Television Department

6-16 续 表 continued

序号 No.	企业名称	Enterprise
51	北京松下电子部品有限公司	Beijing Matsushita Electronics Components Co.,Ltd.
52	北京市华都酿酒食品工业公司	Beijing Huadu Wine-making and Food Industry Company
53	北京联合印刷纸器有限公司	Beijign Lianhe Printing Equipment CO.,LTD.
54	北京天坛生物制品股份有限公司	Beijing Tiantan Biological Product CO.,LTD
55	北京鹏翼包装制品公司	Beijing Pengyi Packing Products Corp.
56	北京可口可乐饮料有限公司	Beijing Coca-Cola Beverage Co.,Ltd.
57	北京万辉药业集团	Beijing Wanhui Pharmaceutical Group
58	北京市顺义区肉类联合加工厂	Beijing Shunyi District Meat United Processing Factory
59	中国大恒（集团）有限公司	China Daheng Group,Inc.
60	北京市皮件厂	Beijing Leather Factory.
61	北京路桥机械厂	Beijing Luqiao Machinery Factory.
62	北京三环亚太啤酒有限公司	Beijing Three Ring Asia Pacific Beer CO.,LTD.
63	北京万东医疗装备股份有限公司	Beijing Wandong Medical Equipment CO.,Ltd
64	北京普莱克斯实用气体有限公司	Beijing Pulaikesi Practical Gas CO.,Ltd
65	北京诺基亚航星通讯系统有限公司	Beijing Noka Hang Xing Telecom Munications Systems Co.,Ltd.
66	北京飞机维修工程有限公司	Aircraft Maintenanc And Engineering Corporation Beijing
67	北京科化化学新技术公司	Beijing Kehua Chemical New Technology Corp.
68	北京广东健力宝饮料有限公司	Beijing Guangdong Jianlibao Beverage CO.,Ltd.
69	北京邮电通信设备厂	Beijing Post&Telecom Equipment Factory
70	北京石油机械厂	Beijing Petroleum Machinery Factory
71	北京王致和食品集团有限公司	Beijing WangZhiHe Food Group Co.,Ltd.
72	中科实业集团（控股）公司	Zhongke Industry Group(Holding) Corp.
73	北京贝利控制有限公司	Beijing Beili Control CO.,Ltd
74	北京双桥制药公司	Beijing Shuangqiao Pharmaceatical Corp
75	北京汇能亚澳通讯设备厂	Beijing Huineng Yaao Communication Equipment Factory
76	中国人民解放军解放军报印刷厂	The PLA Daily Printing Factory.
77	北京化二股份有限公司	Beijing Huaer Co.,Ltd.
78	北京神州摩奇食品饮料有限公司	Beijing ShenZhou Moqi Food & Beveragh Co.,Ltd.
79	中国科学院印刷厂	Printing House,Chinese Academy of Sciences(CAS)
80	北京云岗热电厂	Beijing Yungang Heat and Power Plant
81	北京旅行车股份有限公司	Beijign Caravan Corp.
82	北京计算机三厂	Beijing 3RD Computer Factory
83	北京星海乐器有限责任公司	Beijing XinHai Musical Instruments Company Ltd.
84	北京正大饲料有限公司	Beijing Chia Tai Feedmill Ltd.
85	北京汽车摩托车联合制造公司	Beijing Automobile & Motorcycle Union Manufacturing Co
86	北京佳乐食品厂	Beijing Jiale Food Factory.
87	清华同方股份有限公司	Tsinghua TongFang CO.,LTD
88	北京中科三环高技术股份有限公司	Beijing Three Ring Asia High-tech CO.,LTD. Of CAS
89	拜耳医药保健有限公司	Bayer Healthcare Company LTD.
90	北京北方生物技术研究所	Beijing North Biological Technology Research Institute
91	北汽福田车辆股份有限公司	Beiqifutian Auto Corp.
92	清华紫光（集团）总公司	Tsinghua ZiGuang (Group) Corp.
93	密云县粮食局加工厂	Miyun County Grain Bureau Processing Plant
94	北京印刷集团有限责任公司印刷二厂	Beijing 2ND Printing Factory of Beijing Printing Group
95	北京松下彩色显像管有限公司	Beijing National Color Kinescope Co.,Ltd
96	北京印刷集团有限责任公司京华印刷厂	Beijing Jing Hua Printing Factory
97	平谷县水泥二厂	Pinggu 2ND Cement Factory.
98	中国北京同仁堂集团公司	Tongrentang Group Co.
99	北京市东方罗门哈斯有限公司	Beijing Eastern Tohm&Haas CO.,Ltd.
100	北京市顺义飞达玻璃厂	Beijing Shunyi Feida Glass Factory

6-17 大中型工业企业按资产总额排序
ARRANGING IN TOTAL ASSETS OF LARGE AND MEDIUM INDUSTRIAL ENTERPRISES

序号 No.	企业名称	Enterprise
1	首钢总公司	Shougang Group
2	中国华北电力集团公司(在京单位)	NORTH China Power Group Co.
3	中国石化集团北京燕山石油化工有	Beijing Yangshan Petrochemical Group Co.,Ltd
4	北京化学工业集团有限责任公司	Beijing Chemical Industry Group Corp.
5	北京市自来水集团有限责任公司	Beijing Running Water Group Corp.
6	北京诺基亚移动通信有限公司	Beijing Nokia Mobile Telecom Munications Ltd.
7	北京市热力集团有限责任公司	Beijing District Fleating Group Go.,Ltd.
8	北京市燃气集团有限责任公司	Beijing Gas Group Co.,Ltd.
9	北京建筑材料集团有限责任公司	Beijing Building Materials Group Corp.
10	北京燕京啤酒集团公司	Beijing Yanjing Beer Group Corp.
11	联想（北京）有限公司	LEGEND(Beijing) Group Co.,Ltd
12	北京国际交换系统有限公司	Beijing International Switching Corp.
13	北京东方电子集团股份有限公司	Beijing East Electronics Group Corp.
14	清华同方股份有限公司	Tsinghua TongFang CO.,LTD
15	北京松下彩色显像管有限公司	Beijing National Color Kinescope Co.,Ltd
16	中国北京同仁堂集团公司	Tongrentang Group Co.
17	北京牡丹电子集团公司	Beijing Peony Electronics Group Co.
18	北汽福田车辆股份有限公司	Beiqifutian Auto Corp.
19	北京矿务局	Beijing Mining Ministry
20	北内集团总公司	Beinei Group Corp.
21	北新建材（集团）有限公司	Beijing New Building Materials Co.,Ltd.
22	北京诺基亚航星通讯系统有限公司	Beijing Noka Hang Xing Telecom Munications Systems Co.,Ltd.
23	北京兆维电子(集团)有限责任公司	Beijing C&W electronics(Group) CO.,LTD.
24	北京吉普汽车有限公司	Beijing Jeep Corp.
25	北京汽车摩托车联合制造公司	Beijing Automobile & Motorcycle Union Manufacturing Co
26	北京飞机维修工程有限公司	Aircraft Maintenanc And Engineering Corporation Beijing
27	北京京能热电股份有限公司	Beijing JingNeng Thermal Towercoltd Co.,Ltd.
28	北京化二股份有限公司	Beijing Huaer Co.,Ltd
29	北京轻型汽车有限公司	Beijing Light Automobile Co., Ltd
30	北京汽车工业集团总公司	Beijing Automobile Industry Group Co.
31	北京玻璃集团公司	Beijing Glass Group Co.
32	北京水泥厂有限责任公司	Beijing Cement Plant Co.,Ltd.
33	北人集团公司	Beiren Group Corp.
34	北京万辉药业集团	Beijing Wanhui Pharmaceutical Group
35	北京电子管厂	Beijing Electron Tube Factory
36	北京京棉集团有限责任公司	Beijing jingmian Group Corp.
37	首都航天机械公司	Capital Aviation Machinery Co.
38	清华紫光（集团）总公司	Tsinghua ZiGuang (Group) Corp.
39	北人印刷机械股份有限公司	Beiren Printing mechanic Corp.
40	北京邮电通信设备厂	Beijing Post&Telecom Equipment Factory
41	北京轮胎厂	Beijing Tire Factory(Beijing Capital Tire CO.,Ltd.)
42	北京市汽车修理公司	Beijing Automobile Repair Company
43	北京第一机床厂	Beijing 1ST Machine Tool Factory.
44	北京雪花电器集团公司	Beijing Snowflake Electric Appliance Group Corp.
45	北京首钢宝生带钢厂	Beijing Shougang Posheng Strip Co.,Ltd.
46	北京大唐发电股份有限公司	Beijing Datang Electric Power Co.,Ltd
47	北京双鹤药业股份有限公司	Beijing Double-crane Medicine CO.,LTD
48	北京朗讯科技光缆有限公司	Lucent Technolojief Fiber Optic Cable Co.,Ltd.
49	北京电力设备总厂	Beijing Power Equipment Group.
50	清华紫光股份有限公司	TsingHua Unisplendour Corp.Ltd.

6-17 续 表 continued

序 号 No.	企 业 名 称	Enterprise
51	和路雪(中国)有限公司	Walls(China) CO.,Ltd
52	北京市造纸包装工业公司	Beijing Paper&Package Industry Corp.
53	北京亚洲双合盛五星啤酒有限公司	Beijing Asia ShuangHeSheng Five Star Beer CO.,LTD.
54	北京印钞厂	Beijing Printing Bill Factory.
55	北京市平板玻璃集团公司	Beijing Plate-glass Group Corp.
56	北京航星机器制造公司	Beijing Hangxing Machine Building Corp.
57	北京北大方正电子有限公司	Beijing Founder Electronics Co.,Ltd.
58	北京市客车总厂	Beijing Coach General Factory
59	北京电视设备厂	Beijing Television Equipment Factory
60	北京松下通信设备有限公司	Beijing Matsushita Communictian Equipment
61	SMC(中国)有限公司	SMC(China) CO.,Ltd
62	北京市三露厂	CHINA Beijing Sanlu Factory
63	北京市液化石油气公司	Beijing Liquefied Petroleum Gas Company
64	北京亚都科技股份有限公司	Beijing Yadu Science Technology CO.,Ltd
65	北京北方车辆制造厂	Beijing North Auto Factory.
66	北京广播器材厂(七六一厂)	Beijing Broadcast Equipment Factory
67	北京可口可乐饮料有限公司	Beijing Coca-Cola Beverage Co.,Ltd.
68	北京第三制药厂	Beijing 3RD Pharmaceutical Factory
69	北京市顺义宏利钢管有限公司	Shunyi Hongli Steel Tube CO.,Ltd
70	北京华德液压工业集团有限责任公司	Beijing Huade Hydraulic Industry CO.,Ltd
71	航卫通用电器医疗系统有限公司	Ge HangWei Medical Systems Company Ltd.
72	北京化工实验厂	Beijing Chemical Engineering Experimental Plant
73	北京华北电力实业总公司	North China Power Industry Corp.
74	北京卷烟厂	Beijing Tobacco Factory
75	中国大恒（集团）有限公司	China Daheng Group,Inc.
76	北京雪莲羊绒有限公司	Beijing Snow_Lotus Cashmere Co.,Ltd.
77	北京王致和食品集团有限公司	Beijing WangZhiHe Food Group Co.,Ltd.
78	北京啤酒朝日有限公司	Beijing Beer Asahi Co.,Ltd
79	密云县冶金矿山公司	Minyun Metallurgy and Mine Co.
80	北京星海乐器有限责任公司	Beijing XinHai Musical Instruments Company Ltd.
81	北京万东医疗装备股份有限公司	Beijing Wandong Medical Equipment CO.,Ltd
82	北京二七机车厂	Beijing Erqi Auto Factory.
83	北京恩布拉科雪花压缩机有限公司	Beijing Embraco Snowflake Compressor Company Led.
84	北京正东电子动力集团有限公司	Beijing Zhengdong Electronic Power Group Co.
85	北京松下电子部品有限公司	Beijing Matsushita Electronics Components Co.,Ltd.
86	北京福田车辆股份有限公司怀柔汽车厂	Beijing Futian Auto Corp.Huairou Auto Factory
87	北京燕化高新技术股份有限公司	Beijing Yanhua Updated High-teeh Co.,Ltd.
88	北京煤矿机械厂	Beijing Coal Mining Machinery Factory.
89	北京起重机器厂	Beijing Crane Factory.
90	北京重型电机厂	Beijing Heavy-duty Electrical Machinery Factory.
91	北京南口机车车辆工厂	Beijing Nankou Rolling stock Plant
92	北京白菊电器集团	Beijing Baiju Electric Appliance Group
93	北京青云航空仪表有限公司	Beijing Qingyun Air Meter CO.,Ltd
94	北京天坛生物制品股份有限公司	Beijing Tiantan Biological Product CO.,LTD
95	北京三环亚太啤酒有限公司	Beijing Three Ring Asia Pacific Beer CO.,LTD.
96	北京北化精细化学品有限责任公司	Beijing Beihua Fine Chemicals CO.,Ltd.
97	北京合成纤维实验厂(北京华英纶化纤公司)	Beijing Sythetic Fibre Experimental Factory.
98	北京金鹰铜业有限责任公司	Beijing Golden Hawk Copper Industry Corp.
99	北京村田电子有限公司	Beijing Murata Electronics Co.,Ltd.
100	北京二七车辆厂	Beijing Erqi Auto Factory.

主要统计指标解释

工业 指从事自然资源的开采，对采掘品和农产品进行加工和再加工的物质生产部门。具体包括：（1）对自然资源的开采，如采矿、晒盐、森林采伐等（但不包括禽兽捕猎和水产捕捞）；（2）对农副产品的加工、再加工，如粮油加工、食品加工、扎花、纺织、制革等；（3）对采掘品的加工、再加工，如炼铁、炼钢、化工生产、石油加工、机器制造、木材加工等，以及电力、自来水、煤气的生产和供应等；（4）对工业品的修理、翻新，如机器设备的修理、交通运输工具（包括小卧车）的修理等。

1984 年以前农村的村及村以下办工业归属农业，1984 年以后划归工业。

独立核算工业企业 非独立核算工业生产单位 工业企业按其行政和财务是否独立，分为核算工业企业和非独立核算工业生产单位。

独立核算工业企业应同时具备下列三个条件：（1）行政上有独立的组织形式；（2）经济上独立核算、自负盈亏、编制独立的资金平衡表；（3）有权与其他单位签订合同，并在银行社有独立帐户。独立核算工业企业不论是单一性生产或联合性生产的企业，均以整个企业作为一个基层单位进行统计，而不按分厂、车间统计。

非独立核算工业生产单位是指不同时具备独立核算工业企业三个条件，附设与其他企业、事业、机关、团体、学校、科研机构、部队等单位的工业生产单位。非独立核算工业生产单位必须同时具备下列三个条件，才能列入工业统计范围，即：（1）有固定的生产场所和生产设备；（2）有固定的生产工人和学徒在十人以上；（3）一般单位常年生产，季节性生产的单位全年开工时间在三个月以上。

轻工业 指主要提供生活消费品和制作手工工具的工业。按其所使用的原料不同，可分为两大类：（1）以农业为原料的轻工业，是指直接或间接以农产品为基本原料的轻工业。主要包括食品制造、饮料制造、烟草加工、纺织、缝纫、皮革和毛皮制作、造纸以及印刷等工业；（2）以非农产品为原料的轻工业，是指以工业品为原料的轻工业。主要包括文教体育用品、化学药品制造、合成纤维制造、日用化学制品、日用玻璃制品、日用金属制品、手工工具制造、医疗器械制造、文化和办公用机械制造等工业。

重工业 是指为国民经济各部门提供物质技术基础的主要生产资料的工业。按其生产性质和产品用途，可以分为下列三类：（1）采掘（伐）工业，是指对自然资源的开采，包括石油开采、煤炭开采、金属矿开采、非金属矿开采和木材采伐等工业；（2）原材料工业，指向国民经济各部门提供基本材料、动力和燃料的工业。包括金属冶炼及加工、炼焦及焦炭化学、化工原料、水泥、人造板以及电力、石油和煤炭加工等工业；（3）加工工业，是指对工业原材料进行再加工制造的工业。包括装备国民经济各部门的机械设备制造工业、金属结构、水泥制品等工业，以及为农业提供的生产资料如化肥、农药等工业。

根据上述划分原则，修理业中以重工业产品为修理作业对象的划为重工业，反之划为轻工业。

工业总产值 是以货币表现的工业在一定时期内生产的已出售或可供出售工业产品总量，它反映一定时期内工业生产的总规模和总水平。它包括：在本企业内不再进行加工，经检验、包装入库（规定不需包装的产品除外）的成品价值，工业性作业价值，自制半成品、在产品期末初差额价值。工业总产值采用“工厂法”计算，即以工业作业为一个整体，按企业生产活动的最终成果来计算，企业内部不允许重复计算，不能把企业内部各个车间（分厂）生产的成果相加。但在企业之间、行业之间、地区之间存在着重复计算。

轻重工业总产值的划分也是按“工厂法”计算的，即一个工业企业在正常情况下生产的主要产品的性质属于轻工业，则该企业的全部总产值作为轻工业总产值；一个工业企业生产的主要产品的性质属于重工业，则该企业的全部总产值作为重工业总产值。

工业增加值 是指工业行业在报告期内以货币表现的工业生产活动的最终成果。

工业销售产值 是以货币表现的工业企业在一定时期内销售的本企业生产的工业产品产量。包括已销售的成品、半成品价值，对外提供的工业性作业价值和对本单位基本建设部门、生活福利部门等提供的产品和工业性作业及自制设备的价值。已销售的成品、半成品不论是本期生产的、还是上期生产的，只要是本期销售出去的均包括在内。对外提供的工业性作业是指企业按合同对外提供的工业性劳务。企业为本单位基本建设部门、生活福利部门等提供的产品和工业性作业及自制设备也应视同销售，这部分也应作为销售统计。

工业销售产值的计算范围、计算价格和计算方法与工业总产值一致，但两者计算的基础不同，工业销售产值计算的基础是产品销售总量，工业总产值计算的基础是工业产品生产总量。

固定资产原价　指企业在建造、购置、安装、改建、扩建、技术改造某项固定资产时所支出的全部货币总额。它一般包括买价、包装费、运杂费和安装费。

固定资产净值　是指固定资产原价减去历年亿提折旧额后的净值。

新产品　指采用新技术原理、新设计构思、生产的全新产品或在结构、材质、工艺等某一方面比老产品有明显改进，从而显著提高了生产性能或扩大了使用功能的产品。

出口交货值　指工业企业交给外贸部门或自营（委托）出口（包括销往香港、澳门、台湾），用外汇价格结算的批量销售，在国内或边境批量出口的产品价值，还包括外商来样、来料加工、来件装配和补偿贸易等生产的产品价值。

工业品自销零售额　指各种经济类型的制造业生产单位，将本单位生产的产品直接售给居民（包括本企业职工）和社会集团取得的零售额。

工业企业主要财务指标和经济效益指标

1. 资本金合计　是企业在工商行政管理部门登记的注册资金。资本金合计包括国家资本金、法人资本金、个人资本金、外商资本金和集体资本金等。

（1）国家资本金　是指有权代表国家投资的政府部门或者机构以国有资产投入企业形成的资本金。不论企业的资本金是哪个政府部门或机构投入的，只要是以国家资金进行投资的，均作为国家资本金。

（2）法人资本金　是指其他法人单位以其依法可以支配的资产投入企业形成的资本金。

（3）个人资本金　是指社会个人或者企业内部职工以个人合法财产投入企业形成的资本金。

（4）外商资本金　是指外国投资者以及香港、澳门、台湾地区投资者投入企业形成的资本金。

（5）集体资本金　是指集体所有制企业投入企业形成的资本金。

2. 资产合计　指企业拥有或控制的全部资产。包括流动资产、长期投资、固定资产、无形及递延资产、其他长期资产、递延税项等，即为企业资产负债表的资产总计项。

（1）流动资产　指企业可以在一年内或者超过一年的一个生产周期内变现或耗用的资产合计。包括现金及各种存款、短期投资、应收及预付款项、存货等。

（2）固定资产　指企业固定资产净值、固定资产清理、在建工程、待处理固定资产损失所占用的资金合计。

（3）无形资产　指企业长期使用而没有实物形态的资产。包括专利权、非专利技术、商标权、著作权、土地使用权、商誉等。

3. 负债合计　指企业承担并需要偿还的全部债务。包括流动负债和长期负债、递延税项等，即为企业资产负债表的负债合计项。

（1）流动负债　指企业在一年内或者超过一年的营业周期内需要偿还的债务合计，其中包括短期借款、应付及预收款项、应付工资、应交税金和应交利润等。

（2）长期负债　指企业在一年以上或者超过一年的生产周期以上需要偿还的债务合计，其中包括长期借款、应付债务、长期应付款项等。

4. 利税总额　指企业利润总额、产品销售税金及附加和应交增值税之和。

5. 产品销售收入　指企业销售产品的销售收入和提供劳务等主要经营业务取得的业务总额。

6. 产品销售成本　指企业销售产品和提供劳务等主要经营业务的实际成本。

7. 产品销售税金及附加　指企业销售产品和提供工业性劳务等主要经营业务应负担的城市维护建设税、消费税、资源税和教育费附加。

8. 产品销售利润　指企业销售产品和提供工业性劳务等主要经营业务收入扣除其成本、费用、税金后的利润。

9. 利润总额　指企业实现的利润。

10. 所有制者权益　指企业投资人对企业净资产的所有权。企业净资产等于企业全部资产减去全部负债后余额，其中包括投资者对企业的最初投入，以及资本公积金、盈余公积金和未分配利润，对股份制企业即为股东权益。

11. 工业经济效益综合指数　是综合衡量工业经济效益各方面在数量上总体水平的一种特殊相对数，是反映工业经济运行质量的总量指数，是以各项工业经济效益指数实际数值分别除以该项指标的全国标准值并乘以各自权数求得。计算公式：

$$工业经济效益综合指数=\frac{某项经济效益指标报告期数值}{该项指标全国标准值}\times（权数）\div 总权数$$

计算工业经济效益综合指数时，各项经济效益指标的分子、分母应按报告期止累计数（如产品销售收入为报告期止累计产品销售收入）或序时平均数（如平均流动资产为报告期止各月平均流动资产之和除以累计月数）计算。全国的标准值：是根据“八五”期间全国乡及乡以上工业企业每项指标实际完成数值加权平均计算出来的。权数：是根据上述各项工业经济效益指标在综合经济效益中的重要程度，由专家调查法确定的。

12．工业产品销售率　指报告期工业销售产值与同期全部工业总产值之比。计算公式：

$$工业产品销售率（\%）=\frac{报告期现价工业销售产值}{报告期现价工业总产值}\times 100\%$$

13．工业资金利税率　指报告期已实现的利润、税金与同期的资产（流动资产和固定资产净值）之比，反映每单位（通常是每万元）资金所提供的利润税金额。它是考察和评价部门或企业资金运用的经济效益，分析资金投入效果的主要分析指标。计算公式：

$$工业资金利税率（\%）=\frac{报告期累计实现利税总额}{流动资产平均余额+固定资产净值平均余额}\times 100\%$$

14．工业增加值率　指报告期工业增加值占工业总产值的比重，反映降低中间消耗的经济效益。计算公式：

$$工业增加值率（\%）=\frac{报告期现价工业增加值}{报告期现价工业总产值}\times 100\%$$

15．工业成本费用利润率　指在一定时期内实现的利润与成本费用之比，是反映工业生产成本及费用投入的经济效益指标，同时也是反映降低成本的经济效益的指标。计算公式：

$$工业成本费用利润率（\%）=\frac{利润总额}{全部职工平均人数}\times 100\%$$

16．工业全员劳动生产率　指根据产品的价值量指标计算的平均每一个职工在单位时间内的产品生产量。是考核企业经济活动的重要指标，是企业生产技术水平、经济管理水平、职工技术熟练程度和劳动积极性的综合表现。目前我国的全员劳动生产率是将工业企业的工业增加值除以同一时期全部职工的平均人数来计算的。计算公式：

$$工业全员劳动生产率（元/人）=\frac{工业增加值（现价）}{全部职工平均人数}$$

17．流动资产周转次数　指在一定时期内流动资产完成的周转次数，反映流动资产的周转速度。计算公式：

$$流动资产周转次数（次）=\frac{产品销售收入}{流动资产平均余额}$$

18．销售收入利税率　指报告期已实现的利润、税金总额（包括利润总额、产品销售税金及附加和应交增值税）占同期全部销售收入的百分比。计算公式：

$$销售收入利税率（\%）=\frac{利税总额}{销售收入}\times 100\%$$

19．流动比率　是反映企业每百元流动负债中，有多少元流动资产作后盾。计算公式：

$$流动比率=\frac{流动资产总额}{流动负债总额}$$

20．速动比率　是衡量企业流动资产中可以立即用于偿付流动负债的能力。计算公式：

$$速动比率 = \frac{速动资产}{流动负债}$$

注：速动资产是流动资产中流动性相对更强的部分，通常等于现金，短期有价证券与应收款之和。

21. 资产负债率　是反映在企业资产总额中有多少资产是通过借债而得的，也可以用于衡量企业利用债权人提供资金进行经营活动的能力以及企业在清算时保护债权人利益的程度。计算公式：

$$资产负债率 = \frac{负债总额}{资产总额}$$

22. 总资产贡献率　反映企业全部资产的获利能力，是企业经营业绩和管理水平的集中体现，是评价和考核企业盈利能力的核心指标。计算公式为：

$$总资产贡献率 = （利润总额+税金总额+利息支出）\div 平均资产总额 \times \frac{12}{累计月数}$$

其中：税金总额为产品销售税金及附加与应交增值税之和；平均资产总额为期初期末资产总计的算术平均值。

23. 资本保值增值率　反映企业净资产的变动状况，是企业发展能力的集中体现。计算公式为：

资本保值增值率 = 报告期期末所有者权益/上年同期期末所有者权益

Explanatory Notes On Main Statistical Indicators

Industry refers to the physical production concerning extraction of natural resources, processing and reprocessing of minerals and agricultural products: (1) extraction of natural resources, such as mining, salt production, logging(but excluding hunting and fishing）; （2）processing and reprocessing of farm and sideline products, such as rice husking, flour milling, wine making, oil pressing, cotton ginning, silk reeling, spinning and weaving, and leather making; （3）manufacturing of industrial products, such as steel making, iron smelting, chemicals production, petroleum processing, machine building, timber processing; production and supply of water, gas and electricity; （4）repairing of industrial products such as the repairing of machine and vehicles for transportation（including cars）.

Prior to 1984, the rural industrial run by villages and cooperative organizations under village was classified into agriculture. Since 1984, it has been grouped into industry.

Independent Accounting Industrial Enterprises and Non-Independent Accounting Industrial Production Units are distinct by whether they have independent administration and accounting system.

An independent accounting industrial enterprises should satisfy all the following three conditions:（1）having an independent organization for administration;（2）having independent accounting system and filling independent balance sheets, being responsible for its own profits and losses;（3）being able to sign contracts with outside units and having independent bank accounts. An independent accounting industrial enterprise, no matter it is a single-business company or multi-business corporation, is counted as a basic statistical unit and its branch factories and workshops are no longer counted separately.

A non-independent accounting industrial production units is an industrial production unit with one or more of the three conditions unsatisfied. They usually attach to some enterprises, institutions, government departments, organizations, schools, scientific research institutions, or army units. A non-independent accounting industrial production units become a basic units of industrial statistics only when it can satisfy all the following three conditions:（1）having stable production sites and production equipment;（2）having more than 10 permanent workers and apprentices;（3）operating all-year-round for normal production or more than three months a year for seasonal production.

Light Industry refers to the industry that produces consumer goods and hand tools. Depending on the materials used, it is classified into two categories:

(1) Industries using farm products as raw materials directly or indirectly input farm products as basic raw materials, including the production of foods and beverages, tobacco processing, textile, clothing, fur and leather manufacturing, paper making, printing, etc..

(2) Industries using non-farm products as raw materials input manufactured goods as raw materials, including the manufacture of cultural, educational articles and sports goods, chemicals, synthetic fiber, daily use chemical products, glass products, metal products, hand tools, medical apparatus and instruments, and the manufacturing of cultural and office equipment.

Heavy Industry refers to the industry that produces capital goods. It provides various sectors of the national economy with necessary material and technical basis. According to the nature of production and the use of products, it is classified into three groups:

(1) Mining, quarrying and logging industry refers to the extraction of natural resources, including petroleum, coal, metal and non-metal ores and logging.

(2) Raw materials industry refers to the industry that provides various sectors of the national economy with raw materials, fuels and power. It includes smelting and processing of metals, coke and coke chemistry, chemical materials and building materials such as cement, plywood, power, petroleum refining and coal dressing, etc..

(3) Manufacturing industry refers to the industry that processes raw materials. It includes machine-building industry that equips sectors of the national economy, industries of metal structure and cement products, industries producing means of agricultural production, such as chemical fertilizers and pesticides.

According to the above principle of classification, the repairing mainly for heavy industry products are classified into heavy industry while these mainly for light industry products are put into light industry.

Gross Industrial Output Value is the total volume of industrial products sold or available for sale in value terms which reflects the total achievements and overall scale of industrial production during a given period. It includes the value of the finished products, which are not to be further processed in the enterprises and have been inspected, packed and put in storage, the value of industrial services rendered to other units and the differences in the value of the semi-finished products and products in process between the beginning and closing of the period. The gross industrial output value is calculated with "factory method". Based on the final products of every enterprise, there is no double calculation within every enterprise. However, double calculation does occur among different enterprises as well as different sectors and different regions.

Gross output value of light and heavy industries is also classified with the "factory" method. Under normal conditions, if the major products of an industrial enterprise belong to light industry products, the gross output value of the enterprise is put into light industry; the same principle apples to the contrary case.

Value Added of Industry refers to the final results of industrial production in money terms during the reference period.

Sales Value of Industry refers to total sales value of products produced by industrial enterprises during a given period, including sales of finished goods, semi-finished products, value of industrial services provided to outside units, value of products, industrial services and self-produced equipment provided for internal capital construction and welfare. Sales of finished goods and semi-finished products in current period are taken into account regardless whether the production is in the same period. Gross output value of industry is based on output of products while sales value of industry is based on sales of products.

Original Value of Fixed Assets refers to the total value of fixed assets calculated at the cost paid for purchase, installation, reconstruction, expansion, innovation and replacement of the fixed assets, which is normally classified into expenses on purchase, package, transportation, and installation.

Net Value of Fixed Assets is obtained by deducting cumulative depreciation over years from the original value of fixed assets.

New Products refers to new products using new technological principal, new designing ideas or be improved than old products in structure, materials or technology, and so improve production performance or exploited using function.

Delivery Value of Exports refers to value of products which delivered to foreign trade department or self exported(including selled to Hongkong, Macao and Taiwan) by industrial enterprises, and batch selled at exchange prices, batch exported within country or at border, also including value of sample from foreigners, materials received processing, scripts received assembling and compensation trade.

Retail Sales of Self-selling Industrial Products refers to retails sales of products which directly selled to residents(including staff and workers of enterprises) and social groups by manufacturing production units of various ownership.

The Main Financial Indexes and Economic Efficiency Indexes of Industrial Enterprises

1. Total Equity Capital refers to capital of an enterprise registered in Administrative Bureau for Industry and Commerce, which includes the state equity capital, the legal entity equity capital, individuals equity capital, foreign equity capital and collective equity capital.

State equity capital refers to the equity capital formed with the state-owned assets input by government departments or organizations that have the right to invest on behalf of the state. As long as the equity capital formed with the state-owned assets, it belongs to state equity capital, regardless which government department or organization the investor is.

Legal entity equity capital refers to the equity capital formed with the legal assets of a company or organization.

Individual equity capital is the equity capital formed with the legal individual assets from outside persons or internal employees.

Foreign equity capital is the equity capital formed with the legal assets from foreign parties, including parties or investors from Hong Kong, Macao and Taiwan.

Collective equity capital is the equity capital formed with the legal assets from collective enterprises.

2. Total Assets refers to all assets owned or controlled by an enterprises, including current assets, long-term investment, fixed assets, intangible assets and deferred assets, other long-term assets, and deferred taxes, etc. The summation of above items is equal to total assets shown in the balance sheet of the enterprise.

(1) current assets (working capital) refer to assets which can be cashed in or consumed in one year or an operating cycle over one year, including cash, all kinds of deposits, short term investment, receivable, advance payment, inventory, etc..

(2) Fixed assets refer to the total net value of fixed assets, clearance of fixed assets, project under construction, fixed assets losses in suspense. These are corporations' fund holdings.

(3) Intangible assets refer to the assets without physical form used by enterprises over a long time, such as patents, know-how, trade marks, copyright, usufruct of land, good-will, etc..

3. Total Liabilities refers to the debts that enterprises are responsible for repayment, including liquid liabilities, long-term liabilities and deferred taxes, etc. Total liabilities correspond to the summation item of liabilities shown in the balance sheets of the enterprises.

(1) Current liabilities refer to enterprises total debt payable within one year or an operating cycle over one year, including short term loans, payables and advance receipts, wages payable, taxes payable and profit payable, etc..

(2) Long-term liabilities refers to total debt payable within an operating cycle of one year or over one year, including long-term loans, long-term debts, long-term payables, etc..

4. Total Value of Profit and Tax (Pre-tax Profits) refers to the sum of the total net profits, products sales tax and surcharges and the value added tax payable of industrial enterprises, namely pre-tax profits.

5. Product Sales Income refers to the total income obtained by an enterprise via selling its products and providing industrial services.

6. Sales Cost of Industrial Products refers to actual cost of the products sold and the industrial services provided. etc..

7. Sales Tax and Surcharges of Products refers to the tax of city maintenance and construction, consumption tax, resources tax and extra charges for education, which levied on enterprises providing products and industrial services.

8. Sales Profit of Products refers to the profit earned by the enterprises after deducting cost, charges and taxes from the business income with selling products and providing industrial services.

9. Total Profits refer to the total profits gained by the enterprises.

10. Owners' Equity refers to investors' claim for net assets of the enterprise, which equals to the total assets of the enterprise minus its total liabilities, including the initial capital from investors, capital accumulation fund, surplus accumulation fund and undistributed profit. It is the share holders' equity in share holding companies.

11. Aggregate Index of Industrial Economic Efficiency is a special relative value for comprehensively measuring the overall levels in quantitative terms of the industrial economic efficiency from various aspects. It is also a total quantity index reflecting the economic performance quality of the industry. It is the result of the actual value of the industrial economic efficiency index divided by the national standard value in the same field and then multiplied by the weight. The formula is as follows:

$$\text{Aggregate index of industrial economic deficiency (\%)} = \left(\frac{\text{Value of an economic deficiency index}}{\text{National standard value in the same field}} \times \text{weight}\right)(\text{overall weight})$$

12. Sales Rate of Industrial Products refers to the ratio of the sales value of industry to the gross industrial output value in the same period. The formula is as follows:

$$\text{Sales Rate of Industrial Products (\%)} = \frac{\text{Sales value of industry}}{\text{Gross industrial output value}} \times 100\%$$

13. Ratio of Profit and Tax to Capital in Industry refers to the ratio of the total realized profits and taxes to total assets（net fixed assets plus working capital）, often expressed as pre-tax profit earned per 10000 yuan capital, which reflects the utilization efficiency of the assets and is calculated as follows:

$$\text{Ratio of Profit and Tax to Capital in Industry (\%)} = \frac{\text{Total realized pre-tax profit}}{\text{Average current assets} + \text{Average net value of fixed assets}} \times 100\%$$

14. Value Added Rate of industry refers to the ratio of value added of industry to the gross output value in the same period, which reflects the economic efficiency of productive consumption and is calculated as follows:

$$\text{Value Added Rate of industry (\%)} = \frac{\text{Value Added of Industry}}{\text{Gross industrial Output Value}} \times 100\%$$

15. Ratio of Profits to Total Industrial Costs refers to the ratio of profits realized to the total costs occurred in the same period, which reflects the economic efficiency of input in costs and expenses and is calculated as follows:

$$\text{Ratio of Profits to Total Industrial Costs (\%)} = \frac{\text{Total Profits}}{\text{Total Costs}} \times 100\%$$

16. Overall Labor Productivity of Industrial Enterprises refers to the average output per staff and worker in industrial enterprises in value terms within a given period, which reflects comprehensively the technological level, the management level, the skills and initiatives of the staff or workers. At present, the overall labor productivity is gotten via dividing the value added by the average number of staff and workers of an industrial enterprises in a given period. The formula:

$$\text{Overall Labor Productivity (yuan/person)} = \frac{\text{Value Added of Industry}}{\text{Average Number of Staff and Workers}}$$

17. Current Assets Turnover refers to times of the current assets turnover in a given period, which reflects the speed of the turnover of current assets and is calculated as follows:

$$\text{Current Assets Turnover (time)} = \frac{\text{Product Sales Income}}{\text{Average Balance of Circulating Assets}}$$

18. Ratio of Pre-tax Profits to Sales Revenue refers to the ratio of the total amount of pre-tax profits（including total profits, products sales tax and surcharges as well as the value added tax payable）to the total sales revenue in the same period. The formula is as follows:

$$\text{Ratio of Pre-tax Profits to Sales Revenue (\%)} = \frac{\text{Total Pre-tax Profits}}{\text{Total Sales Revenue}} \times 100\%$$

19. Current Ratio refers to how many times of the current assets can cover the current liabilities. The formula is as follows:

$$\text{Current Ratio} = \frac{\text{Total Current Assets}}{\text{Total Current Liabilities}}$$

20. Quick Ratio reflects to the capability of an enterprise to repay its current liabilities immediately. The equation is as follows:

$$\text{Quick Ratio} = \frac{\text{Total Quick Assets}}{\text{Total Current Liabilities}}$$

Note: Quick Assets is the more liquid part of current assets, usually equals to the sum of cash, short-term securities and receivable.

21. Debt - Asset Ratio refers to the proportion of debts as an enterprise's total assets, which reflects the enterprise's capability in utilizing debts for operation and also to what extent the interest of the creditors be protected at the expiration. The formula:

$$\text{Debt - Asset Ratio} = \frac{\text{Total Debt}}{\text{Total Assets}}$$

22. EBIT to Total Assets reflects the profitability of total assets, depending on performance in various aspects of an enterprise, therefore, became a central indicators for evaluate an enterprise. The formula:

$$\text{EBIT to Total Assets} = \frac{\text{Net profit} + \text{Total tax} + \text{Interest payment}}{\text{Average total Assets}} \times 100\%$$

23. Ratio of Capital Increment and Preservation refers to the change of owner's net assets,and presents corporations' strength.The formula：

$$\text{Capital Increment and Preservation Ratio} = \frac{\text{Owner's Capital of the end of Reference Period}}{\text{Owner's Capital of the previous end of Reference Period}}$$

北京统计年鉴——2001

BEIJING STATISTICAL YEARBOOK

能源生产与消费

7

ENERGY PRODUCTION AND CONSUMPTION

7-1 能 源 消 费 总 量
TOTAL CONSUMPTION OF ENERGY

单位：万吨标准煤 (10000 tons of SCE)

项目	Item	2000		1999	
		数量 Quantity	构成(%) Composition(%)	数量 Quantity	构成(%) Composition(%)
合 计	**Total**	**4211.5**	**100.0**	**3895.6**	**100**
第一产业	Primary Industry	104.9	2.5	86.9	2.2
第二产业	Secondary Industry	2565.9	60.9	2498.4	64.1
# 工业	Industry	2497.5	59.3	2436.2	62.5
第三产业	Tertiary Industry	1007.2	23.9	923.1	23.7
# 交通邮电	Transportation,Posts and Telecommunications	313.1	7.4	283.0	7.3
生活消费	Living Consumption	533.5	12.7	477.2	12.2
城 镇	Urban	388.1	9.2	330.5	8.5
农 村	Rural	145.4	3.5	146.6	3.8

注：电力、热力按等价热值折算标准煤，其他能源品种均按其当量热值折算标准煤，以下各表同。

Note: The coefficient for conversion of electricity and heat into SCE(standard coal) is calculated on equivalent heat and other energy conversed to SCE according to calorific value(the followings are the same) .

7-2 能 源 生 产 量
PRODUCTION OF ENERGY

项目		Item		2000	1999	2000年为1999年% 2000 as % of 1999
一次能源	**(吨标煤)**	**Primary Energy**	**(ton of SCE)**	**523.7**	**595.6**	**87.9**
原 煤	(万吨)	Coal	(10000 tons)	690.0	792.1	87.1
水 电	(亿千瓦时)	Hydropower	(100 million kwh)	9.1	9.4	96.8
二次能源	**(吨标煤)**	**Secondary Energy**	**(ton of SCE)**	**2461.6**	**2156.8**	**114.1**
洗 精 煤	(万吨)	Clean Coal	(10000 tons)		25.8	
其他洗煤	(万吨)	Other Clean Coal	(10000 tons)		3.8	
煤 制 品	(万吨)	Coal Products	(10000 tons)	4.9	10.4	47.1
焦 炭	(万吨)	Coke	(10000 tons)	402.1	395.7	101.6
焦炉煤气	(亿立方米)	Coking Gas	(100 million cu.m)	18.4	17.3	106.4
其他煤气	(亿立方米)	Other Gas	(100 million cu.m)	1.7	3.0	56.7
汽 油	(万吨)	Gasoline	(10000 tons)	146.2	124.3	117.6
柴 油	(万吨)	Diesel Oil	(10000 tons)	183.9	170.1	108.1
燃 料 油	(万吨)	Fuel Oil	(10000 tons)	78.6	75.5	104.1
液化石油气	(万吨)	Liquefied Petroleum	(10000 tons)	40.0	35.6	112.4
炼厂干气	(万吨)	Gas of Plant	(10000 tons)	16.8	18.1	92.8
其他石油制品	(万吨)	Other Petroleum Products	(10000 tons)	209.9	223.3	94.0
其他焦化产品	(万吨)	Other Coking Products	(10000 tons)	21.4	21.0	101.9
热 力	(万百万千焦)	Heat	(10 billion kilo-joules)	8758.8	7885.4	111.1
电 力	(亿千瓦时)	Electricity	(100 million kwh)	180.7	164.9	109.6

7-3 能源平衡表（实物量）（简表）

单位：万吨

项目	Item	原煤 Coal	洗精煤 Clean Coal	其他洗煤 Other Washing Coal	煤制品 Coal Products	焦炭 Coke	焦炉煤气（亿立方米） Coking Gas (100 million cu.m)	其它煤气（亿立方米） Other Gas (100 million cu.m)	原油 Crude Oil
可供本地区消费的能源量	**Total Energy Available for Consumption**	**2068.44**	**569.80**	**8.85**		**46.45**			**755.20**
加工转换投入(-)产出(+)量	**Input(-) or Output(+) in Processing and Transformation**	**-922.96**	**-543.83**	**-3.16**	**4.94**	**398.43**	**16.99**	**0.12**	**-694.68**
火力发电	Thermal Power	-707.09		-2.28			-0.23		-0.26
供　　热	Heating	-205.62		-0.88			-1.16		
洗选煤	Washing-dressing Coal								
炼　　焦	Coking		-543.83			402.07	17.75	-1.54	
炼　　油	Petroleum Refining								-694.42
制　　气	Gas Production	-5.47				-3.64	0.63	1.66	
# 焦炭再投入量(-)	Coke Re-input(-)								
煤制品加工	Coal Products Processing	-4.78			4.94				
损 失 量	**Losses**						**1.26**		**3.95**
# 运输和输配损失	in Transportation and Transmission						1.26		3.95
终端消费量	**Final Consumption**	**1237.79**	**5.8**	**5.79**	**4.94**	**445.4**	**15.01**	**0.02**	**56.08**
第一产业	Primary Industry	44.64							
农、林、牧、渔业	Farming, Forestry, Animal Husbandry and Fishery	44.64							
第二产业	Secondary Industry	692.13	5.80	5.79	0.51	445.44	11.30	0.02	56.08
工　业	Industry	683.08	5.80	5.79	0.51	445.44	11.30	0.02	56.08
# 用作原料、材料	use in Materials	11.71		5.71		13.71			56.00
建 筑 业	Construction	9.05							
第三产业	Tertiary Industry	212.45					2.01		
# 交通运输、仓储及邮电通迅业	Transportation, Storage, Posts and Telecommunications	22.45							
生活消费	Residential Consumption	288.57			4.43		1.70		
城　　镇	Urban	123.57			4.43		1.70		
乡　　村	Rural	165.00							
平衡差额	Balance	-92.31	20.17	-0.10		-0.56	0.72	0.10	0.49
消费量合计	**Total Energy Consumption**	**2160.75**	**549.63**	**8.95**	**4.94**	**449.08**	**17.66**	**1.56**	**754.71**

ENERGY BALANCE(ABRIDGED EDITION)

(10000 tons)

汽油 Gasoline	煤油 Kerosene	柴油 Diesel Fuel Oil	燃料油 Fuel Oil	液 化 石油气 Liquefied Petroleum	炼厂干气 Net Gas of Plant	天然气 (亿立方米) Natural Gas (100 million cu.m)	其它石油制品 Other Petroleum Products	其它焦化产品 Other Coking Products	热力 (万百万千焦) Heat (10000 million kilo-joule)	电力 (亿千瓦时) Electricity (100 million kwh)	其它能源 (万吨标准煤) Others (10000 tons of SCE)	合计 (万吨标准煤) Total (10000 tons of SCE)
-24.30	**116.22**	**-100.50**	**11.04**	**-8.49**		**10.97**	**-19.86**	**-1.41**		**204.94**	**175.57**	**4201.9**
146.2		**183.35**	**17.03**	**39.96**	**10.9**	**-3.70**	**198.44**	**21.37**	**8758.82**	**180.73**	**-42.41**	**377.17**
												-35.46
		-0.50	-18.04							180.73	-19.00	
		-0.07	-38.45		-5.86	-3.70	-11.49		8758.82		-23.41	
								21.18				-25.18
146.20		183.92	78.55	39.96	16.75		209.93					-1.99
			-5.03					0.19				-8.29
0.72		**0.57**		**1.16**		**1.38**			**335.00**	**34.14**		**162.26**
0.72		0.57		1.16		1.38			335.00	34.14		162.26
105.88	**117.6**	**80.03**	**28.10**	**27.83**	**10.9**	**5.81**	**180.98**	**19.77**	**8423.82**	**350.34**	**133.16**	**4013.81**
3.18		9.79								16.14		104.86
3.18		9.79								16.14		104.86
17.03	0.33	21.55	26.80	5.97	10.89	1.19	180.98	19.77	5109.27	172.33	133.16	2397.89
11.41	0.26	15.13	26.79	5.92	10.89	0.52	180.98	19.77	5109.27	161.76	133.16	2329.54
0.05			0.88				177.65	19.76				384.41
5.62	0.07	6.42	0.01	0.05		0.68				10.57		68.35
55.67	117.27	43.66	1.30	3.89		2.47			1968.14	114.22		977.5
8.80	117.27	25.68	0.60			0.43				11.41		283.42
30.00		5.03		17.97		2.15			1346.41	47.65		533.56
30.00		5.03		17.97		2.15			1346.41	38.54		388.15
										9.11		145.44
15.30	-1.38	2.25	-0.03	2.48		0.07	-2.40	0.19		1.19		-9.56
106.60	**117.60**	**81.17**	**89.62**	**28.99**	**16.75**	**10.90**	**192.47**	**19.77**	**8758.82**	**384.48**	**175.57**	**4211.53**

7-4 工业分行业能源终端消费量(实物量)

单位：万吨

项目	Item	原煤 Coal	洗精煤 Clean Coal	其他洗煤 Other Washing Coal	焦炭 Coke	焦炉煤气(亿立方米) Coking Gas (100 million cu.m)	其他煤气(亿立方米) Other Gas (100 million cu.m)	原油 Crude Oil
工业	**Industry**	**683.08**	**5.80**	**5.79**	**445.44**	**11.30**	**0.02**	**56.08**
轻工业	Light Industry	122.10			0.18	0.08		
重工业	High Industry	560.98	5.80	5.79	445.26	11.22	0.02	56.08
采掘业	**Excavation**	**12.10**			**0.05**			
煤炭采选业	Coal Mining and Dressing	9.62						
石油和天然气开采	Petroleum and Natural Gas Extraction							
黑色金属矿采选业	Ferrous Metals Mining and Dressing	1.20						
有色金属矿采选业	Nonferrous Metals Mining and Dressing							
非金属矿采选业	Nonmetal Minerals Mining and Dressing	1.28						
其他矿采选业	Other Minerals Mining and Dressing				0.05			
木材及竹材采运业	Timber and Bamboo Cutting and Shipping							
制造业	**Manufacturing**	**647.05**	**5.80**	**5.79**	**445.39**	**11.30**	**0.02**	**56.08**
食品加工业	Food Processing	9.23						
食品制造业	Food Making	17.60			0.09	0.03		0.08
饮料制造业	Beverage Making	30.28						
烟草加工业	Tobacco Processing	1.38						
纺织业	Textile Industry	17.72				0.01		
服装及其他纤维制品制造业	Garments and Other Fiber Products	9.33						
皮革、毛皮、羽绒及其制品业	Leather,Furs,Down and Related Products	1.40						
木材加工及竹、藤、棕、草制品业	Timber Processing,Bamboo,Cane,Palm Fiber and Straw Products	1.47						
家具制造业	Furniture Manufacturing	2.96						
造纸及纸制品业	Papermaking and Paper Products	9.08						
印刷业、记录媒介的复制	Printing and Record Medium Re-produced	7.91				0.03		
文教体育用品制造业	Stationery,Educational and Sports Goods	1.10			0.07			
石油加工及炼焦业	Petroleum Processing and Coking Products	1.94						
化学原料及化学制品制造业	Raw Chemical Materials and Chemical Products	28.50	0.08	5.72	14.04	4.27		56.00
医药制造业	Medical and Pharmaceutical Products	9.79				0.01		
化学纤维制造业	Chemical Fibers	1.59						
橡胶制品业	Rubber Products	10.11						
塑料制品业	Plastic Products	5.92			0.06			
非金属矿物制品业	Nonmetal Mineral Products	242.47			1.45	0.27		
黑色金属冶炼及压延加工业	Smelting and Pressing of Ferrous Metals	155.47	5.72	0.06	423.65	6.51		
有色金属冶炼及压延加工业	Smelting and Pressing of Nonferrous Metals	1.89			0.36			
金属制品业	Metal Products	7.50			1.95	0.07		
普通机械制造业	Ordinary Machinery	11.31			3.08	0.02		
专用设备制造业	Equipment for Special Purpose	12.49			0.14	0.01		
交通运输设备制造业	Transportation Equipment	25.83			0.34	0.03	0.02	
武器弹药制造业	Weapon and Ammunition	3.53						
电气机械及器材制造	Electric Equipment and Machinery	9.19		0.01	0.13	0.02		
电子及通信设备制造	Electronic and Telecommunications	4.64				0.02		
仪器仪表及文化、办公用机械制造业	Instruments,Meters,Cultural and Office Machinery	3.30			0.01			
其他制造业	Other Manufacturing	2.12			0.02			
电力、煤气及水的生产和供应业	**Electricity,Gas and Water Production and Supply**	**23.93**						
电力、蒸汽、热水的生产和供应业	Electricity,Steam and Hot Water Production and Supply	23.29						
煤气生产和供应业	Gas Production and Supply	0.03						
自来水的生产和供应	Water Production and Supply	0.61						

ENERGY TERMINAL CONSUMPTION IN KIND OF INDUSTRY BY SECTOR

(10000 tons)

汽 油 Gasoline	煤 油 Kerosene	柴 油 Diesel Fuel Oil	燃料油 Fuel Oil	液 化 石油气 Liquefied Petroleum	炼 厂 干 气 Net Gas of Plant	天然气 (亿立方米) Natural Gas (100 million cu.m)	其 他 石油制品 Other Petroleum Products	其他焦 化产品 Other Coking Product	热 力 (万百万千焦) Heat (10 billion kilo-joule)	电 力 (亿千瓦时) Electricity (100 million kwh)	能源合计 (万吨 标准煤) Total (10000 tons of SCE)
11.41	**0.26**	**15.13**	**26.79**	**5.92**	**10.89**	**0.52**	**180.98**	**19.77**	**5109.27**	**161.76**	**2329.58**
3.51	0.05	2.36	0.57	0.20		0.05			351.31	17.17	167.42
7.90	0.21	12.77	26.22	5.72	10.89	0.47	180.98	19.77	4757.96	144.59	2162.16
0.29		**0.78**								**2.44**	**18.32**
0.22		0.22								1.64	12.91
0.02		0.13								0.54	2.88
0.05		0.03								0.01	0.14
		0.40								0.25	2.33
											0.05
10.57	**0.26**	**14.24**	**25.38**	**5.91**	**10.89**	**0.51**	**180.98**	**19.77**	**4974.21**	**128.05**	**2180.01**
0.41		0.19	0.10	0.01		0.01			4.62	1.31	12.22
0.52		1.31		0.16		0.01			30.61	1.81	22.93
0.51		0.14							27.42	2.09	30.09
										0.10	1.29
0.28	0.01	0.15		0.01					175.34	3.11	30.11
0.41		0.13				0.01			9.10	0.96	11.00
0.04									0.07	0.13	1.47
0.05		0.02							1.42	0.13	1.63
0.18		0.03								0.33	3.53
0.21	0.01	0.16	0.47						7.00	1.06	11.42
0.45	0.02	0.11				0.02			28.10	2.01	14.64
0.12		0.02							8.17	0.16	1.90
0.89	0.02	1.41	3.17	5.04	10.89		176.07		2615.73	16.36	443.99
0.75	0.01	0.37	4.38	0.26		0.10	4.12	10.50	800.61	15.94	255.22
0.19		0.06							43.98	0.90	11.99
0.02									15.54	0.55	3.59
0.14		0.02							1.01	0.84	10.14
0.30		0.31		0.01					1.73	1.48	10.18
1.18	0.09	3.04	3.27	0.15		0.21	0.79		56.10	14.91	239.32
0.49	0.01	4.36	13.43						789.27	45.70	900.67
0.05		0.12						9.26		0.72	16.40
0.72	0.01	0.18	0.20	0.18		0.01			1.41	2.19	17.09
0.50	0.03	0.35	0.01	0.01				0.01	72.36	2.30	22.85
0.43	0.01	0.51		0.02		0.03			54.40	2.65	21.70
0.77	0.02	0.69	0.25	0.01		0.01			142.93	3.47	38.22
0.03		0.12	0.08			0.05			11.85	0.52	5.60
0.46	0.01	0.27		0.03					36.92	1.57	14.48
0.25		0.09	0.02	0.01		0.04			26.61	3.94	18.78
0.12		0.04				0.01			10.55	0.57	4.99
0.10	0.01	0.04		0.01					1.36	0.24	2.59
0.55		**0.11**	**1.41**	**0.01**		**0.01**			**135.06**	**31.27**	**131.26**
0.34		0.09	1.41			0.01			133.60	28.79	121.93
0.14									1.46	0.07	0.53
0.07		0.02		0.01						2.41	8.79

7-5 平均每万元国内生产总值能源消费量
ENERGY CONSUMPTION PER 10000 YUAN GROSS DOMESTIC PRODUCT

项 目 Item				2000	1999
能源总消费量	**(吨标煤/万元)**	**Total**	**(ton of SCE/10000 yuan)**	**1.71**	**1.83**
煤 炭	(吨/万元)	Coal	(ton/10000 yuan)	1.11	1.22
电 力	(万千瓦时/万元)	Electricity	(10000 kwh/10000 yuan)	0.16	0.14
石 油	(吨/万元)	Petroleum	(ton/10000 yuan)	0.28	0.31

7-6 人均生活用能量
PER CAPITA ENERGY CONSUMPTION FOR NON-PRODUCTION PURPOSE

项 目 Item				2000	1999
人均生活用能量	**(千克标准煤)**	**Non-productive Consumption Per Capita**	**(kg of SCE)**	**482.1**	**433.8**
煤 炭	(千克)	Coal	(kg)	260.6	254.6
电 力	(千瓦时)	Electricity	(kwh)	430.3	324.2
液化石油气	(千克)	Liquefied Petroleum	(kg)	16.2	16.8
天 然 气	(立方米)	Natural Gas	(cu.m)	19.4	16.3
煤 气	(立方米)	Gas	(cu.m)	15.3	19.1

主 要 统 计 指 标 解 释

能源总消费量 指报告期内社会各行业和居民生活所消费的各种能源数量，是观察本地区能源消费水平、构成和发展速度的总量指标，能源总消费量包括终端能源消费量、加工转换损失量和损失量三部分。

一次能源生产量 指报告期内生产一次能源的企业将自然界现存的能源资源经过开采而产出的合格产品，主要包括原煤、原油、天然气、水电等。

二次能源生产量 指报告期内将一次能源经过各种加工转换设备生产出的另一种形式的各种合格的能源产品。如火电、热力、洗煤、焦碳、各种石油制品、焦炉煤气、城市煤气等。

工业终端消费量 又称最终消费量。它反映报告期内工业企业作为原料、燃料和动力消费的能源及其去向。它们的消费过程体现了能源消费的终止。不包括用于加工转换投入量、加工转换损失量和损失量。

平均每万元国内生产总值能源消费量 能源总消费量或分品种能源消费量与国内生产总值之比。

人均生活用能量 指用于生活消费的各种能源数量与人口总数之比。

Explanatory Notes On Main Statistical Indicators

Total Energy Consumption refers to the total consumption of all sectors and households in a given period. It is a comprehensive indicator to show the scale, composition and trend of energy consumption of some region. The total energy consumption can be divided into three parts: Final Energy Consumption, Loss During the Process of Energy Conversion and Loss.

Production Volume of Directly-use Energy refers to qualified products through excavation and production from energy source in stock of nature , mainly include coal, crude oil, natural gas, water and electricity and so on.

Production Volume of Indirectly-use Energy refers to qualified energy products in another form through pressing and changing-over from directly-use energy, such as thermal power, heat, clean coal, coke, petroleum products, coking gas, city gas and so on.

Terminal Consumption of Industry named final consumption, too. It reports energy consumped as raw materials, fuels and power by industrial enterprises and the direction that has gone. The process of consumption reflects the end of energy consumption, exclude input in pressing and changing-over, loss in pressing and changing-over and loss.

Energy Consumption Per 10000 yuan GDP refers to ratio of total consumption or consumption put into different categories to Gross Domestic Product(GDP).

Living Consumption of Energy Per Capita refers to ratio of living consumption to total population.

建筑业

8

CONSTRUCTION

独立核算建筑施工企业总产值 （单位：亿元）

Gross Output Value of Construction by Enterprises with Independent Accounting System (100 million yuan)

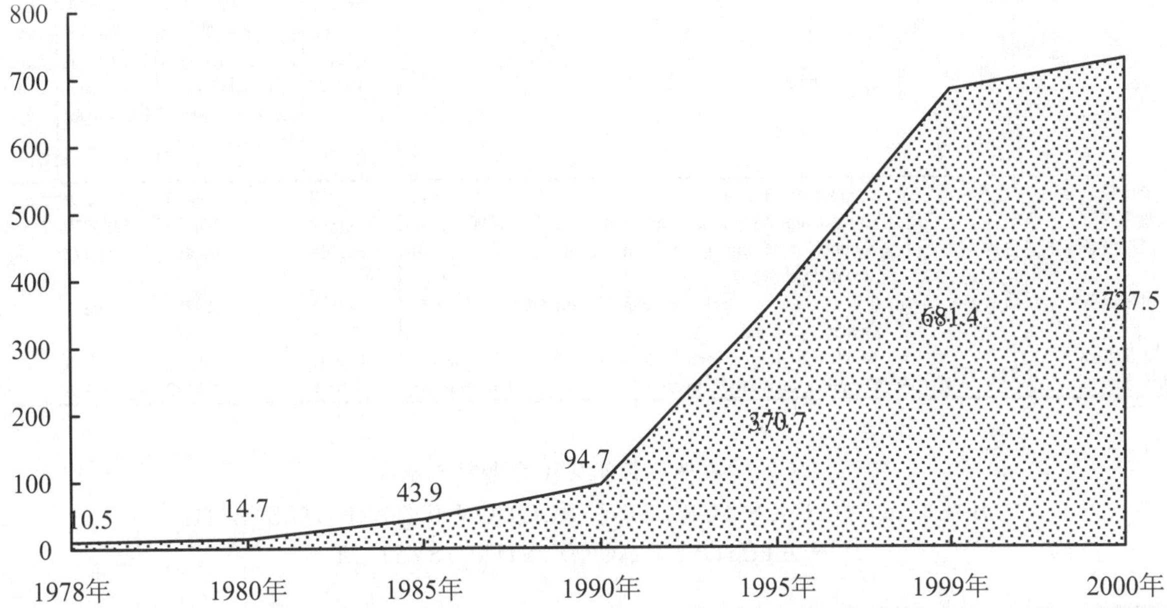

2000年独立核算建筑施工企业工程质量 （单位：%）

Project Quality of Enterprises with Independent Accounting System (%)

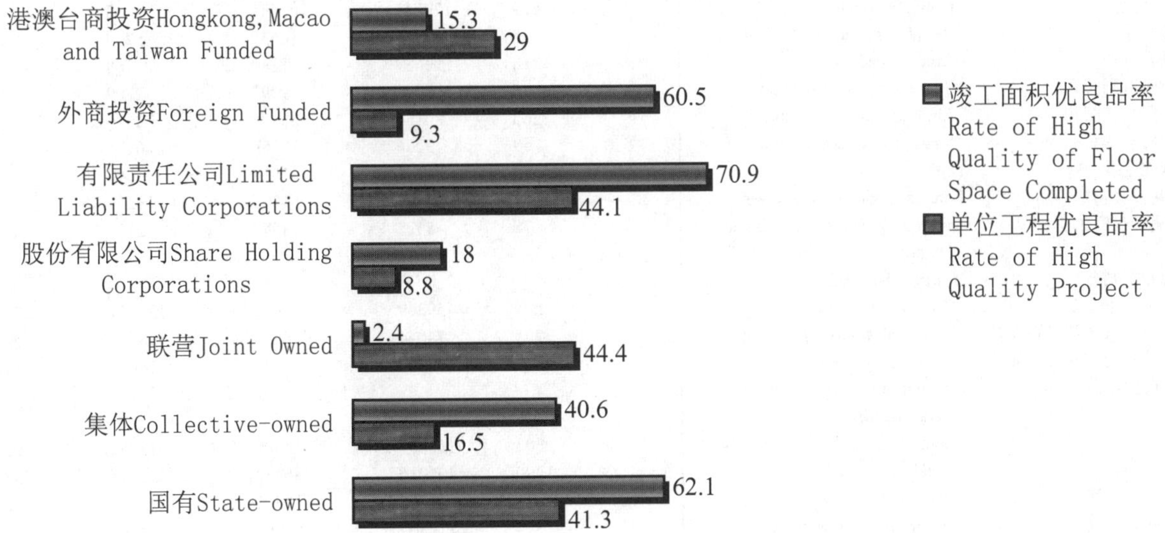

8-1 全市建筑施工企业主要经济指标
MAIN ECONOMIC INDICATORS ON CONSTRUCTION ENTERPRISES

项目 Item				全市总计 Total	独立核算建筑施工企业 Construction Enterprises with Independent Accounting System	#大中型企业 Large and Medium Enterprises	建筑业活动单位 Construction Units
企业单位数	(个)	Number of Enterprises	(unit)	1712	1697	262	15
建筑业总产值	(万元)	Gross Output Value of Construction	(10000 yuan)	7284899	7274774	5380970	10124
自有机械设备年末总台数	(台)	Number of Machinery and Equipment Owned(year-end)	(unit)	162765	162403	101472	362
自有机械设备年末总功率	(千瓦)	Total Power of Machinery and Equipment Owned (year-end)	(kw)	3392584	3378831	2429681	13753
年末从业人数	(人)	Number of Employment(year-end)	(person)	566592	566023	379738	569
劳动生产率	(元/人)	Overall Labor Productivity	(yuan/person)	88083	88132	101328	62924

8-2 独立核算建筑施工企业基本情况
BASIC STATISTICS FOR CONSTRUCTION ENTERPRISES WITH INDEPENDENT ACCOUNTING SYSTEM

项目	Item	企业单位数(个) Number of Enterprises (unit)	年末从业人员(人) Employment (year-end) (person)	年末自有机械设备 Machinery and Equipment Owned(year-end) 净值(万元) Net Value (10000 yuan)	总台数(台) Total Number (unit)	总功率(千瓦) Total Power (kw)
总计	**Total**	1697	566023	440441	162403	3378831
按企业登记注册类型分	**Grouped by Registration Status of Enterprises**					
内资企业	Domestic Investment Enterprises	1566	557204	432587	157011	3348244
国有企业	State-owned	342	259597	211420	64997	1590761
集体企业	Collective-owned	629	179743	101545	53832	940655
私营企业	Private Business	198	13554	10658	5270	44706
联营企业	Joint-owned	18	2089	1289	768	9318
股份有限公司	Share Holding Company	46	8040	9397	2709	75952
有限责任公司	Limited-Liability Company	265	80164	85406	22656	578586
股份合作企业	Share Holding Cooperative	58	9266	10259	6131	77705
其他企业	Others	10	4751	2614	648	30561
外商投资企业	Foreign Funded Enterprises	53	3497	4307	3257	22057
港澳台投资企业	HongKong,Macao and Taiwan Funded	78	5322	3547	2135	8530
按行业类别分	**Grouped by Sector**					
土木工程	Civil Engineering	875	459369	355919	125251	2784233
线路、管道和设备安装	Line and equipment Installation	275	74044	66698	23494	483801
建筑物的装修装饰业	Building Decoration	547	32610	17824	13658	110797
按隶属关系分	**Grouped by Administrative Relationship**					
中央	Central	207	161007	154689	38728	1039175
地方	Local	1490	405016	285752	123675	2339656
市属	City Owned	311	158704	135505	42788	962068
区县属	District and County Owned	314	112865	66062	38592	676537
街道	Subdistrict Owned	79	11526	4018	4011	49268
镇	Town Owned	176	47678	26358	14973	206004
其他	Others	610	74243	53810	23311	445779
按企业规模分	**Grouped by Size of Enterprises**					
大型	Large Enterprises	117	304105	251512	75460	1826528
中型	Medium Enterprises	139	75436	66292	25963	602502
小型	Small Enterprises	1435	186285	122593	60931	949150

8-3 独立核算建筑施工企业总产值和劳动生产率
GROSS OUTPUT VALUE AND LABOR PRODUCTIVITY OF CONSTRUCTION ENTERPRISES WITH INDEPENDENT ACCOUNTING SYSTEM

项目	Item	总产值(万元) Gross Output Value (10000 yuan)		劳动生产率(元/人) Overall Labor Productivity (yuan/person)	
		2000	1999	2000	1999
总计	**Total**	**7274774**	**6814102**	**88132**	**82465**
按企业登记注册类型分	**Grouped by Registration Status of Enterprises**				
内资企业	Domestic Investment Enterprises	7025721	6581812	86989	81553
国有企业	State-Owned	3259032	3529405	81639	85286
集体企业	Collective Owned	1576469	1536495	75625	62612
私营企业	Private	109687	54127	69731	64452
联营企业	Joint Owned	31722	20733	71349	59854
股份有限公司	Share Holding Company	120208	688383	87019	127750
有限责任公司	Limited-Liability Company	1629969	567657	109920	85908
股份合作企业	Share Holding Cooperative	206519	176854	173051	118186
其他企业	Others	92115	8158	159313	78520
外商投资企业	Foreign Funded	148083	131616	158768	123944
港、澳、台商投资企业	Hongkong,Macao and Taiwan Funded	100970	100675	119266	116671
按行业类别分	**Grouped by Sector**				
土木工程	Civil Engineering	5796962	5575647	83823	79339
线路、管道和设备安装	Line and Equipment Installation	1013877	896373	115594	103853
建筑物的装修装饰业	Building Decoration	463935	342082	100497	91879
按隶属关系分	**Grouped by Administrative Relationship**				
中央	Central	2108194	2067214	106794	96993
地方	Local	5166580	4746889	82266	77415
市属	City Owned	2726815	2588927	100648	89130
区县属	District and County Owned	1152469	1055742	83229	66063
街道	Subdistrict Owned	56495	71445	47631	43310
镇	Town Owned	443530	342141	39330	62881
其他	Others	787271	688634	83745	74854
按企业规模分	**Grouped by Size of Enterprises**				
大型	Large Enterprises	4511447	4249406	107704	94327
中型	Medium Enterprises	865611	919739	77415	72406
小型	Small Enterprises	1893804	1644958	64327	66120

8-4 独立核算建筑施工企业竣工率
RATIO OF COMPLETED OF CONSTRUCTION INDEPENDENT ACCOUNTING SYSTEM

单位：%　　(%)

项目	Item	产值竣工率 Ratio of Output Value Completed to Total		面积竣工率 Ratio of Floor Space of Building Completed	
		2000	1999	2000	1999
总计	**Total**	**66.8**	**69.0**	**38.8**	**38.6**
按企业登记注册类型分	**Grouped by Registratiaon Status of Enterprises**				
内资企业	Domestic Investment Enterprises	67.1	69.3	38.9	38.5
国有企业	State-Owned	72.4	71.7	39.4	38.7
集体企业	Collective Owned	66.3	70.4	44.8	49.2
私营企业	Private	64.0	63.0	54.3	54.1
联营企业	Joint Owned	64.0	67.8	43.1	45.3
股份有限公司	Share Holding Company	54.4	66.2	23.4	27.0
有限责任公司	Limited-Liability Company	60.2	60.1	31.9	23.2
股份合作企业	Share Holding Cooperative	66.3	55.2	53	41.0
其他企业	Others	34.6	99.4	22.8	100.0
外商投资企业	Foreign Funded	48.3	59.5	19.5	38.6
港、澳、台商投资企业	Hongkong,Macao and Taiwan Funded	72.6	62.3	61.2	71.1
按行业类别分	**Grouped by Sector**				
土木工程	Civil Engineering	68.4	69.9	38.5	38.5
线路、管道和设备安装	Line and Equipment Installation	57.6	68.5	65.2	41.1
建筑物的装修装饰业	Building Decoration	66.5	56.1	50.5	55.6
按隶属关系分	**Grouped by Administrative Relationship**				
中央	Central	66.0	71.4	36.3	37.2
地方	Local	67.1	68.0	39.5	39.0
市属	City Owned	66.6	67.9	33.4	31.0
区县属	District and County Owned	64.7	68.1	43.4	46.6
街道	Subdistrict Owned	74.0	79.5	39.9	63.2
镇	Town Owned	65.7	65.4	52.4	49.0
其他	Others	72.4	68.1	48.5	51.6
按企业规模分	**Grouped by Size of Enterprises**				
大型	Large Enterprises	64.2	65.7	34.6	34.6
中型	Medium Enterprises	71.0	68.0	40.7	39.6
小型	Small Enterprises	71.0	78.2	52.9	52.0

8-5 独立核算建筑施工企业工程质量
PROJECTS QUALITY OF CONSTRUCTION ENTERPRISES WITH INDEPENDENT ACCOUNTING SYSTEM

单位：% (%)

项目	Item	单位工程优良品率 Rate of High Quality Project		竣工面积优良品率 Rate of High Quality of Floor Space Completed	
		2000	1999	2000	1999
总计	**Total**	**25.6**	**18.7**	**55.3**	**49.2**
按企业登记注册类型分	**Grouped by Registration Stutus of Enterprises**				
内资企业	Domestic Investment Enterprises	25.7	18.7	55.4	49.1
国有企业	State-Owned	41.3	33.5	62.1	58.4
集体企业	Collective Owned	16.5	11.9	40.6	28.0
私营企业	Private	26.3	8.9	3.1	0.3
联营企业	Joint Owned	44.4	16.3	2.4	12.3
股份有限公司	Share Holding Company	8.8	20.8	18.0	70.3
有限责任公司	Limited-Liability Company	44.1	30.6	70.9	60.5
股份合作企业	Share Holding Cooperative	11.7	13.1	43.1	65.2
其他企业	Others	15.6			
外商投资企业	Foreign Funded	9.3	13.9	60.5	47.1
港、澳、台商投资企业	Hongkong,Macao and Taiwan Funded	29.0	22.6	15.3	61.2
按行业类别分	**Grouped by Sector**				
土木工程	Civil Engineering	30.1	26.7	55.8	49.2
线路、管道和设备安装	Line and Equipment Installation	21.5	12.1	36.2	35.2
建筑物的装修装饰业	Building Decoration	3.2	6.8	21.5	48.3
按隶属关系分	**Grouped by Administrative Relationship**				
中央	Central	50.9	39.4	67.9	62.5
地方	Local	20.2	14.0	51.6	44.8
市属	City Owned	29.4	20.4	71.4	66.9
区县属	District and County Owned	18.5	14.7	38.2	29.0
街道	Subdistrict Owned	8.6	10.5	18.7	37.6
镇	Town Owned	18.7	13.0	30.7	21.6
其他	Others	17.1	10.6	36.2	31.2
按企业规模分	**Grouped by Size of Enterprises**				
大型	Large Enterprises	41.9	46.6	68.2	62.0
中型	Medium Enterprises	15.1	18.6	50.8	41.2
小型	Small Enterprises	19.9	9.4	26.7	22.8

8-6 独立核算建筑施工企业主要财务指标

单位：万元

项目	Item	资产总计 Total Assets	流动资产 合计 Total Circulating Assets	#货币资金 Cash	#应收帐款 Accounts Receivable	#存货 Stock
总计	**Total**	**10864580**	**8588493**	**1153147**	**2964033**	**2413283**
按企业登记注册类型分	**Grouped by Registration Status of Enterprises**					
内资企业	Domestic Investment	10562641	8326943	1087843	2906798	2354475
国有企业	State-Owned	6290436	4863943	618262	1769527	1214189
集体企业	Collective Owned	1534264	1211708	227193	274923	497430
私营企业	Private	118341	86439	16251	23301	30387
联营企业	Joint Owned	74039	61311	8380	22839	12179
股份有限公司	Share Holding Company	237049	197207	22834	43418	80620
有限责任公司	Limited-Liability Company	2007268	1665340	155074	698411	438091
股份合作企业	Share Holding Cooperative	179226	134889	18615	39265	52138
其他企业	Others	122017	106108	21234	35114	29441
外商投资企业	Foreign Funded	131814	108238	35761	12308	26365
港、澳、台商投资企业	Hongkong,Macao and Taiwan Funded	170126	153311	29542	44927	32443
按行业类别分	**Grouped by Sector**					
土木工程	Civil Engineering	8498059	6782089	772105	2595397	1859781
线路、管道和设备安装	Line and Equipment Installation	1845417	1392820	298369	290667	423024
建筑物的装修装饰业	Building Decoration	521104	413583	82673	77968	130477
按隶属关系分	**Grouped by Administrative Relationship**					
中央	Central	3135268	2333273	382281	920818	456918
地方	Local	7729313	6255220	770865	2043215	1956365
市属	City Owned	5152223	4229627	417723	1532451	1194706
区县属	District and County Owned	1065071	823957	110448	230303	303824
街道	Subdistrict Owned	95700	83620	11911	19127	38999
镇	Town Owned	375258	278782	41448	100434	96668
其他	Others	1041062	839235	189336	160901	322168
按企业规模分	**Grouped by Size of Enterprises**					
大型	Large Enterprises	7226040	5619527	637036	2156109	1438079
中型	Medium Enterprises	1326354	1101228	162761	375521	325844
小型	Small Enterprises	2307847	1863576	352575	432251	647756

MAIN FINANCIAL INDICATORS FOR CONSTRUCTION ENTERPRISES WITH INDEPENDENT ACCOUNTING SYSTEM

(10000 yuan)

#在建工程 under Construction	长期投资 Long-term Investment	固定资产合计 Total Fixed Assets	固定资产原价合计 Original Value of Fixed Assets	#生产经营用 for Production Use	累计折旧 Accumulative Depreciation	#本年折旧 of this Year	专项工程 Special Projects	无形及递延资产合计 Intangible and Deffered Assets	#无形资产 Intangible
987501	**684330**	**1244720**	**1888611**	**1309412**	**664101**	**106035**	**183746**	**86965**	**55784**
957378	680068	1220613	1848301	1283923	647317	102634	181207	82152	52164
473511	476231	738692	1128677	744118	402230	62888	134055	34648	24512
161419	63798	224113	319182	222021	97704	16127	15806	13698	7410
8543	3691	24952	31216	22261	6585	1890	2096	789	28
5919	827	8295	11147	7499	2851	491	199	2985	2959
14069	15975	19274	24659	15437	5353	1399	3043	1394	832
261602	110328	169938	280642	237306	115060	17812	20047	22201	13791
30058	7426	28715	39781	25106	11090	1259	2069	3412	2144
2257	1794	6634	12998	10175	6446	769	3891	3024	489
11730	1682	14324	22365	11695	8566	1849	2500	1353	727
18392	2579	9783	17945	13793	8217	1553	39	3460	2893
741080	538258	948238	1441288	1011547	510746	82495	110930	58104	38025
185123	125899	227887	354951	234914	128912	18028	69926	18047	10977
61298	20173	68595	92373	62950	24443	5512	2890	10815	6782
256780	239200	462740	724750	496985	271284	41750	56315	15758	9760
730720	445130	781980	1163861	812427	392817	64285	127431	71208	46024
453649	343606	414536	653792	463287	246997	37581	95933	34510	24605
136054	36168	166102	231149	157869	66615	11549	14787	21350	13943
26946	1708	8653	15540	11338	6977	951	952	404	279
16652	12179	66047	86895	61060	21661	4317	6745	9743	4914
97420	51468	126642	176486	118873	50568	9887	9014	5201	2282
556663	568684	783090	1219453	847352	451548	65783	151224	54499	36769
172048	37679	155364	233243	161544	79616	16240	14274	10125	5149
257587	77966	306131	435746	300396	132905	23986	18249	22299	13866

8-6 续表1 continued

单位：万元

项 目	Item	其他资产合计 Other Assets	负债合计 Total Liability	流动负债合计 Total Circulating Liability	#短期借款 Short-term Loans	#应付帐款 Accounts Payable
总 计	**Total**	76327	8275634	7822187	1187742	2098540
按企业登记注册类型分	**Grouped by Registration Status of Enterprises**					
内资企业	Domestic Investment	71658	8097565	7646866	1170821	2039065
国有企业	State-Owned	42867	5043366	4676394	722058	1217288
集体企业	Collective Owned	5141	1021754	1011024	134873	255522
私营企业	Private	375	52884	49041	6441	15651
联营企业	Joint Owned	423	55641	54615	6417	11472
股份有限公司	Share Holding Company	156	145797	121764	32875	28985
有限责任公司	Limited-Liability Company	19414	1550784	1510592	247367	438628
股份合作企业	Share Holding Cooperative	2715	121277	117722	15996	32074
其他企业	Others	566	106063	105715	4795	39445
外商投资企业	Foreign Funded	3716	75531	74776	10719	16672
港、澳、台商投资企业	Hongkong,Macao and Taiwan Funded	953	102538	100544	6203	42803
按行业类别分	**Grouped by Sector**					
土木工程	Civil Engineering	60441	6595498	6267676	1080810	1782102
线路、管道和设备安装	Line and Equipment Installation	10839	1394511	1279867	73457	251774
建筑物的装修装饰业	Building Decoration	5048	285625	274643	33475	64664
按隶属关系分	**Grouped by Administrative Relationship**					
中 央	Central	27982	2445609	2266712	279209	646868
地 方	Local	48345	5830024	5555475	908533	1451672
市 属	City Owned	34011	4161247	3922277	675577	984300
区县属	District and County Owned	2707	716177	696088	112966	233223
街 道	Subdistrict Owned	362	70237	69611	1454	24359
镇	Town Owned	1763	209149	202599	56920	72119
其 他	Others	9501	673215	664900	61616	137671
按企业规模分	**Grouped by Size of Enterprises**					
大 型	Large Enterprises	49016	5721228	5319192	928393	1352697
中 型	Medium Enterprises	7685	1021459	998961	91145	324620
小 型	Small Enterprises	19626	1530407	1501494	168182	421087

8-6 续表2 continued

(10000 yuan)

长期负债合计 Total Long-term Liability	#长期借款 Long-term Loans	所有者权益合计 Ownership Interest	实收资本 Contributed Capital	国家资本 State	集体资本 Collective	法人资本 Institutionnal Units	个人资本 Individuals	港澳台资本 Hongkong, Macao and Taiwan	外商资本 Foreign	工程结算收入 Revenue of Settlement of Projects
453447	161868	2588947	1776282	702209	356968	528473	129685	33142	25806	7069836
450699	159736	2465075	1658718	690214	353273	485577	129655			6771875
366972	112993	1247070	767357	610351		157006				3497059
10730	6326	512510	353859		310051	43808				1246990
3843	3272	65458	57407			24594	32812			91275
1026	280	18399	12771	8476	2425	1870				28356
24033	22352	91252	80561	2590	3188	65483	9300			107835
40193	12287	456484	332204	68687	19289	172601	71627			1581545
3555	2227	57949	43793	110	17320	10446	15916			165506
348		15954	10768		1000	9768				53309
754	480	56283	50672	3645	1957	19033		231	25806	159182
1993	1653	67588	66893	8349	1739	23864	30	32911		138779
327822	123352	1902562	1266576	533458	291327	366252	57583	8232	9725	5615898
114644	33256	450906	291050	136794	43951	88203	18032	3570	500	1026690
10982	5260	235479	218657	31957	21690	74019	54070	21339	15582	427249
178898	70567	689658	470985	350274	7933	94398	5137	7948	5295	2298404
274549	91302	1899288	1305297	351934	349035	434076	124548	25193	20511	4771432
238970	69055	990976	616676	265794	33778	263317	32738	10352	10697	2760139
20089	11584	348894	257536	79291	110232	41719	19702	2225	4367	886366
626	331	25463	19723		16542	2504	207	156	315	57340
6550	5268	166109	108908	40	67595	30571	9358	99	1245	372496
8315	5064	367847	302454	6809	120888	95965	62543	12361	3887	695091
402036	138127	1504812	941625	503733	130041	278290	25245	698	3618	4448374
22498	8768	304896	211420	62936	51591	74381	15435	3599	3478	858790
28912	14974	777440	621400	135539	175336	174890	88205	28844	18585	1759028

8-6 续表3 continued

单位：万元

项目	Item	工程结算成本 Cost of Settlement of Projects	工程结算税金及附加 Tax and Extra Charges of Settlement of Projects	工程结算利润 Profits of Settlement of Projects	其他业务收入 Revenue of Other Business	其他业务利润 Profits of Other Business
总计	**Total**	**6121176**	**212745**	**735915**	**569644**	**91008**
按企业登记注册类型分	**Grouped by Registration Status of Enterprises**					
内资企业	Domestic Investment	5859526	204595	707754	567013	90068
国有企业	State-Owned	3060032	105193	331834	474310	70366
集体企业	Collective Owned	1063984	40569	142437	12036	3739
私营企业	Private	75194	3117	12965	1472	537
联营企业	Joint Owned	24539	916	2901	200	225
股份有限公司	Share Holding Company	83497	3629	20710	26237	3571
有限责任公司	Limited-Liability Company	1364124	43491	173930	43408	10527
股份合作企业	Share Holding Cooperative	142409	5962	17135	1254	936
其他企业	Others	45747	1720	5843	8095	167
外商投资企业	Foreign Funded	137503	3941	17738	197	185
港、澳、台商投资企业	Hongkong,Macao and Taiwan Funded	124146	4210	10423	2434	756
按行业类别分	**Grouped by Sector**					
土木工程	Civil Engineering	4879472	169327	567099	511269	79367
线路、管道和设备安装	Line and Equipment Installation	876083	30672	119935	51763	9606
建筑物的装修装饰业	Building Decoration	365620	12747	48882	6612	2035
按隶属关系分	**Grouped by Administrative Relationship**					
中央	Central	2039648	66088	192668	146735	11217
地方	Local	4081528	146657	543247	422909	79791
市属	City Owned	2364101	81384	314654	398841	69229
区县属	District and County Owned	766851	28541	90974	8675	5760
街道	Subdistrict Owned	48205	1908	7227	899	211
镇	Town Owned	311642	12612	48242	4003	1934
其他	Others	590728	22212	82150	10490	2657
按企业规模分	**Grouped by Size of Enterprises**					
大型	Large Enterprises	3866766	131399	450209	503570	74477
中型	Medium Enterprises	744125	26939	87727	23994	9151
小型	Small Enterprises	1507172	54287	197569	42080	7336

8-6 续表4 continued

(10000 yuan)

管理费用 Overhead Cost	税金 Taxes	财产保险费 Premium of Property	劳动待业保险费 Premium for Employment	财务费用 Financial Expense	#利息支出 Interest Expenditure	营业利润 Operating Profits	投资收益 Investment Income	营业外收入 Out-business Income	营业外支出 Out-business Expenditure	利润总额 Total Profits
608811	**9408**	**2803**	**71593**	**64809**	**53145**	**153304**	**10114**	**30830**	**24617**	**163561**
583061	9244	2632	71229	64453	53124	150308	10100	30210	24140	160389
329636	4137	1413	48737	35197	27315	37367	7422	23649	18669	46722
87101	3465	867	2248	6812	5555	52263	1436	2400	2428	52794
10931	261	14	78	122	49	2449	26	162	93	2622
2647	28	18	404	27	23	452		244	7	692
11283	100	40	173	2119	2028	10878	311	54	48	11134
125269	1118	240	18537	19213	17312	39975	584	2304	2222	38632
11365	77	17	146	880	817	5825	300	1358	515	6754
4828	60	23	907	83	26	1099	21	40	159	1040
13617	87	94	95	244	-21	4061		249	340	4096
12133	77	77	269	111	43	-1066	13	370	138	-924
449979	7299	2120	60611	62829	52823	133659	4602	19946	15988	138303
113690	1689	504	10001	565	-816	15286	5506	7029	8179	20426
45143	420	179	981	1415	1138	4360	6	3855	450	4831
162843	1766	490	22505	15745	12177	25297	1553	5154	7974	25874
445968	7642	2314	49088	49064	40968	128007	8561	25676	16644	137687
291337	3381	1202	44304	37832	32656	54714	6623	16821	12544	61809
64700	1504	391	3808	5436	4348	26599	263	1803	2327	26376
6774	228	31	223	-21	-13	685	51	74	85	723
22504	1903	521	70	3571	2292	24102	3	1546	185	24835
60653	626	169	683	2246	1686	21908	1621	5433	1502	23944
381845	5067	1287	56462	53963	44836	88878	7167	17543	19520	92908
72397	1524	701	9288	3970	3459	20511	618	5486	1899	21769
154186	2816	815	5839	6881	4854	43839	2330	7801	3198	48809

8-6 续表5 continued

单位：万元

项目 Item		应交所得税 Income Tax Payable	转作奖金的利润 Profits Distributed as Bonus	提取盈余公积 Surplus Accumulation Funds Drawn	应付利润 Profits Payable	# 已分配股利 Divided Payment
总计	**Total**	**53149**	**3400**	**34774**	**24945**	**5670**
按企业登记注册类型分	**Grouped by Registration Status of Enterprises**					
内资企业	Domestic Investment	51483	3647	34110	23115	5305
国有企业	State-Owned	16438	162	18041	4963	4
集体企业	Collective Owned	15381	3092	10322	7973	718
私营企业	Private	953	24	717	142	49
联营企业	Joint Owned	190		196	41	
股份有限公司	Share Holding Company	2142		115	680	678
有限责任公司	Limited-Liability Company	13623	250	3595	8605	3833
股份合作企业	Share Holding Cooperative	1940	119	636	308	23
其他企业	Others	817		488	404	
外商投资企业	Foreign Funded	1297	-247	481	1316	24
港、澳、台商投资企业	Hongkong,Macao and Taiwan Funded	369		183	514	341
按行业类别分	**Grouped by Sector**					
土木工程	Civil Engineering	41101	3071	28391	18509	4576
线路、管道和设备安装	Line and Equipment Installation	8696	324	4715	3386	625
建筑物的装修装饰业	Building Decoration	3352	6	1667	3051	469
按隶属关系分	**Grouped by Administrative Relationship**					
中央	Central	9420	-28	5709	3718	
地方	Local	43730	3428	29065	21227	5670
市属	City Owned	21520	235	15596	8013	2227
区县属	District and County Owned	7437	-59	5372	4538	1645
街道	Subdistrict Owned	389	15	179	483	
镇	Town Owned	6730	1440	4798	4364	881
其他	Others	7653	1798	3121	3830	917
按企业规模分	**Grouped by Size of Enterprises**					
大型	Large Enterprises	28256	290	20728	9439	1554
中型	Medium Enterprises	7572	355	5572	3798	963
小型	Small Enterprises	17279	2755	8460	11653	3107

8-6 续表6 continued

(10000 yuan)

未分配利润 Profits Undistributed	本年应付工资总额 Total Wages Payable in the Year	# 主营业务应付工资 Wage Payable of Major Business	本年应付福利费总额 Welfares Payable in the Year	# 主营业务应付福利费 of Major Business	建筑业增加值 Value Added of Construction	流动比率(%) Circulating Assets /Liquid Liabilities(%)	速动比率(%) Quick-circulating Assets /Liquid Lia-bilities(%)	资产负债率(%) Liabilities/ Total Assets (%)	存货周转率(%) Turnover Rate of Stock (%)	资本金利润率(%) Profits/ Capital (%)
55474	**718884**	**655229**	**78583**	**70724**	**1858248**	**1.10**	**0.79**	**0.76**	**2.91**	**0.09**
56550	704991	641700	76582	69003	1802513	1.09	0.78	0.77	2.86	0.10
1112	368461	329298	43305	37690	919615	1.04	0.78	0.80	2.86	0.06
37994	173649	161224	15123	14326	377304	1.20	0.71	0.67	2.34	0.15
743	12434	12131	987	949	31367	1.76	1.14	0.45	2.96	0.05
855	3019	2976	250	247	7961	1.12	0.90	0.75	2.14	0.05
1974	10423	9804	962	896	36709	1.62	0.96	0.62	1.53	0.14
9518	123770	113339	14048	13031	381008	1.10	0.81	0.77	3.77	0.12
3980	9398	9121	877	834	34414	1.15	0.70	0.68	3.16	0.15
375	3838	3808	1030	1030	14135	1.00	0.73	0.87	1.76	0.10
1656	6860	6596	962	888	31439	1.45	1.10	0.57	5.38	0.08
-2732	7033	6933	1039	833	24297	1.53	1.20	0.60	4.11	-0.01
43072	558598	503428	59917	53299	1440486	1.08	0.79	0.78	3.05	0.11
16516	128446	120584	15187	14076	314660	1.09	0.76	0.76	2.27	0.07
-4114	31840	31217	3479	3350	103102	1.51	1.03	0.55	3.14	0.02
2237	204692	188532	23392	21516	534853	1.03	0.83	0.78	4.66	0.06
53236	514192	466697	55191	49208	1323395	1.13	0.77	0.75	2.45	0.11
4508	273408	240602	33160	28354	750024	1.08	0.77	0.81	2.41	0.10
19389	100936	92167	10365	9786	238388	1.18	0.75	0.67	2.75	0.10
-168	9848	9736	1034	1017	21275	1.20	0.64	0.73	1.29	0.04
14352	50694	49849	3642	3523	119076	1.38	0.90	0.56	3.78	0.23
15155	79305	74343	6990	6527	194632	1.26	0.78	0.65	2.05	0.08
17331	436345	384553	49493	43271	1136453	1.06	0.79	0.79	3.13	0.10
18157	101626	96001	10661	9938	247301	1.10	0.78	0.77	2.60	0.10
19995	180689	174452	18402	17488	473682	1.24	0.81	0.66	2.60	0.08

8-7 全市建筑施工企业利税总额前50名
THE FIRST FIFTY PLACES OF TOTAL PRE-TAX PROFITS OF CONSTRUCTION ENTERPRISES

名次 No.	企业名称	Enterprises
1	北京市市政工程总公司	Beijing Municipal Engineering Corporation
2	北京韩村河建筑集团总公司	Beijing Hancunhe Construction Engineering Group Co.
3	铁道部第十六工程局	16th Engineering Bureau of Ministry of Railways
4	北京中关村开发建设股份有限公司	Beijing Centergate Development And Construction Co.
5	北京市第四城市建设工程公司	Beijing No.4 Urban Construction Company
6	中国新兴建设开发总公司	China Xin Xing Construction & Development General Co.
7	北京怀柔建筑企业集团总公司	Beijing Huairou Construction Group Corp
8	中国建筑第一工程局第四建筑公司	China Construction First Division 4th Construction Co.
9	北京城建二建设工程有限公司	Beijing No.2 Urban Construction Company
10	北京城建一建设工程有限公司	Beijing No.1 Urban Construction Company
11	北京城建五建设工程有限公司	Beijing No.5 Urban Construction Company
12	北京建雄建筑集团	Beijing Jianxiong Construction Group
13	北京中铁建筑工程公司	Beijing Zhong-Tie Construction Engineering Group
14	中国路桥集团第一公路工程局	The First Highway Engineering Bureau Of China Road and Bridge Group
15	北京市房山区建筑企业集团总公司	Beijing Fangshan Construction General Company (Group) Corp
16	中国四海工程公司	China Sihai Engineering Corporation
17	中国建筑二局第三建筑公司	The Third Construction Company Of China construction Second Engineering
18	北京城建八道桥工程有限公司	Beijing Urban Construction & Road Bridge Engineering Company
19	北京市第六建筑工程公司	Beijing No.6 Construction Engineering Company
20	北京市第五建筑工程公司	Beijing No.5 Construction Engineering Company
21	光大国际交通工程总公司	Everbringht International Construction Corporation
22	北京市第一建筑工程公司	Beijing No.1 Construction Engineering Company
23	北京市朝阳田华建筑集团公司	Beijing Chaoyang Tianhua Construction Group Co.
24	北京市第三建筑工程公司	Beijing No.3 Construction Engineering Company
25	北京华威建筑工程有限公司	Beijing Huawei Construction Limited Company
26	北京燕山石油化工公司建筑安装工程公司	Beijing Yanshan Co. Construction And Installation Engineering Company
27	中国建筑第一工程局第三建筑公司	China Construction First Division 3th Construction Co.
28	北京市第三住宅建筑工程公司	Beijing 3th Residential Construction Engineering Co.
29	北京市平谷县建筑工程总公司	Beijing Pinggu Construction Engineering Co.
30	北京市第二住宅建筑工程公司	Beijing 2th Residential Construction Engineering Co.
31	房山建工企业集团总公司	Fangshan Construction & Industry Enterprise (FCIE) Group Corp
32	北京城乡建设集团有限责任公司	Beijing Urban & Rural Construction Group Co., Ltd
33	延庆县建筑安装公司	Beijing Badaling Construction Group The Former Yanqing Co.
34	中建第一工程局第五建筑公司	China Construction First Division 5th Construction Co.
35	北京天源建筑工程有限责任公司	Beijing Tianyuan Construction Engineering C0.Ltd
36	中建一局华江建设有限公司	CCFDG,Huajiang Construction Corporation Limited
37	北京市第六住宅建筑工程公司	Beijing 6th Residential Construction Engineering Co.
38	北京市第五住宅建筑工程公司	Beijing 5th Residential Construction Engineering Co.
39	北京市房山城乡建筑企业集团总公司	Beijing Fangshan Urban & Rural Construction Group Co.
40	北京铁路工程总公司	Beijing Ralway Construction Engineering Co.
41	北京城建九建设安装工程有限公司	Beijing No.9 Urban Construction Company
42	北京万兴建筑集团公司	Beijing Wanxing Construction Group Co.
43	北京城建七建设工程有限公司	Beijing No.7 Urban Construction Company
44	北京住总正华建设工程有限责任公司	Beijing Zhuzong Zhenghua Construction Engineering Co.Ltd
45	北京市设备安装工程公司	The Beijing Machinery Equipment And Installation Engineering Company
46	中国建筑第一工程局第二建筑公司	China Construction First Group The Second Construction co.
47	北京铁道建筑工程中心	Beijing Construction Engineering Center Of Tunnei Engineering Bureau Under Minnstry Of Railways
48	北京正荣建筑工程有限责任公司	Beijing Zhengrong Construction Ehgineering Co.Ltd
49	北京城建地铁地基市政工程有限公司	Beijing Bucg Metro & Foundation & Municipal Engineering Company
50	北京城建三建设工程有限公司	Beijing No.5 Urban Construction Company

8-8 外埠进京施工单位主要指标
MAIN INDICATORS ON NON-LOCAL CONSTRUCTION UNITS IN BEIJING

项目 Item			2000	1999
单位个数	(个) Number of Units	(unit)	331	216
职工人数	(万人) Number of Staff and Workers	(10000 persons)	6.8	6.4
施工产值	(亿元) Output Value of Construction	(100 million yuan)	81.9	51.8
施工面积	(万平方米) Floor Space of Buildings under Construction	(10000 sq.m)	451.7	528.8
竣工面积	(万平方米) Floor Space of Buildings Completed	(10000 sq.m)	209.1	234.6

主要统计指标解释

建筑业统计单位 是指从事房屋、构筑物建造和设备安装活动以及建筑物的装修装饰的生产单位。根据不同的组织方式，建筑业统计的调查单位可分为法人建筑业企业和附营建筑施工单位。法人建筑业企业是指专门组织的独立核算的法人建筑业企业。它应同时具备的条件是：（1）依法成立，有自己的名称、组织机构和场所，能够承担民事责任；（2）独立拥有和使用资产，承担负债，有权与其他单位签订合同；（3）独立核算盈亏，能够编制资产负债表。附营建筑施工单位是指建筑业以外行业的企业、事业单位为完成本单位固定资产建造任务而自行组织的建筑施工单位。它应同时具备的条件是：（1）具有一个场所，从事或主要从事建筑安装活动；（2）单独组织生产经营活动；（3）在企业内部单独核算收支。

建筑业总产值（即自行完成施工产值） 是指建筑业企业或附营建筑施工单位自行完成的按工程进度计算的建筑安装生产总值。建筑业产值包括：

（1）建筑工程产值 指列入建筑工程预算内的各种工程价值。

（2）设备安装工程产值 指设备安装工程价值。

（3）房屋、构筑物修理产值 指房屋构筑物修理所完成的价值，但不包括被修理房屋、构筑物本身的价值和生产设备的修理价值。

（4）非标准设备制造产值 指加工制造没有定型的、非标准的生产设备的加工费和原材料价值，不论是现场还是附属加工厂为本单位承建工程制造的非标准设备的价值，都应计算产值。

自有机械设备年末总台数 是指归本企业（或单位）所有，属于本企业固定资产的生产性机械设备年末总台数。包括施工机械、生产设备、运输设备以及其他设备。

自有机械设备年末总功率 是指本企业（或单位）自有施工机械、生产设备、运输设备以及其他设备等列为在册固定资产的生产性机械设备年末总功率，按设定能力或查定能力计算。包括机械本身的动力和为该机械服务的单独动力设备，如电动机等。计算单位用千瓦，动力换算可按 1 马力=0.735 千瓦折合成千瓦数。电焊机、变压器、锅炉不计算动力。

企业总收入 是指与企业生产经营直接有关的各项收入，包括工程结算收入和其他业务收入，即：

企业总收入=工程结算收入+其他业务收入

Explanatory Notes On Main Statistical Indicators

Statistical Unit of Construction refers to the establishment engaged in the construction of buildings, structures or the installation of equipment and decoration of buildings. Depending upon the way of organization, they can be divided into two categories: corporate construction enterprises and affiliated construction units,. A corporate construction enterprise is a legal entity with independent accounting system, especially set up to undertake construction activities. It should meet the following three conditions: (1) being set up in line with relevant legal basis, having its full name, organization and location, and capable of taking civil liabilities; (2) independently possessing and using its assets and assuming its liabilities, and entitled to sign contracts with other institutions; and (3) making independent accounts of its profits and losses, and capable of compiling its own balance sheet. On the other hand, the affiliated construction units are subsidiary constructing units that are established by enterprises or institutions in other industries to take construction projects to build up their fixed assets. They should also meet three conditions: (1) engaged exclusively or mainly in construction and installation activities with a stable sits; (2) organizing independently their production/management; and (3) with independent accounting capability in the enterprises to which they are attached.

Gross Output Value of Construction（Output Value of Projects Under Construction） refers to the gross output value of construction and installation projects that are undertaken by construction enterprises or affiliated constructing units, calculated in line with the planned schedule. It includes:

(1) Output value of construction projects, which is the value of projects covered by the project budgets;

(2) Output value of installation projects, which is the value of the installation of equipment;

(3) Output value of repair of buildings and structures, which is the value created through the repairs, exclude the value of

buildings or structures being repaired or the value of the repair of production equipment;

(4) Output value of manufactured non-standard equipment, that is the value of non-standard production equipment (including raw materials and manufacturing cost) made for the construction project, irrespective of whether the equipment is manufactured on the construction site or in subsidiary workshops.

Total Number of Self-Owned Machinery at Year End refers to the number of machines and equipment owned by the enterprises (or units), and listed as the fixed assets of the enterprises (or units) by the end of the year, including machinery and equipment for construction, production, transportation and other purposes.

Total Power of Self-Owned Machinery at Year End refers to the total power of machines and equipment owned by the enterprises (or units), and listed as the fixed assets of the enterprises (or units) by the end of the year, including machines and equipment for construction, production, transportation and other purposes. The power of the machinery is calculated on basis of the designed or verified capacity, covering the power of the machinery/equipment and the separate power equipment serving the machinery/equipment (such as electric motors), but excluding welders, transformers and boilers. The unit used for the calculation of power is kilowatt, with horsepower converted to kilowatt by 1 horsepower = 0.735 kilowatt.

Total Revenue of Enterprises refers to the sum of income from production and operation of enterprises, including income from settlement of projects and other operational income, namely:

Total Revenue of Enterprises = Income from Settlement of Projects + Other Operation Income

交通运输、邮电通信业

9

TRANSPORTATION, POSTS AND TELECOMMUNICATIONS

全社会客货运输量（单位：万人，万吨）
Passenger and Freight Traffic (10000 persons,10000 tons)

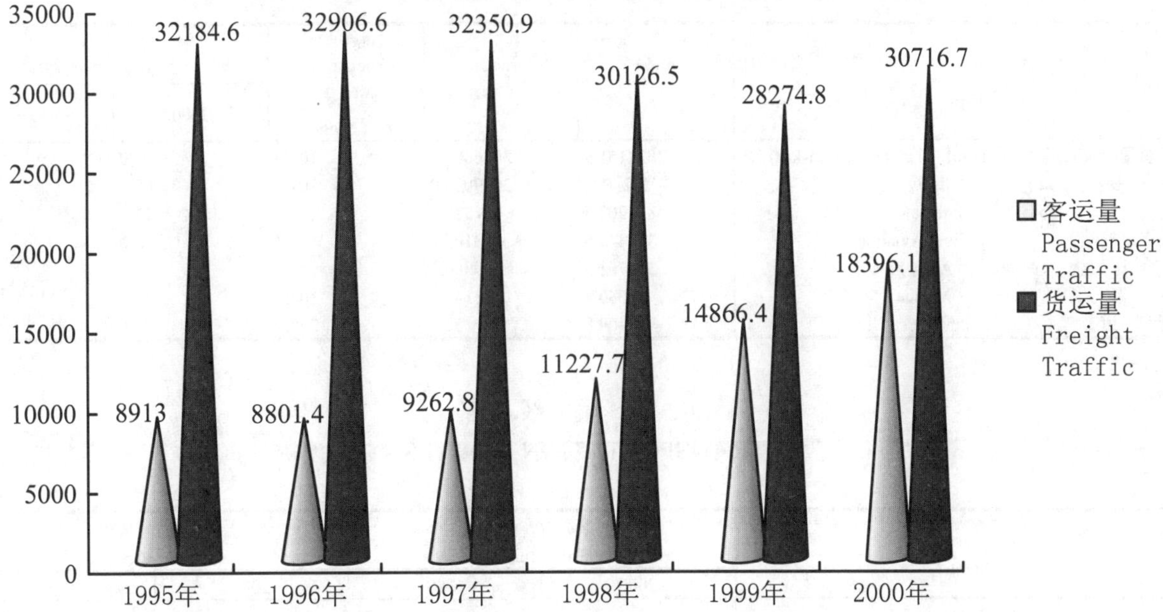

邮电业务总量（单位：亿元）
Revenue of Post and Telecommunication (100 million yuan)

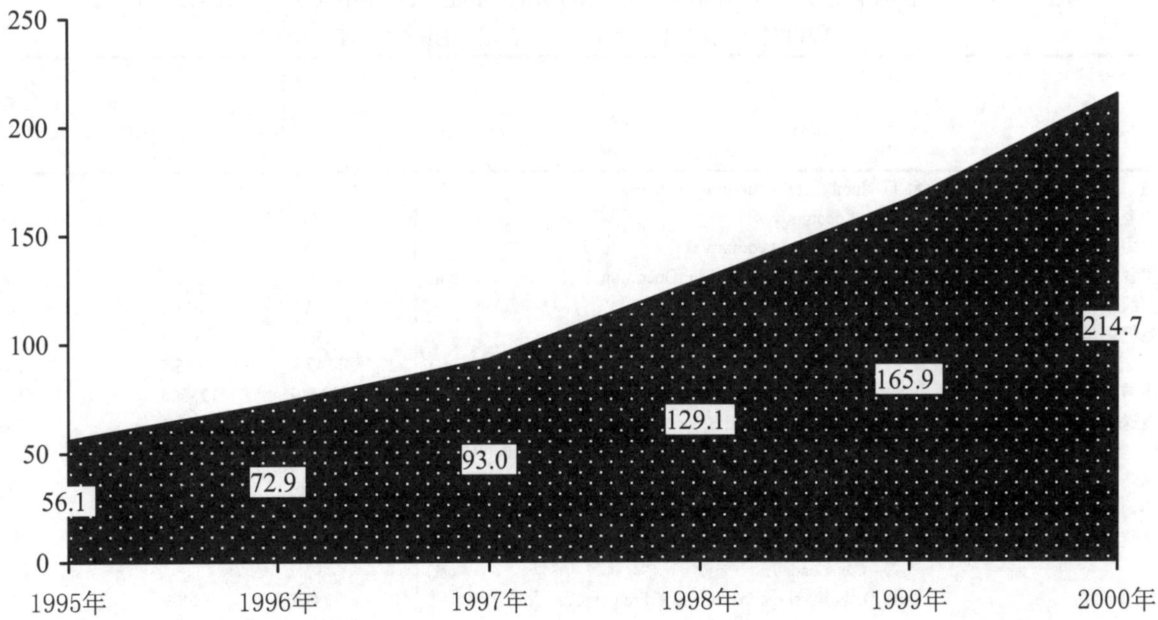

9-1 社 会 客 货 运 总 量 (换算周转量)
PASSENGER AND FREIGHT TRAFFIC(CONVERTED INTO TURNOVER VOLUME)

项 目 Item		2000	1999	2000年为1999年% 2000 as % of 1999	构 成(%) Composition(%)	
					2000	1999
运输总量(万吨公里)	**Total (10000 tn-km)**	**3824151.9**	**3586609.3**	**106.6**	**100**	**100**
铁 路	Railway	2629097	2509028.0	104.8	68.7	70.0
公 路	Highway	879202.5	794323.7	110.7	23.0	22.1
民 航	Civil Aviation	**315442.6**	**283105.1**	**111.4**	**8.2**	**7.9**
# 国 航	Air China	301761.9	269960.0	111.8		
新 华	Xinhua	13680.7	13145.1	104.1		
管 道	Pipeline	409.8	152.5	268.7	…	…

9-2 运 输 线 路
TRANSPORTATION ROUTES

项 目 Item		条 数 (条) Routes(unit)		长 度 (公里) Length(km)	
		2000	1999	2000	1999
铁 路	Railway	26	26	1879.5	1879.7
公 路	Highway	2989	2685	13597	12825
民 航	Civil Aviation	156	173		
# 国 航	Air China	112	133		
新 华	Xinhua	44	40		
管 道	Pipeline	8	8	28.8	28.8

注：民航包括国际航空公司,新华航空公司。
Note: Data of civil aviation include those of Air China and China Xinhua Airlines.

9-3 铁路运输量及主要技术经济指标(铁路分局范围)
RAILWAY TRAFFIC AND MAIN ECONOMIC AND TECHNICAL INDICATORS (WITHIN RAILWAY BUREAU BRANCH)

项 目 Item				2000	1999	2000年为1999年% 2000 as % of 1999
机车数	(台)	Number of Locomotives		598	602	99.3
# 内燃机车		Diesel Locomotives		510	509	100.2
电力机车		Electric Locomotives		88	93	94.6
营业里程	(公里)	Length of Railways in Operation	(km)	1879.5	1879.7	100.0
# 复线里程		Double-tracking Length		653.3	653.3	100.0
电气化里程		Length of Electrified Railways		434.1	434.1	100.0
旅客发送量	(万人)	Passengers Dispatched	(10000 persons)	5742.4	5335.5	107.6
旅客周转量	(万人公里)	Passenger-Kilometers	(10000 passenger-km)	1313440	1195566	109.9
货物发送量	(万吨)	Freight Dispatched	(10000 tons)	4274.7	4122.4	103.7
货物到达量	(万吨)	Freight Arrived	(10000 tons)	7111.2	7014.2	101.4
货物周转量	(万吨公里)	Freight Ton-Kilometers	(10000 ton-km)	4669826	4478635	104.3
货物平均净载重	(吨)	Average Net Load of Freight	(ton)	56.5	56.1	100.7
平均日装车数	(辆)	Daily Average Number of Freight Car Loaded	(car)	2066	2013	102.6
平均日卸车数	(辆)	Daily Average Number of Freight Car Unloaded	(car)	3429	3409	100.6
货车周转时间	(天)	Turnover Time of Freight Train	(day)	1.79	1.9	95.2
电力机车万吨公里耗电	(千瓦时)	Electricity Consumption of Electric Locomotives Per 10000 Ton-km	(kwh)	92.9	93.5	99.4
内燃机万吨公里耗油	(公斤)	Oil Consumption of Diesel Locomotives Per 10000 Ton-km	(kg)	28.7	28.7	100.0

9-4 全社会客、货运输量及周转量
PASSENGER AND FREIGHT TRAFFIC AND TURNOVER VOLUME

项目 Item	2000	1999	2000年为1999年% 2000 as % of 1999	构成(%) Composition(%) 2000	1999
旅客运输量 (万人) Passenger Traffic (10000 persons)	**18396.1**	**14866.4**	**123.7**	**100**	**100**
铁路 Railway	4458.4	4200.5	106.1	24.2	28.3
公路 Highway	13009	9878.0	131.7	70.7	66.4
民航 Civil Aviation	928.7	787.9	117.9	5.0	5.3
旅客周转量 (万人公里) Passenger-Kilometers (10000 passenger-km)	**3139918.1**	**2701470.8**	**116.2**	**100**	**100**
铁路 Railway	627222	579759.0	108.2	20.0	21.5
公路 Highway	527645	400597.0	131.7	16.8	14.8
民航 Civil Aviation	1985051.1	1721114.8	115.3	63.2	63.7
货运量 (万吨) Freight Traffic (10000 tons)	**30716.7**	**28274.8**	**108.6**	**100**	**100**
铁路 Railway	2611.7	2582.8	101.1	8.5	9.1
公路 Highway	28010	25635.0	109.3	91.2	90.7
民航 Civil Aviation	34.7	29.9	116.0	0.1	0.1
管道 Pipeline	60.3	27.1	222.4	0.2	0.1
货物周转量 (万吨公里) Freight Ton-Kilometers (10000 ton-km)	**2996413.9**	**2838856.6**	**105.6**	**100**	**100**
铁路 Railway	2001875	1929269.0	103.8	66.8	68.0
公路 Highway	826438	754264.0	109.6	27.6	26.6
民航 Civil Aviation	167691.1	155171.1	108.1	5.6	5.5
管道 Pipeline	409.8	152.5	268.7	…	…

9-5 公路、民航、邮电主要技术经济指标
MAIN TECHNICAL AND ECONOMIC INDICATORS OF HIGHWAY,CIVIL AVIATION, POSTS AND TELECOMMUNICATIONS

项目 Item	2000	1999	2000年为1999年% 2000 as % of 1999
公路货运 Highway Freight Traffic			
货车百吨公里耗汽油 (升) Petroleum Consumption of Trucks Per 100 Ton-km (liter)	6.7	6.7	100.0
货车百吨公里耗柴油 (升) Diesel Consumption of Trucks Per 100 Ton-km (liter)	4.5	4.5	100.0
货车里程利用率 (%) Intact Rate of Trucks (%)	52.7	52.1	101.2
民　航 Civil Aviation			
每吨公里耗航空油 (公斤) Aviation-oil Consumption Per Kilometer (kg)			
# 国　航 Air China	0.33	0.34	97.1
新　华 Xinhua	0.5	0.53	94.3
邮　电 Posts and Telecommunications			
总包邮件损失 (个) Loss of Parcels (piece)	1.0	1.0	100.0
邮件全程时限延误率 (%) Lossing Rate of Time Limit of Postal Matter Mailed during Whole Course (%)	0.09	0.02	450.0

注：民航包括国际航空公司，新华航空公司。

Note: Data of civil aviation include those of Air China and China Xinhua Airlines.

9-6 邮 电 业 务 总 量
POSTS AND TELECOMMUNICATIONS SERVICES

项目		Item		2000	1999	2000年为1999年% 2000 as % of 1999
邮电业务量	**(万元)**	**Sales Revenue of Posts and Telecommunications**	**(10000 yuan)**	**2147495.5**	**1659132.7**	**129.4**
邮　政		Post		152465.0	131891.0	115.6
电　信		Telecommunications		1995030.5	1527241.7	130.6
邮电业务总量		**Sales Volume of Posts and Telecommunications**				
函件	(万件)	Letters	(10000 pcs)	57695	55071	104.8
包件	(万件)	Parcels	(10000 pcs)	518	445	116.4
汇票	(万件)	Postal Money Order	(10000)	911	888	102.6
报纸累计	(万份)	Newspaper	(10000 copies)	146395	148039	98.9
杂志累计	(万份)	Magazines	(10000 copies)	5592	5480	102.0
公众电报	(万份)	Public Telegrams	(10000 pcs)	27.4	21.4	128.0
用户电报	(万次)	Telex	(10000 times)	58.7	88.4	66.4
长途电话	(万次)	Long-Distance Calls	(10000 times)	71212.8	70849.1	100.5
移动电话用户	(万户)	Mobil Telephone Subscribers	(10000 subscribers)	347.2	186.2	186.4
本地电话用户	(万户)	Local Telephone Subscribers	(10000 subscriber)	451.2	376.3	119.9
公用电话	(部)	Public Telephone	(unit)	70011	60519	115.7

注：1. 本地电话用户包括市内电话用户和农村电话用户，以后农村电话指标不再单独反映。

2. 从2000年起，邮电业务量、移动电话用户包括联通北京分公司数据，1999年数据做相应调整。

a) Data of local telephone subscribers included urban and rural areas,and rural telephones won't be reported separately any more.

b) From 2000, data of sales revenue of posts and telecommunications and mobil telephone subscribers include those of Beijing Branch of China Unicom, and the related data of 1999 has been adjusted according to the changes of 2000.

9-7 邮电局、所及邮路
POSTS AND TELECOMMUNICATIONS OFFICES AND POSTAL ROUTES

单位：公里　　(km)

项目	Item	2000	1999	2000年为1999年% 2000 as % of 1999	结构(%) Composition(%) 2000	1999
邮电局所 (处)	**Number of Posts and Telecommunications Offices (unit)**	**767**	**750**	**102.3**		
邮路单程总长度	**Length of Postal Route**	**121427**	**109838**	**110.6**	**100**	**100**
航空邮路	Air Routes	49646	47029	105.6	40.9	42.8
铁路邮路	Railway Routes	20071	20789	96.5	16.5	18.9
自办汽车邮路	Highway Routes	50344	40232	125.1	41.5	36.6
其　他	Others	1366	1788	76.4	1.1	1.7

9-8 邮电局、所地区分布
POSTS AND TELECOMMUNICATIONS OFFICES BY REGION

单位：个 (unit)

地区 Region		邮电局、所 Posts and Telecommunications Offices		# 设在农村 In Rural Areas	
		2000	1999	2000	1999
全市	**Total**	**767**	**750**	**273**	**276**
城区	**City Proper**	**112**	**104**		
东城区	Dongcheng	42	37		
西城区	Xicheng	41	38		
崇文区	Chongwen	10	10		
宣武区	Xuanwu	19	19		
近郊区	**Near Suburbs**	**295**	**286**		
朝阳区	Chaoyang	114	112		
丰台区	Fengtai	110	51		
石景山区	Shijingshan	14	13		
海淀区	Haidian	57	110		
远郊区	**Outer Suburbs**	**220**	**218**	**171**	**170**
门头沟区	Mentougou	22	22	15	15
房山区	Fangshan	68	68	52	56
通州区	Tongzhou	48	49	34	35
昌平区	Changping	41	41	39	36
顺义区	Shunyi	41	38	31	28
各县	**Counties**	**140**	**142**	**102**	**106**
大兴县	Daxing	44	43	31	32
平谷县	Pinggu	23	23	16	16
怀柔县	Huairou	25	26	20	21
密云县	Miyun	24	25	18	19
延庆县	Yanqing	24	25	17	18

9-9 各种车辆
VARIOUS VEHICLES

单位：辆 (unit)

项目 Item		2000	1999	2000年为1999年% 2000 as % of 1999	构成(%) Composition(%)	
					2000	1999
机动车	**Motor Vehicles**	**1364718**	**1241719**	**109.9**	**100**	**100**
在机动车中:	Of Motor Vehicles					
汽车	Automobiles	1031874	948506	108.8	75.6	76.4
货车	Trucks	206100	202195	101.9	20.0	21.3
# 大货	Heavy Trucks	58020	57932	100.2	28.2	28.7
客车	Coaches	821580	742299	110.7	79.6	78.3
# 小客车	Small Coaches	797296	719837	110.8	97.0	97.0
特种车	Special Purpose Vehicles	4194	4012	104.5	0.4	0.4
机动脚踏车(摩托车)	Motorcycles	332161	292621	113.5	24.3	23.6
# 轻便	Light	131093	121676	107.7	39.5	41.6
电车	Trolleys	683	592	115.4	0.1	0.0
在机动车中:	Of Motor Vehicles					
私人机动车	Private Automobiles	855321	762361	112.2	100	100
# 小轿车	Cars	243377	206152	118.1	28.5	27.0
非机动车	**Nonmotor Vehicles**	**10555058**	**10308466**	**102.4**	**100**	**100**
自行车	Bicycles	9886875	9678544	102.2	93.7	93.9
三轮车	Tricycles	668183	629922	106.1	6.3	6.1

主要统计指标解释

铁路营业里程 又称营业长度，指办理客货运输业务的铁路正线总长度。凡是全线或部分建成双线及以上的线路，以第一线的实际长度计算；复线、站线、段管线、岔线和特殊用途线以及不计算运费的联络线都不计算营业里程。铁路营业里程是反映铁路运输业基础设施发展水平的重要指标，也是计算客货周转量、运输密度和机车车辆运用效率等指标的基础资料。

货（客）运量 指在一定时期内，各种运输工具实际运送的货物（旅客）数量。是反映运输业为国民经济和人民生活服务的数量指标，也是制定和检查运输生产计划，研究运输发展规模和速度的重要指标。货运按吨计算，客运按人计算。货物不论运输距离长短，货物类别，均按实际重量统计；旅客不论行程远近或票价多少，均按一人一次作为客运量统计。半价票、小孩票也按一人统计。

货物（旅客）周转量 指在一定时期内，由各种运输工具运送的货物（旅客）数量与其相应运输距离的乘积之总和，是反映运输业生产总成果的重要指标，也是编制和检查运输生产计划，计算运输效率、劳动生产率以及核算运输单位主要基础资料。通常以吨公里和人公里为计算单位。计算货物周转量通常按发出站与到达站之间的最短距离，也就是计费距离计算。

邮电业务总量 指以货币表现的邮电部门用于传递信息和提供其他邮电服务的总数量。它综合反映了一定时期邮电工作的总成果，是研究邮电业务量构成和发展趋势的重要指标。根据邮电管理体制不同，分为中央国营业务总量和地方国营业务总量。它用各种邮电分类业务量，如函件件数、电报份数、长话张数、市内电话和农村电话的年均户数、订销报刊累计份数等，分别乘以相应的平均单价（不变价），加总后再加上出租电路和设备的收入、代用户维护电话交换机和线路等设备的收入、其他业务收入求得。

Explanatory Notes On Main Statistical Indicators

Length of Railways in Operation refers to the total length of the trunk line for passenger and freight transportation. The calculation is based on the actual length of the first line if the line has a full or partial double track or more tracks, excluding double tracks, station sidings, tracks under the charge of stations, branch lines, specialpurpose lines and the non-payable connecting lines. The length of railways in operation is an important indicator to show the development of the infrastructure for the railway transport, and also the essential data to calculate volume of passenger freight , traffic density and utilization of the locomotives and carriages.

Freight （Passenger）Traffic refers to the volume of freight （passenger）transported with various means. Freight transport is calculated in tons and passenger traffic is calculated in the number of persons. Despite the type of freight and traveling distance, the freight traffic is calculated by weight. Similarly, the passenger traffic is calculated by person regardless he/she travels with a half-price ticket or a child ticket or an adults ticket or how long his/her trip is. The freight（passenger）traffic provides a quantitative measure to show how the transport industry serves the national economy and people, and is also an important indicator for planning the transport industry and for studying the development scale and speed of the transport industry.

Freight Ton-kilometers（Passenger -kilometers） refer to the sum of the products of the volume of transported cargo（passengers）multiplying by the transport distance, usually using ton-kilometer and passenger-kilometers as units for measurement. Normally , the shortest distance between the departure station and the destination station（I. e., the payable distance）is the bases to calculate the freight ton-kilometers. This is an important indicator to show the total results of the transport industry, to prepare and examine the transport plan and to measure the efficiency, the labour productivity and the unit cost of transport.

Business Volume of Posts and Telecommunications refers to the total value of the information delivered and other posts and telecommunications services provided by the posts and telecommunications departments for the customers. It is derived by first multiplying the business volume of different types, such as number of letters, telegrams, long distance calls., city and rural telephone subscribers and accumulated number of newspapers and journals subscribed and sold, etc. by their respective average unit price（fixed price）, and then adding these products together, and then plus the income from the rent of line and equipment, the income from maintenance of telephone exchanges and lines, and the income from other business operations. The business volume of posts and telecommunication indicates the total achievements made by the posts and telecommunications department during a given period of time in a comprehensive way, and is an important indicator to study the composition and development of the posts and telecommunications business.

批发零售贸易业和餐饮业

10

WHOLESALE, RETAIL AND CATERING

社会消费品零售额　（单位：亿元）
Retail Sales of Consumer Goods (100 million yuan)

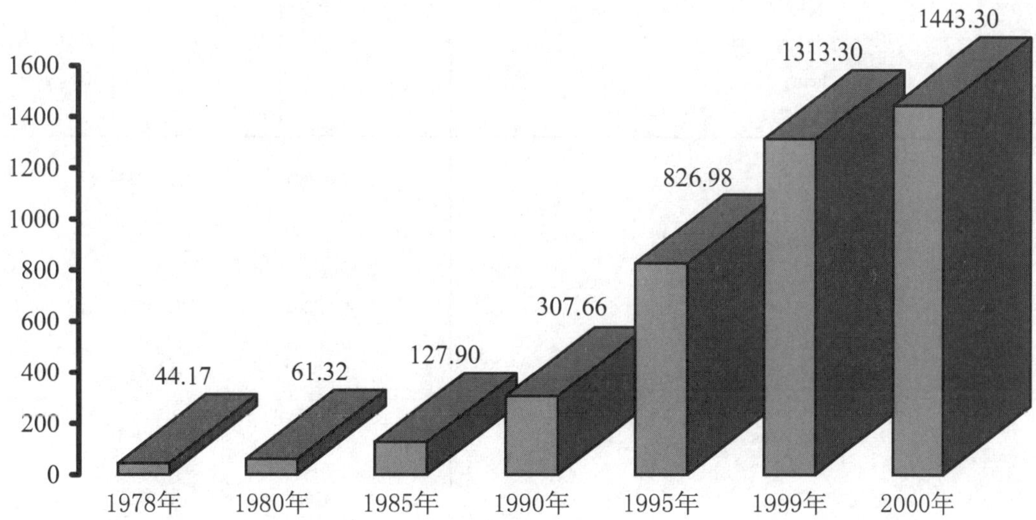

社会消费品零售额构成
Composition of Retail Sales of Consumer Goods

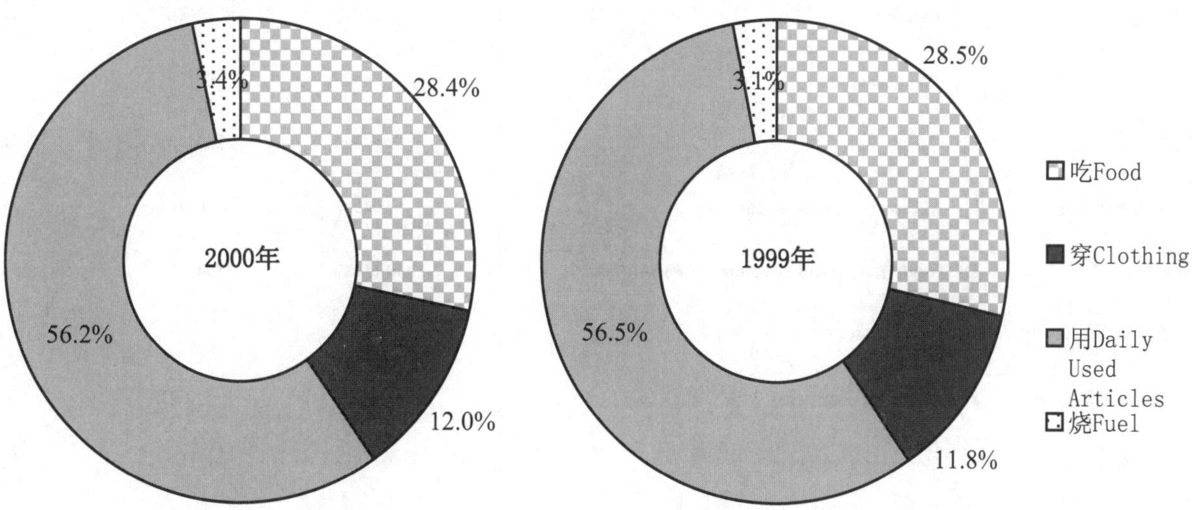

10-1 社会消费品零售额
TOTAL RETAIL SALES OF CONSUMER GOODS

单位：万元 (10000 yuan)

项目	Item	2000	1999	2000年为1999年% 2000 as % of 1999
总　计	**Total**	**14433001**	**13133233**	**109.9**
按用途分	**Grouped by Purpose**			
吃的商品	Food	4102262	3744976	109.5
穿的商品	Clothing	1730119	1556487	111.2
用的商品	Daily Used Articles	8108560	7421048	109.3
烧的商品	Fuels	492060	410722	119.8
按地区分	**Grouped by Region**			
城镇零售额	Town	12310857	11216745	109.8
农村零售额	Rural	2122144	1916488	110.7
按行业分	**Grouped by Sectors**			
批发零售贸易业	Wholesale and Retail Trade	10255131	9261776	110.7
餐饮业	Catering	864010	812690	106.3
制造业	Manufacturing	868870	798169	108.9
其　他	Others	2444990	2260598	108.2
#农民对非农民	Peasant to Non-peasant	64181	76180	84.2
在总计中：　大中型批发零售贸易业	**Of Total: Large and Medium Wholesale and Retail Sales**	**6611447**	**5554995**	**119.0**
按登记注册类型分	Grouped by Registered Type			
内资企业	Domestic Investment	6071539	5098587	119.1
# 国有企业	State-owned	2749739	2551678	107.8
集体企业	Collective-owned	920083	792314	116.1
股份有限公司	Share Holding Company	838158	727343	115.2
港澳台商投资企业	Hongkong, Macao and Taiwan Funded Enterprises	52943	42539	124.5
外商投资企业	Foreign Funded Enterprises	486966	413869	117.7

10-2 各区县消费品零售额

RETAIL SALES OF CONSUMER GOODS IN DISTRICTS AND COUNTIES

单位：万元 (10000 yuan)

地区	Region	合计 Total	按用途分 Grouped by Purpose			
			吃的商品 Food	穿的商品 Clothing	用的商品 Daily Used Articles	烧的商品 Fuels
全　市	**Total**	**10869512**	**3255921**	**1379604**	**5773866**	**460121**
城　区	**City Proper**	**2836087**	**809023**	**557106**	**1448184**	**21774**
东城区	Dongcheng	771989	248306	146624	371799	5260
西城区	Xicheng	1075125	242617	269252	559542	3714
崇文区	Chongwen	463293	177929	68221	216024	1119
宣武区	Xuanwu	525680	140171	73009	300819	11681
近郊区	**Near Suburbs**	**5533413**	**1445720**	**452431**	**3408389**	**226873**
朝阳区	Chaoyang	1791519	543023	224162	862838	161496
丰台区	Fengtai	737843	395201	99593	212365	30684
石景山区	Shijingshan	351544	153758	12671	177950	7165
海淀区	Haidian	2652507	353738	116005	2155236	27528
远郊区	**Outer Suburbs**	**1573066**	**602016**	**211899**	**617988**	**141163**
门头沟区	Mentougou	180147	81330	13058	78643	7116
房山区	Fangshan	483890	138936	83658	204538	56758
通州区	Tongzhou	338569	167250	41930	119783	9606
昌平区	Changping	220045	126426	56580	127294	40115
顺义区	Shunyi	350415	88074	16673	87730	27568
各　县	**Counties**	**926946**	**399162**	**158168**	**299305**	**70311**
大兴县	Daxing	273295	137699	30970	75955	28671
平谷县	Pinggu	136225	54217	25910	38743	17355
怀柔县	Huairou	140118	44209	30726	56015	9168
密云县	Miyun	157096	72907	23807	56946	3436
延庆县	Yanqing	220212	90130	46755	71646	11681

注：本表中区县商业企业为中央属及区县属口径。

Note: Data of districts and counties refers to that of central units,districts and counties.

10-3 社会批发零售贸易业商品购、销、存总值

TOTAL PURCHASES,SALES AND INVENTORY OF WHOLESALE AND RETAIL SALE TRADES

单位：万元 (10000 yuan)

项目	Item	2000	1999	2000年为1999年% 2000 as % of 1999
商品购进总额	**Total Purchases of Goods**	**28083561**	**23271293**	**120.7**
市内纯购进	In the City	11200384	11603478	96.5
市外购进	From Outside	10634914	7404008	143.6
进　口	Import	6248263	4263807	146.5
商品销售总额	**Total Sales**	**32632051**	**26585799**	**122.7**
市内纯销售	In the City	19253080	17914608	107.5
市外销售	To Outside	7134676	3324421	214.6
出　口	Export	6244295	5346770	116.8
年末库存	**Inventory (year-end)**	**4961564**	**5207716**	**95.3**

10-4 批发零售贸易业商品购、销、存总值

PURCHASES,SALES AND INVENTORY OF WHOLESALE AND RETAIL SALE TRADES

单位：万元 (10000 yuan)

项目	Item	2000	1999	2000年为1999年% 2000 as % of 1999
商品购进总额	**Total Purchases of Goods**	**24479325**	**20193079**	**121.2**
市内纯购进	In the City	7629105	8399383	90.8
市外购进	From Outside	10634914	7372452	144.3
进　口	Import	6215306	4421244	140.6
商品销售总额	**Total Sales**	**26717679**	**21575476**	**123.8**
市内纯销售	In the City	13374776	13064834	102.4
市外销售	To Outside	7101556	3292687	215.7
出　口	Export	6241347	5217955	119.6
年末库存	**Inventory (year-end)**	**4991036**	**5496141**	**90.8**

10-5 商委各局大中型批发零售贸易业商品购、销、存总值

PURCHASES,SALES AND INVENTORY OF LARGE AND MEDIUM ENTERPRISES IN WHOLESALE AND RETAIL SALE TRADES OF COMMERCIAL COMMITTEE

单位：万元 (10000 yuan)

项目	Item	北京一商集团有限责任公司 Beijing Yishang Group CO.,LTD	北京二商集团有限责任公司 Beijing Ershang (Group) CO.,LTD	北京粮食局 Beijing Grain Bureau	北京市供销合作社 The Supply And Marketing Cooperatives In Beijing	北京燕莎集团有限责任公司 Beijing Yansha Group CO.,LTD	中国烟草总公司北京市公司 China National Tobacco Corp., Beijing Corp.,
商品购进总额	**Total Purchases**	**281287**	**262623**	**26776**	**174081**	**145457**	**680344**
从生产者购进	From Producers	139238	99628	2723	103039	75465	97257
# 农副产品	Farm and Sideline Products		2266	2723	31891		
市外购进	From Outside	96938	76403		69508	22596	335
从批发零售贸易业购进	From Wholesalers and Retailers	136726	128968	24053	58206	69878	582385
# 市外购进	From Outside	63074	43761		13017	4349	265804
进口额	Import	4730			12757	114	
其他	Others	593	34027		79		702
商品销售总额	**Total Sales**	**306485**	**284774**	**105259**	**198055**	**199102**	**729278**
对生产经营单位销售额	To Producers	30407	33831	2980	39887		
# 生产资料销售	Capital Goods	92			147		
市外销售	To Outside	6593	3835		10911		
对批发零售贸易业批发	To Wholesalers and Retailers	217220	193384	102279	107526	19842	712468
# 市外批发	From Outside	46117	9306	3835	26314	1228	43775
出口额	Export						
对居民的商品零售额	To Residents	45871	55741		42993	174884	
对集团的商品零售额	To Organizations	12987	1818		7649	4376	16810
年末库存	**Inventory(year-end)**	**36208**	**56473**	**165145**	**22007**	**17317**	**30958**

项目	Item	北京王府井百货(集团)股份有限公司 Beijing Wangfujing Department Store (Group) CO.,LTD	北京西单商场股份有限公司 Beijing Xidan Shopping CO.,LTD	北京东安集团公司 Beijing Dongan Group CO.,LTD	北京友谊商店股份有限公司 Beijing Friendship Store CO.,LTD	中盐北京市盐业公司 Beijing Salt Corp., China General industry Corp.,	北京粮食集团有限责任公司 Beijing Grain Group CO.,LTD
商品购进总额	**Total Purchases**	**118611**	**158915**	**199548**	**13973**	**5611**	**47508**
从生产者购进	From Producers	43221	96917	116613	7071	5611	
# 农副产品	Farm and Sideline Products			513			
市外购进	From Outside	17635	18693	57215	2850	5611	
从批发零售贸易业购进	From Wholesalers and Retailers	74225	61990	82809	6902		34245
# 市外购进	From Outside	11621	11108	18491	797		4504
进口额	Import	1052		126			13262
其他	Others	113	8				1
商品销售总额	**Total Sales**	**142450**	**189104**	**234370**	**19393**	**8214**	**45114**
对生产经营单位销售额	To Producers	1817	4340			2343	5503
# 生产资料销售	Capital Goods						116
市外销售	To Outside	1413	1773				
对批发零售贸易业批发	To Wholesalers and Retailers	21725	21718	1141	2225	5722	27838
# 市外批发	From Outside	436	266	298	81		2809
出口额	Export	2643					
对居民的商品零售额	To Residents	108109	158701	216997	16794	53	5981
对集团的商品零售额	To Organizations	8156	4345	16232	374	96	5792
年末库存	**Inventory (year-end)**	**5710**	**14517**	**10017**	**3406**	**1097**	**11129**

10-6 大中型批发零售贸易业商品购、销、存总值(按行政区划分)

PURCHASES,SALES AND INVENTORY LARGE AND MEDIUM ENTERPRISES IN WHOLESALE AND RETAIL SALE TRADES(BY ADMINISTRATIVE REGION)

单位：万元 (10000 yuan)

项目	Item	东城 Dongcheng	西城 Xicheng	崇文 Chongwen	宣武 Xuanwu	朝阳 Chaoyang	丰台 Fengtai	石景山 Shijingshan	海淀 Haidia
商品购进总额	**Total Purchases**	**4567828**	**7780701**	**1433852**	**3392063**	**4824915**	**1200770**	**392238**	**2810735**
从生产者购进	From Producers	3040485	2071177	707714	2711055	2425414	740328	230899	1627511
# 农副产品	Farm and Sideline Products	101212	133258	1063	12836	38844	13445	125	57840
市外购进	From Outside	2476020	914696	293275	1968927	833815	190029	12150	796680
从批发零售贸易业购进	From Wholesalers and Retailers	671369	1832444	591761	452258	1549045	433284	157140	833412
# 市外购进	From Outside	149121	1117370	79482	130727	853427	79066	11431	129805
进口额	Import	846976	3850124	125396	227064	810686	23344		328100
其他	Others	8998	26956	8981	1686	39770	3814	4199	21712
商品销售总额	**Total Sales**	**4764603**	**7655893**	**1624252**	**3625701**	**5036036**	**1297852**	**415229**	**3362750**
对生产经营单位销售额	To Producers	1378520	2913498	134460	1281495	1243168	490907	104642	1095220
# 生产资料销售	Capital Goods	1186	139053		955	5356	29		46580
市外销售	To Outside	1132450	1720404	7312	836728	252687	30437	3755	537597
对批发零售贸易业批发	To Wholesalers and Retailers	656383	1669965	940069	1530671	1453335	202690	60728	545710
# 市外批发	From Outside	127076	743359	119064	1077137	358614	26400	2026	96785
出口额	Export	2122870	1936028	88951	309102	1032062	47150		694001
对居民的商品零售额	To Residents	477239	977405	222797	410560	976860	368682	210915	823131
对集团的商品零售额	To Organizations	129591	158997	237975	93873	330611	188423	38944	204688
年末库存	**Inventory(year-end)**	**442651**	**1478602**	**214096**	**505452**	**789856**	**145209**	**38096**	**312254**

项目	Item	门头沟 Mentou-gou	房山 Fang-shan	通州 Tong-zhou	顺义 Shunyi	昌平 Chang-ping	大兴 Daxing	平谷 Pinggu	怀柔 Huairou	密云 Miyun	延庆 Yanqing
商品购进总额	**Total Purchases**	**55463**	**435166**	**193504**	**289001**	**186310**	**239138**	**81795**	**113496**	**78570**	**66694**
从生产者购进	From Producers	14835	180203	78694	134674	52642	120828	56274	33721	21328	20303
# 农副产品	Farm and Sideline Products	-37	5010	1	10947	269	9715	45	999	802	46
市外购进	From Outside	1018	8407	10684	36274	4495	21546	1077	9814	11713	6047
从批发零售贸易业购进	From Wholesalers and Retailers	39742	252332	114764	151936	130886	117987	24480	79623	53982	46075
# 市外购进	From Outside	1182	5740	6507	7087	11744	16705	240	1427	3795	7366
进口额	Import				1132					2485	
其他	Others	886	2631	46	1259	2782	323	1041	152	775	316
商品销售总额	**Total Sales**	**69362**	**436195**	**228277**	**309143**	**200919**	**276544**	**85872**	**148339**	**86776**	**72949**
对生产经营单位销售	To Producers	16002	128280	79530	45034	26418	80753	2415	26546	19795	4906
# 生产资料销售	Capital Goods	104	4192	3020	6519	1506	10248	1021	1656	5566	1384
市外销售	To Outside	3123	1830	19	7818	239	1963		6	950	120
对批发零售贸易业批发	To Wholesalers and Retailers	14522	213811	60434	98953	56396	109829	63797	38996	33025	22995
# 市外批发	From Outside	9	281	1628	1326	223	7111	56	1034	1243	749
出口额	Export				30	7324			300	3530	
对居民的商品零售额	To Residents	33677	78552	77106	131444	83762	67352	12397	64846	18368	39613
对集团的商品零售额	To Organizations	5161	15552	11207	33682	27019	18610	7263	17651	12058	5435
年末库存	**Inventory(year-end)**	**5086**	**33939**	**14552**	**29072**	**24848**	**24605**	**11016**	**11791**	**15521**	**6346**

10-7 批发零售贸易企业商品分类销售库存

SALES AND INVENTORY BY CATEGORY OF ENTERPRISES IN WHOLESALE AND RETAIL TRADES

单位：万元 (10000 yuan)

项目	Item	合计 Total 商品总销售 Total Sales	# 零售额 Retail	年末库存 Inventory (year-end)	# 大型企业 Large Enterprises 商品总销售 Total Sales	# 零售额 Retail	年末库存 Inventory (year-end)
合计	**Total**	**32737544**	**7915418**	**4991036**	**14247882**	**3515046**	**2196320**
食品、饮料、烟酒类	Food,Beverage,Tobacco and Liquor	4166528	1343642	665796	1356986	638667	133525
# 肉禽蛋类	Meat,Poultry and Eggs	318216	153898	33799	100786	79273	3909
其他食品类	Other Food	2300362	799896	492363	870003	391873	77440
饮料类	Beverage	289606	175094	27542	107040	78403	8174
烟酒类	Tobacco and Liquor	1258344	214754	112092	279157	89118	44002
服装鞋帽、针、纺织品类	Garments,Shoes,Hats and Knitwear	2556123	1207206	243914	1070490	762674	72726
# 服装类	Garments	1252354	809495	113861	702499	523626	44061
鞋帽类	Shoes and Hats	286582	194929	28379	173970	126583	16516
针、纺织品类	Knitwear	1017187	202782	101674	194021	112465	12149
化妆品类	Cosmetics	317455	158723	29562	216700	102711	13362
金银珠宝类	Jewelry	366379	205410	88519	219169	144407	38010
日用品类	Articles for Daily Use	866289	543915	96842	396090	262348	28451
# 洗涤用品类	Detergents	185670	118944	19737	79829	54853	6931
儿童玩具类	Toys for Children	29869	27604	2798	20432	18623	863
五金、电料类	Hardware and Electrical Appliances	417844	133709	81890	40013	25665	3193
体育、娱乐用品类	Sports and Recreation Articles	203649	114817	27968	65071	52993	5023
书报、杂志类	Book and Newspaper	360961	192300	165772	127147	14714	67422
电子出版物及音像制品类	Electronic Publication and Sound-video Products	74636	57381	8640	42070	41060	1142
家用电器和音像器材类	Household Appliances and Sound-video Equipments	1327578	889632	167792	663663	601234	56849
中西药品类	Medicines	1348438	706302	203788	440532	247259	53991
# 西药类	Western Medicines	811895	420056	128866	366930	188437	49067
中草药及中成药类	Chinese Herbal and Patent Medicines	305778	189550	57413	51085	46710	4070
文化、办公用品类	Culture and Office Articles	460779	243922	71723	131024	85715	7226
家具类	Furniture	140563	107500	15831	44300	36791	4937
通讯器材类	Communication Equipments	1773777	140320	128273	1476808	19373	101110
煤炭及制品类	Coal and Coal Products	1245477	29360	15437	91670	19	3555
木材及制品类	Timber and Related Products	278122	17769	59732	84927	3032	20069
石油及制品类	Petroleum and Related Products	2588683	524580	179504	1070115	38353	104426
化工材料及制品类	Chemical Materials and Products	2602936	49554	290450	1417141	1704	150351
# 化肥类	Chemical Fertilizer	428511	69	50738	390070		47169
金属材料类	Ferrous Metal Materials	3148124	38072	385166	1031884	380	74323
建筑及装潢材料类	Construction and Decoration Materials	326989	97798	114975	10625	1759	2204
机电设备及零件类	Mechanical and Electrical Instruments and Components	4165738	772757	748715	2056352	366698	343460
# 农机类	Agricultural Machinery	38475	8714	4327	11144	1999	522
汽车类	Motor Vehicles	958129	548051	95069	483964	305537	42344
种子饲料类	Seeds and Forage	188522	1288	127335	93352		94006
棉麻类	Cotton and Flax	1478385	58	726939	1298544	1	715936
其他类	Others	2333569	339403	346473	803209	67489	101023

10-7 续表 continued

单位：万元 (10000 yuan)

项目	Item	# 中型企业 Medium Enterprises 商品总销售 Total Sales	# 零售额 Retail	年末库存 Inventory (year-end)	# 小型企业 Small Enterprises 商品总销售 Total Sales	# 零售额 Retail	年末库存 Inventory (year-end)
合计	**Total**	**15448809**	**3096402**	**1906669**	**3040853**	**1303970**	**888047**
食品、饮料、烟酒类	Food,Beverage,Tobacco and Liquor	2517030	612953	479051	292512	92022	53220
# 肉禽蛋类	Meat,Poultry and Eggs	191933	66381	28195	25497	8244	1695
其他食品类	Other Food	1266369	358969	375836	163990	49054	39087
饮料类	Beverage	138563	86193	13966	44003	10498	5402
烟酒类	Tobacco and Liquor	920165	101410	61054	59022	24226	7036
服装鞋帽、针、纺织品类	Garments,Shoes,Hats and Knitwear	1359638	373923	127896	125995	70609	43292
# 服装类	Garments	496811	245982	53568	53044	39887	16232
鞋帽类	Shoes and Hats	102003	61044	9101	10609	7302	2762
针、纺织品类	Knitwear	760824	66897	65227	62342	23420	24298
化妆品类	Cosmetics	94898	51927	14961	5857	4085	1239
金银珠宝类	Jewelry	132377	52904	33080	14833	8099	17429
日用品类	Articles for Daily Use	354313	218258	47921	115886	63309	20470
# 洗涤用品类	Detergents	96822	56982	9492	9019	7109	3314
儿童玩具类	Toys for Children	8227	8449	1080	1210	532	855
五金、电料类	Hardware and Electrical Appliances	227650	40755	21437	150181	67289	57260
体育、娱乐用品类	Sports and Recreation Articles	103857	38429	7808	34721	23395	15137
书报、杂志类	Book and Newspaper	196397	147202	70140	37417	30384	28210
电子出版物及音像制品类	Electronic Publication and Sound-video Products	22980	11715	4435	9586	4606	3063
家用电器和音像器材类	Household Appliances and Sound-video Equipments	555791	224359	79095	108124	64039	31848
中西药品类	Medicines	811327	385235	126413	96579	73808	23384
# 西药类	Western Medicines	388136	193026	67538	56829	38593	12261
中草药及中成药类	Chinese Herbal and Patent Medicines	228783	122009	46304	25910	20831	7039
文化、办公用品类	Culture and Office Articles	234047	109895	39144	95708	48312	25353
家具类	Furniture	72476	50199	7757	23787	20510	3137
通讯器材类	Communication Equipments	189554	64664	16000	107415	56283	11163
煤炭及制品类	Coal and Coal Products	1142051	24803	10691	11756	4538	1191
木材及制品类	Timber and Related Products	168466	5130	21933	24729	9607	17730
石油及制品类	Petroleum and Related Products	1211122	227423	28752	307446	258804	46326
化工材料及制品类	Chemical Materials and Products	1008009	6657	103939	177786	41193	36160
# 化肥类	Chemical Fertilizer	33645	69	3183	4796		386
金属材料类	Ferrous Metal Materials	1798249	17651	183286	317991	20041	127557
建筑及装潢材料类	Construction and Decoration Materials	145546	29268	26954	170818	66771	85817
机电设备及零件类	Mechanical and Electrical Instruments and Components	1641639	273699	290438	467747	132360	114817
# 农机类	Agricultural Machinery	25744	5754	3187	1587	961	618
汽车类	Motor Vehicles	430738	211719	45514	43427	30795	7211
种子饲料类	Seeds and Forage	77288	23	13635	17882	1265	19694
棉麻类	Cotton and Flax	165575	57	9539	14266		1464
其他类	Others	1218529	129273	142364	311831	142641	103086

10-8 社会农副产品购进、销售、库存数量
PURCHASES,SALES AND INVENTORY OF FARM AND SIDELINE PRODUCTS

单位：百公斤 (100 kg)

项目	Item	从生产者购进 Purchase from Producers	市外购进 Purchase from Outside	商品总销售 Total Sales	# 对生产经营单位销售 To Producer	# 出口 Export	# 零售量 Retail Sales	年末库存 Inventory (year-end)
粮食	Grain	20344712	15654501	79582198	16466615	4121902	6862171	37736460
食用植物油	Edible Vegetable Oil	3826334	4213211	11962884	3060992	13630	1394635	1018242
猪和猪肉	Hog and Pork	2823369	1403150	3562472	779076	9344	1867809	158095
牛和牛肉	Oxes and Beef	782691	251846	818751	137446	12640	503660	34269
羊和羊肉	Goat,Sheep and Mutton	621497	208729	701562	83233	1126	488555	43385
家禽	Poultry	1798257	283676	1871530	937375	432074	386651	62014
鲜蛋	Fresh Eggs	1029010	277373	1049821	128879		808341	2451
鲜菜	Fresh Vegetable	45318582	13742361	45401957	15418672	23936	14285038	22485
鲜瓜果	Fresh Melon and Fruit	17128525	5757085	17239161	5315033	32360	5451123	3736
水产品	Aquatic Products	2438178	1001920	2491742	700010	68825	1246780	92247

10-9 大中型批发零售贸易企业商品购进、销售、库存数量
PURCHASES,SALES AND INVENTORY VOLUME OF LARGE AND MEDIUM ENTERPRISES IN WHOLESALE AND RETAIL SALE TRADES

项目		Item		从生产者购进 Purchase from Producers	市外购进 Purchase from Outside	商品总销售 Total Sales	# 对生产经营单位销售 To Producer	# 出口 Export	# 零售量 Retail Sales	年末库存 Inventory (year-end)
粮 食	(百公斤)	Grain	(100 kg)	3090575	8508222	32432491	5770922	4121902	1522970	1.9E+07
食用植物油	(百公斤)	Edible Vegetable Oil	(100 kg)	659240	2961836	6770960	1625044		516397	773392
猪和猪肉	(百公斤)	Hog and Pork	(100 kg)	716823	659650	1202076	350087	9214	333090	149965
牛和牛肉	(百公斤)	Cattle and Beef	(100 kg)	41840	26827	68410	450	12570	43330	30919
羊和羊肉	(百公斤)	Goat,Sheep and Mutton	(100 kg)	26787	25457	75682	271	1076	50378	39455
家 禽	(百公斤)	Poultry	(100 kg)	222842	159538	279095	1324	179004	93138	9274
鲜 蛋	(百公斤)	Fresh Eggs	(100 kg)	33836	4939	42747	245		40384	981
鲜 菜	(百公斤)	Fresh Vegetable	(100 kg)	449997	196432	542982	20088	14936	341311	20165
鲜瓜果	(百公斤)	Fresh Melon and Fruit	(100 kg)	1202792	994790	1299538	229	15270	161447	2726
水产品	(百公斤)	Aquatic Product	(100 kg)	562282	441818	596336	334708	68825	94077	83637
食 糖	(百公斤)	Sugar	(100 kg)	962685	1321946	5667483	460539	2946294	124319	1086357

10-9 续表1 continued

项目 Item	从生产者购进 Purchase from Producers	市外购进 Purchase from Outside	商品总销售 Total Sales	# 对生产经营单位销售 To Producer	# 出口 Export	# 零售量 Retail Sales	年末库存 Inventory (year-end)
卷烟 (箱) Cigarettes (case)	1055118	2282497	6116530	5443	143791	232124	179531
酒 (百公斤) Alcoholic Beverage (100 kg)	670976	258281	1080497	13098	22015	457586	141196
茶叶 (百公斤) Tea (100 kg)	222047	178525	246992	326	158884	59899	13850
棉花 (百公斤) Cotton (100 kg)	2582293	5756748	9511533	8672119	680379	183	3840708
鞋 (百双) Shoe (100 pairs)	249092	139178	359819	6456	128019	176582	52040
# 皮鞋 (百双) Leather Shoe (100 pairs)	97805	43844	138052		23687	89700	24952
布 (百米) Cloth (100 m)	2949678	2575750	2643652	452529	2107025	57192	399236
# 棉布 (百米) Cotton Cloth (100 m)	1551065	1386468	1440697	278350	1131232	24745	195213
各种服装 (百件) All Garments (100 pieces)	1443771	432844	1524527	22095	796495	571340	166964
手表 (百个) Watches (100)	4175	2634	11754		400	10089	1388
黄金饰品 (千元) Gold Ornament (1000 yuan)	1618722	684874	2366516	200373	810610	1166604	488212
照相机 (台) Cameras (unit)	413661	487232	675728	35478	6289	284682	58397
自行车 (辆) Bicycle (unit)	253245	180742	352499	17600	112870	211273	20466
电视机 (台) TV Sets (unit)	1095295	432015	1483596	5271	177463	796116	120968
# 彩色电视机 Color TV Set	1056672	410216	1287947	5050	11380	771500	117725
# 64厘米及以上 64 centimeter and above	756657	267380	875796	2789		566114	80478
组合音响 (台) Hi-Fi (unit)	41414	14528	79136	21		59049	16212
摄像机 (架) Pickup Camera (set)	14621	7677	29319	20		26209	4083
录相机 (台) Video-corders (unit)	9739	5376	16786	1380		12304	8211
影碟机 (台) Video CD (unit)	328737	116933	506316	212	12643	432366	38671
家用电风扇 (台) Electrical Fans (unit)	229873	95113	404190	438	2220	293052	71382
家用电冰箱 (台) Refrigerators (unit)	281165	149750	409432	112338		221647	61053
家用洗衣机 (台) Washing Machine (unit)	378814	147023	457505	1334	5875	318019	94739
房间空调器 (台) Air Conditioners (unit)	598368	271735	809233	8215		512570	80028
微波炉 (台) Microwave Oven (unit)	344952	178655	441452	3		296945	56735

10-9 续表2 continued

项目 Item			从生产者购进 Purchase from Producers	市外购进 Purchase from Outside	商品总销售 Total Sales	# 对生产经营单位销售 To Producer	# 出口 Export	# 零售量 Retail Sales	年末库存 Inventory (year-end)
热水淋浴器	(台) Showers	(unit)	228476	82305	323490	160		300153	35618
冰柜	(台) Ice Cabinet	(unit)	31779	22696	54556	3699		37938	10909
吸尘器	(台) Dust Catcher	(unit)	62260	40783	145522	48	36906	97535	14523
抽油烟机	(台) Range Hoods	(uhit)	251082	53108	340290	45094	5766	221574	17453
电饭锅	(个) Electric Rice Cooker	(unit)	319351	122056	500819	27		346353	106910
微型计算机	(台) Micro Computers	(unit)	71662	11387	95336	7816		60461	1951
普通电话机	(部) Telephones	(unit)	756469	407635	1003974	136072	2420	430053	93034
移动电话机	(部) Mobilphone	(unit)	7379111	4484111	8059426	1788657		211626	741450
寻呼机	(部) BP	(unit)	165560	28363	275600	158101		98515	55442
化学肥料	(吨) Chemical Fertilizer	(ton)	1510448	1400005	2679296	1951157	58642	2800	446945
化学农药	(吨) Farm Chemical	(ton)	10570	12559	20061	5120	3911	1006	2843
农用塑料薄膜	(吨) Agricultural Plastic Film	(ton)	16957	8133	15421	3822	1	956	4044
煤炭	(吨) Coal	(ton)	43652301	42357562	47553574	3144958	39285043	1231308	895243
木材	(立方米) Timber	(cu.m)	697550	467212	1045236	693976	322166	4770	616560
汽油	(吨) Gasoline	(ton)	734638	1152183	2340665	435582	337125	578973	738545
煤油	(吨) Kerosene	(ton)	1074146	1178808	1256162	1053539	67600	7218	109833
柴油	(吨) Diesel Oil	(ton)	518983	566599	1164662	292526	66558	192282	214881
钢材	(吨) Steel Products	(ton)	4768385	2474823	6774865	4840131	46950	86262	545680
铜	(吨) Copper	(ton)	57136	56013	71272	55755	282		3267
铝	(吨) Aluminum	(ton)	64473	19793	72974	61986		1100	4032
水泥	(吨) Cement	(ton)	1116419	526304	1230787	1112726	43815	19589	336488
汽车	(辆) Automobile	(unit)	43841	36283	72296	10099		39450	9358
# 小轿车	(辆) Cars	(unit)	21905	20742	39692	2332		23885	4671
摩托车	(辆) Motorcycle	(unit)	58588	37094	68734	6202	13261	38615	9807
拖拉机	(台) Tractors	(unit)	237	1628	290	200	12	65	69

10-10 重点零售商业企业主要经济指标

单位：万元

商业企业	Enterprise	商品销售收入 Sales Revenue	
		2000	1999
百货类	**Department Store**		
北京百盛轻工发展有限公司	Beijing Parkson Light Industry Development CO.,LTD	83929	68420
城乡贸易中心股份有限公司	Beijing Urban-Rural Trade Center CO.,LTD	57357	69529
北京北辰购物中心	Beijing North Star Shopping Center	105140	81051
北京燕莎友谊商城	YouYI Shopping City CO.,LTD	93649	88488
赛特购物中心	Scitech Plaza Scitech Group CO.,LTD	74714	67852
北京双安商场	Shuangan Department Store CO.,LTD	98317	87544
王府井百货大楼	Beijing Wangfujing Department Store (Group) CO.,LTD	123509	77138
北京华联商厦有限公司	Hualian Mansion CO.,LTD	60039	37637
西单商场股份有限公司	Beijing Xidan Shopping CO.,LTD	136918	125980
菜市口百货有限责任公司	Caishiko Department Store C0.,LTD	41308	36063
北京市复兴商业城	Fuxing Shopping City	44262	43730
北京翠微集团	Cuiwei Tower	93879	79083
北京蓝岛大厦	Blue island Mansion	92017	97094
北京市西单购物中心	Beijing Xidan Shopping CO.,LTD	24891	34112
北京东安集团公司长安商场	Changan Market	64967	55347
北京城乡华懋商厦有限公司	Beijing Chenxianghuamao Mansion CO.,LTD	16837	17181
中贸联万客隆商业有限公司	CTA Makro Commercial CO.,LTD	69450	84012
北京世都百货有限责任公司	Beijing World Department Store CO.,LTD	23996	27183
北京庄胜崇光百货商场	Beijing Junefield Sogo Department Store	62365	41893
北京华普吉商业贸易有限公司	Beijing Huapu Commercial CO.,LTD	55390	31588
北京中旭三利百货公司	Beijing Zhongxu Sunry Shopping Center	19739	24117
北京贵友大厦有限公司	Beijing Mansion Guiyou CO.,LTD	36007	39117
北京东安集团公司	Beijing Sun Dong An CO.,LTD	40518	36460
北京创益佳商场	Carrefour	45025	46293
北京燕莎望京购物中心	Beijing Yansha Wangjing Wholesale Warehouse	42498	31639
国华商场有限责任公司	Guohua Department Store CO.,LTD	17094	17112
西单赛特商城有限责任公司	Xidan Scitech Shopping City	24355	27277
北京小白羊超市	Beijing Little White Sheep Supermarkt	34817	12140
北京锐步体育用品中心	Beijing Reebok Sporting Goods Center	8866	6079
北京兴城商厦	Beijing Xingcheng Market	24497	22063
白广路百货有限责任公司	Baiguang Road Department Store CO.,LTD	11676	11217
北京市大明眼镜公司	Beingjing Daming Glasses CO.,LTD	9045	7665
亿客隆商业股份有限公司	Beijing Yikelong Commercial Limited Company	41321	48389
方庄购物中心股份有限公司	Fangzhuang Shopping Center CO.,LTD	12110	14231
北京市京北大世界商贸集团	Beijing Jingbei Great World Commercial Trade Group	18028	12917
百盛购物中心百盛商场	Parkson Shopping Center, Parkson Department Store	11473	10901
北京友谊商店股份有限公司	Beijing Friendship Store CO.,LTD	16594	17232
北京中友百货有限责任公司	Beijing Zhongyou Department Store CO.,LTD	42366	23669
北京市星座商厦	Beijing Constellation Market CO.,LTD	13929	15677
北京市朝阳商业大楼	Chaoyang Commercial Mansion	10285	10281
北京金伦股份有限公司	Beijing Jinlun CO.,LTD	18076	22011
北京大百商贸集团	Beijing DaBai Commodity Trading Group	22685	23140
北京市成文厚帐簿卡片公司	Chengwenhou Account Book Paper Company	3972	4759

MAIN ECONOMIC INDICATORS FOR MAJOR RETAIL ENTERPRISES

(10000 yuan)

利税总额 Total Profits		人均销售额 Sales Value Per Capita		人均创利税 Pre-tax Per Capita		销售利税率(%) Ratio of Pre-tax to Sales Revenue(%)		存货周转率(%) Turnover Rate of Stock(%)	
2000	1999	2000	1999	2000	1999	2000	1999	2000	1999
11382	5928	127.7	94.5	15.5	8.2	12.2	8.7	2658.1	2243.5
13566	20250	51.9	36.7	12.2	10.7	23.7	29.1	774.3	685.4
7946	5360	106.0	83.6	8.0	5.5	7.6	6.6	1321.0	1151.2
13486	12609	56.1	49.0	8.1	7.0	14.4	14.2	909.4	745.5
7737	7180	92.9	70.3	9.6	7.4	10.4	10.6	1254.8	1107.9
5646	4207	54.8	44.5	3.1	2.1	5.7	4.8	1856.8	1283.2
7511	1679	40.5	22.5	2.5	0.5	6.1	2.2	2196.8	1158.3
6386	590	96.5	59.2	10.3	0.9	10.6	1.6	1324.6	310.4
11526	12358	43.2	38.3	3.6	3.8	8.4	9.8	553.5	618.6
4105	3916	86.4	82.7	8.6	9.0	9.9	10.9	3433.6	468.6
3633	3402	53.1	50.3	4.4	3.9	8.2	7.8	1651.0	1311.0
5496	3852	41.5	32.9	2.4	1.6	5.9	4.9	734.2	753.2
3776	6360	35.7	35.2	1.5	2.3	4.1	6.6	1044.1	550.1
3203	4074	45.4	43.2	5.8	5.2	12.9	11.9	1752.9	1977.0
3557	2095	35.8	28.8	2.0	1.1	5.5	3.8	1025.5	1230.0
2101	2067	84.6	71.3	10.6	8.6	12.5	12.0	4192.0	2075.2
1105	1623	120.2	113.8	1.9	2.2	1.6	1.9	1294.9	1671.8
2784		53.2	32.5	6.2		11.6		892.4	652.3
658		105.7	61.7	1.1		1.1		2099.5	1229.9
1417		36.7	24.1	0.9		2.6		1472.5	944.9
1322	173	82.6	46.6	5.5	0.3	6.7	0.7	908.9	981.8
1280	2394	47.2	48.5	1.7	3.0	3.6	6.1	1420.2	1023.0
1385	1283	33.6	25.2	1.1	0.9	3.4	3.5	1784.8	2686.4
481	98	73.1	68.6	0.8	0.1	1.1	0.2	2174.8	1818.0
923	655	44.7	39.2	1.0	0.8	2.2	2.1	1169.4	1150.5
1399	1580	49.3	47.5	4.0	4.4	8.2	9.2	793.2	835.2
572	1405	69.8	64.2	1.6	3.3	2.3	5.2	3024.1	2470.2
1485	433	43.9	32.3	1.9	1.2	4.3	3.6	420.9	454.0
1504	1037	286.0	184.2	48.5	31.4	17.0	17.1	876.4	521.5
586	416	39.6	35.7	0.9	0.7	2.4	1.9	2226.9	1366.9
529	547	58.4	51.9	2.6	2.5	4.5	4.9	2332.6	1425.5
2622	2121	18.1	14.4	5.2	4.0	29.0	27.7	1005.4	517.9
901	1117	25.2	25.8	0.5	0.6	2.2	2.3	660.9	684.3
845	1207	25.2	26.6	1.8	2.3	7.0	8.5	959.1	
1061	122	25.2	18.3	1.5	0.2	5.9	0.9	533.7	421.5
595		56.2	42.7	2.9		5.2		880.8	657.1
1841	1597	15.2	14.9	1.7	1.4	11.1	9.3	162.1	206.5
		91.1	65.4					13073.1	5814.5
524	758	20.4	23.8	0.8	1.2	3.8	4.8	1848.0	1386.5
359	350	33.6	33.6	1.2	1.1	3.5	3.4	2574.1	1051.4
565	718	18.7	20.9	0.6	0.7	3.1	3.3	554.0	547.5
802	750	13.7	14.0	0.5	0.5	3.5	3.2	303.7	264.4
633	742	38.6	43.7	6.1	6.8	15.9	15.6	543.0	342.9

10-10 续表 1 continued

单位：万元

商业企业	Enterprise	商品销售收入 Sales Revenue 2000	1999
西城区新街口百货商场	Xinjiekou Department Store	8057	11402
北京物美商城有限责任公司	Wumei Department Store CO.,LTD	47392	41383
北京西单商场顺义联营大楼	Xidan Shopping Shunyi Commercial Mansion	14475	17467
北京顺义隆华购物中心	Beijing Shunyi Longhua Shopping Center	18095	13101
北京市隆福大厦	Beijing Longfu Department Store	38268	49751
北京市顺义国泰商业大厦	Beijing Shunyi Guotai Trade Building	11206	10408
北京市昌平新世纪商城	Beijing Changping New Century Business city	14052	12162
华奥商厦有限责任公司	Huaao Department Store	10051	13618
北京市天桥百货商场	Tianqiao Department Store	10418	15408
北京利生体育商厦	Beijing Tianyuan Lisheng Sports Trade Tower	7296	9439
怀柔百货大楼股份有限公司	Department Store CO.,LTD Huairou Beijing	12099	12324
北京当代商城实业公司	Modern Plaza	33338	36116
北京市海淀金五星商业大厦	Haidian Jinwuxing Commercial Mansion	9289	9301
北京市超音波总公司	Super Wave Chain	20060	27764
北京工美艺术世界大厦	Beijing Arts & Crafts World	7548	4714
北京麒麟大厦	Beijing Kyin-Plaza	11769	10746
北京市西四电器公司	Xisi Electrical Appliance Company	2453	3044
北京中商西友大厦有限公司	Beijing Zhongshang Seiyu Mansion CO.,LTD	12450	12865
德福瑞百货超市有限公司	Defurui Department CO.,LTD	6934	2890
北京市昌平商业大厦	Beijing Changping Commercial Building	8375	7029
华光商厦有限责任公司	Huaguang Department Store	4659	5971
光明百货市场	The Bright Department Store	3407	6092
北京市丰台百货商场	Beijing Fengtai Department Store	5588	8894
北京天元和平商业大厦	Beijing Tianyuan Heping Commercial House	5025	12864
北京市劲松商场	Beijing Jinsong Department Store	4758	6106
北京市房山商业大楼	Fangshan Commercial Building	2014	2223
北京银岛商厦有限责任公司	Beijing Silver Island Commercial House CO.,LTD	3714	4842
北京恒中超市有限责任公司	Beijing Hengzhong Supermart CO.,LTD	3051	1225
北京雪银大厦	Xueyin Mansion	5459	9049
北京地百商贸股份有限公司	Beijing Dibai Commerce And Trading CO.,LTD	9372	8172
北京市东高地百货商场	Donggaodi Department Store	2154	3027
北京市宣武区内联升鞋店	Neiliansheng Shoes Store	1392	1558
京西旅游公司百货商场	Department Store Of Beijing Jingxi Tourism Development CO.,LTD	2708	3168
北京市东门仓第一百货商场	Dongcanmeng No.1 Department Store	2808	2811
北京丝绸商店	Beijing Silk Store	1240	1390
北京市鼓楼电器公司	Beijing Gulou Electrical Appliance Company	2851	3288
三环毛纺织集团三友商场	Beijing Sanyou Market CO.,LTD	3226	4169
北京正阳商城	Zhengyang Shopping City	1277	1825
房山区良乡商场	Liangxiang Market	1675	1618
前门文化体育用品公司	Qianmen Culture & Sport Branch Company	1509	1740
朝阳区团结湖百货商场	Tuanyiegu Department Store	1928	2608
宣武菜市口文化用品商店	Caishiko Stationery Store	768	833
北京市西四商场	Xisi Department Store	1952	1939

10-10 续表 2 continued

(10000 yuan)

利税总额 Total Profits		人均销售额 Sales Value Per Capita		人均创利税 Pre-tax Per Capita		销售利税率(%) Ratio of Pre-tax to Sales Revenue(%)		存货周转率(%) Turnover Rate of Stock(%)	
2000	1999	2000	1999	2000	1999	2000	1999	2000	1999
550	585	17.5	24.5	1.2	1.3	6.8	5.1	1042.7	1539.1
	1217	21.6	20.8		0.6		2.9	900.2	781.8
372	584	20.1	24.2	0.5	0.8	2.6	3.3	698.2	
199	54	35.1	25.7	0.4	0.1	1.1	0.4	560.8	554.8
		21.8	22.1					1046.5	1269.8
411	331	35.6	19.1	1.3	0.6	3.7	3.2	280.7	278.0
445	558	19.6	19.3	0.6	0.9	3.2	4.6	390.6	298.6
465	739	15.0	19.6	0.7	1.1	4.6	5.4	687.2	772.1
414	518	13.1	21.6	0.5	0.7	4.0	3.4	776.4	580.5
843	728	9.4	11.3	1.1	0.9	11.6	7.7		
100	50	41.9	41.1	0.3	0.2	0.8	0.4	793.4	1015.1
	450	38.9	31.5		0.4		1.2	279.5	294.9
236	231	21.7	20.7	0.6	0.5	2.5	2.5	560.1	509.3
	572	63.5	67.6		1.4		2.1	238.9	327.7
512	310	10.8	5.8	0.7	0.4	6.8	6.6	226.1	117.7
370	370	11.9	10.7	0.4	0.4	3.1	3.4	399.3	292.5
208	347	30.3	35.0	2.6	4.0	8.5	11.4	543.9	856.2
22	5	20.5	20.1			0.2		1572.1	1184.9
		121.6	10.1					62470.0	383.5
190	166	22.2	15.4	0.5	0.4	2.3	2.4	575.1	419.2
193	263	13.9	15.3	0.6	0.7	4.1	4.4	757.9	785.9
92	150	17.0	16.9	0.5	0.4	2.7	2.5	5932.7	818.9
142	216	11.9	12.8	0.3	0.3	2.5	2.4	1849.4	2795.5
410	1179	7.8	18.6	0.6	1.7	8.2	9.2		
200	287	10.3	12.5	0.4	0.6	4.2	4.7	624.1	692.8
115	106	14.9	14.1	0.9	0.7	5.7	4.8	902.0	907.8
129	263	13.8	13.6	0.5	0.7	3.5	5.4	646.8	692.6
39		25.0	10.0	0.3		1.3		2245.4	355.4
220	311	5.6	8.5	0.2	0.3	4.0	3.4	536.5	
	278	20.7	15.8	0.0	0.5		3.4	526.7	11058.1
129	193	10.6	13.5	0.6	0.9	6.0	6.4	574.4	613.2
175	149	9.2	9.0	1.2	0.9	12.6	9.6	408.6	308.0
146	313	8.6	9.7	0.5	1.0	5.4	9.9	314.6	379.8
41	65	14.6	13.1	0.2	0.3	1.5	2.3	1271.1	2049.2
159	133	10.7	11.5	1.4	1.1	12.8	9.6	228.2	247.0
	57	16.7	17.6		0.3		1.7	1068.7	3137.1
119		5.9	6.7	0.2		3.7		356.7	406.4
70	77	10.9	11.4	0.6	0.5	5.5	4.2	504.0	609.0
71	60	8.5	7.0	0.4	0.3	4.2	3.7	490.2	283.6
81	89	8.7	9.7	0.5	0.5	5.4	5.1	254.5	249.4
59	92	10.1	11.5	0.3	0.4	3.1	3.5	415.5	3374.1
44		9.0	9.4	0.5		5.7		667.8	504.8
		10.3	8.6					821.6	842.3

10-10 续表 3 continued

单位：万元

商业企业	Enterprise	商品销售收入 Sales Revenue	
		2000	1999
北京密云燕赛购物中心	Beijing Yansai Shopping Center	2160	2033
北京亿客发商贸集团	Yikefa Commerce and Trading Group	2644	3344
北京快乐城堡购物中心	Beijing Happy Castle Supermart	751	180
八角西单商场有限责任公司	Baijiao Xidan Shopping Center	1446	1990
北京三里河百货商场	Sanlihe Department Store	808	1100
北京天元安定门百货商场	Beijing Tianyuan Andingmen Department Store	308	2282
北京绿屋百货有限责任公司	Green House Department Store CO.,LTD	1630	2782
北京市新汇奥尼尔百货商场	Xinhuiaonier Department Store	1543	1699
北京燕京前门商厦	Yanjing Qianmen Commercial company	1718	9607
北京市西直门五金批发商店	Xizhimen Hardware Wholesale Store	1122	2069
北京西四万方超级市场	Xisi Wanfang Supermart	1237	1781
万方西单商场有限责任公司	Beijing Wanfang Xidan Shopping CO.,LTD	1543	12454
北京市宣武和平门百货商场	Hepingmen Department Store	634	592
元隆丝绸股份有限公司	Yuanlong Silk CO.,LTD	1077	1280
延庆县百货大楼	Yanqing Department Store	210	995
新时代妇女儿童用品公司	Newtime Articles for Women and Children	62	154
北京市平谷银座购物中心	Pinggu Yinzuo Shopping Center	7	26
副食类	**Grocery**		
北京稻香村食品集团	Beijing Daoxiangcun Food Group	39728	38090
北京市崇文门菜市场	Chongwenmen Food Market of Beijing	24173	23927
北京吴裕泰茶叶公司	Wuyutai Tea Company	5011	3954
奥士凯集团公司朝内菜市场	Inside-Chaoyangmen Food Market	6954	6552
北京京客隆商厦	Jingkelong Market	118561	70069
北京东城区王府井食品商场	Wangfujing Food Store	2852	990
北京市朝阳区燕丰商场	Yanfeng Department Store	10876	11192
北太平庄商场有限责任公司	Beitaipingzhuang Department Store	6193	9001
北京市朝阳区万惠商场	Wanhui Department Store	8845	8898
北京市老白广路商场	Old Baiguang Road Department Store	1869	2404
北京市西城和平门菜市场	Hepingmen Food Market	2340	2610
东城区奥之光银龙商贸公司	Yinlong Commerce and Trading Company	1485	1831
西城区地安门副食商场	Di'anmen Food Store	3354	4235
宣武西珠市口副食商店	Xuanwumen Food Store	1365	1831
北京市宣武宣武门副食商场	Xizhushikou Food Store	1616	1491
北京市新街口购物中心	Xinjiekou Shopping Center	1702	2167
北京市金顶街碧泉食品商场	Jindingjie Biquan Food Store	1183	1285
东城区奥之光宝龙商贸公司	Baolong Commerce and Trading Company	1102	1172
北京奥士凯裕龙商贸公司	Yulong Commerce and Trading Company	760	809
北京市奥士凯万龙商贸公司	Wanlong Commerce and Trading Company	692	1326
北京西四万方超级市场	Xisi Wanfang Supermart	1237	1781
东城区奥之光富龙商贸公司	Fulong Commerce and Trading Company	541	733
北京市海淀区海淀菜市场	Haidian Food Market	1147	2314
北京桂香村食品中心	Fragrant Village Food Shop	956	1334
北京博兰特北大地副食商场	Beidadi Food Store	715	1390
北京市京沪食品商场	Jinghu Food Store	726	

10-10 续表 4 continued

(10000 yuan)

利税总额 Total Profits		人均销售额 Sales Value Per Capita		人均创利税 Pre-tax Per Capita		销售利税率(%) Ratio of Pre-tax to Sales Revenue(%)		存货周转率(%) Turnover Rate of Stock(%)	
2000	1999	2000	1999	2000	1999	2000	1999	2000	1999
		7.0	7.0					807.8	1011.2
		7.0	4.7					602.6	441.4
		10.9	1.8					3475.0	342.5
		4.5	5.8					1429.9	1613.3
34	90	4.2	5.4	0.2	0.4	4.2	8.2	811.9	1170.7
75	376	0.9	6.4	0.2	1.1	24.4	16.5		
	437	11.4	15.9		2.5		15.7		214600.0
		10.0	11.0					273.8	335.4
	135	6.0	16.0		0.2		1.4	240.9	364.4
	110	15.6	17.1		0.9		5.3	420.8	494.9
45	24	5.0	7.0	0.2	0.1	3.6	1.3		
	492	3.0	24.6		1.0		4.0	102.4	1275.5
		7.6	6.4					587.8	474.3
	102	4.6	8.8		0.7		8.0	101.9	122.6
	36	1.3	6.0		0.2		3.6	107.3	505.2
		0.8	1.6					44.5	31.8
			0.1					2.2	8.0
4042	3933	51.3	50.3	5.2	5.2	10.2	10.3	6084.5	1972.3
1033	1398	25.4	17.0	1.1	1.0	4.3	5.8	1361.9	1343.5
879	730	32.3	25.8	5.7	4.8	17.5	18.5	1271.5	641.0
447	410	27.6	27.3	1.8	1.7	6.4	6.3	1421.7	1419.3
3488	1616	25.5	11.8	0.8	0.3	2.9	2.3	706.1	436.6
357		21.1	6.9	2.6		12.5		5518.4	1332.3
419	449	20.9	22.3	0.8	0.9	3.9	4.0	1014.3	922.6
379	528	19.5	25.1	1.2	1.5	6.1	5.9	1718.6	2007.9
278	206	20.1	20.6	0.6	0.5	3.1	2.3	1292.5	1230.4
69	63	27.9	24.3	1.0	0.6	3.7	2.6	1682.1	1154.0
86	148	20.3	17.9	0.7	1.0	3.7	5.7	1503.9	1542.3
117	139	6.5	4.1	0.5	0.3	7.9	7.6	2500.0	1572.8
53	94	9.1	11.7	0.1	0.3	1.6	2.2	1862.2	2437.6
32	74	80.3	16.6	1.9	0.7	2.3	4.0	25260.0	2695.0
39	39	25.7	19.4	0.6	0.5	2.4	2.6	1535.2	1548.1
66	170	6.1	7.6	0.2	0.6	3.9	7.8		3503.9
44	36	25.2	21.4	0.9	0.6	3.7	2.8	732.6	945.8
66	75	4.4	4.4	0.3	0.3	6.0	6.4	578.8	514.4
49	31	2.9	2.7	0.2	0.1	6.4	3.8	2064.5	1175.9
93	60	2.4	4.4	0.3	0.2	13.4	4.5	1070.9	1091.4
45	24	5.0	7.0	0.2	0.1	3.6	1.3		
41	40	3.6	4.2	0.3	0.2	7.6	5.5	2700.0	3918.8
	69	5.9	8.9		0.3		3.0	3460.7	1148.8
39	146	3.3	4.3	0.1	0.5	4.1	10.9	445.5	
	73	8.9	11.4		0.6		5.3	2144.4	11350.0
21		4.7		0.1		2.9		422.9	

10-11 商委各局大中型批发零售贸易业财务状况

单位：万元

企业名称	Enterprise	商品销售收入 Sales Revenue	商品销售收入净额 Net Value of Sales Revenue
北京一商集团有限责任公司	Beijing Yishang Group CO.,LTD	254982	254982
北京二商集团有限责任公司	Beijing Ershang(Group) CO.,LTD	238441	238427
北京粮食集团有限责任公司	Beijing Grain Group CO.,LTD	35905	35905
北京市粮食局	Beijing Grain bureau	108910	108910
北京市供销合作社	The Supply And Marketing Cooperatives In Beijing	153998	153840
北京燕莎集团有限责任公司	Beijing Yansha Group CO.,LTD	179825	176012
中国烟草总公司北京市公司	China National Tobacco Corp., Beijing Corp.,	643665	643665
北京王府井百货(集团)股份有限公司	Beijing Wangfujing Department Store (Group) CO.,LTD	123509	123509
北京西单友谊集团	Beijing Xidan Friendship Group	173711	173711
北京东安集团公司	Beijing Dongan Group CO.,LTD	206419	206419
中盐北京市盐业公司	Beijing Salt Corp., China General industry Corp.,	8820	8820

企业名称	Enterprise	财务费用 Financial Expense	利润总额 Total Profits
北京一商集团有限责任公司	Beijing Yishang Group CO.,LTD	2521	649
北京二商集团有限责任公司	Beijing Ershang(Group) CO.,LTD	4166	-311
北京粮食集团有限责任公司	Beijing Grain Group CO.,LTD	-515	3187
北京市粮食局	Beijing Grain bureau	39929	
北京市供销合作社	The Supply And Marketing Cooperatives In Beijing	1885	102
北京燕莎集团有限责任公司	Beijing Yansha Group CO.,LTD	923	1867
中国烟草总公司北京市公司	China National Tobacco Corp., Beijing Corp.,	2740	20718
北京王府井百货(集团)股份有限公司	Beijing Wangfujing Department Store (Group) CO.,LTD	-1636	3877
北京西单友谊集团	Beijing Xidan Friendship Group	-10	7550
北京东安集团公司	Beijing Dongan Group CO.,LTD	1160	2807
中盐北京市盐业公司	Beijing Salt Corp., China General industry Corp.,	141	144

FINANCIAL INDICATORS OF LARGE AND MEDIUM ENTERPRISES IN WHOLESALE AND RETAIL SALE TRADES OF COMMERCIAL COMMITTEE

(10000 yuan)

商　品 销售成本 Sales Cost	经营费用 Operating Expense	商品销售 税金及附加 Sales Tax and Extra Charges	商　品 销售利润 After-tax Profits	主　营 业务利润 Profits from Major Business	其　他 业务利润 Profits from Other Business	管理费用 Overhead Cost
235398	8817	613	10155	10155	4788	14003
213456	16532	731	7709	7709	4242	12068
37037	2446	278	-3856	-3856	2821	4414
120051			-11142	-11142		141
142357	8477	193	2813	2813	8330	9944
143107	17294	187	15425	15427	476	13966
602386	8675	490	32113	32113	486	9343
105030	5321	490	12668	12668	1459	10707
147694	6960	509	18548	18548	2183	13926
170314	14998	1166	19942	19942	989	17245
6165	650	38	1968	1968	345	2013

应付工资 Wages Payable	资产总计 Total Assets	流动资产 合　计 Total Circulating Assets	固定资产 合　计 Total Fixed Assets	流动负债 合　计 Total Liquid Liability	长期负债 合　计 Total Long-term Liability	实　收 资　本 Total Capital
7433	204462	110128	74034	122294	26203	44236
8326	247572	187190	47599	191343	22667	35875
1484	112613	71743	21258	55498	3282	30926
20	655204	655137	67	613115	41939	150
5370	93465	54305	30545	66817	3911	18123
8642	62549	46278	11110	41578	3601	19049
3718	156808	88747	49320	61105	21	12129
5858	230134	140671	35567	74699	421	39297
4751	172419	73848	65721	65471	900	53183
11835	148221	57276	33851	82020	-849	40985
577	12516	3957	7384	5826	1528	2946

10-12 大中型批发零售贸易业财务状况

单位：万元

项目	Item	流动资产合计 Total Circulating Assets	#货币资金 Cash	#应收帐款 Accounts Receivable	#存货 Stock	长期投资 Long-term Investment
合计	**Total**	18284625	2519856	3797386	4313726	4638355
按企业登记注册类型分	**Grouped by Type of Enterprises Registered**					
内资企业	Domestic Investment	18126962	2462171	3774456	4281953	4634648
国有企业	State-Owned	13757276	1932964	3251073	2730936	4130550
集体企业	Collective Owned	1530707	101711	95825	826296	65882
私营企业	Private Owned	215819	34395	33948	90601	3717
联营企业	Joint Owned	275511	23682	17860	125434	6112
股份合作企业	Share Holding Cooperative	125023	15379	8659	52998	12976
股份有限公司	Share Holding Company	720227	128578	89812	177848	208224
有限责任公司	Limited-Liability Company	1502400	225461	277280	277839	207188
其他企业	Others					
港澳台商投资企业	Hongkong,Macao and Taiwan Funded Enterprises	14473	4732	1072	5417	1280
外商投资企业	Foreign Funded Enterprises	143189	52953	21858	26356	2427
按国民经济行业分	**Grouped by Sectors**					
批发业	Wholesale	15998595	2070036	3552594	3637275	4316767
食品饮料烟草和家庭用品批发业	Food,Beverage,Tobacoo and Family Use Goods	5189509	578017	719006	2006751	1566438
食品饮料烟草批发业	Food,Beverage and Tobacoo	2259590	337878	261556	919409	287836
棉麻、土畜产品批发业	Cotton,Flax,Local and Animal Products	1372571	38859	106200	720200	142148
纺织品、服装和鞋帽批发业	Textile,Garments,Shoes and Hats	559162	68527	125925	105139	1026544
日用百货批发业	Daily Use Goods	349029	25173	50820	68486	27503
日用杂品批发业	Grocery	14021	3148	1518	6155	87
五金交电化工批发业	Hardware,Electrical Appliance and Chemical	222575	35629	56170	55119	32289
药品及医疗器械批发业	Medicine and Medical Appliance	412562	68804	116818	132243	50031
能源、材料和机械电子设备批发业	Energy,Materials,Machinery and Electronic Equipments	7158858	987889	1954983	1041337	2025450
能源批发业	Energy	1120602	160173	346931	126558	180986
化工材料批发业	Chemical Materials	580860	95836	144815	117294	215587
木材批发业	Timbers	75188	7547	17420	16497	17990
建筑材料批发业	Building Materials	184024	35123	45970	27276	24486
矿产品批发业	Mineral Products	1125795	123535	290345	90263	296251
金属材料批发业	Metal Materials	1624793	163092	411640	227738	773632
机械、电子设备批发业	Machinery and Electronic Equipments	2071853	341046	637043	327070	433415
汽车摩托车及零配件批发业	Spares and Fittings of Automobile and Motorcycle	335319	57421	54670	104450	70171
再生物资回收批发业	Recovery of Reclaimed Materials	40425	4115	6150	4191	12933
其他批发业	Others	3650228	504130	878605	589187	724879
工艺美术品批发业	Handicrafts	308197	27250	60277	28325	145024
图书报刊批发业	Books,Newspaper and Magazines	166156	41575	26639	43867	36037
农业生产资料批发业	Agricultural Capital Goods	663435	48586	128312	180643	124070
其他类未包括的批发	Others	2512441	386719	663377	336352	419747
零售业	Retail	2286029	449820	244792	676452	321588
食品、饮料和烟草零售业	Food,Beverage and Tobacoo	286196	66395	5070	89494	20739
日用百货零售业	Daily Use Goods	1065417	235603	32176	259427	198541
纺织品、服装和鞋帽零售业	Textile,Garments,Shoes and Hats	70762	6094	4043	29743	4129
日用杂品零售业	Grocery	7820	1875	261	3308	257
五金交电化工零售业	Hardware,Electrical Appliance and Chemical	218290	39509	25872	78420	25097
药品及医疗器械零售业	Medicine and Medical Appliance	44676	11404	6671	17862	8136
图书报刊零售业	Books,Newspaper and Magazines	64668	20723	4410	34243	12473
其他零售业	Others	528202	68218	166290	163955	52216
按规模划分	**Grouped by Size**					
大型企业	Large Enterprises	7862039	1091652	1585788	2070868	1216407
中型企业	Medium Enterprises	10422585	1428204	2211598	2242858	3421948

FINANCIAL INDICATORS OF LARGE AND MEDIUM ENTERPRISE IN WHOLESALE AND RETAIL SALE TRADES

(10000 yuan)

固定资产合计 Total Fixed Assets	固定资产原价合计 Original Value of Fixed Assets	#生产经营用 for Production Use	累计折旧 Accumulative Depreciation	#本年折旧 of this Year	无形及递延资产合计 Intangible and Deferred Assets	#无形资产 Intangible	其他资产合计 Other Assets	资产合计 Total Assets	流动负债合计 Total Circulating Liability
3116282	3233168	2898740	757622	132545	455961	241771	1629486	28124708	15863298
3015072	3111596	2779649	730688	125519	391596	182386	1624369	27792646	15672562
2087142	2127657	1887681	487132	79619	217068	105475	59903	20251938	11935748
260434	293565	253884	64910	12356	39970	21968	1505674	3402667	1379066
27891	25279	19212	6157	2416	4024	760	266	251717	198034
74634	96573	89397	24040	4871	36051	29699		392308	294715
40552	44046	30544	7113	1382	9198	7262	49	187797	110354
336978	329964	318090	100415	14387	48373	7998	54418	1368219	467674
187441	194512	180842	40921	10487	36911	9224	4060	1937999	1286972
6884	13417	12943	7157	475	1826	859	318	24781	14752
94326	108155	106148	19777	6552	62540	58527	4799	307282	175984
1774905	1894433	1673238	464361	72906	154055	89603	1606035	23850357	13330264
598040	660535	621606	181348	23999	50159	32928	1596047	9000193	4438132
268250	307918	291557	115969	11978	20964	12870	58695	2895335	1814591
81822	90691	90484	15930	2645	12881	10493	1502722	3112144	1238545
114906	107966	104842	10554	1787	1706	1318	479	1702797	485585
33457	32610	29823	8098	956	6027	4842		416016	341924
2462	3244	3136	799	84	255			16825	11066
38836	47000	35174	11077	2340	5799	2293	1589	301088	202458
58307	71107	66590	18922	4210	2527	1112	32562	555988	343963
782209	774232	657765	191435	30153	63708	40068	7875	10038100	6095364
157816	179533	163790	46820	7099	14280	4216	1847	1475531	883306
46957	45150	37569	13921	2425	2791	1527	987	847180	475970
4419	3663	3493	715	133	1162	758		98759	76607
55229	67337	63094	17052	2140	5558	1251	16	269313	211379
123014	69998	18888	16634	1754	563	244	31	1545654	1141010
184465	182654	173036	38950	5181	14682	12045	960	2598531	1407636
161158	170576	145448	41879	8595	15357	11892	4017	2685801	1538811
44467	49339	47331	13355	2564	8891	7808	18	458865	325870
4684	5982	5116	2111	262	425	329		58466	34775
394656	459666	393868	91578	18753	40188	16607	2113	4812064	2796768
45036	46669	41420	10073	1343	5901	5610		504158	321381
36134	44148	25191	11929	1583	1281	881		239607	110165
43998	53273	47594	15571	3167	7684	7426		839186	627537
269489	315576	279664	54006	12661	25324	2690	2113	3229113	1737685
1341377	1338735	1225502	293261	59640	301906	152169	23451	4274351	2533034
171778	191548	168743	46934	9189	36896	24492	1487	517094	334356
916673	857138	785168	166993	34525	206850	84947	18810	2406289	1317981
24262	23234	22877	7174	1150	2842	885		101995	65373
2555	3027	2496	1081	182	292			10925	5528
34388	40263	38768	10126	1471	7877	4342	72	285724	206798
13809	17404	16570	4777	1065	2113	653	18	68752	39362
22913	22559	21526	6775	1292	1402	496		101456	63643
154999	183563	169353	49402	10765	43634	36355	3065	782116	499995
1409232	1483960	1361046	358188	62425	271759	146091	1569093	12328530	6327723
1707049	1749208	1537694	399435	70120	184203	95681	60393	15796178	9535575

10-12 续表 1 continued

单位：万元

项目	Item	#短期借款 Short-term Loans	#应付帐款 Accounts Payable	长期负债合计 Total Long-term Liability	#长期借款 Long-term Loans	负债合计 Total Liabilities
合计	**Total**	**6406179**	**2699150**	**3884589**	**1764005**	**19747886**
按企业登记注册类型分	**Grouped by Type of Enterprises Registered**					
内资企业	Domestic Investment	6365294	2614686	3869954	1751805	19542516
国有企业	State-Owned	4515260	1935382	1952122	1639830	13887870
集体企业	Collective Owned	1138259	184680	1730235	22538	3109301
私营企业	Private Owned	32963	53307	5254	4629	203288
联营企业	Joint Owned	76403	87854	3349	3312	298064
股份合作企业	Share Holding Cooperative	20621	20450	9541	3781	119895
股份有限公司	Share Holding Company	115761	103850	20684	13168	488358
有限责任公司	Limited-Liability Company	466027	229163	148770	64548	1435742
其他企业	Others					
港澳台商投资企业	Hongkong,Macao and Taiwan Funded Enterprises	7500	3163	2034	2026	16786
外商投资企业	Foreign Funded Enterprises	33385	81302	12601	10175	188585
按国民经济行业分	**Grouped by Sectors**					
批发业	Wholesale	5732569	2126334	3690484	1648811	17020748
食品饮料烟草和家庭用品批发业	Food,Beverage,Tobacoo and Family Use Goods	2665476	562336	1930953	71895	6369085
食品饮料烟草批发业	Food,Beverage and Tobacoo	993390	117060	171097	53462	1985688
棉麻、土畜产品批发业	Cotton,Flax,Local and Animal Products	1158380	102649	1680673	500	2919217
纺织品、服装和鞋帽批发业	Textile,Garments,Shoes and Hats	226118	101639	4523	4009	490108
日用百货批发业	Daily Use Goods	139477	67565	13158	5469	355083
日用杂品批发业	Grocery	1308	7162	115		11180
五金交电化工批发业	Hardware,Electrical Appliance and Chemical	85762	30296	8065	5556	210523
药品及医疗器械批发业	Medicine and Medical Appliance	61042	135966	53324	2900	397286
能源、材料和机械电子设备批发业	Energy,Materials,Machinery and Electronic Equipments	1918269	1182108	1024294	857634	7119658
能源批发业	Energy	205355	310819	165254	61370	1048559
化工材料批发业	Chemical Materials	161446	88290	11319	10001	487289
木材批发业	Timbers	38775	5360	8901	8439	85508
建筑材料批发业	Building Materials	52418	35798	2044	13262	213423
矿产品批发业	Mineral Products	409322	161650	115744	69696	1256754
金属材料批发业	Metal Materials	445592	190814	104856	101695	1512493
机械、电子设备批发业	Machinery and Electronic Equipments	448855	309635	598310	589499	2137121
汽车摩托车及零配件批发业	Spares and Fittings of Automobile and Motorcycle	134627	73103	17641	3672	343511
再生物资回收批发业	Recovery of Reclaimed Materials	21878	6638	225		35000
其他批发业	Others	1148824	381890	735237	719283	3532005
工艺美术品批发业	Handicrafts	192334	17447	29066	29477	350447
图书报刊批发业	Books,Newspaper and Magazines	23950	33870	6996	-1	117161
农业生产资料批发业	Agricultural Capital Goods	292308	115001	19840	18087	647377
其他类未包括的批发	Others	640231	215572	679335	671720	2417020
零售业	Retail	673611	572817	194105	115194	2727139
食品、饮料和烟草零售业	Food,Beverage and Tobacoo	52312	83720	35081	20936	369436
日用百货零售业	Daily Use Goods	382651	294352	114268	78889	1432248
纺织品、服装和鞋帽零售业	Textile,Garments,Shoes and Hats	17208	20471	3638	2989	69010
日用杂品零售业	Grocery	1173	2248	419	34	5948
五金交电化工零售业	Hardware,Electrical Appliance and Chemical	50156	33578	4877	1563	211675
药品及医疗器械零售业	Medicine and Medical Appliance	5768	17231	1662	1174	41024
图书报刊零售业	Books,Newspaper and Magazines	6257	34395	34		63676
其他零售业	Others	158085	86822	34126	9609	534121
按规模划分	**Grouped by Size**					
大型企业	Large Enterprises	2717806	1105700	2745148	914304	9072871
中型企业	Medium Enterprises	3688374	1593451	1139441	849701	10675016

10-12 续表 2 continued

(10000 yuan)

所有者权益合计 Ownership Interest	# 实收资本 Proceeds of Capital	国家资本 State	集体资本 Collective	法人资本 Institutional Units	个人资本 Individual	港澳台资本 Hongkong,Macao and Taiwan	外商资本 Foreign	商品销售收入 Sales Revenue
8376822	**5442179**	**3643270**	**220883**	**1298170**	**209480**	**4725**	**65651**	**24464228**
8250130	5308989	3635177	218882	1243319	209480	100	2030	24026609
6364069	4177684	3469351	59021	638343	10969			16114448
293366	236591	9089	137491	55537	33474		1000	2539297
48429	56287	550	2599	13140	39999			658145
94244	86356	24238	2975	52953	5191		1000	330058
67902	63948	1025	1743	37519	23661			253891
879862	346107	54096	1465	214314	76232			1262804
502258	342015	76829	13589	231513	19954	100	30	2867968
7995	10291	4743	255	70		4349	873	59088
118697	122900	3349	1746	54781		276	62748	378530
6829610	4328471	3271461	130767	869854	54679	506	1204	18985559
2631109	1715153	1399325	32326	270163	12280	30	1030	7065611
909648	364766	258696	10375	95355	310		30	2834803
192927	85708	59512	10417	15210	570			1516722
1212689	1054059	982082	1844	67453	1680		1000	831886
60933	72938	14237	923	55171	2578	30		445294
5645	1860	76	1522	260	3			35095
90565	64050	40894	3843	13994	5319			540309
158702	71772	43829	3403	22720	1820			861503
2918442	1861191	1214147	83609	522225	40806	230	174	9551706
426971	140969	81334	6616	50088	2701	230		2179573
359891	186801	135289	4144	34850	12518			1098514
13251	21548	13537		5511	2500			105835
55890	47581	23890	7771	15161	760			155438
288900	101717	39704	50434	11579				1142650
1086039	854477	642998	3465	203789	4225			2262679
548680	404461	239261	5471	153580	5975		174	1958566
115355	94143	31686	2663	47666	12128			594326
23467	9495	6450	3045					54127
1280059	752127	657990	14832	77466	1592	246		2368242
153710	71550	68237	240	2123	950			225335
122446	44458	43957		500				182618
191809	98954	79747	12688	6120	400			567417
812094	537166	466049	1905	68723	242	246		1392873
1547212	1113708	371809	90116	428316	154801	4219	64446	5478668
147658	99874	35359	13483	32522	7543		10968	768269
974041	669245	207041	34154	294461	83340	494	49756	2644895
32985	26292	3838	3478	15662	3214	100		90683
4977	2875	10	2544	133	188			14799
74049	71419	7108	13342	13040	37930			539633
27728	11689	5658	954	4020	376	683		181775
37780	29688	3499	270	25792	127			94087
247995	202627	109297	21892	42687	22085	2943	3722	1144528
3255660	1920764	1110853	35450	608162	103058	1392	61849	11612854
5121162	3521414	2532416	185434	690008	106422	3333	3802	12851373

10-12 续表 3 continued

单位：万元

项目	Item	商品销售收入净额 Net Value of Sales Revenue	商品销售成本 Sales Cost	经营费用 Operating Expense	# 运杂及装卸费 Traffic Related Expense	商品销售税金及附加 Sales Tax and Extra Charges
合计	**Total**	**24363271**	**22554378**	**894021**	**146916**	**35748**
按企业登记注册类型分	**Grouped by Type of Enterprises Registered**					
内资企业	Domestic Investment	23929417	22195615	848119	146481	35279
国有企业	State-Owned	16027251	14911008	540449	101727	22262
集体企业	Collective Owned	2536214	2401152	79179	5608	3115
私营企业	Private Owned	658130	594351	43387	2660	1316
联营企业	Joint Owned	327970	288728	17210	1416	1043
股份合作企业	Share Holding Cooperative	253252	230926	15782	1115	513
股份有限公司	Share Holding Company	1259665	1114242	54993	13933	4034
有限责任公司	Limited-Liability Company	2866934	2655207	97119	20023	2996
其他企业	Others					
港澳台商投资企业	Hongkong,Macao and Taiwan Funded Enterprises	58982	51830	2790	104	91
外商投资企业	Foreign Funded Enterprises	374872	306934	43112	331	378
按国民经济行业分	**Grouped by Sectors**					
批发业	Wholesale	18906666	17790343	488687	127432	17907
食品饮料烟草和家庭用品批发业	Food,Beverage,Tobacoo and Family Use Goods	7060893	6674106	160334	32469	5294
食品饮料烟草批发业	Food,Beverage and Tobacoo	2834788	2692114	54563	16292	2362
棉麻、土畜产品批发业	Cotton,Flax,Local and Animal Products	1516722	1500225	10713	2987	116
纺织品、服装和鞋帽批发业	Textile,Garments,Shoes and Hats	831875	757201	28196	4930	402
日用百货批发业	Daily Use Goods	445163	414334	17538	2443	585
日用杂品批发业	Grocery	35095	28780	4217	1628	27
五金交电化工批发业	Hardware,Electrical Appliance and Chemical	540169	506034	10383	1003	508
药品及医疗器械批发业	Medicine and Medical Appliance	857081	775418	34723	3186	1295
能源、材料和机械电子设备批发业	Energy,Materials,Machinery and Electronic Equipments	9512911	9026772	231816	78594	9025
能源批发业	Energy	2179573	2070787	48226	14461	2111
化工材料批发业	Chemical Materials	1098504	1039209	28753	18892	594
木材批发业	Timbers	105835	93304	9377	2645	6
建筑材料批发业	Building Materials	155435	140826	10032	1601	311
矿产品批发业	Mineral Products	1142650	1085679	35167	13397	3281
金属材料批发业	Metal Materials	2262570	2173108	41083	13531	1267
机械、电子设备批发业	Machinery and Electronic Equipments	1920343	1803885	43269	12686	974
汽车摩托车及零配件批发业	Spares and Fittings of Automobile and Motorcycle	593874	568993	14175	871	384
再生物资回收批发业	Recovery of Reclaimed Materials	54127	50981	1735	510	98
其他批发业	Others	2332862	2089465	96537	16369	3588
工艺美术品批发业	Handicrafts	225320	202306	11668	4188	57
图书报刊批发业	Books,Newspaper and Magazines	147302	116301	14150	1833	252
农业生产资料批发业	Agricultural Capital Goods	567417	544444	20669	1532	177
其他类未包括的批发	Others	1392824	1226413	50050	8815	3103
零售业	Retail	5456605	4764036	405335	19484	17841
食品、饮料和烟草零售业	Food,Beverage and Tobacoo	767460	680484	73618	1369	1940
日用百货零售业	Daily Use Goods	2631262	2219046	209139	3293	11522
纺织品、服装和鞋帽零售业	Textile,Garments,Shoes and Hats	90679	71764	10801	417	428
日用杂品零售业	Grocery	14783	12547	1505	170	52
五金交电化工零售业	Hardware,Electrical Appliance and Chemical	539118	506045	26632	1471	828
药品及医疗器械零售业	Medicine and Medical Appliance	180554	156647	9900	339	378
图书报刊零售业	Books,Newspaper and Magazines	88774	64341	11858	250	377
其他零售业	Others	1143977	1053162	61881	12175	2316
按规模划分	**Grouped by Size**					
大型企业	Large Enterprises	11532155	10623325	402988	66692	17443
中型企业	Medium Enterprises	12831116	11931053	491033	80224	18305

10-12 续表 4 continued

(10000 yuan)

商品销售利润 Sales Profits	代购代销收入 Revenue from Agency Activity	主营业务利润 Profits of Major Business	其他业务利润 Profits of Other Business	管理费用 Overhead Expense	# 税金 Taxes	#财产保险费 Premium of Property	# 劳动待业保险 Premium for Employment	财务费用 Financial Expense	# 利息支出 Interest Expenditure	营业利润 Operating Profits
879124	**100663**	**979787**	**284487**	**857789**	**22236**	**5052**	**68374**	**287544**	**351663**	**138005**
850405	100660	951065	278473	829375	21578	4838	67710	283169	348004	135783
553532	90744	644276	188202	538079	15570	2006	49770	238039	285569	66472
52769	350	53118	22596	68199	2371	721	5845	11853	12241	-1070
19077	15	19091	6689	23743	112	216	361	2687	2769	-559
20988	3	20991	2993	22939	363	128	1790	2715	2741	1806
6031		6031	4481	11577	291	123	917	2308	2253	-3172
86396	5091	91488	22787	69576	1419	842	5866	-939	13600	46173
111612	4457	116069	30726	95263	1451	802	3161	26506	28832	26133
4271		4271	81	4419	61	11	66	438	374	-231
24448	3	24450	5933	23995	597	203	598	3937	3285	2453
609730	100091	709821	158037	512990	13885	3713	30298	252797	306950	112912
221159	7900	229060	44006	177512	4788	1603	11892	102267	109637	-800
85749	2797	88547	28318	62180	2201	763	4671	55639	63359	4009
5667	1154	6821	2342	16339	734	191	862	15552	16542	-22724
46076	1941	48017	2081	32592	387	162	1756	12122	11861	5931
12706	912	13618	2964	16305	389	142	980	8724	9031	-8394
2072		2072	82	1537	28	13	104	294	306	324
23244	412	23656	3634	12350	497	85	1080	5466	4557	9520
45645	683	46328	4586	36210	553	247	2439	4471	3982	10534
245298	61890	307187	83341	242232	6139	1578	13311	104288	126445	47650
58449	19302	77751	18909	43339	813	505	2034	6689	16212	46887
29949	9428	39377	4841	21173	375	91	1139	8277	8381	14846
3148	519	3667	264	3243	48	22	138	2586	2748	-1897
4267	1586	5853	9769	15329	301	67	707	2328	2910	-2035
18523	10328	28851	6247	27237	670	153	698	27182	28369	-18982
47113	4962	52075	22967	53659	1275	190	3570	23397	27722	-1598
72215	14885	87101	13677	65049	2455	435	3869	25089	33834	12181
10321	878	11199	4867	10756	156	82	699	7240	4777	-921
1313		1313	1802	2448	46	34	458	1500	1495	-833
143273	30301	173574	30690	93246	2959	533	5095	46242	70868	66062
11288	225	11513	3374	9435	311	221	524	8887	9966	-2712
16599	1690	18289	2515	12628	313	64	1830	1110	1824	7347
2126	4244	6370	3858	11842	280	68	757	7467	8549	-9080
113259	24143	137402	20943	59341	2054	180	1983	28777	50529	70508
269394	572	269966	126451	344798	8351	1339	38076	34747	44713	25093
11418		11418	30598	39347	1003	-2248	9845	4113	4833	-1344
191555	177	191731	67191	218789	5777	2170	20040	20717	30434	23539
7686	59	7745	2964	10202	108	173	1228	763	746	467
679		679	1095	1812	31	22	366	38	53	-76
5613	77	5690	8399	13241	292	136	1263	1310	1605	-201
13629	71	13700	857	11272	251	72	1290	230	451	3063
12197		12197	2851	12070	170	142	1809	161	346	2932
26617	189	26806	12497	38066	719	872	2234	7415	6246	-3287
488399	38019	526417	104865	333758	8137	3933	28421	89184	125072	213904
390726	62644	453370	179623	524031	14099	1119	39952	198360	226591	-75900

10-12 续表 5 continued

单位：万元

项目	Item	投资收益 Investment Income	补贴收入 Subsidy Income	营业外收入 Out-business Income	营业外支出 Out-business Expenditure	利润总额 Total Profits	应交所得税 Income Tax Payable
合计	**Total**	**121249**	**138235**	**69279**	**42937**	**432199**	**168262**
按企业登记注册类型分	**Grouped by Type of Enterprises Registered**						
内资企业	Domestic Investment	120946	138235	69048	42661	430094	165065
国有企业	State-Owned	105483	128900	51978	34498	322238	115474
集体企业	Collective Owned	1359	8796	5453	4679	9547	5487
私营企业	Private Owned	-81	142	1511	93	886	2783
联营企业	Joint Owned	278	13	600	332	4708	1985
股份合作企业	Share Holding Cooperative	8	123	777	59	-1353	576
股份有限公司	Share Holding Company	6394		3783	1011	55815	15631
有限责任公司	Limited-Liability Company	7505	262	4946	1989	38253	23128
其他企业	Others						
港澳台商投资企业	Hongkong,Macao and Taiwan Funded Enterprises	215		103	52	-223	287
外商投资企业	Foreign Funded Enterprises	88		128	224	2328	2910
按国民经济行业分	**Grouped by Sectors**						
批发业	Wholesale	118526	133841	50468	33102	384718	138327
食品饮料烟草和家庭用品批发业	Food,Beverage,Tobacoo and Family Use Goods	39311	98778	23057	14376	150240	52214
食品饮料烟草批发业	Food,Beverage and Tobacoo	21676	74709	11053	7628	106341	25450
棉麻、土畜产品批发业	Cotton,Flax,Local and Animal Products	2516	22293	4098	3124	-56	2234
纺织品、服装和鞋帽批发业	Textile,Garments,Shoes and Hats	1479	1595	1524	497	11592	7638
日用百货批发业	Daily Use Goods	1021		582	1349	-4958	3613
日用杂品批发业	Grocery			220	14	521	176
五金交电化工批发业	Hardware,Electrical Appliance and Chemical	1450		3789	615	14116	7132
药品及医疗器械批发业	Medicine and Medical Appliance	11169	180	1792	1149	22683	5973
能源、材料和机械电子设备批发业	Energy,Materials,Machinery and Electronic Equipments	64521	19336	18707	15787	130039	48414
能源批发业	Energy	8862	181	5221	3817	57664	17030
化工材料批发业	Chemical Materials	5794	149	678	1770	33134	7134
木材批发业	Timbers	489	4	110	30	-1325	523
建筑材料批发业	Building Materials	479		752	368	-2877	460
矿产品批发业	Mineral Products	8444	15420	1060	2795	3520	1155
金属材料批发业	Metal Materials	10190	1960	5085	1479	14093	4649
机械、电子设备批发业	Machinery and Electronic Equipments	25192	1451	3777	3433	24978	16995
汽车摩托车及零配件批发业	Spares and Fittings of Automobile and Motorcycle	4376	76	1954	1944	967	467
再生物资回收批发业	Recovery of Reclaimed Materials	696	96	70	151	-116	
其他批发业	Others	14694	15727	8703	2938	104439	37699
工艺美术品批发业	Handicrafts	921	1954	789	161	131	1461
图书报刊批发业	Books,Newspaper and Magazines	1480	1757	170	148	10733	4084
农业生产资料批发业	Agricultural Capital Goods	602	10955	1959	193	5887	4975
其他类未包括的批发	Others	11691	1060	5785	2436	87687	27180
零售业	Retail	2723	4394	18811	9836	47481	29935
食品、饮料和烟草零售业	Food,Beverage and Tobacoo	-239	3973	3426	1576	4095	3473
日用百货零售业	Daily Use Goods	1624	21	9216	5435	37116	17690
纺织品、服装和鞋帽零售业	Textile,Garments,Shoes and Hats	112	15	566	221	668	595
日用杂品零售业	Grocery	-13	3	144	45	28	28
五金交电化工零售业	Hardware,Electrical Appliance and Chemical	513	44	1318	141	1280	1774
药品及医疗器械零售业	Medicine and Medical Appliance	-391	11	1486	1397	2778	1023
图书报刊零售业	Books,Newspaper and Magazines	244	22	37	56	3102	1066
其他零售业	Others	873	307	2619	965	-1587	4286
按规模划分	**Grouped by Size**						
大型企业	Large Enterprises	30025	24767	15731	11599	268756	88453
中型企业	Medium Enterprises	91224	113468	53548	31338	163443	79809

10-12 续表 6 continued

(10000 yuan)

转作奖金的利润 Profits Distributed as Bonus	应付利润 Profits Payable	本年应付工资总额 Total Wages Payable in the Year	# 主营业务应付工资 Wage Payable of Major Business	本年应付福利费总额 Welfares Payable in the Year	# 主营业务应付福利费 of Major Business	本年应交增值税 Value Added Payable in the Year	本年进项税额 Tax included in Purchasing Cost	本年销项税额 Tax included in Sales Value
787	**106780**	**434875**	**389635**	**56040**	**50433**	**316964**	**3146755**	**3112342**
787	102756	420405	375726	52809	47258	304287	3085253	3039260
276	77797	286931	260118	33797	30332	98786	2053672	1852805
263	3877	37687	31962	5041	4357	148541	225762	356163
	1064	10611	10314	1410	1366	10135	100109	109162
5	2202	9077	9015	2558	2551	6967	46774	52857
203	69	6954	6542	863	842	2797	36256	39167
4	10563	34055	27234	4618	3711	20083	174338	188937
36	7184	35090	30541	4522	4101	16978	448342	440168
	106	2304	1744	316	260	297	9138	8387
	3918	12166	12166	2915	2915	12380	52364	64695
522	95021	222274	196053	25755	22608	207303	2396002	2268888
273	41788	69602	60495	9475	8040	156510	816809	871024
30	18516	26692	25018	3623	3362	14046	350500	356637
	2096	4557	3745	522	386	127392	67504	165908
27	5254	9349	7363	1385	1110	-1889	132323	68246
8	4305	6739	6375	865	828	3514	51128	53232
4	331	675	610	84	84	1202	4518	5685
1	2958	5067	4380	774	591	2294	91451	92724
203	8328	16522	13006	2223	1680	9951	119385	128594
249	36995	123736	112009	12333	11139	45052	1341150	1192537
	8515	14973	14035	1892	1751	11399	229656	240197
	9528	5234	4593	1134	1054	4718	170271	161856
	20	696	575	81	72	-193	11765	9826
199	172	5453	4946	738	693	1897	20774	22596
	9646	8904	6995	1275	1249	4830	212093	165062
43	1116	16032	13531	2118	1804	9292	291266	284582
7	7590	66950	63062	4431	4019	10940	314945	214629
	407	4397	3295	481	332	1675	82285	84628
		1098	977	184	165	493	8095	9162
	16239	28936	23549	3946	3429	5741	238043	205327
	3298	4789	2537	466	354	-1524	25941	5434
	1061	7122	5757	1096	905	1818	12641	14147
	2959	3917	3833	571	557	183	15957	15465
	8921	13108	11421	1813	1613	5264	183504	170281
266	11759	212601	193582	30285	27825	109662	750753	843454
95	557	45484	44488	5822	5716	15046	103672	118319
10	9746	117991	103461	17719	15761	68922	355499	423655
4	99	6607	6490	682	666	2308	12335	12820
		1082	820	147	118	360	2002	2359
24	506	9962	8561	1307	1158	4426	83228	87383
5	317	6558	6403	846	828	3410	26138	29703
	163	6864	6733	1092	1066	3748	8677	12398
128	372	18054	16627	2671	2513	11442	159201	156816
3	50507	156822	136393	23590	20579	223569	1396530	1587759
784	56272	278052	253242	32450	29854	93396	1750225	1524583

10-13 大中型餐饮业财务状况

单位：万元

项目	Item	合计 Total	按登记注册类型分				
			国有企业 State-Owned	集体企业 Collective Owned	私营企业 Private Owned	联营企业 Joint-Owned	股份合作企业 Share Holding Cooperative
流动资产合计	Total Circulating Assets	175678	34646	14121	6222	4629	4907
# 货币资金	Cash	49176	15028	3238	1059	572	682
应收帐款	Accounts Receivable	19195	2703	2354	262	349	1340
存　货	Inventory	18994	3365	1390	914	672	1170
长期投资	Long-term Investment	36150	3484	3127	20		890
固定资产合计	Total Fixed Assets	211878	65137	11730	2457	1440	3171
固定资产原价合计	Total Original Value of Fixed Assets	272279	72677	14044	2890	2062	4458
# 生产经营用	For Production and Business Use	261701	71065	13939	2699	2062	3575
累计折旧	Accumulative Depreciation	82879	16204	5485	972	662	1349
# 本年折旧	of this Year	17609	3194	843	372	96	335
无形及递延资产合计	Total Intangible and Deferred Assets	66224	11237	4747	4557	888	2244
# 无形资产	Intangible Assets	16041	2537	910		4	749
其他资产合计	Other Assets	14003	87	2	33		15
资产合计	Total Assets	503934	114591	33727	13289	6956	11226
流动负债合计	Total Liquid Liabilities	288165	61241	21651	8731	4269	7513
# 短期借款	Short-term Loans	64865	5531	5868	3149	290	2500
应付帐款	Payment Payable	40810	6313	4966	1191	286	2106
长期负债合计	Total Long-term Liabilities	24461	4332	2730	1422		240
# 长期借款	Long-term Loans	17025	1369	1492	507		
负债合计	Total Liabilities	312625	65573	24381	10153	4269	7753
所有者权益合计	Total Ownership Interest	191308	49018	9347	3136	2687	3473
# 实收资本	Capital Stock	221323	29480	16360	6630	2081	4703
国家资本	State	40086	19397	110		215	1888
集体资本	Collective	29015	531	10300		260	891
法人资本	Institutional Units	68299	8549	5476	2580	1226	213
个人资本	Individual	9483	1003	475	4050	380	1710
港澳台资本	Hongkong,Macao and Taiwan	42145					
外商资本	Foreign	32296					
营业收入	Business Revenue	442251	70443	33298	12048	4234	13896
营业成本	Business Cost	210791	35054	18199	5969	1846	8405
营业费用	Business Expenses	153256	24389	10357	4941	1672	3896
营业税金及附加	Business Tax and Extra Charges	21523	3620	1758	670	211	526
主营业务利润	Profits of Major Business	56680	7379	2984	470	504	1068
其他业务利润	Profits of Other Business						
管理费用	Overhead Expenses	51719	9572	3401	1527	467	1711
# 税　金	Taxes	2102	530	109	49	11	5
财产保险费	Premium of Property	553	105	39	2	5	1
劳动待业保险费	Premium for Employment	5281	3167	129	7	96	14
财务费用	Financial Expenses	3509	-650	165	104	39	212
# 利息支出	Interest Expenditure	4367	385	135	160	15	196
营业利润	Operating Profits	1453	-1544	-582	-1161	-2	-854
投资收益	Investment Income	1185	896	19			2
补贴收入	Subsidy Income	5					
营业外收入	Out-business Income	3499	1474	180	75	2	5
营业外支出	Out-business Expenditure	2504	470	62	11	1	4
利润总额	Total Profits	3816	347	-414	-1006		-850
应交所得税	Income Tax Payable	6338	852	223	7	63	43
应付利润	Profits Payable	7747	55	132		6	
转作奖金的利润	Profits Distributed as Bonus	46		20			
本年应付工资总额	Total Wages Payable of this Year	50314	12409	4235	1530	641	1302
# 主营业务应付工资	of Major Business	47503	11862	3737	1329	598	1044
本年应付福利费总额	Total Welfares Payable of this Year	6917	1757	456	121	81	107
# 主营业务应付福利费	of Major Business	6457	1708	404	115	81	94

FINANCIAL INDICATORS OF LARGE AND MEDIUM ENTERPRISES IN CATERING TRADE

(10000 yuan)

By Registered Type					按行业划分 By Sectors			按规模划分 By Size	
股份有限公司 Share Holding Company	有限责任公司 Limited-liabilities	其他企业 Others	港澳台商投资企业 Hongkong,Macao, Taiwan Funded	外商投资企业 Foreign Funded	正餐 Dinner	快餐 Fast Food	其他餐饮业 Others	大型企业 Large	中型企业 Medium
1416	25964		33880	49895	1E+05	33598	3619	74255	101423
904	6940		5822	14933	42085	6920	172	20668	28508
219	3249		2968	5753	18094	1059	42	9502	9693
231	2657		2839	5757	13386	4998	610	6312	12682
125	12865		8732	6907	35460	650	40	21547	14603
1358	26019		16462	84105	2E+05	58718	2237	64450	147428
1557	32727		26953	114911	2E+05	78352	2849	85950	186329
1557	32526		25097	109181	2E+05	74203	2816	82683	179018
320	8606		12538	36744	57228	24947	705	26586	56293
170	2087		2260	8255	11599	5768	242	6731	10878
1252	8190		13282	19827	42924	23150	150	23242	42982
	932		6874	4035	8696	7345		11137	4904
394	73		6430	6969	10024	2506	1474	7628	6375
4545	73110		78786	167704	4E+05	118622	7520	191122	312812
2881	34902		57159	89819	2E+05	62183	4160	91029	197136
778	6865		4634	35251	39330	23087	2447	22932	41933
570	4150		5622	15607	32939	6807	1063	15301	25509
	4527		4246	6963	17637	6724	100	6362	18099
	4558		2724	6375	10324	6701		4111	12914
2881	39429		61405	96782	2E+05	68907	4260	97390	215235
1664	33681		17381	70922	1E+05	49715	3260	93731	97577
1681	24945		51944	83500	2E+05	53003	5488	98305	123018
	6505		2056	9915	32816	7270		7918	32168
	168		3142	13723	28172	713	130	14644	14371
1584	15075		19236	14360	50621	17216	461	45440	22859
96	1145		277	347	8436	1047		1544	7939
	2052		26179	13915	29256	7992	4897	24354	17791
			1055	31240	13531	18764		4406	27890
7140	53027		46075	202091	3E+05	159354	5455	148657	293594
3153	25039		18561	94565	1E+05	74190	1824	73453	137338
2425	17033		20990	67554	90786	59812	2658	47215	106041
384	2536		2220	9600	13481	7786	256	6554	14969
1177	8420		4306	30375	38397	17566	718	21434	35246
943	6668		6770	20660	40036	10606	1077	18187	33532
77	147		168	1004	1536	564	1	547	1555
3	64		127	205	316	227	9	249	304
39	1126		154	552	4736	537	7	2258	3023
80	643		167	2749	1600	1901	7	1127	2382
80	656		135	2605	2343	1973	50	1523	2844
154	1109		-2632	6963	-3239	5059	-367	2120	-667
	780		-516	5	1105	80		1295	-110
				5	5				5
12	410		86	1254	2210	1289		847	2652
3	108		333	1515	909	1548	48	811	1693
163	2192		-3330	6712	-726	4956	-414	3465	351
72	1128		200	3751	3915	2423		2394	3944
14	949		-146	6736	3592	4155		1827	5920
			9	16	46			9	37
775	6930		6904	15591	38945	10725	645	17817	32497
719	6927		6740	14549	36304	10554	645	16800	30703
97	900		877	2523	5300	1471	146	2706	4211
89	899		835	2234	4853	1458	146	2497	3960

10-14 商业、饮食业、服务业经营机构及人员
OPERATING UNITS AND PERSONNEL OF COMMERCE,CATERING AND SERVICES

项　目 Item		经营机构(个) Operating Units (unit)		人　员(人) Personnel (person)	
		2000	1999	2000	1999
总　计	**Total**	**248065**	**255900**	**1232671**	**1231619**
商　业	Commerce	186233	188809	831225	828393
批　发	Wholesale	11586	11949	280459	282723
零　售	Retail	174647	176860	550766	545670
饮食业	Catering	29018	32120	163965	166031
服务业	Services	32814	34971	237481	237195

10-15 商业、饮食业、服务业营业网点及人员(按所有制形式分)
OUTLETS AND PERSONNEL OF COMMERCE,CATERING AND SERVICES (BY OWNERSHIP)

单位：个、人　　(unit,person)

项　目 Item		合计 Total	国有 State-owned	集体 Collective-owned	个体 Individuals	其他 Others
营业网点	**Outlets**	**236479**	**7102**	**8030**	**213160**	**8187**
人　员	**Personnel**	**952212**	**260441**	**137811**	**295732**	**258228**
商　业	Commerce					
零售网点	Retail Outlets	174647	4586	5005	159343	5713
人　员	Personnel	550766	145175	77625	200398	127568
饮食业	Catering					
营业网点	Outlets	29018	878	1345	25532	1263
人　员	Personnel	163965	26878	24189	57104	55794
服务业	Services					
营业网点	Outlets	32814	1638	1680	28285	1211
人　员	Personnel	237481	88388	35997	38230	74866

10-16 批发业网点及人员
OUTLETS AND PERSONNEL OF WHOLESALE TRADE

单位：个、人 (unit,person)

项目	Item	网点 Outlets	人员 Personnel
总计	**Total**	**11586**	**280459**
食品、饮料、烟草批发业	Food,Beverage and Tobacoo	1412	48655
棉、麻、土畜产品批发业	Cotton,Fiber,Local and Livestock Products	56	2877
纺织品、服装和鞋帽批发业	Textile Products,Garments,Shoes and Hats	642	14293
日用百货批发业	Daily Use Goods	1095	22206
日用杂品批发业	Daily Use Groceries	117	2614
五金、交电、化工批发业	Hardware,Electrical Appliances and Chemical	1625	27632
药品及医疗器械批发业	Medicines and Medical Appliances	448	18204
工艺美术品批发业	Handicraft Articles	121	2954
图书报刊批发业	Books,Newspapers and Magazines	78	3171
农业生产资料批发业	Agricultural Capital Goods	169	5463
其他批发业	Others	5823	132390

10-17 商业零售网点及人员
OUTLETS AND PERSONNEL OF RETAIL SALE TRADE

单位：个、人 (unit,person)

项目	Item	网点 Outlets	人员 Personnel
总计	**Total**	**174647**	**550766**
食品、饮料、烟草零售业	Food,Beverage and Tobacoo	40638	110443
日用百货零售业	Daily Use Goods	27982	210393
纺织品、服装和鞋帽零售业	Textile Products,Garments,Shoes and Hats	6573	25228
日用杂品零售业	Daily Use Groceries	3036	6748
五金、交电、化工零售业	Hardware,Electrical Appliances and Chemical	36221	68934
药品及医疗器械零售业	Medicines and Medical Appliances	7110	18026
图书报刊零售业	Books,Newspapers and Magazines	5261	13632
其他零售业	Others	47826	97362

10-18 饮食业营业网点及人员
OUTLETS AND PERSONNEL OF CATERING TRADE

单位：个、人 (unit,person)

项目	Item	网点 Outlets	人员 Personnel
总计	**Total**	**29018**	**163965**
正餐	Dinner	23774	136510
快餐	Fast Food	2764	23573
其他	Others	2480	3882

10-19 服务业营业网点及人员
OUTLETS AND PERSONNEL OF SERVICES

单位：个、人 (unit,person)

项目	Item	网点 Outlets	人员 Personnel
总计	**Total**	**32814**	**237481**
理发及美容化妆业	Services of Haircut,Beauty and Making-up	7457	14687
沐浴业	Bath Service	452	5370
洗染业	Cleaning and Dyeing	1148	3256
摄影及扩印业	Photography and Large-printing	1829	5593
日用品修理业	Repairs of Daily Use Articles	10706	16905
其他居民服务业	Other Residential Services	8455	37218
旅馆业	Hotels	2767	154452

10-20 个体工商业户数及人数

OUTLETS AND PERSONNEL OF SELF-EMPLOYMENT BUSINESS

单位：个、人 (unit,person)

项 目 Item			2000 全 市 Total	2000 城 镇 Urban	2000 农 村 Rural	1999 全 市 Total	1999 城 镇 Urban	1999 农 村 Rural
总 户 数		**Total Outlets**	**245241**	**143018**	**102223**	**257416**	**141551**	**115865**
总 人 数		**Total Persons**	**345332**	**201864**	**143468**	**359077**	**199253**	**159824**
农林牧渔业								
Farming,Forestry,Animal	户 数	Units	1015	246	769	1436	164	1272
Husbandry and Fishery	人 数	Persons	1809	390	1419	2110	212	1898
工 业	户 数	Units	15564	6852	8712	16831	6838	9993
Industry	人 数	Persons	31012	10535	20477	33719	11298	22421
建 筑 业	户 数	Units	624	241	383	592	246	346
Construction	人 数	Persons	1712	646	1066	1956	701	1255
交通运输业	户 数	Units	12751	5734	7017	17330	6119	11211
Transportation	人 数	Persons	12286	5955	6331	19151	6750	12401
商 业	户 数	Units	159343	93634	65709	160547	91230	69317
Commerce	人 数	Persons	200398	116917	83481	199414	111847	87567
饮 食 业	户 数	Units	25532	16742	8790	28276	17750	10526
Catering	人 数	Persons	57104	40952	16152	60440	42934	17506
服 务 业	户 数	Units	19066	13705	5361	18990	12485	6505
Services	人 数	Persons	27753	19026	8727	25351	16802	8549
修 理 业	户 数	Units	10392	5487	4905	12066	6333	5733
Repairs	人 数	Persons	12026	6945	5081	15146	8193	6953
其 他 行 业	户 数	Units	954	377	577	1348	386	962
Others	人 数	Persons	1232	498	734	1790	516	1274

主要统计指标解释

社会消费品零售额　指各种经济类型的批发零售贸易业、餐饮业、制造业及其他业对城乡居民、社会集团的消费品零售额。这个指标反映通过各种商品流通渠道向居民和社会集团供应的生活消费品以满足他们生活需要，是研究人民生活、社会消费品购买力、货币流通等问题的重要指标。社会消费品零售额包括：（1）售给城乡居民作为生活用的商品和修建房屋用的建筑材料；（2）售给机关、团体、学校、部队、企业、事业单位的职工食堂和旅店（招待所）附设专门供本店旅客食用、不对外营业的食堂的各种食品、饮料；企业、单位和国营农场直接售给本单位职工和职工食堂的自己生产的产品；（3）售给部队、战士生活用的粮食、副食品、衣着品、日用品、燃料；（4）售给来华的外国人、华侨、港澳台同胞的消费品；（5）居民自费购买的中、西药品、中药材及医疗用品；（6）报社、出版社直接给居民和社会集团的报纸、图书、杂志、集邮公司出售的新、旧纪念邮票、特种邮票、首日封、集邮册、集邮工具等；（7）旧货寄售商店自购、自销部分的商品；（8）煤气公司、液化石油气站售给居民和社会团体的煤气灶具和罐装液化石油气；（9）农民售给非农业居民和社会团体的商品。不包括售给国民经济各部门企业、事业单位（包括国有经济的农场）生产经营用的各种原材料、燃料、设备、工具等和售给批发零售贸易业、餐饮业作为转卖用的商品、旧货寄售商店受托寄售卖出的商品、服务业的营业收入、邮局出售邮票的收入、自来水、电力、煤气生产（供应）单位的产品供应收入，也不包括农民之间的商品销售。

批发零售贸易业商品购、销、存总额　指以各种经济类型的批发、零售贸易业（不包括个体）为总体的商品购、销、存。

商品购进总额　指从本企业（单位）以外的单位和个人购进（包括从国外直接购进）作为转卖或加工后转卖的商品。这个指标反映批发零售贸易业从国内、国外市场上购进商品的总量。商品购进总额包括：（1）从工农业生产者购进的商品；（2）从出版社、报社的发行部门购进的图书、杂志和报纸；（3）从各种经济类型的批发零售贸易企业（单位）购进的商品，如从机关、团体、企业、单位购进的剩余物资，从餐饮业、服务业购进的商品，从海关、市场管理部门购进的缉私和没收的商品，从居民收购的废旧商品等；（5）从国（境）外直接进口的商品。不包括企业（单位）为自身经营用，和未通过买卖行为而收入的商品以及销售退回、商品升溢等。

商品销售总额　指对本企业（单位）以外的单位和个人出售（包括对国（境）外直接出口）的商品。这个指标反映批发零售贸易业在国内市场上销售商品以及出口商品的总量。商品销售总额包括：（1）售给城乡居民和社会集团消费用的商品；（2）售给工业、农业、建筑业、运输邮电业、批发零售贸易业、餐饮业、服务业等作为生产、经营使用的商品；（3）售给批发零售贸易业作为转卖或加工后转卖的商品；（4）对国（境）外直接出口的商品。不包括：出售本企业（单位）自用的废旧包装用品，为通过买卖行为付出的商品，经本单位介绍，由买卖双方直接结算，本单位只收取手续费的业务，购货退出的商品以及商品损耗和损失等。

批发零售贸易业年末库存　指年末各种经济类型的批发零售贸易企业（单位）已取得所有权的商品。它反映各地区、各批发零售企业（单位）的库存情况，和对市场商品供应的保证程度。年末库存包括：（1）存放在批发零售贸易经营单位（如门市部、批发站、经营处）仓库、货场、货柜和货架中的商品；（2）挑选、整理、包装中的商品；（3）已计入购进而尚未运到本单位的商品，即发货单或银行承兑凭证已到而货未到部分；（4）寄放他处的商品，如因购货方拒绝承付而暂时存放在购货方的商品和已办完加工成品收回手续而未提回的商品；（5）委托其他单位代销（未作销售或调出）尚未售出的商品；（6）代其他单位购进尚未交付的商品。不包括所有权不属于本单位的商品、拨付除批发零售贸易业以外的其他行业所属独立核算加工等加工生产尚未收回成品的商品、代国家物资储备部门保管的商品等。年末库存总额计算方法是：农副产品采购单位按购进价计算，批发单位按进货价计算，零售单位按什么价格核算就按什么价格计算。

网点　指本批发零售贸易企业（单位）设立的从事批发、零售贸易业务的自然单位[包括本企业（单位）自身]，具有独立固定的营业场所，配备一定的业务人员，不论单位大小，不论是否单独核算，均按自然网点计算，即有一个点就算一个网点。不包括同一营业场所内各柜组以及派出的流动推销小组，流动售货车等。

人员　指在批发、零售贸易网点工作并取得劳动报酬的从业人员。包括职工、聘请的离退休人员等。

Explanatory Notes On Main Statistical Indicators

Total Retail Sales of Consumer Goods refer to the sum of retail sales of consumer goods to urban and rural residents and social groups by the establishments in wholesale, retail, catering, manufacturing and other industries of various ownerships. This indicator is used to show the supply of consumers goods through various channels to households and institutions to meet their demands, and is therefore very important for the study of the issues on people's livelihood , on the purchasing power of consumer goods and on the circulation of money. The retail sales of consumer goods include: (1)commodities sold to urban and rural residents for residential use and building materials sold to them for the construction or repair of houses; (2) food and Beverage sold to canteens of institutions, enterprises, schools, military units and to canteens of hotels that only serve their guests, and commodities produced by enterprises, institutions or state farms and sold directly to their employees or their canteens; (3) grain and non-staple food, clothing, daily articles and fuels sold to military and soldiers; (4) consumer goods sold to foreigners, overseas Chinese and Chinese compatriots from Taiwan, Hong Kong and Macao during their stay in the mainland of China; (5) Chinese and western medicines, herbs and medical facilities purchased by residents; (6) newspapers, books and magazines directly sold to residents and social groups by publishers, new and old commemorative stamps, special stamps, first-day envelope, stamp albums and other stamp-collection articles sold by stamp companies; (7) consumer goods purchased and then sold by second-hand shops; (8) stoves and other heating facilities and liquefied gas sold by gas companies to households and institutions; and (9) commodities sold by farmers to non-agricultural residents and social groups. But sales like followings are not included in total retail sales of consumer goods: (1) raw materials, fuels, equipment, tools sold to enterprises, institutions and state farms for production purpose; (2) commodities sold to trade establishments for re-selling; (3) commissioned sales at second-hand shops; (4) operational income of various services; (5) stamps sold at post offices; (6) income of water, power, gas production and supply establishments from the supply of their products; (7) and sales of commodities among farmers.

Purchase, Sales and Stock of Commodities by Wholesalers and Retailers refer to the purchase, sales and stock of commodities by wholesale and retail establishments of different ownership (excluding individual sellers) .

Total Purchases of Commodities refer to the purchases of commodities by the establishments from other establishments or individuals (including direct import from abroad) for the purpose of re-selling, with or without further processing of the commodities purchased. This indicator is used to show the total value of purchases of commodities by wholesale and retail establishments from domestic and overseas markets. The total purchases include: (1) agricultural and industrial products purchased from producers; (2) books, magazines and newspapers purchased from distribution departments of the publishers; (3) commodities purchased from wholesale and retail establishments of various ownership; (4) commodities purchased from other units, such as surplus materials purchased from government agencies, enterprises or institutions, commodities purchased from catering and service establishments, confiscated goods purchased from customs authorities or market management agencies, second-hand goods and wastes purchased from residents; and (5) commodities directly imported from abroad. Excluded are commodities purchased by establishments (units) for use in their own business operation, commodities obtained without buying or selling procedures, rejected commodities, etc.

Total Sales of Commodities refer to selling of commodities by the establishments to other establishments and individuals (including direct export) . This indicator is used to show the total value of sales of commodities at domestic markets and export, The total sales include: (1)commodities sold to urban and rural residents and social groups for final consumption; (2)commodities sold to establishments in industry, agriculture, construction, transportation, post and telecommunications, wholesale and retail trades, catering and public utility for productive consumption; (3) commodities sold to wholesale and retail establishments for re-selling, with or without further processing; and (4) commodities for direct export to other countries. Excluded are sales of self-used waste packaging materials, commodities transferred without buying or selling procedures, commission income from brokerage in transactions whose settlement is directly handled by buyers and sellers, rejected commodities in the purchase, loss in commodities, etc.

Commodity Stock of Wholesale and Retail Enterprises at Year-end refers to total commodities possessed by wholesale and retail enterprises (units) of various ownership, which reflects the inventory level of various wholesale and retail enterprises and the potential for market supply. It includes: （1）Commodities put in storage, garages, counters, and shelves of operating units（such as stores, wholesale centers, and operating offices）of wholesale and retail enterprises; （2）commodities in the process of selecting, sorting, and packing ; （3）commodities not arrived but recorded as purchase in the account, i. e. Commodities not arrived but payment receipts for the commodities from the sellers or the banks arrived; （4） specially deposited commodities, for instance, commodities in the hold of purchasers temporarily due to the refusal of payment and commodities not taken back after going through the formalities; （5）commodities entrusted to other units to sell but not sold yet; （6）commodities purchased for other units but not delivered yet. Commodities not included as stock are those not owned by the enterprise（units）, those allocated to financially independent factories rather than wholesale and retail enterprises for processing but not taken back yet, and finally those put in stock by wholesale and retail enterprises on behalf of the state material reserves units. In the calculation of the value of commodities stock at the end of period, the value is calculated at purchasing prices for agricultural goods purchasing units and wholesale units, and at the market prices for retail units.

Commercial Front Site refers to the operating site (shop, store or supply center) of the wholesale or retail sale enterprise engaged in the wholesaling or retailing, including the enterprise itself. Every front site has its own independent location and a number of personnel for commercial operation, regardless of the size and with or without independent accounting system. But the different counters in a front site, the mobile selling groups of a front site no longer counted as a front site.

Personnel refers to the persons who are employed in wholesale or retail front sites and receive remuneration payments, including staff and workers as well as the retires invited to work in wholesale or retail front sites.

对外经济贸易

11

FOREIGN ECONOMY AND TRADE

地方企业进出口总额（单位：亿美元）
Imports and Exports of Local Enterprises (USD 100 million)

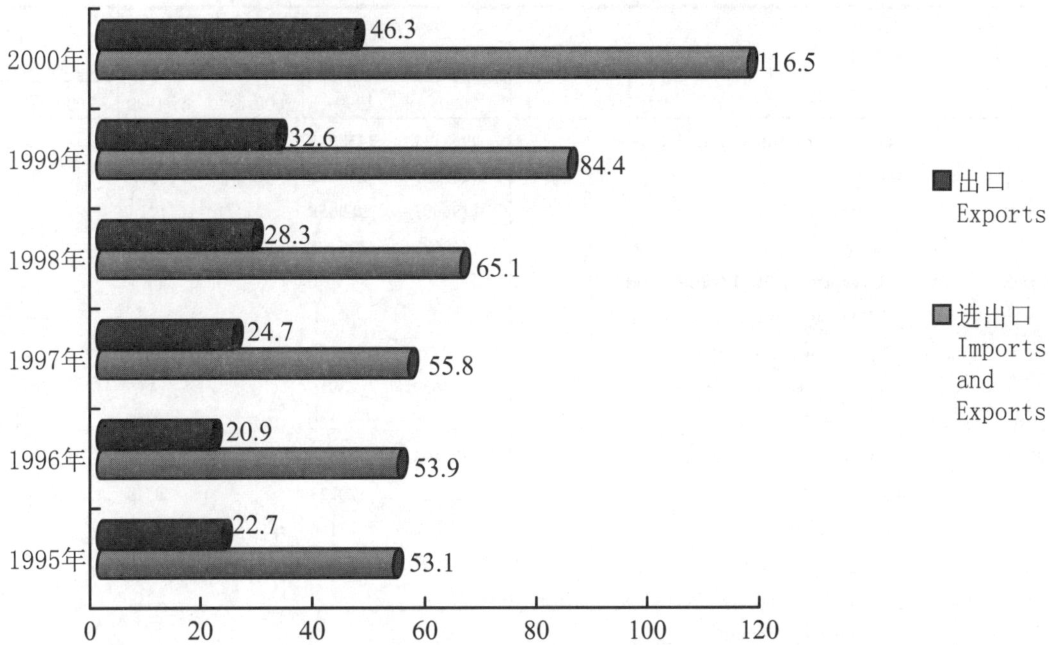

利 用 外 资（单位：亿美元）
Foreign Capital Utilized (USD 100 million)

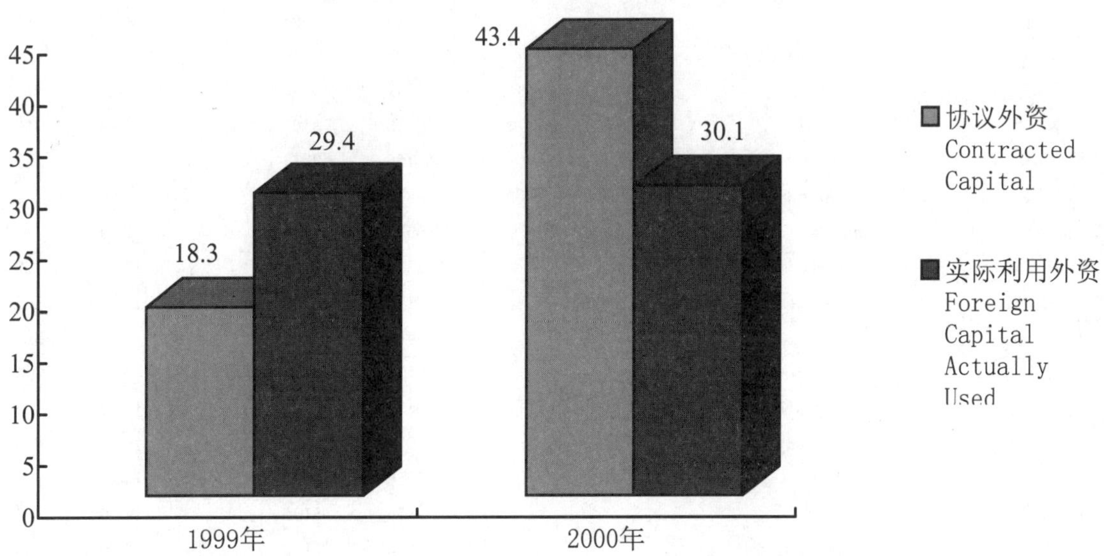

11-1 海关进出口贸易总额
TOTAL VALUE OF IMPORTS AND EXPORTS AT CUSTOMS

项　目	Item	金　额(万美元) Value (USD 10000) 2000	1999	2000年为1999年% 2000 as % of 1999	构　成(%) Composition(%) 2000	1999
进出口总额	**Total Value of Imports and Exports**	**4962177**	**3433845**	**144.5**		
# 地　方	**Local**	**1165059**	**844212**	**138.8**		
出口总额	**Exports**	**1196801**	**989059**	**121.0**		
# 地　方	**Local**	**462683**	**326101**	**141.9**	**100**	**100**
按登记注册类型分	**Grouped by Registration Status**					
内资企业	Domestic Investment Enterprises					
国有企业	State-owned Enterprises	169775	175357	96.8	36.7	53.8
集体企业	Collective-owned Enterprises	5629	3916	143.7	1.2	1.2
其　他	Others	171	200	85.5	…	…
外商投资企业	Foreign Funded Enterprises	287108	146628	195.8	62.1	45.0
中外合资	Joint Venture	255324	120223	2.1倍	55.2	36.9
中外合作	Cooperative	3622	3164	114.5	0.8	1.0
外商独资	Foreign Enterprises	28162	23241	121.2	6.1	7.1
外商投资股份有限公司	Foreign Funded Share Holding Company					
按国别(地区)分	**Grouped by Country (Region)**					
# 香港地区	Hongkong	80645	41721	193.3	17.4	12.8
澳门地区	Macao	85	172	49.5	…	…
日　本	Japan	100080	72643	137.7	21.6	22.3
新加坡	Singapore	6198	4263	145.4	1.3	1.3
英　国	United Kingdom	15021	7169	2.1倍	3.2	2.2
德　国	Germany	24926	13491	184.7	5.4	4.1
法　国	France	3701	2506	147.6	0.8	0.8
意大利	Italy	5081	4569	111.2	1.1	1.4
瑞　士	Switzerland	1782	1529	116.5	0.4	0.5
波　兰	Poland	2726	3064	89.0	0.6	0.9
俄罗斯联邦	Russia Union	23103	40836	56.6	5.0	12.5
埃　及	Egypt	1241	782	158.6	0.3	0.2
加拿大	Canada	4310	3104	138.8	0.9	1.0
美　国	United States	61156	47033	130.0	13.2	14.4
澳大利亚	Australia	6818	4480	152.1	1.5	1.4
进口总额	**Imports**	**3765376**	**2444785**	**154.0**		
# 地　方	**Local**	**702376**	**518111**	**135.6**	**100**	**100**
# 香港地区	Hongkong	19171	18161	105.5	2.7	3.5
日　本	Japan	143411	99713	143.8	20.4	19.2
新加坡	Singapore	10553	11314	93.3	1.5	2.2
英　国	United Kingdom	10810	10116	106.8	1.5	2.0
德　国	Germany	48074	29047	165.5	6.8	5.6
法　国	France	15558	11071	140.5	2.2	2.1
意大利	Italy	5870	5192	113.0	0.8	1.0
瑞　士	Switzerland	4554	4179	108.9	0.6	0.8
比利时	Belgium	2468	2614	94.5	0.4	0.5
俄罗斯联邦	Russia Union	1582	2441	64.9	0.2	0.5
加拿大	Canada	2476	4093	60.5	0.4	0.8
美　国	United States	76798	56947	147.8	10.9	11.0
澳大利亚	Australia	13132	8873	148.0	1.9	1.7

11-2 海关进出口商品类别及构成(地方企业)
VALUE AND COMPOSITION OF IMPORTS AND EXPORTS AT CUSTOMS BY CATEGORY OF COMMODITIES(LOCAL)

项目	Item	金额(万美元) Value (USD 10000) 2000	1999	构成(%) Composition(%) 2000	1999
出口总额	**Exports**	**462683**	**326101**	**100**	**100**
初级产品	Primary Goods	27841	24871	6.0	7.6
食品及主要供食用的活动物	Food and Lively Animals Chiefly for Food	15745	15968	3.4	4.9
饮料及烟草	Beverage and Tabacco	440	523	0.1	0.2
非食用原料（燃料除外）	Non-edible Raw Materials(excluding Fuel)	6590	4802	1.4	1.5
矿物燃料、润滑油及有关原料	Mineral Fuels,Lubricants and Related Materials	4965	3449	1.1	1.0
动植物油、脂及蜡	Animal and Vegetable Oils,Fats and Waxes	101	129	…	…
工业制成品	Manufactured Goods	434842	301230	94.0	92.4
化学品及有关产品	Chemicals and Related Products	17677	9841	3.8	3.0
按原料分类的制成品	Finished Products Grouped by Materials	47384	39529	10.2	12.1
机械及运输设备	Machinery and Transport Equipment	233903	110863	50.6	34.0
杂项制品	Miscellaneous Products	135878	140963	29.4	43.3
未分类商品	Products Not Classified		34	…	…
进口总额	**Imports**	**702376**	**518111**	**100**	**100**
初级产品	Primary Goods	37582	35471	5.4	6.8
食品及主要供食用的活动物	Food and Lively Animals Chiefly for Food	11745	9769	1.8	1.9
饮料及烟草	Beverage and Tabacco	1589	1259	0.2	0.2
非食用原料（燃料除外）	Non-edible Raw Materials(excluding Fuel)	23065	20961	3.3	4.0
矿物燃料、润滑油及有关原料	Mineral Fuels,Lubricants and Related Materials	628	518	0.1	0.1
动植物油、脂及蜡	Animal and Vegetable Oils,Fats and Waxes	555	2964	…	0.6
工业制成品	Manufactured Goods	664794	482640	94.6	93.2
化学品及有关产品	Chemicals and Related Products	34786	26274	5.0	5.1
按原料分类的制成品	Finished Products Grouped by Materials	66107	51490	9.4	9.9
机械及运输设备	Machinery and Transport Equipment	512648	367840	73.0	71.0
杂项制品	Miscellaneous Products	50813	36635	7.2	7.1
未分类商品	Products Not Classified	440	401	…	0.1

11-3 进出口商品检验
TEST OF IMPORTS AND EXPORTS COMMODITIES

项目	Item	2000	1999	2000年为1999年% 2000 as % of 1999
进口商品检验	**Imports Test**			
批数 (批)	Batches (batch)	10853	2789	3.9倍
金额 (万美元)	Value (USD 10000)	110519	69840	158.2
# 不合格商品	Substandard			
批数 (批)	Batches (batch)	377	517	72.9
金额 (万美元)	Value (USD 10000)	1259	1723	73.1
出口商品检验	**Exports Test**			
批数 (批)	Batches (batch)	45918	36762	124.9
金额 (万美元)	Value (USD 10000)	260661	102467	2.5倍
# 不合格商品	Substandard			
批数 (批)	Batches (batch)	140	180	77.8

11-4 海关主要商品出口量
MAJOR EXPORTS COMMODITIES IN VOLUME(CUSTOMS STATISTICS)

品　名 Item	2000	1999	品　名 Item	2000	1999
冻　鸡　(吨) Frozen Chicken (ton)	26615	24445	棉　纱　(吨) Cotton Yarn (ton)	2759	4273
蔬　菜　(万吨) Vegetable (10000 tons)	1	1	棉　布　(万米) Cotton Cloth (10000 m)	5183	8925
干鲜果　(万吨) Dry and Fresh Fruit (10000 tons)	1	1	铅　笔　(吨) (Pencils) (ton)	1245	993
			洗衣粉　(吨) Detergents (ton)	672	122
栗　子　(吨) Chestnuts (ton)	4715	4281	彩色电视机　(万美元) Color TV Sets (USD 10000)	29	11
罐　头　(吨) Canned Food (ton)	297	140			
啤　酒　(万升) Beer (10000 liters)	302	170	收录机　(万台) Recorders (10000)	48	14
中成药　(万美元) Chinese Medicines (USD 10000)	571	737	照相机　(万架) Cameras (10000)	38	75
			地　毯　(万平方米) Carpets (10000 sq.m)	62	54
真丝绸缎　(万米) Silk and Satins(10000 m)	214	760	首　饰　(万美元) Jewelry (USD10000)	3195	5478
手　表　(万只) Watches (10000)	227	178	玻璃制品　(万美元) Glass Ware (USD 10000)	1409	1092
服装及衣着附件　(万美元) Garments (USD 10000)	78535	90537	石　蜡　(万美元) Paraffin Wax (USD 10000)	23	651
皮　鞋　(万双) Leather Shoes (10000 pairs)	1842	1628	钢　材　(万美元) Rolled-ste`' (USD 10000)	2756	1965
			铜　材　(吨) Copper Products (ton)	349	337
胶或塑料底布鞋　(万双) Cloth Shoes with Outer Soles of Rubber or Artificial Plastic Materials (10000 pairs)	1711	1303	铝　材　(吨) Aluminum Products (ton)	656	133
			机　床　(万台) Machine Tools (10000)	305	184
			汽　车　(辆) Motor Vehicle (unit)	469	365

11-5 海关主要商品进口量
MAJOR IMPORTS COMMODITIES IN VOLUME(CUSTOMS STATISTICS)

品名 Item	2000	1999	品名 Item	2000	1999
食糖 (万吨) Sugar (10000 tons)	1	1	复印机 (台) Duplicators (unit)	187	555
谷物及谷物粉 (万吨) Cereal and Cereal Powder (10000 tons)	3	10	食品加工机械 (万美元) Food Processing Machine (USD 10000)	1320	1009
纺织用合成纤维 (万吨) Synthetic Fibers Suitable for Spinning (10000 tons)	1	1	聚乙烯 (吨) Polyethylene (ton)	17213	13606
合成纤维纱线 (吨) Synthetic Fibers, Continuous Filament And Yarn (ton)	5463	849	聚丙烯 (吨) Polypropylene (ton)	4651	2372
羊毛及羊毛条 (吨) Wool and Wool Top (ton)	7159	3514	聚苯乙烯及共聚物 (吨) Polystyrene and Copolymer (ton)	9341	6981
纸及纸板 (万吨) Paper and Paperboard (10000 tons)	3	5	钢材 (万吨) Rolled-steel (10000 tons)	15	8
空气调节器 (台) Air Conditioners (unit)	945	833	铝材 (吨) Aluminum Products (ton)	19722	20543
彩色电视机 (台) Color TV Set (unit)	821	3422	机床 (台) Machine Tools (unit)	1174	1751
电视摄像机 (台) Television Camera (unit)	31196	8681	汽车 (辆) Motor Vehicle (unit)	336	445
			成套数字式数据处理设备 (台) Complete Sets of Digital Data Processing Equipment (unit)	62148	77556
			成套数字式中央处理机 (台) Complete Sets of Digital Central Processing (unit)	8826	16915

11-6 利用外资签约情况
UTILIZATION OF FOREIGN CAPITAL

项目 Item		合同数(个) Number of Contracts (unit)		合同外资金额(万美元) Contracted Foreign Capital(USD 10000)	
		2000	1999	2000	1999
合计	**Total**	**1149**	**647**	**433693.9**	**182648.6**
对外借款	Foreign Loans	3	2	610.0	964.0
外商直接投资	Direct Foreign Investments	1146	645	433083.9	181684.6
按投资方式	By Investment Manner				
合资经营	Joint Venture	428	336	135680.2	54613.1
合作经营	Cooperative Operation	144	96	49446.3	63013.4
独资经营	Foreign Enterprises	573	210	246723.8	57337.3
股份制	Share Holding	1		1233.6	3012.8
外资银行	Foreign Banks		3		3708.0

注：1.外商投资企业投资性借款作为外商直接投资统计，对外借款中不再重复统计。

2.合资经营项目合同外资金额为项目注册资本乘以外商出资比例。

a) Loans for investment of foreign funded enterprises are counted as foreign direct investment and not counted in foreign loans any more.

b) Contracted foreign capital of joint venture projects are counted from registered capital multiplied proportion of foreign investment.

11-7 外商投资企业签约情况

STATISTICS ON CONTRACTS OF FOREIGN FUNDED ENTERPRISES

项　　目	Item	项目数（个） Number of Contracts (unit)		合同总金额（万美元） Total Value of Contracts(USD 10000)		# 外资金额 Foreign Capital	
		2000	1999	2000	1999	2000	1999
合　　计	**Total**	**1146**	**645**	**730376.8**	**306212.1**	**433083.9**	**181684.6**
按登记注册类型分	**Grouped by Investment Manner**						
合资经营	Joint Venture	428	336	350020.8	133006.7	135680.2	54613.1
合作经营	Cooperative Operation	144	96	89783.6	99507.0	49446.3	63013.4
独资经营	Foreign Funded Enterprises	573	210	288966.0	62157.2	246723.8	57337.3
股份制	Share Holding	1		1606.4	7833.2	1233.6	3012.8
外资银行	Foreign Banks		3		3708.0		3708.0
按三次产业分	**Grouped by Three Industry**						
第一产业	Primary Industry	30	16	28312.1	6966.4	12219.7	3026.3
第二产业	Secondary Industry	382	372	158960.4	129468.9	89593.6	88565.9
第三产业	Tertiary Industry	734	257	543104.3	170684.7	331270.6	90092.4
按行业分	**By Sector**						
工业	Industry	369	366	160315.3	139920.4	91762.7	92574.1
建筑业	Construction	12	8	2459.4	1421.8	893.9	579.7
交通运输、仓储及邮电通信业	Transportation, Storage, Posts and Telecommunications	4	7	79437.6	2860.9	78641.9	1297.6
批发和零售贸易餐饮业	Wholesale, Retail and Catering Trade	30	23	26407.0	3594.7	10255.9	1909.0
# 零售业	Retail Trade	6		21038.2		7448.4	
餐饮业	Catering Services	20	23	5134.6	3582.7	2737.7	1903.1
金融保险业	Banking and Insurance		3	20.6	3708.0	5.1	3708.0
房地产业	Real Estate	33	36	253750.4	106598.6	106336.3	54243.2
社会服务业	Social Services	658	169	141747.0	36107.7	96328.4	19593.4
# 信息咨询服务业	Information and Consultancy Services	69	54	8022.8	9567.7	5685.3	5390.3
计算机应用服务业	Computer Application	562	96	122650.0	50391.3	85324.9	10434.6
其他行业	Others	40	33	66239.5	12907.9	48859.7	7779.6
按客商国别(地区)分	**Grouped by Country(Region) of Foreign Partner**						
# 日　本	Japan	52	39	41504.0	16809.6	22228.3	10304.1
美　国	United States	201	130	103451.8	50470.1	62425.3	27955.0
香港地区	Hongkong	285	154	179027.2	82282.4	132149.6	45860.5
澳大利亚	Australia	11	20	4326.2	5445.3	5793.8	1991.0
法　国	France	9	11	3617.8	8654.6	2584.1	7602.1
新加坡	Singapore	48	15	30048.7	4918.0	19887.5	2151.9
加拿大	Canada	25	24	2367.3	2090.7	1782.1	850.1
德　国	Germany	21	16	12481.6	15251.2	11005.2	12086.5
西班牙	Spain	2	2	521.2	1075.6	313.5	479.7
台　湾	Taiwan	47	58	4387.4	9068.8	2582.2	3586.9
瑞　典	Sweden	6	2	9252.9	3227.5	8802.5	3220.0
泰　国	Thailand	4	2	949.9	32.0	437.6	17.8
比利时	Belgium			310.0	25.0	155.0	25.0
丹　麦	Denmark		3	6760.0	116.1	6760.0	79.5
韩　国	Korea	90	45	10964.3	4417.8	7318.9	3160.4
俄罗斯	Russia	2	3	160.0	159.9	119.2	42.0

注：合资企业外资金额是以项目注册资本乘以外商出资比例。

Note: Foreign capital of joint venture are counted from registered capital multiplied proportion of foreign investment.

11-8 外商投资企业生产经营情况
STATISTICS ON PRODUCTION AND BUSINESS OF FOREIGN ENTERPRISES

单位：万元 (10000 yuan)

项 目	Item	销售营业收入 Business Revenue 2000	1999	利润总额 Total Profits 2000	1999	交纳税金总额 Taxes 2000	1999
合 计	**Total**	**18313347**	**13515429**	**544133**	**148830**	**1140361**	**938605**
按登记注册类型分	**Grouped by Registration Status**						
外商投资企业	Foreign Funded Enterprises	12000760	8695071	553888	224875	829235	681634
中外合资	Joint Venture	9154450	6929639	489901	186957	603675	517456
中外合作	Cooperative	542174	297588	12157	-7004	43107	22846
外商独资	Foreign Enterprises	2242616	1436437	55590	46506	175381	126114
外商投资股份有限公司	Foreign Funded Share Holding Company	61520	31407	-3760	-1584	7072	15218
港澳台商投资企业	Hongkong,Macao and Taiwan Funded Enterprises	6312587	4820358	-9755	-76045	311126	256971
港澳台合资	Joint Venture	3110032	2803554	-60477	-118471	199362	183633
港澳台合作	Cooperative	361979	331774	-49956	15751	43422	29446
港澳台商独资	Hongkong,Macao and Taiwan Enterprises	2766713	1629489	84357	20402	62784	38168
港澳台商投资股份有限公司	Hongkong,Macao and Taiwan Funded Share Holding Company	73863	55541	16321	6273	5558	5724
按行业分	**Grouped by Sector**						
农林牧渔水利业	Farming,Forestry,Animal Husbandry, Fishery and Water Conservancy	160361	131375	1226	-1184	731	267
工 业	Industry	12475757	9157936	572259	190420	687545	599824
运输邮电业	Transportation,Post and Telecommunications	101830	35746	5082	1507	5852	1012
商业饮食业	Commerce and Catering Services	790957	639512	-3520	-33802	37849	32817
居民服务业	Residential Services	994738	960410	-962	-30351	85714	81398
其他行业	Others	3789704	2590450	-29952	22240	322670	223287
按客商国别(地区)分	**Grouped by Country(Region) of Foreign Partner**						
# 香港地区	Hongkong	5881607	4378955	-10488	-68438	287275	233153
澳门地区	Macao	35123	34773	628	1007	1028	999
台湾地区	Taiwan	395857	406630	105	-8614	22823	22819
朝鲜民主主义人民共和国	Democratic People's Republic of Korea	10191	11859	726	1096	370	329
日 本	Japan	2426071	1826234	163283	31711	135122	101118
泰 国	Thailand	262141	223817	8935	6905	8860	5442
新加坡	Singapore	399928	306356	21441	28137	40456	21035
印度尼西亚	Indonesia	2172	869	-330	-331	506	62
法 国	France	266044	196457	43250	13893	26208	16483
意大利	Italy	24413	17844	-1802	-1488	1036	677
荷 兰	The Holland	395571	209521	-25842	-36627	41905	9178
瑞 典	Sweden	1163366	849447	10727	28584	50648	52280
西班牙	Spain	10607	9598	1855	-2092	1260	1052
美 国	United States	2586156	2108890	85982	35058	226709	181881
德 国	Germany	863583	706031	147506	80054	92980	124545
丹 麦	Denmark	21574	16785	-2073	-6127	2677	2227
菲律宾	Philippines	13938	17829	-7545	-5964	3342	2781
澳大利亚	Australia	124538	60571	-8031	-9490	7538	3396
新西兰	New Zealand	3065	3754	-787	-918	93	101
韩 国	Korea	150149	132905	-2791	-3654	8186	7612
英 国	United Kingdom	137070	95908	-31942	-5287	13311	18835
瑞 士	Switzerland	182915	162567	17626	18	17671	11240
奥地利	Austria	6727	6995	714	-203	299	100
加拿大	Canada	85371	73613	-3650	5425	3769	2786

11-9 外商投资企业利用外资情况
UTILIZATION OF FOREIGN CAPITAL OF FOREIGN FUNDED ENTERPRISES

单位：万美元 (USD 10000)

项目	Item	实际利用外资额 Amount of Foreign Capital Actually Used	客商实际投资 Auctual Foreign Investment	企业对外借款投资 Foreign Loans for Investment
合计	**Total**	**245849.1**	**218728.7**	**27120.4**
按登记注册类型分	**Grouped by Investment Manner**			
合资经营	Joint Venture	44555.4	41686.0	2869.4
合作经营	Cooperative Operation	48571.8	24622.0	23949.8
独资经营	Foreign Funded Enterprises	152721.9	152420.7	301.2
股份制	Share Holding			
其他	Others			
按行业分	**Grouped by Sector**			
工业	Industry	25798.7	24023.9	1774.8
建筑业	Construction	893.6	893.6	
商业饮食业	Commerce and Catering	5713.9	5693.9	20.0
居民服务业	Residential Services	197031.8	171751.4	25280.4
# 房地产业	Real Estate	43182.2	18672.8	24509.4
其他行业	Others	16411.1	16365.9	45.2
按客商国别(地区)分	**Grouped by Country(Region) of Foreign Partner**			
香港地区	Hongkong	59488.9	36763.4	22725.5
台湾地区	Taiwan	3251.3	2651.3	600.0
日本	Japan	50001.8	49953.5	48.3
新加坡	Singapore	949.5	949.5	
法国	France	14915.8	14885.8	30.0
美国	United States	40806.4	40437.5	368.9
德国	Germany	23096.1	22466.4	629.7
韩国	Korea	7832.9	6855.1	977.8
英国	United Kingdom	10209.5	9609.5	600.0
奥地利	Austria	924.7	410.0	514.7
加拿大	Canada	2124.8	1999.3	125.5
其他	Others	32247.4	31747.4	500.0

注：包括对外借款及其他形式，全年实际利用外资30.1亿美元。

Note: Including foreign loans and other investments,amount of foreign capital actually used is 30.1 USD 100 million.

11-10 外商投资企业投产开业情况
STATISTICS FOR OPENING OF FOREIGN FUNDED ENTERPRISES

项 目	Item	企业单位数 (个) Number of Enterprises (unit)		企业职工人数(人) Number of Staff and Workers (person)	
		2000	1999	2000	1999
合 计	**Total**	**5082**	**5118**	**454411**	**436316**
按登记注册类型分	**Grouped by Registration Status**				
外商投资企业	Foreign Funded Enterprises	2702	2596	246678	229565
中外合资	Joint Venture	1725	1814	182435	183651
中外合作	Cooperative	170	138	15100	11630
外商独资	Foreign Enterprises	804	642	45187	32254
外商投资股份有限公司	Foreign Funded Share Holding Company	3	2	3956	2030
港澳台商投资企业	Hongkong,Macao and Taiwan Funded Enterprises	2380	2522	207733	206751
港澳台合资	Joint Venture	1718	1909	167503	172116
港澳台合作	Cooperative	192	185	12621	10723
港澳台商独资	Hongkong,Macao and Taiwan Enterprises	469	427	25651	20653
港澳台商投资股份有限公司	Hongkong,Macao and Taiwan Funded Share Holding Company	1	1	1958	3259
按行业分	**Grouped by Sector**				
农林牧渔水利业	Farming,Forestry,Animal Husbandry,Fishery and Water Conservancy	42	40	3205	3347
工 业	Industry	2832	3231	275066	282532
运输邮电业	Transportation,Posts and Telecommunications	31	26	2995	1943
商业饮食业	Commerce and Catering	275	293	28130	27774
居民服务业	Residential Services	246	254	55871	60810
其他行业	Others	1656	1274	89144	59910
按客商国别(地区)分	**Grouped by Country (Region) of Foreign Partner**				
# 香港地区	Hongkong	1900	1999	177755	177971
澳门地区	Macao	32	36	2519	2668
台湾地区	Taiwan	448	487	27459	26112
朝鲜民主主义人民共和国	Democratic People's Republic of Korea	8	8	566	411
日 本	Japan	551	576	62417	61978
泰 国	Thailand	36	47	3792	4036
新加坡	Singapore	180	189	14011	13972
印度尼西亚	Indinesia	10	8	439	329
法 国	France	77	77	6299	5735
意大利	Italy	23	22	1325	1658
荷 兰	The Holland	38	36	5930	4461
瑞 典	Sweden	29	22	3915	3308
西班牙	Spain	12	14	602	652
美 国	United States	840	797	72993	66597
德 国	Germany	118	110	14705	14242
丹 麦	Denmark	10	9	891	880
菲律宾	Philippines	9	10	1450	1621
澳大利亚	Australia	63	67	3334	3037
新西兰	New Zealand	16	16	394	515
韩 国	Korea	158	145	11572	11090
英 国	United Kingdom	100	77	7035	5673
瑞 士	Switzerland	29	27	4536	5112
奥地利	Austria	12	11	388	310
加拿大	Canada	98	100	4641	3852

11-11 对外承包工程和劳务合作
CONTRACTED PROJECTS AND LABOR SERVICES COOPERATION WITH FOREIGN COUNTRIES

地区	Region	签定合同份数(份) Number of Contracts (unit)		签定合同金额(万美元) Contracted Value (USD 10000)		营业额(万美元) Fulfilled Value (USD 10000)	
		2000	1999	2000	1999	2000	1999
合计	**Total**	**104**	**90**	**16285**	**25229**	**19798**	**26165**
对外承包工程	**Constructed Projects**	**18**	**17**	**9520**	**18404**	**13296**	**19342**
# 斯里兰卡	Sri Lanka					757	1483
马来西亚	Malaysia	1		157			
巴基斯坦	Pakistan						2248
新加坡	Singapore	3	5	4954	7393	5551	7292
对外劳务合作	**Labor Services**	**50**	**62**	**6349**	**6516**	**6256**	**6477**
# 日本	Japan	12	23	344	401	120	223
香港地区	Hongkong		2		140	42	72
马来西亚	Malaysia					1	2
新加坡	Singapore	1	1	8	6	1	8
韩国	Korea						
埃及	Egypt						1
美国	United States						4
德国	Germany		1		4		
塞浦路斯	Cyprus		1		2		3
尼日利亚	Nigeria		8		8		15
泰国	Thailand		3		3		1
巴林	Bahrain						1
澳门地区	Macao						90
沙特阿拉伯	Saudi Arabia		3		75		5
斯里兰卡	Sri Lanka						126
设计咨询	**Consulting Services for Designing**	**36**	**11**	**416**	**309**	**246**	**346**

11-12 海外企业审批情况
STATISTICS ON EXAMINING AND APPROVING OF CONTRACTS OF OVERSEAS ENTERPRISES

项目	Item	审批项目数(个) Number of Projects Examined and Approved (unit)		# 中方投资金额(万美元) Investment by Chinese Partner(USD 10000)	
		2000	1999	2000	1999
合计	**Total**	**20**	**13**	**2314.8**	**395.0**
按登记注册类型分	**Grouped by Investment Manner**				
合资经营	Joint Venture	7	4	1446.8	119.2
合作经营	Cooperative Operation				
独资经营	Foreign Enterprises	13	9	868.0	275.8
按生产性、非生产性分	**Grouped by Production and Non-production**				
生产性企业	Productive Enterprises	4	1	662.6	13.0
非生产性企业	Non-productive Enterprises	16	12	1652.2	382.0
按投资国别(地区)分	**Grouped by Country(Region) of Investment**				
美国	United States	6	3	1565.0	133.0
澳大利亚	Australia		1		96.0
日本	Japan	1			
蒙古	Mongolia	1		24.0	
俄罗斯	Russia	2	2	25.0	1.8
德国	Germany		1		8.4
罗马尼亚	Romania		1		0.1
秘鲁	Peru		1		50.0
阿尔及利亚	Algeria		1		
波兰	Poland		1		0.3
新加坡	Singapore		1		95.0
多米尼克	Dominica		1		10.0

11-13 外国企业及华侨、港澳地区企业驻京代表机构
REPRESENTATIVE OFFICES IN BEIJING OF FOREIGN,OVERSEAS CHINESE HONGKONG AND MACAO ENTERPRISES

项目	Item	数量(个) Number(unit) 2000	1999	构成(%) Composition(%) 2000	1999
总计	**Total**	**6758**	**6107**	**100**	**100**
#日本	Japan	613	593	9.1	9.7
港澳地区	Hongkong and Macao	1833	1698	27.1	27.8
美国	United States	1296	1152	19.2	18.9
德国	Germany	381	345	5.6	5.6
法国	France	192	185	2.8	3.0
英国	United Kingdom	191	181	2.8	3.0
意大利	Italy	160	146	2.4	2.4
瑞士	Switzerland	97	94	1.4	1.5
瑞典	Sweden	57	55	0.8	0.9
加拿大	Canada	211	176	3.1	2.9
澳大利亚	Australia	141	128	2.1	2.1
比利时	Belgium	37	38	0.5	0.6
新加坡	Singapore	268	232	4.0	3.8
荷兰	The Holland	91	89	1.3	1.5
奥地利	Austria	44	41	0.7	0.7

11-14 区县对外经济基本情况
FOREIGN ECONOMY OF DISTRICTS AND COUNTIES

项目	Item	合计 Total	城区 City Proper	近郊区 Near Suburbs	远郊区 Outer Suburbs	各县 Counties
利用外资	**Utilization of Foreign Capital**					
签约项目 (个)	Projects Signed (unit)	1017	130	671	110	106
合同外资金额 (万美元)	Contracted Foreign Capital (USD 10000)	138445	19147.9	93811.4	17472.6	8012.8
外商实际投资额 (万美元)	Foreign Actual Investment (USD 10000)	95130.6	39876.0	27491.8	15929.7	11833.1
出口商品交货	**Export Delivery**					
交货总额 (万元)	Total Value (10000 yuan)	542396	3653.0	49185.7	235395	254161.7
直接交货 (万元)	Direct Delivery (10000 yuan)	385486	3653.0	29824.4	157487	194521.8
#交本市外贸收购 (万元)	Purchased by Local Foreign Trade (10000 yuan)	182041	2559.7	29142.4	93114.3	57224.5
间接交货 (万元)	Indirect Delivery	156909		19361.3	77908.0	59639.9

11-15 生产型"三资"企业按销售收入

ARRANGING IN SALES REVENUE OF PRODUCTIVE FOREIGN FUNDED ENTERPRISES

排 名 No.	单 位 名 称	Enterprise
1	联想(北京)有限公司	LEGEND(BEIJING)LIMITED
2	北京诺基亚移动通信有限公司	BEIJING NOKIA MOBILE TELECOMMUNICATIONS LTD
3	北京爱立信移动通信有限公司	BEIJING ERICSSON MOBILE COMMUNICATIONS CO., LTD.
4	联想神州数码有限公司	LEGEND DIGITAL CHINA CO.,LTD.
5	北京诺基亚航星通讯系统有限公司	BEIJING NOKIA HANGXING TELECOMMUNICATIONS SYSTEMS CO.,LTD.
6	北京国际交换系统有限公司	BEIJING INTERNATIONAL SWITCHING SYSTEM CORPORATION LTD.
7	北京·松下彩色显象管有限公司	BEIJING·MATSUSHITA COLOR CRT,CO.,LTD
8	UT斯达康（中国）有限公司	UTSTARCOM （CHINA）CO.,LTD.
9	北京松下通信设备有限公司	BEIJING MATSUSHITA COMMUNICATION EQUIPMENT CO.,LTD.
10	北京朗讯科技光缆有限公司	LUCENT TECHNOLOGIES FIBER OPTIC CABLE CO.LTD.,BEIJING
11	北京东方冠捷电子有限公司	BEIJING ORIENT TOP VICTORY ELECTRONICS
12	北京大发正大有限公司	BEIJING DAFA CHIA TAI CO.,LTD.
13	三菱四通集成电路有限公司	MITSUBISHI STONE SEMICONDUCTOR CO.,LTD.
14	北京飞机维修工程有限公司	AIRCRAFT MAINTENANCE AND ENGINEERING CORPORATION，BEIJING
15	北京北大方正电子有限公司	BEIJING FOUNDER ELECTRONICS CO.,LTD.
16	首钢日电电子有限公司	SHOUGANG NEC ELECTRONICS CO., LTD.
17	北京恒基伟业电子产品有限公司	BEIJING HI-TECH WEALTH ELECTRONIC PRODUCT CO.,LTD
18	北京吉普汽车有限公司	BEIJING JEEP CORPORATION,LTD.
19	北京村田电子有限公司	BEIJING MURATA EIECTRONICS CO., LTD.
20	北京JVC电子产业有限公司	JVC BEIJING ELECTRONIC INDUSTRIES CO., LTD.
21	北京.松下电子部品有限公司	BEIJING MATSUSHITA ELECTRONIC COMPONENTS CO.,LTD.
22	北京三元食品有限公司	BEIJING SANYUAN FOOD CO., LTD.
23	爱芬食品（北京）有限公司	EFFEM FOODS (BEIJING) CO., LTD.
24	安捷伦科技有限公司	AGILENT TECHNOLOGIES COMPANY LIMITED
25	北京可口可乐饮料有限公司	BEIJING COCA-COLA BEVERAGE CO., LTD.
26	北京首钢宝生带钢有限公司	BEIJING SHOUGANG-POHSENG STRIP STEEL CO.,LTD.
27	北京金远见电脑技术有限公司	BEIJING GOLDEN GLOBAL VIEW COMPUTER TECHNOLOGY CO.,LTD
28	北京轻型汽车有限公司	BEIJING LIGHT AUTOMOBILE CO.LTD
29	北京甲骨文软件系统有限公司	BEIJING ORACLE SOFTWARE SYSTEM CO.,LTD.
30	北京飞利浦有限公司	BEIJING PHILIPS AUDIO & VIDEO CO.,LTD.
31	北京索鸿电子有限公司	BEIJING SUOHONG ELECTRONICS CO.,LTD.
32	北京地杰通信设备有限公司	BEIJING D&G TELECOMMUNICATION EQUIPMENT CO.,LTD.
33	北京ABB高压开关设备有限公司	ABB HIGH VOLTAGE SWITCHGEAR CO.,LTD. BEIJING
34	北京金裕兴电子技术有限公司	BEIJING GOLDEN YU XING ELECTRONIC CO.,LTD.
35	北京大田联邦快递有限公司	FEDEX-DPW CORPORATION CO.,LTD
36	施耐德（北京）中压电器有限公司	SCHNEIDER (BEIJING) MEDIUM VOLTAGE CO.,LTD.
37	北京四通松下电工有限公司	BEIJING STONE MATSUSHITA ELECTRIC WORKS LTD.
38	北京统一食品有限公司	BEIJING PRESIDENT FOOD CO.,LTD.
39	北京金长科国际电子有限公司	BEIJING GKI ELECTRONICS CO.,LTD.
40	红牛维他命饮料有限公司	RED BULL VITAMIN DRINK CO.,LTD.
41	北京诺华制药有限公司	BEIJING NOVARTIS PHARMA CO.,LTD.
42	三伍电子系统(北京)有限公司	THREE－FIVE SYSTEMS (BEIJING) CO.,LTD.
43	北京顺美服装股份有限公司	BEIJING SMART GARMENTS CO.LTD
44	北京恩布拉科雪花压缩机有限公司	BEIJING EMBRACO SNOWFLAKE COMPRESSOR CO.,LTD.
45	吉百利(中国)食品有限公司	CADBURY FOOD CO.,LTD.（CHINA）
46	北京宏棋讯息有限公司	BEIJING ACER INFORMATION CO.,LTD.
47	北京利乐包包装有限公司	BEIJING TETRA PAK PACKAGING CO.,LTD.
48	资生堂丽源化妆品有限公司	SHISEIDO LIYUAN COSMETICS CO.,LTD.
49	北京松下控制装置有限公司	BEIJING MATSUSHITA AUTOMATION CONTROLS CO.,LTD.
50	北京富特波尔容器有限公司	BEIJING FTB PACKAGING LTD.

11-16 非生产型"三资"企业按销售收入排序
ARRANGING IN SALES REVENUE OF NON-PRODUCTIVE FOREIGN FUNDED ENTERPRISES

排 名 No.	单 位 名 称	Enterprise
1	松下电器（中国）有限公司	MATSUSHITA ELECTRIC （CHINA）CO., LTD.
2	国际商业机器中国有限公司	IBM CHINA COMPANY LTD.
3	爱立信（中国）有限公司	ERICSSON （CHINA）COMPANY LIMITED
4	中国惠普有限公司	CHINA HEWLETT－PACKART
5	西门子（中国）有限公司	SIEMENS LTD., CHINA
6	朗讯科技(中国)有限公司	LUCENT TECHNOLOGIES (CHINA) CO.,LTD.
7	中国国际金融有限公司	CHINA INTERNATIONAL CAPITAL CORPORATION LIMITED
8	赛特集团有限公司	SCITECH GROUP COMPANY LIMITED'
9	北京燕莎友谊商城有限公司	YOU YI SHOPPING CITY CO., LTD. BEIJING LUFTHANSA CENTER
10	北京百盛轻工发展有限公司	BEIJING PARKSON LIGHT INDUSTRY DEVELOPMENT COMPANY LIMITED
11	北京北辰实业股份有限公司	BEIJING NORTH STAR COMPANY LIMITED
12	中贸联万客隆商业有限公司	CTA MAKRO COMMERCIAL CO.,LTD.
13	北京麦当劳食品有限公司	BEIJING MCDONALD'S FOOD CO.,LTD.
14	中外运－敦豪国际航空快件有限公司	DHL－SINOTRANS INTERNATIONAL AIR COURIER LTD.
15	施耐德电气（中国）投资有限公司	SCHNEIDER ELECTRIC （CHINA） INVESTMENT CO., LTD.
16	微软（中国）有限公司	MICROSOFT (CHINA) CO.,LTD.
17	中国国际贸易中心有限公司	CHINA WORLD TRADE CENTER LTD.
18	北京肯德基有限公司	BEIJING KENTUCKY CO.,LTD.
19	东陶机器(中国)有限公司	TOTO (CHINA) CO., LTD.
20	北京电通广告有限公司	BEIJING DENTSU ADVERTISING CO，LTD
21	华糖洋华堂商业有限公司	HUA TANG YOKADO COMMERCIAL CO., LTD.
22	北京燕莎中心有限公司	BEIJING LUFTHANSA CENTER CO.,LTD.
23	北京怡海花园房地产开发有限公司	BEIJING YIHAI GARDEN PROPERTY DEVELOPMENT CO.,LTD.
24	索尼（中国）有限公司	SONY （CHINA）CO.,LTD.
25	丽都饭店有限公司	LIDO HOTEL CO.,LTD.
26	北京三菱移动通信设备有限公司	BEIJING MITSUBISHI MOBILE COMMUNICATION EQUIPMENT CO.,LTD
27	大通国际运输有限公司	EAS INTERNATIONAL TRANSPORTATION LTD.
28	北京敬远房地产开发有限公司	BEIJING JING YUAN PROPERTY DEVELOPMENT CO.,LTD.
29	北京贵友大厦有限公司	BEIJING MANSION GUIYOU CO.,LTD.
30	北京冠海房地产有限公司	BEIJING GUANHAI REAL ESTATE CO.,LTD.
31	松下电工（中国）有限公司	MATSUSHITA ELECTRIC WORKS （CHINA） CO.,LTD.
32	北京紫竹花园房地产开发有限公司	BEIJING ZIZHU GARDEN REAL ESTATE DEVELOPMENT CO.,LTD.
33	纽科租赁有限公司	NEWCOURT LEASING CORPORATION
34	亚信科技(中国)有限公司	ASIAINFO TECHNOLOGY (CHINA) CO.,LTD.
35	三井物产(中国)有限公司	MITSUI & CO. (CHINA) LTD.
36	金光林浆纸业贸易（北京）有限公司	APP CO.,LTD.
37	通标标准技术服务有限公司	SGS－CSTC STANDARDS TECHNICAL SERVICES CO.,LTD.
38	北京市长城饭店公司	GREAT WALL HOTEL JOINT VENTURE OF BEIJING
39	北京长庆房地产开发有限公司	BEIJING CHANG QING REAL ESTATE DEVELOPMENT CO.,LTD.
40	北京通成推广公交广告有限公司	BEIJING TOP RESULT PUBLIC TRANSPORTATION ADVERTISING CO.,LTD
41	北京裕京花园别墅有限公司	BEIJING YU JING GARDEN VILLA CO.,LTD.
42	北京北瑞家具有限公司	BEIJING BEI RUI FURNISHINGS COMPANY LIMITED
43	北京昆仑饭店有限公司	BEIJING KUNLUN HOTEL COMPANY LIMITED
44	北京香江花园别墅房产开发有限公司	BEIJING RIVIERA ESTATE MANAGEMENT OFFICE
45	王府饭店有限公司	THE PALACE HOTEL CO.,LTD
46	北京香格里拉饭店有限公司	BEIJING SHANGRI－LA HOTEL CO.,LTD.
47	北京市华远房地产股份有限公司	BEIJING HUAYUAN PROPERTY COMPANY LIMITED
48	北京四通电工营销有限公司	BEIJING STONE ELECTRIC WORKS MARKETING CO.,LTD.
49	北京金龙兴业房地产有限公司	BEIJING DRAGON STATES PROPERTIES CO.,LTD.
50	北京国际俱乐部有限公司	BEIJING INTERNATIONAL CLUB CORPORATION LTD.

主要统计指标解释

进出口总额 海关进出口总额指实际进、出我国关境并能引起我国境内物质资源增加或减少的进出口货物总金额。包括我国境内法人和其他组织以一般贸易、易货贸易、加工贸易、补偿贸易、寄售代销贸易等方式进出口的货物、租赁期一年及以上的租赁进出口货物、边境小额贸易货物、国际援助物资或捐赠品、保税区和保税仓库进出口货物等的金额合计。进出口总额用以观察一个国家在对外贸易方面的总规模。我国规定出口货物按离岸价格统计，进口货物按到岸价格统计。

利用外资 指我国各级政府、部门、企业和其他经济组织通过对外借款、吸收外商直接投资以及用其他方式筹措的境外现汇、设备、技术等。

对外借款 是我国利用外资的主要部分。包括我国通过外国政府贷款，国际金融组织贷款，外国银行商业贷款，出口信贷以及对外发行债券，股票等方式，从境外筹措的资金。

外商直接投资 是指外国企业和经济组织或个人（包括华侨、港澳台同胞以及我国在境外注册的企业）按我国有关政策、法规，用现汇、实物、技术等在我国境内开办外商独资企业、与我国境内的企业或经济组织共同举办中外合资经营企业、合作经营企业或合作开发资源的投资（包括外商投资收益的再投资）以及经政府有关部门批准的项目投资总额内，企业从境外借入的资金。

对外承包工程 包括各对外承包公司以招标议标承包方式承揽的下列业务（1）承包国外工程建设项目；（2）承包我国对外经援项目；（3）承包我国驻外机构的工程建设项目；（4）承包我国境内利用外资进行建设的工程项目；（5）与外国承包公司合营或联合承包工程项目时我国公司分包部分；（6）以服务成果向业主收费的技术服务项目（包括承担地形地貌测绘；地质资源勘探与普查；建设区域规划；提供设计文件、图纸、生产工艺技术资料和工程技术经济咨询；工程项目的可行性考察、研究和评估；进行技术指导和培训人员等）；（7）对外承包兼营的房屋开发业务。对外承包工程的营业额是以货币表现的本期内完成的对外承包工程的工作量，包括以前年度签定的合同和本年度新签定的合同在报告期完成的工作量。

对外劳务合作 指以收取工资的形式向业主承包商提供技术和劳动服务的活动。我国对外承包公司在境外开办的合营企业，中国公司同时又提供劳务的，其劳务部分也纳入劳务合作统计。劳务合作营业额按报告期内向雇主提交的结算数（包括工资、加班费和奖金等）统计。

Explanatory Notes On Main Statistical Indicators

Total Imports and Exports at Customs refer to the value of commodities imported and exported across the boundary of China and cause increase or decrease of material resource within the boundaries of our country. It includes imports and exports in manner of general trade, barter trade, processing trade, compensation trade, consignment and commission agent trade, leasing commodities with renting period in one year and above, imports and exports in border trade, donations and gifts between governments, imported and exported goods in China from bonded warehouses. The indicator of the total imports and exports at customs can be used to observe the total size of external trade in a country . In accordance with the stipulation of the Chinese government, imports are calculated at CIF, while exports are calculated at FOB.

Utilization of Foreign Capital refers to foreign exchange, equipment and technology financed with foreign loans, foreign direct investment and other ways undertaken by the Chinese governments at all levels, by various departments, enterprises and other economic units.

Foreign Loans refers to funds borrowed from abroad, including loans of foreign governments, loans of international financial institutions, commercial loans of foreign banks, export credit, and funds raised via bonds and shares issued abroad. It is a major part of China's utilization of foreign capital.

Direct Investment by Foreign Enterprises refers to the investments in foreign enterprises, Sino-foreign joint ventures and Sino-foreign cooperative enterprises in China and in Sino-foreign co-operative exploration of resources in China by foreign enterprises, economic organizations or individuals（including overseas Chinese, compatriots from Hong Kong, Taiwan and Macao, and Chinese enterprises registered abroad）, following the relevant policies and laws of China. It includes the re-investment of the foreign parties with the return of the investment and the funds that enterprises borrow from abroad for the investment of projects approved by the relevant government department.

Overseas Projects Contracted refer to projects undertaken by Chinese contractors（project contracting companies）through bidding process, which include:

(1) overseas civil engineering construction projects financed by foreign investor;

(2) overseas projects financed by the Chinese government foreign-aid programs;

(3) construction projects of Chinese institutions functioning abroad;

(4) construction projects in China financed by foreign investment;

(5) sub-contracted projects to be taken by Chinese contractors through a joint umbrella project with foreign contractors;

(6) technical assistance projects charged from the foreign owners according to service results（such as topographic surveying, geological prospecting, development zone programming, provision of designing documents, blueprint, materials on production process, technical consultation, project feasibility studies and evaluation, personnel training , etc.）;

(7) house development projects.

The business income from overseas projects contracted is the work volume of contracted projects completed in the reference period, including completed projects signed contracts in previous years.

Overseas Labor Service Co-operation refers to the activities of providing technology and labor services to employers or contractors and getting salaries and wages in return. Labor services providing by contractual joint ventures of Chinese international contracting corporations should be included in the statistics of overseas labor service co-operation. The business income of labor service co-operation is the total income of wages, salaries, over-time pay, bonuses and other remuneration received from the employers during the reference period.

北京统计年鉴——2001

BEIJING STATISTICAL YEARBOOK

旅游业

TOURISM

12

接待入境旅游人数（单位：万人）
Tourists (10000 persons)

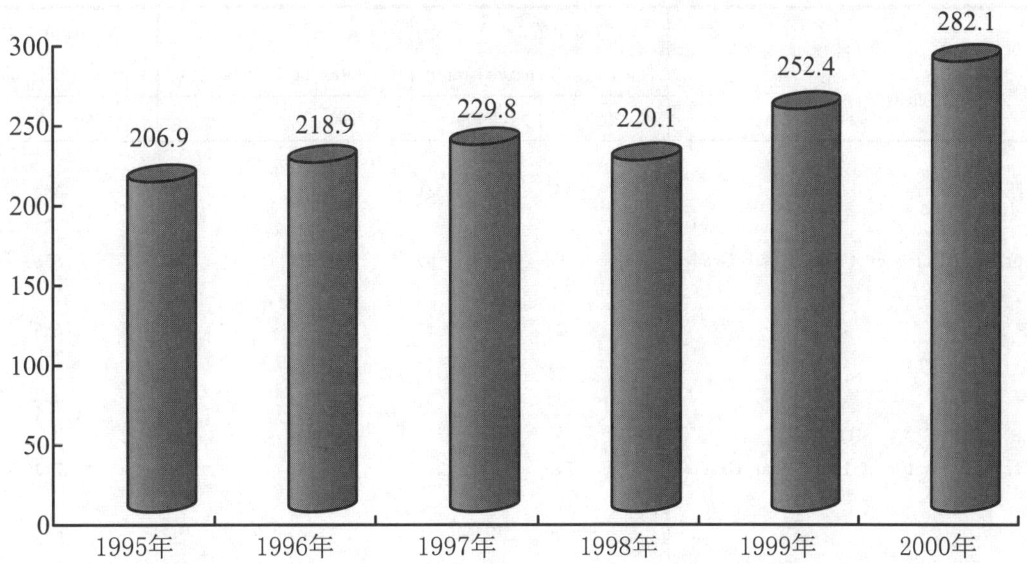

旅游外汇收入　　（单位：亿美元）
Foreign Exchange Earning from Tourism (USD 100 million)

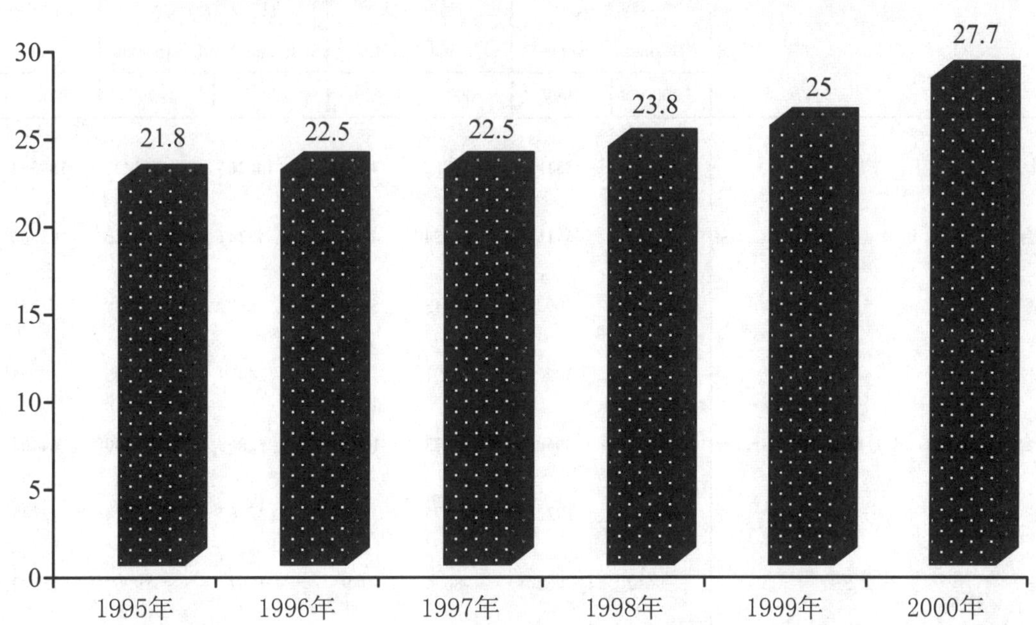

12-1 涉外饭店(公寓)主要经济指标
MAIN ECONOMIC INDICATORS OF TOURIST HOTELS(APARTMENTS)

项目	Item	企业个数（个） Number of Enterprises(unit)		出租率（%） Renting Rate(%)		平均房价（元/间天） Average Price(yuan/room.day)	
		2000	1999	2000	1999	2000	1999
总计	**Total**	**347**	**331**	**61**	**57**	**394**	**395**
四星、五星合计	**Hotels of 4 and 5 Star Grade**	**54**	**49**	**71**	**65**	**535**	**519**
五星	5 Star	21	17	69	65	655	660
四星	4 Star	33	32	72	64	446	436
一星至三星合计	**Hotels of 1 to 3 Star Grade**	**240**	**214**	**54**	**52**	**243**	**243**
三星	3 Star	97	68	62	58	273	287
二星	2 Star	114	111	46	46	198	198
一星	1 Star	29	35	46	46	181	173
其他	**Others**	**53**	**68**	**61**	**55**	**517**	**530**

单位：万元 (10000 yuan)

项目	Item	营业收入 Business Revenue		利润总额 Total Profits		职工人数（人） Staff and Workers(person)		工资总额 Total Wages	
		2000	1999	2000	1999	2000	1999	2000	1999
总计	**Total**	**1281243**	**1231942**	**27822**	**48683**	**106265**	**112427**	**187562**	**185684**
四星、五星合计	**Hotels of 4 and 5 Star Grade**	**752859**	**691673**	**67634**	**48610**	**43247**	**45825**	**102366**	**100166**
五星	5 Star	373274	309378	47243	54280	18807	17530	45221	48666
四星	4 Star	379585	382295	20391	-5670	24440	28295	57145	51500
一星至三星合计	**Hotels of 1 to 3 Star Grade**	**346880**	**306062**	**-36973**	**-15110**	**52868**	**50240**	**64460**	**59010**
三星	3 Star	235546	192237	-28075	-3769	32267	26504	42245	36131
二星	2 Star	96120	96508	-8025	-9893	17647	19967	18543	18939
一星	1 Star	15214	17317	-873	-1448	2954	3769	3672	3940
其他	**Others**	**181504**	**234207**	**-2839**	**15183**	**10150**	**16362**	**20736**	**26508**

注：2000年数据不包括写字楼的数据。

Note: Data of 2000 excludes that of office buildings.

12-2 国际旅行社经营情况
BUSINESS OF INTERNATIONAL TRAVEL AGENCIES

单位：万元 (10000 yuan)

项目		Item		2000	1999	2000年为1999年% 2000 as % of 1999
企业个数	（个）	Number of Enterprises	(unit)	127	120	105.8
营业收入		Business Revenue		576244.6	485678.8	118.6
营业成本		Business Cost		503222.6	427345.7	117.8
营业费用		Business Expense		27911.9	19546.1	142.8
营业税及附加		Business Tax and Extra Charges		3897.1	3233.1	120.5
经营利润		Operating Profits		41213.0	35553.9	115.9
管理费用		Overhead Expense		22788.7	19761.8	115.3
营业利润		Business Profits		16843.5	13923.2	121.0
利润总额		Total Profits		28744.7	26572.0	108.2
平均从业人员	（人）	Average Employed Persons	(person)	6280	…	…
工资总额		Total Wages		11408.1	10833.3	105.3

12-3 国际旅行社外联、接待海外旅游者人数及人天数
PERSONS AND PERSON-DAY OF OVERSEAS GROUP AND RECEIVED BY INTERNATIONAL TRAVEL AGENCIES

单位：人次，人天 (person.time, person-day)

项目	Item	2000	1999	2000年为1999年% 2000 as % of 1999
外联人数	Persons of Overseas Travel Groups	1236629	1031289	119.9
外国人	Foreigners	1158393	950822	121.8
港　澳	Hongkong and Macao Tourists	46335	49721	93.2
台　湾	Taiwan Tourists	31901	30746	103.8
接待人数	Tourists Received	1009849	929416	108.7
外国人	Foreigners	937303	834727	112.3
港　澳	Hongkong and Macao Tourists	42208	53480	78.9
台　湾	Taiwan Tourists	30338	41209	73.6
外联人天数	Person-day of Overseas Travel Groups	6702122	5457656	122.8
外国人	Foreigners	6317527	5096125	124.0
港　澳	Hongkong and Macao Tourists	219377	208293	105.3
台　湾	Taiwan Tourists	165218	153238	107.8
接待人天数	Person-day Received	4075529	3388847	120.3
外国人	Foreigners	3745868	3025467	123.8
港　澳	Hongkong and Macao Tourists	199060	211835	94.0
台　湾	Taiwan Tourists	130601	151545	86.2

注：国际旅行社组团、接待国内游客情况为：2000年组团人数414963人次，接待人数513432人次；1999年组团人数294679人次，接待人数352879人次。

Note: There are 414963 person.times of home groups organized and 513432 person.times received by international travel agencies in 2000, and 294679 person.times organized, 352879 person.times received in 1999.

12-4 国际旅行社组织国内居民出境旅游人数
HOME TOURISTS TRAVELLING OUT-BOUNDARY ORGANIZED BY INTERNATIONAL TRAVEL AGENCIES

项目	Item	2000	1999	2000年为1999年% 2000 as % of 1999
总人数（人）	**Total Tourists**	137106	110505	124.1
出国游	Travel abroad	99011	…	…
港澳游	to Hongkong and Macao	38095	…	…
前往国别及地区（人次）	**Country or Region Travel to(persontime.time)**			
#香　港	Hongkong	49710	47028	105.7
澳　门	Macao	22237	21777	102.1
泰　国	Thailand	39426	36441	108.2
新加坡	Singapore	22402	12308	182.0
马来西亚	Malaysia	20963	11031	190.0
菲律宾	the Philippines	285	485	58.8
韩　国	Republic of Korea	30811	…	…
日　本	Japan	667	…	…
澳大利亚	Australia	10345	…	…
新西兰	New Zealand	1991	…	…

注：目前有特许经营出境旅游业务权的国际旅行社有9家。
Note: Now, there are nine international services specially permitted to operate out-boundary travelling.

12-5 接待海外旅游人数
FOREIGN TOURISTS

单位：人次　(person.time)

项目	Item	2000	1999	项目	Item	2000	1999
合　计	**Total**	**2820911**	**2523943**	法　国	France	95831	78772
外国人	**Foreigner**	**2379637**	**2083375**	德　国	Germany	121091	105305
#日　本	Japan	543319	456451	意大利	Italy	51132	39178
菲律宾	Philippines	8267	11760	瑞　典	Sweden	32364	29458
新加坡	Singapore	73111	72824	瑞　士	Switzerland	24413	25302
泰　国	Thailand	43844	41113	俄罗斯	Russia	38678	45763
印度尼西亚	Indonesia	20637	20774	澳大利亚	Australia	45045	48537
马来西亚	Malaysia	105312	109546	新西兰	New Zealand	7529	10046
蒙　古	Mongolia	26208	21817	荷　兰	The Holland	32804	30496
韩　国	Korea	278055	191539	西班牙	Spain	19052	14992
印　度	India	9361	7018	**港澳台胞**	**Hongkong,Macao and Taiwan Chinese**	**441274**	**440568**
美　国	United States	310515	240924				
加拿大	Canada	52310	54498	#台　胞	Taiwan Chinese	176374	175318
英　国	United Kingdom	96827	88148				

12-6 旅游外汇收入
FOREIGN EXCHANGE EARNING FROM INTERNATIONAL TOURISM

单位：亿美元　(USD 100 million)

项目	Item	2000	1999	2000年为1999年% 2000 as % of 1999	项目	Item	2000	1999	2000年为1999年% 2000 as % of 1999
合　计	**Total**	**27.7**	**25.0**	**110.8**	住　宿	Accommodation	4.2	3.5	120.0
长途交通费	Long-distance Transportation Expenses	8.4	8.2	102.4	餐　饮	Catering Service	2.5	2.1	119.0
					商　品	Commodity	5.2	4.6	113.0
#民　航	Civil Aviation	7.7	7.3	105.5	邮政电讯	Posts and Telecommunications	1.3	0.5	260.0
铁　路	Railway	0.3	0.4	75.0	景点门票	Tickets of Tourism Spots	1.3	1.2	108.3
汽　车	Motor Vehicles	0.3	0.4	75.0	文化娱乐	Culture and Entertainment	1.6	1.3	123.1
市内交通费	Local Transpotation Expense	1.2	1.2	100.0	其　他	Others	2.0	2.4	83.3

12-7 北京市旅游住宿设施一览表
LIST OF ACCOMMODATION INSTALLATION FOR TOURISM
三星级及以上涉外饭店
TOURIST HOTELS OF 3 AND ABOVE STAR GRADE

星 级 Star Grade	饭 店 名 称 Hotel	地 址 Address	邮政编码 Postcode	电 话 Telephone
5	北京饭店	北京市东城区东长安街33号	100004	65137766
5	长城饭店	北京市朝阳区亮马桥东环北路甲6号	100026	65905566
5	长富宫中心	北京市朝阳区建国门外大街26号	100022	65125555
5	钓鱼台宾馆	北京市阜成路 2号	100830	68590077
5	港澳中心瑞士酒店	北京市朝阳区北大街2号	100027	65012288
5	贵宾楼饭店	北京市东城区东长安街35号	100006	65137788
5	国际饭店	北京市东城区建国门内大街9号	100005	65126688
5	华侨大厦	北京市东城区王府井大街2号	100006	65136666
5	皇冠假日饭店	北京市东城区王府井大街48号	100006	65133388
5	嘉里中心饭店	北京市朝阳区光华路1号	100020	65618833
5	京都信苑饭店	北京市海淀区什坊院6号	100036	63901963
5	京广中心	北京市朝阳区呼家楼	100020	65978888
5	京瑞大厦	北京市朝阳区东三环南路	100021	67668866
5	凯宾斯基饭店	北京市朝阳区亮马桥路50号	100016	64653388
5	昆仑饭店	北京市朝阳区亮马桥21号	100004	65903388
5	天伦王朝饭店	北京市东城区王府井大街50号	100006	65138888
5	王府饭店	北京市东城区金鱼胡同8号	100006	65128899
5	希尔顿酒店	北京市朝阳区东三环北路东方路1号	100027	64662288
5	香格里拉饭店	北京市海淀区紫竹院路29号	100081	68412211
5	新世纪饭店	北京市海淀区首体南路6号	100046	68492001
5	中国大饭店	北京市建外大街1号	100004	65052266
4	大观园酒店	北京市宣武区南菜园街57号	100054	63538899
4	德宝饭店	北京市西城德宝新园22号	100044	68318866
4	东方花园饭店	北京市东城区东直门南大街6号	100027	64168866
4	广州大厦	北京市西城区西单横二条甲3号	100031	66078866
4	国都大饭店	北京市朝阳区首都机场南小天竺	100621	64565588
4	国贸饭店	北京市建外大街1号	100004	65052277
4	海逸酒店	北京市朝阳区将台西路8号	100016	64362288
4	和平宾馆	北京市东城区金鱼胡同3号	100004	65128833
4	河南大厦	北京市朝阳区潘家园华威里28号	100021	67751188
4	华润饭店	北京市朝阳区建国路35号	100025	85772233
4	皇家大饭店	北京市朝阳区北三环东路甲6号	100028	64663388
4	建国饭店	北京市朝阳区建国门外大街5号	100020	65002233
4	金都假日饭店	北京市西城区阜外北礼士路98号	100037	68338822
4	金台饭店	北京市东城区地安门西大街38号	100035	63099111
4	京伦饭店	北京市朝阳区建国门外大街3号	100020	65002266
4	凯莱大酒店	北京市朝阳区建国门南大街2号	100022	65158855
4	丽都假日饭店	北京市朝阳区首都机场路将台路口	100004	64376688
4	亮马河大厦	北京市朝阳区东三环北路8号	100004	65906688
4	民族饭店	北京市西城区复兴门内大街51号	100046	66014466
4	赛特饭店	北京市朝阳区建国门外大街22号	100004	65123388
4	深圳大厦	北京市宣武区广外大街1号	100055	63241188
4	首都大酒店	北京市东城区前门东大街3号	100006	65129988
4	五洲大酒店	北京市朝阳区安外北辰东路8号	100101	64915588
4	西苑饭店	北京市海淀区三里河路1号	100046	68313388

12-7 续表 1 continued

星 级 Star Grade	饭 店 名 称 Hotel	地 址 Address	邮政编码 Postcode	电 话 Telephone
4	香山饭店	北京市海淀区香山公园内	100093	62591166
4	新大都饭店	北京市西城区车公庄21号	100044	68319988
4	新联酒店	北京市崇文门外大街3号	100062	67181188
4	燕山大酒店	北京市海淀区海淀路甲138号	100086	62563388
4	友谊宾馆	北京市海淀区白石桥路3号	100873	68498888
4	渔阳饭店	北京市朝阳区新源西里中街18号	100027	64669988
4	月亮河度假村	北京市通洲月亮河河滨路1号	101100	89523737
4	兆龙饭店	北京市朝阳区工体北路2号	100027	65972299
4	中旅大厦	北京市朝阳区北三环东路2号	100028	64622288
4	中苑宾馆	北京市海淀区高梁桥斜街18号	100081	62178888
3	安徽大厦	朝阳区惠新西街1号	100029	64965588
3	奥林匹克饭店	北京市海淀区海淀区白石桥52号	100081	62176688
3	八达岭长城温泉度假村	北京市延庆县沩水北街35号	102100	69148833
3	八达岭华风温泉大城堡	北京市延庆镇庆园街2号	102100	69183396
3	宝辰饭店	北京市东城区建国门内甲18号	100005	65274025
3	宝灵城饭店	北京市海淀区志新路16号	100083	62326655
3	保利大厦	北京市东城区东直门南大街14号	100027	65001188
3	北方长城宾馆	北京市昌平1023信箱	102202	69771368
3	北人大酒店	北京市东三环南路48号	100022	67716600
3	北展宾馆	北京市西城区西直门外大街135号	100044	68316633
3	碧湖宾馆	北京市怀柔县湖光小区37号	101400	69626793
3	碧溪温泉饭店	北京市房山长阳镇张家场	102401	80352288
3	昌平财会之家	北京市昌平区城区镇北环路	102200	69716688
3	昌平华能培训中心	北京市昌平区小汤山镇常兴乡264号	102211	61781166
3	城市宾馆	北京市朝阳区工体东路4号	100027	65007799
3	崇文门饭店	北京市崇文区崇文门西大街2号	100062	65122211
3	翠明庄宾馆	北京市东城区南河沿大街1号	100006	65136622
3	大宝饭店	北京市崇文区龙潭路4号	100061	67188822
3	大兴宾馆	北京市大兴县黄村兴丰大街	102600	69242354
3	大雁楼供电培训中心	北京市怀柔雁栖湖南岸	101407	69662569
3	地铁度假村	北京市昌平区水库路东侧	102200	60713490
3	东方饭店	北京市宣武区万明路11号	100050	63014466
3	二十一世纪饭店	北京市朝阳区亮马桥路40号	100016	64663311
3	丰泽园饭店	北京市宣武珠市口西大街83号	100050	63186688
3	光明饭店	北京市朝阳区小亮马桥路	100016	64678822
3	贵州大厦	北京市朝阳区和平西桥樱花西街18号	100029	64436678
3	国门路大饭店	北京市朝阳区和平路2号	100015	64378866
3	哈德门饭店	北京市崇文区崇外大街甲2号	100062	67112244
3	海特饭店	北京市石景山区苹果园北路海特花	100041	68861188
3	和平里大酒店	北京市和平里北街16号	100001	84225577
3	鸿翔大厦	北京市海淀区龙翔路15号	100083	62013355
3	湖北饭店	北京市海淀区中关村南路36号	100081	62172288
3	华北大酒店	北京市朝阳区鼓楼外大街19号	100011	62028888
3	华都饭店	北京市朝阳区新源南路8号	100027	65971166
3	华风宾馆	北京市前门东大街5号	100006	65247311
3	华汇金润酒店	北京市朝阳区惠忠北里214号	100012	64809988
3	华美伦酒店	北京市东城区苏州胡同59号	100005	65285566

12-7 续表 2 continued

星级 Star Grade	饭店名称 Hotel	地址 Address	邮政编码 Postcode	电话 Telephone
3	华油陶然商贸中心	北京市崇文区马家堡路1号	100077	87286688
3	皇苑大酒店	北京市海淀区西三环北路厂洼19号	100081	68413388
3	黄河京都大酒店	北京市崇文区夕照寺中街29号	100061	67135588
3	惠侨饭店	北京市朝阳区惠新东街19号	100101	64918811
3	吉利大厦	北京市朝阳区雅宝路街5号	100020	85628888
3	吉林大厦	北京市朝阳区安苑北里25号楼	100029	64916677
3	建银大厦	北京市丰台区太平桥东里九号	100073	63266633
3	江苏大厦	北京市安外大街88号	100011	64271188
3	金安皇都大酒店	北京市北京站东街6号	100005	65265588
3	金健饭店	北京市东城区东直门外察慈2号	100027	64652255
3	金朗大酒店	北京市东城区崇内大街75号	100005	65132288
3	金三环宾馆	北京市丰台区木西园18号	100075	67237711
3	金世纪大酒店	北京市朝阳东三环南路1号	100022	67782255
3	金雁饭店	北京市怀柔县雁栖湖雁水路18号	101407	69662759
3	京滨饭店	北京市西城区阜外大街24号	100037	68582233
3	京都苑宾馆	北京市建国门南大街8号	100022	65291900
3	京蒙蒙电大厦	北京市丰台路骆驮湾188号	100073	63487755
3	京民大厦	北京市朝阳华严里10号	100029	62020011
3	京闽饭店	北京市朝阳区十八里店周庄	100023	67326699
3	九华山庄国际保健俱乐部	北京市昌平区小汤山镇葫芦河村北	102211	61782261
3	军都旅游度假村	北京市昌平区水库路东	102200	60713744
3	凯迪克大酒店	北京市朝阳北辰东路18号	100101	64921188
3	空港花园酒店	北京市首都机杨道口	100621	64563388
3	劳动大厦	北京市朝阳德外北沙滩大屯路甲1号	100101	64874433
3	岭南饭店	北京市海淀区岭南路34号	100046	68412288
3	龙泉宾馆	北京市门头沟区三家店水闸北路	102300	69843366
3	梅地亚中心	北京市海淀区复兴路乙11号	100038	68514422
3	诺林大酒店	北京市宣武区枣林前街145号	100053	63547540
3	培新宾馆	北京市崇文区培新街5号	100061	68398494
3	平安府宾馆	北京市东城区东四十条100号	100007	64010389
3	平谷渔阳酒店	北京市平谷渔阳大街39号	101200	69989988
3	栖湖饭店	北京市怀柔雁栖湖北岸	101408	69661188
3	奇然大酒店	北京市宣武区陶然亭路2号	100050	63532288
3	前门饭店	北京市宣武区永安路175号	100050	63016688
3	日坛宾馆	北京市朝阳区日坛路1号	100020	65125588
3	商务会馆	北京市丰台右安门外玉林里一号楼	100054	63292244
3	神路圆大酒店	北京市朝外大街甲77号	100020	65041188
3	胜利饭店	北京市德盛门外北沙滩3号	100085	64871155
3	十三陵石油工人疗养院	北京市昌平长陵镇礁石口村	102213	89721468
3	实创西山科技培训中心	北京市海淀区聂各庄凤凰岭路13号	100039	62459811
3	顺成饭店	北京市西城区金融大街甲16号	100032	66216688
3	松鹤大酒店	北京市东城区灯市口大街78-98号	100006	65138822
3	苏源锦江大厦	北京市宣武区广安门外大街3号	100055	63267788
3	台湾饭店	北京市东城区王府井金鱼胡同5号	100006	65136688
3	太伟饭店	北京市海淀区西三旗建材城	100096	82920661
3	泰山饭店	北京市海淀区西三旗安宁北里8号	100085	62919988
3	陶然大厦	北京市崇文区马家堡路1号	100077	87286688

12-7 续表 3 continued

星 级 Star Grade	饭 店 名 称 Hotel	地 址 Address	邮政编码 Postcode	电 话 Telephone
3	天龙宾馆	北京市顺义县天竺镇	101300	64573377
3	天坛饭店	北京市崇文区体育馆路1号	100061	67112277
3	天佑丰顺宾馆	北京市海淀区北蜂窝路甲15号	100038	63219000
3	天照饭店	北京市朝阳区工体东路18号	100020	65080088
3	铁道大厦	北京市海淀区北蜂窝102号	100038	63229199
3	通联大酒店	北京市海淀区北蜂窝中路17号	100038	63966688
3	万商大厦	北京市石景山路22号	100043	68681188
3	温特莱酒店	北京市朝阳西大望路甲1号	100026	65812288
3	西藏大厦	北京市北西环东路118号	100029	64981133
3	西郊宾馆	北京市海淀区学院路13号	100083	62322288
3	西岭宾馆	北京市怀柔湖光小区甲26号	101400	69626011
3	希赛迪大酒店	北京市昌平县沙河定泗路	102206	69735533
3	锡华海体酒店	北京市海淀区西苑操场15号	100081	62646688
3	峡谷宾馆	北京市怀柔县青龙峡旅游区	101408	69663999
3	新北纬饭店	北京市宣武区西经路11号	100050	63012266
3	新侨饭店	北京市东城区东交民巷2号	100004	65133366
3	新兴宾馆	北京市海淀区西三环中路17号	100036	68166688
3	信人度假村	北京市怀柔雁栖湖	101408	69663888
3	亚洲大酒店	北京市朝阳区工体北路新中西街8号	100027	65007788
3	燕化昌平培训部	北京市昌平水库路	102200	60713015
3	燕京饭店	北京市西城区复外大街19号	100046	68536688
3	燕翔饭店	北京市朝阳区将台路甲2号	100016	64376666
3	洋桥大厦	北京市丰台区马家堡东路88号	100075	87256622
3	瑶台山庄	北京市昌平九里山	100221	60721548
3	颐泉山庄宾馆	北京市海淀区黑山沪农场1号	100094	62895778
3	银龙苑宾馆	北京市西城区展览路甲5号	100037	68351166
3	育新苑宾馆	北京市平谷县金海湖西侧	101201	69991723
3	裕龙大酒店	北京市海淀区阜成路40号	100046	68415588
3	圆山大酒店	北京市西城区德外裕民东里20号	100029	62010033
3	悦都大酒店	北京市丰台区六里桥甲1号	100073	63497722
3	越秀大饭店	北京市宣武区宣武门东大街24号	100051	63014499
3	云佛山旅游度假村	北京市密云溪翁庄镇	101512	89032600
3	云湖度假村	北京市密云水库内湖	101512	61021982
3	云岫山庄	北京市怀柔雁栖湖东侧	101408	69662338
3	运河苑度假村	北京市通州宋庄镇白庙村	101118	65956941
3	章丘大厦	北京市丰台南蜂窝水口子33号	100055	63496688
3	职工之家	北京市西城区真武庙路一号	100045	68539988
3	中彩饭店	北京市宣武广安门南街48号	100053	63567733
3	中建鸿达物业管理	北京市怀柔雁栖湖雁秀路1号	101408	69662292
3	中粮龙泉山庄	北京市门头沟区龙泉村北	102300	60811803
3	中土大厦	北京市海淀区北蜂窝6号	100038	63246666
3	中烟金山饭店	北京市崇文区永外彭庄乙58号	100054	63163377
3	中盐饭店	北京市丰台区西客站南广场驻京办1号楼	100055	63273366
3	中银酒店	北京市延庆县庆园街12号	102100	69171701
3	重庆饭店	北京市朝阳区光西门北里15号	100028	64228888
3	竹园宾馆	北京市西城区旧鼓楼大街小石桥24号	100009	64032229

12-7 续表 4 continued

二、涉外公寓

FOREIGN APARTMENT HOUSES

单位名称 Unit	地　　址 Address	邮政编码 Postcode	电　话 Telephone
朝阳公寓	北京市朝阳区农展馆北里2号	100026	64677119
东苑公寓	北京市朝阳区枣营路25号	100026	64678678
东直门国际公寓	北京市东城区东直门外大街35号	100027	64678221
国际汇园公寓	北京市朝阳区安外安立路8号	100101	64933456
国际网球中心	北京市崇文区天坛东路50号	100061	67142370
国泰饭店松榆公寓	北京市朝阳区松榆西里	100021	67331988
华墅渡假村	北京市朝阳区十八里店老君堂	100023	67383555
华乡公寓	北京市朝阳区高碑店北路6号	100025	65001133
华威大厦	北京市西城区西单北大街130号	100032	66028888
汇园公寓	北京市朝阳区北四环中路8号	100101	64992662
京城大厦	北京市朝阳区新源南路6号	100004	64660088
九花山公寓	北京市海淀区半壁街南路甲1号	100081	68414440
万春园	北京市海淀区圆明园管理处内	100084	62616611
万泉公寓	北京市海淀区西三环北路甲1号	100081	68415813
紫金宫饭店	北京市东城区南河沿华龙街	100006	65130088

注：涉外公寓共15家。

Note: Number of foreign apartment houses is fifteen.

12-7 续表 5 continued

三、涉外写字楼

FOREIGN OFFICE-BUILDINGS

单位名称 Unit	地　　址 Address	邮政编码 Postcode	电　话 Telephone
发展大厦	北京市朝阳区东三环北路5号	100004	65908811
光华园大厦	北京市朝阳区东三环北路38号	100020	65018816
国际大厦	北京市朝阳区建外大街19号	100004	65001159
国际会议中心	北京市朝阳区北辰东路8号	100101	64922328
国际俱乐部有限公司	北京市朝阳区建国门外大街21号	100020	65023975
国际贸易中心	北京市朝阳区建成国门外大街1号	100004	65052288
华鹏大厦	北京市朝阳区东三环北路19号	100020	65975168
汇宾大厦	北京市朝阳区北辰东路8号	100101	64993873
凯威大厦	北京市朝阳区雅宝路10号	100020	65942288
太丰惠中大厦	北京市宣武区珠市口西大街120号	100050	63186068
幸福大厦	北京市朝阳区顺源街5号	100027	64669805
亚太大厦	北京市朝阳区雅宝路8号	100020	65139988
紫金宾馆	北京市崇文区崇文门西大街9号	100005	65136655

注：涉外写字楼共13家。

Note: Number of foreign office-buildings is thirteen.

主要统计指标解释

海外旅游者 指来华入境的海外游客中，在我国旅游住宿设施内至少停留一夜的外国人、港澳台同胞。海外旅游者不包括以下人员：（1）应邀来华访问的政府部长以上官员及其随行人员；（2）外国驻华使领馆官员、外交人员以及随行的家庭服务人员和受赡养者；（3）常住我国一年以上的外国专家、留学生、记者、商务机构人员等；（4）乘坐国际航班过境不需要通过护照检查进入我国口岸的中转旅客；（5）边境地区往来的边民；（6）回大陆定局的港澳台同胞；（7）已在我国定居的外国人和原已出境又返回在我国定居的外国侨民；（8）归国的我国出国人员。

国际旅游（外汇）收入 指海外旅游者在中国（大陆）境内旅行、游览过程中用于交通、参观游览、住宿、餐饮、购物、娱乐等全部花费。

Explanatory Notes On Main Statistical Indicators

Overseas Tourists refers to the entry tourists including foreigners, Hongkong, Macao and Taiwan Chinese who stay in accommodation installation for tourism one night at least. It excludes the following personnel: (a) personnel visit China by invitation whose duty above government minister and their entourage; (b) official to China of embassies and consulates and their entourage for family service and persons supported by them; (c) foreign resident experts, students, correspondents and commercial personnel in China above one year; (d) transfer passengers enter the port of china by international flight not need through passport check; (e) inhabitants of a border area; (f) Hongkong, Macao and Taiwan Chinese come back to settle down in the mainland of China; (g) foreigners have settled down in China and overseas Chinese come back to settle down in China after leaving; (h) returned personnel gone abroad.

Foreign Exchange Receipt from International Tourism refers to the total expenditures of the foreigners, overseas Chinese, compatriots from Hongkong, Macao and Taiwan during their staying in the mainland of China.

金融、保险 13

BANKING AND INSURANCE

存款余额（单位：亿元）
Deposits (100 million yuan)

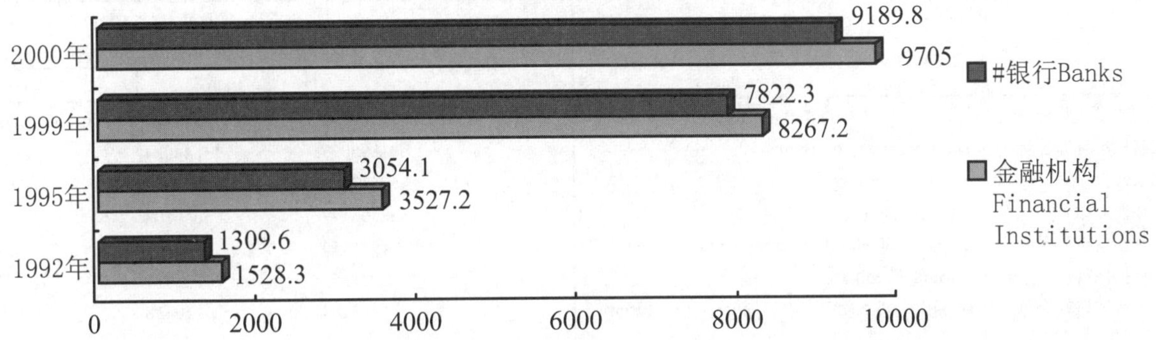

贷款余额（单位：亿元）
Loans (100 million yuan)

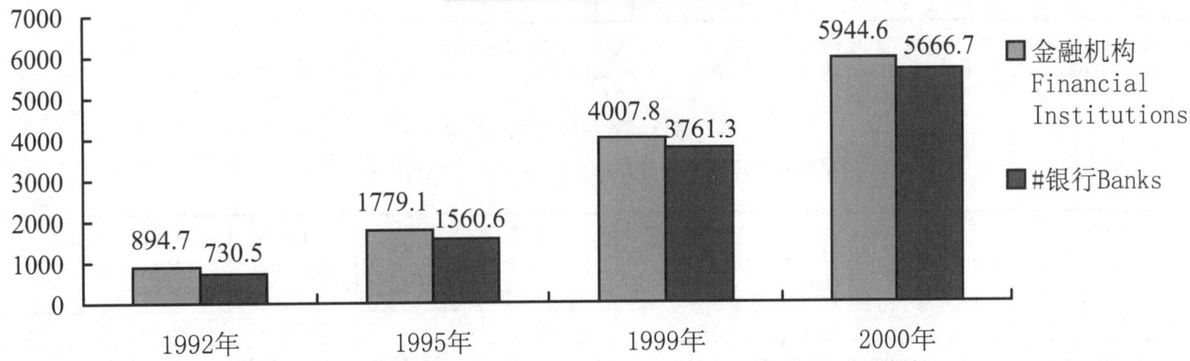

城乡居民储蓄存款余额（单位：亿元）
Saving Deposits of Urban and Rural Residents (100 million yuan)

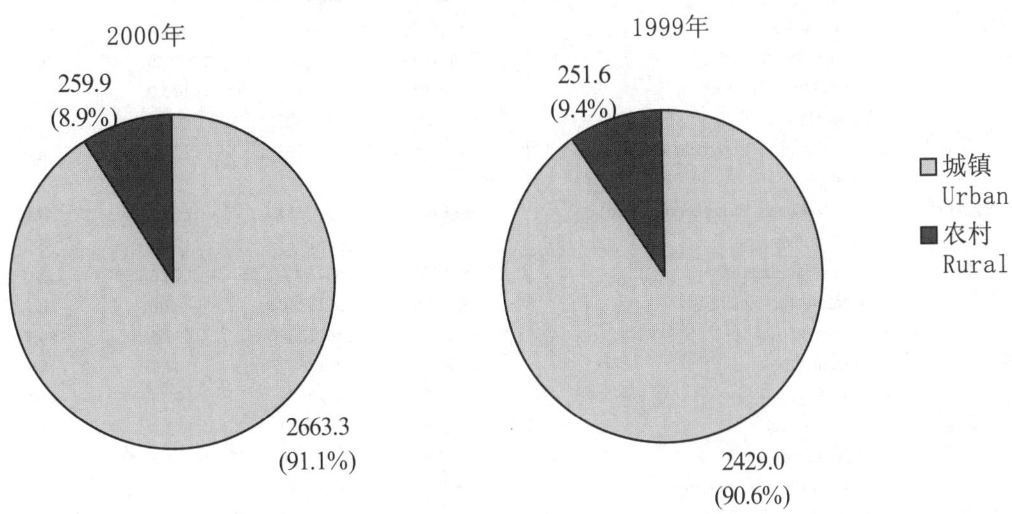

13-1 北京地区金融机构存贷款
DEPOSITS AND LOANS OF FINANCIAL INSTITUTIONS IN BEIJING

单位：万元 (10000 yuan)

项目	Item	2000年余额 Balance of 2000	比年初增减额(+、-) Increase or Decrease than Year-beginning 2000	1999
存 款 总 计	**All Deposits**	**97049590**	**14347357**	**14289313**
全市各银行存款合计	**Total Deposits of Banks**	**91898097**	**13644084**	**13769050**
国家银行小计	National Banks	69532948	7997976	9951854
其他商业银行	Other Commercial Banks	22365149	5646108	3817196
信用合作机构存款	**Deposits of Credit Cooperatives**	**4921359**	**723711**	**597212**
农村信用社	Rural Credit Cooperatives	4921359	723711	597212
非银行金融机构存款	**Deposits of Non-bank Financial Institutions**	**230134**	**-20438**	**-76949**
贷 款 总 计	**All Loans**	**59446110**	**11161284**	**5595885**
全市各银行贷款合计	**Total Loans of Banks**	**56667403**	**10847645**	**5134199**
国家银行小计	National Banks	42940621	5902010	3369910
其他商业银行	Other Commercial Banks	13726782	4945635	1764289
信用合作机构贷款	**Loans of Credit Cooperatives**	**2524679**	**358157**	**479785**
农村信用社	Rural Credit Cooperatives	2524679	358157	479785
非银行金融机构贷款	**Deposits of Non-bank Financial Institutions**	**254028**	**-44518**	**-18099**

注：本表各金融机构存款中，不包含其代理财政存款、汇出汇入款、委托存款及委托投资基金。
Note: All deposits exclude agent financial deposits, remittance, trust deposits and trust investment-fund.

13-2 银行存款及贷款余额
DEPOSITS AND LOANS OF BANKS

项目	Item	绝对数(万元) Amount (10000 yuan) 2000	1999	2000年为1999年% 2000 as % of 1999	构成(%) Composition (%) 2000	1999
年末各项存款合计	**Deposits Balance(year-end)**	**91898097**	**78223288**	**117.5**	**100**	**100**
#地方存款	Local Deposits	70473979	59892419	117.7	76.7	76.6
# 地方工业企业存款	Industrial Enterprise	3326153	3116038	106.7	3.6	4.0
地方商业企业存款	Commercial Enterprise	4401865	3541272	124.3	4.8	4.5
#企业存款	Enterprise Deposits	54252792	44475637	122.0	59.0	56.9
# 工业存款	Industry	6832556	6081437	112.4	7.4	7.8
商业存款	Commerce	5140037	4027515	127.6	5.6	5.1
建筑业存款	Construction	3548325	2792950	127.0	3.9	3.6
城镇储蓄存款	Urban Savings Deposits	26632980	24290306	109.6	29.0	31.1
农业存款	Agricultural Deposits	304646	271969	112.0	0.3	0.3
信托存款	Trust Deposits	1050	507	207.1	…	…
机关团体存款	Deposits of Government Organs and Bodies	4016390	2997893	134.0	4.4	3.8
年末各项贷款合计	**Loans Balance(year-end)**	**56667402**	**37612521**	**150.7**	**100**	**100**
#地方贷款	Local Loans	41480406	30850111	134.5	73.2	82.0
# 地方工业贷款	Industrial Enterprise	6818875	6916918	98.6	12.0	18.4
地方商业贷款	Commercial Enterprise	5938662	6119240	97.0	10.5	16.3
#短期贷款	Short-term Loans	32138281	25601364	125.5	56.7	68.1
# 工业贷款	Industry	10382307	9917578	104.7	18.3	26.4
商业贷款	Commerce	6546045	6722679	97.4	11.6	17.9
建筑业企业贷款	Construction	2217508	1967942	112.7	3.9	5.2
农业贷款	Agriculture	368199	505578	72.8	0.6	1.3
中长期贷款	Mid-term and Long-term Loans	21569860	8229492	262.1	38.1	21.9
# 基本建设贷款	Capital Construction	15495466	3195413	484.9	27.3	8.5
技术改造贷款	Technical Updates and Transformation	4794528	4533975	105.7	8.5	12.1
信托贷款	Trust Loans	14763	1020	1447.4	…	…

13-3 城乡居民储蓄存款余额
SAVINGS DEPOSIT BALANCE IN URBAN AND RURAL AREAS

项目	Item	绝对数(万元) Amount (10000 yuan) 2000	1999	2000年为1999年% 2000 as % of 1999	构成(%) Composition(%) 2000	1999
年末储蓄存款余额	**Savings Deposit Balance**	**29232063**	**26806646**	**109.0**	**100**	**100**
定期	Fixed Deposits	20960674	20604805	101.7	71.7	76.9
活期	Current Deposits	8271389	6201841	133.4	28.3	23.1
城镇居民存款	Urban Savings Deposit	26632980	24290306	109.6	91.1	90.6
农民存款	Rural Savings Deposit	2599083	2516340	103.3	8.9	9.4

13-4 银行、保险系统机构及人员
INSTITUTIONS AND PERSONNEL OF BANK AND INSURANCE SYSTEM

项目	Item	银行系统 Bank System 机构(个) Institution(unit)	人员(人) Personnel(person)	保险系统 Insurance System 机构(个) Institution(unit)	人员(人) Personnel(person)
全市	**Total**	**2676**	**52478**	**130**	**4841**
城区	City Propers	646	20150	47	2748
郊区	Suburbs	1604	26852	67	1774
各县	Counties	426	5476	16	319

13-5 保险费收入
PREMIUMS INCOME

项目	Item	绝对数(万元) Amount (10000 yuan) 2000	1999	2000年为1999年% 2000 as % of 1999	构成(%) Composition(%) 2000	1999
保费总计	**Total**	**880328**	**864954**	**101.8**	**100**	**100**
产险	**Property Insurance**	**299734**	**270963**	**110.6**	**34.0**	**31.3**
#企业财产险	Enterprise Property	36439	35386	103.0	4.1	4.1
家庭财产险	Family Property	7578	7666	98.9	0.9	0.9
运输工具及责任险	Transportation Equipment and Responsibility	214296	193365	110.8	24.3	22.4
货物运输险	Freight Transport	15815	15686	100.8	1.8	1.8
农业险	Agricultural Insurance	54	79	68.0	0.0	0.0
人身险	**Personal Insurance**	**580593**	**593991**	**97.7**	**66.0**	**68.7**
#短期人身险	Short Term Insurance	40552	32055	126.5	4.6	3.7
中长期人寿险	Long Term and Medium Term Insurance	540042	561937	96.1	61.3	65.0

注：保险费收入中不含中国人民保险公司营业部、中国人寿保险公司营业部数据。
Note: Premium income excludes that of salesdepartment of PICC and Chinalife Insurance Company.

13-6 金融市场交易量
FINANCIAL MARKET TRANSACTIONS

单位：万元 (10000 yuan)

项目	Item	2000	1999	2000年为1999年% 2000 as % of 1999
合计	**Total**	**144569773**	**106944575**	**135.2**
国家债券	Treasury Bonds	4356893	5936815	73.4
股票交易	Stock Transactions	91365234	52681881	173.4
国债回购	Repurchase of Treasury Bonds	43902177	44118337	99.5
基金	Funds	3460217	3417393	101.3
其他	Others	1485252	790149	188.0

主 要 统 计 指 标 解 释

信贷资金 国家银行用于发放贷款的资金叫信贷资金。中国人民银行信贷资金的来源有各项存款、对国际金融机构负债、流通中货币、银行自有资金及当年结益等。信贷资金的运用有各项贷款、黄金占款、外汇占款、财政借款及在国际金融机构中的资产等。

存款 企业、机关、团体或居民根据可以收回的原则，把货币资金存入银行或其他信用机构保管并取得一定利息的一种信用活动形式。根据存款对象的不同可划分为企业存款、财政存款、机关团体存款、城镇储蓄存款、农村存款等科目。它是银行信贷资金的主要来源。

贷款 银行或其他信用机构根据必须归还的原则，按一定利率，为企业、个人等提供资金的一种信用活动形式。我国银行贷款分为流动资金贷款、固定资产贷款、城乡个体工商户贷款以及农业贷款等科目。

保费 又叫保险费。是保险人根据保险合同的有关规定，为被保险人取得因约定危险事故发生所造成的经济损失补偿（或给付）权利，付给保险人的代价。包括财产险和人身险收入。

Explanatory Notes On Main Statistical Indicators

Credit Funds refer to the funds issued as loans by state banks. The sources of credit funds of the People's Bank of China included deposits, liabilities to international financial institutions, currency in circulation, self-owned funds and current retained profits, etc. The credit funds can be used in forms of loan, gold, foreign exchange, government debt and assets in the international financial institutions.

Deposit is a form of credit by which enterprises, institutions, organizations or residents can put money into banks and other credit institutions for safekeeping and interest earning under the principle of free withdrawal. According to different depositors, deposits are divided into enterprise deposits, treasury deposits, deposits of government organs and institutions, urban savings deposits, rural deposits and other deposits. Deposits are major sources of the credit funds of banks.

Loan is a form of credit by which banks and other credit institutions provide funds at certain interest rate to enterprises and individuals in the light of the principle of unconditional repayment. Loans from Chinese banks include circulating capital loans, fixed assets loans, loans to urban and rural individuals engaged in industrial and commercial business and agricultural loans.

Premium is the fee paid by the insured based on a proportion of the benefit he or she may get from the insurance plus the insurance value. It includes the income from property insurance and personal insurance.

物 价 14

PRICE INDEX

商品零售价格指数（上年=100）（单位：%）
Retail Price Index (preceding year=100) (%)

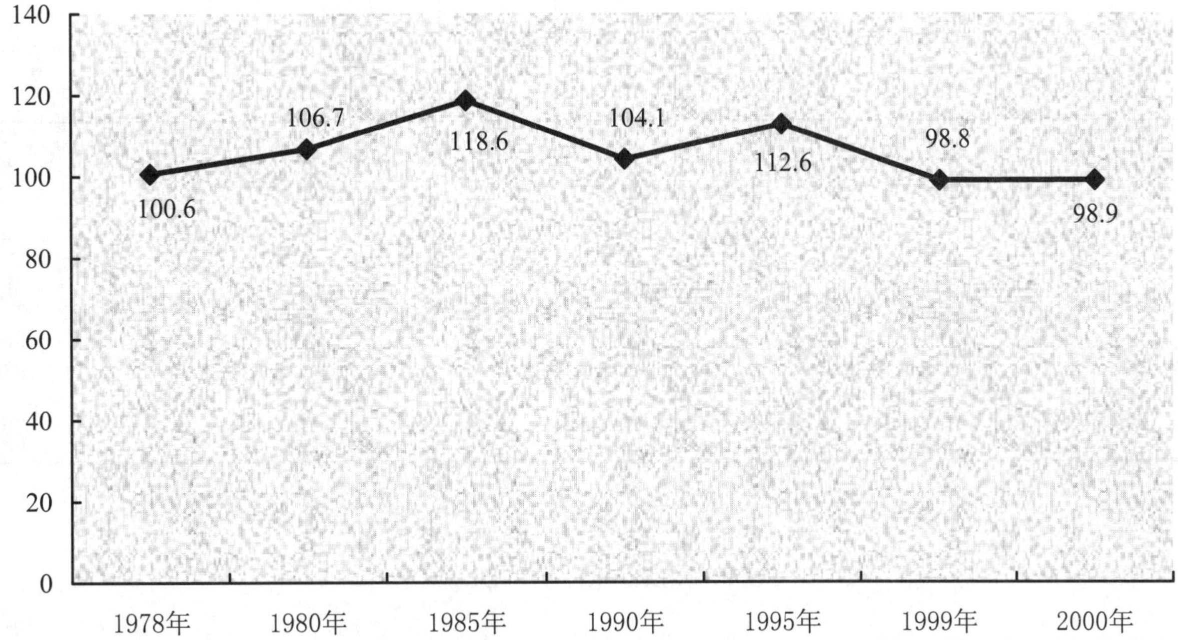

居民消费价格指数（上年=100）（单位：%）
Comsumer Price Index (preceding year=100) (%)

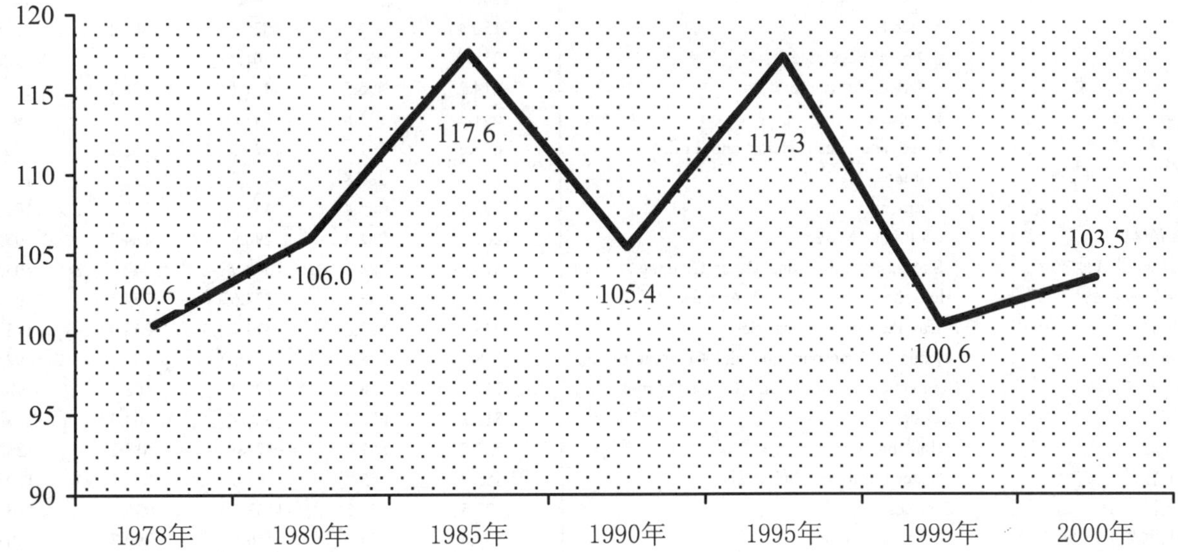

14-1 各种物价总指数
OVERALL PRICE INDICES

单位：% (%)

项目	Item	1978=100	1980=100	1985=100	1990=100	1999=100
居民消费价格总指数	Consumer Price Index	622.9	577.0	463.3	268.6	103.5
商品零售价格总指数	Retail Price Index	465.5	428.2	340.3	195.0	98.9
农副产品收购价格总指数	Farm and Sideline Products Purchasing Price Index	420.0	363.6	266.7	158.5	95.0
农业生产资料价格总指数	Means of Agricultural Production Price Index	356.6	365.3	324.2	195.4	101.7
郊区工业品零售价格总指数	Industrial Products of Suburb Retail Price Index	377.5	373.5	341.3	200.5	103.3
工业品出厂价格总指数	Industrial Products Producer Price Index					102.5
原材料、燃料、动力购进价格指数	Raw Material,Fuels and Motive Power Purchasing Price Index					100.0
固定资产投资额价格指数	Investment in Fixed Assets Price Index					101.0
建筑安装工程价格指数	Building Installation Price Index	484.3	346.5	280.0	103.1	101.3

14-2 居民消费价格指数
CONSUMER PRICE INDICES

单位：% (%)

项目	Item	1978=100	1980=100	1985=100	1990=100	1999=100
总指数	**Aggregate Index**	**622.9**	**577.0**	**463.3**	**268.6**	**103.5**
食品类	Food	647.5	586.3	414.2	234.8	97.9
#粮食	Grain	643.4	643.4	618.5	436.0	91.4
油脂类	Oil	510.0	510.0	435.9	200.2	85.8
肉禽及其制品	Meat,Poultry and Related Products	625.2	506.0	372.1	217.2	98.4
水产品	Aquatic Products	1580.9	1123.1	448.0	176.5	107.3
菜类	Vegetable	1150.4	1017.7	527.9	280.1	98.7
#鲜菜	Fresh Vegetable	1213.7	1062.2	501.2	264.1	98.4
干菜	Dried Vegetable	514.2	495.3	431.1	238.1	101.2
调味品	Flavoring	691.3	711.8	647.6	350.6	98.3
干鲜瓜果类	Dried and Fresh Melon and Fruits	632.6	591.2	324.8	162.2	89.8
衣着类	Clothing	379.2	387.8	410.0	232.1	102.6
服装	Garments	392.8	405.4	448.2	237.5	102.5
衣着材料	Clothing Material	261.2	262.2	296.9	184.7	97.8
鞋袜帽及其他衣着	Shoes,Socks,Hats and Other Clothing	418.0	424.1	398.9	247.8	103.9
家庭设备及用品	Household Facilities and Articles	295.1	293.4	274.6	154.5	96.3
医疗保健	Medicine and Medical Services	635.0	583.8	474.7	258.9	113.5
交通和通讯工具	Means of Transportation and Communications	128.7	128.7	145.1	108.5	92.3
娱乐教育文化用品	Recreation,Education and Cultural Articles	210.1	204.5	198.9	108.1	97.8
居住	Residence	512.3	688.8	660.7	504.7	117.9
住房	Housing	557.5	881.2	874.0	618.2	125.2
水电燃料	Water,Electricity and Fuels	455.9	455.9	402.8	376.1	110.5
服务项目	Services	2177.5	2172.1	1933.3	935.1	116.2
#电讯费	Communication	569.0	569.0	440.5	299.7	100.0
交通费	Transportation	654.7	654.7	635.0	466.3	137.6
文娱费	Recreation	18277.7	18277.7	16752.7	7435.7	118.7
学杂保育费	Education and Nursery	1820.8	1820.8	1820.8	1054.0	122.5
修理及其他服务费	Repair and Other Services	1096.9	1083.3	734.0	388.7	94.5
医疗保健服务	Medicine and Medical Service	1428.0	1428.0	1428.0	793.2	128.6

14-3 商品零售价格指数
RETAIL PRICE INDICES

单位：%　　　　　　　　　　　　　　　　　　　　　　　　　　　　　　（%）

项目	Item	1999=100	项目	Item	1999=100
商品零售价格指数	**Aggregate Index**	**98.9**	呢　绒	Woolen Fabric	98.1
食品类	Food	97.5	绸　缎	Silk	97.6
粮　食	Grain	92.0	其他纺织品	Other Textiles	98.5
油脂类	Oil	85.8	中西药品类	Traditional Chinese and Western Medicines	113.6
肉蛋禽	Meat,Egg and Poultry	96.6	中　药	Traditional Chinese Medicines	136.4
水产品	Aquatic Products	107.3	西　药	Western Medicine	98.1
鲜　菜	Fresh Vegetable	98.5	医疗用品	Medicine and Medical Articles	100.8
干　菜	Dried Vegetable	98.1	化妆品类	Cosmetics	95.3
鲜　果	Fresh Fruit	88.4	书报杂志类	Book,Newspaper and Magazine	107.9
干　果	Nuts	94.9	文化体育用品	Stationery and Sports Goods	99.9
其他食品类	Other Foods	98.8	文化用品	Stationery	100.1
饮食业	Catering	101.2	体育用品	Sports Goods	97.0
饮料烟酒类	Beverage,Tobacco and Liquor	101.9	日用品类	Daily Use Articles	98.3
饮　料	Beverage	99.1	一般日用品	Ordinary Daily Use Articles	96.7
烟　酒	Tobacco and Liquor	103.6	家具类	Furnitures	100.5
服装鞋帽类	Garments,Shoes,Hats	102.9	日用杂品	Daily Use Sundiries	101.3
服　装	Garments	102.5	家用电器类	Household Appliances	92.1
鞋	Shoes	104.4	首饰类	Jewelry	89.6
其他衣着	Other Clothing	99.8	燃料类	Fuels	109.4
纺织品类	Textile	98.3	建筑装潢材料类	Building Decoration Materials	97.7
棉　布	Cotton Cloth	97.9	机电产品类	Mechanical and Electrical Products	97.1
棉花化纤混纺布	Blend Cloth	104.3			
化纤布	Chemical Fiber Cloth	97.1			

14-4 居民货币购买力指数
INDICES OF MONETARY PURCHASING POWER OF RESIDENTS

单位：%　　　　　　　　　　　　　　　　　　　　　　　　　　　　　　（%）

基期 Base Period	2000	1999
1957=100	15.6	16.2
1965=100	16.2	16.8
1970=100	15.9	16.5
1975=100	15.9	16.5
1978=100	16.0	16.6
1980=100	17.4	18.0
1985=100	21.6	22.4
1990=100	37.4	38.7
以上年为100 Preceding Year=100	96.6	99.4

14-5 农副产品收购价格总指数
PURCHASING PRICE INDICES FOR FARM AND SIDELINES PRODUCTS

单位：% (%)

项目	Item	1978=100	1985=100	1990=100	1999=100
总指数	**Aggregate Index**	**420.0**	**266.7**	**158.5**	**95.0**
粮食类	Grain	266.5	183.0	116.9	87.0
经济作物类	Industrial Crops	545.4	326.0	140.1	103.7
畜禽产品类	Livestock Products,Poultry and Eggs	478.7	325.2	187.8	98.4
生猪	Pigs	539.5	367.2	185.8	101.4
鸡蛋	Chicken Eggs	258.5	179.2	108.1	75.0
干鲜果类	Dried and Fresh Fruits	485.1	272.8	175.1	102.1
鲜瓜果	Fresh Melons and Fruits	472.6	297.7	206.3	103.5
鲜果	Fresh Fruits	423.9	231.0	169.2	109.0
西瓜	Water Melon	285.3	208.0	132.1	91.7
鲜菜类	Fresh Vegetable	679.6	335.5	190.0	97.6
水产品类	Aquatic Products	749.6	263.6	169.2	101.5

14-6 郊区工业品零售价格指数
RETAIL PRICE INDICES OF INDUSTRIAL PRODUCTS IN SUBURBS

单位：% (%)

项目	Item	1978=100	1985=100	1990=100	1999=100
总指数	**Aggregate Index**	**377.5**	**341.3**	**200.5**	**103.3**
日用消费品	**Daily Use Articles**	**372.6**	**345.1**	**200.1**	**103.8**
食品类	Food	454.2	375.0	223.6	97.9
衣着类	Clothing	314.3	330.4	179.7	102.6
日用杂品类	Daily Use Sundries	287.9	274.8	167.9	107.9
农业生产资料	**Agricultural Capital Goods**	**365.8**	**324.2**	**195.4**	**101.7**
农业机械	Agricultural Machinery	305.3	292.5	183.8	98.2
化学肥料	Chemical Fertilizer	424.5	355.1	231.7	95.1
化学农药	Agricultural Chemicals	219.9	209.5	87.6	101.0
农机用油	Oil for Agricultural Machinery		536.3	436.6	133.6
种子	Seed		215.3	133.7	94.0
饲料	Forage		503.5	263.6	102.2

14-7 工农业产品综合比价指数

AGGREGATE PRICE PARITY INDEX OF INDUSTRIAL AND AGRICULTURAL PRODUCTS

单位：% (%)

基　　期 Base Period	农副产品收购价格总指数 Purchasing Price Indices of Farm and Sidelining Products	农村工业品零售价格总指数 Retail Price Index of Industrial Products in in Rural Area	工农业产品综合比价指数 Aggregate Parity Index of Industrial and Agricultural Products	
			以农产品指数为100 Agricultural Products Index=100	以工业品指数为100 Industrial Products Index=100
1957=100	515.6	360.7	70.0	142.9
1965=100	463.2	350.4	75.6	132.2
1970=100	462.5	372.1	80.5	124.3
1975=100	430.4	382.8	88.9	112.4
1978=100	420.0	377.5	89.9	111.3
1980=100	363.6	373.5	102.7	97.3
1985=100	266.7	341.3	128.0	78.1
1990=100	158.5	200.5	126.5	79.1
1995=100	81.7	106.9	130.8	76.4
1999=100	95.0	103.3	108.7	92.0

14-8 工业品出厂价格指数（以上年为100）

INDUSTRIAL PRODUCTS PRODUCER PRICE INDICES（PRECEDING YEAR=100）

单位：% (%)

项　目	Item	2000	1999
总指数	**Aggregate Index**	**102.5**	**97.7**
# 轻工业	Light Industry	98.0	97.8
以农产品为原料	Using Farm Products as Raw Materials	97.5	98.4
以非农产品为原料	Using Non-farm Products as Raw Materials	99.4	96.4
重工业	Heavy Industry	104.2	97.7
采　掘	Excavation	101.3	93.6
原　料	Raw Material	107.8	98.6
加　工	Processing	100.7	95.5
# 生产资料	Capital Goods	103.4	96.5
采　掘	Excavation	101.3	93.6
原　料	Raw Material	106.7	98.3
加　工	Processing	99.3	93.2
生活资料	Living Goods	98.8	100.7
食　品	Food	97.6	100.3
衣　着	Clothing	97.8	98.8
一般日用品	Articles for Daily Use	98.4	99.4
耐用消费品	Durable Consumer Goods	104.2	104.3

14-9 原材料、燃料、动力购进价格指数（以上年为100）

PRICE INDICES OF RAW MATERIAL, FUEL PURCHASING（PRECEDING YEAR=100）

单位：% （%）

项目	Item	2000	1999
总指数	**Aggregate Index**	**100.0**	**95.8**
燃料、动力类	Fuel and Motive Power	104.3	97.4
黑色金属材料类	Ferrous Metal Materials	100.5	96.8
#钢材	Steel Products	101.5	96.6
其他	Others	98.2	
有色金属材料类	Nonferrous Metal Materials	106.9	94.5
化工原料类	Industrial Chemicals	103.4	94.7
木材及纸浆类	Timber and Paper Pulp	94.8	102.5
建筑材料及非金属类	Construction Materials and Nonmetals	101.9	98.0
其它工业原材料及半成品类	Other Industrial Materials and Semi-manufactured Goods	98.4	95.5
农副产品类	Farming and Sideline Products	94.5	90.1
纺织原料类	Textile Materials	91.5	90.5

14-10 固定资产投资额价格指数

PRICE INDICES OF INVESTMENT IN FIXED ASSETS

单位：% （%）

项目	Item	1992=100	1993=100	1994=100	1999=100
总指数	**Aggregate Index**	**189.4**	**149.7**	**128.7**	**101.0**
建筑安装工程	Building Installation	214.4	163.5	136.5	101.3
设备、工器具购置	Purchase of Equipment, Tools and Instruments	146.4	127.4	124.8	100.5
其他费用	Others	159.4	130.6	105.6	100.6

注：按国家统计局的有关规定，固定资产投资额价格指数从1992年开始计算。

Note: According to rules of State Statistical Bureau, price indices of investment in fixed assets are counted from 1992.

14-11 建筑安装工程价格指数

PRICE INDICES OF BUILDING INSTALLATION

单位：% （%）

项目	Item	1978=100	1985=100	1990=100	1999=100
总指数	**Aggregate Index**	**484.3**	**346.5**	**280.0**	**101.3**
直接费用价格指数	**Price Index of Direct Cost**	**607.4**	**383.9**	**311.0**	**101.3**
人工费	Labor Cost	1028.1	706.9	758.6	105.7
材料费用	Material Cost	511.8	360.9	260.2	100.2
其他费用价格指数	**Price Index of Other Cost**	**333.0**	**240.0**	**190.5**	**101.3**

14-12 建筑安装工程中主要材料费用价格指数

PRICE INDICES OF MAJOR MATERIALS IN BUILDING INSTALLATION

单位：%　　　　(%)

项目	Item	1978=100	1985=100	1990=100	1999=100
总 指 数	**Aggregate Index**	**511.8**	**360.9**	**260.2**	**100.2**
钢　材	Rolled-steel Products	460.6	364.9	326.9	101.0
木　材	Timber	802.5	413.5	302.2	96.6
水　泥	Cement	693.5	493.5	314.5	98.9
地方材料	Local Materials	515.1	347.4	233.9	100.6
其他材料	Other Materials	537.8	381.9	268.9	100.2

14-13 房地产价格指数(以上年为100)

PRICE INDICES OF REAL ESTATE(PRECEDING YEAR=100)

单位：%　　　　(%)

项目	Item	2000	1999
土地交易价格指数	**Price Indices of Land Transaction**	**100.0**	**100.2**
居民住宅用地	Residential Building	100.0	100.2
工业用地	Industry	100.0	100.1
商业旅游娱乐用地	Commerce,Tourism and Recreation	100.0	100.3
其他用地	Others	100.0	100.3
房地产销售价格指数	**Price Indices of Real Estate Sales**	**99.5**	**100.1**
商品房	Commodity Building	98.7	98.7
住宅	Residence	98.8	98.3
非住宅	Non-residence	97.2	100.6
旧房交易	Transaction of Old Residence	100.4	99.2
公有住房	Public Residence	100.6	101.8
房地产租赁价格指数	**Price Indices of Real Estate Rent**	**166.6**	**98.5**
住宅	Residence	199.4	100.4
公房	Public	202.6	100.0
私房	Private	132.8	103.8
办公用房	Office	97.0	87.3
商业用房	Commerce	96.0	95.8
厂房仓库	Plant		100.0
旅店饭店客房	Guest Room of Hotel	99.0	91.9

14-14 36个大中城市物价指数(以上年价格为100)

PRICE INDEX OF THE 36 LARGE AND MEDIUM CITIES(PRECEDING YEAR=100)

单位：%　　　　(%)

城市	City	2000		1999	
		居民消费价格指数 Consumer Price Index	商品零售价格指数 Retail Price Index	居民消费价格指数 Consumer Price Index	商品零售价格指数 Retail Price Index
平均指数	**Average Index**	**101.3**	**98.3**	**99.2**	**97.0**
北京	Beijing	103.5	98.9	100.6	98.8
天津	Tianjin	99.6	98.6	98.9	97.5
石家庄	Shijinazhuang	101.7	99.9	99.8	98.7
太原	Taiyuan	103.6	96.0	100.1	97.3
呼和浩特	Huhehaote	103.0	98.4	102.1	98.4
沈阳	Shenyang	100.0	98.0	97.6	95.4
大连	Dalian	99.6	97.8	99.5	95.3
长春	Changchun	98.8	97.5	98.5	96.4
哈尔滨	Haerbin	100.2	98.8	97.2	96.9
上海	Shanghai	102.5	96.4	101.5	97.3
南京	Nanjing	100.0	99.2	98.6	97.1
杭州	Hangzhou	100.8	98.3	100.4	98.2
宁波	Ningbo	100.3	98.3	100.0	97.3
合肥	Hefei	101.3	97.2	97.7	96.5
福州	Fuzhou	102.9	98.8	99.3	96.8
厦门	Xiamen	106.3	98.4	99.0	95.2
南昌	Nanchang	102.6	97.8	99.8	96.9
济南	Jinan	100.6	98.0	99.1	96.9
青岛	Qingdao	103.3	99.7	100.2	96.5
郑州	Zhengzhou	99.0	99.1	98.7	96.8
武汉	Wuhan	100.6	97.4	96.1	93.7
长沙	Changsha	101.7	100.7	100.2	98.4
广州	Guangzhou	102.8	99.4	98.5	96.8
深圳	Shenzhen	102.8	100.6	99.3	96.1
南宁	Nanning	100.0	98.3	95.9	95.9
海口	Haikou	101.5	101.0	99.2	98.0
重庆	Chongqing	96.7	95.5	99.3	96.5
成都	Chengdu	100.2	98.2	98.3	97.1
贵阳	Guiyang	98.7	95.8	97.6	96.6
昆明	Kunming	97.5	97.0	98.9	97.2
拉萨	Lasa	100.2	99.5	98.7	97.9
西安	Xian	100.2	98.7	96.8	97.4
兰州	Lanzhou	99.3	99.0	96.9	97.5
西宁	Xining	99.9	99.3	99.5	98.7
银川	Yinchuan	99.2	97.7	100.1	98.7
乌鲁木齐	Wulumuqi	100.7	99.2	97.1	96.4

主要统计指标解释

居民消费价格指数 是反映居民家庭所购买的生活消费品和支付的服务项目价格变动总趋势和程度的一种综合价格指数，分为城市居民消费价格指数和农村居民消费价格指数。通过编制居民消费价格指数，可以全面观察居民消费价格变动对居民生活的影响。居民消费价格指数还是反映通货膨胀的重要指标。按国家规定我市只编制上报城市居民消费价格指数。

商品零售价格指数 是反映工业、商业、餐饮业和其他零售业向城乡居民、机关团体出售生活消费品和办公用品价格变动总趋势和程度的一种综合价格指数。通过编制商品零售价格指数，可以全面掌握市场商品零售价格的变动情况。

农产品收购价格指数 是反映国有商业、集体商业、个体商业、外贸部门、国家机关、社会团体等各种经济类型的商业企业和有关部门收购农产品价格的变动趋势和程度的相对数。农产品收购价格指数可以观察和研究农产品价格总水平的变化情况，以及对农民货币收入的影响，作为制定和检查农产品价格政策的依据。计算指数所选的商品有 11 各大类、包括 276 种农副土特产品。采用加权倒数平均公式（即按报告期实际收购金额加权综合法）计算。

工业产品出厂价格指数 是反映全部工业产品出厂价格总水平的变动趋势和程度的相对数。其中包括工业企业售给商业、外贸、物资部门的产品外，还包括售给工业和其他部门的生产资料以及直接售给居民的生活消费品。通过工业生产价格指数能观察出厂价格变动对工业总产值的影响。

固定资产投资价格指数 是反映固定资产投资额价格变动趋势和程度的相对数。固定资产投资额是由建筑安装工程投资完成额、设备、工器具购置投资完成额和其他费用投资完成额三部分组成的。编制固定资产投资价格指数应首先分别编制上述三部分投资的价格指数，然后采用加权算术平均法求出固定资产投资价格总指数。编制固定资产投资价格指数可以准确地反映固定资产投资中涉及的各类商品和取费项目价格变动趋势和变动幅度，消除按现价计算的固定资产投资指标中的价格变动因素，真实地反映固定资产投资的规模、速度、结构和效益，为国家科学地制定，检查固定资产投资计划并提高宏观调控水平，为完善国民经济核算体系提供科学的，可靠的依据。

原材料、燃料、动力购进价格指数 是反映全部工业原材料、燃料、动力购进价格总水平的变动趋势和程度的相对数。用其可以观察和研究工业企业原材料价格变动对生产的影响，以及企业对原材料涨价的消化能力和承受能力，为制订价格政策提供依据。

房地产价格指数 是反映全部房地产价格总水平的变动趋势和程度的相对数。包括土地出让价格指数、房地产销售价格指数、房地产租赁价格指数。

土地交易价格指数 是指房地产开发商或其他建设单位在进行商品房开发前为取得土地使用权而实际支付的价格的变动趋势和程度的相对数。

房地产销售价格指数 是指房地产销售价格总水平变动趋势和程度的相对数。

房地产租赁价格指数 是指房地产租赁价格总水平变动趋势和程度的相对数。

Explanatory Notes On Main Statistical Indicators

Consumer Price Index reflects the general trend and extent in prices of consumer goods and services purchased by urban and rural residents, including that of urban residents and rural residents. Consumer price index can be used to analyze the impact of consumer price change on actual living expenditures of urban and rural residents. And it also an important indicator reflects inflation.

Retail Price Index reflects the general trend and extent in prices of consumer goods and office articles sold to urban and rural residents, organs and social bodies by industry, commerce, catering service and other retail trade. The calculation of retail price index is useful to analyze the changes of retail prices on market.

Purchasing Price Index of Farm Products reflects the relative change in purchasing prices of farm products purchased by state-owned, collective-owned, and individual commercial enterprises, foreign trade sectors, government agencies, social organizations and other units of various types of ownership. It is used to observe the impact of change in purchasing prices of farm products on money income of peasants and is calculated with the method of weighted harmonic mean, taking the amount of purchases during a given period as the weight. Number of products involved in the current calculation totaled 276 in 11 categories.

Ex-factory Price Index of Industrial Products reflects the relative change in general ex-factory prices of all industrial products, including sales of industrial products to commercial enterprises, foreign trade sectors , materials supplying and distributing sectors as well as sales of production means to industry and other sectors and sales of consumer goods to residents. It can be used to analyze the impact of ex-factory prices on gross industrial output value.

Price Index of Investment in Fixed Asses reflects the change in prices of investment in fixed assets. The investment in fixed assets consists of three components, namely the investment in construction and installation, the investment in purchases of equipment and instrument, and the investment in other items. Price index of investment in fixed assets is calculated as the weighted arithmetic mean of the price indices of the three components.

Price index of investment in fixed asses reflects the change of price in various goods and services involved in investment in fixed assets and therefore can be used to observe the actual size, speed, structure, and efficiency of investment in fixed assets and provides reliable and rational data for government planning, management, decision making, and further improving the current national accounting system.

Purchase Price Index of Raw Materials, Fuel and Power reflects relative changes in the general purchase price of all industrial raw materials, fuel and power. The index can be used to study and analyze the impact of price changes of industrial raw materials of the production and enterprises capability to bear and digest the price increase of raw materials, so as to provide basis for the government to formulate price policies.

Price Indices of Real Estate reflects the trend and extent of price changes of real estate, including price indices of land sale, price indices of real estate sale and price indices of real estate rent.

Price Indices of Land Transaction reflects the changing trend and extent of price which paid actually by developing enterprises or construction units to get land use rights before development of commodity buildings.

Price Indices of Real Estate Sale reflects the trend and extent of price changes of real estate sale

Price Indices of Real Estate Rent reflects the trend and extent of price changes of real estate rent.

教育、文化 15

EDUCATION AND CULTURE

2000年学校及在校学生数（单位：个，万人）
Number of Schools and Students Enrollment in 2000 (uint, 10000 persons)

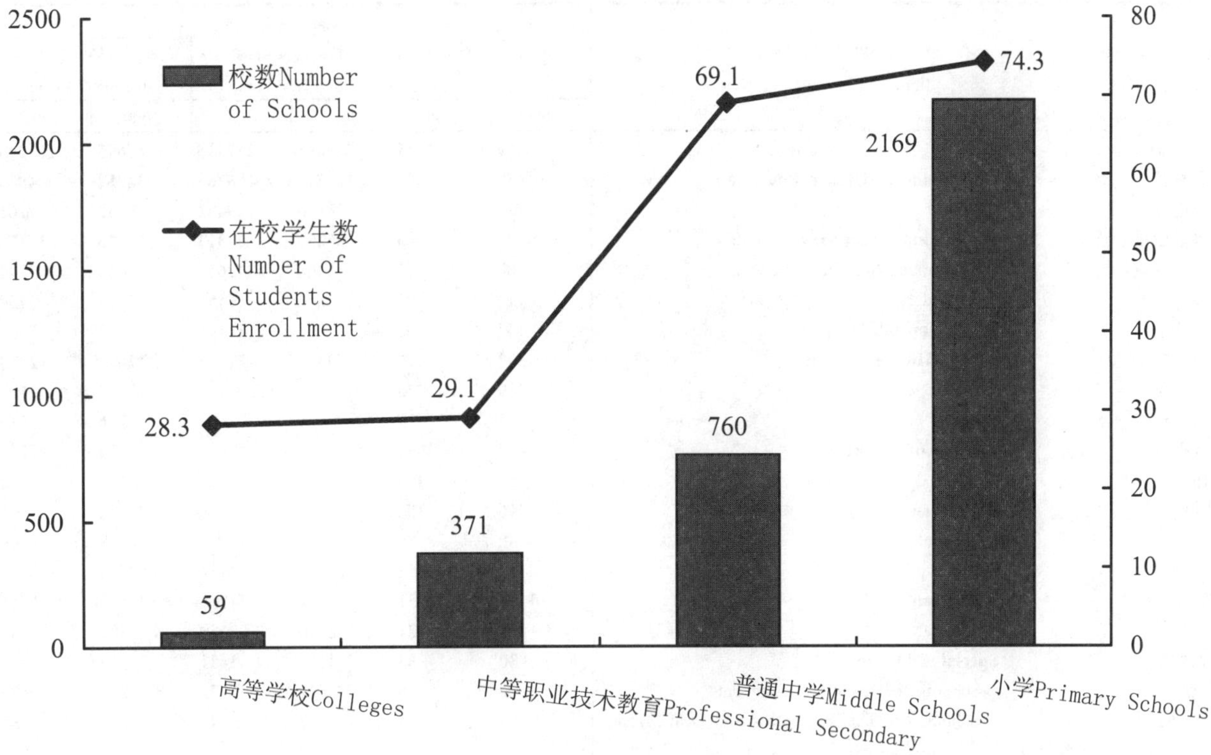

平均每万人口在校学生数（单位：人）
Students Enrollment Per 10000 Population (person)

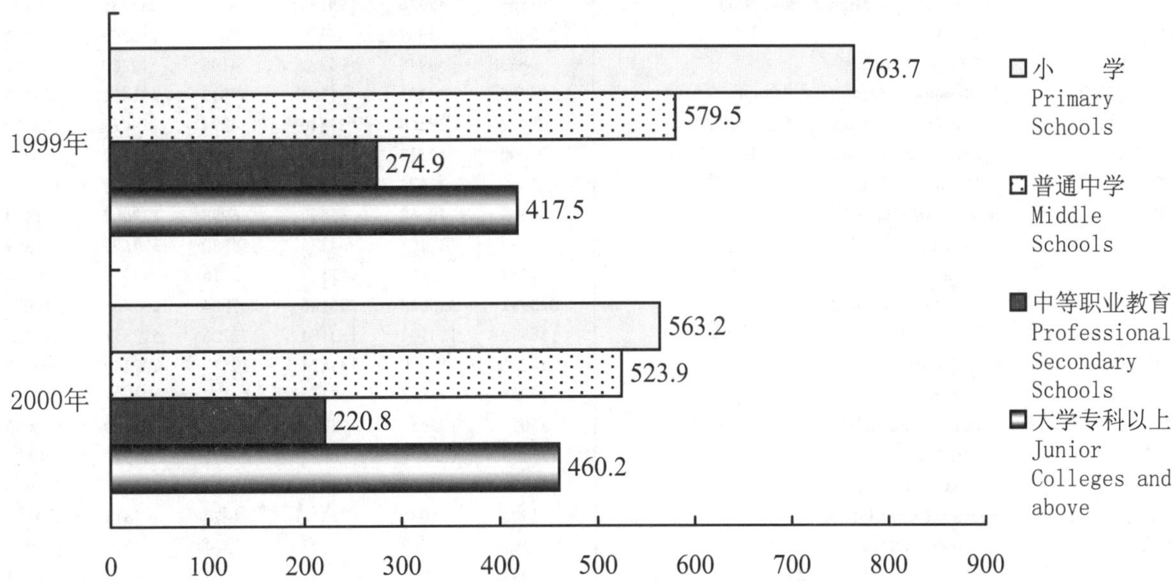

15-1 各类学校基本情况
BASIC STATISTICS FOR EDUCATION

单位：人 (person)

类别	Item	校数(所) Number of Schools (unit) 2000	1999	教职工数 Teachers,Staff and Workers 2000	1999	# 专任教师 Full-time Teachers 2000	1999
总计	**Total**	**3389**	**3611**	**279611**	**287935**	**157605**	**162363**
高等学校	**Institutions of Higher Education**	**59**	**64**	**104814**	**106766**	**34952**	**34976**
# 地方	Local	27	19	24488	19482	9632	7261
中等职业技术教育	**Professional Secondary Schools**	**371**	**406**	**28289**	**33312**	**14875**	**17175**
中等专业学校	Specialized Secondary Schools	108	111	10468	12658	4648	5780
技工学校	Secondary Technical Schools	119	127	5846	7459	3160	3704
职业学校	Vocational Schools	144	168	11975	13195	7067	7691
普通高中	**Senior Middle Schools**	**302**	**275**	**73492**	**72312**	**12873**	**12023**
城镇	Urban	289	258			12477	11507
农村	Rural	13	17			396	516
义务教育	**Compulsory Education**	**2627**	**2831**			**94032**	**97263**
初中	Junior Middle Schools	458	479			36030	36142
城镇	Urban	316	304			28202	27343
农村	Rural	142	175			7828	8799
小学	Primary Schools	2169	2352	71701	74114	58002	61121
城镇	Urban	1290	1231	52711	51855	41619	41941
农村	Rural	879	1121	18990	22259	16383	19180
特殊教育	**Special Education**	**30**	**35**	**1315**	**1431**	**873**	**926**
工读学校	Schools for Juvenile Delinquents	6	6	421	422	229	197
盲聋哑学校	Schools for The Blind,Deaf and Deaf-Mutes	7	7	367	440	252	287
弱智儿童辅读学校(班)	Schools(Classes) for Less Intelligent Children	17	22	527	569	392	442
民办学校	**Non-state Owned Schools**	**71**	**59**	**3414**	**3439**	**2129**	**2106**

类别	Item	毕业生数 Graduates 2000	1999	招生数 New Students Enrollment 2000	1999	在校学生数 Students Enrollment 2000	1999
总计	**Total**	**509804**	**500762**	**513080**	**494699**	**2017266**	**2015940**
高等学校	**Institutions of Higher Education**	**51556**	**49936**	**99397**	**78354**	**282585**	**234033**
# 地方	Local	19000	15989	42390	27028	112507	76496
外国留学生	Foreign Students	4825	3945	4882	4198	9260	8203
中等职业技术教育	**Professional Secondary Schools**	**84780**	**79252**	**71291**	**90813**	**291401**	**301199**
中等专业学校	Specialized Secondary Schools	28113	27266	27816	34294	119427	123379
技工学校	Secondary Technical Schools	21000	17512	21510	25515	81691	70856
职业学校	Vocational Schools	35667	34474	21965	31004	90283	106964
普通高中	**Senior Middle Schools**	**47569**	**40660**	**65890**	**56998**	**179002**	**161473**
城镇	Urban	46185	38793	64375	54880	174653	155309
农村	Rural	1384	1867	1515	2118	4349	6164
义务教育	**Compulsory Education**	**323991**	**328828**	**275186**	**267064**	**1255460**	**1310077**
初中	Junior Middle Schools	138932	153172	183184	172706	512351	473422
城镇	Urban	114206	119299	145824	129577	409449	360427
农村	Rural	24726	33873	37360	43129	102902	112995
小学	Primary Schools	185059	175656	92002	94358	743109	836655
城镇	Urban	137139	123049	70677	69171	557541	578595
农村	Rural	47920	52607	21325	25187	185568	258060
特殊教育	**Special Education**	**1908**	**2086**	**1316**	**1470**	**8818**	**9158**
工读学校	Schools for Juvenile Delinquents	561	548	492	514	1011	912
盲聋哑学校	Schools for The Blind,Deaf and Deaf-Mutes	291	282	263	207	1272	1412
弱智儿童辅读学校(班)	Schools(Classes) for Less Intelligent Children	1056	1256	561	749	6535	6834
民办学校	**Non-state Owned Schools**	**4939**	**3890**	**8754**	**7998**	**25440**	**24035**

注：教职工数中，普通高中人数为初中和高中合计数。
Note: Number of teachers,staff and workers of senior middle schools includes those of junior and senior middle schools.

15-2 高等学校基本情况
BASIC STATISTICS FOR INSTITUTION OF HIGHER EDUCATION

单位：人 (person)

类别	Item	校数(所) Number of Schools (unit)	毕业生数 Graduates	招生数 New Students Enrollment	在校学生数 Students Enrollment	教职工数 Teachers, Staff and Workers	#专任教师 Full-time Teachers
总计	**Total**	**59**	**51556**	**99397**	**282585**	**104814**	**34952**
综合大学	Comprehensive Universities	3	7685	11426	36637	23589	7990
理工院校	Science and Engineering	19	22948	44812	128971	37004	13400
农业院校	Agriculture	2	1965	5007	12815	3341	1279
林业院校	Forestry	1	907	2672	6238	1274	449
医药院校	Medicine	3	1351	1944	6687	12671	1038
师范院校	Teacher Training	3	3389	5378	16649	6288	2540
语文院校	Literature	7	3138	7115	17577	5349	2296
财经院校	Economics and Finance	4	3847	6926	20539	5072	1971
政法院校	Politics and Law	4	2588	5674	15632	3677	1159
体育院校	Physical Culture	1	616	964	2982	919	358
艺术院校	Art	7	780	1723	4477	2665	1114
民族院校	National Colleges	1	1062	1195	3881	1591	700
职业技术学院	Professional Institute	4	1280	4561	9500	1374	658
在总计中：	**Of Total:**						
市属院校	Municipal						
综合大学	Comprehensive Universities	1	2991	6089	16887	3325	1284
理工院校	Science and Engineering	10	8130	17669	48754	9712	3737
农业院校	Agriculture	1	259	1363	3153	495	195
医药院校	Medicine	1	709	1053	3585	1342	435
师范院校	Teacher Training	2	2032	3162	9965	3108	1273
语文院校	Literature	2	958	2581	5247	1150	512
财经院校	Economics and Finance	2	1835	3878	10864	2514	914
政法院校	Politics and Law		269	817	1609		
艺术院校	Art	4	537	1217	2943	1468	624
职业技术学院	Professional Institute	4	1280	4561	9500	1374	658

15-3 高等学校分科学生数
NUMBER OF STUDENTS BY DEPARTMENTS IN INSTITUTIONS OF HIGHER EDUCATION

单位：人 (person)

学科	Item	毕业生数 Graduates	招生数 New Students Enrollment	在校学生数 Students Enrollment
总计	**Total**	**51556**	**99397**	**282585**
哲学	Philosophy	96	162	590
经济学	Economics	9639	18584	50673
法学	Law	3935	8578	23117
教育学	Education	2182	3328	9538
文学	Literature	7011	14660	38571
历史学	History	501	666	2074
理学	Science	3375	6733	19222
工学	Engineering	21551	41412	121573
农学	Agriculture	929	2198	6211
医学	Medicine	2337	3076	11016

15-4 高等学校及科研机构分科研究生数
NUMBER OF POSRGRADUATE BY FIELD OF STUDY IN INSTITUTIONS OF HIGHER EDUCATION AND SCIENTIFIC RESEARCH INSTITUTIONS

单位：人 (person)

学科 Item		攻读博士学位研究生 Postgraduate for Doctor Degree			攻读硕士学位研究生 Postgraduate for Master Degree			研究生班研究生数 Postgraduates in Class
		毕业生数 Graduates	招生数 New Students Enrollment	在学研究生数 Postgraduate Enrollment	毕业生数 Graduates	招生数 New Students Enrollment	在学研究生数 Postgraduate Enrollment	
总　计	**Total**	**3322**	**6829**	**18343**	**9916**	**19672**	**45565**	**82**
# 市属院校	Municipal	48	178	377	804	1739	3880	
哲　学	Philosophy	90	133	347	106	201	469	
经济学	Economics	266	522	1453	1255	2540	5947	
法　学	Law	230	575	1540	1187	1932	4786	
教育学	Education	68	197	432	235	526	1147	
# 体育学	Physical Culture	12	36	96	60	125	294	
文　学	Literature	117	299	762	669	1331	3127	82
# 艺　术	Art	27	68	156	93	299	684	82
历史学	History	80	137	346	119	263	614	
理　学	Science	740	1373	3528	1123	2210	5073	
工　学	Engineering	1177	2749	7755	4505	9316	21050	
# 力　学	Mechanics	82	110	367	160	227	515	
农　学	Agriculture	146	274	683	251	442	1015	
# 林　学	Forestry	23	63	162	66	409	233	
医　学	Medicine	408	570	1497	466	911	2337	

15-5 高等学校专任教师学历情况
EDUCATIONAL BACKGROUND OF FULL-TIME TEACHERS IN INSTITUTIONS OF HIGHER EDUCATION

单位：人 (person)

学历 Educational Background		总计 Total	正高级 Senior Title	副高级 Asso. Senior Title	中级 Middle Title	初级 Junior Title	无职称 No Title
合　计	**Total**	**34952**	**5899**	**11828**	**12015**	**4189**	**1021**
研究生毕业	Postgraduate						
博　士	Doctor Degree	5514	1476	2473	1379	104	82
硕　士	Master Degree	11173	1126	3282	4800	1608	357
未获博士硕士学位	Not Obtained Degrees	860	282	283	264	22	9
本科毕业	Undergraduate						
学　士	Bachelor	12672	1379	3798	4785	2216	494
研究生肄业	Not Pass the Postgraduate Study	140	8	52	60	15	5
未获学士学位	Not Obtained Degree	3594	1530	1591	357	89	27
专科毕业及本专科肄业两年及以上	Graduate from Junior College and Undergraduate Study for Two Years above	841	67	313	324	121	16
本专科肄业未满两年	Undergraduate Study for Less than Two Years	158	31	36	46	14	31

15-6 中等专业学校基本情况
BASIC STATISTICS ON SPECIALIZED SECONDARY SCHOOLS

单位：人 (person)

类别	Item	校数(所) Number of Schools (unit)	毕业生数 Graduates	招生数 New Students Enrollment	在校学生数 Students Enrollment	教职工数 Teachers, Staff and Workers	#专任教师 Full-time Teachers
总计	**Total**	**108**	**28113**	**27816**	**119427**	**10468**	**4648**
中等技术学校	**Secondary Technical Schools**	**92**	**26988**	**27567**	**117928**	**9658**	**4309**
工业学校	Industry	29	16702	17443	77566	4608	1953
农业学校	Agriculture	1	850	1279	3853	362	146
林业学校	Forestry	1	175	266	711	91	35
医药学校	Medicine	35	2867	1468	7588	1516	693
财经学校	Economics and Finance	8	3646	4806	17983	1262	548
政法学校	Politics and Law	4	1246	237	2977	287	119
体育学校	Physical Culture	7	459	693	1666	673	265
艺术学校	Art	6	766	1194	4443	778	486
其他学校	Others	1	277	181	1141	81	64
中等师范学校	**Teacher Training School**	**16**	**1125**	**249**	**1499**	**810**	**339**
# 幼儿师范	Kindergarten	1	207	160	446	133	53

15-7 中等专业学校专任教师学历
EDUCATIONAL BACKGROUND OF FULL-TIME TEACHERS IN SPECIALIZED SECONDARY SCHOOLS

单位：人 (person)

学历	Educational Background	中等专业学校 Secondary Specialized Schools		#中等专业技术学校 Secondary Technical Schools		# 中等专业师范学校 Teacher Training Schools	
		人数 Number of Persons	构成(%) Composition (%)	人数 Number of Persons	构成(%) Composition (%)	人数 Number of Persons	构成(%) Composition (%)
合计	**Total**	**4648**	**100**	**4309**	**100**	**339**	**100**
本科毕业及以上	Undergraduate and the Level above	3629	78.1	3327	77.2	302	89.1
专科毕业及本专科肄业两年及以上	Graduate from Junior College and Undergraduate Study for Two Years above	767	16.5	734	17.0	33	9.7
本专科肄业未满两年	Undergraduate Study for Less than Two Years	15	0.3	15	0.3		
中专、高中毕业及以下	Specialized Secondary School, Senior Middle School and the Level below	237	5.1	233	5.4	4	1.2

15-8 中等专业学校分学科学生数
NUMBER OF STUDENTS IN SPECIALIZED SECONDARY SCHOOLS BY FIELD OF STUDY

单位：人 (person)

学科	Item	毕业生数 Graduates 2000	1999	招生数 New Students Enrollment 2000	1999	在校学生数 Students Enrollment 2000	1999
总计	**Total**	**28113**	**27266**	**27816**	**34294**	**119427**	**123379**
工科	Engineering	11730	10471	14251	16710	59877	57931
农科	Agriculture	394	411	514	537	1735	1625
林科	Forestry	208	61	309	155	730	632
医药卫生	Medicine	2789	2985	1434	1858	7517	9088
财经	Economics and Finance	4958	4155	2331	3256	11445	14668
管理	Administration	3807	3458	5401	7736	24358	22918
政法	Politics and Law	1345	952	237	937	3112	4236
艺术	Art	1209	864	2308	1862	7249	6329
体育	Physical Culture	501	263	782	660	1832	1720
师范	Teacher Training	1172	3646	249	583	1572	4232
# 幼儿师范专业	Kindergarten	238	339	164	94	466	580
特教师范专业	Special Education		157		181		431

15-9 普通中学分课程专任教师数
NUMBER OF FULL-TIME TEACHERS BY SUBJECTS OF REGULAR SECONDARY SCHOOLS

单位：人 (person)

学科	Item	合计 Total 2000	1999	高中 Senior Middle School 2000	1999	初中 Junior Middle School 2000	1999
总计	**Total**	**48903**	**48165**	**12873**	**12023**	**36030**	**36142**
政治	Politics	3231	3241	922	871	2309	2370
语文	Chinese	7972	7663	1865	1746	6107	5917
数学	Math	7989	7818	1903	1809	6086	6009
物理	Physics	3906	3869	1418	1320	2488	2546
化学	Chemical	2814	2795	1382	1302	1432	1493
生物	Biology	1839	1813	377	352	1462	1461
地理	Geography	1748	1735	381	359	1367	1376
历史	History	2318	2277	741	687	1577	1590
英语	English	7604	7328	1898	1711	5706	5617
俄语	Russian	2		1		1	
日语	Japanese	15	13	8	8	7	5
体育	Physical Education	2962	2920	768	729	2194	2191
生理卫生	Physiology	64	94	11	1	53	93
音乐	Music	1067	1038	142	135	925	903
美术	Art	979	974	117	111	862	863
计算机	Computer	975	864	320	312	655	552
职业劳动	Vocational Labor	586	650	47	43	539	607
其他	Others	396	406	110	80	286	326

15-10 职业高中分科学生数

NUMBER OF STUDENTS BY FIELD OF STUDY IN VOCATIONAL SCHOOLS

单位：人 (person)

学科 Item		毕业生数 Graduates		招生数 New Students Enrollment		在校学生数 Students Enrollment	
		2000	1999	2000	1999	2000	1999
总计	**Total**	**35644**	**34380**	**21965**	**31004**	**90283**	**106941**
工科	Engineering	11481	9784	8268	8685	30969	30019
农科	Agriculture	115	105	102	100	463	230
林科	Forestry	377	352	107	487	689	1426
医药卫生	Medical Health	1222	889	667	897	3616	3968
财经	Economics and Finance	4671	6090	2149	4469	10938	17053
管理	Administration	13564	13618	6120	11621	29409	40609
政法	Politics and Law	179	216	18	214	485	615
艺术	Art	2917	2285	3605	3332	10720	9655
体育	Physical Culture	315	254	506	455	1333	1026
师范	Teacher Training	803	787	423	744	1661	2340

15-11 普通中学、职业中学、小学校舍情况

STATISTICS FOR SCHOOLHOUSES OF REGULAR SECONDARY SCHOOLS, VOCATIONAL SCHOOLS AND PRIMARY SCHOOLS

单位：万平方米 (10000 sq.m)

类别 Item		学校占地面积 Areas of Schools	校舍建筑面积 Floor Space of Schoolhouses	教学及辅助用房 Teaching and Auxiliary Houses	行政办公用房 Administrative Houses	生活福利用房 Houses for Welfare and Life
合计	**Total**	**4105.3**	**1201.3**	**651.5**	**213.5**	**336.2**
城市	Urban	1250.2	665.1	351.3	123.7	190.2
县镇	Towns	1598.7	342.9	185.2	56.1	101.5
农村	Rural	1256.4	193.3	115	33.7	44.5
普通中学	**Regular Secondary Schools**	**1920.2**	**602.9**	**296.3**	**105.5**	**201**
城市	Urban	682.2	354.6	172.1	63	119.5
县镇	Towns	819.9	180.1	87.5	29.9	62.6
农村	Rural	418.1	68.2	36.7	12.6	18.9
职业中学	**Vocational Schools**	**315.3**	**121.5**	**61.3**	**22.3**	**37.9**
城市	Urban	131.8	81	41.4	16.6	23.1
县镇	Towns	119.0	29.3	13.5	4.7	11.1
农村	Rural	64.5	11.2	6.4	1	3.7
小学	**Primary Schools**	**1869.8**	**476.9**	**293.9**	**85.7**	**97.3**
城市	Urban	436.2	229.5	137.8	44.1	47.6
县镇	Towns	659.8	133.5	84.2	21.5	27.8
农村	Rural	773.8	113.9	71.9	20.1	21.9

15-12 普通中小学专任教师学历
EDUCATIONAL BACK OF FULL-TIME TEACHERS IN PRIMARY AND SECONDARY SCHOOLS

单位：人 (person)

学历	Educational Background	高中 Senior Middle Schools 人数 Number of Persons	构成(%) Composition (%)	初中 Junior Middle School 人数 Number of Persons	构成(%) Composition (%)	小学 Primary School 人数 Number of Persons	构成(%) Composition (%)
总计	**Total**	**12873**	**100**	**36030**	**100**	**58002**	**100**
本科毕业及以上	Undergraduate and The Level above	11201	87.0	15651	43.4	1522	2.6
大专毕业	College for Professional Training	1580	12.3	17838	49.5	20045	34.6
中专毕业	Specialized Secondary School	62	0.5	1817	5.0	30774	53.1
高中及以下	Senior Middle School and the Level below	30	0.2	724	2.0	5661	9.8

15-13 平均每万人口在校学生数
AVERAGE NUMBER OF STUDENT ENROLLMENT PER 10000 POPULATION

单位：人 (person)

类别	Item	2000	1999
大学专科以上	Junior Colleges and above	460.2	417.5
中等职业教育	Professional Secondary Schools	220.8	274.9
普通中学	Regular Secondary Schools	523.9	579.5
小学	Primary Schools	563.2	763.7

15-14 平均每一专任教师负担学生数
AVERAGE NUMBER OF STUDENTS INSTRUCTED BY A FULL-TIME TEACHER

单位：人 (person)

类别	Item	2000	1999
普通高校	Institutions of Regular Higher Education	13.7	11.7
成人高校	Institutions of Adult Higher Education	9.0	10.0
普通中专	Specialized Secondary Schools	26.0	21.0
职业中学	Vocational Secondary Schools	12.8	13.9
高中	Senior Middle Schools	13.9	13.4
初中	Junior Middle Schools	14.2	13.1
小学	Primary Schools	12.8	13.7

15-15 小 学 学 龄 儿 童 入 学 率
ENROLLMENT RATE OF CHILDREN AT SCHOOL-AGE

单位：人 (person)

项 目 Item		校内外学龄人口总数 Number of Children at School-age	# 女 Female	在校学龄人口总数 Number of Children at School-age in Schools	# 女 Female	入 学 率(%) Enrollment Rate(%)	# 女 Female
合 计	**Total**	**705854**	**341549**	**705527**	**341372**	**99.95**	**99.95**
城 市	Urban	315712	154384	315695	154381	99.99	100.00
县 镇	Towns	216263	103997	216057	103890	99.90	99.90
农 村	Rural	173879	83168	173775	83101	99.94	99.92

15-16 中、小学校外教育
AFTER-SCHOOL EDUCATION OF SECONDARY AND PRIMARY SCHOOLS

单位：人 (person)

项 目 Item		单 位 数 (个) Number of Units(unit)	活 动 小 组 数(个) Activities Groups(unit)	参加小组 学 生 数 Students Join Groups	教 职 工 人 数 Staff and Workers	# 辅导员 Counselors	兼 职 辅 导 员 Part-time Counselors
总 计	**Total**	**1251**	**5756**	**113043**	**2228**	**1656**	**1985**
少 年 宫	Children's Palace	17	2202	44375	**903**	536	92
少年科技馆(站)	Children's Scientific Museums (Centers)	8	503	8738	201	131	30
少年之家	Children's Home	38	1148	16608	414	279	129
少年活动站	Children's Club	1188	1903	43322	710	710	1734

15-17 幼 儿 园 基 本 情 况
STATISTICS FOR KINDERGARTENS

单位：人 (person)

项 目 Item		总 计 Total	# 女 Female	城 市 Urban	县 镇 Towns	农 村 Rural
园数 (所)	Number of Kindergartens (unit)	2047		631	519	897
班数 (个)	Number of Classes (unit)	8636		4697	1860	2079
# 学前班	Preschool Classes	1129		303	398	428
在园幼儿数	Children Enrollment	229012	106188	125250	56621	47141
# 学前班	Preschool Classes	31616	15299	9848	10050	11718
教职工数	Teachers,Staff and Workers	27257	25692	19679	5231	2347
# 园长	Headmaster	1851	1800	1163	456	232
教师	Teachers	12595	12504	8653	2671	1271
保健员	Health Workers	1059	1045	810	191	58

15-18 各类成人教育毕业生、招生、在校学生数
NUMBER OF GRADUATES NEW STUDENTS ENROLLMENT AND STUDENTS ENROLLMENT OF ADULT EDUCATION

单位：人 (person)

类别	Item	校数(教学点)(所) Number of Schools(unit)	毕(结)业生数 Graduates	招生数 New Students Enrollment	在校学生数 Students Enrollment
高等教育	**Higher Education**	**61**	**71309**	**103918**	**260624**
广播电视大学	Radio and TV Universities	2	1456	1567	4939
职工高等学校	Schools for Staff and Workers	34	9120	8737	25277
管理干部学院	Management Colleges	23	7843	8645	21014
教育学院	Pedagogical Colleges	1	2852	4146	10339
独立函授学院	Independent Correspondence Colleges	1	291		154
普通高校函授部	Correspondence Department Run by Institutions of Higher Education		27834	41976	109983
普通高校夜大学	Evening Universities Run by Institutions of Higher Education		12904	21274	55599
普通高校成人脱产班	Full Time Adult Class Run by Institutions of Higher Education		9009	17573	33319
中等专业教育	**Specialized Secondary Education**	**102**	**21646**	**15166**	**49782**
广播电视中专	Radio and TV Specialized Secondary Schools	1	4082	3061	10818
职工中专学校	Specialized Secondary Schools for Staff and Workers	61	9122	7494	24589
干部中专学校	Specialized Secondary School for Cadres	8	898	317	1184
农民中专学校	Specialized Secondary School for Peasants	15	5054	1987	8290
函授中专学校	Specialized Correspondence Secondary Schools	1	1702	2098	4038
教师进修学校	Teacher Training Schools	16	788	209	863
中等文化教育	**Secondary Education**	**28**	**4436**	**2881**	**9560**
职工中学	Middle Schools for Staff and Workers	27	4436	2850	9323
农民中学	Middle Schools for Peasants	1		31	237

15-19 各类成人教育教职工数
NUMBER OF TEACHERS,STAFF AND WORKERS IN ADULT EDUCATION

单位：人 (person)

类别	Item	合计 Total		# 专任教师 Full-time Teachers		# 兼任教师 Part-time Teachers	
		2000	1999	2000	1999	2000	1999
高等教育	**Higher Education**	**17047**	**16952**	**7529**	**7281**	**3737**	**3873**
广播电视大学	Radio and TV Universities	1336	1121	465	392	820	809
职工高等学校	School of Higher Education for Staff and Workers	9057	9793	4377	4510	2561	2442
管理干部学院	Management Colleges	4254	5406	1618	2103	271	622
教育学院	Pedagogical Colleges	717	530	263	213	85	
独立函授学院	Independent Correspondence Colleges		102		63		
普通高校函授部、夜大学	Correspondence Department or Evening Universities Run by Institutions of Higher Education	1683		806			
中等专业教育	**Specialized Secondary Education**	**5858**	**7133**	**2632**	**3277**	**922**	**1787**
广播电视中专	Radio and TV Specialized Secondary Schools	35	823	5	450		746
职工中专学校	Specialized Secondary Schools for Staff and Workers	2575	2899	1028	1176	532	564
干部中专学校	Specialized Secondary Schools for Cadres	435	458	171	146	69	87
农民中专学校	Specialized Secondary Schools for Peasants	921	913	432	432	318	362
函授中专学校	Specialized Correspondence Secondary Schools	265	205	106	98		14
教师进修学校	Teacher Training Schools	1627	1835	889	975	3	14

15-20 民办教育基本情况
STATISTICS FOR NON-STATE EDUCATION

单位：人 (person)

类别	Item	校数(所) Number of Schools (unit)	毕业生数 Number of Graduates	招生数 New Students Enrollment	在校学生数 Students Enrollment	教职员工数 Teachers,Staff and Workers	专任教师数 Full-time Teachers	代课、兼任教师数 Full-time Teachers
普通中学	**Regular Secondary Schools**	**51**	**3286**	**7305**	**19274**	**2259**	**1366**	**142**
城 市	Urban	31	2230	5180	13552		920	
县 镇	County and Township	19	1056	2037	5634		442	
农 村	Rural	1		88	88		4	
职业中学	**Vocational Secondary Schools**	**16**	**757**	**1019**	**2633**	**363**	**195**	**244**
城 市	Urban	13	757	910	2497		185	226
县 镇	County and Township	2		9	54			
农 村	Rural	1		100	82		10	18
小 学	**Primary Schools Schools**	**4**	**896**	**430**	**3533**	**792**	**568**	**7**
城 市	Urban	2	540	221	1988		281	7
县 镇	County and Township	1	340	207	1483		272	
农 村	Rural	1	16	2	62		15	
幼儿园	**Kindergartens**	**113**		**1972**	**5878**	**1312**	**572**	

15-21 各类学校教育经费来源和支出情况(1999年)
SOURCES AND EXPENDITURE OF EDUCATIONAL FUNDS IN VARIOUS SCHOOLS(1999)

单位：万元 (10000 yuan)

学校类型	Type of Schools	合计 Total	国家财政性教育经费 Government Appropriation for Education	# 预算内教育经费 Budgetary	社会团体和公民个人办学经费 Funds of Social Organizations and Citizens for Running Schools	社会捐资和集资办学经费 Donations and Fund-raising for Running Schools	学费和杂费 Tuition and Miscellaneous Fee	其他教育经费 Other Educational Funds
总　计	**Total**	**2503068**	**1698275**	**1534734**	**28930**	**88387**	**230580**	**456896**
# 中央	Central	1254876	795655	758147		40423	90674	328124
地方	Local	1248192	902620	776587	28930	47964	139906	128772
按学校类别分组	Grouped by Type of Schools							
高等学校	Institutions of Higher Education	1477860	973292	931671		41788	150446	312334
普通高等学校	Regular Institutions of Higher Education	1437242	954557	913486		41788	141516	299381
成人高等学校	Institutions of Higher Education for Adults	40618	18735	18185			8930	12953
中等专业学校	Specialized Secondary Schools	82224	56046	52664	429	266	18239	7244
中等技术学校	Technical Schools	67486	47350	44163		185	15373	4578
中等师范学校	Teacher Training Schools	6199	4669	4586		81	156	1293
成人中专学校	Specialized Secondary Schools for Adults	8539	4027	3915	429		2710	1373
技工学校	Technical Schools	33575	33575					
中　学	Secondary Schools	360124	249264	205784	17988	27262	33755	31855
普通中学	Regular Secondary Schools	359472	249033	205553	17988	27262	33340	31849
高级中学	Senior Secondary Schools	69059	45337	29385	5434	6476	6331	5481
完全中学	Whole Secondary Schools	139473	93593	80006	8988	9860	13976	13056
初级中学	Junior Secondary Schools	150940	110103	96162	3566	10926	13033	13312
# 农村	Rural	47384	39331	36314		1776	2824	3453
成人中学	Secondary Schools for Adults	652	231	231			415	6
职业中学	Vocational Schools	56464	35604	32815	1980	2206	11550	5124
小　学	Primary Schools	253073	201665	179177	8533	11487	10681	20707
普通小学	Regular Primary Schools	253073	201665	179177	8533	11487	10681	20707
# 农村	Rural	75362	67390	64460		708	2736	4528
成人小学	Primary Schools for Adults							
特殊教育学校	Special Education Schools	5836	4500	3749		596	119	621
幼儿园	Kindergartens	22969	12345	11661		2356	5790	2478
其　他	Others	210943	131984	117213		2426		76533

15-22 公 共 图 书 馆
PUBLIC LIBRARIES

项目 Item			总计 Total	中央属 Central	市属 Municipal	区县属 District and County
个数	(个) Number	(unit)	26	1	2	23
从业人员	(人) Employment	(person)	2787	1698	306	783
总藏数	(万册、件) Total Collections	(10000 volumes)	3020	2249	323	448
# 图书	(万册、件) Books	(10000 volumes)	1353	683	252	418
建筑面积	(平方米) Floor Space of Building	(sq.m)	270430	164000	10442	95988
阅览座席	(个) Seats for Reading	(unit)	10895	3000	330	7565
外借人次	(万人次) Person-times of Lending	(10000)	283	72	16	195
外借册次	(万册次) Volume-times Lending	(10000)	663	217	44	402

15-23 艺 术 剧 团
ART TROUPES

项目	Item	个数 (个) Number (unit)	从业人员 (人) Perons Employed (person)	国内演出场次 (场) Domestic Perfor-mances	#农村 In Rural Areas	国内观众人数 (万人次) Domestic Spectator (10000 person.time)	总收入 (千元) Total Revenue (1000 yuan)	# 演出收入 from Performances
总计	**Total**	**31**	**5089**	**7610**	**161**	**926**	**257280**	**48944**
按隶属关系分组	**Grouped by Administrative Relationship**							
中央属	Central	11	2840	1448		247	150606	26298
市属	Municipal	11	1905	4818	161	659	98316	19545
区县属	District and County	9	344	1344		20	8358	3101
按剧种分	**Grouped by Art Troupes**							
话剧、儿童剧团	Drama,Children's Play	5	753	896	35	45	28807	3834
歌剧、舞剧、歌舞剧团	Opera,Dance Drama and Song and Dance Troupe	3	911	241		37	39246	7236
歌舞团、轻音乐团	Song and Dance Ensembles and Light Music Troupes,	3	709	790	36	543	49874	11088
乐团	Philharmonic Troupes	3	559	304		39	40136	9218
文工团	Cultural Troupes							
戏曲剧团	Local Opera Troupes	12	1697	2543	79	100	79539	9117
# 京剧团	Local Beijing Opera Troupes	3	954	1143	8	40	48753	6166
曲、杂、木、皮影剧团	Recitation and Ballad Troupe,Acrobatics and Circus Troupe,Puppet Show Troupe and Shadow Puppet Troupe	5	460	2836	11	163	19678	8451

15-24 电影摄制情况
STATISTICS FOR FILM PRODUCTION

类别 Item		合计 Total 部 Film	合计 Total 本 Reel	#长片 Long Film 部 Film	#长片 Long Film 本 Reel	#短片 Short Film 部 Film	#短片 Short Film 本 Reel
合计	**Total**	**50**	**177**	**13**	**91**	**37**	**86**
故事片	Feature Film	7	55	7	55		
纪录片	Documentary Film	1	2			1	2
科教片	Popular Science Film	36	84			36	84
译制片	Dubbed Film	6	36	6	36		
美术片	Puppet Film						

15-25 报纸出版情况
NEWSPAPER PUBLICATION

门类 Item		种数 (种) Number of Publications (kind)	平均期印数 (万份) Average Printed Copies Per Issue (10000)	总印数 (万份) Total Printed Copies (10000)	总印张 (千印张) Total Signature (1000)
总计	**Total**	**240**	**3343**	**686740**	**15257844**
综合报	Comprehensive	51	1541	395325	9793978
专业报	Professional	189	1802	291415	5463866

15-26 杂志出版情况
MAGAZINES PUBLICATION

门类 Item		种数 (种) Number of Publications (kind)	平均期印数 (万册) Average Copies Per Issue (10000)	总印数 (万册) Total Copies (10000)	总印张 (千印张) Total Signatures (1000)
总计	**Total**	**2352**	**5909**	**79124**	**3295599**
综合	Comprehensive	135	950	13358	529375
哲学、社会科学	Philosophy and Social Sciences	571	2608	35456	1175452
自然科学技术	Natural Sciences and Technology	1286	1289	16100	872077
文化、教育	Culture and Education	200	577	7567	469905
文学、艺术	Literature and Art	109	214	2468	125290
少年儿童读物	Juvenile and Children's Books	16	189	3144	80457
画刊	Pictorial	35	82	1031	43043

15-27 图书出版情况
BOOKS PUBLICATION

门类	Item	出版图书种数 合计 (种) Number of Publications(kind)	#新书 New Publications	总印数 (万册、张) Total Copies (10000)	总印张 (千印张) Total Signatures(1000)
总计	**Total**	**55130**	**35285**	**91006**	**8877059**
书籍合计	**Books**	**54597**	**35107**	**89039**	**8837902**
马列主义、毛泽东思想	Maxism-Leninism-Mao Zedong Thought	82	53	351	35155
哲学	Philosophy	615	443	612	80850
社会科学总论	General Social Sciences	855	713	759	105295
政治、法律	Politics and Law	3624	2533	5886	687561
军事	Military	307	268	248	28175
经济	Economics	4934	3721	5513	713781
文化、科学、教育、体育	Culture,Science,Education and Sports	13737	7790	47071	2958841
语言、文字	Languages	2885	1637	5304	804565
文学	Literature	2955	2195	3677	519934
艺术	Art	1892	1283	1585	138874
历史、地理	History and Geography	1706	1367	1490	182320
自然科学总论	General Natural Sciences	128	96	109	9110
数学科学、化学	Mathematics and Chemistry	1228	492	1581	218875
天文学、物理科学	Astronomy and Physics	427	376	107	13937
生物科学	Biology	296	157	164	29038
医药、卫生	Medicine and Health Care	3137	2039	2739	470323
农业科学	Agricultural Science	1907	1169	1821	147511
工业技术	Industrial Technology	11238	6814	7758	1410857
交通运输	Transportation	785	443	857	108567
航空、航天	Aeronautics and Aerospace	67	62	23	4125
环境科学	Environmental Science	299	233	173	17909
综合性图书	General Books	1493	1223	1211	152299
图片合计	**Pictures**	**533**	**178**	**1967**	**39157**

15-28 电视台情况
BASIC STATISTICS ON TELEVISION STATIONS

项目 Item				2000 中央 Central	2000 地方 Local	1999 中央 Central	1999 地方 Local
基本情况		**Basic Statistics**					
电视台	(座)	Television Stations	(unit)	1	1	1	1
电视发射台、转播台	(座)	Transmission Stations and Relay Stations	(unit)	1	10	1	10
电视差转台	(座)	Transformation Stations	(unit)		47		62
节目套数	(套)	Programs	(set)	9	12	8	12
平均每周播出时间(按12月份第三周计算)	(时：分)	Program Hours Per Week(according to the third week of December)	(hour:minute)	1086:00	857:11	1020:54	828:30
播放节目情况		**Shows of TV Programs**					
自办节目时间	(时：分)	Self-Produced Programs	(hour:minute)	1086:00	755:03	1021:54	716:25
新闻节目	(时：分)	News Programs	(hour:minute)	178:00	79:06	177:10	81:11
专题节目	(时：分)	Special Topic Programs	(hour:minute)	328:00	147:36	317:59	163:31
教育节目	(时：分)	Educational Programs	(hour:minute)	28:00	29:20	28:45	29:00
文艺节目	(时：分)	Entertainment Programs	(hour:minute)	417:00	400:48	419:45	350:24
服务性节目	(时：分)	Service Programs	(hour:minute)	82:00	98:13	78:15	92:19

注：电视台数不包括区县电视台。
Note: Number of television stations excludes those of districts and counties.

15-29 广播电台情况
BASIC STATISTICS ON BROADCASTING STATIONS

项目 Item				2000 中央 Central	2000 地方 Local	1999 中央 Central	1999 地方 Local
基本情况		**Basic Statistics**					
电　台	(座)	Broadcasting Stations	(unit)	2	1	2	1
发射台、转播台	(座)	Transmission Stations and Relay Stations	(unit)	5	9	5	10
节目套数	(套)	Programs	(set)	9	16	7	16
平均每日播音时间(按12月份计算)	(时：分)	Program Hours Per Week(according to December)	(hour:minute)	367:00	188:55	320:00	178:12
播放节目情况		**Shows of TV Programs**					
自办节目时间	(时：分)	Self-Produced Programs	(hour:minute)	367:00	176:00	310:15	164:32
新闻节目	(时：分)	News Programs	(hour:minute)	108:00	13:45	85:10	12:45
专题节目	(时：分)	Special Topic Programs	(hour:minute)	126:00	64:35	89:05	28:15
教育节目	(时：分)	Educational Programs	(hour:minute)	17:00	10:15	26:30	17:15
文艺节目	(时：分)	Entertainment Programs	(hour:minute)	91:00	56:40	85:55	83:15
服务性节目	(时：分)	Service Programs	(hour:minute)	16:00	30:45	23:35	23:02

注：广播电台数不包括区县电台。
Note: Number of broadcasting stations excludes those of districts and counties.

15-30 文化产业活动单位情况
STATISTICS OF CULTURAL INDUSTRIAL UNITS

单位：个 (unit)

行业类别	Sector	合计 Total	按隶属关系分 Grouped by Administrative Relationship	
			地方属 Local	中央属 Central
合　计	**Total**	**3570**	**2577**	**993**
出版业	Publication	446	58	388
印刷业	Printing	869	748	121
图书报刊批发、零售业	Wholesale and Retail of Books and Newspapers	495	407	88
文化体育用品制造业	Stationery,Educational and Sports Goods Making	113	108	5
文化体育用品零售业	Retail of Stationery,Educational and Sports Goods	426	320	106
艺术业	Arts	81	48	33
文物保护业	Protection of Historical Relics	74	59	15
图书馆、档案馆	Libraries and Archives	42	29	13
群众文化业及其他文化业	Mass Culture and Others	154	125	29
广播电影电视业（含新闻）	Radio,Film and Television(including News)	123	78	45
体育	Sports	88	61	27
娱乐服务业	Recreational Services	115	100	15
摄影及扩印业	Photography and Large-printing	41	33	8
园林业	Parks	140	132	8
广告业	Advertisement	363	271	92

15-31 文化产业活动单位从业人员
EMPLOYMENT OF CULTURAL INDUSTRIAL UNITS

单位：人 (person)

行业类别	Sector	合计 Total	按隶属关系分 Grouped by Administrative Relationship	
			地方属 Local	中央属 Central
合　计	**Total**	**213458**	**117882**	**95576**
出版业	Publication	42064	7196	34868
印刷业	Printing	61849	40079	21770
图书报刊批发、零售业	Wholesale and Retail of Books and Newspapers	5567	3011	2556
文化体育用品制造业	Stationery,Educational and Sports Goods Making	4717	4543	174
文化体育用品零售业	Retail of Stationery,Educational and Sports Goods	4491	4185	306
艺术业	Arts	10238	4008	6230
文物保护业	Protection of Historical Relics	4968	1929	3039
图书馆、档案馆	Libraries and Archives	3730	1522	2208
群众文化业及其他文化业	Mass Culture and Others	5622	4154	1468
广播电影电视业（含新闻）	Radio,Film and Television(including News)	19911	5324	14587
体育	Sports	8724	5757	2967
娱乐服务业	Recreational Services	10636	8629	2007
摄影及扩印业	Photography and Large-printing	2604	2055	549
园林业	Parks	19596	19307	289
广告业	Advertisement	8741	6183	2558

15-32 文化产业活动单位资产情况
ASSETS OF CULTURAL INDUSTRIAL UNITS

单位：万元 (10000 yuan)

行业类别	Sector	合计 Total	按隶属关系分 Grouped by Administrative Relationship 地方属 Local	中央属 Central
合　计	**Total**	**7208034.2**	**2602898.1**	**4605136.1**
出版业	Publication	1945282.0	383717.1	1561564.9
印刷业	Printing	825118.8	418280.8	406838.0
图书报刊批发、零售业	Wholesale and Retail of Books and Newspapers	290284.0	63557.0	226727.0
文化体育用品制造业	Stationery,Educational and Sports Goods Making	85230.0	75663.2	9566.8
文化体育用品零售业	Retail of Stationery,Educational and Sports Goods	101456.0	93401.0	8055.0
艺术业	Arts	164315.2	46844.5	117470.7
文物保护业	Protection of Historical Relics	133219.5	54642.3	78577.2
图书馆、档案馆	Libraries and Archives	203267.5	64864.2	138403.3
群众文化业及其他文化业	Mass Culture and Others	89213.8	53482.0	35731.8
广播电影电视业（含新闻）	Radio,Film and Television(including News)	1808062.8	368168.7	1439894.1
体育	Sports	330028.1	122676.2	207351.9
娱乐服务业	Recreational Services	408104.2	334388.6	73715.6
摄影及扩印业	Photography and Large-printing	21943.7	10346.8	11596.9
园林业	Parks	300363.3	295102.7	5260.6
广告业	Advertisement	502145.3	217763.0	284382.3

15-33 文化产业活动单位创造增加值情况
VALUE ADDED OF CULTURAL INDUSTRIAL UNITS

行业类别	Sector	合计 (万元) Total (10000 yuan)	人均增加值 (元/人) Value Added Per Capita (yuan/person)
合　计	**Total**	**1128566.9**	**52870.7**
出版业	Publication	364996.2	86771.6
印刷业	Printing	220891.8	35714.7
图书报刊批发、零售业	Wholesale and Retail of Books and Newspapers	41053.1	73743.7
文化体育用品制造业	Stationery,Educational and Sports Goods Making	30653.4	64984.9
文化体育用品零售业	Retail of Stationery,Educational and Sports Goods	7358.8	16385.7
艺术业	Arts	30647.8	29935.3
文物保护业	Protection of Historical Relics	17596.4	35419.5
图书馆、档案馆	Libraries and Archives	15774.8	42291.7
群众文化业及其他文化业	Mass Culture and Others	26256.8	46703.7
广播电影电视业（含新闻）	Radio,Film and Television(including News)	164626.4	82681.1
体育	Sports	27385.9	31391.4
娱乐服务业	Recreational Services	28414.4	26715.3
摄影及扩印业	Photography and Large-printing	5426.1	20837.6
园林业	Parks	53164.8	27130.4
广告业	Advertisement	94320.2	107905.5

15-34 文化产业活动单位经营收入情况
OPERATING REVENUE OF CULTURAL INDUSTRIAL UNITS

单位：万元 (10000 yuan)

行 业 类 别	Sector	合 计 Total	按隶属关系分 Grouped by Administrative Relationship 地方属 Local	中央属 Central
合 计	**Total**	**2584340.6**	**1028690.2**	**1555650.4**
出版业	Publication	1024175.2	202842.6	821332.6
印刷业	Printing	488770.7	253093.1	235677.6
图书报刊批发、零售业	Wholesale and Retail of Books and Newspapers	214650.0	59882.0	154768.0
文化体育用品制造业	Stationery,Educational and Sports Goods Making	32855.1	29376.8	3478.3
文化体育用品零售业	Retail of Stationery,Educational and Sports Goods	94087.0	83555.0	10532.0
艺术业	Arts	5879.5	3320.4	2559.1
文物保护业	Protection of Historical Relics	4763.6	4652.0	111.6
图书馆、档案馆	Libraries and Archives	1337.4	139.0	1198.4
群众文化业及其他文化业	Mass Culture and Others	28619.4	14686.7	13932.7
广播电影电视业（含新闻）	Radio,Film and Television(including News)	143491.4	21353.0	122138.4
体育	Sports	20204.1	17300.2	2903.9
娱乐服务业	Recreational Services	87723.2	69156.6	18566.6
摄影及扩印业	Photography and Large-printing	19869.9	14908.2	4961.7
园林业	Parks	35444.2	32320.7	3123.5
广告业	Advertisement	382469.9	222103.9	160366.0

15-35 文化产业活动单位人均经营收入情况
BUSINESS REVENUE PER CAPITA OF CULTURAL INDUSTRIAL UNITS

单位：元/人 (yuan/person)

行 业 类 别	Sector	合 计 Total	按隶属关系分 Grouped by Administrative Relationship 地方属 Local	中央属 Central
合 计	**Total**	**121070.2**	**87264.4**	**162765.8**
出版业	Publication	243480.2	281882.4	235554.8
印刷业	Printing	79026.5	63148.6	108258.0
图书报刊批发、零售业	Wholesale and Retail of Books and Newspapers	385575.7	198877.4	605508.6
文化体育用品制造业	Stationery,Educational and Sports Goods Making	69652.5	64663.9	199902.3
文化体育用品零售业	Retail of Stationery,Educational and Sports Goods	209501.2	199653.5	344183.0
艺术业	Arts	5742.8	8284.4	4107.7
文物保护业	Protection of Historical Relics	9588.6	24116.1	367.2
图书馆、档案馆	Libraries and Archives	3585.5	913.3	5427.5
群众文化业及其他文化业	Mass Culture and Others	50906.1	35355.6	94909.4
广播电影电视业（含新闻）	Radio,Film and Television(including News)	72066.4	40107.1	83731.0
体育	Sports	23159.2	30050.7	9787.3
娱乐服务业	Recreational Services	82477.6	80144.4	92509.2
摄影及扩印业	Photography and Large-printing	76305.3	72546.0	90377.0
园林业	Parks	18087.5	16740.4	108079.6
广告业	Advertisement	437558.5	359217.0	626919.5

主 要 统 计 指 标 解 释

普通高等学校 指按照国家规定的设置标准和审批程序批准举办， 通过国家统一招生考试， 招收高中毕业生为主要培养对象， 实施高等教育的全日制大学、独立设置的学院和高等专科学校、短期职业大学。

成人高等学校 指按照国家有关规定审批， 招收通过全国成人高教统一招生考试的具有高中毕业或同等学历的在职从业人员，利用脱产、半脱产、业余或函授等多种形式对其实施高等学历教育， 培养高等教育专科或本科毕业水平的专门人才， 修业年限、课程设置和总学时数均按高等学历教育要求付诸实施的学校。包括广播电视大学、职工高等学校、农民高等学校、管理干部学院、教育学院、独立设置的函授学院等。

小学学龄儿童入学率 指调查范围内已入小学学习的学龄儿童占校内外学龄儿童总数（包括弱智儿童在内，但不包括聋哑儿童）的比重。计算公式：

$$\text{小学学龄儿童入学率}=\frac{\text{已入学的小学学龄儿童数}}{\text{校内外小学学龄儿童总数}}\times 100\%$$

艺术剧团 指从事戏曲、音乐、舞蹈、杂技等专业艺术表演，有独立帐户、实行独立核算的团体。不包括半工半艺和民间职业剧团。

艺术表演观众人数（人次） 指售票、包场演出或民族地区免费演出的艺术表演观众人次数。不包括彩排审查和内部观摩演出的观众人次数。

Explanatory Notes On Main Statistical Indicators

Regular Institutions of Higher Education refer to full-time universities, colleges, high professional schools and short-term professional universities set up according to the government standards and approval procedures, enrolling graduates from senior secondary schools through nation-wide unified examination and providing higher education courses and training.

Institutions of Higher Education for Adults refer to Radio and TV universities, staff colleges, peasants colleges, colleges for management cadres, educational colleges and independent correspondence colleges set up in line with relevant government policies, enrolling staff and workers with senior secondary school or equivalent education, and providing higher education courses in various forms of full-time, part-time, spare-time, or correspondence for adults. There are government regulations on various aspects for institutions of higher education for adults, such as the courses and total learning hours.

Enrollment Rate of School-Age Children refers to the proportion of primary school-age children enrolled at primary schools to the total number of primary school-age children both in and outside primary schools （including retarded children, but excluding blind, deaf and mute children）. The formula is:

$$\text{Enrollment Rate of School-age Children}=\frac{\text{Total school-age children in schools}}{\text{Total school-age children in and outside schools}}\times 100\%$$

Art Troupe refers to the troupe which is engaged in drama, opera, music, dance, acrobatics or other art performance, opens independent accounts in banks and has independent accounting system; excluding the troupes which are engaged partly in industrial or agricultural activities, partly in art performance or the non-governmental troupes.

Number of Spectators at Art Performance refers to the number of attendants at commercial shows, completely booked shows or free shows given in minority national areas, and does not include the number of spectators at rehearsals and internal shows.

科　技　16

SCIENCE AND TECHNOLOGY

专业技术人员人数（单位：万人）
Number of Professional Technical Personnel (10000 persons)

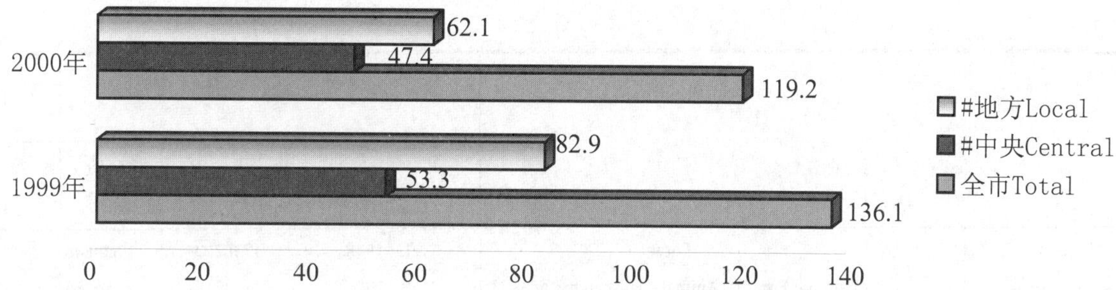

每万从业人员拥有专业技术人员（单位：人）
Number of Professional Technical Personnel Per 10000 Employed Persons (perosn)

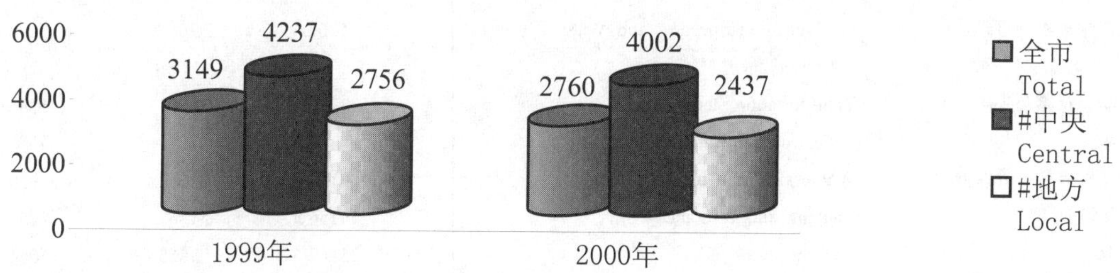

高新技术产业工业总产值构成（按领域分）
Composition of Gross Output Value for High-grade Technological Industry (by field)

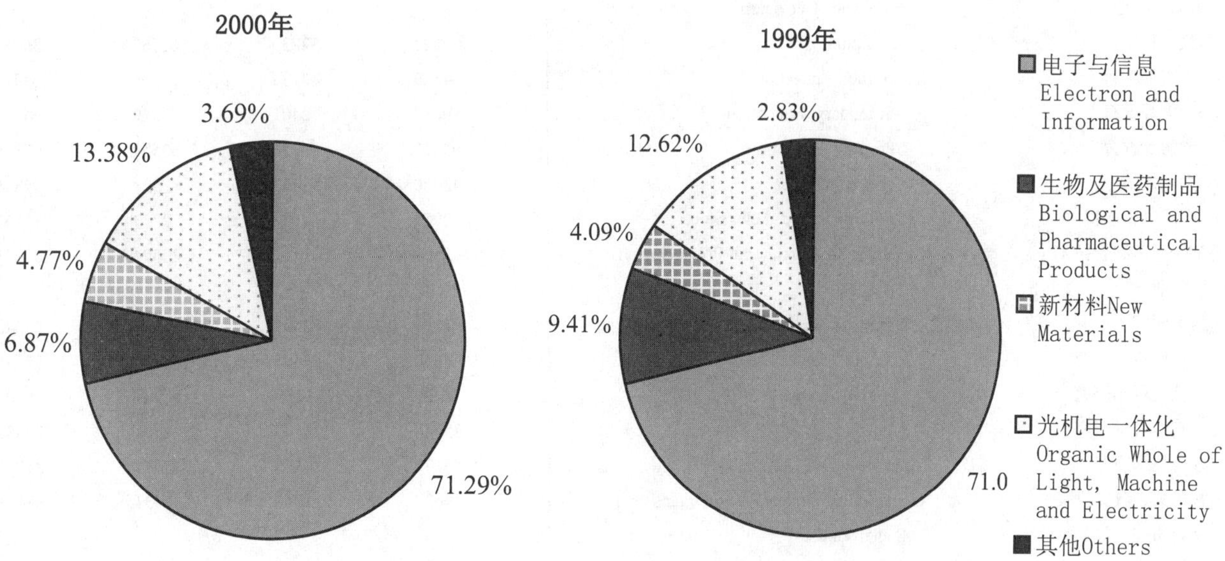

16-1 国民经济各行业专业技术人员
NUMBER OF PROFESSIONAL TECHNICAL PERSONNEL BY SECTORS OF NATIONAL ECONOMY

单位：人　　(person)

项　目	Item	2000			1999
		全　市 Total	# 中　央 Central	# 地　方 Local	全　市 Total
合　计	**Total**	**1191948**	**473622**	**620848**	**1361168**
农、林、牧、渔业	Farming,Forestry,Animals Husbandry and Fishery	7376	891	6383	8202
采掘业	Excavation	3204	32	3172	4114
制造业	Manufacturing	173527	38405	126058	219042
电力、煤气及水的生产和供应业	Electricity,Gas and Water Production and Supply	8804	2771	6033	10713
建筑业	Construction	115023	28739	68650	112203
地质勘查业、水利管理业	Geological Prospecting and Water Conservancy	5865	3667	2198	5173
交通运输、仓储及邮电通讯业	Transportation,Storage,Posts and Telecommunications	33270	26091	5886	37026
批发和零售贸易、餐饮业	Wholesale,Retail and Catering	86134	26681	38936	111092
金融、保险业	Banking and Insurance	54156	51367	2250	58910
房地产业	Real Estate	25147	3865	15066	24466
社会服务业	Social Services	96585	30240	37813	120629
卫生、体育和社会福利业	Health Care,Sports and Social Welfare	94249	29172	64769	94995
卫　生	Health Care	91378	28607	62519	92296
体　育	Sports	1333	412	867	1449
社会福利保障业	Social Welfare	1538	153	1383	1250
教育、文化艺术和广播电影电视业	Education,Culture and Arts and Radio, Film and Television	273995	93875	177538	291663
教　育	Education	222021	52839	167767	236165
高等教育	Higher Education	64543	47133	17204	69979
中等教育	Secondary Education	80684	2401	77949	84557
初等教育	Primary Education	63327	721	62559	67328
文化艺术	Culture and Art	42020	33464	7528	44331
广播电影电视	Radio,Film and Television	9954	7572	2243	11167
科学研究和综合技术服务业	Scientific Research and Polytechnical Services	132369	101871	20594	169975
科学研究	Scientific Research	79194	72509	5521	88242
自然科学研究	Natural Science	48018	43593	3773	53745
社会科学研究	Social Science	5428	5169	247	6608
其他科学研究	Others	25748	23747	1501	27889
综合技术服务	Polytechnical Services	53175	29362	15073	81733
国家机关、政党机关和社会团体	Government Organs,Party Organs and Social Bodies	59637	21068	38433	68041
其他行业	Others	22607	14887	7069	24924

注：按劳动工资年报口径，专业技术人员调整为在岗职工的其中项（下表同）。

Note: Professional technica personnel has been adjusted to one of staff and workers at their posts according to the caliber of annual report on labor force and wages.(the following is the same).

16-2 国民经济各行业每万从业人员拥有专业技术人员

NUMBER OF SCIENTIFIC AND TECHNICAL PERSONNEL PER 10000 EMPLOYMENT BY SECTORS OF NATIONAL ECONOMY

单位：人 (person)

项目	Item	2000			1999
		全市 Total	#中央 Central	#地方 Local	全市 Total
合计	**Total**	**2760**	**4002**	**2437**	**3149**
农、林、牧、渔业	Farming,Forestry,Animals Husbandry and Fishery	2555	5260	2410	2633
采掘业	Excavation	1241	8421	1231	1428
制造业	Manufacturing	1837	2370	1753	2142
电力、煤气及水的生产和供应业	Electricity,Gas and Water Production and Supply	2207	2759	2021	2554
建筑业	Construction	2264	2661	2652	2243
地质勘查业、水利管理业	Geological Prospecting and Water Conservancy	3914	6339	2389	3116
交通运输、仓储及邮电通讯业	Transportation,Storage,Posts and Telecommunications	1817	2030	1171	1898
批发和零售贸易、餐饮业	Wholesale,Retail and Catering	1785	4275	1367	2144
金融、保险业	Banking and Insurance	7601	7719	6228	7978
房地产业	Real Estate	2045	1869	2140	2344
社会服务业	Social Services	1524	2542	1016	2107
卫生、体育和社会福利业	Health Care,Sports and Social Welfare	5930	6962	6798	7024
卫生	Health Care				
体育	Sports	7381	7364	7458	7526
社会福利保障业	Social Welfare	1519	1541	1494	1813
教育、文化艺术和广播	Education,Culture and Arts and Radio,	583	4016	2448	2705
电影电视业	Film and Television	6567	6053	7056	6854
教育	Education	6844	5936	7317	7099
高等教育	Higher Education	5706	6025	5189	6090
中等教育	Secondary Education	7379	6174	7479	7579
初等教育	Primary Education	8873	7441	8915	8862
文化艺术	Culture and Art	5692	6335	4424	6054
广播电影电视	Radio,Film and Television	5243	5715	4210	5682
科学研究和综合技术服务业	Scientific Research and Polytechnical Services	4047	6271	1476	5908
科学研究	Scientific Research	6202	6293	5116	6456
自然科学研究	Natural Science	6116	6235	4891	6417
社会科学研究	Social Science	7026	7090	6237	7281
其他科学研究	Others	6211	6245	5599	6362
综合技术服务	Polytechnical Services	2667	6217	1171	5412
国家机关、政党机关和社会团体	Government Organs,Party Organs and Social Bodies	2412	3248	2117	2262
其他行业	Others	2020	2002	2432	3632

16-3 市属国有企事业单位专业技术人员

NUMBER OF SCIENTIFIC AND TECHNICAL PERSONNEL IN LOCAL STATE-OWNED ENTERPRISES AND INSTITUTIONS

单位：人 (person)

项目	Item	总计 Total	# 高级 Senior	# 中级 Middle	# 初级 Junior
总计	**Total**	**495834**	**40707**	**158018**	**263953**
工程技术人员	Engineering	114354	10109	35187	60582
农业技术人员	Agriculture	5064	257	1509	3068
科研实验人员	Scientific Research and Experimentation	3974	1145	1885	671
卫生技术人员	Health Care	68021	5077	17537	43107
教学人员	Teaching	165489	18547	66912	69562
经济人员	Economy	49649	1404	10570	31260
会计人员	Accountant	42376	648	6287	32115
统计人员	Statistician	7657	79	1567	5497
翻译人员	Translator	1205	69	620	456
图书档案人员	Librarian and Archvist	6543	322	2433	3366
新闻出版人员	News Publisher	3306	533	1286	1141
律师公证人员	Law and Notarization	254	12	79	106
播音人员	Broadcasting	174	13	50	85
工艺美术人员	Industrial Art	595	41	156	360
体育人员	Sports	856	151	335	305
艺术人员	Art	2722	518	1411	653
政工人员	Political Staff	23595	1782	10194	11619

16-4 专利申请及授权情况

PATENT APPLICATIONS EXAMINED AND CERTIFIED

单位：项 (item)

项目	Item	申请量 Total Applications Examined		批准量 Total Applications Certified	
		2000	1999	2000	1999
合计	**Total**	**10344**	**7716**	**5905**	**5829**
按种类分	**Grouped by Type**				
发明	Creations and Inventions	3409	2055	1074	573
实用新型	Utility Models	4984	4045	3463	3948
外观设计	Designs	1951	1616	1368	1308
按对象分	**Grouped by Applicator**				
工矿企业	Industrial and Mineral Enterprises	2547	1850	1497	1339
大专院校	Universities and Colleges	465	288	241	227
科研单位	Scientific Research Institution	870	726	583	549
机关团体	Government Organs and Associations	25	39	66	82
个人	Individuals	6437	4813	3518	3632

16-5 技术合同签定及执行情况
CONCLUSION AND IMPLEMENTATION OF TECHNICAL CONTRACTS

项　　目	Item	签定合同数(项) Contracts Concluded (item)		合同金额(万元) Amount of Contracts (10000 yuan)	
		2000	1999	2000	1999
合　　计	**Total**	**21270**	**20711**	**1402871.3**	**921889.4**
按合同类别分类	**Grouped by Type**				
技术开发合同	Technological Development	5068	3750	655773.5	386291.2
技术转让合同	Technology Transfer	3103	4469	288270.0	129643.8
技术咨询合同	Technical Consultation	1946	1931	41768.1	34721.4
技术服务合同	Technical Service	11153	10561	417059.7	371233.1
按合同卖方类别分类	**Grouped by Type of Seller**				
科研机构	Scientific Research Institutions	10214	11865	457255.7	363760.8
高等院校	Institutions of Higher Education	1454	1227	99255.8	31924.9
工业企业	Industrial Enterprises	443	1265	93015.6	124774.6
技术贸易机构	Technology Trade Institutions	1679	1897	114796.0	37012.1
个人及个人合伙	Individual and Individual Partnership	176	48	3025.5	2703.9
其　他	Others	7304	4409	635524.8	361713.1
按合同买方类别分类	**Grouped by Type of Buyer**				
工业企业	Industrial Enterprises	13919	12360	885130.6	620899.4
科研机构	Scientific Research Institutions	3322	4132	130875.6	70671.9
各级管理部门	Management Departments	2089	1796	229423.5	127165.0
技术贸易机构	Technology Trade Institutions	346	860	31822.1	53018.4
个人及个人合伙	Individual and Individual Partnership	146	246	385.7	1387.8
其　他	Others	1448	1317	125233.7	48746.8
按服务社会经济目标分类	**Grouped by Social and Economic Service Objection**				
陆地、海洋和大气的开发与估价	Development and Appraisal of Lands,Seas and Atmosphere	64	65	4776.1	2399.2
民用宇宙空间	Civil Universal Space	255	337	17634.6	18600.7
农业、林业和渔业的发展	Development of Agriculture, Forestry and Fishery	310	225	23958.7	12726.5
促进工业的发展	Promoting Industrial Development	5160	4199	241039.3	192502.4
能源的生产、储存和分配	Production,Stockpile and Distribution of Energy	1798	1479	98803.2	77254.4
交通、通讯事业的发展	Development of Transportation and Telecommunication	3808	2401	382891.8	163804.8
教育事业的发展	Development of Education	207	132	8502.1	7549.8
卫生事业的发展	Development of Health Care	1054	916	68449.4	22718.9
社会发展和社会经济服务	Social Development and Economic Service	4181	6132	328158.0	246500.4
环境保护	Environmental Protextion	1010	1091	24656.1	23369.7
知识的全面发展	All-round Development of Knowledge	61	110	2491.6	2736.6
其他目标	Others	3039	3427	157782.1	128539.3
国　防	National Defence	323	197	43728.4	23186.7
按技术流向分类	**Grouped by Spread Area**				
北　京	Beijing	9984	8963	731446.1	426543.5
外　地	Outside Beijing	11286	11748	671425.2	495345.9

16-6 科学技术协会及所属学会工作情况

BASIC STATISTICS OF SCIENCE AND TECHNOLOGY ASSOCIATION AND SUBORDINATE INSTITUTES

项目		Item		合计 Total	市科协 Municipal Science and Technology Association	市级学会 Institutes at Municipal Level
机构与人员		**Institutions and Personnel**				
机　构	(个)	Institutions		142	1	141
人　员	(人)	Personnel	(person)	230831	52	230779
学术交流		**Academic Exchange**				
国内学术会议	(次)	Domestic Academic Meeting	(time)	450	10	440
参加人数	(人次)	Participants	(person.time)	34048	412	33636
交流论文	(篇)	Papers Presented	(article)	5672	63	5609
国际学术会议	(次)	International Academic Meeting	(time)	43	1	42
参加人数	(人次)	Participants	(person.time)	4110	300	3810
交流论文	(篇)	Papers Presented	(article)	565	20	545
民间科技交流		**Non-governmental Scientific and Technological Exchange**				
出国科学考察	(人次)	Scientific Visit abroad	(person.time)	173	83	90
出国参加国际会议	(人次)	Scientific Meeting abroad	(person.time)	125	21	104
出国参加技贸活动	(人次)	Technology Trade abroad	(person.time)	11	11	0
外派科技研修生	(人次)	Study abroad	(person.time)	29	27	2
接待海外科技团组	(个)	Foreign Scientic and Technology Visit	(unit)	84	31	53
接待人次	(人次)	Participants	(person.time)	613	176	437
举办国际学术报告	(场)	International Academic Meeting	(unit)	49	9	40
听报告人次	(人次)	Participants	(person.time)	4461	707	3754
科学普及		**Scientific Promoting**				
科普讲座	(次)	Lectures	(time)	446	60	386
参加人次	(人次)	Participants	(person.time)	145189	10700	134489
科普展览	(次)	Exhibitions	(time)	63	11	52
参观人次	(人次)	Participants	(person.time)	184170	40000	144170
科技培训		**Training Program**				
培训班数	(个)	Classes	(time)	322	97	225
培训人数	(人次)	Participants	(person.time)	30758	3801	26957
科技咨询服务		**Consultative Services**				
完成咨询合同	(项)	Contracts Completed	(item)	763	560	203
咨询合同实现金额	(万元)	Contracts Revenue	(10000 yuan)	18810	16277	2533
无偿咨询项目	(项)	Free Consultative Project	(item)	1825	105	1720
决策合同	(项)	Contracts of Concluded	(item)	44	2	42
青少年科技活动		**Activity of Teenagers Science Technology**				
科技夏(冬)令营	(个)	Summer/Winter Science and Technology Camp	(time)	25	7	18
参加人数	(人次)	Participants	(person.time)	3883	424	3459
青少年科技竞赛	(个)	Science and Technology Competetions	(unit)	36	11	25
参加人数	(人次)	Participants	(person.time)	221723	19952	201771

16-7 计量器具检定情况

STATISTICS FOR MEASURING IMPLEMENTS TEST

单位：台、件、套 (unit)

地区	Region	合计 Total	长度 Length	温度 Temperature	力学 Mechanics	#衡器 Weighing Apparatus	电学 Electricity
总计	**Total**	**827281**	**106190**	**20145**	**573753**	**98273**	**67003**
市属小计	**Municipal**	**255450**	**29921**	**2912**	**206145**	**982**	**4638**
区县属小计	**District and County**	**571831**	**76269**	**17233**	**367608**	**97291**	**62365**
东城区	Dongcheng	58459	12737	1033	23298	5355	5169
西城区	Xicheng	55549	28281	548	23099	6550	2818
崇文区	Chongwen	20499	3904	444	14285	1960	1515
宣武区	Xuanwu	10130			9316	4361	387
朝阳区	Chaoyang	84956	7030	4326	61907	6509	11693
丰台区	Fengtai	19156	1616	1046	16494	3100	
石景山区	Shijingshan	27088	1348	1446	19477	2898	4159
海淀区	Haidian	68531	3375	2399	58780	22254	2953
门头沟区	Mentougou	7413	509		6810	857	69
房山区	Fangshan	47704	4616	1328	16548	7213	19414
通州区	Tongzhou	39713	2644	893	28294	3320	7669
昌平区	Changping	23982	15	150	11613	3314	
顺义区	Shunyi	24091	5578	1585	10264	1900	1739
大兴县	Daxing	22268	1081	1848	14704	2846	255
平谷县	Pinggu	23212	958	56	21755	17918	327
怀柔县	Huairou	14426	649		11591	4168	976
密云县	Miyun	16792	1311	94	12179	1545	3208
延庆县	Yanqing	7862	617	37	7194	1223	14

地区	Region	光学 Optics	声学 Acoustics	化学 Chemistry	电离辐射 Ionization Radition	无线电 Radio	时间频率 Time Frequency	其他 Other
总计	**Total**	**19101**	**1946**	**5763**	**1413**	**3789**	**1293**	**26885**
市属小计	**Municipal**	**1505**	**1819**	**3946**	**1342**	**2202**	**1020**	
区县属小计	**District and County**	**17596**	**127**	**1817**	**71**	**1587**	**273**	**26885**
东城区	Dongcheng	12562		620				3040
西城区	Xicheng			339		464		
崇文区	Chongwen			127		224		
宣武区	Xuanwu	125		32		231		39
朝阳区	Chaoyang							
丰台区	Fengtai							
石景山区	Shijingshan	642		16				
海淀区	Haidian	149		438		437		
门头沟区	Mentougou							25
房山区	Fangshan							5798
通州区	Tongzhou	140	35	38				
昌平区	Changping	40	50	95	50	100	273	11596
顺义区	Shunyi							4925
大兴县	Daxing	3938		81		109		252
平谷县	Pinggu		42	31	21	22		
怀柔县	Huairou							1210
密云县	Miyun							
延庆县	Yanqing							

16-8 高新技术产业情况
STATISTICS ON HIGH-GRADE TECHNOLOGICAL INDUSTRY

单位：亿元 (100 million yuan)

项目	Item	工业总产值(现价) Gross Output Value of Industry (at constant prices) 2000	1999	2000年为1999年% 2000 as % of 1999
合计	**Total**	**867.6**	**610.8**	**142.0**
按登记注册类型分	**Grouped by Registered Type**			
国有经济	State-owned	263.5	219.1	120.3
集体经济	Collective-owned	42.1	26.8	157.1
"三资"及港澳台经济	Chinese-foreign, Hongkong, Macao and Taiwan Enterprises	482.1	339.7	141.9
股份制及其他经济	Share Holding and Others	79.9	25.2	317.1
按行业类别分	**Grouped by Sectors**			
医药制造业	Medicine and Pharmaceutical Products	37.0	31.1	119.0
专用设备制造业	Special Purpose Equipment	17.0	7.8	217.9
交通运输设备制造业	Transportation Equipment	38.1	21.6	176.4
电气机械及器材制造业	Electric Equipment and Machine	42.0	24.2	173.6
电子及通讯设备制造业	Electronic and Telecommunication	621.8	437.2	142.2
仪器仪表制造业	Instruments and Meters	37.2	28.1	132.4
其他	Others	74.5	60.8	122.5
按高新技术领域分	**Grouped by the Field of Highgrade Technology**			
电子与信息	Electron and Information	618.5	433.9	142.5
生物及医药制品	Biological and Pharmaceutical Products	59.6	57.5	103.7
新材料	New Materials	41.4	25.0	165.6
光机电一体化	Organic Whole of Light, Machine and Electricity	116.6	77.1	151.2
新能源	New Energy	11.2	2.0	560.0
环保设备	Equipment for Environmental Protection	3.1	1.7	182.4
航空航天及地球空间技术	Technology on Aerospace and Earth Space	17.2	13.6	126.5

主 要 统 计 指 标 解 释

专业技术人员 指已取得专业技术职称，或大学、中专毕业，以及从工作实践中提拔，从事研究、教学、生产的专业人员和在机关、企业、事业中从事管理工作的专业人员。

工程技术人员 指从事工程技术工作的专业技术人员，包括：高级工程师、工程师、助理工程师、技术员和未评定职称的技术人员。

农业技术人员 指从事农业技术工作的专业技术人员，包括：高级农艺师、农艺师、助理农艺师、技术员和未评定职称的技术人员。

发明 指专利法及其实施细则所称的发明，指对有关产品、方法或其改进所提出的新的技术方案。

实用新型 指专利法及其实施细则所称的实用新型，指对产品的形状、构造或者其结合所提出的适于实用的新的技术方案。

外观设计 指专利法及其实施细则所称的外观设计，指对产品的形状、图案、色彩或者其结合所作出的富有美感并适于工业上应用的新设计。

Explanatory Notes On Main Statistical Indicators

Professional and Technical Personnel refers to those professionals with technical titles, or those being graduated from colleges and specialized secondary schools, or those being promoted in practice and working on research, teaching and production , or the professionals doing administrative work in government agencies, enterprises and institutions.

Engineering Professionals refer to the persons who are engaged in engineering science and technology, including senior engineers, engineers, assistant engineers, technicians and technical personnel without professional titles.

Agricultural Professionals refer to the persons who are working on the science of agriculture, including senior agronomists, agronomists, assistant agronomists, technicians and technical personnel without professional titles.

Inventions refer to the inventions as specified by the patent law and its detailed rules and regulations for implementation, including the new technical proposals or modifications for products or the methods.

Utility Models refer to the utility models as specified by the patent law and its detailed rules and regulations for implementation, including the practical and new technical proposals on the shape and structure of the product or the combination of both .

External Form Design refer to the external form design specified by the patent law and its detailed rules and regulations for implementation, including the practical and new technical proposals on the structure, shape and color of the product or the combination of them.

卫生、体育 17

HEALTH AND SPORTS

卫生机构、床位及卫生技术人员数（单位：个，张，人）
Number of Health Care Institutions,Beds and Medical Technical Personnel (unit, perosn)

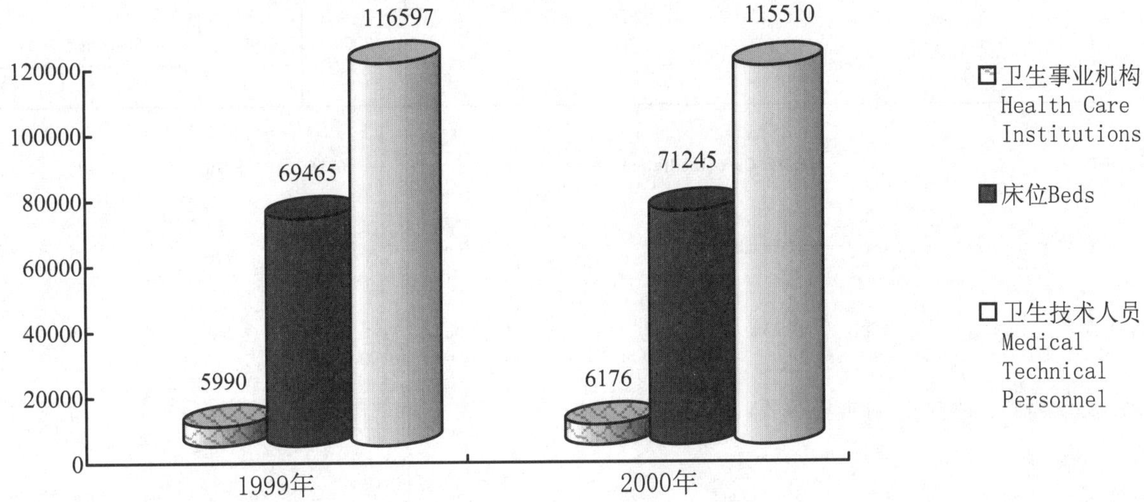

平均每千人拥有床位及医生数（单位：张，人）
Number of Beds and Doctors Per 1000 Persons (uint, perosn)

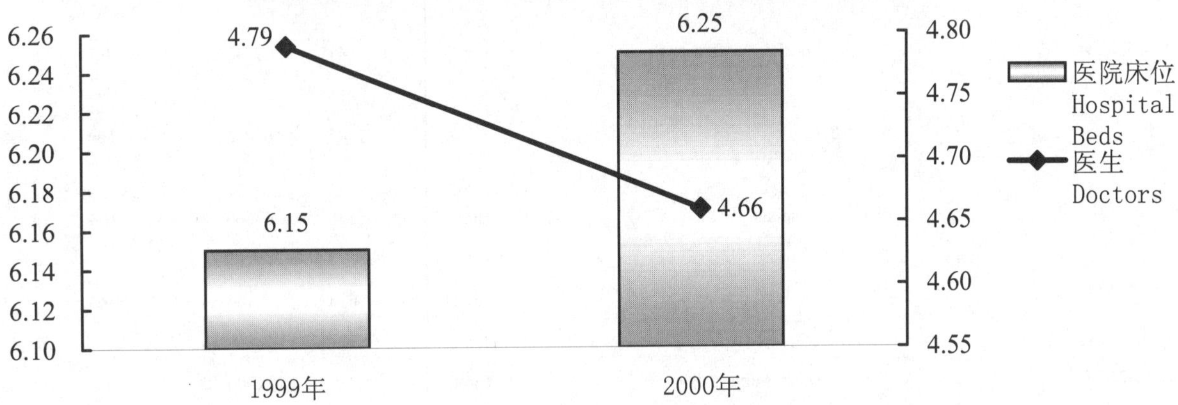

2000年运动员获奖牌情况（单位：块）
Medals Won in 2000 (piece)

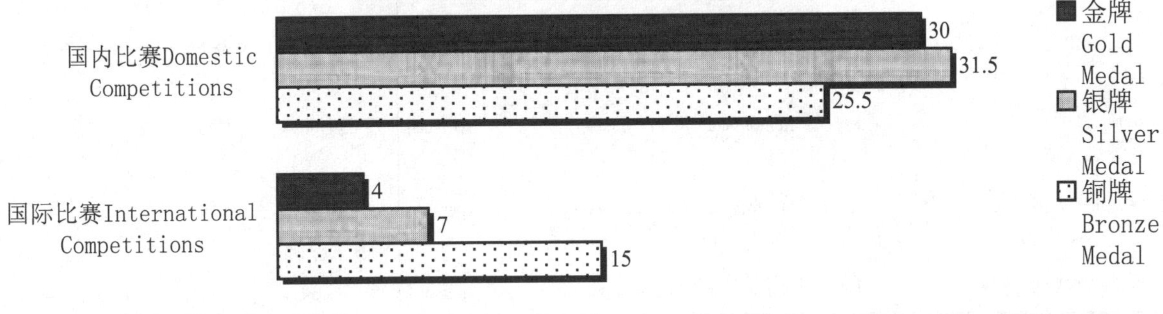

17-1 医疗卫生机构基本情况

BASIC STATISTICS FOR INSTITUTIONS OF PUBLIC HEALTH

项目		Item		2000	1999	构成(%) Composition(%) 2000	1999
卫生事业机构		**Health Care Institutions**		**6176**	**5990**	**100**	**100**
# 医　院	（个）	Hospitals	(unit)	458	460	7.4	7.8
门 诊 部	（个）	Clinics	(unit)	216	210	3.5	3.4
诊所、卫生保健所、医务室	（个）	Clinics and Health Stations	(unit)	5061	4859	81.9	80.6
疗 养 院	（个）	Sanatoriums	(unit)	4	5	0.1	0.1
卫生防疫站	（个）	Sanitation and Antiepidemic Stations	(unit)	21	22	0.3	0.4
妇幼保健所、站	（个）	Maternity and Child Care Centers	(unit)	8	8	0.1	0.2
专科防治所、站	（个）	Specialized Stations	(unit)	41	41	0.7	0.7
床　位		**Beds**		**71245**	**69465**	**100**	**100**
# 医　院	（张）	Hospitals	(unit)	65138	63660	91.4	91.4
门 诊 部	（张）	Clinics	(unit)	634	186	0.9	0.1
疗养院、所	（张）	Sanatoriums	(unit)	820	1000	1.2	1.8
平均每千人拥有医院床位	（张）	Hospitals Beds per 1000 Population	(unit)	6.25	6.15		
卫生技术人员		**Medical Technical Personnel**		**115510**	**116597**	**100**	**100**
# 医　生	（人）	Doctors	(person)	51570	52646	44.6	44.8
护师（士）	（人）	Senior and Junior Nurses	(person)	39900	39625	34.5	33.5
平均每千人拥有医生	（人）	Doctors per 1000 Population	(person)	4.66	4.79		
平均每千人拥有护士	（人）	Nurses per 1000 Population	(person)	3.60	3.60		

注：1996年开始，医院数仅包括县及县以上医院和其他医院，乡镇卫生院不再作为医院统计（下同）。
Note: Number of hospitals only included hospitals at county level and above and other hospitals from 1996, and township hospitals were no longer taken into account(the following as the same).

17-2 农村医疗卫生机构基本情况
HEALTH INSTITUTIONS IN RURAL AREA

项目		Item		2000	1999	构成（%）Composition(%) 2000	1999
卫生事业机构		**Health Care Institutions**		**838**	**861**	**100**	**100**
#医院	（个）	Hospitals	(unit)	62	63	7.4	7.3
乡（镇）卫生院	（个）	Township Hospitals	(unit)	110	117	13.1	13.6
床位		**Beds**		**11686**	**10385**	**100**	**100**
#医院	（张）	Hospitals	(unit)	8949	8413	76.6	81.0
乡（镇）卫生院	（张）	Township Hospitals	(unit)	1794	1609	15.4	15.5
卫生技术人员		**Medical Technical Personnel**		**14064**	**13733**	**100**	**100**
#医生	（人）	Doctors	(person)	7026	6931	50.0	50.5
护师（士）	（人）	Senior and Junior Nurses	(person)	3992	3836	28.4	27.9
乡村医生和卫生员		**Doctors and Health Workers**		**5617**	**5705**	**100**	**100**
#会接生的	（人）	Midwife	(person)	309	221	5.5	3.9
乡村医生	（人）	Doctors	(person)	5278	5391	94.0	94.5
卫生员	（人）	Health Workers	(person)	339	314	6.0	5.5

17-3 全市各饮食单位食品卫生合格率情况

FOOD QUALIFIED RATE OF FOOD AND BEVERAGE DEALERS

单位：% (%)

地区	Region	合计 Total	生产加工业 Processing	批发零售业 Wholesale and Retail	饮食服务业 Catering Services	集体食堂 Canteen	食品摊贩 Food Street Pedlar
合计	**Total**	**89.98**	**91.81**	**93.16**	**86.14**	**88.52**	**91.20**
东城区	Dongcheng	90.02	98.15	95.48	83.12	94.04	95.18
西城区	Xicheng	81.14	86.15	86.88	75.28	90.83	76.90
崇文区	Chongwen	98.68	93.93	97.52	92.08	97.56	90.64
宣武区	Xuanwu	89.66	83.72	80.74	88.00	79.93	96.03
朝阳区	Chaoyang	96.27	84.93	91.03	81.53	91.78	99.32
丰台区	Fengtai	84.47	88.94	88.61	86.63	76.97	84.26
石景山区	Shijingshan	94.33	89.90	95.35	88.14	96.12	96.34
海淀区	Haidian	79.91	70.87	79.74	64.16	67.48	82.33
门头沟区	Mentougou	98.64	88.40	99.73	98.26	98.75	96.64
房山区	Fangshan	99.54	99.69	99.82	99.38	98.88	99.46
通州区	Tongzhou	90.34	90.34	91.95	86.64	88.96	91.35
昌平区	Changping	96.67	97.36	98.49	97.16	98.83	93.44
顺义区	Shunyi	94.10	92.24	94.68	94.42	94.62	93.20
大兴县	Daxing	97.69	94.26	99.43	95.55	97.70	100.00
平谷县	Pinggu	98.53	95.11	99.31	98.19	98.38	98.29
怀柔县	Huairou	87.08	89.40	89.20	87.03	90.57	82.32
密云县	Miyun	84.59	85.63	91.93	83.05	91.24	80.03
延庆县	Yanqing	88.70	71.28	94.49	88.75	82.48	81.43

17-4 全市医院基本情况
BASIC STATISTICS FOR HOSPITALS

项目	Item	医院数（个）Hospitals (unit)	床位数（张）Beds (unit)	职工人数（人）Staff and Workers (person)	# 卫生技术人员 Medical Technical Personnel	中医师 Doctors of Chinese Medicine	西医师 Doctors of Western Medicine	中医士 Junior Doctors of Chinese Medicine
总计	**Total**	**458**	**65138**	**115629**	**87151**	**4191**	**28142**	**164**
县及县以上医院	**Hospitals at and above County Level**	**280**	**57931**	**104021**	**78281**	**3550**	**25346**	**97**
城市	Urban	228	49365	93179	69915	3121	22408	65
农村	Rural	52	8566	10842	8366	429	2938	32
其他医院	**Other Hospitals**	**178**	**7207**	**11608**	**8870**	**641**	**2796**	**67**
在县及县以上医院中	**Of Hospitals at and above County Level**							
综合医院	Comprehensive Hospitals	198	35968	66698	50575	1267	17870	45
中医医院	Hospitals of Chinese Medicine	22	3982	8144	6231	1629	880	39
医学院校附属医院	Hospitals Attached to Medical College	10	5513	11153	8715	499	2366	2
传染病院	Infectious Disease Hospitals	3	1193	1446	1061	8	301	
精神病院	Mental Hospitals	9	3809	2800	1988	24	470	4
结核病院	Tuberculosis Hospitals	1	518	598	406	1	94	
妇幼保健院	Hospitals for Maternity and Child Care	13	663	1726	1425	11	698	2
妇产医院	Hospitals for Gynecology and Obstetrics	2	439	1075	762	7	249	
儿童医院	Children's Hospitals	3	990	2341	1759	27	573	
职业病院	Hospitals for Occupational Diseases	1	250	250	126	3	39	
肿瘤医院	Tumor Hospitals	3	1363	2250	1398	2	454	
康复医院	Recovery Hospitals	5	911	1233	676	17	170	3
口腔医院	Stomatologital Hospitals	1	80	624	427		208	
骨科医院	Hospitals of Orthopedics	1	240	345	239	2	66	1
整形医院	Plastically Hospitals	1	328	445	210	1	85	
中西医结合医院	Hospitals which Integrate Traditional Chinese Therapeutics with Western Therapeutics in Practice	2	400	572	484	36	161	
其他专科医院	Other Specialized Hospitals	5	1284	2321	1799	16	662	1

17-4 续表 continued

项目	Item	西医士 Junior Doctors of Western Medicine	中西医结合医师 Doctors who Integrate Traditional Chinese Therapeutics with Western Therapeutics in Practice	其他中医 Other Doctors of Chinese Medicine	药师 Pharmacists	检验师 Laboratory Technicians	助产士 Midwifes	护师（士） Nurses
总计	**Total**	**1794**	**326**	**37**	**5142**	**2830**	**212**	**35487**
县及县以上医院	**Hospitals at and above County Level**	**1261**	**267**	**20**	**4519**	**2555**	**201**	**32831**
城市	Urban	1014	255	16	4041	2293	185	29569
农村	Rural	247	12	4	478	262	16	3262
其他医院	**Other Hospitals**	**533**	**59**	**17**	**623**	**275**	**11**	**2656**
在县及县以上医院中	**Of Hospitals at and above County Level**							
综合医院	Comprehensive Hospitals	902	52	8	2816	1749	120	21433
中医医院	Hospitals of Chinese Medicine	72	148	12	607	184	8	2030
医学院校附属医院	Hospitals Attached to Medical College	115	45		566	193	4	3561
传染病院	Infectious Disease Hospitals	15			54	77		511
精神病院	Mental Hospitals	48	1		84	32	1	1153
结核病院	Tuberculosis Hospitals				17	22		255
妇幼保健院	Hospitals for Maternity and Child Care	47	1		52	49	15	467
妇产医院	Hospitals for Gynecology and Obstetrics	10	1		28	44	49	319
儿童医院	Children's Hospitals	3	9		112	69		844
职业病院	Hospitals for Occupational Diseases	2			7	10		53
肿瘤医院	Tumor Hospitals		5		42	32		650
康复医院	Recovery Hospitals	5	2		31	19		301
口腔医院	Stomatologital Hospitals				12	8		117
骨科医院	Hospitals of Orthopedics	25			5	4		81
整形医院	Plastically Hospitals				6	5		105
中西医结合医院	Hospitals which Integrate Traditional Chinese Therapeutics with Western Therapeutics in Practice	6	1		33	15	4	215
其他专科医院	Other Specialized Hospitals	11	2		47	43		736

17-5 医院、卫生院工作情况
WORKS OF HOSPITALS

项目	Item	医院、卫生院（个）Hospiatls (unit)	诊疗人次数（万人次）Patients Treated (10000 person.time)	#门诊 Out-patients	健康检查人数（人）Health Check (person)	平均开放病床数（张）Beds in Use (unit)	入院人数（人）In-patients (person)
总计	**Total**	**654**	**6308.3**	**5563.9**	**2032736**	**65994**	**850388**
县及县以上医院合计	**Hospitals at and above County Level**	**277**	**5289.8**	**4651.0**	**1387161**	**56099**	**754316**
卫生部门医院合计	Hospitals of Health Care Department	118	3888.2	3486.7	674322	37286	579776
综合医院	Comprehensive Hospitals	50	2435.6	2135.9	382393	18579	333479
# 县医院	Countyship Hospitals	12	234.6	187.9	41343	2909	59503
中医医院	Hospitals of Chinese Medicine	18	355.1	332.5	48215	3440	39856
医学院校附属医院	Hospitals Attached to Medical College	10	616.5	565.0	30949	5430	98376
传染病院	Infectious Disease Hospitals	3	18.5	17.0	742	1050	8455
精神病院	Mental Hospitals	7	27.9	25.4	10253	2654	5690
结核病院	Tuberculosis Hospitals	1	3.1	3.0	300	521	3382
妇幼保健院	Hospitals for Maternity and Child Care	12	82.5	77.5	151086	592	20684
妇产医院	Hospitals for Gynecology and Obstetrics	2	31.1	30.3	1500	440	10038
儿童医院	Children's Hospitals	3	187.3	175.8	9488	955	22518
肿瘤医院	Tumor Hospitals	2	32.7	31.9	8197	1265	14527
康复医院	Recovery Hospitals	2	2.2	2.1		450	525
口腔医院	Stomatologital Hospitals	1	32.8	31.6	8750	80	634
整形医院	Plastically Hospitals	1	2.7	2.6	55	329	4295
中西医结合医院	Hospitals which Integrate Traditional Chinese Therapeutics with Western Therapeutics in Practice	1	33.9	31.4	11979	236	4078
其他专科医院	Other Specialized Hospitals	5	26.3	24.7	10415	1265	13239
工业及其他部门医院	Hospitals of Industry and Other Departments	151	1306.5	1098.5	649784	17374	160071
集体所有制医院	Collective-owned Hospitals	7	94.4	65.2	63058	1417	14454
其他医院合计	**Other Hospitals**	**167**	**465.6**	**398.2**	**306162**	**6398**	**36054**
卫生院合计	**Total Township Hospitals**	**210**	**553.0**	**514.7**	**339413**	**3497**	**60018**

17-5 续表 continued

项 目 Item		出院人数 (人) Leaving Hospital (person)	治愈率 (%) Recovering Rate (%)	好转率 (%) Mending Rate (%)	病死率 (%) Rate of Death of Illness (%)	病床周转次数 (次) Turnover Beds (times)	病床使用率 (%) Utilization Rate (%)	出院者平均住院日 (日) Average Hospitalization Period (day)
总 计	**Total**	**847503**	**57.89**	**35.59**	**2.40**	**12.84**	**68.82**	**18.18**
县及县以上医院合计	**Hospitals at and above County Level**	**753626**	**56.71**	**36.36**	**2.53**	**13.43**	**73.12**	**18.84**
卫生部门医院合计	Hospitals of Health Care Department	581514	56.59	36.27	2.38	15.60	80.50	18.35
综合医院	Comprehensive Hospitals	334011	56.31	36.69	2.56	17.98	80.72	16.06
# 县医院	Countyship Hospitals	59119	55.84	38.71	1.56	20.32	67.01	11.63
中医医院	Hospitals of Chinese Medicine	40913	40.88	51.43	3.39	11.89	73.77	22.00
医学院校附属医院	Hospitals Attached to Medical College	98230	58.68	33.48	2.05	18.09	84.50	16.83
传染病院	Infectious Disease Hospitals	8372	54.65	33.20	5.23	7.97	64.77	29.03
精神病院	Mental Hospitals	5640	40.56	55.32	1.12	2.13	99.57	157.23
结核病院	Tuberculosis Hospitals	3360	19.42	55.33	5.51	6.45	72.31	41.38
妇幼保健院	Hospitals for Maternity and Child Care	20492	95.31	3.50	0.08	34.61	68.90	6.92
妇产医院	Hospitals for Gynecology and Obstetrics	10867	84.13	13.16	0.31	24.70	87.41	11.37
儿童医院	Children's Hospitals	22440	58.31	35.64	0.72	23.50	84.32	12.37
肿瘤医院	Tumor Hospitals	14475	51.52	37.81	2.95	11.44	96.72	30.96
康复医院	Recovery Hospitals	523	63.29	32.54	1.39	1.16	18.13	51.37
口腔医院	Stomatologital Hospitals	619	91.52	7.94		7.74	44.33	20.70
整形医院	Plastically Hospitals	4295	92.66	7.05	0.10	13.05	71.27	21.45
中西医结合医院	Hospitals which Integrate Traditional Chinese Therapeutics with Western Therapeutics in Practice	4045	48.83	46.11	2.34	17.14	83.44	17.54
其他专科医院	Other Specialized Hospitals	13232	44.82	47.10	2.25	10.46	65.13	21.87
工业及其他部门医院	Hospitals of Industry and Other Departments	157846	56.66	37.07	3.10	9.09	58.43	20.88
集体所有制医院	Collective-owned Hospitals	14251	63.00	30.90	2.56	10.06	60.13	16.15
其他医院合计	**Other Hospitals**	**33273**	**51.13**	**41.86**	**3.41**	**5.20**	**48.89**	**25.02**
卫生院合计	**Total Township Hospitals**	**60604**	**75.26**	**23.35**	**0.29**	**17.33**	**36.37**	**6.30**

17-6 全市居民前十位死因顺位、死亡率及构成

顺位 No	死因名称	Cause of Death	死亡率（1/10万） Death Rate (1/100 thousand)	构成（%） Composition(%)
	全市	**Total**	**577.39**	**93.74**
1	脑血管病	Cerebrovasular Disease	164.85	26.76
2	心脏病	Heart Trouble	139.85	22.71
3	恶性肿瘤	Malignant Tumour	117.92	19.14
4	呼吸系病	Respiratory Disease	67.88	11.02
5	损伤和中毒	Trauma and Toxicosis	35.09	5.70
6	内分泌、营养、代谢及免疫病	Internal System, Nutrition, Metabolite And Immunity Disease	20.68	3.36
7	消化系病	Gigestive Disease	14.22	2.31
8	泌尿生殖系病	Urinary Disease	8.64	1.40
9	神经系病	Neuropathy	4.49	0.73
10	传染病	Infection Disease	3.77	0.61
	市	**District**	**561.24**	**94.33**
1	脑血管病	Cerebrovasular Disease	142.02	23.87
2	心脏病	Heart Trouble	140.83	23.67
3	恶性肿瘤	Malignant Tumour	127.28	21.39
4	呼吸系病	Respiratory Disease	66.26	11.13
5	损伤和中毒	Trauma and Toxicosis	26.81	4.51
6	内分泌、营养、代谢及免疫病	Internal System, Nutrition, Metabolite And Immunity Disease	23.61	3.97
7	消化系病	Gigestive Disease	16.26	2.73
8	泌尿生殖系病	Urinary Disease	9.09	1.53
9	神经系病	Neuropathy	4.98	0.84
10	传染病	Infection Disease	4.1	0.69
	县	**County**	**613.24**	**92.59**
1	脑血管病	Cerebrovasular Disease	215.56	32.55
2	心脏病	Heart Trouble	137.68	20.79
3	呼吸系病	Respiratory Disease	97.11	14.66
4	恶性肿瘤	Malignant Tumour	71.49	10.79
5	损伤和中毒	Trauma and Toxicosis	53.49	8.08
6	内分泌、营养、代谢及免疫病	Internal System, Nutrition, Metabolite And Immunity Disease	14.15	2.14
7	消化系病	Gigestive Disease	9.69	1.46
8	泌尿生殖系病	Urinary Disease	7.65	1.15
9	神经系病	Neuropathy	3.39	0.51
10	传染病	Infection Disease	3.03	0.46

17-7 全市0-6岁儿童系统管理情况

STATISTICS FOR SYSTEMATIC CARE OF CHILDREN AT AGE 0-6

地区 Region		0-6岁儿童数（人）Number of Children at Age 0-6 (person)	系统管理人数（人）Children Under Systematic Care (person)	体检人数（人）Children Having Health Check (person)	0-2岁儿童佝偻病患病率（%）Suffering Rate from Rickets of Children at Age 0-2 (%)	0-2岁儿童贫血患病率（%）Suffering Rate from Amenia of Children at Age 0-3 (%)	3-6岁儿童贫血患病率（%）Suffering Rate from Amenia of Children at Age 3-6 (%)	0-6岁儿童系统管理覆盖率（%）Covering Rate of Systematic Care of Children at Age 0-6 (%)
合　计	**Total**	**440132**	**430340**	**422877**	**0.63**	**4.99**	**1.52**	**97.78**
东城区	Dongcheng	16810	16810	16638	0.04	3.92	0.44	100.00
西城区	Xicheng	19022	19022	18975	0.03	3.30	0.61	100.00
崇文区	Chongwen	12261	12261	12140	0.00	6.41	0.69	100.00
宣武区	Xuanwu	10733	10733	10724	0.02	1.44	0.35	100.00
朝阳区	Chaoyang	54885	54419	54214	0.23	4.27	0.99	99.15
丰台区	Fengtai	32992	32992	32529	0.29	4.31	1.29	100.00
石景山区	Shijingshan	11712	11434	11313	0.14	4.06	0.88	97.63
海淀区	Haidian	61226	61196	60025	0.92	5.05	0.61	99.95
门头沟区	Mentougou	10701	10232	9353	2.60	7.35	2.28	95.62
房山区	Fangshan	39063	37305	37266	0.93	8.75	4.16	95.50
通州区	Tongzhou	26779	26779	25024	0.68	6.34	2.01	100.00
昌平区	Changping	19895	18809	18577	1.01	3.85	1.22	94.54
顺义区	Shunyi	21393	20751	21027	0.19	4.36	2.06	97.00
大兴县	Daxing	26184	26161	25532	0.66	3.43	0.75	99.91
平谷县	Pinggu	21593	19972	19640	1.00	9.43	4.50	92.49
怀柔县	Huairou	13774	13192	12427	0.34	6.85	2.56	95.77
密云县	Miyun	26832	24162	24418	1.70	2.71	0.98	90.05
延庆县	Yanqing	14277	14110	13055	0.90	5.42	1.71	98.83

17-8 全市婴儿、新生儿死亡率

DEATH RATE OF INFANT AND NEWBORN BABY

单位：%　　　　（%）

地区 Region		婴儿死亡率 Death Rate of Infant		新生儿死亡率 Death Rate of Newborn Baby	
		2000	1999	2000	1999
合　计	**Total**	**5.36**	**7.95**	**3.70**	**5.94**
区	District	6.29	7.78	4.26	5.74
县	County	4.05	8.38	2.91	6.45

17-9 农村改水情况
STATISTICS FOR WATER-CHANG IN RURAL AREA

项目		Item		2000	1999
农村总人口	（万人）	Total Rural Population	(10000 persons)	373.4	373.4
已改水累计受益人口	（万人）	Accumulative Population Benefited from Water-changing	(10000 persons)	372.8	372.8
饮用自来水		Using Tap Water			
现有水厂	（座）	Water Plants	(10000)	3848	3839
累计受益人口	（万人）	Accumulative Benefited Population	(10000 persons)	366.8	365.9
饮用水压机井水		Using Motor-pumped Water			
现有机井	（万台）	Motor-pumped Wells	(10000)	1.4	1.6
累计受益人口	（万人）	Accumulative Benefited Population	(10000 persons)	4.4	5.0
其他形式		Others			
累计受益人口	（万人）	Accumulative Benefited Population	(10000 persons)	1.7	1.9

17-10 体育场馆数
STADIUMS AND GYMNASIUMS

单位：个 (unit)

项目	Item	2000	1999
总　计	**Total**	**4673**	**4670**
体育场	**Stadiums**	**45**	**44**
甲级	First Class	2	2
乙级	Second Class	2	2
丙级	Third Class	5	4
丁级	Fourth Class	36	36
体育馆	**Gymnasiums**	**23**	**23**
甲级	First Class	2	2
乙级	Second Class	3	3
丙级	Third Class	8	8
丁级	Fourth Class	10	10
# 游泳跳水馆	Natatoriums	6	6
游泳池	Swimming Pools	208	206
有固定看台的灯光球场	Illuminated Fields with Fixed Seating	13	13
田径房	Athletic House	4	4
保龄球房	Bowling House	29	29
台球房	Billiards House	50	50
运动场	Sports Field	116	116
足球场	Football Field	49	49
网球场	Tennis Field	93	93
射击场	Shooting Field	18	18
轮滑场	Wheel-skating Field	5	5
篮球场	Basketball Field	2749	2749

注：各年份数据为截止到年底的累计体育场馆数。
Note: Data of each year is the accumulative one at the year-end.

17-11 群众体育活动情况
ACTIVITIES OF MASS SPORTS

项目		Item		2000	1999
举办县以上运动会次数	（次）	Sports Meetings above County Level	(time)	1840	3497
体委系统		Physical Culture and Sports Commissions		424	261
其他系统		Other Departments		1416	3236
参加县以上运动会运动员人数	（人次）	Athletes Attending Sports Meetings above County Level	(person.time)	1123907	3481313
体委系统		Physical Culture and Sports Commissions		632648	801271
其他系统		Other Departments		491259	2680042
举办乡镇运动会次数	（次）	Sports Meetings at Town and Township Level	(time)	266	413
参加乡镇运动会运动员人数	（人次）	Athletes Attending Sports Meetings at Town and Township Level	(person.time)	101227	116709
《国家体育锻炼标准达标人数》	（万人）	Number of Persons Who Have Come up to the State Physical Training Standards	(10000 persons)	142	143
优秀级	（万人）	Excellent	(10000 persons)	42	42
良好级	（万人）	Good	(10000 persons)	53	52
及格级	（万人）	Pass	(10000 persons)	47	49

17-12 分等级运动员发展人数情况
NUMBER OF CERTIFIED ATHLETES ADMITTED

单位：人 (person)

项目 Item		合计 Total	国家级健将 National Master	运动健将 Master Athletes	一级 First Grade Athletes	二级 Second Grade Athletes	三级 Third Grade Athletes	少年级 Juvenile Grade Athletes
总计	**Total**	**1817**	**5**	**62**	**256**	**982**	**274**	**238**
# 女性	Female	702	4	30	95	309	137	127

17-13 专职教练员获职称人数情况
NUMBER OF PROFESSIONAL TRAINERS GAINED TITLE

单位：人 (person)

项目 Item		合计 Total	高级职称 Senior	中级职称 Middle	初级职称 Junior
总计	**Total**	**533**	**99**	**216**	**218**
# 女性	Female	162	19	64	79

17-14 分等级裁判员发展人数情况
NUMBER OF CERTIFIED REFEREES ADMITTED

单位：人 (person)

项目 Item		合计 Total	国家级 National Referees	一级 First Grade Referees	二级 Second Grade Referees	三级 Third Grade Referees
总计	**Total**	**1103**	**47**	**99**	**526**	**431**
# 女性	Female	265	12	37	112	104

17-15 运动员获奖牌情况
STATISTICS ON MEDALS WON

单位：块 (piece)

项目 Item		金牌 Gold	银牌 Silver	铜牌 Bronze
合计	**Total**	**40.5**	**38.5**	**34**
国际比赛	International competitions	15	7	4
国内比赛	Domestic Competitions	25.5	31.5	30

17-16 北京市运动员获全国冠军名单
LIST OF NATIONAL CHAMPIONSHIPS BY ATHLETES OF BEIJING

比 赛 名 称 Matches		大项名称 Item		小 项 名 称 Item	姓 名 Name
全国田径锦标赛	The National Track-and-field Championships	田径	Track and Field	男子跳高	周忠革
全国田径锦标赛	The National Track-and-field Championships	田径	Track and Field	男子铅球	刘昊
全国田径锦标赛	The National Track-and-field Championships	田径	Track and Field	男子马拉松	战东林
全国田径冠军赛	The National Track-and-field Championships	田径	Track and Field	女子标枪	李蕾
全国花样游泳锦标赛	The National Figure Swimming Championships	花样游泳	Figure Swimming	八人集体	夏晔等8人
全国花样游泳冠军赛	The National Figure Swimming Championships	花样游泳	Figure Swimming	八人集体	夏晔等8人
全国跳水冠军赛	The National Diving Tournament	跳水	Diving	女子团体	
全国跳水冠军赛	The National Diving Tournament	跳水	Diving	女子双人跳台	李娜
全国武术个人套路锦标赛	The National Wushu Personal-way Championships	武术	Wushu	男子刀术	赵庆建
全国武术个人套路锦标赛	The National Wushu Personal-way Championships	武术	Wushu	男子棍术	简增蛟
全国武术个人套路锦标赛	The National Wushu Personal-way Championships	武术	Wushu	男子刀棍全能	赵庆建
全国武术个人套路锦标赛	The National Wushu Personal-way Championships	武术	Wushu	男子枪术	张继东
全国武术个人套路锦标赛	The National Wushu Personal-way Championships	武术	Wushu	女子长拳	刘清华
全国武术个人套路锦标赛	The National Wushu Personal-way Championships	武术	Wushu	女子刀术	王晓娜
全国武术个人套路锦标赛	The National Wushu Personal-way Championships	武术	Wushu	女子棍术	王晓娜
全国武术个人套路锦标赛	The National Wushu Personal-way Championships	武术	Wushu	女子刀棍全能	王晓娜
全国古典式摔跤冠军赛	The National Classical-wrestling Tournament	摔跤	Wrestling	58公斤级	张洋
全国古典式摔跤冠军赛	The National Classical-wrestling Tournament	摔跤	Wrestling	63公斤级	崔鹏
全国古典式摔跤冠军赛	The National Classical-wrestling Tournament	摔跤	Wrestling	76公斤级	高云飞
全国自由式摔跤冠军赛	The National Free-wrestling Tournament	摔跤	Wrestling	58公斤级	张帆
全国自由式摔跤冠军赛	The National Free-wrestling Tournament	摔跤	Wrestling	85公斤级	连春超
全国男子柔道冠军赛	The National Male Judo Tournament	柔道	Judo	66公斤级	康凯
全国男子柔道冠军赛	The National Male Judo Tournament	柔道	Judo	73公斤级	谢建华
全国男子柔道冠军赛	The National Male Judo Tournament	柔道	Judo	81公斤级	于志军
全国跆拳道锦标赛	The National Teekwondo Championships	跆拳道	Teekwondo	72公斤级	卢涛
全国射击（步枪）个人锦标赛	The National Personal Shooting(Rifle) Championships	射击	Shooting	男子自选步枪卧射	刘志伟
全国射击（飞碟）个人锦标赛	The National Personal Shooting(Flying Saucer) Championships	射击	Shooting	女子飞碟双多向	李清念
全国赛艇锦标赛	The National Rowing Championships	赛艇	Rowing	女子轻量级双人双桨	余华 傅凤君
全国自行车锦标赛	The National Cycling Championships	山地车	Cycling	女子越野赛	王慧敏
全国垒球总决赛	The National Finals of Soft-ball	垒球	Soft-ball	女子	北京
全国乒乓球锦标赛	The National Table Tennis Championships	乒乓球	Table Tennis	男子单打	侯英超
全国网球巡回赛总决赛	The National Circuit Finals of Tennis	网球	Tennis	男子双打	张宇 鲁凌
全国网球巡回赛总决赛	The National Circuit Finals of Tennis	网球	Tennis	男子团体	北京
首届全国体育大会	The First-run Sports Meeting	国际象棋	Chess	男子个人	叶江川
首届全国体育大会	The First-run Sports Meeting	围棋	Weiqi	男子个人	孔杰
全国围棋个人锦标赛	The National Personal Weiqi Championships	围棋	Weiqi	女子个人	徐莹
全国体操冠军赛	The National Gymnastics Tournament	体操	Gymnastics	男子吊环	谢建辉
全国体操冠军赛	The National Gymnastics Tournament	体操	Gymnastics	女子平衡木	白春月
全国棒球冠军赛	Zz	棒球	Baseball	棒球	北京队
全国曲棍球冠军赛	The National Hockey Tournament	曲棍球	Hockey	女子	北京队
全国射箭冠军赛	The National Archery Tournament	射箭	Archery	女团淘汰赛	张晓颖等4人
全国射箭冠军赛	The National Archery Tournament	射箭	Archery	男团淘汰赛	高宇等4人
全国射箭冠军宽	The National Archery Tournament	射箭	Archery	男子个人淘汰赛	张 峥

主要统计指标解释

等级运动员人数 指经考核正式批准授予等级运动员称号的人数。运动员等级分为国际级运动健将、运动健将、一级运动员、二级运动员、三级运动员、少年级运动员。

等级裁判员人数 指经考核正式批准授予等级裁判员称号的人数。裁判员等级分为国际级裁判、国家级裁判、一级裁判、二级裁判、三级裁判。

卫生技术人员 指卫生机构支付工资的全部固定职工和合同制职工中现任职务为卫生技术工作的专业人员。包括中医师、西医师、中西医结合医师、护师、中药师、西药师、检验师、其他技师、中医士、西医士、护士、助产士、中药剂士、西药剂士、检验士、其他技士、其他中医、护理员、中药剂员、西药剂员、检验员，其他初级卫生技术人员。

Explanatory Notes On Main Statistical Indicators

Number of Athletes in Grades refers to the number of athletes who have been given titles through examination. The titles of athletes include international masters of sports, masters of sports, first-grade, second-grade and third-grade sportsmen and young athletes.

Number of Referees in Grades refers to the number of referees who have been given titles through examination. They are classified as international referees, national referees and referees of the first, second and third grades.

Medical Technical Personnel refers to all permanent medical staff and workers employed by medical institutions, including doctors of Chinese and Western medicine, doctors who integrate traditional Chinese therapeutics with Western therapeutics in practice, senior nurses, pharmacists of Chinese and Western medicine, laboratory specialists, other specialists, paramedics of Chinese and Western medicine, nurses, midwives, druggists in Chinese and Western medicine, laboratory technicians, other technicians, other practitioners of Chinese medicine , nursing attendants, pharmacological workers of Chinese and Western medicine, laboratory workers, and other primary medical personnel.

城市公用事业 18

URBAN PUBLIC UTILITIES

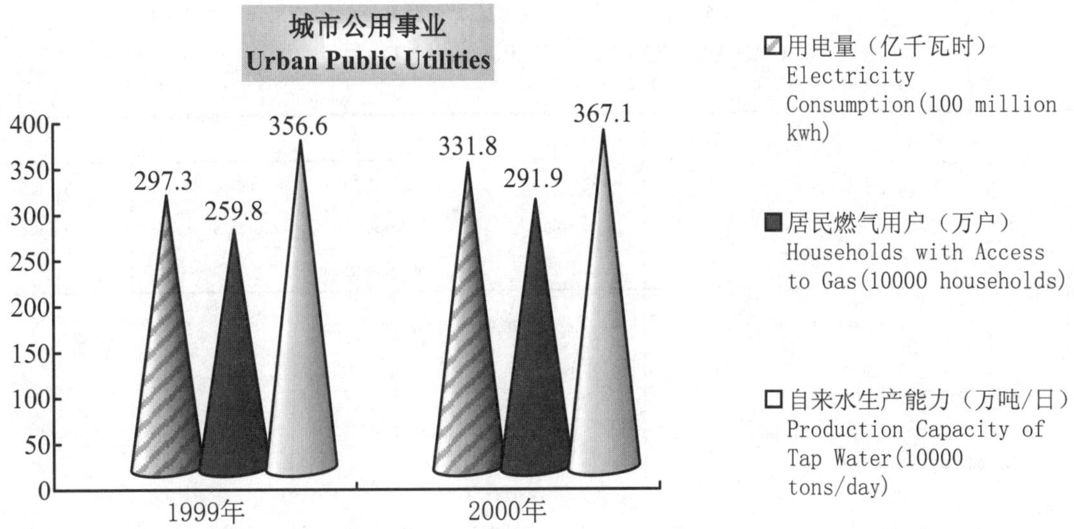
城市公用事业
Urban Public Utilities
400
350
300
250
200
150
100
50
0
297.3
259.8
356.6
331.8
291.9
367.1
1999年
2000年
用电量（亿千瓦时）
Electricity Consumption(100 million kwh)
居民燃气用户（万户）
Households with Access to Gas(10000 households)
自来水生产能力（万吨/日）
Production Capacity of Tap Water(10000 tons/day)

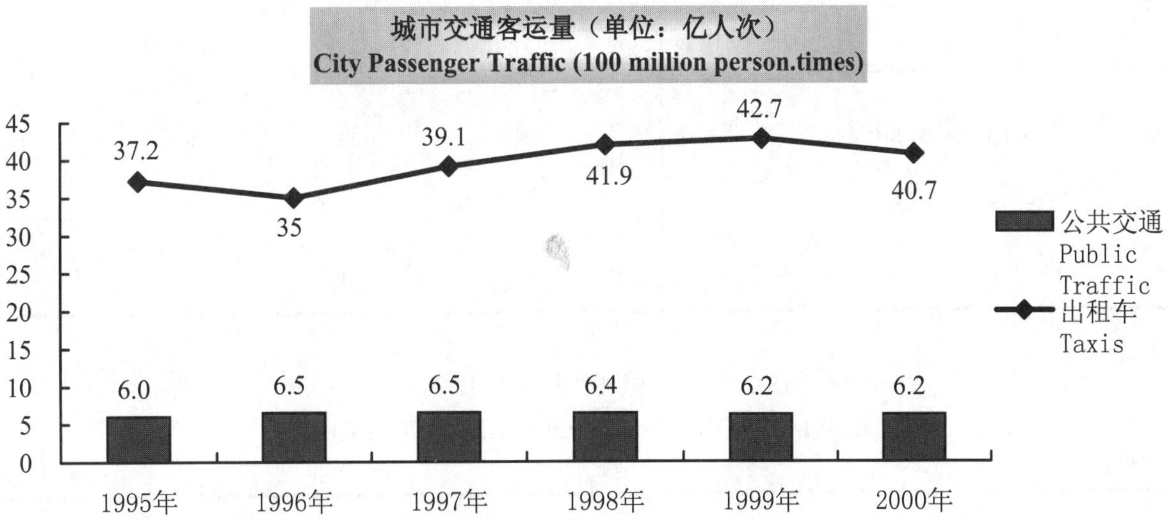
城市交通客运量（单位：亿人次）
City Passenger Traffic (100 million person.times)
45
40
35
30
25
20
15
10
5
0
37.2
35
39.1
41.9
42.7
40.7
6.0
6.5
6.5
6.4
6.2
6.2
1995年
1996年
1997年
1998年
1999年
2000年
公共交通
Public Traffic
出租车
Taxis

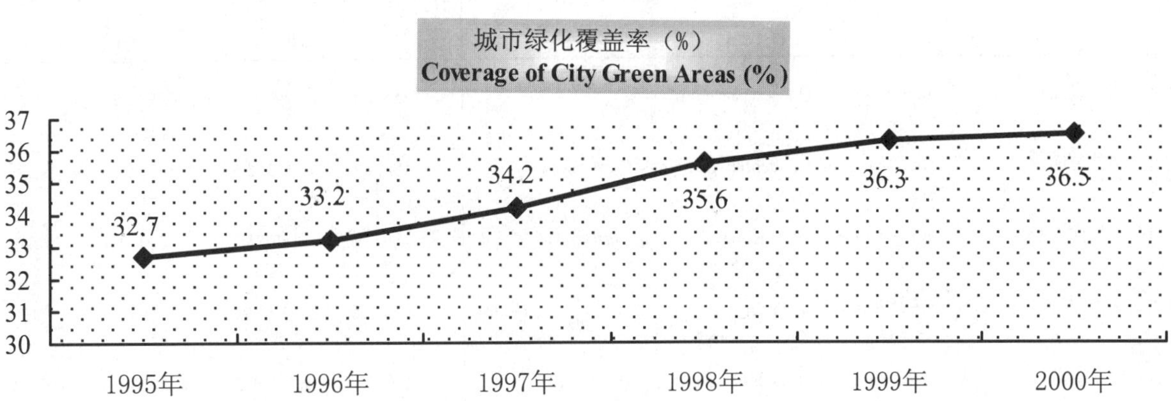
城市绿化覆盖率（%）
Coverage of City Green Areas (%)
37
36
35
34
33
32
31
30
32.7
33.2
34.2
35.6
36.3
36.5
1995年
1996年
1997年
1998年
1999年
2000年

18-1 城镇建设用地
URBAN CONSTRUCTION LAND

单位：公顷 (hectare)

项目	Item	全市 Total	城近郊区 City Proper and Near Suburbs	远郊区 Outer Suburbs	各县 Counties
合计	**Total**	**1379.9**	**672.8**	**331.0**	**376.1**
商业服务业用地	Commerce and Services	87.9	87.9		
工业和仓储用地	Industry and Stock	31.3	2.3	29.0	
交通用地	Transportation	581.8	237.4	184.2	160.3
市政公用设施及绿化用地	Municipal Public Facilities and Green Areas	200.1	121.6	42.3	36.2
公共建筑用地	Public Construction	138.1	7.1	2.3	128.7
住宅用地	Residential Buildings	159.9	112.3	30.5	17.2
特殊用地	Special Purposes	8.6	1.4	7.3	
其他用地	Others	172.3	102.9	35.6	33.7

18-2 城市居民居住水平
RESIDENTIAL CONDITIONS OF URBAN RESIDENTS

单位：万平方米 (10000 sq.m)

项目	Item	2000	#市区 City Proper and Near Suburbs	1999	#市区 City Proper and Near Suburbs
年末实有房屋建筑面积	Floor Space of Houses(year-end)	35530.6	29109.3	33272.5	27429.8
年末实有住宅建筑面积	Floor Space of Residential Buildings (year-end)	18638.6	15195.5	17234.4	14211.5
年末实有住宅居住面积	Living Space of Residential Building (year-end)	8623.6	7075.3	8046.9	6669.9
平均每人居住面积(平方米)	Per Capita Living Space (sq.m)	11.15	10.91	10.63	10.43
年末实有住宅使用面积	Using Space of Residential Buildings (year-end)	12961.7	10709.5	12026.4	10036.1
平均每人使用面积(平方米)	Per Capita Using Space (sq.m)	16.75	16.52	15.88	15.69

18-3 用　电　量 (北京地区)

ELECTRICITY CONSUMPTION(BEIJING AREA)

单位：万千瓦小时 (10000 kwh)

项目	Item	2000	1999	2000年为1999年% 2000 as % of 1999
合　计	**Total**	**3318171**	**2972629**	**111.6**
农、林、牧、渔、水利业	Farming,Forestry,Animals Husbandry,Fishery and Water Conservancy	130865	121242	107.9
# 排灌	Irrigation and Drainage	77393	71635	108.0
工业	Industry	1540797	1178523	130.7
按轻重工业分	Grouped by Heavy and Light Industry			
轻工业	Light Industry	304022	282405	107.7
重工业	Heavy Industry	1236775	1196118	103.4
按行业分	Grouped by Sectors			
采掘业	Excavation	73956	73236	101.0
采矿业	Minerals Mining	48960	47584	102.9
制造业	Manufacturing	1466841	1405287	104.4
食品、饮料和烟草制造业	Food,Beverage and Tobacco Production	66200	62677	105.6
纺织业	Textile Industry	40140	37832	106.1
石油加工业	Petroleum Processing	157429	132866	118.5
炼焦、煤气及煤制品业	Coking,Gas and Coal Products	19367	16226	119.4
化学工业	Chemical Industry	154514	169310	91.3
建筑材料及其他非金属矿制品业	Construction Materials and Other Nonmetal Minerals Products	160460	152980	104.9
黑色金属冶练及压延加工业	Smelting and Pressing of Ferrous Metals	370366	374178	99.0
金属制品业	Metal Products	35501	32866	108.0
机械工业	Machinery Manufacturing	50155	48726	102.9
交通运输、电气、电子设备制造业	Transportations,Electric and Electronic Equipment Manufacturing	117081	108403	108.0
电力、蒸汽热水生产和供应业	Electricity,Steam and Hot Water Production and Supply	117778	108283	108.8
自来水生产和供应	Tap Water Production and Supply	24968	25596	97.5
建筑业	Construction	105712	103454	102.2
地质普查和勘探业	Geological Survey and Prospecting	1027	1383	74.3
交通运输、邮电通信业	Transportations,Posts and Telecommunications	114135	98521	115.8
商业、公共饮食业、物资供销和仓储业	Commerce,Catering,Capital Goods Distribution and Storage	341443	266741	128.0
其他事业	Others	607717	546189	111.3
# 市内公共交通业	Municipal Public Transportation	22717	8667	262.1
# 路灯业	Road Lamps	9155	7964	115.0
城乡居民生活用电	Electricity Consumption by Urban and Rural Households	476475	356576	133.6
乡　村	Rural	91079	79934	113.9
城　市	Urban	385396	276642	139.3

18-4 供　　热
HEAT SUPPLY

项　目		Item		2000	1999	2000年为1999年% 2000 as % of 1999
全市采暖面积合计	**（万平方米）**	**Total Heating Area**	**(10000 sq.m)**	**10859.6**	**9991.7**	**108.7**
集中供热		Central Heat Supply				
热力供应能力	（百万千焦/小时）	Supply Capacity	(10^9 joule/hour)	16998	15198	111.8
采暖单位	(户)	Heat Users	(unit)	3304	3142	105.2
采暖面积	(万平方米)	Heating Area	(10000sq.m)	5012.6	4145.4	120.9
管道长度	(公里)	Length of Pipeline	(km)	254	242	105.0
销售量	(万百万千焦)	Volume Supplied	(10^13 joule)	2414.7	1986.5	121.6
小区集中供热		Central Heat Supply in Residential Districts				
采暖面积	(万平方米)	Heating Area	(10000 sq.m)	5657.5	5622.9	100.6
余热供热		Surplus Heat Supply				
采暖面积	(万平方米)	Heating Area	(10000 sq.m)	189.5	223.4	84.8

注：小区集中供热、联片供热、余热供热统计范围为市区10万平米以上的供热面积。

Note: Figures for central heat supply in residential districts,joint heat supply and surplus heat supply only include those who heating areas are more than 100000 sq.m.

18-5 供　　气
STEAM SUPPLY

项　目		Item		2000	1999	2000年为1999年% 2000 as % of 1999
蒸气供应能力	(吨／小时)	Supply Capacity	(ton/hour)	1350	1350	100.0
用气单位	(个)	Steam Users	(unit)	130	119	109.2
# 工　业	(个)	Industry	(unit)	130	119	109.2
管道长度	(公里)	Length of Pipeline	(km)	42	42	100.0
销售量	(万吨)	Volume Supplied	(10000 tons)	359.2	352.2	102.0
# 工　业	(万吨)	Industry	(10000 tons)	359.2	352.2	102.0

18-6 煤气、液化石油气及天然气
GAS,LIQUEFIED PETROLEUM GAS AND NATURAL GAS

项目		Item		2000	1999	2000年为1999年% 2000 as % of 1999
煤　气		**Gas**				
管道长度	(公里)	Length of Pipeline	(km)	544.8	1217.7	44.7
供应量	(万立方米)	Gas Supply	(10000 cu.m)	60066.0	74682.2	80.4
销售量	(万立方米)	Gas Sale	(10000 cu.m)	46718.9	61845.6	75.5
# 工业用	(万立方米)	for Industrial Use	(10000 cu.m)	8833.8	9581.1	92.2
生活用	(万立方米)	for Living Use	(10000 cu.m)	36430.7	47385.3	76.9
用　户	(万户)	Consumer	(10000 households)	35.9	48.9	73.4
# 家庭用户	(万户)	Household	(10000 households)	35.6	46.9	75.9
液化石油气		**Liquefied Petroleum Gas**				
储气能力	(吨／罐)	Storage Capability	(ton/tank)	22100/82	21803/81	
# 燃气集团	(吨／罐)	Gas Group	(ton/tank)	18000/49	18000/49	
供应站	(个)	Supply Units	(unit)	220	216	101.9
# 燃气集团	(个)	Gas Group	(unit)	84	80	105.0
液化气钢瓶	(万个)	Tanks	(10000)	147.0	142.9	102.9
销售量	(吨)	Gas Sales	(ton)	190570.7	188450.0	101.1
# 工业用	(吨)	for Industrial Use	(ton)	2472.0	2458.5	100.5
生活用	(吨)	for Living Use	(ton)	186518	185959	100.3
用　户	(万户)	Consumer	(10000 households)	124.5	113.9	109.3
# 家庭用户	(万户)	Household	(10000 households)	122.1	109.5	111.5
天然气		**Natural Gas**				
管道长度	(公里)	Length of Pipeline	(km)	4231.6	3277.3	129.1
供应量	(万立方米)	Gas Supply	(10000 cu.m)	109725.2	75833.7	144.7
销售量	(万立方米)	Gas Sales	(10000 cu.m)	95918.6	64833.0	147.9
# 工业用	(万立方米)	for Industrial Use	(10000 cu.m)	3967.4	3759.0	105.5
生活用	(万立方米)	for Living Use	(10000 cu.m)	90997.9	61040.4	149.1
用　户	(万户)	Consumer	(10000 households)	135.4	105.0	129.0
# 家庭用户	(万户)	Household	(10000 households)	134.2	103.4	129.8
居民燃气用户	**(万户)**	**Household with Access to Gas**	**(10000 households)**	**291.9**	**259.8**	112.4
气化率	(%)	Percentage of Population Using Gas	(%)	99.3	97.1	

18-7 自来水及自备水源
TAP WATER AND SELF-PROVIDED SOURCE OF WATER

项目		Item		2000	# 城近郊区 City Propers and Near Suburbs	1999	# 城近郊区 City Propers and Near Suburbs
自来水		**Tap Water**					
水　厂	(个)	Water Plants	(unit)	20	10	20	10
生产能力	(万吨／日)	Production Capacity	(10000 tons/day)	367.1	310.7	356.6	304.6
管线长度	(公里)	Length of Pipelines	(km)	7610.4	6042.6	7178.5	5741.3
供水面积	(平方公里)	Area of Water Supply	(sq.km)	725.3	558.9	722.9	549.9
售水量	(万吨)	Sales in Volume	(10000 tons)	75363.9	65880.9	78098.0	67533.7
# 工业用	(万吨)	for Industrial Use	(10000 tons)	12516.4	9798.4	13432.9	10983.8
生活用	(万吨)	for Living Use	(10000 tons)	58850.7	52720.7	60243.2	53059.1
平均每人每日生活用水	(公斤)	Living Consumption Per Day	(kg)	240.2	259.6	250.1	266.8
自来水普及率	(%)	Percentage of Population Using Tap Water	(%)	100	100	100	100
自备水源		**Self-provided Source of Water**					
生产能力	(万吨／日)	Production Capacity	(10000 tons/day)	594.9	279.4	291.7	202.7
用水量	(万吨)	Consumption	(10000 tons)	54717.0	34754.2	46426.4	36251.2
# 生产用	(万吨)	Production	(10000 tons)	24599.7	14238.5	23922.1	16760.7
生活用	(万吨)	Living	(10000 tons)	26041.9	16699.2	22472.3	19458.4

18-8 节　　水
WATER SAVING

项目		Item		2000	1999	2000年为1999年% 2000 as % of 1999
节水量	(万吨)	Volume Saved	(10000 tons)	4450.7	2051.0	217.0
自来水	(万吨)	Tap Water	(10000 tons)	2076.1	1469.0	141.3
自备水井	(万吨)	Self-Provided Well	(10000 tons)	2374.6	582.0	408.0
完成节水措施	(项)	Save Measures Completed	(item)	381	141	270.2

注：节水量中未包括河水节水量。
Note:Volume saved excluded river water.

18-9 公共交通
PUBLIC TRAFFIC

项目		Item		2000	# 城近郊区 City Propers and Near Suburbs	1999	# 城近郊区 City Propers and Near Suburbs
年末营运车辆	**(辆)**	**Operating Vehicles (year-end)**	**(unit)**	**14191**	**12741**	**12509**	**11029**
公共汽车	(辆)	Buses	(unit)	12976	11526	11472	9992
# 小公共汽车	(辆)	Mini-Buses	(unit)	3251	2178	3886	2721
无轨电车	(辆)	Trolley Buses	(unit)	628	628	546	546
地铁机车	(辆)	Subways	(unit)	587	587	491	491
营运线路		**Operating Routes**					
条　数	(条)	Number	(line)	682	611	750	602
公共汽车	(条)	Buses	(line)	666	595	735	587
# 小公共汽车	(条)	Mini-Buses	(line)	222	159	340	200
无轨电车	(条)	Trolley Buses	(line)	14	14	13	13
地　铁	(条)	Subways	(line)	2	2	2	2
长　度	(公里)	Length	(km)	15638.8	15514.2	16566.2	12641.6
公共汽车	(公里)	Buses	(km)	15411.1	15286.5	16354.5	12429.9
# 小公共汽车	(公里)	Mini-Buses	(km)	4151.7	2441.7	6800.0	3000.0
无轨电车	(公里)	Trolley Buses	(km)	173.7	173.7	158.0	158.0
地　铁	(公里)	Subways	(km)	54.0	54.0	53.7	53.7
里程利用率		**Utilization Rate of Mileage**					
公共汽车	(%)	Buses	(%)	95.3	96.5	93.6	93.9
# 小公共汽车	(%)	Mini-Buses	(%)	90.3	90.5	89.4	89.1
无轨电车	(%)	Trolley Buses	(%)	100	100	99.8	99.8
地　铁	(%)	Subways	(%)	99.6	99.6	99.8	99.8
客运量	**(万人次)**	**Passengers Carried**	**(10000 person.times)**	**406691.0**	**396121.7**	**426706.0**	**415919.2**
按车种分		By Type of Vehicles					
公共汽车及无轨电车	(万人次)	Buses and Trolley Buses	(10000 person.times)	363213.0	352643.7	378483.0	367696.3
# 小公共汽车	(万人次)	Mini-Buses	(10000 person.times)	15717.9	12098.9	19087.2	15157.6
地　铁	(万人次)	Subways	(10000 person.times)	43478.0	43478.0	48222.9	48222.9
按购票方式分		By Ways of Payment					
普　票	(万人次)	Common	(10000 person.times)	133277.0	129095.7	116189.0	111631.8
月　票	(万人次)	Monthly	(10000 person.times)	266036	260189.0	305570	299894.7
包　车	(万人次)	Hire	(10000 person.times)	2833.5	2379.0	3287.2	2802.9
旅　游	(万人次)	Tourism	(10000 person.times)	390.0	361.0	381.1	358.3
免　费	(万人次)	Free of Charge	(10000 person.times)	4153.8	4098.0	1279.2	1231.4
售出月票	**(万张)**	**Monthly Ticket Sales**	**(10000)**	**1875.8**	**1836.4**	**1969.4**	**1931.3**
客运收入	**(万元)**	**Revenue of Passengers Traffic**	**(10000 yuan)**	**258004.6**	**243446.6**	**182704**	**172586.0**

18-10 客运出租汽车
TAXIS SERVICE

项目		Item		2000	1999	2000年为1999年% 2000 as % of 1999
出租汽车营运单位		**Operating Units**		**1811**	**2185**	**82.9**
国有单位	(个)	State-Owned	(unit)	204	398	51.3
集体单位	(个)	Collective-Owned	(unit)	293	469	62.5
个体户	(个)	Individuals	(unit)	1164	1164	100.0
中外合资	(个)	Joint Venture	(unit)		4	
其他	(个)	Others	(unit)	150	150	100.0
营运车辆	**(辆)**	**Operating Vehicles**	**(unit)**	**65127**	**61920**	**105.2**
小轿车	(辆)	Cars	(unit)	62613	59485	105.3
旅行车	(辆)	Wagon Cars	(unit)	501	1162	43.1
大轿车	(辆)	Coaches	(unit)	2013	1273	158.1
客运量		**Passengers Carried**		**62406**	**61817**	**101.0**
小轿车	(万人次)	Cars	(10000 person.times)	59770	59111	101.1
旅行车	(万人次)	Wagon Cars	(10000 person.times)	483	1145	42.2
大轿车	(万人次)	Coaches	(10000 person.times)	2153	1561	137.9
里程利用率		**Utilization Rate of Mileage**				
小轿车	(%)	Cars	(%)	66	67	
旅行车	(%)	Wagon Cars	(%)	84	85	
大轿车	(%)	Coaches	(%)	88	87	

18-11 交通管理设施
UTILITIES OF TRANSPORTATION ADMINISTRATION

项目		Item		2000	1999	2000年为1999年% 2000 as % of 1999
交通警岗	(个)	Police Boxes	(unit)	1880	2760	68.1
灯岗	(个)	Lamp Posts	(unit)	105	940	11.2
巡逻岗	(个)	Patrol Posts	(unit)	1775	1820	97.5
信号灯	(座)	Traffic Lights	(unit)	1036	940	110.2
# 自动信号灯	(座)	Automatic	(unit)	1036	940	110.2
安全示意线	(公里)	Signal Lines for Safety	(km)	9320	7469	124.8
交通标志	(面)	Transportation Signal	(unit)	48221	46289	104.9
隔离墩	(套)	Separate Blocks	(set)	4590	8453	54.3
护栏	(米)	Protective Fences	(m)	227947	204403	111.5

18-12 道路及桥梁
ROADS AND BRIDGES

项目		Item		2000	# 城近郊区 City Proper and and Near Suburb	1999	# 城近郊区 City Proper and and Near Suburb
道　路		**Roads**					
道路长度	(公里)	Length	(km)	4125.8	3623.9	3753.2	3277.3
按质量分		By Quality					
# 高　级	(公里)	Senior	(km)	1876.0	1705.9	1777.4	1616.2
次高级	(公里)	Secondary Senior	(km)	1681.1	1353	1481.9	1170.2
按车辆运行方式分		By Operating Ways of Vehicles					
# 快慢车分行路	(公里)	Separate Routes of Quick and Slow Vehicles	(km)	513.1	336.0	417.7	276.0
道路面积	(万平方米)	Areas of Roads	(10000 sq.m)	4921.4	4198.8	4353.0	3654.4
按质量分		By Quality					
# 高　级	(万平方米)	Senior	(10000 sq.m)	3243.1	2960.3	2864.1	2592.3
次高级	(万平方米)	Secondary Senior	(10000 sq.m)	1354.4	906.5	1288.9	867.1
按车辆运行方式分		By Operating Ways of Vehicles					
# 快慢车分行路	(万平方米)	Separate Routes of Quick and Slow	(10000 sq.m)	1519.6	1144.0	1196.4	878.0
铺装步路	(万平方米)	Paved Roads	(10000 sq.m)	739.2	588.1	628.6	486.9
桥　梁		**Bridges**					
城市桥梁	(座)	City Bridges	(unit)	834	715	787	665
# 大型道路立交桥	(座)	Large Flyovers	(unit)	149	121	141	113
行人过街天桥	(座)	Overpass	(unit)	182	180	149	147
地下通道	**(座／处)**	**Underpass**	**(unit/place)**	**183/138**	**155/110**	**174/131**	**147/104**

18-13 城市路灯设施
STREET LAMPS

项目		Item		2000	# 城近郊区 City Proper and and Near Suburb	1999	# 城近郊区 City Proper and and Near Suburb
路灯盏数	**(盏)**	**Number of Road Lamps**	**(unit)**	**200384**	**156733**	**183576**	**148143**
# 白炽灯	(盏)	Incandescent Lamps	(unit)	21164	16290	20129	16547
汞　灯	(盏)	Mercury Lamps	(unit)	81364	69390	79803	67818
钠　灯	(盏)	Sodium Lamps	(unit)	95364	69625	81718	63149
线路长度	**(公里)**	**Length of Lines**	**(km)**	**5159.4**	**3684.9**	**4952.4**	**3560.2**

18-14 城市园林绿化
GARDENS AND PLANTED AREAS

项目		Item		2000	# 城近郊区 City Proper and and Near Suburb	1999	# 城近郊区 City Proper and and Near Suburb
年末公共绿地面积	(公顷)	Public Green Areas(year-end)	(hectare)	7140	5513	6457	4989
平均每人占有公共绿地面积(包括水面)	(平方米)	Per Capita Public Green Areas (including water surface)	(sq.m)	9.7	8.7	9.1	8.2
城市绿化覆盖率	(%)	Coverage of City Green Areas	(%)	36.5	36.3	36.3	35.3
道路绿化总长度	(公里)	Total Length of Green Roads	(km)	2301	1795	2600	2115
年末实有树木	(万株)	Trees(year-end)	(10000)	4150	3191	4865	3758
# 本年新植	(万株)	Newly Planted	(10000)	481	344	309	224
全年出圃苗木	(万株)	Total Nursery Stage	(10000)	119	115	118	118
苗圃面积	(公顷)	Areas of Nursery	(hectare)	413	326	651	651
草坪面积	(万平方米)	Areas of Lawn	(10000 sq.m)	5648	4573	4602	3526
# 本年新植	(万平方米)	Newly Planted	(10000 sq.m)	423	251	565	427
公园个数	(个)	Parks	(unit)	128	96	117	95
公园面积	(公顷)	Areas of Parks	(hectare)	4848	4192	4320	3856
全年游园人数	(万人次)	Visitors to Parks and Zoos	(10000 person.times)	8540	7849	8756	8284

注：根据2000年开展的全市范围的园林普查，1999年数据有所调整。
Note: Data of 1999 has been adjusted according to gardens survey of Beijing in 2000.

18-15 城 市 排 水
DRAINAGE

项目 Item				2000	# 城近郊区 City Proper and and Near Suburb	1999	# 城近郊区 City Proper and and Near Suburb
下水道长度	**(公里)**	**Length of Sewer**	**(km)**	**4846.9**	**4146.1**	**4737.1**	**4067.2**
雨水管	(公里)	Rain Pipes	(km)	1477.7	1342.7	1391.0	1273.8
污水管	(公里)	Sewage Pipes	(km)	1852.1	1691.2	1753.7	1631.9
雨污合流管	(公里)	Rain and Sewage Pipes	(km)	1517.1	1112.2	1592.4	1161.5
污水处理		**Dispose of Sewage**					
处理厂	(个)	Disposal Plants	(unit)	4	4	4	4
处理能力	(万吨／日)	Disposal Capability	(10000 tons/day)	128.5	128.5	58.5	58.5
处理量	(万吨)	Disposed Volume	(10000 tons)	37031.1	35094.8	25440.5	23725.0
处理率	(%)	Disposal Rate	(%)	39.4	39.4	25.0	25.0
平均每日污水量	(万吨)	Daily Sewage	(10000 tons)	257.5	244.3	278.8	260.0

18-16 城 市 环 境 卫 生
MUNICIPAL ENVIRONMENT AND SANITATION

项目 Item				2000	# 城近郊区 City Proper and and Near Suburb	1999	# 城近郊区 City Proper and and Near Suburb
工作量		**Work Load**					
清扫街道面积	(万平方米／日)	Area Cleaned	(10000 sq.m/day)	6014.7	5098.4	5574.0	4705.0
清运垃圾	(万吨)	Garbage Disposal	(10000 tons)	583.9	489.3	505.0	449.5
清运粪便	(万吨)	Night Soil Disposal	(10000 tons)	274.0	249.2	298.0	273.5
环卫机械数量	**(辆)**	**Number of Environmental Sanitation Equipment**	**(unit)**	**2998**	**2592**	**3184**	**2868**
大中型扫尘车	(辆)	Large and Medium Road Sweepers	(unit)	165	149	170	151
大中型洒水车	(辆)	Large and Medium Watering Cars	(unit)	125	115	136	125
大中型垃圾车	(辆)	Large and Medium Dustcarts	(unit)	1552	1320	1892	1671
真空吸粪车	(辆)	Vacuum Dung-drawer Carts	(unit)	543	484	497	444
其他环卫车辆	(辆)	Others	(unit)	613	524	489	477
环卫设施		**Environmental Sanitation Facilities**					
垃圾桶	(个)	Garbage Cans	(unit)	12717	5100	12327	5092
果皮箱	(个)	Dustbins	(unit)	11729	9500	12643	10877
公共厕所	(座)	Lavatories	(unit)	5488	5096	6535	5900
密闭式集装箱垃圾站	(座)	Airtight Container Caerbage Stations	(unit)	734	715	791	757

注：由于环卫部门机构调整，2000年环卫指标的统计口径有所变化。
Note: Data calibre of 2000 has been adjusted because of the agency changing.

18-17 北京市环境保护基本情况
BASIC STATISTICS FOR ENVIRONMENT PROTECTION

项 目 Item			2000	1999
工业废水排放量达标率	(%) Percentage of Industrial Waste Water up to the Standards for Discharge	(%)	92.6	83.7
工业固体废物综合利用率	(%) Percentage of Industrial Solid Wastes Utilized	(%)	72.4	
烟尘控制区面积	(平方公里) Soot Controlling Area	(sq.km)	490.1	488.3
环境噪声达标区面积	(平方公里) Area of Environmental Noise up to the Standard	(sq.km)	348.9	321.8
自然保护区面积	(万公顷) Nature Protection Area	(10000 hectare)	6.8	5.0

18-18 空气污染指数监测情况
MINITORING STATISTICS FOR AIR POLLUTION INDEX

单位：天 (day)

首要污染物 First Pollutant / 污染指数 Pollution Index		可吸入颗粒物 Pellet can be Breathe in	二氧化氮 Nitrogen Dioxide	二氧化硫 Sulphur Dioxide	合 计 Total
合 计	**Total**	**312**	**6**	**48**	**366**
一 级	First Grade	9	2	3	14
二 级	Second Grade	133	2	28	163
三 级	Third Grade	147	2	17	166
四 级	Fourth Grade	16			16
五 级	Fifth Grade	7			7

单位：毫克/立方米 (mg/cu.m)

污染物 Pollutant / 年 份 Year	可吸入颗粒物 Pellet can be Breathe in	二氧化氮 Nitrogen Dioxide	二氧化硫 Sulphur Dioxide
2000	0.353	0.123	0.071
1999	0.364	0.14	0.08
2000年为1999年% 2000 as % of 1999	90	92	89

注：上表反映全年被监测的三种主要污染物成为首要污染物的天数分布。

Note: The top table indicates day-distribution of the three main pollutant supervised in the whole year.

主 要 统 计 指 标 解 释

年底自来水生产能力 是指城市供水设施取水、净水、送水、出厂输水干管等环节的综合生产能力，按设计能力（以四个环节中最薄弱环节为主）计算。在设计生产能力的基础上，经挖、革、改增加的生产能力，应按一次或数次增加的设计生产能力总和加原设计生产能力求得。

气化率 是指使用燃气（包括人工煤气、液化石油气、天然气）的城市非农业人口数（不包括临时人口和流动人口）与城市非农业人口总数之比。计算公式：

$$\text{气化率} = \frac{\text{城市非农业用气人口数}}{\text{城市非农业人口总数}} \times 100\%$$

城市桥梁 是指城市范围内，修建在河道上的桥梁和道路与道路立交、道路跨越铁路的立交桥，以及人行天桥。包括永久性桥和半永久性桥，不包括临时性桥、铁路桥、涵洞。

城市下水道总长度 是指汇集和排放污水、废水和雨水的管渠及其附属设施所组成的系统。长度按所有排水总管、干管、支管及检查井，联接井进出水口等长度之和计算，不包括雨水口至排水管道间的联接管、进户管及明渠。

城市污水日处理能力 是指污水处理厂每昼夜处理污水量的设计能力。

营运线路长度 是指公共交通全部运营线路的长度之和。

公共绿地 是指向公众开放的各级各类公园，小游园、街头绿地等，包括其范围内的水域。

Explanatory Notes On Main Statistical Indicators

Production Capacity of Tap Water at Year-end refers to the comprehensive production capacity such as water inflow, purification, conveyance and outflow of the trunk pipelines into account of the urban water-suppling construction, counted according to designed capacity(taking the weakest link of the above four as the principal one). The incremental capacity through innovation and reproduction on the bases of designed capacity, will be the sum of original designed capacity and incremental ones through one time or several times.

Percentage of Urban Gas Users refers to the ratio of the urban non-agricultural population using gas（including gas, liquefied petroleum gas and natural gas ）to the total of urban non-agricultural population （excluding temporary and mobile population）. The formula is:

$$\text{Percentage of Urban Gas Users} = \frac{\text{Urban Non-agricultural gas users}}{\text{Urban Non-agricultural Population}} \times 100\%$$

Urban Bridges refer to bridges over river courses, great separated junctions and overpasses in urban areas, including permanent bridges and semi-permanent bridges, excluding temporary bridges, railway bridges and culverts.

Length of Urban Sewage Pipes refers to the total length of general drainage, trunks, branches and blind drainage, inspection wells, connection wells, inlets and outlets, etc.

Daily Disposal Capacity of Urban Sewage refers to the designed 24-hour capacity of sewage disposal at the sewage works.

Length of Routes in Operation refers to the sum length of all routes in operation of public traffic.

Public Green Area refers to green areas of various parks, amusement parks and green-land streets opened to the public, including waters within the above region.

北京统计年鉴——2001

BEIJING STATISTICAL YEARBOOK

人民生活 19

PEOPLE'S LIVELIHOOD

居民人均收入（单位：元）
Income Per Capita (yuan)

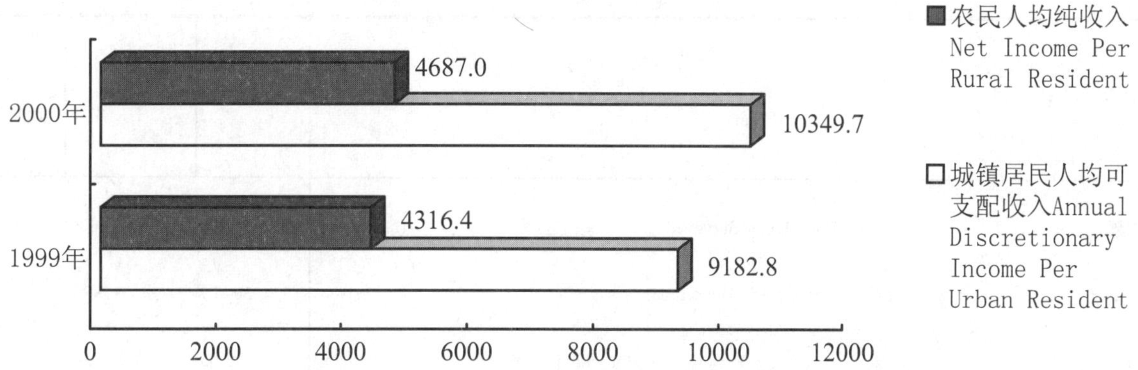

居民人均消费性支出（单位：元）
Annual Living Expenditures Per Capita (yuan)

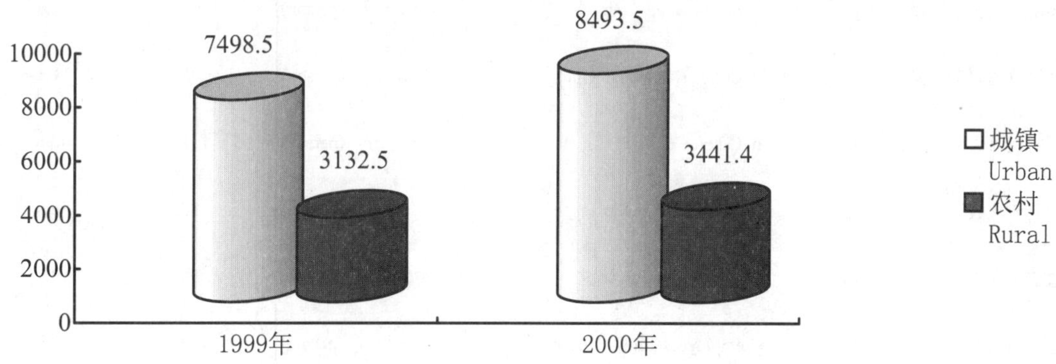

居民人均住房情况（单位：平方米）
Living Conditions Per Capita (sq.m)

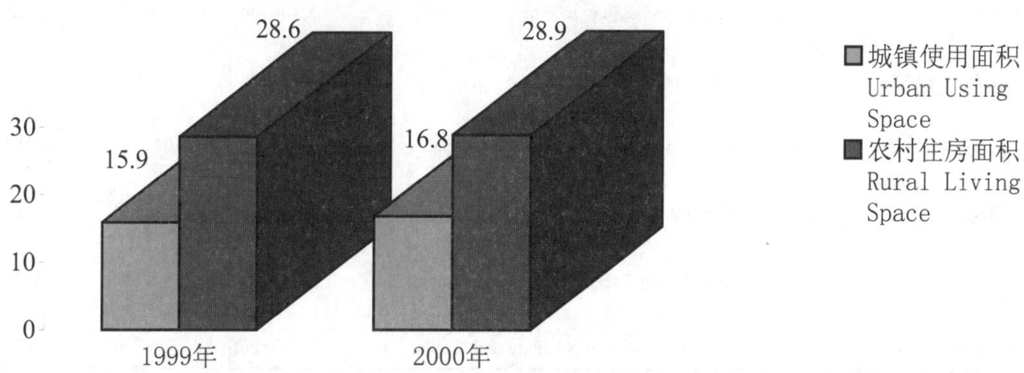

19-1 1000户城镇居民家庭基本情况
BASIC STATISTICS OF 1000 SAMPLED URBAN HOUSEHOLDS

项目 Item				2000	1999	2000年为1999年% 2000 as % of 1999
调查户数	(户)	Households Surveyed	(household)	1000	1000	
家庭人口数	(人)	Persons of Households	(person)	3046.9	3089.7	98.6
平均每户人口	(人)	Average Persons Per Household	(person)	3.05	3.09	98.7
有收入者	(人)	Persons Having Income	(person)	2346.4	2364.5	99.2
就业人口数	(人)	Employees	(person)	1743.7	1764.8	98.8
平均每户就业人口数	(人)	Average Employees Per Household	(person)	1.74	1.76	98.9
国有经济单位职工人数	(人)	in State-owned Units	(person)	1285.4	1317.8	97.5
集体经济单位职工人数	(人)	in Collective-owned Units	(person)	96.7	111.3	86.9
其他所有制单位职工人数	(人)	in Other Units	(person)	161.2	140.6	114.7
个体经营者人数	(人)	Individual Employer	(person)	16.0	16.8	95.2
个体被雇者人数	(人)	Individual Employee	(person)	15.9	9.7	163.9
离、退休再就业人数	(人)	Reemployees after retirement	(person)	160.7	159.9	100.5
其他就业者人数	(人)	Others	(person)	7.8	8.8	88.6
离退休人员数	(人)	Retirees	(person)	596.6	594.7	100.2
其他有收入者人数	(人)	Others	(person)	6.1	4.9	124.5
无收入者人数	(人)	Persons having no Income	(person)	700.5	725.2	96.6
平均每一就业者负担人数	(人)	Dependents Per Employee	(person)	1.4	1.4	100.0
平均每人年可支配收入	(元)	Annual Discretionary Income Per Capita	(yuan)	10349.7	9182.8	112.7
平均每人月可支配收入	(元)	Monthly Discretionary Income Per Capita	(yuan)	862.5	765.2	112.7
平均每人年消费性支出	(元)	Annual Living Expenditure Per Capita	(yuan)	8493.5	7498.5	113.3
平均每人月消费性支出	(元)	Monthly Living Expenditure Per Capita	(yuan)	707.8	624.9	113.3

注：1.有收入者指就业者和16岁以上的、当月财产性收入、转移性收入和零星劳动收入在100元以上的无职业者。
2.离、退休人员不包括离、退休后再就业人员，这类人员计为就业人员。

a) Persons having income refers to employees and unemployees over 16-year-old and month property-income, transfer-income and odd income totaled to more than 100 yuan.

b) Retirees exclude reemployees after retirement.

19-2 1000户城镇居民家庭基本情况(按收入水平分)
BASIC STATISTICS OF 1000 SAMPLED URBAN HOUSEHOLDS(BY INCOME LEVEL)

项目 Item				全市合计 Total	低收入户 Low Income	中等偏下收入户 Medium-Low Income	中等收入户 Medium Income	中等偏上收入户 Medium-High Income	高收入户 High Income
调查户数	(户)	Households Surveyed	(household)	1000	200	200	200	200	200
家庭人口数	(人)	Persons of Households	(person)	3046.9	664.7	628.4	619.1	581.3	553.4
平均每户人口	(人)	Average Persons Per Household	(person)	3.1	3.3	3.1	3.1	2.9	2.8
有收入者	(人)	Persons Having Income	(person)	2346.4	459.6	463.6	485.3	474.2	463.8
就业人口数	(人)	Employees	(person)	1743.7	353.4	334.3	360.2	347.3	348.6
平均每户就业人口数	(人)	Average Employees Per Household	(person)	1.7	1.8	1.7	1.8	1.7	1.7
国有经济单位职工人数	(人)	in State-owned Units	(person)	1285.4	261.4	264.6	249.9	267.3	242.2
集体经济单位职工人数	(人)	in Collective-owned Units	(person)	96.7	34.5	20.2	21.2	12.1	8.7
其他所有制单位职工人数	(人)	in Other Units	(person)	161.2	29.6	14.7	47.8	23.8	45.2
个体经营者人数	(人)	Individual Employer	(person)	16.0	4.3	3.0	2.5	2.4	3.8
个体被雇者人数	(人)	Individual Employee	(person)	15.9	2.3	2.2	3.8	4.0	3.6
离、退休再就业人数	(人)	Reemployees after retirement	(person)	160.7	16.5	29.0	33.2	37.7	44.4
其他就业者人数	(人)	Others	(person)	7.8	4.8	0.6	1.8		0.7
离退休人员数	(人)	Retirees	(person)	596.8	102.6	128.3	124.4	126.1	115.2
其他有收入者人数	(人)	Others	(person)	6.1	3.6	1.0	0.7	0.8	
无收入者人数	(人)	Persons having no Income	(person)	700.5	205.1	164.8	133.8	107.1	89.6
平均每一就业者负担人数	(人)	Dependents Per Employee	(person)	1.4	1.6	1.5	1.4	1.3	1.3
平均每人年可支配收入	(元)	Annual Discretionary Income Per Capita	(yuan)	10349.7	5774.6	7916.4	9624.0	11861.2	17831.2
平均每人月可支配收入	(元)	Monthly Discretionary Income Per Capita	(yuan)	862.5	481.2	659.7	802.0	988.4	1485.9
平均每人年消费性支出	(元)	Annual Living Expenditure Per Capita	(yuan)	8493.5	5412.7	6763.1	8369.4	9687.2	13043.4
平均每人月消费性支出	(元)	Monthly Living Expenditure Per Capita	(yuan)	707.8	451.1	563.6	697.5	807.3	1086.9

19-3 1000户城镇居民家庭每人每年现金收入
ANNUAL CASH INCOME PER CAPITA OF THE 1000 URBAN HOUSEHOLDS

单位：元 (yuan)

项目	Item	总平均 Average	低收入户 Low Income	中等偏下收入户 Medium-Low Income	中等收入户 Medium Income	中等偏上收入户 Medium-High Income	高收入户 High Income	2000年为1999年% 2000 as % of 1999
现金收入	**Cash Income**	**12560.32**	**7084.28**	**9040.03**	**11699.46**	**13964.29**	**22622.01**	**117.9**
实际收入	Real Income	10416.39	5824.60	7972.40	9685.31	11932.44	17931.36	112.7
# 可支配收入	Discretionary Income	10349.69	5774.64	7916.37	9624.04	11861.15	17831.19	112.7
职工收入	Staff and Workers	6816.34	3905.31	5089.16	6388.42	7902.90	11610.96	110.3
个体经营劳动者收入	Individuals	119.40	49.20	49.74	154.70	121.31	241.30	181.9
离退休再就业者收入	Reemployee after Retirement	252.74	108.70	171.17	236.62	318.10	467.72	106.4
其他就业者收入	Other Employee	9.14	16.99	4.86	13.50		9.29	176.1
其他劳动收入	Other Income from Work	244.28	147.24	155.51	240.67	188.16	524.54	127.6
财产性收入	Property Income	112.25	17.07	64.97	81.29	72.71	356.36	122.1
转移性收入	Transfer Income	2862.24	1580.09	2436.99	2570.11	3329.26	4721.19	116.0
#离退休金	Pension	2429.74	1386.82	2152.23	2226.88	2960.18	3667.19	117.1
赡养收入	Maintenance Income	100.05	38.76	48.31	90.33	83.40	260.76	106.9
赠送收入	Gift Income	123.68	67.84	100.05	101.37	70.62	298.20	102.9
亲友搭伙费	Poor Funds	41.87	19.41	33.86	39.16	66.75	54.83	77.6
记帐补贴	Subsidies of Account	53.83	48.76	51.97	52.89	60.37	56.21	110.0
出售财物收入	Proceeds from Sales of Belongings	3.89	3.95	2.90	1.73	0.61	10.77	30.1
其　他	Others	106.61	14.37	40.96	57.44	83.85	370.80	185.4
借贷收入	Credit Income	2143.93	1259.68	1067.63	2014.15	2031.85	4690.65	151.4

19-4 1000户城镇居民家庭每人每年现金支出
ANNUAL CASH EXPENDITURES PER CAPITA OF THE 1000 URBAN HOUSEHOLDS

单位：元 (yuan)

项目	Item	总平均 Average	低收入户 Low Income	中等偏下收入户 Medium-Low Income	中等收入户 Medium Income	中等偏上收入户 Medium-High Income	高收入户 High Income	2000年为1999年% 2000 as % of 1999
现金支出合计	**Total**	**11690.41**	**6716.18**	**8534.92**	**11049.56**	**13085.60**	**20498.41**	**118.2**
实际支出	Actual Expenditures	10083.62	6225.37	7581.77	9778.09	11435.97	16479.36	119.3
消费性支出	Living Expenditures	8493.49	5412.73	6763.12	8369.35	9687.15	13043.40	113.3
非消费支出	Non-Living Expenditures	1590.13	812.64	818.65	1408.74	1748.82	3435.96	166.5
贷款利息	Loan Interets							
个人所得税	Individual Income-tax	12.87	1.20	4.06	8.38	10.92	43.95	181.4
各种税金	Taxes	4.02	1.53	2.18	4.79	2.89	9.43	35.8
非储蓄性保险	Non-saving-deposits Insurance	37.40	16.50	35.76	32.98	41.10	65.39	103.6
赡养支出	Support Expenditures	145.35	82.37	110.12	164.63	164.08	219.76	91.5
赠送支出	Gift Expenditures	379.05	182.31	236.44	363.24	465.30	704.33	115.1
购房与建房支出	Expenditures on Purchasing and Building Houses	973.92	520.33	402.74	803.86	1013.35	2315.93	292.8
其他非消费性支出	Others	37.52	8.39	27.34	30.85	51.18	77.18	43.5
借贷支出	Credit Expenditures	1606.79	490.81	953.15	1271.47	1649.63	4019.05	111.6
存入储蓄款	Saving Deposits	1185.18	300.55	592.99	951.12	1232.83	3131.57	109.2
存入储金会款	Reserve Fund	2.48	1.31	7.32	1.28	1.72	0.54	44.4
归还借款	Returning Loans	46.71	40.28	34.69	9.69	69.69	85.39	117.1
其他	Others	126.32	50.72	100.44	118.43	119.72	262.24	119.6

19-5 1000户城镇居民家庭平均每人年消费性支出
ANNUAL LIVING EXPENDITURE PER CAPITA OF THE 1000 URBAN HOUSEHOLDS

单位：元 (yuan)

项目	Item	总平均 Average	低收入户 Low Income	中等偏下收入户 Medium-Low Income	中等收入户 Medium Income	中等偏上收入户 Medium-High Income	高收入户 High Income	2000年为1999年% 2000 as % of 1999
消费性支出	**Living Expenditures**	**8493.49**	**5412.73**	**6763.12**	**8369.35**	**9687.15**	**13043.40**	**113.3**
食　品	Food	3083.37	2385.19	2842.40	3206.29	3379.24	3747.34	104.2
衣　着	Clothing	755.03	374.11	569.13	789.98	919.66	1211.60	103.3
家庭设备用品及服务	Household Facilities, Articles and Services	1097.82	522.98	632.07	943.83	1067.85	2520.61	146.5
医疗保健	Medicine and Medical Services	588.80	453.53	461.90	597.07	671.74	798.99	114.7
交通通讯	Transportation and Communication	604.69	321.69	435.66	524.40	732.27	1092.33	129.2
娱乐、教育文化服务	Recreation,Education And Culture Services	1283.85	713.60	1042.85	1284.44	1546.77	1965.56	112.4
居住	Residence	587.42	451.57	453.25	557.84	679.43	839.37	122.8
杂项	Miscellaneous	492.51	190.06	325.86	465.50	690.19	867.60	107.6

19-6 1000户城镇居民家庭平均每人年购买食品支出
ANNUAL EXPENDITURE OF FOOD PER CAPITA OF THE 1000 URBAN HOUSEHOLDS

单位：元 (yuan)

项目	Item	总平均 Average	低收入户 Low Income	中等偏下收入户 Medium-Low Income	中等收入户 Medium Income	中等偏上收入户 Medium-High Income	高收入户 High Income	2000年为1999年% 2000 as % of 1999
食　品	**Food**	**3083.37**	**2385.19**	**2842.40**	**3206.29**	**3379.24**	**3747.34**	**104.2**
粮　食	Grain	224.38	215.04	231.46	224.89	222.48	228.96	91.9
淀粉及薯类	Starches and Tuber	23.65	21.15	24.28	23.80	23.98	25.44	97.3
干豆类及豆制品	Bean and Bean Products	44.20	38.19	43.49	42.89	47.64	50.09	106.7
油脂类	Oil	70.35	72.28	78.98	68.75	72.12	58.16	96.3
肉禽及制品	Meat,Poultry and Related Products	553.55	478.99	566.19	548.91	579.01	607.25	102.4
蛋类	Eggs	66.69	59.40	68.31	66.61	68.77	71.49	85.4
水产品类	Aquatic Products	132.00	93.61	117.15	141.46	145.50	170.21	100.8
菜类	Vegetable	235.72	208.78	227.87	237.71	245.32	264.69	95.0
调味品	Flavorings	54.85	47.59	54.10	56.83	53.98	63.13	96.5
糖类	Sugar	40.76	30.04	35.50	42.93	45.53	52.19	94.6
烟草类	Tabacco	97.51	85.92	90.45	102.92	101.24	109.49	101.4
酒和饮料	Liquor and Beverage	214.92	181.52	205.70	226.98	225.66	240.75	113.3
干鲜瓜果类	Dried and Fresh Melon and Fruits	216.47	168.16	200.71	223.06	238.74	261.64	96.8
坚果和果仁	Nuts and Kernel	56.01	44.54	52.55	58.62	57.91	68.78	109.3
糕点类	Cake	107.27	83.70	99.68	116.61	113.47	127.24	107.7
奶及奶制品	Milk and Dairy Products	178.33	127.81	156.66	184.30	200.02	234.14	125.1
其他食品	Others	99.69	67.95	81.36	89.89	118.83	149.47	96.2
在外用餐	Dinning Out	666.75	360.26	507.63	748.93	818.80	963.93	116.5
食品加工费	Food Processing Service	0.27	0.26	0.33	0.20	0.24	0.29	112.6

19-7 1000户城镇居民家庭平均每人年购买衣着、家庭设备用品及服务、医疗保健支出
ANNUAL PURCHASES OF CLOTHING,HOUSEHOLDS ARTICLES AND SERVICES, MEDICINE AND MEDICAL SERVICES PER CAPITA OF THE 1000 URBAN HOUSEHOLDS

单位：元 (yuan)

项目	Item	总平均 Average	低收入户 Low Income	中等偏下收入户 Medium-Low Income	中等收入户 Medium Income	中等偏上收入户 Medium-High Income	高收入户 High Income	2000年为1999年% 2000 as % of 1999
衣　着	**Clothing**	**755.03**	**374.11**	**569.13**	**789.98**	**919.66**	**1211.60**	**103.3**
服　装	Garments	497.23	224.61	351.15	528.37	609.67	837.58	103.4
衣着材料	Clothing Materials	36.60	23.46	34.92	35.76	41.65	49.92	83.1
棉　布	Cotton Cloth	8.00	4.57	9.03	6.67	8.46	11.95	96.9
棉化纤混纺布	Cotton/Chemical Fabric Blend Cloth	3.58	0.93	1.85	4.35	3.43	8.00	86.9
化纤布	Chemical Fabric Cloth	5.69	2.99	5.65	5.79	6.87	7.62	52.4
呢　绒	Woolen Fabric	5.14	0.83	4.09	5.40	8.45	7.76	79.7
绸　缎	Silk and Stain	3.28	1.69	4.15	2.42	2.91	5.58	105.1
毛　线	Knitting Wool	7.31	8.52	7.92	7.81	6.84	5.10	105.9
其　他	Others	3.60	3.94	2.24	3.31	4.68	3.91	83.3
鞋袜帽及其他	Shoes,Socks,Hats and Others	202.73	116.56	167.12	208.58	245.94	294.73	109.1
衣着加工费	Clothing Processing	18.47	9.48	15.94	17.27	22.40	29.37	91.6
家庭设备用品及服务	**Households Articles and Services**	**1097.82**	**522.98**	**632.07**	**943.83**	**1067.85**	**2520.61**	**146.5**
耐用消费品	Durable Consumer Goods	725.95	314.65	414.19	596.95	739.53	1703.85	157.6
家　具	Furniture	168.79	91.63	58.44	87.84	168.97	477.07	139.6
住房装饰	House Decorate	147.22	31.23	24.45	111.08	92.85	523.39	227.5
家庭设备	Households Facility	409.94	191.78	331.30	398.03	477.71	703.39	149.1
室内装饰品	Room Ornament	27.20	7.81	9.11	28.39	24.28	72.79	120.9
床上用品	Articles for Bed	29.65	16.48	21.91	27.40	35.06	51.10	100.4
家庭日用杂品	Groceries for Households Daily Use	190.45	126.48	152.85	188.45	192.07	310.52	113.2
家具材料	Furniture Materials	14.48	0.64	2.06	0.30	9.07	66.75	524.6
家庭服务	Households Services	110.09	56.92	31.95	102.34	67.84	315.60	167.4
医疗保健	**Medicine and Medical Services**	**588.80**	**453.53**	**461.90**	**597.07**	**671.74**	**798.99**	**114.7**
医疗器具	Medical Implements	8.69	1.58	6.42	12.63	13.46	10.42	114.5
保健用品	Health Appliance	14.77	5.33	9.23	12.27	27.75	21.55	104.1
医药费	Medicine Expenses	392.93	326.10	302.71	416.63	425.37	515.04	115.7
补药品	Tonic	69.60	34.58	50.47	52.55	105.07	115.21	158.5
医疗保健服务	Medical Services	89.91	76.65	79.11	91.36	78.53	128.43	94.9
其　他	Others	12.90	9.28	13.96	11.63	21.57	8.34	96.9

19-8 1000户城镇居民家庭平均每人年交通通讯、娱乐文教服务支出
ANNUAL EXPENDITURE OF TRANSPORTATION,COMMUNICATION, RECREATION,CULTURE AND EDUCATION SERVICES PER CAPITA OF THE 1000 URBAN HOUSEHOLDS

单位：元 (yuan)

项目	Item	总平均 Average	低收入户 Low Income	中等偏下收入户 Medium-Low Income	中等收入户 Medium Income	中等偏上收入户 Medium-High Income	高收入户 High Income	2000年为1999年% 2000 as % of 1999
交通和通讯	**Transportation and Communication**	**604.69**	**321.69**	**435.66**	**524.40**	**732.27**	**1092.33**	**129.2**
交　通	Transportation	230.39	124.35	176.98	192.66	247.94	442.13	112.5
#家庭交通工具	Means of Transport for Household	26.84	14.10	20.51	27.25	23.71	52.17	44.2
交通费	Transport Fare	171.51	98.11	134.83	143.19	181.02	322.99	145.0
维修服务费	Fare for Repair	26.92	11.18	20.67	17.50	31.57	58.57	112.7
通　讯	Communication	374.30	197.34	258.68	331.74	484.32	650.20	142.2
#通讯工具	Means	90.05	35.94	30.21	91.34	142.63	166.32	157.9
电讯费	Telecommunication Fare	274.20	158.92	217.76	231.85	335.15	460.11	140.4
邮　费	Post Fare	4.46	0.91	3.35	4.20	3.51	11.27	76.9
其　他	Others	5.59	1.57	7.36	4.35	3.03	12.51	111.1
娱乐文教服务	**Recreation,Culture and Education Services**	**1283.85**	**713.60**	**1042.85**	**1284.44**	**1546.27**	**1965.56**	**112.4**
耐用消费品	Durable Consumer Goods	367.05	150.49	268.67	395.48	507.19	559.85	97.8
#彩　电	Color TV	77.38	31.39	64.76	80.40	101.35	118.40	64.5
影碟机	Video CD	13.72	7.29	13.34	16.12	19.23	13.39	51.7
录放象机	Video-corder	0.33		1.50				132.0
家用电脑	Game-computer	195.97	75.66	121.11	222.01	288.65	298.98	146.1
录音机	Recorder	6.86	3.35	5.10	7.01	8.91	10.78	97.7
组合音响	Hi-Fi System	3.87	5.76	3.98		5.08	4.52	22.3
摄象机	Pickup Camera							
照相机	Camera	8.92	3.62	10.00	18.58	5.21	7.17	120.9
照相器材	Photographic Equipment	2.60	0.46		8.17	1.64	2.92	2888.9
钢　琴	Piano							
中高档乐器	Secondary and Top Grade Musical Instrument	3.23	1.17	2.07	4.33	8.26	0.51	54.6
其　他	Others	38.46	13.80	25.22	32.45	50.77	76.89	121.0
修理服务费	Fare for Repairs	14.21	6.63	20.43	5.47	15.91	24.22	99.4
教　育	Education	616.27	411.30	544.79	603.29	674.53	896.94	125.0
#教学参考书	Teaching Reference Book	42.93	38.18	46.32	38.55	37.85	55.02	108.0
学杂费	Tuition and Incidentals	390.76	270.96	382.73	395.01	476.35	449.11	129.2
托幼费	Child-care Fare	24.17	24.72	12.59	23.37	27.45	34.09	73.5
成人教育	Adult Education	46.84	11.97	27.47	19.85	26.83	161.89	198.6
其　他	Others	111.58	65.47	75.68	126.50	106.06	196.83	118.1
文化娱乐	Culture and Recreation	300.54	151.81	229.39	285.68	365.05	508.77	109.9
#文娱用品	Appliance	93.40	38.62	65.81	85.83	106.06	185.68	107.3
书报杂志	Book,Newspaper and Magazine	80.11	43.36	63.08	74.95	102.57	125.75	105.1
文娱费	Fare	127.02	69.83	100.50	124.89	156.41	197.33	115.4

19-9 1000户城镇居民家庭平均每人年居住、杂项商品和服务支出
ANNUAL EXPENDITURE OF RESIDENCE,MISCELLANEOUS COMMODITIES AND SERVICES PER CAPITA OF THE 1000 URBAN HOUSEHOLDS

单位：元 (yuan)

项目	Item	总平均 Average	低收入户 Low Income	中等偏下收入户 Medium-Low Income	中等收入户 Medium Income	中等偏上收入户 Medium-High Income	高收入户 High Income	2000年为1999年% 2000 as % of 1999
居住	**Residence**	**587.42**	**451.57**	**453.25**	**557.84**	**679.43**	**839.37**	**122.8**
住房	House	265.38	193.44	152.82	241.84	316.37	452.34	133.2
#建筑材料	Construction Materials	107.95	69.48	40.89	100.29	103.18	243.82	137.8
房租	Rent	88.58	87.00	80.06	104.71	76.87	94.42	149.4
维修服务	Repairs	68.85	36.96	31.87	36.84	136.32	114.10	111.8
水电燃料	Fare for Water,Electricity and Fuel	322.04	258.13	300.43	316.00	363.06	387.03	115.3
#水费	Water	48.67	38.52	46.70	47.83	52.47	60.11	132.0
电费	Electricity	149.59	112.44	135.49	153.06	169.74	185.10	119.6
燃料	Fuel	109.65	96.72	110.52	104.29	117.14	122.31	107.1
煤炭	Coal	28.62	31.08	33.13	31.02	27.55	19.00	112.0
液化石油气	Liquefied Petroleum Gas	21.95	22.08	25.43	23.34	23.46	14.68	92.1
管道煤气	Pipeline Gas	53.02	42.00	49.45	48.47	53.12	75.20	107.0
其他	Others	6.06	1.56	2.51	1.47	13.01	13.44	175.7
其他	Others	13.75	8.76	7.72	10.82	23.61	19.47	92.8
杂项商品和服务	**Miscellaneous Commodities and Service**	**492.51**	**190.06**	**325.86**	**465.50**	**690.19**	**867.60**	**107.6**
个人消费	Personal Consumption	433.76	170.64	292.11	401.06	623.55	747.96	105.4
个人用品	Personal Articles	133.30	72.24	97.80	130.20	160.00	220.32	100.9
#金银珠宝饰品	Golden,Silver and Jewelry Ornament	26.70	2.16	9.00	23.16	48.96	56.88	105.1
纸张文具	Paper and Stationery	17.33	14.16	17.04	17.28	16.92	21.84	95.2
其他日用品	Other Articles for Daily Use	82.62	52.44	66.36	84.36	91.32	126.12	99.4
理发、美容用品	Articles for Haircut Improving one's Looks	68.22	44.28	51.60	73.68	75.36	102.24	109.0
#理发美容用品	Articles for Haircut Improving one's Looks	1.92	1.32	1.20	2.16	2.40	2.76	89.7
美容化妆品	Cosmetics	63.12	41.28	48.72	68.40	68.88	93.60	109.1
旅游	Tourism	199.84	37.20	121.68	159.36	347.64	373.92	104.6
#火车费	Train Fare	35.58	7.68	24.00	24.84	70.08	57.96	105.9
其他交通费	Other Fare for Transport	31.17	2.40	4.56	38.18	43.24	75.36	144.8
住宿费	Fare for Accmmodation	19.16	1.20	11.76	17.28	25.44	44.64	160.3
其他	Others	100.23	21.96	72.96	73.68	186.84	164.16	89.9
服务费	Services	32.41	16.92	21.03	37.68	38.52	51.60	124.8
#理发洗澡费用	Fare for Hair-cut and Bath	19.10	12.48	15.96	20.52	24.48	23.40	106.9
美容费	Fare for Improving one's Looks	6.82	2.40	2.16	5.28	8.64	17.16	188.4
其他商品	Other Commodities	14.30	3.24	7.68	25.20	16.56	20.40	103.3
其他服务	Other Services	44.45	16.20	26.04	39.24	50.04	99.24	138.5

19-10 1000户城镇居民家庭平均每百户耐用消费品年购买量

PER 100 HOUSEHOLDS ANNUAL PURCHASES OF DURABLE CONSUMER GOODS OF THE 1000 URBAN HOUSEHOLDS

项目	Item		总平均 Average	低收入户 Low Income	中等偏下收入户 Medium-Low Income	中等收入 Medium Income	中等偏上收入户 Medium High Income	高收入户 High Income	2000年为1999年% 2000 as % of 1999
组合家具	(套) Combined Furniture	(set)	1.4	1.5	0.5	0.5	1.5	3.0	73.7
沙发床	(个) Bed with Mattress	(unit)	5.4	5.5	2.0	4.5	4.5	10.5	120.0
沙　发	(个) Sofas	(unit)	9.2	10.5	1.5	7.5	8.5	18.0	119.5
摩托车	(辆) Motorcyles	(unit)	0.3					1.5	100.0
自行车	(辆) Bicycles	(unit)	16.9	14.5	15.5	24.5	18.0	12.0	106.3
家用汽车	(辆) Cars	(unit)							
电风扇	(台) Electric Fans	(set)	8.9	10.5	10.5	8.5	7.0	8.0	93.7
电冰箱	(台) Refrigerators	(set)	7.7	4.5	9.0	9.0	9.5	6.5	163.8
洗衣机	(台) Washing Machines	(set)	7.3	5.5	8.5	6.0	8.0	8.5	121.7
缝纫机	(台) Sewing Machine	(set)	0.1			0.5			100.0
冰　柜	(台) Freezers	(set)	0.1					0.5	33.3
微波炉	(台) Microwave Stove	(set)	8.2	4.0	8.5	8.5	8.5	11.5	113.9
空调器	(台) Air-Conditioners	(set)	18.0	7.5	13.5	18.0	22.0	29.0	191.5
电炊具	(台) Electric Cooking Appliances	(set)	13.7	9.0	13.5	17.5	11.0	17.5	97.9
淋浴热水器	(个) Showers	(set)	10.5	8.5	9.0	7.5	12.5	15.0	147.9
脱排油烟机	(台) Range Hoods	(set)	8.1	7.0	5.5	7.0	10.0	11.0	188.4
吸尘器	(台) Dust Catcher	(set)	1.4	1.0	1.5	0.5	1.0	3.0	350.0
彩　电	(台) Color TV Sets	(set)	10.3	7.0	12.0	9.5	10.5	12.5	79.8
影碟机	(台) Video CD	(set)	4.9	2.5	6.0	6.0	5.5	4.5	72.1
录放像机	(台) Videorecorders	(set)	0.1		0.5				100.0
家用电脑	(台) Game-Computers	(set)	7.3	3.0	5.0	8.5	10.5	9.5	149.0
组合音响	(套) Hi-Fi Systems	(set)	0.8	1.0	1.0		1.0	1.0	36.4
录音机	(台) Recorders	(set)	4.7	2.5	3.0	4.5	8.5	5.0	78.3
摄像机	(台) Pickup Camera	(set)							
钢　琴	(台) Piano	(set)							
其他中高档乐器	(件) Secondary and Top Grade Musical Instrume	(unit)	1.1	0.5	1.5	1.5	1.5	0.5	100.0
照相机	(架) Camera	(set)	2.2	2.5	2.0	3.5	1.5	1.5	84.6

19-11 1000户城镇居民家庭平均每百户耐用消费品年拥有量
PER 100 HOUSEHOLDS ANNUAL POSSESSION OF DURABLE CONSUMER GOODS OF THE 1000 URBAN HOUSEHOLDS

项目 Item			总平均 Average	低收入户 Low Income	中等偏下收入户 Medium-Low Income	中等收入户 Medium Income	中等偏上收入户 Medium-High Income	高收入户 High Income	2000年为1999年% 2000 as % of 1999
组合家具	(套) Combined Furniture	(set)	78.0	71.0	69.5	78.0	80.5	91.0	103.9
沙发床	(个) Bed with Mattress	(unit)	83.6	71.0	63.5	87.5	89.5	106.5	108.2
沙 发	(个) Sofas	(unit)	154.1	133.0	119.5	129.0	159.0	229.5	100.4
摩托车	(辆) Motorcycles	(unit)	5.7	9.0	3.0	3.0	7.5	6.0	95.0
自行车	(辆) Bicycles	(unit)	230.7	230.0	237.5	234.0	229.5	222.5	104.8
家用汽车	(辆) Cars	(unit)	2.5	2.0	2.0	1.0	2.0	5.5	100.0
电风扇	(台) Electric Fans	(set)	153.4	143.5	153.0	151.5	155.5	163.5	105.5
电冰箱	(台) Refrigerators	(set)	107.4	105.0	105.0	109.5	108.0	109.5	104.5
洗衣机	(台) Washing Machines	(set)	102.8	97.0	103.0	99.0	105.0	110.0	103.2
健身器材	(件) Health Equipment	(set)	9.3	4.0	6.5	9.5	8.5	18.0	93.0
冰 柜	(台) Freezers	(set)	16.3	11.0	10.5	13.0	22.0	25.0	95.3
微波炉	(台) Microwave Stove	(set)	58.4	40.0	56.5	57.0	64.5	74.0	119.7
空调器	(台) Air-Conditioners	(set)	69.6	50.0	57.5	61.5	77.0	102.0	139.5
电炊具	(台) Electric Cooking Appliances	(set)	104.0	74.0	97.0	100.0	103.5	145.5	124.3
淋浴热水器	(个) Showers	(set)	74.4	67.0	64.0	70.5	79.0	91.5	110.9
脱排油烟机	(台) Range Hoods	(set)	67.9	54.5	58.5	62.5	76.5	87.5	107.9
吸尘器	(台) Dust Catcher	(set)	24.9	15.5	20.0	23.5	28.0	37.5	107.8
彩 电	(台) Color TV Sets	(set)	145.5	134.5	143.5	142.0	149.0	158.5	102.9
影碟机	(台) Video CD	(set)	46.1	34.0	40.0	46.5	53.0	56.5	120.7
录放像机	(台) Videorecorders	(set)	56.9	46.0	55.5	54.0	57.0	72.0	105.2
家用电脑	(台) Game-Computers	(set)	32.1	17.0	24.0	35.0	36.5	48.0	136.6
组合音响	(套) Hi-Fi Systems	(set)	30.1	25.0	20.0	25.5	39.0	41.0	117.6
录音机	(台) Recorders	(set)	72.7	64.5	77.0	64.0	70.5	87.5	104.0
摄像机	(台) Pickup Camera	(set)	5.4	2.5	4.0	4.5	5.0	11.0	96.4
钢 琴	(台) Piano	(set)	2.2	1.0	1.0	2.0	3.5	3.5	75.9
其他中高档乐器	(件) Secondary and Top Grade Musical Instrument	(unit)	13.7	7.5	12.0	13.0	15.5	20.5	112.3
照相机	(架) Camera	(set)	95.7	78.5	96.5	90.0	97.5	116.0	100.7
移动电话	(台) Mobilphone	(unit)	27.6	16.0	13.5	24.0	34.0	50.5	214.0

19-12 1000户城镇居民家庭居住情况
HOUSING CONDITIONS OF THE 1000 URBAN HOUSEHOLDS

项　　目 Item		2000	1999	2000年为1999年% 2000 as % of 1999
平均每户居室间数 (间) Number of Rooms Per Household	(room)	2.12	2.14	99.1
平均每人使用面积 (平方米) Per Capita Using Space	(sq.m)	13.76	12.93	106.4
平均每人居住面积 (平方米) Per Capita Living Space	(sq.m)	9.36	8.90	105.2
平均每人辅助面积 (平方米) Per Capita Auxiliary Space	(sq.m)	4.40	4.03	109.2
按居住面积分 Grouped by Living Space				
无房户 (户) No House	(household)			
4平方米以下 (户) below 4 sq.m	(household)	35	44	79.5
4-6平方米 (户) 4-6 sq.m	(household)	177	173	102.3
6-8平方米 (户) 6-8 sq.m	(household)	198	229	86.5
8-10平方米 (户) 8-10 sq.m	(household)	206	225	91.6
10-12平方米 (户) 10-12 sq.m	(household)	128	115	111.3
12-14平方米 (户) 12-14 sq.m	(household)	89	97	91.8
14平方米以上 (户) above 14 sq.m	(household)	167	117	142.7
按自来水使用情况分 Grouped by Using of Tap Water				
无自来水 (户) No Tap Water	(household)		3	
独用自来水 (户) Using by oneself	(household)	812	751	108.1
公用自来水 (户) Public Tap Water	(household)	188	246	76.4
按卫生设备拥有情况分 Grouped by Possession of Sanitary Equipment				
无卫生设备 (户) No Sanitary Equipment	(household)	272	289	94.1
有浴室厕所 (户) Having Bathroom and Lavatory	(household)	96	74	129.7
有厕所无浴室 (户) Having Lavatory and No Bathroom	(household)	553	501	110.4
公用卫生设备 (户) Public Sanitary Equipment	(household)	79	136	58.1
按取暖设备拥有情况分 Grouped by Possession of Heating Equipment				
无取暖设备 (户) No Heating Equipment	(household)	2	2	100.0
空调设备 (户) Air Conditioner	(household)	4	15	26.7
暖　气 (户) Central Heating	(household)	678	655	103.5
其　他 (户) Others	(household)	316	328	96.3

19-12 续表 continued

单位：户 (household)

项目	Item	2000	1999	2000年为1999年% 2000 as % of 1999
按厨房使用情况分	**Grouped by Using of Kitchen**			
无厨房	No Kitchen	159	196	81.1
独用厨房	Using Kitchen by oneself	802	691	116.1
公用厨房	Public Kitchen	39	113	34.5
按房屋产权分	**Grouped by House Property Rights**			
公房	Public House	532	639	83.3
租赁私房	Rent Private House	16	17	94.1
自有房	Self-house	216	121	178.5
部分产权自有房	Self-house with Part Property Rights	234	221	105.9
其他	Others	2	2	100.0
按燃料使用情况分	**Grouped by Using of Fuel**			
管道煤气	Pipeline Gas	564	536	105.2
液化石油气	Liquefied Petroleum Gas	390	403	96.8
煤	Coal	25	39	64.1
其他	Others	21	22	95.5
按电话拥有情况分	**Grouped by Possession of Telephone**			
无电话	No Telephone	94	146	64.4
公费电话	Free Telephone	53	60	88.3
自费电话	Telephone at one's Own Expenses	827	786	105.2
公用电话	Public Telephone	26	8	325.0
按住房建筑式样分	**Grouped by Style of House Construction**			
家庭单栋配套楼房	Individual Storied Building of a Family		1	
单元式配套楼房	Storied Building on Unit Style	627	610	102.8
一居室	One-room	64	99	64.6
二居室	Two-room	411	358	114.8
三居室	Three-room	132	133	99.2
四居室以上	Four-room and above	20	20	100.0
普通楼房	Ordinary Storied Building	49	55	89.1
普通平房及其他	Ordinary Single-story Building	324	334	97.0

19-13 35个大中城市居民人均收支对比
CONTRAST ON PER CAPITA INCOME AND EXPENDITURE OF URBAN RESIDENTS OF 35 LARGE AND MEDIUM CITIES

单位：元 (yuan)

城市 City		人均可支配收入 Annual Discretionary Income Per Capita			人均消费性支出 Annual Living Expenditure Per Capita		
		2000	1999	2000年为1999年% 2000 as % of 1999	2000	1999	2000年为1999年% 2000 as % of 1999
北京	Beijing	10349.7	9182.8	112.7	8493.5	7498.5	113.3
天津	Tianjin	8140.5	7649.8	106.4	6121.0	5851.5	104.6
石家庄	Shijiazhuang	6443.5	6131.0	105.1	5246.7	5002.8	104.9
太原	Taiyuan	6018.6	5627.4	107.0	5340.6	4693.4	113.8
呼和浩特	Huhehaote	5581.9	5167.4	108.0	4612.9	4172.8	110.5
沈阳	Shenyang	5850.5	5364.3	109.1	5103.0	4652.2	109.7
大连	Dalian	6860.6	6274.0	109.3	6073.0	5530.3	109.8
长春	Changchun	5568.2	5110.2	109.0	5113.3	4571.2	111.9
哈尔滨	Haerbin	5632.0	5032.3	111.9	4508.3	4215.8	106.9
上海	Shanghai	11718.0	10931.6	107.2	8868.2	8247.7	107.5
南京	Nanjing	8233.0	7693.8	107.0	7047.5	6448.6	109.3
杭州	Hangzhou	9668.1	9084.5	106.4	7789.7	7423.7	104.9
宁波	Ningbo	10921.3	9491.7	115.1	7997.4	7493.3	106.7
合肥	Hefei	6389.3	5812.9	109.9	5039.8	4551.7	110.7
福州	Fuzhou	8300.4	7413.8	112.0	6416.6	5732.9	111.9
厦门	Xiamen	10813.0	9625.6	112.3	9047.1	7889.6	114.7
南昌	Nanchang	5733.5	5287.5	108.4	3924.8	4077.4	96.3
济南	Jinan	8471.3	7162.5	118.3	6891.8	6415.4	107.4
青岛	Qingdao	8016.4	7281.7	110.1	6676.5	5980.8	111.6
郑州	Zhengzhou	6457.8	6147.7	105.0	5443.9	5064.7	107.5
武汉	Wuhan	6760.6	6262.1	108.0	6074.8	5452.8	111.4
长沙	Changsha	7985.5	7297.1	109.4	7370.1	6538.3	112.7
广州	Guangzhou	13621.8	12326.0	110.5	10989.0	10272.3	107.0
深圳	Shenzhen	21577.2	20548.4	105.0	18200.7	15726.1	115.7
南宁	Nanning	7448.0	6846.4	108.8	6705.5	6320.5	106.1
海口	Haikou	7103.5	7058.9	100.6	5423.9	5569.3	97.4
成都	Chengdu	7649.1	7098.0	107.8	6423.5	5798.0	110.8
重庆	Chongqing	6276.0	5896.0	106.4	5569.8	5444.2	102.3
贵阳	Guiyang	6453.3	6082.2	106.1	5550.2	5327.1	104.2
昆明	Kunming	7563.3	7239.4	104.5	6844.6	6371.1	107.4
西安	Xi'an	6364.2	5998.8	106.1	5445.7	5361.0	101.6
兰州	Lanzhou	5850.2	5127.5	114.1	5047.6	4505.6	112.0
西宁	Xining	5297.9	4764.9	111.2	4244.7	3966.3	107.0
银川	Yinchuan	5621.5	5167.7	108.8	5369.1	4484.4	119.7
乌鲁木齐	Wulumuqi	7252.0	6676.0	108.6	5643.7	5183.6	108.9

19-14 2710户农民家庭基本情况
SAMPLING STATISTICS FOR 2710 RURAL HOUSEHOLDS

项目 Item		总平均 Average	按人均年纯收入水平分组 Grouped by Annual Net Income Per Capita				2000年为1999年% 2000 as % of 1999
			2000元以下 below 2000 yuan	2000～3500	3500～5000	5000元以上 above 5000 yuan	
调查户数 (户)	Households Surveyed (household)	2710	278	737	689	1006	121.0
常住人口 (人)	Permanent Residents (person)	9545	1069	2757	2486	3233	117.8
平均每户 (人)	Average Per Household (person)	3.52	3.85	3.74	3.61	3.21	97.2
整半劳动力 (个)	Full-time and Part-time Labors(person)	6305	673	1760	1625	2247	110.9
平均每户 (个)	Average Per Household (person)	2.33	2.42	2.39	2.36	2.23	91.7
平均每一劳动力负担人口 (人)	Dependents Per Labor Force (person)	1.51	1.59	1.57	1.53	1.44	105.6
学龄前儿童人数 (人)	Number of Preschool Children(person)	359	53	108	104	94	172.6
家庭经营耕地面积 (公顷)	Cultivated Land Area Runned by Households (hectare)	447.44	57.97	145.11	108.86	135.50	88.0
家庭经营山地面积 (公顷)	Mountain Land Area Runned by Households (hectare)	48.52	9.24	17.76	10.71	10.81	43.9
人均生产性固定资产原值 (元)	Original Value of Productive Fixed Assets Per Capita (yuan)	1473.85	2149.20	808.48	1418.09	1860.82	139.8
人均住房面积 (平方米)	Per Capita Living Space (sq.m)	28.91	22.11	25.00	27.41	34.81	101.1
人均总收入 (元)	Per Capita Total Revenue (yuan)	5537.59	2436.94	3245.01	4977.67	8948.41	111.9
# 现金收入 (元)	Cash Income (yuan)	5136.89	2202.38	2970.85	4619.84	8351.89	110.1
人均纯收入 (元)	Net Income Per Capita (yuan)	4687.03	1301.34	2751.86	4196.92	7833.65	108.6
人均生活消费支出 (元)	Per Capita Annual Living Expenditures (yuan)	3441.35	1734.34	2256.17	3239.19	5171.91	109.9
# 现金支出 (元)	Cash Expenditures (yuan)	3352.94	1653.19	2152.24	3149.17	5095.58	111.9
平均每个劳动力创造纯收入 (元)	Average Net Income Per Labor Force (yuan)	6477.08	1805.23	4061.26	5937.90	10158.45	113.1

19-15 2710户农民家庭平均每人年纯收入
ANNUAL NET INCOME PER CAPITA OF THE 2710 RURAL HOUSEHOLDS

单位：元 (yuan)

项目	Item	总平均 Average	按人均年纯收入水平分组 Grouped by Annual Net Income Per Capita				2000年为1999年% 2000 as % of 1999
			2000元以下 below 2000 yuan	2000～3500	3500～5000	5000元以上 above 5000 yuan	
合计	**Total**	**4687.03**	**1301.34**	**2751.86**	**4196.92**	**7833.65**	**108.6**
基本收入	**Basic Income**	**4278.47**	**1136.50**	**2592.61**	**3881.37**	**7060.33**	**106.5**
工资性收入	Wage	2937.73	984.68	1750.15	2711.89	4769.92	101.9
在非企业组织中劳动的报酬	From Non-enterprise Organizations	1024.98	248.20	541.63	939.34	1759.85	92.0
在企业劳动得到的报酬	From Enterprises	1779.26	657.52	1081.08	1635.62	2856.02	105.2
在其他单位劳动得到的报酬	From Other Units	133.49	78.96	127.44	136.93	154.05	175.9
家庭经营纯收入	Net Income from Family Business	1340.74	151.82	842.46	1169.48	2290.41	118.0
从第一产业得到	from Primary Industry	742.12	58.20	596.69	738.37	1141.11	100.8
从第二产业得到	from Secondary Industry	58.26	-77.21	30.81	39.34	141.00	186.1
从第三产业得到	from Tertiary Industry	540.36	170.83	214.96	391.77	1008.30	146.6
转移性和财产性收入	**Transfer and Property Income**	**408.56**	**164.84**	**159.25**	**315.55**	**773.32**	**136.9**
在外人口寄、带回	Transferring from Family Members	11.19	5.09	5.51	8.15	20.38	103.6
农村外部亲友赠送	Gifts from Relatives and Friends	38.74	32.27	9.97	21.45	78.72	251.6
退休金收入	Pension	81.22	15.45	28.18	94.94	137.65	149.8
财产性收入	Property Income	174.63	40.63	53.01	134.34	353.63	170.0

19-16 2710 户农民家庭平均每人年生活费支出

ANNUAL LIVING EXPENDITURES PER CAPITA OF THE 2710 RURAL HOUSEHOLDS

单位：元 (yuan)

项目	Item	总平均 Average	按人均年纯收入水平分组 Grouped by Annual Net Income Per Capita 2000元以下 below 2000 yuan	2000～3500	3500～5000	5000元以上 above 5000 yuan	2000年为1999年% 2000 as % of 1999
合计	**Total**	**3441.35**	**1734.34**	**2256.17**	**3239.19**	**5171.91**	**109.9**
食品支出	**Food Expenditure**	**1263.62**	**712.65**	**945.27**	**1314.38**	**1678.26**	**100.8**
#主食	Staple Food	222.97	190.24	219.28	221.59	237.99	84.7
副食	Non-Staple Food	538.21	285.57	382.79	622.89	689.18	105.1
其他食品	Others	345.97	179.89	242.70	322.29	507.14	102.8
衣着支出	**Clothing Expenditure**	**261.73**	**107.01**	**151.43**	**233.54**	**428.64**	**102.0**
#服装支出	Garments	123.26	44.37	64.97	102.80	214.79	97.0
居住支出	**Residence**	**539.11**	**256.17**	**298.45**	**475.10**	**887.12**	**129.5**
#住房	Housing	320.45	138.69	140.14	264.31	577.47	160.1
燃料	Fuel	124.41	69.51	92.87	131.80	163.76	119.2
家庭设备用品及服务支出	**Household Facilities,Articles and Services**	**252.16**	**95.26**	**127.31**	**198.22**	**451.97**	**95.8**
#耐用消费品	Durable Consumer Goods	154.43	41.42	60.41	110.73	305.57	107.1
家庭日用杂品	Daily Use Household Articles	75.88	37.01	52.70	71.22	112.09	78.7
医疗保健支出	**Medicines and Medical Services**	**276.11**	**137.05**	**171.40**	**257.44**	**425.73**	**123.8**
交通和通讯支出	**Transportation and Communications**	**217.46**	**90.87**	**118.87**	**196.53**	**359.48**	**131.4**
#交通工具	Transportation Means	55.34	18.00	25.73	56.76	91.83	79.9
交通费	Transportation	30.13	10.00	19.55	23.90	50.60	147.0
邮电费	Posts and Telecommunications	80.71	39.54	45.41	72.64	130.64	186.0
文教娱乐用品及服务支出	**Cultural,Education and Recreation Articles and Services**	**495.26**	**285.76**	**377.78**	**463.05**	**689.48**	**107.3**
#文娱用机电消费品	Mechanical and Electric Consumer Goods of Culture and Recreation	97.86	17.28	49.14	71.62	186.23	93.7
书报杂志	Books,Newspapers and Magazines	6.74	1.92	4.58	4.66	11.79	129.6
学杂费	Tuition and Incidentals	339.57	247.86	293.01	335.58	412.67	113.4
文娱费	Recreation	5.17	1.86	2.23	4.07	9.61	30.1
其他商品及服务支出	**Other Commodity and Services**	**135.90**	**49.57**	**65.66**	**100.93**	**251.23**	**146.3**
#商品性支出	Commodity Expenditures	36.10	11.65	15.58	25.92	69.50	190.0

19-17 2710户农民家庭平均每人年粮食收支情况

BROUGHT IN AND SENT OUT OF GRAIN PER CAPITA OF THE 2710 HOUSEHOLDS

单位：公斤 (kg)

项目	Item	总平均 Average	按人均年纯收入水平分组 Grouped by Annual Net Income Per Capita 2000元以下 below 2000 yuan	2000～3500	3500～5000	5000元以上 above 5000 yuan	2000年为1999年% 2000 as % of 1999
年内粮食收入	**Brought in within this Year**	**603.01**	**565.48**	**483.83**	**574.62**	**738.87**	**112.7**
家庭经营生产	Household Production	427.89	357.58	359.57	400.11	530.77	99.0
购入	Purchasing	171.35	205.15	120.03	171.34	203.93	171.5
其他	Others	3.77	2.75	4.23	3.17	4.17	139.6
年内粮食支出	**Sent out within this Year**	**441.53**	**456.43**	**358.91**	**421.21**	**522.69**	**111.4**
生活用粮	Living Consumption	141.35	127.96	149.79	139.70	139.85	86.1
#稻谷	Rice	34.68	33.49	30.01	33.11	40.25	102.6
小麦	Wheat	80.94	64.85	86.79	82.06	80.42	82.3
出售粮食	Selling	202.57	202.06	161.43	180.22	255.01	98.8
其他	Others	97.61	126.41	47.69	101.29	127.83	361.5

19-18 2710户农民家庭主要生活消费品平均每人消费量
CONSUMPTION OF MAJOR LIVING CONSUMER GOODS PER CAPITA OF THE 2710 RURAL HOUSEHOLDS

项目 Item			总平均 Average	按人均年纯收入水平分组 Grouped by Annual Net Income Per Capita				2000年为1999年% 2000 as % of 1999
				2000元以下 below 2000 yuan	2000～3500	3500～5000	5000元以上 above 5000 yuan	
粮　食	(公斤) Grains	(kg)	141.35	127.96	149.79	139.70	139.85	86.1
豆制品	(公斤) Bean Products	(kg)	5.03	3.09	4.28	5.92	5.62	130.6
蔬　菜	(公斤) Vegetables	(kg)	106.09	82.47	97.15	104.17	122.99	102.5
植物油	(公斤) Vegetable Oil	(kg)	8.90	7.07	8.00	8.88	10.30	104.6
动物油	(公斤) Animal Oil	(kg)	0.41	0.44	0.50	0.38	0.33	89.1
猪牛羊肉	(公斤) Pork,Beef,Mutton	(kg)	15.18	8.59	12.43	15.21	19.67	103.6
家　禽	(公斤) Poultry	(kg)	2.09	0.89	1.42	1.85	3.23	112.4
蛋　类	(公斤) Eggs	(kg)	9.10	6.19	7.83	9.11	11.14	112.5
奶及奶制品	(公斤) Milk and Diary Products	(kg)	6.02	2.16	3.81	4.99	9.97	174.5
水产品	(公斤) Aquatic Products	(kg)	3.83	2.47	2.69	3.72	5.36	91.4
食　糖	(公斤) Sugar	(kg)	1.41	0.84	1.15	1.44	1.81	93.4
糖　果	(公斤) Candy	(kg)	0.34	0.19	0.22	0.27	0.54	130.8
酒　类	(公斤) Liquor	(kg)	17.86	11.58	15.46	19.14	21.02	104.6
茶　叶	(公斤) Tea	(kg)	0.81	0.46	0.77	0.86	0.93	77.9
糕　点	(公斤) Cake	(kg)	1.88	1.47	1.42	1.74	2.53	78.0
瓜　果	(公斤) Melons and Fruits	(kg)	37.94	19.50	30.10	36.80	51.62	102.1
棉布服装	(件) Cotton Cloth and Related Clothing	(piece)	0.51	0.28	0.31	0.45	0.81	283.3
化纤布服装	(件) Chemical Fiber Cloth and Related Clothing	(piece)	0.84	0.54	0.71	0.81	1.06	115.1
毛料服装	(件) Fur-material Garment	(piece)	0.08	0.02	0.03	0.07	0.15	200.0

19-19 2710户农民家庭平均每百户耐用消费品拥有量
DURABLE CONSUMER GOODS POSSESSION PER 100 HOUSEHOLDS OF THE 2710 HOUSEHOLDS

项目 Item			总平均 Average	按人均年纯收入水平分组 Grouped by Annual Net Income Per Capita				2000年为1999年% 2000 as % of 1999
				2000元以下 below 2000 yuan	2000～3500	3500～5000	5000元以上 above 5000 yuan	
自行车	(辆) Bicycles	(unit)	220	194	212	226	228	91.3
电风扇	(台) Electric Fans	(set)	143	108	130	149	157	100.0
洗衣机	(台) Washing Machines	(set)	85	66	80	88	92	98.8
电冰箱	(台) Refrigerators	(set)	84	62	71	87	99	103.7
摩托车	(辆) Motorcycles	(unit)	34	22	30	36	39	100.0
黑白电视机	(台) Black and White TV Sets	(set)	18	21	20	20	15	52.9
彩色电视机	(台) Color TV Sets	(set)	107	94	97	109	116	105.9
收录机	(台) Recorders	(set)	34	22	32	33	39	57.6
照相机	(架) Cameras	(set)	26	12	13	22	43	89.7
录像机	(台) Videorecorders	(set)	16	5	9	14	24	106.7
抽油烟机	(台) Range Hoods	(set)	22	9	9	19	37	129.4
吸尘器	(台) Vacuum Cleaners	(set)	4	1	2	3	8	80.0

主要统计指标解释

城镇居民家庭就业人口 指城镇居民从事社会劳动并取得劳动报酬或经营收入的人口。就业人口包括通过国家统筹规划和指导由劳动部门介绍就业，自愿组织起来就业和自谋职业等方式，在国有制、集体所有制、中外合资、中外合作、外资在华独资的企事业单位和私营企业单位工作或从事个体劳动的有固定性职业或临时性职业的人口。被聘用和留用的离退休人员也计入就业人口。本指标可以反映城镇居民的就业情况，是计算就业面、负担系数的重要资料。

城镇居民家庭全部收入 指被调查城镇居民家庭全部的实际现金收入，包括经常或固定的收入和一次性收入。不包括周转性收入，如提取银行存款、向亲友借入款、收回借出款以及其他各种暂收款。

城镇居民家庭可支配收入 指居民家庭在支付个人所得税后，所余下的实际收入。计算公式为：

可支配收入=实际收入－个人所得税－家庭副业生产支出－记帐补贴

城镇居民家庭消费性支出 指被调查的城镇居民家庭用于日常生活的全部支出，包括八类：食品、衣着、家庭设备用品及服务、医疗保健、交通通讯、娱乐教育文化服务、居住、杂项商品和服务。服务支出是指城镇居民用于社会提供的各种文化和生活服务方面的支出。不包括罚没、丢失款和缴纳的各种税款（如个人所得税、牌照税、房产税等），也不包括个体劳动者经营过程中发生的各项费用。

农村居民家庭纯收入 指农村居民家庭总收入中，扣除从事生产和非生产经营费用支出、缴纳税款和上交承包集体任务金额以后剩余的，可直接用于进行生产性、非生产性建设投资、生活消费和积蓄的那一部分收入。它是反映农民家庭实际收入水平的综合性的主要指标。农民家庭纯收入，既包括从事生产性和非生产性的经营收入，又包括取自在外人口寄回带回和国家财政救济、各种补贴等非经营性收入；既包括货币收入，又包括自产自用的实物收入。但不包括向银行、信用社和向亲友借款等属于借贷性的收入。

农村居民家庭整半劳动力 指农村常住居民家庭成员中有劳动能力并经常参加实际劳动的人员。是生产的基本要素指标之一，是发展生产增加农民家庭收入的重要源泉。按规定，农村男 18 周岁至 50 周岁、女 18 周岁至 45 周岁为整劳动力；男 16 周岁至 17 周岁、51 周岁到 60 周岁，女 16 周岁到 17 周岁、46 周岁至 55 周岁为半劳动力。农民家庭整半劳动力既包括在上述规定劳动年龄内和在劳动年龄以外有劳动能力并经常参加实际劳动的男女整半劳动力；也包括农民家庭常住人员中属于职工的劳动力。但不包括在劳动年龄内已丧失劳动能力的人员。

农村居民家庭生活消费支出 指农村常住居民家庭年内用于日常生活的全部开支。它是用来反映和研究农民家庭实际生活消费水平高低的重要指标。农民家庭生活消费支出，包括用于吃、穿、住、烧、用等生活消费品开支和文化、生活服务费用开支两大部分。

Explanatory Notes On Main Statistical Indicators

Employed Population in Urban Households refers to urban residents engaged in certain work and receiving payment for their labor or income from their business operation, including those who work in state-owned or collective units, joint ventures, foreign-owned units and private units with permanent or temporary jobs, self-employed individuals and re-employed retirees. The indicator reflects the situation of urban employment and is the basic data for calculating employment rate and dependency ratio.

Total Income of Urban Households refers to the total actual cash income of the sample households, including regular or fixed income and occasional income, excluding temporary transferred income, such as withdrawal from bank deposits, borrowed money from relatives or friends, repayment of loans received and various temporary receipts of money.

Discretionary Income of Urban Households refers to the total actual income of households after individual income tax turned over.The formula：

Discretionary Income=Actual Income－Individual Income Tax－Expenditure of Sideline Production－Subsidies of Account

Expenditure on Consumption of Urban Households refers to total expenditure of the sample households on consumption in daily life, including expenditure on eight kinds such as food, clothing, households facilities, articles and services, medicine and medical services, transportation and communication, recreation, education and culture services, residence and miscellaneous. Service expenditure refers to that on various of culture and living by urban residents. The expenditure exclude fines and confiscation, loss, tax payments（such as income tax, license tax, real estates tax, etc.）or various operating expenses in individual business.

Net Income of Rural Households refers to the total income of the permanent residents of the rural households with deduction of the operating expenses in productive and non-productive business, the tax payment and the payment to collective units for their contracted tasks. The net income can be used for investments in productive and non-productive construction, for consumption in daily life and for savings deposit. It is a comprehensive indicator to show the actual income level of the peasants' household, which includes not only the income from the productive and non-productive work, but also the transferred income, such as the money remitted or brought back by household members who are in other places, the government relief and various subsidies, not only the money income, but also the income in kind. But the money borrowed from banks, friends and relatives is excluded.

Full and half Labors of Rural Households refer to permanent residents of rural households who are able to work and actually engaged in social labor, which are factors of production and sources of rural household income. According to the relevant regulations, male aged 18-50 and female aged 18-45 are considered as full labors; male aged 16-17 and 51-60, female aged 16-17 and 46-55 are considered as half labors. Those who are not in the above age range but able to work and actually engaged in social labor are also considered as full or half labors.

Expenditure on Consumption of Rural Households refers to total expenditure of rural households on daily life , including expenses on food, clothing, housing , fuel, articles for daily use, and expenses on cultural life and services. This indicator is used to show the actual consumption level of peasants.

北京统计年鉴——2001

BEIJING STATISTICAL YEARBOOK

社会福利、政法及其他

SOCIAL WELFARE, POLITICS AND LAW AND OTHERS

20

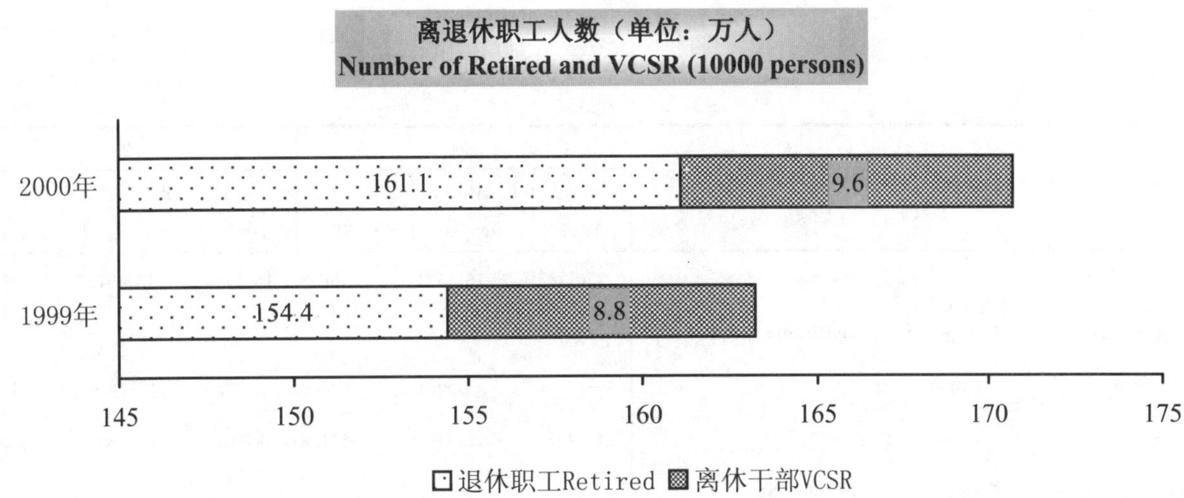
离退休职工人数（单位：万人）
Number of Retired and VCSR (10000 persons)
2000年
1999年
161.1
9.6
154.4
8.8
145
150
155
160
165
170
175
退休职工Retired
离休干部VCSR

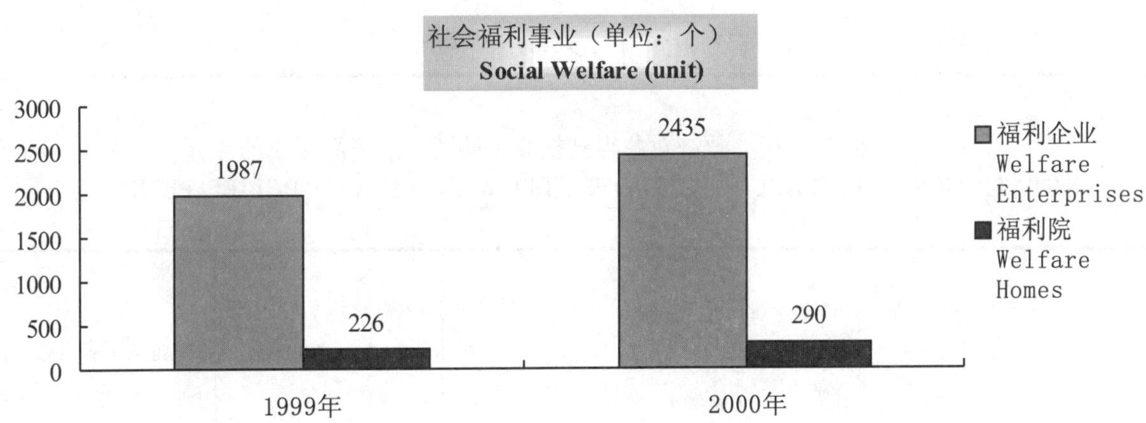
社会福利事业（单位：个）
Social Welfare (unit)
3000
2500
2000
1500
1000
500
0
1987
226
2435
290
1999年
2000年
福利企业 Welfare Enterprises
福利院 Welfare Homes

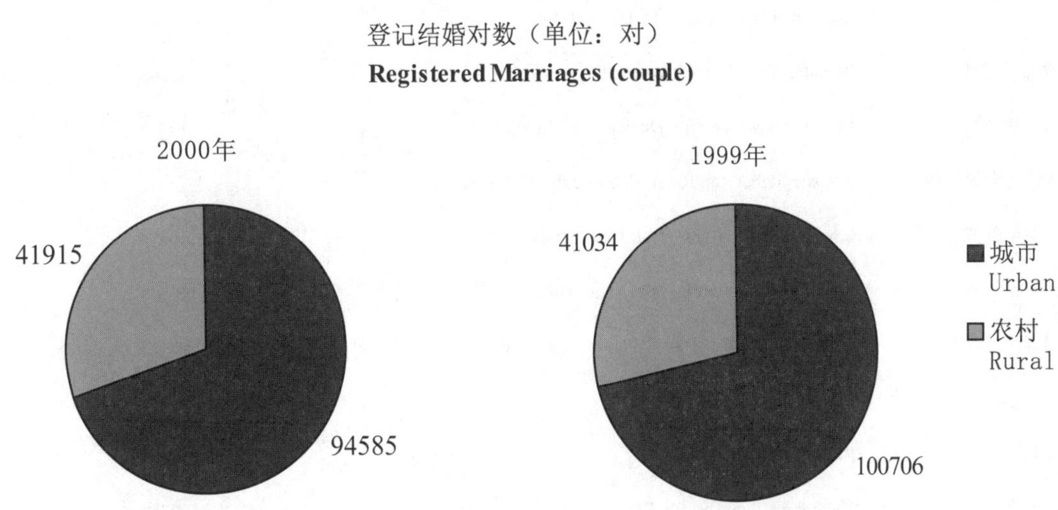
登记结婚对数（单位：对）
Registered Marriages (couple)
2000年
41915
94585
1999年
41034
100706
城市 Urban
农村 Rural

20-1 离休、退休职工人数
NUMBER OF RETIRED AND VCSR

单位：人 (person)

行业 Sector		2000 合计 Total	2000 # 退休职工 Retired	2000 # 离休干部 VCSR	1999 合计 Total	1999 # 退休职工 Retired	1999 # 离休干部 VCSR
总 计	**Total**	**1762283**	**1611374**	**96048**	**1685968**	**1544041**	**88253**
按隶属关系分	**Grouped by Administrative Relationship**						
中央单位	Central Units	367751	315683	44909	347952	295850	45586
地方单位	Local Units	1394532	1295691	51139	1338016	1248191	42667
按登记注册类型分	**Grouped by Registration Status**						
国有经济	State-Owned	1421805	1307140	89397	1334456	1227468	83651
集体经济	Collective-Owned	249760	217906	4574	310733	277314	3917
其 他	Others	90718	86328	2077	40779	39259	685

20-2 优抚、救济对象得到抚恤、补助、救济情况
STATISTICS FOR SPECIAL PENSIONS,ALLOWANCES AND RELIEF FUNDS

项目 Item		人数 (人) Number of Persons (person)	抚恤、补助、救济金额 (千元) Amount of Pensions, Subsidies and Relief Funds (1000 yuan)
烈属牺牲病故军人家属抚恤	Pensions for Members of Revolutionary Martyr's Family, Armymen Sacrificed and Died of Illness	3330	16299
革命伤残人员抚恤	Pensions for Disabled Veterans	12142	7444
复退军人生活补助	Living Allowances for Demobilized Soldiers	15378	73629
农村五保户定期救济补助	Register Relief for Rural Households with Five-guarantees	3342	6791
农村低保对象救济	Low Relief for Rural Poor Households	16144	4332
城镇低保对象救济	Low Relief for Urban Poor Households	64674	81833
精简退职老职工救济	Relief for Old Staff and Workers Reduced and Discharged	8353	13386
自然灾害救济 (人次)	Relief for Natural Calamity (person.time)	14.5	17685
临时救济困难户 (人次)	Temporary Relieves for Households with Living Difficulties (person.time)	69769	12826
离退休人员	VCSR and RRSW	30781	359513
# 离 休	VCSR	2957	52585

20-3 优抚及主要救济对象情况
STATISTICS FOR PERSONS RECEIVING SPECIAL PENSIONS AND RELIEF

单位：人 (person)

项目	Item	人数 Number of Persons 2000	1999	2000年为1999年% 2000 as % of 1999
优抚对象合计	**Persons Receiving Special Pensions**	**248476**	**278256**	**89.3**
烈属	Members of A Revolutionary Martyr's Family	12625	14552	86.8
牺牲、病故军人家属	Families of Soldiers Sacrificed or Died of Illness	2562	2381	107.6
现役军人家属	Servicemen's Families	100685	124280	81.0
革命伤残人员	Revolutionary Disabled	12142	12168	99.8
在乡复员军人	Demobilized Soldiers in Hometown	12691	14405	88.1
在乡退伍军人	Veterans in Hometown	107767	110466	97.6
在乡退伍红军老战士	Demobilized Old Red Army Men in Hometown	4	4	100.0
社会救济对象合计	**Total Persons Receiving Special Relief**	**138978**	**115719**	**120.1**
城镇救济对象	Urban	68454	46877	146.0
# 低保对象人数	Persons Receiving Low Relief	64674	42901	150.8
农村救济对象合计	Rural	70524	68842	102.4
# 困难人口数	Population with Living Difficulties	59910	58831	**101.8**
散居孤老残幼人数	Scattered Orphans and Widows,Disabled, the Old and the Youth	4659	5756	80.9

20-4 社会福利事业情况
BASIC STATISTICS FOR SOCIAL WELFARE PROJECTS

项目		Item		2000	1999	2000年为1999年% 2000 as % of 1999
建立农村社会保障网络数	(个)	Number of Rural Social Security Network	(unit)	118	165	71.5
社会福利企业	(个)	Social Welfare Enterprises	(unit)	2435	1987	122.5
职工人数	(人)	Number of Staff and Workers	(person)	67847	55055	123.2
# 残疾职工	(人)	Disabled Persons	(person)	29603	23397	126.5
城镇社区服务设施	(个)	Urban Welfare Facilities	(unit)	813	1051	77.4

20-5 城乡各种福利院情况
STATISTICS FOR URBAN AND RURAL WELFARE HOMES

项目 Item	合计 Total	光荣院 Homes for Disabled Veterans	社会福利院 Social Welfare Homes	儿童福利院 Welfare Homes for Children	精神病院 Mental Homes	城镇老年福利机构 Welfare Homes for Urban Old People	农村老年福利机构 Welfare Homes for Rural Old People
福利院单位数 (个) Welfare Homes (unit)	290	10	5	3	2	135	135
职工人数 (人) Staff and Workers (person)	3921	234	621	318	263	1411	1074
床位数 (张) Beds (bed)	18680	606	1232	525	620	8957	6740
收养人数 (人) Persons Adopted (person)	11087	452	1145	495	568	4142	4285
# 自 费 (人) at One's Own Expense(person)	6518	27	804	14	313	2878	2482
国家拨款 (千元) Financial Allocation (1000 yuan)	89530	29668	18890	19990	10718	2916	7348

20-6 北京市历年社会保障相关待遇标准
SOCIAL WELFARE TREATMENT STANDARD OF BEIJING

单位：元/月 (yuan/month)

年份 Year \ 标准 Standard	职工最低工资 Lowest Wage of Staff and Workers	失业保险 Unemployment Insurance	下岗职工基本生活费 Basic Cost-of-living of Staff and Workers off their Posts	城镇居民最低生活保障标准 Urban Lowest Cost-of-living
1996	270	189-229.5	180	170
1997	290	203-247	200	190
1998	310	217-264	210	200
1999年第一次 First-time in 1999	320	224-272	220	210
1999年第二次 Second-time in 1999	400	291-374	286	273
2000	412	300-385	296	280

年份 Year \ 标准 Standard	基本养老金平均水平 Average Standard of Basic Old-age Pension	最低退休金 Lowest Pensions of Retired Persons	最低退职金 Lowest Resignation Allowances	最低退养金 Lowest Pensions of Persons Withdraw
1996	60	263	202	170
1997	55	293	232	200
1998	50	336	265	233
1999年第一次 First-time in 1999	40			
1999年第二次 Second-time in 1999	80	396	335	288
2000	30	421	360	308

20-7 社会保险基金统筹情况
SOCIAL BLANKET INSURANCE FUNDS

项　目 Item		退休(养老)基金统筹 Retirement Funds(Old-age)			失业保险基金统筹 Unemployment Insurance Funds		
		单位个数 (个) Number of Units (unit)	人　数 (人) Number of Persons (person)	应缴金额 (万元) Amount Drawn (10000 yuan)	单位个数 (个) Number of Units (unit)	人　数 (人) Number of Persons (person)	应缴金额 (万元) Amount Drawn (10000 yuan)
合　计	**Total**	**21647**	**3916608**	**787640**	**28937**	**3061994**	**84754**
按登记注册类型分	**Grouped by Registered Type**						
国　有	State-Owned	8491	2882388	586053	7262	1633885	45564
集　体	Collective-Owned	4687	465359	1592	4594	212196	2880
其　他	Others	8469	568861	199995	17081	1215913	36310
按隶属关系划分	**Grouped by Administrative Relationship**						
# 中央单位	Central Units	1520	673588	181445	5123	796949	22036
地方单位	Local Units	20127	3243020	606195	23814	2265045	62718

20-8 婚 姻 登 记 情 况
BASIC STATISTICS FOR MARRIAGE REGISTRATIONS

项　目		Item		2000	1999	2000年为1999年% 2000 as % of 1999
登记结婚对数	**(对)**	**Registered Marriages**	**(couple)**	**79519**	**82464**	**96.4**
初婚人数	(人)	First Marriages	(person)	136500	141740	96.3
城　市	(人)	Urban	(person)	94585	100706	93.9
男初婚人数	(人)	Male	(person)	49880	53028	94.1
# 22-24岁	(人)	Age 22-24	(person)	5431	5513	98.5
25岁以上	(人)	Age 25 and above	(person)	44449	47515	93.5
女初婚人数	(人)	Female	(person)	44705	47678	93.8
# 20-22岁	(人)	Age 20-22	(person)	4991	4238	117.8
23岁以上	(人)	Age 23 and above	(person)	39714	43440	91.4
农　村	(人)	Rural	(person)	41915	41034	102.1
男初婚人数	(人)	Male	(person)	17883	17346	103.1
# 22-24岁	(人)	Age 22-24	(person)	8799	8620	102.1
25岁以上	(人)	Age 25 and above	(person)	9084	8726	104.1
女初婚人数	(人)	Female	(person)	24032	23688	101.5
# 20-22岁	(人)	Age 20-22	(person)	9415	8604	109.4
23岁以上	(人)	Age 23 and above	(person)	14617	15084	96.9
再婚人数	(人)	Remarriages	(person)	22538	23188	97.1
男　性	(人)	Male	(person)	11756	11813	99.5
女　性	(人)	Female	(person)	10782	11375	94.8
登记离婚对数	**(对)**	**Registered Divorces**	**(couple)**	**26651**	**23905**	**111.5**

20-9 律 师 工 作
STATISTICS FOR LAWYERS

项 目 Item				2000	1999	2000年为1999年% 2000 as % of 1999
律师事务所	(个)	Law Offices	(unit)	345	319	108.2
律师工作人员	(人)	Lawyers	(person)	5495	5017	109.5
专职律师	(人)	Full-time Lawyers	(person)	3159	2317	136.3
兼职律师	(人)	Part-time Lawyers	(person)	1082	1092	99.1
特邀律师	(人)	Lawyers Specially Invited	(person)	173	270	64.1
其 他	(人)	Others	(person)	1081	1338	80.8
聘请常年法律顾问的单位	(个)	Units with Permanent Legal Advisers	(unit)	4474	4112	108.8
民事代理	(件)	Civil Case	(case)	9094	8971	101.4
经济案件	(件)	Economic Case	(case)	8836	8362	105.7
行政案件	(件)	Administrative Case	(case)	207	169	122.5
刑事辩护	(件)	Criminal Defense	(case)	4300	4320	99.5
非诉讼法律事务	(件)	Off-court Case	(case)	15180	12489	121.5

20-10 部分市属律师事务所主要业务情况
STATISTICS FOR MAJOR MUNICIPAL LAW OFFICES

律师事务所 Law Office	担任常年法律顾问(家) Acted as Permanent Legal Advisers (unit)	律协诉讼案件(件) Lawsuit Cases(case)			办理非诉讼法律事务(件) Off-court Case (case)
		刑 事 Criminal	民 事 Civil	经 济 Economic	
竞天公诚	43	1	26	47	820
君 合				16	89
中伦金通	65			75	49
金 杜	15	5	5	10	77
尚 公	7			6	
海 问	3			5	21
北 斗	79	75	173	207	96
隆 安	37	6	41	110	49
嘉 和	45	8	21	42	65
陆 通	90	26	33	41	467
天 元	41		3	55	50
共 和	3	3	1	27	37
通 商	4				10
观 韬	6	4	15	28	33
炜 衡	25	27	31	38	5
博景泓	21	5	18	74	
时 代	10	6	15	36	6
金 诚	96	2	15	77	112

20-11 部分基层法律服务所主要工作情况
STATISTICS FOR MAJOR LAW SERVICE OFFICES AT BASIC-LEVEL

基层法律服务所 Basic-Level Law Service Office		担任常年法律顾问 (家) Acted as Permanent Legal Advisers (unit)	民事代理 (件) Civil Case (case)	代写法律文书 (份) Legal Document Written on Behalf of Client (unit)	协办公证 (件) Deal Notarization Jointly (case)	解答法律咨询 (人次) Legal Advisory Services (person.time)
东城区	Dongcheng	67	382	408	16	6525
西城区	Xicheng	51	1050	1941	150	13698
崇文区	Chongwen	112	272	245	31	1572
宣武区	Xuanwu	85	566	764	20	6891
朝阳区	Chaoyang	293	690	1560	118	7956
丰台区	Fengtai	106	201	507	4	2157
石景山区	Shijingshan	41	281	848	44	4016
海淀区	Haidian	282	1544	1921	805	7708
门头沟区	Mentougou	12	62	265	3	771
房山区	Fangshan	210	1095	2193	78	9840
通州区	Tongzhou	668	1264	2001	273	7480
顺义区	Shunyi	247	1070	1216	31	3345
昌平区	Changping	502	1005	1518	56	4670
大兴区	Daxing	132	715	1687	32	3234
平谷县	Pinggu	82	350	511	19	1959
怀柔县	Huairou	24	285	537	10	1623
密云县	Miyun	235	787	1254	10	7620
延庆县	Yanqing	76	397	551	15	1961

20-12 历 届 律 师 资 格 考 试 情 况
STATISTICS FOR LAWYER QUALIFICATION EXAMINATION

单位：人 (person)

年份 Year	报考人数 Number of Persons Registered	实考人数 Number of Persons Scattered	录取人数 Number of Persons Passed	录取人数占实考人数比例 (%) Percentage of Passed in Persons Attended (%)
1988	4280	2782	1329	47.8
1990	3735	2549	46	1.8
1992	2732	1882	510	27.1
1993	4769	3400	1068	31.4
1994	5653	4480	533	11.9
1995	5842	4661	1204	25.8
1996	5873	4445	317	7.1
1997	6350	4760	1126	23.7
1998	7946	6188	1436	23.2
1999	9736	7911	1727	21.8
2000	10649	8594	1637	19.0

20-13 乡镇(街道)法律服务情况
STATISTICS FOR TOWNSHIP(URBAN SUBDISTRICT) LAW SERVICES

项目 Item				2000	1999	2000年为1999年% 2000 as % of 1999
法律服务所	(个)	Law Service Offices	(unit)	356	352	101.1
法律工作者	(人)	Law Personnel	(person)	1916	2285	83.9
调解纠纷	(件)	Disputes Mediated	(case)	6494	6258	103.8
协办公证	(件)	Deal Notarization Jointly	(case)	1685	1726	97.6
担任法律顾问	(家)	Act as Legal Advisers	(unit)	3225	3479	92.7
民事代理	(件)	Civil Cases	(case)	12016	13531	88.8

20-14 法院行政案件收、结案情况
STATISTICS FOR ADMINISTRATIVE CASES ACCEPTED AND CLOSED BY COURT

单位：件 (case)

项目 Item		收案 Cases Accepted	结案 Cases Closed	#维持 Affirm	#调解 Mediation	#判决 Jadgement
合计	**Total**	**1136**	**1135**	**363**	**97**	**381**
公安	Security	188	182	45	8	64
工商	Industry and Commerce	48	46	8	6	10
卫生	Health Care	15	15			6
土地	Land	88	85	22	12	40
税务	Tax	4	5	2	1	2
城建	Urban Construction	426	426	206	48	98
环保	Environmental Protection	5	5			2
林业	Forestry	2	2	1		1
专利	Patent	25	29	21	4	4
民政	Civil Affairs	4	4		1	1
其他	Others	331	336	58	17	153

20-15 刑事案件情况
STATISTICS FOR CRIMINAL CASES

单位：起 (case)

项目 Item		2000	1999	2000年为1999年% 2000 as % of 1999
刑事案件	**Criminal Cases**			
立案	Cases Registered	82849	65750	126.0
破案	Cases Solved	32707	21285	153.7

20-16 法院刑事案件收、结案情况
STATISTICS FOR CRIMINAL CASES ACCEPTED AND CLOSED BY COURT

项目	Item	收案 (件) Cases Accepted (case)	结案 (件) Cases Closed (case)	排挤判决发生法律效力 Judgment with Legal Force 件数(件) Number of Cases (case)	人数(人) Number of Persons (person)
合计	**Total**	**11501**	**11609**	**9946**	**14679**
危害国家安全罪	Offense against State Security	7	10	5	7
危害公共安全罪	Offense against Public Security	643	644	594	676
破坏社会主义市场经济秩序罪	Offense against the Socialist Market Economic Order	550	564	465	668
侵犯公民人身权利、民主权利罪	Infringement of Civil Personal Rights and Democratic Rights	2978	3015	2343	2979
侵犯财产罪	Infringement Property	5240	5277	4748	7651
妨害社会管理秩序罪	Interference with Public Function	1818	1826	1602	2467
危害国防利益罪	Offense against National Defense Interest	12	12	12	22
贪污贿赂罪	Corruption and Bribery Crime	233	239	167	196
渎职罪	Malpraetice Duty	20	22	10	13

20-17 法院民事案件收、结案情况
STATISTICS FOR CIVIL CASES ACCEPTED AND CLOSED BY COURT

单位：件 (case)

项目	Item	收案 Cases Accepted	结案 Cases Closed	#调解 Mediation	#判决 Judgment
合计	**Total**	**98756**	**98898**	**34272**	**32367**
离婚	Divorce	31256	31302	17716	5705
抚养	Foster	2627	2622	1061	854
继承	Inherit	814	789	204	342
房屋	House	5109	5171	680	1785
相邻关系	Relation of Neighborhood	1842	1842	278	702
赔偿	Compensation	10424	10388	2546	5007
债务	Debt	31648	31774	8798	11414
著作权	Copyright	383	407	40	224
人身权	Personal Right	289	280	21	147
其他	Others	14364	14323	2928	6187

20-18 法院经济纠纷案件收、结案情况
STATISTICS FOR ECONOMIC DISPUTE CASES ACCEPTED AND CLOSED BY COURT

单位：件 (case)

项目	Item	收案 Cases Accepted	结案 Cases Closed	#调解 Mediation	#判决 Judgment
合计	**Total**	**24220**	**24720**	**6605**	**8133**
购销合同	Purchases and Sales Contracts	10867	10975	3493	2996
加工承揽合同	Processing Contracts	1978	1989	601	601
借款合同	Debt Contracts	2763	2955	557	1637
企业承包经营合同	Contracts of Enterprises	310	332	57	134
联营合同	Joint Business Contracts	231	247	34	115
财产租赁合同	Property Leases Contracts	865	845	215	290
建筑工程承包合同	Construction Project Contracts	93	90	20	27
交通运输纠纷	Transportation Dispute	216	220	57	53
农村承包合同	Foreign,Hongkong,Macao and	291	298	137	75
其他	Others	6606	6769	1434	2205

20-19 检察机关办理各类案件情况
STATISTICS FOR CASES HANDLED BY PROCURATORIAL ORGAN

项目	Item	受案(受理) Cases Accepted 件 Case	受案(受理) Cases Accepted 人 Person	审结案合计 Cases Closed 件 Case	审结案合计 Cases Closed 人 Person	# 重特大案 Important Cases 人 Person
审查批捕	**Examine for Arrest**	**11164**	**16771**	**10691**	**15942**	**3675**
# 批准逮捕	Approve			10171	15027	3675
不批准逮捕	Disapprove			520	915	
审查起、免诉	**Examine for Sue**	**12542**	**18783**	**11433**	**16730**	**2421**
# 起诉	Sue	12533	18773	11212	16389	2421
不起诉	Immunity from Suit	9	10	221	341	
举报控告案件	**Prosecution Cases**	**7401**		**7432**		
申诉案件	**Appeal Cases**	**436**		**415**		
民事、行政检察	**Civil and Administrative Procuratorial Work**	**1887**		**1738**		
民事案	Civil Cases	1451		1355		
知识产权案	Intellectual Property	18		8		
经济纠纷案	Economic Disputes	257		222		
行政案	Administrative Cases	161		153		

20-20 检察机关自侦经济、法纪案件情况
CASES SELF-INVESTIGATION OF ECONOMY,LAW AND DISCIPLINE BY PROCURATORIAL ORGAN

项目	Item	自侦经济案件 Self-investigate Economic Cases 合计 Total	贪污 Corruption	受贿 Accepting Bribes	行贿 Bribe	#挪用公款 Misappropriate Public Funds	其他 Others	自侦法纪案件 Self-Investigate Law and Discipline Cases
受案 (件)	**Cases Accepted (case)**	**1368**	**650**	**375**	**33**	**281**	**29**	**128**
立案 (件)	**Cases Registered (case)**	**419**	**161**	**89**	**21**	**143**	**5**	**33**
# 重特大案	Important Cases							9
5至10万元	50000-100000 Yuan	65	34	11	3	15	2	
10至50万元	100000-500000 Yuan	115	44	18	5	46	2	
50至100万元	500000-1000000 Yuan	31	6	5	5	15		
100万元以上	Over 1000000 Yuan	73	9	7	3	53	1	
结案	**Cases Closed**							
件数 (件)	Number of Cases (case)	306	121	64	11	104	6	30
人数 (人)	Number of Persons (person)	345	143	65	11	117	9	43
# 移送起诉	Hand over to Suit							
件数 (件)	Number of Cases (case)	281	117	56	10	92	6	26
人数 (人)	Number of Persons (person)	315	137	57	10	103	8	34
挽回经济损失 (万元)	**Retrieve Pecuniary Losses (10000 yuan)**	**57800**	**1903.2**	**336.3**	**85.2**	**55163.3**	**312**	

20-21 查处治安案件情况
STATISTICS FOR INVESTIGATING AND HANDLING PUBLIC ORDER CASES

项目	Item	查处(起) Investigating and Handling (case)	构成(%) Composition (%)
合计	**Total**	**154702**	**100**
扰乱工作、公共秩序	Disturb Working or Public Order	40927	26.5
结伙斗殴、寻衅滋事	Gang Fighting	1823	1.2
侮辱妇女及其他流氓活动	Insult Woman and Other Immoral Behavior	300	0.2
阻碍国家工作人员执行公务	Interference with Government Function	700	0.5
违反枪支管理规定	Violate Regulatory Regime for Firearms	100	0.1
违反爆炸物品管理规定	Violate Regulatory Regime for Explosive Goods	618	0.4
殴打他人	Beat up Others	15633	10.1
偷窃财物	Steal	9595	6.2
骗取、抢夺、敲诈勒索财物	Cheat,Rob and Extort Property	2271	1.4
哄抢公私财物	Rob Public Property	88	0.1
故意损坏公私财物	Damage Public and Private Properties Intentionally	681	0.4
伪造倒卖票券、证件	Forge,Resell Bill,Ticket and Credentials	426	0.3
利用迷信扰乱秩序或骗财	Disturb Public Order or Defraud sb.of His Belongings by Superstitions	2029	1.3
卖淫、嫖娼	Prostitution,Visit Prostitution	1681	1.1
赌博	Gambling	2322	1.5
违反户口、居民身份证管理	Violate Regulations for Residence Cards or ID	36240	23.4
其他	Others	39268	25.3

20-22 调解工作
MEDIATION

项目 Item				2000	1999	2000年为1999年% 2000 as % of 1999
专职司法助理员	(人)	Full-time Judicial Assistants	(person)	534	646	82.7
人民调解委员会	(个)	People's Mediation Committees	(unit)	10933	12517	87.3
调解人员	(万人)	Intermediators	(10000 persons)	14	16	87.5
调解委员	(万人)	Members of the Mediation Institution	(10000 persons)	4.9	5.5	89.1
调解各类纠纷	(万件)	Disputes Mediated	(10000 cases)	11.5	12.1	95.0
防止民间纠纷激化	(件)	Prevent Intensification of Civil Disputes	(case)	2133	2546.0	83.8

20-23 公证工作
NOTARIZATIONS

项目 Item				2000	1999	2000年为1999年% 2000 as % of 1999
公证处	(个)	Notary Offices	(unit)	24	24	100.0
公证人员	(人)	Notary Personnel	(person)	272	237	114.8
办理国内民事公证	(件)	Notarized Domestic Civil Affairs	(case)	76563	64325	119.0
办理国内经济公证	(件)	Notarized Domestic Economic Affairs	(case)	26711	34418	77.6
办理涉外公证	(件)	Notarized Foreign Affairs	(case)	205982	192503	107.0

20-24 2000年全市公证处总办证量情况对比表
STATISTICS FOR WORK OF NOTARY OFFICES IN 2000

单位：件 (case)

区 县 District and County		总办证量 Notary Documents	# 国内民事 Domestic Civil Affairs	# 国内经济 Domestic Economic Affairs
东城区	Dongcheng	18470	16883	1587
西城区	Xicheng	3754	3673	81
崇文区	Chongwen	1736	1706	30
宣武区	Xuanwu	2999	2892	107
朝阳区	Chaoyang	3775	3554	221
丰台区	Fengtai	1296	1152	144
石景山区	Shijingshan	1838	1834	4
海淀区	Haidian	14349	13187	1162
门头沟区	Mentougou	554	524	30
房山区	Fangshan	1160	613	547
通州区	Tongzhou	1961	1750	211
顺义区	Shunyi	1348	1202	146
昌平区	Changping	672	500	172
大兴县	Daxing	2175	2110	65
平谷县	Pinggu	409	281	128
怀柔县	Huairou	752	317	435
密云县	Miyun	1141	1055	86
延庆县	Yanqing	308	277	31

20-25 国内公证文书分类
CLASSIFIED STATISTICS FOR DOMESTIC NOTARY DOCUMENTS

单位：件 (case)

项目	Item	民事公证数 Civil Notarization
收养	Adoption	200
解除收养	Dissolution of Adoption	4
继承权	Rights of Inheritance	3650
遗嘱	Testaments	3576
产权	Property Rights	180
亲属关系	Kinship	538
死亡	Death Certificates	8
房屋买卖	House Purchase and Sale	982
房屋租赁	House Leases	17
留学协议	Agreements on Studying abroad	476
遗赠扶养协议	Agreements on Bequeath and Fostering	122
委托书	Certificate of Entrustment	15012
赠与书	Deed of Gift	4268
声明书	Declarations	2513
现场监督	Spot Supervision	12667
签名印鉴属实	True Signature	323
文本相符	Confirmation of Copies to the Original	3401
宅基地使用权	Using House Site Rights	4
证据保全	Evidence Preservation	1399
拆迁协议	Dismantle,Move Agreement	315
计划生育	Family Planning Agreemen	398
赡养协议	Support Agreements	236
合伙协议	Partnership Agreements	5
夫妻财产协议	Agreements on Estates by the Entirety	262
其他民事协议	Other Civil Agreements	6845
其他	Others	19162
合计	**Total**	**76563**

项目	Item	经济公证数 Economic Notarization
购销	Purchases and Sales	8
联营	Joint Business	4
拍卖	Actions	34
贷款	Loans	187
担保	Guarantees	162
招标投标	Bidding	134
科技协作	Scientific and Technological Cooperation	14388
供用电	Electricity Supply or Use	
劳务合同	Labor Contracts	1023
建筑工程承包	Construction Projects Contracts	3
工商服务业承包	Contracts of Industry,Commerce and Services	7
农林牧副渔业承包	Contract of Farming,Forestry, Animal Husbandry,Sideline And Fishery	226
乡镇企业承包	Contracts of Township Enterprises	34
财产租赁	Property Leases	208
企业租赁	Enterprise Leases	106
资产经营责任制	Asset Business Contracts	4
还款协议	Agreements on Paying off Loans	197
土地使用权出让转让	Selling and Transferring of Land Using Right	40
其他经济合同	Other Economic Contracts	1532
法人(代表人)资格	Identification of Institutional Units(Agent)	56
法人委托书	Trust Deeds of Institutional Units	2892
公司章程	Corporation Constitutions	19
执行许可证明	Operating Permits	1
提存	Drawings	28
抵押登记	Mortgage Registration	1332
公司会议记录	Records of Corporation Conference	10
其他	Others	4076
合计	**Total**	**26711**

20-26 消 防 建 设 情 况
STATISTICS FOR FIRE FIGHTING

项 目 Item				2000	1999	1998	1997	1996	1995
消防队数	(队)	Number of Fire Brigades	(unit)	47	77	41	38	36	35
消防车辆	(辆)	Number of Fire Engines	(unit)	259	236	210	190	180	180
义务消防团	(个)	Voluntary Fire Brigades	(unit)					20	20
队数	(万个)	Fire Bridges	(10000)	3.9				3.9	3.9
人数	(万人)	Persons	(10000 persons)	77				77	77

20-27 火 灾 及 损 失
FIRE AND LOSSES

项 目 Item				数 量 Amount		直接经济损失(万元) Direct Pecuniary Loss (10000 yuan)	
				2000	1999	2000	1999
总 计	**(起)**	**Total**	**(unit)**	**5037**	**5395**	**1435.9**	**3165.0**
# 特大火灾		Extraordinarily Serious			1		1736.0
重大火灾		Heavy		4	5	179.4	1808.0
起火原因		**Cause of Fire**					
# 电 器		Electric Appliances		1480	1216	607.5	2254.8
违反安全规定		Violate Safety Regulation		165	149	147.7	62.5
吸 烟		Smoking		612	969	55.9	139.4
生活用火不慎		Careless		1377	1354	104.5	129.1
玩 火		Play with Fire		296	191	44.9	21.9
伤 人	(人)	**Injuries**	**(person)**	**107**	**92**		
死 人	(人)	**Deaths**	**(person)**	**42**	**53**		

20-28 交 通 事 故 及 损 失
STATISTICS FOR TRAFFIC ACCIDENTS AND LOSSES

项 目 Item				2000	1999	2000年为1999年% 2000 as % of 1999
总 计	**(起)**	**Total**	**(case)**	**32378**	**32291**	**100.3**
伤 人	(人)	Injuries	(person)	10583	10607	99.8
死 亡	(人)	Deaths	(person)	1459	1502	97.1
在总计中：机动车事故	**(起)**	**Of Total:Motor Vehicle Accident**	**(case)**	**30121**	**29923**	**100.7**
伤 人	(人)	Injuries	(person)	8660	8577	101.0
死 亡	(人)	Deaths	(person)	1070	1101	97.2
直接经济损失	**(万元)**	**Direct Pecuniary Losses**	**(10000 yuan)**	**13777.5**	**15539.3**	**88.7**
每万辆机动车死亡	(人)	Deaths Per 10000 Motor Vehicles	(persons)	9.8	10.8	90.7

20-29 妇联组织状况
STATISTICS FOR WOMAN FEDERATION ORGANIZATIONS

单位：个，人 (unit,person)

项目	Item	2000	1999
区妇联数	Number of District Women Organizations	13	13
区妇联干部数	Cadres in District Women Organization Cadres	161	161
县妇联数	Number of County Women Organizations	5	5
县妇联干部数	Cadres in County Women Organization Cadres	43	43
乡妇联组织数	Number of Township Women Organizations	240	240
街妇联组织数	Number of Street Women Organizations	116	116
乡、街妇联干部数	Cadres of Township and Street Women Organization	434	434
城市基层妇代会组织数	Number of Urban Basic Women Congress	4050	4548
农村基层妇代会组织数	Number of Rural Basic Women Congress	4320	4332
机关及事业单位妇委会组织数	Number of Women Committees in Organs and Institutions	415	556
乡、镇企业妇委会组织数	Number of Women Committees in Township and Village Enterprises	1044	1044
各类妇女联谊组织数	Women Connection Organizations	14	14

20-30 各级工会情况
LABOR UNIONS

项目	Item	基层以上工会组织（个） Labor Union above Basic-level(unit)		工会专职干部人数（人） Full-time Cadre(person)	
		2000	1999	2000	1999
市总工会	Municipal Federation of Labor Union	1	1	163	163
区县级工会	Labor Union at District and County Level	18	18	393	407
产业及局总公司集团工会	Labor Union of Industry and General Company Group	130	89	610	553
二级公司工会	Labor Union of Second-level Company	443	514	871	1074
其他	Others	209	135	224	136

20-31 工会组织建设情况
WORKERS CONGRESS BUILDING

项目 Item			国有企业 State-owned	集体企业 Collective-owned	股份合作企业 Share Holding Cooperative	联营企业 Joint-owned	国有独资公司 Enterprises with exclusively State Investment
基层工会组织	(个) Workers Congress at Basic-level	(unit)	3097	2236	397	45	65
职工人数	(人) Staff and Workers	(person)	1187478	219802	37471	8150	37566
# 女职工	(人) Female	(person)	454913	97515	14385	4101	14859
工会专职干部	(人) Full-time Cadre of Workers Congress	(person)	4712	950	173	37	164

项目 Item			其他有限责任公司 Limited-Liability Company	国有控股公司 State-owned Holding Company	其他股份有限公司 Other Share Holding Coporations	私营企业 Private Owned	其他内资企业 Other Domestic Investment Enterprises
基层工会组织	(个) Workers Congress at Basic-level	(unit)	401	121	160	641	10
职工人数	(人) Staff and Workers	(person)	35654	86944	30043	23358	579
# 女职工	(人) Female	(person)	14007	31227	11495	8953	47
工会专职干部	(人) Full-time Cadre of Workers Congress	(person)	165	333	55	70	1

20-32 职工民主管理情况

STATISTICS FOR WORKERS DEMOCRACY MANAGEMENT

单位：个 (unit)

项目	Item	国有企业 State-owned	集体企业 Collective-owned	股份合作企业 Share Holding Cooperative	联营企业 Joint-owned	国有独资公司 Enterprises with exclusively State Investment
建立职工代表大会制度的单位	Number of Units with Workers	2851	1318	185	35	55
建立女职工工作委员会的单位	Number of Units with Working Committee for Female Workers	2408	965	132	24	51
召开职工代表大会的单位	Number of Units Hold Workers Congress	2778	1240	180	33	48
实行厂务公开的单位	Number of Units Business Brought into the Open	2743	1254	173	31	51
建立劳动法律监督组织的单位	Number of Units with Supervise Organization for Labor Law	1234	402	59	8	16
开展民主评议企业领导的单位	Number of Enterprises Carry out Democratic Appraise Cadre	2627	1127	163	28	43

项目	Item	其他有限责任公司 Limited-Liability Company	国有控股公司 State-owned Holding Company	其他股份有限公司 Other Share Holding Coporations	私营企业 Private Owned	其他内资企业 Other Domestic Investment Enterprises
建立职工代表大会制度的单位	Number of Units with Workers Congress	183	112	71	86	5
建立女职工工作委员会的单位	Number of Units with Working Committee for Female Workers	135	103	70	101	1
召开职工代表大会的单位	Number of Units Hold Workers Congress	169	108	67	74	5
实行厂务公开的单位	Number of Units Business Brought into the Open	161	113	65	73	2
建立劳动法律监督组织的单位	Number of Units with Supervise Organization for Labor Law	65	52	39	16	
开展民主评议企业领导的单位	Number of Enterprises Carry out Democratic Appraise Cadre	140	99	54	39	2

20-33 职工经济技术活动情况
ECONOMIC AND TECHNICAL ACTIVITIES OF STAFF AND WORKERS

项目 Item	国有企业 State-owned	集体企业 Collective-owned	股份合作企业 Share Holding Cooperative	联营企业 Joint-Owned	国有独资公司 Enterprises with exclusively State Investment
本年度提出合理化建议件数 (件) Number of Rationlization Proposal Presented in this Year (unit)	221697	6551	1602	726	2687
本年度已实施的合理化建议创造的经济效益 (万元) Economic Benefits Created by Rationlization Proposal Carried out (10000 yuan)	147863	2984	2230	74	1653
开展劳动竞赛活动的单位 (个) Units Hold Labor Emulation (unit)	2013	635	102	17	40
劳动竞赛创造的可计算的经济效益 (万元) Calculable Economic Benefits Created by Labor emulation (10000 yuan)	283666	12520	17624	526	3653

项目 Item	其他有限责任公司 Limited-Liability Company	国有控股公司 State-owned Holding Company	其他股份有限公司 Other Share Holding Coporations	私营企业 Private Owned	其他内资企业 Other Domestic Investment Enterprises
本年度提出合理化建议件数 (件) Number of Rationlization Proposal Presented in this Year (unit)	2097	5659	1680	177	2
本年度已实施的合理化建议创造的经济效益 (万元) Economic Benefits Created by Rationlization Proposal Carried out (10000 yuan)	836	4310	159	82	
开展劳动竞赛活动的单位 (个) Units Hold Labor Emulation (unit)	109	92	58	88	3
劳动竞赛创造的可计算的经济效益 (万元) Calculable Economic Benefits Created by Labor emulation (10000 yuan)	42470	22608	2699	91	1

20-34 参加社会保障的单位情况
STATISTICS FOR UNITS ATTEND SOCIAL SECURITY

单位：个 (unit)

项目 Item	国有企业 State-owned	集体企业 Collective-owned	股份合作企业 Share Holding Cooperative	联营企业 Joint-owned	国有独资公司 Enterprises with exclusively State Investment
参加养老保险社会统筹的单位 Units Attend Social Overall Endowment Insurance	2928	1306	198	34	61
参加医疗保险社会统筹的单位 Units Attend Medical Insurance	2582	1238	187	32	50
足额交纳养老保险金的单位 Units Pay Full Endowment Insurance Pension	2884	1268	196	32	59
足额交纳医疗保险金的单位 Units Pay Full Medical Insurance Pension	2517	1193	186	29	48
职工互助保险参加人数 (人) Persons Attend Mutual aid and Supplementary Insurance (person)	189275	6299	1501	625	5509
职工医疗互助保险参加人数 (人) Persons Attend Medical Mutual aid and Supplementary Insurance (person)	80949	2191	1271		1003

项目 Item	其他有限责任公司 Limited-Liability Company	国有控股公司 State-owned Holding Company	其他股份有限公司 Other Share Holding Coporations	私营企业 Private Owned	其他内资企业 Other Domestic Investment Enterprises
参加养老保险社会统筹的单位 Units Attend Social Overall Endowment Insurance	285	117	115	129	6
参加医疗保险社会统筹的单位 Units Attend Medical Insurance	262	106	108	117	6
足额交纳养老保险金的单位 Units Pay Full Endowment Insurance Pension	281	114	112	127	5
足额交纳医疗保险金的单位 Units Pay Full Medical Insurance Pension	257	102	105	112	6
职工互助保险参加人数 (人) Persons Attend Mutual aid and Supplementary Insurance (person)	567	5739	2112	4	
职工医疗互助保险参加人数 (人) Persons Attend Medical Mutual aid and Supplementary Insurance (person)	297	676	618	4	

20-35 《九十年代中国儿童发展规划纲要》监测统计资料(目标指标)

SUPERVISORY STATISTICS FOR 《PROGRAM OUTLINE OF CHINESE CHILDREN DEVELOPMENT IN 1990S》 (OBJECT INDICATORS)

项目	Item	1990	1999	2000
婴儿死亡率 (‰)	Infant Death Rate (‰)	11.66	7.95	5.36
城　市	Urban	11.15	7.78	6.29
农　村	Rural	12.27	8.38	4.05
五岁以下儿童死亡率 (‰)	Death Rate of Children below 5-year-old (‰)	13.72	9.97	6.78
城　市	Urban	13.06	9.64	
农　村	Rural	14.51	10.81	
孕产妇死亡率 (1/10万)	Death Rate of Pregnant Woman and Lying-in Woman (10/million)	24.99	17.53	9.70
城　市	Urban	20.92	15.69	7.10
农　村	Rural	29.89	22.06	13.38
五岁以下儿童中重度营养不良患病率 (%)	Rate of Heavy Malnutrition of Children below 5-year-old (%)	2.44	0.61	0.54
城　市	Urban	1.04	0.62	0.52
农　村	Rural	3.49	0.59	0.58
年龄别体重	Weight by Stages of Age	2.44	0.61	0.54
年龄别身高	Height by Stages of Age		0.79	0.71
身高别体重	Weight by Stages of Height		0.38	0.33
缺水地区农村饮用水受益人口 (万人)	Population Benefited from Drinking Water in Rural Water Deficient Area (10000 persons)	62		
城市污水处理率 (%)	Disposal Rate of Urban Sewage (%)	6.60	24.69	39.40
城市卫生厕所覆盖率 (%)	Covering Rate of Urban Toilet (%)	99.50	99.83	99.85
农村享有卫生厕所的人口比重 (%)	Rate of Rural Population Use Toilet (%)	8.54	75.79	80.90
学龄儿童入学率 (%)	Enrollment Rate of Children at School-age (%)	99.50	99.95	99.95
城　市	Urban	99.70	99.96	99.99
农　村	Rural	99.60	99.93	99.94
小学毕业率 (%)	Graduate Rate of Primary School (%)	99.20	100.05	99.96
小学巩固率 (%)	Stronging Rate of Primary School (%)	100.23	99.83	99.94
小学辍学率 (%)	Rate of Leaving off Study of Primary School (%)	-0.17	0.06	0.07
男	Male		0.07	0.06
女	Female		0.04	0.09
初中入学率 (%)	Enrollment Rate of Junior Middle School (%)	99.24	97.85	99.99
初中毕业率 (%)	Graduate Rate of Junior Middle School (%)	91.43	96.04	
初中巩固率 (%)	Stronging Rate of Junior Middle School (%)	93.69	97.83	98.88
小学专任教师学历合格率 (%)	Qualified Rate of Educational Background of Full-time Teacher of Primary School (%)	89.00	97.72	99.50
3-6岁儿童入园率 (%)	Enrollment Rate of Kindergarten of Children at Age 3-6 (%)	71.20	80.80	81.00
城　市	Urban	94.10	90.80	90.80
农　村	Rural	50.80	71.10	72.12
青壮年文盲率 (%)	Illiteracy Rate of Young People (%)	1.60		4.90
校外教育活动场所数 (个)	Number of Locations of After-school Education (unit)	1434	1594	1251
家长受教育率 (%)	Rate of Parents Educated (%)		97.30	98.50
科学育儿知识普及率 (%)	Spreading Rate of Raising Children with Scientific Method (%)	59.40	96.11	97.08
出生缺陷儿发生率 (‰)	Rate of Defect New-borns (‰)	7.36	10.60	9.78
城　市	Urban	5.34	11.31	10.85
农　村	Rural	6.34	9.88	7.86
婚前医学检查率 (%)	Rate of Physic Pre-martial Check-up (%)	54.70	98.70	99.90
城　市	Urban	77.00	99.77	99.90
农　村	Rural	23.30	95.79	96.17
残疾儿童入学率 (%)	Enrollment Rate of Deformed Children (%)	64.15	99.00	98.40

20-36 《九十年代中国儿童发展规划纲要》监测统计资料(措施指标)

SUPERVISORY STATISTICS FOR 《PROGRAM OUTLINE OF CHINESE CHILDREN DEVELOPMENT IN 1990S》(MEASURE INDICATORS)

项目	Item	1990	1999	2000
人口自然增长率 (‰)	Natural Growth Rate of Population (‰)	6.62	0.90	0.90
节育手术并发症发生率 (1/万)	Rate of Complication from Birth Control Operation (1/ten thousand)	2.50	2.28	1.40
城市	Urban	3.50	2.34	1.28
农村	Rural	2.70	2.12	1.69
预算内卫生事业经费增长速度 (%)	Growth Rate of Budgetary Health Fund (%)		24.00	31.00
妇幼保健费增长速度(卫生局系统) (%)	Growth Rate of Maternal and Child Hygiene Subsidies(Health Bureau System) (%)		-10.00	25.2
卫生防疫费增长速度(卫生局系统) (%)	Growth Rate of Epidemic Prevention Subsidies (Health Bureau System) (%)		1.00	25.2
新法接生率 (%)	Rate of Delivering Children with New Method (%)	99.70	99.68	100.00
城市	Urban	99.90	99.61	100.00
农村	Rural	99.60	99.84	100.00
孕产妇住院分娩率 (%)	Childbirth Rate of Pregnant Woman and Lying-in Woman in Hospital (%)	83.79	98.82	99.56
城市	Urban	99.90	99.09	99.63
农村	Rural	67.30	98.15	99.44
产后出血死亡率 (1/10万)	Death Rate of Birth Hemorrhage (10/million)	9.28	3.19	1.39
孕妇缺铁性贫血患病率 (%)	Rate of Iron-deficiency Anemia of Pregnant Woman (%)		6.39	5.84
城市	Urban		6.78	5.23
农村	Rural		5.10	7.09
母乳喂养率(0-4个月) (%)	Rate of Feeding on Mother Milk(0-4 months) (%)		90.99	91.37
城市	Urban	13.60	87.96	88.69
农村	Rural	67.00	95.37	95.39
七岁以下儿童保健复盖率 (%)	Health Protection Rate of Children below 7-year-old (%)	59.40	96.11	97.78
城市	Urban		97.62	98.89
农村	Rural	82.73	93.79	96.02
孕产妇保健复盖率 (%)	Covering Rate of Health Protection for Pregnant Woman and Lying-in Woman (%)		95.38	97.58
城市	Urban		96.75	98.43
农村	Rural		91.95	96.15
一岁以内儿童计划免疫"四苗"接种率 (%)	Inoculation Rate of Immunity Four-Vaccine of Children within 1-year-old (%)	98.73	91.60	99.63
卡介苗	BCG Vaccine	99.50	93.60	99.80
麻疹疫苗	Measles Vaccine	99.20	98.50	99.81
百白破三联制剂	Pertussis,Diphtheria and Tetanus Vaccine	99.10	98.70	99.92
脊髓灰质炎疫苗	Poliomyelitis Polio Vaccine	99.30	98.80	99.87
小儿脊髓灰质炎发病率 (1/10万)	Rate of Poliomyelitis Polio of Children (10/million)	0.04		0.00
新生儿破伤风发病率 (‰)	Rate of Tetanus of New-borns (‰)	0.04	0.00	0.00
新生儿破伤风死亡专率 (‰)	Death Rate of Tetanus of Newborns (‰)	0.5	0.00	0.00
麻疹死亡专率 (1/10万)	Death Rate of Measles (10/million)			0.00
麻疹发病率 (1/10万)	Rate of Measles (10/million)	0.51	1.93	2.13
儿童腹泻发病率 (‰)	Rate of Diarrhea of Children (‰)		1.17	1.22
五岁以下儿童因腹泻死亡的人数比例 (1/10万)	Proportion of Children below 5-year-old Died of Diarrhea (10/million)	4.46	3.69	3.67
急性呼吸道感染标准病例管理率 (%)	Managing Rate of Standard Case of Acute Infection of Respiratory Tract (%)		90.31	91.91
急性呼吸道感染临床管理率 (%)	Clinical Managing Rate of Acute Infection of Respiratory Tract (%)		99.31	99.33
五岁以下儿童因急性呼吸道感染死亡的人数 (人)	Number of Children below 5-year-old Died of Infection of Respiratory Tract (person)	92	39	29
地方性甲状腺肿大率 (%)	Rate of Local Goitre (%)	1.90	3.40	1.70
城市三岁以上儿童入园率 (%)	Enrollment Rate in Kindergarten of Urban Children over 3-year-old (%)		90.80	90.80
农村学前一年幼儿入园(班)率 (%)	Enrollment Rate in Kindergarten of Rural Children at Age Preschool a Year (%)		95.00	95.00

主要统计指标解释

社会福利事业单位 指为社会上丧失劳动能力、无依无靠、无生活来源的孤老残幼、家庭无力照管的老人、残疾儿童、精神病人和优抚对象、困难户、社区居民提供收养、帮助、服务的福利机构和福利设施。

社会福利企业 指以集中安置有一定劳动能力的残疾人就业为目的、带有社会福利性质的特殊企业的总称（残疾职工占生产人员10%以上）。

社会收养单位 指国有优抚（休）疗养院、福利院以及集体所有制和其他所有制的光荣院、敬老院事业单位的总称。

收养人数 指优抚疗养院、福利院报告期末实际收养的优抚对象、社会“三无”对象和自费人员在院的总人数。

律师 指受聘参加律师事务所工作，提任法律顾问、刑（民）事代理人、刑事辩护人，办理非诉讼事件、解答法律询问，代写法律事务文书等主要从事律师业务的专职法律工作者和兼职律师。

公证人员 指在国家公证机关依法办理公证事务的司法人员。包括公证员、助理公证员和在公证处工作的其他人员。

办理公证文书 指公证处在一定时期内办结的公证文书件数。公证文书系按司法部规定或批准的格式制作。包括国内公证和涉外公证两部分。其中国内公证分为经济公证和民事法律关系公证两大类。

调解人员 指人民调解委员会担负调解民间一般民事纠纷和轻微违法行为所引起的纠纷的工作人员。包括调解委员会的委员和调解小组调解员。

调解民间纠纷 指调解委员会依照法律规定，根据自愿原则，用说服教育的方法调解民间发生的有关民事权利和义务的争执，促成当事双方达到协议和谅解，解决纠纷。包括婚姻家庭纠纷，财产权益纠纷等。不包括法院受理调解的民事案件数。

离休、退休、退职人员 指正式办理了离休、退休、退职手续，并享受相应的离休、退休、退职待遇的人员。

保险福利费用 指企业、事业、机关单位再工作以外实际支付给职工和离休、退休、退职人员个人以及用于集体的劳动保险和福利费用。

1．职工保险福利费用具体包括：

（1）医疗卫生费 指实行公费医疗企业的职工及其供养的直系亲属的医疗费、医务经费、职工因工伤就医路费以及住院伙食补助费等；卫生部门开支的事业及机关单位职工的公费医疗经费；未参加公费医疗的企业、事业和机关单位职工的医疗费。

（2）丧葬抚恤救济费 指因职工死亡而支付的丧葬费、丧葬补助费和所遗供养直系亲属的抚恤费、救济费、生活补助费以及职工供养直系亲属死亡时的丧葬补助费等。

（3）生活困难补助 指对生活困难的职工实际支付的定期补助和临时性补助。

（4）文体宣传费 指企业、事业和机关单位实际支付的文体宣传费。不包括学习费。

（5）集体福利事业补贴费 指对职工浴室、理发室、洗衣房、哺乳室、托儿所等集体福利设施各项支出与收入相抵后的差额补助费。

（6）集体福利设施费 指按照国家规定开支的集体福利设施费用。如职工食堂炊事用具的购置费、修理费、职工宿舍的修缮费用。不包括由企业、事业和机关单位自筹经费开支的职工福利设施的基本建设费用。

（7）计划生育补贴 指发给职工独生子女的补贴费和保健营养费。

（8）其他 指上述费用以外，单位支付给职工的保险福利费。

2．离休、退休、退职人员保险福利费用具体包括：

（1）离休金 指发给离休人员的工资和按 1982 年国务院发布的“关于老干部离职休养制度的几项规定”发给符合规定的离休干部相当于 1—2 个月标准工资的生活补贴和按有关文件规定提高离休人员的待遇所增加的费用及粮油价格补贴等。

（2）退休金 指按照国家有关规定发给退休人员的退休费和按有关文件规定提高退休人员的待遇所增加的费用及粮油价格补贴等。

（3）职工生活费 指按照 1978 年国务院《关于工人退休、退职的暂行办法》规定定期发给退职人员的生活费用和按有关文件规定提高退职人员的待遇所增加的费用及粮油价格补贴等。

（4）医疗卫生费 指离休、退休、退职人员的医疗费、住院费以及住院伙食补助等费用。

（5）护理费　指因工致残、饮食起居需人扶助的离休、退休人员的护理费以及因病不能自理的离休人员的护理费。

（6）生活补贴　指按照 1985 年国务院《关于发给离退休人员生活补贴费的通知》规定，发给离休、退休人员的生活补贴费。

（7）交通费补贴　指按月发给离休人员的交通费补贴。

（8）丧葬抚恤救济费　指离休、退休、退职人员死亡的丧葬费、丧葬补助费和所遗供养直系亲属的抚养费、救济费、生活补助费以及供养直系亲属死亡时的丧葬补助费等。

（9）其他　包括易地安置的离休、退休、退职人员的安家补助费；离休、退休、退职人员的生活困难补助费、书报费、洗理费、副食品价格补贴、房租价格补贴、水电补贴、少数民族补贴以及老干部活动经费开支的旅游费用等。

Explanatory Notes On Main Statistical Indicators

Social Welfare Institutions refer to institutions providing adoption,help and services to persons such as (1)those who have no kith and kin and can not support themselves, (2)the old,deformed children,mental patients with no cares of family (3)persons receiving special pensions or with living difficulties,etc.

Social Welfare Enterprises refer to special enterprises which centralized employing deformed man with ability to work（the proportion of deformed staff and workers to all production personnel above 10%）.

Adoption Units including state-owned sanatoriums for persons receiving special pensions,social welfare homes, collective-owned and other ownership homes for disable veterans and old people.

Number of People Adopted by Social Welfare Institutions refers to the number of persons receiving special pensions,those who have no ability to work,no dependent and no living source and persons at one's expenses taken in by social welfare institutions at the end of reported period.

Lawyers include full or part-time lawyers and full-time legal workers employed by law office to act as law advisers, agents in criminal or civil lawsuits, defenders in criminal lawsuits, or to handle non-litigious legal affairs, to advise on legal matters, or to write legal papers for others.

Notary Personnel refer to judicial officials of the state notary offices handling notarization work according to law. They include notaries, assistant notaries, and other people working for notary offices.

Notarized Documents refer to the notary documents finished by notary offices in a year. The notary documents are drawn up in accordance with the regulations of the Ministry of Justice, including domestic documents and foreign-related documents.

Domestic documents are divided into two major categories: documents on economy and documents on civil legal relations.

Mediators refer to workers in people's mediation committees responsible for mediating in civil disputes and cases of slight infraction of the law, including members of the mediation committees and mediators in mediation groups.

Mediation of Civil Disputes refers to mediation committees' work in mediating of civil disputes concerning civil rights and responsibilities through persuasion and education in accordance with the provisions of law on a voluntary basis, so as to solve disputes by helping the parties involved come to an agreement and understanding . The disputes include divorce cases and disputes over property ownership , but exclude the civil cases to be handled by the court.

Retired or Resigned Personnel refers to the persons who have formally gone through the formalities for their retirement or quitting work and enjoy the corresponding treatments.

Insurance and Welfare Funds refers to labor insurance and welfare fund paid by enterprises, organizations and institutions to their staff and workers as well as retired and quitted persons in addition to their wages and salaries.

1. **Insurance and Welfare Funds for Staff and Workers** include:

（1）Medical Care Allowance includes cost of medical care of staff and workers and their dependent family members covered by the medical care system of enterprises, traveling expenses of injured employees to hospital and their food subsidies during hospitalization; the cost of medical care of employees covered by the medical care system of institutions and organizations; the cost of medicine of employees in enterprises, institutions and organizations not covered by the medical care system.

（2） Funeral Expenses and Pensions for Family of the Deceased refer to funeral expenses of staff and workers, pensions and allowance for their dependent family members, as well as subsidies to funeral expenses of staff and workers' dependent family members.

（3） Allowance for Living refers to regular or temporary allowance to staff and workers with difficulties in making living.

（4） Expenses on Recreation, Sports and Publicity Activities refer to actual payment made by enterprises and institutions in recreational , sports and publicity activities, excluding training cost .

（5） Subsidies to Collective Welfare refer to the expenditures on making up the loss of welfare operations, such as public bathrooms, barber shops, laundries, nurseries and kindergartens.

（6）Expenses on Collective Welfare Facilities refer to expenditures on collective welfare facilities in line with state regulations, such as the purchase and repair of cooking utensils for canteens, and repair of living quarters of staff and workers, but excluding the expenses on welfare projects financed with self-raised funds.

（7） Family Planning Subsidy refers to subsidy of health allowance paid to staff and workers in one-child family.

（8） Others refer to other insurance and welfare funds paid to staff and workers.

2. Insurance and Welfare Funds for Retired and quitted Staff and Workers include:

(1) Merit Retirement Pensions refer to pensions and other subsidies paid to merit retired in line with relevant government documents.

（2） Retirement Pensions refer to pensions and other subsidies paid to retired staff and workers in line with the relevant government documents.

（3） Quitted Allowances for Living refer to living allowances and subsidies paid to quitted staff and workers in line with relevant government instructions.

（4） Expenses for Medical Care refer to the costs for medical treatment, hospitalization and food subsidies in hospitals for merit retired, retired and quitted staff and workers.

（5） Nursing Cost refers to cost for nursing retired or quitted staff and workers without ability to take care of themselves and need the help of nurses.

（6） Living Subsidy refers to living subsidy paid to merit retired and retired employees in line with the instructions in a 1985 State Council document.

（7） Traffic Subsidy refers to the traffic subsidy paid monthly to merit retired staff.

（8）Funeral Expenses and Pensions for Family of the Deceased refer to the funeral expenses of merit retired, retired and quitted staff and workers, pensions and allowances for their dependent family members, as well as subsidies to funeral expenses of their dependent family members.

（9）Others refer to other expenses, including moving and settlement allowance, living allowance for difficult families, book and newspaper allowance, subsidy for non-staple foods, allowance for bath and haircut, housing subsidy, water and electricity subsidy, special allowance for staff and workers of national minorities, travelling cost for senior retired staff, etc.

21

服务业

SERVICE

2000年服务业企业流动资产与固定资产状况（单位：亿元）
Ciuculating and Fixed Assets of Servives in 2000 (100 million yuan)

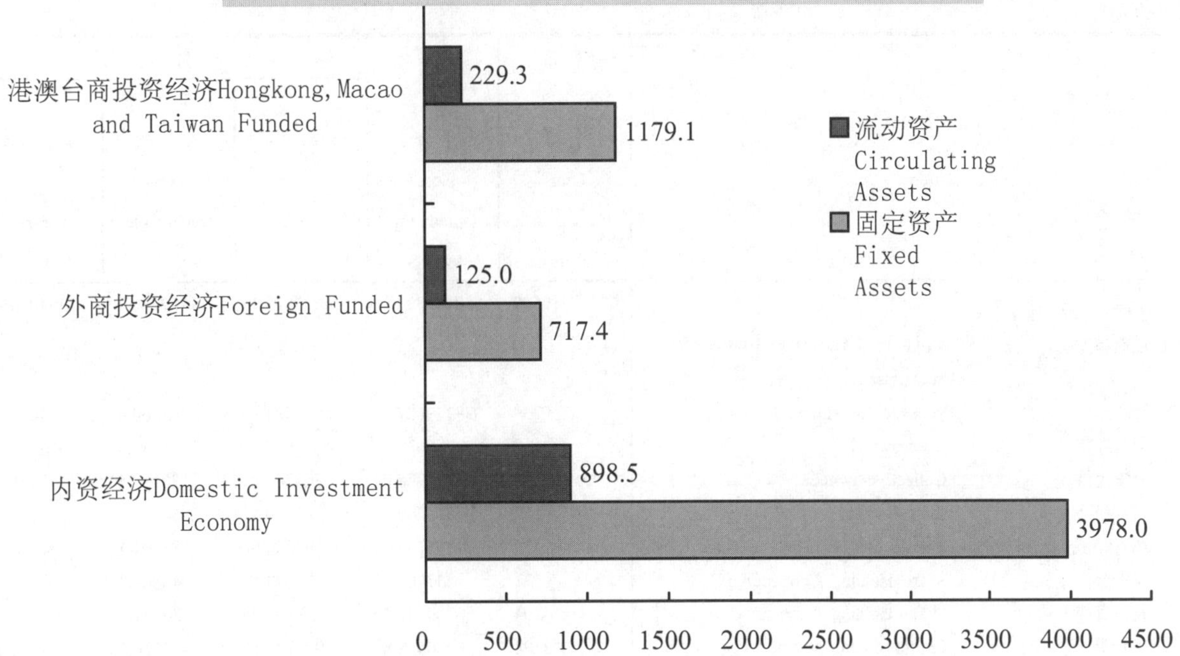

2000年服务业企业营业收入状况（单位：亿元）
Operating Income of Services in 2000 (100 million yuan)

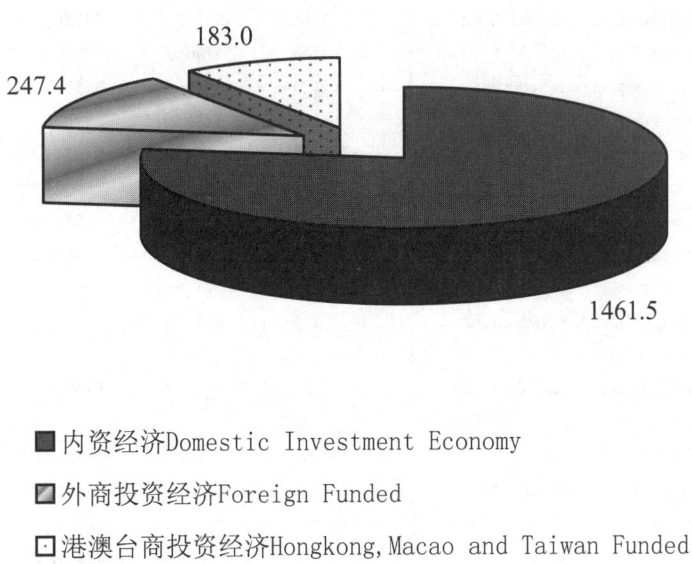

21-1 服务业企业财务状况

单位：万元

项目	Item	单位个数 Units (unit)	流动资产 合计 Total Circulating Assets	#货币资金 Cash	#应收帐款 Accounts Receivable	#存货 Stock
合计	**Total**	**10509**	**58744300.2**	**10835628.1**	**4669066.7**	**23940463.6**
按登记注册类型分	**Grouped by Registation Status of Enterprises**					
内资经济	Domestic Investment Economy	9259	39779657.0	8589481.8	3763560.0	12248454.6
# 国有经济	State-owned	3113	19785638.4	4656527.7	2088083.0	5168794.5
集体经济	Collective-owned	1548	1257978.0	263269.8	120118.3	512014.8
联营经济	Joint Owned	162	563260.3	87290.3	52084.2	237265.1
私营经济	Private Owned	1479	1398459.5	195650.0	83004.1	644869.4
股份合作企业	Share Holding Cooperative	471	437869.3	77673.4	48869.2	147917.4
股份有限公司	Share Holding Company	304	3769742.2	912195.8	580331.5	1095707.5
有限责任公司	Limited-LiabilityCompany	2104	8470656.8	1957734.6	495520.1	2786421.3
国有独资公司	State Funded	63	4089720.9	438334.0	295307.5	1654249.3
其他	Others	15	6331.6	806.2	242.1	1215.3
外商投资经济	Foreign Funded	690	7173984.3	1314390.8	769108.1	2995786.6
港澳台商投资经济	Hongkong,Macao and Taiwan Funded	560	11790658.9	931755.5	136398.6	8696222.4
按国民经济行业分	**Grouped by Sector**					
房地产业	Real Estate	1426	33669907.5	2909381.5	107883.0	22046536.5
公共服务业	Public Services	615	860141.5	298883.8	299252.9	34113.1
居民服务业	Personal Services	353	98826.7	29984.8	17531.7	10036.2
旅馆业	Hotel	837	952299.5	411593.1	89029.6	59973.6
旅游业	Tourism	247	367729.3	90432.5	71939.6	4357.7
交通运输辅助业	Logistic Support for Transportation	112	164490.2	74510.0	58118.3	2929.9
仓储业	Storage	94	94360.1	24546.6	12682.3	14605.4
商业经纪与代理业	Commercial Brokerage and Agencies	42	1394169.0	277545.6	661597.9	74033.3
租赁服务业	Rental Services	148	557408.6	128413.7	220145.3	29903.5
计算机应用服务业	Computer Application Services	1333	2289481.1	575767.2	317079.1	374498.2
娱乐服务业	Entertainment Services	110	87846.3	19806.6	11931.4	6853.8
信息咨询服务业	Consulting Services	1665	2217975.1	940249.2	386769.8	89365.5
# 广告业	Advertisement	361	386168.5	155697.5	77441.7	8128.3
其他社会服务业	Other Social Services	502	2313307.0	823796.0	311495.0	89814.8
卫生、体育和社会福利业	Health,Sports and Social Welfare	55	131366.7	28641.6	70035.3	9975.7
教育文化艺术和广播电影电视业	Education,Culture,Arts,Radio,Film and Television	433	1153084.3	425183.2	140751.4	255019.1
科学研究和综合技术服务业	Scientific Research and Polytechnical Services	2028	5783111.4	1674619.1	1064576.2	532936.1
农林牧渔服务业	FFAF Services	66	25167.9	6203.8	6544.8	6399.3
地质勘察和水利管理业	Geological Prospecting and Water Conservancy	32	192490.9	41734.0	8614.4	1210.6
其他	Others	411	6391137.1	2054335.8	813088.7	297901.3

注：服务业企业包括 (1)农林牧渔服务业；(2)地质勘察、水利管理业；(3)交通运输辅助业、其他交通运输业；(4)仓储业；(5)商业经纪与代理业；(6)房地产业；(7)社会服务业；(8)卫生、体育和社会福利业；(9)教育、文化艺术及广播电影、电视业；(10)科学研究和综合技术服务业；(11)其他行业。

FINANCIAL INDICATORS FOR SERVICES ENTERPRISES

(10000 yuan)

长期投资 Long-term Investment	固定资产合计 Total Fixed Assets	固定资产原价合计 Original Value of Fixed Assets	#生产经营用 for Production Use	累计折旧 Accumulative Depreciation	#本年折旧 of this Year	无形及递延资产合计 Intangible and Deffered Assets	#无形资产 Intangible	其他资产合计 Other Assets
15417645.4	**12527589.2**	**17008191.4**	**8205988.7**	**4480602.2**	**699727.6**	**2042481.7**	**1122700.3**	**1652404.3**
13655043.3	8985324.0	11760050.2	5799837.4	2774726.2	470003.7	1220982.4	613450.6	1042380.2
10652492.2	5628432.6	7384103.9	3807855.5	1755671.3	249345.0	553982.6	259347.2	551584.6
193038.2	559923.1	768029.4	397327.5	208106.3	43743.1	163570.5	90386.1	20645.4
56955.7	137211.1	172083.9	68641.2	34872.8	5428.0	32929.0	21341.6	5996.4
72121.6	182974.6	230616.3	122697.0	47641.7	16456.2	46755.9	9589.9	62769.8
68365.6	167365.5	217786.1	154034.0	50420.6	12154.9	57981.1	37781.0	7046.8
823892.7	886119.5	1125240.7	654551.4	239121.2	64581.3	87009.0	48112.2	30274.2
646276.7	917018.5	1131458.8	504736.6	214440.3	70701.0	221990.5	123467.2	357705.5
1141814.9	488005.2	701795.2	62026.6	213790.0	6568.6	55335.1	22024.7	6220.4
85.7	18273.9	28935.9	27967.6	10662.0	1025.6	1428.7	1400.7	137.1
1351906.8	1249726.9	1905849.0	924349.1	656122.1	103811.9	251905.7	165528.6	312108.9
410695.3	2292538.3	3342292.2	1481802.2	1049753.9	125912.0	569593.6	343721.1	297915.2
1924704.0	2751587.7	3447270.7	1588429.6	695683.0	108820.2	813525.3	469211.9	502002.4
201493.2	1312844.7	1809749.2	931085.5	496904.5	123592.9	82063.4	63349.8	29111.7
12333.3	54761.9	79519.6	46400.3	24757.7	4952.1	9274.1	2993.8	4106.2
445998.9	2631835.6	3909042.9	2049781.9	1277207.3	149966.7	286027.3	125301.3	132936.5
262991.2	149337.8	202159.3	110039.8	52821.5	16881.6	24938.7	13272.5	39406.8
47942.0	69938.0	100451.0	81726.7	30513.0	7520.3	3132.3	2302.9	1225.4
12363.8	123663.0	173407.7	77077.4	49744.7	8670.4	16098.2	6766.3	245.3
587645.2	124198.6	148699.5	72235.6	24500.9	5037.4	8708.3	6420.6	1093.1
90164.6	172093.5	215099.9	90492.4	43006.4	9755.9	42165.4	20296.5	283759.3
507421.3	425559.5	606144.4	283759.5	180584.9	46660.3	139811.1	108404.2	35683.4
3320.1	242533.3	350469.9	198106.7	107936.6	17046.8	49400.1	23914.6	24547.2
858958.8	386826.4	532403.4	235939.6	145577.0	27531.1	55208.0	23989.2	27616.0
44768.7	53983.2	98209.5	61773.0	44226.3	6690.9	11937.8	5926.6	3403.8
3082002.5	752503.6	1000790.9	568320.9	248287.3	37246.6	66290.0	37267.2	26214.1
2939.1	65420.8	80850.5	42510.3	15429.7	2502.4	1340.9	282.2	4840.6
165770.8	673331.2	893514.7	487872.4	220183.5	34950.8	40222.0	20197.2	11378.8
2470898.3	1312301.9	1831841.3	656131.8	519539.4	63308.4	226483.3	125629.2	84290.1
5269.2	20782.9	26486.8	16794.3	5703.9	733.4	1663.5	618.9	6.0
795417.9	153698.3	236553.1	168168.7	82854.8	5519.0	4250.5	970.8	548.9
3940011.2	1104370.5	1363736.6	501115.3	259366.1	29031.3	171879.3	71511.2	443392.5

Note: Service enterprises include(a)FFAF services, (b)geographical prospecting and water conservancy, (c)logistic support for transportation and other transportation, (d)storage,(e)commercial brokerage and agencies, (f)real estate, (g)social services,(h)health,sports and social welfares, (i)education,culture,arts,radio,film and television, (j)scientific research and polytechnical services, (k)other services.

21-1 续表 1 continued

单位：万元

项目	Item	资产合计 Total Assets	流动负债合计 Total Circulating Liability	# 短期借款 Short-term Loans	# 应付帐款 Accounts Payable	长期负债合计 Total Long-term Liability
合　计	**Total**	**90384420.8**	**43114880.6**	**8707096.2**	**6606788.1**	**14855271.0**
按登记注册类型分	**Grouped by Registation Status of Enterprises**					
内资经济	Domestic Investment Economy	64683386.9	31221906.6	6026056.9	4902036.1	8173021.8
# 国有经济	State-owned	37172130.4	16111265.7	3150785.0	2889967.4	4719159.9
集体经济	Collective-owned	2195155.2	1304783.7	251459.9	266970.0	123064.8
联营经济	Joint Owned	796352.5	527192.0	117979.5	88735.3	57642.9
私营经济	Private Owned	1763081.4	1194717.0	193401.7	183107.5	58885.7
股份合作企业	Share Holding Cooperative	738628.3	391342.4	96396.1	88397.3	89670.8
股份有限公司	Share Holding Company	5597037.6	2364636.4	963850.4	250999.0	584521.1
有限责任公司	Limited-LiabilityCompany	10613648.0	6057164.5	894253.3	741398.8	1708542.6
国有独资公司	State Funded	5781096.5	3243246.7	356151.0	388976.3	831253.0
其　他	Others	26257.0	27558.2	1780.0	3484.5	281.0
外商投资经济	Foreign Funded	10339632.6	4760243.0	1181998.5	679360.9	1672086.2
港澳台商投资经济	Hongkong,Macao and Taiwan Funded	15361401.3	7132731.0	1499040.8	1025391.1	5010163.0
按国民经济行业分	**Grouped by Sector**					
房地产业	Real Estate	39661726.9	23523077.8	4720981.9	2945906.1	7785231.9
公共服务业	Public Services	2485654.5	1084964.7	279651.7	412976.4	227569.5
居民服务业	Personal Services	179302.2	87198.7	9149.5	14959.8	15813.0
旅馆业	Hotel	4449097.8	1750253.4	416234.4	181252.2	1299250.2
旅游业	Tourism	844403.8	271228.9	83227.4	80555.6	43919.4
交通运输辅助业	Logistic Support for Transportation	286727.9	170397.4	10266.7	112700.0	3928.9
仓储业	Storage	246730.4	123506.1	45893.5	9291.7	6876.5
商业经纪与代理业	Commercial Brokerage and Agencies	2115814.2	1187802.3	526301.8	221801.5	65888.7
租赁服务业	Rental Services	1145591.4	386166.6	64062.2	128164.0	591023.2
计算机应用服务业	Computer Application Services	3397956.4	1642592.5	405827.6	225086.3	216490.1
娱乐服务业	Entertainment Services	407647.0	221752.2	65598.9	23605.5	83272.1
信息咨询服务业	Consulting Services	3546584.3	1565779.5	192891.7	482174.4	186273.7
# 广告业	Advertisement	500262.0	341340.7	38535.6	144187.5	7695.3
其他社会服务业	Other Social Services	6240317.2	1520529.9	225398.3	236374.8	1069837.0
卫生、体育和社会福利业	Health,Sports and Social Welfare	205908.1	117345.3	15063.7	11335.3	2026.3
教育文化艺术和广播电影电视业	Education,Culture,Arts,Radio,Film and Television	2043787.1	655611.3	76692.9	134749.5	76425.0
科学研究和综合技术服务业	Scientific Research and Polytechnical Services	9877085.0	4177651.2	1030183.0	1025468.6	1281707.1
农林牧渔服务业	FFAF Services	52889.5	23828.4	5732.9	7319.3	5457.6
地质勘察和水利管理业	Geological Prospecting and Water Conservancy	1146406.5	117867.3	58203.6	2402.3	328929.8
其　他	Others	12050790.6	4487327.1	475734.5	350664.8	1565351.0

21-1 续表 2 continued

(10000 yuan)

#长期借款 Long-term Loans	负债合计 Total Liabilities	所有者权益合计 Ownership Interest	#实收资本 Proceeds of Capital	#国家资本 State	#集体资本 Collective	#法人资本 Institutional Units	#个人资本 Individual	#港澳台资本 Hongkong, Macao and Taiwan
9933943.2	**57970151.6**	**32414269.2**	**23470590.0**	**9610198.9**	**1179511.4**	**6460168.1**	**821235.5**	**2666444.0**
5905450.0	39394928.4	25288458.5	16471291.8	9256517.2	1051543.4	5288802.0	819508.3	20200.6
3594200.4	20830425.6	16341704.8	10079895.6	8145747.8	30747.2	1843085.7	36335.1	6019.2
74339.4	1427848.5	767306.7	506403.0	19925.0	338065.7	109728.3	36376.2	1055.3
46496.3	584834.9	211517.6	176124.1	59422.6	33707.1	74471.8	5443.5	86.0
44752.5	1253602.7	509478.7	409027.0	11605.0	2900.6	177326.7	216728.6	413.9
38013.6	481013.2	257615.1	221993.8	1552.3	22944.7	90282.4	97158.3	109.4
475863.6	2949157.5	2647880.1	1618399.8	110235.4	74468.8	1286338.2	147010.5	346.9
825412.8	7765707.1	2847940.9	2719708.3	293523.4	547454.3	1583884.6	280160.9	12169.9
806081.4	4074499.7	1706596.8	736998.9	614495.7	145.0	122334.7	23.5	
290.0	27839.2	-1582.2	2741.3	10.0	1110.0	1349.6	271.7	
1429743.6	6432329.2	3907303.4	3486226.9	132653.0	25154.5	452518.1	678.6	322217.6
2598749.6	12142894.0	3218507.3	3513071.3	221028.7	102813.5	718848.0	1048.6	2324025.8
4718807.8	31308309.7	8353417.2	6819421.2	1001603.8	220670.4	2736725.8	146379.1	2011696.5
110228.4	1312534.2	1173120.3	797600.0	528177.2	72853.3	161678.9	27744.7	4675.7
11410.9	103011.7	76290.5	64836.8	19364.7	11319.1	15919.4	7416.3	6694.6
1093628.4	3049503.6	1399594.2	1949189.4	919819.8	99706.0	428973.0	18456.8	331899.0
25150.6	315148.3	529255.5	305217.9	170623.1	6080.9	99379.4	18237.8	10435.3
3657.3	174326.3	112401.6	68250.2	28498.6	2038.6	27092.5	1879.7	3467.9
4963.2	130382.6	116347.8	88552.8	31491.9	8391.8	20452.7	656.2	9023.1
46513.5	1253691.0	862123.2	592939.0	228452.0	595.0	128853.5	640.0	
466524.8	977189.8	168401.6	159339.5	27663.2	18526.1	64004.9	16649.0	8231.2
197651.2	1859082.6	1538873.8	1401056.4	154524.9	478293.4	307416.3	143412.5	50082.9
46401.5	305024.3	102622.7	186387.9	47554.0	11546.1	30857.1	2549.6	40931.0
115972.0	1752053.2	1794531.1	1460234.4	250720.0	69231.6	411776.5	102606.6	55128.5
2633.5	349036.0	151226.0	109582.5	36553.9	20807.9	26508.5	16701.5	3056.5
992134.9	2590366.9	3649950.3	1815735.6	1349701.6	41631.6	336428.3	25307.4	4340.2
960.1	119371.6	86536.5	26304.5	6801.8	3865.3	1546.5	1596.4	2134.2
57111.3	732036.3	1311750.8	543165.2	420052.5	3418.6	38018.4	12885.6	59602.2
1042897.7	5459358.3	4417726.7	2651943.7	1231921.5	88629.3	897883.0	192453.5	40278.1
4124.2	29286.0	23603.5	17768.0	4636.4	5407.1	6907.3	817.2	
298146.5	446797.1	699609.4	590891.2	287676.2	586.6	302133.2	495.2	
697658.9	6052678.1	5998112.5	3931756.3	2900915.7	36720.6	444121.4	101051.9	27823.6

21-1 续表 3 continued

单位：万元

项目 Item		#外商资本 Foreign	营业收入 Operating Income	营业成本 Operating Cost	营业费用 Operating Expenses	营业税金及附加 Operating Tax and Extra Charges
合计	Total	2733032.1	18919876.6	12999282.8	1846136.8	556561.2
按登记注册类型分	Grouped by Registation Status of Enterprises					
内资经济	Domestic Investment Economy	34720.3	14615308.9	10607068.5	1192502.7	391687.0
# 国有经济	State-owned	17960.6	7616890.5	5603982.1	578044.9	195892.5
集体经济	Collective-owned	1252.5	745850.0	484096.6	115672.2	24024.7
联营经济	Joint Owned	2993.1	201865.5	143786.0	21443.4	5307.0
私营经济	Private Owned	52.2	789465.2	484462.1	121820.5	25716.3
股份合作企业	Share Holding Cooperative	9946.7	332201.4	207146.4	47525.4	9073.8
股份有限公司	Share Holding Company		1167606.1	866140.2	51043.4	32227.0
有限责任公司	Limited-LiabilityCompany	2515.2	2502259.4	1817861.8	212192.6	74192.5
国有独资公司	State Funded		1252687.4	996498.7	43329.0	24941.0
其他	Others		6483.4	3094.6	1431.3	312.2
外商投资经济	Foreign Funded	2553005.1	2474442.4	1399172.0	368347.6	81700.0
港澳台商投资经济	Hongkong,Macao and Taiwan Funded	145306.7	1830125.3	993042.3	285286.5	83174.2
按国民经济行业分	Grouped by Sector					
房地产业	Real Estate	702345.6	4323732.8	3259477.6	318455.9	217229.9
公共服务业	Public Services	2470.2	622544.2	479267.1	46842.2	33603.0
居民服务业	Personal Services	4122.7	93729.3	42555.0	31522.6	3277.4
旅馆业	Hotel	150334.8	1113697.9	157220.9	397934.3	57516.8
旅游业	Tourism	461.4	609411.8	517265.5	31152.6	4706.7
交通运输辅助业	Logistic Support for Transportation	5272.9	147816.7	100247.4	19877.2	3210.5
仓储业	Storage	18537.1	114497.3	78853.0	22311.6	2041.0
商业经纪与代理业	Commercial Brokerage and Agencies	234398.5	639392.5	515775.1	16164.9	6377.2
租赁服务业	Rental Services	24265.1	122906.3	78236.5	18661.1	3473.5
计算机应用服务业	Computer Application Services	267326.4	1672308.2	1161410.3	188837.7	22658.7
娱乐服务业	Entertainment Services	52950.1	87226.5	17344.3	35300.8	6322.7
信息咨询服务业	Consulting Services	570771.2	1507786.2	858646.9	201444.4	50853.2
# 广告业	Advertisement	5954.2	380094.3	228603.7	42387.6	16237.3
其他社会服务业	Other Social Services	58326.5	984815.0	664059.0	133401.4	22466.3
卫生、体育和社会福利业	Health,Sports and Social Welfare	10360.3	47354.6	19645.5	11824.1	780.0
教育文化艺术和广播电影电视业	Education,Culture,Arts,Radio,Film and Television	9187.9	990255.9	553575.2	103798.5	27886.4
科学研究和综合技术服务业	Scientific Research and Polytechnical Services	200778.3	3675555.1	2930805.6	119249.5	52483.8
农林牧渔服务业	FFAF Services		22702.5	15428.0	2752.9	270.5
地质勘察和水利管理业	Geological Prospecting and Water Conservancy		47306.7	31515.2	1560.9	1666.4
其他	Others	421123.1	2096837.1	1517954.7	145044.2	39737.2

21-1 续表 4 continued

(10000 yuan)

经营利润 Business Profits	其他业务利润 Profits of Other Business	管理费用 Overhead Expense	# 税金 Taxes	#财产保险费 Premium of Property	# 劳动待业保险 Premium for Employment	财务费用 Financial Expense	# 利息支出 Interest Expenditure	营业利润 Operating Profits
3517895.8	**260779.4**	**3080813.4**	**82172.9**	**17525.7**	**82216.5**	**524728.7**	**664885.5**	**173133.1**
2424050.7	180712.5	1927729.9	47153.8	10724.8	76961.0	299473.3	423236.7	377560.0
1238971.0	111033.6	1040351.2	31280.4	5957.9	61378.0	157566.2	269145.0	152087.2
122056.5	14798.5	127415.3	5084.4	1715.1	2273.4	13707.1	11953.1	-4267.4
31329.1	2548.7	30542.3	442.0	186.8	475.8	4419.9	6435.4	-1084.4
157466.3	3746.7	114645.0	1910.4	478.1	798.5	4875.6	2789.9	41692.4
68455.8	2305.4	34609.3	378.3	134.4	341.5	5242.4	5366.6	30909.5
218195.5	10054.8	115854.8	1696.1	369.9	2993.7	53142.9	54234.3	59252.6
398012.5	25505.4	305677.1	4511.4	1609.3	5130.6	36798.9	42387.9	81041.9
187918.7	10715.4	157497.0	1816.2	244.4	3552.4	23637.2	30835.3	17499.9
1645.3	4.0	1137.9	34.6	28.9	17.1	83.1	89.2	428.3
625222.8	66214.5	672789.2	17384.5	2665.3	2495.3	83964.5	89221.1	-65316.4
468622.3	13852.4	480294.3	17634.6	4135.6	2760.2	141290.9	152427.7	-139110.5
528569.4	37637.7	514462.3	23168.4	4579.3	7707.5	264927.0	327233.5	-213182.2
62831.9	-935.2	141735.8	2537.9	1723.0	25137.5	14542.7	14914.1	-94381.8
16374.3	787.7	19432.0	269.4	110.6	1390.9	831.6	783.4	-3101.6
501025.9	5114.2	472382.0	24496.4	4823.9	9514.9	125419.1	118556.4	-91661.0
56287.0	1706.7	39929.0	725.9	313.6	946.5	5207.1	6764.5	12857.6
24481.6	1203.9	23218.1	401.9	246.1	429.0	-533.0	580.1	3000.4
11291.7	2401.4	27648.8	500.1	264.0	2497.3	3082.9	3174.9	-17038.6
101075.3	28211.8	59236.1	793.1	122.3	840.0	22574.2	27961.9	47476.8
22535.2	773.9	22990.4	475.7	476.9	464.4	2959.8	3156.0	-2641.1
299401.5	58746.5	299386.2	1450.2	502.7	2662.0	16768.8	11413.9	41993.0
28258.7	258.7	43672.6	798.3	291.9	270.1	872.4	3480.8	-16027.6
396841.7	18784.2	334567.1	4306.0	913.3	3160.6	-8872.9	12445.3	89931.7
92865.7	2121.9	55782.4	560.6	73.2	430.9	-1337.5	910.2	40542.7
164888.3	12262.6	136799.3	7659.2	593.1	4250.7	5554.1	16380.8	34797.5
15105.0	181.8	13567.6	63.4	11.8	58.9	398.5	514.7	1320.7
304995.8	28608.3	182102.8	8402.6	993.0	9761.9	1370.3	5080.6	150131.0
573016.2	34812.5	460032.5	3159.9	1028.5	9700.3	42097.9	66049.9	105698.3
4251.1	611.7	2679.0	45.2	21.5	54.1	685.9	682.4	1497.9
12564.2	83.4	18252.8	162.0	37.2	965.1	284.2	9348.9	-5889.4
394101.0	29527.6	268719.0	2757.3	473.0	2404.8	26558.1	36363.4	128351.5

21-1 续表 5 continued

单位：万元

项目	Item	投资收益 Investment Income	补贴收入 Subsidy Income	营业外收入 Out-business Income	营业外支出 Out-business Expenditure	利润总额 Total Profits
合计	**Total**	**545292.4**	**209945.1**	**106763.0**	**107237.5**	**1062045.7**
按登记注册类型分	**Grouped by Registation Status of Enterprises**					
内资经济	Domestic Investment Economy	434457.5	209840.0	80514.9	79337.2	1175262.7
# 国有经济	State-owned	277543.2	162034.7	42415.7	42020.7	744776.8
集体经济	Collective-owned	4190.9	1683.4	7156.8	17879.0	1839.4
联营经济	Joint Owned	2002.3	274.1	447.4	381.6	7823.8
私营经济	Private Owned	2016.8	848.9	1684.7	1792.8	54508.5
股份合作企业	Share Holding Cooperative	2567.1	538.6	2421.1	3170.8	32352.1
股份有限公司	Share Holding Company	52834.6	42308.9	5834.7	6125.4	162285.3
有限责任公司	Limited-LiabilityCompany	50303.8	2025.4	10708.8	6490.2	108246.9
国有独资公司	State Funded	42998.8	126.0	9828.7	1469.7	62962.7
其他	Others			17.0	7.0	467.2
外商投资经济	Foreign Funded	96996.0	89.4	18511.5	8396.9	-17719.2
港澳台商投资经济	Hongkong,Macao and Taiwan Funded	13838.9	15.7	7736.6	19503.4	-95497.8
按国民经济行业分	**Grouped by Sector**					
房地产业	Real Estate	66284.4	7311.1	25886.2	28269.0	-140837.2
公共服务业	Public Services	10783.4	107824.2	7925.2	16206.6	20606.1
居民服务业	Personal Services	227.9	1353.9	1928.2	488.2	361.2
旅馆业	Hotel	8127.7	1967.3	8120.6	229.8	-17815.2
旅游业	Tourism	13515.6	0.1	1523.0	1316.1	30476.5
交通运输辅助业	Logistic Support for Transportation	1823.0		1079.2	356.3	6614.6
仓储业	Storage	306.3	16443.8	505.3	446.2	-730.1
商业经纪与代理业	Commercial Brokerage and Agencies	68806.1	117.6	614.2	4346.5	108696.9
租赁服务业	Rental Services	1020.8	81.9	1596.8	1933.7	-5030.1
计算机应用服务业	Computer Application Services	23690.3	2148.1	13722.0	8497.4	67510.4
娱乐服务业	Entertainment Services	39.2		603.0	116.3	-15910.3
信息咨询服务业	Consulting Services	50403.3	1771.0	9603.8	5129.4	156773.2
# 广告业	Advertisement	9755.9	9.6	1841.6	403.4	52091.8
其他社会服务业	Other Social Services	70454.2	147.3	3194.4	7544.1	94812.0
卫生、体育和社会福利业	Health,Sports and Social Welfare	2.3	10.6	506.2	3742.6	-1723.5
教育文化艺术和广播电影电视业	Education,Culture,Arts,Radio,Film and Television	7385.5	22240.3	7257.2	5901.0	176848.0
科学研究和综合技术服务业	Scientific Research and Polytechnical Services	114111.3	10614.6	17763.7	8788.1	280058.2
农林牧渔服务业	FFAF Services	206.3	141.3	181.5	219.1	1574.8
地质勘察和水利管理业	Geological Prospecting and Water Conservancy	12639.3	59.0	363.3	79.4	9575.3
其他	Others	95465.5	37713.0	4389.2	13627.7	290184.9

21-1 续表 6 continued

(10000 yuan)

应交所得税 Income Tax Payable	转作奖金的利润 Profits Distributed as Bonus	应付利润 Profits Payable	# 已分配股利 Divided Payment	本年应付工资总额 Total Wages Payable in the Year	# 主营业务应付工资 Wage Payable of Major Business	本年应付福利费总额 Welfares Payable in the Year	# 主营业务应付福利费 of Major Business
423248.2	**4959.2**	**250660.2**	**16279.4**	**1527332.8**	**1155442.8**	**229388.0**	**171215.1**
343701.6	4918.3	192077.8	7512.7	1109189.4	839251.4	146129.0	106513.4
204592.8	1721.4	51914.8	673.1	588646.3	402594.4	85772.9	57942.0
9110.1	1032.5	7437.2	300.6	154011.1	140908.1	10942.8	9053.7
3263.3	183.1	2444.8	1101.0	13461.4	10475.5	2172.8	1648.6
18616.3	340.4	12017.5	836.6	60129.0	48797.1	7455.1	6228.7
6297.1	1800.1	3003.5	261.7	25084.5	20218.5	3376.6	2725.3
34580.7	-368.8	67014.2	576.9	76928.3	62286.4	9263.4	7559.6
48816.1	102.3	43689.0	3433.4	150600.9	120903.1	22504.7	17665.4
18395.6	107.3	4553.9	329.4	39719.7	32569.6	4527.5	3586.0
29.6	0.0	2.9		608.2	498.7	113.2	104.1
38503.9	-108.8	15233.3	2056.3	259768.1	218165.5	46342.6	40371.5
41042.7	149.7	43349.1	6710.4	158375.3	98025.9	36916.4	24330.2
82653.7	-325.8	36754.0	2442.2	204263.4	70216.6	33281.7	11916.6
7533.2	162.0	14736.2	396.6	164799.5	68337.6	21805.9	8684.7
1442.8	237.6	808.7	238.8	19905.0	18059.4	2996.0	1963.8
17391.7	590.7	29087.0	2009.0	188995.5	150199.5	41653.9	31871.1
9283.3	12.1	581.5	29.4	18565.0	15517.6	2526.3	1907.8
3569.2	13.9	2037.8		15244.8	12701.1	1955.9	1475.3
594.6	1.6	436.5	86.9	15118.5	12010.8	2392.8	2092.4
23502.1	130.9	2660.4	1100.0	14024.2	13334.0	2524.7	2423.9
1259.7	78.3	1154.9	252.6	84128.5	83197.4	1366.7	1064.0
20441.0	51.9	9034.3	1520.7	158866.8	147434.4	27326.3	26697.4
1069.2	-95.4	1876.8	1650.5	16474.7	12946.9	2684.7	1968.0
48138.8	683.9	27928.6	730.4	147474.6	125133.7	19599.5	16554.0
25512.1	211.4	4329.8	217.8	24250.7	22172.4	3424.5	3145.2
19785.7	2460.0	22698.8	3265.9	114642.8	106622.1	15031.7	13841.8
185.0	50.4	377.5	87.3	7248.1	5079.0	507.8	440.8
66598.0	234.9	4404.3	34.6	82077.9	71365.9	12691.1	11263.0
45893.7	99.9	21279.4	1347.8	160720.0	141660.9	24716.7	22673.9
76.6	160.2	623.7	4.1	1978.0	1671.2	189.6	160.8
2583.2	69.6	5602.9		7397.8	4856.7	965.8	668.4
71246.7	342.5	68576.9	1082.6	105407.7	95098.0	15170.9	13547.4

21-2 金融业企业财务状况

单位：万元

项目	Item	单位个数 Units (unit)	流动资产合计 Total Circulating Assets	# 货币资金 Cash	# 应收帐款 Accounts Receivable	# 短期投资 Short-term Investment
合　计	**Total**	**88**	**188194332.8**	**66604548.0**	**18520301.6**	**5567697.4**
按登记注册类型分	**Grouped by Registation Status of Enterprises**					
内资经济	Domestic Investment Economy	75	186951516.2	66391586.0	18395714.9	4871999.6
国有经济	State-owned	34	151481334.6	57266727.2	17504915.4	2665909.6
集体经济	Collective-owned	2	6742525.7	357384.5	89556.3	1716054.2
联营经济	Joint Owned	1	143491.0	1270.2	10735.3	2.7
股份合作企业	Share Holding Cooperative	2	7139561.2	3074352.4	17366.6	115681.9
股份有限公司	Share Holding Company	8	10318105.8	134215.9	51203.5	1690.4
有限责任公司	Limited-LiabilityCompany	23	6281307.3	1605508.4	409400.8	334954.1
国有独资公司	State Funded	5	4845190.6	3952127.4	312537.0	37706.7
外商投资经济	Foreign Funded	12	1217171.4	209241.2	102662.3	695697.8
港澳台商投资经济	Hongkong,Macao and Taiwan Funded	1	25645.2	3720.8	21924.4	

项目	Item	流动负债合计 Total Circulating Liability	# 短期借款 Short-term Loans	# 应付帐款 Accounts Payable	长期负债合计 Total Long-term Liability	# 长期借款 Long-term Loans
合　计	**Total**	**220902234.7**	**80408643.5**	**26039272.9**	**77466558.2**	**27205908.8**
按登记注册类型分	**Grouped by Registation Status of Enterprises**					
内资经济	Domestic Investment Economy	219588374.7	79553046.6	25968767.9	77414615.2	27155144.7
国有经济	State-owned	183068297.4	75132743.6	25137033.0	70151738.2	26242147.1
集体经济	Collective-owned	7882614.4	3463653.4	21606.7	699025.8	564113.6
联营经济	Joint Owned	134295.0		110.5	25776.4	322.8
股份合作企业	Share Holding Cooperative	7319897.1		128453.2	2036754.8	
股份有限公司	Share Holding Company	13229288.2	30683.0	58266.0	1109300.7	12358.2
有限责任公司	Limited-LiabilityCompany	3204085.5	875246.8	281504.0	3218327.5	317265.0
国有独资公司	State Funded	4749897.1	50719.8	341794.5	173691.8	18938.0
外商投资经济	Foreign Funded	1276690.5	855596.9	33335.5	51943.0	50764.1
港澳台商投资经济	Hongkong,Macao and Taiwan Funded	37169.5		37169.5		

FINANCIAL INDICATORS FOR BANKING SERVICES

(10000 yuan)

长期资产合计 Long-term Assets	# 固定资产合计 Total Fixed Assets	# 固定资产原价合计 Original Value of Fixed Assets	# 累计折旧 Accumula-tive Depre-ciation	# 本年折旧 of this Year	无形递延其它资产合计 Intangible and Deffer-ed Assets	# 无形资产 Intangible	资产合计 Total Assets
123315434.2	**3077000.2**	**3759081.4**	**682081.2**	**109560.8**	**14312642.3**	**120930.7**	**325822409.3**
122683179.0	3028014.5	3688578.8	660564.3	104203.5	14272647.5	120700.0	323907342.7
112323546.5	2445410.1	2844399.5	398989.4	57041.8	13781181.6	85421.1	277586062.7
1656338.3	139491.0	164492.8	25001.8	44.7	257494.7	6407.7	8656358.7
14140.7	42.1	230.0	187.9	13.0	303.3	279.3	157935.0
2362044.6	152745.3	245608.4	92863.1	12640.0	30109.4		9531715.2
4384410.7	123389.1	175397.9	52008.8	12169.7	92104.2	2523.9	14794620.7
1211659.8	74877.6	106380.1	31502.5	7528.6	47311.8	12453.8	7540278.9
731038.4	92059.3	152070.1	60010.8	14765.7	64142.5	13614.2	5640371.5
610828.3	46178.1	66087.1	19909.0	5065.2	39827.4	230.7	1867827.1
21426.9	2807.6	4415.5	1607.9	292.1	167.4		47239.5

负债合计 Total Liabilities	所有者权益合计 Ownership Interest	# 实收资本 Proceeds of Capital	国家资本 State	集体资本 Collective	法人资本 Institutional Units	个人资本 Individual	港澳台资本 Hongkong, Macao and Taiwan	外商资本 Foreign
298368792.9	**27453616.4**	**18299611.4**	**15476283.0**	**228014.2**	**2095784.3**	**47243.7**	**135385.9**	**316900.3**
297002989.9	26904352.8	17934191.2	15469976.6	228014.2	2050143.8	47243.7	119203.9	19609.0
253220035.6	24366027.1	16660159.3	15070684.0	1200.0	1449462.4		119203.9	19609.0
8581640.2	74718.5	11209.1		11209.1				
160071.4	-2136.4	7361.2			7361.2			
9356651.9	175063.3	142877.1		142877.1				
14338588.9	456031.8	187761.5	36397.4		104245.4	47118.7		
6422413.0	1117865.9	617154.8	114727.0	72728.0	429574.8	125.0		
4923588.9	716782.6	307668.2	248168.2		59500.0			
1328633.5	539193.6	355463.3	6306.4		45640.5		6225.1	297291.3
37169.5	10070.0	9956.9					9956.9	

21-2 续表

单位：万元

项目 Item		营业收入 Operating Income	#利息收入 Interest	#金融企业往来收入 from Banking Enterprises	#手续费收入 Factorge	营业支出 Operating Expenditure
合　计	**Total**	**13224015.9**	**5469780.2**	**6464146.7**	**767511.5**	**12265599.6**
按登记注册类型分	**Grouped by Registation Status of Enterprises**					
内资经济	Domestic Investment Economy	12974206.1	5408925.6	6462953.5	763353.6	12070495.4
国有经济	State-owned	11119129.4	4668277.5	5903993.6	407909.6	10513658.6
集体经济	Collective-owned	385096.2	161765.7	213126.8	9001.9	332600.1
联营经济	Joint Owned	46.6	26.0	20.6		625.0
股份合作企业	Share Holding Cooperative	305306.8	213369.9	42470.3	2662.9	312407.3
股份有限公司	Share Holding Company	550295.2	312501.6	195641.2	16086.2	499939.2
有限责任公司	Limited-LiabilityCompany	267116.5	45549.6	63671.7	62661.6	179687.5
国有独资公司	State Funded	347215.4	7435.3	44029.3	265031.4	231577.7
外商投资经济	Foreign Funded	245433.6	57785.9	79.9	3963.7	190940.6
港澳台商投资经济	Hongkong,Macao and Taiwan Funded	4376.2	3068.7	1113.3	194.2	4163.6

项目 Item		营业利润 Operating Profuts	#投资收益 Investment Income	#股票投资收益 Stock	国家补贴收入 State Subsidies Income	营业外收入 Out-business Income
合　计	**Total**	**587830.9**	**2478550.9**	**18855.6**	**45652.1**	**39022.2**
按登记注册类型分	**Grouped by Registation Status of Enterprises**					
内资经济	Domestic Investment Economy	544715.5	2442234.9	18855.6	45652.1	36552.4
国有经济	State-owned	347386.5	2137149.5	18855.6	45601.2	18967.0
集体经济	Collective-owned	38000.2	3846.7			1828.5
联营经济	Joint Owned	-580.6	9.0			
股份合作企业	Share Holding Cooperative	-22299.0	73214.5			6336.6
股份有限公司	Share Holding Company	20297.3	133180.3			1922.2
有限责任公司	Limited-LiabilityCompany	70761.6	68835.2			5563.5
国有独资公司	State Funded	91149.5	25999.7		50.9	1934.6
外商投资经济	Foreign Funded	42957.9	36316.0			2469.8
港澳台商投资经济	Hongkong,Macao and Taiwan Funded	157.5				

continued

(10000 yuan)

# 利息支出 Interest	#居民利息支出 to Residents	金融企业往来支出 For Business among Banking	营业费用 Operating Expense	# 税金 Taxes	# 财产保险费 Premium of Property	# 劳动待业保险 Premium for Employment	# 住房公积金 Housing Accumulation Funds	# 排污费养路费 Fees for Dirt Disposal and Road Toll	营业税金及附加 Operation Tax and Extra Charges
4344043.8	**1130598.5**	**5681959.0**	**1344497.2**	**23711.9**	**3923.8**	**38901.0**	**14345.7**	**7997.3**	**370585.4**
4299557.2	1123408.4	5679189.7	1214910.3	23575.4	3897.9	37012.1	13258.4	7994.7	358995.2
3800095.0	972916.9	5320484.4	680329.7	17613.0	1984.0	19420.3	7156.7	3828.4	258084.3
106030.9		149151.1	66185.3	2034.2	386.0	3151.8	895.2	1944.9	14495.9
			624.8			8.6	5.8		2.2
152557.1	103248.9	30156.5	69753.3	1319.6	722.5	2188.5	2145.2		15198.5
182285.1	47008.9	110474.8	161959.4	1318.0	680.0	10275.6	2063.3	2203.3	30058.7
32730.7	233.7	61939.1	65614.0	677.4	112.8	1956.1	940.1	18.1	16667.4
25858.1		6983.8	170443.8	613.2	12.6	11.2	52.1		24488.2
44220.2	7190.1	40.0	128419.0	81.4	10.3	1878.5	1080.2	1.9	11535.1
266.4		2729.3	1167.9	55.1	15.6	10.4	7.1	0.7	55.1

营业外支出 Out-business Expenditure	利润总额 Total Profits	# 应交所得税 Income Tax Payable	# 应付利润 Profits Payable	# 已分配股利 Divided Payment	# 转作奖金的利润 Profits Distributed as Bonus	本年应付工资总额 Total Wages Payable in the Year	# 主营业务应付工资 Wage Payable of Major Business	本年应付福利费总额 Welfares Payable in the Year	# 主营业务应付福利费 of Major Business
81440.6	**3015158.4**	**614512.9**	**129531.6**	**6356.1**	**8.3**	**250393.6**	**202775.2**	**43324.6**	**39054.0**
80644.2	2937995.1	608838.2	128269.0	6025.0		212240.0	164621.6	37841.8	33571.2
69310.3	2468212.6	494894.8	74802.5			137081.4	94244.4	15134.6	11854.7
424.1	30034.1	10001.0				17235.1	16472.1	2540.2	2101.0
0.4	-572.0					68.3	68.3	16.3	16.3
1901.0	55351.2	2586.9	25190.3			13832.1	13832.1	4868.2	4868.2
3578.2	161488.1	33694.3				31233.3	27478.4	13178.7	12683.4
3319.1	106499.4	21662.4	28276.2	6025.0		9958.1	9694.6	1405.0	1348.8
2111.1	116981.7	45998.8				2831.7	2831.7	698.8	698.8
796.4	77005.8	5630.2	1262.6	331.1	8.3	37785.4	37785.4	5450.6	5450.6
	157.5	44.5				368.2	368.2	32.2	32.2

21-3 保险业财务状况

单位：万元

项目	Item	单位个数 Units (unit)	流动资产合计 Total Circulating Assets	#货币资金 Cash	#应收分保帐款 Accounts Receivable	#短期投资 Short-term Investment
合计	**Total**	**12**	**3312735.2**	**888929.6**	**8460.7**	**832237.7**
按登记注册类型分	**Grouped by Registation Status of Enterprises**					
内资经济	Domestic Investment Economy	11	3308698.8	886662.8	6745.1	832237.7
国有经济	State-owned	4	1737004.4	797895.7	3240.2	555255.0
股份有限公司	Share Holding Company	6	1570686.0	88659.2	3504.9	276982.7
有限责任公司	Limited-LiabilityCompany	1	1008.4	107.9		
外商投资经济	Foreign Funded	1	4036.4	2266.8	1715.6	

项目	Item	流动负债合计 Total Circulating Liability	#短期借款 Short-term Loans	#应付分保帐款 Accounts Payable	长期负债合计 Total Long-term Liability	#长期借款 Long-term Loans
合计	**Total**	**853115.2**		**4032.6**	**2611131.0**	
按登记注册类型分	**Grouped by Registation Status of Enterprises**					
内资经济	Domestic Investment Economy	851013.3		4032.6	2611131.0	
国有经济	State-owned	498795.1		3378.4	1366905.2	
股份有限公司	Share Holding Company	352207.0		654.2	1244225.8	
有限责任公司	Limited-LiabilityCompany	11.2				
外商投资经济	Foreign Funded	2101.9				

FINANCIAL INDICATORS FOR INSURANCE SERVICES

(10000 yuan)

长期投资 Long-term Investment	#债券投资 Bond	固定资产合计 Total Fixed Assets	固定资产原价合计 Original Value of Fixed Assets	累计折旧 Accumulative Depreciation	#本年折旧 of this Year	无形及其它资产合计 Intangible and Deffered Assets	#无形资产 Intangible	资产合计 Total Assets
178162.6	**138529.0**	**204591.8**	**236624.6**	**32032.8**	**9184.4**	**55846.8**	**1605.5**	**3751336.4**
178162.6	138529.0	204471.3	236437.0	31965.7	9159.5	55776.1	1605.5	3747108.8
108945.7	71334.8	173153.5	198335.0	25181.5	6534.2	47003.8	1448.1	2066107.4
69216.9	67194.2	31317.4	38101.6	6784.2	2625.3	8767.9	157.4	1679988.2
		0.4	0.4			4.4		1013.2
		120.5	187.6	67.1	24.9	70.7		4227.6

负债合计 Total Liabilities	所有者权益合计 Ownership Interest	#实收资本 Proceeds of Capital	国家资本 State	集体资本 Collective	法人资本 Institutional Units	个人资本 Individual	港澳台资本 Hongkong, Macao and Taiwan	外商资本 Foreign
3464246.2	**287090.2**	**267500.0**	**263000.0**	**2500.0**	**700.0**	**300.0**		**1000.0**
3462144.3	284964.5	266500.0	263000.0	2500.0	700.0	300.0		
1865700.3	200407.1	130000.0	130000.0					
1596432.9	83555.4	135500.0	133000.0	2500.0				
11.2	1002.0	1000.0			700.0	300.0		
2101.9	2125.7	1000.0						1000.0

21-3 续表

单位：万元

项目 Item		保费业务收入 Premiums Business Income	#保费收入 Premiums	#分保费收入 Premiums Transferred into	保费业务支出 Premiums Expenditure	#赔款支出 Reparations	#死伤医疗年金给付及退保金 Annuity for Casualty and Insurance-quit
合计	**Total**	**2302171.8**	**893109.4**	**1406534.2**	**1677797.9**	**161356.9**	**166652.1**
按登记注册类型分	**Grouped by Registration Status of Enterprises**						
内资经济	Domestic Investment Economy	2300197.1	893109.4	1406534.2	1676767.4	161356.9	166652.1
国有经济	State-owned	1685059.8	280617.3	1404282.9	1368470.0	91326.4	55707.8
股份有限公司	Share Holding Company	614873.9	612492.1	1987.9	308046.5	70030.5	110944.3
有限责任公司	Limited-LiabilityCompany	263.4		263.4	250.9		
外商投资经济	Foreign Funded	1974.7			1030.5		

项目 Item		准备金提转差 Balance of Reserve Extracted and Transfer	承保利润 Insurance Profits	#投资收益 Investment Income	#利息收入 Interest Income	#利息支出 Interest Expenditure	营业利润 Operating Profits
合计	**Total**	**576367.1**	**19461.9**	**40685.3**	**30561.5**	**1694.3**	**122711.9**
按登记注册类型分	**Grouped by Registration Status of Enterprises**						
内资经济	Domestic Investment Economy	576367.1	18616.4	40685.3	30533.5	1694.3	121749.6
国有经济	State-owned	212641.1	87237.9	24329.4	28900.3	1297.6	157388.1
股份有限公司	Share Holding Company	363726.0	-68622.6	16355.9	1633.2	396.7	-35630.1
有限责任公司	Limited-LiabilityCompany		1.1				-8.4
外商投资经济	Foreign Funded		845.5		28.0		962.3

continued

(10000 yuan)

# 佣金支出 Commission	# 分保赔款支出 Reparations Shared	# 营业费用 Operating Expense	# 税金 Taxes	# 财产保险费 Premium of Property	# 劳动待业保险 Premium for Employment	# 住房公积金 Housing Accumulation Funds	# 排污费养路费 Fees for Dirt Disposal and Road Toll	营业税金及附加 Operation Tax and Extra Charges	提取保险保障基金 Ensurance Funds Extracted
44350.6	**692245.0**	**107622.0**	**1248.2**	**375.9**	**325.9**	**1812.6**	**127.6**	**28544.9**	**16094.9**
44350.6	692245.0	106690.2	1247.6	368.3	325.9	1793.2	127.6	28446.2	16094.9
6687.0	695814.6	44857.5	855.1	276.3	302.1	260.6	107.4	16710.8	15307.5
37663.6	-3569.6	61832.7	392.5	92.0	23.8	1532.6	20.2	11724.0	787.4
								11.4	
		931.8	0.6	7.6		19.4		98.7	

营业外收入 Out-business Income	营业外支出 Out-business Expenditure	利润总额 Total Profits	#应交所得税 Income Tax Payable	# 应付利润 Profits Payable	# 已分配股利 Divided Payment	# 转作奖金的利润 Profits Distribut-	本年应付工资总额 Total Wages Payable in the Year	本年应付福利费总额 Welfares Payable in the Year
82.4	**2987.4**	**119806.9**	**1060.0**	**6665.0**			**26047.7**	**3588.0**
82.4	2849.9	118982.1	854.0	6665.0			25693.4	3588.0
42.0	2602.8	154827.3					11676.4	1999.9
40.4	247.1	-35836.8	854.0	6665.0			13977.6	1585.2
		-8.4					39.4	2.9
	137.5	824.8	206.0				354.3	

22 企业及企业集团

ENTERPRISE AND ENTERPRISE GROUP

22-1 地方企业集团按销售收入排序
ARRANGING IN SALES REVENUE ORDER OF LOCAL BUSINESS GROUP

序 号 No.	企 业 名 称	Enterprises
1	北京邮电通信设备厂	BEIJING TELECOMMUNICATION EQUIPMENT FACTORY
2	北京汽车工业集团	BEIJING AUTOMOTIVE INDUSTRY CORP
3	北京化学工业集团有限责任公司	BEIJING CHEMICAL INDUSTRY GROUP CO.,LTD.
4	北京建工集团	BEIJING CONSTRUCTION ENGINEERING GROUP CO.,LTD.
5	北京二商集团有限责任公司	BEIJING ERSHANG （GROUP）CO.,LTD.
6	北京首都创业集团	CAPITAL GROUP
7	北京住宅开发建设集团总公司	BEIJING ZHUZONG GROUP CO.,LTD.
8	北京建筑材料集团有限责任公司	BEIJING BUILDING MATERIALS GROUP
9	北京市公共交通总公司	BEIJING PUBLIC TRAFFIC GROUP CO.,LTD.
10	北京一商集团有限责任公司	BEIJING YI SHANG GROUP CO.,LTD.
11	北京旅游集团有限责任公司	BEIJING TOURISM GROUP CO.,LTD.
12	北京市燃气集团有限责任公司	BEIJING GAS GROUP CO.,LTD.
13	北京东方电子集团股份有限公司	BEIJING ORIENT ELECTRONICS GROUP CO.,LTD.
14	北京天鸿集团公司	BEIJING TIANHONG GROUP CORPORATION
15	北京王府井东安集团有限责任公司	BEIJING WANGFUJING-DONGAN GROUP CO.,LTD.
16	北京西单友谊集团	BEIJING XIDAN MARKET GROUP
17	北京燕莎集团有限责任公司	BEIJING YANSHA GROUP CO.,LTD.
18	北京燕京啤酒集团公司	BEIJING YANJING BEER GROUP CORPORATION
19	北京城乡建设集团有限责任公司	BEIJING URBAN & RURAL CONSTRUCTION GROUP CO.,LTD.
20	北京市热力集团有限责任公司	BEIJING DISTRICT FLEATING GROUP CO.,LTD.
21	北京城市开发集团有限责任公司	BEIJING URBAN DEVELOPMENT GROUP CO.,LTD.
22	北京一轻集团有限责任公司	BEIJING YIQING GROUP CO.,LTD.
23	北京市自来水集团有限责任公司	BEIJING WATER WORKS GROUP CO.,LTD.
24	北京牡丹电子集团公司	BEIJING PEONY ELECTRONIC GROUP CO.,LTD.
25	北京华都集团有限责任公司	BEIJING HUADU GROUP CO.,LTD.
26	北京雪花电器集团公司	BEIJING SNOWFLAKE ELECTRIC APPLIANCE GROUP CROP
27	北人集团	BEIREN GROUP CORPORATION
28	北京首都旅游汽车股份有限公司	BTG AUTOMOBILE SERVICE CO.,LTD.
29	北京市针棉织品进出口集团公司	BEIJING KNITWEAR IMP. & EXP. GROUP CORPORATION
30	北内集团	BEIJING GROUP CORPORATION
31	北京粮食集团有限责任公司	BEIJING GRAIN GROUP CO.,LTD.
32	北京兆维电子（集团）有限责任公司	BEIJING C&W ELECTRONICS (GROUP)CO.,LTD.
33	北京北辰实业集团公司	BEIJING NORTH STAR INDUSTRIAL GROUP
34	首汽集团	SHOUQI GROUP
35	北京外企服务集团有限责任公司	BEIJING FOREIGN ENTERPRISE SERVICE GROUP CO.,LTD.
36	北京市九达纺织集团公司	BEIJING JIU DA TEXTILE GROUP CORP.
37	北京印刷集团有限责任公司	BEIJING PRINTING GROUP CO.,LTD.
38	北京建筑材料经贸集团总公司	BEIJING CONSTRUCTION MATERIAL ECONOMIC TRADE GROUP CO.,LTD.
39	中国北京全聚德集团有限责任公司	CHINA BEIJING QUANJUDE GROUP CO.,LTD.
40	北京飞达电子集团公司	BEIJING FEIDA ELECTRONICS GROUP COMPANY
41	北京饮食服务集团有限责任公司	BEIJING CATERING & SERVICES GROUP CO.,LTD.
42	北京轻联包装印刷集团	BEIJING LIGHT INDUSTRY PACKING PRINTING GROUP CORPORATION
43	北京五洲染织集团公司	BEIJING WUZHOU DYEING AND WEAVING GROUP CORPORATION
44	北京厨房设备集团公司	BEIJING KITCHEN EQUIPMENT GROUP CORPORATION
45	北京华讯集团	BEIJING HUAXUN GROUP
46	北京青年实业集团公司	BEIJING YOUTH INDUSTRIAL(GROUP)CO.,LTD.
47	北京北奥有限责任公司	BEIJING BEI AO INCORATION
48	北京百花集团	BEIJING BAIHUA GROUP
49	北京标准件工业集团公司	BEIJING STANDARD FASTENERS INDUSTRIAL GROUP CO.,LTD.
50	北京市京工服装工业集团公司	BEIJING JING GONG GARMENT INDUSTRY GROUP CORPORATION
51	北京轻联皮革集团公司	BEIJING QING LIAN LEATHER GROUP CORPORATION
52	北京用友软件股份有限公司	BEIJING UFSOFT CO.,LTD.
53	北京章光101集团公司	BEIJING ZHANG GUANG 101 GROUP CO.,LTD.
54	北京首都科技集团有限责任公司	BEIJING CAPITAL SCIENCE TECHNOLOGY GROUP CO.,LTD.

22-2 地方企业集团按利润总额排序
ARRANGING IN TOTAL PROFITS OF LOCAL BUSINESS GROUP

序号 No.	企业名称	Enterprises
1	北京邮电通信设备厂	BEIJING TELECOMMUNICATION EQUIPMENT FACTORY
2	北京首都创业集团	CAPITAL GROUP
3	北京燕京啤酒集团公司	BEIJING YANJING BEER GROUP CORPORATION
4	北京旅游集团有限责任公司	BEIJING TOURISM GROUP CO.,LTD.
5	北京天鸿集团公司	BEIJING TIANHONG GROUP CO.,LTD
6	北京住宅开发建设集团总公司	BEIJING ZHUZONG GROUP CO.,LTD.
7	北京东方电子集团股份有限公司	BEIJING ORIENT ELECTRONICS GROUP CO.,LTD.
8	北京燕莎集团有限责任公司	BEIJING YANSHA GROUP CO.,LTD.
9	北京城市开发集团有限责任公司	BEIJING URBAN DEVELOPMENT GROUP CO.,LTD.
10	北京建筑材料集团有限责任公司	BEIJING BUILDING MATERIALS GROUP
11	北京建工集团	BEIJING CONSTRUCTION ENGINEERING GROUP CO.,LTD.
12	北人集团	BEIREN GROUP CO.,LTD
13	北京西单友谊集团	BEIJING XIDAN MARKET GROUP
14	北京用友软件股份有限公司	BEIJING UFSOFT CO.,LTD.
15	北京兆维电子（集团）有限责任公司	BEIJING C&W ELECTRONICS (GROUP)CO.,LTD.
16	北京城乡建设集团有限责任公司	BEIJING URBAN & RURAL CONSTRUCTION GROUP CO.,LTD.
17	中国北京全聚德集团有限责任公司	CHINA BEIJING QUANJUDE GROUP CO.,LTD.
18	北京市燃气集团有限责任公司	BEIJING GAS GROUP CO.,LTD.
19	北京首都旅游汽车股份有限公司	BTG AUTOMOBILE SERVICE CO.,LTD.
20	北京北辰实业集团公司	BEIJING NORTH STAR INDUSTRIAL GROUP
21	首汽集团	SHOUQI GROUP
22	北京市公共交通总公司	BEIJING PUBLIC TRAFFIC GROUP CO.,LTD.
23	北京王府井东安集团有限责任公司	BEIJING WANGFUJING-DONGAN GROUP CO.,LTD.
24	北京市九达纺织集团公司	BEIJING JIU DA TEXTILE GROUP CORP.
25	北京华都集团有限责任公司	BEIJING HUADU GROUP CO.,LTD.
26	北京雪花电器集团公司	BEIJING SNOWFLAKE ELECTRIC APPLIANCE GROUP CO.,LTD.
27	北京华讯集团	BEIJING HUAXUN GROUP
28	北京轻联包装印刷集团	BEIJING LIGHT INDUSTRY PACKING PRINTING GROUP CORPORATION
29	北京百花集团	BEIJING BAIHUA GROUP
30	北京北奥有限责任公司	BEIJING BEI AO INCORATION
31	北京市自来水集团有限责任公司	BEIJING WATER WORKS GROUP CO.,LTD.
32	北京一商集团有限责任公司	BEIJING YI SHANG GROUP CO.,LTD.
33	北京印刷集团有限责任公司	BEIJING PRINTING GROUP CO.,LTD.
34	北京饮食服务集团有限责任公司	BEIJING CATERING & SERVICES GROUP CO.,LTD.
35	北京建筑材料经贸集团总公司	BEIJING CONSTRUCTION MATERIAL ECONOMIC TRADE GROUP CO.,LTD.
36	北京五洲染织集团公司	BEIJING WUZHOU DYEING AND WEAVING GROUP CORPORATION
37	北京市京工服装工业集团公司	BEIJING JING GONG GARMENT INDUSTRY GROUP CORPORATION
38	北京牡丹电子集团公司	BEIJING PEONY ELECTRONIC GROUP CO.,LTD
39	北京飞达电子集团公司	BEIJING FEIDA ELECTRONICS GROUP COMPANY
40	北京标准件工业集团公司	BEIJING STANDARD FASTENERS INDUSTRIAL GROUP CO.,LTD.
41	北京轻联皮革集团公司	BEIJING QING LIAN LEATHER GROUP CORPORATION
42	北京首都科技集团有限责任公司	BEIJING CAPITAL SCIENCE TECHNOLOGY GROUP CO.,LTD.
43	北京章光101集团公司	BEIJING ZHANG GUANG 101 GROUP CO.,LTD
44	北京外企服务集团有限责任公司	BEIJING FOREIGN ENTERPRISE SERVICE GROUP CO.,LTD.
45	北京一轻集团有限责任公司	BEIJING YIQING GROUP CO.,LTD.
46	北京厨房设备集团公司	BEIJING KITCHEN EQUIPMENT GROUP CORPORATION
47	北京青年实业集团公司	BEIJING YOUTH INDUSTRIAL(GROUP)CO.,LTD.
48	北京粮食集团有限责任公司	BEIJING GRAIN GROUP CO.,LTD.
49	北京市针棉织品进出口集团公司	BEIJING KNITWEAR IMP. & EXP. GROUP CORPORATION
50	北京二商集团有限责任公司	BEIJING ERSHANG （GROUP）CO.,LTD.
51	北京化学工业集团有限责任公司	BEIJING CHEMICAL INDUSTRY GROUP CO.,LTD.
52	北内集团	BEIJING GROUP CORPORATION
53	北京市热力集团有限责任公司	BEIJING DISTRICT FLEATING GROUP CO.,LTD.
54	北京汽车工业集团	BEIJING AUTOMOTIVE INDUSTRY CORP

22-3 地方企业集团按资产总额排序
ARRANGING IN TOTAL ASSETS OF LOCAL BUSINESS GROUP

序号 No.	企业名称	Enterprises
1	北京首都创业集团	CAPITAL GROUP
2	北京化学工业集团有限责任公司	BEIJING CHEMICAL INDUSTRY GROUP CO.,LTD.
3	北京城市开发集团有限责任公司	BEIJING URBAN DEVELOPMENT GROUP CO.,LTD.
4	北京旅游集团有限责任公司	BEIJING TOURISM GROUP CO.,LTD.
5	北京天鸿集团公司	BEIJING TIANHONG GROUP CORPORATION
6	北京住宅开发建设集团总公司	BEIJING ZHUZONG GROUP CO.,LTD.
7	北京汽车工业集团	BEIJING AUTOMOTIVE INDUSTRY CORP
8	北京建筑材料集团有限责任公司	BEIJING BUILDING MATERIALS GROUP
9	北京建工集团	BEIJING CONSTRUCTION ENGINEERING GROUP CO.,LTD.
10	北京市公共交通总公司	BEIJING PUBLIC TRAFFIC GROUP CO.,LTD.
11	北京邮电通信设备厂	BEIJING TELECOMMUNICATION EQUIPMENT FACTORY
12	北京一轻集团有限责任公司	BEIJING YIQING GROUP CO.,LTD.
13	北京市自来水集团有限责任公司	BEIJING WATER WORKS GROUP CO.,LTD.
14	北京市燃气集团有限责任公司	BEIJING GAS GROUP CO.,LTD.
15	北京市热力集团有限责任公司	BEIJING DISTRICT FLEATING GROUP CO.,LTD.
16	北京北辰实业集团公司	BEIJING NORTH STAR INDUSTRIAL GROUP
17	北京二商集团有限责任公司	BEIJING ERSHANG （GROUP）CO.,LTD.
18	北京燕京啤酒集团公司	BEIJING YANJING BEER GROUP CORPORATION
19	北京东方电子集团股份有限公司	BEIJING ORIENT ELECTRONICS GROUP CO.,LTD.
20	北京一商集团有限责任公司	BEIJING YI SHANG GROUP CO.,LTD.
21	北京城乡建设集团有限责任公司	BEIJING URBAN & RURAL CONSTRUCTION GROUP CO.,LTD.
22	北内集团	BEIJING GROUP CORPORATION
23	北京外企服务集团有限责任公司	BEIJING FOREIGN ENTERPRISE SERVICE GROUP CO.,LTD.
24	北人集团	BEIREN GROUP CORPORATION
25	北京牡丹电子集团公司	BEIJING PEONY ELECTRONIC GROUP CO.,LTD
26	北京西单友谊集团	BEIJING XIDAN MARKET GROUP
27	北京粮食集团有限责任公司	BEIJING GRAIN GROUP CO.,LTD.
28	北京燕莎集团有限责任公司	BEIJING YANSHA GROUP CO.,LTD.
29	北京兆维电子（集团）有限责任公司	BEIJING C&W ELECTRONICS (GROUP)CO.,LTD.
30	北京雪花电器集团公司	BEIJING SNOWFLAKE ELECTRIC APPLIANCE GROUP CROP
31	北京王府井东安集团有限责任公司	BEIJING WANGFUJING-DONGAN GROUP CO.,LTD.
32	北京华都集团有限责任公司	BEIJING HUADU GROUP CO.,LTD.
33	北京首都旅游汽车股份有限公司	BTG AUTOMOBILE SERVICE CO.,LTD.
34	首汽集团	SHOUQI GROUP
35	北京市针棉织品进出口集团公司	BEIJING KNITWEAR IMP. & EXP. GROUP CORPORATION
36	北京饮食服务集团有限责任公司	BEIJING CATERING & SERVICES GROUP CO.,LTD.
37	北京建筑材料经贸集团总公司	BEIJING CONSTRUCTION MATERIAL ECONOMIC TRADE GROUP CO.LTD.
38	北京印刷集团有限责任公司	BEIJING PRINTING GROUP CO.,LTD.
39	北京飞达电子集团公司	BEIJING FEIDA ELECTRONICS GROUP COMPANY
40	中国北京全聚德集团有限责任公司	CHINA BEIJING QUANJUDE GROUP CO.,LTD.
41	北京五洲染织集团公司	BEIJING WUZHOU DYEING AND WEAVING GROUP CORPORATION
42	北京市九达纺织集团公司	BEIJING JIU DA TEXTILE GROUP CORP.
43	北京青年实业集团公司	BEIJING YOUTH INDUSTRIAL(GROUP)CO.,LTD
44	北京标准件工业集团公司	BEIJING STANDARD FASTENERS INDUSTRIAL GROUP CO.,LTD
45	北京轻联皮革集团公司	BEIJING QING LIAN LEATHER GROUP CORPORATION
46	北京轻联包装印刷集团	BEIJING LIGHT INDUSTRY PACKING PRINTING GROUP CORPORATION
47	北京北奥有限责任公司	BEIJING BEI AO INCORATION
48	北京厨房设备集团公司	BEIJING KITCHEN EQUIPMENT GROUP CORPORATION
49	北京百花集团	BEIJING BAIHUA GROUP
50	北京市京工服装工业集团公司	BEIJING JING GONG GARMENT INDUSTRY GROUP CORPORATION
51	北京用友软件股份有限公司	BEIJING UFSOFT CO.,LTD.
52	北京章光101集团公司	BEIJING ZHANG GUANG 101 GROUP CO.,LTD
53	北京华讯集团	BEIJING HUAXUN GROUP
54	北京首都科技集团有限责任公司	BEIJING CAPITAL SCIENCE TECHNOLOGY GROUP CO.,LTD.

22-4 企业集团主要经济指标（2000年）

单位：万元

项目	Item	集团个数（个）Number of Groups (unit)	所属企业数（个）Number of Enterprises Belonged to (unit)	资产总计 Total Assets
总计	**Total**	**94**	**1250**	**95220260**
按审批部门划分	**By Departments Responsible for Approval**			
国务院	The State Council	1	41	35860984
国务院主管部门	Competent Authorities of the State Council	39	573	33769133
省级政府	Municipal Government	43	562	20896481
省级政府主管部门	Competent Authorities of Municipal Government	8	58	3833453
其他	Others	3	16	860208
按控股情况划分	**By Share Holding**			
国有绝对控股	State-owned Absolute Holding Enterprises	84	1164	92472171
国有相对控股	State-owned Relative Holding Enterprises	6	52	2647102
集体绝对控股	Collective-owned Absolute Holding Enterprises	1	7	24446
其他	Others	3	27	76540
按行业划分	**By Sector**			
农、林、牧、渔业	Farming,Forestry,Animal Husbandry and Fishery	2	31	211242
采掘业	Excavation		2	
制造业	Manufacturing	32	351	13871859
电力煤气等供应业	Electricity,Gas Production and Supply	4	9	2475355
建筑业	Construction	8	86	6257458
运输邮电业	Transportation,Posts and Telecommunications	3	23	15432656
批发零售贸易餐饮业	Wholesale,Retail and Catering	26	318	4298002
金融保险业	Banking and Insurance	1	8	35860984
房地产业	Real Estate	4	96	4157591
其他	Others	14	326	12655110
按登记注册类型划分	**By Registration Status**			
国有企业	State-owned	21	329	13640526
国有独资公司	Exclusive State-owned	58	741	62510455
其他有限责任公司	Other Limited-liability Corporations Ltd.	7	125	17747610
股份有限公司	Share Holding Corporations Ltd.	5	34	1261698
其他	Others	3	21	59969

MAIN ECONOMIC INDICATORS OF BUSINESS GROUP（2000）

(10000 yuan)

固定资产原价 Original Value of Fixed Assets	流动资产平均余额 Average Balance of Circulating Funds	负债合计 Total Liabilities	所有者权益 Ownership Interest	主营收入 Major Business Revenue	利润总额 Total Profits	从业人员（人） Number of Employed Persons (person)	从业人员报酬 Remuneration for Employed Persons	研究开发费用 Research and Exploit Expenses
23938297	**45062371**	**67686046**	**27534214**	**24493701**	**1180723**	**900281**	**1452781**	**254268**
2520113	17944297	31338059	4522925	2755673	308317	53829	97228	4508
11341433	13570402	20346746	13422387	12264364	550838	367969	617870	130392
8531194	10805301	13068652	7827830	6472154	125022	375265	584589	30138
1407126	2038242	2312495	1520957	1173939	100461	97282	138797	8499
138429	704127	620094	240113	1827569	96083	5936	14295	80730
23581472	43306910	65879582	26592589	23542271	1096720	871322	1388375	234344
328837	1704733	1753920	893183	910602	77774	26548	58485	13551
10986	13333	8798	15648	5969	656	315	428	11
17002	37394	43746	32794	34858	5571	2096	5492	6362
83430	117134	145349	65895	112092	3114	9282	12352	
5817914	6066935	8399641	5472218	7081767	266427	290318	391640	173991
2133005	600534	539839	1935515	640905	5940	23319	47978	20953
1145555	4680161	4897652	1359806	3010404	68549	130620	236789	2048
7284528	3882352	8238032	7194624	2958651	219978	154265	271671	500
1288517	2562549	3016517	1281485	2432064	53732	74337	121440	6437
2520113	17944297	31338059	4522925	2755673	308317	53829	97228	4508
307043	3394404	3487864	669727	540681	42200	15858	26868	78
3358188	5814001	7623093	5032017	4961460	212462	148453	246812	45752
4153612	6384363	8795246	4845280	8610775	281251	210634	329100	163550
11425209	33038887	48441113	14069341	11147815	581768	519944	807225	57650
7953512	5044687	9771553	7976057	3982753	263687	148879	274958	3632
374571	563514	651815	609885	731299	52422	18669	38962	28924
31392	30918	26319	33650	21058	1594	2155	2534	511

22-5 建立现代企业制度企业主要经济指标（2000年）

MAIN ECONOMIC INDICATORS OF ENTERPRISES WITH MODERN ENTERPRISE SYSTEM（2000）

单位：万元　　　　(10000 yuan)

项　　目	Item	单位数（个）Number of Enterprises (unit)	资产总计 Total Assets	固定资产原价 Original Value of Fixed Assets	累计折旧 Accumulative Depreciation in this Year
总　计	**Total**	**191**	**191915178**	**90913074**	**29194045**
按确定企业改制的主管部门划分	**By Department Responsible for Enterprises Restructure**				
国家经贸委	State Economic and Trade Commission	10	6988411	4171857	1780220
国家体改委	State Commission for Restructuring Economy	6	1885383	337719	117419
市经贸委	Municipal Economic and Trade Commission	13	9232224	3047392	1309571
市体改委	Municipal Commission for Restructuring Economy	93	20347359	10369075	3020597
企业主管部门	Departments in Charge of Enterprises	16	6075836	4382092	1439944
其　他	Others	53	147385964	68604938	21526293
按控股情况划分	**By Share Holding**				
国有绝对控股	State-owned Absolute Holding Enterprises	160	190384815	90557998	29078492
国有相对控股	State-owned Relative Holding Enterprises	12	740928	158281	59401
集体绝对控股	Collective-owned Absolute Holding Enterprises	9	198615	47629	14807
集体相对控股	Collective-owned Relative Holding Enterprises	3	54704	24193	5230
其　他	Others	7	536114	124971	36113
按企业规模划分	**By Size**				
特大型	Oversized	29	121187361	69170456	23183955
大　型	Large-sized	110	45908304	13624359	4179656
中　型	Medium-sized	34	4575402	490712	129625
小　型	Small-sized	9	2258597	267242	67059
其　他	Others	9	17985513	7360303	1633748
按行业划分	**By Sector**				
农、林、牧、渔业	Farming,Forestry,Animal Husbandry and Fishery	3	268522	81854	28466
采掘业	Excavation	5	1272296	467003	151255
制造业	Manufacturing	91	34875493	14732608	5448135
电力、煤气及水的生产和供应业	Electricity,Gas,Water Production and Supply	5	101199160	61179162	19692640
建筑业	Construction	8	10233685	1370384	457020
运输邮电业	Transportation,Posts and Telecommunications	11	22964691	10756200	2781909
批发零售贸易餐饮业	Wholesale,Retail and Catering	44	5217240	819828	216370
金融保险业	Banking and Insurance				
房地产业	Real Estate	3	1600431	117444	22850
其　他	Others	21	14283660	1388590	395399
按登记注册类型划分	**By Registration Status**				
国有企业	State-owned	97	140399117	75203765	24773506
国有独资公司	Exclusive State-owned	43	33624176	8135736	2760211
其他有限责任公司	Other Limited-liability Corporations Ltd.	16	15518618	6862629	1445291
股份有限公司	Share Holding Corporations Ltd.	25	2175445	609617	187489
中外合资企业	Joint Venture	3	100705	59591	16390
港澳台合资企业	Hongkong,Macao ang Taiwan Venture	1	24324	16558	2556
其　他	Others	6	72790	25176	8600

22-6 建立现代企业制度企业主要经济指标（1999年）

MAIN ECONOMIC INDICATORS OF ENTERPRISES WITH MODERN ENTERPRISE SYSTEM（1999）

单位：万元 （10000 yuan)

项目	Item	单位数（个）Number of Enterprises (unit)	资产总计 Total Assets	固定资产原价 Original Value of Fixed Assets	累计折旧 Accumulative Depreciation in this Year
总计	**Total**	**195**	**168775200**	**82068738**	**26437206**
按确定企业改制的主管部门划分	**By Department Responsible for Enterprises Restructure**				
国家经贸委	State Economic and Trade Commission	10	6698615	3801376	1565531
国家体改委	State Commission for Restructuring Economy	7	1850963	389376	123492
市经贸委	Municipal Economic and Trade Commission	10	8660647	2927948	1157633
市体改委	Municipal Commission for Restructuring Economy	88	18751957	9961509	2974133
企业主管部门	Departments in Charge of Enterprises	25	7537587	3965967	1255843
其他	Others	55	125275430	61022562	19360573
按控股情况划分	**By Share Holding**				
国有绝对控股	State-owned Absolute Holding Enterprises	167	167581608	81769200	26324726
国有相对控股	State-owned Relative Holding Enterprises	9	577212	111761	49379
集体绝对控股	Collective-owned Absolute Holding Enterprises	9	200156	48418	27549
集体相对控股	Collective-owned Relative Holding Enterprises	3	52702	19085	4066
其他	Others	7	363521	120272	31484
按企业规模划分	**By Size**				
特大型	Oversized	43	111915309	65974100	21567921
大型	Large-sized	109	41231826	11076622	3719754
中型	Medium-sized	26	4168461	426845	115237
小型	Small-sized	10	2324994	244067	68437
其他	Others	7	9134608	4347103	965855
按行业划分	**By Sector**				
农、林、牧、渔业	Farming,Forestry,Animal Husbandry and Fishery	4	239404	78923	24074
采掘业	Excavation	5	1250944	453998	148981
制造业	Manufacturing	84	30569596	12174065	4812067
电力、煤气及水的生产和供应业	Electricity,Gas,Water Production and Supply	5	91871746	58377189	18462929
建筑业	Construction	11	9939091	1361771	446828
运输邮电业	Transportation,Posts and Telecommunications	7	15617253	7406025	2006067
批发零售贸易餐饮业	Wholesale,Retail and Catering	58	4820328	895902	201392
金融保险业	Banking and Insurance	1			
房地产业	Real Estate	2	1490731	86492	13793
其他	Others	18	12976107	1234372	321073
按登记注册类型划分	**By Registration Status**				
国有企业	State-owned	88	128543826	69875819	23101053
国有独资公司	Exclusive State-owned	50	31849451	7770543	2381944
其他有限责任公司	Other Limited-liability Corporations Ltd.	16	6468777	3772363	755698
股份有限公司	Share Holding Corporations Ltd.	35	1712832	549323	175073
中外合资企业	Joint Venture	2	110548	64003	14696
港澳台合资企业	Hongkong,Macao ang Taiwan Venture	2	24181	12779	1872
其他	Others	2	65584	23907	6867

22-7 建立现代企业制度企业主要财务指标（2000年）

单位：万元

项目	Item	流动资产年平均余额 Average Balance of Circulating Funds	年末负债合计 Total Liabilities	年末股东权益合计 Ownership Interest
总计	**Total**	**66655852**	**106293876**	**85621302**
按确定企业改制的主管部门划分	**By Department Responsible for Enterprise Restructure**			
国家经贸委	State Economic and Trade Commission	2645572	3939710	3048701
国家体改委	State Commission for Restructuring Economy	1015314	1369539	515844
市经贸委	Municipal Economic and Trade Commission	4870175	5899758	3332466
市体改委	Municipal Commission for Restructuring Economy	6238377	8880518	11466841
企业主管部门	Departments in Charge of Enterprises	2027439	4837469	1238367
其他	Others	49858975	81366881	66019082
按控股情况划分	**By Share Holding**			
国有绝对控股	State-owned Absolute Holding Enterprises	66001576	105437934	84946881
国有相对控股	State-owned Relative Holding Enterprises	308616	457557	283371
集体绝对控股	Collective-owned Absolute Holding Enterprises	120138	120658	77956
集体相对控股	Collective-owned Relative Holding Enterprises	28668	38974	15730
其他	Others	196852	238752	297362
按企业规模划分	**By Size**			
特大型	Oversized	36786070	65206697	55980664
大型	Large-sized	20195452	25826843	20081461
中型	Medium-sized	2081849	3190765	1384636
小型	Small-sized	1817624	1886675	371921
其他	Others	5774854	10182895	7802618
按行业划分	**By Sector**			
农、林、牧、渔业	Farming,Forestry,Animal Husbandry and Fishery	138400	204599	63923
采掘业	Excavation	741121	868574	403722
制造业	Manufacturing	14683253	18085435	16790058
电力、煤气及水的生产和供应业	Electricity,Gas,Water Production and Supply	28742593	53983203	47215957
建筑业	Construction	7432114	7771637	2462048
运输邮电业	Transportation,Posts and Telecommunications	6055456	13271079	9693612
批发零售贸易餐饮业	Wholesale,Retail and Catering	3047672	3423507	1793732
金融保险业	Banking and Insurance			
房地产业	Real Estate	1266847	1102481	497950
其他	Others	4548396	7583359	6700300
按登记注册类型划分	**By Registration Status**			
国有企业	State-owned	45891847	76393695	64005421
国有独资公司	Exclusive State-owned	15629386	20158641	13465535
其他有限责任公司	Other Limited-liability Corporations Ltd.	4100351	8526457	6992161
股份有限公司	Share Holding Corporations Ltd.	939291	1101540	1073905
中外合资企业	Joint Venture	36218	50286	50419
港澳台合资企业	Hongkong,Macao ang Taiwan Venture	9022	16765	7559
其他	Others	49734	46490	26300

MAIN FINANCIAL INDICATORS OF ENTERPRISES WITH MODERN ENTERPRISE SYSTEM (2000)

(10000 yuan)

股 本 Capital Stock	主营业务收入 Major Business Revenue	出口额 Total Exports	主营业务成本 Major Business Cost	利润总额 Total Profits	累计对外投资 Accumulative External Investment	投资收益 Investment Income	从业人员年末人数(人) Employed Persons (person)	从业人员劳动报酬 Remuneration of Employed Persons
35964362	**70941654**	**3548632**	**59820145**	**2784207**	**32635617**	**1476978**	**2070668**	**3658993**
1268286	4161117	69577	3725673	60225	894723	70830	71785	148045
242403	600278	192842	511425	41119	198161	44931	25516	39773
1400419	3357109	117352	2866962	80411	1482495	27417	118612	237866
6261598	11210278	448116	8772973	311552	3980409	205549	396004	628316
589137	2121915	156248	1718512	-117358	469524	31277	47347	104422
26202518	49490957	2564496	42224599	2408257	25610304	1096973	1411404	2500570
35682780	69451118	3384885	58495484	2733978	32496459	1463743	2039550	3615858
107352	971207	72	877885	23741	49080	5869	13218	22108
55517	155985	1200	131629	7276	11141	1174	5327	5229
16384	59911	25382	50732	1128	147	-158	3755	4055
102328	303431	137092	264413	18082	78789	6350	8818	11741
22879848	43086472	186609	38544986	990474	20833888	949124	1238745	2346452
8776926	22529782	2102649	17415925	1521017	9751447	467102	657033	1008964
1296858	555425	160384	477153	13100	857313	22351	30978	38947
215387	853489	513629	739557	5315	193746	10020	5515	12893
2795342	3916485	585360	2642523	254300	999222	28381	138397	251735
76569	200346	31709	188140	-1092	54581	355	3154	3058
225843	574121	28203	459836	19506	107594	3083	58483	73536
7870525	22177733	2462344	17093740	1460209	4546251	220682	539715	853217
19803085	35231489		31758309	978518	16370716	810845	927090	1869414
648944	4428260	13426	3883355	60137	1264067	18036	272892	349392
3557725	4209112	7049	2866861	6348	2708558	59552	107653	236474
768675	2886483	825427	2521303	77981	952852	57843	47200	86674
132000	211809		165637	40885	230404	42765	7374	15956
2880996	1022301	180473	882964	141715	6400593	263817	107107	171270
27729305	56581987	2505541	48089778	2127678	22924942	1092010	1484194	2747526
5830671	9275661	868288	7955674	356999	8741262	349377	429829	643153
1817940	2960665	10471	1904087	214795	789278	17333	103648	197853
516532	1971769	158034	1740784	78283	177571	18182	42566	59857
41867	47820	2644	39969	607			5536	6663
7384	19316		18720	233			1039	897
20662	84434	3653	71130	5610	2563	75	3856	3041

22-8 建立现代企业制度企业主要财务指标（1999年）

单位：万元

项目	Item	流动资产年平均余额 Average Balance of Circulating Funds	年末负债合计 Total Liabilities	年末股东权益合计 Ownership Interest
总计	**Total**	**56252143**	**92235732**	**76539467**
按确定企业改制的主管部门划分	**By Department Responsible for Enterprise Restructure**			
国家经贸委	State Economic and Trade Commission	2153686	3695631	3002984
国家体改委	State Commission for Restructuring Economy	906074	1326580	524383
市经贸委	Municipal Economic and Trade Commission	4289225	5345817	3314830
市体改委	Municipal Commission for Restructuring Economy	5797874	8053986	10697970
企业主管部门	Departments in Charge of Enterprises	2086833	4767728	2769859
其他	Other	41018450	69045990	56229440
按控股情况划分	**By Share Holding**			
国有绝对控股	State-owned Absolute Holding Enterprises	55738584	91570263	76011344
国有相对控股	State-owned Relative Holding Enterprises	236724	333080	244132
集体绝对控股	Collective-owned Absolute Holding Enterprises	122134	122237	77919
集体相对控股	Collective-owned Relative Holding Enterprises	27994	35356	17346
其他	Others	126705	174796	188725
按企业规模划分	**By Size**			
特大型	Oversized	33138765	57088171	54827138
大型	Large-sized	18495398	24355481	16876345
中型	Medium-sized	1572757	2729238	1439223
小型	Small-sized	875922	1886343	438651
其他	Others	2169299	6176498	2958110
按行业划分	**By Sector**			
农、林、牧、渔业	Farming,Forestry,Animal Husbandry and Fishery	143052	203917	35487
采掘业	Excavation	737034	839241	411703
制造业	Manufacturing	11476771	16622040	13947556
电力、煤气及水的生产和供应业	Electricity,Gas,Water Production and Supply	26202501	46942322	44929424
建筑业	Construction	6885704	7586378	2352713
运输邮电业	Transportation,Posts and Telecommunications	3102523	9409070	6208183
批发零售贸易餐饮业	Wholesale,Retail and Catering	2979567	3085503	1734824
金融保险业	Banking and Insurance			
房地产业	Real Estate	1033771	916572	574159
其他	Others	3691220	6630689	6345418
按登记注册类型划分	**By Registration Status**			
国有企业	State-owned	40397673	67997429	60546396
国有独资公司	Exclusive State-owned	14602850	18916006	12933445
其他有限责任公司	Other Limited-liability Corporations Ltd.	331843	4409733	2059044
股份有限公司	Share Holding Corporations Ltd.	830812	803654	909177
中外合资企业	Joint Venture	38371	53482	57065
港澳台合资企业	Hongkong,Macao ang Taiwan Venture	6908	12968	11213
其他	Others	43684	42458	23126

MAIN FINANCIAL INDICATORS OF ENTERPRISES WITH MODERN ENTERPRISE SYSTEM (1999)

(10000 yuan)

股本 Capital Stock	主营业务收入 Major Business Revenue	出口额 Total Exports	主营业务成本 Major Business Cost	利润总额 Total Profits	累计对外投资 Accumulative External Investment	投资收益 Investment Income	从业人员年末人数（人） Employed Persons (person)	从业人员劳动报酬 Remuneration of Employed Persons
33190642	**58236922**	**2767965**	**50428309**	**1974147**	**28239198**	**1166846**	**2134676**	**3321922**
1261618	2613713	37394	2168866	105363	968951	54994	74912	135239
244793	537724	174389	387309	33027	208039	24175	31998	39152
1322050	3311754	54789	2846659	82452	1196723	43904	132521	227684
5054470	8102737	378982	7253863	234243	3594886	157616	425866	595233
550193	2028785	197148	1617874	-102316	369673	28407	52132	94373
24757517	41642208	1925262	36153738	1621378	21900926	857749	1417247	2230239
32926901	57252414	2708583	49580167	1954237	28112495	1159138	2101871	3281487
92516	616655	57	540103	428	43565	1948	13628	21404
58713	169755	1600	144847	7683	8699	669	6024	5327
15619	45085	18438	36903	-1228	643	-189	3109	2823
96892	153011	39287	126287	13026	73796	5279	10044	10879
22636299	36110305	70511	32174837	1008823	18603619	798740	1364867	2166040
7356200	18101333	1415766	15237950	692714	8652002	333487	589131	880993
1211588	616505	208340	525105	8312	555012	13215	33894	37110
221941	687586	468796	594145	5045	191879	6286	8857	14009
1764613	2721191	604551	1896270	259251	236685	15117	137927	223767
52115	192988	25015	182446	-833	33728	1296	3162	3711
231069	551493	34088	439194	14172	106063	3079	61365	73096
6899495	15706847	1604848	13119952	661208	3609199	212273	588546	772547
19724322	30063499		27139327	929600	14399455	647207	1011303	1729598
634384	5035377	15406	4406168	107605	1142190	10456	203849	286324
2473608	3076193	8303	2146276	70243	1783525	65422	104158	200274
618193	2472125	852593	2095822	74453	729356	46796	49779	85645
129438	242289		198811	35566	300348	28217	6554	13888
2428017	896109	227711	700312	82131	6135333	152100	105960	156837
25959821	45391565	1919423	39767188	1385946	19856903	903567	1603296	2524621
5107273	9353666	781514	8037871	299824	8167386	240702	384595	570024
1541994	1861801	7579	1234215	227823	39604	14076	95300	163237
514182	1491647	54015	1272557	54479	172742	8375	41265	54650
42183	46587	1985	38899	814			5660	6243
7384	12811		10796	102			618	537
17803	78843	3448	66781	5157	2562	125	3942	2607

开发区 23

DEVELOPMENT ZONES

23-1 各类开发区基本情况
BASIC STATISTICS FOR DEVELOPMENT ZONES

项目 Item		合计 Total	国家级 Of State	市级 Of City	其他 Others
开发区个数 (个)	Number of Development Zones (unit)	30	5	10	15
累计完成征用土地面积 (平方公里)	Accumulative Area of Requisitions Realized (sq.km)	48.4	12.8	19.0	16.6
累计"七通一平"土地开发面积 (平方公里)	Accumulative Area of Began Seven-through-One-Flat (sq.km)	41.4	12.7	17.0	11.7
累计完成"七通一平"土地开发面积 (平方公里)	Accumulative Area of Seventhrough-One-Flat Realized (sq.km)	37.8	12.3	14.7	10.8
累计招商占用土地面积 (平方公里)	Accumulative Area Spared for Business (sq.km)	23.7	5.9	10.9	6.9
# 三资企业占用 (平方公里)	Foreign Funded Enterprises (sq.km)	7.9	1.8	3.8	2.3
累计建成区土地面积 (平方公里)	Accumulative Completed Area (sq.km)	28.6	10.1	11.0	7.5
# 工业用地 (平方公里)	For Industrial Use (sq.km)	15.3	3.9	7.2	4.2
累计招商个数 (个)	Accumulative Number of Hirer Leaseholder (unit)	13257	9003	2393	1861
累计项目总投资 (亿元)	Accumulative Investment (100 million yuan)	1149.5	347.2	340.8	461.5
累计注册资本 (亿元)	Accumulative Registered Capital (100 million yuan)	716.9	308.4	158.6	249.9
# 外方 (亿元)	Foreign Partner (100 million yuan)	434.6	178.9	81.2	174.5
累计协议外资金额 (亿美元)	Accumulative Contracted Foreign Capital (USD 100 million)	107.6	16.4	13.6	77.6
外商累计入资 (亿美元)	Accumulative Foreign Capital Inflow (USD 100 million)	37.6	11.1	8.9	17.6

说明：1.累计完成征用土地面积中包括原建成区面积。
2.表内"七通"指：上水、下水、煤气、热力、电力、通讯和道路通；"一平"指：场地自然平整。
3.表内"累计"指自开始至2000年末的累计数。

a) Accumulative requisition area of included original completed area.
b) Seven-through refers to water,drainage,gas,heat,electricity,communications and transportation,and one-flat refers to flat ground.
c) Accumulative data of this table refers to that from the beginning to the end of 2000.

23-2 各类开发区主要指标完成情况
STATISTICS FOR FULFILLMENT OF MAJOR INDICATORS OF DEVELOPMENT ZONES

项目 Item		2000	1999	2000年为1999年% 2000 as % of 1999
完成固定资产投资 (亿元)	Investment in Fixed Assets Completed (100 million yuan)	108.0	84.1	128.4
新增固定资产 (亿元)	Incremental Fixed Assets (100 million yuan)	35.8	31.3	114.4
房屋建筑施工面积 (万平方米)	Floor Space of Buildings under Construction (10000 sq.m)	462.4	407.4	113.5
房屋建筑竣工面积 (万平方米)	Floor Space of Buildings Completed (10000 sq.m)	184.8	143.1	129.1
完成增加值 (亿元)	Value Added Completed (100 million yuan)	412.5	281.5	146.5
实现销售收入 (亿元)	Sales Revenue Completed (100 million yuan)	2006.7	1173.3	171.0
实现利润总额 (亿元)	Total Profits Completed (100 million yuan)	119.1	66.5	179.1
应缴税金总额 (亿元)	Total Taxes Turned over (100 million yuan)	110.2	53.6	205.6

23-3 各类开发区一览表
DEVELOPMENT ZONES LIST

名　称 Name	通讯地址 Address	主要负责人 Chairman	邮编 Post Code	电话 Telephone
北京经济技术开发区	北京经济技术开发区万源街4号	李凤玲	100176	67681207
北京市王府井地区开发建设办公室	王府井大街99号世纪大厦A608室	陈　平	100006	65129999
北京西三旗高新建材城	海淀区西三旗	蒋卫平	100096	82910873
北京市朝阳望京工业区	朝阳区东湖渠甲3号	佟克克	100102	64724723
朝阳东部旅游经济开发区	朝阳区农展南路9号	田　锦	100026	65940942
中关村科技园区海淀园	海淀中关村南大街3号海淀科技大厦	马　林	100080	62569636
中关村科技园区丰台园	丰台科学城海鹰路2号	汪　洪	100070	63725608
北京八大处高科技园区	石景山路22号万商大厦	李云涛	100043	68686665
北京市门头沟区石龙工业区	门头沟区石龙南路6号	韩立宝	102308	69843664
北京良乡工业开发区	良乡凯旋大街金光路2号	李建民	102488	39351867
北京市燕山东流水工业区	北京市燕山东流水工业区管委会	黄祖团	102500	69347332
北京大兴工业开发区	北京大兴工业开发区广茂大街9号	蔡连军	102600	69244179
北京埝坛工业区	大兴县黄村镇念坛村	刘宝岩	102600	69245165
通州工业开发区	通州区张家湾镇光华路西	唐　钰	101113	69541700
北京永乐经济开发区	通州区永乐店小甸屯村南	张　洪	101105	69544479
北京次渠工业区	通州区次渠工业区	张　华	101111	69502049
中关村科技园区昌平园	昌平城区镇超前路9号	洪起忠	102200	69709140
北京雁栖工业开发区	怀柔县雁栖工业开发区	孟昭霞	101407	61668124
北京凤翔科技开发区	怀柔县杨宋镇	线继文	101400	61679488
北京怀柔农业经济开发区	怀柔县富乐小区北里26号	唐爱民	101400	69641848
北京中国乡镇企业城	海淀复兴路甲23号城乡华懋商厦14层	曹　林	101400	68298317
怀柔民营经济开发区	怀柔龙山宾馆北二楼万通公司	许　立	101400	60693701
平谷县滨河工业开发区	平谷县府前西大街22号	王新海	101200	69963791
平谷县兴谷经济开发区	平谷县乐园西小区7号	李宝峰	101200	69964071
北京市密云县工业开发区	密云工业开发区	李永军	101500	69041550
北京林河工业开发区	顺义区林河工业区	张东生	101300	89493610
北京天竺空港工业区	顺义区天竺镇	李友生	101312	64565745
北京市延庆经济技术开发区	延庆县城东外大街15号	张德福	102100	69142562
北京八达岭工业开发区	延庆县西大街2号	李志民	102100	69141563
北京电子城科技园	北京朝阳区酒仙桥路12号北门	鲍玉桐	100016	64377993

23-4 各类开发区招商、入资情况

STATISTICS ON HIRER LEASEHOLDER AND CAPITAL INFLOW OF DEVELOPMENT ZONES

名　　称 Name	自开始至报告期累计 Accumulative Number from Beginning					
	招商个数 (个) Number of Hirer Leaseholder (unit)	项　目 总投资 (万元) Total Investment (10000 yuan)	注册资本 (万元) Registered Capital (10000 yuan)	# 外方 Foreign Partner	协议外资 金　额 (万美元) Contracted Foreign Capital (USD 10000)	外　商 实际投资 (万美元) Foreign Actual Investment (USD 10000)
北京经济技术开发区	817	2229297	1498590	1E+06	109938	87786
王府井商业区	26	2852288	1472004	1E+06	738229	145779
北京西三旗高新建材城	22	155552	94226	87966	9612	9612
望京工业区	87	405873	105134	32176	2749	2749
东部旅游经济开发区	5	201939	70384	70384	5111	4121
中关村科技园区海淀园	5711					
中关村科技园区丰台园	1427	495241	495241	244417	14007	12043
八大处高科技园区	640	236452	225181	45195	4753	3427
北京石龙工业区	1006	446105	388484	99287	7875	7656
良乡卫星城工业开发区	305	163791	59543	6702	317	769
燕山东流水工业区	13	2677	1389	570	100	20
北京大兴工业开发区	263	191103	109420	43369	2898	2505
北京念坛工业区						
通州工业开发区	77	133200	85227	52210	4160	3879
永乐工业开发区	30	43091	26105	10880	3980	1225
北京次渠工业区	13	184600	67208	5344	600	600
中关村科技园区昌平园	947	747000	473965	186412	15430	10821
雁栖工业开发区	53	208132	74550	70700	22000	22000
凤翔科技开发区	224	75910	40610	17435	2930	2350
怀柔农业经济开发区	26	12997	11022	4532	498	498
中国乡镇企业城	36	86313	58977	24600	5300	3500
怀柔民营经济开发区	40	86275	86275			
滨河工业区	383	180142	180106	20679	1724	1724
兴谷经济开发区	141	210943	101573	81883	14808	14808
密云县工业开发区	86	900000	238000	54000	6300	4100
顺义林河工业开发区	48	149234	70277	52307	5500	4889
天竺空港工业区	113	910206	403340	350900	71000	27400
延庆经济技术开发区	316	91681	60289	19322	762	762
八达岭经济开发区	301	95000	56000	232	778	778
北京电子城科技园	101		615989	346651	24279	

23-5 各类开发区投资、生产情况
INVESTMENT AND PRODUCTION OF DEVELOPMENT ZONES

单位：平方米、万元 (sq.m,10000 yuan)

名　称 Name	自年初累计 Accumulative Number from Year-beginning					
	完成固定资产投资 Investment in Fixed Assets	新增固定资产 Incremental Fixed Assets	房屋建筑施工面积 Floor Space of Buildings under Construction	房屋建筑竣工面积 Floor Space of Buildings Completed	完成产值 Gross Output Value Completed	完成销售收入 Sales Revenue Completed
北京经济技术开发区	201954	111287	1145219	488518	838792	984108
王府井商业区	130886					56371
北京西三旗高新建材城	11911	6293	172766	42198	57018	92549
望京工业区	176104	111129	1160462	467353	36512	37555
东部旅游经济开发区	3797	3797	14289	14289		8331
中关村科技园区海淀园	44443	21331	385766	70798	6401200	10849500
中关村科技园区丰台园	20754	1138	150000	103771	307682	865863
八大处高科技园区	8569	11049	132458	82048	23424	246520
北京石龙工业区	7295		52098	25535	185824	471056
良乡卫星城工业开发区	4340	2340	16300	9600	154500	206000
燕山东流水工业区					2531	4363
北京大兴工业开发区	11888	1600	143771	6575	72187	104916
北京念坛工业区						
通州工业开发区	3515	3515	35105	15046	11281	34686
永乐工业开发区	2605	1900	10031		8	5
北京次渠工业区	13550	1200	37184	37184	183136	14299
中关村科技园区昌平园	16229	10941	146482	58744	317766	392670
雁栖工业开发区	500	400	2000	2000	76496	64798
凤翔科技开发区	1200	500	14900	13800	73865	95000
怀柔农业经济开发区						
中国乡镇企业城	1138	1138			36884	35618
怀柔民营经济开发区						
滨河工业区					30809	31340
兴谷经济开发区	2050	900	40720	12890	78801	66877
密云县工业开发区	260000	122	150000	86000	195500	181684
顺义林河工业开发区	6802	495	62794	3200	20901	23131
天竺空港工业区	6450	8600	81591	81591	1306772	1511523
延庆经济技术开发区	4582	4582	37170	37170	97746	120473
八达岭经济开发区	51000	20000	164917	122014	27015	567916
北京电子城科技园	88022	33306	468307	68141	2950000	3000000

23-6 北京经济技术开发区主要经济指标
MAIN ECONOMIC INDICATORS FOR BEIJING ECONOMIC-TECHNOLOGICAL DEVELOPMENT AREA

项 目 Item				2000	1999	2000年为1999年% 2000 as % of 1999
规划面积	（公顷）	Area Planned	(hectare)	1586.7		
累计征用土地面积	（公顷）	Accumulative Land Area Requisitioned	(hectare)	882.6		
生产总值	（亿元）	Gross Output Value	(100 million yuan)	29.1	13.8	2.1倍
工业总产值	（亿元）	Gross Output Value of Industry	(100 million yuan)	83.9	45.3	185.0
销售（营业）收入	（亿元）	Sales(Business) Revenue	(100 million yuan)	98.4	53.1	185.0
利润总额	（亿元）	Total Profits	(100 million yuan)	7.4	0.6	13倍
进出口总值	（亿美元）	Total Imports and Exports Value	(USD 100 million)	6.0	2.6	2.3倍
出口	（亿美元）	Exports	(USD 100 million)	1.4	0.8	182.0
进口	（亿美元）	Imports	(USD 100 million)	4.6	1.8	2.5倍
财政收入	（亿元）	Financial Revenue	(100 million yuan)	11.1	9.4	118.0
# 税收	（亿元）	Tax	(100 million yuan)	9.8	5.7	171.8
土地收入	（亿元）	from Land	(100 million yuan)	1.3	3.7	34.0
财政支出	（亿元）	Financial Expenditure	(100 million yuan)	5.4	4.1	131.0
批准企业个数	（个）	Number of Enterprises Ratified	(unit)	355	223	159.0
入区企业投资额	（亿美元）	Investment of Enterprises Entered	(USD 100 million)	5.9	5.5	108.0
注册资本	（亿美元）	Registered Capital	(USD 100 million)	4.0	3.0	134.0
合同外资金额	（亿美元）	Contracted Foreign Capital	(USD 100 million)	1.5	1.7	90.0
实际利用外资	（亿美元）	Foreign Capital Actually Used	(USD 100 million)	0.7	1.2	58.0
固定资产投资	（亿元）	Investment in Fixed Assets	(USD 100 million)	20.2	9.8	2.1倍
从业人员	（人）	Number of Employed Persons	(person)	23452	16446	143.0
劳动者报酬	（亿元）	Laborer Remuneration	(100 million yuan)	5.6	3.6	154.0

资料来源：北京经济技术开发区。

Sources: Beijing Economic-technological Development Area.

区县资料 24

DISTRICTS AND COUNTIES

24-1 东城区、西城区国民经济主要指标
MAIN NATIONAL ECONOMIC INDICATORS FOR DONGCHENG AND XICHENG DISTRICTS

项目	Item	东城区 Dongcheng 2000	1999	2000年为1999年% 2000 as% of 1999	西城区 Xicheng 2000	1999	2000年为1999年% 2000 as% of 1999
综合	**General Survey**						
国内生产总值 (万元)	Gross Domestic Product (10000 yuan)	314520.5	268175.6	117.3	453992	388605	116.8
第一产业	Primary Industry						
第二产业	Secondary Industry	40269.6	37675.0	106.9	28152	27842	101.1
第三产业	Tertiary Industry	274250.9	230500.6	119.0	425840	360763	118.0
财政收入 (万元)	Fiscal Revenue (10000 yuan)	179309	163238	109.8	229891	136294	168.7
#增值税	Increased Value Tax	12314	10838	113.6	21443		
营业税	Operating Tax	80880	70303	115.0	117476	65439	179.5
个人所得税	Private Income Tax		18772			16743	
企业所得税	Enterprise Income Tax	35181	31919	110.2	25238	36557	69.0
财政支出 (万元)	Fiscal Expenditure (10000 yuan)	157184	159733	98.4	173827	160983	108.0
#基本建设支出	Capital Construction	10343	11499	89.9	25468	16698	152.5
支援农业生产支出	Supporting Agriculture						
文教卫生事业费	Culture,Education and Health	38055	37523	101.4	44484	41271	107.8
人口和劳动力	**Population and Labor Force**						
总人口 (人)	Total Population (person)	712603	709733	100.4	856444	859262	99.7
常住户籍人口 (人)	Permanent Registered Population (person)	625596	628665	99.5	781437	787261	99.3
#非农业人口	Non-agriculture	625596	628665	99.5	781435	787259	99.3
男	Male	311739	313418	99.5	391057	394379	99.2
女	Female	313857	315247	99.6	390378	392880	99.4
出生率 (‰)	Birth Rate (‰)	4.21	4.15		4.46	4.14	
死亡率 (‰)	Death Rate (‰)	6.46	6.02		6.75	5.54	
自然增长率 (‰)	Natural Growth Rate (‰)	-2.25	-1.87		-2.29	-1.40	
从业人员 (人)	Employment (person)	123027	127268	96.7	150897	141323	106.8
按职工非职工分	Grouped by Staff and Workers or Non-staff-and-worker						
职工人数 (人)	Staff and Worker (person)	115988	120096	96.6	123147	121904	101.0
#国有单位	State-owned	53384	56603	94.3	65036	63811	101.9
集体单位	Collective-owned	19428	25147	77.3	16187	20074	80.6
城镇个体劳动者	Urban and Rural Individuals	13831	24880	55.6	16909	15673	107.9
劳动工资	**Wages**						
工资总额 (万元)	Total Wages (10000 yuan)	169860.7	147517.9	115.1	176049	160650	109.6
#国有单位	State-owned	84994.1	78778.8	107.9	93903	90127	104.2
集体单位	Collective-owned	18399.2	21325.1	86.3	15976	18016	88.7
职工平均工资 (元)	Average Wage (yuan)	14934	12357	120.9	15605	14426	108.2
固定资产投资	**Investment in Fixed Assets**						
全社会固定资产投资 (万元)	Total Investment in Fixed Assets(10000 yuan)	442462	446137	99.2	446651	434403	102.8
按建设性质分	Grouped by Type of Construction						
#基本建设投资	Capital Construction	46046	40828	112.8	28216	19589	144.0
更新改造投资	Innovation and Replacement	17408	28086	62.0	27513	54384	50.6
按登记注册类型分	Grouped by Registered Type						
# 国有单位	State-owned	103019	113755	90.6	104466	104428	100.0
集体单位	Collective-owned	1112	759	146.5			

注：因北京市2000年实行分税制改革，故本表中财政收入及其构成项的同期数按可比口径调整（其他区县情况相同）。

Note: Fiscal revenue of 1999 has been changed to the same statement with 2000 because of the tax reform in 2000(other districts and counties are the same).

24-1 续表 1 continued

项目		Item	东城区 Dongcheng 2000	1999	2000年为1999年% 2000 as% of 1999	西城区 Xicheng 2000	1999	2000年为1999年% 2000 as% of 1999
新增固定资产	(万元)	Incremental Fixed Assets (10000 yuan)	159449	211790	75.3	256262	349130	73.4
#国有单位		State-owned	84494	103743	81.4	74359	51751	143.7
集体单位		Collective-owned	1412	623	226.6			
房屋施工面积	(万平方米)	Floor Space of Buildings under Construction (10000 sq.m)	221.3	244.7	90.4	264.7	274.3	96.5
#国有单位		State-owned	42.9	60.3	71.1	31.4	39.6	79.3
集体单位		Collective-owned	0.8	1.5	53.3			
房屋竣工面积	(万平方米)	Floor Space of Buildings Completed (10000 sq.m)	26.2	44.6	58.7	66.6	77.5	85.9
#国有单位		State-owned	9.3	24.1	38.6	15.4	11.6	132.8
#住宅		Residence	3.6	13.8	26.1	11.5	6.6	174.2
#集体单位		Collective-owned	0.8	0.2	400.0			
#住宅		Residence						
工业		**Industry**						
全部工业企业单位数	(个)	Number of Enterprises (unit)	261	266	98.1	265	319	83.1
国有		State-owned	47	55	85.5	49	78	62.8
集体		Collective-owned	90	98	91.8	94	107	87.9
其他		Others	124	113	109.7	122	134	91.0
全部工业总产值(现价,万元)		Gross Output Value of Industry (at current prices,10000 yuan)	76679.3	65700.0	116.7	71020	83385	85.2
国有		State-owned	7414.8	12377.9	59.9	9501	15088	63.0
集体		Collective-owned	29023.4	30321.0	95.7	9954	10194	97.6
其他		Others	40241.1	23001.1	175.0	51565	58103	88.7
全部工业总产值(1990年不变价,万元)		Gross Output Value of Industry (at constant prices of 1990,10000 yuan)	60415.3	52181.0	115.8	64467	72418	89.0
国有		State-owned	6637.9	10825.5	61.3	9501	10784	88.1
集体		Collective-owned	20642.1	22544.6	91.6	9954	8979	110.9
其他		Others	33135.3	18810.9	176.1	45012	52655	85.5
全部轻工业总产值(现价,万元)		Gross Output Value of Light Industry (at current prices,10000 yuan)	61641.4	50754.9	121.4	34053	40731	83.6
以农产品为原料		Using Farm Products as Raw Materials	52823.7	40760.9	129.6	22051	27687	79.6
以非农产品为原料		Using Non-farm Products as Raw Materials	8817.7	9994.0	88.2	12002	13044	92.0
全部重工业总产值(现价,万元)		Gross Output Value of Heavy Industry (at current prices,10000 yuan)	15037.9	14945.1	100.6	36967	42654	86.7
采掘工业		Excavation						
原料工业		Raw Materials Industry	206.9	51.5	401.7	1826	1879	97.2
制造工业		Manufacturing Industry	14831.0	14893.6	99.6	35141	40775	86.2
独立核算工业企业工业增加值	(万元)	Value Added of Enterprises with Independent Accounting System (10000 yuan)	25722.8	20850.0	123.4	16442	31246	52.6
独立核算工业企业平均职工人数	(人)	Average Number of Staff and Workers in Enterprises with Independent Accounting System (person)	10214	12326	82.9	10249	12555	81.6

24-1 续表 2 continued

项目	Item	东城区 Dongcheng 2000	1999	2000年为1999年% 2000 as % of 1999	西城区 Xicheng 2000	1999	2000年为1999年% 2000 as % of 1999
#国有	State-owned	1757	2544	69.1	2629	3135	83.9
集体	Collective-owned	5582	7119	78.4	3507	2960	118.5
独立核算工业企业总产值(现价,万元)	Gross Output Value of Enterprises with Independent Accounting System (at current prices, 10000 yuan)	76679.3	65700.0	116.7	71020	83385	85.2
#国有	State-owned	7414.8	12377.9	59.9	9501	15088	63.0
集体	Collective-owned	29023.4	30321.0	95.7	9954	10194	97.6
独立核算工业企业财务指标	Financial Indicators for Enterprises with Independent Accounting System						
产品销售收入 (万元)	Sales Revenue (10000 yuan)	76926.3	66666.3	115.4	92499	93912	98.5
#国有	State-owned	7139.6	10173.6	70.2	13622	14737	92.4
产品销售成本 (万元)	Cost of Sales (10000 yuan)	53719.7	49740.8	108.0	75333	73841	102.0
#国有	State-owned	4891.5	7161.3	68.3	10565	11649	90.7
固定资产原价 (万元)	Original Value of Fixed Assets (10000 yuan)	57312.0	46883.2	122.2	46162	48105	96.0
#国有	State-owned	8345.0	9015.9	92.6	11541	13469	85.7
固定资产净值 (万元)	Net Value of Fixed Assets (10000 yuan)	38249.9	31217.8	122.5	28320	29544	95.9
#国有	State-owned	5638.4	6201.6	90.9	7080	9759	72.5
全部流动资金年平均余额 (万元)	Annual Average Balance of Circulating Funds (10000 yuan)	100873.9	75186.0	134.2	113894	114322	99.6
#国有	State-owned	10165.6	12878.5	78.9	19362	19438	99.6
利润总额 (万元)	Total Profits (10000 yuan)	3127.5	936.3	334.0	-2196	-2266	96.9
#国有	State-owned	-645.7	1119.3		499	413	120.8
资金利税率 (%)	Ratio of Pre-tax Profits to Total Capital (%)	4.8	4.4		1.2	1.2	
产品销售率 (%)	Ratio of Sales Value to Gross Output Value (%)	96.4	96.1		102.1	95.8	
增加值率 (%)	Ratio of Added Value to Gross Output Value (%)	25.9	22.6		23.2	37.5	
独立核算工业企业全员劳动生产率 (元/人)	Overall Labor Productivity of Enterprises with Independent Accounting System (yuan/person)	25184	16915	148.9	69295	66416	104.3
#国有	State-owned	16177	18683	86.6	36139	48128	75.1
集体	Collective-owned	21865	16929	129.2	28383	34439	82.4
商业	**Commerce**						
社会消费品零售额 (万元)	Retail Sales of Consumer Goods (10000 yuan)	589493	548189	107.5	905398	809619	111.8
按登记注册类型分	Grouped by Registered Type						
国有	State-owned	147971	143916	102.8	362159	348136	104.0
集体	Collective-owned	70142	70696	99.2	27162	37450	72.5
其他	Others	371380	333577	111.3	516077	424033	121.7
按类别分	Grouped by Type of Goods						
吃的商品	Food	218613	240969	90.7	204620	194308	105.3

24-1 续表 3 continued

项目	Item	东城区 Dongcheng 2000	1999	2000年为1999年% 2000 as % of 1999	西城区 Xicheng 2000	1999	2000年为1999年% 2000 as % of 1999
穿的商品	Clothing	104812	85410	122.7	226350	170020	133.1
用的商品	Daily Used Articles	261551	217697	120.1	474428	445291	106.5
烧的商品	Fuel	4517	4113	109.8			
网点数 (个)	Number of Outlets (unit)	10320	15637	66.0	11114	11042	100.7
#商业	Wholesale and Retail	6758	11395	59.3	6815	6952	98.0
饮食业	Catering	1594	2578	61.8	2074	2057	100.8
服务业	Services	1968	1664	118.3	2225	1963	113.3
#宾馆、饭店	Hotels	135	133	101.5	63	67	94.0
营业人员 (人)	Personnel (person)	94176	104737	89.9	55368	58635	94.4
#商业	Wholesale and Retail	43204	56389	76.6	32676	35158	92.9
饮食业	Catering Service	14632	17335	84.4	11002	10399	105.8
服务业	Services	36340	31013	117.2	11690	10265	113.9
#宾馆、饭店	Hotels	4311	4587	94.0	3230	3335	96.9
外经、外贸	**Foreign Economy and Trade**						
出口商品交货额 (万元)	Delivery Value of Exports (10000 yuan)	1154.4			1130	2230	50.7
利用外资签订协议(合同)数 (个)	Number of Signed Agreements and Contracts of Foreign Capital to be Utilized (unit)	55	43	127.9	56	41	136.6
利用外资签订协议(合同)金额 (万美元)	Amount of Foreign Capital to be Utilized through Agreements and Contracts (USD 10000)	18899.2	5630.3	335.7	2107	2845	74.1
实际利用外资 (万美元)	Amount of Foreign Capital Actually Used (USD 10000)	25281.8	40584.8	62.3	2780	3516	79.1
旅游人数 (万人)	Number of Tourists (10000 persons)	1916.4	2232.0	85.9	2413	2495	96.7
教育	**Education**						
学校数 (个)	Number of Schools (unit)	109	113	96.5	122	134	91.0
小学	Primary Schools	61	64	95.3	73	77	94.8
普通中学	Regular Secondary Schools	38	33	115.2	46	52	88.5
中等专业教育	Specialized Secondary Schools	10	16	62.5	3	5	60.0
招生数 (人)	New Student Enrollment (person)	22280	21966	101.4	24631	24356	101.1
小学	Primary Schools	4369	4689	93.2	4388	4865	90.2
初级中等学校	Junior Secondary Schools	9934	9511	104.4	10449	10529	99.2
高级中等学校	Senior Secondary Schools	6290	5372	117.1	9794	8795	111.4
中等专业教育	Specialized Secondary Schools	1687	2394	70.5		167	
在校学生 (人)	Student Enrollment (person)	89247	92511	96.5	100942	99493	101.5
小学	Primary Schools	34749	38527	90.2	36752	42055	87.4
初级中等学校	Junior Secondary Schools	29110	28627	101.7	31049	30752	101.0

24-1 续表 4 continued

项目 Item		东城区 Dongcheng 2000	1999	2000年为1999年% 2000 as % of 1999	西城区 Xicheng 2000	1999	2000年为1999年% 2000 as % of 1999
高级中等学校	Senior Secondary Schools	17361	15660	110.9	32309	25564	126.4
中等专业教育	Specialized Secondary Schools	8027	9697	82.8	832	1122	74.2
毕业生 (人)	Graduates (person)	25950	25898	100.2	31346	29920	104.8
小学	Primary Schools	8960	8796	101.9	10235	10329	99.1
初级中等学校	Junior Secondary Schools	9142	9769	93.6	10007	11352	88.2
高级中等学校	Senior Secondary Schools	4642	4049	114.6	10841	7891	137.4
中等专业教育	Specialized Secondary Schools	3206	3284	97.6	263	348	75.6
达到"国家体育标准"学生数 (人)	Number of Students Come to the Standard for State Physical Training (person)	84353	76023	111.0	92778	96152	96.5
幼儿园、托儿所个数 (个)	Number of Kindergardens (unit)	57	66	86.4	75	82	91.5
幼儿入托数 (人)	New Enrollment (person)	9280	10013	92.7	12780	13140	97.3
文化	**Culture**						
文化馆、站 (个)	Cultural Centers (unit)	11	11	100.0	149	141	105.7
公共图书馆 (个)	Public Libraries (unit)	2	2	100.0	2	2	100.0
公共图书馆藏书 (万册)	Collection (10000 volume)	317	298	106.4	40.7	37	109.7
电影放映单位 (个)	Film Projection Units (unit)	9	8	112.5	10	13	76.9
区级以上重点文物保护单位 (个)	Cultural Relics Preserved at District Level and above (unit)	130	130	100.0	108	108	100.0
卫生	**Health**						
卫生机构数 (个)	Number of Health Institutions (unit)	83	86	96.5	630	603	104.5
#医院	Hospitals	30	30	100.0	24	24	100.0
卫生院	Clinics						
床位数 (张)	Number of Beds (unit)	6695	6691	100.1	7368	7977	92.4
#医院	Hospitals	6695	6691	100.1	7268	7877	92.3
卫生院	Clinics						
平均每千人拥有床位数 (张)	Average Number of Beds Per 1000 Persons (unit)	10.7	10.6	100.9	9.4	10	93.1
卫生技术人员 (人)	Medical Technical Personnel (person)	13366	13945	95.8	18609	13322	139.7
#医生	Doctors	5474	5877	93.1	5587	5100	109.5
公用设施	**Public Utilities**						
区级以上公园 (个)	Parks at District Level and above (unit)	7	7	100.0	10	10	100.0
体育场馆 (个)	Stadiums and Gymnasiums (unit)	9	9	100.0	217	217	100.0
道路长度 (公里)	Length of Roads (km)	99.1	98.0	101.1	245	243	100.8

24-2 崇文区、宣武区国民经济主要指标
MAIN NATIONAL ECONOMIC INDICATORS FOR DONGCHENG AND XICHENG DISTRICTS

项目		Item		崇文区 Chongwen 2000	1999	2000年为1999年% 2000 as% of 1999	宣武区 Xuanwu 2000	1999	2000年为1999年% 2000 as% of 1999
综合		**General Survey**							
国内生产总值	(万元)	Gross Domestic Product	(10000 yuan)	170300.0	128171.9	132.9	184452	179193.0	102.9
第一产业		Primary Industry							
第二产业		Secondary Industry		20814.0	27295.0	76.3	48380.4	47675.6	101.5
第三产业		Tertiary Industry		149684.0	100876.9	148.4	136072	131517.4	103.5
财政收入	(万元)	Fiscal Revenue	(10000 yuan)	50292	45163	111.4	101527	97896	103.7
#增值税		Increased Value Tax		4635	4355	106.4	17840	18141	98.3
营业税		Operating Tax		16747	15230	110.0	41243	41267	99.9
个人所得税		Private Income Tax							
企业所得税		Enterprise Income Tax		12212	9936	122.9	10947	8004	136.8
财政支出	(万元)	Fiscal Expenditure	(10000 yuan)	67003	52907	126.6	119988	109987	109.1
#基本建设支出		Capital Construction		2511	3437	73.1	15486	18408	84.1
支援农业生产支出		Supporting Agriculture							
文教卫生事业费		Culture,Education and Health		20289	17392	116.7	24810	23928	103.7
人口和劳动力		**Population and Labor Force**							
总人口	(人)	Total Population	(person)	462564	463427	99.8	605416	595706	101.6
常住户籍人口	(人)	Permanent Registered Populatio	(person)	412911	417247	99.0	536290	536813	99.9
#非农业人口		Non-agriculture		412860	417188	99.0	536275	536797	99.9
男		Male		206313	208598	98.9	270416	270990	99.8
女		Female		206547	208649	99.0	265859	265807	100.0
出生率	(‰)	Birth Rate	(‰)	3.44	3.30		3.7	3.6	
死亡率	(‰)	Death Rate	(‰)	7.48	5.40		7.7	6.9	
自然增长率	(‰)	Natural Growth Rate	(‰)	-4.04	-2.10		-4.1	-3.3	
从业人员	(人)	Employment	(person)	66594	71972	92.5	104798	87553	119.7
按职工非职工分		Grouped by Staff and Workers or Non-staff-and-worker							
职工人数	(人)	Staff and Worker	(person)	70532	75804	93.0	101909	85310	119.5
#国有单位		State-owned		32277	35555	90.8	50092	37845	132.4
集体单位		Collective-owned		14814	19803	74.8	27049	26792	101.0
城镇个体劳动者		Urban and Rural Individuals							
劳动工资		**Wages**							
工资总额	(万元)	Total Wages	(10000 yuan)	86405.6	78047.5	110.7	122753.8	93599.3	131.1
#国有单位		State-owned		4677.2	41967.3	11.1	66378.8	48279.5	137.5
集体单位		Collective-owned		12582.9	14591.9	86.2	26393.2	22716.6	116.2
职工平均工资	(元)	Average Wage	(yuan)	12251	10296	119.0	12182	11102	109.7
固定资产投资		**Investment in Fixed Assets**							
全社会固定资产投资	(万元)	Total Investment in Fixed Assets	(10000 yuan)	398431	141616	281.3	413781	201205	205.7
按建设性质分		Grouped by Type of Construction							
#基本建设投资		Capital Construction		187263	13227	1415.8	187926	14870	1263.8
更新改造投资		Innovation and Replacement		19330	28148	68.7	18651	51523	36.2
按登记注册类型分		Grouped by Registered Type							
#国有单位		State-owned	(10000 yuan)	234935	44856	523.8	379309	125508	302.2

24-2 续表 1 continued

项目	Item	崇文区 Chongwen 2000	1999	2000年为1999年% 2000 as% of 1999	宣武区 Xuanwu 2000	1999	2000年为1999年% 2000 as% of 1999
集体单位	Collective-owned	1817	1577	115.2	140	5678	2.5
新增固定资产 (万元)	Incremental Fixed Assets (10000 yuan)	400698	164373	243.8	576292	341393	168.8
#国有单位	State-owned	82170	46357	177.3	444133	216156	205.5
集体单位	Collective-owned	240	2349	10.2	450	18591	2.4
房屋施工面积 (万平方米)	Floor Space of Buildings under Construction (10000 sq.m)	145.6	92.0	158.3	209.2	261.8	79.9
#国有单位	State-owned	52.0	26.2	198.5	158.7	160.6	98.8
集体单位	Collective-owned	2.0	2.9	69.0	1.7	19.4	8.8
房屋竣工面积 (万平方米)	Floor Space of Buildings Completed (10000 sq.m)	15.6	11.5	135.7	83.4	97.9	85.2
#国有单位	State-owned	9.2	7.2	127.8	74.0	45.1	164.1
#住宅	Residence	3.4	2.9	117.2	50.3	23.3	215.9
#集体单位	Collective-owned	0.2	1.0	20.0	0.3	13.4	2.2
#住宅	Residence		0.7		0.3	9.3	3.2
工业	**Industry**						
全部工业企业单位数 (个)	Number of Enterprises (unit)	158	184	85.9	221	257	86.0
国有	State-owned	29	30	96.7	36	46	78.3
集体	Collective-owned	83	96	86.5	79	118	66.9
其他	Others	46	58	79.3	106	93	114.0
全部工业总产值 (现价,万元)	Gross Output Value of Industry (at current prices,10000 yuan)	43533.7	49716.7	87.6	61272.0	56097.3	109.2
国有	State-owned	5596.5	5732.0	97.6	8403.8	10468.0	80.3
集体	Collective-owned	16187.4	16710.5	96.9	16561.9	18436.5	89.8
其他	Others	21749.8	27274.2	79.7	36306.3	27192.4	133.5
全部工业总产值 (1990年不变价,万元)	Gross Output Value of Industry (at constant prices of 1990,10000 yuan)	38133.6	43521.2	87.6	59586.6	54619.7	109.1
国有	State-owned	4193.8	4440.2	94.5	8461.5	9747.5	86.8
集体	Collective-owned	16013.2	15336.7	104.4	16379.8	18474.4	88.7
其他	Others	17926.6	23744.3	75.5	34745.3	26397.8	131.6
全部轻工业总产值 (现价,万元)	Gross Output Value of Light Industry (at current prices,10000 yuan)	29084.6	31999.6	90.9	40784.6	40238.8	101.4
以农产品为原料	Using Farm Products as Raw Materials	16320.4	19554.5	83.5	21800.8	22168	98.3
以非农产品为原料	Using Non-farm Products as Raw Materials	12764.2	12445.1	102.6	18983.8	18071	105.1
全部重工业总产值 (现价,万元)	Gross Output Value of Heavy Industry (at current prices,10000 yuan)	14449.1	17717.1	81.6	20487.4	15858.5	129.2
采掘工业	Excavation						
原料工业	Raw Materials Industry	1731.1	1770.5	97.8	1081.0	816.9	132.3
制造工业	Manufacturing Industry	12718.0	15946.6	79.8	19406.4	15042	129.0
独立核算工业企业工业增加值 (万元)	Value Added of Enterprises with Independent Accounting System (10000 yuan)	10299.5	16113.4	63.9	17314.2	19346.0	89.5
独立核算工业企业平均职工人数 (人)	Average Number of Staff and Workers in Enterprises with Independent Accounting System (person)	11989	11275	106.3	10856	12245	88.7

24-2 续表 2 continued

项目	Item	崇文区 Chongwen 2000	1999	2000年为1999年% 2000 as% of 1999	宣武区 Xuanwu 2000	1999	2000年为1999年% 2000 as% of 1999
#国有	State-owned	2208	2523	87.5	2279	2902	78.5
集体	Collective-owned	7268	5904	123.1	5339	7054	75.7
独立核算工业企业总产值(现价,万元)	Gross Output Value of Enterprises with Independent Accounting System (at current prices,10000 yuan)	43533.7	49716.7	87.6	61272.0	56097.3	109.2
#国有	State-owned	5596.5	5732.0	97.6	8403.8	10468.4	80.3
集体	Collective-owned	16187.4	16710.5	96.9	16561.9	18436.5	89.8
独立核算工业企业财务指标	Financial Indicators for Enterprises with Independent Accounting System						
产品销售收入 (万元)	Sales Revenue (10000 yuan)	51164.1	52511.2	97.4	62374.7	66918.3	93.2
#国有	State-owned	7786.1	7997.7	97.4	8312.0	10354.1	80.3
产品销售成本 (万元)	Cost of Sales (10000 yuan)	39770.1	38781.1	102.6	47811.3	51787.9	92.3
#国有	State-owned	6032.1	5600.0	107.7	7377.7	8751.1	84.3
固定资产原价 (万元)	Original Value of Fixed Assets (10000 yuan)	26833.9	27578.4	97.3	47979.4	43620.4	110.0
#国有	State-owned	8057.7	8050.8	100.1	11072.9	12211.1	90.7
固定资产净值 (万元)	Net Value of Fixed Assets (10000 yuan)	14495.0	16400.3	88.4	26643.2	23399.5	113.9
#国有	State-owned	3803.3	5370.5	70.8	6556.8	7446.3	88.1
全部流动资金年平均余额 (万元)	Annual Average Balance of Circulating Funds (10000 yuan)	53633.9	61992.6	86.5	90854.0	90016.6	100.9
#国有	State-owned	10378.0	12424.9	83.5	14937.8	16932.9	88.2
利润总额 (万元)	Total Profits (10000 yuan)	-1898.4	748.7		-2548.8	-1406.1	
#国有	State-owned	-1377.1	-275.7		-351.4	-128.2	
资金利税率 (%)	Ratio of Pre-tax Profits to Total Capital (%)	2.5	6.1		1.2	1.5	
产品销售率 (%)	Ratio of Sales Value to Gross Output Value (%)	103.3	97.5		104.2	103.6	
增加值率 (%)	Ratio of Added Value to Gross Output Value (%)	23.7	32.4		28.3	34.5	
独立核算工业企业全员劳动生产率 (元/人)	Overall Labor Productivity of Enterprises with Independent Accounting System (yuan/person)	8590.8	14291.0	60.1	15948.9	16012.3	99.6
#国有	State-owned	8196.6	6418.0	127.7	11053.9	11649.9	94.9
集体	Collective-owned	5983.9	6238.0	95.9	7723.0	10223.8	75.5
商业	**Commerce**						
社会消费品零售额 (万元)	Retail Sales of Consumer Goods (10000 yuan)	345747	345431	100.1	450880	394507	114.3
按登记注册类型分	Grouped by Registered Type						
国有	State-owned	115871	103203	112.3	83413	72984	114.3
集体	Collective-owned	12587	25849	48.7	129853	113618	114.3
其他	Others	217286	216379	100.4	337614	207905	162.4
按类别分	Grouped by Type of Goods						
吃的商品	Food	177799	170465	104.3	178727	156381	114.3

24-2 续表 3 continued

项目		Item		崇文区 Chongwen 2000	1999	2000年为1999年% 2000 as % of 1999	宣武区 Xuanwu 2000	1999	2000年为1999年% 2000 as % of 1999
穿的商品		Clothing		67717	66431	101.9	50860	44501	114.3
用的商品		Daily Used Articles		99112	107078	92.6	217133	189985	114.3
烧的商品		Fuel		1119	1457	76.8	4160	3640	114.3
网点数	(个)	Number of Outlets	(unit)	8993	7364	122.1	8297	8602	96.5
#商业		Wholesale and Retail		7218	5404	133.6	7017	6872	102.1
饮食业		Catering		598	717	83.4	560	1024	54.7
服务业		Services		1148	1243	92.4	720	706	102.0
#宾馆、饭店		Hotels		29	19	152.6	131	133	98.5
营业人员	(人)	Personnel	(person)	55944	42789	130.7	78174	94405	82.8
#商业		Wholesale and Retail		34901	34479	101.2	39766	56776	70.0
饮食业		Catering Service		4591	4901	93.7	8825	11667	75.6
服务业		Services		13705	3409	402.0	29583	25962	113.9
#宾馆、饭店		Hotels		2747	2383	115.3	7203	5746	125.4
外经、外贸		**Foreign Economy and Trade**							
出口商品交货额	(万元)	Delivery Value of Exports	(10000 yuan)	2111.9	6936.3	30.4	2094.7	149.5	1401.1
利用外资签订协议(合同)数	(个)	Number of Signed Agreements and Contracts of Foreign Capital to be Utilized	(unit)	13	10	130.0	16	6	266.7
利用外资签订协议(合同)金额	(万美元)	Amount of Foreign Capital to be Utilized through Agreements and Contracts	(USD 10000)	4786.6	19775.0	24.2	4050.0	…	
实际利用外资	(万美元)	Amount of Foreign Capital Actually Used	(USD 10000)	2822.3	13165.3	21.4	1276.4	968.0	131.9
接待国内外旅游者	(万人次)	Number of Tourists	(10000 persons)	900			140.6		
教育		**Education**							
学校数	(个)	Number of Schools	(unit)	66	78	84.6	87	94	92.6
小学		Primary Schools		39	44	88.6	52	54	96.3
普通中学		Regular Secondary Schools		21	25	84.0	31	30	103.3
中等专业教育		Specialized Secondary Schools		6	9	66.7	4	10	40.0
招生数	(人)	New Student Enrollment	(person)	13055	13739	95.0	14678	15639	93.9
小学		Primary Schools		2444	2734	89.4	2902	3298	88.0
初级中等学校		Regular Secondary Schools		5910	5994	98.6	6944	7273	95.5
高级中等学校		Specialized Secondary Schools		3166	2592	122.1	3422	2958	115.7
中等专业教育		Specialized Secondary Schools		1535	2419	63.5	1410	2110	66.8
在校学生	(人)	Student Enrollment	(person)	54597	57940	94.2	62623	67353	93.0
小学		Primary Schools		21552	24698	87.3	25038	29212	85.7
初级中等学校		Junior Secondary Schools		17737	17769	99.8	21129	21177	99.8

24-2 续表 4 continued

项目 Item				崇文区 Chongwen			宣武区 Xuanwu		
				2000	1999	2000年为1999年% 2000 as% of 1999	2000	1999	2000年为1999年% 2000 as% of 1999
高级中等学校		Senior Secondary Schools		8513	7797	109.2	9399	8603	109.3
中等专业教育		Specialized Secondary Schools		6795	7676	88.5	7057	8361	84.4
毕业生	(人)	Graduates	(person)	16572	17583	94.3	18877	19349	97.6
小学		Primary Schools		6023	6036	99.8	6915	7268	95.1
初级中等学校		Junior Secondary Schools		5804	7107	81.7	6790	7894	86.0
高级中等学校		Senior Secondary Schools		2377	1944	122.3	2569	1872	137.2
中等专业教育		Specialized Secondary Schools		2368	2496	94.9	2603	2315	112.4
达到"国家体育标准"学生数	(人)	Number of Students Come to the Standard for State Physical Training	(person)	48286	52789	91.5	63711	65199	97.7
幼儿园、托儿所个数	(个)	Number of Kindergardens	(unit)	30	38	78.9	41	50	82.0
幼儿入托数	(人)	New Enrollment	(person)	6317	6535	96.7	6442	7351	87.6
文化		**Culture**							
文化馆、站	(个)	Cultural Centers	(unit)	10	10	100.0	9	9	100.0
公共图书馆	(个)	Public Libraries	(unit)	1	1	100.0	1	1	100.0
公共图书馆藏书	(万册)	Collection	(10000 volume)	41	40	102.5	25.6	24.0	106.7
电影放映单位	(个)	Film Projection Units	(unit)	2	2	100.0	4	4	100.0
区级以上重点文物保护单位	(个)	Cultural Relics Preserved at District Level and above	(unit)	21	21	100.0	38	38	100.0
卫生		**Health**							
卫生机构数	(个)	Number of Health Institutions	(unit)	336	339	99.1	351	383	91.6
#医院		Hospitals		7	11	63.6	20	20	100.0
卫生院		Clinics							
床位数	(张)	Number of Beds	(unit)	1929	2021	95.4	3802	3894	97.6
#医院		Hospitals		1929	2021	95.4	3802	3894	97.6
卫生院		Clinics							
平均每千人拥有床位数	(张)	Average Number of Beds Per 1000 Persons	(unit)	5.6	4.9	115.1	7	7	95.9
卫生技术人员	(人)	Medical Technical Personnel	(person)	5373	3747	143.4	7461	7658	97.4
#医生		Doctors		2066	1556	132.8	2819	3067	91.9
公用设施		**Public Utilities**							
区级以上公园	(个)	Parks at District Level and above	(unit)	4	4	100.0	4	4	100.0
体育场馆	(个)	Stadiums and Gymnasiums	(unit)	6	6	100.0	2	2	100.0
道路长度	(公里)	Length of Roads	(km)	177.5	176.4	100.6	116.8	116.4	100.3

24-3 朝阳区、丰台区国民经济主要指标
MAIN NATIONAL ECONOMIC INDICATORS FOR CHAOYANG AND FENGTAI DISTRICTS

项目		Item		朝阳区 Chaoyang 2000	1999	2000年为1999年% 2000 as % of 1999	丰台区 Fengtai 2000	1999	2000年为1999年% 2000 as % of 1999
综合		**General Survey**							
国内生产总值	(万元)	Gross Domestic Product	(10000 yuan)	888096	786066.9	113.0	451061	385424	117.0
第一产业		Primary Industry		25533.6	26977.9	94.6	18042	18469	97.7
第二产业		Secondary Industry		206608	191695.3	107.8	132500	125118	105.9
第三产业		Tertiary Industry		655954	567393.7	115.6	300519	241837	124.3
财政收入	(万元)	Fiscal Revenue	(10000 yuan)	375540	337716	111.2	76202	66365	114.8
#增值税		Increased Value Tax		39916	35676	111.9	13393	12054	111.1
营业税		Operating Tax		166175	146042	113.8	30477	26833	113.6
个人所得税		Private Income Tax							
企业所得税		Enterprise Income Tax		87999	84132	104.6	8475	7642	110.9
财政支出	(万元)	Fiscal Expenditure	(10000 yuan)	264427	218963	120.8	126246	113137	111.6
#基本建设支出		Capital Construction		10582	14824	71.4	3004	7322	41.0
支援农业生产支出		Supporting Agriculture		6886	5764	119.5	2429	2009	120.9
文教卫生事业费		Culture,Education and Health		72507	61322	118.2	32617	28549	114.2
人口和劳动力		**Population and Labor Force**							
总人口	(人)	Total Population	son)	1905237	1860558	102.4	1100090	1059740	103.8
常住户籍人口	(人)	Permanent Registered Population	(person)	1530130	1487650	102.9	822633	809487	101.6
#非农业人口		Non-agriculture		1342182	1300513	103.2	674904	661870	102.0
男		Male		778725	757792	102.8	419274	412499	101.6
女		Female		751405	729858	103.0	403359	396988	101.6
出生率	(‰)	Birth Rate	(‰)	5.28	5.1		5.7	5.1	
死亡率	(‰)	Death Rate	(‰)	6.07	5.3		5.38	5.8	
自然增长率	(‰)	Natural Growth Rate	(‰)	-0.79	-0.3		0.32	-0.7	
从业人员	(人)	Employment	(person)	112277	117428	95.6	104907	95566	109.8
按产业分		Grouped by Industry							
第一产业		Primary Industry		22	33	66.7	335	70	478.6
第二产业		Secondary Industry		36027	37008	97.3	28072	29778	94.3
第三产业		Tertiary Industry		76228	80387	94.8	76500	65718	116.4
按职工非职工分		Grouped by Staff and Workers or Non-staff-and-worker							
职工人数		Staff and Worker		111748	117411	95.2	99139	91883	107.9
#国有单位		State-owned		69676	72808	95.7	40381	42613	94.8
集体单位		Collective-owned		36774	39319	93.5	12637	19872	63.6
城镇个体劳动者		Urban and Rural Individuals		40484	38189	106.0	9388	11602	80.9
劳动工资		**Wages**							
工资总额	(万元)	Total Wages	(10000 yuan)	155567	146285.8	106.3	121764	100937	120.6
#国有单位		State-owned		119338.0	111492.7	107.0	61829.0	55068.7	112.3
集体单位		Collective-owned		28264.6	27321.0	103.5	9912.7	12798.8	77.5
职工平均工资	(元)	Average Wage	(yuan)	14059	12682	110.9	12281	11221	109.4
固定资产投资		**Investment in Fixed Assets**							
全社会固定资产投资	(万元)	Total Investment in Fixed Assets	(10000 yuan)	592226	384073	154.2	189451	166037	114.1
按建设性质分		Grouped by Type of Construction							
#基本建设投资		Capital Construction					46656	37973	122.9
更新改造投资		Innovation and Replacement		48688	19415	250.8	38119	31357	121.6

24-3 续表 1 continued

项目	Item	朝阳区 Chaoyang 2000	1999	2000年为1999年% 2000 as% of 1999	丰台区 Fengtai 2000	1999	2000年为1999年% 2000 as% of 1999
按登记注册类型分	Grouped by Registered Type						
#国有单位	State-owned	246862	186481	132.4	111576	94348	118.3
集体单位	Collective-owned	39506	48440	81.6	17477	29466	59.3
新增固定资产 (万元)	Incremental Fixed Assets (10000 yuan)	252910	295412	85.6	155105	161693	95.9
#国有单位	State-owned	193886	154821	125.2	86277	95845	90.0
集体单位	Collective-owned	50196	61757	81.3	23871	23083	103.4
房屋施工面积 (万平方米)	Floor Space of Buildings under Construction (10000 sq.m)	480.2	288.7	166.3	159.7	137.4	116.2
#国有单位	State-owned	135.2	96.0	140.8	48.6	61.9	78.5
集体单位	Collective-owned	66.7	58.4	114.2	13.3	38.3	34.7
房屋竣工面积 (万平方米)	Floor Space of Buildings Completed (10000 sq.m)	87.0	105.5	82.5	50.5	60.3	83.7
#国有单位	State-owned	54.1	47.8	113.2	8.5	23.9	35.6
#住宅	Residence	27.9	28.3	98.6	5.4	15.3	35.3
#集体单位	Collective-owned	25.5	32.6	78.2	9.8	20.7	47.3
#住宅	Residence	23.5	30.7	76.5	7.9	20.7	38.2
农村经济	**Rural Economy**						
农村劳动力 (人)	Labor Force (person)	97376	90957	107.1	72542	71394	101.6
种植业	Planting	13833	14663	94.3	16533	15412	107.3
林业	Forestry	2517	764	329.5	2006	1616	124.1
牧业	Animal Husbandry	1888	2058	91.7	1154	1083	106.6
渔业	Fishery	881	947	93.0	168	192	87.5
农村工业	Rural Industry	28444	29000	98.1	25157	26284	95.7
农村建筑业	Rural Construction	6096	4150	146.9	2649	2042	129.7
农村运输业	Rural Transportation	10049	9027	111.3	5243	4765	110.0
农村商、饮食业、服务	Commerce,Catering and Services	13121	8712	150.6	19632	20000	98.2
耕地面积 (公顷)	Area under Cultivation (hectare)	11307	13656.4	82.8	5875.4	6106	96.2
农业机械总动力 (千瓦)	Total Power of Agricultural Machinery (kw)	203799	233852	87.1	150837	154763	97.5
化肥施用实物量 (吨)	Consumption of Chemical Fertilizers (ton)	7677	10879	70.6	5169	4828	107.1
化肥施用折纯量 (吨)	Consumption of Chemical Fertilizers (100%) (ton)	3032	4074	74.4	1541	1625	94.8
农村用电量 (万千瓦时)	Consumption of Electricity (10000 kwh)	40654.0	36210.1	112.3	26955	26304.8	102.5
农村国内生产总值 (万元)	Rural Gross Domestic Product (10000 yuan)				182120	165977	109.7
第一产业	Primary Industry				16475.7	18468.7	89.2
第二产业	Secondary Industry				57534.8	55101.4	104.4
第三产业	Tertiary Industry				108110	92407.1	117.0
农业总产值 (万元)	Gross Output Value of Agriculture (10000 yuan)	31467	37653.5	83.6	25536.9	27766.5	92.0
种植业	Planting	14376	19215.1	74.8	18505.4	21022.8	88.0
林业	Forestry	496.9	646.1	76.9	315.3	402.9	78.3
牧业	Animal Husbandry	9870	9684.2	101.9	5696.6	5901.8	96.5
渔业	Fishery	6724.4	7944.5	84.6	1019.6	439.0	232.3
农作物总播种面积 (万公顷)	Sown Area of Farm Crops (10000 hectare)	1.3	1.2	108.3	0.7	0.7	100.0
粮食作物	Grain	0.7	1.2	58.3	0.3	0.3	100.0
经济作物	Industrial Crops				0.4	0.4	100.0
其他作物	Other Crops						

24-3 续表2 continued

项目		Item		朝阳区 Chaoyang 2000	1999	2000年为1999年% 2000 as% of 1999	丰台区 Fengtai 2000	1999	2000年为1999年% 2000 as% of 1999
农副产品产量		Yield of Farm and Sideline Crops							
粮食	(万吨)	Grain	(10000 tons)	3.9	6.6	59.1	0.8	1.1	76.4
蔬菜	(吨)	Vegetable	(ton)	174157	176573	98.6	143524	155205	92.5
干鲜果	(吨)	Dry and Fresh Fruits	(ton)	924	770	120.0	4772	4926	96.9
畜产品产量		Output of Livestock Products							
生猪出栏	(头)	Slaughtered Hogs	(head)	251753	262005	96.1	67223	86574	77.6
商品猪	(头)	Commodity Hogs	(head)				67223	86574	77.6
猪牛羊肉	(吨)	Pork,Beef and Mutton	(ton)	17296	17994	96.1	4525	5574	81.2
#猪肉		Pork		16716	17250	96.9	4418	5483	80.6
禽肉		Meat of Poultry	(ton)	381	176	216.5	1036	750	138.1
禽蛋		Poultry Eggs	(ton)	491	753	65.2	4718	5181	91.1
牲畜年底头数	(头)	Number of Livestock(year-end)	(head)						
大牲畜		Large Animals		2764	3010	91.8	1553	1468	105.8
猪		Hogs		118224	136908	86.4	40424	57305	70.5
羊		Goats and Sheep		14042	15766	89.1	11416	11128	102.6
水产品产量	(吨)	Output of Aquatic Product	(ton)	5061	6079	83.3	341	404	84.4
农村集体经济收入	(万元)	Rural Collective Economic Revenue	(10000 yuan)	1390120	1230570	113.0	990095	895380	110.6
农村集体经济利润总额	(万元)	Total Profits of Rural Collective Economy	(10000 yuan)	90953	81594	111.5	89278	80231	111.3
国家税金		State Taxes		45252.6	39394.2	114.9	24292	22154	109.7
集体积累		Collective Accumulation		61554.5	57346.0	107.3	36988	32646	113.3
劳动所得		Income from Work		145744	130383.5	111.8	98564	92111	107.0
乡镇企业单位数	(个)	Number of Township and Village Enterprise	(unit)	1452	1678	86.5	2329	2405	96.8
乡镇企业人数	(人)	Number of Persons of Township and Village Enterprises	(person)	77305	84503	91.5	67096	64559	103.9
乡镇企业纯利润	(万元)	Net Profit of Township and Village Enterprises	(10000 yuan)	23693.7	22466.9	105.5	48194	49681	97.0
乡镇企业固定资产原价	(万元)	Original Value of Fixed Assets of Township and Village Enterprises	(10000 yuan)	355890	333196	106.8	395643	348019	113.7
乡镇企业固定资产净值	(万元)	Net Value of Fixed Assets of Township and Village Enterprises	(10000 yuan)	250980.0	235856.9	106.4	264190	235905	112.0
工业		**Industry**							
全部工业企业单位数	(个)	Number of Enterprises	(unit)	2090	2037	102.6	1183	1242	95.2
国有		State-owned		124	148	83.8	73	86	84.9
集体		Collective-owned		1016	1215	83.6	461	517	89.2
其他		Others		950	674	140.9	649	639	101.6
全部工业总产值(现价,万元)		Gross Output Value of Industry (at current prices,10000 yuan)		731728.0	631750.2	115.8	540807	435865.6	124.1
国有		State-owned		7921.9	15012.8	52.8	41706.7	38067.8	109.6
集体		Collective-owned		325735	311327.2	104.6	127474	128870	98.9
其他		Others		398071	305410.2	130.3	371626	384910.8	96.5

24-3 续表 3 continued

项目	Item	朝阳区 Chaoyang 2000	1999	2000年为1999年% 2000 as % of 1999	丰台区 Fengtai 2000	1999	2000年为1999年% 2000 as % of 1999
全部工业总产值(1990年不变价,万元)	Gross Output Value of Industry(at constant price of 1990,10000 yuan)	677541	575819.3	117.7	488971.0	401377.8	121.8
国有	State-owned	7080.0	11843.8	59.8	37850.9	35499.7	106.6
集体	Collective-owned	293439	283756.3	103.4	120421	121643.4	99.0
其他	Others	377022	280219.2	134.5	330699	244234.7	135.4
全部轻工业总产值(现价,万元)	Gross Output Value of Light Industry (at current prices,10000 yuan)	376647	353784.3	106.5	214045	177367.8	120.7
以农产品为原料	Using Farm Products as Raw Materials	268500	271706.3	98.8	109587	107298.1	102.1
以非农产品为原料	Using Non-farm Products as Raw Materials	108147	82078.0	131.8	104459	70069.7	149.1
全部重工业总产值(现价,万元)	Gross Output Value of Heavy Industry (at current prices,10000 yuan)	334864	277965.9	120.5	326761	258497.8	126.4
采掘工业	Mining and Quarrying				2582.8	3560.2	72.5
原料工业	Raw Materials Industry	33442.9	29186.4	114.6	32158.8	29314.1	109.7
制造工业	Manufacturing Industry	301421	248779.5	121.2	292020	225623.5	129.4
独立核算工业企业平均职工人数 (人)	Average Number of Staff and Workers in Enterprises with Independent Accounting System (person)	80649	87424	92.3	47988	46786	102.6
#国有	State-owned	3178	4728	67.2	4609	4290	107.4
集体	Collective-owned	42001	52350	80.2	22038	24356	90.5
独立核算工业企业总产值(现价,万元)	Gross Output Value of Enterprises with Independent Accounting System (at current prices,10000 yuan)	711511	631750.2	112.6	524226	415132.6	126.3
#国有	State-owned	7987.9	15012.8	53.2	41706.7	38067.8	109.6
集体	Collective-owned	315846	311327.2	101.5	127474	128870	98.9
独立核算工业企业工业增加值 (万元)	Value Added of Enterprises with Independent Accounting System (10000 yuan)				152716.0	136403.2	112.0
独立核算工业企业财务指标	Financial Indicators for Enterprises with Independent Accounting System						
产品销售收入 (万元)	Sales Revenue (10000 yuan)	711511	600820.4	118.4	514965	398845	129.1
#国有	State-owned	7987.9	13430.6	59.5	39874.8	36852.7	108.2
产品销售成本 (万元)	Cost of Sales (10000 yuan)	574408	475343.5	120.8	400915	319531	125.5
#国有	State-owned	6506.7	11060.3	58.8	31769.9	30145.5	105.4
固定资产原价 (万元)	Original Value of Fixed Assets(10000 yuan)				323346	278687.2	116.0
#国有	State-owned				22138.8	15768.7	140.4
固定资产净值 (万元)	Net Value of Fixed Assets (10000 yuan)	281216.0	227110.1	123.8	213034	189605.0	112.4
#国有	State-owned	4927.5	5677.8	86.8	12824.8	9379.2	136.7
全部流动资金年平均余额 (万元)	Annual Average Balance of Circulating Funds (10000 yuan)	629870	500483.4	125.9	509077	396467.4	128.4
#国有	State-owned	17680.7	16515.9	107.1	52973.4	43492.0	121.8
利润总额 (万元)	Total Profits (10000 yuan)	22789	7155.0	318.5	31849.7	8410.2	378.7
#国有	State-owned	-1103	2218.0		861.1	1592.1	54.1

24-3 续表 4 continued

项　目	Item	朝阳区 Chaoyang 2000	朝阳区 Chaoyang 1999	朝阳区 2000年为1999年% 2000 as % of 1999	丰台区 Fengtai 2000	丰台区 Fengtai 1999	丰台区 2000年为1999年% 2000 as % of 1999
资金利税率 (%)	Ratio of Pre-tax Profits to Total of Capital (%)				7.6	4.9	
产品销售率 (%)	Ratio of Sales Value to Gross Output Value (%)	97.2	94.5		96.4	97.0	
增加值率 (%)	Ratio of Added Value to Gross Output Value (%)	32.9	30.7		29.1	32.9	
独立核算工业企业全员劳动生产率 (元/人)	Overall Labor Productivity of Enterprises with Independent Accounting System (yuan/person)	29835	22333	133.6	31824	23609	134.8
#国有	State-owned	9973.0	22341.8	44.6	24800	20081	123.5
集体	Collective-owned	23083.0	17259.6	133.7	13483	12307	109.6
商业	**Commerce**						
社会消费品零售额 (万元)	Retail Sales of Consumer Goods (10000 yuan)	1423488	1281129	111.1	737843	613137	120.3
按登记注册类型分	Grouped by Registered Type						
国有	State-owned	369030	382936.5	96.4	51603	78753	65.5
集体	Collective-owned	106670	120609.3	88.4	72471	86773	83.5
其他	Others	947788.0	777583.2	121.9	613769	447611	137.1
按类别分	Grouped by Type of Goods						
吃的商品	Food	487586	421491	115.7	395201	283987	139.2
穿的商品	Clothing	140177	175515	79.9	99593	64920	153.4
用的商品	Daily Used Articles	735586	588038	125.1	212365	241656	87.9
烧的商品	Fuel	60139	96085	62.6	30684	22574	135.9
网点数 (个)	Number of Outlets (unit)	24710	31444	78.6	25147	26339	95.5
#商业	Wholesale and Retail	14226	24832	57.3	22001	22408	98.2
饮食业	Catering	2850	2638	108.0	1668	2088	79.9
服务业	Services	7634	3974	192.1	1478	1843	80.2
#宾馆、饭店	Hotels				99	68	145.6
营业人员 (人)	Personnel (person)	145151	181397	80.0	71374	66049	108.1
#商业	Wholesale and Retail	83566	94179	88.7	49235	46546	105.8
饮食业	Catering	16742	17905	93.5	7806	8258	94.5
服务业	Services	44843	69313	64.7	14333	11245	127.5
#宾馆、饭店	Hotels				6173	4258	145.0
外经、外贸	**Foreign Economy and Trade**						
出口商品交货额 (万元)	Delivery Value of Exports (10000 yuan)	24521.9	20092	122.0	2813	2977.3	94.5
利用外资签订协议(合同)数 (个)	Number of Signed Agreements and Contracts of Foreign Capital to be Utilized (unit)	188	80	235.0	28	21	133.3
利用外资签订协议(合同)金额 (万美元)	Amount of Foreign Capital to be Utilized through Agreements and Contracts (USD 10000)	11575.7	9338.9	124.0	5662	5153	109.9
实际利用外资 (万美元)	Amount of Foreign Capital Actually Used (USD 10000)	13479.6	7569.1	178.1	2511.0	3037.2	82.7
旅游人数 (万人)	Number of Tourists (10000 persons)				315	295	106.8
教育	**Education**						
学校数 (个)	Number of Schools (unit)	310	320	96.9	174	178	97.8
小学	Primary Schools	211	216	97.7	112	115	97.4

24-3 续表 5 continued

项目		Item		朝阳区 Chaoyang 2000	1999	2000年为1999年% 2000 as % of 1999	丰台区 Fengtai 2000	1999	2000年为1999年% 2000 as % of 1999
普通中学		Regular Secondary School		79	78	101.3	50	62	80.6
中等专业教育		Specialized Secondary Schools		20	26	76.9		1	
招生数	(人)	New Student Enrollment	(person)	34956	35439	98.6	23776	22345	106.4
小学		Primary Schools		9562	9822	97.4	7199	7215	99.8
初级中等学校		Junior Secondary Schools		16081	15728	102.2	10317	9939	103.8
高级中等学校		Senior Secondary Schools		6607	6041	109.4	6260	5191	120.6
中等专业教育		Specialized Secondary Schools		2706	3848	70.3			
在校学生	(人)	Student Enrollment	(person)	147718	154970	95.3	95327	97622	97.6
小学		Primary Schools		71519	79751	89.7	49589	54815	90.5
初级中等学校		Junior Secondary Schools		46034	43977	104.7	29256	27382	106.8
高级中等学校		Senior Secondary Schools		17846	16345	109.2	16482	15228	108.2
中等专业教育		Specialized Secondary Schools		12319	14897	82.7		197	
毕业生	(人)	Graduates	(person)	40671	40923	99.4	24036	24495	98.1
小学		Primary Schools		17270	16934	102.0	10317	10686	96.5
初级中等学校		Junior Secondary Schools		13785	15797	87.3	8795	9005	97.7
高级中等学校		Senior Secondary Schools		4505	3677	122.5	4924	4611	106.8
中等专业教育		Specialized Secondary Schools		5111	4515	113.2		193	
达到"国家体育标准"学生数	(人)	Number of Students Come to the Standard for State Physical Training	(person)	145551	120707	120.6	77111	82344	93.6
幼儿园、托儿所个数	(个)	Number of Kindergardens	(unit)	164	220	74.5	125	136	91.9
幼儿入托数	(人)	New Enrollment	(person)	29953	10923	274.2	18392	17539	104.9
文化		**Culture**							
文化馆、站	(个)	Cultural Centers	(unit)	44	44	100.0	8	17	47.1
公共图书馆	(个)	Public Libraries	(unit)	1	1	100.0	2	1	200.0
公共图书馆藏书	(万册)	Collection	(10000 volume)	48.6	46.5	104.5	28	22	127.3
电影放映单位	(个)	Film Projection Units	(unit)	12	12	100.0	4	2	200.0
区级以上重点文物保护单位	(个)	Cultural Relics Preserved at District Level and above	(unit)	13	13	100.0	25	20	125.0
卫生		**Health**							
卫生机构数	(个)	Number of Health Institutions	(unit)	1110	1112	99.8	617	599	103.0
#医院		Hospitals		107	111	96.4	58	57	101.8
卫生院		Clinics							
床位数		Number of Beds	(unit)	10492	10504	99.9	6283	5475	114.8
#医院		Hospitals		10492	10398	100.9	6283	5475	114.8
卫生院		Clinics							
平均每千人拥有床位数	(张)	Average Number of Beds Per 1000 Persons	(unit)	6.8	7.1	95.8	7.6	6.8	111.8
卫生技术人员	(人)	Medical Technical Personnel	(person)	17678	18217	97.0	8063	9140	88.2
#医生		Doctors	(person)	8062	8417	95.8	3388	3900	86.9
公用设施		**Public Utilities**							
区级以上公园	(个)	Parks at District Level and above	(unit)	25	21	119.0	21	17	123.5
体育场馆	(个)	Stadiums and Gymnasiums	(unit)	9	9	100.0	6	6	100.0
道路长度	(公里)	Length of Roads	(km)	289.3	263.5	109.8	214	214	100.0

24-4 石景山区、海淀区国民经济主要指标
MAIN NATIONAL ECONOMIC INDICATORS FOR SHIJINGSHAN AND HAIDIAN DISTRICTS

项目	Item	石景山区 Shijingshan 2000	1999	2000年为1999年% 2000as% of 1999	海淀区 Haidian 2000	1999	2000年为1999年% 2000as% of 1999
综合	**General Survey**						
国内生产总值 (万元)	Gross Domestic Product (10000 yuan)	143945.0	1232195	116.8	2810657	2192168	128.2
第一产业	Primary Industry	1967.2	1937.1	101.6	20943.1	22049.9	95.0
第二产业	Secondary Industry	26744.7	25671	104.2	1547508	1358219	113.9
第三产业	Tertiary Industry	115233	95612	120.5	1242207	811899.0	153.0
财政收入 (万元)	Fiscal Revenue (10000 yuan)	60002	54813	109.5	281593	221229	127.3
#增值税	Increased Value Tax	19548	17589	111.1	38071	29982	127.0
营业税	Operating Tax	12101	12790	94.6	136737	109906	124.4
个人所得税	Private Income Tax					47645	
企业所得税	Enterprise Income Tax	8956	8123	110.3	41132	28107	146.3
财政支出 (万元)	Fiscal Expenditure (10000 yuan)	74370	58946	126.2	404197	294428	137.3
#基本建设支出	Capital Construction	11592	9667	119.9	48342	52098	92.8
支援农业生产支出	Supporting Agriculture	350	732	47.8	4792	3545	135.2
文教卫生事业费	Culture,Education and Health	17228	17001	101.3	70744	58406	121.1
人口和劳动力	**Population and Labor Force**						
总人口 (人)	Total Population (person)	414155	404292	102.4	1963816	1887778	104.0
常住户籍人口 (人)	Permanent Registered Population (person)	331759	326803	101.5	1616483	1570115	103.0
#非农业人口	Non-agriculture	316008	311153	101.6	1493683	1443213	103.5
男	Male	174627	165399	105.6	775045	749761	103.4
女	Female	157132	145754	107.8	718638	693452	103.6
出生率 (‰)	Birth Rate (‰)	4.7	4.5		5.7	5.2	
死亡率 (‰)	Death Rate (‰)	5.7	4.8		4.5	4.1	
自然增长率 (‰)	Natural Growth Rate (‰)	-1.0	-0.3		1.12	1.1	
从业人员 (人)	Employment (person)	51113	48114	106.2	347904	356886	97.5
按产业分	Grouped by Industry						
第一产业	Primary Industry	15	1322	1.1	12133	16779	72.3
第二产业	Secondary Industry	11274	11780	95.7	69034	101405	68.1
第三产业	Tertiary Industry	39824	35012	113.7	277578	238702	116.3
按职工非职工分	Grouped by Staff and Workers or Non-staff-and-worker						
职工人数	Staff and Worker	45832	43226	106.0	303409	272488	111.3
#国有单位	State-owned	20643	22178	93.1	79365	82279	96.5
集体单位	Collective-owned	6506	8323	78.2	44421	40931	108.5
城镇个体劳动者	Urban and Rural Individuals				34893	32526	107.3
劳动工资	**Wages**						
工资总额 (万元)	Total Wages (10000 yuan)	56139.3	49069.5	114.4	575525.9	410276.3	140.3
#国有单位	State-owned	34181.9	31170.0	109.7	146670.8	128324.1	114.3
集体单位	Collective-owned	5061.7	6106.6	82.9	50574.8	54963.5	92.0
职工平均工资 (元)	Average Wage (yuan)	13064	11331	115.3	19507.4	15164.0	128.6
固定资产投资	**Investment in Fixed Assets**						
全社会固定资产投资 (万元)	Total Investment in Fixed Assets(10000 yuan)	72924	70977	102.7	830631	484044	171.6
按建设性质分	Grouped by Type of Construction						
#基本建设投资	Capital Construction	30857	21218	145.4	248765	211951	117.4
更新改造投资	Innovation and Replacement	7906	6395	123.6	60250	14700	409.9

24-4 续表1 continued

项目		Item		石景山区 Shijingshan 2000	1999	2000年为1999年% 2000as% of 1999	海淀区 Haidian 2000	1999	2000年为1999年% 2000as% of 1999
按登记注册类型分		Grouped by Ownership							
#国有单位		State-owned		66363	65546	101.2	418297	267706	156.3
集体单位		Collective-owned					30729	31348	98.0
新增固定资产	(万元)	Incremental Fixed Assets	(10000 yuan)	86438	59547	145.2	509513	445716	114.3
#国有单位		State-owned		85861	55979	153.4	329395	271421	121.4
集体单位		Collective-owned					11690	11674	100.1
房屋施工面积	(万平方米)	Floor Space of Buildings under Construction	(10000 sq.m)	74.1	71.6	103.5	432.6	336.7	128.5
#国有单位		State-owned		60.3	66.3	91.0	132.7	141.5	93.8
集体单位		Collective-owned					30	30.7	97.7
房屋竣工面积	(万平方米)	Floor Space of Buildings Completed	(10000 sq.m)	23.5	22.0	106.8	116.3	120.2	96.8
#国有单位		State-owned		23.3	21.2	109.9	55.3	55.1	100.4
#住宅		Residence		10.4	17.2	60.5	18.4	30.0	61.3
#集体单位		Collective-owned					8.2	7.1	115.5
#住宅		Residence					7.3	6.1	119.7
农村经济		**Rural Economy**							
农村劳动力	(人)	Labor Force	(person)	7007	7638	91.7	54121	61383	88.2
种植业		Planting		793	859	92.3	8664	12777	67.8
林业		Forestry		285	222	128.4	1078	909	118.6
牧业		Animal Husbandry		108	194	55.7	1108	1389	79.8
渔业		Fishery			6		191	224	85.3
农村工业		Rural Industry		2648	3050	86.8	17908	21287	84.1
农村建筑业		Rural Construction		208	127	163.8	3014	3274	92.1
农村运输业		Rural Transportation		328	303	108.3	2609	2264	115.2
农村商、饮食业、服务业		Commerce,Catering and Services		2637	2877	91.7	6267	6819	91.9
耕地面积	(公顷)	Area under Cultivation	(hectare)	376.1	396.1	95.0	8154	8624.4	94.5
农业机械总动力	(千瓦)	Total Power of Agricultural Machinery	(kw)	11696.3	7075.0	165.3	146000	148168	98.5
化肥施用实物量	(吨)	Consumption of Chemical Fertilizers	(ton)	238	128	185.9	11146	8738	127.6
化肥施用折纯量	(吨)	Consumption of Chemical Fertilizers(100%)	(ton)	81	46	176.1	3715.3	2955	125.7
农村用电量	(万千瓦时)	Consumption of Electricity	(10000 kwh)	2362	2244	105.3	17812	20477.9	87.0
农村国内生产总值	(万元)	Rural Gross Domestic Product	(10000 yuan)	21363.3	19118.8	111.7	190741	169265.7	112.7
第一产业		Primary Industry		1967.2	1937.1	101.6	20943.1	22049.9	95.0
第二产业		Secondary Industry		7127.1	6867.2	103.8	54461.3	52058.6	104.6
第三产业		Tertiary Industry		12269.0	10314.5	118.9	115336	95157.2	121.2
农业总产值	(万元)	Gross Output Value of Agriculture	(10000 yuan)	4248.7	4401.4	96.5	50695	45019.8	112.6
种植业		Planting		1108.7	902.4	122.9	34167.9	28251.0	120.9
林业		Forestry			80.0		1978.6	864.0	229.0
牧业		Animal Husbandry		3110.0	3397.8	91.5	10230.2	11655.4	87.8
渔业		Fishery		30.0	21.2	141.5	4318.3	4249.4	101.6
农作物总播种面积	(万公顷)	Sown Area of Farm Crops	(10000 hectare)	0.2	0.1	200.0	0.7	0.9	77.8
粮食作物		Grain					0.5	0.6	83.3
经济作物		Industrial Crops		0.2	0.1	200.0			
其他作物		Other Crops					0.2	0.3	66.7

24-4 续表 2 continued

项目		Item		石景山区 Shijingshan 2000	1999	2000年为1999.年% 2000 as% of 1999	海淀区 Haidian 2000	1999	2000年为1999年% 2000 as% of 1999
农副产品产量		Yield of Farm and Sideline Crops							
粮食	(万吨)	Grain	(10000 tons)				3.0	3.6	83.3
蔬菜	(吨)	Vegetable	(ton)	9148	8825	103.7	106515	139312	76.5
干鲜果	(吨)	Dry and Fresh Fruits	(ton)	999	770	129.7	11187	11112	100.7
畜产品产量		Output of Livestock Products							
生猪出栏	(头)	Slaughtered Hogs	(head)	28667	37687	76.1	52456	111613	47.0
商品猪	(头)	Commodity Hogs	(head)	28667	37687	76.1	52456	111613	47.0
猪牛羊肉	(吨)	Pork,Beef and Mutton	(ton)	1200	2374	50.5	3388	6731	50.3
#猪肉		Pork		1200	2374	50.5	3285	6627	49.6
禽肉		Meat of Poultry	(ton)	120	74	162.2	1336	2327	57.4
禽蛋		Poultry Eggs	(ton)	1540	1540	100.0	2212	2861	77.3
牲畜年底头数	(头)	Number of Livestock(year-end)	(head)	10155	16814	60.4			
大牲畜		Large Animals		545	523	104.2	1014	1108	91.5
猪		Hogs		9610	16291	59.0	33090	40672	81.4
羊		Goats and Sheep					8806	8053	109.4
水产品产量	(吨)	Output of Aquatic Product	(ton)	40	40	100.0	2644	2171	121.8
农村集体经济收入	(万元)	Rural Collective Economic Revenue	(10000 yuan)	188229	176467	106.7	713589	769660	92.7
农村集体经济利润总额	(万元)	Total Profits of Rural Collective Economy	(10000 yuan)	5774	4923	117.3	19294	20161	95.7
国家税金		State Taxes					20059	20317	98.7
集体积累		Collective Accumulation					35198	35881	98.1
劳动所得		Income from Work					64023	63859	100.3
乡镇企业单位数	(个)	Number of Township and Village Enterprise	(unit)	216	239	90.4	974	1231	79.1
乡镇企业人数	(人)	Number of Persons of Township and Village Enterprises	(person)	8104	7975	101.6	43551	44104	98.7
乡镇企业纯利润	(万元)	Net Profit of Township and Village Enterprises	(10000 yuan)	3059	1864	164.1	18413	23337	78.9
乡镇企业固定资产原价	(万元)	Original Value of Fixed Assets of Township and Village Enterprises	(10000 yuan)	37099	37099	100.0	207422	204265	101.5
乡镇企业固定资产净值	(万元)	Net Value of Fixed Assets of Township and Village Enterprises	(10000 yuan)				140934	133580.0	105.5
工业		**Industry**							
全部工业企业单位数	(个)	Number of Enterprises	(unit)	376	366	102.7	1006	1030	97.7
国有		State-owned		43	45	95.6	101	161	62.7
集体		Collective-owned		149	166	89.8	517	544	95.0
其他		Others		184	155	118.7	388	325.0	119.4
全部工业总产值(现价,万元)		Gross Output Value of Industry (at current prices,10000 yuan)		95994.1	80272.5	119.6	4131199.9	3958418.5	143.3
国有		State-owned		1878.5	1837.8	102.2	246408.0	1946855.9	21.3
集体		Collective-owned		27994.9	30474.8	91.9	182785.8	254272.5	79.9
其他		Others		66120.7	47959.9	137.9	3702006.0	1757290.1	247.2

24-4 续表 3 continued

项目	Item	石景山区 Shijingshan 2000	1999	2000年为1999年% 2000 as% of 1999	海淀区 Haidian 2000	1999	2000年为1999年% 2000 as% of 1999
全部工业总产值(1990年不变价,万元)	Gross Output Value of Industry(at constant price of 1990,10000 yuan)	97833.1	76728.0	127.5	5773867.3	3615324.2	159.7
国有	State-owned	1880.9	1829.6	102.8	233007.0	1208843.2	19.3
集体	Collective-owned	25030.1	27422.9	91.3	167731.5	227416.8	73.8
其他	Others	70922.1	46475.5	152.6	5373128.8	2179064.2	246.6
全部轻工业总产值(现价,万元)	Gross Output Value of Light Industry (at current prices,10000 yuan)	46493.1	28422.9	163.6	283213.4	321670.6	88.0
以农产品为原料	Using Farm Products as Raw Materials	28214.3	20091.1	140.4	129662.0	149586.0	86.7
以非农产品为原料	Using Non-farm Products as Raw Materials	18278.8	7485.6	244.2	153551.4	172084.6	89.2
全部重工业总产值(现价,万元)	Gross Output Value of Heavy Industry (at current prices,10000 yuan)	49501.0	52695.8	93.9	3847986.5	2560308.8	150.3
采掘工业	Mining and Quarrying	127.3	74.8	170.2	915.9	246.9	371.0
原料工业	Raw Materials Industry	6965.1	8512.6	81.8	227747.6	145879.6	156.1
制造工业	Manufacturing Industry	42408.6	44108.4	96.1	3619323.0	2413682.3	150.0
独立核算工业企业平均职工人数 (人)	Average Number of Staff and Workers in Enterprises with Independent Accounting System (person)	11943	12316	97.0	83312	81650	102.0
#国有	State-owned	414	513	80.7	9658	17396	55.5
集体	Collective-owned	6064	7423	81.7	23941	29234	81.9
独立核算工业企业总产值(现价,万元)	Gross Output Value of Enterprises with Independent Accounting System (at current prices,10000 yuan)	95994.1	80272.5	119.6	4131199.9	2881979.4	143.3
#国有	State-owned	1878.5	1837.8	102.2	246408.1	1155524.0	12.7
集体	Collective-owned	27994.9	30474.8	91.9	182785.8	254272.5	71.9
独立核算工业企业工业增加值 (万元)	Value Added of Enterprises with Independent Accounting System (10000 yuan)	34501.6	22473.6	153.5	1126573	1223151.3	92.1
独立核算工业企业财务指标	Financial Indicators for Enterprises with Independent Accounting System						
产品销售收入 (万元)	Sales Revenue (10000 yuan)	92609.4	86289.1	107.3	3951730	3297419.6	119.8
#国有	State-owned	1908.1	1899.6	100.4	229924.4	1257879.1	18.3
产品销售成本 (万元)	Cost of Sales (10000 yuan)	73242.4	68181.4	107.4	3077123	2703579.7	113.8
#国有	State-owned	1566.2	1487.1	105.3	178102.5	1058849.2	16.8
固定资产原价 (万元)	Original Value of Fixed Assets(10000 yuan)	69223.1	67143.6	103.1	817185.9	823485.2	99.2
#国有	State-owned	943.3	998.3	94.5	73675.7	188916.8	39.0
固定资产净值 (万元)	Net Value of Fixed Assets (10000 yuan)	43386.3	47663.0	91.0	489759.1	423308.0	115.7
#国有	State-owned	641.5	602.8	106.4	47286.5	82238.8	57.5
全部流动资金年平均余额 (万元)	Annual Average Balance of Circulating Funds (10000 yuan)	121579	101703.9	119.5	2604642.2	2441751.6	106.7
#国有	State-owned	1618.6	1447.2	111.8	263600.9	599808.9	43.9
利润总额 (万元)	Total Profits (10000 yuan)	-1823.8	-2813.4		390717.8	180920.8	216.0
#国有	State-owned	36.6	76.5	47.8	35096.1	59282.0	59.2

24-4 续表 4 continued

项目	Item	石景山区 Shijingshan 2000	1999	2000年为1999年% 2000as% of 1999	海淀区 Haidian 2000	1999	2000年为1999年% 2000as% of 1999
资金利税率 (%)	Ratio of Pre-tax Profits to Total of Capital(%)	1.7	-1.6		17.4	4.9	
产品销售率 (%)	Ratio of Sales Value to Gross Output Value (%)	99.8	98.1		92.8	95.6	
增加值率 (%)	Ratio of Added Value to Gross Output Value (%)	35.9	28.0		27.3	30.9	
独立核算工业企业全员劳动生产率 (元/人)	Overall Labor Productivity of Enterprises with Independent Accounting System (yuan/person)	28014.0	18247.5	153.5	135223.4	149804	90.3
#国有	State-owned	11937.0	11333.0	105.3	91139.16	345814	26.4
集体	Collective-owned	15835.0	14241.0	111.2	28990.73	26876	107.9
商业	**Commerce**						
社会消费品零售额 (万元)	Retail Sales of Consumer Goods (10000 yuan)	351544.2	319603.1	110.0	2543373	2400543	105.9
按登记注册类型分	Grouped by Registered Type						
国有	State-owned				494021		
集体	Collective-owned				183193		
其他	Others				1866159		
按类别分	Grouped by Type of Goods						
吃的商品	Food	153758.1	178753.0	86.0	348235	371857	93.6
穿的商品	Clothing	12671.0	14076.0	90.0	115567	106660	108.4
用的商品	Daily Used Articles	177950.1	121800.0	146.1	2061542	1910316	107.9
烧的商品	Fuel	8003.0	4974.1	160.9	18029	11710	154.0
网点数 (个)	Number of Outlets (unit)	9641	11746	82.1	38217	36212	105.5
#商业	Wholesale and Retail	7105	7534	94.3	27770	26545	104.6
饮食业	Catering	609	1788	34.1	4047	3730	108.5
服务业	Services	1927	2424	79.5	6400	5937	107.8
#宾馆、饭店	Hotels				188	188	100.0
营业人员 (人)	Personnel (person)	46493	48065	96.7	146612	137869	106.3
#商业	Wholesale and Retail	22065	22779	96.9	76496	72777	105.1
饮食业	Catering	3415	8944	38.2	18438	17098	107.8
服务业	Services	21013	16342	128.6	51678	47994	107.7
#宾馆、饭店	Hotels				7766	8525	91.1
外经、外贸	**Foreign Economy and Trade**						
出口商品交货额 (万元)	Delivery Value of Exports (10000 yuan)	4947.9	4971.9	99.5	268445.1	221414.5	121.2
利用外资签订协议(合同)数 (个)	Number of Signed Agreements and Contracts of Foreign Capital to be Utilized (unit)	14	2	700.0	441	138	319.6
利用外资签订协议(合同)金额 (万美元)	Amount of Foreign Capital to be Utilized through Agreements and Contracts (USD 10000)	760	46	1652.2	50506	17005	297.0
实际利用外资 (万美元)	Amount of Foreign Capital Actually Used (USD 10000)	230.0	782.4	29.4	23842.4	9877.8	241.4
旅游人数 (万人)	Number of Tourists (10000 persons)	267.8	281.6	95.1	1718.66	1489.4	115.4
教育	**Education**						
学校数 (个)	Number of Schools (unit)	78	77	101.3	278	246	113.0
小学	Primary Schools	42	44	95.5	163	142	114.8

24-4 续表 5 continued

项目		Item		石景山区 Shijingshan 2000	1999	2000年为1999年% 2000 as % of 1999	海淀区 Haidian 2000	1999	2000年为1999年% 2000 as % of 1999
普通中学		Regular Secondary School		31	28	110.7	114	104	109.6
中等专业教育		Specialized Secondary Schools		5	5	100.0			
招生数	(人)	New Student Enrollment	(person)	9136	9784	93.4	49174	47777	102.9
小学		Primary Schools		2366	2514	94.1	13577	14222	95.5
初级中等学校		Junior Secondary Schools		4044	4142	97.6	20023	18012	111.2
高级中等学校		Senior Secondary Schools		1733	1728	100.3	15574	15543	100.2
中等专业教育		Specialized Secondary Schools		993	1400	70.9			
在校学生	(人)	Student Enrollment	(person)	38775	40623	95.5	197312	199946	98.7
小学		Primary Schools		17703	19603	90.3	94339	100437	93.9
初级中等学校		Junior Secondary Schools		11967	11476	104.3	55400	51663	107.2
高级中等学校		Senior Secondary Schools		5141	4800	107.1	47573	47846	99.4
中等专业教育		Specialized Secondary Schools		3964	4744	83.6			
毕业生	(人)	Graduates	(person)	10568	11185	94.5	51186	47033	108.8
小学		Primary Schools		4237	4204	100.8	18331	17788	103.1
初级中等学校		Junior Secondary Schools		3572	4229	84.5	17065	17225	99.1
高级中等学校		Senior Secondary Schools		1317	1134	116.1	15790	12020	131.4
中等专业教育		Specialized Secondary Schools		1442	1528	94.4			
达到"国家体育标准"学生数	(人)	Number of Students Come to the Standard for State Physical Training	(person)	37877			123743	115426	107.2
幼儿园、托儿所个数	(个)	Number of Kindergardens	(unit)	44	75	58.7	203	215	94.4
幼儿入托数	(人)	New Enrollment	(person)	2976	2851	104.4	39736	40687	97.7
文化		**Culture**							
文化馆、站	(个)	Cultural Centers	(unit)	7	7	100.0	11	27	40.7
公共图书馆	(个)	Public Libraries	(unit)	2	2	100.0	2	2	100.0
公共图书馆藏书	(万册)	Collection	(10000 volume)	42	39	107.7	2277.9	2221	102.6
电影放映单位	(个)	Film Projection Units	(unit)	1	1	100.0	1	3	33.3
区级以上重点文物保护单位	(个)	Cultural Relics Preserved at District Level and above	(unit)	2	2	100.0	4	4	100.0
卫生		**Health**							
卫生机构数	(个)	Number of Health Institutions	(unit)	204	209	97.6	162	163	99.4
#医院		Hospitals		23	22	104.5	88	88	100.0
卫生院		Clinics		1	1	100.0	8	8	100.0
床位数		Number of Beds	(unit)	3924	3746	104.8	8718	8863	98.4
#医院		Hospitals		3224	3026	106.5	8568	8533	100.4
卫生院		Clinics			20		494	530	93.2
平均每千人拥有床位数	(张)	Average Number of Beds Per 1000 Persons	(unit)	11.8	11.4	103.5	5.4	5.8	93.1
卫生技术人员	(人)	Medical Technical Personnel	(person)	4924	5170	95.2	12469	12753	97.8
#医生		Doctors	(person)	2115	2231	94.8	5325	5362	99.3
公用设施		**Public Utilities**							
区级以上公园	(个)	Parks at District Level and above	(unit)	9	10	90.0	6	6	100.0
体育场馆	(个)	Stadiums and Gymnasiums	(unit)	4	4	100.0	3	3	100.0
道路长度	(公里)	Length of Roads	(km)	178.1	177.9	100.1	735	672.9	109.2

24-5 门头沟区、房山区国民经济主要指标
MAIN NATIONAL ECONOMIC INDICATORS FOR MENTOUGOU AND FANGSHAN DISTRICTS

项目		Item		门头沟区 Mentougou 2000	1999	2000年为1999年% 2000as% of 1999	房山区 Fanshan 2000	1999	2000年为1999年% 2000as% of 1999
综合		**General Survey**							
国内生产总值	(万元)	Gross Domestic Product	(10000 yuan)	202251.6	173555.6	116.5	843387.3	751012.8	112.3
第一产业		Primary Industry		4947.8	4821.9	102.6	82652.0	73177.2	112.9
第二产业		Secondary Industry		70860.3	65861.3	107.6	366030.0	334833.6	109.3
第三产业		Tertiary Industry		126443.5	102872.4	122.9	394705.3	343002.0	115.1
财政收入	(万元)	Fiscal Revenue	(10000 yuan)	28378	23340	121.6	50106	41595	120.5
#增值税		Increased Value Tax		4803	3652	131.5	10785	10335	104.4
营业税		Operating Tax		10368	8273	125.3	16283	12358	131.8
个人所得税		Private Income Tax			1403				
企业所得税		Enterprise Income Tax		7650	6176	123.9	5601	5012	111.8
财政支出	(万元)	Fiscal Expenditure	(10000 yuan)	82906	65346	126.9	96893	68719	141.0
#基本建设支出		Capital Construction		4835	1036	466.7	5608	2330	240.7
支援农业生产支出		Supporting Agriculture		5347	4557	117.3	7096	6137	115.6
文教卫生事业费		Culture,Education and Health		15319	12813	119.6	27847	25600	108.8
人口和劳动力		**Population and Labor Force**							
总人口	(人)	Total Population	(person)	255440	256203	99.7	751772	752185	99.9
常住户籍人口	(人)	Permanent Registered Population	(person)	234003	235146	99.5	751772	752185	99.9
#非农业人口		Non-agriculture		152740	151853	100.6	272654	267403	102.0
男		Male		122037	122770	99.4	377748	378393	99.8
女		Female		111966	112376	99.6	374024	373792	100.1
出生率	(‰)	Birth Rate	(‰)	6.5	6.2		7.5	7.6	
死亡率	(‰)	Death Ratc	(‰)	10.2	8.4		7.4	6.4	
自然增长率	(‰)	Natural Growth Rate	(‰)	-3.7	-2.2		0.1	1.2	
从业人员	(人)	Employment	(person)	89311	86613	103.1	337810	305851	110.4
按产业分		Grouped by Industry							
第一产业		Primary Industry		12916	11729	110.1	77973	78891	98.8
第二产业		Secondary Industry		21073	21804	96.6	125740	101856	123.4
第三产业		Tertiary Industry		55322	53080	104.2	134097	125104	107.2
按职工非职工分		Grouped by Staff and Workers or Non-staff-and-worker							
职工人数		Staff and Worker		38896	37603	103.4	94894	89862	105.6
#国有单位		State-owned		19923	20390	97.7	44887	44356	101.2
集体单位		Collective-owned		5397	5771	93.5	40296	39986	100.8
城镇个体劳动者		Urban and Rural Individuals		8119	6182	131.3	11497	10265	112.0
劳动工资		**Wages**							
工资总额	(万元)	Total Wages	(10000 yuan)	44519.9	37067.9	120.1	107346.8	87130	123.2
#国有单位		State-owned		29350.9	24298.7	120.8	57423.3	49892	115.1
集体单位		Collective-owned		4887.7	4676.4	104.5	41278.5	35139	117.5
职工平均工资	(元)	Average Wage	(yuan)	12816	10547	121.5	10549	9402	112.2
固定资产投资		**Investment in Fixed Assets**							
全社会固定资产投资	(万元)	Total Investment in Fixed Assets	(10000 yuan)	41479	23352	177.6	207063	165784	124.9
按建设性质分		Grouped by Type of Construction							
#基本建设投资		Capital Construction		20341	14496	140.3	32797	18431	177.9
更新改造投资		Innovation and Replacement		544	320	170.0	1261	3499	36.0

24-5 续表1 continued

项目	Item	门头沟区 Mentougou 2000	1999	2000年为1999年% 2000as% of 1999	房山区 Fanshan 2000	1999	2000年为1999年% 2000as% of 1999
按登记注册类型分	Grouped by Registered Type						
#国有单位	State-owned	34064	14955	227.8	63985.0	56479.2	113.3
集体单位	Collective-owned	550	1417	38.8	66143.0	60849.3	108.7
新增固定资产 (万元)	Incremental Fixed Assets (10000 yuan)	27281	18092	150.8	117597.0	129677.4	90.7
#国有单位	State-owned				31963	58818	54.3
集体单位	Collective-owned						
房屋施工面积 (万平方米)	Floor Space of Buildings under Construction (10000 sq.m)	37.5	31.4	119.4			
#国有单位	State-owned						
集体单位	Collective-owned				74.5	65.6	113.6
房屋竣工面积 (万平方米)	Floor Space of Buildings Completed (10000 sq.m)	14.1	18.9	74.6	85.4	85.5	99.9
#国有单位	State-owned				26.5	44.1	60.1
#住宅	Residence				16.2	27.1	59.8
#集体单位	Collective-owned				31.1	33.8	92.0
#住宅	Residence				19.5	20.0	97.5
农村经济	**Rural Economy**						
农村劳动力 (人)	Labor Force (person)	42332	43210	98.0	223141	213154	104.7
种植业	Planting	8854	8284	106.9	57494	60215	95.5
林业	Forestry	1850	1547	119.6	6535	5766	113.3
牧业	Animal Husbandry	2162	1849	116.9	12459	11472	108.6
渔业	Fishery	50	49	102.0	809	678	119.3
农村工业	Rural Industry	8106	7723	105.0	44207	46018	96.1
农村建筑业	Rural Construction	2705	2304	117.4	30778	28585	107.7
农村运输业	Rural Transportation	7711	7159	107.7	27931	24489	114.1
农村商、饮食业、服务业	Commerce,Catering and Services	5510	4167	132.2	42928	35931	119.5
耕地面积 (公顷)	Area under Cultivation (hectare)	2845.6	2855	99.7	39778.5	41225.9	96.5
农业机械总动力 (千瓦)	Total Power of Agricultural Machinery (kw)	117541	120701	97.4	613175	637144	96.2
化肥施用实物量 (吨)	Consumption of Chemical Fertilizers (ton)	1363	1774	76.8	45361	49230	92.1
化肥施用折纯量 (吨)	Consumption of Chemical Fertilizers (100%) (ton)	455	628	72.5	14894	16940	87.9
农村用电量 (万千瓦时)	Consumption of Electricity(10000 kwh)	7179	5897.5	121.7	29927	27372.4	109.3
农村国内生产总值 (万元)	Rural Gross Domestic Product (10000 yuan)	71732.9	65396.1	109.7	593393.6	541464.4	109.6
第一产业	Primary Industry	5262.3	5015.0	104.9	82652	73177.2	112.9
第二产业	Secondary Industry	25737.1	26113.2	98.6	249964.2	250902.7	99.6
第三产业	Tertiary Industry	40733.5	34267.9	118.9	260777.4	217384.5	120.0
农业总产值 (万元)	Gross Output Value of Agriculture (10000 yuan)	7176.7	6663.7	107.7	121606.7	77774.9	156.4
种植业	Planting	2614.3	2478.5	105.5	44319.6	38098	116.3
林业	Forestry	663.5	538.1	123.3	2440.5	1432.8	170.3
牧业	Animal Husbandry	3341.9	3235.2	103.3	73795.5	37336.8	197.6
渔业	Fishery	557	411.8	135.3	1051.1	907.3	115.8
农作物总播种面积 (万公顷)	Sown Area of Farm Crops (10000 hectare)	0.5	0.5	100.0	5.3	5.7	93.0
粮食作物	Grain	0.4	0.4	100.0	4.4	5.3	83.0
经济作物	Industrial Crops				0.2	0.1	200.0
其他作物	Other Crops	0.1	0.1	100.0	0.7	0.3	233.3

24-5 续表2 continued

项目		Item		门头沟区 Mentougou 2000	1999	2000年为1999年% 2000as% of 1999	房山区 Fanshan 2000	1999	2000年为1999年% 2000as% of 1999
农副产品产量		Yield of Farm and Sideline Crops							
粮食	(万吨)	Grain	(10000 tons)	0.6	0.8	75.0	20.7	27.9	74.2
蔬菜	(吨)	Vegetable	(ton)	21786	22989	94.8	239703	206200	116.2
干鲜果	(吨)	Dry and Fresh Fruits	(ton)	6461	5442	118.7	67480	51413	131.3
畜产品产量		Output of Livestock Products							
生猪出栏	(头)	Slaughtered Hogs	(head)	330022	37959	869.4	344896	314223	109.8
商品猪	(头)	Commodity Hogs	(head)						
猪牛羊肉	(吨)	Pork,Beef and Mutton	(ton)	2909	3292	88.4	32659	26861	121.6
#猪肉		Pork		2226	2659	83.7	24638	23362	105.5
禽肉		Meat of Poultry	(ton)	545	254	214.6	17677	8665	204.0
禽蛋		Poultry Eggs	(ton)	1087	1339	81.2	14048	13645	103.0
牲畜年底头数	(头)	Number of Livestock(year-end)	(head)	103679	90875	114.1	532545	480611	110.8
大牲畜		Large Animals		2672	2521	106.0	17235	11510	149.7
猪		Hogs		19549	21572	90.6	236878	201613	117.5
羊		Goats and Sheep		81458	66782	122.0	278432	263488	105.7
水产品产量	(吨)	Output of Aquatic Product	(ton)	450	400	112.5	2100	2054	102.2
农村集体经济收入	(万元)	Rural Collective Economic Revenue	(10000 yuan)	144792	125844	115.1	773492.1	735083	105.2
农村集体经济利润总额	(万元)	Total Profits of Rural Collective Economy	(10000 yuan)	9189	8144	112.8	46534.8	41755	111.4
国家税金		State Taxes		5261	4888	107.6	21740	19920	109.1
集体积累		Collective Accumulation		1684	1640	102.7	9348	14316	65.3
劳动所得		Income from Work					46457.5	51038.0	91.0
乡镇企业单位数	(个)	Number of Township and Village Enterprise	(unit)	8703	7953	109.4	33903	30271	112.0
乡镇企业人数	(人)	Number of Persons of Township and Village Enterprises	(person)	32356	31373	103.1	176520	173525	101.7
乡镇企业纯利润	(万元)	Net Profit of Township and Village Enterprises	(10000 yuan)	23018	18413	125.0	137067	101919	134.5
乡镇企业固定资产原价	(万元)	Original Value of Fixed Assets of Township and Village Enterprises	(10000 yuan)	63186	56289	112.3	443243	410387	108.0
乡镇企业固定资产净值	(万元)	Net Value of Fixed Assets of Township and Village Enterprises	(10000 yuan)	45579	40962	111.3	335618	312836	107.3
工业		**Industry**							
全部工业企业单位数	(个)	Number of Enterprises	(unit)	824	880	93.6	3547	3469	102.2
国有		State-owned		5	23	21.7	24	20	120.0
集体		Collective-owned		228	315	72.4	846	1037	81.6
其他		Others		591	542	109.0	2677	2412	111.0
全部工业总产值(现价,万元)		Gross Output Value of Industry (at current prices,10000 yuan)		181976.0	162004.8	112.3	662462	586643.2	112.9
国有		State-owned		5374.7	11897.1	45.2	18729	19265	97.2
集体		Collective-owned		76489.0	50151.3	152.5	371132	375432.6	98.9
其他		Others		100112	99956.4	100.2	272601	191945.6	142.0

24-5 续表3 continued

项目	Item	门头沟区 Mentougou 2000	1999	2000年为1999年% 2000 as % of 1999	房山区 Fanshan 2000	1999	2000年为1999年% 2000 as % of 1999
全部工业总产值(1990年不变价,万元)	Gross Output Value of Industry(at constant price of 1990,10000 yuan)	172517	148420.5	116.2	600315.4	538617.7	111.5
国有	State-owned	4736.7	11663.9	40.6	14287.6	14717.7	97.1
集体	Collective-owned	57334.1	57466.9	99.8	333500.3	342231.0	97.4
其他	Others	110446	79289.7	139.3	252527.5	181669.0	139.0
全部轻工业总产值(现价,万元)	Gross Output Value of Light Industry (at current prices,10000 yuan)	70991.0	64862.7	109.4	271609.4	200976.1	135.1
以农产品为原料	Using Farm Products as Raw Materials	48293.7	44815.1	107.8	176546.2	130634.5	135.1
以非农产品为原料	Using Non-farm Products as Raw Materials	22697.3	20047.6	113.2	95063.2	70341.6	135.1
全部重工业总产值(现价,万元)	Gross Output Value of Heavy Industry (at current prices,10000 yuan)	110985.0	83557.8	132.8	390852.6	385667.1	101.3
采掘工业	Mining and Quarrying	17021.5	21295.4	79.9	71977.2	71022.3	101.3
原料工业	Raw Materials Industry	27033.5	13403.6	201.7	112498.3	111005.8	101.3
制造工业	Manufacturing Industry	66930	48858.8	137.0	206377.1	203639.0	101.3
独立核算工业企业平均职工人数 (人)	Average Number of Staff and Workers in Enterprises with Independent Accounting System (person)	9302	12029	77.3	48637	51468	94.5
#国有	State-owned	1162	2361	49.2	3997	4912	81.4
集体	Collective-owned	9574	5196	184.3	36084	40590	88.9
独立核算工业企业总产值(现价,万元)	Gross Output Value of Enterprises with Independent Accounting System (at current prices,10000 yuan)	124854	106446.0	117.3	276057.7	258314.1	106.9
#国有	State-owned	5374.7	10951.5	49.1	18729.0	19265.0	97.2
集体	Collective-owned	52480.0	38587.4	136.0	191398.3	187683.1	102.0
独立核算工业企业工业增加值 (万元)	Value Added of Enterprises with Independent Accounting System (10000 yuan)	36063.9	34188.5	105.5	119188.4	80783.7	147.5
独立核算工业企业财务指标	Financial Indicators for Enterprises with Independent Accounting System						
产品销售收入 (万元)	Sales Revenue (10000 yuan)	86532.5	89729.1	96.4	251713.1	230856.8	109.0
#国有	State-owned	4027.4	6562.3	61.4	17801.6	18253.3	97.5
产品销售成本 (万元)	Cost of Sales (10000 yuan)	66836.5	70999.6	94.1	211547.8	194950.0	108.5
#国有	State-owned	2897.4	5254.0	55.1	13979.8	14485.9	96.5
固定资产原价 (万元)	Original Value of Fixed Assets(10000 yuan)	92343.7	92682.4	99.6	228645.5	220187.2	103.8
#国有	State-owned	7384.9	17043.1	43.3	32528.0	30566.0	106.4
固定资产净值 (万元)	Net Value of Fixed Assets (10000 yuan)	69612.7	74433.8	93.5	155152.3	149718.6	103.6
#国有	State-owned	8018.8	13789.0	58.2	17841.6	18170.4	98.2
全部流动资金年平均余额 (万元)	Annual Average Balance of Circulating Funds (10000 yuan)	103915	104077.5	99.8	192456.4	189083.2	101.8
#国有	State-owned	7387.9	14223.5	51.9	17081.4	16235.2	105.2
利润总额 (万元)	Total Profits (10000 yuan)	670.5	-2913.2		6196.5	3947.7	157.0
#国有	State-owned	-121.9	-1703.1		-728.8	-1019.7	

24-5 续表4 continued

项目		Item	门头沟区 Mentougou 2000	门头沟区 Mentougou 1999	门头沟区 Mentougou 2000年为1999年% 2000as% of 1999	房山区 Fanshan 2000	房山区 Fanshan 1999	房山区 Fanshan 2000年为1999年% 2000as% of 1999
资金利税率	(%)	Ratio of Pre-tax Profits to Total of Capital(%)	8.8	2.6		4.7	6.5	
产品销售率	(%)	Ratio of Sales Value to Gross Output Value (%)	99.4	93.4		94.0	90.7	
增加值率	(%)	Ratio of Added Value to Gross Output Value (%)	30.5	37.3		43.2	31.3	
独立核算工业企业全员劳动生产率	(元/人)	Overall Labor Productivity of Enterprises with Independent Accounting System (yuan/person)	23989	25642	93.6	24506	15696	156.1
#国有		State-owned	20752	26810	77.4	17702	10123	174.9
集体		Collective-owned	24512	20676	118.6	24501	15952	153.6
商业		**Commerce**						
社会消费品零售额	(万元)	Retail Sales of Consumer Goods (10000 yuan)	180147.0	161720.8	111.4	483889.6	457476.2	105.8
按登记注册类型分		Grouped by Registered Type						
国有		State-owned	52209.6	49177.0	106.2	85552.3	83737.2	102.2
集体		Collective-owned	6198.7	21380.9	29.0	289498.4	271621.2	106.6
其他		Others	121739	91162.9	133.5	108838.9	102117.8	106.6
按类别分		Grouped by Type of Goods						
吃的商品		Food	81330.0	74626.7	109.0	138935.4	124578.3	111.5
穿的商品		Clothing	13057.7	10971.7	119.0	83658.4	79058.8	105.8
用的商品		Daily Used Articles	78643.1	70976.7	110.8	204538	205149.5	99.7
烧的商品		Fuel	7116.2	5145.7	138.3	56757.8	48689.6	116.6
网点数	(个)	Number of Outlets (unit)		8041		11272	10809	104.3
#商业		Wholesale and Retail		6526		7515	7255	103.6
饮食业		Catering		671		2473	2387	103.6
服务业		Services		530		1284	1167	110.0
#宾馆、饭店		Hotels		4		67	66	101.5
营业人员	(人)	Personnel (person)		26588		29118	29860	97.5
#商业		Wholesale and Retail		17072		21618	22485	96.1
饮食业		Catering		2257		3943	4099	96.2
服务业		Services		6770		3557	3276	108.6
#宾馆、饭店		Hotels		842		2860	2726	104.9
外经、外贸		**Foreign Economy and Trade**						
出口商品交货额	(万元)	Delivery Value of Exports (10000 yuan)	9194.6	6236.6	147.4	36654.8	25785.5	142.2
利用外资签订协议(合同)数	(个)	Number of Signed Agreements and Contracts of Foreign Capital to be Utilized (unit)	15	15	100.0	15	15	100.0
利用外资签订协议(合同)金额	(万美元)	Amount of Foreign Capital to be Utilized through Agreements and Contracts (USD 10000)	847.8	1200.9	70.6	3147.5	1201.9	261.9
实际利用外资	(万美元)	Amount of Foreign Capital Actually Used (USD 10000)	301.2	453.3	66.4	1885.6	2087.9	90.3
旅游人数	(万人)	Number of Tourists (10000 persons)	302.6	300.6	100.7	318.3	270.2	117.8
教育		**Education**						
学校数	(个)	Number of Schools (unit)	97	109	89.0	322	346	93.1
小学		Primary Schools	69	79	87.3	249	275	90.5

24-5 续表5 continued

项目		Item		门头沟区 Mentougou 2000	1999	2000年为1999年% 2000 as % of 1999	房山区 Fanshan 2000	1999	2000年为1999年% 2000 as % of 1999
普通中学		Regular Secondary School		22	24	91.7	69	67	103.0
中等专业教育		Specialized Secondary Schools		6	6	100.0	4	4	100.0
招生数	(人)	New Student Enrollment	(person)	7890	7662	103.0	29363	25355	115.8
小学		Primary Schools		1992	2026	98.3	7477	7604	98.3
初级中等学校		Junior Secondary Schools		3816	3953	96.5	17882	14134	126.5
高级中等学校		Senior Secondary Schools		1182	937	126.1	3940	3032	129.9
中等专业教育		Specialized Secondary Schools		900	746	120.6	64	585	10.9
在校学生	(人)	Student Enrollment	(person)	31355	32072	97.8	125277	132470	94.6
小学		Primary Schools		14468	16391	88.3	66696	77863	85.7
初级中等学校		Junior Secondary Schools		11542	11051	104.4	45816	40104	114.2
高级中等学校		Senior Secondary Schools		2942	2408	122.2	11693	11672	100.2
中等专业教育		Specialized Secondary Schools		2403	2222	108.1	1072	2831	37.9
毕业生	(人)	Graduates	(person)	8186	8572	95.5	33520	30764	109.0
小学		Primary Schools		3759	3984	94.4	18343	14709	124.7
初级中等学校		Junior Secondary Schools		3191	3489	91.5	11367	11994	94.8
高级中等学校		Senior Secondary Schools		600	543	110.5	3394	3273	103.7
中等专业教育		Specialized Secondary Schools		636	556	114.4	416	788	52.8
达到"国家体育标准"学生数	(人)	Number of Students Come to the Standard for State Physical Training	(person)	25707	26732	96.2	117296	121364	96.6
幼儿园、托儿所个数	(个)	Number of Kindergardens	(unit)	22	20	110.0	111	176	63.1
幼儿入托数	(人)	New Enrollment	(person)	1975	1882	104.9	8856	7986	110.9
文化		**Culture**							
文化馆、站	(个)	Cultural Centers	(unit)	15	15	100.0	24	13	184.6
公共图书馆	(个)	Public Libraries	(unit)	1	1	100.0	1	1	100.0
公共图书馆藏书	(万册)	Collection	(10000 volume)	22	22	100.0	12	7	171.4
电影放映单位	(个)	Film Projection Units	(unit)	5	5	100.0	8	12	66.7
区级以上重点文物保护单位	(个)	Cultural Relics Preserved at District Level and above	(unit)	74	74	100.0	68	68	100.0
卫生		**Health**							
卫生机构数	(个)	Number of Health Institutions	(unit)	28	28	100.0	44	44	100.0
#医院		Hospitals		5	5	100.0	6	6	100.0
卫生院		Clinics		15	15	100.0	26	26	100.0
床位数		Number of Beds	(unit)	722	736	98.1	1719	1730	99.4
#医院		Hospitals		603	623	96.8	1139	1098	103.7
卫生院		Clinics		93	93	100.0	554	596	93.0
平均每千人拥有床位数	(张)	Average Number of Beds Per 1000 Persons	(unit)	3.1	3.1	100.0	2.3	2.3	100.0
卫生技术人员	(人)	Medical Technical Personnel	(person)	1171	1192	98.2	2726	2536	107.5
#医生		Doctors	(person)	585	599	97.7	1871	1506	124.2
公用设施		**Public Utilities**							
区级以上公园	(个)	Parks at District Level and above	(unit)	4	4	100.0	8	4	200.0
体育场馆	(个)	Stadiums and Gymnasiums	(unit)	2	2	100.0	281	257	109.3
道路长度	(公里)	Length of Roads	(km)	393	367.4	107.1	1865.2	1796	103.9

24-6 昌平区、顺义区国民经济主要指标
MAIN NATIONAL ECONOMIC INDICATORS FOR CHANGPING AND SHUNYI DISTRICTS

项目		Item		昌平区 Changping 2000	1999	2000年为1999年% 2000as% of 1999	顺义区 Shunyi 2000	1999	2000年为1999年% 2000as% of 1999
综合		**General Survey**							
国内生产总值	(万元)	Gross Domestic Product	(10000 yuan)	581047	510631.1	113.8	1029373.2	868554.2	118.5
第一产业		Primary Industry		49515.9	48281.9	102.6	171453	157252.4	109.0
第二产业		Secondary Industry		221914	194474.9	114.1	536815	431094.7	124.5
第三产业		Tertiary Industry		309618	267874.3	115.6	321105	280207.7	114.6
财政收入	(万元)	Fiscal Revenue	(10000 yuan)	30183	21105	143.0	49210	36002	136.7
#增值税		Increased Value Tax		5772	4749	121.5	8827		
营业税		Operating Tax		10090	7301	138.2	13763	16263	84.6
个人所得税		Private Income Tax			2039			5572	
企业所得税		Enterprise Income Tax		2655	2326	114.1	15171	13845	109.6
财政支出	(万元)	Fiscal Expenditure	(10000 yuan)	70913	53407	132.8	111891	85936	130.2
#基本建设支出		Capital Construction		2637	2170	121.5	7228	4486	161.1
支援农业生产支出		Supporting Agriculture		6043	5141	117.5	18549	17613	105.3
文教卫生事业费		Culture,Education and Health		18637	15518	120.1	26416	24481	107.9
人口和劳动力		**Population and Labor Force**							
总人口	(人)	Total Population	(person)	501166	475945	105.3	540288	540398	100.0
常住户籍人口	(人)	Permanent Registered Population	(person)	427771	424919	100.7	540288	540398	100.0
#非农业人口		Non-agriculture		180196	173669	103.8	117999	109920	107.3
男		Male		212517	211780	100.3	266191	266275	100.0
女		Female		215254	213139	101.0	274097	274123	100.0
出生率	(‰)	Birth Rate	(‰)	9.72	9.30		7.15	9.86	
死亡率	(‰)	Death Rate	(‰)	9.68	5.27		7.95	7.60	
自然增长率	(‰)	Natural Growth Rate	(‰)	0.04	4.03		-0.8	2.2	
从业人员	(人)	Employment	(person)	188475	199076	94.7	271894	271051	100.3
按产业分		Grouped by Industry							
第一产业		Primary Industry		45544	49182	92.6	59856	63765	93.9
第二产业		Secondary Industry		61517	54072	113.8	102518	97281	105.4
第三产业		Tertiary Industry		80412	95822	83.9	109520	110005	99.6
按职工非职工分		Grouped by Staff and Workers or Non-staff-and-worker							
职工人数		Staff and Worker		70692	65744	107.5	70658	63749	110.8
#国有单位		State-owned		33839	36848	91.8	45198	46040	98.2
集体单位		Collective-owned		15342	16382	93.7	10024	11073	90.5
城镇个体劳动者		Urban and Rural Individuals		3414	1545	221.0	17720	19916	89.0
劳动工资		**Wages**							
工资总额	(万元)	Total Wages	(10000 yuan)	79381.2	62027.9	128.0	95993.4	68865.3	139.4
#国有单位		State-owned		43541.2	38175.1	114.1	59237.9	51634.1	114.7
集体单位		Collective-owned		13044.0	12264.1	106.4	9320.4	9059.4	102.9
职工平均工资	(元)	Average Wage	(yuan)	11024	9406	117.2	13621	10674	127.6
固定资产投资		**Investment in Fixed Assets**							
全社会固定资产投资	(万元)	Total Investment in Fixed Assets	(10000 yuan)	182978.0	92691.2	197.4	241710	210000	115.1
按建设性质分		Grouped by Type of Construction							
#基本建设投资		Capital Construction		158796.0	74763.7	212.4	158340	140000	113.1
更新改造投资		Innovation and Replacement		24182.0	17927.5	134.9	83370	70000	119.1

24-6 续表1 continued

项目	Item	昌平区 Changping			顺义区 Shunyi		
		2000	1999	2000年为1999年% 2000as% of 1999	2000	1999	2000年为1999年% 2000as% of 1999
按登记注册类型分	Grouped by Registered Type						
#国有单位	State-owned	33629.0	39698.5	84.7	125000	105000	119.0
集体单位	Collective-owned	44126.0	28488.2	154.9	96600	84000	115.0
新增固定资产 (万元)	Incremental Fixed Assets(10000 yuan)	93096.0	95466.0	97.5	174938	149000	117.4
#国有单位	State-owned	32351.0	45775.5	70.7	63250	55000	115.0
集体单位	Collective-owned	26529.0	24541.0	108.1	18400	16000	115.0
房屋施工面积 (万平方米)	Floor Space of Buildings under Construction (10000 sq.m)	145.2	92.2	157.5	243	120	202.5
#国有单位	State-owned	44.7	46.4	96.3	102	70	145.7
集体单位	Collective-owned	43.9	26.5	165.7	58	42	138.1
房屋竣工面积 (万平方米)	Floor Space of Buildings Completed (10000 sq.m)	56.7	52.0	109.0	105.5	88.7	118.9
#国有单位	State-owned	21.5	26.3	81.7	60.1	51.0	117.8
#住宅	Residence	12.4	21.2	58.5	44.1	37.5	117.6
#集体单位	Collective-owned	21.4	19.2	111.5	38.2	32.0	119.4
#住宅	Residence	6.6	7.2	91.7	12.0	10.5	114.3
农村经济	**Rural Economy**						
农村劳动力 (人)	Labor Force (person)	118524	118142	100.3	184199	189018	97.5
种植业	Planting	32270	35370	91.2	70706	45398	155.7
林业	Forestry	6000	5690	105.4	2866	2185	131.2
牧业	Animal Husbandry	6523	5839	111.7	12902	13001	99.2
渔业	Fishery	751	862	87.1	1873	2204	85.0
农村工业	Rural Industry	22315	22491	99.2	53682	55423	96.9
农村建筑业	Rural Construction	8888	8057	110.3	15713	15476	101.5
农村运输业	Rural Transportation	13083	12414	105.4	13783	12311	112.0
农村商、饮食业、服务业	Commerce,Catering and Services	9291	7650	121.5	11901	11742	101.4
耕地面积 (公顷)	Area under Cultivation (hectare)	23953.4	24178.9	99.1	46988.1	50290.7	93.4
农业机械总动力 (千瓦)	Total Power of Agricultural Machinery (kw)	212822	206464	103.1	531617	537816.0	98.8
化肥施用实物量 (吨)	Consumption of Chemical Fertilizers (ton)	20731	25500	81.3	83777.7	88613.0	94.5
化肥施用折纯量 (吨)	Consumption of Chemical Fertilizers (100%) (ton)	8259	10339	79.9	30988	34484	89.9
农村用电量 (万千瓦时)	Consumption of Electricity (10000 kwh)	26613.0	24841.4	107.1	34137.6	34923.2	97.8
农村国内生产总值 (万元)	Rural Gross Domestic Product (10000 yuan)	325879.2	276095.9	118.0	518967	462727.0	112.2
第一产业	Primary Industry	49515.9	48281.9	102.6	169020	156083.2	108.3
第二产业	Secondary Industry	107779.3	88363.2	122.0	187140	165067.9	113.4
第三产业	Tertiary Industry	168584.0	139450.8	120.9	162807	141575.9	115.0
农业总产值 (万元)	Gross Output Value of Agriculture (10000 yuan)	118875.8	115565.9	102.9	276464	231542.8	119.4
种植业	Planting	52889.0	51295.1	103.1	126752	76253.3	166.2
林业	Forestry	4305.6	4292.2	100.3	2738.4	1342.4	204.0
牧业	Animal Husbandry	54695.2	53141.5	102.9	134724	143084.3	94.2
渔业	Fishery	6986.0	6483.1	107.8	12249.5	10862.8	112.8
农作物总播种面积 (万公顷)	Sown Area of Farm Crops (10000 hectare)	3.1	3.6	86.1	7.5	9.2	81.5
粮食作物	Grain	2.6	3.2	81.3	5.1	7.7	66.2
经济作物	Industrial Crops						
其他作物	Other Crops	0.3	0.3	100.0	2.4	1.5	160.0

24-6 续表2 continued

项目	Item	昌平区 Changping 2000	1999	2000年为1999年% 2000as% of 1999	顺义区 Shunyi 2000	1999	2000年为1999年% 2000as% of 1999
农副产品产量	Yield of Farm and Sideline Crops						
粮食 (万吨)	Grain (10000 tons)	11.8	16.3	72.4	23.9	37.8	63.2
蔬菜 (吨)	Vegetable (ton)	126923	122148	103.9	1008552	850208.0	118.6
干鲜果 (吨)	Dry and Fresh Fruits (ton)	55005	52805	104.2	45616.8	41968.0	108.7
畜产品产量	Output of Livestock Products						
生猪出栏 (头)	Slaughtered Hogs (head)	246146	250817	98.1	1481711	1340344	110.5
猪牛羊肉 (吨)	Pork,Beef and Mutton (ton)	16740	14507	115.4	1481711	1340344	110.5
#猪肉	Pork	13795	12610	109.4	115599.9	123057.0	93.9
禽肉	Meat of Poultry (ton)	15221	16021	95.0	99960.5	108843.0	91.8
禽蛋	Poultry Eggs (ton)	6893	8122	84.9	79298.6	72024.0	110.1
牲畜年底头数 (头)	Number of Livestock (year-end) (head)	201629	207050	97.4	21340.2	22408.0	95.2
大牲畜	Large Animals	14335	13350	107.4	41912	30988	135.3
猪	Hogs	108287	124359	87.1	857426	824362	104.0
羊	Goats and Sheep	79007	69341	113.9	159600	119326	133.8
水产品产量 (吨)	Output of Aquatic Product (ton)	8048.3	8046.0	100.0	16072.5	16036.8	100.2
农村集体经济收入 (万元)	Rural Collective Economic Revenue (10000 yuan)	395823.4	346022.5	114.4	1233882	1125968	109.6
农村集体经济利润总额 (万元)	Total Profits of Rural Collective Economy (10000 yuan)	35955.6	27282.5	131.8	325104	296678	109.6
国家税金	State Taxes	21500.0	19591.1	109.7	19784	17683	111.9
集体积累	Collective Accumulation	14913.1	8852.1	168.5	33876	28405	119.3
劳动所得	Income from Work	129799.0	112642.4	115.2	221390	210707	105.1
乡镇企业单位数 (个)	Number of Township and Village Enterprise (unit)	1018	1078	94.4	835	922	90.6
乡镇企业人数 (人)	Number of Persons of Township and Village Enterprises (person)	45163	43862	103.0	82395	82396	100.0
乡镇企业纯利润 (万元)	Net Profit of Township and Village Enterprises (10000 yuan)	21749	14826	146.7	24913	25964	96.0
乡镇企业固定资产原价 (万元)	Original Value of Fixed Assets of Township and Village Enterprises (10000 yuan)	212653	167890	126.7	344276	334505	102.9
乡镇企业固定资产净值 (万元)	Net Value of Fixed Assets of Township and Village Enterprises (10000 yuan)	159570	121758	131.1	243644	244103	99.8
工业	**Industry**						
全部工业企业单位数 (个)	Number of Enterprises (unit)	1203	1207	99.7	2430	2971	81.8
国有	State-owned	58	57	101.8	60	60	100.0
集体	Collective-owned	688	793	86.8	525	624	84.1
其他	Others	457	357	128.0	1845	2287	80.7
全部工业总产值 (现价,万元)	Gross Output Value of Industry (at current prices,10000 yuan)	556300.8	453914.9	122.6	2273333	1154822.3	196.9
国有	State-owned	46569.5	45879.2	101.5	375294.0	311883.4	120.3
集体	Collective-owned	195649.0	194083.8	100.8	284743.3	282013.5	101.0
其他	Others	314082.3	213951.9	146.8	1613295	560925.4	287.6

24-6 续表3 continued

项目	Item	昌平区 Changping 2000	昌平区 Changping 1999	昌平区 Changping 2000年为1999年% 2000as% of 1999	顺义区 Shunyi 2000	顺义区 Shunyi 1999	顺义区 Shunyi 2000年为1999年% 2000as% of 1999
全部工业总产值(1990年不变价,万元)	Gross Output Value of Industry(at constant price of 1990,10000 yuan)	526004.8	440411.5	119.4	2421751	1065147.4	227.4
国有	State-owned	37158.8	38000.0	97.8	296031.6	239046.3	123.8
集体	Collective-owned	197096.0	193410.0	101.9	264466.0	265390.8	99.7
其他	Others	291750.0	209001.5	139.6	1861253.0	560710.3	331.9
全部轻工业总产值(现价,万元)	Gross Output Value of Light Industry (at current prices,10000 yuan)	269262.2	232477.1	115.8	894597.3	780505.6	114.6
以农产品为原料	Using Farm Products as Raw Materials	153488.5	141999.1	108.1	613297.3	572521.2	107.1
以非农产品为原料	Using Non-farm Products as Raw Materials	115773.7	90478.0	128.0	281300.0	207984.4	135.3
全部重工业总产值(现价,万元)	Gross Output Value of Heavy Industry (at current prices,10000 yuan)	287038.6	221437.8	129.6	1378735	374316.7	368.3
采掘工业	Mining and Quarrying	42535.5	10187.9	417.5	1218.3	2710.7	44.9
原料工业	Raw Materials Industry	19981.3	15615.3	128.0	84960.2	81601.1	104.1
制造工业	Manufacturing Industry	224521.8	195634.6	114.8	1292557	29004.9	4456.3
独立核算工业企业平均职工人数 (人)	Average Number of Staff and Workers in Enterprises with Independent Accounting System (person)	51179	52315	97.8	99914	100654	99.3
#国有	State-owned	2943	3486	84.4	21537	19581	110.0
集体	Collective-owned	27902	32472	85.9	41802	49557	84.4
独立核算工业企业总产值(现价,万元)	Gross Output Value of Enterprises with Independent Accounting System (at current prices,10000 yuan)	532075.0	431737.3	123.2	2196815	1070257.1	205.3
#国有	State-owned	22765.4	24667.7	92.3	375294.0	311883.4	120.3
集体	Collective-owned	195651.0	191710.9	102.1	284743.3	282013.5	101.0
独立核算工业企业工业增加值 (万元)	Value Added of Enterprises with Independent Accounting System (10000 yuan)	166638.7	148898.8	111.9	405237.3	255111.6	158.8
独立核算工业企业财务指标	Financial Indicators for Enterprises with Independent Accounting System						
产品销售收入 (万元)	Sales Revenue (10000 yuan)	503147.8	390318.6	128.9	2349153	1026557.6	228.8
#国有	State-owned	25894.8	27878.2	92.9	373318.5	316974.0	117.8
产品销售成本 (万元)	Cost of Sales (10000 yuan)	400481.1	312673.9	128.1	1982604	801995.2	247.2
#国有	State-owned	18946.0	21570.3	87.8	249663.6	210504.8	118.6
固定资产原价 (万元)	Original Value of Fixed Assets(10000 yuan)	318256.0	289388.7	110.0	1101171	892364.6	123.4
#国有	State-owned	30061.6	21962.1	136.9	471323.5	339970.1	138.6
固定资产净值 (万元)	Net Value of Fixed Assets (10000 yuan)	216007.3	200725.7	107.6	813432.0	685640.1	118.6
#国有	State-owned	18794.0	13243.3	141.9	352521.9	267190.7	131.9
全部流动资金年平均余额 (万元)	Annual Average Balance of Circulating Funds (10000 yuan)	408891.8	336758.1	121.4	1286124	700776.9	183.5
#国有	State-owned	23629.3	23734.8	99.6	247983.1	195229.5	127.0
利润总额 (万元)	Total Profits (10000 yuan)	30953.2	16375.4	189.0	143433.2	55797.8	257.1
#国有	State-owned	-100.5	-1606.1		48950.6	48328.0	101.3

24-6 续表4 continued

项目	Item	昌平区 Changping 2000	1999	2000年为1999年% 2000as% of 1999	顺义区 Shunyi 2000	1999	2000年为1999年% 2000as% of 1999
资金利税率 (%)	Ratio of Pre-tax Profits to Total of Capital(%)	8.1	6.5		9.7	10.0	
产品销售率 (%)	Ratio of Sales Value to Gross Output Value (%)	96.9	94.7		99.0	95.9	
增加值率 (%)	Ratio of Added Value to Gross Output Value (%)	31.3	34.5		20.6	24.5	
独立核算工业企业全员劳动生产率 (元/人)	Overall Labor Productivity of Enterprises with Independent Accounting System (yuan/person)	32559	28461	114.4	40558.6	25345.4	160.0
#国有	State-owned	25676	22477	114.2	53303.5	68455.8	77.9
集体	Collective-owned	23637	20861	113.3	13250.7	11238.0	117.9
商业	**Commerce**						
社会消费品零售额 (万元)	Retail Sales of Consumer Goods (10000 yuan)	220045	185147	118.8	350415	323403	108.4
按登记注册类型分	Grouped by Registered Type						
国有	State-owned	39792	27171	146.5	94525	85797	110.2
集体	Collective-owned	103505	79020	131.0	81995	77875	105.3
其他	Others	76748	78956	97.2	173895	159731	108.9
按类别分	Grouped by Type of Goods						
吃的商品	Food	88074	74798	117.7	121000	113191	106.9
穿的商品	Clothing	16673	17871	93.3	71000	48510	146.4
用的商品	Daily Used Articles	87730	76334	114.9	137000	129361	105.9
烧的商品	Fuel	27568	16144	170.8	21415	32341	66.2
网点数 (个)	Number of Outlets (unit)	10508	9984	105.2	7455	5436	137.1
#商业	Wholesale and Retail	8057	6616	121.8	4304	3764	114.3
饮食业	Catering	1226	2638	46.5	991	630	157.3
服务业	Services	1200	704	170.5	2160	1042	207.3
#宾馆、饭店	Hotels	2	2	100.0	14	14	100.0
营业人员 (人)	Personnel (person)	35875	28093	127.7	52875	33665	157.1
#商业	Wholesale and Retail	26880	18326	146.7	36091	21845	165.2
饮食业	Catering	6104	7091	86.1	6072	3633	167.1
服务业	Services	2662	2406	110.6	10715	8187	130.9
#宾馆、饭店	Hotels	309	350	88.3	1786	1701	105.0
外经、外贸	**Foreign Economy and Trade**						
出口商品交货额 (万元)	Delivery Value of Exports (10000 yuan)	65074.4	59642.2	109.1	593226	225353.6	263.2
利用外资签订协议(合同)数 (个)	Number of Signed Agreements and Contracts of Foreign Capital to be Utilized (unit)	22	24	91.7	39	23	169.6
利用外资签订协议(合同)金额 (万美元)	Amount of Foreign Capital to be Utilized through Agreements and Contracts (USD 10000)	3383.6	2453.4	137.9	6032.0	1792.7	336.5
实际利用外资 (万美元)	Amount of Foreign Capital Actually Used (USD 10000)	1603.7	2488.5	64.4	10162.3	10272.5	98.9
旅游人数 (万人)	Number of Tourists (10000 persons)	1107	1055	104.9	63.7	72.5	87.9
教育	**Education**						
学校数 (个)	Number of Schools (unit)	179	184	97.3	169	187	90.4
小学	Primary Schools	134	141	95.0	128	146	87.7

24-6 续表5 continued

项目		Item		昌平区 Changping 2000	1999	2000年为1999年% 2000 as % of 1999	顺义区 Shunyi 2000	1999	2000年为1999年% 2000 as % of 1999
普通中学		Regular Secondary School		44	42	104.8	39	39	100.0
中等专业教育		Specialized Secondary Schools		1	1	100.0	4	2	200.0
招生数	(人)	New Student Enrollment	(person)	13661	13033	104.8	24310	22990	105.7
小学		Primary Schools		3845	3538	108.7	4984	5003	99.6
初级中等学校		Junior Secondary Schools		7313	6878	106.3	15803	13619	116.0
高级中等学校		Senior Secondary Schools		2503	2554	98.0	3523	2792	126.2
中等专业教育		Specialized Secondary Schools			63		1074	1576	68.1
在校学生	(人)	Student Enrollment	(person)	55463	58690	94.5	104987	110209	95.3
小学		Primary Schools		26609	30019	88.6	54768	64810	84.5
初级中等学校		Junior Secondary Schools		20836	19652	106.0	40977	34134	120.0
高级中等学校		Senior Secondary Schools		4883	8588	56.9	9242	7720	119.7
中等专业教育		Specialized Secondary Schools		135	431	31.3	3020	3545	85.2
毕业生	(人)	Graduates	(person)	15725	15992	98.3	27176	27188	100.0
小学		Primary Schools		7321	7043	103.9	15480	13749	112.6
初级中等学校		Junior Secondary Schools		5370	6055	88.7	9183	9613	95.5
高级中等学校		Senior Secondary Schools		2915	2603	112.0	2513	2236	112.4
中等专业教育		Specialized Secondary Schools		119	291	40.9	1580	1590	99.4
达到"国家体育标准"学生数	(人)	Number of Students Come to the Standard for State Physical Training	(person)	54196	57931	93.6	86182	85645	100.6
幼儿园、托儿所个数	(个)	Number of Kindergardens	(unit)	170	183	92.9	105	113	92.9
幼儿入托数	(人)	New Enrollment	(person)	9737	10502	92.7	8836	9155	96.5
文化		**Culture**							
文化馆、站	(个)	Cultural Centers	(unit)	21	26	80.8	20	20	100.0
公共图书馆	(个)	Public Libraries	(unit)	1	1	100.0	1	1	100.0
公共图书馆藏书	(万册)	Collection	(10000 volume)	15.0	17.8	84.3	16	15	106.7
电影放映单位	(个)	Film Projection Units	(unit)	41	41	100.0	10	30	33.3
区级以上重点文物保护单位	(个)	Cultural Relics Preserved at District Level and above	(unit)	73	73	100.0	9	9	100.0
卫生		**Health**							
卫生机构数	(个)	Number of Health Institutions	(unit)	58	57	101.8	47	47	100.0
#医院		Hospitals		18	18	100.0	14	14	100.0
卫生院		Clinics		26	26	100.0	23	23	100.0
床位数		Number of Beds	(unit)	5162	4398	117.4	1955	1901	102.8
#医院		Hospitals		3902	3759	103.8	1592	1498	106.3
卫生院		Clinics		432	341	126.7	332	371	89.5
平均每千人拥有床位数	(张)	Average Number of Beds Per 1000 Persons	(unit)	12.4	10.4	119.2	3.1	3.5	88.6
卫生技术人员	(人)	Medical Technical Personnel	(person)	4010	3696	108.5	2771	2879	96.2
#医生		Doctors	(person)	1682	1509	111.5	1404	1533	91.6
公用设施		**Public Utilities**							
区级以上公园	(个)	Parks at District Level and above	(unit)	8	8	100.0	3	3	100.0
体育场馆	(个)	Stadiums and Gymnasiums	(unit)	2	2	100.0	7	4	175.0
道路长度	(公里)	Length of Roads	(km)	1335.4	1323.9	100.9	1565	1516	103.2

24-7 通州区、大兴县国民经济主要指标
MAIN NATIONAL ECONOMIC INDICATORS FOR TONGZHOU DISTRICT AND DAXING COUNTY

项目	Item	通州区 Tongzhou 2000	1999	2000年为1999年% 2000 as% of 1999	大兴县 Daxing 2000	1999	2000年为1999年% 2000 as% of 1999
综合	**General Survey**						
国内生产总值 (万元)	Gross Domestic Product (10000 yuan)	571282.0	500564	114.1	534245	447552.7	119.4
第一产业	Primary Industry	106736.0	100695	106.0	111283	106926.1	104.1
第二产业	Secondary Industry	193394.0	158137	122.3	174573	135517.8	128.8
第三产业	Tertiary Industry	271152.0	241733	112.2	248389	205108.8	121.1
财政收入 (万元)	Fiscal Revenue (10000 yuan)	35164	30319	116.0	30182	23986	125.8
#增值税	Increased Value Tax				3749	2761	135.8
营业税	Operating Tax	13312	15314	86.9	11710	8666	135.1
个人所得税	Private Income Tax		2444			1861	
企业所得税	Enterprise Income Tax	5736	6915	83.0	4759	4124	115.4
财政支出 (万元)	Fiscal Expenditure (10000 yuan)	96363	60740	158.6	92435	65975	140.1
#基本建设支出	Capital Construction	6140	1579	388.9	5392	4295	125.5
支援农业生产支出	Supporting Agriculture	9790	6417	152.6	9378	5445	172.2
文教卫生事业费	Culture,Education and Health	18516	15765	117.5	26097	20655	126.3
人口和劳动力	**Population and Labor Force**						
总人口 (人)	Total Population (person)	653126	642139	101.7	657630	604800	108.7
常住户籍人口 (人)	Permanent Registered Population (person)	597395	597139	100.0	527630	523800	100.7
#非农业人口	Non-agriculture	190763	184977	103.1	155952	149240	104.5
男	Male	294219	294140	100.0	263832	262092	100.7
女	Female	303176	302999	100.1	263798	261708	100.8
出生率 (‰)	Birth Rate (‰)	6.21	5.37		6.0	6.2	
死亡率 (‰)	Death Rate (‰)	7.51	6.98		7.3	5.4	
自然增长率 (‰)	Natural Growth Rate (‰)	-1.30	-1.61		-1.3	0.8	
从业人员 (人)	Employment (person)	243673	243225	100.2	267211	253226.0	105.5
按产业分	Grouped by Industry						
第一产业	Primary Industry	81474	83900	97.1	125079	128073.0	97.7
第二产业	Secondary Industry	82188	78444	104.8	60763	53326.0	113.9
第三产业	Tertiary Industry	80011	80881	98.9	81369	71827.0	113.3
按职工非职工分	Grouped by Staff and Workers or Non-staff-and-worker						
职工人数	Staff and Worker	55257	53521	103.2	87627	60937	143.8
#国有单位	State-owned	33814	37287	90.7	32736	32576	100.5
集体单位	Collective-owned	6441	8950	72.0	17113	8826	193.9
城镇个体劳动者	Urban and Rural Individuals	4682	5101	91.8	4045	2221	182.1
劳动工资	**Wages**						
工资总额 (万元)	Total Wages (10000 yuan)	61563.6	51536.4	119.5	78614.5	58627.1	134.1
#国有单位	State-owned	43928.4	39481.2	111.3	41970.5	35376.8	118.6
集体单位	Collective-owned	5197.8	6025.5	86.3	6804.4	6423.1	105.9
职工平均工资 (元)	Average Wage (yuan)	10937	9468	115.5	11241	9659	116.4
固定资产投资	**Investment in Fixed Assets**						
全社会固定资产投资 (万元)	Total Investment in Fixed Assets (10000 yuan)	137838	61984	222.4	145510	77193	188.5
按建设性质分	Grouped by Type of Construction						
#基本建设投资	Capital Construction	100111	41747	239.8	12718	17630	72.1
更新改造投资	Innovation and Replacement	37727	20237	186.4	1387	2338	59.3

24-7 续表 1 continued

项目 Item	通州区 Tongzhou 2000	1999	2000年为1999年% 2000 as % of 1999	大兴县 Daxing 2000	1999	2000年为1999年% 2000 as % of 1999
按登记注册类型分 Grouped by Registered Type						
#国有单位 State-owned	37283	25022	149.0	34042	27267	124.8
集体单位 Collective-owned	20775	10806	192.3	2743	2488	110.2
新增固定资产 (万元) Incremental Fixed Assets (10000 yuan)	97670	52086	187.5	71761	63311	113.3
#国有单位 State-owned	29828	26988	110.5	30724	43305	70.9
集体单位 Collective-owned	18297	10762	170.0	16930	2038	8.3倍
房屋施工面积 (万平方米) Floor Space of Buildings under Construction (10000 sq.m)	133.3	65.8	202.6	133.3	71.5	186.4
#国有单位 State-owned	26.6	28.9	92.0	34.0	38.8	87.6
集体单位 Collective-owned	16.2	9.0	180.0	1.7	2.6	65.4
房屋竣工面积 (万平方米) Floor Space of Buildings Completed (10000 sq.m)	70.9	46.3	153.1	37.4	39.3	95.2
#国有单位 State-owned	12.9	22.6	57.1	13.3	27.6	48.2
#住宅 Residence	10.7	21.2	50.5	31.5	20.0	157.5
#集体单位 Collective-owned	16.0	8.9	179.8	1.7	2.0	85.0
#住宅 Residence	0.4	0.7	57.1	1.0	1.6	62.5
农村经济 Rural Economy						
农村劳动力 (人) Labor Force (person)	183734	184599	99.5	195532	191692	102.0
种植业 Planting	64634	69844	92.5	106948	112834	94.8
林业 Forestry	3072	2111	145.5	8199	5943	138.0
牧业 Animal Husbandry	10006	8544	117.1	8607	8105	106.2
渔业 Fishery	2604	2353	110.7	555	539	103.0
农村工业 Rural Industry	43725	44452	98.4	19607	20833	94.1
农村建筑业 Rural Construction	15693	14875	105.5	7269	6220	116.9
农村运输业 Rural Transportation	13180	12751	103.4	9498	7417	128.1
农村商、饮食业、服务业 Commerce,Catering and Services	30820	29669	103.9	9083	7880	115.3
耕地面积 (公顷) Area under Cultivation (hectare)	49180.9	49867	98.6	50935.8	52308.3	97.4
农业机械总动力 (千瓦) Total Power of Agricultural Machinery (kw)	369852	381362	97.0	585097	581800	100.6
化肥施用实物量 (吨) Consumption of Chemical Fertilizers (ton)	93173	99244	93.9	106612	109350	97.5
化肥施用折纯量 (吨) Consumption of Chemical Fertilizers (100%) (ton)	34380	34862	98.6	31594	31870	99.1
农村用电量 (万千瓦时) Consumption of Electricity (10000 kwh)	36415	23762	153.2	29393	28034.2	104.8
农村国内生产总值 (万元) Rural Gross Domestic Product (10000 yuan)	400746	339030	118.2	389705	334709.1	116.4
第一产业 Primary Industry	106736	100695	106.0	110814	106926.1	103.6
第二产业 Secondary Industry	172509	135203	127.6	134962	100264.3	134.6
第三产业 Tertiary Industry	121501	130133	93.4	143930	127518.7	112.9
农业总产值 (万元) Gross Output Value of Agriculture (10000 yuan)	120425	111279	108.2	154904	141717.7	109.3
种植业 Planting	67817.3	69132.8	98.1	101978	97909.7	104.2
林业 Forestry	1147.1	756.1	151.7	1510.9	1397.7	108.1
牧业 Animal Husbandry	41191.7	33328.4	123.6	49112.6	40476.4	121.3
渔业 Fishery	9354.2	7711.4	121.3	2302.2	1933.9	119.0
农作物总播种面积 (万公顷) Sown Area of Farm Crops (10000 hectare)	6.8	9.2	73.9	8.3	8.4	98.8
粮食作物 Grain	4.4	7.3	60.3	4.5	5.4	83.3
经济作物 Industrial Crops	0.3	0.2	150.0	0.5	0.4	125.0
其他作物 Other Crops	2.1	1.7	123.5	3.3	2.6	126.9

24-7 续表 2 continued

项目		Item	通州区 Tongzhou 2000	1999	2000年为1999年% 2000 as% of 1999	大兴县 Daxing 2000	1999	2000年为1999年% 2000 as% of 1999
农副产品产量		Yield of Farm and Sideline Crops						
粮食	(万吨)	Grain (10000 tons)	22.4	38.3	58.5	23.1	28.3	81.6
蔬菜	(吨)	Vegetable (ton)	859169	756107	113.6	1112582	984891	113.0
干鲜果	(吨)	Dry and Fresh Fruits (ton)	42441	33065	128.4	95488	85106	112.2
畜产品产量		Output of Livestock Products						
生猪出栏	(头)	Slaughtered Hogs (head)	443301	426598	103.9	395543	382075	103.5
商品猪	(头)	Commodity Hogs (head)						
猪牛羊肉	(吨)	Pork,Beef and Mutton (ton)	36994	34996	105.7	30116	28051	107.4
#猪肉		Pork	31160	31098	100.2	25016	24140	103.6
禽肉		Meat of Poultry (ton)	18622	9345	199.3	26046	15137	172.1
禽蛋		Poultry Eggs (ton)	13725	14795	92.8	29441	28419	103.6
牲畜年底头数	(头)	Number of Livestock(year-end) (head)	383493	352577	108.8	437516	385585	113.5
大牲畜		Large Animals	21847	14552	150.1	17507	14031	124.8
猪		Hogs	254041	245650	103.4	253984	231538	109.7
羊		Goats and Sheep	107605	92375	116.5	166025	140016	118.6
水产品产量	(吨)	Output of Aquatic Product (ton)	11669	13460	86.7	4646	4634	100.3
农村集体经济收入	(万元)	Rural Collective Economic Revenue (10000 yuan)	489345	444857	110.0	1225235.5	1009331.2	121.4
农村集体经济利润总额	(万元)	Total Profits of Rural Collective Economy (10000 yuan)	34796	33010	105.4	69206.2	53541.7	129.3
国家税金		State Taxes	24248	20914	115.9	35827.2	26756.1	133.9
集体积累		Collective Accumulation	20153	15668	128.6	28652.4	23738.3	120.7
劳动所得		Income from Work	47286	45974	102.9	198543.0	175094.9	113.4
乡镇企业单位数	(个)	Number of Township and Village Enterprise (unit)	14077	12816	109.8	1340	1291	103.8
乡镇企业人数	(人)	Number of Persons of Township and Village Enterprises (person)	115944	109652	105.7	63289	51663	122.5
乡镇企业纯利润	(万元)	Net Profit of Township and Village Enterprises (10000 yuan)	65430	55934	117.0	37183	29055	128.0
乡镇企业固定资产原价	(万元)	Original Value of Fixed Assets of Township and Village Enterprises (10000 yuan)	475154	367728	129.2	445515	291097	153.0
乡镇企业固定资产净值	(万元)	Net Value of Fixed Assets of Township and Village Enterprises (10000 yuan)	370390	266534	139.0	364378	231530	157.4
工业		**Industry**						
全部工业企业单位数	(个)	Number of Enterprises (unit)	3524	2794	126.1	2541	2292	110.9
国有		State-owned	38	26	146.2	217	213	101.9
集体		Collective-owned	861	2405	35.8	906	944	96.0
其他		Others	2625	363	723.1	1418	1135	124.9
全部工业总产值(现价, 万元)		Gross Output Value of Industry (at current prices,10000 yuan)	573339	542952	105.6	705405.7	577266.5	122.2
国有		State-owned	29323.8	26379.5	111.2	37484.0	38211.8	98.1
集体		Collective-owned	216894	379977.0	57.1	179958.9	177315.9	101.5
其他		Others	327122	136596	239.5	492962.8	361738.8	136.3

24-7 续表 3 continued

项目	Item	通州区 Tongzhou 2000	通州区 Tongzhou 1999	通州区 Tongzhou 2000年为1999年% 2000 as % of 1999	大兴县 Daxing 2000	大兴县 Daxing 1999	大兴县 Daxing 2000年为1999年% 2000 as % of 1999
全部工业总产值(1990年不变价,万元)	Gross Output Value of Industry (at constant price of 1990,10000 yuan)	558729.7	529044	105.6	678295	556802.5	121.8
国有	State-owned	25516.8	21205.6	120.3	34108.4	35173.4	97.0
集体	Collective-owned	211484.3	378765	55.8	180478	177090.0	101.9
其他	Others	321728.6	129073	249.3	463709	344539.1	134.6
全部轻工业总产值(现价,万元)	Gross Output Value of Light Industry (at current prices,10000 yuan)	337789.3	321118	105.2	438310	349038.6	125.6
以农产品为原料	Using Farm Products as Raw Materials	200735.1	200413	100.2	220362	161631.1	136.3
以非农产品为原料	Using Non-farm Products as Raw Materials	137054.2	120705	113.5	217949	187407.5	116.3
全部重工业总产值(现价,万元)	Gross Output Value of Heavy Industry (at current prices,10000 yuan)	235549.8	221834	106.2	267095	228227.9	117.0
采掘工业	Mining and Quarrying				809.8	569.0	142.3
原料工业	Raw Materials Industry	59647.5	41271.5	144.5	55473.4	45584.3	121.7
制造工业	Manufacturing Industry	175902.3	180563	97.4	210812	182074.6	115.8
独立核算工业企业平均职工人数 (人)	Average Number of Staff and Workers in Enterprises with Independent Accounting System (person)	28278	31390	90.1	59041	55710	106.0
#国有	State-owned	4839	4300	112.5	5169	7614	67.9
集体	Collective-owned	10901	16719	65.2	20029	22927	87.4
独立核算工业企业总产值(现价,万元)	Gross Output Value of Enterprises with Independent Accounting System (at current prices,10000 yuan)	211216.1	177592	118.9	673382	537739.6	125.2
#国有	State-owned	29323.8	26379.5	111.2	37484	38211.8	98.1
集体	Collective-owned	59353.8	66689.5	89.0	179958	177657.9	101.3
独立核算工业企业工业增加值 (万元)	Value Added of Enterprises with Independent Accounting System (10000 yuan)				137883	115781.5	119.1
独立核算工业企业财务指标	Financial Indicators for Enterprises with Independent Accounting System						
产品销售收入 (万元)	Sales Revenue (10000yuan)	180748	141736	127.5	635663	504759.6	125.9
#国有	State-owned	22104.4	19054.8	116.0	40931.3	34328.9	119.2
产品销售成本 (万元)	Cost of Sales (10000 yuan)		12583.8		496063	404743.1	122.6
#国有	State-owned		23107.6		34128.5	27588.1	123.7
固定资产原价 (万元)	Original Value of Fixed Assets (10000 yuan)	192007.5	162421	118.2	371798	308586.8	120.5
#国有	State-owned	31577	34759.3	90.8	36550.5	46586.1	78.5
固定资产净值 (万元)	Net Value of Fixed Assets (10000 yuan)	135870.6	101597	133.7	282664	221878.6	127.4
#国有	State-owned	21637.9	21587.2	100.2	26546.6	22821.7	116.3
全部流动资金年平均余额 (万元)	Annual Average Balance of Circulating Funds (10000 yuan)	177367.5	146913	120.7	417466	342543.6	121.9
#国有	State-owned	24242.1	25541.1	94.9	32404.3	37927.0	85.4
利润总额 (万元)	Total Profits (10000 yuan)	-362.0	-6170.3		30099.6	23717.6	126.9
#国有	State-owned	-972.8	-834.5		922.5	803.1	114.9

24-7 续表 4 continued

项目 Item	通州区 Tongzhou 2000	1999	2000年为1999年% 2000 as% of 1999	大兴县 Daxing 2000	1999	2000年为1999年% 2000 as% of 1999
资金利税率 (%) Ratio of Pre-tax Profits to Total of Capital (%)	6.0	1.9		6.9	8.7	
产品销售率 (%) Ratio of Sales Value to Gross Output Value (%)	93.0	105.5		94.7	93.6	
增加值率 (%) Ratio of Added Value to Gross Output Value (%)	33.0	21.2		17.5	18.4	
独立核算工业企业全员劳动生产率 (元/人) Overall Labor Productivity of Enterprises with Independent Accounting System (yuan/person)	25307.2	14835.9	170.6	23353.7	20782.8	112.4
#国有 State-owned	24810.7	12981.1	191.1			
集体 Collective-owned	21859.4	14486.7	150.9			
商业 Commerce						
社会消费品零售额 (万元) Retail Sales of Consumer Goods (10000 yuan)	338569	330069	102.6	294028	263515	111.6
按登记注册类型分 Grouped by Registered Type						
国有 State-owned	30471	30002.7	101.6	85347	82508	103.4
集体 Collective-owned	44014	44011	100.0	66563	64411	103.3
其他 Others	264084	256055	103.1	142118	116596	121.9
按类别分 Grouped by Type of Goods						
吃的商品 Food	167250	166025	100.7	145741	126630	115.1
穿的商品 Clothing	41930	23765	176.4	30989	28609	108.3
用的商品 Daily Used Articles	119783	134008	89.4	86747	88398	98.1
烧的商品 Fuel	9606	6271	153.2	30551	19878	153.7
网点数 (个) Number of Outlets (unit)	9821	12924	76.0	11178	13119	85.2
#商业 Wholesale and Retail	7710	9839	78.4	7143	9757	73.2
饮食业 Catering	919	1658	55.4	1926	1565	123.1
服务业 Services	818	674	121.4	2109	1797	117.4
#宾馆、饭店 Hotels	2	2	100.0	8	7	114.3
营业人员 (人) Personnel (person)	20632	26362	78.3	31393	25755	121.9
#商业 Wholesale and Retail	16129	19089	84.5	22873	19034	120.2
饮食业 Catering	2098	4013	52.3	4900	4076	120.2
服务业 Services	1707	1519	112.4	3620	2645	136.9
#宾馆、饭店 Hotels	581	622	93.4	458	464	98.7
外经、外贸 Foreign Economy and Trade						
出口商品交货额 (万元) Delivery Value of Exports (10000 yuan)	71968.2	60400.3	119.2	85569.5	62948.6	135.9
利用外资签订协议(合同)数 (个) Number of Signed Agreements and Contracts of Foreign Capital to be Utilized (unit)	31	28	110.7	40	35	114.3
利用外资签订协议(合同)金额 (万美元) Amount of Foreign Capital to be Utilized through Agreements and Contracts (USD 10000)	2638.7	1954.2	135.0	3916.9	1918.6	2倍
实际利用外资 (万美元) Amount of Foreign Capital Actually Used (USD 10000)	5048.1	4503.0	112.1	4447	2948.4	150.8
旅游人数 (万人) Number of Tourists (10000 persons)	146.0	133.5	109.4	46.1	41.0	112.4
教育 Education						
学校数 (个) Number of Schools (unit)	203	208	97.6	227	245	92.7
小学 Primary Schools	153	162	94.4	173	192	90.1

24-7 续表 5 continued

项目 Item		通州区 Tongzhou 2000	1999	2000年为1999年% 2000 as % of 1999	大兴县 Daxing 2000	1999	2000年为1999年% 2000 as % of 1999
普通中学	Regular Secondary School	44	42	104.8	48	52	92.3
中等专业教育	Specialized Secondary Schools	6	4	150.0	1	1	100.0
招生数 (人)	New Student Enrollment (person)	20772	19551	106.2	21893	22468	97.4
小学	Primary Schools	5649	5959	94.8	5680	5839	97.3
初级中等学校	Junior Secondary Schools	12106	10524	115.0	12932	12827	100.8
高级中等学校	Senior Secondary Schools	2733	2276	120.1	2053	3621	56.7
中等专业教育	Specialized Secondary Schools	284	792	35.9		181	
在校学生 (人)	Student Enrollment (person)	94871	96553	98.3	98731	102842	96.0
小学	Primary Schools	54017	60650	89.1	51394	58805	87.4
初级中等学校	Junior Secondary Schools	31409	27533	114.1	35720	31851	112.1
高级中等学校	Senior Secondary Schools	7545	5840	129.2	5596	11271	49.6
中等专业教育	Specialized Secondary Schools	1900	2530	75.1	453	915	49.5
毕业生 (人)	Graduates (person)	24179	23373	103.4	24768	24242	102.2
小学	Primary Schools	12321	11014	111.9	13023	13020	100.0
初级中等学校	Junior Secondary Schools	8715	9975	87.4	8052	8176	98.5
高级中等学校	Senior Secondary Schools	2255	1537	146.7	1454	2775	52.4
中等专业教育	Specialized Secondary Schools	888	847	104.8	76	271	28.0
达到"国家体育标准"学生数 (人)	Number of Students Come to the Standard for State Physical Training (person)	80499	98509	81.7			
幼儿园、托儿所个数 (个)	Number of Kindergartens (unit)	168	141	119.1	172	222	77.5
幼儿入托数 (人)	New Enrollment (person)	13759	16478	83.5	5613	4635	121.1
文化	**Culture**						
文化馆、站 (个)	Cultural Centers (unit)	19	23	82.6	15	22	68.2
公共图书馆 (个)	Public Libraries (unit)	1	1	100.0	1	1	100.0
公共图书馆藏书 (万册)	Collection (10000 volume)	15.1	15	100.7	11.2	10.9	102.8
电影放映单位 (个)	Film Projection Units (unit)	22	19	115.8	14	21	66.7
区级以上重点文物保护单位 (个)	Cultural Relics Preserved at District Level and above (unit)	28	28	100.0	15	15	100.0
卫生	**Health**						
卫生机构数 (个)	Number of Health Institutions (unit)	172	171	100.6	45	45	100.0
#医院	Hospitals	12	11	109.1	11	11	100.0
卫生院	Clinics	16	16	100.0	27	27	100.0
床位数	Number of Beds (unit)	2294	1987	115.5	2366	2077	113.9
#医院	Hospitals	1698	1603	105.9	1630	1410	115.6
卫生院	Clinics	375	365	102.7	705	647	109.0
平均每千人拥有床位数 (张)	Average Number of Beds Per 1000 Persons (unit)	3.8	3.3	115.2	4	4	100.0
卫生技术人员 (人)	Medical Technical Personnel (person)	2995	2954	101.4	3276	2495	131.3
#医生	Doctors	1499	1467	102.2	1247	1236	100.9
公用设施	**Public Utilities**						
区级以上公园 (个)	Parks at District Level and above (unit)	1	1	100.0	2	2	100.0
体育场馆 (个)	Stadiums and Gymnasiums (unit)	1	1	100.0	2	2	100.0
道路长度 (公里)	Length of Roads (km)	2153.5	1722.7	125.0	1410	1390	101.4

24-8 平谷县、怀柔县国民经济主要指标
MAIN NATIONAL ECONOMIC INDICATORS FOR PINGGU AND HUAIROU COUNTIES

项目		Item		平谷县 Pinggu 2000	平谷县 Pinggu 1999	平谷县 Pinggu 2000年为1999年% 2000as% of 1999	怀柔县 Huairou 2000	怀柔县 Huairou 1999	怀柔县 Huairou 2000年为1999年% 2000as% of 1999
综合		**General Survey**							
国内生产总值	(万元)	Gross Domestic Product	(10000 yuan)	331118	299447	110.6	379223.7	339925.3	111.6
第一产业		Primary Industry		75836	75616.0	100.3	38529.4	37609.0	102.4
第二产业		Secondary Industry		134900	119050	113.3	203574.7	185608.8	109.7
第三产业		Tertiary Industry		120382	104781	114.9	137119.6	116707.5	117.5
财政收入	(万元)	Fiscal Revenue	(10000 yuan)	26014	21866.0	119.0	27380	22345	122.5
#增值税		Increased Value Tax		3681			4461	4737	94.2
营业税		Operating Tax		9589	13408	71.5	9988	7868	126.9
个人所得税		Private Income Tax			1301		2792	1889	147.8
企业所得税		Enterprise Income Tax		6807	14313	47.6	8701	6149	141.5
财政支出	(万元)	Fiscal Expenditure	(10000 yuan)	97182	66489	146.2	105006	81827	128.3
#基本建设支出		Capital Construction		6071	3153	192.5	13932	4036	345.2
支援农业生产支出		Supporting Agriculture		6968	4475	155.7	11623	7901	147.1
文教卫生事业费		Culture,Education and Health		19899	14896	133.6	19476	16393	118.8
人口和劳动力		**Population and Labor Force**							
总人口	(人)	Total Population	(person)	400201	398565	100.4	265314	265215	100.0
常住户籍人口	(人)	Permanent Registered Population	(person)	387108	389092	99.5	263271	262699	100.2
#非农业人口		Non-agriculture		97456	92981	104.8	81831	78160	104.7
男		Male		50860	48740	104.3	133076	133225	99.9
女		Female		46596	44241	105.3	130195	129474	100.6
出生率	(‰)	Birth Rate	(‰)	6.6	6.1		7.4	7.1	
死亡率	(‰)	Death Rate	(‰)	8.8	4.8		8.1	6.1	
自然增长率	(‰)	Natural Growth Rate	(‰)	-2.1	1.3		-0.7	1.0	
从业人员	(人)	Employment	(person)	194466	202063	96.2	140771	140403	100.3
按产业分		Grouped by Industry							
第一产业		Primary Industry		82610	80395	102.8	36905	36860	100.1
第二产业		Secondary Industry		60262	66621	90.5	52277	52080	100.4
第三产业		Tertiary Industry		51594	55047	93.7	51589	51463	100.2
按职工非职工分		Grouped by Staff and Workers or Non-staff-and-worker							
职工人数		Staff and Worker		42441	47013	90.3	35994	34597	104.0
#国有单位		State-owned		32089	37017	86.7	20754	19896	104.3
集体单位		Collective-owned		3137	3327	94.3	5139	5562	92.4
城镇个体劳动者		Urban and Rural Individuals		5202	9745	53.4	20419	16600	123.0
劳动工资		**Wages**							
工资总额	(万元)	Total Wages	(10000 yuan)	44709.6	42106.1	106.2	47069.7	40014.2	117.6
#国有单位		State-owned		37161.2	35213.7	105.5	27833.5	22916.5	121.5
集体单位		Collective-owned		929.7	1015.4	91.6	4361.2	4747.0	91.9
职工平均工资	(元)	Average Wage	(yuan)	9923	8889	111.6	13077	11472	114.0
固定资产投资		**Investment in Fixed Assets**							
全社会固定资产投资	(万元)	Total Investment in Fixed Assets	(10000 yuan)	65376	38895	168.1	97528	94688	103.0
按建设性质分		Grouped by Type of Construction							
#基本建设投资		Capital Construction		31019	12931	239.9	49279	31450	156.7
更新改造投资		Innovation and Replacement		10734	7092	151.4	6420	37362	17.2

24-8 续表1 continued

项目 Item		平谷县 Pinggu 2000	1999	2000年为1999年% 2000as% of 1999	怀柔县 Huairou 2000	1999	2000年为1999年% 2000as% of 1999
按登记注册类型分	Grouped by Registered Type						
#国有单位	State-owned	31424	15991	196.5	26050	24464	106.5
集体单位	Collective-owned	27023	18172	148.7	30963	29600	104.6
新增固定资产 (万元)	Incremental Fixed Assets (10000 yuan)	57200	34854	164.1	92584	72584	127.6
#国有单位	State-owned	28404	13723	207.0	26050	24649	105.7
集体单位	Collective-owned	27566	17099	161.2	28309	36051	78.5
房屋施工面积 (万平方米)	Floor Space of Buildings under Construction (10000 sq.m)	48.6	53.8	90.3	71.1	67.9	104.7
#国有单位	State-owned	27.7	20.3	136.5	26.7	26.9	99.3
集体单位	Collective-owned	20.9	15.5	134.8	31.7	29.1	108.9
房屋竣工面积 (万平方米)	Floor Space of Buildings Completed (10000 sq.m)	34.5	39.2	88.0	41.3	41.1	100.5
#国有单位	State-owned	19.0	8.6	220.9	14.7	15.6	94.2
#住宅	Residence	15.8	5.4	292.6	10.1	7.8	129.5
#集体单位	Collective-owned	10.0	12.8	78.1	19.0	18.9	100.5
#住宅	Residence	5.1	5.7	89.5	11.2	12.2	91.8
农村经济	**Rural Economy**						
农村劳动力 (人)	Labor Force (person)	150456	149169	100.9	81885	81752	100.2
种植业	Planting	68879	67947	101.4	22665	25445	89.1
林业	Forestry	2763	2717	101.7	10248	7796	131.5
牧业	Animal Husbandry	7664	6310	121.5	3068	2759	111.2
渔业	Fishery	2262	2261	100.0	451	330	136.7
农村工业	Rural Industry	31522	32263	97.7	11167	11938	93.5
农村建筑业	Rural Construction	13541	13427	100.8	6369	5950	107.0
农村运输业	Rural Transportation	6432	6099	105.5	6464	5659	114.2
农村商、饮食业、服务业	Commerce,Catering and Services	17393	18145	95.9	6262	5470	114.5
耕地面积 (公顷)	Area under Cultivation (hectare)	18985.9	19063.1	99.6	14937.2	15101.9	98.9
农业机械总动力 (千瓦)	Total Power of Agricultural Machinery (kw)	320391	336108	95.3	211621	211088	100.3
化肥施用实物量 (吨)	Consumption of Chemical Fertilizers(ton)	57478	63298	90.8	19745	20650	95.6
化肥施用折纯量 (吨)	Consumption of Chemical Fertilizers (100%) (ton)	18001	19340	93.1	7534	8330	90.4
农村用电量 (万千瓦时)	Consumption of Electricity (10000 kwh)	19221.0	18240.5	105.4	17084.0	14919.9	114.5
农村国内生产总值 (万元)	Rural Gross Domestic Product (10000 yuan)	233006	214146	108.8	243677	210774.0	115.6
第一产业	Primary Industry	75836	75616	100.3	38529.4	37609.0	102.4
第二产业	Secondary Industry	106367	88214.8	120.6	126788	107150.7	118.3
第三产业	Tertiary Industry	50803.4	50315.2	101.0	78360.2	66014.3	118.7
农业总产值 (万元)	Gross Output Value of Agriculture (10000 yuan)	88403.2	84212.4	105.0	48536.4	46048.0	105.4
种植业	Planting	43701.6	47653.2	91.7	19266.4	21223.3	90.8
林业	Forestry	1100.9	1167.5	94.3	3947.6	3910.8	100.9
牧业	Animal Husbandry	36006.9	28012.6	128.5	19814.5	18059.0	109.7
渔业	Fishery	7593.9	7379.1	102.9	5507.9	2854.9	192.9
农作物总播种面积 (万公顷)	Sown Area of Farm Crops (10000 hectare)	2.8	3.4	82.4	2.1	2.3	91.3
粮食作物	Grain	1.9	2.6	73.1	1.6	2.0	80.0
经济作物	Industrial Crops	0.1	0.1	100.0	0.2	0.1	200.0
其他作物	Other Crops	0.8	0.7	114.3	0.3	0.2	150.0

24-8 续表 2 continued

项目	Item	平谷县 Pinggu			怀柔县 Huairou		
		2000	1999	2000年为1999年% 2000 as % of 1999	2000	1999	2000年为1999年% 2000 as % of 1999
农副产品产量	Yield of Farm and Sideline Crops						
粮食 (万吨)	Grain (10000 tons)	7.2	10.9	66.1	7.8	11.3	69.0
蔬菜 (吨)	Vegetable (ton)	360682	330697	109.1	54240	51183	106.0
干鲜果 (吨)	Dry and Fresh Fruits (ton)	150145	146911	102.2	45818	47915	95.6
畜产品产量	Output of Livestock Products						
生猪出栏 (头)	Slaughtered Hogs (head)	260623	248650	104.8	195410	192760	101.4
商品猪 (头)	Commodity Hogs (head)				189000	188900	100.1
猪牛羊肉 (吨)	Pork,Beef and Mutton (ton)	19209	18182	105.6	18616	15089	123.4
#猪肉	Pork	16547	15681	105.5	16280	13425	121.3
禽肉	Meat of Poultry (ton)	10548	6811	154.9	9721	6283	154.7
禽蛋	Poultry Eggs (ton)	22666	20953	108.2	7647	6749	113.3
牲畜年底头数 (头)	Number of Livestock (year-end) (head)	249244	223678	111.4	161476	159536	101.2
大牲畜	Large Animals	10693	9775	109.4	21031	15006	140.2
猪	Hogs	177070	165904	106.7	102185	109864	93.0
羊	Goats and Sheep	61481	47999	128.1	38260	34666	110.4
水产品产量 (吨)	Output of Aquatic Product (ton)	14365	13997	102.6	2045	2004	102.0
农村集体经济收入 (万元)	Rural Collective Economic Revenue (10000 yuan)	406639	388082	104.8	592611	564756	104.9
农村集体经济利润总额 (万元)	Total Profits of Rural Collective Economy (10000 yuan)	24949	25504	97.8	41774.2	34764	120.2
国家税金	State Taxes	17753	21375	83.1	30055.6	28304.0	106.2
集体积累	Collective Accumulation	11350	9303	122.0	16288	12387	131.5
劳动所得	Income from Work	20338	20116.3	101.1	89500.4	79091.0	113.2
乡镇企业单位数 (个)	Number of Township and Village Enterprise (unit)	699	818	85.5	704	675	104.3
乡镇企业人数 (人)	Number of Persons of Township and Village Enterprises (person)	48899	49933	97.9	46603	42203	110.4
乡镇企业纯利润 (万元)	Net Profit of Township and Village Enterprises (10000 yuan)	33352	25217	132.3	43520	35859	121.4
乡镇企业固定资产原价 (万元)	Original Value of Fixed Assets of Township and Village Enterprises (10000 yuan)	178627	186814	95.6	233274	183204	127.3
乡镇企业固定资产净值 (万元)	Net Value of Fixed Assets of Township and Village Enterprises (10000 yuan)	125596	121257	103.6	183099	145524	125.8
工业	**Industry**						
全部工业企业单位数 (个)	Number of Enterprises (unit)	496	523	94.8	537	652	82.4
国有	State-owned	51	65	78.5	36	57	63.2
集体	Collective-owned	321	357	89.9	322	426	75.6
其他	Others	124	101	122.8	179	169	105.9
全部工业总产值 (现价,万元)	Gross Output Value of Industry (at current prices,10000 yuan)	471442	428418.1	110.0	887994	874521.0	101.5
国有	State-owned	42815	45284.4	94.5	39908.8	41976.0	95.1
集体	Collective-owned	174014	142105.9	122.5	272015	211291.0	128.7
其他	Others	254613	241027.8	105.6	576070	521254.0	110.5

24-8 续表 3 continued

项目	Item	平谷县 Pinggu 2000	1999	2000年为1999年% 2000 as % of 1999	怀柔县 Huairou 2000	1999	2000年为1999年% 2000 as % of 1999
全部工业总产值(1990年不变价,万元)	Gross Output Value of Industry(at constant price of 1990,10000 yuan)	488376	430112.0	113.5	902943	890122	101.4
国有	State-owned	71788.1	58300.6	123.1	42641.3	43899	97.1
集体	Collective-owned	172211	140757.0	122.3	256297	269396	95.1
其他	Others	244377	231054.4	105.8	604005	576827	104.7
全部轻工业总产值(现价,万元)	Gross Output Value of Light Industry (at current prices,10000 yuan)	266068	295947.3	89.9	558310	549344	101.6
以农产品为原料	Using Farm Products as Raw Materials	205857	179397.9	114.7	364617	358762	101.6
以非农产品为原料	Using Non-farm Products as Raw Materials	60210.9	116549.4	51.7	193693	190582	101.6
全部重工业总产值(现价,万元)	Gross Output Value of Heavy Industry (at current prices,10000 yuan)	205374	132470.8	155.0	344633	340778	101.1
采掘工业	Mining and Quarrying	1742.8	1305.2	133.5	18499.8	20567.0	89.9
原料工业	Raw Materials Industry	17229.1	14817.9	116.3	30414	38974	78.0
制造工业	Manufacturing Industry	186402.0	116347.7	160.2	295719	281237	105.1
独立核算工业企业平均职工人数 (人)	Average Number of Staff and Workers in Enterprises with Independent Accounting System (person)	45350	45248	100.2	33720	38038	88.6
#国有	State-owned	5223	5593	93.4	2334	3296	70.8
集体	Collective-owned	22901	23727	96.5	14735	23932	61.6
独立核算工业企业总产值(现价,万元)	Gross Output Value of Enterprises with Independent Accounting System (at current prices,10000 yuan)	470077	427133.9	110.1	887994	869521	102.1
#国有	State-owned	42165.0	44295.0	95.2	39908.8	41976.0	95.1
集体	Collective-owned	173320	141879.1	122.2	272015	309291	87.9
独立核算工业企业工业增加值 (万元)	Value Added of Enterprises with Independent Accounting System (10000 yuan)	132494	115906.7	114.3	166148	151520.2	109.7
独立核算工业企业财务指标	Financial Indicators for Enterprises with Independent Accounting System						
产品销售收入 (万元)	Sales Revenue (10000 yuan)	425555	364933.7	116.6	799934	771836.4	103.6
#国有	State-owned	35013.7	37997.8	92.1	35649.1	29565.8	120.6
产品销售成本 (万元)	Cost of Sales (10000 yuan)	352286	290865.0	121.1	635641	615930	103.2
#国有	State-owned	29670.9	32290.4	91.9	31018.3	27192.6	114.1
固定资产原价 (万元)	Original Value of Fixed Assets(10000 yuan)	307251	295045.6	104.1	433778	329419.5	131.7
#国有	State-owned	29064.9	27999.6	103.8	33044.0	27292.4	121.1
固定资产净值 (万元)	Net Value of Fixed Assets (10000 yuan)	232567	229436.6	101.4	325664	302736.3	107.6
#国有	State-owned	19765	18136.3	109.0	22691.2	21201.4	107.0
全部流动资金年平均余额 (万元)	Annual Average Balance of Circulating Funds (10000 yuan)	264536	258437.6	102.4	390837	391469.5	99.8
#国有	State-owned	20464.2	28435.2	72.0	23368.1	27921.0	83.7
利润总额 (万元)	Total Profits (10000 yuan)	24826.1	20847.3	119.1	42186.7	33967.5	124.2
#国有	State-owned	574.3	700.0	82.0	-95.3	348.1	

24-8 续表 4 continued

项目		Item		平谷县 Pinggu 2000	1999	2000年为1999年% 2000 as% of 1999	怀柔县 Huairou 2000	1999	2000年为1999年% 2000 as% of 1999
资金利税率	(%)	Ratio of Pre-tax Profitsto Total of Capital(%)		8.4	8.0		11.6	11.6	
产品销售率	(%)	Ratio of Sales Value to Gross Output Value	(%)	93.0	90.3		98.6	97.6	
增加值率	(%)	Ratio of Added Value to Gross Output Value	(%)	27.3	26.2		17.2	16.3	
独立核算工业企业全员劳动生产率	(元/人)	Overall Labor Productivity of Enterprises with Independent Accounting System	(yuan/person)	29216	25616	114.1	267777	234009	114.4
#国有		State-owned		27333	27223	100.4	182696	158537	115.2
集体		Collective-owned		17534	12132	144.5	173937	142515	122.0
商业		**Commerce**							
社会消费品零售额	(万元)	Retail Sales of Consumer Goods	(10000 yuan)	136225	128418	106.1	140118	137223	102.1
按登记注册类型分		Grouped by Registered Type							
国有		State-owned		38505	37241	103.4	28023.6	31073	90.2
集体		Collective-owned		18072	17979	100.5	39233	45044	87.1
其他		Others		79648	73198	108.8	72861.4	61106	119.2
按类别分		Grouped by Type of Goods							
吃的商品	(万元)	Food	(10000 yuan)	54217	44004	123.2	44209	49861	88.7
穿的商品	(万元)	Clothing	(10000 yuan)	25910	23629	109.7	30726	23915	128.5
用的商品	(万元)	Daily Used Articles	(10000 yuan)	38743	49099	78.9	56015	61265	91.4
烧的商品	(万元)	Fuel	(10000 yuan)	17355	11686	148.5	9168	2182	420.2
网点数	(个)	Number of Outlets	(unit)	3937	7595	51.8	10155	9335	108.8
#商业		Wholesale and Retail		3109	4277	72.7	7074	6531	108.3
饮食业		Catering		279	462	60.4	1533	1354	113.2
服务业		Services		402	1033	38.9	1548	1450	106.8
#宾馆、饭店		Hotels		28	23	121.7	35	30	116.7
营业人员	(人)	Personnel	(person)	10226	14869	68.8	20180	18207	110.8
#商业		Wholesale and Retail		7483	8783	85.2	14330	12882	111.2
饮食业		Catering		1209	1500	80.6	3373	3215	104.9
服务业		Services		1384	1431	96.7	2477	2110	117.4
#宾馆、饭店		Hotels		1332	1383	96.3	1077	984	109.5
外经、外贸		**Foreign Economy and Trade**							
出口商品交货额	(万元)	Delivery Value of Exports	(10000 yuan)	92839.4	76470.4	121.4	41229.5	37120.6	111.1
利用外资签订协议(合同)数	(个)	Number of Signed Agreements and Contracts of Foreign Capital to be Utilized	(unit)	18	27	66.7	20	20	100.0
利用外资签订协议(合同)金额	(万美元)	Amount of Foreign Capital to be Utilized through Agreements and Contracts	(USD 10000)	1396.0	2781.8	50.2	1754	1622	108.1
实际利用外资	(万美元)	Amount of Foreign Capital Actually Used	(USD 10000)	903.9	246.5	366.7	3929.4	3075.4	127.8
旅游人数	(万人)	Number of Tourists	(10000 persons)	324.3	281.0	115.4	592	554.2	106.8
教育		**Education**							
学校数	(个)	Number of Schools	(unit)	194	208	93.3	107	119	89.9
小学		Primary Schools		157	172	91.3	82	97	84.5

24-8 续表 5 continued

项目		Item		平谷县 Pinggu 2000	1999	2000年为1999年% 2000 as % of 1999	怀柔县 Huairou 2000	1999	2000年为1999年% 2000 as % of 1999
普通中学		Regular Secondary School		36	35	102.9	24	21	114.3
中等专业教育		Specialized Secondary Schools		1	1	100.0	1	1	100.0
招生数	(人)	New Student Enrollment	(person)	18796	17977	104.6	10830	11141	97.2
小学		Primary Schools		4643	4804	96.6	3329	3139	106.1
初级中等学校		Junior Secondary Schools		11469	10572	108.5	4822	5010	96.2
高级中等学校		Senior Secondary Schools		2684	2601	103.2	1728	1147	150.7
中等专业教育		Specialized Secondary Schools						40	
在校学生	(人)	Student Enrollment	(person)	78443	80458	97.5	45175	45809	98.6
小学		Primary Schools		40660	47575	85.5	22264	23781	93.6
初级中等学校		Junior Secondary Schools		30124	25343	118.9	14614	14020	104.2
高级中等学校		Senior Secondary Schools		7579	7350	103.1	4141	3434	120.6
中等专业教育		Specialized Secondary Schools		80	190	42.1	118	113	104.4
毕业生	(人)	Graduates	(person)	20415	20378	100.2	11606	11716	99.1
小学		Primary Schools		11593	10862	106.7	4266	5070	84.1
初级中等学校		Junior Secondary Schools		6331	7260	87.2	4720	4151	113.7
高级中等学校		Senior Secondary Schools		2381	2096	113.6	1164	929	125.3
中等专业教育		Specialized Secondary Schools		110	160	68.8		39	
达到"国家体育标准"学生数	(人)	Number of Students Come to the Standard for State Physical Training	(person)	74666	76218	98.0	32670	43749	74.7
幼儿园、托儿所个数	(个)	Number of Kindergardens	(unit)	211	211	100.0	93	100	93.0
幼儿入托数	(人)	New Enrollment	(person)	9388	11656	80.5	5336	5456	97.8
文化		**Culture**							
文化馆、站	(个)	Cultural Centers	(unit)	18	22	81.8	16	15	106.7
公共图书馆	(个)	Public Libraries	(unit)	1	1	100.0	1	1	100.0
公共图书馆藏书	(万册)	Collection	(10000 volume)	14.6	12	121.7	11.8	11.0	107.3
电影放映单位	(个)	Film Projection Units	(unit)	12	12	100.0	32	30	106.7
区级以上重点文物保护单位	(个)	Cultural Relics Preserved at District Level and above	(unit)	17	18	94.4	16	14	114.3
卫生		**Health**							
卫生机构数	(个)	Number of Health Institutions	(unit)	72	76	94.7	447	440	101.6
#医院		Hospitals		7	6	116.7	10	9	111.1
卫生院		Clinics		16	20	80.0	11	11	100.0
床位数		Number of Beds	(unit)	1088	960	113.3	1098	1034	106.2
#医院		Hospitals		804	676	118.9	1023	961	106.5
卫生院		Clinics		274	259	105.8	75	73	102.7
平均每千人拥有床位数	(张)	Average Number of Beds Per 1000 Persons	(unit)	2.8	2.5	112.0	4.2	3.9	107.7
卫生技术人员	(人)	Medical Technical Personnel	(person)	1793	1804	99.4	1516	1441	105.2
#医生		Doctors	(person)	965	910	106.0	841	774	108.7
公用设施		**Public Utilities**							
区级以上公园	(个)	Parks at District Level and above	(unit)	1	1	100.0	8	8	100.0
体育场馆	(个)	Stadiums and Gymnasiums	(unit)	1	1	100.0	4	4	100.0
道路长度	(公里)	Length of Roads	(km)	934.5	841.1	111.1	1154.9	1153.8	100.1

24-9 密云县、延庆县国民经济主要指标
MAIN NATIONAL ECONOMIC INDICATORS FOR MIYUN AND YANQING COUNTIES

项目		Item		密云县 Miyun 2000	1999	2000年为1999年% 2000 as% of 1999	延庆县 Yanqing 2000	1999	2000年为1999年% 2000 as% of 1999
综合		**General Survey**							
国内生产总值	(万元)	Gross Domestic Product	(10000 yuan)	358692	306261.8	117.1	218208	197936.7	110.2
第一产业		Primary Industry		67427.2	60704.9	111.1	77007.9	72968.4	105.5
第二产业		Secondary Industry		163170	126224.6	129.3	70082.5	60417.5	116.0
第三产业		Tertiary Industry		128095	119332.3	107.3	71117.8	64550.8	110.2
财政收入	(万元)	Fiscal Revenue	(10000 yuan)	20821	19083	109.1	17714	13063	135.6
#增值税		Increased Value Tax		5017	4068	123.3	1562	1488	105.0
营业税		Operating Tax		7035	5612	125.4	5362	3554	150.9
个人所得税		Private Income Tax					1613	923	174.7
企业所得税		Enterprise Income Tax		4801	4779	100.5	4328	2728	158.7
财政支出	(万元)	Fiscal Expenditure	(10000 yuan)	94599	84148	112.4	70732	52688	134.2
#基本建设支出		Capital Construction		6046	2151	281.1	772	1975	39.1
支援农业生产支出		Supporting Agriculture		12330	10082	122.3	9718	6899	140.9
文教卫生事业费		Culture,Education and Health		21547	17091	126.1	17076	14704	116.1
人口和劳动力		**Population and Labor Force**							
总人口	(人)	Total Population	(person)	421730	430711	97.9	271634	271790	99.9
常住户籍人口	(人)	Permanent Registered Population	(person)	414981	425495	97.5	268942	269252	99.9
#非农业人口		Non-agriculture		97242	96609	100.7	61859	57836	107.0
男		Male		208706	214232	97.4	137739	138040	99.8
女		Female		206275	211263	97.6	133895	133750	100.1
出生率	(‰)	Birth Rate	(‰)	8.1	8.8		15.2	14.0	
死亡率	(‰)	Death Rate	(‰)	11.6	7.7		8.5	7.0	
自然增长率	(‰)	Natural Growth Rate	(‰)	-3.5	1.1		6.8	7.0	
从业人员	(人)	Employment	(person)	217019	214175	101.3	123898	129851	95.4
按产业分		Grouped by Industry							
第一产业		Primary Industry		76752	79096	97.0	52376	52660	99.5
第二产业		Secondary Industry		71745	63530	112.9	30076	25193	119.4
第三产业		Tertiary Industry		68522	71549	95.8	41446	51998	79.1
按职工非职工分		Grouped by Staff and Workers or Non-staff-and-worker							
职工人数		Staff and Worker		46346	43483	106.6	33717	32463	103.9
#国有单位		State-owned		29438	29926	98.4	21722	25578	84.9
集体单位		Collective-owned		4325	4328	99.9	2819	3587	78.6
城镇个体劳动者		Urban and Rural Individuals		4620	3846	120.1	7240	7584	95.5
劳动工资		Wages							
工资总额	(万元)	Total Wages	(10000 yuan)	52505.2	42996.5	122.1	40172.4	31334.4	128.2
#国有单位		State-owned		35418.2	32515.1	108.9	28903.8	26661.3	108.4
集体单位		Collective-owned		3013.7	2650.4	113.7	2547.5	2281.7	111.7
职工平均工资	(元)	Average Wage	(yuan)	11595	9846	117.8	11638	9652	120.6
固定资产投资		**Investment in Fixed Assets**							
全社会固定资产投资	(万元)	Total Investment in Fixed Assets	(10000 yuan)	81254	66065	123.0	70882	43499	163.0
按建设性质分		Grouped by Type of Construction							
#基本建设投资		Capital Construction		23043	24422	94.4	65029	43499	149.5
更新改造投资		Innovation and Replacement		3155	2879	109.6	864		

24-9 续表 1 continued

项目 Item		密云县 Miyun			延庆县 Yanqing		
		2000	1999	2000年为1999年% 2000as% of 1999	2000	1999	2000年为1999年% 2000as% of 1999
按登记注册类型分	Grouped by Registered Type						
#国有单位	State-owned	36437	35381	103.0	60315	29209	206.5
集体单位	Collective-owned	15734	19688	79.9	4759	9014	52.8
新增固定资产 (万元)	Incremental Fixed Assets (10000 yuan)	59346	87986	67.5	68976	28932	238.4
#国有单位	State-owned	31179	38565	80.8	58629	24517	239.1
集体单位	Collective-owned	17017	22111	77.0	4621	3651	126.6
房屋施工面积 (万平方米)	Floor Space of Buildings under Construction (10000 sq.m)	81.2	79.4	102.3	42.1	38.7	108.8
#国有单位	State-owned	40.9	35.5	115.2	35.8	27.9	128.3
集体单位	Collective-owned	16.5	21.5	76.7	2.8	10.8	25.9
房屋竣工面积 (万平方米)	Floor Space of Buildings Completed (10000 sq.m)	54.8	57.2	95.8	23.7	19.1	124.1
#国有单位	State-owned	26.2	26.8	97.8	20.1	10.4	193.3
#住宅	Residence	20.8	19.3	107.8	2.5	8.0	31.2
#集体单位	Collective-owned	14.3	21.9	65.3	1.6	3.9	41.0
#住宅	Residence	11.2	19.1	58.6	1	3.9	25.6
农村经济	**Rural Economy**						
农村劳动力 (人)	Labor Force (person)	154363	156183	98.8	93193	97388	95.7
种植业	Planting	49843	59103	84.3	42567	43890	97.0
林业	Forestry	10407	8206	126.8	4022	3512	114.5
牧业	Animal Husbandry	15243	10356	147.2	5293	4818	109.9
渔业	Fishery	896	939	95.4	494	448	110.3
农村工业	Rural Industry	20083	20084	100.0	6613	7734	85.5
农村建筑业	Rural Construction	13538	11489	118.2	12944	11294	114.6
农村运输业	Rural Transportation	9911	8862	111.8	6294	5277	119.3
农村商、饮食业、服务业	Commerce,Catering and Services	8369	7004	119.5	14966	20415	73.3
耕地面积 (公顷)	Area under Cultivation (hectare)	23428.5	23503.7	99.7	32501.1	32607.8	99.7
农业机械总动力 (千瓦)	Total Power of Agricultural Machinery (kw)	329433	316279	104.2	229841	230025	99.9
化肥施用实物量 (吨)	Consumption of Chemical Fertilizers (ton)	40610	48517	83.7	42667	39858	107.0
化肥施用折纯量 (吨)	Consumption of Chemical Fertilizers (100%) (ton)	9891	12219	90.9	11244	12082	93.1
农村用电量 (万千瓦时)	Consumption of Electricity(10000 kwh)	11479	10467.8	109.7	7650	6800.6	112.5
农村国内生产总值 (万元)	Rural Gross Domestic Product (10000 yuan)	205005	167566.6	122.3	165486	140571.4	117.7
第一产业	Primary Industry	57529.3	45736.4	125.8	77007.9	72968.4	105.5
第二产业	Secondary Industry	73848.8	55373.1	133.4	46438.8	33670.1	137.9
第三产业	Tertiary Industry	73627.1	66457.1	110.8	42038.9	33932.9	123.9
农业总产值 (万元)	Gross Output Value of Agriculture (10000 yuan)	67722.5	59848.0	113.2	6844301	59257.2	115.5
种植业	Planting	19523.1	21206.0	92.1	32963.3	29133.2	113.1
林业	Forestry	1894.9	1854.3	102.2	3975.8	2753.6	144.4
牧业	Animal Husbandry	44354.2	34951.5	126.9	27129.8	22219.3	122.1
渔业	Fishery	1950.4	1836.2	106.2	1398.8	1383.1	101.1
农作物总播种面积 (万公顷)	Sown Area of Farm Crops (10000 hectare)	3.0	3.2	93.8	3.3	3.1	106.5
粮食作物	Grain	2.2	2.5	88.0	2.2	2.4	91.7
经济作物	Industrial Crops	0.5	0.4	125.0	1.0	0.6	166.7
其他作物	Other Crops	0.3	0.3	100.0	0.1	0.1	100.0

24-9 续表 2 continued

项目	Item	密云县 Miyun 2000	1999	2000年为1999年% 2000as% of 1999	延庆县 Yanqing 2000	1999	2000年为1999年% 2000as% of 1999
农副产品产量	Yield of Farm and Sideline Crops						
粮食 (万吨)	Grain (10000 tons)	5.4	9.8	55.1	14.6	14.0	104.3
蔬菜 (吨)	Vegetable (ton)	182385	159061	114.7	481029	423024	113.7
干鲜果 (吨)	Dry and Fresh Fruits (ton)	35905	38000	94.5	45236	40677	111.2
畜产品产量	Output of Livestock Products						
生猪出栏 (头)	Slaughtered Hogs (head)	320078	308285	103.8	152505	146492	104.1
商品猪 (头)	Commodity Hogs (head)				152505	146492	104.1
猪牛羊肉 (吨)	Pork,Beef and Mutton (ton)	26392	24164	109.2	14784	13656	108.3
#猪肉	Pork	22028	20844	105.7	11606	11406	101.8
禽肉	Meat of Poultry (ton)	18265	14140	123.2	11409	10904	104.6
禽蛋	Poultry Eggs (ton)	19549	16653	117.4	12692	12198	104.0
牲畜年底头数 (头)	Number of Livestock(year-end) (head)				164055	155649	105.4
大牲畜	Large Animals	29682	21674	136.9	23644	21653	109.2
猪	Hogs	194155	201071	96.6	70155	77200	90.9
羊	Goats and Sheep	124710	104785	119.0	70256	56796	123.7
水产品产量 (吨)	Output of Aquatic Product (ton)	4309	4114	104.7	2811.9	2716.2	103.5
农村集体经济收入 (万元)	Rural Collective Economic Revenue(10000 yuan)	537985	449370	119.7	220080	183923.0	119.7
农村集体经济利润总额 (万元)	Total Profits of Rural Collective Economy (10000 yuan)	9419.1	9291.9	101.4	13857.9	11649.0	119.0
国家税金	State Taxes	11077.3	9224.3	120.1	11987	10792.0	111.1
集体积累	Collective Accumulation				3490.6	4702.0	74.2
劳动所得	Income from Work	114625	99902.8	114.7	92630.7	80842.0	114.6
乡镇企业单位数 (个)	Number of Township and Village Enterprise(unit)	10508	9544	110.1	5202	4121	126.2
乡镇企业人数 (人)	Number of Persons of Township and Village Enterprises (person)	58667	56749	103.4	35278	34202	103.1
乡镇企业纯利润 (万元)	Net Profit of Township and Village Enterprises (10000 yuan)	16896	13568	124.5	13452	8691	154.8
乡镇企业固定资产原价 (万元)	Original Value of Fixed Assets of Township and Village Enterprises (10000 yuan)	140117	144606	96.9	62955	62541	100.7
乡镇企业固定资产净值 (万元)	Nct Valuc of Fixcd Assets of Township and Village Enterprises (10000 yuan)	104650	110189	95.0	49002	47557	103.0
工业	**Industry**						
全部工业企业单位数 (个)	Number of Enterprises (unit)	1470	1354	108.6	196	223	87.9
国有	State-owned	20	21	95.2	19	22	86.4
集体	Collective-owned	190	239	79.5	106	169	62.7
其他	Others	1260	1094	115.2	76	32	237.5
全部工业总产值 (现价,万元)	Gross Output Value of Industry (at current prices,10000 yuan)	531576	401314.2	132.5	190588	152084.6	125.3
国有	State-owned	32604.3	32431.9	100.5	11027.3	11813.1	93.3
集体	Collective-owned	67594.2	84363.7	80.1	29682.8	40264.0	73.7
其他	Others	431377	284518.6	151.6	149878	100007.5	149.9

24-9 续表 3 continued

项目	Item	密云县 Miyun 2000	密云县 Miyun 1999	密云县 Miyun 2000年为1999年% 2000 as% of 1999	延庆县 Yanqing 2000	延庆县 Yanqing 1999	延庆县 Yanqing 2000年为1999年% 2000 as% of 1999
全部工业总产值(1990年不变价,万元)	Gross Output Value of Industry(at constant price of 1990,10000 yuan)	514918	378963.5	135.9	184705	145170.3	127.2
国有	State-owned	25831.3	21619.6	119.5	8366.2	8757.8	98.6
集体	Collective-owned	59594.5	78486.3	75.9	29163.7	37823.7	77.1
其他	Others	429493	278857.6	154.0	147175	98588.8	149.3
全部轻工业总产值(现价,万元)	Gross Output Value of Light Industry (at current prices,10000 yuan)	311503	155408.7	200.4	134881	127429.2	105.8
以农产品为原料	Using Farm Products as Raw Materials	146406	139675.3	104.8	113560	107286.2	105.8
以非农产品为原料	Using Non-farm Products as Raw Materials	165097	15733.4	1049.3	21321	20143	105.8
全部重工业总产值(现价,万元)	Gross Output Value of Heavy Industry (at current prices,10000 yuan)	220072	196283.2	112.1	55706.4	24655.4	225.9
采掘工业	Mining and Quarrying	19800	54810.2	36.1	1132.0	501.0	225.9
原料工业	Raw Materials Industry	6600	29331.3	22.5	13834.4	6123.0	225.9
制造工业	Manufacturing Industry	193672	111141.7	174.3	40740.0	18031.4	225.9
独立核算工业企业平均职工人数 (人)	Average Number of Staff and Workers in Enterprises with Independent Accounting System (person)	53233	39029	136.4	12702.0	13015.0	97.6
#国有	State-owned	5922	6498	91.1	1755	1724	101.8
集体	Collective-owned	16994	18409	92.3	5223	5809	89.9
独立核算工业企业总产值(现价,万元)	Gross Output Value of Enterprises with Independent Accounting System (at current prices,10000 yuan)	528671	263604.6	200.6	70906	63535.4	111.6
#国有	State-owned	32604.3	32431.9	100.5	11027.3	14505.0	76.0
集体	Collective-owned	64689.8	49417.4	130.9	29682.8	26372.0	113.2
独立核算工业企业工业增加值 (万元)	Value Added of Enterprises with Independent Accounting System (10000 yuan)	141070	86639.6	162.8	17059.7	16389.6	104.1
独立核算工业企业财务指标	Financial Indicators for Enterprises with Independent Accounting System						
产品销售收入 (万元)	Sales Revenue (10000 yuan)	509106	309562.4	164.5	78402.3	65582.0	119.5
#国有	State-owned	32356.1	36098.8	89.6	9920.6	10212.4	97.1
产品销售成本 (万元)	Cost of Sales (10000 yuan)	369025	242700.7	152.0	64198.1	53946.4	119.0
#国有	State-owned	28363.5	28375.2	100.0	6979.3	7547.8	92.5
固定资产原价 (万元)	Original Value of Fixed Assets(10000 yuan)	227451	205694.1	110.6	46285.3	54122.4	85.5
#国有	State-owned	43632.3	55108.8	79.2	9576.5	13333.0	71.8
固定资产净值 (万元)	Net Value of Fixed Assets (10000 yuan)	180550	135096.6	133.6	29574.7	38229.9	77.4
#国有	State-owned	35974.4	35484.5	101.4	5550.3	8927.2	62.2
全部流动资金年平均余额 (万元)	Annual Average Balance of Circulating Funds (10000 yuan)	244263	210494.7	116.0	65730.0	56709.1	115.9
#国有	State-owned	45008	39625	113.6	11296.0	11836.4	95.4
利润总额 (万元)	Total Profits (10000 yuan)	23655.3	14890.4	158.9	-70	-939.8	
#国有	State-owned	777.7	-837.5		-848.8	-1002.0	

24-9 续表 4 continued

项目		Item	密云县 Miyun 2000	1999	2000年为1999年% 2000 as% of 1999	延庆县 Yanqing 2000	1999	2000年为1999年% 2000 as% of 1999
资金利税率	(%)	Ratio of Pre-tax Profits to Total of Capital(%)	6.7	5.9		7.1	4.3	
产品销售率	(%)	Ratio of Sales Value to Gross Output Value (%)	96.7	99.0		94.3	94.9	
增加值率	(%)	Ratio of Added Value to Gross Output Value (%)	26.6	29.2		24.0	25.4	
独立核算工业企业全员劳动生产率	(元/人)	Overall Labor Productivity of Enterprises with Independent Accounting System (yuan/person)	99200	67541	146.9	55822	48817	114.3
#国有		State-owned	55055	49911	110.3	62833	84135	74.5
集体		Collective-owned	28984	26844	108.0	56830	45398	125.1
商业		**Commerce**						
社会消费品零售额	(万元)	Retail Sales of Consumer Goods (10000 yuan)	158046	148629	106.3	223002	192332	115.9
按登记注册类型分		Grouped by Registered Type						
国有		State-owned	22126	21527	102.8	56216	45146	124.5
集体		Collective-owned	12000	12602	95.2	60208	49370	121.9
其他		Others	123920	114500	108.2	106578	97816	108.9
按类别分		Grouped by Type of Goods						
吃的商品		Food	73382	82078	89.4	91604	81064	113.0
穿的商品		Clothing	23807	16551	143.8	46755	40922	116.5
用的商品		Daily Used Articles	57433	41616	138.0	72193	62385	115.7
烧的商品		Fuel	3436	8384	41.0	12450	7961	156.4
网点数	(个)	Number of Outlets (unit)	9044	8293	109.1	6010	5761	104.3
#商业		Wholesale and Retail	6294	5435	115.8	4044	3974	101.8
饮食业		Catering	956	1139	83.9	1109	1080	102.7
服务业		Services	1794	1719	104.4	857	707	121.2
#宾馆、饭店		Hotels	131	130	100.8	16	16	100.0
营业人员	(人)	Personnel (person)	20509	18890	108.6	13609	13309	102.3
#商业		Wholesale and Retail	14185	13283	106.8	6872	6491	105.9
饮食业		Catering	2117	2055	103.0	3886	3788	102.3
服务业		Services	4207	3552	118.4	2851	3030	94.1
#宾馆、饭店		Hotels	2280	1920	118.8	1439	1258	114.4
外经、外贸		**Foreign Economy and Trade**						
出口商品交货额	(万元)	Delivery Value of Exports (10000 yuan)	42786.7	38086.8	112.3	30000.7	26412.2	113.6
利用外资签订协议(合同)数	(个)	Number of Signed Agreements and Contracts of Foreign Capital to be Utilized (unit)	31	20	155.0	8	7	114.0
利用外资签订协议(合同)金额	(万美元)	Amount of Foreign Capital to be Utilized through Agreements and Contracts (USD 10000)	1439.8	1578.8	91.2	387.5	643.3	60.2
实际利用外资	(万美元)	Amount of Foreign Capital Actually Used (USD 10000)	1703.8	152.0	1120.9	3446.4	47.5	7254.7
旅游人数	(万人)	Number of Tourists (10000 persons)	450.2	400.2	112.5	824.2	672.9	122.5
教育		**Education**						
学校数	(个)	Number of Schools (unit)	200	226	88.5	170	201	84.6
小学		Primary Schools	152	174	87.4	130	161	80.7

24-9 续表 5 continued

项目		Item		密云县 Miyun 2000	密云县 Miyun 1999	密云县 Miyun 2000年为1999年% 2000 as % of 1999	延庆县 Yanqing 2000	延庆县 Yanqing 1999	延庆县 Yanqing 2000年为1999年% 2000 as % of 1999
普通中学		Regular Secondary Schools		34	38	89.5	33	32	103.1
中等专业教育		Specialized Secondary Schools		6	6	100.0	7	8	87.5
招生数	(人)	New Student Enrollment	(person)	15054	14212	105.9	10262	10847	94.6
小学		Primary Schools		4801	4240	113.2	3038	2939	103.4
初级中等学校		Junior Secondary Schools		8073	7952	101.5	5432	5975	90.9
高级中等学校		Senior Secondary Schools		1531	1219	125.6	1445	1088	132.8
中等专业教育		Specialized Secondary Schools		204	512	39.8	747	845	88.4
在校学生	(人)	Student Enrollment	(person)	64320	65905	97.6	48615	50003	97.2
小学		Primary Schools		35500	39314	90.3	25646	28259	90.8
初级中等学校		Junior Secondary Schools		22829	20584	110.9	16939	16092	105.3
高级中等学校		Senior Secondary Schools		3874	3370	115.0	3483	2934	118.7
中等专业教育		Specialized Secondary Schools		842	1139	73.9	2547	2718	93.7
毕业生	(人)	Graduates	(person)	15917	17139	92.9	11441	11080	103.2
小学		Primary Schools		8237	8148	101.1	5483	5994	91.5
初级中等学校		Junior Secondary Schools		5575	6566	84.9	4270	3667	116.4
高级中等学校		Senior Secondary Schools		1002	1070	93.6	847	855	99.1
中等专业教育		Specialized Secondary Schools		458	444	103.2	841	564	149.1
达到"国家体育标准"学生数	(人)	Number of Students Come to the Standard for State Physical Training	(person)	63765	67700	94.2	39055	38261	102.1
幼儿园、托儿所个数	(个)	Number of Kindergardens	(unit)	220	223	98.7	53	53	100.0
幼儿入托数	(人)	New Enrollment	(person)	10286	10207	100.8	3767	5092	74.0
文化		**Culture**							
文化馆、站	(个)	Cultural Centers	(unit)	20	20	100.0	16	19	84.2
公共图书馆	(个)	Public Libraries	(unit)	1	1	100.0	1	1	100.0
公共图书馆藏书	(万册)	Collection	(10000 volume)	10	17	58.8	12.9	12.8	100.8
电影放映单位	(个)	Film Projection Units	(unit)	22	22	100.0	5	12	41.7
区级以上重点文物保护单位	(个)	Cultural Relics Preserved at District Level and above	(unit)	44	30	146.7	106	106	100.0
卫生		**Health**							
卫生机构数	(个)	Number of Health Institutions	(unit)	82	82	100.0	28	32	87.5
#医院		Hospitals		10	10	100.0	6	6	100.0
卫生院		Clinics		17	17	100.0	13	17	76.5
床位数		Number of Beds	(unit)	1065	1015	104.9	907	795	114.1
#医院		Hospitals		820	778	105.4	742	655	113.3
卫生院		Clinics		197	189	104.2	110	100	110.0
平均每千人拥有床位数	(张)	Average Number of Beds Per 1000 Persons	(unit)	4.6	4.2	109.5	3.3	2.9	113.8
卫生技术人员	(人)	Medical Technical Personnel	(person)	1903	1782	106.8	1228	1243	98.8
#医生		Doctors	(person)	920	909	101.2	559	582	96.0
公用设施		**Public Utilities**							
区级以上公园	(个)	Parks at District Level and above	(unit)	2	2	100.0	2	2	100.0
体育场馆	(个)	Stadiums and Gymnasiums	(unit)		1		1	1	100.0
道路长度	(公里)	Length of Roads	(km)	1176	1173	100.3	918.4	918.4	100.0

主要统计指标解释

国内生产总值 为区县及以下单位创造的国内生产总值。不包括民航、铁路、及中央属、市属单位。

财政收入、财政支出 为区县财政局提供的地方财政收支数字。

人口 为公安局户籍人口按地域范围统计的数据。

从业人员 为在区县及以下各单位中工作人员，包括在岗职工、聘用留用的离退休人员、外方和港澳台方人员以及人事档案关系保留在原单位的人员以及农村劳动力和城镇个体。

职工人数 为区县及以下各单位职工人数，即在岗职工和不在岗职工。

工资总额 与“职工人数”同口径。

全社会固定资产投资 为区县及以下各单位基本建设、更新改造、城镇集体单位投资及商品房投资。

工业增加值 为区县及以下各独立核算工业企业进行的工业经济活动，不包括中央和市属各工业企业的经济活动。

轻、重工业总产值 与“工业增加值”同口径。

商业 为区县及以下各商业活动单位数据。

外经、外贸 为各区县外经委数据。

教育 用区县教育局数据，不包括成人教育。其中高级中学包括普通高中和职业高中，中等专业教育含师范学校。

文化 按地域统计。海淀区图书馆数和藏书应包括北京图书馆、东城区应包括首都图书馆。

卫生 为各区县卫生局地域统计数据。

公园 按地域统计。

体育场馆 指专门用于体育训练、比赛和健身活动，有专人管理和一定投资的体育建筑设施。用于经营性和非经营性比赛训练和健身锻炼、长期闲置和临时被占用的体育场地均予统计，按地域统计。

道路长度 为市政管理系统道路长度和公路局系统公路长度之和。

旅游人数 按地域统计（包括海外旅游者及国内旅游者）。

Explanatory Notes On Main Statistical Indicators

Gross Domestic Product refers to that created by units at district and county level and below，exclude units of civil aviation，railway and central ，municipal units.

Fiscal Revenue or Expenditure refers to local fiscal revenue or expenditure provided by Bureau of Finance of district and county.

Population refers to registered statistics counted according to scope of region by Public Security Bureau.

Employment refers to those worked in units at district and county level and below，include staff and workers at their posts，retired and VCSR engaged and kept on，foreign，Hongkong，Macao and Taiwan employee and personnel who organizational affiliation reserved in reformer units and rural labor force, urban individuals.

Staff and Workers refers to those at and off their posts in units at district and county level and below.

Total Wages the same account as “staff and workers”.

Total Investment in Fixed Assets include investment in capital construction，innovation，real estate and urban collective-owned investment of units at district and county level and below.

Value Added of Industry refers to that created by enterprises with independent accounting system at district and county level，exclude central and municipal industrial enterprises.

Gross Output Value of Light or Heavy Industry：the same account as“Value Added of Industry”.

Commerce refers to data of commercial units at district and county level and below.

Foreign Economy and Trade refers to data provide by Committee of Foreign Economics and Trade.

Education refers to data provided by Bureau of Education of district and county，exclude adult education. And senior middle school include regular secondary school and vocational school, special secondary school include teacher training school.

Culture refers to data counted according to scope of region. Libraries and collections of Haidian District include Beijing Library，and those of Dongcheng District include Capital Library.

Health refers to data counted according to scope of region by Health Bureau of district and county.

Parks refers to data counted according to scope of region.

Stadiums and Gymnasiums refers to data counted according to scope of region， include physical construction with special management and some investment specially used in training，match and body-building，also include long-time idle and temporarily occupied places used in managing or non-managing training，match and body-building.

Length of Roads refers to the sum of length of roads of Municipal Management System and Highway Bureau System.

Tourists refers to data counted according to scope of region， include foreign and domestic tourists.

北京统计年鉴——2001

BEIJING STATISTICAL YEARBOOK

附 录

APPENDIX

附录1：历史资料

APPENDIX 1：HISTORICAL STATISTICS

附1-1 人 口 状 况

POPULATION

年 份 Year	年 底 总人口 (万人) Total Population (10000 persons)	按性别分 By Sex		按农业、非农业分 By Agriculture and Non-agriculture		人口出生率 (‰) Birth Rate (‰)	人口死亡率 (‰) Death Rate (‰)	人口自然增长率 (‰) Natural Growth Rate (‰)
		男 Male	女 Female	农业人口 Agriculture	非农业人口 Non-agriculture			
1978	872	443	429	393	479	12.93	6.12	6.81
1979	897	455	442	387	510	13.67	5.92	7.75
1980	904	458	446	383	521	15.56	6.30	9.26
1981	919	466	453	386	533	16.93	6.02	10.91
1982	935	474	461	391	544	20.04	5.68	14.36
1983	950	483	467	393	557	15.63	5.49	10.14
1984	965	491	474	395	570	16.74	5.53	11.21
1985	981	500	481	395	586	15.45	5.75	9.70
1986	1028	524	504	407	621	15.82	4.47	11.35
1987	1047	525	522	410	637	17.29	5.40	11.89
1988	1061	534	527	411	650	14.43	5.08	9.35
1989	1075	538	537	431	664	12.84	5.53	7.49
1990	1086	545	541	413	673	13.04	5.75	7.23
1991	1094	547	547	411	683	8.03	5.82	2.21
1992	1102	554	548	410	692	9.22	6.11	3.11
1993	1112	559	553	405	707	9.35	6.16	3.19
1994	1125	564	561	400	725	8.96	5.76	3.20
1995	1251	627	624	436	815	7.92	5.12	2.80
1996	1259	639	620	430	829	8.02	5.34	2.68
1997	1240	629	611	414	826	7.91	6.02	1.89
1998	1246	631	615	408	838	6.00	5.30	0.70
1999	1257	636	621	403	854	6.50	5.60	0.90
2000	1364	711	653	427	937	6.20	5.30	0.90

注：1. 1982-1989年数据是根据1982、1990年两年人口普查数据调整的，1990年以后数据是人口变动抽样调查数,其余年份数据为户籍统计数。
2. 2000年数为2000年北京市第五次全国人口普查快速汇总推算数。

a) Data from 1982 to 1989 were obtained from adjustment of cencus of 1982 and 1990,data after 1990 were those from sample survey of population changes, and data of other years were those of registered permanent population.

b) Data of 2000 is estimated through the quick collections of 2000 Beijing Population Census.

附1-2 按城乡分从业人员(年底数)
EMPLOYEE BY URBAN AND RURAL AREA(YEAR-END)

单位：万人 (10000 persons)

年份 Year	合 计 Total	城 镇 Urban	#国有经济单位 State-Owned	# 集体经济单位 Collective-Owned	#联营经济单位 Joint Owned	#股份制经济单位 Share Holding	#外商投资经济单位 Foreign Funded	# 港澳台投资经济单位 Hongkong, Macao and Taiwan Funded	# 个 体 Individuals	乡 村 Rural
1978	291.6	291.6	240.9	50.7						
1979	312.0	312.0	254.2	57.8						
1980	484.2	326.8	269.4	57.1					0.3	157.4
1981	511.7	345.2	283.1	61.3					0.8	166.5
1982	535.2	361.1	293.0	67.1					1.0	174.1
1983	552.0	373.8	303.4	68.5					1.9	178.2
1984	556.2	377.6	302.5	71.6			1.3		2.2	178.6
1985	558.7	384.8	308.1	72.6			1.6		2.5	173.9
1986	572.7	400.5	324.4	71.1			2.4		2.6	172.2
1987	580.3	408.4	331.8	70.7			2.8		3.1	171.9
1988	603.1	413.9	336.4	69.9	0.2		3.4		3.5	189.2
1989	593.9	424.0	343.8	67.4	3.4		3.7		5.6	169.9
1990	627.1	461.2	357.9	86.8	5.1		4.6		6.3	165.9
1991	634.0	477.2	367.8	89.0	0.5		7.7	0.2	7.2	156.8
1992	649.3	490.6	371.5	90.5	0.4		11.4	0.2	14.0	158.7
1993	627.8	481.4	362.3	79.7	2.8		11.0	6.4	14.0	146.4
1994	664.3	492.7	363.5	73.3	3.5	6.3	15.0	9.4	20.9	171.6
1995	665.3	492.7	358.1	72.1	3.7	8.0	17.4	10.4	21.9	172.6
1996	660.2	495.7	355.1	68.6	3.4	14.8	20.7	10.1	22.9	164.5
1997	655.8	498.8	354.7	68.5	3.2	19.3	21.2	10.2	21.2	157.1
1998	622.2	463.2	308.1	51.0	5.2	44.5	21.2	13.1	20.1	158.9
1999	618.6	456.1	287.6	49.7	4.8	24.9	20.6	13.5	23.7	162.5
2000	619.3	456.3	266.2	48.3	4.0	14.0	23.8	14.2	24.4	163.0

附1-3 从业人员和职工人数(年底数)
NUMBER OF EMPLOYED PEROSNS,STAFF AND WORKERS(YEAR-END)

单位：万人 (10000 persons)

年 份 Year	从业人员 Employed Persons	第一产业 Primary Industry	第二产业 Secondary Industry	第三产业 Tertiary Industry	职工人数 Staff and Workers	国有经济单位 State-Owned	城镇集体经济单位 Urban Collective Owned	其他经济单位 Others
1978	444.1	125.9	177.9	140.3	291.6	240.9	50.7	
1979	470.5	121.4	195.2	153.9	311.9	254.2	57.7	
1980	484.2	118.0	207.3	158.9	326.5	269.4	57.1	
1981	511.7	117.2	220.4	174.1	344.4	283.1	61.3	
1982	535.2	115.1	228.6	191.5	360.1	293.0	67.1	
1983	552.0	117.1	240.2	194.7	371.9	303.4	68.5	
1984	566.5	106.7	246.5	213.3	375.4	302.5	71.6	1.3
1985	574.8	97.1	254.3	223.4	382.3	308.1	72.6	1.6
1986	590.0	93.3	260.8	235.9	397.9	324.4	71.1	2.4
1987	598.2	91.8	264.1	242.3	405.2	331.8	70.7	2.7
1988	584.1	88.4	267.6	228.1	410.4	336.4	69.9	4.1
1989	593.9	91.0	266.3	236.6	418.4	343.8	67.4	7.2
1990	627.1	90.7	281.6	254.8	454.9	357.9	86.8	10.2
1991	634.0	90.8	279.7	263.5	470.0	367.8	89.0	13.2
1992	649.3	84.5	281.6	283.2	476.6	371.5	90.5	14.6
1993	627.8	65.1	279.4	283.3	467.3	362.3	79.6	25.4
1994	664.3	73.2	272.2	318.9	471.8	363.5	73.4	34.9
1995	665.3	70.6	271.0	323.7	470.9	358.2	72.1	40.6
1996	660.2	72.5	260.1	327.6	460.6	349.0	64.8	46.8
1997	655.8	71.0	257.6	328.1	465.3	348.7	65.0	51.6
1998	622.2	71.5	226.0	324.7	450.1	321.7	50.8	77.6
1999	618.6	74.5	216.2	327.9	438.0	303.0	49.6	85.4
2000	619.3	72.9	208.2	338.2	434.2	283.0	46.0	105.2

附1-4 国民生产总值
GROSS NATIONAL PRODUCT

单位：亿元 (100 million yuan)

年份 Year	国民生产总值 Gross National	国内生产总值 Gross Domestic Product	第一产业 Primary Industry	第二产业 Secondary Industry	#工业 Industry	#建筑业 Construction	第三产业 Tertiary Industry	#运输邮电业 Transportation, Post and Telecommunication	#商业 Commerce	人均国内生产总值(元) Per Capita Gross Domestic Product (yuan)
1978	108.84	108.84	5.63	77.43	70.22	7.21	25.78	7.00	8.28	1290
1979	120.11	120.11	5.17	85.18	77.37	7.81	29.76	6.55	8.79	1396
1980	139.07	139.07	6.07	95.79	86.94	8.85	37.21	6.96	11.01	1584
1981--1985	**950.95**	**950.95**	**62.46**	**589.30**	**515.41**	**73.89**	**299.19**	**48.08**	**80.80**	
1981	139.15	139.15	6.61	92.52	82.71	9.81	40.02	7.60	11.86	1558
1982	154.94	154.94	10.34	99.79	89.30	10.49	44.81	8.25	11.05	1704
1983	183.13	183.13	12.85	112.65	98.76	13.89	57.63	9.06	13.63	1979
1984	216.61	216.61	14.85	130.68	113.99	16.69	71.08	10.43	18.37	2306
1985	257.12	257.12	17.81	153.66	130.65	23.01	85.65	12.74	25.89	2702
1986--1990	**1978.48**	**1978.68**	**162.93**	**1084.23**	**917.29**	**166.94**	**731.52**	**94.39**	**172.89**	
1986	284.86	284.86	19.14	165.75	141.17	24.58	99.97	14.98	27.99	2953
1987	326.82	326.82	24.31	182.59	154.54	28.05	119.92	17.70	27.21	3336
1988	410.22	410.22	37.07	221.27	189.48	31.79	151.88	19.03	39.07	4124
1989	455.86	455.96	38.53	252.23	212.83	39.40	165.20	18.72	34.77	4509
1990	500.72	500.82	43.88	262.39	219.27	43.12	194.55	23.96	43.85	4878
1991--1995	**4650.47**	**4650.44**	**303.97**	**2167.24**	**1791.38**	**375.86**	**2179.23**	**247.74**	**586.26**	
1991	598.79	598.89	45.52	291.53	255.59	35.94	261.84	29.61	65.65	5782
1992	709.00	709.10	48.67	345.91	292.97	52.94	314.52	35.49	85.41	6804
1993	863.23	863.53	53.57	414.79	334.00	80.79	395.17	37.58	113.88	8239
1994	1084.33	1084.03	74.77	499.84	405.11	94.73	509.42	61.51	146.62	10261
1995	1395.12	1394.89	81.44	615.17	503.71	111.46	698.28	83.55	174.70	13085
1996--2000	**10092.58**	**10090.35**	**432.32**	**3992.29**	**3135.09**	**857.20**	**5665.74**	**761.68**	**1026.34**	
1996	1616.03	1615.73	83.46	683.14	541.41	141.73	849.13	113.78	187.59	15044
1997	1810.49	1810.09	84.85	738.56	588.36	150.20	986.68	135.79	202.45	16735
1998	2011.77	2011.31	86.56	786.85	610.66	176.19	1137.90	154.45	207.33	18478
1999	2174.97	2174.46	87.48	840.23	649.34	190.89	1246.75	167.54	210.43	19846
2000	2479.32	2478.76	89.97	943.51	745.32	198.19	1445.28	190.12	218.54	22460

注：本表按当年价格计算。

Note: Data of this table is calculated at current prices.

附1-5 国民生产总值指数(1978=100)
INDEX OF GROSS NATIONAL PRODUCT(1978=100)

单位：%　　(%)

年份 Year	国民生产总值 Gross National	国内生产总值 Gross Domestic Product	第一产业 Primary Industry	第二产业 Secondary Industry	#工业 Industry	#建筑业 Construction	第三产业 Tertiary Industry	#运输邮电业 Transportation, Post and Telecommunication	#商业 Commerce	人均国内生产总值(元) Per Capita Gross Domestic Product (yuan)
1978	100	100	100	100	100	100	100	100	100	100
1979	109.7	109.7	105	109.2	110.1	108.4	113.2	93.5	104.3	107.6
1980	122.6	122.6	114.8	120.2	121.2	119.6	134.1	96.7	124.5	117.8
1981	120.8	120.8	139.0	113.4	119.2	127.2	142.3	104.1	132.3	115.1
1982	129.7	129.7	157.6	116.9	123.0	141.3	167.5	117.5	151.7	121.4
1983	150.2	150.2	169.4	134.9	137.1	187.0	199.3	113.9	159.1	138.1
1984	176.7	176.5	180.9	157.8	158.6	222.1	242.4	130.1	210.5	159.9
1985	191.9	191.7	192.2	174.6	173.4	277.0	252.8	149.2	249.7	171.4
1986	209.0	208.8	192.4	178.9	178.2	278.1	320.3	152.1	255.4	184.3
1987	229.0	228.8	217.9	187.5	186.3	295.6	379.6	168.2	227.8	198.8
1988	258.3	258.1	242.3	213.0	210.5	314.9	424.0	166.7	268.9	220.9
1989	269.7	269.5	245.0	228.8	228.2	353.3	421.9	227.2	204.6	226.9
1990	284.3	284.0	253.3	231.1	232.5	337.7	480.9	241.3	244.9	235.5
1991	311.3	311.0	262.5	248.8	261.8	275.6	543.5	313.4	239.0	257.8
1992	347.4	347.1	270.3	279.0	288.8	346.4	611.4	344.4	283.5	286.0
1993	389.4	389.1	278.7	314.9	319.1	445.1	689.1	379.2	328.0	318.8
1994	442.0	441.6	286.0	360.9	362.2	537.7	783.5	471.0	359.5	359.0
1995	497.2	496.4	262.2	388.4	390.0	578.6	947.2	658.9	422.0	399.9
1996	543.0	542.0	254.4	417.1	413.8	659.0	1063.7	783.4	444.8	433.5
1997	595.1	594.1	256.9	450.9	449.8	692.6	1189.2	883.7	468.0	471.7
1998	653.4	652.3	260.8	494.2	489.0	791.0	1317.7	972.1	486.7	514.6
1999	720.0	718.8	267.3	553.5	551.6	854.3	1437.6	1058.6	499.8	563.5
2000	799.3	797.9	278.0	616.6	624.4	872.2	1597.1	1174.0	524.8	621.0

注：本表按可比价格计算。
Note：Data of this table are calculated at constant prices.

附1-6 国民生产总值指数(上年=100)

INDEX OF GROSS NATIONAL PRODUCT(PRECEDING YEAR=100)

单位：% (%)

年份 Year	国民生产总值 Gross National	国内生产总值 Gross Domestic Product	第一产业 Primary Industry	第二产业 Secondary Industry	# 工业 Industry	# 建筑业 Construction	第三产业 Tertiary Industry	#运输邮电业 Transportation, Post and Telecommunication	# 商业 Commerce	人均国内生产总值(元) Per Capita Gross Domestic Product (yuan)
1979	109.7	109.7	105.0	109.2	110.1	108.4	113.2	93.5	104.3	107.6
1980	111.8	111.8	109.3	110.1	110.1	110.3	118.5	103.4	119.4	109.5
1981	98.5	98.5	121.1	94.3	98.3	106.4	106.1	107.7	106.2	97.7
1982	107.4	107.4	113.4	103.1	103.2	111.1	117.7	112.8	114.7	105.5
1983	115.8	115.8	107.5	115.4	111.5	132.3	119.0	97.0	104.9	113.7
1984	117.6	117.5	106.8	117.0	115.7	118.8	121.6	114.2	132.3	115.8
1985	108.6	108.6	106.2	110.6	109.3	124.7	104.3	114.7	118.6	107.2
1986	108.9	108.9	100.1	102.5	102.8	100.4	126.7	101.9	102.3	107.5
1987	109.6	109.6	113.3	104.8	104.5	106.3	118.5	110.6	89.2	107.9
1988	112.8	112.8	111.2	113.6	113.0	106.5	111.7	99.1	118.0	111.1
1989	104.4	104.4	101.1	107.4	108.4	112.2	99.5	136.3	76.1	102.7
1990	105.4	105.4	103.4	101.0	101.9	95.6	114.0	106.2	119.7	103.8
1991	109.5	109.5	103.6	107.7	112.6	81.6	113.0	129.9	97.6	109.5
1992	111.6	111.6	103.0	112.1	110.3	125.7	112.5	109.9	118.6	110.9
1993	112.1	112.1	103.1	112.9	110.5	128.5	112.7	110.1	115.7	111.5
1994	113.5	113.5	102.6	114.6	113.5	120.8	113.7	124.2	109.6	112.6
1995	112.5	112.4	91.7	107.6	107.7	107.6	120.9	139.9	117.4	111.4
1996	109.2	109.2	97.0	107.4	106.1	113.9	112.3	118.9	105.4	108.4
1997	109.6	109.6	101.0	108.1	108.7	105.1	111.8	112.8	105.2	108.8
1998	109.8	109.8	101.5	109.6	108.7	114.2	110.8	110.0	104.0	109.1
1999	110.2	110.2	102.5	112.0	112.8	108.0	109.1	108.9	102.7	109.5
2000	111.0	111.0	104.0	111.4	113.2	102.1	111.1	110.9	105.0	110.2

注：本表按可比价格计算。

Note: Data of this table are calculated at constant prices.

附1-7 国内支出总额
GROSS DOMESTIC EXPENDITURE

单位：亿元 (100 million yuan)

年份 Year	国内支出总额 Gross Domestic Expenditure	最终消费 Final Consumption	居民消费 Residenrtial Consumption	农民 Peasant	非农业居民 Non-Peasant	政府消费 Government Consumption	资本形成总额 Total Capital Formation	固定资产 Fixed Assets	存货 Stock
1978	108.84	40.98	30.47	7.32	23.15	10.51	31.67	24.84	6.83
1979	102.11	49.34	36.24	8.63	27.61	13.10	37.40	29.76	7.64
1980	139.07	57.44	44.35	10.53	33.82	13.09	43.69	35.63	8.06
1981--1985	**950.95**	**424.69**	**306.14**	**87.83**	**218.31**	**118.55**	**343.04**	**271.97**	**71.07**
1981	139.15	63.72	47.66	11.98	35.68	16.06	38.85	29.53	9.32
1982	154.94	71.22	51.24	13.64	37.60	19.98	34.43	26.10	8.33
1983	183.13	81.31	56.45	16.57	39.88	24.86	54.76	49.04	5.72
1984	216.61	96.14	67.65	21.05	46.60	28.49	78.57	68.60	9.97
1985	257.12	112.30	83.14	24.59	58.55	29.16	136.43	98.70	37.73
1986--1990	**1978.68**	**880.15**	**640.93**	**188.47**	**452.46**	**239.22**	**1218.96**	**925.87**	**293.09**
1986	284.86	125.16	92.40	26.10	66.30	32.76	156.33	129.75	26.58
1987	326.82	147.87	107.73	29.12	78.61	40.14	208.33	170.12	38.21
1988	410.22	178.49	131.98	37.25	94.73	46.51	250.01	197.79	52.22
1989	455.96	197.67	138.99	46.78	92.21	58.68	297.00	200.26	96.74
1990	500.82	230.96	169.83	49.22	120.61	61.13	307.29	227.95	79.34
1991--1995	**5274.68**	**1701.59**	**1177.92**	**276.13**	**901.79**	**523.67**	**3530.54**	**2119.49**	**1411.05**
1991	560.21	225.47	153.62	37.59	116.03	71.85	322.77	184.37	138.40
1992	681.43	262.97	177.08	40.11	136.97	85.89	423.71	200.98	222.73
1993	1019.55	310.28	207.21	52.95	154.26	103.07	625.15	326.82	298.33
1994	1318.60	396.29	264.55	66.95	197.60	131.74	902.63	519.01	383.62
1995	1694.89	506.58	375.46	78.53	296.93	131.12	1256.28	888.31	367.97
1996--2000	**10248.98**	**4306.50**	**2950.75**	**537.84**	**2412.91**	**1355.75**	**6775.65**	**5706.55**	**1069.10**
1996	1678.52	617.85	451.96	92.89	359.07	165.89	1107.06	922.48	184.58
1997	1870.93	703.36	492.88	97.25	395.63	210.48	1228.65	1001.73	226.92
1998	2046.31	809.82	563.62	109.26	454.36	246.20	1396.40	1171.90	224.50
1999	2174.46	954.14	633.76	112.52	521.24	320.38	1526.16	1233.46	292.70
2000	2478.76	1221.33	808.53	125.92	682.61	412.80	1517.38	1376.98	140.40

注：本表按当年价格计算。

Note: Data of this table is calculated at current prices.

附1-8 全社会固定资产投资
TOTAL INVESTMENT IN FIXED ASSETS

单位：亿元 (100 million yuan)

年 份 Year	合 计 Total	国有经济单位 State-Owned	#基本建设 Capital Construction	#更新改造 Innovation	集体经济单位 Collective Owned	#农 村 Rural	其他经济单位 Others	私营个体经济 Private and Individuals	#农 村 Rural
1985	94.0	73.6	50.7	21.7	16.2	10.8		4.2	3.8
1986--1990	**724.1**	**609.6**	**378.2**	**201.3**	**83.1**	**49.1**		**31.4**	**27.5**
1986	106.2	88.7	54.2	33.4	13.3	6.4		4.2	4.0
1987	136.2	115.8	71.7	43.1	15.2	8.3		5.2	4.5
1988	163.0	133.2	87.7	43.6	21.4	13.7		8.4	7.6
1989	139.5	117.7	79.8	36.5	15.1	9.0		6.7	5.7
1990	179.2	154.2	84.8	44.7	18.1	11.7		6.9	5.7
1991--1995	**2358.7**	**1764.2**	**808.7**	**567.9**	**188.7**	**134.8**	**381.0**	**24.8**	**19.3**
1991	192.0	165.0	86.8	52.4	20.2	14.6		6.8	6.4
1992	266.0	230.1	114.9	79.2	27.3	19.8		8.6	7.4
1993	410.4	340.1	157.1	116.1	37.4	28.8	30.9	2.0	1.2
1994	648.8	514.8	229.2	179.2	44.6	33.7	86.3	3.1	2.0
1995	841.5	514.2	220.7	141.0	59.2	37.9	263.8	4.3	2.3
1996--2000	**5461.7**	**3380.8**	**1699.2**	**865.2**	**261.8**	**156.1**	**1704.7**	**114.4**	**74.6**
1996	876.9	545.7	241.8	156.4	57.6	41.1	268.8	4.8	2.5
1997	961.2	605.7	294.1	174.4	54.7	38.5	296.8	4.0	2.1
1998	1155.6	727.9	369.1	196.5	48.7	24.3	349.0	30.0	17.5
1999	1170.6	735.7	389.0	164.6	55.8	25.7	344.3	34.8	23.4
2000	1297.4	765.8	405.2	173.3	45.0	26.5	445.8	40.8	29.1

年 份 Year	固定资产投资来源 Source of Investment in Fixed Assets					固定资产投资 Investment in Fixed Assets					
	国家预算内投资 State Budgetary Investment	国内贷款 Domestic Loan	利用外资 Foreign Capital	自筹投资 Selfraised investment	其他投资 Other Investment	第一产业 Primary Industry	第二产业 Secondary Industry	#工业 Industry	#能源工业 Energy	第三产业 Tertiary Industry	#运输邮电业 Transportation, Post and Telecommunications
1985	30.4	11.5	5.1	26.4	4.4	1.6	32.4	28.8	4.4	43.8	5.3
1986--1990	**184.9**	**90.3**	**69.1**	**245.6**	**39.5**	**9.4**	**218.8**	**209.1**	**43.1**	**384.2**	**47.7**
1986	33.0	17.0	4.6	37.4	2.5	1.5	41.4	38.8	5.5	51.6	6.6
1987	43.1	19.5	8.8	49.1	5.7	1.6	46.9	44.3	10.0	72.9	9.7
1988	37.4	18.2	22.3	62.3	9.2	2.0	48.8	47.2	9.9	87.9	7.8
1989	35.6	12.8	18.2	44.5	12.0	1.9	38.4	37.0	8.5	81.9	10.0
1990	35.8	22.8	15.2	52.3	10.1	2.4	43.3	41.8	9.2	89.9	13.6
1991--1995	**254.5**	**274.8**	**189.6**	**888.4**	**127.3**	**15.5**	**624.1**	**585.1**	**154.8**	**973.5**	**256.2**
1991	35.5	28.2	13.9	65.5	8.0	2.7	51.3	49.3	11.8	90.4	13.0
1992	42.2	40.1	14.9	109.9	9.6	3.9	82.9	80.2	22.0	114.2	28.4
1993	46.4	71.0	28.0	168.9	35.9	2.1	150.4	134.6	28.2	165.7	51.7
1994	62.5	70.9	87.8	283.7	44.8	3.7	185.8	175.9	40.2	318.4	81.2
1995	67.9	64.6	45.0	260.4	29.0	3.1	153.7	145.1	52.6	284.8	81.9
1996--2000	**492.2**	**501.1**	**195.2**	**1706.3**	**182.6**						
1996	73.1	71.1	53.8	265.7	39.8	2.8	174.9	167.3	69.8	319.7	99.5
1997	82.8	89.7	51.3	322.4	41.3	0.9	201.1	192.1	93.3	380.1	113.4
1998	93.9	108.4	41.2	382.9	43.0	1.5	201.7	192.6	96.2	479.7	169.8
1999	135.7	96.9	34.5	359.1	31.4	1.7	179.4	166.6	85.1	470.4	108.2
2000	106.7	135.0	14.4	374.9	26.9	3.0	157.2	148.0	57.8	510.3	124.4

注：1.全社会固定资产投资来源中,1985和1986年为固定资产投资完成额资金来源分组。
2.按资金来源和三次产业划分的固定资产投资不含房地产开发投资。

a) In source of total investment of fixed assets,data of 1985 and 1986 are grouped by source of investment completed.
b) Data of investment grouped by source of funds and three industry excluded real estate development.

附1-9 基本建设投资额
INVESTMENT IN CAPITAL CONSTRUCTION

年 份 Year	基本建设投资额 (万元) Investment (10000 yuan)	按隶属关系分 Grouped by Administrative Relationship		按建设性质分 Grouped by Type of Construction			新增固定资产 (万元) Incremental Fixed Assets (10000 yuan)	固定资产交付使用率 (%) Rate of Fixed Assets Put into Operation (%)
		中央 Central	地方 Local	新建 Newly-built	扩建、改建 Expanding, Replacement	其他 Others		
1978	198908	90498	108410				169148	85.0
1979	234741	124132	110609	107611	105561	21569	212111	90.4
1980	265185	139843	125342	123520	135064	6601	231715	87.4
1981--1985	**1672352**	**926161**	**746191**	**670739**	**827830**	**173783**	**1421535**	**85.0**
1981	238693	130589	108104	111150	121431	6112	309203	129.5
1982	259866	121116	138750	119196	130002	10668	199313	76.7
1983	271126	141087	130039	93471	172287	5368	236816	87.3
1984	360756	210516	150240	136480	161372	62904	360997	100.1
1985	541911	322853	219058	210442	242738	88731	315206	58.2
1986--1990	**4000931**	**2506444**	**1494487**	**1888490**	**1641503**	**470938**	**2662712**	**66.6**
1986	587030	358562	228468	249512	254774	82744	354264	60.3
1987	763286	494817	268469	297042	359192	107052	463887	60.8
1988	926549	590549	336000	454766	365721	106062	455230	49.1
1989	835661	521340	314321	419002	323336	93323	512484	61.3
1990	888405	541176	347229	468168	338480	81757	876847	98.7
1991--1995	**9314619**	**5081070**	**4233549**	**3940498**	**4651510**	**722611**	**5263959**	**56.5**
1991	902052	481844	420208	390091	412787	99174	779764	86.4
1992	1185313	646031	539282	458089	618029	109195	726984	61.3
1993	1726260	934439	791821	640690	962772	122798	805405	46.7
1994	2851219	1329286	1521933	1340373	1306164	204682	1386866	48.6
1995	2649775	1689470	960305	1111255	1351758	186762	1564940	59.1
1996--2000	19974274	10874857	9099417	6454909	11602297	1917068	16793905	84.1
1996	3138456	1892321	1246135	1213019	1675846	249591	2625211	83.6
1997	3743212	2233708	1509504	1250778	2124370	368064	2639688	70.5
1998	4295514	2506556	1788958	1337033	2559533	398948	3000077	69.8
1999	4327251	2420060	1907191	1294950	2481402	550899	3569318	82.5
2000	4469841	1822212	2647629	1359129	2761146	349566	4959611	111.0

附1-10 国有单位基本建设投资额
INVESTMENT IN CAPITAL CONSTRUCTION OF STATE-OWNED UNITS

年 份 Year	基本建设投资额 (亿元) Investment (100 million yuan)	按隶属关系分 Grouped by Administrative Relationship		按建设性质分 Grouped by Type of Construction			新增固定资产 (亿元) Incremental Fixed Assets (100 million yuan)	固定资产交付使用率 (%) Rate of Fixed Assets Put into Operation (%)
		中央 Central	地方 Local	新建 Newly-built	扩建、改建 Expanding, Replacement	其他 Others		
1981--1985	**160.2**						**132.6**	**82.8**
1981	23.4						24.9	106.4
1982	25.0	12.1	12.9				19.4	77.6
1983	26.4	14.1	12.3				23.2	87.9
1984	34.7	21.0	13.7	13.0	15.9	5.8	35.0	100.9
1985	50.7	32.3	18.4	18.8	23.9	8.0	30.1	59.4
1986--1990	**378.2**	**250.4**	**127.8**	**177.6**	**160.6**	**40.0**	**251.2**	**66.4**
1986	54.2	35.8	18.4	22.7	24.6	6.9	32.9	60.7
1987	71.7	49.5	22.2	26.8	35.5	9.4	43.7	60.9
1988	87.7	58.9	28.8	42.4	36.0	9.3	42.3	48.2
1989	79.8	52.1	27.7	40.1	31.7	8.0	48.3	60.5
1990	84.8	54.1	30.7	45.6	32.8	6.4	84.0	99.1
1991--1995	**808.7**	**480.8**	**327.9**				**457.9**	**56.6**
1991	86.8	48.2	38.6	38.1	40.4	8.3	75.6	87.1
1992	114.9	64.6	50.3	45.2	60.1	9.6	67.4	58.7
1993	157.1	89.7	67.4				53.5	34.1
1994	229.2	125.6	103.6				124.3	54.2
1995	220.7	152.7	68.0				137.1	62.1
1996--2000	**1699.2**	**976.9**	**722.3**	**370.5**	**925.7**	**161.2**	**1445.0**	**85.0**
1996	241.8	165.8	76.0				229.8	95.0
1997	294.1	193.0	101.1	64.5	194.0	35.6	221.0	75.1
1998	369.1	224.5	144.6	93.3	237.3	38.5	207.5	56.2
1999	389.0	218.7	170.3	98.8	235.9	54.3	308.8	79.4
2000	405.2	174.9	230.3	113.9	258.5	32.8	477.9	117.9

附1-11 更新改造投资额
INVESTMENT IN INNOVATIONS

年 份 Year	更新改造投资额(万元) Investment (10000 yuan)	按隶属关系分 Grouped by Administrative Relationship		按建设性质分 Grouped by Type of Construction			新增固定资产(亿元) Incremental Fixed Assets (100 million yuan)	固定资产交付使用率(%) Rate of Fixed Assets Put into Operation (%)
		中央 Central	地方 Local	新建 Newly-built	扩建、改建 Expanding, Replacement	其他 Others		
1980	66542						48089	72.3
1981--1985	**671784**						**479560**	**71.4**
1981	75545						56527	74.8
1982	84818	16044	68774				63785	75.2
1983	114327	26087	88240				88582	77.5
1984	161276	35069	126207	3354	138963	18959	110265	68.4
1985	235818	44706	191112	14281	208010	13527	160401	68.0
1986--1990	**2123897**	**331964**	**1791933**	**133715**	**1710681**	**279501**	**1511075**	**71.1**
1986	358357	57582	300775	26619	289075	42663	230940	64.4
1987	450629	79105	371524	11550	386744	52335	335159	74.4
1988	460025	66340	393685	29480	366311	64234	317796	69.1
1989	386827	58418	328409	26969	307067	52791	283194	73.2
1990	468059	70519	397540	39097	361484	67478	343986	73.5
1991--1995	**6178916**	**1888982**	**4289934**	**237180**	**5256320**	**685416**	**4378783**	**70.9**
1991	541624	86149	455475	11578	460759	69287	448861	82.9
1992	824518	169979	654539	17901	731095	75522	600487	72.8
1993	1218170	367869	850301	33269	1092674	92227	687026	56.4
1994	2022193	669408	1352785	36723	1855312	130158	1625303	80.4
1995	1572441	595577	976834	137709	1283375	151327	1017106	64.7
1996--2000	**9318081**	**4140784**	**5177297**	**453518**	**7807172**	**1057391**	**7646213**	**82.1**
1996	1680479	636918	1043561	222645	1318904	138930	1553521	92.4
1997	1911525	894052	1017473	180134	1550027	181364	1301241	68.1
1998	2114549	1003398	1111151	27792	1822482	264275	1412362	66.8
1999	1752093	646454	1105639	10618	1536248	205227	1990395	113.6
2000	1859435	959962	899473	12329	1579511	267595	1388694	74.7

附1-12 国有单位更新改造投资额
INVESTMENT IN INNOVATIONS OF STATE-OWNED UNITS

年份 Year	更新改造投资额 (亿元) Investment (100 million yuan)	按隶属关系分 Grouped by Administrative Relationship		按建设性质分 Grouped by Type of Construction			新增固定资产 (亿元) Incremental Fixed Assets (100 million yuan)	固定资产交付使用率 (%) Rate of Fixed Assets Put into Operation (%)
		中央 Central	地方 Local	新建 Newly-built	扩建、改建 Expanding, Replacement	其他 Others		
1981--1985	**62.5**						**44.7**	**71.5**
1981	6.8						5.3	77.9
1982	7.9	1.6	6.3				5.9	74.7
1983	10.8	2.6	8.2				8.1	75.0
1984	15.3	3.5	11.8	0.3	13.2	1.8	10.3	67.3
1985	21.7	4.5	17.2	1.3	19.3	1.1	15.1	69.6
1986--1990	**201.3**	**33.2**	**168.1**	**12.8**	**163.1**	**25.4**	**143.2**	**71.1**
1986	33.4	5.7	27.7	2.4	27.1	3.9	21.9	65.6
1987	43.1	7.9	35.2	1.1	37.1	4.9	32.1	74.5
1988	43.6	6.6	37.0	2.8	34.9	5.9	29.5	67.7
1989	36.5	5.9	30.6	2.6	29.2	4.7	26.8	73.4
1990	44.7	7.1	37.6	3.9	34.8	6.0	32.9	73.6
1991--1995	**567.9**	**185.1**	**382.8**				**418.3**	**73.7**
1991	52.4	8.6	43.8	1.2	44.9	6.3	43.1	82.3
1992	79.2	17.0	62.2	1.8	70.5	6.9	57.8	73.0
1993	116.1	36.3	79.8				66.7	57.5
1994	179.2	65.9	113.3				154.9	86.4
1995	141.0	57.3	83.7				95.8	67.9
1996--2000	**865.2**	**406.0**	**459.2**	**20.2**	**577.2**	**111.4**	**702.5**	**81.2**
1996	156.4	61.8	94.6				138.4	88.5
1997	174.4	87.8	86.6	10.1	112.8	51.5	123.6	70.9
1998	196.5	98.9	97.6	8.5	172.2	15.8	131.7	67.0
1999	164.6	63.8	100.8	0.4	144.4	19.8	181.8	110.4
2000	173.3	93.7	79.6	1.2	147.8	24.3	127.0	73.3

附1-13 房 地 产 投 资 额
INVESTMENT IN REAL ESTATE DEVELOPMENT

年份 Year	投资总额 (亿元) Total Investment (100 million yuan)	商品房屋施工面积 (万平方米) Floor Space of Commodity Buildings under Construction (10000 sq.m)	# 本年新开工面积 Construction of this Year	商品房屋竣工面积 (万平方米) Floor Space of Commodity Buildings Completed (10000 sq.m)	商品房销售建筑面积 (万平方米) Floor Space of Commodity Buildings Sales (10000 sq.m)
1990	22.5	774.0	249.1	271.6	142.2
1991--1995	**568.4**	**7501.6**	**3022.6**	**2061.7**	**855.6**
1991	24.0	815.1	317.6	275.2	154.0
1992	33.7	1021.1	508.6	331.4	159.1
1993	58.4	1262.0	524.8	356.4	182.0
1994	99.5	1593.2	659.4	445.7	168.6
1995	352.8	2810.2	1012.2	653.0	191.9
1996--2000	**1979.5**	**17432.3**	**5359.2**	**4762.6**	**2416.7**
1996	328.2	2824.6	578.7	663.4	215.3
1997	330.3	2869.6	848.4	682.3	290.9
1998	377.4	3499.1	1193.4	842.8	409.2
1999	421.5	3784.0	1061.8	1208.5	544.4
2000	522.1	4455.0	1676.9	1365.6	956.9

附1-14 地方财政收支

LOCAL FINANCIAL REVENUE AND EXPENDITURE

单位：亿元 (100 million yuan)

年份 Year	地方财政收入 Local Financial Revenue	#各项税收 Taxes	地方财政支出 Local Financial Expenditure	#基本建设 Capital Construction	#农业生产和农业事业费 Agricultural Production and Operating Expenses	#文教科卫事业费 Culture,Education, Science and Health Expenses	#教育事业费 Education	#科学事业费 Scientific Research
1978	50.46	18.25	20.38	10.89	0.84	2.43	1.46	0.22
1979	47.75	19.41	20.06	10.07	0.86	2.94	1.77	0.24
1980	51.29	21.22	14.87	5.65	0.75	3.22	1.93	0.26
1981--1985	**234.27**	**149.21**	**111.40**	**39.75**	**4.69**	**24.82**	**14.04**	**1.64**
1981	49.12	22.47	14.85	5.95	0.71	3.65	2.15	0.29
1982	47.25	24.40	16.80	6.44	0.80	4.17	2.37	0.27
1983	39.84	26.45	19.61	6.47	0.83	4.63	2.65	0.36
1984	45.62	31.49	27.15	10.06	1.12	5.53	3.00	0.37
1985	52.44	44.40	32.99	10.83	1.23	6.84	3.87	0.37
1986--1990	**337.13**	**335.42**	**272.89**	**55.78**	**12.72**	**59.36**	**30.48**	**2.99**
1986	60.34	49.82	44.27	11.22	1.57	8.20	4.45	0.49
1987	63.62	55.16	49.67	10.47	1.91	9.21	4.79	0.58
1988	68.11	67.27	52.93	10.53	2.88	11.46	6.04	0.58
1989	71.05	79.30	59.50	11.70	3.15	13.67	7.00	0.57
1990	74.01	83.87	66.52	11.86	3.21	16.82	8.20	0.76
1991--1995	**456.48**	**586.35**	**473.64**	**51.07**	**22.74**	**131.86**	**73.30**	**7.36**
1991	77.02	92.02	67.98	9.35	3.67	17.58	9.41	1.01
1992	80.25	104.14	71.74	8.57	3.98	19.72	10.56	1.10
1993	84.10	136.77	80.99	10.35	4.33	24.08	13.10	1.30
1994	99.85	107.48	98.53	9.37	4.93	29.81	17.22	1.62
1995	115.26	145.94	154.40	13.43	5.83	40.67	23.01	2.34
1996--2000	**1345.25**	**1402.32**	**1655.37**	**182.00**	**57.35**	**376.87**	**216.14**	**21.91**
1996	150.90	203.07	187.45	21.66	7.42	51.66	29.57	2.94
1997	209.91	239.13	262.20	24.89	9.85	63.83	35.97	3.74
1998	265.61	272.23	316.84	32.50	10.70	72.79	41.31	4.11
1999	320.44	315.10	398.53	45.46	13.13	84.52	49.22	4.91
2000	398.39	372.79	490.34	57.49	16.25	104.07	60.07	6.21

注：1. 地方财政收支数为决算数。

2. 1996-2000年各项税收中含企业所得税。

a) Data is the final one.

b) Taxes from 1996 to 2000 include those from enterprise income.

附1-15 北京市各银行各项存款年末余额
YEAR-END BALANCE OF DEPOSITS OF BANKS OF BEIJING

单位：万元 (10000 yuan)

年份 Year	合计 Total	企业存款 Enterprises	财政存款 Financial	机关团体、部队存款 Government Organs Bodies and Army	城镇储蓄存款 Urban Saving Deposits	农村存款 Rural
1978	1146580	527922	40273	389409	88991	46749
1979	1390517	649013	49342	463723	104400	57357
1980	1679891	834102	71486	566547	133310	67679
1981	2204737	1131870	65544	750606	157369	89070
1982	2792318	1432034	87904	974105	191882	105168
1983	3212851	1660027	85297	1087862	251065	128364
1984	3755220	2254153	129052	927955	321447	122081
1985	4109535	2454797	182064	890667	422447	137390
1986	5087562	3116297	165906	1027730	556249	179889
1987	6107619	3555956	150093	1335385	751854	205995
1988	6099142	3328559	97147	1180338	905519	295712
1989	7176132	3709770	259761	1218831	1337629	317000
1990	8689227	4293690	290365	1503878	1879081	297212
1991	11060952	5484293	333025	1879611	2498786	367665
1992	13095965	7005468	112779	1422621	3282099	534536
1993	16492164	8351199	142235	1551093	4824810	804791
1994	23111169	10377956	227561	2004247	7414350	932779
1995	30541198	16074288	359667	2116841	11034549	184283
1996	37818707	19705705	483317	2364532	15060889	199136
1997	51036605	29211539	381652	3303945	17709062	252358
1998	63691737	36289291	970772	5134092	20631876	266550
1999	79068543	44475637	1968641	7252845	24290306	271969
2000	92610099	54252792	2023219	8354037	26632980	304646

注：1997-2000年存款合计中含代理财政存款。

Note: Deposits from 1997 to 2000 include agent financial deposits.

附1-16 北京市各银行各项贷款年末余额
YEAR-END BALANCE OF LOANS OF BANKS BEIJING

单位：万元 (10000 yuan)

年份 Year	合计 Total	工业生产企业贷款 Industrial Production	商业企业贷款 Commerce	建筑企业贷款 Construction	农业贷款 Agriculture	固定资产贷款 Fixed Assets	短期贷款 Short-term	中长期贷款 Mid,Long-term
1978	539078	214352	319239		5484	3		
1979	742332	216791	475507		6133	43901		
1980	873420	252528	495423	2198	7442	110685		
1981	912591	265718	517190	3624	8642	102540		
1982	1090686	346081	522596	10508	9479	178107		
1983	1494770	687371	552268	21486	14350	189486		
1984	1933724	774286	646218	76085	55606	304220		
1985	2534647	926420	697008	90789	61870	428020		
1986	3127010	1126873	814253	109423	96030	528287		
1987	3623937	1237457	896170	120812	126462	608207		
1988	4157237	1401628	1133718	162539	72292	753177	2777141	
1989	4870606	1740436	1407018	175324	99980	776477		
1990	5526782	2113813	1613340	187509	147878	946906	4159282	946906
1991	6326887	2407065	1810436	201089	193636	1159300	4724335	1159300
1992	7304636	2662278	2091350	218154	232829	1473004	5325684	1473004
1993	9715379	3372431	2519224	262157	271067	2344437	6713712	2344437
1994	10703251	3887403	1954192	284100	274209	3124624	7155394	3124624
1995	15605875	4643921	3592487	358327	339788	3563697	10159790	3563697
1996	18096848	5747916	4327060	483578	386784	3918864	12463119	3918864
1997	25444738	7412815	5632541	1000396	477519	5524730	18353500	5524730
1998	31269744	8919232	5892568	1383505	530789	7281840	20993880	7281840
1999	37612521	9917578	6722679	1967942	505578	8229492	25601364	8229492
2000	56667402	10382307	6546045	2217508	368199	21569860	32138281	21569860

附1-17 各种物价总指数
AGGREGATE PRICE INDICES

年份 Year	商品零售价格总指数(上年=100) Aggregate Retail Price Index (preceding year=100)	居民消费价格总指数(上年=100) Aggregate Consumer Price Index (preceding year=100)	农副产品收购价格总指数(上年=100) Purchasing Price Index of Farm and Sideline Products (preceding year=100)	农业生产资料价格指数(上年=100) Price Index of Agricultural Capital Goods (preceding year=100)	商品零售价格总指数(1978=100) Aggregate Retail Price Index (1978=100)	居民消费价格总指数(1978=100) Aggregate Consumer Price Index (1978=100)	农副产品收购价格总指数(1978=100) Purchasing Price Index of Farm and Sideline Products (1978=100)	农业生产资料价格指数(1978=100) Price Index of Agricultural Capital Goods (1978=100)
1978	100.6	100.6			100.0	100.0	100.0	100.0
1979	101.8	101.8	109.5	100.0	101.5	101.4	109.5	100.0
1980	106.7	106.0	105.5	100.2	108.6	107.9	115.5	100.3
1981	101.4	101.3	109.4	100.1	110.2	109.2	126.4	100.3
1982	102.0	101.8	101.9	100.1	112.3	111.2	128.7	100.4
1983	100.6	100.5	101.8	101.6	113.0	111.8	131.0	102.0
1984	102.1	102.2	102.3	109.7	115.4	114.2	133.9	111.9
1985	118.6	117.6	117.6	100.9	136.8	134.4	157.5	112.9
1986	106.7	106.8	108.1	102.7	145.9	143.5	170.3	115.9
1987	108.7	108.6	116.1	110.8	158.6	155.8	197.6	128.4
1988	121.9	120.4	123.2	117.6	193.3	187.6	243.4	151.0
1989	118.5	117.2	106.8	121.5	229.1	219.9	260.0	183.5
1990	104.1	105.4	101.9	102.1	238.5	231.8	264.9	187.4
1991	108.5	111.9	101.7	102.5	258.8	259.4	269.4	192.1
1992	108.3	109.9	102.4	103.6	280.3	285.1	275.9	199.0
1993	116.9	119.0	107.0	109.1	327.7	339.3	295.2	217.1
1994	117.9	124.9	133.4	120.1	386.4	423.8	393.8	260.7
1995	112.6	117.3	130.6	133.2	435.1	497.1	514.3	347.3
1996	107.3	111.6	101.5	106.8	466.9	554.8	522.0	370.9
1997	103.8	105.3	92.8	100.4	484.6	584.2	484.4	372.2
1998	98.3	102.4	93.6	102.6	476.4	598.2	484.4	372.2
1999	98.8	100.6	97.5	94.2	470.7	601.8	442.1	359.7
2000	98.9	103.5	95.0	101.7	465.5	622.9	420.0	365.8

附1-18 职工工资总额和保险福利费

TOTAL WAGES,INSURANCE AND WELFARES OF STAFF AND WORKERS

年 份 Year	职工工资总额(亿元) Total Wages (100 million yuan)	国有经济单位 State-Owned	城镇集体经济单位 Urban Collective Owned	其他经济单位 Others	职工保险福利费用总额(亿元) Total Insurance and Welfares (100 million yuan)	国有经济单位 State-Owned	城镇集体经济单位 Urban Collective Owned	其他经济单位 Others
1978	18.7	16.2	2.5		2.6	2.6		
1979	22.4	19.4	3.0		3.1	3.1		
1980	26.9	23.3	3.6		4.3	4.3		
1981--1985	**183.7**	**153.7**	**29.6**	**0.4**	**39.5**	**39.5**		
1981	28.3	24.2	4.1		5.2	5.2		
1982	30.5	25.9	4.6		5.8	5.8		
1983	33.8	28.5	5.3		7.7	7.7		
1984	40.4	33.7	6.6	0.1	9.3	9.3		
1985	50.7	41.4	9.0	0.3	11.5	11.5		
1986--1990	**421.1**	**349.7**	**64.4**	**7.0**	**95.7**	**91.5**	**3.6**	**0.6**
1986	58.0	48.5	9.1	0.4	13.9	13.9		
1987	66.7	56.0	10.1	0.6	17.0	17.0		
1988	81.2	68.1	12.1	1.0	24.3	24.3		
1989	96.3	81.0	13.4	1.9	19.5	17.4	1.8	0.3
1990	118.9	96.1	19.7	3.1	21.0	18.9	1.8	0.3
1991--1995	**1198.1**	**950.3**	**156.6**	**91.2**	**156.0**	**138.9**	**10.9**	**6.2**
1991	132.2	106.1	21.5	4.6	25.3	22.6	2.1	0.6
1992	158.5	128.6	23.9	6.0	30.6	27.4	2.4	0.8
1993	218.9	176.6	28.5	13.8	36.0	32.2	2.5	1.3
1994	306.5	243.4	36.2	26.9	30.4	27.0	1.9	1.5
1995	382.0	295.6	46.5	39.9	33.7	29.7	2.0	2.0
1996-2000	**2825.4**	**1988.5**	**236.5**	**600.4**				
1996	442.4	339.4	46.2	56.8	37.3	31.7	2.8	2.8
1997	514.8	383.6	53.8	77.4	48.1	41.6	2.8	3.7
1998	558.2	391.9	45.0	121.3	54.5	47.5	3.0	4.0
1999	614.5	420.0	44.8	149.7	60.2	50.1	4.0	6.2
2000	695.5	453.6	46.7	195.2				

附1-19 职工平均工资及指数

AVERAGE WAGE AND INDEX OF STAFF AND WORKERS

年 份 Year	职工平均工资(元) Average Wage (yuan)	国有经济单位 State-Owned	城镇集体经济单位 Urban Collective Owned	其他经济单位 Others	职工实际工资指数(1978=100) Index of Actual Wage	国有经济单位 State-Owned	城镇集体经济单位 Urban Collective Owned	其他经济单位 Others
1978	673	703	471		100	100	100	100
1979	742	778	556		108.3	108.7	116.0	
1980	848	889	635		116.8	117.3	125.0	
1981	837	880	685		113.9	114.6	133.1	
1982	863	896	715		115.3	114.6	136.5	
1983	931	964	785		123.7	122.6	149.0	
1984	1086	1127	946	1170	141.3	140.3	175.8	
1985	1343	1367	1231	1768	148.5	144.7	194.5	112.5
1986	1488	1530	1287	2080	154.1	151.7	190.4	123.9
1987	1670	1712	1449	2267	159.3	156.3	197.5	124.4
1988	2000	2048	1738	2661	158.4	155.3	196.7	121.2
1989	2312	2366	1992	2761	156.2	153.1	192.3	107.3
1990	2653	2713	2334	3243	170.1	166.5	213.8	119.6
1991	2877	2937	2504	3713	164.8	161.1	205.0	122.3
1992	3402	3500	2828	4289	177.3	174.6	210.6	128.6
1993	4780	4920	3834	5469	209.3	206.3	239.9	137.8
1994	6540	6695	5009	8179	229.3	224.7	250.9	165.0
1995	8144	8237	6516	10278	243.4	235.7	278.3	176.7
1996	9579	9645	7133	13851	256.5	247.3	273.0	213.4
1997	11019	10917	8259	15370	280.2	265.6	300.2	224.9
1998	12285	11971	8800	15989	306.1	285.5	313.3	229.1
1999	13778	13483	8928	17748	335.2	314.0	310.3	248.4
2000	15726	15483	9844	19165	375.1	353.6	335.5	263.0

附1-20 居民生活
PEOPLE'S LIVELIHOOD

年份 Year	城镇居民家庭平均每人每年(元) Annual Per Capita of Urban Households(yuan)					农村居民家庭平均每人每年(元) Annual Per Capita of Rural Households(yuan)				
	全部收入 Total Income	可支配收入 Discretionary Income	可支配收入指数(1978=100) Index of Discretionary Income (1978=100)	生活消费支出 Living Expenditures	#食品 Food	纯收入 Net Income	纯收入指数(1978=100) Index of Net Income (1978=100)	总支出 Total Expenditures	生活消费支出 Living Expenditures	#食品 Food
1978	450.2	365.4	100.0	359.9	211.2	224.8	100.0	219.0	185.4	116.7
1979	491.5	415.0	111.6	408.7	236.7	250.0	110.9	235.0	204.7	131.1
1980	599.4	501.4	127.2	490.4	271.0	308.1	135.4	290.0	256.8	140.2
1981	619.6	514.1	128.8	511.4	295.1	361.4	158.5	351.0	307.2	160.6
1982	668.1	561.1	138.0	534.8	317.6	430.2	186.1	411.0	345.5	181.1
1983	716.6	590.5	144.5	574.1	337.7	519.5	225.1	499.0	384.4	193.8
1984	837.7	693.7	166.1	666.8	379.1	664.2	282.9	559.0	435.0	222.5
1985	1158.8	907.7	134.8	923.3	466.9	775.1	324.0	726.0	510.0	240.5
1986	1317.3	1067.5	203.5	1067.4	543.4	823.1	335.6	857.0	645.3	292.4
1987	1413.2	1181.9	207.5	1147.6	605.0	916.4	357.4	943.0	705.5	340.9
1988	1767.7	1437.0	209.3	1455.6	743.4	1062.6	368.8	1246.0	883.3	407.9
1989	1899.6	1787.1	198.5	1520.4	841.3	1230.7	376.8	1356.0	976.3	484.3
1990	2067.3	1787.1	210.8	1646.1	892.2	1297.1	384.8	1372.0	980.7	496.8
1991	2359.9	2040.4	215.3	1860.2	1016.8	1422.3	391.3	1585.0	1100.1	537.0
1992	2813.1	2363.7	226.9	2134.7	1126.3	1568.8	399.4	1684.0	1179.0	573.8
1993	3935.4	3296.0	265.9	2939.6	1404.7	1854.8	419.8	1714.0	1308.9	611.7
1994	5585.9	4731.2	305.5	4134.1	1919.0	2422.1	457.8	2175.0	1676.5	824.8
1995	6748.7	5868.4	322.9	5019.8	2436.5	3208.5	486.3	3080.0	2433.0	1206.0
1996	7945.8	6885.5	378.9	5729.5	2671.5	3562.7	509.8	3272.0	2655.5	1233.1
1997	8741.7	7813.1	365.9	6531.8	2854.4	3762.4	535.8	3379.0	2795.4	1248.4
1998	10098.2	8472.0	387.6	6970.8	2865.7	4028.9	571.7	3617.0	2945.5	1241.9
1999	10654.8	9182.8	417.6	7498.5	2959.2	4316	612.9	3938.0	3132.5	1253.5
2000	12560.3	10349.7	454.7	8493.5	3083.4	4687.0	657.6	4517.9	3441.4	1263.6

年份 Year	每一城镇就业者负担人数(人) Dependents Per Urban Employee (person)	每一农村劳动力负担人数(人) Dependents Per Rural Labor Force (person)	城市人均居住面积(平方米) Urban Per Capita Living Space (sq.m)	农村人均住房面积(平方米) Rural Per Capita Living Space (sq.m)	城乡储蓄存款余额(亿元) Balance of Saving Deposits (100 million yuan)	城镇储蓄 Urban	农户储蓄 Rural	人均储蓄(元) Per Capita Saving Deposits (yuan)
1978	1.86	2.15	4.55	9.25	9.33	8.90	0.43	107.09
1979	1.83	2.16	4.57	9.67	11.07	10.44	0.63	123.04
1980	1.80	2.13	4.79	10.09	14.39	13.33	1.06	159.20
1981	1.72	2.13	5.08	12.35	17.39	15.74	1.65	189.23
1982	1.66	1.97	5.38	13.01	21.77	19.19	2.58	232.55
1983	1.65	1.82	5.68	14.09	29.81	25.11	4.70	312.49
1984	1.63	1.79	5.92	14.08	38.82	32.14	6.67	401.42
1985	1.66	1.64	6.17	16.37	51.70	42.24	9.45	522.70
1986	1.66	1.66	6.46	17.17	68.58	55.62	12.95	664.52
1987	1.65	1.64	6.82	18.38	92.98	75.19	17.79	871.38
1988	1.71	1.63	7.17	19.23	111.64	90.55	21.09	1033.98
1989	1.52	1.62	7.45	20.09	162.01	133.75	28.26	1597.76
1990	1.52	1.61	7.72	20.62	226.62	188.03	38.59	2208.73
1991	1.47	1.59	8.01	21.92	298.18	249.88	48.30	2878.21
1992	1.43	1.58	8.31	22.67	387.82	328.21	59.61	3721.93
1993	1.42	1.51	8.51	23.7	560.66	482.48	78.18	5349.78
1994	1.41	1.49	8.73	24.42	853.21	745.88	107.33	8079.62
1995	1.41	1.47	9.03	24.74	1253.95	1111.50	142.46	11757.61
1996	1.41	1.45	9.33	25.74	1706.98	1528.41	178.56	15839.09
1997	1.43	1.48	9.66	27.39	1975.23	1770.90	204.36	18196.80
1998	1.40	1.44	10.03	27.64	2287.19	2063.19	224.00	20954.54
1999	1.41	1.43	10.63	28.65	2680.67	2429.03	251.63	24374.11
2000	1.41	1.51	11.15	28.91	2923.21	2663.30	259.91	26394.64

附1-21 城镇居民家庭平均每百户主要耐用消费品拥有量

POSSESSION OF MAIN DURABLE CONSUMER GOODS OF PER 100 URBAN HOUSEHOLDS

年 份 Year	自行车 (辆) Bicycles (unit)	录放像机 (台) Videocorders (set)	淋 浴 热水器 (台) Showers (unit)	洗衣机 (台) Washing Machines (unit)	彩 色 电视机 (台) Color TV Sets (set)	黑 白 电视机 (台) Black and White (set)	收录机 (台) Recorders (set)	电冰箱 (台) Refrige- rators (unit)	照相机 (架) Cameras (set)
1978	135.8					19.2	0.6		7.5
1979	145.7			0.1		41.8	2.4		9.8
1980	150.9			1.9		65.8	9.5	0.3	11.4
1981	153.8			12.3	1.7	80.0	20.0	1.7	13.3
1982	166.5			18.8	1.7	84.8	28.0	2.7	17.2
1983	175.8			28.7	4.3	86.6	40.5	7.0	20.6
1984	183.0			42.3	8.0	86.5	51.5	15.3	29.1
1985	177.0			57.5	32.2	80.7	70.3	41.9	34.6
1986	193.9			75.9	50.9	69.2	80.1	61.5	47.4
1987	210.2			82.6	57.5	70.5	87.0	71.8	55.5
1988	193.7			86.0	69.7	57.8	91.8	81.2	59.6
1989	233.0	10.1		89.7	80.5	55.4	95.5	89.4	62.2
1990	228.3	19.9		93.2	90.9	51.2	99.6	96.4	66.5
1991	233.8	28.4		93.0	97.1	44.0	100.0	101.7	72.7
1992	229.2	41.7	17.0	96.1	101.4	39.5	104.1	101.3	77.2
1993	243.2	45.6	23.2	99.8	107.2	39.2	113.0	100.8	82.4
1994	246.8	49.8	38.8	102.8	111.8	37.4	107.8	104.4	85.4
1995	243.6	54.2	45.4	100.4	113.6	33.8	110.2	104.4	86.8
1996	249.0	57.8	52.0	101.4	119.2	30.8	113.8	105.4	87.2
1997	209.4	56.0	58.4	100.6	123.8		65.0	104.2	88.2
1998	221.0	59.8	65.4	102.2	133.2			105.4	95.2
1999	220.1	54.1	67.1	99.6	141.4		69.9	102.8	95.0
2000	230.7	56.9	74.4	102.8	145.5		72.7	107.4	95.7

附1-22 农民家庭平均每百户主要耐用消费品拥有量
POSSESSION OF MAIN DURABLE CONSUMER GOODS OF PER 100 RURAL HOUSEHOLDS

年 份 Year	自行车 (辆) Bicycles (unit)	缝纫机 (架) Sewing Machines (set)	手 表 (只) Watches (unit)	黑 白 电视机 (台) Black and White TV Sets (set)	彩 色 电视机 (台) Color TV Sets (set)	录音机 (台) Recorders (set)	照相机 (架) Cameras (set)	电风扇 (台) Electric Fans (unit)	洗衣机 (台) Washing Machines (unit)	电冰箱 (台) Refrige-rators (unit)
1978	109	36	46							
1979	98	32	67	1						
1980	123	39	103	5						
1981	135	46	136	14						
1982	141	50	169	33		2		11	2	
1983	167	55	192	41		7		17	6	
1984	187	58	211	57		14		28	15	1
1985	182	57	201	53	7	21	2	32	23	2
1986	191	56	211	59	12	28	4	42	39	5
1987	204	60	226	63	15	34	5	52	48	9
1988	218	61	231	66	20	41	7	61	56	14
1989	224	63	232	66	25	47	8	67	61	19
1990	235	65	243	65	29	47	8	73	63	23
1991	232	63	217	58	42	48	11	84	69	36
1992	245	64	229	60	46	50	14	92	73	40
1993	249	68	223	56	56	53	15	98	76	47
1994	254	69	239	54	65	59	17	109	80	53
1995	251	67	214	46	74	56	21	115	81	63
1996	250	68	217	44	79	58	21	117	83	67
1997	248	68	221	43	85	58	25	127	84	72
1998	249	70	227	39	92	58	26	133	85	75
1999	241	69	225	34	101	59	29	143	86	81
2000	220	69		18	107	34	26	143	85	84

附1-23 农 业 基 本 情 况
BASIC STATISTICS FOR AGRICULTURE

年 份 Year	农林牧渔业从业人员(万人) Labors Force of Farming,Freostry Animal Husbandry and Fishery (10000 persons)	年末实有耕地面积(万公顷) Cultivated Area (year-end) (10000 hectare)	当年减少耕地面积(万公顷) Decresae of Cultivated Area of this Year (10000 hectare)	播种面积(万公顷) Sown Area (10000 hectare)	# 粮食作物 Grain Crops	# 经济作物 Cash Crops	造林面积(万公顷) Afforestation Area (10000 hectare)	受灾面积(万公顷) Disaster Area (10000 hectare)	成灾面积(万公顷) Infested Area (10000 hectare)
1978	117.7	42.9	0.3	69.1	56.1	4.9	1.4		
1979	115.5	42.7	0.2	67.7	56	3.7	1.6		
1980	113.3	42.6	0.1	65.7	54.9	3.3	2.4		
1981	112.6	42.5	0.1	64.3	53.0	3.2	2.7		
1982	110.1	42.4	0.1	64.2	52.7	2.9	2.8		
1983	112.2	42.3	0.1	63.8	53.0	2.8	3.3	16.2	8.9
1984	101.1	42.2	0.1	63.3	52.3	2.7	3.2	18.0	14.0
1985	90.3	42.1	0.1	61.8	51.1	2.9	3.0	14.0	8.0
1986	86.1	41.9	0.2	60.5	49.9	2.4	1.4	7.0	3.0
1987	84.6	41.8	0.1	59.8	49.5	2.0	2.0	3.0	1.0
1988	80.9	41.6	0.2	59.5	48.8	1.9	1.6	11.0	5.0
1989	83.4	41.4	0.2	58.9	48.3	1.6	0.8	21.0	9.0
1990	82.5	41.3	0.1	59	48.4	1.6	4.1	17.8	8.7
1991	80.3	41.1	0.2	59.0	48.3	1.7	1.5	16.9	7.7
1992	74.6	40.9	0.2	58.6	47.7	1.7	1.5	3.8	0.8
1993	72.5	40.6	0.3	56.5	45.6	1.8	4.8	11.9	5.3
1994	68.7	40.2	0.4	55.1	43.0	1.7	5.5	19.3	4.6
1995	65.5	39.9	0.3	55.3	43.4	1.5	4.7	12.1	3.7
1996	66.9	39.9	0.3	53.8	42.7	1.4	4.0	12.3	5.0
1997	65.3	34.2	0.3	53.6	42.5	1.2	3.8		
1998	67.7	34.1	0.3	53.5	42.3	1.2	3.7		
1999	71.1	33.8	0.3	52.7	41.0	1.3	3.0		
2000	69.7	32.9	1.1	45.6	30.8	1.9	2.6		

注：1995、1996、1997年耕地面积由市土地局提供。

Note：Data of cultivated area of 1995 and 1996 are provided by Municipal Land Bureau.

附1-24 农业生产条件
PRODUCTIVE CONDITIONS OF AGRICULTURE

年份 Year	农用机械总动力 (万千瓦) Total Power of Agricultural Machinery (10000kw)	农用大中型拖拉机 (台) Large Medium Tractors (unit)	小型拖拉机 (台) Mini-Tractors (unit)	灌溉面积 (千公顷) Irrigated Area (1000 hectare)	化肥施用量 (万吨) Consumption of Chemical Fertilizers (10000 tons)	农村用电量 (万千瓦小时) Rural Electricity Consumption (10000 kwh)	农村居民家庭每户生产性固定资产 (元) Productive Fixed Assets Per Rural Households (yuan)	每公顷面积产量(公斤) Yield Per Hectare(kg) 粮食 Grain	棉花 Cotton	油料 Oilbearing Crops
1978	189.4	5568	23412	341.7	1.2	58802	5.0	3315	255	788
1979	212.2	6496	24724	340.8	1.1	59531	6.5	3090	278	855
1980	234.6	7705	24952	340.3	1.2	76753	8.0	3390	443	1118
1981	244.8	8284	23465	341.3	1.1	91843	10.9	3413	338	810
1982	242.2	9032	22843	339.3	1.2	96960	22.3	3518	503	953
1983	262.1	9855	22652	343.3	1.2	104608	95.3	3803	593	1065
1984	291.3	10859	26563	342.7	1.1	119287	163.0	4155	900	1500
1985	320.4	11319	35051	338.4	8.2	126830	394.3	4298	848	1928
1986	345.5	11664	37023	337.9	9.1	180640	419.2	4335	735	1530
1987	388.4	12170	37319	337.9	10.0	159450	444.0	4590	908	2085
1988	399.7	12596	45013	338.1	10.6	163986	549.7	4800	810	2055
1989	423.9	12344	47546	338.4	11.8	128414	543.3	4950	960	2220
1990	416.2	12844	47020	335.1	14.4	122711	595.6	5460	1035	2565
1991	384.8	12906	44610	328.7	14.4	111347	700.4	5787	885	2685
1992	399.8	12752	44525	331.1	14.4	143963	844.9	5907	1051	2760
1993	450.5	12701	44200	314.7	14.9	169911	951.6	6236	1043	3009
1994	459.2	12475	44500	323.4	19.8	172042	2194.6	6420	910	3051
1995	468.1	12228	42100	292.4	18.8	201731	2776.5	5985	825	2794
1996	468.4	12272	38200	301.9	18.9	275871	2394.2	5659	924	2741
1997	433.2	12088	30000	323.3	19.7	301655	2818.9	5594	1040	2736
1998	415.5	12032	30000	323.7	19.3	290859	3411.8	5661	854	2941
1999	410.4	11852	27295	322.1	19.0	330069	3814.0	4905	1016	2647
2000	399.2	11781	25004	322.7	17.9	572257	5191.1	4677	983	2461

注：1.化肥施用量为折纯量。
2.农村居民家庭每户生产性固定资产为抽样调查数。

a) Consumption of chemical fertilizers are those converted into pure.

b) Data of productive fixed assets per rural household refers to those from sample survey.

附1-25 农林牧渔业总产值和指数

GROSS OUTPUT VALUE OF FARMING,FORESTRY,ANIMAL HUSBANDRY FISHERY AND THEIR INDEX

年 份 Year	农林牧渔业总产值(亿元) Gross Output Value of Farming, Forestry, Animal Husbandry and Fishery (100 million yuan)	农 业 Farming	林 业 Forestry	牧 业 Animal Husbandry	渔 业 Fishery	农林牧渔业总产值指数(1978=100) Index of Gross Output Value of FFAF (1978=100)	农 业 Farming	林 业 Forestry	牧 业 Animal Husbandry	渔 业 Fishery
1978	11.5	8.9	0.2	2.4	0.01	100.0	100.0	100.0	100.0	100.0
1979	12.3	8.8	0.2	3.3	0.02	99.1	95.8	87.5	108.5	200.0
1980	14.2	9.7	0.5	3.9	0.05	101.2	92.9	137.5	122.0	200.0
1981--1985	**98.2**	**63.0**	**4.2**	**30.1**	**0.80**					
1981	14.9	10.1	0.7	4.1	0.05	100.6	92.1	137.5	120.7	200.0
1982	16.7	11.2	0.7	4.7	0.05	108.5	96.3	137.5	140.2	200.0
1983	19.4	12.5	0.8	6.0	0.10	123.6	107.1	150.0	168.3	400.0
1984	22.2	14.4	0.9	6.7	0.20	137.6	120.0	150.0	182.9	600.0
1985	25.9	16.1	0.8	8.6	0.40	146.4	126.3	137.5	198.8	1200.0
1986--1990	**242.4**	**138.8**	**4.1**	**91.6**	**7.9**					
1986	28.1	17.2	0.8	9.4	0.7	147.0	125.0	125.0	202.4	1464.4
1987	34.4	20.3	0.8	12.3	1.0	160.0	134.2	137.5	224.4	2185.4
1988	52.6	31.4	0.9	18.6	1.7	179.4	140.8	125.0	278.0	2907.4
1989	60.4	34.2	0.7	23.3	2.2	198.2	151.3	112.5	324.4	3236.8
1990	70.2	39.0	0.9	28.0	2.3	210.3	154.2	125.0	348.8	3622.8
1991--1995	**567.9**	**291.0**	**11.2**	**244.6**	**21.1**					
1991	76.4	39.5	1.5	32.8	2.6	229.1	164.6	162.5	395.1	4211.4
1992	84.5	43.2	1.6	36.3	3.4	244.5	172.5	150.0	431.7	5092.8
1993	100.4	51.1	2.3	42.7	4.3	257.3	183.3	162.5	443.9	5887.7
1994	144.3	72.5	3.1	64.0	4.7	276.7	193.8	187.5	487.8	6131.4
1995	164.4	86.8	2.7	68.8	6.1	273.9	195.4	200.0	462.2	7500.8
1996--2000	**895.9**	**447.7**	**18.5**	**394.2**	**35.5**					
1996	168.9	89.2	2.8	71.1	5.8	271.5	190.0	212.5	473.2	7000.0
1997	170.9	87.0	2.9	74.8	6.2	273.8	199.7	226.9	466.2	6522.4
1998	176.6	89.2	3.2	76.6	7.6	283.0	201.5	202.3	484.4	7374.0
1999	184.3	91.2	4.2	81.1	7.8	301.8	204.6	225.0	529.3	9502.0
2000	195.2	91.1	5.4	90.6	8.1	340.8	225.9	282.9	617.5	10599.0

注：绝对数按现价计算，指数按可比价计算。

Note：Value are calculated at current prices and index are calculated at constant prices.

附1-26 主要农业产品产量
OUTPUT OF MAJOR AGRICULTURAL PRODUCTS

年份 Year	粮食(万吨) Grain (10000 tons)	# 谷物 Cereal	棉花(万吨) Cotton (10000 tons)	油料(万吨) Oilbearing Crops (10000 tons)	猪牛羊肉(万吨) Pork,Beef and Mutton (10000 tons)	禽蛋(万吨) Poultry Eggs (10000 tons)	水产品(万吨) Aquatic Products (10000 tons)	大牲畜年底头数(万头) Large Animals (year-end) (10000 heads)	# 役畜 Draught Animals	猪年底头数(万头) Hogs (year-end) (10000 heads)
1978	186.0	180.4	0.3	2.6	11.9	0.5	0.2	30.4	21.5	248.3
1979	172.8	168.4	0.1	2.6	13.2	1.0	0.3	29.2	20.4	246.7
1980	186.0	182.2	0.1	3.1	15.1	3.4	0.4	27.9	19.3	232.5
1981--1985	**1004.8**	**984.1**	**1.4**	**13.1**	**70.7**	**44.3**	**4.0**	**119.5**	**89.7**	**927.0**
1981	180.7	177.7	0.1	2.2	14.3	3.7	0.4	26.3	19.2	210.9
1982	185.5	182.5	0.1	2.3	14.1	5.4	0.4	24.9	18.2	206.4
1983	201.5	198.3	0.2	2.1	14.9	8.9	0.6	24.3	18.1	190.3
1984	217.4	211.5	0.6	2.6	13.9	12.2	1.0	22.8	17.6	161.8
1985	219.7	214.1	0.4	3.9	13.5	14.1	1.6	21.2	16.6	157.6
1986--1990	**1181.9**	**1154.1**	**1.4**	**15.2**	**77.3**	**103.8**	**18.8**	**115.2**	**82.7**	**805.0**
1986	216.5	211.2	0.2	3.0	13.3	14.7	2.2	21.9	16.6	145.6
1987	227.0	220.9	0.3	3.3	13.0	16.8	3.0	23.1	16.9	120.4
1988	234.6	229.2	0.3	3.0	13.4	21.8	3.9	23.1	16.3	145.3
1989	239.2	233.7	0.3	2.8	17.2	24.7	4.6	23.8	16.6	187.7
1990	264.6	259.1	0.3	3.1	20.4	25.8	5.1	23.3	16.3	206.0
1991--1995	**1381.6**	**1349.3**	**1.9**	**17.6**	**138.0**	**139.3**	**34.7**	**130.6**	**61.3**	**1276.5**
1991	279.7	274.7	0.3	3.3	24.8	25.0	5.6	27.9	15.0	241.7
1992	281.9	276.7	0.5	3.4	27.3	26.5	6.4	26.9	13.6	269.1
1993	284.1	278.2	0.4	3.8	28.2	28.1	7.0	26.2	12.8	252.2
1994	249.2	267.0	0.4	3.8	30.7	31.2	7.6	26.7	10.9	260.1
1995	259.8	252.7	0.3	3.3	27.0	28.5	8.1	22.9	9.0	253.4
1996--2000	**1059.3**	**963.4**	**1.1**	**15.1**	**153.0**	**98.2**	**38.2**	**101.3**	**26.3**	**1233.8**
1996	237.4	231.8	0.3	3.0	27.6	24.7	7.8	20.5	7.4	240.0
1997	237.5	232.3	0.2	2.7	27.9	23.8	7.7	19.7	6.0	241.0
1998	239.2	234.0	0.2	2.8	31.2	17.9	7.6	18.5	5.3	254.5
1999	201.0	196.1	0.2	2.8	32.3	15.8	7.6	19.0	4.1	248.3
2000	144.2	136.1	0.2	3.8	34.0	16.0	7.5	23.6	3.5	250.0

附1-27 每一农林牧渔业从业者农业生产量
PRODUCTION VOLUME PER EMPLOYEE OF FARMING,FORESTRY, ANIMAL HUSBANDRY AND FISHERY

年 份 Year	农林牧渔业总产值(元) Gross Output Value of Farming, Forestry, Animal Husbandry and Fishery (yuan)	粮 食(公斤) Grain (kg)	# 谷物 Cereal	棉 花(公斤) Cotton (kg)	油 料(公斤) Oilbearing Crops (kg)	猪牛羊肉(公斤) Pork,Beef and Mutton (kg)	禽 蛋(公斤) Poultry Eggs (kg)	水产品(公斤) Aquatic Products (kg)
1978	977.9	1580.1	1529.3	2.9	22.2	101.1	4.6	1.5
1979	1066.7	1496.2	1458.3	0.6	22.2	114.0	8.5	2.4
1980	1248.9	1641.7	1608.1	0.8	27.3	133.2	29.6	3.6
1981	1318.8	1604.4	1577.7	0.6	19.8	127.1	32.7	3.8
1982	1512.3	1684.6	1657.5	0.9	20.7	128.3	51.1	3.4
1983	1729.1	1795.8	1767.1	1.8	18.3	132.6	79.2	4.9
1984	2146.4	2150.0	2092.4	5.6	26.2	137.5	120.9	10.0
1985	2823.9	2432.5	2370.5	4.8	43.6	149.3	156.1	17.6
1986	3228.8	2514.2	2453.3	2.5	35.4	155.0	170.6	25.6
1987	3995.3	2683.3	2610.9	3.1	38.7	153.1	198.4	35.5
1988	6415.3	2900.0	2833.6	3.4	37.0	166.0	269.1	48.2
1989	7146.3	2868.5	2801.6	3.1	34.1	205.8	296.3	55.2
1990	8400.0	3207.5	3140.5	4.2	37.5	247.0	312.4	61.9
1991	9402.2	3483.3	3421.0	4.3	40.9	309.1	311.5	69.4
1992	11166.2	3779.2	3708.9	6.5	45.6	366.5	355.1	86.0
1993	13848.3	3917.4	3837.8	5.9	52.2	389.1	387.7	96.9
1994	21004.4	4019.6	3886.2	5.4	55.2	447.4	453.8	111.1
1995	25099.2	3965.8	3858.3	4.2	50.2	412.0	435.7	122.9
1996	25232.6	3545.7	3465.4	3.8	44.0	411.6	368.8	117.0
1997	26152.0	3634.8	3556.1	3.4	41.8	426.8	363.9	117.3
1998	26076.0	3532.4	3454.0	2.7	41.9	460.8	264.0	129.1
1999	23904.0	2827.0	2758.1	2.6	39.4	454.3	222.2	106.9
2000	28015.7	2069.2	1952.7	2.2	54.5	488.0	229.9	107.7

附1-28 工业总产值
GROSS OUTPUT VALUE OF INDUSTRY

单位：亿元 (100 million yuan)

年份 Year	工业总产值 Gross Output Value	# 国有工业 State-owned	# 集体工业 Collective-owned	# 乡及乡以上 at Township Level and above	轻工业 Light Industry	重工业 Heavy Industry	# 大中型工业 Large and Medium Industry
1984	276.20	217.27	54.14	276.20	117.99	158.22	178.66
1985	324.19	248.48	69.43	324.19	135.75	188.44	213.73
1986--1990	**2618.45**	**1491.40**	**516.39**	**2521.45**	**1070.73**	**1450.73**	**1741.65**
1986	344.95	268.20	68.80	344.95	144.34	200.61	237.43
1987	399.09	305.99	81.08	399.09	164.80	234.29	280.16
1988	508.69		104.06	508.69	218.16	290.53	354.45
1989	622.37	450.88	134.46	622.37	272.66	349.71	421.68
1990	743.35	466.33	127.99	646.35	270.77	375.59	447.93
1991--1995	**6866.31**	**3737.35**	**1139.43**	**5862.75**	**1952.32**	**3910.41**	**3799.15**
1991	880.79	527.78	146.53	757.05	309.08	447.96	526.02
1992	1085.37	627.84	170.07	915.50	326.31	589.19	625.27
1993	1513.59	797.13	227.78	1242.56	385.44	857.12	796.27
1994	1721.13	906.56	243.61	1456.85	460.06	996.79	915.45
1995	1665.43	878.04	351.44	1490.79	471.43	1019.35	936.14
1996--2000	**10808.67**	**4268.63**	**1284.07**	**10221.13**	**2984.43**	**7236.7**	**5676.57**
1996	1853.34	887.00	277.38	1632.17	522.43	1109.74	987.48
1997	1963.83	960.04	179.76	1744.98	554.07	1190.91	958.61
1998	2027.02	863.46	301.14	1991.96	612.02	1379.94	1084.25
1999	2190.26	769.54	263.17	2144.61	610.68	1533.93	1071.44
2000	2774.22	788.59	262.62	2707.41	685.23	2022.18	1574.79

注：总产值按现价计算，乡及乡以上工业总产值从1998年开始调整为不含个体工业企业口径（以下乡及乡以上口径变化与此相同）。

Note: Gross output value is calculated at current prices, that at township level and above changed to that of enterprises except individual industry from 1998 (the followings have the same change).

附1-29 工业总产值指数(1978=100)
INDEX OF GROSS OUTPUT VALUE OF INDUSTRY(1978=100)

单位：%　　(%)

年份 Year	工业总产值 Gross Output Value	# 国有工业 State-owned	# 集体工业 Collective-owned	# 乡及乡以上 at Township Level and above	轻工业 Light Industry	重工业 Heavy Industry	# 大中型工业 Large and Medium Industry
1978	100.0	100.0	100.0	100.0	100.0	100.0	100.0
1979	110.5	110.1	112.1	121.3	113.1	109.1	110.9
1980	121.3	118.6	134.3	122.0	134.9	113.9	118.5
1981	112.1	119.5	139.8	123.3	154.5	106.4	121.2
1982	118.4	125.9	147.9	130.2	159.6	114.5	134.7
1983	129.7	136.3	170.4	142.7	171.9	127.2	151.4
1984	145.9	148.7	204.2	160.4	188.5	146.0	175.3
1985	159.2	158.4	240.2	175.1	204.7	159.9	199.1
1986	166.6	167.0	242.4	183.2	214.9	166.9	212.1
1987	184.9	182.6	278.0	203.4	233.5	188.4	239.0
1988	216.6	207.0	337.9	238.2	280.5	216.3	274.8
1989	232.2	215.7	373.2	255.3	301.2	231.6	286.4
1990	257.0	215.7	396.3	268.3	312.2	245.9	297.7
1991	398.1	230.3	447.2	299.1	340.9	278.3	329.7
1992	454.8	252.2	514.5	341.8	353.8	338.2	365.1
1993	516.1	277.9	651.4	413.8	418.4	415.0	381.0
1994	532.2	269.0	657.1	444.6	447.8	446.9	393.3
1995	569.5	290.6	665.9	494.1	432.3	533.6	472.6
1996	624.7	290.6	771.5	512.1	443.3	559.4	470.0
1997	694.0	325.9	485.9	574.1	487.0	628.5	442.3
1998	819.4	353.2	475.7	679.7	497.7	792.6	633.2
1999	936.6	290.7	460.0	774.9	513.1	940.0	695.1
2000	1229.5	264.0	446.5	1013.9	598.3	1278.7	1111.5

注：指数按可比价计算（下表同）。

Note：Index are calculated at constant prices(the following table is the same) .

附1-30 工业总产值指数(上年=100)

INDEX OF GROSS OUTPUT VALUE OF INDUSTRY(PRECEDING YEAR=100)

单位：% (%)

年份 Year	工业总产值 Gross Output Value	# 国有工业 State-owned	# 集体工业 Collective-owned	# 乡及乡以上 at Township Level and above	轻工业 Light Industry	重工业 Heavy Industry	# 大中型工业 Large and Medium Industry
1978	111.5	114.5	112.5	114.2	110.8	116.1	100.0
1979	111.2	110.1	112.1	110.5	113.1	109.1	110.9
1980	110.4	107.7	119.7	109.8	119.3	104.5	106.9
1981	101.8	100.8	104.2	101.7	114.5	93.4	102.7
1982	106.1	105.4	105.8	105.6	103.3	107.6	111.2
1983	111.0	108.3	115.2	109.6	107.7	111.2	112.4
1984	113.8	109.1	119.9	112.4	109.6	114.7	115.7
1985	110.8	106.5	117.6	109.2	108.6	109.6	113.6
1986	105.9	105.5	100.9	104.6	104.9	104.4	106.5
1987	113.4	109.3	114.7	111.0	108.7	112.8	112.7
1988	121.1	113.3	121.6	117.1	120.1	114.8	114.9
1989	109.0	104.2	110.4	107.2	107.4	107.1	104.2
1990	106.1	100.0	106.2	105.1	103.7	106.2	104.0
1991	113.5	106.8	112.9	111.5	109.2	113.2	110.7
1992	118.0	109.5	115.0	114.3	103.8	121.5	110.7
1993	122.3	110.2	126.6	121.1	118.3	122.7	104.4
1994	104.2	96.8	100.9	107.4	107.0	107.7	103.2
1995	107.0	107.9	101.3	111.1	96.5	119.4	120.2
1996	109.7	103.8	126.1	109.2	109.7	109.7	102.5
1997	111.1	112.1	63.0	112.1	109.9	112.4	94.1
1998	118.1	108.4	97.9	118.4	102.2	126.1	142.4
1999	114.3	82.3	96.7	114.0	103.1	118.6	109.8
2000	131.1	90.8	97.1	130.8	116.6	136.0	159.9

附1-31 独立核算工业企业主要指标
MAIN INDICATORS FOR INDUSTRIAL ENTERPRISES WITH INDEPENDENT ACCOUNTING SYSTEM

年份 Year	平均职工人数(万人) Average Number of Staff and Workers (10000 persons)	总产值(万元) Gross Output Value (10000 yuan)	固定资产原价(万元) Original Value of Fixed Assets (10000 yuan)	产品销售收入(万元) Sales Revenue (10000 yuan)	利税总额(万元) Total Pre-tax Profits (10000 yuan)	国有工业 State-owned Industry				
						平均职工人数(万人) Average Number of Staff and Workers (10000 persons)	总产值(万元) Gross Output Value (10000 yuan)	固定资产原价(万元) Original Value of Fixed Assets (10000 yuan)	产品销售收入(万元) Sales Revenue (10000 yuan)	利税总额(万元) Total Pre-tax Profits (10000 yuan)
1978	114.79	1654593	1305271	1098279		89.0	1397086	1211739	919313	435095
1979	116.79	1843056	1371335	1186497		92.3	1543621	1262408	984888	
1980	140.91	2061664	1495083	1987967	604241	95.3	1694298	1366890	1647908	520978
1981--1985		**12511777**	**9642045**	**12561630**	**3383077**		**9940322**	**8614039**	**10117128**	**2852798**
1981	152.90	2105591	1622035	2054862	599452	103.7	1716072	1474519	1693086	518716
1982	158.70	2205469	1750727	2183458	604372	107.6	1794192	1581902	1796342	521452
1983	161.98	2389253	1886857	2408893	642437	109.3	1918673	1693586	1961803	545140
1984	165.50	2702857	2045344	2728866	707360	109.4	2117273	1812660	2179349	589607
1985	165.63	3108607	2337082	3185551	829456	110.1	2394112	2051372	2486548	677883
1986--1990		**24483553**	**17321757**	**24054442**	**4825016**		**18108076**	**14798805**	**18384654**	**3925489**
1986	169.85	3365481	2627346	3385055	813979	111.5	2601751	2281006	2659067	676895
1987	170.52	3875977	3008917	3935004	885303	112.6	2970928	2604582	3065446	732447
1988	170.54	4956478	3412765	5032042	1081370	112.8	3695388	2949027	3835082	882479
1989		6026646	3890267	5597829	1087017		4352862	3294245	4258859	885038
1990	173.46	625897.1	4382462	6104512	957347	115.4	4487147	3669945	4566200	748630
1991--1995		**57607603**	**44341698**	**57731437**	**8051832**		**35547109**	**35600600**	**37861701**	**5876833**
1991	172.39	7302060	5052285	7271529	1106009	112.2	5080426	4210383	5274088	837566
1992	175.48	8600195	5754181	8526860	1347058	116.3	5834134	4757957	6054470	1027279
1993	167.90	11666047	9986886	12822058	1811556	114.6	7598865	8471018	8977254	1379167
1994	179.50	15536585	9648050	13207344	1857476	109.9	8599364	7493956	7815491	1224709
1995	176.16	14502716	13900296	15903646	1929733	107.3	8434320	10667286	9740398	1408112
1996--2000		**100791594**	**105474337**	**103617473**	**8655552**		**40144235**	**66553723**	**46027770**	**4130797**
1996	166.63	15222854	16319878	15801389	1225314	97.7	8366714	12273744	9303959	762024
1997	157.52	17161951	18503218	17070867	1405499	91.2	9355501	14106270	9570024	878170
1998	167.11	19886587	22213387	20345380	1617338	70.3	8615543	13621321	9532486	823114
1999	161.10	21446119	23121446	22186280	1846310	62.4	5920611	13276604	8423097	873620
2000	145.60	27074083	25316408	28213557	2561091	56.8	7885866	13275784	9198204	793869

注：利税总额包括增值税。

Note：Total pre-tax profits included added value tax.

附1-32 独立核算工业企业效益指标

BENEFICIAL INDICATORS FOR INDUSTRIAL ENTERPRISES WITH INDEPENDENT ACCOUNTING SYSTEM

年份 Year	百元固定资产实现利税(元) Pre-tax Profits/Fixed Assets (yuan)	资金利税率(%) Pre-tax Profits/Total Assets (%)	产值利税率(%) Pre-tax Profits/Gross Output Value (%)	百元销售收入实现利润(元) After-tax Profits/Sales Revenue (yuan)	增加值劳动生产率(元/人) Labor Productivity at Value Added (yuan/person)	国有工业 State-owned Industry 百元固定资产实现利税(元) Pre-tax Profits/Fixed Assets (yuan)	资金利税率(%) Pre-tax Profits/Total Assets (%)	产值利税率(%) Pre-tax Profits/Gross Output Value(%)	百元销售收入实现利润(元) After-tax Profits/Sales Revenue (yuan)	增加值劳动生产率(元/人) Labor Productivity at Value Added (yuan/person)
1978				33.76		35.91		31.14	34.71	
1979				34.92					36.24	
1980	40.42	38.50	29.31	22.79		38.11	38.00	20.75	23.65	
1981	36.96	34.70	28.47	21.45		35.18	34.40	30.23	22.53	
1982	34.52	32.60	27.40	20.15		32.96	32.50	29.06	21.16	
1983	34.05	34.80	26.89	19.48		32.19	34.70	28.41	20.27	
1984	34.58	35.30	26.17	18.51		32.53	35.33	27.85	19.24	
1985	35.49	35.47	26.68	17.30		33.05	35.34	28.31	17.68	
1986	30.98	28.13	24.19	15.48		29.68	30.79	26.02	16.11	
1987	29.42	29.98	22.84	14.50		28.12	28.85	24.65	15.21	
1988	31.69		21.82	13.94		29.92	30.38	23.88	14.64	
1989	27.94	25.03	18.04	11.40		26.87	25.95	20.33	11.79	
1990	21.84	19.21	15.30	8.02		20.40	19.33	16.68	7.72	
1991	21.89	19.50	15.15	8.02		19.89	19.07	16.49	7.70	
1992	23.41	16.46	15.66	8.77		21.59	16.98	17.61	8.92	
1993	18.14	12.37	15.53	8.54	24364	16.28	12.10	18.15	9.26	20197
1994	19.25	13.05	11.96	7.28	31294	16.34	12.78	14.24	7.73	25144
1995	13.89	9.92	13.31	5.36	26068	13.20	10.95	16.70	6.32	27241
1996	9.30	5.41	8.05	2.09	23445	7.88	5.19	9.11	1.82	19571
1997	9.36	5.44	8.19	2.37	28220	7.80	5.39	9.39	2.40	27534
1998	9.15	4.99	8.13	2.38	35033	7.69	5.10	9.55	2.31	36926
1999	10.15	5.65	8.61	3.15	36347	8.49	5.57	11.35	3.11	33567
2000	13.29	7.03	9.46	4.50	51469	8.04	5.02	10.06	2.25	44223

注：增加值劳动生产率按工业增加值计算。

Note: Labor productivity at value added is calculated by value added of industry.

附1-33 工业产品产量
OUTPUT OF INDUSTRIAL PRODUCTS

年份 Year	布 (万米) Cloth (10000 m)	纱 (万吨) Yarn (10000 m)	机制纸及纸板 (万吨) Machine-made Paper and Paperboard (10000 tons)	合成洗涤剂 (万吨) Synthetic Detergents (10000 tons)	饮料酒 (万吨) Soft Drinking (10000 tons)	家用电冰箱 (万台) Household Refrigerators (10000)	家用洗衣机 (万台) Household Washing Machines (10000)	电视机 (万台) TV Sets (10000)	#彩色 Color TV Sets
1978	25436	5.4	12.1	2.1	8.4			3.9	0.0
1979	27297	5.8	13.9	2.2	9.9	2.0	0.7	12.5	0.3
1980	28940	6.5	14.0	2.4	11.6	2.6	5.8	28.0	1.2
1981--1985	**142080**	**34.5**	**86.9**	**18.9**	**87.3**	**41.6**	**211.7**	**262.3**	**79.5**
1981	28635	6.8	14.5	2.4	13.4	3.1	18.7	43.0	7.2
1982	29758	6.9	15.8	3.0	14.9	4.5	32.1	43.4	8.0
1983	30068	6.9	17.1	3.7	17.4	6.4	44.3	41.4	10.3
1984	27621	7.1	18.9	4.8	20.3	10.3	51.4	59.1	15.5
1985	25998	6.9	20.6	5.1	21.3	17.3	65.2	75.4	38.5
1986--1990	**153032**	**38.8**	**120.5**	**29.6**	**131.4**	**96.4**	**237.4**	**410.5**	**248.8**
1986	27503	7.4	21.9	5.8	21.5	18.1	70.0	67.5	34.2
1987	29738	7.7	24.1	5.4	22.7	19.4	57.7	85.1	48.5
1988	32262	8.1	23.3	5.7	23.9	23.6	58.0	92.9	57.9
1989	32271	7.9	25.8	6.4	28.7	24.7	31.9	88.9	57.6
1990	31258	7.7	25.4	6.4	34.6	10.7	19.7	76.1	50.7
1991--1995	**133994**	**38.6**	**116.5**	**38.1**	**347.3**	**27.0**	**81.7**	**369.9**	**299.4**
1991	31497	7.7	27.2	5.7	43.8	7.1	21.9	91.6	58.2
1992	29717	8.0	22.6	6.6	56.6	9.1	14.7	64.1	64.1
1993	26816	8.7	19.1	7.9	72.6	4.2	14.1	56.9	56.9
1994	21440	6.9	21.0	7.3	83.1	6.6	20.0	90.0	70.0
1995	24524	7.4	26.6	10.7	91.2		11.0	67.4	50.2
1996--2000	**96005**	**28.1**	**70.0**	**34.5**	**436.6**	**15.9**	**72.5**	**102.4**	**92.9**
1996	22585	6.8	15.3	9.3	102.2	6.3	13.1	37.2	31.2
1997	25185	6.4	18.1	9.5	...	...	12.0	40.8	38.2
1998	21299	6.1	13.1	6.3		0.3	6.4	12.1	11.1
1999	14753	4.7	13.0	5.8	148.8	5.8	20.0	11.7	11.7
2000	12183	4.1	10.6	3.7	185.6	3.6	21.0	0.6	0.6

年份 Year	原煤 (万吨) Coal (10000 tons)	发电量 (万千瓦时) Electricity (10000 kwh)	钢 (万吨) Steel (10000 tons)	成品钢材 (万吨) Rolled-steel (10000 tons)	水泥 (万吨) Cement (10000 tons)	硫酸 (万吨) Sulphuric Acid (10000 tons)	烧碱 (万吨) Caustic Soda (10000 tons)	化肥 (万吨) Chemical Fertilizer (10000 tons)	化学农药 (万吨) Chemical Pesticide (10000 tons)
1978	818.7	990750	191.0	116.8	191.5	14.95	5.47	10.70	1.28
1979	711.1	1042870	196.5	137.5	196.9	14.05	6.68	12.01	1.08
1980	791.0	1065060	200.9	152.1	217.4	13.01	8.13	12.41	0.93
1981—1985	**4269.1**	**5101356**	**1114.2**	**907.9**	**1355.7**	**61.85**	**42.56**	**57.68**	**2.32**
1981	788.7	993071	190.3	149.5	225.7	13.02	7.81	12.19	0.76
1982	811.3	1003446	200.4	159.4	249.1	12.64	8.24	12.00	0.60
1983	840.5	1028826	214.1	177.9	270.8	15.20	8.41	13.04	0.41
1984	884.3	1038842	241.7	200.1	291.6	13.24	8.92	12.36	0.42
1985	944.3	1037171	267.7	221.0	318.5	7.75	9.18	8.09	0.13
1986—1990	**4745.3**	**5656282**	**1837.8**	**1556.7**	**1649.3**	**50.49**	**51.89**	**45.77**	**0.10**
1986	917.2	1043208	303.6	255.5	310.5	7.87	9.25	8.26	0.04
1987	899.8	1057493	335.5	283.4	319.6	11.86	9.61	9.02	
1988	906.0	1110758	369.0	314.9	334.3	13.07	11.04	9.53	0.02
1989	1016.8	1191269	386.0	327.9	345.9	10.64	11.26	9.74	0.02
1990	1005.5	1253554	443.7	375.0	339.0	7.05	10.73	9.22	0.02
1991--1995	**4851.0**	**6772732**	**3411.0**	**2613.9**	**2364.7**	**38.57**	**55.69**	**46.41**	**0.43**
1991	996.5	1318000	499.7	402.9	377.6	7.12	11.00	6.94	0.05
1992	1015.2	1423000	575.0	438.3	403.0	8.23	11.38	9.70	0.11
1993	835.4	1410900	702.7	525.3	477.9	3.96	11.23	9.61	0.14
1994	1008.5	1298718	828.7	617.6	531.7	9.29	10.76	9.57	0.10
1995	995.4	1322114	804.9	629.8	574.2	9.97	11.32	10.59	0.03
1996--2000	**4360.0**	**7330814**	**3937.5**	**3343.3**	**3758.9**	**44.25**	**48.52**	**51.47**	**0.14**
1996	1013.7	1415555	794.7	654.3	666.0	10.85		12.72	0.14
1997	1011.7	1464302	801.7	652.4	700.9	9.26	11.36	11.92	
1998	989.5	1566621	803.2	676.1	762.0	7.75	10.28	11.25	
1999	792.1	1431772	734.5	663.8	803.0	8.42	11.74	8.79	
2000	553.0	1452564	803.4	696.7	827	7.97	15.14	6.79	

附1-34 独立核算建筑业企业基本情况

BASIC STATISTICS FOR CONSTRUCTION ENTERPRISES WITH INDEPENDENT ACCOUNTING SYSTEM

年份 Year	建筑施工企业单位数(个) Construction Enterprises (unit)	建筑施工企业从业人员(万人) Employed Persons (10000 persons)	建筑施工企业总产值(亿元) Gross Output Value (100 million yuan)	建筑施工企业全员劳动生产率(元/人) Overall Labor Productivity (yuan/person)	建筑施工企业工程优良品率(%) Rate of High Quality Projects (%)	建筑施工企业利润总额(万元) Total Profits (10000 yuan)
1978	64	25.4	10.5	4397	72.9	7017
1979	70	26.4	12.7	4680	67.9	9256
1980	71	27.8	14.7	5249	65.5	14543
1981	71	27.0	14.5	5264	65.9	15778
1982	91	30.7	17.3	5404	81.2	17169
1983	116	37.2	22.6	6128	68.3	25489
1984	2765	53.0	33.4	6345	45.3	32342
1985	2549	62.8	43.9	7197	31.8	39277
1986	2361	61.3	51.3	8702	56.3	33084
1987	2292	64.4	67.0	10832	61.3	41202
1988	1659	64.2	81.6	12992	58.2	38679
1989	1545	60.0	89.0	14539	53.8	38189
1990	994	60.2	94.7	16340	54.5	33762
1991	922	60.3	99.6	17031	47.7	27690
1992	976	62.7	122.6	19786	25.0	30984
1993	1098	75.9	210.7	27739	21.9	61432
1994	1259	73.4	301.5	41099	26.7	94385
1995	1332	82.6	370.7	44852	23.3	77857
1996	1292	82.5	468.1	56750	17.5	88896
1997	1297	80.3	519.2	64633	19.8	104320
1998	1482	75.6	624.7	73644	21.4	123744
1999	1588	82.6	681.4	82465	18.7	135595
2000	1697	82.5	727.5	88132	25.6	163561

注：（1）1994年以后从业人员为计算劳产率的年平均人数；1996年以后全部指标不包括建筑业活动单位及四级以下施工企业。

（2）工程优良品率按单位工程个数计算。

a) Data of number of employment after 1994 refers to annual average number for calculating labor productivity; indicators after 1996 exclude construction units and enterprises below fourth grade.

b) Rate of high quality projects is calculated by number of unit project.

附1-35 运输邮电业基本情况
TRANSPORTATON,POSTS AND TELECOMMUNICATIONS

年 份 Year	铁路里程 (公里) Railway Operating Length (km)	公路里程 (公里) Highway Operating Length (km)	客运量 (万人) Passenger Traffic (10000 persons)	#铁 路 Railway	#公 路 Highway	# 民 航 Civil Aviation	货运量 (万吨) Freight Traffic	# 铁 路 Railway	# 公 路 Highway
1978	699	6562		2264		46.5	7394.4	3370	4023
1979	700	7278		2504		53.2	7763.7	3485	4277
1980	707	7339		2762		58.4	7571.0	3356	4213
1981--1985				**17688**		**544.0**	**37500.1**	**15425**	**22061**
1981	858	7427		2982		70.7	6895.1	3046	3847
1982	858	7543		3205		78.8	7379.2	3065	4312
1983	860	2906		3546		78.3	7639.6	3152	4485
1984	864	8131		3877		169.1	7897.2	3133	4761
1985	876	8487		4078		147.1	7689.0	3029	4656
1986--1990			**38505.7**	**21290**	**16160**	**1055.9**	**75409.6**	**15518**	**59324**
1986	876	8849	7336.7	4106	3059	171.7	7994.3	3030	4958
1987	876	8956	7763.4	4418	3117	228.4	7985.0	3125	4852
1988	876	9124	8491.4	4782	3460	249.4	7598.1	3168	4421
1989	876	9218	7433.9	4214	3034	186.1	25184.3	3144	21767
1990	876	9648	7480.3	3770	3490	220.3	26647.9	3051	23326
1991--1995			**40918.8**	**20615**	**18010**	**2292.4**	**152109**	**14923**	**136497**
1991	876	10259	7703.8	4036	3378	289.4	29347.5	2983	26099
1992	875	10827	8158.0	4196	3593	369.0	29887.2	2912	26881
1993	875	11242	7607.5	4374	2781	451.5	29864.6	3048	26730
1994	875	11532	8536.5	3992	4008	536.5	30824.6	3006	27700
1995	875	11532	8913.0	4017	4250	646.0	32184.6	2974	29087
1996--2000			**62554.4**	**19683.1**	**38888**	**3983.26**	**154376**	**13491.3**	**140455**
1996	922.0	11682	8801.4	3650.0	4395	756.4	32906.6	2851	29960
1997	923.5	12306	9262.8	3612.6	4902	748.2	32350.9	2883.3	29360
1998	923.5	12498	11227.7	3761.6	6704	762.1	30126.5	2562.5	27490
1999	997.1	12825	14866.4	4200.5	9878	787.9	28274.8	2582.8	25635
2000	996.9	13597	18396.1	4458.4	13009	928.7	30716.7	2611.7	28010

附1-35 续表1 continued

年 份 Year	# 民 航 Civil Aviation	旅 客 周转量 (万人公里) Passenger-Kilometers (10000 passenger-km)	# 铁 路 Railway	# 公路 Highway	# 民航 Civil Aviation	货 物 周转量 (万吨公里) Freight Ton-Kilometers (10000 ton-km)	# 铁 路 Railway	# 公 路 Highway	# 民 航 Civil Aviation
1978	1.4			59367				92247	
1979	1.7			64033				97616	
1980	2.0			73692				93899	
1981--1985	**14.1**							**437318**	
1981	2.1			81879				93254	
1982	2.2			90092				106767	24173
1983	2.6			103742				110118	26713
1984	3.2			113871				113871	20896
1985	4.0	1187072	473328	109184	604560	2128868	1992247	109184	27437
1986--1990	**40.7**	**6333894**	**2608550**	**629210**	**3076133**	**13732367**	**11007906**	**2496086**	**191715**
1986	6.3	1133620	496288	119065	518267	2579647	2133836	405645	28281
1987	8.0	1281763	534720	113735	613308	2802099	2282106	471393	37966
1988	9.1	1503508	588947	141625	772936	2896715	2344684	498391	42612
1989	7.8	1216981	521263	122435	573283	2765660	2179878	546022	38194
1990	9.5	1198022	467332	132350	598339	2688246	2067402	574635	44662
1991--1995	**79.7**	**8690002**	**2645880**	**842807**	**5201313**	**14535984**	**11382191**	**3488944**	**346841**
1991	11.9	1383465	506431	139041	737993	2799731	2153176	591187	54929
1992	14.4	1666810	531574	161735	973501	2938746	2230406	642200	65614
1993	17.3	1656130	551392	127461	977277	2458751	2301941	767790	73216
1994	19.1	1906718	547488	180030	1179199	3107722	2303265	725740	78142
1995	17.0	2076879	508995	234540	1333343	3231034	2393403	762027	74940
1996--2000	**125.2**	**12523195.8**	**2649587**	**1744526**	**8129083**	**14984163**	**10458031**	**3918017**	**606427**
1996	18.0	2107834	459514	250488	1397832	3174846	2311011	784888	78595
1997	20.2	2154186	477538	261204	1415444	3127394	2263274	769190	94500
1998	22.4	2419787	505554	304592	1609641	2846652	1952602	783237	110470
1999	29.9	2701471	579759	400597	1721115	2838857	1929269	754264	155171
2000	34.7	3139918	627222	527645	1985051	2996414	2001875	826438	167691

附1-35 续表 2 continued

年份 Year	机动车拥有量(辆) Possession of Motor Vehicles (unit)	# 公路部门 Highway Department	# 私人 Individuals	邮电局所(处) Post and Telecommunications Offices (unit)	邮电业务总量(万元) Revenue of Post and Telecommunications (10000 yuan)	市话交换机容量(万门) City Switchboards Capacity (10000)	电话机拥有量(部) Possession of Telephones (unit)	城市 Urban	农村 Rural
1978	77059			415	9050.6	26.2	87428	75597	11831
1979	89447			418	9986.8	31.5	93012	80365	12647
1980	103826			427	11403.7	35.0	99104	86057	13047
1981--1985									
1981	116360			427	12781.7	39.0	107310	94415	12895
1982	130332			437	13986.5	43.3	114908	101163	13745
1983	139756			450	15724.0	46.4	124907	111048	13859
1984	167028			472	18357.4	53.1	136481	123137	13344
1985	224272			479	22413.3	62.1	151861	138130	13731
1986--1990									
1986	266706			476	25347.7	69.6	178527	163377	15150
1987	272290	5983	7148	478	29282.3	83.8	209294	193865	15929
1988	312174			475	35478.5	101.6	238122	236389	1733
1989	353315	6195	24029	470	43922.3	119.9	277967	276234	1733
1990	384451			479	77205.6	136.2	332946	331188	1758
1991--1995									
1991				484	157417.7	165.0	394837	393046	1791
1992	341015	5813	48643	494	215768.9	193.9	479937	478024	1913
1993	563690	5298	66883	507	311251.3	226.2	664676	662449	2227
1994	664355	5280	85474	536	418773.9	303.5	1890224		
1995	804229	5237	127568	633	561296.4	369.3	2417207		
1996--2000									
1996	798392		351835	681	729022.4	442.0	2923042		
1997	1019042		540564	701	930136.7	546.4	3577825		
1998	1163338		697707	728	1290966.5	686.8	5225253		
1999	1241719		762361	750	1659132.7	748.3	6545155		
2000	1364718		855321	767	2147495.5	803.7	9094594		

注：1.公路货运量1988年以前为交通运输部门数据。

2.铁路是北京市辖范围。

a) Data of freight traffic of highway before 1988 was provided by transport department.

b) Railway refers to that within the jurisdiction of Beijing.

附1-36 社会消费品零售额

TOTAL RETAIL SALES OF CONSUMER GOODS

单位：亿元 (100 million yuan)

年份 Year	社会消费品零售额 Retail Sales of Consumer Goods	按地区分 By Region 市 City	县 County	县以下 Below County Level	按经济类型分 By Ownership 国有经济 State-Owned	集体经济 Collective Owned	合营经济 Joint Owned	个体经济 Individuals	其他经济 Others
1978	44.2	34.5	5.3	4.4	37.2	7.0			
1979	52.2	41.6	5.8	4.8	44.2	7.9		0.1	
1980	61.3	49.3	6.6	5.4	49.1	11.8		0.4	
1981--1985	**455.3**	**364.0**	**48.3**	**43.0**	**301.7**	**143.5**	**1.0**	**9.1**	
1981	68.8	55.6	7.3	5.9	48.7	19.2	0.2	0.7	
1982	73.3	58.6	8.1	6.6	51.0	21.2	0.2	0.9	
1983	83.6	66.6	9.3	7.7	56.0	26.1	0.1	1.4	
1984	101.7	81.1	10.4	10.2	67.7	32.1	0.2	1.7	
1985	127.9	102.1	13.2	12.6	78.3	44.9	0.3	4.4	
1986--1990	**1131.8**	**943.0**	**103.4**	**85.5**	**617.7**	**401.1**	**6.4**	**106.7**	
1986	146.5	121.7	12.1	12.7	84.5	51.0	0.4	10.6	
1987	176.6	145.7	16.2	14.7	97.1	64.5	0.6	14.5	
1988	234.3	195.0	21.2	18.1	129.4	84.5	0.6	19.7	
1989	266.7	221.5	25.0	20.2	143.8	92.2	2.6	28.2	
1990	307.7	259.1	28.9	19.7	162.9	108.9	2.2	33.7	
1991--1995	**2813.6**	**2215.9**	**373.6**	**224.1**	**1332.7**	**792.6**	**76.3**	**530.3**	**81.7**
1991	357.8	301.2	33.4	23.2	191.8	122.9	2.6	40.5	
1992	430.0	360.2	41.1	28.7	230.6	139.6	3.3	56.5	
1993	531.8	430.9	60.6	40.3	273.0	162.5	8.1	88.2	
1994	667.0	525.1	90.6	51.3	299.3	171.2	23.1	152.3	21.1
1995	827.0	598.5	147.9	80.6	338.0	196.4	39.2	192.8	60.6
1996--2000	**5927.0**	**4694.1**	**409.6**	**823.4**	**1920.6**	**1111.5**	**488.5**	**1265.0**	**1141.2**
1996	923.7	664.5	95.6	163.6	314.8	217.3	70.5	241.8	79.3
1997	1051.5	808.3	88.2	155.0	368.8	247.9	83.4	236.5	114.9
1998	1195.2	952.5	77.0	165.7	344.8	231.5	114.3	243.0	261.6
1999	1313.3	1037.7	84.0	191.6	436.1	200.8	105.7	258.0	312.7
2000	1443.3	1231.1	64.7	147.5	456.1	214.1	114.6	285.8	372.7

年份 Year	按行业分 By Sector 批发零售贸易业 Wholesale and Retail Sales	餐饮业 Catering	制造业 Manufacturing	其他行业 Others	按类别分 By Category 食品类 Food	衣着类 Clothing	日用品类 Daily Use Articles	燃料类 Fuels	农业生产资料零售额 Retail Sales of Agricultural Capital Goods	集市贸易成交额 Value of Country Fair Trade
1978	40.7	1.7	1.2	0.6	18.0	8.9	12.4	1.3	3.6	
1979	47.3	2.1	2.1	0.7	20.4	11.1	15.7	1.5	3.5	0.2
1980	53.5	2.7	3.5	1.6	24.4	12.9	18.8	1.6	3.6	0.7
1981--1985	**381.7**	**21.9**	**34.0**	**17.7**	**174.3**	**82.0**	**161.3**	**10.3**	**27.4**	**8.2**
1981	57.8	3.5	5.1	2.4	27.2	14.1	21.9	1.7	3.9	0.9
1982	61.4	3.7	5.5	2.7	28.9	13.3	24.2	1.7	5.2	1.1
1983	70.4	4.0	6.0	3.2	32.9	15.2	27.9	1.9	5.7	1.3
1984	85.6	4.7	7.8	3.6	38.1	18.0	37.0	2.2	6.4	1.5
1985	106.5	6.0	9.6	5.8	47.2	21.4	50.3	2.8	6.2	3.4
1986--1990	**906.7**	**70.7**	**64.5**	**89.9**	**451.8**	**152.4**	**447.9**	**24.1**	**55.6**	**71.1**
1986	119.3	8.1	8.9	10.2	57.4	21.6	57.1	3.3	7.1	6.4
1987	140.2	10.7	12.0	13.7	72.4	25.6	67.3	3.7	7.6	8.5
1988	186.4	16.1	13.9	17.9	92.0	33.0	93.9	4.1	11.3	14.1
1989	213.1	16.5	15.4	21.7	108.0	31.6	106.3	5.8	14.9	18.4
1990	247.7	19.3	14.3	26.4	122.0	40.6	123.3	7.2	14.6	23.6
1991--1995	**2079.3**	**215.5**	**119.8**	**399.0**	**1095.5**	**418.1**	**1195.0**	**64.9**	**83.4**	**514.9**
1991	286.2	22.9	16.8	31.9	138.6	47.1	146.6	7.7	17.8	31.0
1992	333.7	30.8	19.4	46.1	165.5	57.2	174.8	10.3	22.2	55.3
1993	393.0	44.6	28.7	65.5	192.0	84.0	241.5	14.3	17.6	83.4
1994	481.5	54.2	25.3	106.0	246.4	109.0	294.6	17.0	12.4	150.1
1995	584.9	63.0	29.6	149.5	353.0	120.9	337.5	15.6	13.4	195.1
1996--2000	**4183.9**	**390.4**	**324.9**	**1027.8**	**1894.3**	**747.3**	**3111.8**	**173.5**	**60.7**	**1539.2**
1996	657.1	68.4	38.1	160.1	372.0	132.7	401.8	17.2	11.6	250.8
1997	709.4	72.5	56.3	213.3	389.7	140.6	492.2	29.1	9.5	285.3
1998	865.7	81.8	63.8	183.9	347.9	145.5	664.9	36.9	10.5	323.8
1999	926.2	81.3	79.8	226.0	374.5	155.6	742.1	41.1	10.5	307.0
2000	1025.5	86.4	86.9	244.5	410.2	173.0	810.9	49.2	22.8	372.3

注：1993年以前是社会商品零售总额，1993年以后是社会消费品零售总额。

Note: Data before 1993 refers to total retail sales of commodity and data after 1993 refers to total retail sales of consumer goods.

附1-37 北京市对外经济贸易和国际旅游
FOREIGN ECONOMICS,TRADE AND TOURISM

年 份 Year	进出口总额(万美元) Total Value of Imports and Exports (USD 10000)	# 出口 Exports	签订利用外资协议项目(个) Contracts Signed of Foreign Capital Utilization (unit)	# 对外借款 Foreign Loans	# 外商直接投资 Direct Foreign Investment	签订利用外资协议金额(万美元) Contracted Foreign Capital (USD10000)	对外借款 Foreign Loans	外商直接投资 Direct Foreign Investment	外商其他投资 Other Foreign Investment
1978	29751	28524							
1979	45036	41757							
1980	66280	59277							
1981--1985	**382296**	**308276**							
1981	70091	63230							
1982	68921	61339							
1983	69621	59009							
1984	76303	62623	55	2	31	13826	1600	11660	566
1985	97360	62075	108	1	83	40788	130	39649	1009
1986--1990	**940420**	**457112**	**853**	**58**	**709**	**171046**	**26952**	**138628**	**5467**
1986	166847	65252	85	2	63	55888	9700	41952	4236
1987	154470	78239	97	6	72	66515	3322	62414	779
1988	198846	99121	193	21	148	18533	4144	14202	187
1989	205162	102336	209	10	185	14252	5731	8372	149
1990	215095	112164	269	19	241	15859	4055	11688	116
1991--1995	**1999096**	**836561**	**10987**	**67**	**10911**	**1699801**	**168840**	**1530412**	**549**
1991	258632	123987	735	8	724	47995	19431	28488	76
1992	320171	152555	2231	23	2208	177274	30079	147195	
1993	420029	137056	3765	13	3752	664911	36987	627924	
1994	469339	195936	2688	13	2675	505300	52000	453300	
1995	530925	227027	1568	10	1552	304321	30344	273505	472
1996--2000	**3756584**	**1526807**	**4118**	**18**	**4100**	**1377471**	**5893**	**1371578**	
1996	539201	208624	868		868	179029		179029	
1997	557576	246503	798	8	790	171532	3429	168103	
1998	650536	282896	656	5	651	410567	890	409677	
1999	844212	326101	647	2	645	182649	964	181685	
2000	1165059	462683	1149	3	1146	433694	610	433084	

注：1. 进出口总额1986年以前为外贸部门口径，从1986年开始为海关口径。

2. 海关进出口数为地方企业数据。

a) Data of total value of imports and exports refers to customs from 1986, while that before 1986 was provided from foreign trade department.
b) Data of imports and exports(customs)refers to that of local enterprises.

附1-37 续表 continued

年 份 Year	实际利用外资金额(万美元) Foreign Capital Actually Used (USD10000)	对外借款 Foreign Loans	外商直接投资 Direct Foreign Investment	外商其他投资 Other Foreign Investment	对外承包工程和劳务合作 Constructed Projects and Labor Services Cooperation with Foreign Countries 合同数(份) Contracts (unit)	合同金额(万美元) Contracted (USD 10000)	完成营业额(万美元) Fulfiled Value (USD 10000)	旅游外汇收入总额(万美元) Tourism Foreign Exchange Earnings (USD 10000)
1978								10000
1979								9000
1980								12000
1981--1985								**94000**
1981								12000
1982								13000
1983					9	218.5	837.1	14000
1984					9	2801.5	1843.2	23000
1985					14	852.8	2083.1	32000
1986--1990					**331**	**7733.7**	**5108.9**	**280901**
1986					30	445.3	1535.5	46000
1987	17725.4	7146.6	9534.0	1044.8	37	548.6	697.6	55000
1988	61943.8	11524.4	50277.9	141.5	46	884.9	802.4	67000
1989	49506.8	17491.0	31845.9	169.9	113	2099.4	1017.5	47195
1990	40641.4	12743.5	27695.5	202.4	105	3755.5	1055.9	65706
1991--1995	**579524.3**	**168401**	**410896.0**	**226.9**	**586**	**79267.8**	**48984.0**	**735519**
1991	36798.1	12303.8	24481.8	12.5	114	3202.2	1896.8	85001
1992	52711.9	17710.8	34984.2	16.9	130	8887.6	3299.6	107286
1993	97619.8	30729.3	66693	197.5	117	36854.0	11442.0	124128
1994	194740.2	50280.2	144460		109	15521.0	18671.0	200904
1995	197654.3	57377.3	140277		116	15613.0	12789.0	218200
1996--2000	**1366753.8**	**266219**	**989964**	**110571**	**601**	**173362**	**164461**	**1214800**
1996	225842.3	70552.3	155290.0		116	67688.0	43057.0	225200
1997	259161.8	73330.4	159286	26545.0	107	35640.0	29629.0	224800
1998	286973.4	57194.5	206415	23364.0	184	28520.0	45812.0	238400
1999	293681.6	43945.5	223124	26612.3	90	25229.0	26165.0	249600
2000	301094.7	21195.8	245849	34049.8	104	16285.0	19798.0	276800

附1-38 教育基本情况
BASIC STATISTICS FOR EDUCATION

年 份 Year	在校学生数(万人) Students Enrollment (10000 persons)				升学率(%) Rate of Entering Higher Grade Schools(%)		学龄儿童入学率(%) Enrollment	平均每一专任教师负担学生数(人) Average Number of Students Instructed by a Professional Teacher(person)		
	合 计 Total	高等学校 Institutions of Higher Education	普通中学 Regular Secondary Schools	小 学 Primary Schools	初中毕业生 Graduates of Junior Middle Schools	小学毕业生 Graduates of Primary Schools	Rate of Children at School-Age (%)	高等学校 Institutions of Higher Education	普通中学 Regular Secondary Schools	小 学 Primary Schools
1978	208.1	4.9	109.5	93.7	79.7	102.6	99.0	2.4	19.9	20.7
1979	186.1	5.5	83.7	96.9	63.0	99.6	98.4	2.3	16.1	21.3
1980	173.5	6.4	71.9	95.2	80.3	99.5	98.7	2.6	14.5	21.7
1981	157.5	7.7	59.8	90.0	57.3	98.8	98.9	3.8	13.4	19.7
1982	144.6	7.2	51.9	85.5	58.6	97.0	98.9	3.2	12.3	19.5
1983	139.1	8.1	47.2	83.8	60.1	97.8	99.0	3.0	11.5	19.6
1984	137.4	9.1	52.0	76.3	61.2	98.7	99.3	3.3	13.2	18.2
1985	139.6	12.0	54.2	73.4	72.6	98.3	99.1	3.6	13.9	17.4
1986	156.0	13.0	56.5	74.9	77.1	97.8	99.49	3.6	13.9	17.4
1987	157.2	13.6	52.3	77.8	65.1	98.6	99.46	3.7	12.8	16.8
1988	160.3	14.5	46.9	85.1	64.3	98.5	99.50	4.0	11.4	17.6
1989	166.0	14.1	43.4	93.5	80.5	99.1	98.97	3.8	11.0	19.1
1990	168.7	14.0	40.9	99.6	81.8	99.3	99.47	3.9	10.1	18.6
1991	171.8	13.7	43.2	101.3	86.4	98.8	99.72	3.1	10.2	18.0
1992	176.2	14.0	47.6	100.2	88.5	99.6	99.65	4.0	11.3	17.4
1993	186.3	15.9	52.3	102.2	93.5	98.7	99.88	4.6	12.1	17.4
1994	196.1	17.5	58.4	102.4	86.7	99.4	99.92	4.9	13.1	16.9
1995	202.8	18.2	62.8	100.7	87.3	99.5	99.93	5.0	13.6	16.5
1996	207.9	19.0	64.9	100.0	88.1	99.3	99.93	5.2	13.7	16.1
1997	207.3	19.6	62.6	97.7	92.3	98.6	99.95	5.4	13.2	15.7
1998	204.7	21.3	61.0	92.0	92.2	98.7	99.96	5.8	12.8	14.9
1999	201.6	23.4	63.5	83.7	94.7	98.3	99.95	6.7	13.2	13.7
2000	201.7	28.3	69.1	74.3	93.92	98.99	99.95			12.8

注：因“平均每一专任教师负担学生数”指标中，高等学校及普通中学分组有所调整，故自2000年起，有关数据请参照“教育文化”章节中的相关指标。

Note: As the groups divided of institutions of higher education and regular secondary schools in indicator of “average number of students by a professional teacher” has been changed,please use the related data in chapter “education and culture” .

附1-39 卫生情况
STATISTICS ON HEALTH

年　份 Year	医院数 (个) Hospital (unit)	医生数 (人) Doctors (person)	医　院 床位数 (张) Beds (unit)	每千人拥有 医生数(人) Doctors Per 1000 Persons (person)	每千人拥有 医院床位(张) Beds Per 1000 Persons (bed)
1978	389	28435	26432	3.35	3.11
1979	387	31842	26808	3.66	3.08
1980	393	34365	28495	3.88	3.22
1981	406	37886	29783	4.21	3.31
1982	413	39385	30940	4.29	3.37
1983	412	41216	32242	4.42	3.46
1984	423	42112	34602	4.46	3.66
1985	376	42498	38180	4.44	3.99
1986	371	43403	40903	4.47	4.21
1987	398	46007	44407	4.66	4.49
1988	445	48216	48711	4.82	4.87
1989	470	49361	51877	4.83	5.08
1990	512	50934	55474	4.93	5.37
1991	525	52309	58747	5.03	5.65
1992	535	53254	59833	5.10	5.73
1993	548	53906	62340	5.13	5.93
1994	629	53865	64416	5.07	6.07
1995	629	54114	64211	5.06	6.00
1996	405	54091	60997	5.02	6.02
1997	435	54909	61865	5.06	6.06
1998	449	51902	63144	4.76	6.13
1999	460	52646	63660	4.79	6.15
2000	458	51570	65138	4.66	6.25

注：1996年起，医院数仅指县及县以上医院和其他医院，乡镇卫生院不再做为医院统计。

Note: From 1996, number of hospitals included hospitals at county level and above and other hospitals, township hospitals were not calculated as hospitals any more.

附1-40 离退休退职人数
NUMBER OF VCSR AND RRSW

年 份 Year	离退休、退职人数(万人) Number of VCSR and RRSW(10000 persons)	国有单位 State-Owned	城镇集体单位 Urban Collective Owned	其他单位 Others	在职职工与离退休退职人员之比 Ratio of Staff and Workers on Their Posts to VCSR and RRSW
1989	75.9	58.4	17.3	0.2	5.3
1990	81.9	64.2	17.5	0.2	5.3
1991	87.7	70.0	17.6	0.2	5.2
1992	94.1	75.8	18.1	0.2	5.1
1993	100.8	82.1	17.9	0.8	4.5
1994	110.5	86.6	23.0	0.9	4.3
1995	120.7	93.6	25.2	1.9	3.9
1996	133.0	103.5	27.1	2.4	3.5
1997	144.3	113.2	28.6	2.5	3.2
1998	155.6	123.3	29.5	2.8	2.9
1999	168.6	133.4	31.1	4.1	2.6
2000	176.2	142.2	25.0	9.1	2.5

注：最后一列以离退休、退职人数为1。

Note: Data of last line are caculated according to number of VCSR and RRSW=1.

附录 2：各类市场情况　APPENDIX 2：VARIOUS　MARKETS

附2-1 房 产 交 易 情 况

HOUSE PROPERTY BUSINESS

项　目 Item		起 Case	建筑面积 (万平方米) Floor Space (10000 sq.m)	# 楼房 Storied Building	立契价 (万元) Contracted Price (10000 yuan)
合　计	**Total**	**72755**	**901.1**	**886.1**	**2667326.0**
市房屋交易所	**Municipal Transaction Department of Houses**	**1602**	**44.1**	**44.0**	**573567.5**
区县交易所	**Transaction Department of District and County**	**71153**	**857.0**	**842.1**	**2093758.5**
东城区	Dongcheng	2182	27.7	24.0	80521.1
西城区	Xicheng	1580	15.2	14.6	41394.5
崇文区	Chongwen	2471	30.7	30.4	92056.1
宣武区	Xuanwu	466	27.4	27.4	153312.6
朝阳区	Chaoyang	12708	140.8	140.8	239810.4
丰台区	Fengtai	2384	71.0	70.8	284044.4
石景山区	Shijingshan	4967	46.3	46.1	66937.9
海淀区	Haidian	16765	206.3	206.2	666036.5
门头沟区	Mentougou	701	4.8	3.1	6265.7
房山区	Fangshan	286	2.8	2.8	3684.6
通州区	Tongzhou	5239	53.0	48.6	81055.8
昌平区	Changping	5448	63.9	63.9	146342.6
顺义区	Shunyi	458	3.8	3.8	6593.7
大兴县	Daxing	7328	80.6	80.3	150576.0
平谷县	Pinggu	2115	20.7	20.2	16325.4
怀柔县	Huairou	1902	18.0	17.5	25814.3
密云县	Miyun	2572	28.4	26.9	18823.0
延庆县	Yanqing	1581	15.6	14.9	14164.0

附2-2 各类商品交易市场基本情况
STATISTICS FOR COMMODITY TRANSACTION MARKETS

单位：个 (unit)

项目	Item	全市 Total	城区 City Proper	近郊区 Near Suburbs	远郊区 Outer Suburbs	各县 Counties
各类商品市场总数	**Total Number of Markets**	**832**	**176**	**356**	**194**	**106**
# 亿元市场数	Million-yuan Markets	78	13	52	7	6
综合市场	**Complex Markets**	**494**	**88**	**187**	**146**	**73**
工业品综合市场	of Industrial Products	34	12	7	5	10
农产品综合市场	of Farm Products	386	69	159	104	54
其它综合市场	Others	74	7	21	37	9
专业市场	**Specialized Markets**	**328**	**81**	**167**	**47**	**33**
纺织品服装鞋帽市场	of Textiles, Garments, Shoes and Hats	66	19	30	10	7
食品饮料烟酒市场	of Food, Beverage, Tobacco and Liquor	8	4	4		
家具市场	of Furniture	35	3	17	10	5
小商品市场	of Small Commodities	31	16	10	2	3
文化、音像、书报杂志市场	of Culture, Audio and Video, Books, Newspaper and Magazines	19	5	14		
旧货市场	of Old Commodities	6	1	4	1	
机动车市场	of Motor Vehicles	4		4		
金属材料市场	of Metal Materials	2		2		
煤炭市场	of Coal	3			2	1
木材市场	of Timber	18		4	9	5
建材装饰材料市场	of Building Materials and Decoration Materials	67	4	53	5	5
粮油市场	of Grain and Edible Oil	7		5	2	
干鲜果品市场	of Dry and Fresh Fruits	4		2	1	1
水产品市场	of Aquatic Products	2	1	1		
蔬菜市场	of Vegetable	9	4	2		3
肉食禽蛋市场	of Meet, Poultry and Eggs	2	1	1		
农业生产资料市场	of Agricultural Capital Goods	1		1		
餐饮业市场	of Catering Trade	5	5			
其他专业市场	Others	39	18	13	5	3
其他市场	**Others**	**10**	**7**	**2**	**1**	
其他市场	Others	10	7	2	1	

附2-3 各类商品交易市场成交额

TRANSACTION VALUE OF COMMODITY TRANSACTION MARKETS

单位：万元 (10000 yuan)

项 目	Item	全市 Total	城区 City Proper	近郊区 Near Suburbs	远郊区 Outer Suburbs	各县 Counties
各类商品市场总数	**Total Number of Markets**	**5555165**	**835776**	**3880717**	**525523**	**313149**
# 亿元市场数	Million-yuan Markets	4464937	660638	3411487	253875	138937
综合市场	**Complex Markets**	**2806349**	**5022895**	**1609073**	**467549**	**226832**
工业品综合市场	of Industrial Products	108306	72055	6409	16814	13028
农产品综合市场	of Farm Products	2483935	419977	1465757	399774	198427
其它综合市场	Others	214108	10863	136907	50961	15377
专业市场	**Specialized Markets**	**2745670**	**330307**	**2271360**	**57686**	**86317**
纺织品服装鞋帽市场	of Textiles, Garments, Shoes and Hats	413826	129848	253072	19252	11654
食品饮料烟酒市场	of Food, Beverage, Tobacco and Liquor	100966	3190	97776		
家具市场	of Furniture	187755	21946	146046	17392	2371
小商品市场	of Small Commodities	180394	115397	57153	548	7296
文化、音像、书报杂志市场	of Culture, Audio and Video, Books, Newspaper and Magazines	278425	10979	267446		
旧货市场	of Old Commodities	14059	24	14020	15	
机动车市场	of Motor Vehicles	749071		749071		
金属材料市场	of Metal Materials	101941		101941		
煤炭市场	of Coal	3590			590	3000
木材市场	of Timber	23364		8099	11511	3754
建材装饰材料市场	of Building Materials and Decoration Materials	338678	12399	309347	7112	9820
粮油市场	of Grain and Edible Oil	108497		107441	1056	
干鲜果品市场	of Dry and Fresh Fruits	13159		6010	150	6999
水产品市场	of Aquatic Products	38889	11573	27316		
蔬菜市场	of Vegetable	41865	2080	167		39618
肉食禽蛋市场	of Meet, Poultry and Eggs	5585	4730	855		
农业生产资料市场	of Agricultural Capital Goods	228		228		
餐饮业市场	of Catering Trade	549	549			
其他专业市场	Others	144829	17592	125372	60	1805
其他市场	**Others**	**3146**	**2574**	**284**	**288**	
其他市场	Others	3146	2574	284	288	

附2-4 消费品市场成交量
TRANSACTION VOLUME OF CONSUMER GOODS MARKETS

单位：百公斤 (100 kg)

项目	Item	成交量 Transaction Volume	零售量 Retail	社会纯销量 Sales	零售量占社会纯销量比重（%） Proportion of Retail in Sales(%)
粮食	Grain	7731997	2311391	23328786	9.9
食用植物油	Edible Vegetable Oil	1655884	553228	4455627	12.4
猪和猪肉	Hog and Pork	1951366	1366689	2646885	51.6
牛和牛肉	Oxes and Beef	719331	446200	641106	69.6
羊和羊肉	Goat, Sheep and Mutton	584640	419157	571788	73.3
家禽	Poultry	404625	243043	1324026	18.4
鲜蛋	Fresh Eggs	900814	695367	937220	74.2
鲜菜	Fresh Vegetable	44578495	13811727	29703710	46.5
鲜瓜果	Fresh Melon and Fruit	15871283	5241716	10766156	48.7
水产品	Aquatic Products	1845706	1117803	1946790	57.4

附2-5 生产资料市场成交情况
STATISTICS FOR TRANSACTION IN CAPITAL GOODS MARKETS

项目 Item				2000	1999	2000年为1999年% 2000 as % of 1999
成交额	**(万元)**	**Transaction Value**	**(10000 yuan)**	**1206953**	**1037397**	**116.3**
成交量		**Transaction Volume**				
新、旧汽车	(辆)	New and Old Automobiles	(unit)	72634	78757	92.2
钢材	(吨)	Rolled Steel	(ton)	299819	293982	102.0
木材	(立方米)	Timber	(cu.m)	329531	367954	89.6
煤炭	(吨)	Coal	(ton)	122453	2235	5478.9

附2-6 消 费 者 投 诉 与 处 理
CONSUMER'S LAWSUITS AND HANDLING

单位：件 (case)

项目	Item	2000 受理投诉件数 Cases Accepted	2000 构成(%) Composition(%)	1999 受理投诉件数 Cases Accepted	1999 构成(%) Composition(%)
总　计	**Total**	**14300**	**100**	**15379**	**100**
按行业分	**By Sector**				
家用电器类	Household Appliances	2159	15.1	1451	9.4
# 电视机	TV Sets	274	12.7	186	12.8
电冰箱	Refrigerators	138	6.4	75	5.2
洗衣机	Washing Machines	72	3.3	32	2.2
收录机	Recorders	64	3.0	71	4.9
家用机械类	Household Machines	770	5.4	745	4.8
# 照相机	Cameras	52	6.8	35	4.7
自行车	Bicycles	67	8.7	118	15.8
摩托车	Motorcycles	171	22.2	158	21.2
钟　表	Clocks and Watches	71	9.2	100	13.4
日用百货类	Articles of Daily Use	4505	31.5	5454	35.5
# 家　具	Furniture	587	13.0	548	10.1
服　装	Garments	1430	31.7	1634	30.0
鞋	Shoes	1817	40.3	2482	45.5
化妆品	Cosmetics	156	3.5	131	2.4
食　品	Food	1445	10.1	2481	16.1
药　品	Medicine	91	0.6	102	0.7
服　务	Services	2810	19.7	2773	18.0
农用资料	Materials for Agricultural Use	224	1.6	207	1.4
邮　购	Mail-order	423	3.0	543	3.5
其　他	Others	1873	13.1	1623	10.6
按内容分	**By Content**				
质　量	Quality	9929	69.4	10698	70.0
价　格	Price	945	6.6	631	4.1
虚假广告	False Advertisements	299	2.1	93	0.6
假冒伪劣商品	Counterfeit Goods	123	0.9	151	0.9
计　量	Measure	613	4.3	1175	7.6
欺诈骗销	Cheating Sales	95	0.7	132	0.8
其　他	Others	2296	16.1	2499	16.0

注：总解决率为98.1%。

Note: Total rate of settlement is 98.1%.

附录3：世界主要国家和地区统计资料
APPENDIX 3: STATISTICS OF MAJOR COUNTRIES AND TERRITORIES
附3-1 1999年世界主要国家和地区人均国民生产总值
GROSS NATIONAL PRODUCT(GNP) PER CAPITA IN MAIN COUNTRIES AND TERRITORIES OF 1999

国家和地区 Country or Territory		人均国民生产总值 GNP Per Capita		购买力平价法计算的GNP GNP Calculated in Purchasing-power-parity Way	
		人均值（美元） Per Capita (US$)	年增长率（%） Growth Rate (%)	总额（十亿美元） Total (US$ 1 billion)	人均值（美元） Per Capita (US$)
中国	China	780	6.3	4112.2	3291
美国	United States	30600	3.1	8350.1	30600
日本	Japan	32230	0.8	3042.9	24041
德国	Germany	25350	1.2	1837.8	22404
英国	United Kingdom	22640	1.6	1234.4	20883
法国	France	23480	2.0	1293.8	21897
意大利	Italy	19710	0.9	1196.3	20751
加拿大	Canada	19320	2.8	726.1	23725
澳大利亚	Australia	20050	2.5	426.4	22448
波兰	Poland	3960	3.3	305.5	7894
罗马尼亚	Romania	1520	-2.8	126.8	5647
保加利亚	Bulgaria	1380	3.5	40.4	4914
印度	India	450	4.9	2144.1	2149
印度尼西亚	Indonesia	580	0.3	505.0	2439
巴基斯坦	Pakistan	470	1.2	236.8	1757
泰国	Thailand	1960	4.1	345.4	5599
菲律宾	Philippines	1020	1.4	292.9	3815
马来西亚	Malaysia	3400	1.9	180.8	7963
韩国	Korea Rep.	8490	10.1	685.7	14637
尼日利亚	Nigeria	310	0.5	92.2	744
巴西	Brazil	4420	-3.2	1061.7	6317
墨西哥	Mexico	4400	2.4	752.0	7719
阿根廷	Argentina	7600	-4.1	414.1	11324
孟加拉国	Bangladesh	370	3.3	188.3	1475
新加坡	Singapore	29610	3.6	87.1	27024
越南	Viet Nam	370	2.9	136.1	1755
阿尔及利亚	Algeria	1550	1.3	142.3	4753
南非	South Africa Rep.	3160	-0.9	350.2	8318
新西兰	New Zealand	13780	1.9	63.3	16566

资料来源：世界银行《2000/2001年世界发展报告》。
Source: World Development Report 2000/2001.

附3-2 世界主要国家和地区经济增长率

GROWTH RATE OF ECONOMY IN MAIN COUNTRIES AND TERRITORIES

单位：% (%)

国家和地区 Country or Territory		1997	1998	1999	2000 *
中国	China	8.8	7.8	7.1	7.5
美国	United States	4.4	4.4	4.2	5.2
日本	Japan	1.6	-2.5	0.2	1.4
德国	Germany	1.4	2.1	1.6	2.9
英国	United Kingdom	3.5	2.6	2.1	3.1
法国	France	2.0	3.2	2.9	3.5
意大利	Italy	1.8	1.5	1.4	3.1
加拿大	Canada	4.4	3.3	4.5	4.7
澳大利亚	Australia	3.9	5.2	4.4	4.0
波兰	Poland	6.8	4.8	4.1	5.0
匈牙利	Hungary	4.6	4.9	4.5	5.5
罗马尼亚	Romania	-6.1	-5.4	-3.2	1.3
印度	India	4.7	6.3	6.4	6.7
印度尼西亚	Indonesia	4.5	-13.0	0.3	4.0
巴基斯坦	Pakistan	1.0	2.6	2.7	5.6
泰国	Thailand	-1.7	-10.2	4.2	5.0
菲律宾	Philippines	5.2	-0.6	3.3	4.0
马来西亚	Malaysia	7.3	-7.4	5.6	6.0
韩国	Korea Rep.	5.0	-6.7	10.7	8.8
埃及	Egypt	5.5	5.6	6.0	5.0
巴西	Brazil	3.6	-0.1	1.0	4.0
墨西哥	Mexico	6.8	4.9	3.5	6.5
阿根廷	Argentina	8.1	3.9	-3.1	1.7
新加坡	Singapore	8.4	0.4	5.4	7.9
南非	South Africa Rep.	2.5	0.6	1.2	3.0
新西兰	New Zealand	2.1	-0.2	3.4	4.0

注：*为预测数。

资料来源：2000年《世界经济展望》。

Note: * indicates the predetermined data.

Source: 2000 Prospects for the World Economy.

附3-3 世界主要国家和地区通货膨胀率
INFLATION RATE OF MAIN COUNTRIES AND TERRITORIES

单位：%　　　　(%)

国家和地区	Country or Territory	1997	1998	1999	2000 *
中国	China	2.8	-0.8	-1.4	0.5
美国	United States	2.3	1.6	2.2	3.2
日本	Japan	1.7	0.6	-0.3	-0.2
德国	Germany	1.5	0.6	0.7	1.7
英国	United Kingdom	2.8	2.7	2.3	2.0
法国	France	1.3	0.7	0.6	1.5
意大利	Italy	1.7	1.7	1.7	2.5
加拿大	Canada	1.6	1.0	1.7	2.3
澳大利亚	Australia	1.7	0.9	1.5	4.8
波兰	Poland	14.9	11.8	7.3	9.5
匈牙利	Hungary	18.3	14.3	10.0	8.3
罗马尼亚	Romania	154.8	59.1	45.8	40.2
印度	India	7.2	13.2	4.7	5.6
印度尼西亚	Indonesia	6.3	58.0	20.8	3.2
巴基斯坦	Pakistan	11.8	7.8	5.7	3.6
泰国	Thailand	5.6	8.1	0.3	1.7
菲律宾	Philippines	5.9	9.7	6.7	5.0
马来西亚	Malaysia	2.7	5.3	2.8	3.2
韩国	Korea Rep.	4.4	7.5	0.8	2.2
埃及	Egypt	6.2	4.7	3.8	2.9
巴西	Brazil	6.9	3.2	4.9	7.5
墨西哥	Mexico	20.6	15.9	16.6	9.5
阿根廷	Argentina	0.8	0.9	-1.2	-0.7
新加坡	Singapore	2.0	-0.3	0.1	1.4
南非	South Africa Rep.	8.6	6.9	5.2	4.7
新西兰	New Zealand	1.7	1.6	1.1	2.3

注：*为预测数。
资料来源：2000年《世界经济展望》。
Note: * indicates the predetermined data.
Source: 2000 Prospects for the World Economy.

附3-4 1999年世界主要国家和地区投资率

INVESTMENT RATE IN MAIN COUNTRIES AND TERRITORIES OF 1999

单位：% (%)

国家和地区	Country or Territory	1995	1996	1997	1998	1999
世界	**World**	**21.8**	**22.0**	**22.0**	**20.0**	**22.0**
中国	China	40.8	39.2	35.0	39.0	40.0
美国	United States	17.7	18.0	18.0	18.0	19.0
日本	Japan	28.5	29.0	29.0		29.0
德国	Germany	22.5	23.0	23.0	21.0	21.0
英国	United Kingdom	16.0	16.0		16.0	16.0
法国	France	18.2	18.0	18.0	17.0	17.0
意大利	Italy	18.1	18.0	18.0	17.0	18.0
加拿大	Canada	18.4	18.0	18.0	18.0	20.0
澳大利亚	Australia	21.5	21.0	21.0	20.0	22.0
波兰	Poland	18.0	20.4	22.0	24.0	28.0
俄罗斯	Russia	23.2	22.2	22.0	20.0	14.0
罗马尼亚	Romania	25.6	25.4	25.0	20.0	15.0
保加利亚	Bulgaria	15.7	14.1	14.0	12.0	16.0
印度	India	26.2	26.5	25.0	23.0	24.0
印度尼西亚	Indonesia	31.1	31.8	31.0	31.0	14.0
巴基斯坦	Pakistan	18.7	18.6	19.0	17.0	15.0
泰国	Thailand	42.3	41.0	41.0	35.0	21.0
菲律宾	Philippines	22.2	24.2	25.0	25.0	21.0
马来西亚	Malaysia	40.6	41.2	43.0	32.0	32.0
韩国	Korea Rep.	37.0	38.2	35.0	35.0	27.0
尼日利亚	Nigeria	18.5	18.7	18.0	20.0	11.0
巴西	Brazil	21.9	19.5	20.0	21.0	21.0
墨西哥	Mexico	19.6	20.9	21.0	26.0	24.0
阿根廷	Argentina	18.3	18.5	19.0	22.0	18.0
孟加拉国	Bangladesh	16.6	17.0	17.0	21.0	20.0
新加坡	Singapore	33.1	35.1	37.0	37.0	33.0
阿尔及利亚	Algeria	32.0	27.0	27.0	27.0	27.0
南非	South Africa Rep.	18.6	17.5	16.0	20.0	16.0
新西兰	New Zealand	21.9	22.0	22.0	22.0	21.0

资料来源：世界银行《2000/2001年世界发展报告》。
Source: World Development Report 2000/2001.

附3-5 1999年世界主要国家和地区储蓄率

SAVING DEPOSITS RATE IN MAIN COUNTRIES AND TERRITORIES OF 1999

单位：% (%)

国家和地区	Country or Territory	1995	1996	1997	1998	1999
世界	**World**	**22.1**	**22.0**	**22.0**	**21.0**	**23.0**
中国	China	42.0	44.0	40.0	43.0	42.0
美国	United States	16.2	16.0	16.0	16.0	17.0
日本	Japan	30.0	30.0	30.0		30.0
德国	Germany	23.4	23.0	23.0	22.0	23.0
英国	United Kingdom	15.0	15.0		15.0	15.0
法国	France	20.5	21.0	21.0	20.0	21.0
意大利	Italy	22.3	22.0	22.0	22.0	22.0
加拿大	Canada	20.9	21.0	21.0	21.0	21.0
澳大利亚	Australia	21.3	21.0	21.0	21.0	21.0
波兰	Poland	19.4	17.6	18.0	20.0	18.0
俄罗斯	Russia	26.8	25.4	25.0	24.0	29.0
罗马尼亚	Romania	21.1	18.9	19.0	13.0	10.0
保加利亚	Bulgaria	17.9	16.7	17.0	17.0	12.0
印度	India	22.7	23.9	22.0	18.0	20.0
印度尼西亚	Indonesia	32.3	33.2	31.0	31.0	24.0
巴基斯坦	Pakistan	15.7	14.2	14.0	13.0	11.0
泰国	Thailand	36.2	35.3	35.0	36.0	32.0
菲律宾	Philippines	14.4	14.4	16.0	15.0	16.0
马来西亚	Malaysia	37.2	41.9	44.0	47.0	45.0
韩国	Korea Rep.	36.0	34.2	34.0	34.0	34.0
尼日利亚	Nigeria	20.9	24.4	24.0	12.0	0.0
巴西	Brazil	21.1	18.2	18.0	19.0	20.0
墨西哥	Mexico	22.5	23.4	23.0	24.0	23.0
阿根廷	Argentina	18.4	18.2	18.0	19.0	16.0
孟加拉国	Bangladesh	8.3	7.2	10.0	15.0	14.0
新加坡	Singapore	50.8	50.5	51.0	51.0	52.0
阿尔及利亚	Algeria	29.0	34.0	27.0	27.0	30.0
南非	South Africa Rep.	18.7	18.3	17.0	17.0	18.0
新西兰	New Zealand	22.9	23.0	23.0	22.0	21.0

资料来源：世界银行《2000/2001年世界发展报告》。
Source: World Development Report 2000/2001.

附3-6 1999年世界主要国家和地区消费率

CONSUMPTION RATE IN MAIN COUNTRIES AND TERRITORIES OF 1999

单位：% (%)

国家和地区	Country or Territory	1995	1996	1997	1998	1999
世界	**World**	**77.9**	**79.0**	**78.0**	**79.0**	**77.0**
中国	China	59.0	58.6	60.0	57.0	58.0
美国	United States	83.8	84.0	84.0	84.0	83.0
日本	Japan	70.0	70.0	70.0		70.0
德国	Germany	76.6	77.0	77.0	78.0	77.0
英国	United Kingdom	85.0	85.0	21.0	85.0	84.0
法国	France	79.5	79.0	79.0	80.0	79.0
意大利	Italy	77.7	77.0	77.0	77.0	78.0
加拿大	Canada	79.1	80.0	80.0	79.0	79.0
澳大利亚	Australia	78.7	79.0	79.0	80.0	79.0
波兰	Poland	80.6	82.4	82.0	81.0	83.0
俄罗斯	Russia	73.2	74.6	74.0	77.0	71.0
罗马尼亚	Romania	78.9	81.1	81.0	87.0	90.0
保加利亚	Bulgaria	82.1	83.3	83.0	82.0	88.0
印度	India	77.3	76.1	78.0	82.0	80.0
印度尼西亚	Indonesia	67.7	66.8	70.0	70.0	76.0
巴基斯坦	Pakistan	84.3	85.8	85.0	87.0	89.0
泰国	Thailand	63.8	64.7	65.0	64.0	68.0
菲律宾	Philippines	85.6	85.6	85.0	86.0	84.0
马来西亚	Malaysia	62.8	58.1	56.0	53.0	54.0
韩国	Korea Rep.	64.0	65.8	66.0	66.0	66.0
尼日利亚	Nigeria	79.1	75.6	82.0	88.0	100.0
巴西	Brazil	78.9	81.8	82.0	81.0	80.0
墨西哥	Mexico	77.5	76.6	76.0	76.0	77.0
阿根廷	Argentina	81.6	81.8	82.0	81.0	84.0
孟加拉国	Bangladesh	91.7	92.8	91.0	84.0	86.0
新加坡	Singapore	49.2	49.5	48.0	49.0	49.0
阿尔及利亚	Algeria	71.0	66.0	73.0	73.0	70.0
南非	South Africa Rep.	81.3	81.7	83.0	83.0	82.0
新西兰	New Zealand	77.1	77.0	77.0	77.0	78.0

资料来源：世界银行《2000/2001年世界发展报告》。
Source: World Development Report 2000/2001.

附3-7 世界主要国家和地区中央政府收入占GDP比重
COMPOSITION OF REVENUE OF CENTRAL GOVERNMENT IN GDP OF MAIN COUNTRIES AND TERRITORIES

单位：%　　　　(%)

国家和地区 Country or Territory		税收 Tax		非税收 Non-tax	
		1990	1998	1990	1998
中国	China	4.0	5.7	2.4	0.2
美国	United States	18.0	20.4	1.5	1.4
日本	Japan	13.7		0.8	
英国	United Kingdom	33.3	36.3	3.2	2.0
法国	France	37.6	39.2	2.8	2.6
意大利	Italy	37.3	38.6	1.2	2.9
加拿大	Canada	18.3		2.7	
澳大利亚	Australia	23.8	22.9	2.1	1.6
波兰	Poland		32.8		2.9
西班牙	Spanish	28.8	28.1	1.6	2.0
罗马尼亚	Romania	30.9	24.4	3.5	2.1
保加利亚	Bulgaria	34.5	27.0	12.6	6.9
印度	India	9.9	8.6	2.4	3.0
印度尼西亚	Indonesia	17.8	15.6	1.0	1.2
巴基斯坦	Pakistan	13.3	12.6	5.8	3.3
泰国	Thailand	17.1	14.4	1.5	1.8
菲律宾	Philippines	14.1	17.0	2.1	2.0
马来西亚	Malaysia	19.6	18.9	7.5	4.1
韩国	Korea Rep.	15.9	17.3	1.7	2.7
埃及	Egypt	16.7	16.6	6.2	9.7
巴西	Brazil	19.0		3.7	
墨西哥	Mexico	13.7	13.0	1.6	1.7
阿根廷	Argentina	9.4	12.4	1.0	1.2
蒙古	Mongolia	15.6	13.5	2.7	6.0
新加坡	Singapore	15.4	16.2	11.5	8.4
南非	South Africa Rep.	24.3	24.5	2.0	1.7
芬兰	Finland	28.3	28.1	2.8	3.9
新西兰	New Zealand	36.3	32.1	6.2	2.1

资料来源：世界银行《2000/2001年世界发展报告》。
Source: World Development Report 2000/2001.

附3-8 世界主要国家和地区中央政府支出占GDP比重

COMPOSITION OF EXPENDITURE OF CENTRAL GOVERNMENT IN GDP OF MAIN COUNTRIES AND TERRITORIES

单位：% (%)

国家和地区 Country or Territory		经常项目支出 Current Expenditure		资本支出 Capital Expenditure	
		1990	1998	1990	1998
美国	United States	21.7	20.4	1.8	0.6
日本	Japan	13.7		2.0	
英国	United Kingdom	34.2	36.3	3.8	1.5
法国	France	40.0	44.6	2.5	2.0
意大利	Italy	43.8	42.2	4.0	2.4
加拿大	Canada	25.3		0.5	
澳大利亚	Australia	22.2	23.3	2.1	1.3
波兰	Poland		35.7		2.0
西班牙	Spanish	30.6	34.2	3.2	1.9
罗马尼亚	Romania	27.9	29.1	5.9	2.9
保加利亚	Bulgaria	53.5	30.5	1.6	3.0
印度	India	14.2	12.8	1.8	1.6
印度尼西亚	Indonesia	10.4	12.2	8.0	5.7
巴基斯坦	Pakistan	19.8	18.8	2.6	2.5
泰国	Thailand	11.5	11.7	2.6	6.7
菲律宾	Philippines	16.5	16.3	3.1	2.2
马来西亚	Malaysia	23.3	15.2	7.3	4.5
韩国	Korea Rep.	13.8	13.7	2.4	3.8
埃及	Egypt	23.0	23.3	4.8	7.4
巴西	Brazil	46.1		0.7	
墨西哥	Mexico	15.5	14.3	2.5	1.9
阿根廷	Argentina	10.1	14.1	0.5	1.2
蒙古	Mongolia	18.7	19.8	2.9	3.2
新加坡	Singapore	16.4	11.8	5.1	5.1
南非	South Africa Rep.	27.0	28.4	3.1	1.2
芬兰	Finland	28.7	34.2	2.1	1.1
新西兰	New Zealand	43.1	32.5	0.9	0.9

资料来源：世界银行《2000/2001年世界发展报告》。

Source: World Development Report 2000/2001.

附3-9 世界主要国家和地区人文发展指数
HUMANE DEVELOPMENT INDEX IN MAIN COUNTRIES AND TERRITORIES

国家和地区 Country or Territory		出生时的预期寿命（岁）Anticipated Age When Born (year)	成人识字率（%）Literacy Rate of Adult (%)	初等、中等和高等教育综合入学率（%）Entrance Rate of Primary,Secondary and Higher Education (%)	实际人均GDP（PPP$）Actual GDP Per Capita（PPP$）	人文发展指数 Humane Development Index
		1998	1998	1998	1998	1998
中国	China	70.1	82.8	72	3105	0.706
美国	United States	76.8	99.0	94	29605	0.929
日本	Japan	80.0	99.0	85	23257	0.924
德国	Germany	77.3	99.0	90	22169	0.911
英国	United Kingdom	77.3	99.0	105	20336	0.918
法国	France	78.2	99.0	93	21175	0.917
意大利	Italy	78.3	98.3	83	20585	0.903
加拿大	Canada	79.1	99.0	100	23582	0.935
澳大利亚	Australia	78.3	99.0	114	22452	0.929
波兰	Poland	72.7	99.7	79	7619	0.814
罗马尼亚	Romania	70.2	97.9	70	5648	0.770
保加利亚	Bulgaria	71.3	98.2	73	4809	0.772
印度	India	62.9	55.7	54	2077	0.563
印度尼西亚	Indonesia	65.6	85.7	65	2651	0.670
巴基斯坦	Pakistan	64.4	44.0	43	1715	0.522
泰国	Thailand	68.9	95.0	61	5456	0.745
菲律宾	Philippines	68.6	94.8	83	3555	0.744
马来西亚	Malaysia	72.2	86.4	65	8137	0.772
韩国	Korea Rep.	72.6	97.5	90	13478	0.854
尼日利亚	Nigeria	50.1	61.1	43	795	0.439
巴西	Brazil	67.0	84.5	84	6625	0.747
墨西哥	Mexico	72.3	90.8	70	7704	0.784
阿根廷	Argentina	73.1	96.7	80	12013	0.837
孟加拉国	Bangladesh	58.6	40.1	36	1361	0.461
新加坡	Singapore	77.3	91.8	73	24210	0.881
越南	Viet Nam	67.8	92.9	63	1689	0.671
阿尔及利亚	Algeria	69.2	65.5	69	4792	0.683
南非	South Africa Rep.	53.2	84.6	95	8488	0.697
新西兰	New Zealand	77.1	99.0	96	17288	0.903

资料来源：联合国《2000年人文发展报告》。

Source: 2000 Humane Development Report of the United Nations.

附3-10 世界主要国家和地区医疗卫生指标统计
MEDICAL AND HEALTH INDICATORS IN MAIN COUNTRIES AND TERRITORIES

国家和地区 Country or Territory		对医疗卫生的公共开支占GDP的% Composition of Public Expenditure for Medical and Health in GDP	获得改善的水源的人口占总人口的% Composition of Population Get the Source of Water Improved in Total Population		获得卫生设施的人口占总人口的% Composition of Population Get Health Facilities in Total Population		婴儿死亡率（每千例活产婴儿在一岁以下死亡人数）Death Rate of Infant (Death Number below 1-year-old of 1000 Live Infants)		总和生育率（每位妇女的生育个数）Fertility Rate (Fertility Number of Per Woman)	
		1990-1998*	1982-1985*	1990-1996*	1982-1986*	1990-1997*	1980	1998	1980	1998
中国	China	2.0		90		21	42	31	2.5	1.9
美国	United States	6.5			98		13	7	1.8	2.0
日本	Japan	5.9	99	96	99	100	8	4	1.8	1.4
德国	Germany	8.3					12	5	1.4	1.4
英国	United Kingdom	5.9	100	100		100	12	6	1.9	1.7
法国	France	7.1	98	100		96	10	5	1.9	1.8
意大利	Italy	5.3	99			100	15	5	1.6	1.2
加拿大	Canada	6.4	100	99	85	95	10	5	1.7	1.6
澳大利亚	Australia	5.5	99	99	99	86	11	5	1.9	1.8
波兰	Poland	4.2	82			100	26	10	2.3	1.4
罗马尼亚	Romania	2.9	71	62		44	29	21	2.4	1.3
保加利亚	Bulgaria	3.2	85			99	20	14	2.0	1.1
印度	India	0.6	54	81	8	16	115	70	5.0	3.2
印度尼西亚	Indonesia	0.6	39	62	30	51	90	43	4.3	2.7
巴基斯坦	Pakistan	0.9	38	60	16	30	127	91	7.0	4.9
泰国	Thailand	1.7	66	89	47	96	49	29	3.5	1.9
菲律宾	Philippines	1.7	65	83	57	77	52	32	4.8	3.6
马来西亚	Malaysia	1.3	71	89	75	94	30	8	4.2	3.1
韩国	Korea Rep.	2.5	83	83	100	100	26	9	2.6	1.6
尼日利亚	Nigeria	0.2	36	39		36	99	76	6.9	5.3
巴西	Brazil	3.4	75	72	24	67	70	33	3.9	2.3
墨西哥	Mexico	2.8	82	83	57	66	51	30	4.7	2.8
阿根廷	Argentina	4.0	55	65	69	75	35	19	3.3	2.6
孟加拉国	Bangladesh	1.6	40	84	4	35	132	73	6.1	3.1
新加坡	Singapore	1.1	100	100	85	100	12	4	1.7	1.5
越南	Viet Nam	0.4		36		21	57	34	5.0	2.3
阿尔及利亚	Algeria	3.3					98	35	6.7	3.5
南非	South Africa Rep.	3.2		70		46	67	51	4.6	2.8
新西兰	New Zealand	5.9	100		88		13	5	2.0	1.9

注：* 指标为该时期内可获得的最近一年的数据。
资料来源：世界银行《2000/2001年世界发展报告》。
Note: * indicaters the recent data obtainable during the period.
Source: World Development Report 2000/2001.

附录4：香港特别行政区主要社会经济指标
APPENDIX 4：MAIN SOCIAL AND ECONOMIC INDICATORS OF HONG KONG

项　　　目		Item		1995	1999	2000
年中人口数	（万人）	Mid-year Population	(10000 persons)	615.6	672.1	679.7
出生率	（‰）	Birth Rate	(‰)	11.2	7.6	8.0
死亡率	（‰）	Death Rate	(‰)	5.1	5.0	4.9
自然增长率	（‰）	Natural Growth Rate	(‰)	6.1	2.6	3.1
平均期望寿命	（岁）	Life Expectancy at Birth	(age)			
男		Male		76.0	77.2	77.2
女		Female		81.5	82.4	82.4
劳动力总人数	（万人）	Active Population Total	(10000 persons)	300.1	334.3	338.3
男		Male		184.1	196.4	196.0
女		Female		116.0	137.9	142.3
失业人数	（万人）	Unemployed	(10000 persons)	9.6	20.9	16.8
失业率	（%）	Unemployment Rate	(%)	3.2	6.3	5.0
国内生产总值		Gross Domestic Product				
以当时市价计算	（亿港元）	At Current Market Prices	(HK$100 million)	10771	12314	12717
以固定（1990）市价计算	（亿港元）	At Constant(1990) Market Prices	(HK$100 million)	7558	8091	8937
人均国内生产总值		Per Capita GDP				
以当时市价计算	（港元）	At Current Market Prices	(HK$)	174972	183219	187105
以固定(1990)市价计算	（港元）	At Constant(1990) Market Prices	(HK$)	122778	120389	131483
国内生产总值部门构成	(%)	Composition of GDP by Kind of Activity	(%)			
农业和渔业		Agriculture and Fishery		0.1	0.1	
采矿业		Mining and Quarrying				
制造业		Manufacturing		8.3	5.7	
电、煤气、水		Electricity,Gas and Water		2.3	3.0	
建筑业		Construction		5.4	5.8	
商业、饭店、旅馆		Whole Sale,Retail Sale and Hotels		26.6	25.2	
运输、仓储、通信		Transport,Storage and Communications		10.1	9.6	
金融、保险、不动产和产业服务		Financing,Insurance, Real Estate and Business Services		24.4	23.2	
房屋所有权		Ownership of Premises		13.3	14.1	
社会团体和个人服务		Community,Social and Personal Services		17.3	21.5	
非直接计算的金融中介服务调整		Adjustment for Financial Intermediation Services Indirectly Measured		-7.8	-8.2	
制造业生产指数		Index of Manufacturing Production Industry		126.2	103.1	100.9
商品进出口贸易总额	（亿港元）	Total Imports and Exports	(HK$100 million)	28353	27417	32307
商品进口额		Imports		14911	13927	16580
商品出口额		Domestic Exports		2317	1706	1810
商品转口额		Re-exports		11125	11784	13917

附录4 续表 continued

项　　目 Item				1995	1999	2000
政府财政收支	（十亿港元）	Government Revenue and Expenditure	(HK$1 billion)			
总收入		Total Revenue		153.2	216.1	233.0
总支出		Total Expenditure		155.9	218.8	214.5
消费者物价指数	(%)	Consumer Price Index	(%)	101.8	96.0	96.3
电力耗用	（兆焦耳）	Electricity Consumption	(terajoules)			
住宅		Domestic		27063	31400	32234
商业		Commercial		59908	76028	80347
工业		Industrial		20222	17547	17769
街灯		Street lighting		284	312	325
出口往中国内地		Export to the mainland of China		5340	2279	4253
总计		Total		112817	127566	134928
抵港及离港旅客人数	（千人次）	Number of Passengers	(1000 person.times)			
抵港		to Hongkong		46112	64560	72035
离港		off Hongkong		46014	64475	71938
公共道路长度	（公里）	Length of Roads	(km)	1717	1885	1904
公共交通乘客人数	（百万人次）	Number of Passengers of Public Traffic	(1 million person.times)	3826	3896	3971
按种类划分的领牌车辆数字	（千辆）	Vehicles grouped by Type	(1000)			
私家车		Individuals		285	322	332
电单车（包括机动三轮车		Motorcycles		21	24	26
的士		Taxi		18	18	18
公共及私家巴士		Public and Private Mini-bus		10	12	13
公共及私家小型巴士		Public and Private Bus		7	6	6
货车		Trucks		118	114	114
特别用途车辆（*少于0.5）		Special-use(*<0.5)		*	*	*
政府车辆		of Government		7	7	7
总计		Total		466	504	517
按主要死亡原因划分的死亡人数及死亡率		Number Deaths and Death Rate by Death Cause				
恶性肿瘤死亡人数	（人）	Malignant Tumour	(person)	9680	10977	11176
死亡率	（人/每十万名人口）	Death Rate	(1/100 thousand persons)	157.2	163.3	164.8
心脏病死亡人数	（人）	Heart Trouble	(person)	4886	5220	5315
死亡率	（人/每十万名人口）	Death Rate	(1/100 thousand persons)	79.4	77.7	78.4
肺炎死亡人数	（人）	Pneumonia	(person)	3266	2977	3031
死亡率	（人/每十万名人口）	Death Rate	(1/100 thousand persons)	53.1	44.3	44.7
脑血管疾病死亡人数	（人）	Cerebrovasular disease	(person)	3310	3491	3554
死亡率	（人/每十万名人口）	Death Rate	(1/100 thousand persons)	53.8	51.9	52.4
受伤及中毒死亡人数	（人）	Injured and Poisoned	(person)	1590	2053	2090
死亡率	（人/每十万名人口）	Death Rate	(1/100 thousand persons)	25.8	30.5	30.8
婴儿死亡率（按每千名出生登记活产婴儿计算）	（‰）	Death Rate of New-borns(according to 1000 New-borns registered)	（‰）	4.4	3.2	2.9

附录5：澳门地区主要社会经济指标

Appendix 5：MAIN SOCIAL AND ECONOMIC INDICATORS OF MACAO

项目		Item		1998	1999	2000
人口总数估计	（人）	Estimate of Population	(person)	430549	437455	437903
男		Male		204734	206563	207197
女		Female		225815	230892	230706
增长率	（%）	Growth Rate	（%）	2.0	1.6	0.1
劳动力总人数	（千人）	Active Population Total	(1000 persons)	210.7	216.2	
男		Male		116.4	115.7	
女		Female		94.3	100.5	
失业人数	（千人）	Unemployed	(1000 persons)	9.6	13.8	
失业率	（%）	Unemployment Rate	(%)	4.6	6.4	
国内生产总值		Gross Domestic Product				
以当时市价计算	（百万澳门元）	At Current Market Prices	(MOP million)	51901.7	49210.2	
以固定（1996）市价计算	（百万澳门元）	At Constant(1996) Market Prices	(MOP million)	52579.9	51074.5	
人均国内生产总值		Per Capita GDP				
以当时市价计算	（澳门元）	At Current Market Prices	(MOP)	121750	113044	
以当时市价计算	（美元）	At Current Market Prices	(USD)	15259	14145	
国内生产总值部门构成	(%)	Composition of GDP by Kind of Activity	(%)			
第二产业		Secondary Sector of Activity		16.1		
采矿业		Mining and Quarrying		0.0		
制造业		Manufacturing		9.3		
电、煤气、水		Electricity,Gas and Water		3.1		
建筑业		Construction		3.7		
第三产业		Tertiary Sector of Activity		90.3		
批发零售、维修、饭店、旅馆		Whole Sale,Retail Sale，Repair,Hotels and Restaurants		9.9		
运输、仓储、通信		Transport,Storage and Communications		6.8		
金融、保险、不动产租赁及商业服务		Financing,Insurance, Real Estate,Renting and Business Services		26.8		
公共行政、社会服务及个人服务（包括博彩业）		Public Administration, Other Community, Social and Personal Services(Including Gambling)		46.8		
非直接计算的金融中介服务调整		Adjustment for Financial Intermediation Services Indirectly Measured		-6.4		
商品进口额	（千澳门元）	Imports	（MOP thousand)	15596446	16300195	18097560
商品出口额	（千澳门元）	Exports	（MOP thousand)	17083615	17579981	20380421
出进口差额	（千澳门元）	Balance of Trade	（MOP thousand)	1487169	1279786	2282861
出进口比例	(%)	Coverage Rate	(%)	110	108	113
再进口	（千澳门元）	Re-imports	（MOP thousand)	1840954	2427696	2975686

附录5 续表 continued

项目		Item		1998	1999	2000
消费物价指数	(%)	Consumer Price Index	(%)	104.46	101.12	99.49
（1999年10月--2000年9月=100）		(October,1999--September,2000=100)				
粮食及不含酒精饮品		Foodstuffs and Beverages		105.91	101.25	99.74
衣履		Clothing & Footwear		103.08	100.84	95.35
维修及住屋开支		Rents Housing Expense		104.41	101.31	99.54
烟酒		Tabacco & Alcoholic Beverages		100.90	100.70	99.95
家居用品		Household Goods		103.59	100.80	99.20
药物及医疗		Health		102.45	99.85	100.46
交通及通讯		Transport & Communications		104.31	102.17	100.49
教育文化及休闲		Education & Leisure		103.03	100.32	99.45
其他物品及服务		Other Goods and Services		102.44	99.30	99.49
通货膨胀率	(%)	Inflation Rate	(%)		-3.20	-1.61
电力	(百万千瓦小时)	Electricity	(1 million kwh)			
净生产量		Net Production		1377.0	1365.7	1408.3
净进口量		Net Imports		172.6	194.4	194.6
本地购入		Local Purchases		54.6	55.9	54.5
总供应量		Gross Available Supply		1604.1	1616.0	1657.4
旅游指标		Tourism				
入境旅客	(千人)	Visitor Arrivals	(1000 persons)	6948.5	7443.9	9162.2
出境旅客	(千人)	Visitor Departures	(1000 persons)	6663.4	7297.6	9211.5
房间入住率	(%)	Hotel Occupancy Rate	(%)	53.11	55.42	59.15
五星酒店		5-stars Hotels		55.01	55.28	61.65
四星酒店		4-stars Hotels		53.84	58.77	59.68
三星酒店		3-stars Hotels		61.97	65.88	68.24
二星酒店		2-stars Hotels		28.54	28.61	32.52
平均留宿时间	(晚数)	Average Length of Stay	(night)	1.43	1.43	1.33
交通事故		Traffic Accidents				
数目	（起）	No. of Accidents	(case)	7935	7950	8278
伤亡人数	（人）	Persons Injured &/or Dead	(person)	2458	2024	2258
每千居民拥有电话数	（部）	Telephones Per 1000 Inhabitants	(unit)	583	686	
移动电话总数（不包括SIM卡用户）	（户）	Mobile Telephones(SIM Card Excluded)	(unit)	67042	92081	120957
互联网用户登记总数	（户）	Internet Subscribers	(unit)	9516	17034	27346
卫生		Health				
平均每一医生服务人数	（人）	Inhabitants Per Doctor	(person)	495	488	
平均每张床位服务人数	（人）	Inhabitants Per Hospital Bed	(person)	407	415	
导致死亡的主要原因构成	（%）	Main Causes of Death	(%)			
循环系统疾病		Diseases of the Circulatory System		37.2	34.4	
肿瘤		Neoplasms		24.7	26.6	
呼吸系统疾病		Diseases of the Respiratory System		12.5	12.2	
消化系统疾病		Diseases of the Digestive System		3.5	3.9	
泌尿生殖系统疾病		Diseases of the Genitourinary System		3.6	3.0	
传染病和寄生虫病		Infectious and Parasitic Diseases		3.2	2.4	
内分泌、营养和代谢疾病及免疫病患		Endocrine, Nutritional and Metabolic Diseases and Immunity Disorders		1.3	2.0	

中国统计出版社最新资料书简目

中国统计年鉴-2001
中国统计摘要-2001
中国城市统计年鉴-2000
中国农村统计年鉴-2001
中国劳动统计年鉴-2001
中国人口统计年鉴-2001
中国社会统计资料-2000
中国市场统计年鉴-2001
中国建筑业统计年鉴-2001
中国固定资产投资统计年鉴-2001
中国价格及城镇居民家庭收支调查统计年鉴-2001
国际统计年鉴-2001
中国对外经济贸易统计年鉴-2000
中国商品交易市场统计年鉴-2001
中国基本单位统计年鉴-2000
中国食品工业年鉴-2000
中国民政统计年鉴-2001
如何使用统计年鉴
北京统计年鉴-2001
天津统计年鉴-2001
河北经济年鉴-2001
山西统计年鉴-2001
内蒙古统计年鉴-2001
辽宁统计年鉴-2001
吉林统计年鉴-2001
黑龙江统计年鉴-2001
上海统计年鉴-2001
江苏统计年鉴-2001
浙江统计年鉴-2001
安徽统计年鉴-2001
福建统计年鉴-2001
江西统计年鉴-2001
山东统计年鉴-2001
河南统计年鉴-2001
湖北统计年鉴-2001
湖南统计年鉴-2001
广东统计年鉴-2001
广西统计年鉴-2001
贵州统计年鉴-2001
云南统计年鉴-2001
海南统计年鉴-2001
四川统计年鉴-2001
重庆统计年鉴-2001
西藏统计年鉴-2001
陕西统计年鉴-2001
甘肃年鉴-2001
青海统计年鉴-2001
宁夏统计年鉴-2001
新疆统计年鉴-2001
新疆生产建设兵团统计年鉴-2001
石家庄统计年鉴-2001
唐山统计年鉴-2001
廊坊统计年鉴-2001
邯郸统计年鉴-2001
衡水统计年鉴-2001
张家口统计年鉴-2001
邢台经济统计年鉴-2001
太原统计年鉴-2001
临汾年鉴-2001
呼和浩特经济统计年鉴-2001
沈阳年鉴-2001
大连统计年鉴-2001
吉林市社会经济统计年鉴-2001
四平统计年鉴-2001
延吉统计年鉴-2001
哈尔滨统计年鉴-2001
齐齐哈尔经经济统计年鉴-2001
双鸭山社会经济统计年鉴-2001
黑龙江垦区统计年鉴-2001
牡丹江统计年鉴-2001
上海浦东新区统计年鉴-2001
宝山年鉴-2001
南京统计年鉴-2001
苏州统计年鉴-2001
无锡统计年鉴-2001
常州统计年鉴-2001
徐州统计年鉴-2001
南通统计年鉴-2001
盐城统计年鉴-2001
连云港统计年鉴-2001
杭州统计年鉴-2001
宁波统计年鉴-2001
绍兴统计年鉴-2001
嘉兴统计年鉴-2001
台州统计年鉴-2001
舟山统计年鉴-2001
金华统计年鉴-2001
温州统计年鉴-2001
福州年鉴-2001
厦门经济特区年鉴-2001
福州经济开发区年鉴-2001
南昌统计年鉴-2001
九江统计年鉴-2001
宜春统计年鉴-2001
济南统计年鉴-2001
青岛统计年鉴-2001
潍坊统计年鉴-2001
泰安统计年鉴-2001
德州统计年鉴-2001
日照统计年鉴-2001
郑州统计年鉴-2001
洛阳统计年鉴-2001
开封统计年鉴-2001
三门峡统计年鉴-2001
平顶山统计年鉴-2001
南阳经济统计年鉴-2001
武汉统计年鉴-2001
宜昌统计年鉴-2001
广州统计年鉴-2001
深圳统计信息年鉴-2001
惠州统计年鉴-2001
珠海统计年鉴-2001
东莞统计年鉴-2001
南宁统计年鉴-2001
桂林经济社会统计年鉴-2001
柳州地区统计年鉴-2001
贵阳统计年鉴-2001
海口统计年鉴-2001
成都统计年鉴-2001
广安统计年鉴-2001
攀枝花统计年鉴-2001
西安统计年鉴-2001
兰州年鉴-2000
西宁统计年鉴-2001
乌鲁木齐统计年鉴-2001
巴音郭楞统计年鉴-2001
吐鲁番统计年鉴-2001
石河子统计年鉴-2001
伊犁统计年鉴-2001
巴州统计年鉴-2001
河北农村统计年鉴-2001
广东农村统计年鉴-2001
福建农村统计年鉴-2001
湖北农村统计年鉴-2001
河南农村统计年鉴-2001
山东城市统计年鉴-2001
湖北工交统计年鉴-2000

编辑部电话：（010）63262276　63266600—30605
欲购以上图书请与中国统计出版社发行部联系。电话：（010）63459084　同楫行书店电话：68585978
通讯地址：北京市西城区三里河月坛南街 75 号。邮政编码：100826

北京有线电视台

2000年北京国际电视周于6月19－21日在北京国际会议中心举行。图为北京有线电视台展台

北京有线台现有三套自办节目、一套合办节目。三个自办频道分别是影视（17频道）、综合（24频道）、体育（19频道），每天共播出54个小时。

影视频道主要以播出影视剧为主，是有线台收视率最高的频道。《欢乐总动员》、《电影与电影人》《中国影视动态》等栏目，均深受广大首都观众喜爱。

2000年5月23日，北京市广播电视局局长李廷芝同志（中）、台长于知峰同志、总编辑张晓爱同志在北京有线电视台首届“我最喜爱的播音员、主持人”颁奖仪式上

综合频道主要以新闻节目为主，辅以科教、经济、文化、音乐等娱乐服务类节目。《科学探索》、《自然探索》、《风格传播》、《童真·花季》等节目形式新颖、既富趣味性，又有知识性。

体育频道是北京地区开办最早的专业频道，主要栏目有《甲A现场直播》、《国安绿茵传真》等。

1999年9月28日，为庆祝国庆50周年，北京有线电视台举办大型庆典晚会《我和我的祖国》

北京有线电视台的娱乐性栏目《欢乐总动员》录制现场

首钢电视台

在首钢电视台台长司金贵（左）陪同下，首钢总公司党委书记董事长罗冰生（右）到首钢电视台慰问

首钢闭路电视以特大企业首钢为后盾，具有充足的一流设备和专业技术人才，是全国首批“双十佳、双十优企业电视台”。其专题片制作、摄像服务、光盘刻录质高价廉；首钢集团自产优质光盘裸盘以低价位批量供应；电视广告把关严格，赢得观众充分信赖。其经营范围广，合作方式活。愿广交四海朋友，共闯双盈市场。

联系电话：88920262

联 系 人：朱女士

北京首钢第一建设有限公司

NO.2Construction & Erection Compan

◀ 领导班子成员：（从左至右）
刘怀荣（副书记）于振山（工程经理）郭延斌（设材经理）陈建基（书记）侯小其（总经理）李智（开发经理）李生涛（人事经理）林雪峰（总工程师）

▲ 公司参加承建的首钢1号高炉工程

真诚奉献
雕塑精品工程

携手同行
创建美好未来

北京首钢第一建设有限公司第二建筑安装工程公司

地　址：北京石景山区古城南路
电　话：(010)88294401
传　真：(010)88292683
邮　编：100043

NO.2CONSTRUCTION &ERECTION COMPANY OF BEIJING
SHOUGANG NO.1 CONSTRUCTION CORORATION
ADD:GUCHENG SOUTH DOAD SHIJINGSHAN BEIJING CHINA
TEL:(010)88294401
FAX:(010)88292683
POST CODE:100043

N0.2Construction & Erection Company of Beijing

安装工程公司

of Beijing Shougang No.1 Construction Corporation

建成了高层民用住宅楼

北京首钢第一建设有限公司第二建筑安装工程公司，是以土建施工为主的综合性建筑安装工程公司。具有冶金、有色建筑工程施工、工业与民用建筑工程（壹级）施工；建筑装修工程施工；市政工程施工的企业资质。

公司前身为原冶金部第十一冶金建设公司，成立于60年代，先后参加了江西省大吉山钨矿、河北省龙烟钢铁公司、甘肃省白银有色金属公司、黄河引水工程等一大批国家重点项目的建设任务。一九七七年成建制并入首钢总公司，先后参加了首钢钢铁主流程的新建、扩建、改建以及北京市第一热电厂等百余项工业项目的施工，并承建了首钢建筑史上第一栋高层民用建筑（老山1#塔楼）及苹果园住宅小区等民用工程。

仅用28天就建成的首钢月季迎宾馆

公司现有职工1092人，拥有各类专业技术人员98人，其中高级工程师6人，工程师19人，技术员73人。公司下属有金属结构分公司、机械设备分公司、汽车维修中心、以及若干个项目经理部，拥有适应现代化工程建设的各类施工机械226台套，公司各部门已实现计算机管理。

“质量第一、信誉至上”是本公司一贯的经营宗旨。公司已通过了ISO9002质量体系认证。多年来，依靠技术进步和推行全面质量保证体系，有力地保证了工程质量，近年来施工的首钢三万立方米制氧、二烧结电除尘工程获冶金部优质工程，石景山建设银行宿舍楼获北京市优质工程。由本公司牵头研制的直径600毫米至1400毫米、高程60米不同模数钢管混凝土倒灌顶升施工工艺，属国内首创，获北京市科技进步奖。

本公司愿以一流的技术、管理、质量和装备为国内外各行各业竭诚服务，用我们的智慧和汗水，雕塑精品工程，奉献一片真情。

各项装饰工程

购物是享受　享受到燕莎

燕莎友谊商城

YOUYI SHOPPING CITY

—— Beijing Lufthansa Center ——

北京燕莎友谊商城是具有国际水准的现代化中外合资商业零售企业，与四周著名的凯宾斯基、昆仑、长城等五星级酒店及众多外交公寓和使馆区交相辉映、共同组成了京东地区的高消费商业圈。

燕莎商场2.2万平方米的营业面积，经营着10万种、40万个花色规格的国内外名牌精品，自1992年6月30日开业以来，累计接待中外宾客逾8500万人次，实现销售总额72亿元。

作为中国首家开业的、中外合资经营的高档购物场所，燕莎商城在同行业中最先全面引进现代化的经营管理技术；最先享有进出口经营权；最先向国内商业企业输出管理技术；最先独创自身经营特色 。“燕莎”的诞生，标志着中国零售商业进入了新的发展阶段。

“购物是享受，享受到燕莎”，北京燕莎友谊商城将以超前的经营理念，准确的市场定位，科学先进的营销方式，以及特色化的商品管理不断地 完善和发展自己，给每一位客人温馨舒适的现代生活享受，为中国现代商业发展做出新的贡献。

- 国内一流、国际水平
- 高中档、系列化
- 尊重理解、体贴入微
- 荟萃国际、国内精品

地　址：北京朝阳区亮马桥路52号　邮　编：100016

电　话：010--64651188　传　真：010-64674532　电子邮件：yansha@public.fhnet.cn.net

藍島大廈

BLUE ISLAND TOWER

蓝岛大厦在世纪末完成了以东西区廊桥贯通经营结构调整和环境装修改造为标志的世纪大调整，将一个崭新的蓝岛带入新世纪。新世纪的新蓝岛，使蓝岛的面貌焕然一新，突出了穿在蓝岛、文化消费、家居生活三大特色经营主题。新增的便民食品日用超市和娱乐休闲服务项目，创新了服务功能。以计算机单品物流管理为核心的管理信息系统开通，实现了经营与管理机制的调整。

京泰實業(集團)有限公司

BEIJING HOLDINGS LIMITED

董 事 长：胡昭广

副董事长、总经理：衣锡群

京泰实业（集团）有限公司，是北京市政府于1979年在香港注册成立的"窗口"公司。20多年来，京泰集团以"繁荣香港、服务北京"为宗旨，对促进京港经济优势互补，共同繁荣和为北京市从国际市场筹集资金、引进技术和管理人才等，作出了积极贡献。1997年，北京市政府对京泰集团和北京市优势产业进行资产重组，打出北京概念，以红筹股在香港成功上市，实现了集团经营主业由贸易为主向资本运营为主的综合性国有控股公司的成功转变。迄今，京泰集团已形成上市、贸易、金融服务和投资四大业务板块。

集团资产总值已经达到167.28亿港元。最近，北京市政府已批准向集团注资8亿元，并批准把京唐港1.6亿元资产和陆港公司9900万元股权分别划拨和注入京泰集团，又为京泰集团的发展增添了新的活力。

香港干诺道中200号信得中心西座34楼

电　　话：(00852)25402086

传　　真：(00852)28581544

通讯地址：北京市崇文门外大街3号B，北京新世界中心北办公大楼12A层

邮　　编：100062

电话中继线：(8610)67089988

传　　真：(8610)67085256　(8610)67080452

网　　址：www.bhl.net.cn

铜牛
TONGNIU
绿色 自然 健康
铜牛内衣的主题
中国环境标志认证的生态纺织品是指采用对周围环境无害或少害的原料,合理利用并对人体健康无害的产品。
铜牛服装在原材料的筛选,染整工艺路线的选择等方面以环境标志认证的技术要求为准。
2000年铜牛牌纯棉内衣、纯毛内衣、混纺内衣在服装领域率先通过环境标志认证,被认定为生态纺织品。充分体现铜牛集团倡导以人为本,以环境为本的经营理念。
选择通过环境标志认证的服装
尤其是童装和内衣对我们的健康非常重要。
北京铜牛针织集团有限责任公司
BEIJING TONGNIU KNITTING GROUP CO.,LTD.
地址:中国·北京朝阳门外小庄6号 电话:010-65025221
传真:010-65004430 邮编:100026 网址:WWW.TONGNIU.COM

中国电信
CHINA TELECOM
北京市电信公司
是北京
北京·宽带网 BBN
世界的距离 因你而近
我们认为，宽带网不仅将世界沟通提升为可能，更将改变人
的服务体系、多种技术支持、长期的运营经验，各类示范工
及的任意范围。让您在对未来世界的探索与认知中的一路领
北京电信已成功为《人民日报》、新华社、国家图书馆、东

门的生活。这正是我们建设北京宽带网（BBN）的原因。我们将以丰富的通信设施，完整的运行维护体系、完善
程让你放心。北京宽带网（BBN）将以高品质的网络支持、高速宽带服务将因特网的共享世界，拓展到你伸手可
先。未来与梦想因宽带网而实现。
亍广场、北京饭店、MOTOROLA、北京教育信息网等提供高速宽带服务。

北京东城园林局

东城区园林局位于北京市东城区东直门内北中街西侧，东邻俄罗斯驻华使馆，是北京市东城区城市绿化工作的业务主管部门。主要负责东城区辖区内部分道路及地坛公园、青年湖公园、柳荫公园、南馆公园及全区主要道路的绿化美化建设管理。指导驻区中央、北京市党政机关、企事业单位和全区各街道办事处开展绿化美化工作。

九五期间，东城园林局遵照“生态园林、精致园林”的思路，突出精品意识，连续推出了许多重点精品绿化工程。如在道路绿化中，以精心规划设计为龙头，不断提高道路绿化效果，建设完成北京站前街、北河沿花街、建国门绿色广场、王府井、平安大街、雍和宫北口、东单路口等优秀街道绿化工程。在公园景观建设中完成被列为北京市重点绿化工程的柳荫公园“又一村”景区、占地31000平方米的地坛一区绿化改造、被市政府列入为群众办的60件实事之一的青年湖北门－东岸区绿改工程等多项重大建设项目。

面对新世纪，东城园林人将播绿不辍，继续为推动首都城市现代化建设，促进人与自然的和谐发展而努力。

局长、党委书记
总公司经理 方少奇

北京市顺义区交通局（北京通达实业总公司）位于顺义府前西街。是一个集行政、事业、企业三位一体的自收自支单位。全局（总公司）共有干部职工2000余人，资产总值4.3亿元。局行政管理部门设有公路运输、汽车维修、客运出租管理所等单位。其主要职能是：根据国家道路运输管理的方针政策及北京市有关地方法规、规章依法对全区客货运输、汽车维修三大市场进行规划、协调、监督、服务，为发展公共交通事业和地区经济建设保驾护航。

顺义区交通局在抓好行业管理的同时，坚持发展是硬道理，开拓进取，不断发展壮大局属企业，现已形成以工业、商业、运输业三大产业为主导，门类涉及交通运输、化工石油、机动车检测、汽车、汽车配件销售、餐饮娱乐、无线寻呼、旅游等二十多个行业组成的经济实体。拥有北方中油石油销售有限公司，北京深顺塑料编织制品有限公司，宝顺汽车销售公司，京顺机动车检测场，深顺、金顺出租汽车公司及顺交运输队、驾校、氧气站等20余家企业。2000年完成销售收入8.6亿元，利润4033万元，取得了明显的经济效益和社会效益。先后被评为“百强企业”“花园式企业”及“精神文明先进单位”。走出了以交通运输主产业带动相关邻近产业共同发展的新路，成为了顺义区及郊区中具有较强实力的经济实体，跨入市交通系统和郊区中具有较强实力的经济实体，跨入市交通系统和区属工业企业先进行列。

北京市顺义区交通局
（北京通达实业公司）

北京深顺塑料制品有限公司

地　址：北京市顺义府前西街
电　话：(010)69444637
传　真：(010)69441208

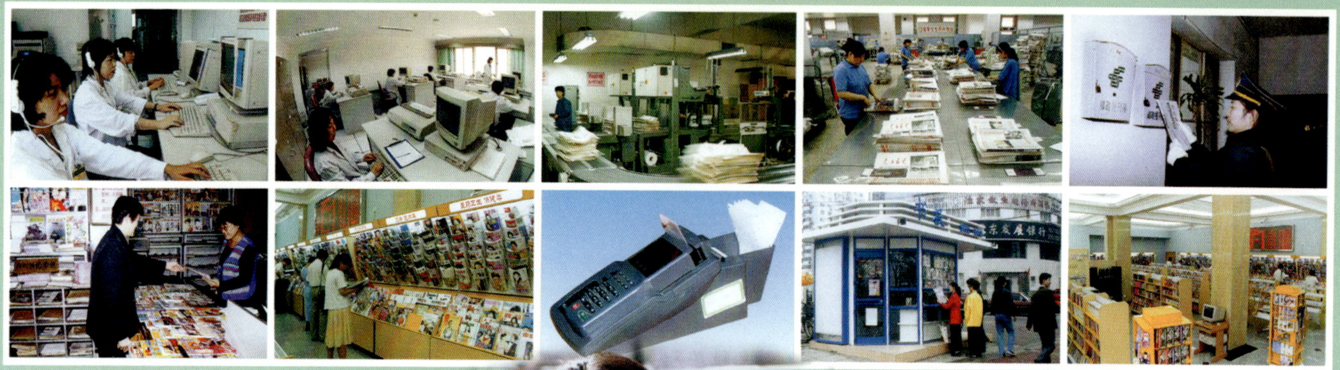

北京报刊发行局

北京报刊发行局位于北京西三环中路莲花桥西侧，东临北京西客站，是北京邮政管理局负责报刊发行业务的专业经营、管理部门。

北京报刊发行局始建于1950年。在报刊发行方面积累了丰富的经验。能够满足报刊出版部门的各项业务需求。目前，与全国近千家报刊社保持着频繁的业务往来。接受报刊社的委托，将北京出版的中央及北京市属的1755种报刊迅速、准确、安全地发往全国8.2万个邮政局（所）；并为北京市的读者订阅、零购全国各地出版的6538种报刊，提供方便的服务，年报刊发行总量逾46亿份（册），是全国报刊发行行业中业务功能最全，经营能力最强的报刊发行企业。

北京报刊发行局依托邮政的网络优势，拥有通达全国的报刊发行网络、拥有现代化的全国联网业务数据处理中心和全国一流的报刊分发、封装设备。遍布全市城区、近、远郊区县的644个邮电局（所）都办理订阅、零售业务；目前北京邮局在全市拥有1000多个邮政报刊亭，报刊零售网点达到3000余处。

北京报刊发行局一贯坚持“人民邮电为人民”的宗旨，坚持邮政普遍服务的原则。为广大读者和报刊社提供一系列优质服务，主要有：随时订阅报刊、集订分送、800邮政报刊订阅咨询免费服务热线、上门取费、北京出版的日报可以次日起订、日报早投、邮电所也可以办理订阅报刊的业务等等。

报刊礼仪订阅、报刊订阅专用卡使报刊消费具有了更高的文化品位；全市通订，使您只要身边有邮局就可以订报刊，想投递到哪里就投递到哪里；上楼（进院）投递，把报刊送到家门口。

北京报刊发行局的网上订阅站点（http//www.bj-bkfx.com.cn）成立于1998年，是全国率先提供网上订阅服务的站点，并于2000年7月重新改建，与北京邮政电子商务平台一同推出。作为北京邮政报刊发行的服务窗口，网站主要面向北京地区的用户提供全国6500余种邮发报刊的查询和订阅服务。

满足用户的需求，是企业的终极目标。北京报刊发行局以满足社会需要、促进社会发展为己任，不断改革创新，为报刊社和读者提供优质、高效的服务，为首都的精神文明和物质文明建设做出更大的贡献。

邮政报刊订阅咨询服务热线电话：8008100351/52

北京首都高速公路发展有限公司

北京控股有限公司，通过其拥有96%权益的附属公司——北京首都高速公路发展有限公司，管理和经营一条收费的首都机场高速公路，将中国最繁忙机场之一的首都国际机场与市中心连接。该高速公路于1992年7月开始施工，并于1993年9月投入服务。

本路西起三元桥，东至首都机场，全长18.735公里，宽34.5米，各方向均有三条车道，设计车速为每小时120公里，设计车流量为每小时6300辆次，该路设计达到了高速公路全封闭、全立交、汽车专用的标准。

本路全线设有从西班牙进口的中央交通监控系统，以及收费系统、通讯系统、供电照明系统、交通工程的设施。

本路由于服务规范，设施完善，管理到位，先后被北京市政府授予文明单位，被交通部授予文明服务示范窗口的荣誉称号。

地　址：北京首都机场高速公路
电　话：64563399　64565620
传　真：64563113
邮　编：100621

北京建筑材料经贸集团总公司

北京建筑材料经贸集团总公司是国有大型物资流通企业。近年来，集团总公司提出并坚持了“上经营、办实业、置产业、求发展”的总体发展思路，一手抓建材经营，一手抓市场建设，推动了集团经营销售业务的发展。1992年获得“中国物资流通百强企业”称号，1993年跨入“中国500家最大服务业，流通业”，1995年在全国建材流通企业综合实力评比排序中，成为全国建材流通十强企业之一，排序第二。

建材流通贸易作为集团的主营业务，设有水泥、玻璃、地方材料、五金水暖、防水材料、新型建材、工程配套供应等专业子公司及新科股份公司、建材经贸大厦等营销机构，拥有各类经营场所70余处，10座综合、专业物资仓库。2000年度建材流通经营额达7亿元，其规模与本市同类企业相比居于领先地位。

此外在建材产品深加工、建筑防水施工、装饰装修工程、工程监理、物资运输、餐饮业、物业管理等方面也有一定发展。

目前我集团立足经营、实业、物业三大产业，投资组合日趋合理，各项经营呈良性发展。集团确定，经过四、五年努力，将成为国内知名、行业领先的现代企业集团。

地　址：北京市朝阳区东土城路14号　　邮　编：100013
电　话：85271066　　传　真：85271065

北辰集团 BNSC
北辰购物中心

北辰购物中心是香港上市公司——北辰实业股份有限公司的骨干企业之一。北辰购物中心成立于1990年，曾成功地接待了第十一届亚运会、远南运动会、世界妇女代表大会等国际盛会，是北京市旅游局定点商店，“北京市消费者满意单位”，“销售服务好先进单位”，1994年跻身于北京市销售亿元商场行列。

北辰购物中心地处亚运村地区，是北京最具发展潜力的地区之一。亚运村周围已落成和在建的居民小区、公寓、别墅、写字楼鳞次栉比，各类公司和社团云集，被海外传媒称为“高速发展的国际商贸社区”，随着亚运村及周边地区消费水平和规模的不断增强，为了最大限度地满足顾客消费需求，1996年5月实施加层改造扩建工程，于1997年9月6日重张。新“北辰”建筑面积30463平方米，营业面积15000平方米，共分五个楼层，开架售货占95%以上，是北京北部地区规模最大的百货商厦之一。

北辰购物中心将遵循高质、名牌、低价位的经营方针和让消费者满意的服务宗旨，向广大顾客提供食品、百货、钟表、首饰、文化用品、家用电器、服装鞋帽、工艺礼品、快餐等四十一个大类，八万余种名、特、优、新产品；八部自动扶梯，全方位的闭路监视及消防系统，计算机网络管理等硬件设施与方便快捷周到的服务配套；以一流环境，一流商品，一流管理，一流服务迎接八方宾客；成为集购物、美食、社区服务等多种功能为一体的大型购物中心，向广大顾客展现现代化商场的风采。

地　址：安定门外安立路八号（亚运村）
邮　编：100101
电　话：64993260
传　真：64910586

北京市住房与社会保障体制改革世行贷款项目办公室

宝晟公司　宝盛里小区

安居公司　蒲华园小区

富民公司　晋元庄小区

为支持我国企业与社会保障体制改革，世界银行向我国政府提供住房与社会保障体制改革项目贷款，总规模为3.5亿美元。其中北京市为1.58亿美元，加上国内配套资金，项目规模为30亿元人民币。世行贷款的根本目的是通过住房商品化、社会化的改革，变住房的“实物分配”为“货币分配”，改善市民的居住条件。

北京市政府组建了8家住房股份公司，利用世界银行贷款开发建设住宅。现已批准的子项目45个、总建筑规模近110多万平方米，总投资规模约25亿元人民币。目前，世行项目已竣工62万平方米，累计完成投资额20多亿元人民币。

开发建设项目	联系电话
宝晟公司	64068482
安居公司	67609524
富民公司	67642898
万发公司	64256536
安苑公司	65520570
瑞德康公司	69256372
嘉业公司	64426969
世安公司	68520683

万发公司　沙板庄北里小区

瑞德康公司　永华北里小区

安苑公司　青塔G区

嘉业公司　石佛营住宅小区

世安公司　望京新城K5住宅小区

北京市农村信用社
BEIJING RURAL CREDIT COOPERATIVES

北京市农村信用合作社联合社成立于2000年1月16日，作为全国第一家省级信用联社，成立一年来，在市委、市政府和人民银行的正确领导下，坚持合作制原则，树立首都意识，充分发挥对全市农村信用社管理、指导、协调和服务的行业管理职能，积极引导信用社端正经营方向，切实加强内部管理，防范和化解农村金融风险，改进金融服务，为支持京郊农民、农业、农村经济发展作出了重要贡献。截至2000年末，全市信用社实现收入26亿元，获纯益2.38亿元，总资产达746亿元，在积极促进首都农村经济腾飞的同时，也发展壮大了信用社自身的实力。

——机构网点遍布京郊农村。截至2000年末，全市信用社拥有机构网点1226个，网点分布在京郊14个区县和部分城区，已经形成了市区（县）有信用合作联社，乡镇有信用社，村屯有信用代办站的合作金融网络体系。

——各项存款大幅增长，贷款规模不断扩大。截至2000年末，全市信用社存款余额达490亿元，各项存款超亿元的信用社149个。各项贷款余额252亿元，贷款支持的集体和个人户数达4.5万户。

——服从国家宏观调控，为平衡国家信贷收支，支持国家经济建设做出了积极贡献。截至2000年末，全市信用社转存银行款124.6亿元，存放人行特种存款5亿元，与人民银行融通资金14.9亿元，购买各种债券103.4亿元，总计达247.9亿元，占各项存款总额的50.4%。

——大力促进首都农村经济发展，农村金融主力军作用得到充分体现。信用社是农民信赖的“农户银行”，始终坚持为农户、农业和农村经济发展服务的宗旨，在坚持优先满足农户和农业生产资金需要的前提下，大力持了京郊农村家庭养殖业、籽种农业、创汇农业、观光农业、农副产品加工业、主导产业以及山区水利富民综合开发工程和首都绿化隔离地区建设。截至2000年末，全市信用社贷款余额达252亿元，其中对农村经济贷款占全市金融机构对农业贷款总额的80%，为促进京郊经济发展，推广社会进步，发挥了主力军作用。

——积极缩小与其它金融机构在结算手段上的差距，信用社电子化建设取得重大进展。2000年，在借鉴深圳市农信联社电子化建设成功经验的基础上，全面启动“北京市农村信用社综合业务网络系统项目”，实现了当年开发、当年上线的目标，并在全系统内分步实现了通存通兑业务，结束了手工传统作业的历史。结算渠道的疏通，为进一步开发信用社的新业务奠定了坚实的基础。

北京市农村信用合作社联合社领导成员
理 事 长：尹凤海
主　　任：陈翰林
副 主 任：陆　萍　郑瑞泉　王　建
主任助理：阮明月

北京赛迪传媒投资股份有限公司

BEIJING CCID MEDIA INVESTMENTS CO.,LTD

一、基本情况

1、公司法定中文名称：北京赛迪传媒投资股份有限公司
公司法定英文名称：BEIJING CCID MEDIA INVESTMENTS CO.,LTD
公司简称：赛迪传媒
英文缩写：CMI
2、公司法定代表人：李　颖
电话：010-68710712,68710713
传真：010-68710711
E-mail:hmi@163bi.com
联系地址：北京市海淀区友谊宾馆苏园写字楼278室

3、公司注册地址：北京市昌平区超前路9号附楼403
办公地址：北京市海淀区中关村南大街1号友谊宾馆苏园写字楼278室
邮政编码：100873
4、公司股票上市交易所：深圳证券交易所
总股本：311,573,902股　　上市流通A股：86,755,932股
公司股票简称：赛迪传媒
公司股票代码：0504

二、公司经营范围

(1)公司行业归属：本公司原属房地产类公司，2000年，公司通过资产重组，将主业定位于资讯科技、信息媒体产业。本公司控股的北京中计报投资有限公司所投资管理的《中国计算机报》属于国内计算机业的行业报，其发行量及市场受众份额居同业媒体前列。

(2)公司经2000年度实施资产重组后，实现公司由房地产行业向资讯传媒产业的转换，主营业务范围变更为高新技术企业资讯、媒体、文化传播项目投资管理，提供信息源服务等。

公司在确立IT传媒主业的同时，加大主营业务的经营力度，保证公司经营业绩的稳定增长；欲确立和巩固在中国IT信息服务领域的领导地位。

加大传媒产业的投入，形成以中计报公司为龙头的集团架构。介入与媒体相关的领域，挖掘媒体产业的附加值。形成出版、发行、销售、服务一体化的多点纵深媒体经营格局。

首都科技集团

（北京科技协作中心）

首都科技集团（北京科技协作中心）理事会是北京市人民政府为发挥首都的科技优势，联合中央在京科研院所、大专院校及北京市属科研院所和北京市有关委办、总（集团）公司组成的科技联合体。现拥有200多理事会成员单位，常设办事机构为北京科技协作中心和北京首科集团公司。

北京是我国最重要的科学研究和教育基地。北京地区科技人才荟萃，研究机构密集，创新实力雄厚，成果专利丰富，具有中国乃至世界上少有的地区科技、人才、信息优势。首都科技集团的宗旨是发挥首都科技优势，促进科技成果产业化，推动首都高新技术产业的发展。实施"立足北京，建好基地；面向全国，辐射联合；发挥优势，开拓外向"的发展战略。

首都科技集团集成了中央近30个部委、局、总公司的科技优势，其中有中国机械科学研究院、钢铁研究总院等9个国家级研究院；清华大学、北京大学等20多所高等院校；共近200家各类科研院所。拥有中科院和工程院院士100多位；国家级数据库10余个；科研设备资产总值约100亿元；每年推出科技成果约1万项；科技成果转化率居全国领先地位。首科集团创建的"中国技术交易网"是沟通科研单位与各界的桥梁。

首科集团以理事单位的强大科技实力为依托，围绕首都经济的发展，面向国内外开展技术中介、技术攻关、资产重组、引资融资、咨询评估、软件评审、技术贸易、展览交流、规划论证等业务，加速科技成果的转化，有效地实现高新技术产业化。

CAPITAL SCIENCE & TECHNOLOGY GROUP

新世界集团是香港十大财团和四大地产商之一，拥有物业、酒店、基建、服务、电讯等多元事业。新世界旗下名动香港的丽晶酒店和君悦酒店一直被著名业内杂志推选为亚洲最佳商务酒店，而闻名世界的香港回归祖国庆典仪式地点——香港会议展览中心，也是本集团承建和管理的综合大厦之一。自1980年以来，新世界集团在内地投资基建、房地产、旧城改造、工业改造等100多个项目，是在内地投资最大的香港企业之一。新世界中国地产是新世界集团全资附属公司，在北京、广州、上海、武汉、天津、沈阳和珠江三角洲等城市开发兴建了大批优质住宅、写字楼、酒店和百货商场，位于京城崇文门的北京新世界中心，亦是新世界中国地产开发建造的物业。新世界集团在物业的发展与管理上为客户提供全球一致的国际水准服务，多年精心打造的品牌使新世界成为一面房地产业鲜明的旗帜，客户信心的保障。

投资商
新世界中国地产有限公司
发展商
北京崇裕房产开发有限公司
北京天竺花园别墅发展有限公司
北京崇文·新世界房地产发展有限公司
北京新康房地产发展有限公司

新世界北京项目管理中心 地址：北京市崇文门外大街3号B 北京新世界中心北办公楼15-16层 电话：010 67087788 传真：010 67085360

北京华威建筑工程有限公司

董事长兼总经理：蔺洪齐

北京华威建筑工程有限公司系1998年转制企业。成立于1976年5月。95年以前曾名“通县建筑集团第二建筑公司”。98年以前曾名“北京宋庄建筑集团”。公司于1995年8月晋升建筑二级资质。97年6月通过ISO9002国际标准认证，11月获三A信用等级。

公司现有职工4000余人。其中有职称人员351人。工程系列有职称288人。高中级职称105人，有资质项目经理40余人。

公司上设董事会、监事会、三总师、十部一室，下辖十四个项目部及四个附属企业、八个分公司。

公司现注册资金8000万元。有大中型施工机械1200台（套），二级试验室、检测仪器50台（件），网络化办公设备70余台（件）。

公司始终秉承“建一项工程、塑一座精品、美化一方环境”、“真诚共事、保证质量”之质量目标、方针。年施工能力三十万平方米，工程合格率100%、优良率近80%。先后有数十项工程被评为市级和国家级优质、样板工程；安全文明生产工程。98年取得银屋奖、金屋奖，2000年荣获结构长城杯。

正在施工工程

地　址：北京市朝阳区
华威里甲48号
邮　编：100021
电　话：(010)67701345
传　真：(010)67722629

知春里科研楼

丰台周庄群体住宅工程

北京·福田汽车

北汽福田车辆股份有限公司

北汽福田车辆股份有限公司成立于1996年8月，是经北京市人民政府批准，由100家法人企业发起设立的跨地区、跨行业、跨所有制、多产经营的上市公司，是国家520家重点企业之一，是北京市优中选优重点支持的企业，是北京汽车工业的重点骨干企业。

福田公司现辖9个事业部、12个职能部，拥有员工13000余人。1998年销售汽车1.7万辆，1999年销售汽车6.4万辆，2000年销售车辆突破8万辆，在全国轻卡行业保持第一位。

福田公司以汽车为主导产业，同时大力发展农业装备和住宅产业。拥有现代化冲压、焊装、涂装、总装生产线，独家同时具有引进日本五十铃公司技术的4JB1，日产公司技术的SD22和丰田公司技术的4Y三条发动机生产线，具有年产发动机12万台能力。

福田公司技术研究院是北京市级企业技术中心，它是集产品分析、研究、开发、试制、管理为一体的技术开发中心。现已研制开发出26个大系列、316个品种，开发手段上通过CAD建设及其推广应用，已经全面实现“甩图板工程”，在整车、车身设计方面引进国际尖端技术和分析软件。

福田营销公司对福田公司车辆产品的市场开发、成车销售、配件供应、技术服务、信息反馈“五位一体”的营销过程实施全方位管理。目前在全国设有7个销售分公司，47个市场部、700余个营销网点覆盖全国除港澳台藏外所有省市和自治区。在全国建立技术服务站188个，特约维修厂268个，技术服务中心16个，配件供应中心28个，配件供应点856个，全方位满足顾客的需求。

2001年，是新世纪的第一年，同时也是福田公司“新三步”战略的第一年。福田公司以市场为导向，相继推出“阳光轿卡”和“福田风景”轻客等系列环保汽车，美观实用的车身，环保动力的配制，舒适豪华的驾驶环境以及大众化的价位，受到了广大消费者的一致好评。新世纪、新福田，福田公司将继续坚持“立足中国，面向世界，发展大众化汽车，造福亿万百姓”这个汽车产业经营宗旨，加快发展步伐，以全新的面貌迎接“入世”的挑战。

北汽福田车辆股份有限公司
电　话：010-80716401
传　真：010-80716402
地　址：北京市昌平区沙河镇沙阳路
邮　编：102206
E-mail:ftgjmyb@public3.bta.net.cn

BEIJING ENTERPRISES HOLDINGS HIGH-TECH.DEVELOPMENT CO.,LTD.

北控高科技发展有限公司

董事长：白金荣

总经理：王思红

北控高科技发展有限公司是经中华人民共和国对外贸易经济合作部批准成立的中外合资的综合性投资公司。由北京控股有限公司与中关村科技园区管理委员会下属企业共同出资组建，注册资金3000万美元。

北京控股有限公司与中关村科技园区管理委员会合作，充分利用双方资金、人才、信息和管理、技术、优惠政策等方面资源的优势，促进北京市高新技术成果尽快转化成生产力，加快高新技术产品商品化、产业化的进程。

北控高科技发展有限公司力求按照国际资本市场的专业规范进行管理，依靠高素质人才、高效灵活的机制，凭借与国内外的广泛联系、雄厚的资金实力，本着振兴民族高科技产业，促进高科技产品产业化、国际化的宗旨，与高科技企业、大专院校、科研院所优势互补，携手合作，利益共享，风险共担，同心协力，共创辉煌。

地　址：北京市朝阳区安翔北里甲11号
电　话：64850345/46/47
传　真：64850334
邮　编：100101
E-mail:bkgk@public2.east.net.cn

北京市市政六建筑工程有限公司

北京市市政六建设工程有限公司是由北京市市政总公司控股的大型市政综合施工企业，具有市政建设、机械化施工一级资质，公路施工一级资信，具备道路、桥梁、高速公路、土石方机械化施工、大型构件吊装运输、垃圾填埋场建设、基础工程、市政综合管线、市政隧道工程、钢结构加工、电器设备安装等多种施工能力。公司技术力量雄厚，设备精良，管理严格，注册资金6000万元，总资产18249万元，各种设备557台，设备总功率23228KW，旅行资信AAA级，年施工能力2亿元以上。1997年，通过了ISO-8002国际质量体系认证。公司的宗旨是："用户至上，质量第一，信守合同，优质服务。"以诚信与社会各界朋友真诚合作。

北京市工程咨询公司

BEIJING ENGINEERING CONSULTING CORPORATION

经　理：刘　义

北京市工程咨询公司经北京市人民政府批准，于1986年8月成立，注册资金2千万元人民币，公司是国家计委颁发的全国第一批具有甲级资格的工程咨询单位，同时也是具有甲级监理、甲级工程造价咨询以及甲级工程招标代理资质的综合性工程咨询机构，系国际咨询工程师联合会（FIDIC）会员和中国工程咨询协会常务理事单位之一。公司拥有近90名专业理论水平较高、实践经验丰富的各类高、中级专业技术人员和管理人员，具有各类执业资格100多人次，专业门类齐全、技术实力雄厚。公司专家委员会是公司的“智囊团”由政府有关部门和社会知名专家、教授、高级管理人员、律师共50多人组成。

公司监理的万博苑小区

公司成立十多年来，秉承“客观、科学、独立、公正”的咨询原则，以投资咨询、工程概预结算审核、工程招投标代理和建设项目监理为主业。截止2000年底，公司已完成了各类咨询项目1315项，涉及投资总额2951亿元，为国家和社会客户节约投资59亿元。

公司承担的北京地铁一线改造及新建复八线可行性研究报告评估

项目覆盖了国民经济各领域的几十个行业，公司具备为客户提供全过程、多方位工程咨询服务的能力。

地　址：北京市西城区复兴门南大街丁2号
（天银大厦c东七层——八层）
邮　编：100031
电　话：66411030
传　真：66411031
http://www.becc.com.cn
E-mail:becc@becc.com.cn

诠释现代生活方式　创造美好生活家园

阳光100国际公寓

锦绣馨园

锦绣园
工体北使馆区

锦绣园公寓－98年北京十大热销项目之一，现已获得涉外租赁许可权，俱乐部各项设施完备，恭迎八方宾客。

公寓涉外租赁：64151320
健身俱乐部：64169916

亚视大厦

中天大厦

永馨公寓

北京银信投资有限公司

北京银信投资有限公司成立于1996年，注册资金1.6亿元，主要经营房地产开发、电讯科技、投资银行等业务。公司倡导以人为本、自然和谐的居住理念，成功开发了永馨公寓、锦绣园、阳光100等优秀项目，赢得了市场好评；目前正在CBD东侧开发超大规模的郊区住宅项目，将为业主提供全新的居住环境与生活方式。

公司拥有一批高素质、年轻化专业人才，实行现代企业管理制度，把“建百年老店”作为长期奋斗目标，愿与社会各届精诚合作，共创美好未来。

地址：北京市朝阳区幸福村中路锦绣园　邮编：100027　电话：64169843　传真：64150035

上海浦東發展銀行北京分行

上海浦东发展银行北京分行是一家国有控股股份制商业银行，于1996年4月20日正式成立。

建行以来，浦发北京分行始终贯彻“为社会主义金融事业闯新路，服务于首都北京的经济建设与发展”的指导思想，积极支持北京的经济建设与发展；以“笃守诚信、创造卓越”的浦发理念，依托科技、人才和机制优势，锐意创新，开拓发展，努力为客户服务，短短五年时间，便在广大客户中树立起了“规范、高效、安全、创新”的新型商业银行形象，取得了良好的经济效益和社会效益，在社会上赢得了良好的口碑，成为北京地区最富活力的商业银行之一。

目前，上海浦东发展银行北京分行在北京东城区、西城区、朝阳区和海淀区开办了13家营业网点，全面办理单位和个人本外币存款、贷款，结算、票据贴现、信用卡、开出信用证、保函、代理发行金融债券和政府债券、代理收付款项及代理保险等金融业务。截止2000年末，本外币存款余额达192亿元，资产总额超过207亿元，累计实现利润8.25亿元，上缴税金1.8亿元，发展速度位居同类商业银行前列。

北京分行积极支持国有骨干优势企业和新兴产业的发展，五年来，累计发放贷款360余亿元，支持了一大批优质企业，为北京市的经济发展和城市建设做出了积极的贡献。

SHANGHAI PUDONG DEVELOPMENT BANK

永远创新的四通

董事会

intel+duan2

四通集团公司是中国著名的民营高新技术企业。

四通主要从事电子信息产业，并涉足生物医药领域。集团注册资本1亿元，下有50余家全资、合资及联营企业，4个海外机构，职工3000多人。至1999年底累计实现销售收入409亿元，利税1.85亿元。

1984年5月，一群辞去公职的科技人员借款2万元创办了四通。依据“自筹资金、自由组合、自主经营、自负盈亏”的“四自”原则，以自行研制生产的MS系列中英文文字处理机为主打，四通迅速崛起于新兴的中国电子行业，国内市场占有率达到85%以上，为中国办公自动化事业的进步做出了重大贡献。

进入90年代，四通在中国企业中率先举起“第二次创业”的旗帜。围绕着“股份化、集团化、产业化、国际化”的目标——整合旗下骨干企业，以“四通电子”在香港股票市场上市，将四通的活动舞台从国内扩展到海外。

牵手国际大公司，合资兴建产业基地，“与巨人同行”，包括与日本松下电工合资的中国最大的照明电器公司，与日本三菱电机合资的大规模集成电路公司，与美国TRW合资的大型系统集成公司，等等。

开发生产打印机、收款机等多种面向部门用户、行业用户的专用电子产品，进入国民经济信息化改造的主战场。

世纪之交，为解决囿于历史因素而存留的产权难题，四通在全集团范围展开大规模的重组改制，完成了中国经济界首例MBO。

基于重组后的崭新格局，四通集团进一步确立了新世纪的战略方向，将核心业务定位于以网络为基础的信息服务，力争抓住新经济革命带来的历史机遇，赢得市场、赢得技术、赢得人才、赢得未来。

四通，正迈向新的高度。

三菱车间

信息技术

北京华方投资经营公司

BEIJING HUAFANG INVESTMENT & OPERATION CO.

董事长、总经理：阎嗣烈

北京华方投资经营公司，是北京市西城区人民政府于1998年投资组建的一家国有资产经营公司，主要从事国有资本营运，进行国有资产的经营、管理、优化配置等。以商业、服务业企业为主导，投资涉及综合百货、餐饮、医药、物业管理、房地产开发、商办加工、证券投资等领域。截至2000年底总资产达27.6亿元人民币，净资产12.8亿元。拥有北京华兴新业商贸有限责任公司、北京金象复星医药股份有限公司、北京华天饮食集团公司、北京万方实业总公司、北京华利佳合实业有限公司（筹）、北京贯通经贸集团等6家商贸企业的全部国有产（股）权，并对其履行“投资、监督、调控、服务”职能。

华方公司诞生之初即确立了“以人为本、本以人为”的企业理念。她顺应知识经济时代的要求，以人为中心，通过人自身价值的升华，实现企业的目标，实现对社会的贡献。

华方公司自成立以来，坚持以“管好资产、盘活存量、培育亮点、深化改革、促进发展”为企业生存与发展的指导方针，以产权制度改革为主线，在抓好国有资产管理的基础上，以其权属企业“老板”的身份，大胆从事资产重组、产权转让和证券投资等资本经营，不仅连续两年超额完成西城区政府（国资委）确定的国有资本保值增值指标，而且初步建立了现代企业制度的基本框架，受到业内人士的广泛关注。

地　　址：北京西城区月坛西街乙2号5号楼
邮　　编：100045
电　　话：010-68037853
传　　真：010-68037241
电子邮件：Lij_601@sina.com
网　　址：//www.huafanginv.com

投资燕山　拥抱成功

北京燕山位于京郊西南，距市中心50公里，总面积43平方公里。这里城市环境优雅，公用设施齐备，交通通信便利。京原铁路穿境而过，距京石高速10公里。

燕山是首都卫星城，是中国特大型石油化工企业——北京燕山石油化工有限公司所在地，是我国石油化工产品的主要集散地，每年区内企业为各级财政上缴税收16亿元。在此投资既有巨大的内在市场，又有广阔的外部市场，置身其中，商机无限。

1992年北京市计委、首都规划委批准建立燕山工业区，工业区规划用地140万平方米，区内公用工程建设完备，1999年被北京市科委批准为燕山星火技术密集区基地，目前注册企业已有58家，该工业区是您投资精细化工、高新技术等企业的好去处。

几年来，政府致力于改善投资环境，一个社会安定、秩序优良、环境优美、服务优质、经济繁荣、文化生活高雅、群众生活方便、公民素质较高、两个文明协调发展的一流首都卫星城，正展现在人们面前。

中共北京市房山区燕山工作委员会
北京市房山区燕山办事处
电　话：(010) 69341628　(010) 69342570
传　真：(010) 69341628　(010) 89342306
邮　编：102500
网　址：燕山工业信息网HTTP://WWW.JJW.GOV.CN

京都菇业开发中心

JING DU DEVELOPMENT CENTRE OF MUSHROOM SPECILITY

北京京都菇业开发中心位于北京通州八里桥开发区，占地面积1936平方米，现有建筑面积1741平方米办公楼一栋，附属平房294平方米，拥有通州、大兴、红星、朝阳、顺义五大生产基地和崇文区中心商务总部，专业菌类生产用温室大棚106栋，并配备菌种厂、礼品加工厂、素食加工厂等。

中心基地在通州占地75亩，全封闭结构，即有品类中试，全面实验的生产功能，又是菌类观赏、品尝、采摘、娱乐等游玩寻趣的仙居乐园。中心注册资金120万元，自有固定资产200万元，长期租赁资产2000万元，年产值1000万元左右。

主要生产平菇、灵芝、香菇、木耳、鸡腿菇等食药用菌品和盒式灵芝礼品、灵芝盆景、京都素食菇品、深加工菇粉精品等，其盒式保鲜菇耳类，早已占据京都各大超市，盒式礼品灵芝是本中心最新推出的年节贺岁礼品，灵芝朵大色正，包装精美新潮，无任何添加成份，既是纯天然保健珍菌，又是新年贺岁的上等馈赠佳品，京都素食是中心加工品类中的拳头产品，灵芝加素食是长寿的基础，京都菇业将为您提供一座良好的生命保养中心。

中心为解决下岗职工的后顾之忧，在无偿提供食用菌种植技术，回收产品的同时，又开办大棚出租业务，年每栋大棚投资7.5万元，年产值保证达到18万元，同时还免费为下岗职工培训技术，提供常年跟踪服务，让食用菌品全面及时地摆上京城市民的餐桌，把一个投产比例大，周期短，效益高，风险小的大农业高科技项目尽快引入产业机制，造福于百姓，回报于社会。

京都菇业开发中心总经理赵启平先生，携全体员工愿与各届有识之士共同发展京都菇业。

北京市前疃蝎产品有限公司

该公司是二十一世纪以蝎子和珍珠獾为载体开发各类生物产品。添补医学药匣子和绿色菜蓝子，促使人体基因转化，提高人类健康水平的生物工程公司。它不仅带有巨大的商业利益，而且有助于中华社会实力的增强。是二十一世纪主要的经济增长点之一。

蝎子是生物中的抗癌之王，补钙之王，该公司有北京强华养蝎基地即天下第一蝎子城，有北京潮河蝎产品研究所有国家级的专家教授，博士，硕士导师等科技人员5名，有适应养蝎的高科技模拟式养蝎技术，总资产为800万元人民币，是集体所有制企业。在全国设有分公司，以具备开发的基础条件，本公司为了适应市场的需求，产生连锁效益。

开发招商引资1000万元－2000万元人民币。我们竭诚欢迎国内外的朋友，仕君前来真诚的合作，共展宏图。

CCPIT PATENT AND TRADEMARK LAW OFFICE

中国国际贸易促进委员会
专利商标事务所

本事务所

是建国以来历史最长、规模最大的涉外知识产权代理机构之一
有为国内外客户多年服务所积累的工作经验，熟悉并适应国内外客户的工作方式、能满足客户的任何要求
以英、法、德、日、俄等语种为工作语言，便于与客户进行交流
有在国内外，特别是在美、英、法、德、日等国系统培训过的机械、化学、物理、电子和电器专利代理人，商标代理人共120余名，其中60人具有律师资格，全体工作人员300余名
有先进的计算机管理系统及现代化的通讯设备

代理业务范围

代理在中国申请专利、代理向国外申请外国专利
代理在中国申请商标注册、代理向国外申请商标注册
代理在台湾、香港、澳门地区专利申请、外观设计登记、商标申请及有关知识产权事宜
代理专利商标侵权及其他知识产权争议的诉讼，行政处理、调解及法律诉讼
代理计算机软件登记、著名权登记、互联网域名登记
代理知识产权海关备案
代理专利检索、商标检索及专利商标监视服务
关于技术贸易及其他知识产权的法律咨询、知识产权领域内的其它服务
本所在日本东京、德国慕尼黑、美国纽约和我国香港设有办事处。

地　址：北京市复兴门内大街158号远洋大厦F10层
电　话：(86-10)6851-6688
传　真：(86-10)6858-7610
邮　编：100031
E-mail:mail@ccpit-patent.com.cn
网　址：www.ccpit-patent.com.cn

北京—清华 工业开发研究院

北京——清华工业开发研究院是在贾庆林同志的提议下，由北京市政府和清华大学共同组建和管理的事业法人单位，实行理事会领导下的院长负责制。北京市市长刘淇任理事长，清华大学副秘书长戴猷元任院长。工研院贯彻“科教兴国”的战略，探索产、学、研结合的新途径，是政府部门和高等学校进行科技创新尝试的新机制。她参考了国际上研究院科技成果孵化器的成功经验，采用市场运作方式，以清华大学科技力量、科研基地、科技成果为基础，为北京市高新技术产业发展、产业结构调整和传统产业改造提供技术支持和项目支撑，使清华大学成为首都经济的重要科技源头和高层管理人员及技术人员的重要培训基地。北京——清华工业开发研究院作为北京市高新技术产业的孵化中心、企业发展的服务中心、科技信息的集散中心和政府决策的咨询中心，发挥着积极的作用。

建院二年多来，按照“边建设、边开发、边转化”的建院思路，在加快科技成果转化，促进首都经济发展方面取得了初步进展。1999年初，已完成了第一批科技成果转化项目的立项工作。另外与北京市科委联手尝试推出了“共同筛选、联合支持”的活动，遴选支持了8项科研转化型项目。工研院还参与了《中关村科技园发展规划》的制订和北京清华（密云）工业园的建设。

北京海淀区清华科技园华业大厦六层
电　话：010-62780501　010-62773259
　　　　010-62773260
传　真：010-62780503
邮　编：100084

北京城建工程承发包有限责任公司

执行董事长兼总经理高登广先生

北京城建工程承发包有限责任公司是隶属北京城建集团的国有独资公司。公司成立于1991年，是经北京市计建二委批准的一家代政府做甲方承担市政基础设施建设与开发，房地产开发经营的专业公司。公司注册资金5030.92万元，具有从事市政工程设计规划、拆迁、代甲方实施招标、工程建设施工管理、直到交付使用后配套物业管理等一整套运作能力。

公司先后完成成寿寺路综合市政工程、“三九一”工程、北太平庄立交桥工程、阜石路、阜外大街、北苑路、牡丹园小区市政拆迁房建设、罗庄小区市政拆迁房建设等一大批项目，累计完成总投资90.68亿元，创出了辉煌业绩，受到市政府及甲方的信任和好评。

目前，随着经营重点的调整，房地产开发已成为公司的主业。217 万平方米的北苑家园自1996年开发建设以来，累计开工90万平方米，完成投资近16亿元。竣工50多万平方米，入住居民已近2000多户。北苑家园作为公司向社会奉献的北京城北“花园大社区”，预计2006年全部建成，总投资约60亿元人民币。

公司感谢市政府以及社会各界近年来给予的大力支持，公司将继续遵循“重信兴利，服务社会”的企业理念，恪首“创建精美工程，提供满意服务”的质量方针，竭诚为社会各界提供更优质的服务。

北京市殡仪服务中心

北京市殡仪服务中心是经过市机构编制委员会批准设立的单位，隶属于北京市殡葬管理处，是本市专门从事殡葬系列服务的部门。

服务中心位于海淀区四道口路7号。北接北三环，毗邻大钟寺批发市场，南临学院南路，交通便利，行车方便。中心设有商务部、业务接待部、市场开发部和电脑网络中心及殡葬用品销售部等服务机构。同时，市属及各区县民政局所辖合法公墓在中心内设有办事处。

殡仪服务中心二楼大厅

殡仪服务中心

服务中心的服务内容包括：提供殡葬咨询，解答疑难问题，联系丧事活动，介绍骨灰安置（包括骨灰堂寄存、墓葬、骨灰墙、廊安放、骨灰撒海及骨灰林安葬）等“一条龙”殡仪服务。同时还提供上门服务，陪同引导服务及各式家庭灵堂布置等项服务。

中心设有24小时全天候快捷的殡仪服务热线，竭诚为社会各界人士提供便捷、高效、优质的服务。

服务热线:62110126

北京市殡葬服务单位一览表

单位名称	联系电话
八宝山殡仪馆	68160313
东郊殡仪馆	65761082
万安公墓	62591545
福田公墓	68872551
八宝山人民公墓	68216204
西静园管理处	62880461
金山陵园	62591604
温泉墓园	62458645
太子峪陵园	83877030
朝阳陵园	84317780
通惠陵园	69591394
天慈墓园	61267869
宝云岭墓园	89011468
八达岭人民公墓	61161944
万佛华侨陵园	69803346
长青园骨灰林基地	65898999
外侨公墓	84311290

北京市殡葬管理处